D1108411

Carpentry

& BUILDING CONSTRUCTION

Sixth Edition

Mark D. Feirer • John L. Feirer

New York, New York   Columbus, Ohio   Chicago, Illinois   Peoria, Illinois   Woodland Hills, California

BRAND DISCLAIMER

Publisher does not necessarily recommend or endorse any particular company or brand name product that may be discussed or pictured in this text. Brand name products are used because they are readily available, likely to be known to the reader, and their use may aid in the understanding of the text. Publisher recognizes that other brand name or generic products may be substituted and work as well or better than those featured in the text.

SAFETY NOTICE

The reader is expressly advised to consider and use all safety precautions described in this book or that might also be indicated by undertaking the activities described herein. In addition, common sense should be exercised to help avoid all potential hazards.

Publisher and Author assume no responsibility for the activities of the reader or for the subject matter experts who prepared this book. Publisher and Author make no representation or warranties of any kind, including but not limited to, the warranties of fitness for particular purpose or merchantability, nor for any implied warranties related thereto, or otherwise. Publisher and Author will not be liable for damages of any type, including any consequential, special or exemplary damages resulting, in whole or in part, from reader's use or reliance upon the information, instructions, warnings or other matter contained in this book.

SAFETY FIRST

Work Safely on the Job

The information in each Safety First feature emphasizes key safety practices in building construction. Make safety a habit by placing safety first.

Publisher gratefully acknowledges the assistance of the Steel Framing Alliance™

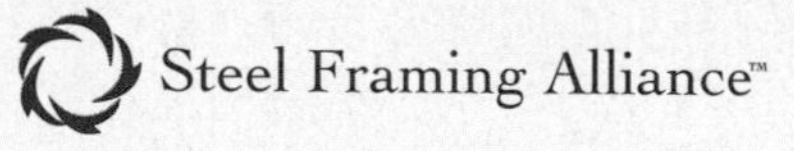

The McGraw·Hill Companies

Copyright © 2004 by Glencoe/McGraw-Hill, a division of The McGraw-Hill Companies. Previous copyrights © 1997, 1993 by Glencoe/McGraw-Hill; previous copyrights © 1986, 1981, 1976 by John L. Feirer and Gilbert R. Hutchings.
All rights reserved. Except as permitted under the United States Copyright Act, no part of this publication may be reproduced or distributed in any form or by any means, or stored in a database or retrieval system, without prior written permission of the publisher, Glencoe/McGraw-Hill.

Send all inquiries to:
Glencoe/McGraw-Hill
3008 W. Willow Knolls Drive
Peoria, IL 61614

ISBN 0-07-822702-X (Student Text)
ISBN 0-07-822703-8 (Carpentry Applications)
ISBN 0-07-825353-5 (Carpentry Math)
ISBN 0-07-825352-7 (Safety Guidebook)
ISBN 0-07-822704-6 (Instructor Resource Guide)
ISBN 0-07-825347-0 (Instructor Productivity CD-ROM)
Printed in the United States of America
2 3 4 5 6 7 8 9 10 071 06 05 04 03

PREFACE

This new edition of *Carpentry & Building Construction* retains its focus as an essential text for students of carpentry and general wood technology. Building on the strengths of the five previous editions, this new edition presents information that has been updated, reorganized, and rewritten. All photographs and drawings are new.

This edition maintains a detailed coverage of wood framing techniques. However, the other major categories of residential building materials are also discussed. Much information has been added on new building materials and construction techniques. For example, an entire chapter is devoted to engineered lumber products such as laminated-veneer lumber and wood I-beams. Information on insulated-concrete foundations has been added. There is improved coverage of building systems such as slab foundations, brick-veneer siding, and stucco siding. Two added chapters on steel framing reflect the growing use of this system. The construction of wood decks is covered in a new chapter.

This edition includes estimating techniques and timesaving carpenter's tips. Regional variations in building practices have been noted. Essential construction procedures are clearly presented in a step-by-step format. As did earlier editions, this edition emphasizes careful work habits and close attention to the best safety practices. Safety First information is highlighted in the style shown on the facing copyright page.

Every illustration has been replaced to reflect the use of current tools, materials, and applications. All photographs are also now full color. Every drawing has been reviewed to ensure accuracy and uniformity of style. Color has been added to drawings to aid understanding by emphasizing points of interest.

For many years, residential construction was governed by several regionally based building codes. In 2000, the organizations publishing these codes joined forces to publish a new building code for application throughout the United States. This code is the *International Residential Code for One- and Two-Family Dwellings*, commonly referred to as the IRC. Building code references in this edition of *Carpentry & Building Construction* are to the 2000 edition of the *IRC*, the most current edition available during the preparation of this new edition. However, readers of this book should always consult the latest edition of their local building codes.

Those who carefully use this book to increase their knowledge of residential construction and develop carpentry skills should be able to:

- Identify career opportunities in the building trades.
- Demonstrate competency in the use of the materials and tools used in building construction.
- Understand the building codes used in residential building construction.
- Read the prints and technical materials used in residential construction.
- Demonstrate carpentry skills meeting or exceeding recognized standards.

A book of this complexity, detail, and depth could not have been completed without the efforts of technical reviewers. These reviewers were construction professionals associated with wood technology and construction programs in high schools, vocational schools, community colleges, and apprenticeship training programs. Through their critique of the text and review of the illustrations, they provided helpful comments. Many manufacturers and trade associations supplied technical advice or provided illustrations. The author gratefully acknowledges all of these contributions.

DEDICATION

This edition is dedicated to John L. Feirer (1915-2000), a nationally recognized authority in technical and industrial education and principal author of the five previous editions of *Carpentry & Building Construction*. Throughout his long career as a respected educator, prolific author, and award-winning editor, my father exemplified integrity and craftsmanship.

Mark D. Feirer

CONTENTS IN BRIEF

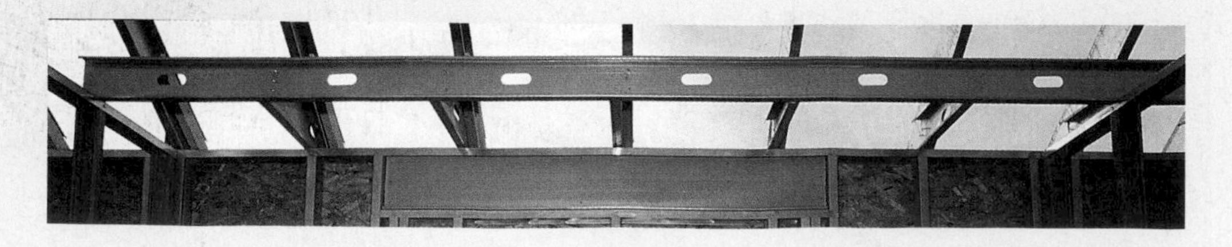

TECHNICAL REVIEWERS

Martin Anderson
Instructor
Associated General
Contractors of America
San Diego, California

Sonny Backs
Carpentry Instructor
Pascagoula Applied Technology Center
Pascagoula, Mississippi

Byron Boyer
Construction Trades Instructor
Newton High School
Newton, Illinois

Kyle Jay Davis
Wood Technology Instructor
Hillsboro High School
Hillsboro, Texas

Basil Espinosa
Instructor & Apprenticeship Coordinator
Associated General Contractors of America
San Diego, California

Mike Fischer
Carpentry Instructor
Lawrence Country High School
Lawrenceburg, Tennessee

Don Fleming
Carpentry Instructor
Okaloosa Applied Technology Center
Fort Walton Beach, Florida

Michael Frederick
Vocational Building Trades Instructor
Walker Career Center
Indianapolis, Indiana

Gary Gray
Carpentry Instructor
Agoura High School
Agoura, California

Glenn Marsteller
Instructor (retired)
Associated General
Contractors of America
San Diego, California

Steve Nicholson
Carpentry Instructor
Cypress High School/Long Beach City College
Cypress, California

Terry D. Pollard
Residential Construction
Instructor/Contributor
Byington Solway Technical Center
Knox, Tennessee

E. Edward Prevatt
Program Director/Instructor
Academy of Construction Technology
W.T. Loften High School
Gainesville, Florida

Marty Stout
Instructor
Associated General Contractors of America
San Diego, California

Kathy C. Swan, Ph.D.
United Brotherhood of Carpenters
Tacoma, Washington

Robert W. Swegle
Coordinator
Regional Council of Carpenters – JATC
United Brotherhood of Carpenters and Joiners
of America
Pekin, Illinois

Todd Turley
Instructor
Winslow High School
Winslow, Arizona

Timothy J. Waite, P.E.
President
Steel Framing Alliance
Washington, D.C.

Daniel F. Williams
Building Construction Instructor
Limestone County Career Technical Center
Athens, Alabama

Robert Ziegler
Carpentry Instructor
Connelley Technical Institute
Pittsburgh, Pennsylvania

CONTENTS

Top and bottom plates on edge
Tack plates together with 8d nails

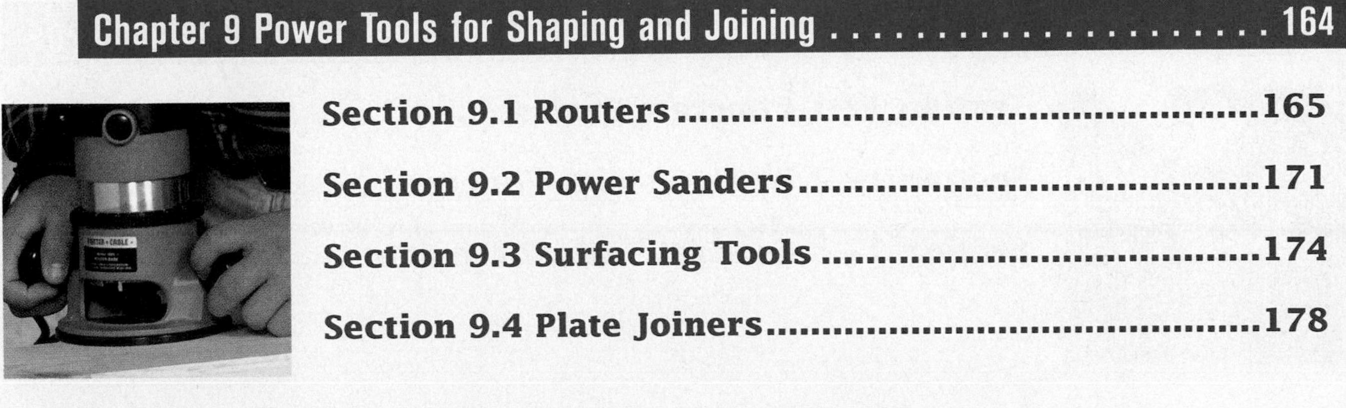

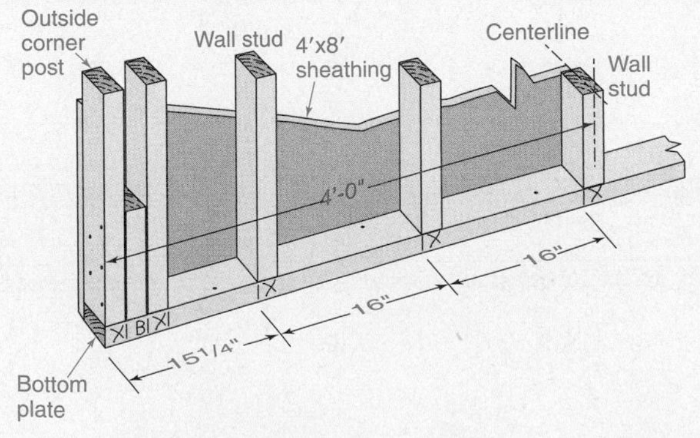
Outside corner post
Wall stud
4′x8′ sheathing
Centerline
Wall stud
4′-0″
16″
16″
15 1/4″
Bottom plate

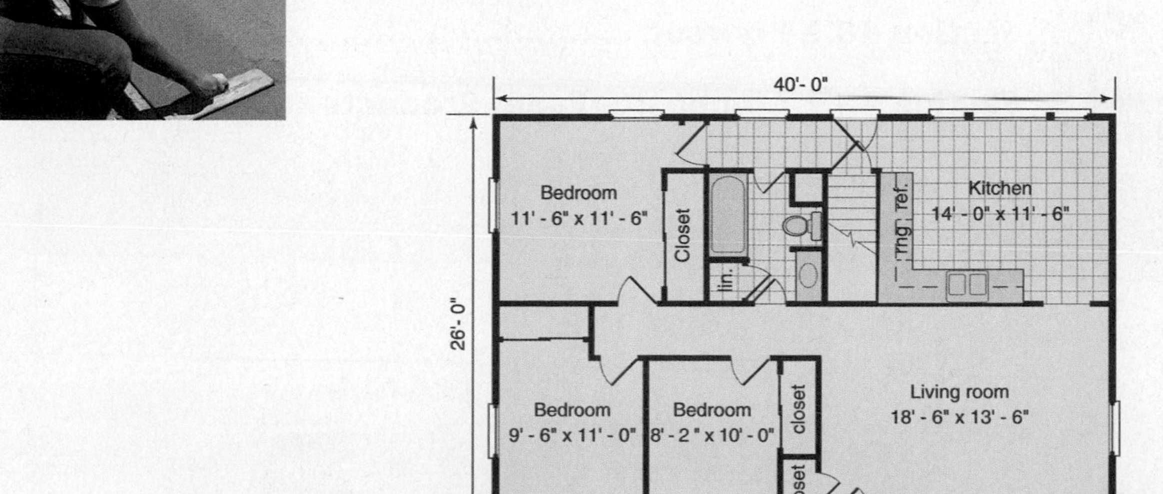

40'- 0"
26'- 0"
Bedroom
11' - 6" x 11' - 6"
Closet
lin.
rng. ref.
Kitchen
14' - 0" x 11' - 6"
Bedroom
9' - 6" x 11' - 0"
Bedroom
8' - 2" x 10' - 0"
closet
closet
Living room
18' - 6" x 13' - 6"

UNIT 4 WOOD FRAME CARPENTRY 286

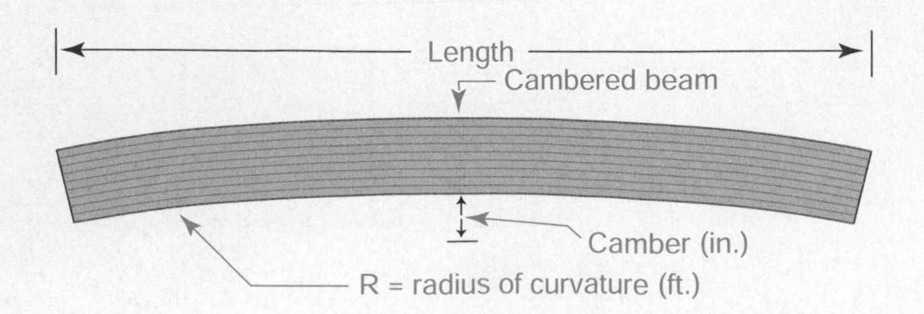

Correctly nailed

Nail too long

Nail at wrong angle

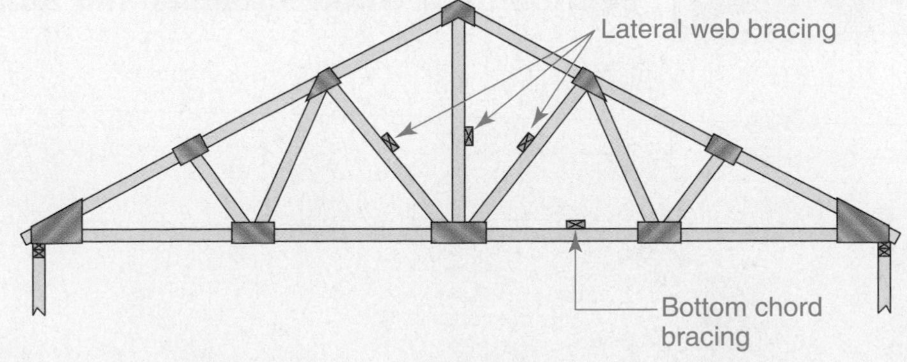
Lateral web bracing
Bottom chord bracing

UNIT 6 CLOSING IN THE STRUCTURE 548

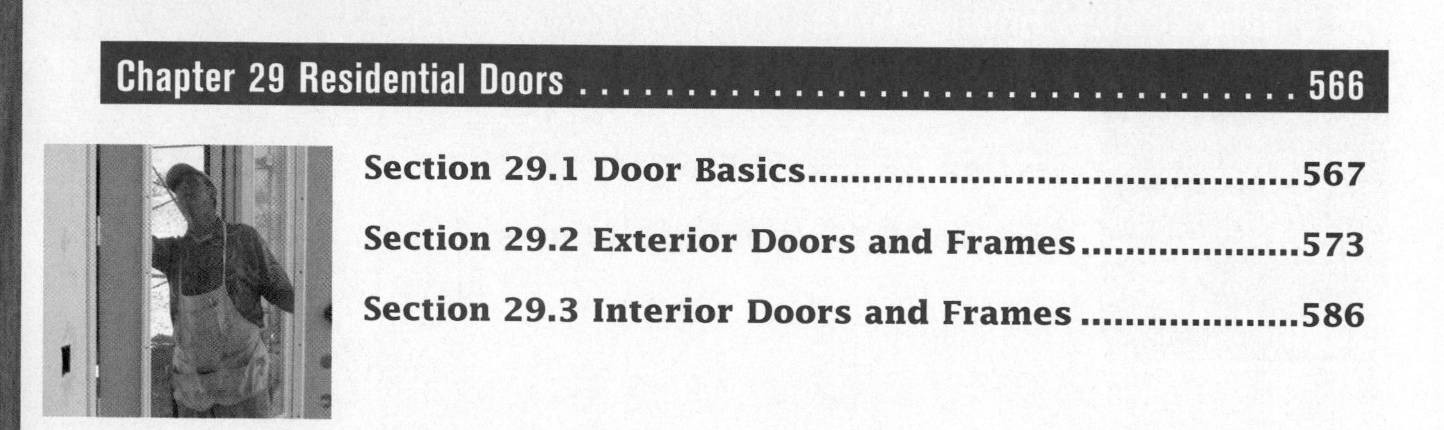

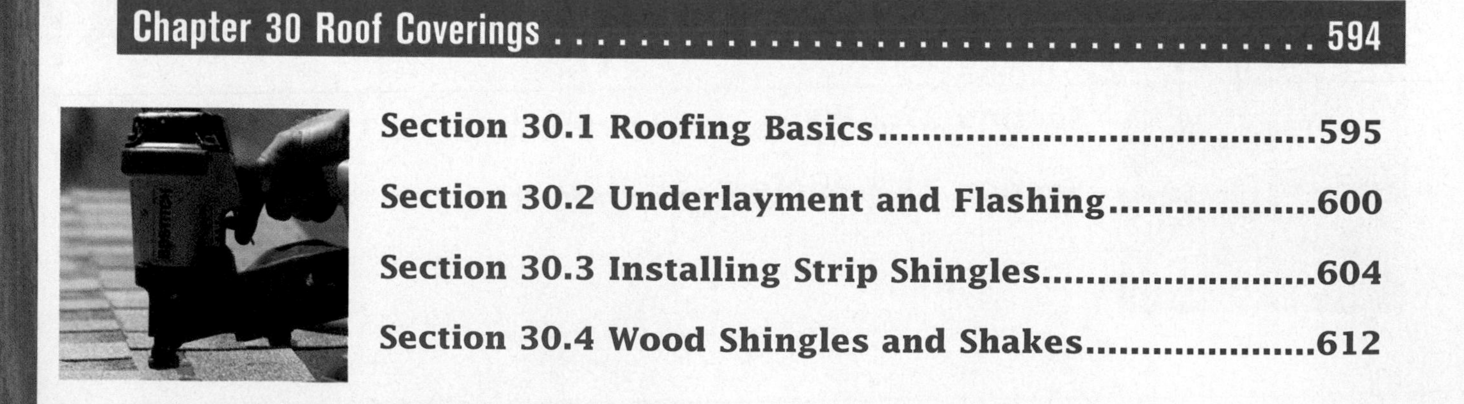

UNIT 7 FINISH CARPENTRY 676

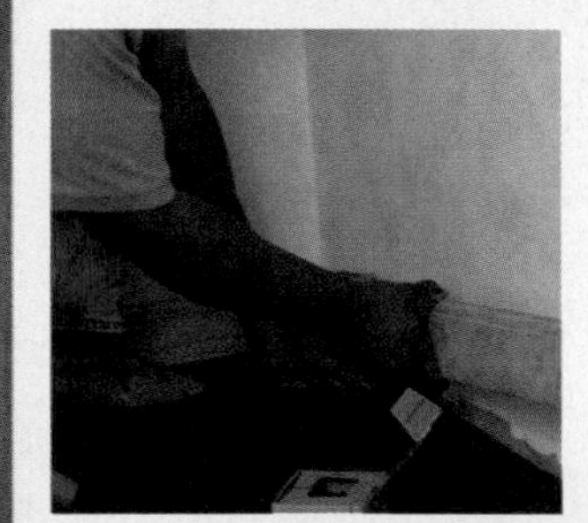

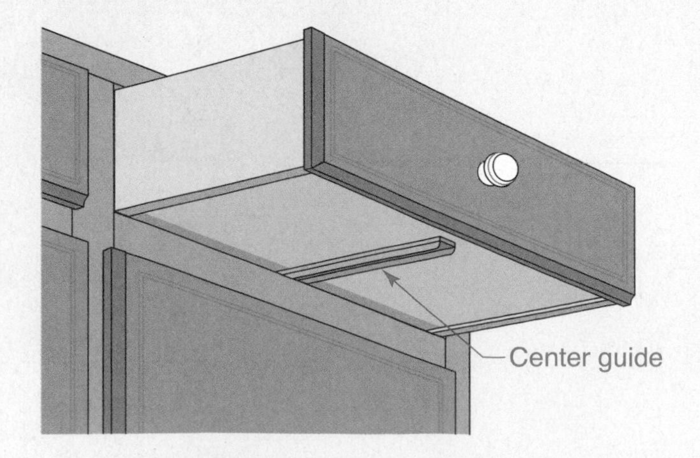

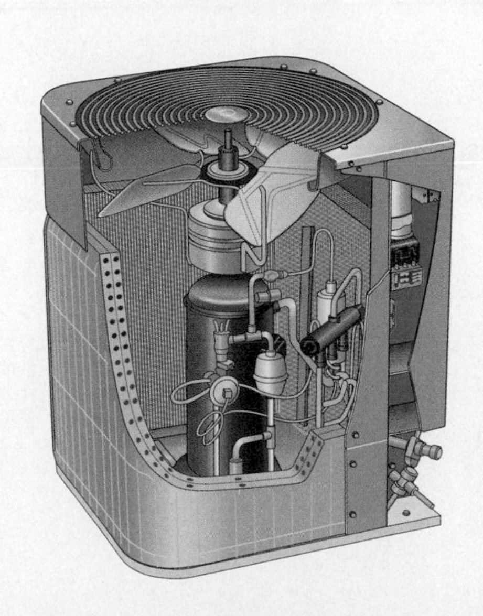

WORKSITE *Know-How*

SAFETY FIRST

This feature stresses safety on the job. It stresses work practices that require special attention to ensure personal safety.

from Another Angle

Some work practices vary from one part of the country to the other. This feature highlights some of those practices.

Carpenter's Tip

This feature presents workplace tips designed to save time and labor, without sacrificing accuracy or quality.

STEP BY STEP

Estimating...

Unit 1

PREPARING TO BUILD

Building Trades

Construction involves both the creation of new structures and the repair or modification of existing structures. Construction can be divided into general building construction, heavy construction, and special trades construction. General building construction deals with residential, industrial, and commercial buildings. Sewers, roads, and bridges are examples of heavy construction. Workers in the special trades include carpenters, plumbers, electricians, painters, and others.

Most construction is overseen by a *general contractor*, who is legally responsible for the entire project. However, general contractors may subcontract part of the work to heavy construction or special trades contractors.

Whatever the area or type of construction, workers must have a high school diploma. They must also be in good physical condition, be willing to learn new skills, and be willing to work under a variety of conditions. More than 60 percent of construction jobs are with specialty contractors, and many construction workers are also self-employed.

For more information, check the *Occupational Outlook Handbook* or look up "construction" on the Internet.

Chapter 1 The Construction Industry

Objectives

After reading this chapter, you'll be able to:

- Describe career specialties in construction.
- Describe educational and training programs that can prepare you for a construction career.
- Explain the function of a business plan for entrepreneurs.
- List the primary employability skills.
- Describe the steps in obtaining a job.
- List several responsibilities of employers and employees.

Terms

apprentice
business plan
certification
entrepreneur
ethics
free enterprise
networking
résumé
trend
work ethic

The construction industry employs over six million people in the United States. The industry builds residential and commercial buildings, among other things. Residential buildings include houses and apartments. Commercial buildings include office and government buildings, schools, and hospitals. Employment in construction is *cyclical*—it rises and falls with the economy.

To advance in construction, you need to obtain training, education, and work experience. Employees who take pride in the quality of their work will find many rewarding opportunities. Someone with a carpenter's license can advance to construction superintendent. The graduate of a technical school may start as a drafter and become a project manager. An assistant architect may work up to full professional status.

SECTION 1.1

Careers in Construction

Much of the work in construction is done by trained specialists.

CONSTRUCTION SPECIALTIES

The three specialized categories are craft, technical, and professional.

Craft Workers

Workers in the building crafts (trades) represent the largest group of skilled workers in the United States. There are more than two dozen skilled building crafts, and carpenters are the largest group. Carpenters erect the wood framework of a building. They install molding, paneling, cabinets, windows, and doors. They build stairs and lay floors.

Members of the building trades often have a high level of skill earned through experience or training. In unions, for example, a worker in the crafts may begin as an *apprentice*. A *journey-level worker* has an intermediate level of skill. The highest level is that of *master*.

Construction craft work is sometimes grouped into three classifications: structural, finish, and mechanical. Occupations concerned mainly with structural work include carpenter, bricklayer, and cement mason. Finish work is done by painters, glaziers, and roofers. Occupations involving mechanical work include plumber and construction electrician. Many of these workers work outdoors. In some regions, the work tends to be seasonal.

Technical Workers

Some careers in building construction require additional training and education at a technical institute or community college. Examples include architectural drafter, estimator, and purchasing agent. A drafter works on building plans. An *estimator* figures the cost of a project. **Fig. 1-1.** A *purchasing agent* buys materials according to current needs.

Professional Workers

College can prepare you for many professional careers related to construction. These include architect, project engineer, and teacher at a trade or vocational school.

Management opportunities in the construction industry are also open to individuals with appropriate work experience, training, and education. For example, the management of a large construction project is the job of a *construction supervisor*, or *construction administrator*. This person schedules workers and inspections and arranges for the delivery of materials.

Related Careers

There are also opportunities for employment in businesses that serve the construction industry. Many people sell or service tools and equipment. Others supply building materials. Some check for building code enforcement. Still others design, repair, or evaluate new products.

TRENDS

To plan for customers' needs, industry experts track trends. A **trend** is a general development

Fig. 1-1. The cost of a project must be accurately estimated to ensure a profit.

or movement in a certain direction. Trends affect job opportunities. For example, as the aging population increases, more people will be living in retirement centers and nursing homes. More companies will be building them. Three factors influencing residential building trends include:

- **Family structure.** Family structure is changing as the number of single and single-parent households increases. This has increased the demand for apartments and smaller, more energy-efficient houses.
- **Work patterns.** The number of people who work and the increased number of hours they work reflect another trend. People want houses that require less maintenance because their time is limited.
- **Personal preferences.** Increasingly, people are moving to warmer climates. This has sparked a construction boom in those areas.

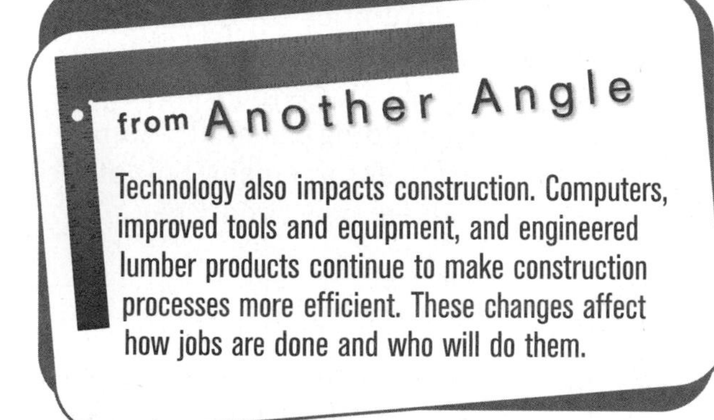

SECTION 1.1

Check Your Knowledge

1. How many people are employed in the construction industry?
2. Name the three categories of specialized workers.
3. What is a trend?
4. What three factors influence residential building trends?

On the Job

Working in teams, search at least five print or Internet sources to identify two current construction trends. Share your findings with the class. Discuss some ways construction operations have already adapted to these trends.

SECTION 1.2

Education and Training

A high school education is a solid foundation on which to build a construction career. Learning excellent communication skills—reading, writing, listening, and speaking—is critical. That, plus mathematics, will teach you the basics you'll need for any job. Courses in science will broaden your understanding of construction methods and materials. You can also take technical education courses and join in activities such as SkillsUSA/VICA (Vocational Industrial Clubs of America).

Another way to learn about the industry is through a part-time, entry-level job in a construction operation. An entry-level position, such as carpenter's helper, requires little or no training or experience. **Fig. 1-2.** You learn on the job. However, many carpenters learn their trade through formal programs. These include certificate programs, apprenticeships, degree programs, and military training programs.

CERTIFICATES

Many community colleges offer certificate programs. These often involve work experience, coursework, and a certification test. Obtaining **certification**, or proof of skill, in any area of construction makes you more employable. Certification is available in several areas, such as building code enforcement, framing carpentry, and construction supervision.

Fig. 1-2. This carpenter's helper is learning essential information about basic carpentry techniques.

Before enrolling, carefully evaluate the program and the reputation of the school or operation. Find out what jobs are available for people with that particular certificate. Remember, certification programs usually focus on particular skills. Advancement opportunities may require that you obtain more formal education.

APPRENTICESHIPS

An **apprentice** works under the guidance of a skilled worker to learn a particular trade. In the construction industry, an apprentice carpenter learns under an experienced carpenter. An apprenticeship involves a combination of hands-on training and classroom instruction. Programs vary in length.

Professional organizations and industry associations often operate apprenticeship programs. These include the United Brotherhood of Carpenters and Joiners of America and the National Association of Home Builders.

ASSOCIATE'S DEGREES

Many colleges and universities offer two-year, or associate's, degrees in the construction field. They provide hands-on experience so you can apply the techniques you've learned in the classroom. Select a program that meets your needs. Evaluate the program, the school's credentials, and the employment rate for graduates before making a decision.

BACHELOR'S DEGREES

Four-year, or bachelor's degree, programs offer a well-rounded education. They begin with general courses in science and the humanities. They also provide in-depth training in one or more areas that prepares students for supervisory and management positions. General degrees in subjects such as marketing, business, and management provide the basis for learning a wide range of skills and information.

Students may be able to take part in a cooperative education or work experience program at the same time. Students are matched with a company whose business is related to their interests.

MILITARY TRAINING

The military offers training in many specialties in the construction trades. They include carpentry specialist, electrician, and plumber. Individuals with training in these areas leave the military with the skills needed to find good jobs in civilian life. **Fig. 1-3.**

Fig. 1-3. Carpentry skills learned in the military can provide a strong base for work in civilian life.

ON-THE-JOB TRAINING

On-the-job training is another option. Some construction managers use a method called *job rotation*. Entry-level workers are rotated through a series of jobs, which allows them to learn a variety of skills. This is similar to cross-training.

Internships are another form of on-the-job training. They combine classroom instruction and work experience. Many people benefit from finding a *mentor*—someone at work whom they can talk to who is willing to guide them.

SECTION 1.2

Check Your Knowledge

1. What is certification?
2. What is the difference between an associate's degree program and a bachelor's degree program?
3. Who is the primary teacher of an apprentice?
4. What is an internship?

On the Job

Locate information on construction-related certificate and apprenticeship programs in your area. Also locate information on the associate's and bachelor's degree programs available in your state. Then visit at least one military Web site to learn about education available. Create a chart that compares all the programs.

SECTION 1.3

Entrepreneurship

An **entrepreneur** (ahn-truh-pruh-NURR) is a person who creates and runs his or her own business. **Fig. 1-4.** Entrepreneurs take personal and financial risks. However, entrepreneurship can lead to great rewards.

Entrepreneurs in the construction industry usually begin by opening a small business, such as one devoted to remodeling. Small businesses are those with fewer than 100 employees. In the United States, more than 53 percent of the workforce works for small businesses.

Do the rewards of entrepreneurship outweigh the costs? **Table 1-A** compares the advantages and disadvantages. You decide!

TYPES OF BUSINESS OWNERSHIP

After you decide to open a business, you must choose the form of ownership. There are three common types of business ownership.

A business with only one owner is called a *sole proprietorship* (proh-PRI-uh-tor-ship). A *partnership* is two or more people who share the ownership of the business. Control and profits of the business are divided among partners according to a partnership agreement.

Fig. 1-4. An entrepreneur is responsible for making sure that all aspects of the job are on schedule.

Table 1-A.	Rewards and Risks for Entrepreneurs
Advantages	
Ownership. You decide what jobs to take. You're the boss.	
Job satisfaction. The rewards are all yours. You can take pride in your accomplishments.	
Earning potential. If you've got what it takes, you might make more working for yourself than you could working for someone else.	
Disadvantages	
Financial risk. If you invest your own money, you could lose it all and even go into debt.	
Competition. Others competing with you may have greater skills or experience.	
No guarantees. New businesses have a high rate of failure.	
Long hours. It is common for entrepreneurs to work evenings and weekends.	

A *corporation* is created when a state grants an individual or a group of people a charter with legal rights. The owners buy *shares*, or parts of the company. These owners, called *shareholders*, earn a profit based on the number of shares they own. If the business fails, the owners lose the money they have invested in the business.

DEVELOPING A BUSINESS PLAN

One of the main reasons start-up businesses fail is that a **business plan** was not followed. A business plan gives specific information about the business. All business plans should include a vision, goals, strategies, and a plan of action.

The entrepreneur's *vision* should include the goods and services the business will offer. It should indicate how much it will cost to start and run the business and the business location. It must also include the targeted customer base and an estimate of the profits.

After the vision is described, *goals* must be stated. These goals must be specific, concrete, and measurable. The plan must also give a timetable for meeting these goals.

A business plan should include *strategies* for meeting its goals. These strategies may include the type of marketing the business will use to attract customers. *Marketing* is the process of promoting and supplying goods and services to customers. It includes packaging, advertising, selling, and shipping.

A business also needs a plan of action. A *plan of action* helps a business reach its goals by identifying a specific course of action.

RULES AND REGULATIONS

The economic system in the United States is known as the free enterprise system. **Free enterprise** means that businesses or individuals may buy, sell, and set prices for goods and services. However, businesses are subject to some government controls. For example, the government passes laws that set safety standards and that affect prices and wages.

Government also has a voice in building codes and zoning requirements. *Zoning* divides land into areas used for different purposes. Only certain types of buildings may be built within these defined zones. **Fig. 1-5.** If you are in the construction business, it is important to understand the zoning process.

Fig. 1-5. This area is zoned for C-2 Commercial. Only C-2 Commercial buildings can be built here.

Before starting a construction business, you must obtain a *license* that grants you permission to open a business. Special *liability insurance* may also be necessary. This protects you from loss in case of damage.

Payment of taxes is another requirement. You must maintain accurate financial records of all income and spending. Many people use record keeping software to set up and store this information electronically.

SECTION 1.3

Check Your Knowledge

1. Name at least one advantage and one disadvantage of being an entrepreneur.
2. What is included in a business plan?
3. Define *free enterprise*.
4. What is zoning?

On the Job

All successful businesses fulfill a need. With a teammate, observe construction needs in your area. If you were to start a construction-related business, what kind would it be? Write a paragraph describing your vision for this business.

SECTION 1.4

Employability Skills

The basic skills you would need for a job in construction are the same skills you would need to find and keep a job in any field. They are the academic skills involving mathematics, communication, and science. Additional skills in interaction, thinking, a work ethic, leadership, and using resources are also important.

BASIC ACADEMIC SKILLS

Every employer expects a worker to have certain basic academic skills. These skills provide you with a strong foundation for finding and keeping employment and advancing on the job.

Mathematics

The ability to calculate, or work with numbers, is a basic part of every construction job. You'll need to be able to add, subtract, multiply, and divide to solve on-the-job problems. For example:

- Carpenters use mathematics skills to measure and cut lumber, plan stairways, and frame roofs. They often have to refer to tables, like **Table 1-B**, and make calculations based on them.
- Construction managers use mathematics skills to estimate lumber quantities, order lumber and other supplies, schedule deliveries, set up employee work rosters, complete payroll and tax forms, prepare bids, and estimate profits.
- All employees use basic mathematics skills to keep track of their work hours and pay rates.

Writing

Your ability to communicate in writing will help you find a job and perform well. Your writing will improve if you pay attention to your audience, your purpose, your style, and the form you use.

Table 1-B. Material Needed for Ceiling Joists

Ceiling Joists	Board Feet Needed for 100 Sq. Ft. of Surface Area	
Size of Joist	16″ OC	24″ OC
2x4	59	42
2x6	88	63
2x8	117	84
2x10	147	104

Before you write anything, picture the person or group who will be reading it. Tailor what you write to the reader's needs. Choose language that suits the purpose of your writing. Read what you have written and decide if you have achieved your purpose. Most business communications are intended for one of the following:

- To inform or give instructions.
- To request or ask for information, seek a decision, or call for action.
- To persuade the reader to agree or to pursue a course of action.
- To complain or to protest.

Style involves your choice of language and tone. Business communications are written in a direct style with a professional tone.

The two most common forms of business writing are memos and business letters. Use the spell check and grammar check features on your word processor to check your writing. Ask someone to proofread your letters before sending them. Be sure your ideas are easy to understand and flow in logical order.

Reading

Much of the information you receive comes through reading. In construction you'll use reading skills to:

- Evaluate building plans by reading schedules and measurements.
- Operate construction equipment by reading instruction manuals and safety precautions.
- Carry out general job duties by reading workplace policies and communications.

Science

Construction is really applied science. For example, all the tools you would use as a carpenter are based on the simple machines you learned about in science courses. Concrete hardens because of a chemical reaction. The frame of a house bears heavy loads based on principles of physics.

Your knowledge of scientific principles can help you on the job. It will help you understand why and how things work.

Practice the following steps to develop your reading skills:

1. Preview. Read the headings and subheads to get an overview.
2. Look for key points. This is called *skimming*.
3. Focus. Pay full attention to what you're reading.
4. Visualize. If the text is not illustrated, imagine what is being described. For example, if a roof is being discussed, try to picture it.
5. Check. Ask yourself how well you understand what you've read. If there are words you don't understand, look them up in a dictionary. Dictionaries that define construction terms are available.

INTERACTIVE SKILLS

The interactive skills include speaking and listening. They, too, are used for communication. They affect how you relate to coworkers and to customers.

Speaking

On a construction site, your safety often depends on making yourself understood. **Fig. 1-6.** How well you are understood depends on how effectively you speak. In speaking, pay attention to the following:

- Pronounce words clearly and correctly.
- Pronounce each syllable of a word.
- Speak at a medium pace.
- Regulate your volume.
- Don't use slang on the job.

When using the telephone, speak clearly at a moderate volume. Your performance on the telephone may be a customer's first or only impression of your business.

Did you know you can speak without saying a word? *Body language*, or how you physically respond, also "speaks" for you. The way you sit, stand, move your hands, look, and smile or frown sends a clear message to the listener(s).

Fig. 1-6. Your ability to get your ideas across to other team members depends on how well you speak.

Listening

The listening skills you need on the job are aimed at promoting understanding. Listening isn't just keeping quiet. It is *active listening*—the skill of paying attention to and interacting with the speaker. Don't let your feelings about the speaker get in the way. Even if you disagree with the speaker, listen. Wait until the speaker has finished before replying.

Practice key steps in the listening process:

1. Think about the purpose of the message. Why is the person speaking?
2. Signal your level of understanding with eye contact and body language, such as nodding your head.
3. Ask questions to help clarify points you do not understand. **Fig. 1-7.**
4. Listen for the speaker's inflections—tones that reveal feelings.
5. Look at the speaker's body language. What is he or she saying with posture, gestures, and facial expressions?
6. Take notes as needed about important points.
7. Listen for the conclusion of the message.

Fig. 1-7. There is more to active listening than simply being quiet.

THINKING SKILLS

On the job, you also need to think critically, make decisions, and solve problems.

- **Thinking critically.** Thinking critically is the ability to analyze and evaluate. It enables you to respond to a variety of situations.
- **Making decisions.** Making good decisions means carefully weighing all the evidence. It also means considering possible outcomes of your decisions.
- **Solving problems.** Problem solving involves clarifying the problem. Then you propose, test, and try out possible solutions.

A WORK ETHIC

Your **work ethic** (EH thick) is your personal commitment to doing your very best on the job. The qualities that mark a strong work ethic can be developed with practice. They include responsibility, flexibility, honesty, cooperation, and commitment.

Think of responsibility as responding to what a particular situation demands of you. Being responsible means showing up for work on time. It means becoming familiar with the tasks that make up your job and carrying them out correctly. It means being someone others can rely on. When you are responsible, you also accept the consequences of your choices and actions instead of blaming others.

Flexibility—the ability to adapt willingly to changing circumstances—can also be a part of your work ethic. Being flexible on the job means adjusting to changes without complaining. The more confident you are in your skills, the easier you'll find it to be flexible when circumstances demand it.

You practice honesty on the job when you're truthful and loyal in your words and actions. For example, if you make a mistake on the job, admit your mistake. Then find out how to prevent the same error in the future. Honesty also means not stealing from the company, either by taking materials or loafing on the job.

As a construction worker, you will often find yourself part of a team. Teamwork means cooperation. You'll practice teamwork on the job by supporting the efforts of your coworkers. **Fig. 1-8.** Teamwork also means trying to get along with everyone.

When you have a strong work ethic, you have a commitment to quality and excellence. In construction, a commitment to quality involves using quality materials and methods. When you're committed to quality, you strive to meet the highest standards.

LEADERSHIP

Employers look for employees with leadership skills, too. *Leadership* is the ability to inspire others to accomplish a common task. It also plays a part in making you a good citizen.

Fig. 1-8. Teamwork is important. It builds efficiency and encourages new ideas.

You don't need to wait until you're employed to develop leadership skills. Many organizations and programs have been designed to help. SkillsUSA-VICA is one example. **Fig. 1-9.** SkillsUSA-VICA is a national organization of high school and college students enrolled in training programs for technical, skilled, and service occupations. They partner students with industry professionals to provide the SkillsUSA Championships.

Construction students can participate in contests that test framing skills. Students are judged on their technical abilities.

Fig. 1-9. The programs sponsored by SkillsUSA-VICA help develop leadership skills.

USE OF RESOURCES

Resources are the raw materials with which you do your work. Making the best use of resources is also a skill. The key resources are:

- Time. You use time effectively when you complete tasks quickly and accurately. You can also learn to *prioritize*, or put tasks in order of importance. Simplifying tasks is another way to use time well.
- Energy. Use personal energy resources effectively by getting the right amount of rest.
- Money. If you're responsible for making purchases, look for good value for the money. If you're receiving money in payment, be honest.
- Materials and equipment. The materials, equipment, and tools associated with your job are resources. Use them properly and with safety in mind. Immediately report any problems with or damage to equipment and supplies. Don't waste materials.
- People. You, too, are a resource. Your employer depends on your labor to accomplish many tasks.
- Information. Information comes in many forms. It is in the building plans you follow or the safety warning on a nailer. **Fig. 1-10.**

Information Resources

On the job, you will acquire, use, and share information. Information comes from many sources. Your boss, your coworkers, a drawing, an instruction manual, and the Internet all provide information.

Look for clues to tell the difference between useful information and idle chatter or false statements. Is it from a reliable source? What evidence is given? Does it seem to make sense? Be careful when using information from the Internet. Some Web sites contain misleading information. Reliable information comes from known sources, such as government agencies or established businesses.

Use information wisely. If you've been asked to frame a wall, use the information on the plans to do it properly. Use hints from coworkers to make the job go faster or more easily. Follow the instructions your boss has given you.

Share information. Don't keep important information to yourself. If you see a problem, tell your supervisor. If you have a suggestion for doing a better job, share it.

Fig. 1-10. Be sure to read the instruction manual for any tool you will be using.

Technology Resources

Technology has brought many improvements to construction. Surveyors now use lasers to lay out a building site. Carpenters use nailers to speed up framing. Supervisors access building plans on their computers.

Stay informed about new technologies. Ask your supervisor if you can be trained to use those that might be helpful. An up-to-date employee is valuable.

SECTION 1.4

Check Your Knowledge

1. What basic academic skills are needed for any job?
2. What qualities contribute to developing a strong work ethic?
3. List the key resources used on the job.
4. How can technology resources help your career?

On the Job

Suppose you have been asked to lead a team that will frame a house. Write a short help-wanted ad, describing the qualities you want in team members.

SECTION 1.5

Seeking Employment

Finding a job means gathering information, applying, going to an interview, and responding to the offer.

GATHERING INFORMATION

Many first-time job seekers think that classified ads are the only place to search for a job. Construction jobs are frequently listed in the newspaper. However, other helpful resources are also available.

Networking

If you've ever followed up on a job tip received from a family member, you have practiced networking. **Networking** means making use of all your personal connections to achieve your career goals. **Fig. 1-11.** When you receive job information from people you know, you can be informed and confident. In addition to family members, you can also network with friends and classmates, teachers and mentors, employers and coworkers, and school and professional organizations.

When you network, be courteous. Don't pressure people for information. Every reference you receive through networking is a personal gift. Treat it with respect. Follow up on job leads in a responsible manner. Be on time for interviews. Return phone calls. Always present yourself professionally. Your grooming, communication skills, and behavior reflect not only on you, but

Fig. 1-11. Networking can provide strong advantages in a job search.

also on the person who recommended you. Remember to return the favor. When you become aware of job information, share it with the members of your network.

Trade Publications

Extend your job search resources by reading construction trade publications. These professional magazines and newsletters are available by subscription. Most of them list job opportunities. Some of these publications can be found in public libraries or on the Internet.

Employment Agencies

There may be times when it's best to use an employment agency to assist in your job search. *Employment agencies* put employers in touch with potential employees. Most employment agencies charge for their services.

The Internet

Thousands of employment resources are available on the Internet. Search engines often list jobs by category. Also, many companies include job opportunities on their own Web sites. You can network, contact professional organizations, read online versions of trade publications, and register with online employment agencies.

APPLYING FOR THE JOB

If you have identified several good leads, rank the jobs in order of preference. Apply for the job you want most first.

Some employers may ask you to begin with a telephone call. Some will ask you to contact them by mail, sending a letter of application and a résumé. A **résumé** is a summary of your career objectives, work experience, job qualifications, education, and training. Others will ask you to come in and fill out an application.

Before you are hired you will be invited to a job interview. Job *interviews* are formal meetings between you and your potential employer. It is important to perform each step of the job application process in a professional manner.

Responding by Telephone

Your job leads may come from listings that give phone numbers and ask you to call for more information. **Fig. 1-12.** When making a phone call, follow these guidelines:

- Tell the person who answers the phone that you are calling in response to a job opening. He or she will direct your call to the contact person.
- When you're connected to the contact person, give your name and the name of the job you are interested in. If you were referred by someone, mention that person's name.
- The contact person will identify the next steps in the application process. These may include asking you to send a letter of application and a résumé. The contact person may offer to send you a job application or set up an appointment for an interview.
- Write down everything you are told to do. Repeat it to the contact person to make sure you understood the steps.
- Ask any questions you may have about the application process. Answer any questions the contact person asks you.
- Thank the contact person for his or her time.

Fig. 1-12. Some information relating to job leads can be obtained by telephoning. Be sure to make careful notes.

Responding in Writing

Write a letter of request when asking for an application form or requesting an interview. Include a brief summary of your education, experience, and other qualifications in the letter. Sign your letter in black ink. Before mailing it, double-check the letter, the contact name, address, and postage.

Preparing Your Résumé

Your résumé gives an employer information about your background. Include work experience, skills, education, and training that will convince an employer that you're the best candidate for the job. Always be truthful. If you are mailing your résumé, include a cover letter. This letter should introduce you to your prospective employer without repeating your résumé.

Here are some guidelines for résumés:

- Keep your résumé brief.
- Include accurate contact information.
- Include your career objective.
- Stress relevant work experience, skills, education, and training.
- If you are responding online, use keywords that describe your work experience. A *keyword* is a significant word that makes it easier for employers to search for relevant information. If your résumé contains a keyword such as *carpentry* or *framing*, employers with construction opportunities will be more likely to call up your résumé in an electronic search.
- Use correct spelling and grammar.
- Present your résumé on quality paper.
- Avoid using decorative graphics and pictures.

Filling Out an Application

You will be asked to complete a job application form at some point during the job application process. Job application forms vary, but they all ask for the same basic information.

Remember to make a good impression from the beginning. Don't enter a potential workplace, even to ask for an application, unless your clothing is neat and appropriate and you're clean and well groomed.

When completing an application:

- Print neatly, using blue or black ink. Use cursive handwriting for your signature only.
- Read the instructions for completing each blank before responding. Try not to make errors. If you need to correct what you have written, draw a line through it.
- Carry important information with you. This includes your Social Security number; driver's license number; and the names, addresses, and phone numbers of previous employers. (If you don't have a driver's license yet, work toward getting one.)
- Don't leave any part of the application form blank unless you're asked to do so. If a question doesn't apply, write *NA*—for *not applicable*—in the space provided.
- Always tell the truth on an application. Submitting false information is illegal.

THE INTERVIEW PROCESS

If the employer is interested in you, you will be asked to come in for a job interview. During this important face-to-face meeting, you'll have a chance to convince an employer that you're the right person for the job. You will be evaluated by your appearance, attitude, and answers to the employer's questions.

Before the Interview

The interview process begins when an employer arranges an appointment. Write down the date, time, and place of the interview. Ask for directions if necessary.

The more you know about the employer and the job, the better you'll do in the interview. Check community business publications, local newspapers, Internet directories, and professional organizations. Try to find out the size of the business, its profitability, and its plans for future growth. Make notes about what you learn. Next, think about your answers to possible questions.

Your prospective employer's first impression of you will be based on your appearance. Your grooming habits can make or break a job interview. Choose appropriate clothing that fits properly and is clean, pressed, and in good condition. You, too, should be clean, your hair well trimmed and conservatively styled, and your fingernails clean and neatly trimmed.

Allow plenty of time to locate your destination. It is best to arrive a few minutes early. As you introduce yourself to anyone before meeting with the interviewer, be polite and respectful.

Common Questions Asked by Interviewers:

- Why would you like to work for this company?
- What do you want to be doing in five years?
- What are your qualifications for this job?
- What are your strengths and weaknesses?
- Why did you leave your last job?
- Tell me about a challenge you met or a problem you solved in school or on the job.
- What do you enjoy doing in your spare time?
- Have you ever been a member of a team or club? What did you like best and least about that experience?
- What questions do you have about the job or this company?
- Why should we hire you?

During the Interview

You'll do well in the interview if you are prepared, positive, and relaxed. The interviewer will introduce himself or herself. Introduce yourself in return, and offer your hand for a firm, confident handshake. Remain standing until the interviewer asks you to be seated. He or she will probably ask a few simple questions to help you feel more at ease. Smiling never hurts.

Throughout the interview, maintain eye contact with the interviewer. Eye contact helps show that you are interested in what the interviewer is saying. When you reply, use correct grammar and speak clearly. The interviewer will ask you questions designed to determine if you are the person needed for the job. Do not interrupt the interviewer. If you don't understand a question or don't know the answer, say so politely. Don't hesitate to ask the interviewer about the nature of the job, your responsibilities, and the work environment. Save questions about pay and benefits, such as vacation time, for the end of the interview.

When the interview ends, thank the interviewer for his or her time. **Fig. 1-13.** Shake hands as you leave. The interviewer will signal the end of the interview in one of the following ways:

- The interviewer may tell you that you will be contacted later. If the interviewer does not specify a time, politely ask, "When may I expect to hear from you?"
- You may be asked to contact the employer later. Note the telephone number, the preferred time to call, and the contact person.
- You may be offered the job. You may be asked to decide right away whether you'll take the job. If you are unsure, ask the interviewer if you may think about the offer. If this option is offered, be sure to follow up by responding promptly.
- You may be turned down for the job. Don't be discouraged. The interviewer is under no obligation to tell you why you are not being offered the job. Accept the decision gracefully.

Fig. 1-13. In leaving an interview, remember that you want to make a good impression.

After the Interview

After each job interview, you have several responsibilities. The next day, send the interviewer a letter thanking him or her for the interview. Do this even if you have been turned down for the job. Be sure the correct address and the correct postage are on the envelope.

If you have been asked to contact the employer, do so at the specified time. Send or deliver any materials or information, such as references, you have agreed to supply. If the employer has promised to contact you, wait the specified amount of time. If this time passes, telephone the employer and politely ask about the status of your application. You may be asked to go through a second interview.

As soon as possible after the interview, go over the session in your mind. Think about the impression you made. Make notes on anything you could do to improve. Note any key information, such as employer expectations and job responsibilities. List any questions you still have about the job.

RESPONDING TO A JOB OFFER

When you receive an offer of employment, you have three options. First, you can accept the offer. The employer will then give you information on when you can begin work. You may be asked to attend an employee orientation or a training session. You will be given specific details on pay, schedules, and other factors.

Second, you can ask for time to consider the offer. This is the time to bring up any unanswered questions that might affect your decision. Come to an agreement on when you will notify the employer of your decision. Do not be late.

Third, you can turn down the job offer. Perhaps the job is not right for you. You may have been offered a better job in the meantime. Whatever the case, if you do not intend to take the job, say so. You don't need to give reasons. Simply say, "Thank you for considering me, but I have decided not to take the job."

SECTION 1.5 Check Your Knowledge

1. What is a job interview?
2. List five sources for job leads.
3. What is the purpose of a résumé?
4. When should you send the interview thank-you letter?

On the Job

Write a résumé and cover letter in response to a job ad from the newspaper or the Internet. Then write a thank-you letter for an interview.

SECTION 1.6 On the Job

When you accept a job, you enter into a relationship in which both parties have rights and responsibilities. In this section, you will learn about your rights as an employee and your responsibilities to your employer. You will become familiar with wages, taxes, and benefits. You will practice skills for getting along with others on the job. You'll also identify some of the qualities required for advancement.

YOUR RESPONSIBILITIES

Your employer will explain company rules and expectations when you begin your job. Your main responsibility is to do the best job possible. Here are some general guidelines:

- Use time responsibly. Be on time for work. Return promptly from authorized breaks and meal periods. Stay at work for your full shift, or specified hours of employment. Keep busy on the job. **Fig. 1-14.** Don't waste time socializing with coworkers. Avoid using company time or resources for personal business.

Fig. 1-14. When on the job, pay attention to the work at hand.

- Respect the rules. Learn and follow your employer's rules and policies. You'll probably be given an employee handbook. If you are in doubt about a company policy, ask your supervisor. Avoid drug and alcohol use, especially on the job.
- Work safely. Familiarize yourself with the safety requirements of your job. Learn how to operate and maintain equipment safely. Report any unsafe conditions or practices to your supervisor immediately.
- Earn your pay. Complete each task you are assigned to the best of your ability. Keep your work area neat and well organized. Respect the value of the equipment and materials you work with. Use company resources responsibly.

Ethical Behavior

Your employer has the right to expect ethical behavior from you. Your **ethics** are your inner guidelines for telling right from wrong. Ethical behavior consists of doing what is right. Much of the time, it's easy to recognize the ethical course of action. Some choices, however, are more difficult. When two choices appear equally right or equally wrong, ask yourself the following questions:

- Does the choice comply with the law?
- Is the choice fair to those involved?
- Does the choice harm anyone?
- Has the choice been communicated honestly?
- Can I live with the choice without embarrassment or guilt?

YOUR EMPLOYER'S RESPONSIBILITIES

Your employer has responsibilities to you, too. Your employer must make sure that you are paid fairly for your work. You must also be given what you need to do your job. This often includes on-the-job training. **Fig. 1-15.** Your employer must also provide safe working conditions and make sure you're treated fairly.

Safe Working Conditions

Federal, state, and local regulations require your employer to provide you with safe working conditions. This includes:

- Eliminating recognized health and safety hazards. Injury prevention is part of this responsibility. For example, employers have supported research into *repetitive stress injuries.* These are ailments that develop among workers who perform the same motions repeatedly. They can affect a person's employability.

Fig. 1-15. On-the-job training (OJT) provides first-hand experience in learning important skills.

- Providing equipment and materials necessary to do the job safely.
- Informing you when conditions or materials pose dangers to health and safety.
- Maintaining records of job-related illnesses and injuries.
- Complying with environmental protection policies for safely disposing of waste materials.
- Contributing to workers' compensation. If you're injured on the job and can't work, your employer has a legal responsibility to provide financial help. This is called *workers' compensation* and it covers medical expenses and lost wages.

Fair Labor Practices

Your employer has a legal responsibility to protect you from unfair treatment on the job. In the United States, labor laws protect the following rights of employees:

- To have an equal opportunity to obtain and keep employment.
- To be paid a fair wage.
- To be considered fairly for promotion.
- To be protected in times of personal and economic change.

Employers must also pay their employees at least the federal *minimum wage.* This is the lowest hourly amount a worker can earn. Employers must give employees who work overtime extra pay or time off. This time off is called *compensatory time.*

American workers are guaranteed the right to join a *labor union*, an organization of workers in a similar field. Labor unions act as the voice of their members in *collective bargaining*. Bargaining is for working conditions, contracts, and other job benefits.

Employers must also protect their employees from *discrimination*—unfair treatment based on age, gender, race, ethnicity, religion, physical appearance, disability, or other factors. For example, *sexual harassment*, any unwelcome behavior of a sexual nature, is prohibited in the workplace. It should be reported to a supervisor.

WAGES AND BENEFITS

When you agree to take a job, you trade your skills and efforts for pay. Your pay is determined by a number of factors. These include your level of experience, the difficulty of the work, and the number of people competing for the same job. Pay periods differ from employer to employer. Some employers pay weekly, others every two weeks, still others once a month.

Your employer will pay you in one of two ways. If you earn an *hourly wage*, you are paid a certain amount for each hour you work. Your pay varies depending on how many hours you work all together. If you receive a *salary*, your employer pays you a set amount of money per year, regardless of the hours worked. This amount is divided up and paid at regular intervals.

Deductions

The amount of money you receive before deductions is known as your *gross pay*. The amount of money you actually receive is called your *net pay*, or *take-home pay*. *Deductions* are the amounts withheld from your gross pay for taxes, insurance, and other fees. Ask your employer to explain the deductions that will be taken from your pay. Some common deductions are shown in **Fig. 1-16**.

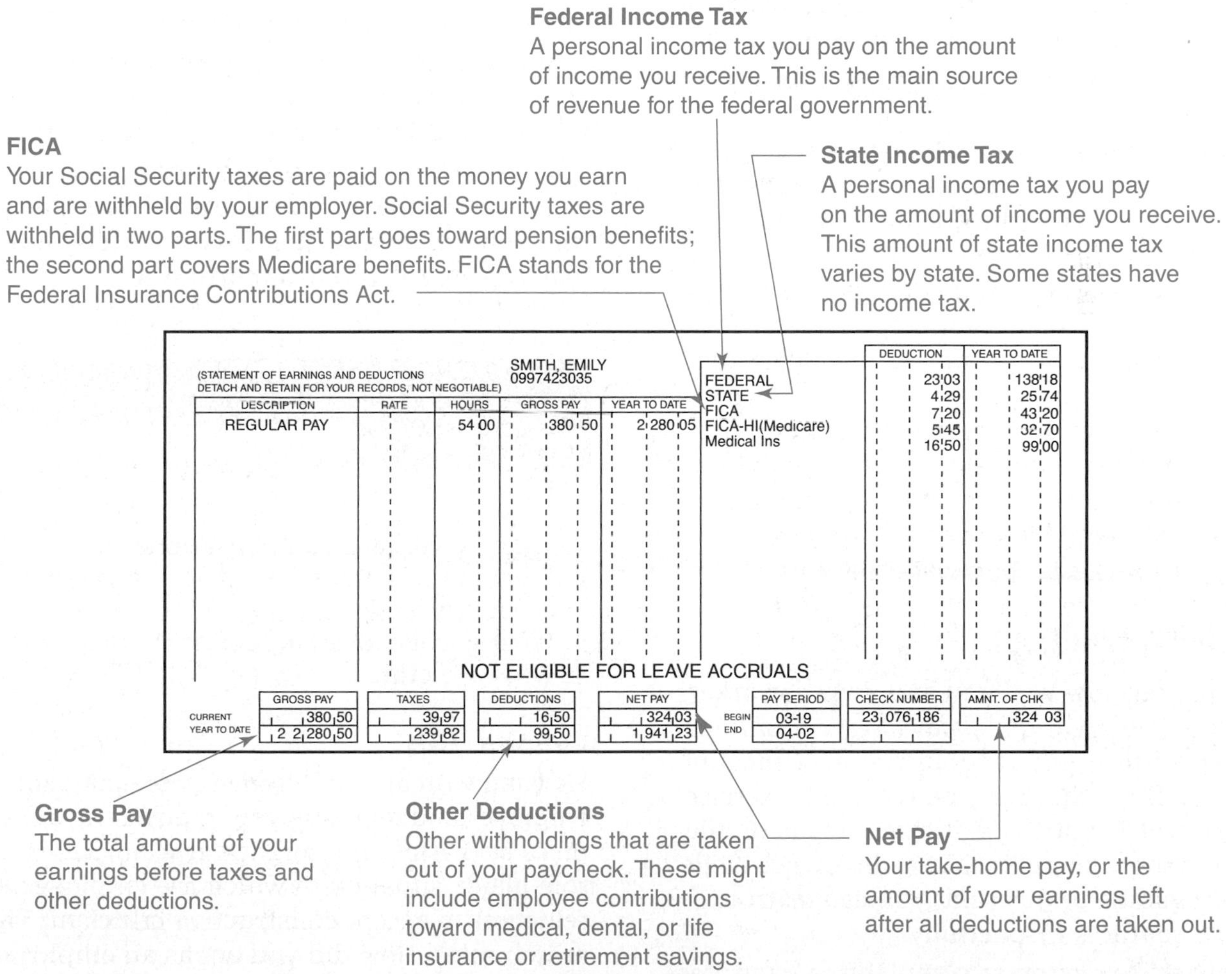

Federal Income Tax
A personal income tax you pay on the amount of income you receive. This is the main source of revenue for the federal government.

FICA
Your Social Security taxes are paid on the money you earn and are withheld by your employer. Social Security taxes are withheld in two parts. The first part goes toward pension benefits; the second part covers Medicare benefits. FICA stands for the Federal Insurance Contributions Act.

State Income Tax
A personal income tax you pay on the amount of income you receive. This amount of state income tax varies by state. Some states have no income tax.

(STATEMENT OF EARNINGS AND DEDUCTIONS DETACH AND RETAIN FOR YOUR RECORDS, NOT NEGOTIABLE)
SMITH, EMILY
0997423035

DESCRIPTION	RATE	HOURS	GROSS PAY	YEAR TO DATE
REGULAR PAY		54 00	380 50	2 280 05

	DEDUCTION	YEAR TO DATE
FEDERAL	23 03	138 18
STATE	4 29	25 74
FICA	7 20	43 20
FICA-HI(Medicare)	5 45	32 70
Medical Ins	16 50	99 00

NOT ELIGIBLE FOR LEAVE ACCRUALS

	GROSS PAY	TAXES	DEDUCTIONS	NET PAY
CURRENT	380 50	39 97	16 50	324 03
YEAR TO DATE	2 2 280 50	239 82	99 50	1 941 23

	PAY PERIOD	CHECK NUMBER	AMNT. OF CHK
BEGIN	03-19	23 076 186	324 03
END	04-02		

Gross Pay
The total amount of your earnings before taxes and other deductions.

Other Deductions
Other withholdings that are taken out of your paycheck. These might include employee contributions toward medical, dental, or life insurance or retirement savings.

Net Pay
Your take-home pay, or the amount of your earnings left after all deductions are taken out.

Fig. 1-16. A pay stub shows you the amount of each deduction taken from your gross pay.

Benefits

In addition to your salary, your employer may offer benefits. Among the possible benefits are:

- Health and accident insurance.
- Paid vacation days.
- Life insurance.
- Disability insurance, which helps pay your expenses if you become disabled and can no longer work.
- Tuition reimbursement, or full or partial repayment of tuition and fees you pay for education directly related to your career.
- Savings and investment plans, such as a 401K, to help you save money for retirement.

Be sure to figure in any benefits when calculating your job compensation. A high wage may make up for few benefits. A good range of benefits, on the other hand, can make up for a lower wage.

COWORKERS AND CUSTOMERS

When you take a job, you also enter into a relationship with your coworkers and customers. Every person is an individual, with his or her own personality traits, strengths, and weaknesses. You will need to get along and work together. You can do this if you:

- **Keep a positive attitude.** An upbeat, positive outlook contributes to team spirit. Complaining can bring the whole team down and affect your job performance.
- **Respect yourself.** You demonstrate self-respect when you accept responsibility for your actions, learn from your mistakes, and take care of your appearance.
- **Respect others.** Disrespectful actions can result in unemployment. Learn to put yourself in another's place. This will help you understand the people you meet at work. Also, show respect for the property of others.

Resolving Conflicts

No matter how well you and your coworkers get along, you will not always agree. Conflicts are part of team interaction. You may encounter some conflicts that can't be resolved. Exercise self-control. If you are criticized, focus on the problem, not the personalities involved. While conflict can be unpleasant, you can learn to resolve conflicts respectfully.

Respond to customer complaints in a professional manner. Don't take them personally. If you can't solve the problem yourself, ask your supervisor to step in.

ADVANCING ON THE JOB

Advancement may involve a promotion. It may also mean staying at the same job level but with more or different responsibilities at a higher rate of pay.

Certain behavior will help you advance. For example, taking on new tasks and levels of responsibility shows initiative (ih-NIH-shuh-tihv). Workers with initiative don't wait to be told what to do next. Continuing your education or training through formal classes, workshops, or independent study will also help. This shows a desire to learn.

LEAVING THE JOB

At some point you may seek a new job. Perhaps work is slow and you have been laid off. Perhaps you think you'd be happier with a different employer. In either case, behave in a professional way when you leave.

If leaving is your choice, give your employer at least two weeks' notice. Thank your employer for the opportunities you have been given.

If there were conflicts, don't criticize your employer during job interviews. If you are asked why you are leaving, just say something like, "I'm looking for better opportunities."

SECTION 1.6

Check Your Knowledge

1. What is worker's compensation?
2. What is the difference between a salary and an hourly wage?
3. What is collective bargaining?
4. What are ethics?

On the Job

Working with another student, role-play an employer and an employee in different workplace scenarios. You might, for example, role-play a situation in which the employee is reluctant to accept constructive criticism. Then switch roles. How did you act as an employee? How did you act differently as an employer?

Chapter 1

Review

Section Summaries

1.1 Construction jobs fall into craft, technical, and professional categories. Customer needs influence construction trends.

1.2 Education for a construction career includes certificate programs, apprenticeships, associate's and bachelor's degree programs, military programs, and on-the-job training.

1.3 An entrepreneur creates and runs his or her own business. Entrepreneurs need a business plan.

1.4 A person's employability skills include academic, interactive, and thinking skills; a work ethic; leadership skills; and use of resources.

1.5 Finding a job means gathering information, applying, going to an interview, and responding to the offer. The application form and résumé provide information about the job seeker.

1.6 Both employers and employees have responsibilities on the job.

Review Questions

1. In what category of construction specialists do carpenters belong?
2. What is the difference between commercial and residential buildings?
3. What is an apprenticeship?
4. What is job rotation?
5. What is a shareholder?
6. Why do you think a business plan would be important to an entrepreneur?
7. A business communication usually has at least one of four main purposes. What are they?
8. Name the basic steps in obtaining a job.
9. List the four general ways a worker can meet his or her responsibilities to an employer.
10. What is the difference between gross pay and net pay?

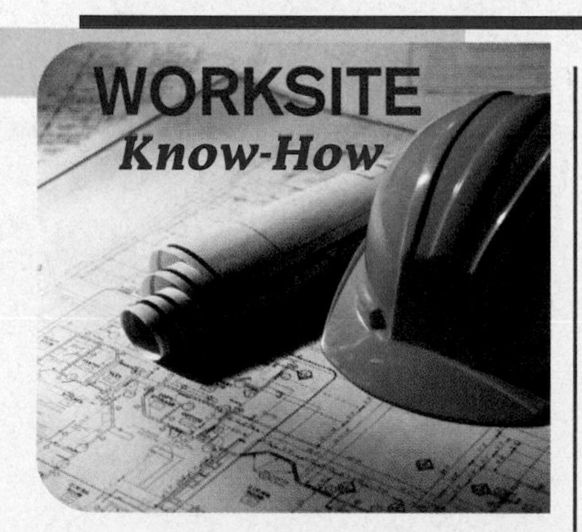

Giving a Technical Presentation Your employer may ask you to present technical information to new employees or even a customer. First, evaluate your audience. How much do they already know? Next, prepare an outline of the material you want to cover. If you're explaining a process, start with the first step and move in order through to the last. Give background information or an overview first. Your audience will then know where the rest of the information fits. If possible, give a demonstration. Then summarize what you've said. When you're finished, ask for questions. You also may be asked to speak *extemporaneously.* This means you will have no time to prepare. However, the same principles apply.

Chapter 2

Building Codes and Planning

Objectives

After reading this chapter, you'll be able to:

- Identify the major model building codes used in the United States.
- List the steps in planning to build a house.
- Name three sources of house plans.
- Explain how financing for construction is obtained.

Terms

building code
building permit
construction loan
floor plan
International Residential Code (IRC)
model building code
mortgage
setback distance
stock plan

A house is a complex assembly of materials that must fit together with precision. Complicated systems distribute power and water and maintain the comfort of the people who live there. Unless construction is planned carefully, the house will not be safe, durable, functional, or comfortable.

House designers and builders must know about regulations that affect the design of a house. Other factors, such as climate, local architectural styles, and the client's budget, also affect house design.

SECTION 2.1

Building Codes

A **building code** is a set of regulations that governs the details of construction. Its purpose is to ensure that buildings are structurally sound and safe from fire and health hazards. Most locations have one or more building codes. The only exceptions are some rural areas.

Building codes establish minimum standards of quality and safety. A builder can construct a house that is better than what the code requires. Many builders who have a reputation for high-quality work do this. However, a builder may not construct a house that falls short of the code requirements. During construction, a building inspector visits the project at various times to ensure that the building codes are being followed.

MODEL BUILDING CODES

Traditionally, local building codes have been based on model building codes. A **model building code** is a set of regulations developed by an independent organization on which local governments can base their own building codes. There are three major model building codes. They cover both residential and commercial construction. They set minimum standards for both residential and commercial construction. The *National Building Code* is published by the Building Officials and Code Administrators International (BOCA). The *Standard Building Code* is published by the Southern Building Code Congress International (SBCCI). The *Uniform Building Code* is published by the International Conference of Building Officials (ICBO). The regions of the United States covered by each code are shown in **Fig. 2-1**. Canada, too,

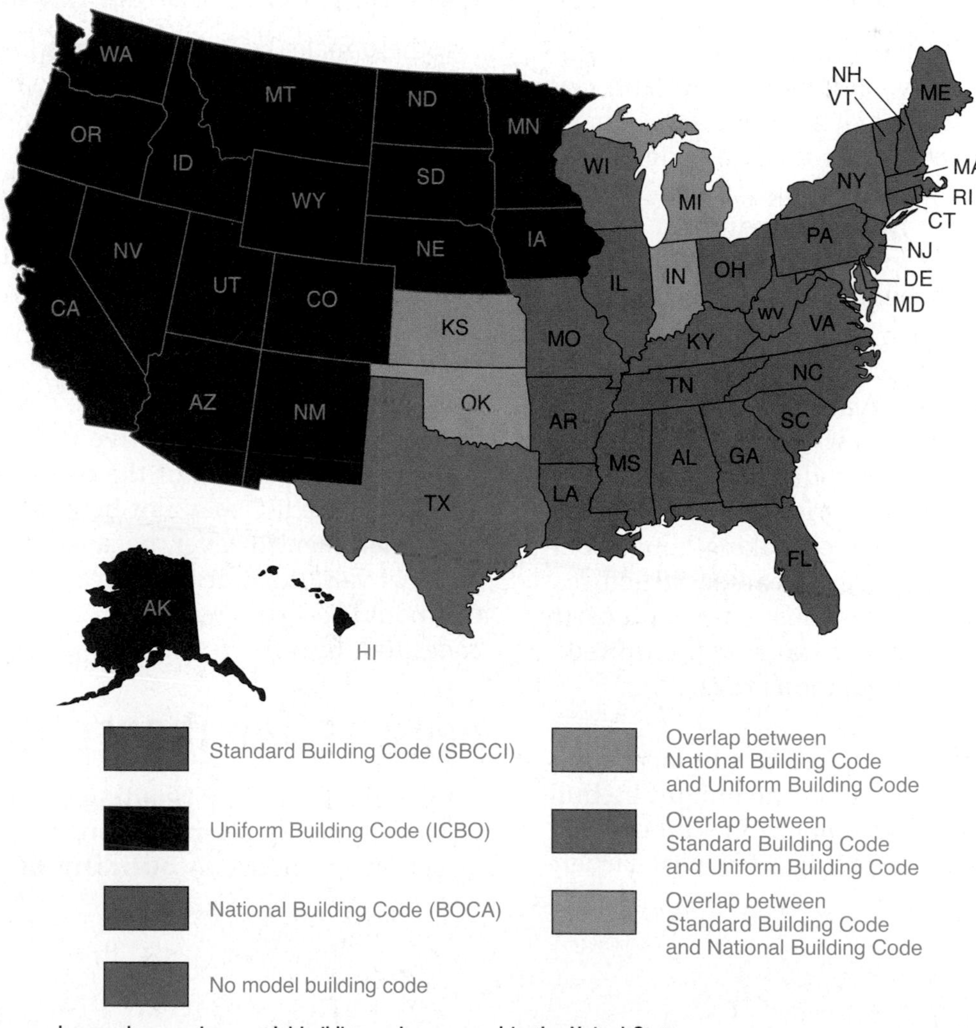

Fig. 2-1. This map shows where various model building codes are used in the United States.

has a number of model codes, including the *National Building Code of Canada.*

The Americans with Disabilities Act (ADA) and the Fair Housing Act contain provisions regarding new construction. Public buildings and certain multi-family dwellings must comply with these provisions to ensure that the building is accessible to people who have disabilities. Model building codes include standards for meeting these provisions.

Work done to install such utilities as electricity and plumbing is also covered by codes. The *National Electrical Code* and the *Uniform Plumbing Code* are two examples.

Building codes cover standard types of construction. However, an architect or builder may decide to use unusual materials and techniques. For example, it is possible to build a house entirely out of concrete. **Fig. 2-2.** The builder or designer must then prove to local officials that the house would meet or exceed standard requirements and that it would be safe.

Fig. 2-2. A concrete home is an example of an alternate form of construction.

Modifying Codes

The building department, which is a part of the town, city, county, or state government, may adopt all the provisions of a model code. If so, it does not need to develop its own code. Sometimes, however, it will adopt only those parts of the model code that fit local conditions. Additional regulations applying to the local area are developed and attached.

For example, some cities in the western United States have developed regulations that encourage water conservation. These are stricter than regulations in areas where lack of water is not a problem. Likewise, codes for areas along the coastlines of Texas, Florida, and other states exposed to hurricanes cover making houses better able to withstand severe weather. Structures in earthquake-prone areas must withstand earthquakes. The northernmost states in the United States have detailed regulations regarding energy conservation.

Because codes are modified to suit local conditions, a house in South Carolina might be built to a different code than a house in Minnesota. This is generally not a problem for local carpenters and builders. They learn what is required during their training. However, if a carpenter or builder moves to another region, he or she must learn how the codes differ. Large companies that handle construction in several different areas must also adapt to suit the local codes.

The International Residential Code

To help make building codes more uniform, several of the model code organizations have jointly produced the *International Residential Code for One- and Two-Family Dwellings.* The **International Residential Code (IRC)** is designed to make up for regional variations. **Fig. 2-3.** It covers detached one- and two-family dwellings and townhouses that are no more than three stories high. It was first published in January, 2000.

Most building departments review and update their codes every three to five years. Some may still choose to use one of the older model codes. Therefore, the IRC may not be widely adopted for some time. However, because it minimizes regional variations, it is referred to throughout this book. *For your own work, always follow the codes that have been adopted in your area.*

PERMITS AND INSPECTIONS

In areas covered by building codes, you must obtain a building permit before beginning construction of a house. A **building permit** is a

PROTECTION AGAINST TERMITES

R324.4 FOAM PLASTIC PROTECTION. In areas where the probability of termite infestation is "very heavy" as indicated in figure R301.2(6), extruded and expanded polystyrene, polyisocyanurate and other foam plastics shall not be installed on the exterior face or under interior or exterior foundation walls or slab foundations located below grade. The clearance between foam plastics installed above grade and exposed earth shall be at least 6 inches (152 mm).

EXCEPTIONS:

1. Buildings where the structural members of walls, floors, cellings, and roofs are entirely of noncombustible materials or pressure preservatively treated wood.
2. When in addition to the requirements of R324.1, an approved method of protecting the foam plastic and structure from subterranean termite damage is provided.
3. On the interior side of the basement walls.

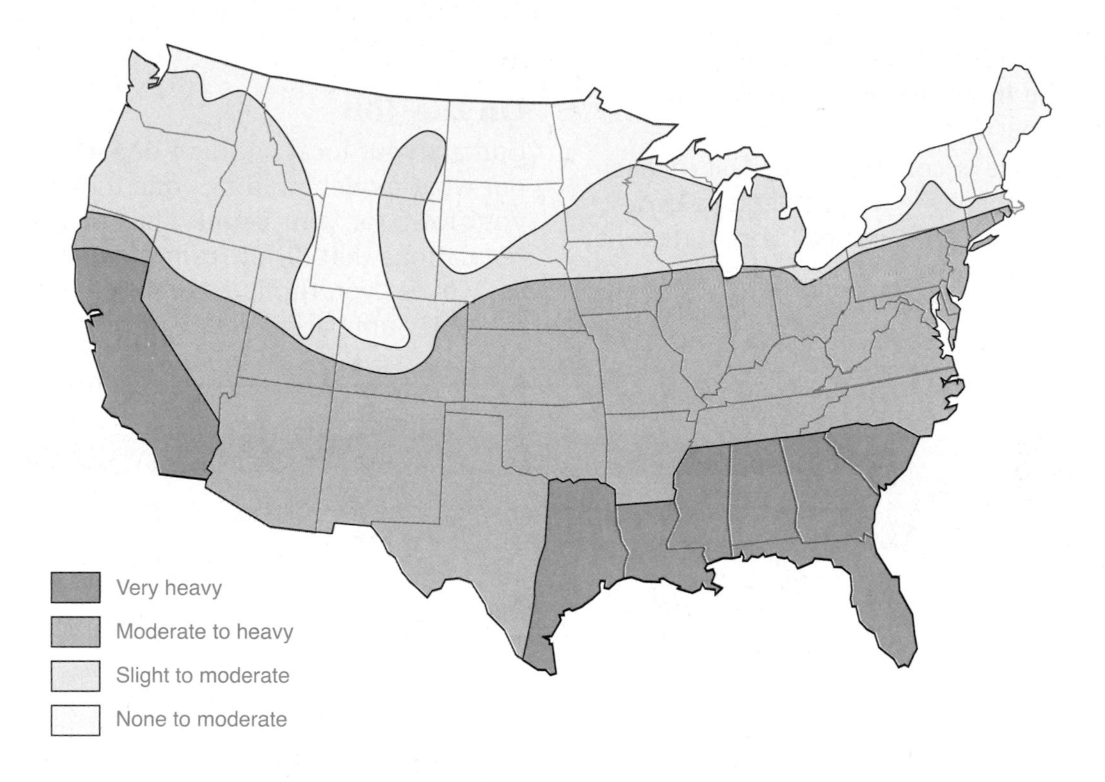

Note: Lines defining areas are approximate only. Local conditions may be more or less severe than indicated by the region classification.

Fig. 2-3. The IRC addresses regional variations. In this example, it covers the need for termite control.

formal, printed authorization for the builder to begin construction. To obtain one, the builder must submit a full set of working drawings, called *plans*, to the local building department. Plans show exactly how a house will be built (see Chapter 3, "Reading and Drawing Plans"). Small remodeling projects may not require a permit, but construction of a new house or an addition almost always does. Check with your local building department for permit requirements. There can be substantial penalties for building without a building permit.

The building department examines the plans to ensure that they meet local codes. If they do, the builder is issued a permit, which must be posted on the building site throughout construction. The cost of a building permit is usually based on the estimated cost of construction.

At key points during construction, a city or county building inspector will visit the job site to examine the work. The inspections vary from town to town. They often include an examination of footing trenches and foundation formwork, framing, wiring, plumbing, and insulation. The builder must contact the building department to schedule an inspection when each part of the job is complete, but before it is covered by other work. The inspector can require that work be done over if it does not meet building codes. If the work has passed inspection, the inspector will initial or "sign off" on the paperwork.

When the house is complete, one last inspection is made. If there are no problems, a *certificate of occupancy* (CO) is issued. This states that the house is ready to live in.

SECTION 2.1

Check Your Knowledge

1. What is a building code, and what is its purpose?
2. What is a model building code?
3. What is a building permit, and what must you provide to apply for one?
4. What document indicates that a house is ready to live in?

On the Job

Contact your local building department to find out what model building code they follow. Ask if your town (or your county) has developed any regulations that differ from those in this code. If so, why do you think different codes were needed? Summarize your findings in a short paper.

SECTION 2.2

Planning to Build

A great deal of planning must occur before a house can be designed and built. **Fig. 2-4.** The process involves more than just deciding what the house will look like. The home has to fit the family's needs, both now and in the future. How construction will be paid for must also be determined.

Sometimes a builder constructs a house before there is a buyer. Such a house is called a *spec house.*

LOT OR HOUSE SELECTION

When it comes to choosing a lot to build on or an existing house to purchase, the following factors are important to consider.

- *Cost.* Generally, not more than 25 percent of gross monthly income should be spent for housing, including mortgage payments, insurance, property taxes, utilities, and repairs. However, some families want to spend more on housing, expecting that their income will rise. Others find that it is wise to spend less because they have other large expenses.

Fig. 2-4. Careful planning is needed to ensure that a building project is completed on time and on budget.

- *Location.* Are jobs, schools, community services, and recreational facilities nearby? **Fig. 2-5.** Is the neighborhood likely to remain fairly stable, or will it change as the surrounding area grows? Are utilities such as water, sewer service, and electricity available?
- *Lot shape and contour.* Is the lot wide enough and deep enough for the desired house? Does it have unusual contours or other features that would make construction difficult or expensive? **Fig. 2-6.** Will neighboring houses be so close that privacy will be a problem?
- *Special conditions.* For example, is the lot on a flood plain? Were there underground mines in the area? Was there industrial contamination?
- *Zoning restrictions.* Most communities are divided into zones in which certain types of buildings are encouraged or restricted. Common zones are those for single-family dwellings, apartments and condominiums, commercial buildings, and industrial buildings. Many people prefer to live in a neighborhood that does not include commercial or industrial buildings.
- *Deed restrictions.* Within any zone there may be deed restrictions on an individual lot. *Deed restrictions* might specify such things as the minimum-size house that can be built on the lot, requirements for certain architectural features, or setback distances. A **setback distance** is the minimum distance allowed from the house to adjacent features, such as other houses or the street. For example, a house near a stream might have to be located a certain distance above flood levels. A house being built in a historic area might be limited to the use of certain exterior colors or roofing materials.

Fig. 2-5. This community was planned to allow access to recreational facilities.

Fig. 2-6. The slope and contour of the building lot will affect the cost of the project.

LEGAL DOCUMENTS

At least four legal documents are involved with the purchase of a house:

- The *official survey*, which shows the boundaries of the property.
- The *deed*, which is evidence of ownership.
- The *abstract of title*, which is a history of the deeds and other papers affecting the ownership of the property.
- The *contract of sale* (sometimes called a *sales contract*), which usually describes all the details relating to the purchase.

Before buying property, the purchaser should have the property surveyed to make certain its dimensions match the dimensions noted on the sales contract.

After the property is purchased, the buyer should retain a copy of the official survey, the deed, and the abstract of title. These are needed to secure financing and permits for new construction.

The contract of sale is required when a house or land is purchased. For an existing house, the contract contains such information as its exact location, the sales price, and a listing of anything inside the house that was not part of the sale. For example, the current owner might want to take the laundry appliances to another house. If a builder is hired to build a new house, the contract specifies such things as when the work will begin and when it will end. It also includes a great deal of detail regarding the house. For example, it might specify the level of quality the construction must reach. (For more on specifications, see Chapter 3, "Reading and Drawing Plans.")

To be valid, a sales contract must have these features:

- It must be written.
- It must clearly state the terms of the agreement, so there will be no disagreement about what is being purchased.
- It must include the price and the terms of payment.
- It must be dated.
- It must be signed by both the buyer and the seller. Both parties must be competent and old enough to sign legal documents.

from Another Angle

The process for purchasing property differs from region to region. In Connecticut, for example, the attorney for the seller of a house draws up a contract. The attorney for the buyer does a title search through local records to make sure the title is free of any other claims on it. In Oregon, a realtor draws up a standardized contract and the title search is done by a title company. A title company specializes in tracing the ownership of property through legal documents. In this case, the buyer and seller do not employ attorneys for the title search.

HOUSE PLANS

House plans can be obtained in several ways. The buyer can purchase a stock plan. A **stock plan** is a standard house plan that can be adapted to fit many different lots. Companies that sell them usually provide floor plans and other drawings to show what the finished house will look like. A **floor plan** is a scale drawing showing the size and location of rooms on a given floor. Once a suitable house plan has been chosen, complete working drawings and materials lists can be purchased. Stock plans are also available on the Internet, from plan books, and from some magazines.

House plans can also be obtained from local builders. Often, a builder specializes in a certain type of house. He or she develops one or two basic plans and then adapts them as needed to suit various buyers. This is why houses in a certain neighborhood often have similar features.

A third way to obtain house plans is to hire an architect or building designer to develop them to the buyer's specifications. This can be time consuming and expensive. A design fee may be based on a percentage of construction costs, or it may be a flat fee. A percentage fee can range from 5 percent to 10 percent. Many people prefer to use an architect or designer, however, because the design can be tailored exactly to their needs. The architect may be hired just to design the house or also to supervise its construction.

FINANCING

After a builder has been chosen, financing must be obtained, usually from a bank or savings and loan company. The loan is for a certain percentage of the total cost. This percentage varies, but 80 percent is common. The borrower provides the balance as a down payment.

Typically, a borrower starts with a **construction loan**. A construction loan is a short-term loan used during construction. The lender provides money periodically as the work progresses. These amounts of money are called advances or *draws*. The borrower pays only the interest on these draws.

After construction is finished, the construction loan is converted to a mortgage. A **mortgage** is a long-term loan (usually 15 to 30 years)

from Another Angle

The design of a house is often influenced by climate, available materials, and local traditions. **Fig. 2-7.** For example, houses in New England must withstand cold winters. Eaves are short or nonexistent, and traditional floor plans tend to feature many small rooms. In the Southwest, houses are often built of dense materials, such as adobe and masonry, which keep the interior cool. In the coastal Northwest, houses often have deep eaves to shield walls and windows from frequent rains.

A

B

Fig. 2-7. The roofing materials shown here are appropriate to the environment. *A.* Clay-tile roof on a Spanish-style house in the Southwest. *B.* Cedar roof shingles on a log house in the Northwest.

that is secured by property. It allows the lender to claim the property if the borrower does not make the mortgage payments. The borrower pays interest and principal over the life of the loan.

Loan providers, as well as some federal agencies, may establish certain requirements for home construction. These requirements are not the same as building codes. They are standards that a builder must meet to obtain a certain type of mortgage.

Once financing has been arranged, contracts are signed for the construction. From then on, it is the responsibility of the builder and/or architect to make sure that the building goes as planned. A loan officer at the bank may also require progress reports to ensure that money loaned by the bank is being used properly.

Builders are usually paid a certain portion of the construction costs before work is started. They are then paid additional amounts at certain stages, such as after the roof is on. These are the draws, or advances, from the construction loan. Final payment is made after the client and lender have inspected and approved the work.

SECTION 2.2 Check Your Knowledge

1. Name the four legal documents having to do with the purchase of a house or land.
2. What is a mortgage?
3. What percentage of the purchase price of a house can usually be financed?
4. What factors can cause actual costs to exceed average house construction costs?

On the Job

A family has a monthly income of $4,600. They want to buy a house listed for $120,900. Discuss with a team member what other facts you need to know before deciding if this family can buy this particular house. Figure their annual income. Using the guidelines in this chapter, determine the maximum amount the family should spend per month and also per year for housing, including mortgage, utilities, and repairs.

Estimating...

Construction Costs

To determine house construction costs, builders and designers often start with the average cost per square foot for residential buildings in their area. They multiply this figure by the number of square feet in the plans to estimate total costs. **Fig. 2-8.** However, actual costs can be higher because of special features, unusual materials, or custom products. **Fig. 2-9.** For example, granite countertops are much more expensive than those made from plastic laminate. Bay windows are more costly than standard windows. Kiln-dried lumber is more expensive than air-dried lumber.

The only way to get an accurate price estimate is to ask builders to bid on the project. They study the plans to arrive at exact costs. It is important to get several written bids for the work and to talk to builders in detail about what their bid includes.

ESTIMATING ON THE JOB

Find out the average construction costs for your area. Then estimate the cost of building houses with the following square footage: 1,500 sq. ft., 3,422 sq. ft., 4,689 sq. ft.

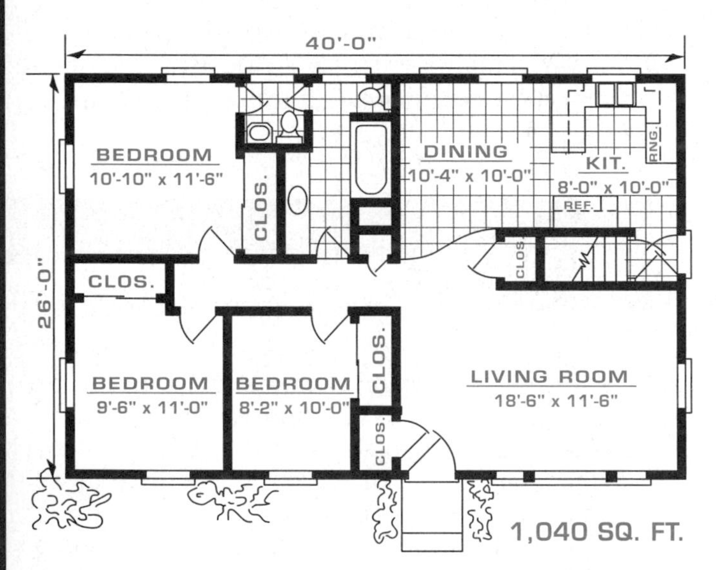

Fig. 2-8. A rough estimate of construction costs can be made by multiplying the number of square feet in the floor plan by the average cost of building (per sq. ft.) in your area.

Fig. 2-9. This woodstove is connected to an insulated, prefabricated chimney.

Chapter 2

Review

Section Summaries

2.1 Building codes establish minimum standards of quality and safety in housing. A building department can develop its own codes or adopt model codes developed elsewhere. In areas that are covered by building codes, it is usually necessary to get a permit before beginning construction.

2.2 Many factors are important when choosing a lot to build on or a house to buy. Various legal documents are required during the process. Stock house plans, plans from a builder, or plans developed by an architect may be used. Financing is obtained in the form of a construction loan and a mortgage. A builder's final payment comes when the house is completed and the client and lender have inspected and approved the work.

Review Questions

1. Name the three major model building codes used in the United States.
2. What is the *International Residential Code*?
3. Identify the model building code used where you live.
4. When must a builder schedule an inspection by the building department?
5. In general, what percentage of a family's income should be spent for housing?
6. When choosing a lot or an existing house, what six important factors must be considered?
7. Name three sources of house plans.
8. What is a floor plan?
9. Based on a percentage, how much might an architect charge to design a house that would cost $250,000 to build?
10. What is the repayment time for most mortgages?

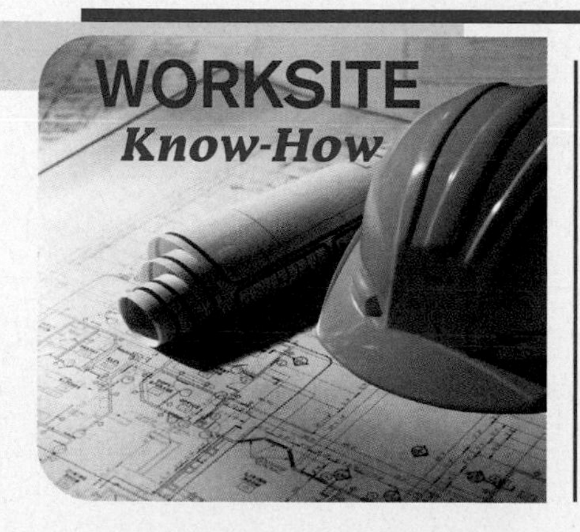

Impacts of Construction A new structure has an impact on the surrounding community and can add to its costs. New houses often mean additional children in the local schools, more traffic on the streets, and a strain on water resources. Parks may get more use, more waste will have to be disposed of, and fire and police departments may need more personnel in order to provide enough services. Some states impose impact fees to cover part of these costs. Typically, such fees fall in the $3,000 to $8,000 range and must be figured into the cost of a new home.

Chapter

Reading and Drawing Plans

Objectives

After reading this chapter, you'll be able to:

- Define ***scale*** and tell how it is used in architectural drawings.
- Name and describe several elements used in architectural drawings.
- Tell the advantages of computer-aided drafting and design.
- Name several of the drawings found in a set of architectural plans and tell their purpose.

Terms

architect's scale
cutting plane
dimensions
elevation
plan view
scale
specifications

The ability to read and understand a set of construction plans is an essential skill. Plans tell you everything you need to know about how to build something. By means of lines, symbols, and words, the ideas of the designer or architect are made clear to those who must work on the project. These people include carpenters and other tradespeople, materials suppliers, and building inspectors. To be successful in most construction-related jobs, you must be able to interpret the plans correctly. You must also be able to measure accurately and read a rule.

SECTION 3.1

Drawing and Measurement

Construction plans consist of drawings of the structure, as well as measurements of each part.

TYPES OF DRAWINGS

A *sketch* of something is a quick and informal drawing. An architect might make a sketch to capture an original idea. He or she might also sketch a house to show clients how it would look. A carpenter might sketch a framing connection as a way of showing an apprentice how to make it.

Architectural plans, sometimes called *construction drawings* or *working drawings*, are a set of more formal drawings. They provide an organized and precise way of showing how an entire structure should be built. **Fig. 3-1.** Copies of original plans are called *prints*. Many people refer to prints as "blueprints." This is because plans used to be printed as white lines on a dark blue background. An architect, an architectural designer, or a drafter usually makes the original drawing from which prints are made.

Carpenter's Tip

Various versions of the plans are produced during the design development of a house. Before construction begins, make sure you have reviewed the latest set of the plans. If you have any doubts, contact the project manager or designer. Make sure any subcontractors that will be working for you also have the latest plans.

MEASURING SYSTEMS

Two common systems of measurement are used worldwide. The United States currently uses the customary (English) system of measurement. All of the other industrial nations use the metric system. Some industries in the United States have changed over to the metric system. In construction, however, the customary system is still used. Some products, such as paint, are often labeled using both systems of measurement.

Fig. 3-1. Plans provide a kind of universal language that even those who don't speak the same language can "read."

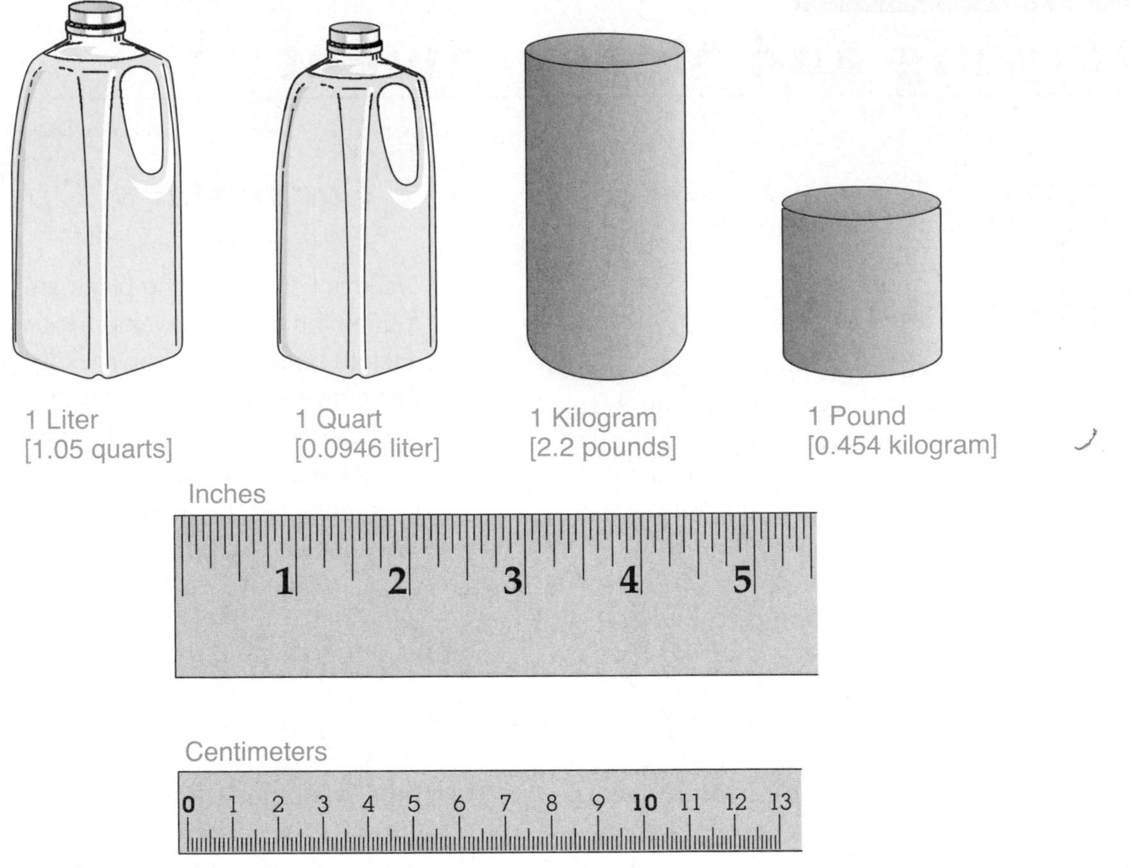

Fig. 3-2. The metric system compared with the customary system.

In the customary system, lengths are given in inches, feet, yards, and miles. In the metric system, lengths are given in millimeters, centimeters, meters, and kilometers. **Fig. 3-2.** A meter, which is the basic unit of length, is slightly longer than a yard (39.37″). One inch is equal to 25.4 millimeters.

The metric system is based on units of ten. The millimeter is equal to 1⁄1000 of a meter, and a centimeter is 1⁄100 of a meter. A kilometer consists of 1000 meters. The two most common length measures in the customary system used for residential construction are the inch and the foot. In the metric system for construction, the two length measurements used are the millimeter and the meter. A customary/metric conversion table titled "Metric Conversion Factors" can be found in the Ready Reference Appendix.

In the customary system, liquids are measured in quarts and gallons. In the metric system, they are measured in liters. A liter is about 5 percent larger than a quart. Liquid finishing materials, including paints, are normally given in liters, half-liters and quarter-liters. Weight in the customary system is given in pounds. In the metric system it is given in kilograms. A kilogram is approximately 2.2 pounds.

In countries that use metric measures, particularly Great Britain, a standard unit is 300 millimeters, which is very close to one foot. On architectural plans, all building dimensions are given in millimeters. All site measurements appear in meters and millimeters. In the United States, building dimensions are given in feet, inches, and fractions of an inch. All site dimensions are given in feet and inches.

Reading a Customary Rule

Measuring devices used in construction are based on multiples of twelve inches (one foot). The skills for measuring are the same, whether you're using a 1′ rule or a 100′ layout tape measure.

Take a look at the drawing shown in **Fig. 3-3**. The distance between 0 and 1 represents 1″. At

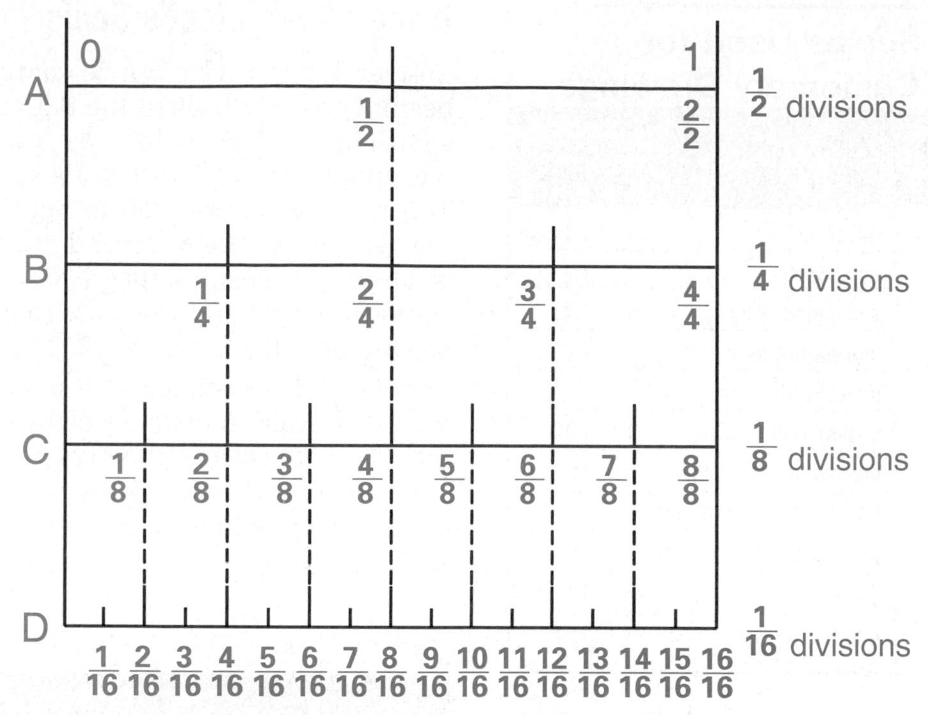

Fig. 3-3. Divisions of an inch. (For ease in reading, this drawing shows an inch larger than it really is.)

A the inch is divided into two equal parts. Each half represents ½″. At *B* the inch is divided into four equal parts. The first marker indicates ¼″, the second marker 2⁄4″ (½″), and the third marker ¾″. At *C* the inch is divided into eight equal parts; each small division is ⅛″. Two of these divisions make 2⁄8″ (¼″). Four make 4⁄8″ (½″). At *D* the inch is divided into sixteen parts. This is usually the smallest division on rules used for drawing. Notice that 4⁄16″ is equal to ¼″. One mark past ¼″ indicates 5⁄16″. Notice on your own rule that between one inch mark and the next, the ½″ mark is the longest. The ¼″ mark is the next longest, then the ⅛″ mark. The 1⁄16″ mark is the shortest.

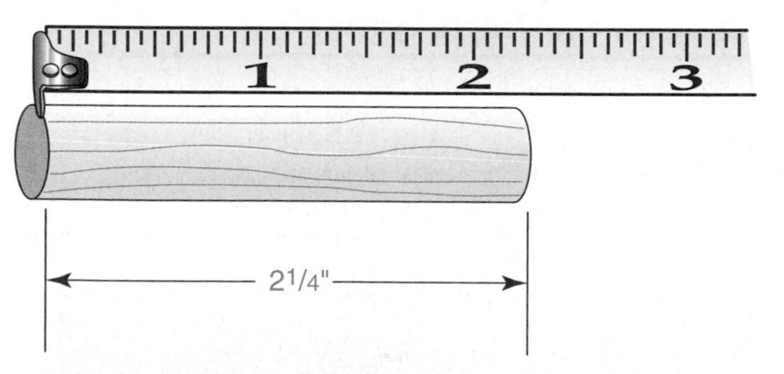

Fig. 3-4. Use a rule to measure this line.

To read a fraction of an inch, count the number of small divisions beyond the inch mark. For example, when measuring the line in **Fig. 3-4**, you will find that it is 2″ plus four 1⁄16″ segments. This is 2 4⁄16″, which is the same as 2¼″.

UNDERSTANDING SCALE

In order to represent large objects on fairly small sheets of paper, architectural plans are drawn to scale. Drawings done "to scale" are drawn with the same proportions as the objects they represent, but at a different size. In the case of architectural plans, the drawings are much smaller than the actual buildings and other objects they represent.

An architect can represent a building of any size on a single piece of paper by drawing it to a certain scale. However, it is important to understand that scale is not a unit of measurement. **Scale** is the ratio between the size of the object as drawn and its actual size. If the drawn object is exactly the same size as the real object, it is called a *full-size* or *full-scale* drawing. If it is reduced, as most drawn objects are, it will probably be drawn to one of the common scales shown in **Table 3-A**. Look at the scale in which

Table 3-A.	Scales Used for Customary Drawings	
Measurements based on...	Scale of drawing	Scale given as a ratio
1′ = 1′	full size	1:1
6″ = 1′	half size	1:2
3″ = 1′	one-fourth size	1:4
1½″ = 1′	one-eighth size	1:8
1″ = 1′	one-twelfth size	1:12
¾″ = 1′	one-sixteenth size	1:16
½″ = 1′	one-twenty-fourth size	1:24
⅜″ = 1′	one-thirty-second size	1:32
¼″ - 1′	one-forty-eighth size	1:48
3⁄16″ = 1′	one-sixty-fourth size	1:64
⅛″ = 1′	one-ninety-sixth size	1:96

3″ = 1′. It is called one-fourth size because there are four sets of 3″ lengths in 1′. What size is a drawing in which ½″ = 1′?

The tool that architects use when making scale drawings is called an **architect's scale**. It allows the measurements in reduced-scale drawings to be measured in feet and inches. **Fig. 3-5.** Several sets of markings representing various scales as ratios can be displayed on its triangular shape. Some of these markings read left to right, while others read right to left. Architect's scales are available in other shapes, however, including flat models.

A scale of ¼″ = 1′-0″ is most often used for drawing houses. A distance of ¼″ on the drawing represents a distance of 1′-0″ on the actual house. For example, if you used a tape measure to measure a window on a house, it might be 4′ high and 3′ wide. If you drew that window to a scale of ¼″ = 1′-0″, its size on the paper would be 1″ high and ¾″ wide. If you wrote its dimensions next to the window on the drawing, however, you would write the size of the real window.

Using an Architect's Scale

An architect's scale can be confusing for a beginner to use. Look at the flat architect's scale shown in **Fig. 3-6**. Its left end is labeled ⅛, meaning that a ⅛″ = 1′-0″ scale starts at this end. This scale reads from left to right beginning at the zero mark. The other end of the instrument is labeled ¼, meaning that a ¼″ = 1′-0" scale starts from that end. It reads from right to left beginning at the zero mark.

In Fig. 3-6, a distance of 8′-6″ is shown on the ¼″ = 1′-0″ scale. A distance of 14′-0″ is shown on the ⅛″ = 1′-0″ scale. Can you see how these distances were arrived at? With practice, you will be able to draw lines of any distance using a scale.

SECTION 3.1 Check Your Knowledge

1. What is another term for architectural plans?
2. On what unit is the metric system based?
3. What is a scale drawing and why is it important for making architectural plans?
4. A drawing in which 6″ = 1′ is called a half-size drawing. What size is a drawing done to a scale of ¼″ = 1′-0″?

On the Job

Using an architect's scale and a drawing triangle or a protractor, draw a rectangle. It should represent a house wall that is 18′-9″ long and 8′-6″ high. Use the ¼″ = 1′ portion of the scale. Draw a line between two diagonally opposite corners of the rectangle. Using the architect's scale, measure this line. Now determine the length it would be if it appeared on the actual wall. Can you measure its length exactly?

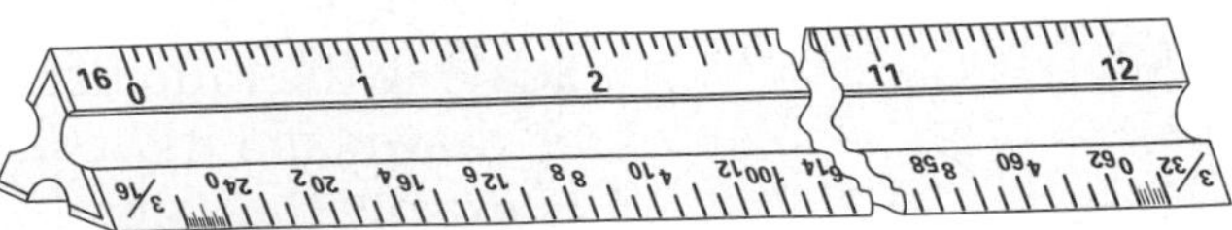

Fig. 3-5. The architect's scale is used when making scale drawings.

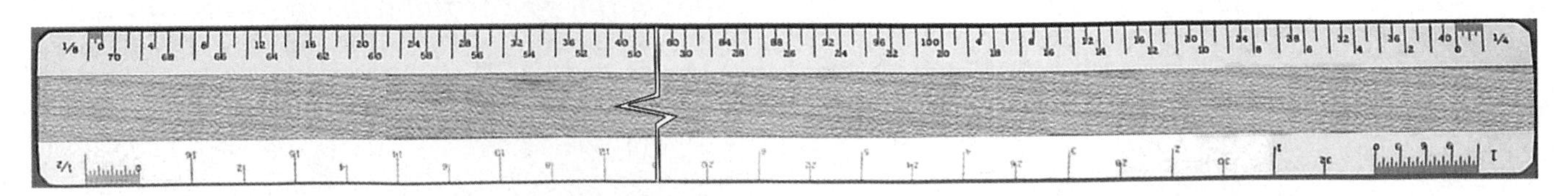

Fig. 3-6. This flat scale is a type of architect's scale but is easier to use.

SECTION 3.2

Making Architectural Drawings

Architectural drawings may be done by hand or on a computer. In either case, the same elements are used.

ELEMENTS OF A DRAWING

An architectural drawing consists of lines, dimensions, symbols, and notes. All four of these elements are very important to understanding, or "reading," the drawing.

Lines

Lines show the shape of an object and are used for many other purposes as well. The lines described below are commonly used for all drawings. **Fig. 3-7.**

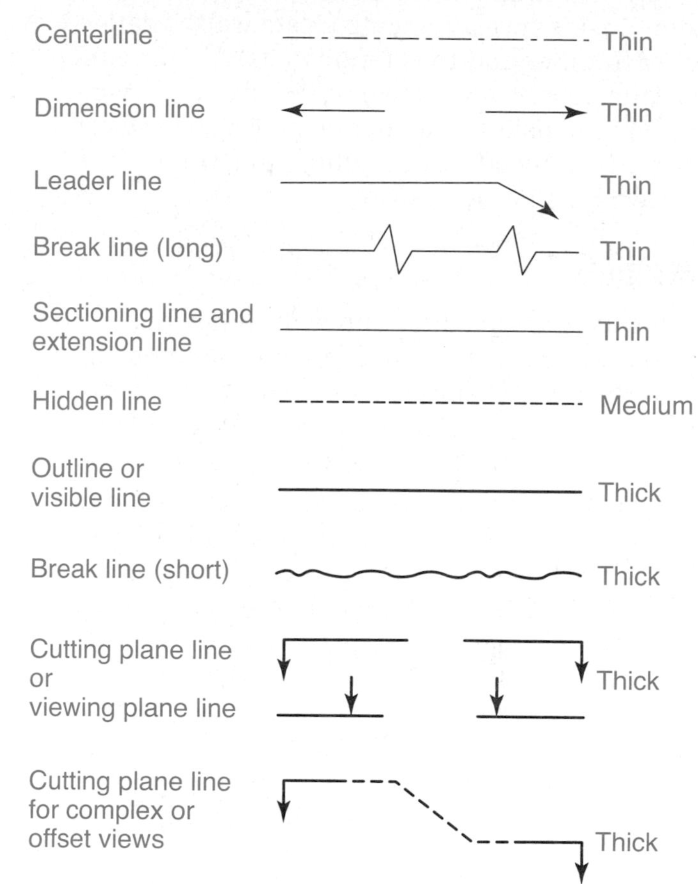

Fig. 3-7. Lines commonly used on architectural plans.

- *Centerlines* are used to indicate the center of an object. They are composed of long and short dashes, alternately and evenly spaced with a long dash at each end. At intersections, the short dashes cross. Very short centerlines may be broken if they will not be confused with other lines.
- *Dimension lines* indicate the start and end point of a particular dimension. They have arrowheads at each end. The dimension is written as a break in the middle of the line.
- *Leader lines* lead to a part to which a note or other reference applies. They usually end in an arrowhead or a large, circular dot. Arrowheads should always end at a line. Dots should be within the outline of an object. Leaders should end at any suitable portion of the note, reference, or dimension.
- *Break lines* may be solid, freehand lines that indicate short breaks. Full, ruled lines with freehand zigzags are used for long breaks.
- *Sectioning lines* indicate the exposed surfaces of an object in a sectional view. They are generally full, thin lines, but they may vary with the kind of material shown.
- *Extension lines* mark the end points of a dimension and should not touch the outline of the object.
- *Hidden lines* are short dashes evenly spaced that show the hidden features of a part. They always begin with a dash in contact with the line from which they start. However, a space is added when such a dash would form the continuation of a full line. Dashes touch at corners.
- *Visible lines* represent those edges of the object which can actually be seen.
- *Cutting plane lines* or *viewing plane lines* show where a section has been taken in the drawing in order to show more detail.

Dimensions

Dimensions are numbers that tell the size of something. The dimension of a particular feature on a plan can be determined by using an architect's scale. However, dimensions are usually written on the plans. Carpenters and other tradespeople must follow the written dimensions when laying out the framing of a structure.

Plans are dimensioned both outside and inside the building lines. Outside dimensions describe openings and other changes in the exterior wall, in addition to its overall dimension. Inside measurements locate walls relative to each other and to exterior walls. All horizontal dimensions are shown in the plan (top) view. Some dimensions may not be shown. These can be derived by adding or subtracting other dimensions in the drawing.

Symbols

Symbols are used to represent things that would be impractical to show in some types of drawings. For example, they are often used to represent doors, windows, electrical receptacles, plumbing fixtures, and heating equipment.

A great many symbols appear on plans. Some of them are easy to interpret, while others are less so. **Fig. 3-8.** Symbol keys are sometimes present. Just as a written language is composed of letters grouped into words, symbols are grouped in various ways to make them easier to interpret. Many electrical symbols, for example, have similar shapes. **Fig. 3-9.** Some symbols are used to indicate objects, while others are used to indicate materials. **Figs. 3-10** and **3-11.**

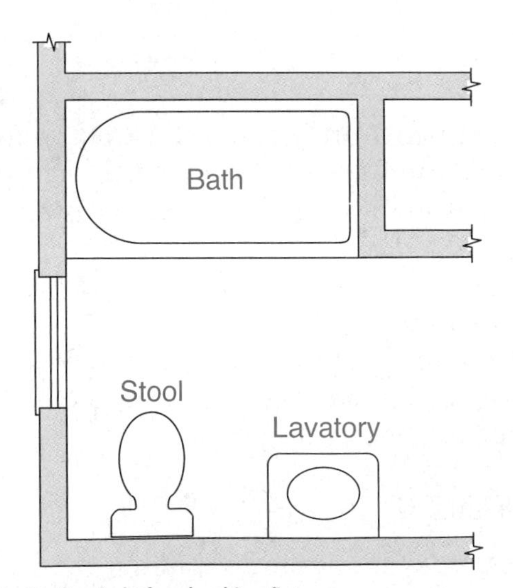

Fig. 3-8. Symbols for plumbing fixtures.

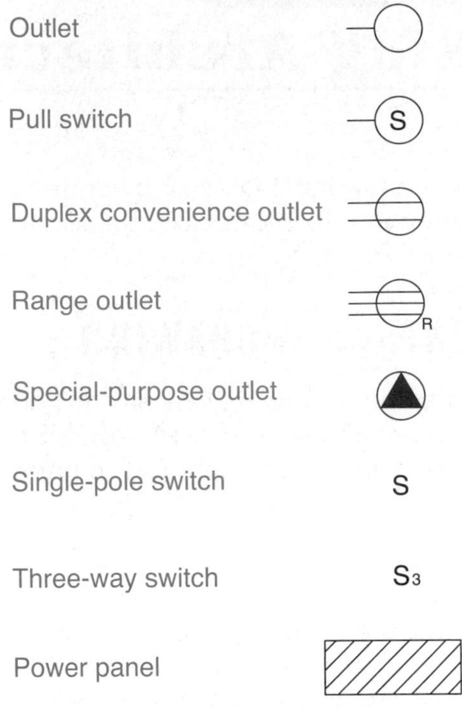

Fig. 3-9. Symbols for electrical wiring.

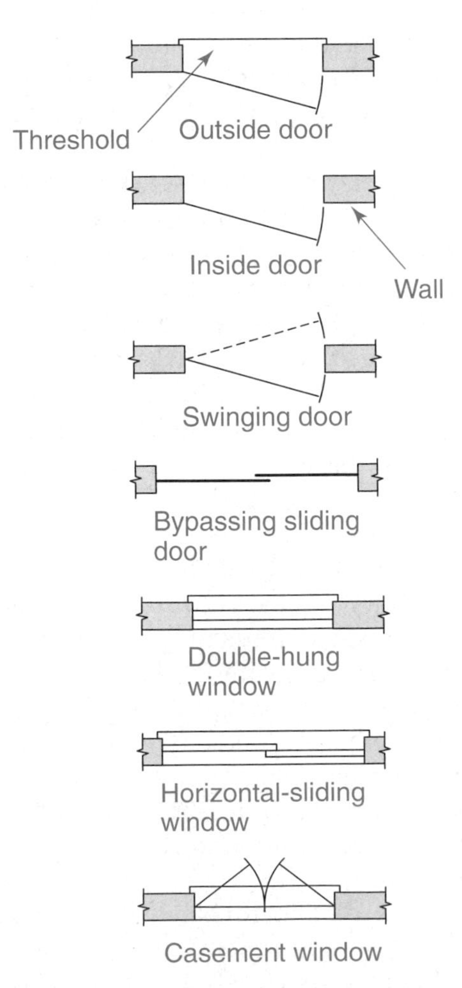

Fig. 3-10. Symbols for doors and windows.

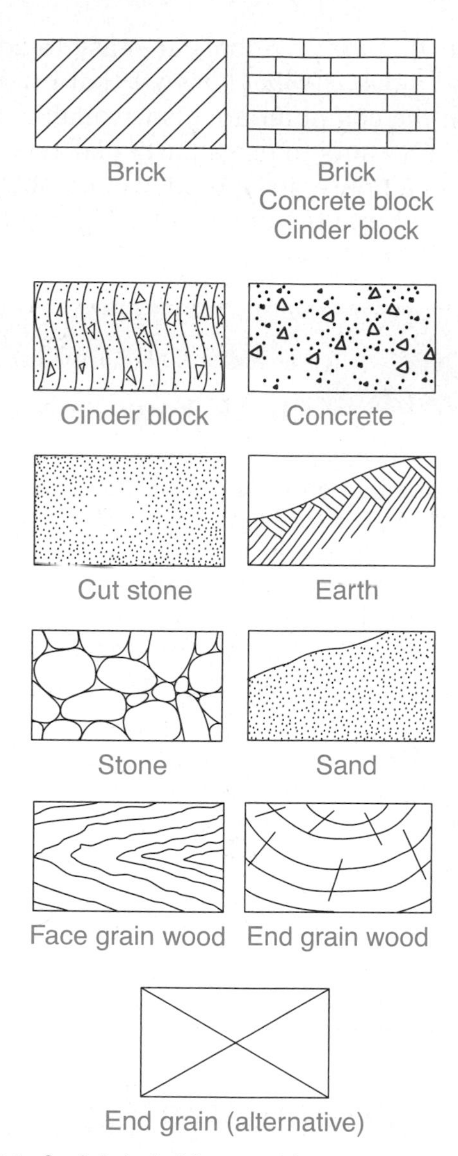

Fig. 3-11. Symbols for building materials.

Notes

Notes are short, written explanations of some feature that might not be clear from the drawing or that requires extra emphasis. Notes give information about such matters as materials, construction, and finish. They are included wherever necessary. There are two kinds of notes: specific and general.

Specific notes might clarify dimensions or suggest a construction technique. For example, a note might be included telling the carpenters to check the dimensions of an unusually shaped bathtub before framing the bathroom walls.

General notes can be added referring to many or all drawings in a set of plans. An example of such a note would be: "All dimensions are given from stud face to stud face." General notes may be underlined to attract attention.

To save space in notes, abbreviations are often used. Standard abbreviations for use on construction drawings can be found in the Ready Reference Appendix table "Architectural Abbreviations."

COMPUTER-AIDED DRAFTING AND DESIGN

For many years, architectural plans were drawn by hand, using pencil or ink. Plastic templates speeded up the drawing of elements used over and over, such as circles and arcs or symbols of plumbing fixtures. Though plans are still drawn this way, computers are increasingly preferred.

SAFETY FIRST

Avoiding Stress Hazards

Anyone who prepares architectural plans may spend many hours in front of a computer. Be sure to arrange the monitor, keyboard, and electronic drawing tablets to minimize the risk of repetitive stress hazards. Eyestrain is another risk with prolonged computer use. Adjust lighting conditions accordingly, particularly to reduce glare.

Computer-aided drafting and design (CADD or just CAD) programs can be used to create site plans, floor plans, elevation drawings, and even perspective (realistic) drawings of a structure. These drawings can be sent electronically to a printer in the architect's office. **Fig. 3-12.**

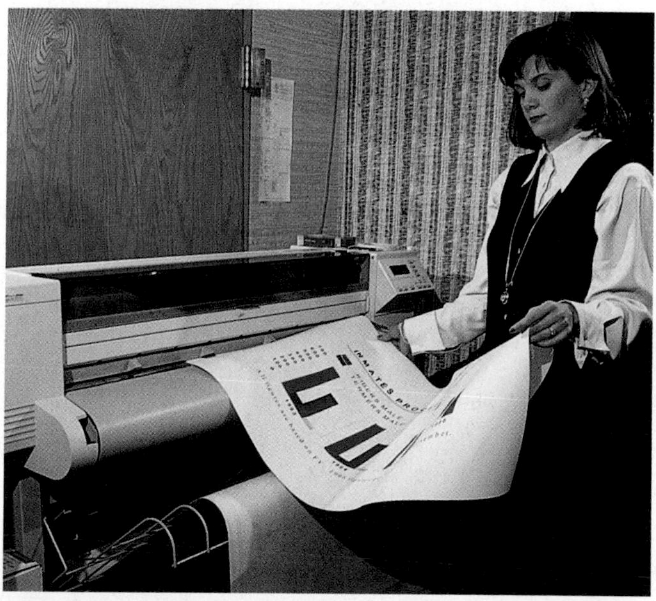

Fig. 3-12. A wide-format printer is required for computer-drawn architectural plans.

from Another Angle

One advantage of using CADD software to prepare architectural plans is that details can be drawn once and reused on subsequent projects. However, software incompatibilities may prevent these drawings from being widely shared. The establishment of uniform CADD standards will reduce or eliminate this problem. In the meantime, verify that details are compatible with your software when you receive files from outside sources.

Electronic drawing files can also be sent via the Internet to a local printing company. These companies have high-quality, high-volume color printers that can process many drawings quickly.

Using a computer offers many advantages. The drawings can be revised with ease. Instead of having to be redrawn, the new version is simply reprinted. Estimating software can be combined with CAD software to produce a list of materials directly from the drawings. Drawing symbols by hand can be quite time consuming.

With a computer, symbols are easy to add, delete, or move. *Symbol libraries* that can be stored in the computer are also available. When an architect wants to use a particular type of window in a house, its symbol can be obtained and inserted into the drawing with the click of a mouse.

SECTION 3.2

Check Your Knowledge

1. What does a centerline look like, and what does it represent?
2. What are extension lines?
3. What two things do symbols usually represent?
4. What does CADD stand for, and why is it important in construction?

On the Job

CADD technology changes rapidly. Using the Internet, locate at least two companies that sell CADD software for making residential architectural drawings. List the minimum computer and printer hardware requirements needed. Find out what the programs cost. Share your findings with the class.

SECTION 3.3

Architectural Plans

A set of architectural plans consists of different views of the site and structure at various stages of construction. Taken together, these views provide the information a carpenter or builder would need to make the structure. Knowing which view is likely to contain certain information is an important part of reading plans.

The views of a building include general drawings and detail drawings. General drawings consist of plan views and elevations. Their purpose is to show large portions of the building. Details are shown with section views and detail drawings. They provide information about how parts fit together. Additional information is often given in the form of schedules and specifications. Other workers, such as estimators, depend on them.

Figure 3-13 is a photograph of a house. Many of the architectural plans shown in the rest of this chapter are for this house.

PLAN VIEW

A **plan view** is a top view. It is also known as a "bird's-eye" view. It allows you to see the width, length, and location of objects as if you were standing on a platform high above them and looking down. It is not possible to see the true height of objects in a plan view. Several types of plan views are commonly used.

Fig. 3-13. The building plans for the house shown here are on the following pages.

- A *site plan*, or *plot plan*, shows the building lot with boundaries, contours, existing roads, utilities, and other details such as existing trees and buildings. **Fig. 3-14.** It is drawn from notes and sketches based upon a survey. This plan shows where the driveway will be located. The outline of the building is often superimposed on the site plan, and corners are located by reference to natural objects or other buildings. The excavation contractor relies on this plan.

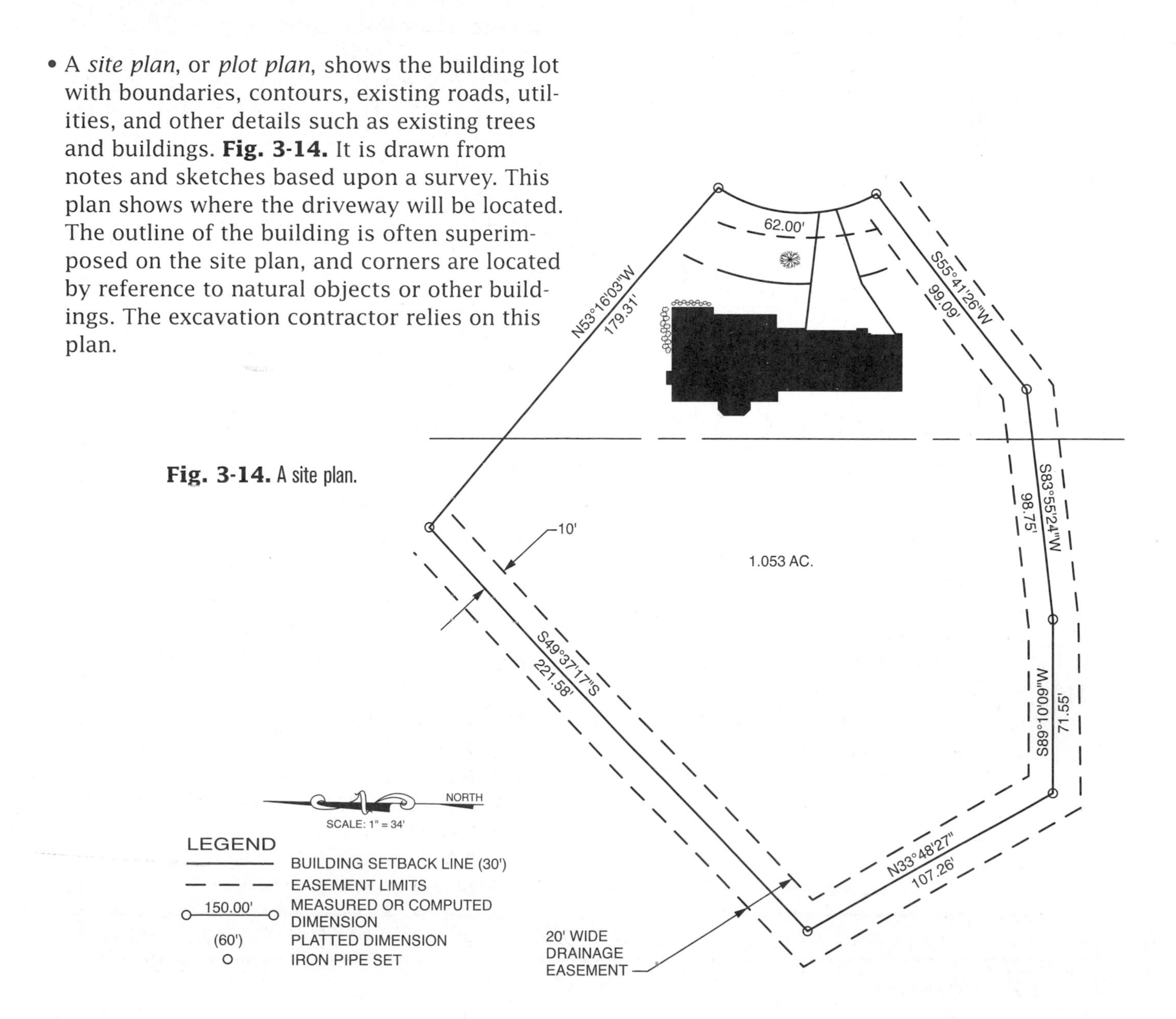

Fig. 3-14. A site plan.

- A *foundation plan* is a top view of the footings and foundation walls. **Fig. 3-15.** It also shows the location of posts and other elements, such as pads needed to support an exterior deck. All openings in foundation walls are labeled and dimensioned. The type and location of foundation anchor bolts are identified. The foundation contractor relies on this plan.
- *Floor plans* are included for each level of the building. **Fig. 3-16.** They are drawn as if the house was sliced horizontally at a level that would include all doors and window openings. This imaginary slicing is referred to as a **cutting plane**. A floor plan shows the outside shape of the building; the arrangement, size, and shape of rooms; types of materials used; thickness of walls; and the types, sizes, and locations of doors and windows. A floor plan may also include details of the structure, although these are usually shown on separate drawings called *framing plans*. Carpenters and many other tradespeople rely on floor plans.
- *Reflected ceiling plans* are drawn as the ceiling would appear in a mirror placed on the floor below it. Reflected plans are used to show complex designs, such as tray ceilings and customized suspended ceilings, or to show the locations of multiple lighting fixtures.
- *Framing plans* show the size, number, and spacing of structural members. Separate framing plans may be drawn for the floors and the roof. The floor framing plan must specify the sizes and spacing of joists, girders, and columns used to support the floor. Doubled framing around openings and beneath bathroom fixtures is also shown. Detail drawings are added, if necessary, to show the methods of anchoring joists and girders to the foundation walls. Roof framing plans show the size and spacing of rafters, as well as information about the roof slope and sheathing. Carpenters rely on these plans.
- The *electrical plan*, which is drawn like a simplified floor plan, shows the location and type of every electrical feature of the building. **Fig. 3-17.** These include switches, ceiling lights, receptacles, and the service panel. It also indicates a schematic view of the electrical wiring that connects individual features to each other. The electrician relies on this plan.

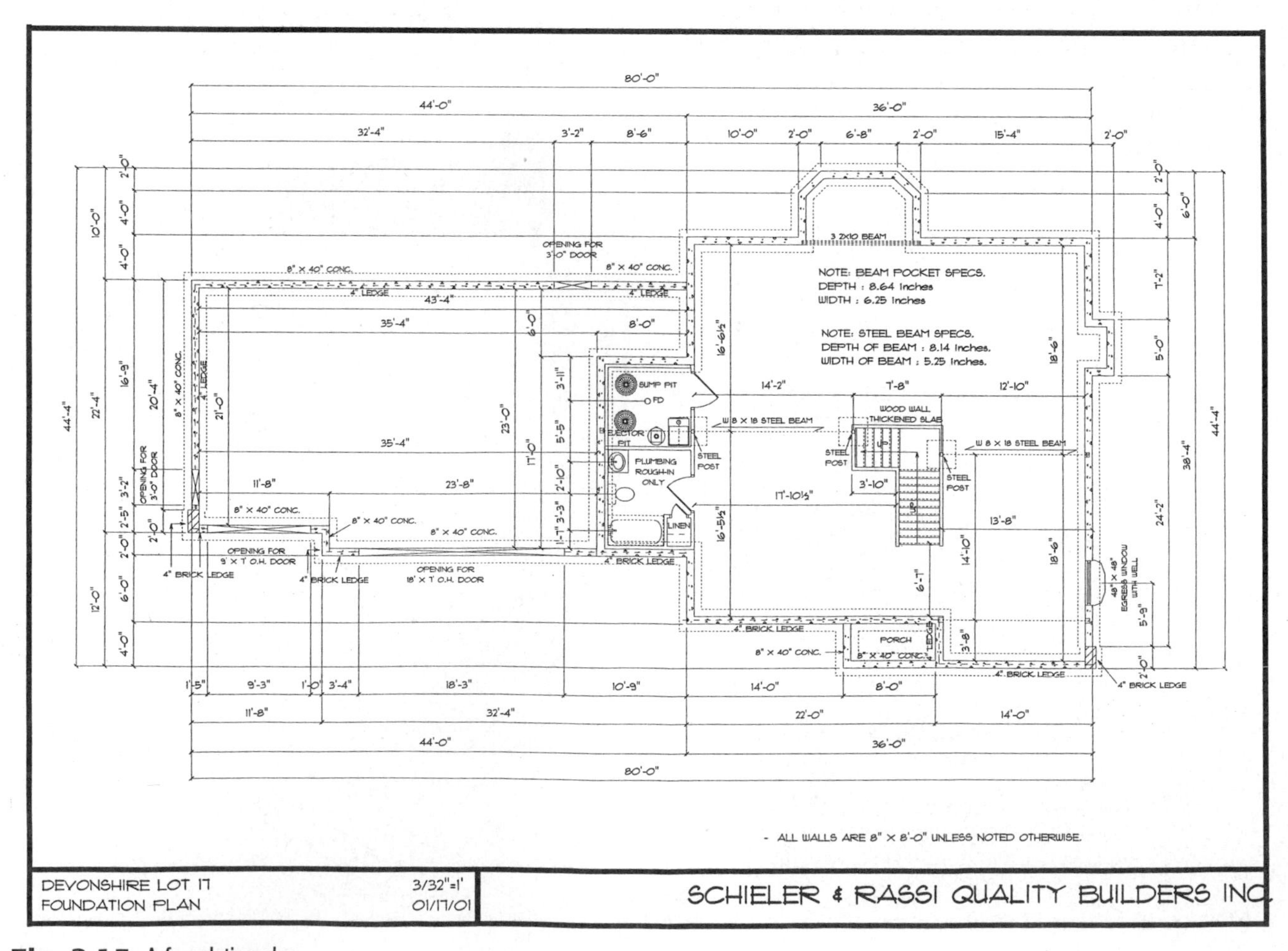

Fig. 3-15. A foundation plan.

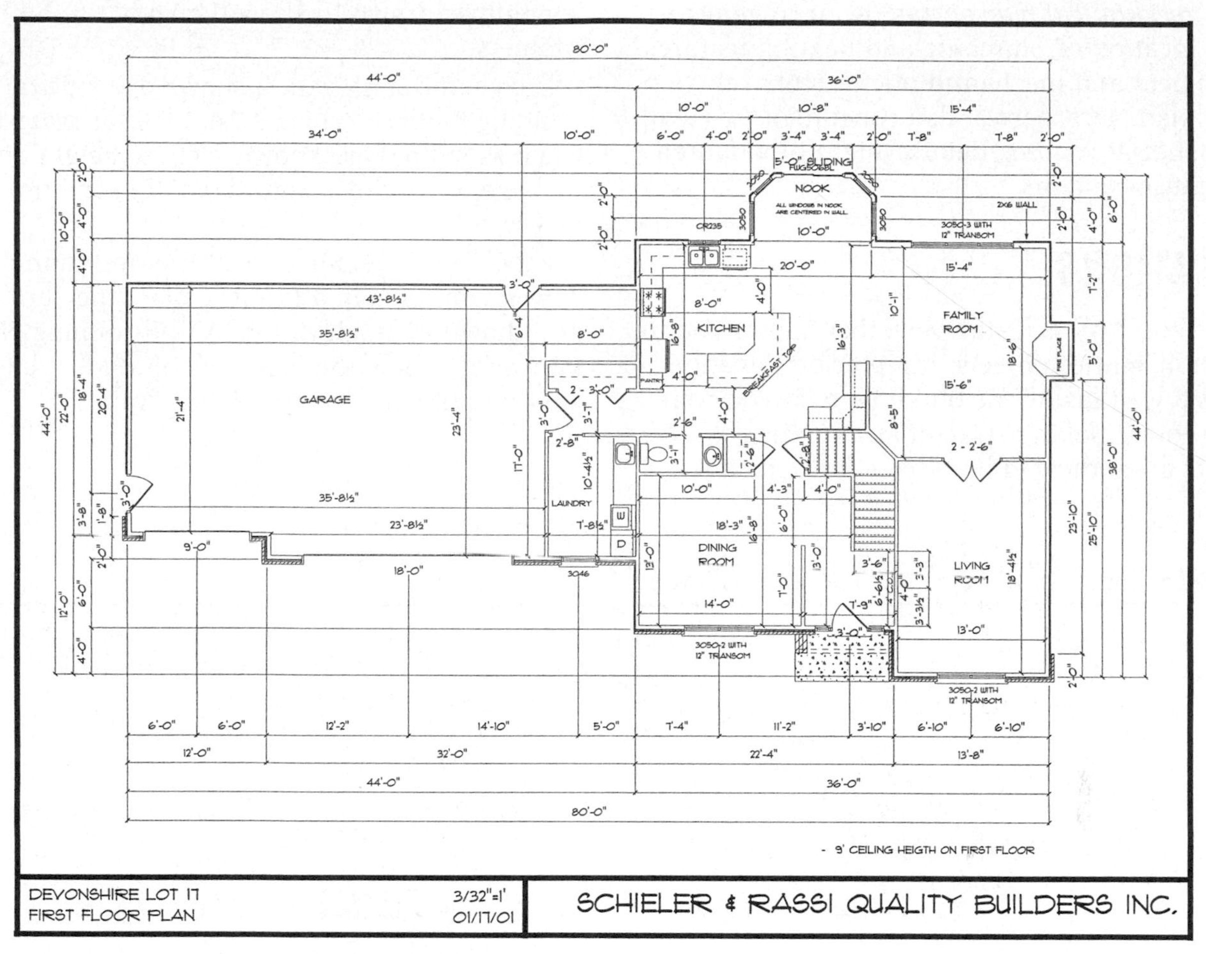

Fig. 3-16. A floor plan. This shows the first floor.

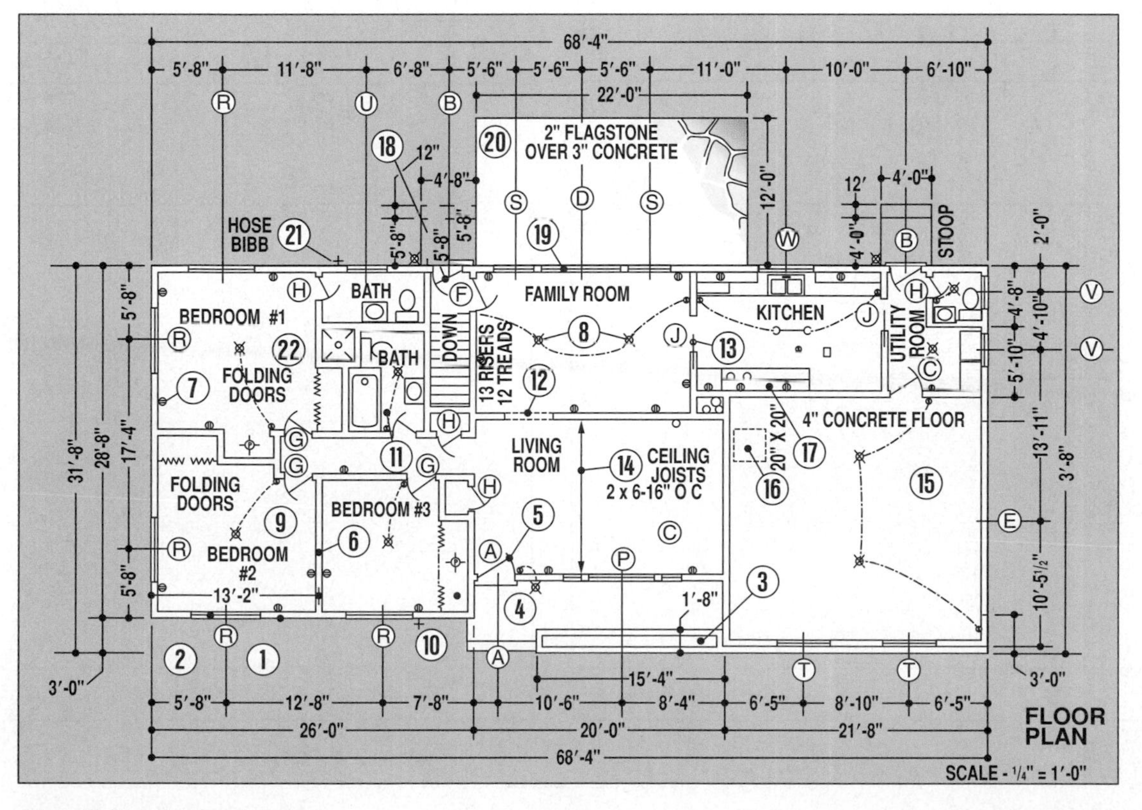

Fig. 3-17. An electrical plan.

- The *mechanical plan* shows the arrangement and location of plumbing and heating features. Plumbers and mechanical contractors rely on this plan. A carpenter also consults it to see if any special framing details might be required for these systems.

ELEVATIONS

An **elevation** is a side view that allows you to see the height of objects. An interior elevation shows a wall inside the building, as if you were in the room looking straight at it. Ceiling heights are indicated. Interior elevations are sometimes drawn to show the layout of built-in cabinets.

Each exterior elevation shows one side of the building's exterior. **Fig. 3-18.** Exterior materials (such as siding) are shown. Ceiling height and the size of windows and doors are sometimes given.

Because the details of wall framing cannot be shown complete in a framing plan, they are usually shown in an elevation. A wall framing elevation would show the locations of studs, plates, sills, and bracing in a particular wall.

Fig. 3-18. Exterior elevations (front, back, right side, and left side).

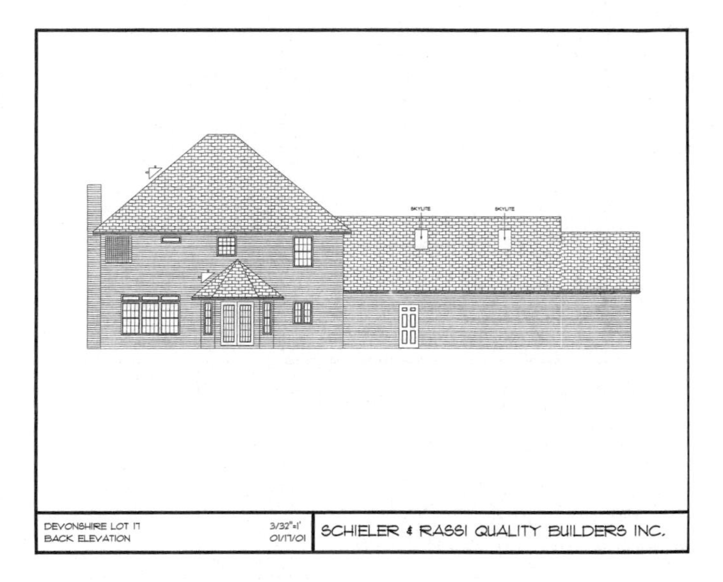

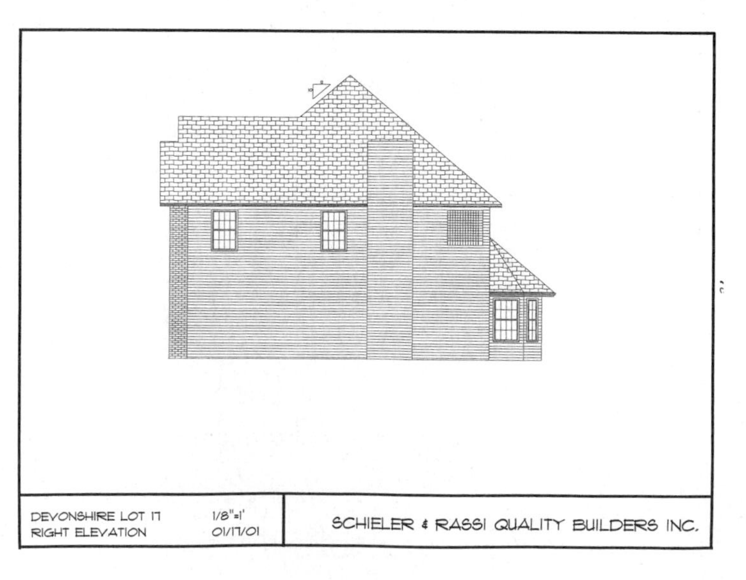

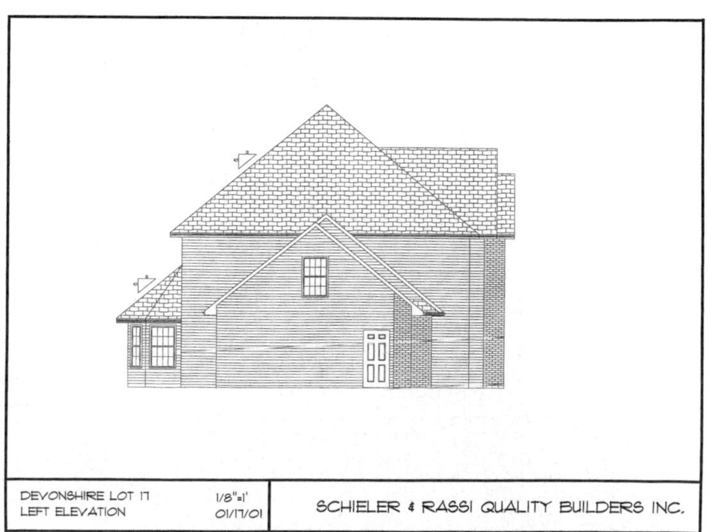

SECTION VIEWS

Section views provide important information about materials, fastening and support systems, and concealed features. They show how an object looks when "cut" vertically by an imaginary cutting plane. **Fig. 3-19.** The cut is not necessarily continuous but may be staggered to include as much construction information as possible.

Where a section view is used to give more information about a larger drawing, the cutting plane is shown on the larger drawing by special lines. These lines, which sometimes have an arrow at each end, are identified with letters or numbers or both, for example, "A-2." The section view is then also labeled A-2. This helps the reader to understand exactly what portion of the house the section view represents.

Sections may be classified as typical or specific. *Typical sections* show construction features that are repeated many times throughout a structure. They are labeled "TYP" or "Typical." When a feature occurs only once and is not shown clearly elsewhere, it is represented by a *specific section.*

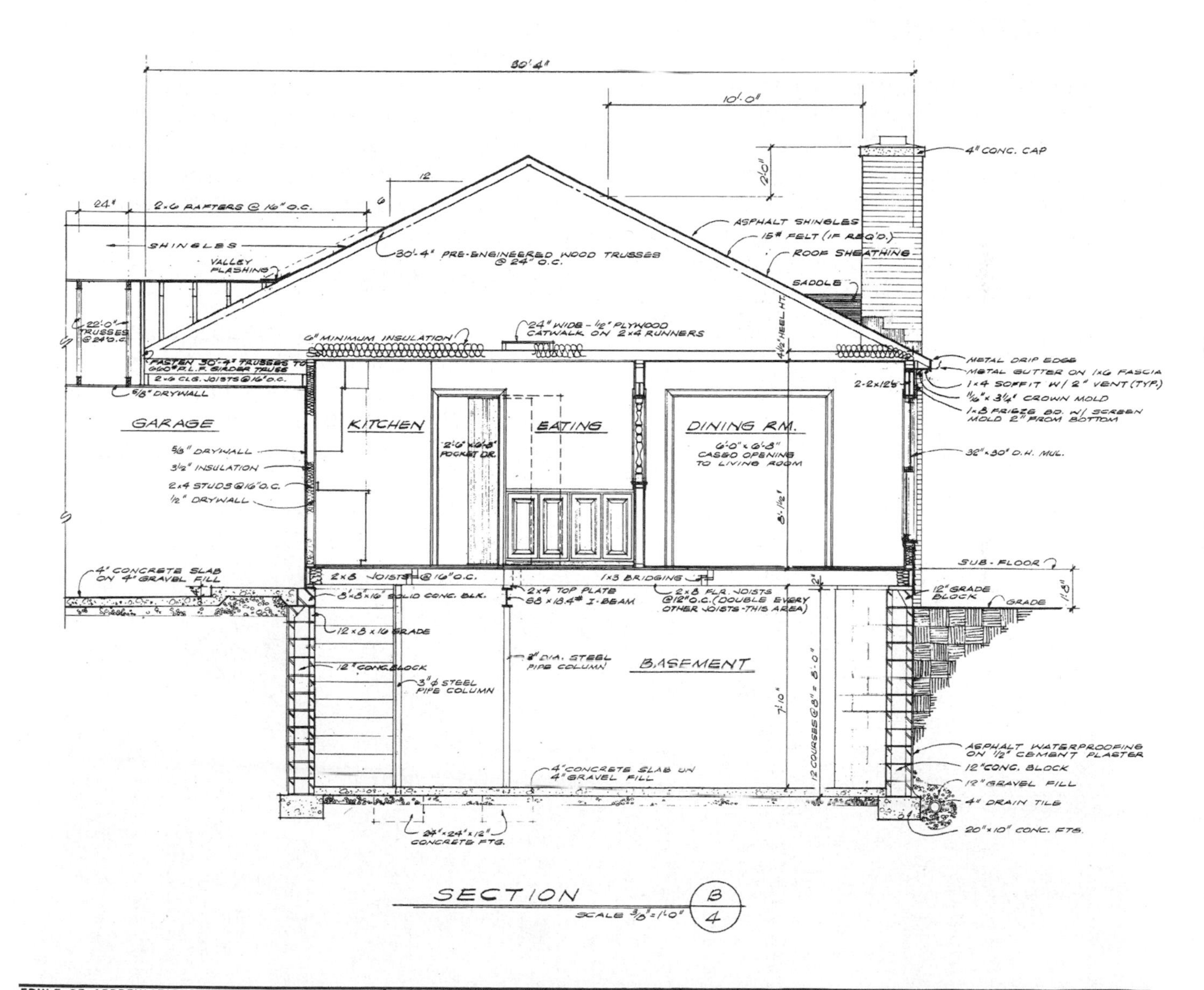

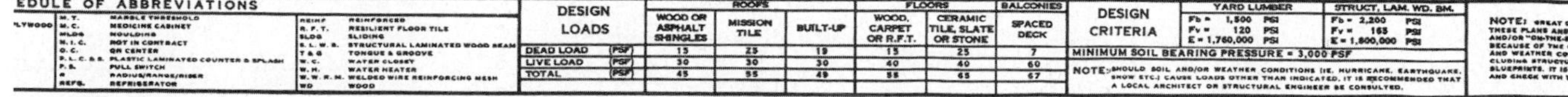

EDULE OF ABBREVIATIONS

LYWOOD	M.T.	MARBLE THRESHOLD	REINF	REINFORCED
	M.C.	MEDICINE CABINET	R.F.T.	RESILIENT FLOOR TILE
	MLDG	MOULDING	SLDG	SLIDING
	N.I.C.	NOT IN CONTRACT	S.L.W.B.	STRUCTURAL LAMINATED WOOD BEAM
	O.C.	ON CENTER	T & G	TONGUE & GROOVE
	P.L.C. & S.	PLASTIC LAMINATED COUNTER & SPLASH	W.C.	WATER CLOSET
	P.S.	PULL SWITCH	W.H.	WATER HEATER
	R	RADIUS/RANGE/RISER	W.W.R.M.	WELDED WIRE REINFORCING MESH
	REFG.	REFRIGERATOR	WD	WOOD

DESIGN LOADS		ROOFS			FLOORS		BALCONIES
		WOOD OR ASPHALT SHINGLES	MISSION TILE	BUILT-UP	WOOD, CARPET OR R.F.T.	CERAMIC TILE, SLATE OR STONE	SPACED DECK
DEAD LOAD	(PSF)	15	25	19	15	25	7
LIVE LOAD	(PSF)	30	30	30	40	40	60
TOTAL	(PSF)	45	55	49	55	65	67

DESIGN CRITERIA	YARD LUMBER	STRUCT. LAM. WD. BM.
	Fb = 1,500 PSI Fv = 120 PSI E = 1,760,000 PSI	Fb = 2,200 PSI Fv = 165 PSI E = 1,800,000 PSI
MINIMUM SOIL BEARING PRESSURE = 3,000 PSF		
NOTE: SHOULD SOIL AND/OR WEATHER CONDITIONS (IE. HURRICANE, EARTHQUAKE, SNOW ETC.) CAUSE LOADS OTHER THAN INDICATED, IT IS RECOMMENDED THAT A LOCAL ARCHITECT OR STRUCTURAL ENGINEER BE CONSULTED.		

NOTE: GREAT CA[illegible] THESE PLANS AND [illegible] AND/OR "ON-THE-SIT[illegible] BECAUSE OF THE G[illegible] AND WEATHER CON[illegible] CLUDING STRUCTUR[illegible] BLUEPRINTS. IT IS [illegible] AND CHECK WITH TO[illegible]

Fig. 3-19. A section view of the house.

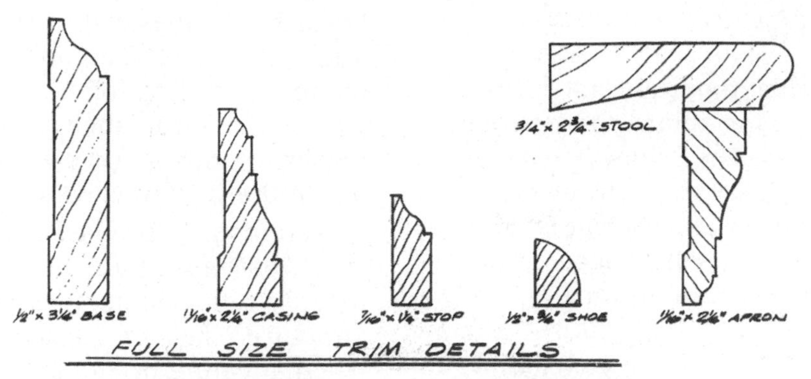

Fig. 3-20. A detail drawing is used to show details of construction.

DETAIL DRAWINGS

When precise information is needed about a small or complex portion of the building, a *detail drawing* is made. **Fig. 3-20.** Such drawings are used whenever the information given in elevations, plans, and sections is not clear enough. The construction at doors, windows, and eaves is often shown in detail drawings. Details are drawn at larger scales than plan views, such as ½″ = 1′-0″, ¾″ = 1′-0″, 1″ = 1′-0″, or 1¼″ = 1′-0″. Detail drawings are usually grouped so that references may be made easily from the general drawings. They are often located near section drawings because they show a particular part of the section.

Detail drawings are sometimes made as isometric drawings. Isometric drawings are constructed around three basic lines that form 120° angles to one another. They sometimes illustrate an assembly detail, such as an interlocking joint in a timber-framed house. The isometric technique gives the detail a three-dimensional look.

RENDERINGS

A *rendering* is sometimes called a *presentation drawing.* It is more like a picture of the structure than any other type of architectural drawing. **Fig. 3-21.** Its purpose is most often to show the exterior of a house as it would look

Fig. 3-21. This is a rendering of the house shown in the preceding drawings.

completed. A rendering often includes such elements as plants, shadowing, and "in use" features that add to a sense of reality.

Renderings are sometimes drawn for clients to help them visualize what the house would look like after all the landscaping has been done. Some renderings are drawn in color.

SCHEDULES

A *schedule* is a list. For example, a window schedule lists all the windows that will be used in the building. **Fig. 3-22.** It contains information about the sizes of rough openings, glazing, finish, trim, manufacturer's name, and window type and size, among other things. It is information that would not necessarily appear in any of the drawings. Each window on the list is keyed to the floor plans with a letter or number. This ensures that windows will be put in the proper locations. A door schedule contains similar information.

When building from architectural plans, always verify that the door and window schedules match dimensions given on the floor plans. It is far easier to correct mistakes before framing begins than after the house has been framed and sheathed.

A *room-finish schedule* identifies the materials and finishes to be used for floors, walls, and ceilings for each room, including hallways. For example, a living room might show on the schedule as having strip-oak flooring, pine baseboard and window trim, painted drywall wall/ceiling surfaces, and wood paneling on two walls.

SCHEDULES							
WINDOWS				DOORS			
MARK	SIZE	TYPE	REMARKS	MARK	SIZE	TYPE	REMARKS
W1	14-3′-4" x 5′-5"	D.H. VINYL		A	9′-0" x 6′-8"	OVERHEAD	GARAGE
W2	3-3′-4" x 4′-9"	D.H. VINYL		B	18′-0" x 6′-8"	OVERHEAD	GARAGE
W3	1-3′-4" x 4′-6"	D.H. VINYL		C	5′-0" x 6′-8"	FWD GLD PAT	NOOK
W4	2-2′-0" x 5′-5"	D.H. VINYL		D	3′-0" x 6′-8"	1/2 LIGHT	MN ENTR
W5	1- 3′-4" x 2′-9"	D.H. VINYL		E	2-1′-0" x 6′-8"	1/2 LT SIDE LT	
W6	1-3′-0" x 3′-0"	D.H. VINYL		F	3-3′-0" x 6′-8"	6 PANEL	
W7	8-3′-0" x 1′-0"	D.H. VINYL	TRANSOMS	G	2 6′-0" x 6′-8"	BYPASS	
W8	2-4′-0" x 4′-0"	D.H. VINYL	FIXED PICT.	H	2-2′-6" x 6′-8"	BIFOLD	
W9	1-2′-2" x 1′-3"	D.H. VINYL	CIRCLE TOP	I	2-3′-0" x 6′-8"	BIFOLD	
W10	5′-0" x 1′-0"	D.H. VINYL	TRANSOM	J	2′-6" x 6′-8"	SGL POCKET	
				K	2′-4" x 6′-8"	SGL POCKET	
				L	2′-8" x 6′-8"	SGL POCKET	
				M	2-2′-6" x 6′-8"	FRENCH	
				N	2-2′-8" x 6′-8"	FRENCH	
				O	1′-8" x 6′-8"	ST 4 PANEL	
				P	2-2′-6" x 6′-8"	ST 4 PANEL	
				Q	4-2′-8" x 6′-8"	ST 4 PANEL	

Fig. 3-22. A window and door schedule.

SPECIFICATIONS

The house is to be built for________________________________ Owner,

residing at (Number)________________(Street) ________________

____

(City or Town) (County) (State)

and is to be built upon the Owner's property located as described below:

____

____

____

LOCATION OF HOUSE ON LOT - The location of the house shall be as shown and dimensioned on the Plot Plan included in the Working Drawings.

GENERAL CONDITIONS OF THE SPECIFICATIONS

GENERAL DESCRIPTION OF THE WORK -The Contractor shall supply all labor, material, transportation, temporary heat, fuel, light, equipment, scaffolding, tools and services required for the complete and proper shaping of the work in strict conformity with the Drawings and Specifications. All work of all trades included in the Specifications shall be Performed in a neat and workmanlike manner equal to the best in current shop and field practice.

BIDS-in receiving bids for the work specified herein, the Owner incurs no obligations to any bidder and reserves the right to reject any and all bids.

CONTRACT DOCUMENTS-The Contract Documents consist of the Drawings, Specifications, Plot Plan and the Agreement. The Contract Documents are complementary and what is called for by one shall be as binding as if called for by all. The intent and purpose of the Contract Documents is to include all labor, material, equipment, transportation and handling neccesary for the complete and proper execution of the work.

PERMITS AND INSPECTIONS-The Contractor shall give all notices, secure and pay for all permits and inspections and shall comply with all laws, ordinances and regulations governing construction, fire prevention, health and sanitation bearing on the conduct of the work.

CLEANING-The Contractor shall at all times keep the premises free from accumulations of waste materials and rubbish, and at the completion of the work all rooms and spaces shall be left broom clean.

WORK NOT INCLUDED-The following items of work are excluded from the Contract, however, may be included if noted under "Special Items Included."

Blasting
Sub-soil Drain
Waterproofing
Driveways and Walks
Finished Grading, Planting and Landscaping
Fences
Furniture and Furnishings
Venetian Blinds
Window Shades
Refrigerator
Cooking Range
Bathroom Accessories
Weatherstripping

EXCAVATION AND GRADING

The General Conditions of the Specifications apply to this Section.

WORK INCLUDED-The work under this Section shall consist of furnishing all equipment and performing all necessary labor to do all excavating and rough grading work shown or specified. Excavate to dimen-

Fig. 3-23. A portion of the specifications for a house.

SPECIFICATIONS

Specifications are written notes arranged in list form. They give instructions about materials and methods of work, especially those having to do with quality standards. **Fig. 3-23.** Specifications may explain the level of quality expected of tradespeople and give the minimum quality for materials and finishes.

In commercial construction, fulltime specification writers often work on complex projects. In residential construction, the specifications are often provided by the architect. Specifications should be clear and brief.

SECTION 3.3 Check Your Knowledge

1. Name the four types of views commonly included in a set of architectural plans.
2. What is a typical section and how is it often identified?
3. Give three pieces of information that you would expect to find on a window schedule.
4. What is found on a room-finish schedule?

On the Job

From the house plans contained in this chapter, determine how many doors there are in the garage.

Chapter 3

Review

Section Summaries

3.1 Construction plans consist of drawings of each part of the structure, as well as its measurements. In order to represent full-size objects on fairly small sheets of paper, objects are drawn to scale, which means they are smaller but in the correct proportions. This is done with an architect's scale.

3.2 The elements of a drawing include lines, dimensions, symbols, and notes. Different kinds of lines and symbols express different kinds of information. Computer-aided drafting and design enables architects to create plans and other drawings electronically. Estimating software can be combined with CADD to produce lists of materials. Electronic libraries provide pre-drawn symbols that save time.

3.3 Plan views include site plans, foundation plans, floor plans, framing plans, electrical plans, and mechanical plans. Elevations, section views, schedules, and specifications give information that does not appear in plan views. Renderings show the finished building.

Review Questions

1. What is a sketch?
2. What is scale and how is it used?
3. What is the most common scale used for drawing houses?
4. Describe a hidden line and tell its purpose.
5. What is the purpose of notes on a construction drawing?
6. What are the advantages of CADD?
7. What information would you find in an exterior elevation that you wouldn't find in a plan view?
8. What part of the house framing is most often shown in an elevation and why?
9. What is the purpose of a rendering?
10. What are specifications?

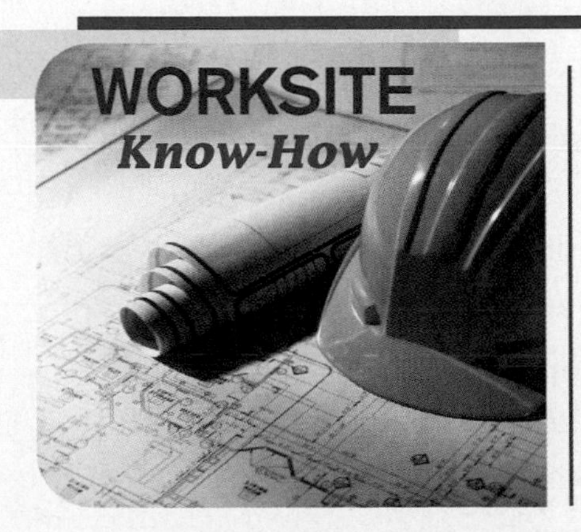

Using the Internet for Building Plans The Internet plays an important role for almost all industries, including construction. For example, there are Web sites that serve as storage and distribution centers for building plans and specifications. Owners, designers, contractors, and subcontractors on a project can view, transfer, download, fax, or print copies, as needed. Distribution of plans is less costly and more efficient. Tracking and record keeping are easier. The sites are secure, and only those working on a particular project can access the material.

Chapter

Estimating and Scheduling

Objectives

After reading this chapter, you'll be able to:

- Name and describe the three basic types of cost estimates.
- Give an example of a direct cost and an indirect cost.
- Draw a simple critical path method (CPM) diagram.

Terms

allowance
bid
board foot
critical path method (CPM)
direct cost
indirect cost
nodes
punch list
quantity takeoff
unit-cost estimate

Estimating and scheduling are two separate tasks. They are often linked, however, because both organize the materials and labor needed to build a house. *Estimating* determines the costs of building a house, particularly the cost of labor and materials. *Scheduling* organizes the construction process so the contractor can make the most efficient use of resources. It also enables the builder to determine when the project is ahead of or behind schedule.

Though these two processes are often intertwined, the estimate generally occurs first. After an estimate has been accepted and construction contracts have been signed, detailed scheduling begins.

This chapter gives a general introduction to estimating and scheduling. Detailed methods will be found where appropriate throughout this book.

SECTION 4.1

Estimating

General contractors and subcontractors alike regularly make estimates. An estimate can determine in advance how much it will cost to build a house. This information is important because it relates directly to how profitable the contractor's business is. If construction costs are *under*estimated all the time, a contractor will eventually go out of business. If they are *over*estimated too often, the contractor may lose jobs to contractors with lower, more accurate bids. A **bid** is a signed proposal to do work and/or supply a material for a specified price. The ability to make accurate estimates is one of the most important skills any builder or contractor can develop.

Typically, a builder contacts suppliers of materials and labor and asks them to bid on the project. This is called competitive bidding. The builder often requests bids from several sources for each portion of the project, such as excavation, framing, and roofing. After receiving all the bids, the builder chooses those that are the best. For example, the goal might be to complete the house quickly. In this case, the builder might choose the company that promised the earliest start date. If the goal was to keep costs as low as possible, the builder might choose those who submitted the lowest of several bids.

A large construction company employs workers who specialize in preparing quantity and cost estimates. Many building material retailers also have at least one estimator on staff. In a small construction company, however, it is the owner who generally prepares the estimates. Anyone who prepares estimates must:

- Be able to read and measure building plans accurately.
- Have an excellent understanding of the materials and techniques used to build houses.
- Have an excellent understanding of the local building codes.
- Be precise in assembling and computing numerical data.

Estimating varies by region. An estimator moving from one region to another must become acquainted with local building practices as well as local building codes.

TYPES OF ESTIMATES

Estimates are used at many different times during the construction process. Some are informal and approximate, while others are detailed and precise. Generally, the earliest estimates are the least accurate. Accuracy increases as estimates are refined to reflect new information.

Pre-Design Estimate

During the early stages of working with a client, a builder is often asked how much a new house will cost. Providing an accurate answer is impossible without spending many hours studying a set of plans. Instead, the builder may multiply the square footage of the house by the approximate construction costs per square foot in that area. This type of estimate is called a *pre-design estimate.* It may also be called a *preliminary, ballpark,* or *conceptual estimate.* It is an estimate made before the exact features of the house are known.

An experienced builder usually knows the range of overall construction costs in the area. For example, a simple house built with modest materials might cost $75 per square foot. A more complex house in which high-quality materials are used might run $120 per square foot. Thus the pre-design estimate for an 1,800-square-foot house could range from $135,000 to $216,000. The cost of land is added to determine a pre-design total cost for the project. This figure would enable the client to determine whether or not new construction was affordable.

An architect may use pre-design estimates to figure his or her design fee. Insurance companies also use pre-design estimates to establish approximate replacement costs after damage has occurred.

Quantity Takeoff

For a detailed understanding of costs, a builder or contractor develops a quantity takeoff. A **quantity takeoff** is a cost estimate in which every piece of material required to build the house is counted and priced. It is also sometimes called a *complete construction cost esti-*

Basement Stair

Part	Unit	Material	Length	Unit Cost	Total Cost
Stringer	LF	2x12 pine	12′		
Treads	PC				
Risers	PC				
Handrail	LF				
Balusters	PC				
Brackets	PC				
Other					

Fig. 4-1. A simple quantity takeoff. In this example, the unit cost for the stringer would be the cost per lineal foot. The unit cost will vary. The total cost would be the unit cost times 12.

mate or a *quantity survey.* **Fig. 4-1.** A takeoff is time-consuming, but, once complete, it has other uses. For example, the builder may refer to the takeoff when ordering materials. Many computer programs are available to prepare quantity takeoffs.

A complete set of building plans is necessary to prepare a quantity takeoff. The estimator must also review the project specifications with great care. There can be a big difference in cost between one grade of material and another, even though the number of pieces does not change. If a quantity takeoff is precise, there will be little or no difference between the estimate and actual construction costs.

Estimators must use the proper measure of quantity when preparing a quantity takeoff. For example, concrete is generally measured by the cubic yard. Framing lumber is measured by the lineal foot, by the piece, or by thousand-board-foot quantities. Carpeting is measured by the square yard and, increasingly, by the square foot. **Table 4-A** shows common abbreviations used in estimating.

Unit-Cost Estimate

Another detailed estimate of construction costs is a **unit-cost estimate**, or *component-cost estimate.* In making a unit-cost estimate the estimator divides the house into components, such as walls or roof. Estimates are made of the cost for each component. This is faster than the quantity takeoff method.

The "unit" of a unit-cost estimate depends on the component. The unit for walls is typically lineal feet (LF) while the unit for floors and roofs is square feet (SF). For example, the 8′ high inte-

Table 4-A. Common Abbreviations Used in Estimating

APPR (approximate)	MISC (miscellaneous)
BDL (bundle)	NA (not applicable)
BF (board foot)	NAT (natural)
CF (cubic foot)	OA (overall)
CY (cubic yard)	OZ (ounce)
EA (each)	PC (piece)
GA (gauge)	PR (pair)
GAL (gallon)	QT (quart)
HR (hour)	R/L (random lengths)
LB (pound)	RH (right hand)
LBS/HR (pounds per hour)	SA (sack)
LF (lineal foot)	SF (square foot)
LH (left hand)	SQ (square)
M2 (square meter)	UNF (unfinished)
M3 (cubic meter)	YD (yard)
MH (man-hour)	

Note: These abbreviations are usually capitalized but may also be seen in other forms. For example, "each" may be written Ea. Some of these abbreviations may also be followed by periods. Some of these abbreviations differ from those used in this text.

rior partition shown in **Fig. 4-2** would be measured in lineal feet. Suppose the wall is 12′ long. The cost of the wall would include the costs of every part, including:

- Plates.
- Studs.
- 16d nails.
- Drywall on both sides of the wall.
- Drywall screws.
- Joint tape.
- Joint compound.
- Drywall primer.
- Interior paint (2 coats).
- Baseboard trim.

The total cost for the wall would be divided by 12 to determine the unit cost. After a unit cost for a partition is figured, the estimator can quickly determine the lineal feet in the whole house by measuring the plans. This figure is then multiplied by the unit cost to determine total costs for the walls. Depending upon the estimator's needs, the unit cost may be for materials only, or it may include labor. A unit cost for labor would include the labor of a carpenter, a drywall installer, and a painter.

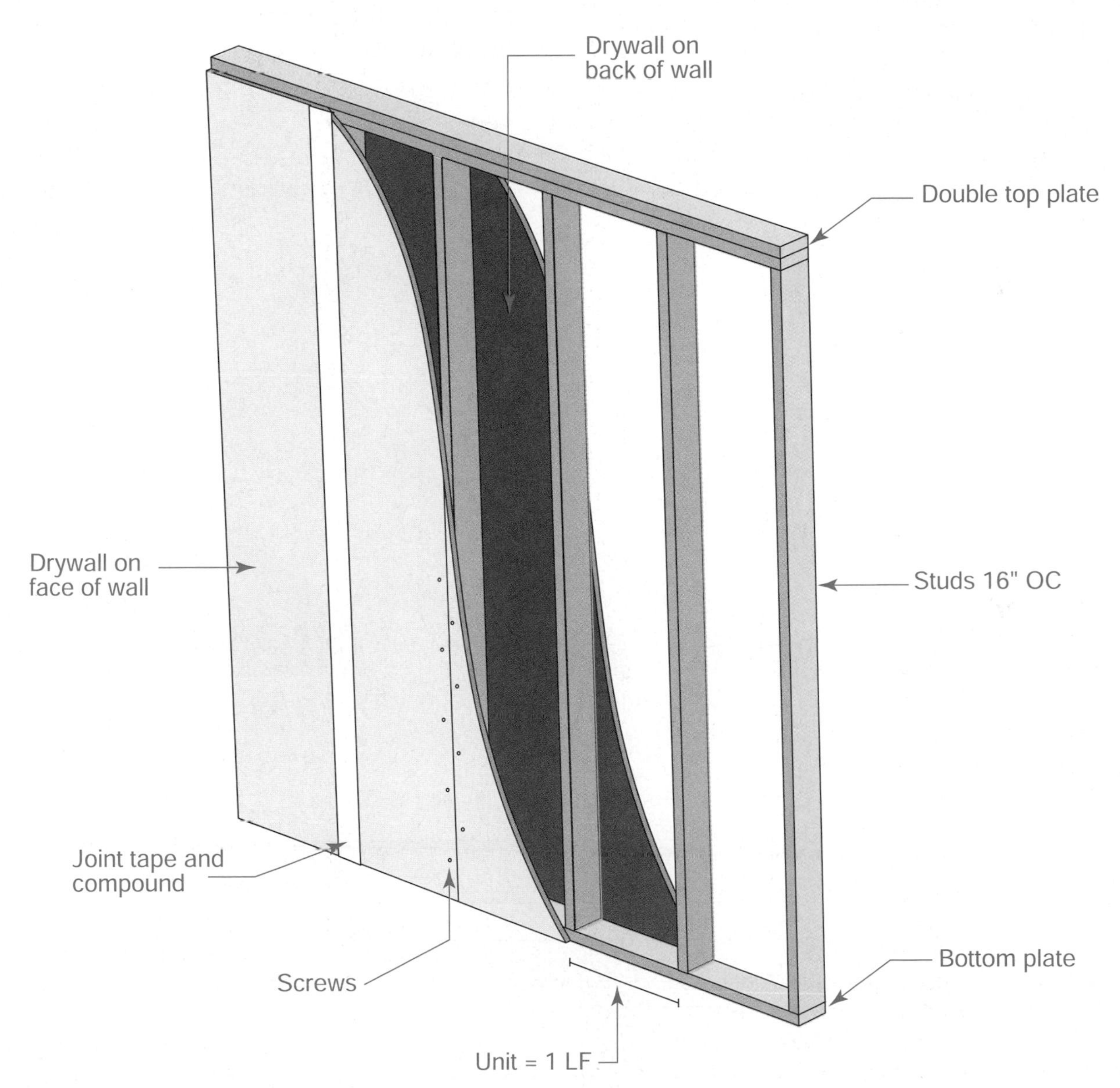

Fig. 4-2. A completed partition. The unit measurement of this wall would be in lineal feet (LF). If the wall included an opening, the cost of those materials would also need to be estimated.

CALCULATING BOARD FEET

A **board foot** is a unit of measure that represents a piece of lumber having a flat surface area of 1 sq. ft. and a thickness of 1″ nominal size. **Fig. 4-3.** The number of board feet can be found by using simple arithmetic or by referring to a table. **Table 4-B.**

To determine the number of board feet in one or more pieces of lumber, use the following formula:

$$\frac{\text{Pieces} \times \text{Thickness (in.)} \times \text{Width (in.)} \times \text{Length (ft.)}}{12}$$

Example 1: Find the number of board feet in a piece of lumber 2″ thick, 10″ wide, and 6′ long. **Fig. 4-4.**

$$\frac{2 \times 10 \times 6}{12} = 10 \text{ bd. ft.}$$

Table 4-B. Rules of Thumb for Estimating Board Feet

Width (inches)	Thickness (inches)	Board Feet
3	1 or less	¼ of the length
4	1 or less	⅓ of the length
6	1 or less	½ of the length
9	1 or less	¾ of the length
12	1 or less	Same as the length
15	1 or less	1¼ of the length

Example 2: Find the number of board feet in 10 pieces of lumber 2″ thick, 10″ wide, and 6′ long.

$$\frac{10 \times 2 \times 10 \times 6}{12} = 100 \text{ bd. ft.}$$

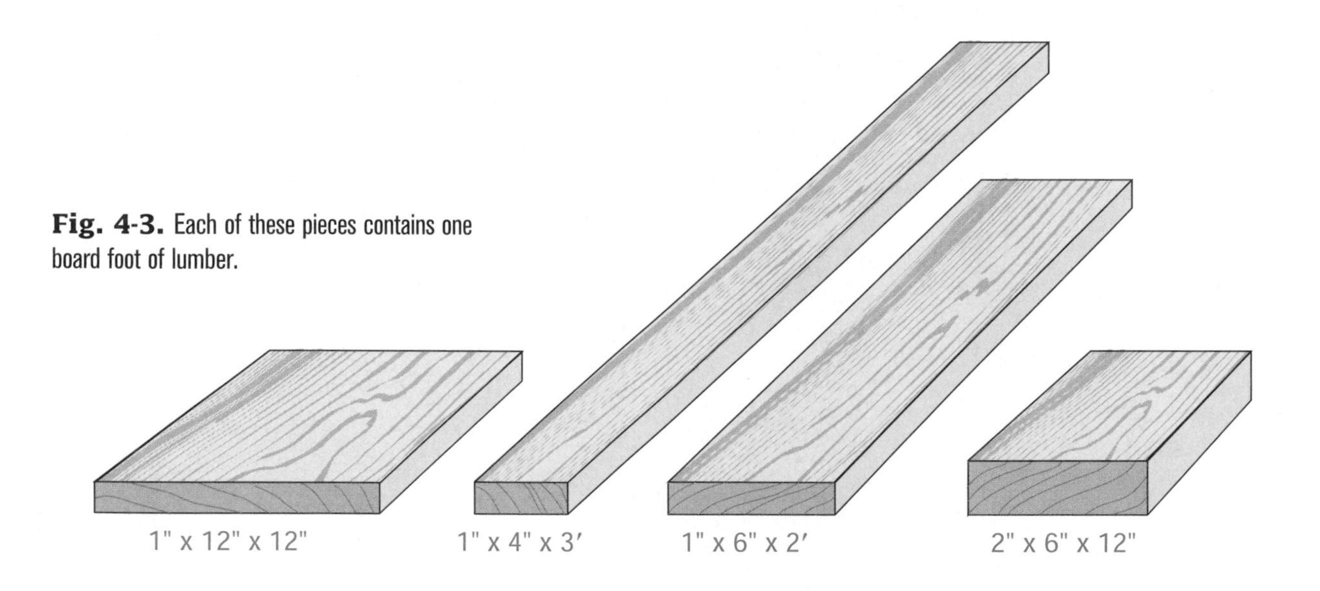

Fig. 4-3. Each of these pieces contains one board foot of lumber.

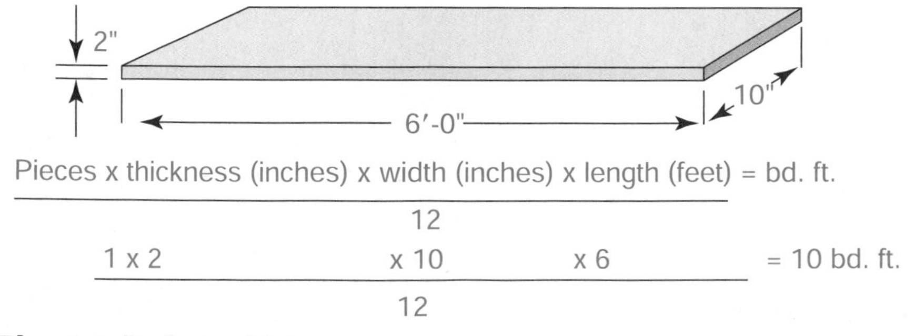

Fig. 4-4. Figuring board feet.

If all three dimensions are expressed in inches, the same formula applies. However, the divisor is changed to 144.

Example 3: Find the number of board feet in one piece of lumber 2″ thick, 10″ wide, and 18″ long.

$$\frac{1 \times 2 \times 10 \times 18}{144} = 2\tfrac{1}{2} \text{ bd. ft.}$$

ALLOWANCES

When an estimate is being prepared for a custom house, some costs may not be known until late in the process. These are usually related to products that the client must choose, such as lighting fixtures, floor coverings, and cabinetry. To account for these items, the estimator includes an **allowance** in the estimate. An allowance is a dollar figure representing the cost of products that have not yet been chosen when a detailed estimate is made. For example, $3,500 might be the builder's allowance for interior and exterior lighting fixtures. If the client later chooses fixtures that cost more, the client must pay the difference.

The advantage of allowances is that the builder can provide an early cost estimate without forcing the client to make difficult product choices. The hazard of allowances is that they can be unrealistically low. The client might be surprised by large expenses late in the process.

Money is usually set aside in a builder's construction budget to cover the costs of unforeseen situations. These might include an unexpected stretch of wet weather. Such weather might require the builder to use pumps to keep the excavation dry. This allocation of money is called a *contingency allowance*. If the money is not required, the builder either adds it to the profit or refunds it to the client.

TYPES OF COSTS

A builder must account for two types of expenses in order to turn a profit. **Direct costs**, or *project costs*, are related to a certain house. They include such costs as those for labor, materials, building permits, temporary power hookups, and some types of insurance. Most direct costs can be determined based on a review of the building plans. The estimating techniques noted throughout this book are those that determine direct costs.

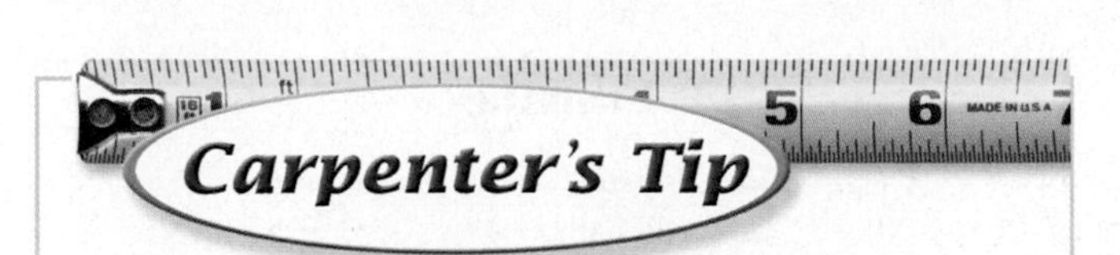

A client approves plans for the house in advance. However, the client may wish to change some aspect of the house after construction has begun. In such a case, the builder and client sign a document that describes the changes exactly and estimates the cost for the extra work. This document is called a change order. A change order helps the builder keep track of extra costs. It also reduces the chances for misunderstandings between builder and client.

Indirect costs, or *overhead*, are not specifically related to a particular house. These costs relate to the organization and supervision of the project. They include the cost of office equipment and supplies and construction tools and equipment, as well as office payroll and taxes.

Some needs involve both direct and indirect costs. For example, the monthly access charge for the phone in a builder's truck would be an indirect cost. Long-distance calls made to a supplier for lumber used on a project could be considered direct costs.

A percentage for profit must be added to every estimate. This percentage may range from 10 to 40 percent, depending on the job size and the work.

CHECKLISTS

The heart of an estimate is a checklist that identifies everything used at every stage of construction. The purpose of a checklist is to ensure that nothing is left out of the estimate.

The builder or estimator reviews each item on the checklist and determines which ones apply to the project. For each item, the estimator calculates the dimensions and quantity of material needed and the cost.

Framing

- ❑ 8d nails
- ❑ 10d nails
- ❑ 16d nails
- ❑ Hold-downs
- ❑ Tie straps
- ❑ Post bases
- ❑ Post caps

Wall Frame

- ❑ Sill plate
- ❑ Top plate
- ❑ Walls, cripple
- ❑ Walls, 2x4
- ❑ Walls, 2x6
- ❑ Walls, other
- ❑ Blocking
- ❑ Sheathing
- ❑ Beams
- ❑ Posts

Headers

- ❑ Door
- ❑ Window

Ceiling Frame

- ❑ Ledgers
- ❑ Joists
- ❑ Blocking
- ❑ Soffits
- ❑ Anchors

Floor Frame

- ❑ Ledgers
- ❑ Girders
- ❑ Beams
- ❑ Joists
- ❑ Joist hangers
- ❑ Rim joists
- ❑ Blocking
- ❑ Sheathing

Roof Frame

- ❑ Ridge
- ❑ Ledgers
- ❑ Plates
- ❑ Rafters
- ❑ Metal anchors
- ❑ Purlins
- ❑ Braces
- ❑ Collar ties
- ❑ Sheathing
- ❑ Blocks
- ❑ Outriggers

Fig. 4-5. An example of a construction-order checklist.

Construction-Order Checklist

Many builders prefer items on a checklist to be in the same order as the jobs to be done. Thus, the first items on a *construction-order checklist* relate to excavation, the next to building the foundation, and so on. Part of the framing portion of such a checklist is shown in **Fig. 4-5**. One advantage of this approach is that it encourages the estimator and the builder to think logically about how the house will be built.

CSI MasterFormat Checklist

The Construction Specifications Institute (CSI) is a professional association that develops standards for writing specifications. CSI has developed a system of organizing specifications for various aspects of commercial construction. This system is called *MasterFormat*. The MasterFormat system organizes all aspects of construction into sixteen main categories. **Fig. 4-6.** Each category consists of many subcategories. Though the system was developed for commercial construction, some residential builders have adapted it for use in developing estimating checklists.

SOURCES FOR COST INFORMATION

Gathering information about the exact cost of materials and labor can be time consuming. The estimator must check various sources.

- **Material suppliers.** The estimator can contact local material suppliers to get the cost of materials. Generally this is done after the quantity is determined. This is because a large quantity of flooring, for example, generally costs less per square foot than a small quantity. Several suppliers may then make bids. For example, several suppliers may bid on supplying all the lumber and sheathing for a project. A builder generally accepts the lowest bid for a given quality and quantity.
- **Prior bids.** If the builder has recently completed another house using similar materials, some of the cost information can be obtained from the previous estimate.

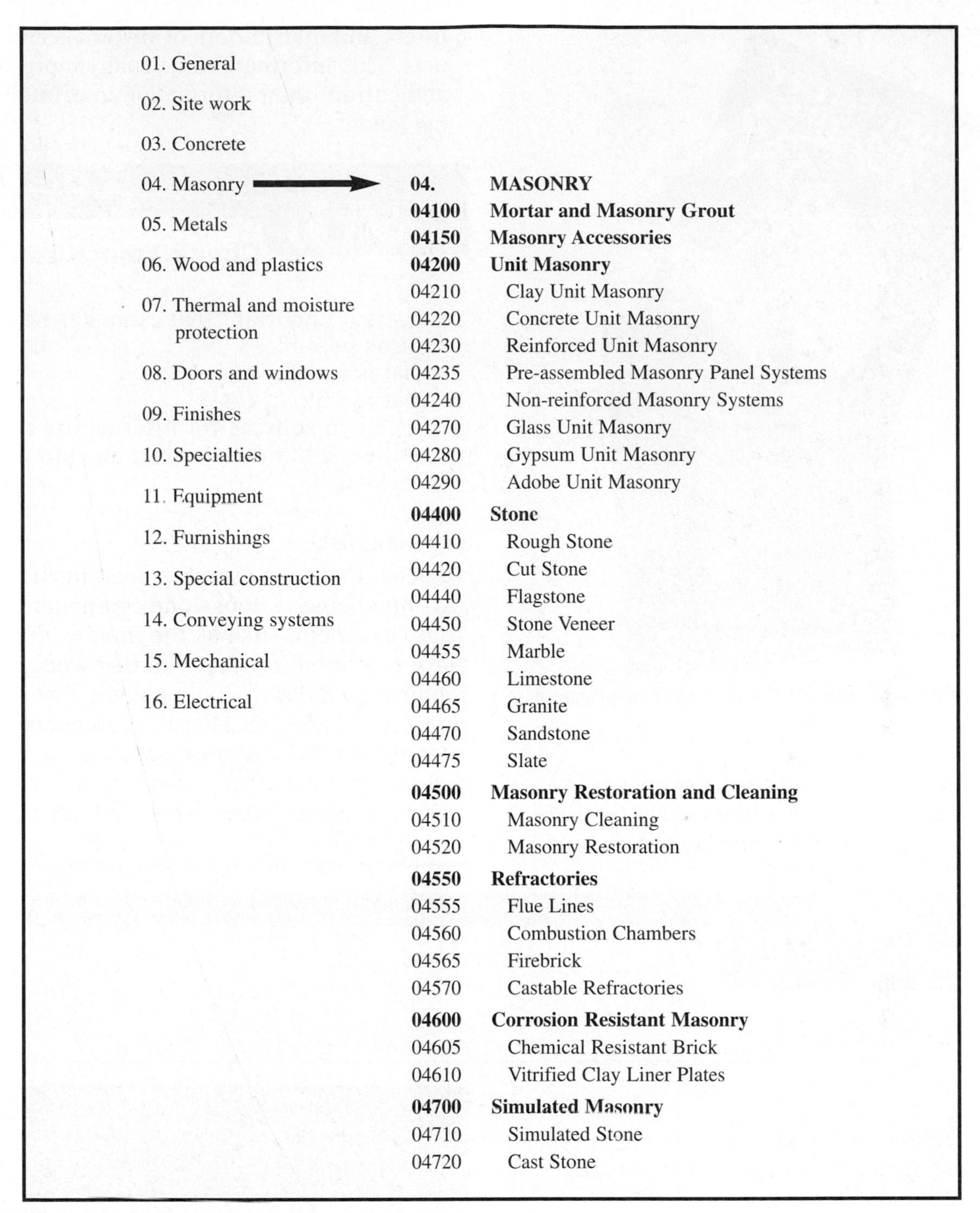

01. General		
02. Site work		
03. Concrete		
04. Masonry →	**04.**	**MASONRY**
	04100	**Mortar and Masonry Grout**
05. Metals	**04150**	**Masonry Accessories**
06. Wood and plastics	**04200**	**Unit Masonry**
	04210	Clay Unit Masonry
07. Thermal and moisture protection	04220	Concrete Unit Masonry
	04230	Reinforced Unit Masonry
08. Doors and windows	04235	Pre-assembled Masonry Panel Systems
	04240	Non-reinforced Masonry Systems
09. Finishes	04270	Glass Unit Masonry
10. Specialties	04280	Gypsum Unit Masonry
	04290	Adobe Unit Masonry
11. Equipment	**04400**	**Stone**
12. Furnishings	04410	Rough Stone
13. Special construction	04420	Cut Stone
	04440	Flagstone
14. Conveying systems	04450	Stone Veneer
15. Mechanical	04455	Marble
	04460	Limestone
16. Electrical	04465	Granite
	04470	Sandstone
	04475	Slate
	04500	**Masonry Restoration and Cleaning**
	04510	Masonry Cleaning
	04520	Masonry Restoration
	04550	**Refractories**
	04555	Flue Lines
	04560	Combustion Chambers
	04565	Firebrick
	04570	Castable Refractories
	04600	**Corrosion Resistant Masonry**
	04605	Chemical Resistant Brick
	04610	Vitrified Clay Liner Plates
	04700	**Simulated Masonry**
	04710	Simulated Stone
	04720	Cast Stone

Fig. 4-6. An example of the CSI MasterFormat checklist.

- **Pricing guides.** Books are available that contain detailed listings of the prices of materials and of the labor to supply them. **Fig. 4-7.** These books are published annually or semi-annually.

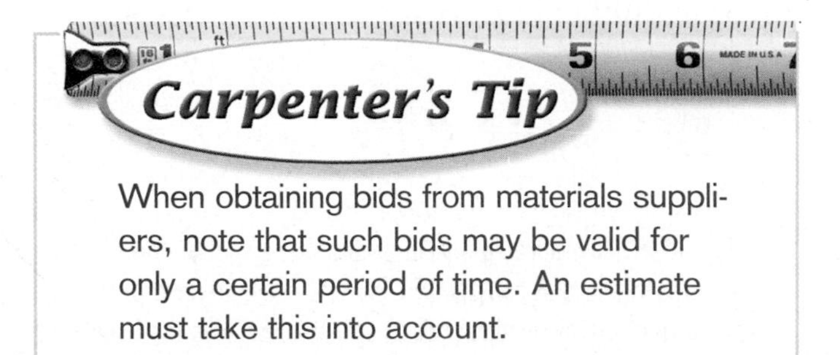

Carpenter's Tip

When obtaining bids from materials suppliers, note that such bids may be valid for only a certain period of time. An estimate must take this into account.

Fig. 4-7. Costs of materials and labor are available for all areas of construction.

- **Databases.** Increasingly, estimators use the Internet to check current prices. These prices are posted on their Web sites by the manufacturers and distributors of materials and products. This information is usually more reliable and current than information in printed pricing guides.

SECTION 4.1

Check Your Knowledge

1. Why is it important that estimates be as accurate as possible?
2. What is an allowance?
3. What is a direct cost?
4. Name two sources for information that can help a builder develop an estimating checklist.

On the Job

To be accurate, an estimate must include every part of a house. Choose one component of your classroom, such as the floor or the walls. Make a list of every material that would be required to build that component. One way to do this is to imagine that the component has been destroyed and must be replaced. Compare your list to the lists of others in your class who were working with the same component. Did you miss anything?

SECTION 4.2

Scheduling

Two elements must be scheduled when building a home: materials and activities. It is the responsibility of the general contractor to set up and monitor these schedules. Naturally, the size of the building project affects the complexity of the scheduling. **Fig. 4-8.**

Fig. 4-8. In a building project of this size, a special crew is responsible for each phase of construction. For example, one crew puts in the footings and the foundation walls. A second crew does the floor framing. A third crew does the wall framing, and so on. Supervisors, who are directly responsible to the general contractor, coordinate material deliveries and scheduling of work crews.

A contractor who is building only a few houses each year with a small crew often works part-time as part of the crew on the job site. The rest of the time is spent in coordinating the delivery of materials and the work of the subcontractors. **Fig. 4-9.** Contractors with many projects may spend all their time on these matters or may hire supervisors to do it.

In residential construction, builders may use several different employment strategies. A builder may:

- Build entirely with his or her own employees.
- Build with a team composed of of employees and subcontractors.
- Build entirely with subcontractors.

It is important that all work is completed on time so as not to delay overall progress. Especially important is coordinating the work of subcontractors, because they work on different projects and for various builders.

MATERIAL SCHEDULING

Proper scheduling of material deliveries can have a major impact on the efficiency and quality of construction. The builder is responsible for ensuring access to the site. The builder must also make sure that delivered materials can be properly stored. For example, if a large load of oak flooring is delivered before the house is closed in, it has to be stored outdoors. There it is exposed to possible weather damage. Also, the bundles of oak are in the way of workers, which reduces worker efficiency.

Material scheduling must be coordinated by builders or general contractors. They work with suppliers to ensure that materials will be available for delivery when needed. **Fig. 4-10.** Materials that are normally kept in stock, such as framing lumber, can usually be ordered on short notice. A non-stock item, such as a custom cabinet or Italian granite of an unusual color, may require a lead time of weeks or months.

Naturally, deliveries vary depending on the type and size of the project. They depend also on the number of people working on it and the time set for completion.

Fig. 4-9. Many homes are built by contractors with only two or three employees. Much of the work is done by specialized subcontractors hired for the project.

Fig. 4-10. General contractors who work on large projects buy large quantities of materials from a single source to obtain a better price. These materials are then delivered to a central receiving area for redistribution at the job site.

Generally, material deliveries are made in the following order:

- *First load:* all items needed to complete the house up to and including the subfloor.
- *Second load:* wall framing and ceiling joists.
- *Third load:* roof framing materials and roof coverings. If roof trusses are used, these will be shipped to the site on a special truck. This truck sometimes has a crane to lift trusses into position.
- *Fourth load:* exterior doors, windows, exterior trim, and siding, as needed. After the building has been enclosed with doors and windows and can be locked up, the interior wall finish is applied. If the walls are plastered, adequate drying time must be allowed before additional material shipments are made.
- *Fifth load:* hardwood flooring and underlayment materials.
- *Sixth load:* interior doors, trim, and built-in cabinet materials.

Materials to be delivered to the job site are placed in the truck in the sequence in which they are to be used. When the materials are unloaded and stacked at the site, those needed first will be on top of the pile.

It is the general contractor's responsibility to check the delivered materials against the original order. If materials are damaged or missing, the supplier should be contacted immediately. If this is not done, construction may be delayed. If materials are left over, the supplier may accept them back for credit but may charge a restocking fee.

The supplier keeps a running tally of the materials shipped to the job site, as well as any credits for returns. The general contractor is expected to pay for materials on a certain time schedule, such as every week or month. In the case of special orders, full or partial payment may be required when the order is placed.

ACTIVITY SCHEDULING

The general contractor is responsible for scheduling subcontractors and other labor and keeps things moving smoothly. Careful scheduling can limit delays caused by subcontractors whose work needs to be done before other subcontractors can begin. For example, if a builder does not arrange for foundation contractors far enough in advance, the entire project may be delayed until a subcontractor can fit the project into his or her schedule.

Following is a list of general steps in house construction. It is the general contractor's responsibility to see that these steps are carried out. However, sometimes jobs must be started ahead of schedule or delayed. Therefore, the steps may not always occur in this order. Note that required inspections must be scheduled at the appropriate time.

1. *Survey.* The job site is surveyed and the abstract of title is brought up to date so that application for title insurance can be made.
2. *Permit.* A building permit is obtained from proper authorities so that work can begin.
3. *Excavation.* The excavator brings in power equipment and strips the topsoil away, piling it in one corner of the lot for future use. If the building will have a basement, it is excavated at this time.

SAFETY FIRST

Call Before You Dig

Before any excavation or trenching is done, the local gas, electric, water, and phone utility companies must be contacted. They then mark the location of utility lines. This "call before you dig" precaution helps to prevent the accidental cutting of buried lines that cross the property. Cutting into a power line is a serious safety hazard! Be sure you know where utilities are located before you enter an excavation.

4. *Temporary power.* The electric company must be contacted to set up a temporary power pole on the building site and hook it up. The electricity is needed for operating power tools.
5. *Temporary water.* On some job sites the plumber makes the temporary water hookup, which must be coordinated with the city utilities. In existing neighborhoods, water can sometimes be obtained from a neighbor. In this case, the permanent hookup for water to the building is not made until the foundation walls have been installed.

6. *Foundation.* Footings and foundation walls are installed by the foundation subcontractor.

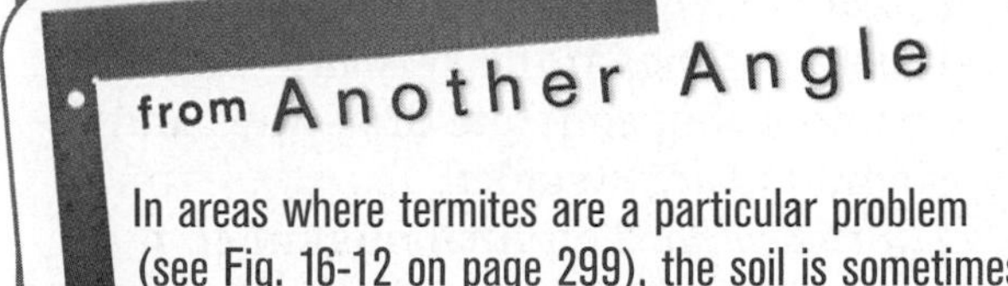

In areas where termites are a particular problem (see Fig. 16-12 on page 299), the soil is sometimes treated with chemicals to prevent infestations. A termite control specialist may treat the soil before the foundation slab is poured.

7. *Plumbing.* Pipelines for the water supply are installed in trenches by the plumbing contractor. If the house will be served by a well, it may be drilled at this time.
8. *Slabs.* If the house has a basement, the concrete floor is poured after the rough plumbing is installed and before the interior finish work. The concrete must cure thoroughly. The garage floor is put in anytime after the backfill is completed. Often this is done at the same time as the basement floor. The concrete is delivered to the site in ready-mix trucks.
9. *Framing.* The carpenters can now frame and sheath the floors, walls, and roof.
10. *Backfilling.* Before any backfilling can be completed, the exterior walls of the foundation must be moisture-proofed and foundation drainage must be in place. Also, backfilling should not be done until the floor system is framed or the foundation walls are otherwise braced. This allows time for the concrete to gain strength and reduces the chance that the pressure of backfill will damage the walls.

    If backfilling is delayed until framing is completed, the workers have the inconvenience of working around a large excavation. However, if backfilling is done before framing begins, extra time and costs are involved in bracing the foundation securely so that it is not damaged by backfill.

SAFETY FIRST

Balancing Act

Keep in mind that if backfilling is delayed until framing is completed, the workers have to work around a large excavation. This can be unsafe because they have to carry materials on planks over the excavation.

11. *Mechanicals.* At this point, a number of activities may be carried out at the same time, or at least in rapid succession. These include plumbing, heating, and electrical work. All mechanical subcontractors must work in two stages: *rough-in work* and *finish work.*

    For example, when the framing is complete, the electrician comes in to do the rough wiring. This includes installing the main circuit panel and outlet boxes and feeding all the wires through the framing. This is the rough-in portion of the work. Later, after the interior walls are completed, the electrician comes back to install the switches, receptacles, and light fixtures. A plumber installs bathtubs during the rough-in phase, because tubs are a built-in feature of the house.
12. *Windows and doors.* While the mechanical subcontractors are doing the rough-in work, the carpenters install exterior doors and windows and complete any remaining details of the framing.

Windows and doors should be installed as soon as possible after they are delivered to the site. This reduces the chance of damage to glass or frames. It also minimizes the number of times doors and windows must be handled. Early installation also keeps these materials out of the way of workers.

13. *Roofing and siding.* To weatherize and protect the house, contractors install roofing and siding. Generally the roofing is installed first.
14. *Insulation.* After all rough-in work is done, insulation is installed in the walls and, as needed, in the ceiling.
15. *Interior and exterior finishes.* Most interiors are finished with drywall or plaster.

Plastering must be done immediately. At the same time, carpenters can work on the exterior of the building installing siding, exterior trim, and the garage door.

Normally, plaster is applied in two stages. Often a week or ten days must be allowed for drying after each stage before proceeding with other interior work. With drywall, the drying period is much shorter since the only wet application is taping the joints and covering nailheads.

16. *Finish carpentry.* At this stage the carpenters are ready to do the interior finishing, provided the plaster and concrete are thoroughly dry. If interior trim is delivered and stored in a house with high humidity due to wet plaster and concrete, the wood will absorb the moisture and swell. Later it will dry out and crack. Wood floors may be installed at this stage but are usually finished later. Built-in shelves, interior doors, and cabinets come next. Finally, the interior moldings are applied, including base, shoe, ceiling, window, and door trim.

Carpenter's Tip

Most general contractors know that it is important to stay in contact with subcontractors as they work on the house. This ensures that the work is done in a timely fashion and at the level of quality agreed to previously. However, it is also important to maintain contact with subcontractors well ahead of the time when their work is to begin. This will often give the general contractor advance warning of any delays that could affect the schedule.

17. *Exterior painting.* As carpenters are working on the inside of the house, painters can be finishing the exterior. The ideal arrangement is for the painters to work closely behind the carpenters so that the wood is properly sealed. If exterior trim has been pre-primed at the factory, timing is not as important.
18. *Finish grading.* While the carpenters are completing the interior of the house, the exterior grading, as well as all flat concrete work such as sidewalks and driveways, is done.
19. *Concrete driveways and sidewalks.* After finish grading, at the very last stages of construction, concrete driveways and sidewalks are installed.
20. *Landscaping.* The final step in completing the exterior of the house is the landscaping.
21. *Interior painting.* After the carpenters have completed the interior of the house, the painting is done.
22. *Floor coverings.* After the paint is dry, floor tile and resilient flooring are installed.
23. *Finish electrical.* At this point the electricians can return to add switches, outlets, and light fixtures. **Fig. 4-11.**
24. *Finish plumbing.* The plumbing fixtures are now installed by the plumbing contractor.
25. *Wood flooring.* One of the last jobs on the interior of the house is to finish the wood flooring. Many homes are completely covered by carpeting and require no floor finishing. However, if hardwood floors are used, sanding should be done after the interior painting to remove any paint drops or spillage. The actual finishing is done as one of the last jobs so that traffic does not raise dust while the finish dries. Hardwood flooring can also be purchased prefinished, which greatly simplifies this part of the job.
26. *Carpeting.* After the wood floors are finished, carpeting is laid.
27. *Cleanup.* The general contractor is responsible for the final cleanup. A responsible contractor will make sure that the windows are washed and all waste materials are removed.
28. *Punch list.* After the entire house has been completed, the general contractor or builder walks through the house with the new owner. This is a chance for the owner to make sure everything has been done to his or her satisfaction. Often, the owner will spot such things as scuffed paint, cracked woodwork, or light fixtures that don't work properly. The contractor then makes a **punch list**. This list identifies all

4-11. The electrician returns to add switches.

the repairs that must be completed before the house is acceptable to the owner.

You can follow the sequence of jobs by looking at the illustrations in **Fig. 4-12** on page 88. The drawings show the steps for a one-story home.

STAYING ON SCHEDULE

A complex project may involve hundreds of individual tasks. Keeping track of scheduled jobs is the key to successful construction management. Many builders use graphic methods to do this, including bar charts and diagrams. Computer software makes it fairly easy to set these up and revise them as needed.

Bar Charts

A bar chart is an easy way to keep track of a project. It shows how long each task will take and when each task will start and end. A calendar format displays the entire job over time. **Fig. 4-13.** Simple bar charts can be used to

Location ______ Lot# ______
Model ______ Start ______ Finish ______

Calendar Days
Working Days 1 2 3 4 5 6 7 8 9 10 11 12 13 14 15 16 17 18 19 19 20 21 22 23 24 25 26 27 28 29 30 31 32 33 34 35 36 37 38 39 40 41 42

ACTIVITY
Permits
Stakeout
Excavation
Footing
Foundation
Sewer lines
Water lines
Framing
Roof framing/sheathing
Roofing
Windows/doors/stairs
Rough HVAC
Rough electrical
Rough plumbing
Insulation
Brickwork
Exterior trim
Siding/gutters
Exterior painting
Backfill/grading
Sidewalks/driveway
Landscaping
Drywall & finish
Finish HVAC
Finish electrical
Finish plumbing
Interior trim
Interior painting
Resilient flooring
Carpeting
Touch-up
Housecleaning

Fig. 4-13. A bar chart shows how long tasks take and presents them in chronological order.

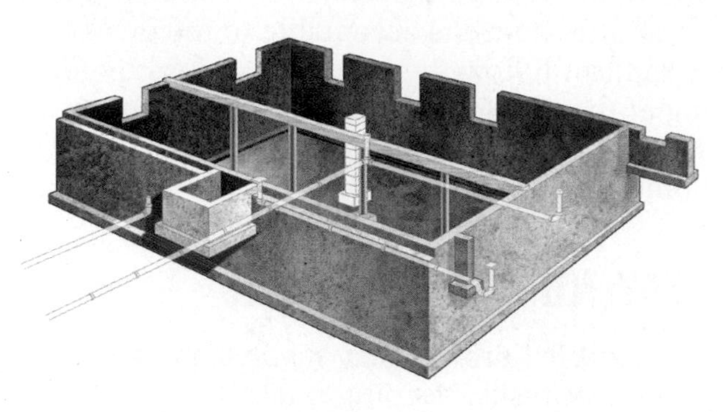

A. Footings and basement walls.

- The basement is excavated and then the footings are placed.
- The foundation walls are either poured or constructed of concrete block. (The fill around the basement is omitted here to show the footings and walls.)
- The supporting columns and the center beam are installed.
- The exterior surface of the walls is moisture-proofed up to the finish grade level.
- The front porch excavation may be filled with sand, ready for the porch and basement floors to be placed.

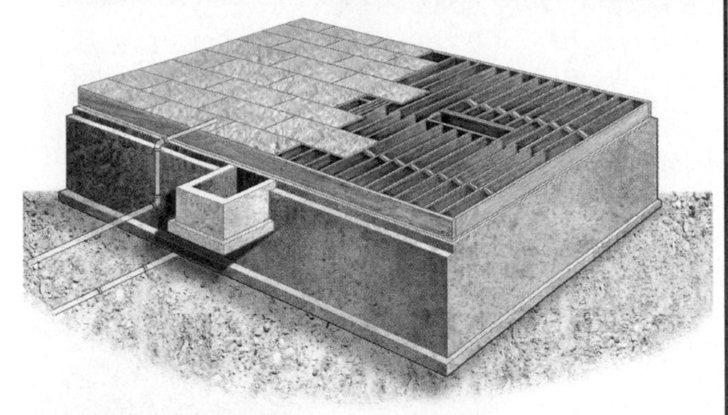

B. First floor construction.

- The rough grading is shown leveled off four inches below the finished grade line.
- The joists are installed. There are double joists at the stairwell and under inside partition walls.
- The double joists are separated with solid bridging. Metal or wood bridging is installed midway between the ends of other joists and the supporting beam.
- The plywood subfloor is laid.

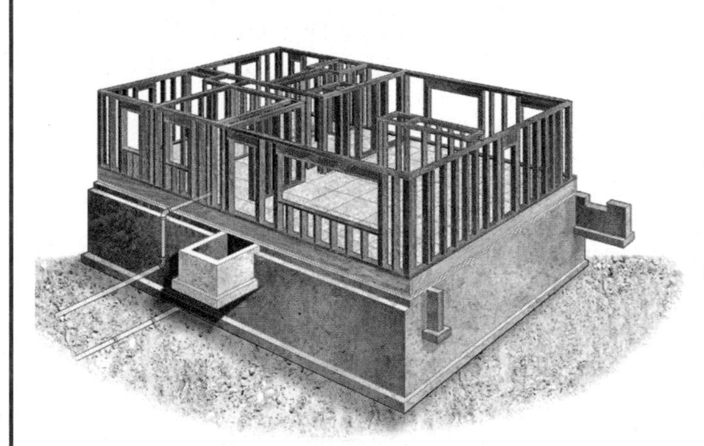

C. Wall framing. Wall framing is completed. If the house has a second story, floor joists and additional wall framing will be added on top of the first-story walls.

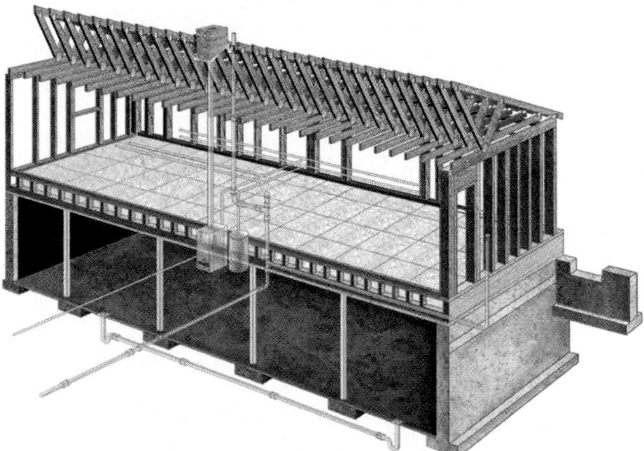

D. Complete framing. Cutaway view of the house showing some finished plumbing and heating. The actual placement of the fixtures and appliances would not be done until the house has been closed in.

E. Rendering of finished home.

Fig. 4-12. The main stages in residential construction.

track small jobs, such as the addition of a bedroom to a house. Expanded versions can track the construction of an entire house.

The value of a bar chart is in its ability to show an overview of the entire project. It also shows how various tasks overlap. However, its simplicity limits its usefulness. A bar chart cannot show complex relationships among various jobs. That is why it is used primarily as a general planning tool.

Critical Path Diagrams

The **critical path method (CPM)** of scheduling shows the relationships among tasks as well as how long they take. It is the most common type of scheduling used in residential construction. The relationships are shown in a CPM diagram.

A CPM diagram's value is in identifying the tasks that are most important (critical) to the success of the project. **Fig. 4-14.** Taken together these tasks identify the minimum amount of time needed. In other words, critical path tasks are those in which any delay will automatically delay completion of the entire project.

To develop a CPM schedule, list all the work that has to be done. The list of tasks under "Activity Scheduling" in this chapter is an example. The following three questions should be answered for each task:

- What tasks come before this one? All tasks have a logical order in which they are performed. For example, the drywall must be taped before it can be painted.
- What tasks cannot start until this one is complete? For example, rough plumbing cannot be installed until the framing is in place.
- What tasks can be conducted at the same time? The job moves quickly when various tradespeople are working at the same time. For example, electricians can be working inside the house while the site is being finish graded.

After these questions have been answered, the tasks can be plotted on a CPM diagram.

The arrows on the diagram indicate tasks. The tail of the arrow represents the start of a task, and the head represents the end. Boxes or cir-

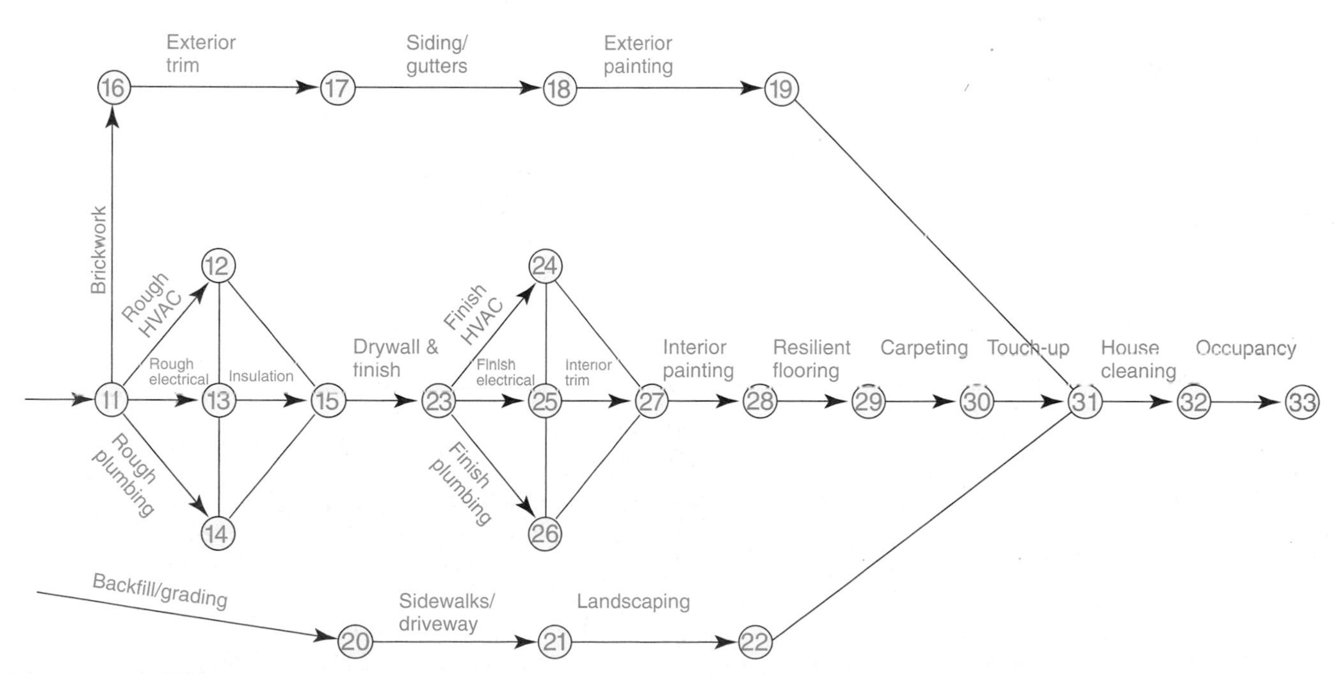

Fig. 4-14. A CPM diagram arranges tasks based on their relationship to one another. The timeline would be placed at the bottom of the diagram and would depend on the schedule for the project.

cles, called **nodes**, represent events that can be recognized, such as "Roof trusses plumbed and braced." Arrows that follow one another along the same path indicate tasks that must end before the next task can begin. Parallel arrows represent tasks that go on at the same time. Arrows can be straight or curved.

from Another Angle

The critical path diagram was originally developed to keep track of maintenance work in an oil and chemical refinery. A similar network diagram, called Program Evaluation and Review Technique (PERT), was developed about the same time to track the construction of nuclear submarines.

SECTION 4.2 Check Your Knowledge

1. What two main elements must be scheduled when building a home?
2. Arrange the following tasks in chronological order, starting with the task that occurs first: A. Interior painting. B. Temporary power. C. Floor coverings. D. Insulation. E. Finish carpentry. F. Floor framing. G. Backfilling.
3. What is a punch list?
4. What do arrows and nodes represent on a CPM diagram?

On the Job

Sketch a CPM diagram for the first twenty-five steps noted under "Activity Scheduling." To keep things simple, assume that each of the steps takes three days.

Begin by identifying the steps that form the critical path. (Refer to Figs. 4-12 and 4-14.) Then identify the steps that may proceed at the same time as the critical tasks. Use arrows to indicate tasks and circles to indicate nodes. When you complete your CPM diagram, compare it with another student's CPM diagram and discuss the differences.

Chapter 4

Review

Section Summaries

4.1 Developing an accurate estimate of materials and costs helps builders ensure a profit. Types of estimates include the pre-design estimate, the quantity take-off, and the unit-cost estimate. Costs may be direct or indirect. Checklists used to make the estimate include the construction-order checklist and the CSI MasterFormat checklist.

4.2 A schedule enables the builder or contractor to keep track of the materials and activities needed for a construction project. There are many steps in building a house. All of the steps progress in a logical order. Some must be complete before others can be started. Builders use bar charts and critical path diagrams to keep track of complicated schedules.

Review Questions

1. Why is it important for estimates to be as accurate as possible?
2. An estimator must have three specialized skills. What are they?
3. Name and describe the three basic types of estimates.
4. What is an allowance?
5. What is an indirect cost?
6. Name the organization that developed the MasterFormat system.
7. List at least three sources estimators use to gather information about costs.
8. Why is it important to contact the local utility companies before the excavation process starts?
9. List the advantages and disadvantages of a bar chart schedule.
10. When developing a CPM diagram, what three questions must be answered for each activity on the schedule?

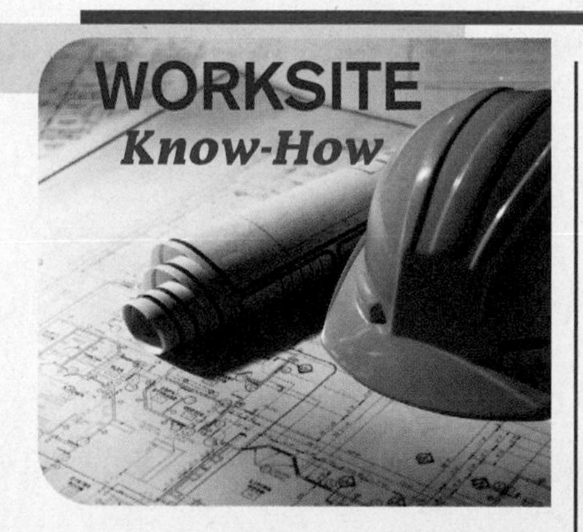

Software Makes It Easier Project managers must keep track of large amounts of data. Several computer software programs are available for estimating and project management. Estimating software makes complex calculations automatically. Accuracy and speed are improved. Project management software, which includes scheduling, makes schedule updates easy. If computers are networked, workers can update their part of the project and inform others of changes simultaneously. Programs include graphic functions that can create charts and schedules that display the information visually.

Unit 2

TOOLS AND EQUIPMENT

Careers in Construction

Apprenticeships

Many construction workers learn their trade through apprenticeship programs. In these programs, they receive instruction both in a classroom and on the job. For example, apprentice carpenters learn about safety, first aid, print reading, sketching, mathematics, and various carpentry techniques in class. On the job, they acquire practical experience in layout, form building, rough framing, and finishing. They also learn to select, use, and maintain hand and power tools.

At a construction site, heavy tools and equipment, such as table saws, compressors, and ladders, are supplied by the general contractor. However, the workers, including apprentices, usually supply their own hand tools and some common power tools, such as circular saws and drills. It is therefore very important to know how to select good tools and how to maintain them properly.

Apprentices should buy the best quality tools they can afford. High-quality tools will perform better and last longer than cheap ones.

For more information, check the *Occupational Outlook Handbook* or look up "apprenticeship AND construction" on the Internet.

Chapter 5

Construction Safety and Health

Objectives

After reading this chapter, you'll be able to:

- Describe the purpose of OSHA.
- Identify practices for keeping a worksite safe.
- Recognize the hazards associated with different types of tools.
- Discuss the need for protective clothing and personal protective devices that suit various weather and job-site conditions.

Terms

conductor
electrical circuit
ergonomics
excavation
grounding
musculoskeletal disorder
repetitive stress injury
wind chill

Construction work is hazardous. A great number of potentially dangerous tools are used. Also, the wide range of working conditions can be difficult to control. For these reasons, workers and supervisors in construction must take extra care to guard their own safety as well as the safety of others.

The best way to avoid accidents is to develop a safe attitude:

- Think about the consequences of your actions, not only for yourself but also for those around you.
- Always decide to follow safe procedures, obey the rules, and act responsibly.
- Keep in mind that you cannot rely on luck to protect you.
- Make safety a habit as you develop your skills.

SECTION 5.1

Ensuring Safety and Health

Did you know that:

- Younger workers are more likely to be injured than older workers. This might be partly due to their inexperience.
- New employees have a higher accident rate than long-time employees. This could be because they are unfamiliar with the job.

Many builders feel that there is a direct relationship between quality work practices and safety. Workers who take the time to do a job carefully and well are safer workers. One reason for this is that it takes a lot of concentration to do a job right. A worker is less likely to be distracted by other workers and more alert to possible hazards. Another reason is that a high degree of craftsmanship slows the pace of construction. Injuries are more likely when workers rush to complete a job.

Fig. 5-1. Inspectors for OSHA may check construction sites for safety and health violations.

OSHA

In 1970, the United States Congress made the federal Occupational Safety and Health Act official. Its purpose is ". . . to assure so far as possible every working man and woman in the Nation safe and healthful working conditions and to preserve our human resources." This act affects all employees who are working in the building trades where one or more workers are employed.

The act is administered by the *Occupational Safety and Health Administration* (OSHA). It issues standards and rules for safe and healthful working conditions, tools, equipment, facilities, and processes. OSHA conducts workplace inspections to ensure the standards are followed. **Fig. 5-1.** It has the legal ability to enforce those standards. Whenever possible, OSHA tries to fix the underlying causes of problems or reduce hazards at their source.

Everyone has a right to a safe workplace. Under OSHA regulations, an employer must:

- Make sure the job and the workplace are free from recognized hazards that are likely to cause death or serious physical harm.
- Comply with OSHA standards, including those for record keeping and accident reporting.

If an employee believes that OSHA standards are not being followed, he or she has the right to contact OSHA and request an inspection. Employees also have responsibilities. They must:

- Comply with OSHA regulations.
- Comply with other occupational safety and health standards that apply.

RESPONDING TO EMERGENCIES

Falls are the most common cause of injury on a construction site. Other common injuries include cuts, puncture wounds, hearing damage, and injuries from falling objects or contact with toxic (poisonous) substances.

If a construction site is not close to a hospital or other source of medical help, OSHA requires that a person certified to give first aid be at the job site. A first-aid kit must also be available.

- Report all injuries immediately to your instructor or supervisor.
- Make sure you know how to summon help. Your instructor or supervisor can give you this information.

- Know the location of first-aid equipment. Even if you are not the one giving first aid, you may be asked to bring the materials.
- Do not give first aid unless you have been trained to do so. Untrained people can make an injury worse or endanger themselves.

WORKER'S COMPENSATION

Even after every effort has been made to ensure a safe workplace, an employee may be injured. Each state has set up a type of insurance program that pays benefits for work-related injuries and illnesses. These are called *worker's compensation programs*. The programs pay for reasonable and necessary medical care if an employee is injured or becomes ill on the job. If an employee is killed on the job, benefits go to his or her family.

Programs in each state vary, but they are designed to handle claims in a prompt and fair way. Worker's compensation laws are complex, but they generally include the following:

- The employee must be given prompt first aid, as well as necessary medical, surgical, rehabilitation, and hospital care.
- If a work-related injury prevents an employee from working for a certain number of days, he or she must be paid disability benefits.
- If an employer denies compensation to a worker, the worker may appeal to state authorities, usually through the worker's compensation program.

If you are injured at work, report your injury to your employer as soon as possible. Afterward, your employer must report the injury to the worker's compensation insurance carrier. You should keep receipts for all expenses associated with your accident. You should also maintain records relating to your care and recovery.

SECTION 5.1 Check Your Knowledge

1. What is the purpose of the Occupational Safety and Health Act?
2. What are the employer's basic responsibilities under OSHA?
3. What are an employee's basic responsibilities under OSHA?
4. What is the most common cause of injury on a construction site?

On the Job

Why do you think that the Occupational Safety and Health Act was developed? Do you think that it is necessary for the government to require that people take safety precautions? Write a one-page essay arguing either for or against government regulation of safety.

SECTION 5.2

Keeping the Worksite Safe

Most injuries can be prevented. Everyone on the job site has some responsibility for keeping the site safe.

HOUSEKEEPING AND SANITATION

A hammer left balanced on a ceiling joist, a bucket left on the stairs, oily rags thrown in a corner—these small acts of carelessness can result in major injuries or property damage. Always practice good housekeeping on the job.

- Keep walkways clear of tools, materials, and clutter.
- Whenever you see protruding nails, remove them or bend them down immediately.
- To prevent fires and reduce hazards, dispose of scraps and rubbish daily. Put oily rags and other highly flammable (able to catch fire easily) waste in approved containers.
- When working above other people, place tools and materials where they will not fall and cause injuries.

Good sanitation (cleanliness) helps prevent the spread of disease. Various OSHA and local regulations apply to sanitation. They cover such things as the supply of drinking water, food service/eating facilities, washing facilities, and toilets.

SIGNS, TAGS, AND BARRICADES

Several kinds of signs and tags are used at construction sites. *Danger signs* warn people about immediate hazards, such as open stairwells. *Caution signs* warn about potential hazards or unsafe practices. **Fig. 5-2.** For example, a caution sign would be used to warn workers entering an area where laser equipment is in use. If a tool or piece of equipment is defective, a temporary tag should be placed on it to warn people that it should not be used. **Fig. 5-3.** A lockout/tagout procedure may be required. *Lockout/tagout* is the use of lockout devices and/or tags to prevent accidental machine startup or release of stored energy.

Barricades, or barriers, can be set up to prevent people from entering a dangerous area. This is often done to guard the outside edges of holes dug for foundations.

The colors used on signs, tags, and barricades have specific meanings. For example, red means "danger," and yellow means "caution." See **Table 5-A** for an explanation of the safety color codes.

Fig. 5-2. Learn to recognize safety signs and colors.

Fig. 5-3. Tags are placed on tools to warn of problems.

Table 5-A. Colors for Safety

Color	Meaning
Red	Danger or emergency
Orange	Be on guard
Yellow	Caution
White	Storage or boundaries
Green	First aid
Blue	Information

FIRE PREVENTION AND EQUIPMENT

Flammable materials are often found at construction sites. These include wood, fuel for generators and other equipment, and paint and solvents. Weeds, grass, and debris (dih-BREE; scraps) around the structure can also catch on fire. To prevent fires:

- Dispose of scraps and rubbish daily.
- Keep the area cleared of weeds and grass.
- Make sure electrical wiring and equipment are properly installed and working correctly.
- Maintain clearance around lights and heaters so that they don't set materials on fire.
- Store materials properly. For example, flammable liquids must be stored in approved, closed containers.
- If a flammable liquid spills or leaks, clean it up promptly and safely.
- Never smoke near flammable materials.
- Do not block exits with materials, equipment, or debris. In case of fire, people need to be able to exit quickly.

Construction sites are required to have fire-fighting equipment on hand. Some fires can be put out with water, so there is usually a water supply as well as fire pails or hoses. Fire extinguishers are also needed, especially for fires that cannot be put out with water. Table 5-B shows the types of fire extinguishers.

MANAGING EXCAVATIONS

An **excavation** is a cut, cavity, trench, or depression made by removing earth. Excavations are dug to prepare the site for footings and foundations. They are also required when installing pipes for site drainage. Workers near an excavation must be careful not to fall in. For those who are working within the excavation, the dangers include cave-ins and the possibility of equipment falling into the excavation. Excavations should be inspected daily for signs of soil movement or other problems. Two basic types of excavations are commonly used on residential job sites: simple slope and benched slope. **Fig. 5-4.** In benching, the soil is excavated to form one or more horizontal levels, or steps. The surfaces between levels are vertical or nearly vertical. Simple slope or benched slope excavations deeper than 20′ must be designated by a registered engineer.

- Before starting an excavation, local utilities must be contacted in order to determine the location of existing underground utility lines.

Table 5-B. Using Fire Extinguishers

Class of Fire	Type of Flammable Material	Type of Fire Extinguisher to Use
Class A	Wood, paper, cloth, plastic	Class A Class A:B
Class B	Grease, oil, chemicals	Class A:B Class A:B:C
Class C	Electrical cords, switches, wiring	Class A:C Class B:C
Class D	Combustible metals	Class D

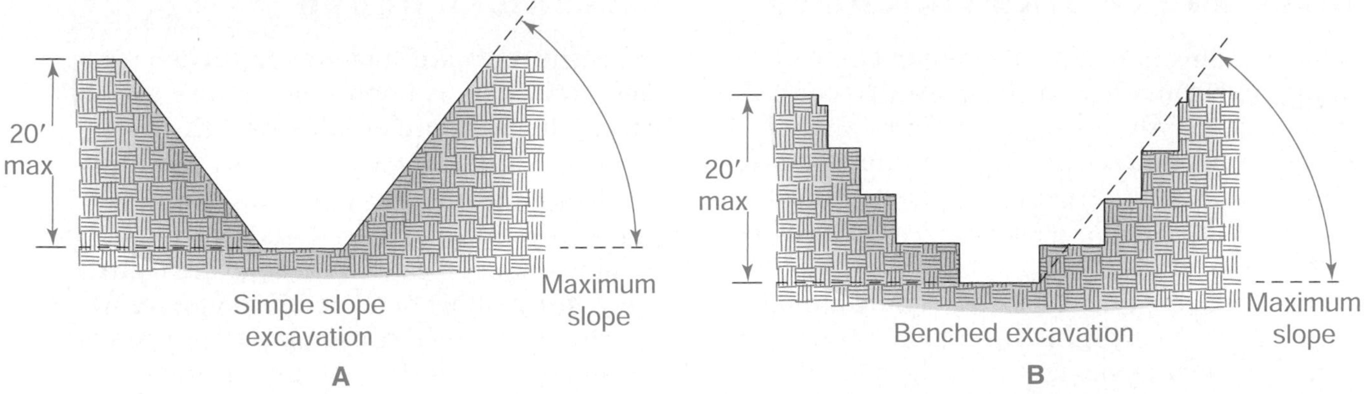

Fig. 5-4. The maximum safe slope for the sides of an excavation is determined by the soil type. *A.* A simple slope excavation is quite common on residential job sites. *B.* A benched slope excavation may also be suitable.

- To minimize the danger of cave-ins, the sides of the excavation should not be too steep. The proper slope depends on the soil type. The maximum safe slope is 53° (¾:1) from the horizontal for Type A soils; 45° (1:1) for Type B soils; and 34° (1½:1) for Type C soils.
- The soil that has been removed must be piled at least 2′ away from the edge of the excavation. Any equipment must also be kept at least 2′ from the edge to minimize the danger of falling in.
- Workers should not be directly underneath the loads being handled by digging or lifting equipment.
- There must be a means for workers to get out of the excavation, such as a ladder or a ramp. The ladder or ramp should be no more than 25′ away from any worker.
- Standing water must be pumped out of the excavation.

SECTION 5.2

Check Your Knowledge

1. What is the purpose of a barricade?
2. The standard colors used on signs, tags, and barricades have specific meanings. Name the colors and their meanings.
3. Why is it important to keep exits clear of materials, equipment, or debris?
4. Describe a benched excavation.

On the Job

Suppose that you have been assigned to improve safety on a job site. Make a poster that explains to workers what the safety colors used on signs mean.

SECTION 5.3

Personal Safety and Health

Be sure you use all suitable safety equipment. Get in the habit of scanning the work area for potential problems. Take immediate steps to prevent any problem from causing injury.

SAFETY FIRST

Safety Is Your Responsibility

A safe worksite is not someone else's responsibility. It's yours. Safety begins with each individual worker. Always consider safety first.

FALLS AND FALLING MATERIALS

Since falling is the most common cause of injury on a construction site, stay alert for possible hazards. Always wear proper footwear. Always walk; do not run. Anyone who works at a height—including carpenters, masons, roofers, and painters—should take extra care. Safety harnesses may be required.

Stairwells must have a safety railing around them at all times. **Fig. 5-5.** Temporary openings in a roof, such as skylight framing, should be covered with a sheet of plywood when not being worked on. Covers over openings must be labeled and mechanically fastened. Roof jacks or other scaffolding should be used whenever necessary (see Chapter 11, "Ladders and Scaffolds").

Many building materials become very slippery when wet or frosty. This is particularly true of plastic, plywood, and housewraps. Keep workplace floors as clean and dry as possible to prevent accidental slips. Be sure to dispose of scraps properly. Never step on any material that is not nailed down.

Whenever construction debris must be dropped from a height of 20 feet or more to any point outside the building, an enclosed chute must be used. This lessens danger to workers below. When debris is dropped through a hole in the floor without the use of chutes, the spot where it lands must be completely enclosed with barricades.

Fig. 5-5. Unprotected stair openings can lead to serious falls. The safety rail at the top of this opening should extend to the end of the opening and should have a full mid-rail. The handrail on the stairway should also include a mid-rail.

ELECTRICAL SHOCK

Electric tools are common on the job site. Electrical safety is important because even a small jolt can injure or kill a worker.

A material that allows electricity to flow through it readily is called a **conductor**. Conductors include most metals. Materials that do not conduct electricity readily are called *insulators.* Rubber is a good insulator. However, moisture can cause some materials to conduct electricity, even if they are poor conductors when dry. This is particularly true of wood.

When electricity flows from a point of origin and returns to that point of origin through a conductor, it makes an **electrical circuit**. Most conductors used in circuits are metal wires insulated with a plastic or rubber casing. The insulation protects the user from the electricity. However, if the insulation is frayed or broken, the conductor is exposed. A person can become part of a circuit by touching both wires in the circuit or by touching the "hot" wire and a ground. (The hot wire is the one bringing electrical power to a device.) You can also become part of the circuit if the tool you are using comes in contact with a wire carrying electricity. This could be a hand tool, such as a screwdriver, or a power tool. When you are part of the circuit, the electricity flows into your body and can cause serious burns, injury, or even death.

For safety, all power tools must be grounded. **Grounding** provides a path for the electricity to flow safely from the tool to the earth. If a person accidentally becomes part of the circuit, electricity will flow through the ground wire, not through the person using the tool. Any break in the grounding system makes it useless, so it is very important to keep the system working properly.

Electric tools typically rely on one or more of these safety systems:

- A three-wire cord with a grounding prong. The grounding prong must never be removed from the plug. When an adapter is used on a two-hole receptacle, the adapter wire must be attached to a known ground.
- A two-wire cord and an insulating plastic shell around the tool's electrical components. The tool is then referred to as a *double-insulated tool.*

- A *ground-fault circuit interrupter (GFCI).* A GFCI is a fast-acting circuit breaker that can protect people from electrical shock. **Fig. 5-6.** A GFCI can be attached to the cord supplying electricity to a power tool. It is particularly important whenever moisture is present. Employers are required to provide GFCIs for all temporary 120-volt, 15- and 20-ampere receptacle outlets on a construction site. A GFCI should also protect any permanent wiring used during the construction process. OSHA requires that GFCIs be used in addition to, not as a substitute for, grounding devices on tools.

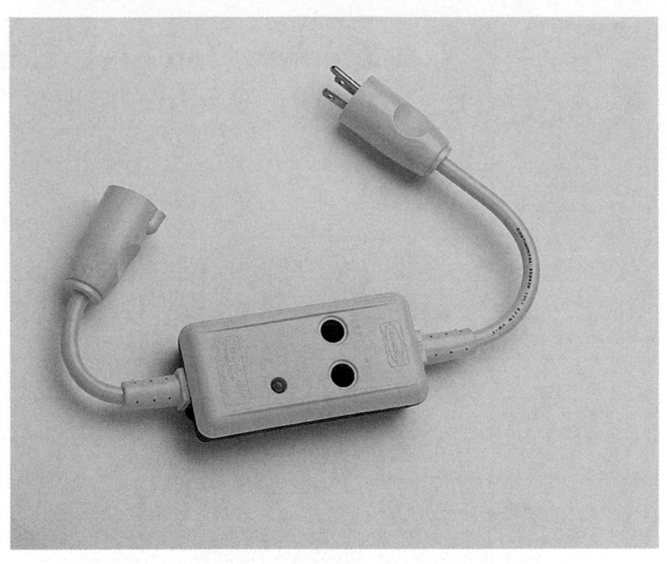

Fig. 5-6. A ground-fault circuit interruptor (GFCI) attached to an extension cord protects workers against electrical shock.

INJURIES FROM TOOLS

Using hand and power tools can create many hazards. Keeping five basic safety rules in mind, however, can help to prevent many injuries:

- Use the proper personal protective equipment, including protective eyewear, in the correct way.
- Use the right tool for the job.
- Examine each tool for damage before use and do not use damaged tools.
- Operate tools according to the manufacturer's instructions.
- Keep all tools in good condition with regular maintenance.

SAFETY FIRST

Power Tools

The following are general safety rules. We strongly advise you to check the manufacturer's manual for each tool for any special safety instructions. In addition, follow the suggestions for power tools given in other chapters of this book.

General Power Tool Safety

- Avoid damaging cords or hoses. Never carry a tool by the cord or hose. Never yank the cord to disconnect it from a receptacle.
- Always use the recommended extension cord size when using portable power tools. See **Table 5-C** on page 102.
- Avoid accidental starts. Do not hold your fingers on the on/off switch while carrying a plugged-in tool. Also, be sure the tool's switch is in the "off" position before plugging the tool in.
- Unplug or disable tools when not using them, before servicing or cleaning them, and when changing or adjusting accessories, such as blades, bits, and cutters.
- Always check lumber for knots, splits, nails, and other defects before machining it.
- Use guards on power equipment and be sure they are installed correctly. Standard safety guards must never be removed when using a portable power tool.
- Keep your fingers away from the cutting edges of tools. Don't try to hold small stock while it is being cut, shaped, or drilled. Secure it with clamps or in a vise whenever possible. This frees both hands to operate the tool.
- Pay attention to the job. Always keep your eyes focused on where the cutting action is taking place. Don't talk with others while you work. Never talk to or interrupt anyone else who is using a power tool.
- Always use a brush, not your hand, to clean sawdust away from a power tool.
- Be sure to keep good footing and maintain good balance when operating power tools.

Table 5-C. Recommended Extension Cord Sizes for Use with Portable Electric Tools

Name-plate Amperes	Cord Length in Feet							
	25	50	75	100	125	150	175	200
1	16	16	16	16	16	16	16	16
2	16	16	16	16	16	16	16	16
3	16	16	16	16	16	16	14	14
4	16	16	16	16	16	14	14	12
5	16	16	16	16	14	14	12	12
6	16	16	16	14	14	12	12	12
7	16	16	14	14	12	12	12	10
8	14	14	14	14	12	12	10	10
9	14	14	14	12	12	10	10	10
10	14	14	14	12	12	10	10	10
11	12	12	12	12	10	10	10	8
12	12	12	12	12	10	10	8	8
13	12	12	12	12	10	10	8	8
14	10	10	10	10	10	10	8	8
15	10	10	10	10	10	8	8	8
16	10	10	10	10	10	8	8	8
17	10	10	10	10	10	8	8	8
18	8	8	8	8	8	8	8	8
19	8	8	8	8	8	8	8	8
20	8	8	8	8	8	8	8	8

Notes: Wire sizes are for 3-CDR Cords, one CDR of which is used to provide a continuous grounding circuit from tool housing to receptacle. Wire sizes shown are A.W.G. (American Wire Gauge). Based on 115V power supply; Ambient Temp. of 30°C, 86°F.

- Loose clothing or jewelry can become caught in moving parts. Wear proper apparel for the task. Tie back long hair.
- Keep work areas well lighted.
- Take steps to ensure that power cords won't create a tripping hazard.
- Never leave tools or materials on any piece of equipment while it is in use. This is especially important with table saws.
- When finished with a power tool, wait until the blade or cutter has come to a complete stop before walking away. Make all adjustments with the power off and the machine at a dead stop.
- Report strange noises or faulty operation of machines to your instructor or supervisor.
- Remove all damaged tools from use and tag them: "Do not use."
- Store electric tools in a dry place when not in use. Do not use them in damp or wet locations unless they are approved for those conditions.

Power Saws

Kickback occurs when the stock being cut or the saw itself is thrown back at the operator at high speed. Because so many workers encounter kickback, the subject is discussed in detail in Chapter 7, "Power Saws."

Always keep your hands clear of the cutting line. Never make adjustments while the saw is running. Disconnect the power source before changing a blade.

Before an abrasive wheel is mounted, inspect it for damage and test it. To test a wheel, tap it gently with a light, non-metallic instrument. An undamaged wheel will give a clear metallic tone or "ring." If you hear a dull "thud" instead, the wheel is cracked or damaged and should not be used.

Portable Tools with Abrasive Wheels

Portable abrasive grinding, cutting, polishing, and wire buffing wheels may throw off flying fragments. They must be equipped with suitable guards.

- Never stand directly in front of the wheel as it accelerates to full speed. An abrasive wheel may disintegrate during start-up.
- Ensure that the operating speed of the tool does not exceed the maximum speed marked on the wheel.
- Allow the tool to reach operating speed before you use it.
- Never clamp a hand-held grinder in a vise.

Gasoline-Powered Tools

Various construction tools are sometimes fueled with gasoline. These include air compressors, chain saws, and portable concrete-cutters. Fuel vapors can burn or explode, and engines create dangerous exhaust fumes.

- Transport and store fuel only in approved containers for flammable liquids.
- Shut down an engine and allow it to cool before filling its fuel tank. This helps prevent vapors from igniting.
- Provide suitable ventilation when the tool is used in an enclosed area. This lessens your exposure to carbon monoxide.
- Keep a fire extinguisher nearby.

Powder-Actuated Tools

Powder-actuated tools are used to install various types of fasteners into steel, concrete, and masonry. **Fig. 5-7.** They operate like a loaded gun to propel the fastener into the material with great speed. These tools must be treated with extreme caution. They should be operated only by employees certified in their proper use. Safety precautions include:

- Wear suitable ear and eye protection.
- Select a powder level that is right for the tool and that is able to do the work without excessive force.
- Faulty cartridges can explode unexpectedly. If a powder-actuated tool misfires, hold it in the operating position for at least 30 seconds before trying to fire it again. If the tool still does not fire, hold it in the operating position for another 30 seconds before removing the cartridge according to the manufacturer's instructions. Immerse the cartridge in water immediately after removal.
- Do not load the tool unless it is to be used immediately.
- Do not leave a loaded tool and cartridges unattended, especially where they might be found by someone not trained in their use.
- Never point the tool at anyone.
- Do not fire fasteners into a material they might pass completely through.
- Do not drive fasteners into very hard or brittle material that might chip or splatter or make the fasteners ricochet (RIK-oh-shay).

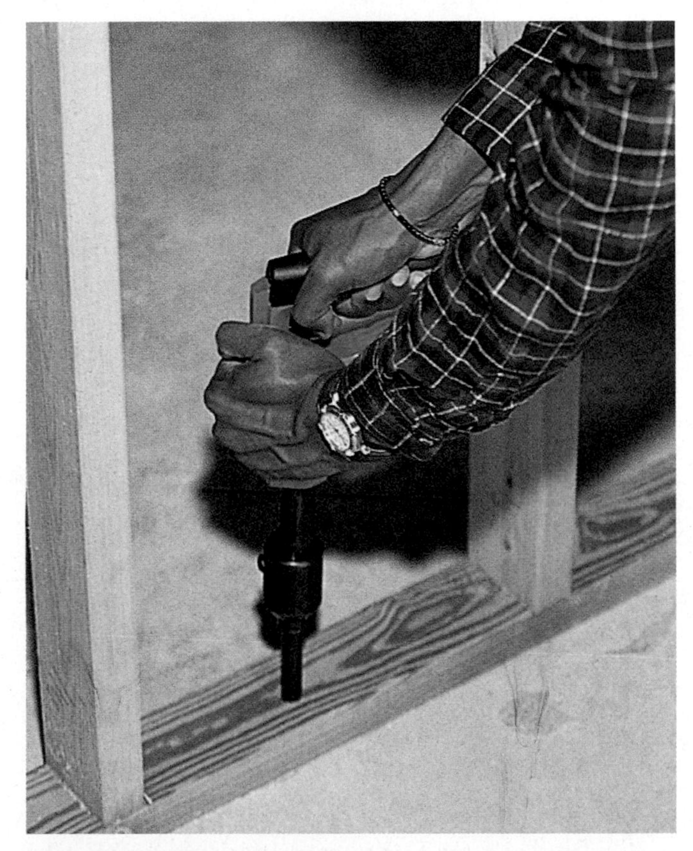

Fig. 5-7. Powder-actuated tools are powerful. Hearing and eye protection are essential when using them.

Hand Tools

The greatest hazards posed by hand tools result from misuse and poor maintenance. Because of the great variety of hand tools, it is impossible to provide a complete guide to their safe use. However, the following examples indicate the types of hazards you may encounter. You will also find safety rules in other chapters of this book, where specific hand tools are discussed.

- Keep your fingers away from cutting edges.
- Do not hold small stock in your hand while it is being cut, shaped, or drilled.
- Do not use a chisel as a screwdriver. The tip of the chisel may break and fly off, hitting someone.
- If the wooden handle on a tool, such as a hammer or an ax, is loose, splintered, or cracked, the head of the tool may fly off and strike someone. Do not use tools in need of repair.
- Make proper adjustments to wrenches. If the jaws of a wrench are not adjusted properly, the wrench might slip.
- If impact tools, such as brick chisels, have a mushroomed head, the head can shatter, sending sharp fragments flying. Be sure heads are properly ground.
- Be sure cutting tools are sharp. If they are not, they require more force to use and are more likely to slip.
- When using a utility knife, consider wearing protective leather gloves. Always cut away from yourself.

MUSCULOSKELETAL DISORDERS

Lifting, fastening materials, and other tasks can cause musculoskeletal disorders (MSDs). A **musculoskeletal disorder** is a disorder of the muscles, tendons, ligaments, joints, cartilage, or spinal discs. **Ergonomics** is the science of designing and arranging things to suit the needs of the human body. Using ergonomically designed tools can lessen the risks of MSDs. Tool features such as cushioned grips and properly angled handles can improve the safety of a tool as well as minimize physical stress and fatigue. **Fig. 5-8.**

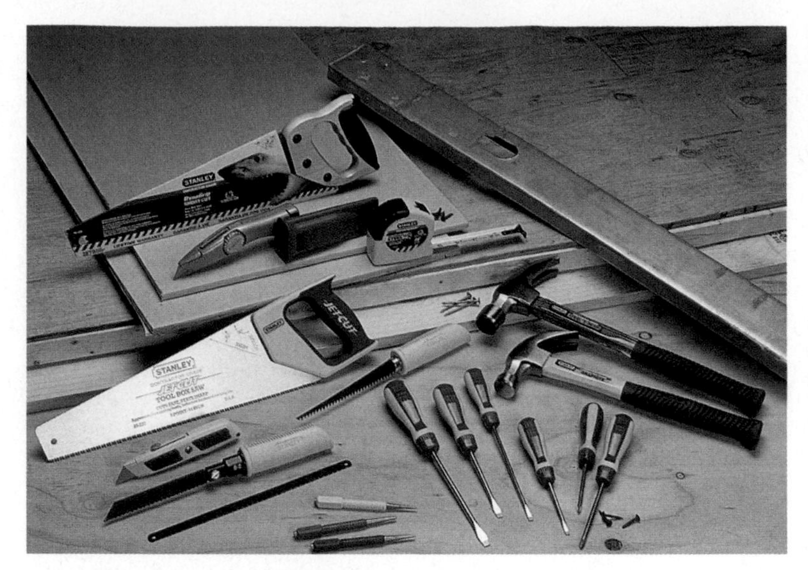

Fig. 5-8. The ergonomic design of tools is important for safety on the job. It also increases a tool's usability.

Repetitive Stress Injuries

A worker's body can be damaged gradually by years of impact or motion. When a task done over and over causes minor irritation to nerves and tissues, the damage is called a **repetitive stress injury** (RSI). Repetitive stress can cause permanent damage. A carpenter, for example, can develop RSI in a wrist after long periods of using a hammer. Hammering with a minimum of wrist movement can help carpenters avoid this problem. Pneumatic nailers also help, although they may bring other health problems.

Other workers, such as trim carpenters and tilesetters, work for long periods on their knees. Special kneepads can protect knees from repetitive stress injuries. In general, whenever work calls for a repeated motion, steps should be taken to lessen its negative effects.

Back Injuries

Proper handling of materials makes any job site safer. Back injuries when handling materials are among the most common injuries suffered by carpenters and masons. Lifting that occurs with objects held below the knee or above the shoulders is more strenuous than lifting from the body's center.

Back injuries can be lessened or avoided if you remember this rule: Lift with your legs, not with your back. This means that you should bend your knees and keep your back straight to prevent back muscles from being strained. **Fig. 5-9.**

Obtain help for lifting loads heavier than you can manage. Whenever possible, stacks of material should be lifted by equipment specially designed for this task. This relieves workers

Fig. 5-9. Lifting properly will reduce the possibility of back injury.

from having to do tiring work, and it also shortens the delivery time.

Back muscles can also be injured if twisted while you're carrying a long piece of material. Long pieces of material should always be carried by two people. Proper support while cutting materials is also important. Whenever possible, the material should be held securely at a comfortable height. Portable sawhorses can be moved around the site for this purpose. **Fig. 5-10.**

HARM FROM HAZARDOUS MATERIALS

Repeated contact with such things as chemicals or dust is often ignored as a threat to a worker's health. However, these materials may affect a worker's health over time. When a worker finally realizes the problem, his or her health may already have suffered permanent damage. Hazardous and toxic substances common on construction sites include dust, fuels, solvents, and chemicals.

OSHA currently regulates many hazardous substances. Manufacturers are required to provide a Material Safety Data Sheet (MSDS) with shipments of their products. These sheets explain the hazards associated with the products. **Fig. 5-11.** The sheets include such information as physical data (melting point, flash point, etc.); toxicity; recommendations for first aid, storage and disposal, and protective equipment; and what to do if a spill or leak occurs.

Fig. 5-10. Sawhorses can be used to position materials at the right height for cutting.

Fig. 5-11. Safety information should be displayed at the job site.

Right to Know

The OSHA standard on Hazard Communication requires employers to inform their workers about dangerous chemicals they may encounter on the job. This requirement is often referred to as the workers' *right to know*. Many states also have their own right-to-know laws.

Every worker must have access to these sheets. Regulations requiring that workers be notified of hazards are often called *right-to-know* laws.

Some of the dangerous substances found in residential construction include asbestos, crystalline silica, formaldehyde, and lead.

Asbestos

Asbestos is a widely used, mineral-based material that resists heat and destructive chemicals. It usually appears as a whitish, fibrous material. It may release these fibers, which range in texture from coarse to silky and which may be too small to see with the naked eye. When asbestos fibers are inhaled or swallowed, they can cause *asbestosis* (az-bess-TOH-sihs; scarring of the lungs) and various types of cancer.

Asbestos is highly regulated by OSHA and other federal agencies. It should be handled or removed only by professionals specially trained for asbestos mitigation work. (*Mitigation* refers to any process that makes a harmful material less dangerous.)

Crystalline Silica

When materials such as concrete, masonry, and rock are cut or ground, the dust may contain extremely fine particles of a mineral called *crystalline silica*. Breathing in these particles can produce permanent lung damage called *silicosis* (sill-ih-KOH-sis). To reduce exposure to crystalline silica, follow these guidelines:

- Always wear a respirator designed to protect against fine, airborne particles. However, do not depend on a respirator as the primary method of protection.
- When sawing concrete or masonry, use saws that spray water on the blade.
- Use a dust collection system whenever possible.

Formaldehyde

Formaldehyde (fohr-MAL-dih-hide) is found in the urea, phenol, and melamine resins used in construction materials and adhesives. Studies indicate that it is a potential cancer-causing agent. When working with liquid products that contain formaldehyde, take care to prevent contact with your skin. When cutting products that contain formaldehyde, wear appropriate breathing protection.

Lead

Many materials containing lead have been eliminated from use in residential building construction because lead has long been recognized as a health hazard. This includes lead-based solders (once used to solder copper-pipe joints) and lead-based paint (see Chapter 41, "Exterior and Interior Finishes"). However, they may still be found during remodeling and demolition work.

The removal of lead-based paint can create large quantities of lead-containing dust. Some states require that materials containing lead be removed only by certified lead-abatement contractors.

PERSONAL PROTECTIVE EQUIPMENT

Throughout this book, you will find references to the need for personal protective equipment. Generally, this refers to hearing protectors, hardhats, safety glasses, hard-toe footwear, and dust masks or respirators. Do not think of these devices as inconveniences. They provide a barrier between the worker and a possible hazard. They are essential tools that help you get the job done safely. The protective equipment you choose should be approved for a given use by the American National Standards Institute (ANSI).

Hearing Protection

Construction workers are regularly exposed to noise. High levels of noise cause hearing loss and may also cause other harmful health effects, such as impaired balance and elevated blood pressure.

Temporary hearing loss results from short-term exposure to noise, with normal hearing returning after a period of rest. Permanent hearing loss is generally due to long exposure to high noise levels over a period of time. Hearing protectors are designed to reduce the noise level. **Fig. 5-12.**

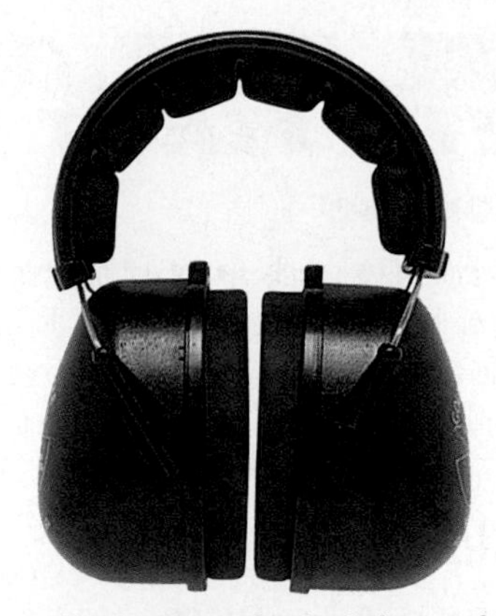

Fig. 5-12. Hearing protection is vital around loud noise.

Head Protection

If there is an overhead hazard at a job site, OSHA requires the use of hardhats. An overhead hazard includes something as common as a falling tool. Though many situations do not expose workers to overhead hazards, wearing a hardhat all the time is a reasonable precaution to take. On some job sites, the project manager requires that everyone who enters the area must wear a hardhat. **Fig. 5-13.**

Fig. 5-13. The hardhat on the top is designed to withstand a blow from directly above. The hardhat on the bottom is designed to withstand a blow from any side.

Eye Protection

Eye hazards are particularly common in construction for workers in all trades. Many eye injuries are caused by sparks, by flying particles smaller than a pinhead, or by chemicals or liquids that splash into a worker's face.

Because you never know when you might be exposed to an eye hazard, you should wear eye protection whenever you are on a job site. **Fig. 5-14.** To be effective, the eyewear must be of the right type for the hazard. It must fit properly and be in good condition. For example, scratched and dirty lenses reduce visibility, cause glare, and may even contribute to accidents.

Respiratory Protection

A dust mask can filter out large particles, such as those created by a circular saw. It cannot protect you against fumes or very fine dust. When exposed to those, wear a respirator approved by the National Institute for Occupational Safety and Health (NIOSH). Respirators contain replaceable filter cartridges designed to protect against a specific hazard. **Fig. 5-15.**

Many tools can also be equipped with a dust collection bag or connected to a vacuum system. Both catch dust before it becomes airborne, a great advantage in enclosed workplaces.

Fig. 5-14. Always wear adequate eye protection for the job to be performed. Sometimes it is necessary also to wear a mask for operations such as spray painting.

Fig. 5-15. Respirators can protect against specific hazards.

Respirator Use

OSHA regulations state that people should not be assigned to tasks requiring the use of respirators unless it has been determined that they are physically able to perform the work and use the equipment. The respirator user's medical status should be reviewed regularly.

Suitable Clothing

What you wear depends partly on the weather. However, you should choose suitable clothing for construction work, just as you would for any job.

- Avoid wearing pants or overalls that are too long or baggy. They tend to catch on your heels and cause falls. Avoid cuffs because they can collect debris, such as sawdust and metal shavings.
- Clothing should not be so loose that it catches on nails or dangles near power tools. Keep the sleeves of shirts or jackets buttoned, or roll them up.
- Keep long hair tied back, or cut it short.
- To protect feet from protruding nails, wear work boots with thick, sturdy soles. When working on a roof, wear boots with slip-resistant soles. Boots with safety toe caps protect feet from injuries caused by falling tools and materials.
- Rings, wristwatches, neck chains, and other jewelry can catch on tools or materials. Avoid wearing them.

PROTECTION FROM THE ENVIRONMENT

Most construction workers work at least part of the time outdoors in a variety of climates and weather conditions. These conditions may vary a great deal from region to region. It is important to take precautions to protect your health and comfort.

Heat

Four factors affect the amount of stress a worker faces in hot weather: over-all temperature, humidity, radiant heat (such as from the sun or a furnace), and air movement. The body reacts to high temperatures by giving off excess heat through the skin and by sweating. If a person cannot dispose of excess heat, various problems such as heat rash, cramps, exhaustion, and heat stroke may then occur.

Heat rash, also known as *prickly heat*, may occur in hot and humid environments where sweat does not easily evaporate. When extensive, heat rash can affect performance or cause temporary disability. It can be prevented by resting in a cool place and allowing the skin to dry.

Heat cramps are painful spasms of the muscles caused when a worker drinks large quantities of water but fails to replace salt in the body. Tired muscles are usually the ones most susceptible to cramps.

Heat exhaustion results from loss of fluid through sweating when a worker has failed to drink enough fluids, take in enough salt, or both. The worker with heat exhaustion still sweats but experiences extreme weakness or fatigue, giddiness, nausea, or headache. The skin is clammy and moist and the body temperature normal or slightly higher. The victim should rest in a cool place and drink an electrolyte beverage. *Electrolyte beverages* are those used by athletes to quickly restore potassium, calcium, and magnesium salts.

Heat stroke is the most serious heat-related health problem. The body can no longer regulate its core temperature. Sweating stops and the body cannot rid itself of excess heat. Signs of heat stroke include mental confusion, delirium, convulsions or coma, and loss of consciousness; a body temperature of 106°F [41°C] or higher; and hot, dry skin that may be red, mottled, or bluish. Heat stroke can be deadly. Summon medical help and remove the victim to a cool area while waiting for help to arrive.

Most heat-related health problems can be prevented or the risk of developing them reduced. Follow these basic precautions:

- Wear suitable clothing.
- Install portable fans when working indoors.
- Drink plenty of water. You may need as much as a quart per hour.
- Alternate work with rest periods in a cool area. If possible, schedule heavy work during the cooler parts of the day.
- Get used to the heat for short periods. New employees and workers returning from a lengthy absence may need five days or more to adjust.

Sunlight

Sunlight is a source of ultraviolet (UV) radiation known to cause skin cancer and various eye problems. People with fair skin or light-colored hair are more sensitive to UV radiation than others.

Skin cancers detected early can almost always be cured. The most important warning sign for skin cancer is a spot that changes in size, shape, or color over a period of one month to two years. The most common skin cancers often take the form of a pale, wax-like, pearly nodule; a red, scaly, sharply outlined patch; or a sore that does not heal. The most serious type of skin cancer, called *melanoma,* often starts as a small, mole-like growth.

When working outdoors, take the following steps to protect yourself from UV radiation:

- Cover up. Wear clothing that protects as much of your skin as possible.
- Use sunscreen. A sunscreen with a *sun protection factor* (SPF) of at least 15 blocks out 93 percent of the burning UV rays. The number represents the level of sunburn protection.
- Wear a hat. A wide-brim hat is ideal because it protects the neck, ears, eyes, forehead, nose, and scalp. A baseball cap provides some protection for the front and top of the head, but not for the back of the neck or the ears, where skin cancers commonly develop.
- Wear sunglasses. UV-absorbent sunglasses can block 99 to 100 percent of UV radiation. The UV protection comes from an invisible chemical applied to the lenses, not from their color or darkness. Choose a lens that is suitable for the work you do.
- Limit direct sun exposure. UV rays are most intense when the sun is high in the sky, between 10 a.m. and 4 p.m.

Cold

When body temperature drops even a few degrees below 98.6°F, a worker is exposed to much stress. The four factors that cause cold-related stress are low temperatures, high/cool winds, dampness, and cold water. **Wind chill** is a combination of temperature and wind speed and increases the chilling effect. For example, when the actual air temperature is 40°F [4°C], a wind of 35 mph creates conditions equivalent to a temperature of 11°F [-12°C].

Estimating...

Clothing Costs

If you live in an area in which weather extremes are common, you will have to invest in the appropriate work clothing. In warm climates, the investment may be small. Outfitting for cold weather, however, can be expensive. In the Midwest, for example, if you work outdoors, your winter clothing needs may include the garments shown in the table, in addition to your everyday garments.

ESTIMATING ON THE JOB

What is the climate like in your area or in an area in which you'd like to work? Determine the most extreme weather conditions for that area. Then, using a catalog that features work clothing or by visiting a local store, estimate the cost of the clothing you would need on a day of bad weather.

Item	Approximate Cost*
Steel-toe insulated boots	$75 – $150
Thermal top and pants	$50 – $75
Thermal socks	$7 – $10
Down jacket with hood	$120 – $200
Wind- and water-resistant insulated pants	$60 – $80

*Costs are for moderately priced items

With *frostbite* the skin tissue actually freezes. Initial effects include uncomfortable feelings of cold and tingling, stinging, or aching in the exposed area followed by numbness. Ears, fingers, toes, cheeks, and noses are commonly affected. Frostbitten areas appear pale and cold to the touch. If you suspect frostbite, seek medical assistance immediately.

Hypothermia occurs when body temperature falls to a level where normal muscle and brain functions are impaired. The first symptoms are shivering, an inability to make complex movements, lack of energy, and mild confusion. In severe cases, the person seems dazed and fails to complete even simple tasks. Speech becomes slurred and behavior may become irrational.

Treatment of hypothermia calls for conserving the victim's remaining body heat and providing additional heat sources. Seek medical assistance immediately.

The proper use of protective clothing is important in avoiding cold-weather health problems. **Fig. 5-16.** Pay special attention to protecting feet, hands, face, and head. Wear at least three layers:

- An outer layer should keep out the wind yet allow some ventilation.
- A middle layer of wool or synthetic fabric should absorb sweat but insulate against dampness.
- An inner layer of cotton or synthetic weave should allow ventilation.

Fig. 5-16. Clothing layers provide the best cold-weather protection.

Lyme Disease

In many areas of the country, people who work outdoors are exposed to an illness called *Lyme disease.* It is transmitted by a particular type of tick. Construction workers, landscapers, and land surveyors are all at risk. Consult local health departments regarding the risk in your area. It can vary within a region and from year to year.

Symptoms are often similar to flu symptoms and may be misdiagnosed. Left untreated, however, Lyme disease can result in severe illness. Consult local health authorities for precautions to take if you are working in a tick-infested area.

SECTION 5.3 Check Your Knowledge

1. How does a conductor differ from an insulator?
2. What are the five most basic safety rules for working with tools?
3. What does MSDS stand for, and why is it important?
4. List five ways to prevent or minimize the risk of heat-related health problems.

On the Job

As safety officials learn more about a hazardous substance, recommendations about safety steps sometimes change. It is always important to use the most up-to-date techniques. Using library or Internet resources, research one of the hazardous substances noted in this section. Summarize the basic requirements of the most recent OSHA regulations for handling the substance.

Chapter 5 Review

Section Summaries

5.1 The purpose of OSHA is to assure safe and healthful working conditions. Workers must take responsibility for safety and know how to handle emergencies. Worker's compensation helps financially after an injury.

5.2 Keeping a worksite safe includes good housekeeping and sanitation; proper use of signs, tags, and barricades; knowing about fire prevention and equipment; and following proper excavation procedures.

5.3 To protect personal safety and health, workers need to take precautions against falls and falling materials, electrical shock, injuries from tools, musculoskeletal disorders, and harm from hazardous materials. They should wear appropriate clothing and personal protective equipment, and they should guard against environmental conditions.

Review Questions

1. What do the initials OSHA stand for, and what is OSHA's purpose?
2. What is the difference between a danger sign and a caution sign? What colors are used for the signs?
3. Why is it important to clear away weeds, grass, and debris at a construction site?
4. What is a GFCI?
5. What dangers are associated with gasoline-powered tools?
6. How should a small piece of stock be held when it is being cut, shaped, or drilled?
7. What is repetitive stress injury and how does it occur?
8. Name three causes of eye injuries.
9. What is a respirator, and why is it sometimes better than a dust mask?
10. List at least three symptoms of heat exhaustion.

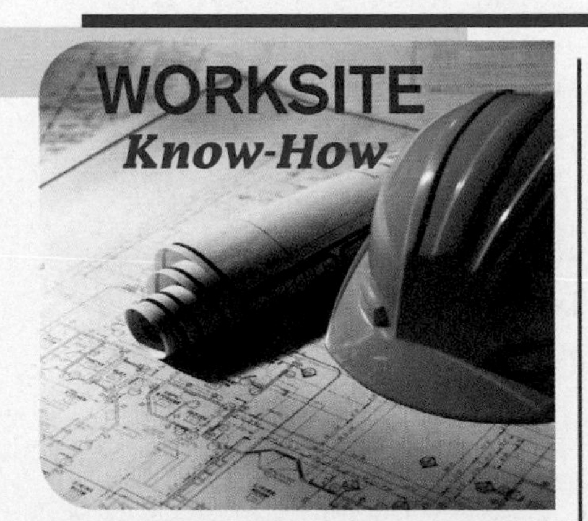

NIOSH: What Is It? NIOSH is the National Institute for Occupational Safety and Health. It is a Federal agency that conducts research and makes recommendations for preventing work-related disease and injury. For example, if many carpenters were to suffer from carpal tunnel syndrome (a painful condition of the wrist), NIOSH would study the scope of the problem to try to determine its cause and prevention. It would investigate working conditions that might lead to the problem. It would then make recommendations about preventing the problem and help train safety and health professionals to combat it. Its sister agency is OSHA, which administers the laws related to workplace health and safety.

Chapter

Hand Tools

Objectives

After reading this chapter, you'll be able to:

- Identify a wide range of hand tools used in carpentry.
- Tell what different hand tools are used for.

Terms

level
pliers
square
wrench

A wide variety of hand tools is necessary for building a house. Some, such as a steel tape measure, are used by all trades. Others are used primarily by one trade. A framing square, for example, is used most often by carpenters.

Most professionals recommend purchasing tools of the highest quality you can afford. High-quality tools work better, hold an edge longer, and are more durable. Also, buying a good tool that will last is more cost-effective than replacing a cheaper tool several times.

Good tools should be cared for properly. Keep them in a toolbox when not in use. Do not leave tools outdoors in wet or damp weather. Inspect hand tools regularly for signs of wear or damage. Keep cutting edges sharp. If the tool cannot be repaired, replace it.

SECTION 6.1

Measuring and Marking Tools

Carpenters must measure, mark, and lay out projects many times a day. A good selection of tools for these tasks is essential. A **square** is used primarily to measure or check angles. A **level** measures the levelness or plumbness of surfaces.

Fig. 6-1. Layout tape measure.

Layout tape measure–A steel or fiberglass tape in a rust-resistant case with a reel-in crank. **Fig. 6-1.** Comes in long lengths of 50′, 100′, and 200′. Uses:

- Laying out foundations and site features, such as walkways and driveways.

Fig. 6-2. Steel tape measure.

Steel tape measure–A steel tape with a hook on the end that adjusts to true zero. The case has a belt clip and a tape-locking button. Comes in various widths and in lengths from 6′ to 33′. The tape most commonly used by carpenters is 25′ or longer. Wide tapes are better for measuring long lengths. **Fig. 6-2.** Uses:

- General measuring tasks.
- Making accurate inside measurements. The measurement is read by adding a specified amount to the reading on the tape. This amount is found on the case.

Chalk line–Powdered chalk and a reel of string in a steel or plastic case. **Fig. 6-3.** A hook/loop is used to secure one end of the string. Uses:

- Quickly creating a straight layout or cutting line over long lengths, as on panel products.
- Indicating the position of walls on a subfloor.

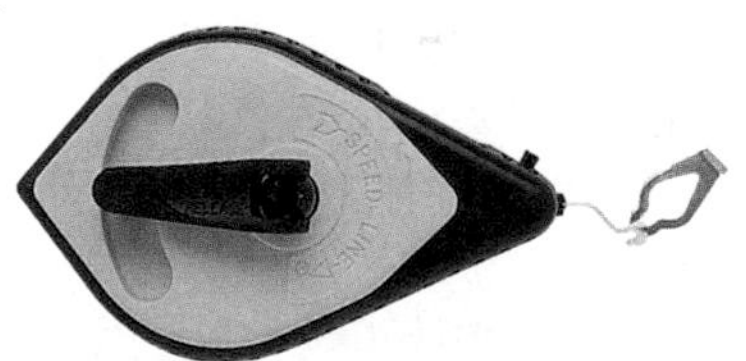
Fig. 6-3. Chalk line.

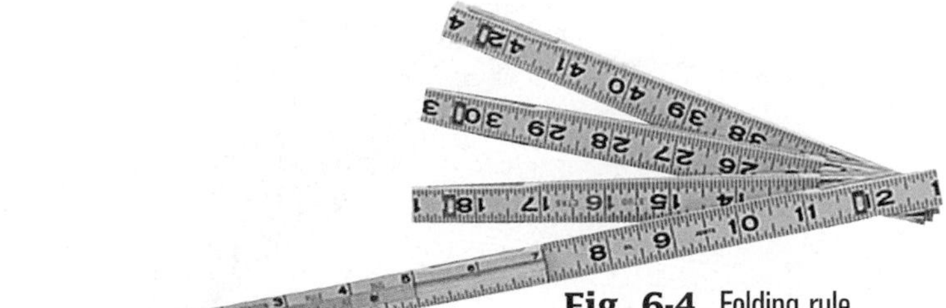
Fig. 6-4. Folding rule.

Fig. 6-5. Carpenter's pencil.

Folding rule–A rigid wood rule 6′ or 8′ long that folds into a compact size. **Fig. 6-4.** A metal slide in one end can be used for measuring depth. Uses:

- Making inside measurements and measuring the depth of a mortise or channel.
- Measuring plumbing runs.

Carpenter's pencil–A sturdy, thick pencil with a wood casing. **Fig. 6-5.** The thick lead resists breakage and can be sharpened with a utility knife. Uses:

- All-purpose marking and layout where great precision is not necessary.

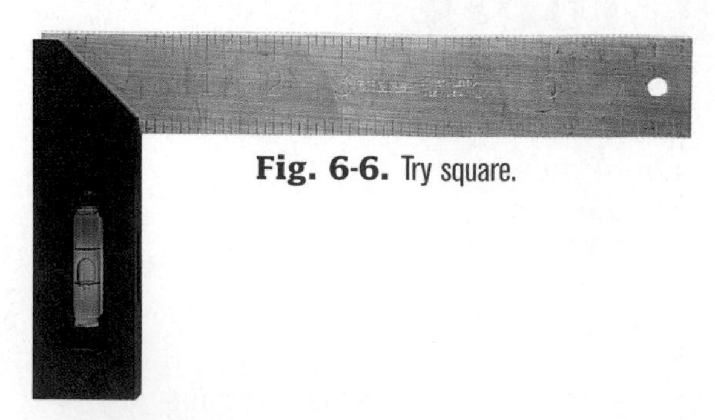

Fig. 6-6. Try square.

Try square–A fixed-blade square with a metal blade and a wood or metal handle. **Fig. 6-6.** The blade may be graduated in inches and is 90° to the handle. Uses:

- Checking adjacent surfaces for squareness.
- Making layout lines across the face or edge of stock.

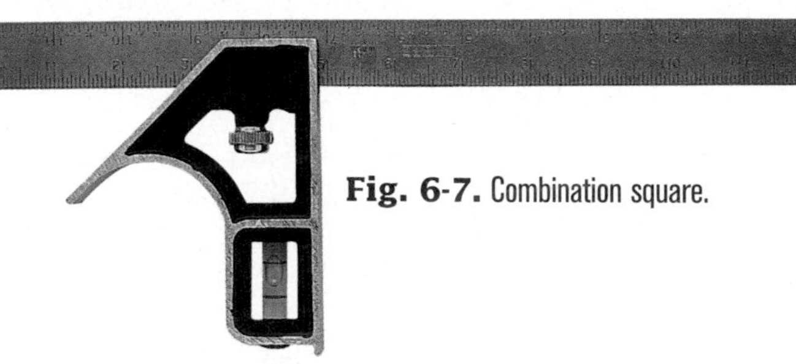

Fig. 6-7. Combination square.

Combination square–A blade that slides along its handle or head. **Fig. 6-7.** The handle may contain a leveling vial and a scriber. The removable blade can be used as a straightedge. Uses:

- Checking adjacent surfaces for a correct angle of 45° or 90°.
- Making layout lines at 45° and 90° across the face or edge of stock.
- Measuring the depth of a mortise or channel.
- Roughly leveling or plumbing a surface.

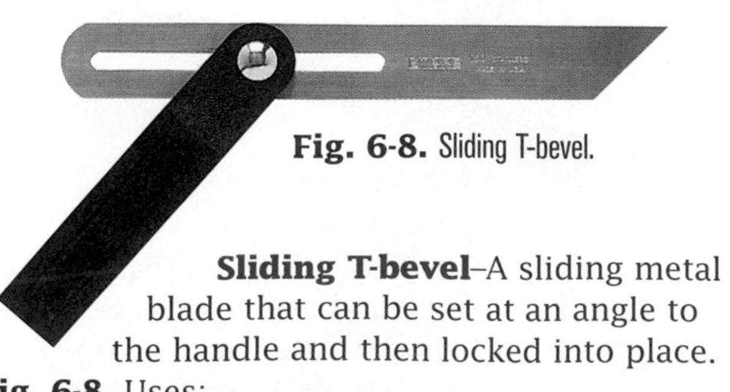

Fig. 6-8. Sliding T-bevel.

Sliding T-bevel–A sliding metal blade that can be set at an angle to the handle and then locked into place. **Fig. 6-8.** Uses:

- Transferring an angle between 0° and 180°.
- Checking or testing a miter cut at other than 45°.

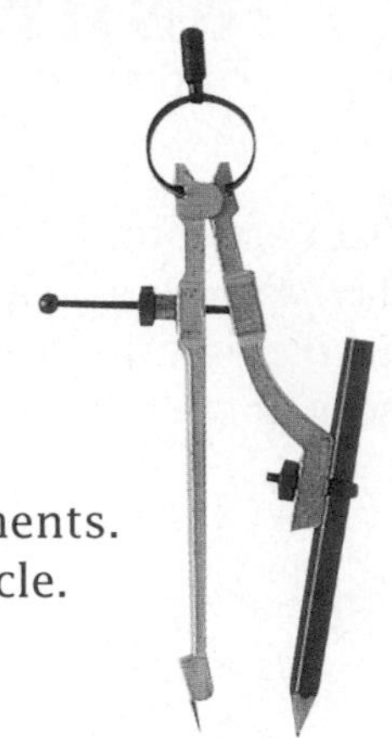

Dividers–A measuring tool with two metal legs. On some, one leg can be removed and replaced with a pencil, forming a compass. **Fig. 6-9.** Uses:

- Stepping off measurements.
- Laying out an arc or circle.

Fig. 6-9. Compass, one type of dividers.

Fig. 6-10A. Framing or carpenter's square.

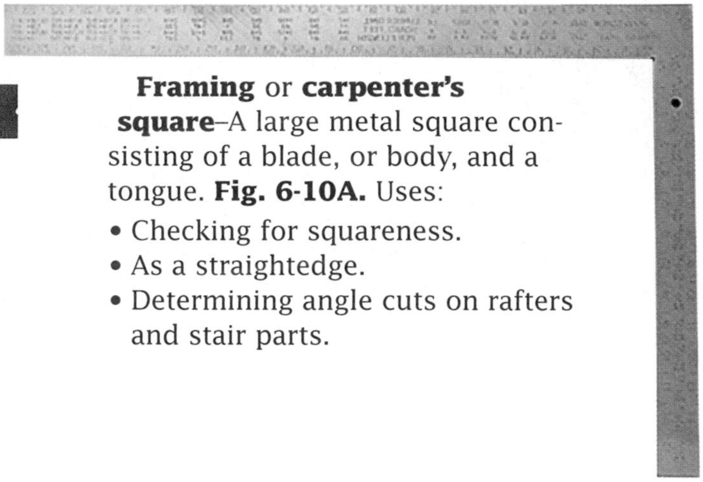

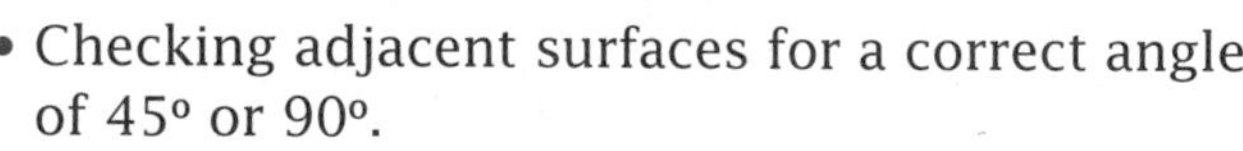

Framing or **carpenter's square**–A large metal square consisting of a blade, or body, and a tongue. **Fig. 6-10A.** Uses:

- Checking for squareness.
- As a straightedge.
- Determining angle cuts on rafters and stair parts.

Fig. 6-10B. Rafter or triangular framing square.

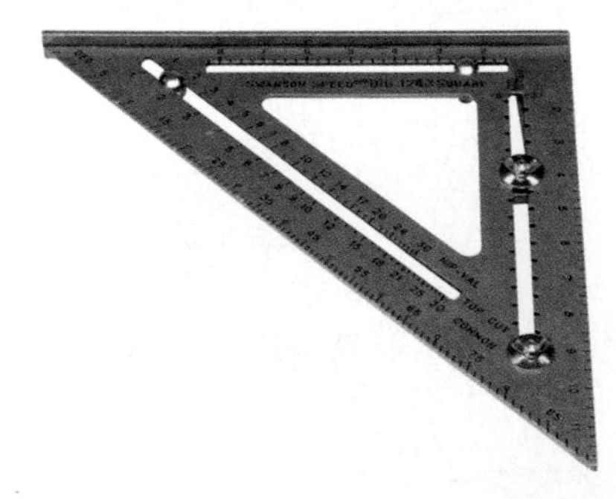

Rafter or **triangular framing square**–A square marked with degrees for fast layouts. Its small size makes it handy. **Fig. 6-10B.** Uses:

- See *Framing* or *carpenter's square.*
- Guides power saws during crosscutting.

Fig. 6-11. Carpenter's level.

Carpenter's level–A long wood, metal, or fiberglass instrument with several glass leveling vials. Sometimes called a *spirit level.* **Fig. 6-11.** Some levels measure electronically instead. Uses:

- Determining whether or not a surface is level (horizontal) or plumb (vertical).

Fig. 6-12. Torpedo level.

Torpedo level–A small spirit level approximately 9" long. **Fig. 6-12.** It has leveling vials for plumb, level, and 45° angles. Sometimes called a *pocket level.* Uses:

- Leveling or plumbing small surfaces, such as pipes, or those that are difficult to reach.

Fig. 6-13. Scratch awl.

Scratch awl–A pointed metal marking tool. **Fig. 6-13.** Uses:

- Scribing a line accurately, particularly on metal.
- Starting a hole before drilling into wood.

Construction calculator–A portable calculator that computes measurements directly in feet and inches. **Fig. 6-15.** Uses:

- Calculating volumes and areas.
- Converting decimals to fractions.
- Solving various roof framing layout problems.

Fig. 6-15. Construction calculator.

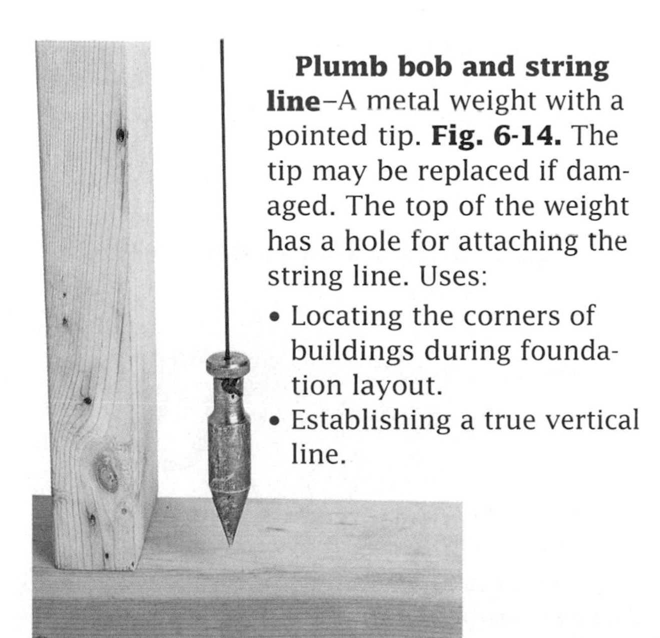

Plumb bob and string line–A metal weight with a pointed tip. **Fig. 6-14.** The tip may be replaced if damaged. The top of the weight has a hole for attaching the string line. Uses:

- Locating the corners of buildings during foundation layout.
- Establishing a true vertical line.

Fig. 6-14. Plumb bob and string line.

Check Your Knowledge

1. What is a layout tape measure used for?
2. What tool can be used to indicate the position of walls on a subfloor?
3. Which type of square can be used to check 45° angles?
4. Which tool would you use to scribe a line on metal?

On the Job

Obtain one of the following tools and learn how to use it properly. Then explain and demonstrate its use to the class: chalk line, combination square, carpenter's level, or plumb bob and stringline.

Saws

A wide variety of saws is available for use in construction. A hand saw can be found for any sawing task.

Fig. 6-16. Utility drywall saw.

Utility drywall saw–A slender saw with a pointed tip, a stiff blade, and large, sharp teeth. **Fig. 6-16.** The blade can be pushed through the drywall surface and does not need an access hole. Uses:

- Making internal cuts in drywall and cutting drywall to irregular shapes.

Backsaw–A fine-tooth crosscut saw with a heavy metal band across the back that strengthens the blade. **Fig. 6-17.** A long model (24″ to 28″) is called a *miter box saw.* Uses:

- Making fine crosscuts and miters in molding and trim. Often used in a miter box.

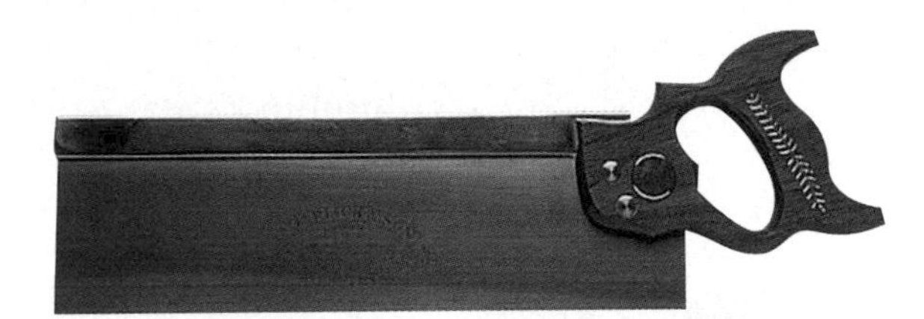

Fig. 6-17. Backsaw.

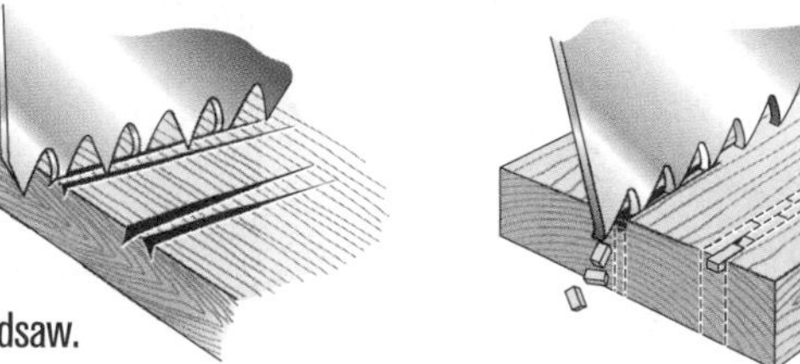

Fig. 6-18. Handsaw.

Handsaw–A saw with a wide blade in lengths from 20″ to 28″. **Fig. 6-18.** The teeth on crosscut models cut *across* the grain. Rip models cut *with* the grain. These cuts are shown above. Uses:

- Cutting wood and completing cuts made by power saws.

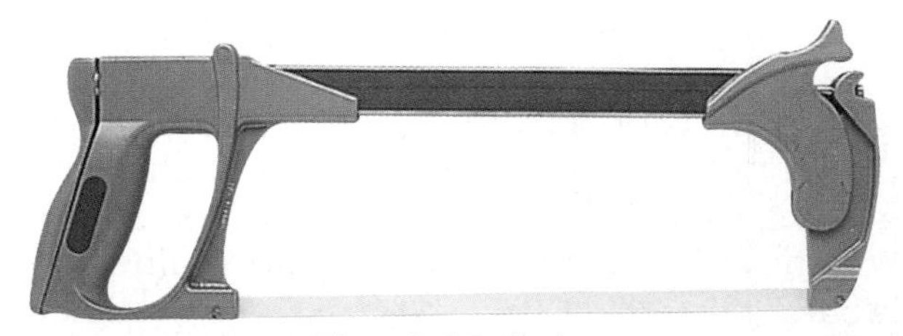

Fig. 6-19. Hacksaw.

Hacksaw–A saw with a U-shaped steel frame fitted with replaceable metal-cutting blades. **Fig. 6-19.** Standard and high-tension models are available. Uses:

- Cutting all types of metal fasteners, hardware, and metal or plastic parts.

Fig. 6-20. Keyhole saw.

Keyhole saw–A narrow saw with a 10″ long replaceable blade with fine teeth. **Fig. 6-20.** The blade tapers to a sharp point. (A compass saw is similar but has slightly bigger teeth and a longer blade.) Uses:

- Cutting curves and enlarging holes.

Toolbox saw–A general purpose handsaw with a flexible blade and hardened teeth. **Fig. 6-21.** It is short enough to fit into a toolbox. Uses:

- Making quick cuts in thin stock.
- Finishing cuts made by a circular saw.

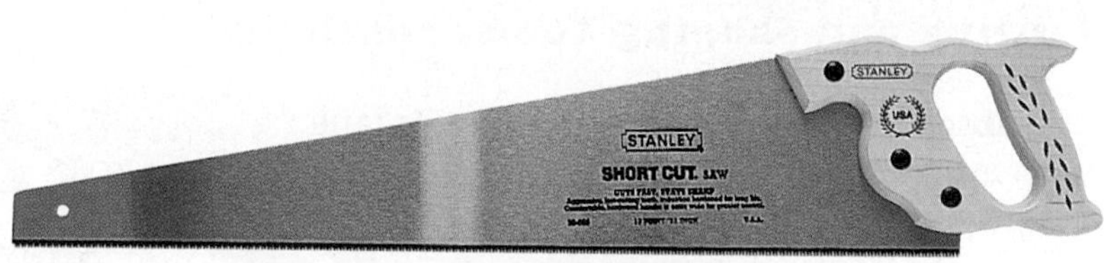

Fig. 6-21. Toolbox saw.

Coping saw–A saw with a U-shaped frame having a deep throat. **Fig. 6-22.** The replaceable ⅛″ wide blade with tiny teeth can be rotated to cut at various angles. Uses:

- Cutting curves in wood molding and trim.
- Shaping the end of molding for joints.
- Cutting scroll work.

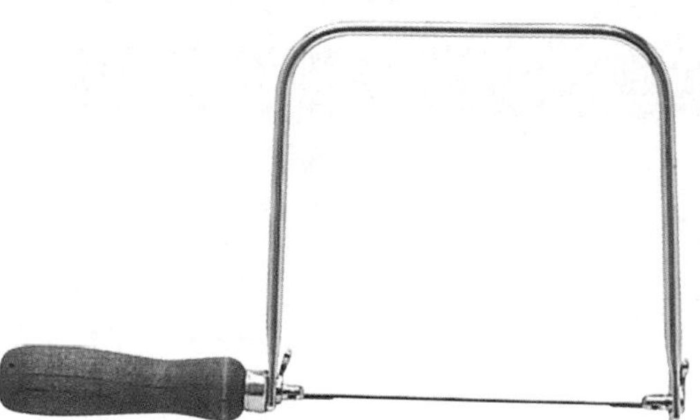

Fig. 6-22. Coping saw.

Fig. 6-23. Dovetail saw.

Dovetail saw–Similar to a backsaw, but the blade is narrower and thinner and has very fine teeth. **Fig. 6-23.** Uses:

- Making short, straight cuts of superior smoothness and accuracy.

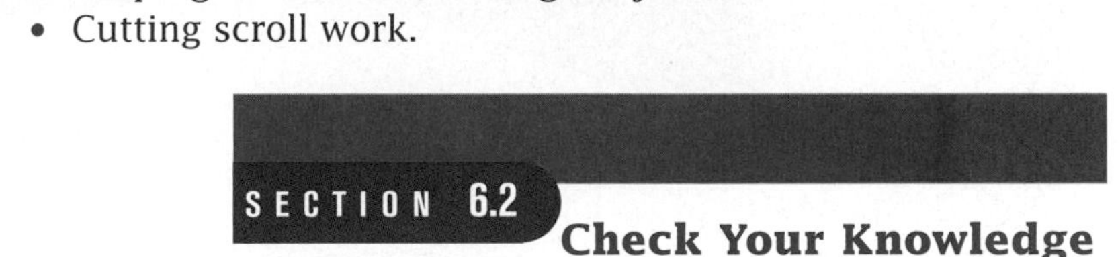

SECTION 6.2

Check Your Knowledge

1. Which type of saw is used for making internal cuts in drywall?
2. Does a ripsaw cut with the grain or across it?
3. A compass saw is a larger version of which type of saw?
4. Which saw has a deep, U-shaped throat?

On the Job

Choose two types of saws discussed in this section. Make sketches showing the tooth configuration of each saw. Write a short paragraph explaining what makes the teeth appropriate for each saw's particular use.

SECTION 6.3

Cutting and Shaping Tools

Cutting, shaping, and drilling tools remove small chips from the workpiece. This makes a high degree of precision possible.

Block plane–A small (about 6″ long) plane with a blade that cuts bevel-side up. **Fig. 6-24.** Standard models have a blade angled 20° to the sole (bottom). Low-angle models are angled at about 12°. Uses:

- Planing end grain.
- Fitting doors.
- Beveling an edge.

Fig. 6-24. Block plane.

Cutting and Shaping Tools, continued

Jointer plane–A long (20″ to 24″) plane with a blade that cuts bevel-side down. Also called a *jack plane*. **Fig. 6-25.** Uses:

- Smoothing and flattening edges for making a close-fitting joint.
- Planing long workpieces, such as the edges of doors.

Fig. 6-25. Jointer plane.

Fig. 6-26. Wood chisel.

Wood chisel–A tool with a steel blade sharpened to a fine edge at one end and a wood or plastic handle at the other. **Fig. 6-26.** Many blade types are available. A set of chisels usually includes blade widths from ¼″ to 1½″. Uses:

- Trimming and shaping wood.

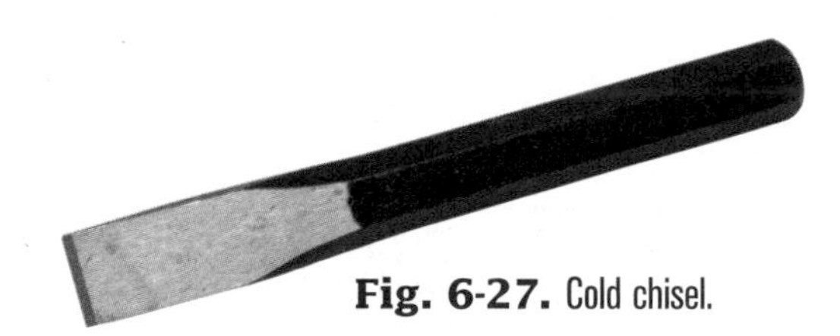

Fig. 6-27. Cold chisel.

Cold chisel–A tool-steel chisel with a hardened and tempered edge for cutting metal. **Fig. 6-27.** The angle of the beveled cutting edge is about 60°. Uses:

- Cutting off a rivet or nail.
- Getting a tight or rusted nut started.

Fig. 6-28. Wood rasp.

Wood rasp–A wood rasp is similar to a metal file but has raised teeth. On some models, the teeth are located on a replaceable, thin metal plate that is attached to the handle. **Fig. 6-28.** In others, the teeth and handle are formed from a solid piece. Uses:

- Rounding corners and edges.
- Quickly removing stock where a smooth edge is not required.

SAFETY FIRST

Sharper Is Safer

Be sure to keep the edge on cutting tools sharp. This makes the tool safer as well as more satisfying to use. Protect sharp edges with a plastic sheath where possible.

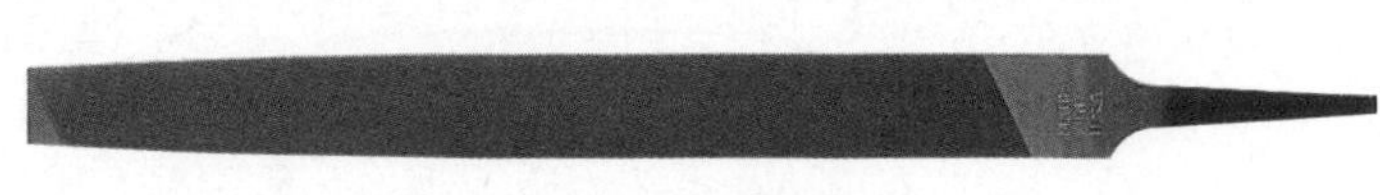

Fig. 6-29. Metal file.

Metal file–A solid metal bar with patterned cutting ridges formed in one or more surfaces and edges. **Fig. 6-29.** Single-cut and double-cut models are most common. Uses:

- Sharpening knives or saws.
- Smoothing the edges of metal products and rounding metal corners.
- Trimming plastic laminate.

Fig. 6-30. Utility knife.

Utility knife–An all-purpose knife with extremely sharp, replaceable blades. **Fig. 6-30.** On some models the blade is retractable. Uses:

- Cutting roof shingles, tarpaper, batt insulation, wood veneer, and many other materials.
- Cutting carpeting when a hooked blade is attached.
- Sharpening a carpenter's pencil.

SECTION 6.3 Check Your Knowledge

1. What is the difference in cutting action between a block plane and a jointer plane?
2. How does a wood rasp differ from a file?
3. What is a utility knife used to cut?
4. What material is cut using a hooked blade on the utility knife?

On the Job

Do a comparison study of the tooth shapes and patterns on the wood rasp and the metal file. Write a short paragraph comparing those tooth shapes and patterns. Discuss the effect of the tooth shape and pattern on each tool's effectiveness when used on the intended materials.

SECTION 6.4

Tools for Assembling and Disassembling

Tools such as hammers help put products together. Tools such as pry bars help take them apart.

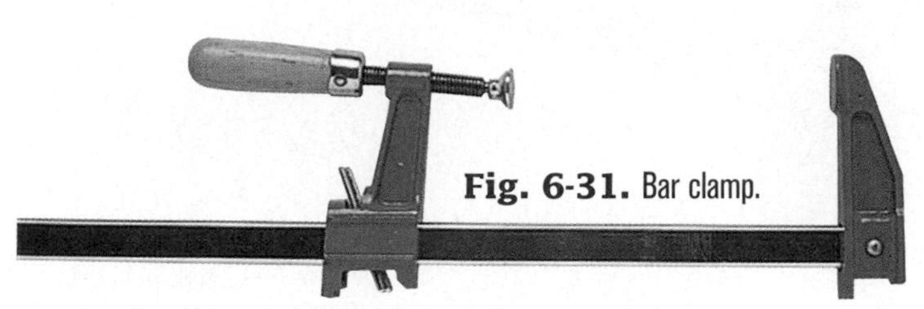

Fig. 6-31. Bar clamp.

Bar clamp–A clamp with a stationary head, a sliding tailstop, and an adjustable screw assembly, all mounted on a flat bar. **Fig. 6-31.** When a pipe is used instead of a bar, the tool is called a *pipe clamp.* Length ranges from 16″ to 5′ or more. Uses:

- Holding materials together as they are being glued.
- Compressing materials temporarily.
- Assembling cabinetry.

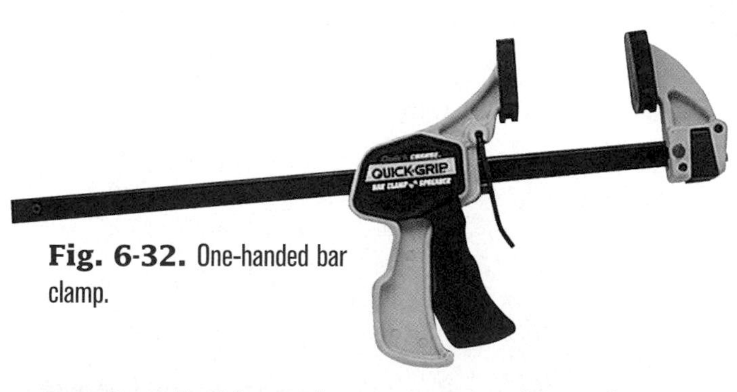

Fig. 6-32. One-handed bar clamp.

One-handed bar clamp–A type of bar clamp with a trigger-handle tailstop that allows quick, one-handed adjustments. **Fig. 6-32.** Uses:

- Securing wood that is being cut with a power saw.
- General light-duty clamping needs.

Because clamps are often used to hold glued items, glue can build up on their surfaces. To prevent this, apply a coat of paste wax to the jaws of the clamp. The wax will also help prevent rust.

Fig. 6-33. Claw hammer.

Claw hammer–A hammer with a curved claw. **Fig. 6-33.** Heads weigh from 8 to 20 oz. A 16 oz. head is suitable for general construction. An 8 oz. head is a good finishing hammer. The face is slightly crowned, with beveled edges. Handles may be of hickory, steel, or fiberglass. Uses:

- Driving or removing nails.

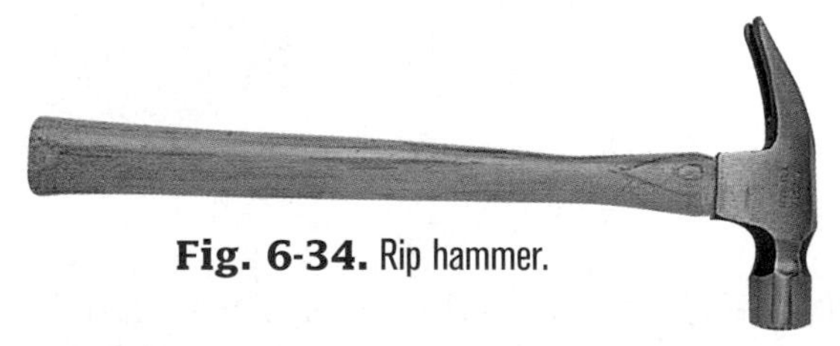

Fig. 6-34. Rip hammer.

Rip hammer–Also called a *straight-claw hammer*, a rip hammer has a wedge-shaped claw. **Fig. 6-34.** Heads weigh from 13 to 25 oz. The handle may be of hickory, steel, or fiberglass. Models used by framing carpenters have longer handles and checkered faces to reduce the chance of glancing blows and flying nails. Uses:

- Driving and removing nails.
- Prying apart pieces that have been nailed together.

Tools for Assembling and Disassembling, continued

Warrington hammer–A hammer with a flattened peen instead of a claw. **Fig. 6-35.** Heads weigh from 3½ to 10 oz. Uses:

- Driving finishing nails into molding and trim and starting brads.

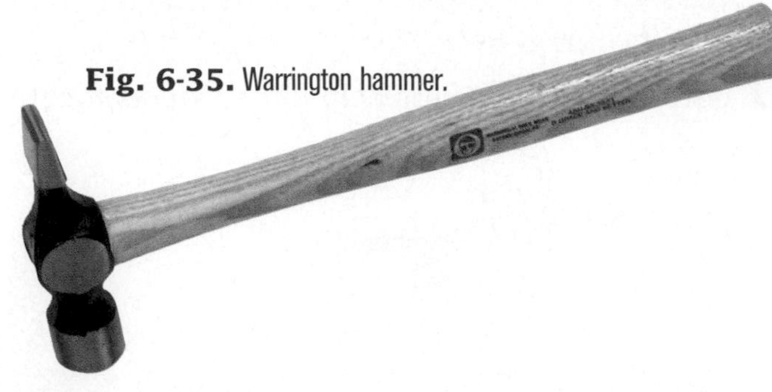

Fig. 6-35. Warrington hammer.

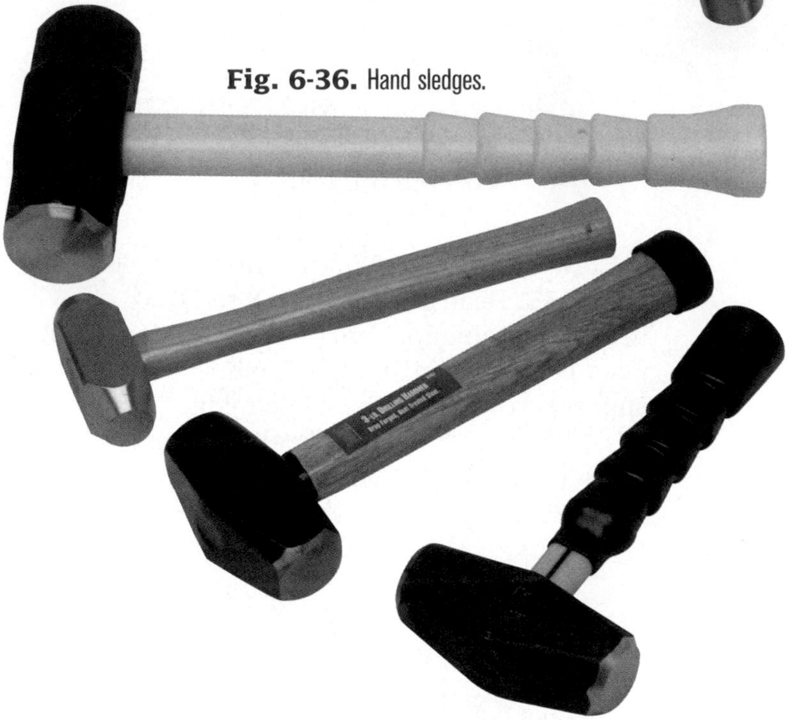

Fig. 6-36. Hand sledges.

Hand sledge–A hammer with a two-faced head weighing between 2 and 4 lbs. **Fig. 6-36.** It has a wood or steel handle. Also called a *hand drilling hammer*. Uses:

- Striking steel tools such as cold chisels, brick chisels, and punches.
- Driving stakes during site layout.

Mallet–A two-headed mallet, often made of wood, rubber, or plastic. The handle is wood. **Fig. 6-37.** Uses:

- Striking blows where steel hammers would mar or damage the surface, as when assembling wood joints.

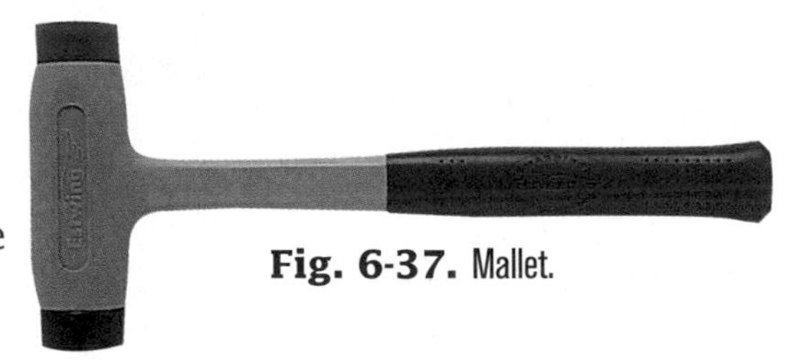

Fig. 6-37. Mallet.

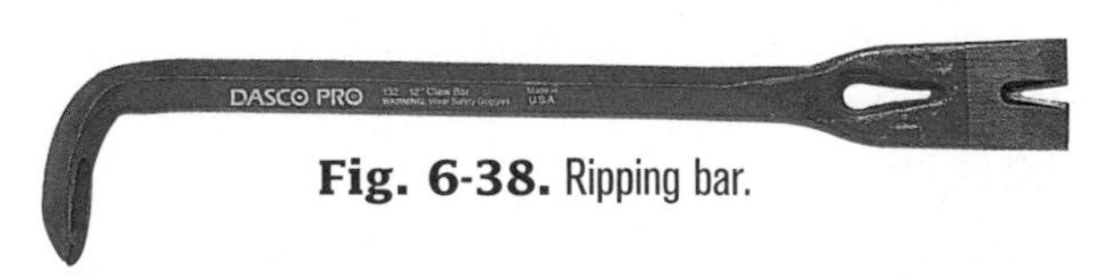

Fig. 6-38. Ripping bar.

Ripping bar–A bar with claws at each end. **Fig. 6-38.** Available in lengths up to 8′. The 3′ bar is suited for general use. Uses:

- Pulling large nails and spikes.
- Prying off old materials during renovation.

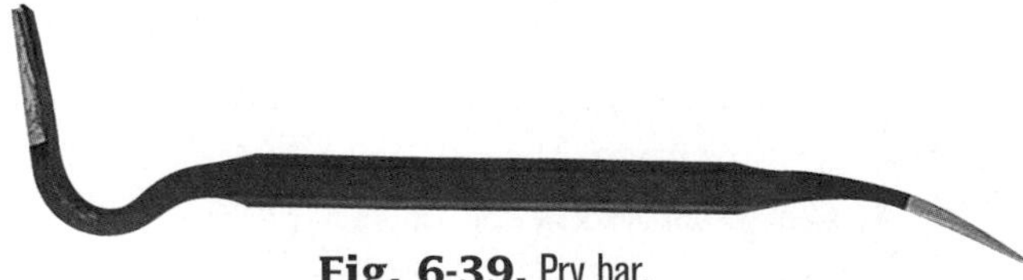

Fig. 6-39. Pry bar.

Pry bar–A steel bar 6″ to 14″ long, with a nail-removing claw at one or both ends. **Fig. 6-39.** Some models have a wide, flattened end for prying molding from a wall. Uses:

- Prying nailed lumber and trim apart.
- Pulling nails.

Fig. 6-40. Nail set.

Nail set–A steel shank 4″ long with a concave tip, a knurled body, and a square striking surface. **Fig. 6-40.** Comes in a set of four that are sized from 1⁄32″ to 1⁄8″ at the tips. Uses:

- Driving finishing nails below the surface of wood. Nail holes can then be filled.

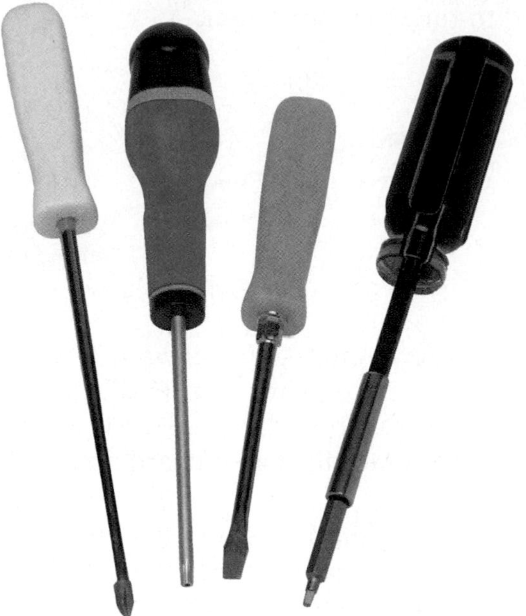

Fig. 6-41. Screwdrivers.

Screwdriver–A steel shank of various lengths with a wood or plastic handle and a tip formed to fit a particular type of screw. **Fig. 6-41.** A standard slotted head widens from tip to shank. A cabinet-slotted head has a uniform width to reach recessed screws. A Phillips head has the shape of an *X* at the tip to reduce slippage. Square-drive and Torx screwdrivers also eliminate slip. Uses:

- Driving and removing screws.

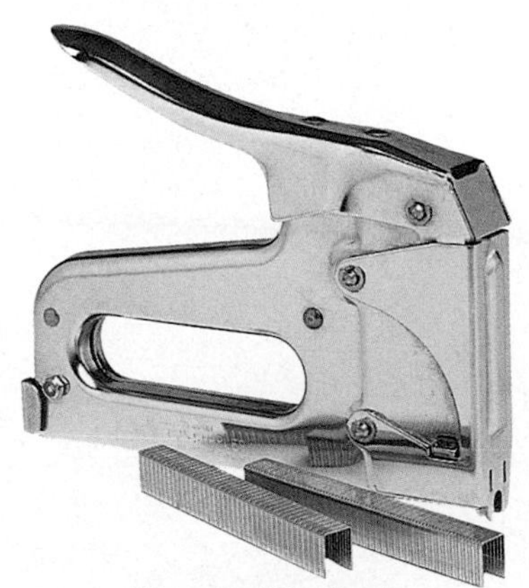

Fig. 6-42. Stapler.

Stapler–Heavy-duty models with spring-driven plungers drive up to 9⁄16″ staples. **Fig. 6-42.** Uses:

- Attaching ceiling tile, screening, and other soft or thin materials.

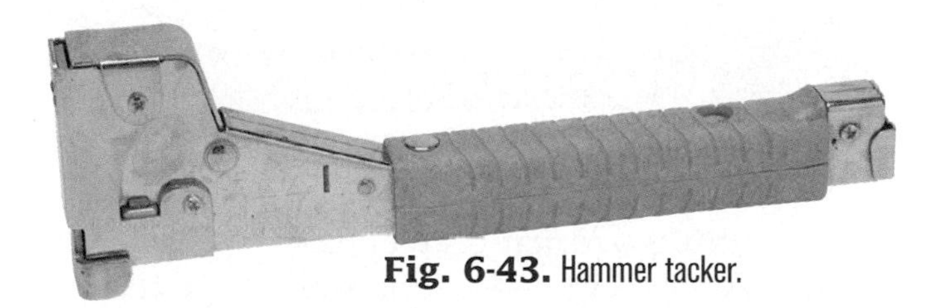

Fig. 6-43. Hammer tacker.

Hammer tacker–A slender magazine for holding staples, with a handle at one end. **Fig. 6-43.** It is used with a striking motion to quickly drive staples. Uses:

- Light-duty, high-volume fastening, such as attaching insulation, roofing felt, and building paper.

SECTION 6.4 Check Your Knowledge

1. Which is the heaviest hammer described in this section?
2. Which tools are used for pulling nails?
3. Which tool is used to drive finishing nails below the surface?
4. A stapler is used to attach which types of materials?

On the Job

Hammer heads are shaped differently. Handle lengths are also different. Conduct a nail-pulling test of curved-claw and straight-claw hammers. Also, compare hammers with different handle lengths. Determine how much the mechanical advantage is increased from one type to another. Report your results to the class.

Wrenches, Pliers, and Snips

Pliers are designed to hold things. They should not be used to turn nuts or bolts because they can damage them. A **wrench** should be used to turn them instead.

Fig. 6-44. Adjustable wrench.

Fig. 6-46. Box wrench.

Adjustable wrench–A steel tool with one adjustable jaw. **Fig. 6-44.** This wrench exerts greatest strength when hand pressure is applied to the side with the fixed jaw. Uses:

- Turning nuts and bolts, when there is plenty of clearance.

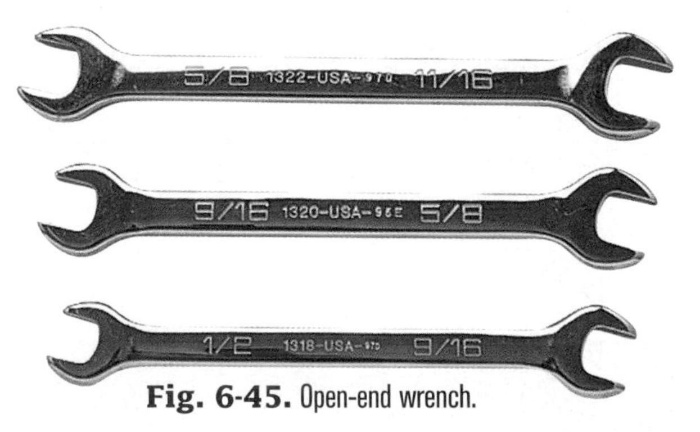

Fig. 6-45. Open-end wrench.

Open-end wrench–A nonadjustable wrench with accurately machined openings on either end. **Fig. 6-45.** For a variety of tasks, a complete set is needed. Sets are available in metric and standard sizes. Uses:

- Turning nuts and bolts in difficult-to-reach areas.

Socket wrench set–A series of metal sockets that fit onto a handle containing a ratcheting mechanism. **Fig. 6-47.** Sets come in metric and standard sizes. A basic set contains ten sockets, a ratcheting handle, and a non-ratcheting handle. Uses:

- Installing or removing nuts, bolts, and lag screws quickly.

Box wrench–A metal wrench with two enclosed ends. **Fig. 6-46.** Heads are offset from 15° to 45°. It is available in metric and standard sizes. Uses:

- Making adjustments where there is limited space for movement.
- Turning nuts and bolts when a secure grip is essential.

Fig. 6-47. Socket wrench set.

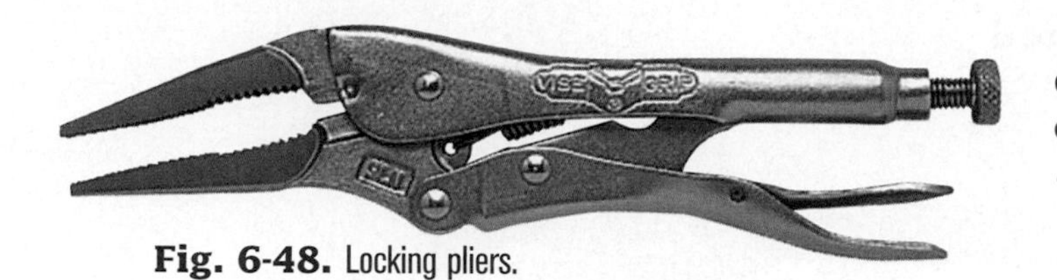
Fig. 6-48. Locking pliers.

Locking pliers–An all-purpose tool with double-lever action that locks the jaws to clamp a workpiece. **Fig. 6-48.** Uses:

- Substitutes for a vise, clamp, pipe wrench, fixed wrench, or adjustable wrench.

Pipe wrench–A tool with hardened, cut teeth on the jaws. **Fig. 6-49.** The jaws tighten as the wrench is turned. Uses:

- Tightening or removing pipes. Should never be used on nuts or bolts.

Fig. 6-49. Pipe wrench.

Fig. 6-50. Allen wrench.
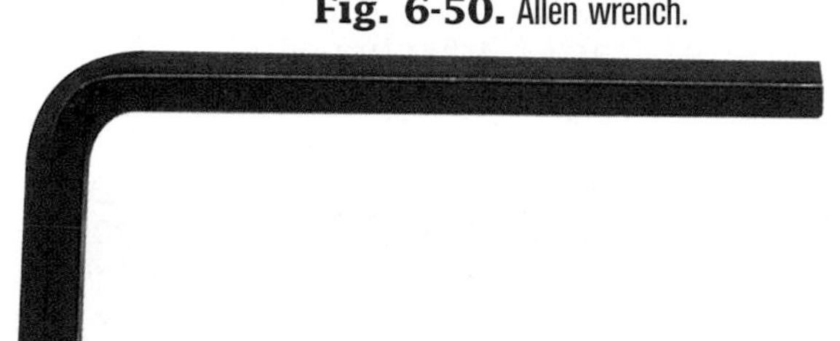

Allen wrench–Hexagonal steel bar with bent ends that fit inside a hexagonal recess in the top of a screw. **Fig. 6-50.** Sometimes called a *hex key*. Uses:

- Tightening and loosening setscrews, some of which secure pulleys and wheels on power tools and equipment.

Slip-joint pliers–An all-purpose adjustable pliers for light-duty gripping. **Fig. 6-51.** Uses:

- Holding and turning round pieces. Should never be used on nuts or the heads of bolts.

Fig. 6-51. Slip-joint pliers.
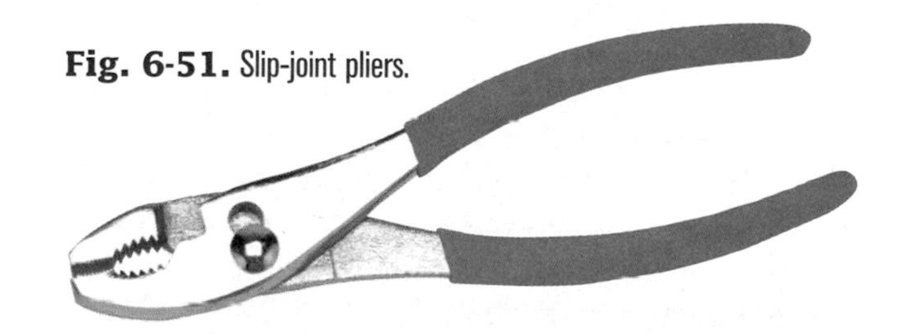

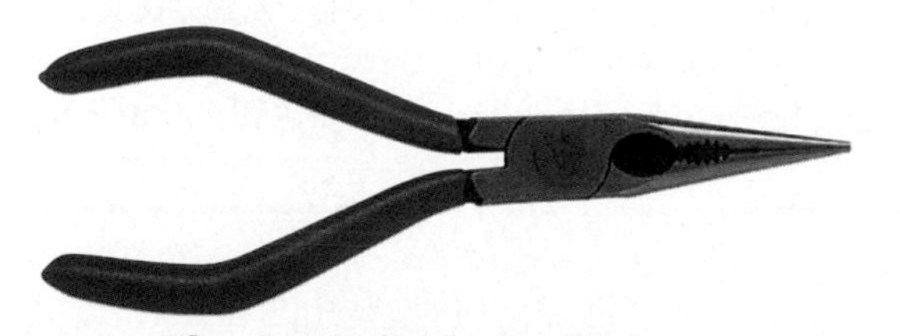
Fig. 6-52. Needle-nose pliers.

Needle-nose pliers–A pliers with a long, thin nose and cutting edges near the joint. **Fig. 6-52.** Uses:

- Holding and bending thin wire and metal fittings.
- Cutting light-gauge electrical wire.

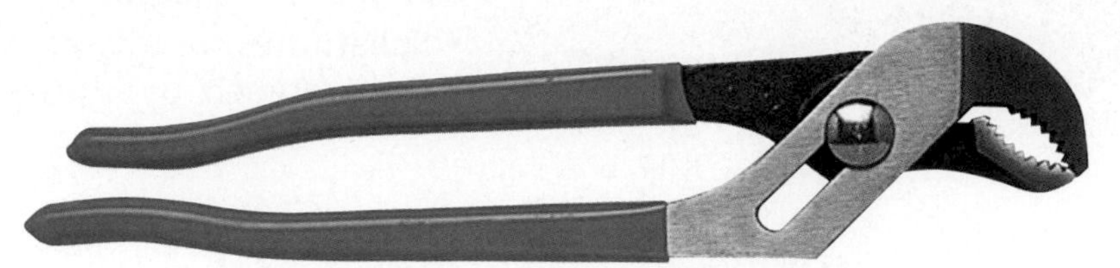

Fig. 6-53. Box-joint utility pliers.

Box-joint utility pliers–A large pliers with a slip joint at four or more positions. **Fig. 6-53.** Sometimes called *groove-joint pliers* or *waterpump pliers.* Uses:

- Holding and turning large, round parts.
- General gripping or turning.

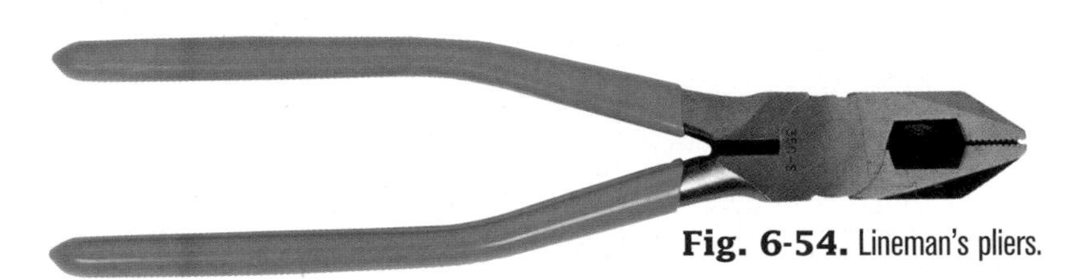

Fig. 6-54. Lineman's pliers.

Lineman's pliers–A pliers with stout, flattened jaws and long, slightly curved handles. Cutting edges are formed into one side of the jaws. Sometimes called *side cutters.* **Fig. 6-54.** Uses:

- Cutting electrical and other wire.
- Twisting or grasping wire.

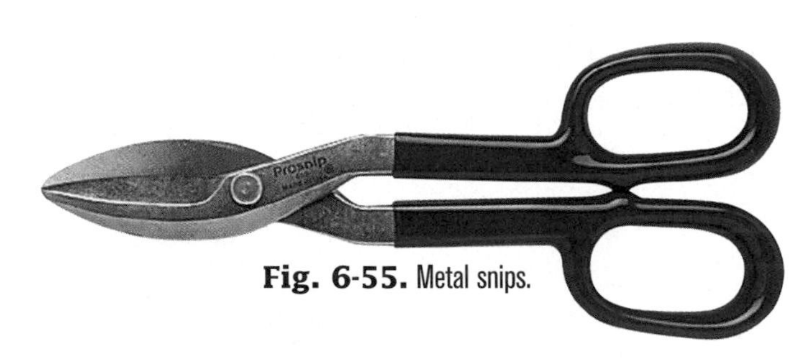

Fig. 6-55. Metal snips.

Metal snips–Steel tool with scissors-like handles. **Fig. 6-55.** Sometimes called *tin snips.* Straight blades are primarily for making straight cuts. Duckbill blades can make curved or straight cuts. Compound-action snips (sometimes called *aviation snips*) can cut thicker stock. Uses:

- Cutting light-gauge metal sheet stock and ducts.

SECTION 6.5 Check Your Knowledge

1. Which general type of tool should be used to turn nuts or bolts?
2. Which tool is used to turn setscrews?
3. Which type of pliers is used to cut light-gauge electrical wire?
4. What other terms are used for metal snips?

On the Job

Obtain sets of socket wrenches in both customary and metric sizes. Make a list of the sizes in the sets. Experiment by using a customary socket wrench on a metric bolt about the same size. What happens? Make the same experiment using a metric socket wrench and a customary bolt. What happens? Should metric and customary sets be used interchangeably? Why or why not?

Chapter 6 Review

Section Summaries

6.1 Measuring and marking tools include layout tape measures, steel tape measures, chalk lines, folding rules, carpenter's pencils, try squares, combination squares, sliding T-bevels, dividers, framing or carpenter's squares, rafter or triangular framing squares, carpenter's levels, torpedo levels, scratch awls, plumb bobs, and construction calculators.

6.2 Saws include utility drywall saws, backsaws, handsaws, hacksaws, keyhole saws, toolbox saws, coping saws, and dovetail saws.

6.3 Cutting and shaping tools include block planes, jointer planes, wood chisels, cold chisels, wood rasps, metal files, and utility knives.

6.4 Assembly, fastening, and disassembly tools include clamps, hammers, mallets, bars, nail sets, screwdrivers, staplers, and tackers.

6.5 Wrenches, pliers, and snips include such tools as adjustable, open-ended, box, pipe, and Allen wrenches; vise-grip, slip joint, needle-nose, box-joint, and lineman's pliers; and metal snips.

Review Questions

1. Which tape measure would you use for measuring the longest lengths?
2. List at least three uses for the combination square.
3. What is the difference between a crosscut saw and a rip saw?
4. What is the most noticeable characteristic of saws used to cut curves?
5. What is the difference between a backsaw and a dovetail saw?
6. What is another term for a jointer plane?
7. What is the best hammer to use for striking metal tools such as cold chisels?
8. What distinguishes a rip hammer used by framing carpenters from other hammers?
9. What are nail sets used for?
10. Name at least two kinds of pliers and identify their uses.

Buying Hand Tools Most carpenters buy their own hand tools. To get the best value for your money, follow these guidelines:

- Before you buy a tool, do some research. Ask experienced carpenters which brands they prefer and why. Check building trades magazines or Web sites for reviews of tools.
- Buy the best quality tool you can afford. Cheap, low-quality tools are a poor investment because they don't last long.
- Keep your tools in good condition. They will work better and last longer if you take good care of them.

Chapter 7 Power Saws

Objectives

After reading this chapter, you'll be able to:

- Follow the safety rules that apply to each type of power saw.
- Explain the causes of kickback on circular saws and table saws.
- Make a rip cut with a circular saw, a table saw, and a jigsaw.
- Maintain a circular saw.
- Maintain a table saw.
- Choose a suitable blade for each type of power saw and material.

Terms

bevel cut
crosscut
feed rate
internal cut
kickback
miter cut
offcut
rip cut

It has been many years since carpenters have had to depend on handsaws to cut framing lumber. On job sites today, carpenters and other tradespeople rely on power saws. A power saw is faster and cuts a wider variety of materials. Like other power tools, power saws are often available in cordless, as well as corded, models.

If used improperly, however, a power saw is much more likely to injure a worker than a handsaw. Its whirling blade can cause a serious injury before the user can react. For this reason, it is very important that you learn the proper use of each type of power saw.

SAFETY FIRST

Power-Saw Safety

Specific safety tips for various types of power saws may be found in the sections dealing with those saws. The following safety tips apply when using any power saw. We strongly advise you to check the manufacturer's manual for any special safety instructions.

GENERAL POWER-SAW SAFETY

- Review the tool-related safety guidelines in Chapter 5, "Construction Safety and Health."
- Always wear safety glasses.
- Wear hearing protection, particularly when using miter saws.
- Avoid wearing loose clothing and jewelry because it could get caught in a blade.
- Make sure that the guard is installed and working properly.
- Never cut while off balance.
- If a loose piece of wood contacts a spinning blade, the wood can be violently ejected from the saw. For this reason, never stand in a direct line with the blade.
- When cutting certain materials, such as fiber-cement, it is important to collect the dust created so it is not inhaled. Most saws can be fitted to collect sawdust. Saws can also be connected to a vacuum hose. Wear a respirator that will protect your lungs.

SECTION 7.1

Circular Saws

A circular saw is one of the most important tools on a job site. It is especially useful for cutting panel products such as plywood and oriented-strand board (OSB) and for crosscutting framing lumber. With the proper blade, even materials such as plastic laminate, masonry, and nonferrous metals can be cut.

Circular saws vary considerably in size, shape, and power. They are generally classified according to the diameter of the blade. A 61⁄20 saw, for example, has a blade with a diameter of 61⁄20. The blades on circular saws range in size from 41⁄20 to over 250. The smallest saws are used for trim work and for cutting panel products such as sheathing. The largest saws, which may require two people to operate, can cut through large timbers and beams in one pass. The most common circular saw is the 71⁄40 model. It is very maneuverable, yet powerful enough to cut a great variety of materials.

Cordless saws that operate on batteries are increasingly popular. As battery technology improves, cordless saws will become even more common on job sites. They may not have the power of a corded saw, but they can operate anywhere. This makes them particularly useful on a roof or for installing wood fencing far from the nearest electrical outlet. In damp conditions, a cordless saw presents less of an electrical hazard than a corded saw. **Fig. 7-1.**

Fig. 7-1. A cordless saw has the great advantage of portability.

SAFETY FIRST

Circular-Saw Safety

The following are general circular-saw safety rules. We strongly advise you to check the manufacturer's manual for any special safety instructions.

CIRCULAR-SAW SAFETY

- Make sure the teeth of the blade are sharp.
- Make sure that the stock is free of nails.
- When working outside or near moisture, make sure that the power source is protected with a GFCI.
- Make sure that any stock that cannot be held safely is clamped to a work surface.
- Never make an adjustment on a saw while it is running.
- Do not stand directly in line with the saw blade. If the blade binds, it may kick the saw back out of the cut. If this happens, turn off the switch immediately.
- Always keep the guard in place and the blade adjusted for the correct depth of cut.
- Use the correct blade for the work to be done.
- Make sure the power cord is clear of the blade.
- Unplug the saw before changing a blade. Make sure that the teeth are pointing in the direction of blade rotation and that the arbor nut is tightened properly.
- Always allow the saw to reach full speed before starting a cut.
- Always keep your hands clear of the cutting line.
- When finished with a cut, release the switch. Wait until the blade comes to a stop before setting the saw down.
- Always support the work in a way that will prevent the blade from being pinched by the material being cut.

PARTS OF A CIRCULAR SAW

The main parts of a circular saw include a motor, a handle, a baseplate or shoe, a fixed guard, an adjustable guard, a blade-guard lever, a blade, a blade-adjustment knob, and an on/off switch. **Fig. 7-2.**

Be certain that the blade is of the correct diameter and that the arbor hole in the blade is of the right size and shape for the saw.

TYPES OF CIRCULAR SAWS

The two basic types of circular saws are the contractor's saw and the worm-drive saw. The motor on a *contractor's saw* is perpendicular to the blade. The blade is usually mounted on the right side of the motor and is driven by a spindle connected directly to it. The contractor's saw is sometimes called a *sidewinder.*

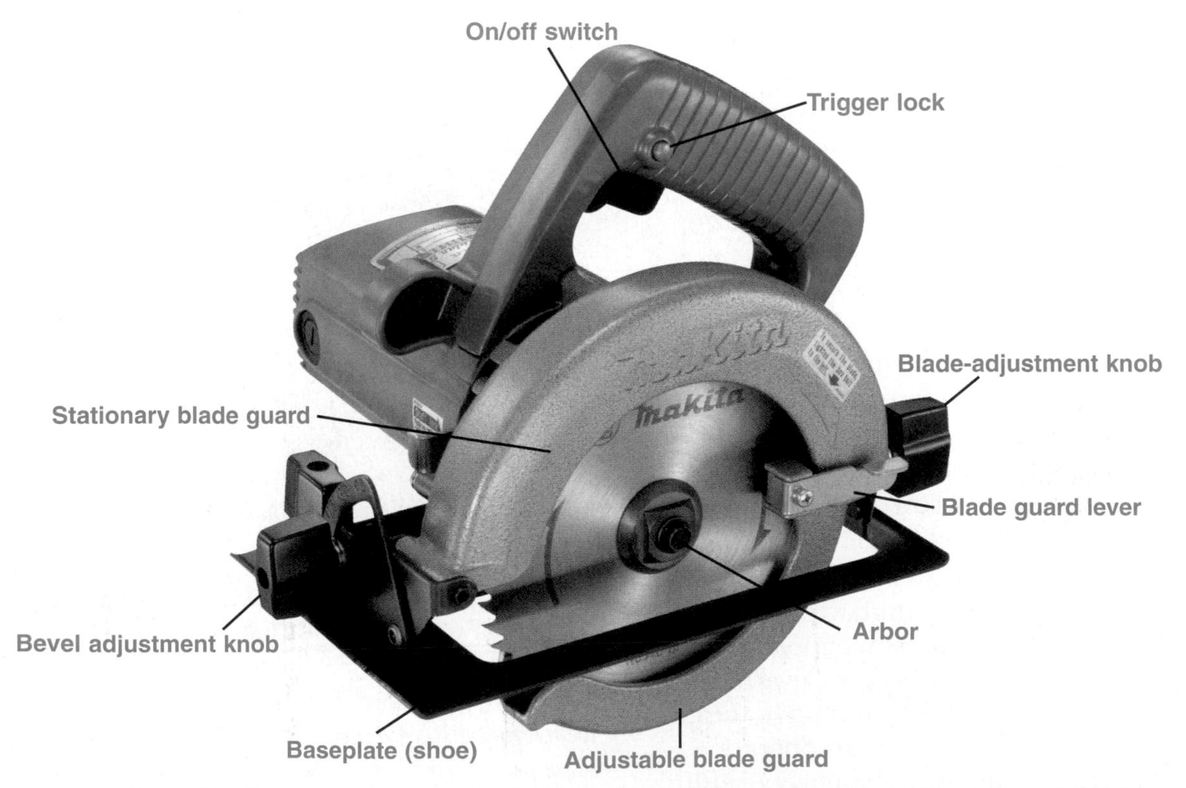

Fig. 7-2. The main parts of a portable circular saw. This model is a contractor's saw with a left-mounted blade.

The motor on a *worm-drive saw* is parallel to the blade. **Fig. 7-3.** The blade is on the motor's left side. Power from the motor is transferred to the blade through two gears mounted at right angles to each other. This arrangement generally results in slower blade speed but higher torque. (*Torque* is the force that produces rotation.) The other parts of a worm-drive saw are similar to those of a contractor's saw.

Fig. 7-3. A worm-drive saw. Note that the saw has two handles. This feature improves operator control.

CIRCULAR-SAW MAINTENANCE

The *owner's manual* is a booklet packaged with a tool. It contains specific instructions on how to use the tool safely and how to maintain it. Keep this manual for reference. Most manufacturers also maintain Web sites.

A saw in good working order is safer and will cut more accurately than a damaged saw. Blade guards are particularly prone to damage.

- Inspect blade guards frequently to ensure that they are working correctly. Never use a saw with a damaged or missing blade guard.
- Check that the baseplate is straight. Sight along the bottom of the plate at the beginning of each day and if the saw has been dropped. If a baseplate cannot be bent back into alignment, replace it.
- Worm-drive saws require a special lubricant to protect the internal gears. Drain the old lubricant periodically and replace it with new lubricant as recommended by the manufacturer.
- Inspect the power cord. A saw's power cord can be damaged by the blade or by other abuse. If the damage extends through the cord's outer casing, the cord should be replaced.

SAFETY FIRST

Power Tool Maintenance

Safety depends on proper tool maintenance. The following are general rules for maintaining power tools:

- Disconnect a tool from its power source before performing any maintenance. If the tool is cordless, remove the battery.
- Check the power cord for cuts and abrasions. Repair any damage before using the tool. If the damage cannot be repaired, replace the entire cordset.
- Replace a power tool's plug if any of the prongs are damaged.
- Brush off or blow off accumulations of sawdust and other debris.
- Replace or sharpen worn blades or bits.
- Use only identical replacement parts when servicing a power tool.
- Consult the owner's manual before applying cleaning agents. Some solvents may damage plastic or rubber parts.

PREVENTING KICKBACK

Kickback is particularly dangerous with a circular saw. **Kickback** occurs when a spinning blade encounters something that stops it while the saw is under full power. Consequently, the saw is violently "kicked back" at the operator. In the split second after this occurs, the operator loses control of the saw and the blade starts spinning again. This combination of events can lead to serious injury.

The following situations can result in kickback:

- The saw may be twisted to the side during the cut or pulled backwards. This causes the blade to bind.
- The material on one or both sides of the cut may bend, pinching the saw blade.
- The saw may also encounter a large knot, which suddenly slows the blade.

To avoid injury from kickback always be sure to follow these precautions:

- Always cut in a straight line.
- Always support the wood in a way that prevents the cut pieces from pressing against the blade.
- Always keep a firm grip on the saw.
- Always work with a sharp blade. Dull blades are more likely to bind or stall.
- When cutting through a knot, push the saw through at a slower rate.
- Never stand in a direct line with the blade.

Fig. 7-4. The wood grid of this panel-cutting table supports plywood as it is being cut. The table rests on sawhorses.

CUTTING TECHNIQUES

Carpenters who cut a lot of plywood can work more safely and quickly by using a panel-cutting table. **Fig. 7-4.** This table is supported by sawhorses and provides a flat surface for cutting plywood and other large panels. Most importantly, it prevents the material being cut from pinching the saw blade. A pinched blade is a major cause of saw kickback. A panel-cutting table can be made on the job site.

Crosscuts and Rip Cuts

The most common cut made with a circular saw is the crosscut. The **crosscut** is made *across* the grain of a board. When using a circular saw to make a crosscut, place the work over sawhorses or support it securely in some other way. Make sure that the area beneath the cutting line is clear.

Because the blade of a circular saw cuts as its teeth enter the *bottom* of a material, it will leave a smoother cut at the bottom than at the top. **Fig. 7-5.** This is why plywood used for cabinetry or siding should be cut with the good side facing down. It is not important to do this when cutting sheathing.

Loosen the blade-adjustment lever to adjust the depth of cut. Only about ⅛″ of the blade should show below the stock. **Fig. 7-6.** Rest the

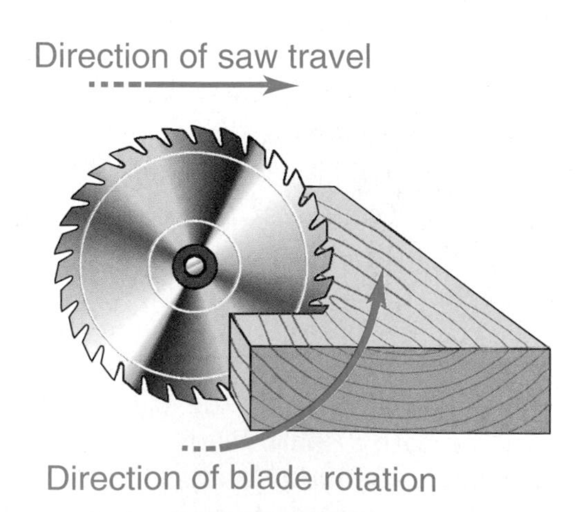

Fig. 7-5. The cutting action of a circular saw blade. The blade cuts from the bottom up.

Fig. 7-6. The blade of a circular saw should extend no more than ⅛″ below the wood.

front of the baseplate flat on the work, but do not let the blade touch the wood yet. Pull the trigger switch and allow the saw to come up to full speed. Guide the saw across the board firmly but without too much pressure.

You can make a long rip cut in much the same way. A **rip cut** is made *along* the direction of the grain. If the cut does not need to be perfectly straight, you can follow a layout line freehand. For the straightest cuts, however, guide the saw with a rip guide. **Fig. 7-7.** The *rip guide* is a metal guide that slips into slots in the saw's baseplate. A circular saw can also be guided by sliding it along a stiff straightedge that has been clamped to the workpiece.

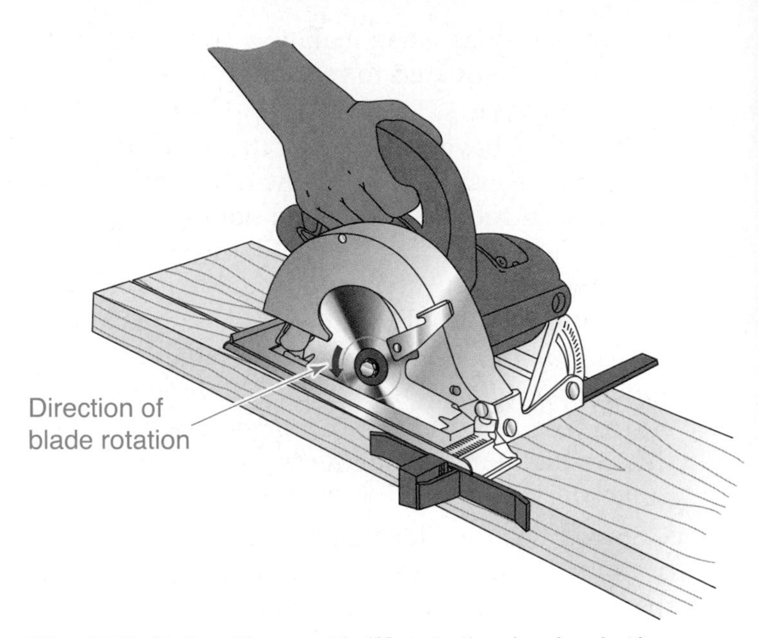

Fig. 7-7. Ripping with a rip guide. When ripping a long board, either walk slowly with the saw or stop the saw and pull it back in the kerf a little way, taking a new position to finish cutting.

Miter Cuts

A **miter cut** is any cut made at an angle across the grain of a board. It is a type of crosscut. Miter cuts can be made freehand, or they can be guided by a saw protractor. **Fig. 7-8.** A saw protractor is a metal guide with two arms that can be adjusted to various angles. It is marked in degrees. To use it, hold the protractor firmly against the workpiece with one hand. Use your other hand to guide the saw's baseplate along the projecting arm.

Bevel Cuts

A **bevel cut** is made at an angle through the thickness of a board or panel. **Fig. 7-9.** When making a bevel cut, the saw does not cut as

Fig. 7-8. Using a saw protractor as a guide for cutting. This can be adjusted to any angle to make miter cuts.

Fig. 7-9. Making a bevel cut. Notice that the guard is partially beneath the board.

deeply as it does when making a crosscut. Most saws can be adjusted to make bevel cuts at angles between 45° and 90°.

To make a bevel cut, loosen the wing nut or adjusting lever and tilt the saw to the desired angle. Then retighten the wing nut or lever. Adjust the saw for the correct depth of cut. Make the bevel cut freehand or guide it with a saw protractor. See Fig. 7-9.

A compound-bevel cut (which is also called a *compound-miter cut*) is made when a bevel is added to a miter cut. It can be created by tilting the blade and using a saw protractor to guide the saw.

Sometimes the blade guard will prevent a bevel cut from starting easily. In that case, using the saw blade lever, raise the guard slightly as you start the cut. Then release the lever.

SECTION 7.1

Check Your Knowledge

1. When using a circular saw, what should you do with a 2x4 that cannot be held safely?
2. What special maintenance does a worm-drive saw require?
3. When making a crosscut with a circular saw, how much of the saw blade should show below the stock?
4. Describe how a bevel cut is made.

On the Job

An instruction manual is always included with a new power tool. The manual includes important information about how to use the tool safely and maintain it properly. Over time, manuals may be lost or discarded, but a missing manual can be replaced.

Identify a particular brand and model of circular saw that you are familiar with. Using the Internet, find at least one source for a printed or downloadable manual that is appropriate for this saw. Summarize your experience for members of your team.

SECTION 7.2

Table Saws

A table saw can be used to crosscut stock, but its primary use is in ripping stock to width. It can rip cut with greater precision than a circular saw. That is why it is often used for ripping framing lumber and wood panel products. With the proper blade, a table saw can also be used to cut materials such as rigid sheet plastic.

Like a circular saw, a table saw is generally classified according to the diameter of the largest blade it will accept. The most common table saw on a job site is the 100 saw.

Because the blade of a table saw cuts as its teeth enter the *top* of the material, it will leave a smoother cut at the top than at the bottom. Material should be cut with the good side facing up. **Fig. 7-10.**

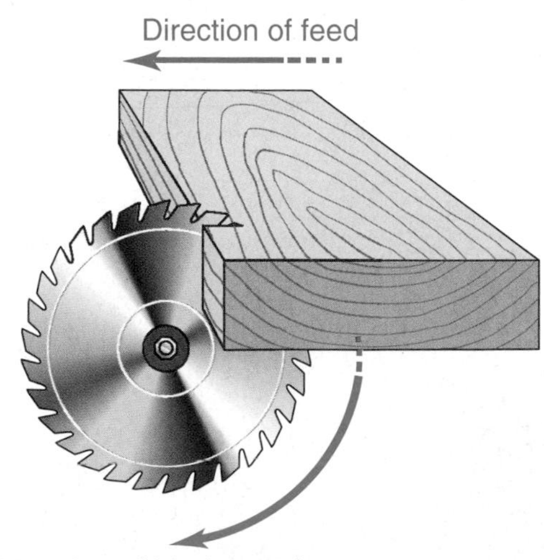

Fig. 7-10. The cutting action of the table saw. The blade cuts from the top down.

SAFETY FIRST

Table-Saw Safety

The following are general table-saw safety rules. We strongly advise you to check the manufacturer's manual for any special safety instructions.

TABLE-SAW SAFETY

- Remove rings, watches, and other items that might catch in the saw. Wear garments with short or tight sleeves. Wear proper eye protection.
- Always keep the area around the table saw clean and uncluttered.
- Never stand directly behind the blade.
- Never cut freehand.
- Do not saw warped or bowed material on the table saw.
- Make sure the stock is free of nails.
- When ripping stock that cannot be fed safely by hand, always push the stock past the blade with a push stick.
- Make all rip fence adjustments after the saw has been turned off and the blade is no longer spinning. Be certain the rip fence is clamped securely while cutting.
- Use the proper saw blade for the operation being performed. Always cut with a sharp blade.
- Unplug the saw before changing blades.
- Always adjust the saw blade so it protrudes just enough above the stock to cut completely through.
- Never reach over a spinning saw blade. Instead, reach around the side of the machine.
- Keep your fingers away from the saw blade at all times.
- Always keep the guard and splitter in place. If the cut you are making doesn't permit use of the guard, use a featherboard or a special guard. A *featherboard* is a piece of stock with a series of long saw cuts on one end. It is used to hold narrow stock against the rip fence when making a rip cut with a table saw.
- When crosscutting with the miter gauge, never use the fence as a stop unless a clearance block is used. A clearance block prevents the wood from becoming trapped between the fence and the blade.
- When ripping, place the jointed edge against the fence.
- Keep the saw table clean. Remove all scraps with a brush or push stick, never with your fingers.
- Always hold the stock firmly against the miter gauge when crosscutting and against the rip fence when ripping. A helper should not pull the stock. The helper only supports the stock.

PARTS OF A TABLE SAW

The main parts of a table saw are the table, the motor, the base, and the on/off switch. **Fig. 7-11.** For safety purposes, the on/off switch should be large and easy to reach. A *miter gauge* or a rip fence guides wood through the blade, and a guard prevents accidental contact. A *splitter* directly behind the blade prevents the stock from pinching the blade as it is being cut.

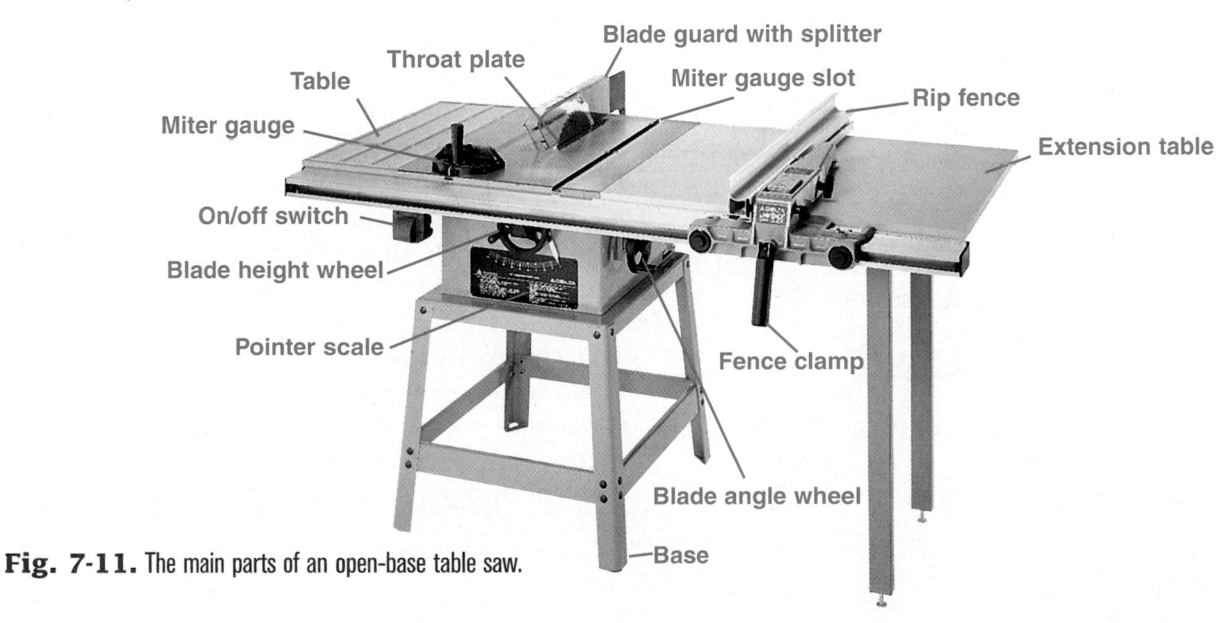

Fig. 7-11. The main parts of an open-base table saw.

An opening in the center of the table allows the blade to be raised above the table surface. The opening is partially covered by a *throat plate.* This plate is an important safety feature that prevents small pieces of wood from being wedged against the blade.

The miter gauge is used during crosscut operations and can be adjusted for various angles. It slides forward and back in one of two grooves in the top of the saw table. Both grooves are parallel to the saw blade. When not in use, the miter gauge should be removed from the table.

The rip fence is used for all ripping operations. It is adjusted by sliding it left or right across the table. When it is ready for use, it is locked in place. When not being used, the fence should be removed or moved well away from the blade and locked.

Also available are table extensions that can be fastened to the sides of the saw table. These are especially convenient when cutting a large panel, such as a sheet of plywood.

The blade guard should be kept in place whenever possible. If a cut cannot be made with the standard guard in place, some other safety method should be used instead.

TYPES OF TABLE SAWS

Most table saws have a fixed, horizontal table and a blade that can be raised, lowered, and angled. This type is called a *tilting-arbor saw.* In contrast, a few saws feature a table that tilts; the blade can only be raised or lowered. This type has limitations on a job site and is rarely used.

Two types of tilting-arbor table saws are commonly used in building construction. *Contractor table saws,* sometimes called *open-base saws,* rest on a metal framework that is light enough for two people to carry and move from site to site. *Portable table saws,* also called *benchtop saws,* are light enough for one person to carry. They are not generally used for heavy-duty cutting. **Fig. 7-12.**

Fig. 7-12. Portable table saws are often used for finish carpentry tasks because they can be easily moved from room to room. This saw is being used to rip a board.

TABLE-SAW MAINTENANCE

A table saw requires little maintenance. The steps for installing a blade are given on page 135. Refer to the manufacturer's instructions for specific recommendations. The following are general guidelines only.

- Keep the table clean and smooth. Remove patches of rust with metal polish. Scrape off paint drips and glue to prevent them from interfering with the movement of stock.
- Unplug the saw, then gently brush or blow accumulated sawdust from the blade-raising-and-tilting mechanism beneath the table. Lubricate the mechanism as recommended by the manufacturer.
- Some saws are driven by a V-belt that links the motor to the arbor. Replace the belt if it becomes worn or damaged.

PREVENTING KICKBACK

Kickback from a table saw can be as dangerous as it is from a circular saw. However, on a table saw, the workpiece is kicked back, not the saw itself. A piece of wood ejected from the saw can become a deadly missile. Kickback can occur:

- When the workpiece is twisted to the side during the cut. This causes the blade to bind.
- When the stock on one or both sides of the cut bends, pinching the saw blade.
- When the rip fence is not parallel to the blade. This causes the blade to bind.
- When wood is being crosscut with a miter gauge and a rip fence. A waste piece, called an **offcut**, can become wedged between the blade and the rip fence. This can produce kickback.

To avoid kickback, always be sure to follow these guidelines:

- Be sure that one edge of the workpiece is always held firmly against the rip fence. Always keep a firm grip on the stock, and hold it flat against the table. Use a push stick when necessary.
- Always support the wood in a way that prevents the cut pieces from pressing against the blade. This might require a table or roller stands placed under the stock where it leaves the table.
- Always work with a sharp blade. Dull blades are more likely to bind or stall.
- When using the miter gauge to crosscut stock, make sure any offcuts cannot become trapped between the blade and the rip fence. To do this, remove the fence or push it well clear of the cutting area.

ADJUSTING THE SAW

To operate a table saw safely, you must carefully adjust the blade, the rip fence, and the miter gauge. Never make adjustments while the saw is running.

STEP BY STEP

Installing a Table-Saw Blade

A blade must often be removed for sharpening or when cutting different materials. Knowing how to change the blade safely is important.

Step 1 Unplug the saw to prevent accidental startup.

Step 2 Remove the throat plate. This usually snaps in and out of position.

Step 3 Select a wrench to fit the arbor nut. On most saws, the arbor has a left-hand thread. The nut must be turned clockwise to loosen it. Hold a piece of scrap wood against the blade to keep the arbor from turning as you work. **Fig. 7-13.**

Step 4 Remove the nut and the collar. Hold them securely or they may drop into the sawdust below and be difficult to find. Take off the old blade, being careful not to bump its teeth against the table.

Step 5 Slip the new blade onto the arbor. The teeth should point in the direction of blade rotation (towards the operator). Replace the collar and nut. Tighten the nut firmly, but not too tight. The nut will tighten further as the saw is used.

Step 6 Replace the throat plate.

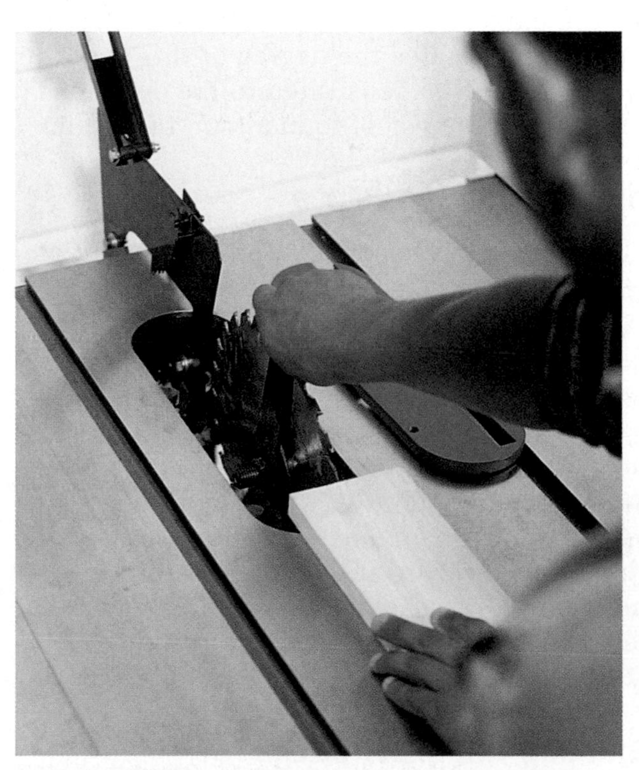

Fig. 7-13. Hold the blade still with a piece of scrap wood. The nut will loosen if turned in the direction in which the teeth are pointing.

An arbor nut always loosens when turned in the direction in which the blade's teeth are pointing. This is the direction of blade rotation.

Setting the Blade Height

To raise the blade, hold the workpiece near the side of the blade and carefully turn the blade-height wheel until the top saw tooth is at the correct height. For most cutting, the top of the blade should extend no more than $\frac{1}{8}$" above the stock. For many joint cuts, however, the blade must be set for the exact depth of cut.

Tilting the Blade

A *blade-angle wheel* on the side of the machine tilts the blade. A *pointer* or *scale* on the front of the saw indicates the degree of tilt. Turn the wheel until the blade is tilted to the desired degree. Lock the wheel to maintain the angle.

Adjusting the Rip Fence

The rip fence is usually placed to the right of the blade. For accurate and safe cutting, set the rip fence exactly parallel to the blade. To check it, align it with one of the miter gauge slots in the table. Then lock the fence. Check again. If the edge of the fence is not parallel to the slot, unlock the fence and readjust it.

To adjust the fence to a specific distance, first move it to the approximate location. Holding a rule or tape measure at a right angle to the fence, carefully measure the distance from the fence to the nearest edge of one tooth. **Fig. 7-14.** Lock the fence.

Fig. 7-14. Adjusting the fence for the correct width of cut. Make a small test cut on the workpiece. Measure it to double-check the setup before making the complete cut. The guard should be in place for all tool operations.

Adjusting the Miter Gauge

The miter gauge, which is used for crosscutting operations, can be used in either groove on the table. There is a pointer and scale on the miter gauge for setting it to any angle to the right or left. Most gauges have automatic stop positions at 30°, 45°, 60°, and 90°.

Before relying on the accuracy of a miter gauge, square it to the blade. Unplug the saw and use a framing square to see if the gauge and the blade form a 90° angle. If they do not, adjust the gauge.

The blade tilt may not be accurate. Make sure the pointer is on 0 when the blade is perpendicular to the table.

CUTTING TECHNIQUES

Many fundamental woodworking operations can be done with the table saw. It can be used not only for cutting stock to size but also for cutting many joints.

Ripping

Make sure the rip fence is properly adjusted for these operations. Whenever possible, place the widest part of the stock between the blade and the fence. The **feed rate** is the speed at which stock is pushed through the saw blade. For ripping thick stock or hardwoods, the feed rate should be slowed.

Stock with a width of 6″ or more is considered wide. To rip wide stock:

1. Adjust the rip fence to the appropriate width and lock it.
2. Turn on the saw. Place the end of the stock flat against the table.

SAFETY FIRST

Avoid Kickback

To avoid kickback, push the stock completely past the blade to complete the cut.

3. Push the wood against the fence with your left hand, and push it forward with the right. If the board is long, use a roller stand as shown in Fig. 7-19 on page 139.
5. Feed the stock into the blade at a slow, steady speed. Hold your right hand close to the fence as you work. Be careful not to overload the saw. **Fig. 7-15.**

To rip narrow stock:

1. When cutting stock narrower than 6″, observe the same general practices as in starting the cut on wide stock.

Fig. 7-15. Ripping on the table saw.

2. As the uncut end of the board reaches the front of the table, use a push stick instead of your hand to guide the board between the blade and the fence. **Fig. 7-16.** Use a featherboard if necessary. Never under any circumstances cut narrow stock without a push stick. It is good practice to hang the push stick conveniently at the side of the saw so that you are not tempted to make a cut without it.

To cut a bevel:

1. Tilt the blade to the correct angle for the bevel.
2. Place the fence on the table so the top of the blade is tilting away from the fence.
3. Adjust the fence for the correct width of cut.
4. Adjust the height of the blade to clear the top of the board slightly.
5. Hold the work firmly against the fence as the cut is made. **Fig. 7-17.**

Crosscutting

Use the miter gauge for most crosscutting operations. Always remove the rip fence or slide it well out of the way.

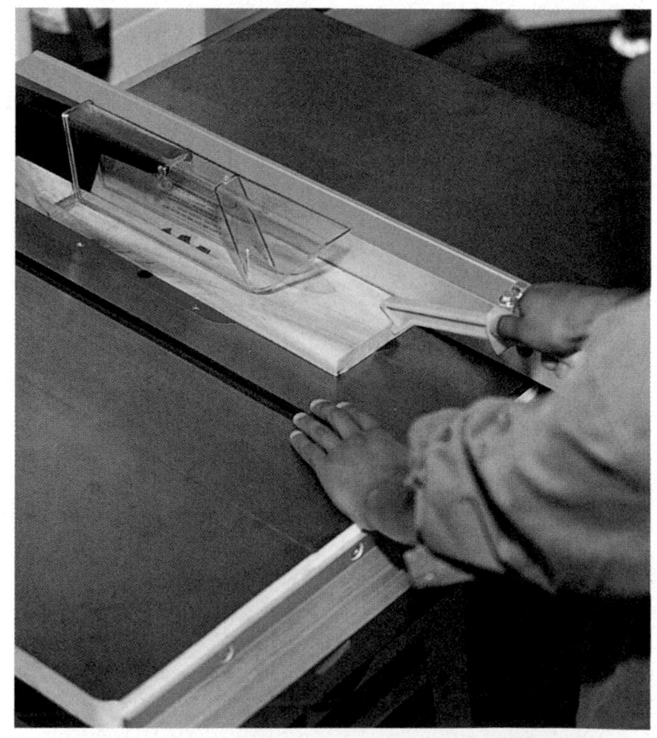

Fig. 7-16. Using a push stick in ripping narrow stock. Note that the push stick is used between the blade and the fence, not on the outside of the blade. The guard should be in place for all tool operations.

To perform crosscutting:

1. Hold the stock firmly against the gauge and advance it slowly into the blade. **Fig. 7-18.**
2. When the cut is complete, slide the stock away from the blade and remove it. Never drag the cut edge back across the blade. Never put your fingers near the blade to remove the offcut.

Fig. 7-17. Cutting a bevel with the grain. The guard is not shown here. This allows the operation to be shown more clearly. The guard should be in place for all tool operations.

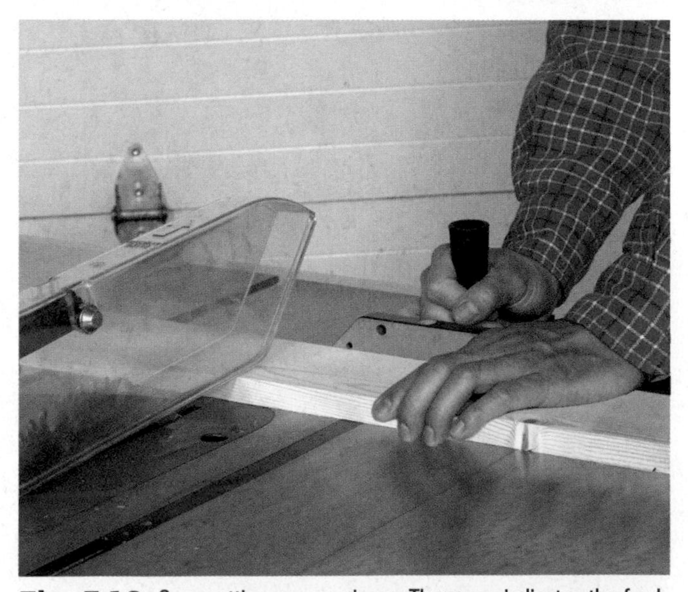

Fig. 7-18. Crosscutting narrow pieces. The arrow indicates the feed direction. The guard should be in place for all tool operations.

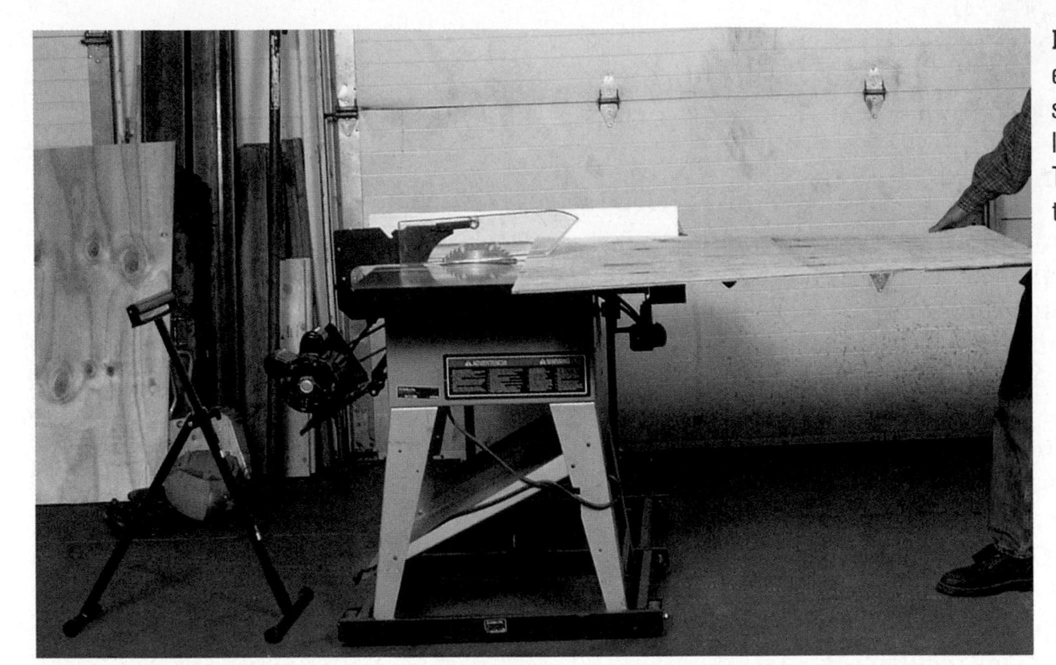

Fig. 7-19. Rest the leading edge of the panel on the front of the saw table. A roller stand can support long stock as it exits a table saw. The guard should be in place for all tool operations.

Cutting Panels

Because of their size, panels such as plywood and oriented-strand board present cutting problems. The workpiece is often too large to fit conveniently on the saw table. The panel and any waste should be fully supported as they leave the top of the table saw. This can be done with a roller stand or an outfeed table.

To cut panels:

1. Adjust the blade to the proper height. Adjust the fence for the width of cut.
2. Make sure the panel edge that will ride against the rip fence is flat and straight. If it is not, the cut will not be accurate. Place a different edge against the fence if necessary.
3. Turn on the saw, and rest the leading edge of the panel on the front of the saw table. The good side should be facing up. **Fig. 7-19.**
4. Push the panel steadily forward, while at the same time applying pressure to keep its edge firmly against the rip fence. Do not allow the panel to move sideways or it will bind on the blade.
5. As you complete the cut, be sure to push the panel and the waste piece completely past the blade.

Carpenter's Tip

Make sure that the wood is flat against the saw table as cutting starts. Before cutting large pieces of stock, rock the wood forward and back on the front surface of the saw table. You will feel it "slap" the table when it is flat.

SECTION 7.2 Check Your Knowledge

1. When you are cutting wood with a table saw, should the good side be facing up or down?
2. Name the two devices that are used to guide stock when cutting with a table saw.
3. List the required steps in installing a table-saw blade.
4. Explain two ways of supporting long stock for ripping on a table saw.

On the Job

During the course of his or her career, a carpenter will purchase various types of saws. What financial investment is required? Visit a home center or tool supplier or consult a mail-order tool catalog to get prices for the following table saws: a 10″ benchtop saw, a 10″ contractor's saw, and a 10″ cabinet saw. List the lowest and the highest price for each. What is the average price for each saw?

Radial-Arm Saw

The radial-arm saw can be used for ripping, dadoing (cutting a groove), and various combination cuts. However, the tool is best suited to crosscutting. For instance, a long board can be cut into shorter lengths easily because the board remains stationary on the table while the saw is pulled forward through the stock. Its primary advantage over other saws is its ability to crosscut unusually wide or thick stock. Since this feature is seldom needed on residential job sites and the saw is awkward to transport, this tool is not as common as it once was.

Like other saws with circular blades, the radial-arm saw is generally classified according to the largest diameter blade it will accept. Heavy-duty saws used in commercial construction might have a 14″ blade. The most common size used in residential construction is the 10" model. The teeth of a radial-arm saw blade point away from the operator and cut from the top. **Fig. 7-20.**

SAFETY FIRST

Radial-Arm Saw Safety

The following are general radial-arm saw safety rules. We strongly advise you to check the manufacturer's manual for any special safety instructions.

RADIAL-ARM SAW SAFETY

- Remove rings, watches, and other items that might catch in the saw. Wear garments with short or tight sleeves. Wear proper eye protection.
- Always keep the safety guard and the anti-kickback device in position unless you are changing the blade.
- Before crosscutting, adjust the anti-kickback device (sometimes called *anti-kickback fingers*) to clear the top of the work by about ⅛″.
- Make sure the clamps and locking handles are tight.
- This saw tends to feed itself into the work. Therefore you will need to regulate the rate of cutting by keeping a firm grip on it.
- Never place your hand closer than 6″ to the blade.
- Use a brush or stick to keep the table clear of all scraps and sawdust.
- When finished with a cut, return the saw head all of the way back past the fence.

PARTS OF A RADIAL-ARM SAW

A radial-arm saw is essentially a circular saw held by a *yoke* that allows it to slide forward and back on a track in the *arm*. The arm is attached to a vertical post that can raise or lower it. The saw takes its name from the fact that the arm moves from side to side or up and down (in other words, radially). Other parts of the radial-arm saw are shown in **Fig. 7-21**.

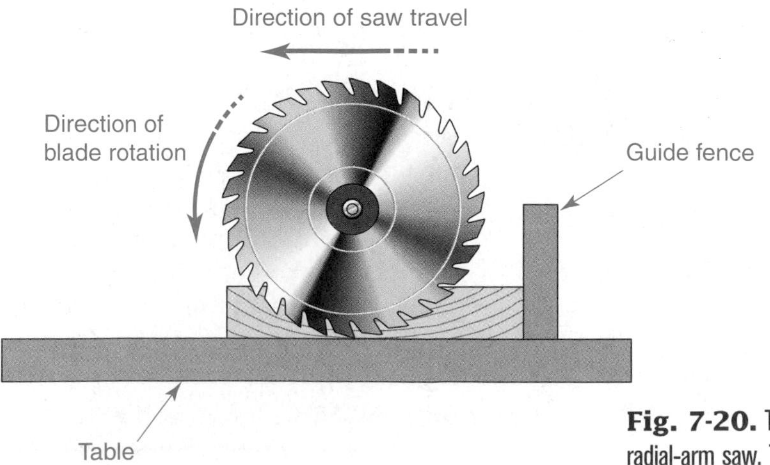

Fig. 7-20. The crosscutting action of the blade of a radial-arm saw. The blade cuts from the top down.

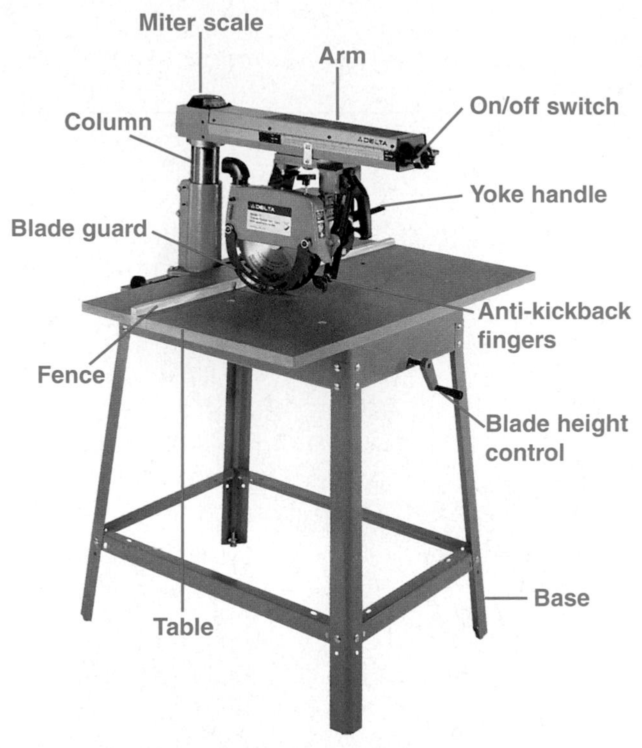

Fig. 7-21. The main parts of a radial-arm saw.

CUTTING TECHNIQUES

To prevent the saw from lurching forward, hold it securely before turning it on and while cutting. **Fig. 7-22.** Hold the stock to be cut tightly against the fence with one hand. With the other hand, grasp the motor yoke handle. For crosscutting and similar operations, pull the saw into the work. Return the saw to the rear of the table after each cut.

SECTION 7.3

Check Your Knowledge

1. What is the greatest advantage of a radial-arm saw over other saws?
2. How close to the workpiece should you set the anti-kickback device?
3. As you crosscut with the saw, where should your hands be?
4. What is the most common size of radial-arm saw found on construction sites?

On the Job

Reread the description of blade rotation for the circular saw and the table saw. Based on what you know of how these saws cut, decide if the good face of a board being cut on a radial-arm saw should face up or down. Explain your answer in a paragraph.

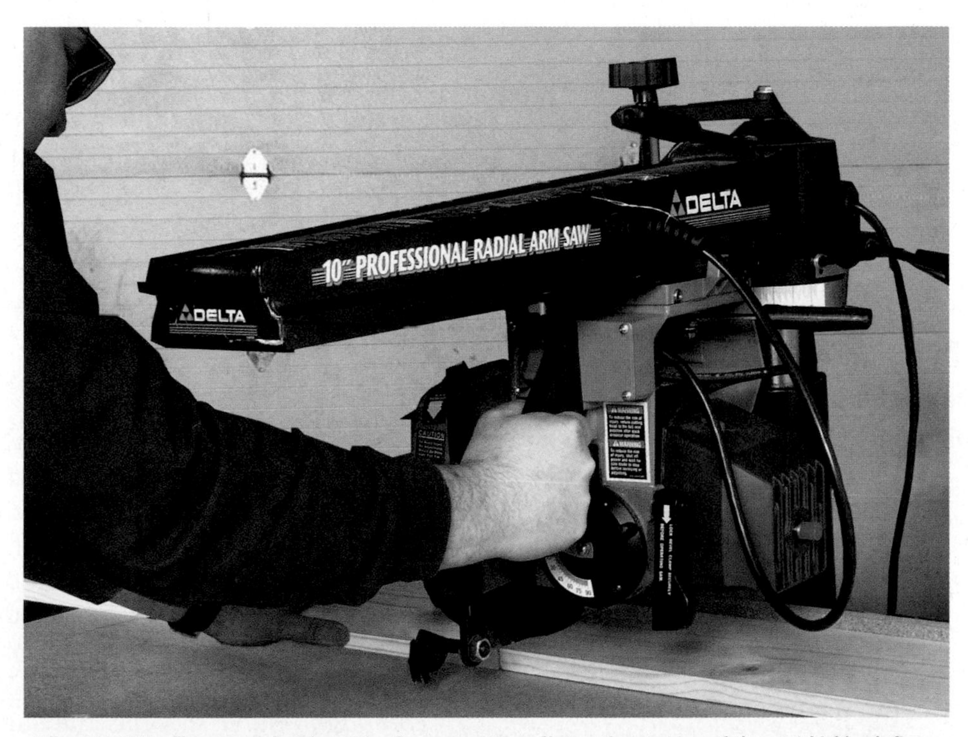

Fig. 7-22. The proper hand position for crosscutting. Notice the position of the anti-kickback fingers. The guard should be in place for all tool operations.

SECTION 7.4

Miter Saws

The miter saw (sometimes called a chop saw) has become a very important tool on the job site. **Fig. 7-23.** Frame carpenters may use the tool for making quick, repetitive crosscuts of framing lumber. The miter saw is essential to finish carpenters, who rely on it for accurate cuts on molding and trim, especially crown molding. (See Chapter 35, "Molding and Trim.")

The miter saw makes a clean cut that is very accurate. It is portable, easy to set up, and maintains its accuracy, which is why it is often preferred over a radial-arm saw. It cannot be used to rip stock. It can be used only for crosscutting. Some miter saws can make compound cuts in one pass. Fitted with a suitable blade, the miter saw can even cut metal pipe and light-gauge metal framing. Also, miter saws can easily be fitted with dust-collection equipment.

The size of a miter saw is determined by its blade diameter. Most miter saws used for residential work are 8¼″, 8½″, 10″, or 12″ models.

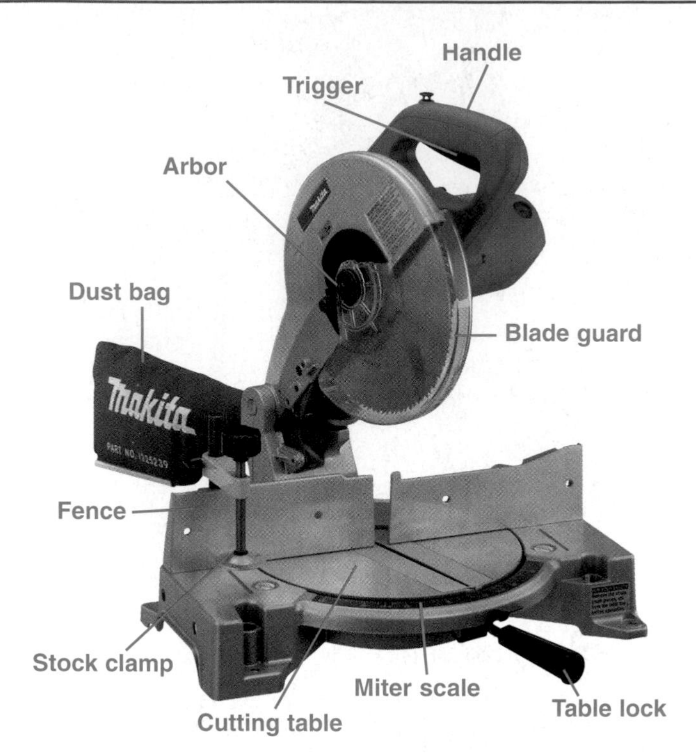

Fig. 7-23. The basic parts of a conventional miter saw.

SAFETY FIRST

Miter-Saw Safety

The following are general miter-saw safety rules. We strongly advise you to check the manufacturer's manual for any special safety instructions.

MITER-SAW SAFETY

- Remove rings, watches, and other items that might catch in the saw. Wear garments with short or tight sleeves. Wear proper eye protection.
- Be sure to use the correct cutting motion. The various types of miter saws have different requirements.
- Make sure that the stock is held firmly against the fence.
- Do not disable the blade guard.
- Make any adjustments to the saw only after the blade has stopped moving.
- Unplug the saw before changing blades.
- Support the stock to be cut along its entire length. Never cut stock that is too short to hold securely.
- Many miter saws operate with a high-pitched whine. Wear hearing protection.
- Do not lift stock into the blade.
- Make sure the saw is equipped with a *blade brake.* A blade brake allows the blade to be stopped quickly. This reduces the chances of hand injuries caused when the blade spins freely.

TYPES OF MITER SAWS

The three basic types of miter saws include conventional miter saws, compound-miter saws, and sliding compound-miter saws. *Conventional miter saws* were the first to become available. The head of the saw pivots up and down and from side to side. Conventional models are typically the simplest and lightest. They are suitable for crosscuts and miter cuts.

A *compound-miter saw* has the same range of motion as conventional models. In addition, however, the head of the saw can be tilted at an angle to one side or the other to create a bevel. **Fig. 7-24.** This allows the saw to make compound cuts in one pass. It is often used when cutting crown moldings, handrails, and other trims that require complex fitting.

A *sliding compound-miter saw* is similar to a compound-miter model, except that it can cut wider stock. **Fig. 7-25.** The head of the saw slides back and forth on one or two metal rails, as well as pivoting up and down. This allows some 10″ saws to crosscut stock up to 12″ wide.

With all three types of miter saw, the direction of blade travel is away from the operator. In other words, the exposed teeth of the saw point toward the fence.

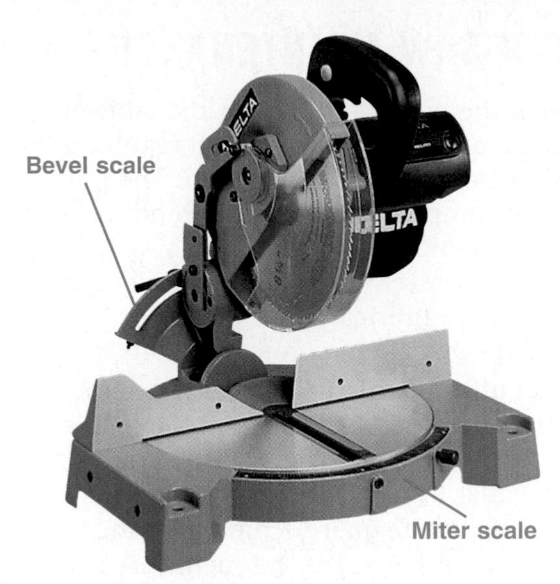

Fig. 7-24. The blade of a compound-miter saw can be tilted away from the vertical plane. This allows it to make a miter cut and a bevel cut at the same time.

PARTS OF A MITER SAW

The saw head may be mounted on a pivoting mechanism or on metal rails. The saw table has a miter scale. Most miter-saw scales contain positive (locked) stops at 90° and 45°. Positive stops allow the saw to be set quickly to commonly used angles. Some saw tables also contain positive stops at 15°, 22.5°, and 30°. On compound saws, the head, too, may contain positive stops.

Miter saws have a split fence that allows the blade to pass through. Miter saws also have retractable blade guards. The guard automatically pivots to shield whatever portions of the blade are not being used in a cut. This safety feature should never be disabled. All miter saws are equipped with a dust bag, a vacuum port, or both.

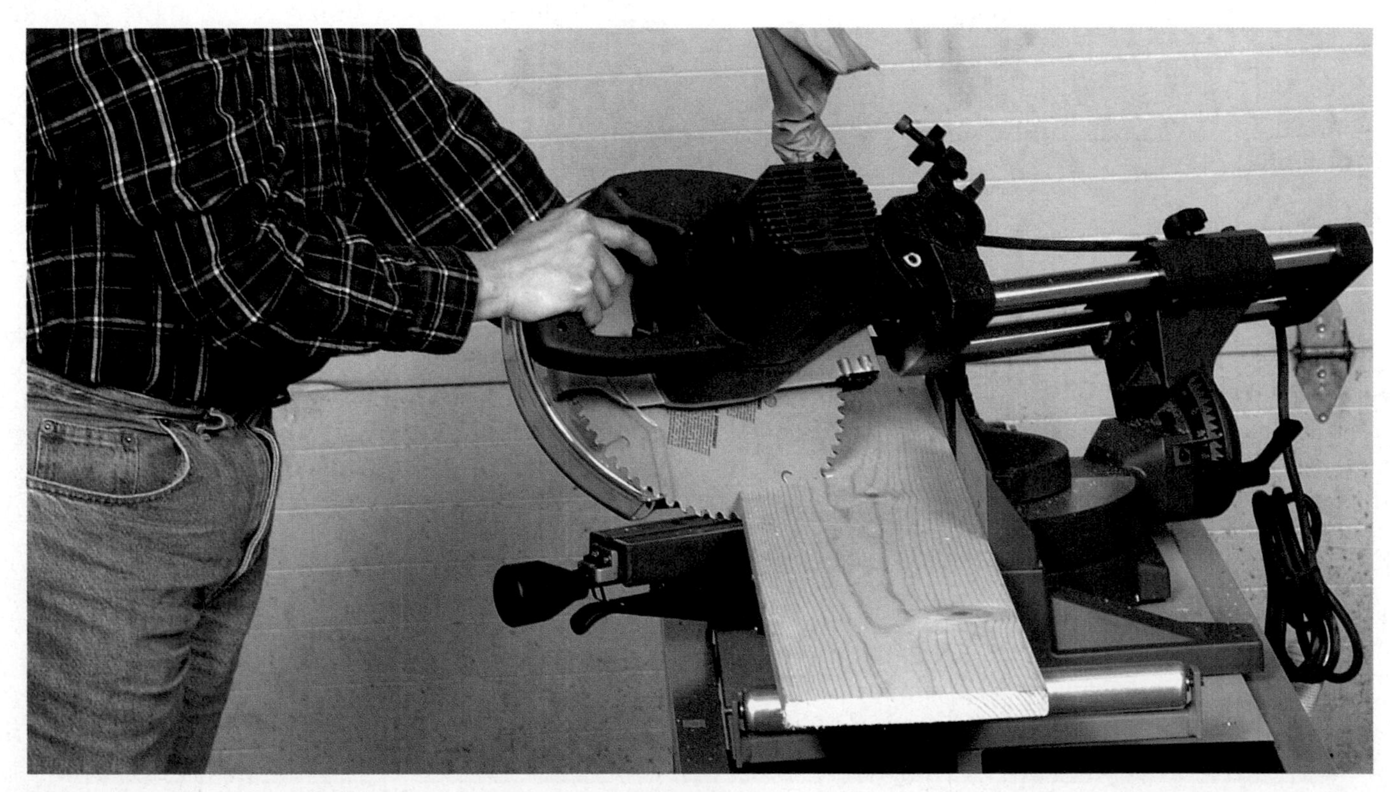

Fig. 7-25. This saw is being used to make a compound cut on wide stock.

MITER-SAW MAINTENANCE

Check the positive stops for the table and the head (on compound models) regularly for accuracy. Adjust them as needed. The rails of a sliding-compound miter saw do not normally require attention other than brushing off excess sawdust. However, the sliding mechanism itself might require lubrication. Consult the owner's manual for specific recommendations.

Brush off the table periodically to remove sawdust and small bits of wood that can interfere with table movement. In addition, remove any sawdust or small pieces of wood that might prevent the blade guard from operating properly. Empty the dust bag frequently. A buildup of sawdust in the bag encourages the release of fine dust into the air. This can lead to respiratory problems for anyone in the area.

Steps for installing a miter-saw blade are given below.

CUTTING TECHNIQUES

Techniques include general operation and crosscutting.

General Operation

The various types of miter saws differ in operation. For safety, be sure you understand the differences.

- All *miter saws:* If the saw has a manually operated blade brake, push down on the brake button when the cut is complete. If the saw has an automatic blade brake, it will engage as soon as the trigger switch is released. The blade will stop quickly.
- *Conventional miter and compound-miter saws:* To turn the saw on, pull the trigger switch. Make the cut by pivoting the saw head down

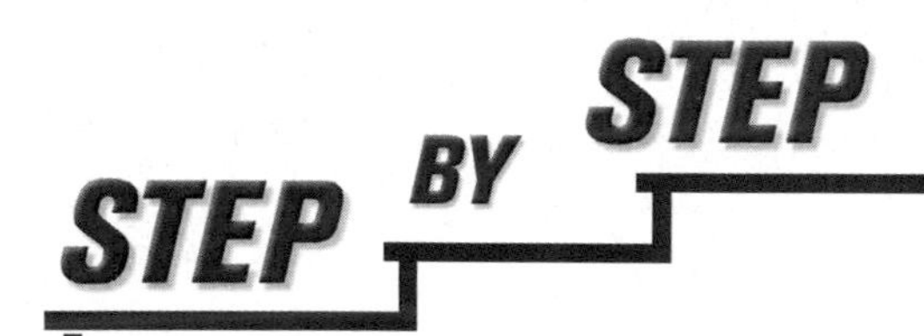

Installing a Miter-Saw Blade

Replace a blade whenever the teeth become dull. A sharp blade improves safety and the quality of a cut.

To replace a blade:

Step 1 Unplug the miter saw from its power source.

Step 2 Remove the blade guard and, if necessary, the blade housing from the saw.

Step 3 Place a hex wrench in the depression in the end of the arbor to hold the arbor stationary. (Many saws have an arbor-lock button instead.)

Step 4 Loosen the arbor nut with an open-end wrench by applying pressure on the wrench in the direction of blade rotation. Remove the nut and the collar.

Step 5 Slide the old blade off the arbor.

Step 6 Slide a new blade onto the arbor. Make certain the teeth at the bottom are pointing away from you and toward the fence.

Step 7 With the recessed side against the blade, replace the collar. Replace and securely tighten the nut. Reinstall the blade housing and blade guard.

Step 8 Plug in the saw and turn it on and off several times without making a cut. This will help you to determine if the blade is properly secured.

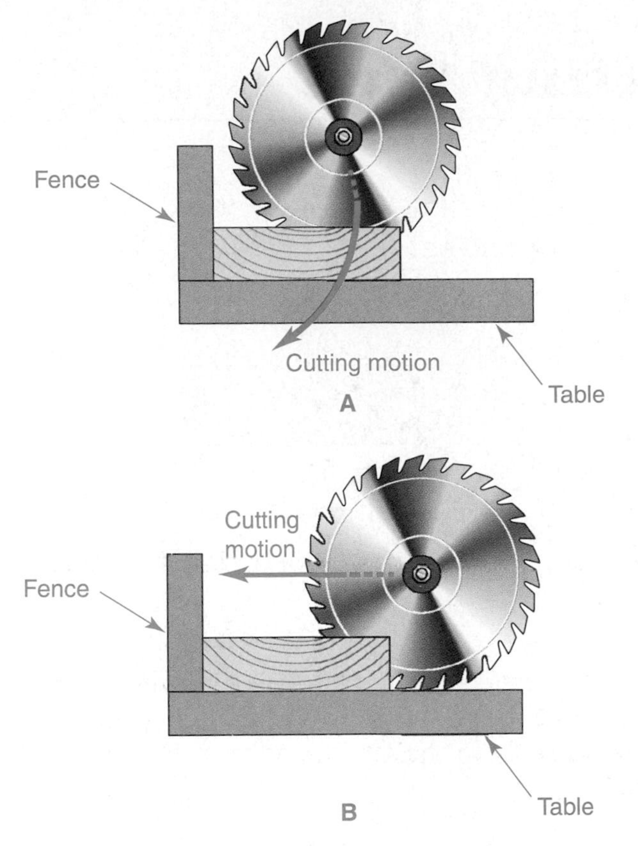

Fig. 7-26. Miter saw cutting motions. *A.* The cutting motion of a conventional miter saw is downward and slightly toward the fence. *B.* The cutting motion of a sliding compound-miter saw is directly toward the fence. The guard is not shown here. This allows the operation to be shown more clearly. The guard should be in place for all tool operations.

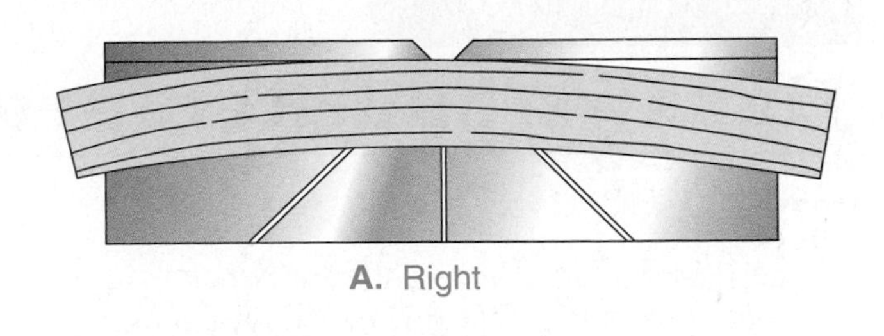

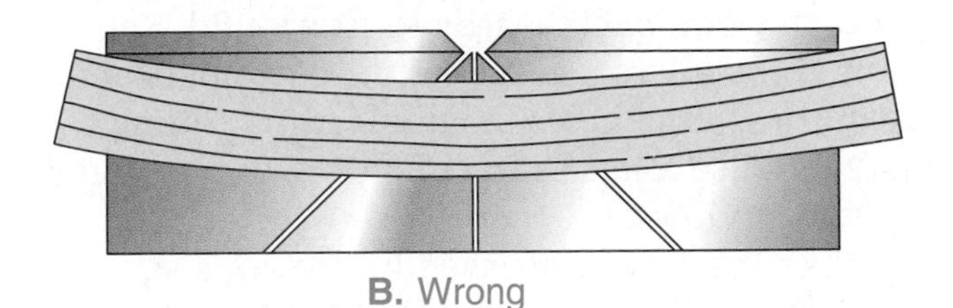

Fig. 7-27. If the material is bowed, position it as shown in *A.* If positioned as shown in *B*, the stock may kick back.

into the wood. As soon as the cut is completed, release the trigger, and return the saw to its starting position. **Fig. 7-26A.**

- *Sliding compound-miter saws:* Slide the saw head outward, past the stock to be cut. **Fig. 7-26B.** Turn the saw on using the trigger switch. To make the cut, pivot the saw head downward all the way and push it forward through the wood. When the blade is completely clear of the stock, release the trigger switch and lift the saw head.

Crosscutting

When cutting flat pieces, first check to see if the material is bowed. If it is, make sure the material is positioned on the table as shown in **Fig. 7-27A.** If the material is positioned as shown in **Fig. 7-27B,** it will pinch the blade near the completion of the cut. This could result in kickback.

Hold the stock flat against the table and tightly against the fence with one hand. Keep it well clear of the blade. Then make the cut by pulling the saw downward.

To make angle cuts, release the table lock. Move the indicator to the angle to be cut and engage the table lock. When making cuts at 45° or 90°, release the table lock and move the handle until the positive stop makes contact. Then engage the table lock.

SECTION 7.4

Check Your Knowledge

1. Explain the basic differences among the three types of miter saws.
2. What is a compound-miter cut, and what is it used for?
3. Why is a blade brake important?
4. Explain the two basic ways in which miter saws cut.

On the Job

Imagine that you have to explain to a coworker what a compound-miter cut is. Sketch a 45° miter cut and a 45° bevel cut. Now sketch a compound-miter cut, using more than one view if necessary. Label the angles.

SECTION 7.5

Jigsaws and Reciprocating Saws

The *jigsaw* (sometimes called a *saber saw* or *bayonet saw*) is the best power saw for making curved or irregular cuts. Carpenters use a jigsaw to notch wood deck boards to fit around a post. Cabinet installers use it for fitting cabinets and for cutting large holes in countertops. Siding installers use a jigsaw to cut siding to fit around curved windows.

Unlike the saws discussed in previous sections, the jigsaw has a straight blade. Teeth are formed into one edge, and, instead of spinning, the blade moves up and down. Fitted with a suitable blade, a jigsaw will cut metal, wood, plastic, and many other materials. It is often used instead of a hacksaw to cut angle iron and various kinds of metal or plastic pipe.

Depending on the blade and the power of the motor, a jigsaw can cut wood up to 3″ thick. The blades cannot be adjusted for depth of cut. Because the teeth of a jigsaw point upward, the best surface of a material should face downward as it is cut. **Fig. 7-28.**

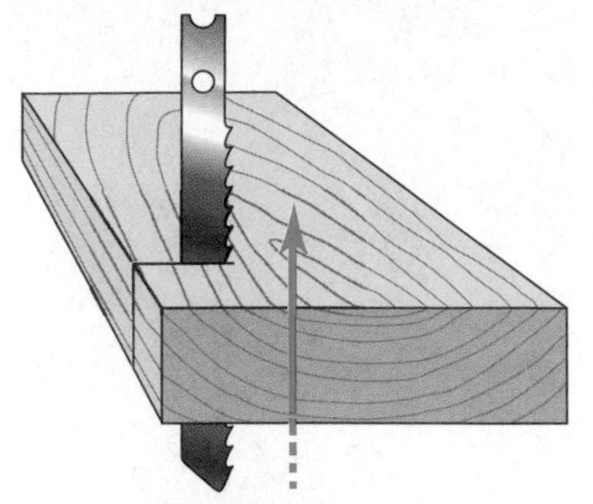

Fig. 7-28. The cutting action of a jigsaw. The blade cuts from the bottom up.

SAFETY FIRST

Jigsaw and Reciprocating-Saw Safety

The following are general jigsaw and reciprocating-saw safety rules. We strongly advise you to check the manufacturer's manual for any special safety instructions.

JIGSAW AND RECIPROCATING-SAW SAFETY

- Select the correct blade for the work and properly secure it in the saw.
- Be certain the material to be sawn is properly clamped.
- Before starting a cut, look under the workpiece to make sure there are no wires or other obstructions near the line of cut.
- Keep the cutting pressure constant, but if you meet resistance, do not force the cut.
- Hold the baseplate firmly against the workpiece when cutting.
- When finished, turn off the power switch and allow the saw to come to a stop before pulling the blade from the cut and setting the saw down.

PARTS OF A JIGSAW

A typical jigsaw has a baseplate, a housing/handle, and a blade-locking mechanism. **Fig. 7-29.** The baseplate on many models can be tilted to one side or the other. This allows the saw to make bevel cuts. Most jigsaws have a variable-speed control. This enables them to cut a wide variety of materials.

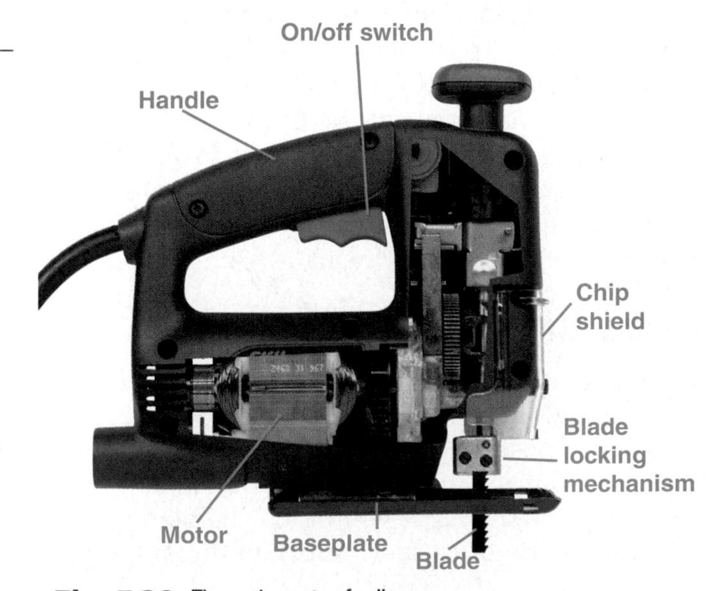

Fig. 7-29. The main parts of a jigsaw.

The blade of a jigsaw is often secured to the shaft by a clamp or mounting screw. To change the blade requires the use of a screwdriver or a hex key. Some jigsaws are fitted with a convenient blade-locking mechanism that does not require a special tool.

TYPES OF JIGSAWS

Two types of jigsaws are commonly used in residential construction. Top-handled models are the most common. The handle contains the trigger switch and is used to guide the tool. Some people prefer the second type: barrel-grip models. Instead of a handle, the user grasps the body of the saw to guide it. Because the hand is held low on the tool and directly behind the blade, they find it easier to control. Mechanically, however, the two types are the same.

On some jigsaws, the blade moves straight up and down. On others, it has a slight orbital motion, during which the material is cut on the up stroke and moves away from the blade on the down stroke. These orbital jigsaws cut much faster through wood. However, orbital motion is a disadvantage when cutting a material such as sheet metal. It causes the metal to vibrate and does not provide as smooth a cut. On some jigsaws the blade can be switched from one type of motion to the other.

CUTTING TECHNIQUES

The blade and the specific cutting technique used with a jigsaw should be adapted to suit the material. The following techniques are commonly used when cutting wood.

Carpenter's Tip

On countertops, use masking tape on cutting lines to keep from chipping Formica.

Straight and Irregular Cutting

If you wish to make an accurate straight cut near the edge of a material, install a rip guide on the jigsaw. **Fig. 7-30.** For straight and irregular cutting, proceed as follows:

1. Mark a layout line on the wood. It must be dark enough to be seen beneath the fine layer of sawdust that will be created around the cutting line.
2. Hold the wood tightly against a work surface, or clamp it in place. **Fig. 7-31.** Make sure the area beneath the cutting line is unobstructed.
3. Rest the front edge of the baseplate on the wood. Start the saw and allow it to come up to full speed.
4. Move the saw blade slowly into the wood. Don't force it. Use only enough pressure to keep the saw cutting at all times.
5. When the cut is complete, stop the saw. Let the blade come to a complete stop before lifting it away from the wood.

Internal Cuts

Sometimes a large hole must be cut in a material without starting at the edge. This is called an **internal cut**. It is easily made with a jigsaw.

1. Mark the outline of the cut on the workpiece, as above.

Fig. 7-30. Using a guide to make an even rip cut with a jigsaw.

Fig. 7-31. Cutting a curve. Notice how the work is clamped to the table.

2. Using a ⅝″ spade bit on an electric drill, drill through the material just inside the layout line. (See Chapter 8, "Electric Drills.") This will be the starting point for the saw. **Fig. 7-32.**
3. Proceed as in steps 2 through 5 in "Straight and Irregular Cutting."

A *plunge cut* is an internal cut that is made without first drilling a hole. This is sometimes done for convenience, particularly with thin stock such as plywood and other sheet goods.

1. Mark the outline of the cut on the workpiece.
2. Choose a convenient starting place inside the waste stock. Tip the saw forward with the baseplate resting on the surface of the material and the top of the blade clear of the work surface. **Fig. 7-33.**
3. Turn on the saw. When the blade reaches full speed, slowly lower the back of the saw until the blade begins to cut through the material. It is important to hold the saw firmly.
4. Continue cutting, using light pressure on the saw blade. When the blade cuts completely through the material, straighten the saw and cut normally.

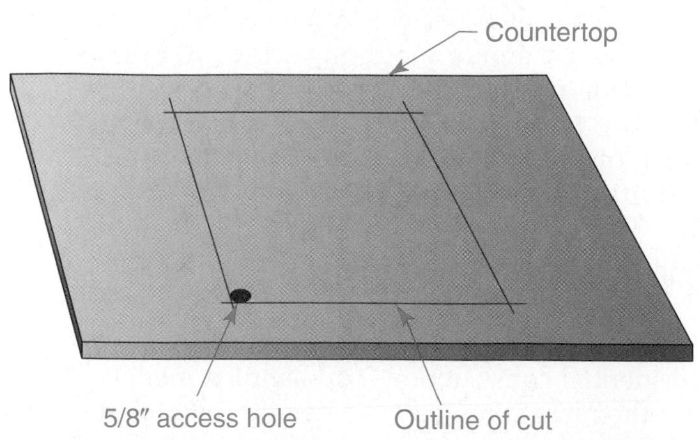

Fig. 7-32. Location of an access hole for an internal cut. The jigsaw blade can cut along two edges.

Fig. 7-33. Tip the saw up on the front of the baseplate. Turn it on and allow it to come to full speed before lowering the blade into the workpiece.

Bevel Cuts

The baseplate of a jigsaw can be adjusted from 0° to 45° for bevel cutting. A bevel cut made with a jigsaw will not be as straight or as smooth as a bevel cut made with a table saw or circular saw. However, a jigsaw can make a bevel cut that follows a curved layout line. After adjusting the baseplate to the bevel angle, follow the instructions for straight cutting.

RECIPROCATING SAWS

A *reciprocating saw* has a straight blade with teeth along one edge. It has many of the characteristics of a jigsaw. **Fig. 7-34.** It cuts with either a straight or an orbital motion. It can be used to make straight or curved cuts and often has variable-speed capability. Fitted with the appropriate blade, a reciprocating saw will cut metal, wood, plastic, and many other materials.

A reciprocating saw is most commonly used in remodeling and demolition work where a smooth finished surface is not required. When more precise control is needed, a jigsaw is often used instead.

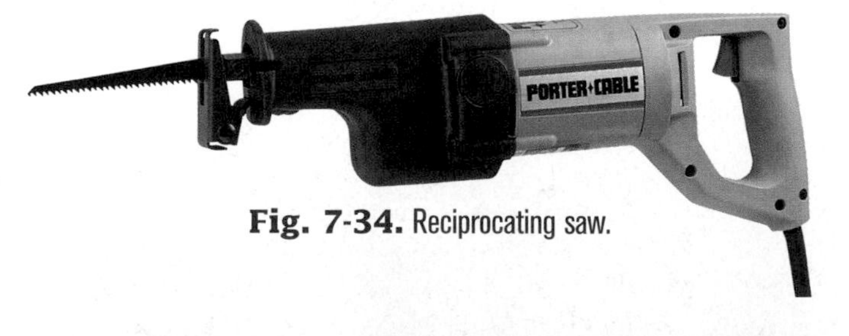

Fig. 7-34. Reciprocating saw.

SAFETY FIRST

Reciprocating Saw

In operating the reciprocating saw, be sure to follow all safety rules. Be sure to wear proper eye protection to protect against dust, debris, and shards from snapped blades.

General Operation

A reciprocating saw is a powerful tool. It is designed to be held with two hands. **Fig. 7-35.** One hand should be on the handle, where it controls the speed of the tool and provides leverage for cutting. The other hand should be placed near the nose of the tool, just behind the blade. The operator should hold the saw's baseplate firmly against the material being cut. Otherwise, the saw may vibrate excessively.

Because the saw can accept blades as long as 12″, it is important to check the area behind and to either side of the cutting line before starting the saw. This will reduce the chance of cutting something accidentally. Many electrical wires and water pipes have been severed by a reciprocating saw that was used carelessly. Before cutting into walls during remodeling work, use a keyhole saw to cut a small access panel. This will enable you to look into the wall cavity and locate hidden pipes, wires, or other obstructions. Avoid using a blade that is longer than necessary for the cut.

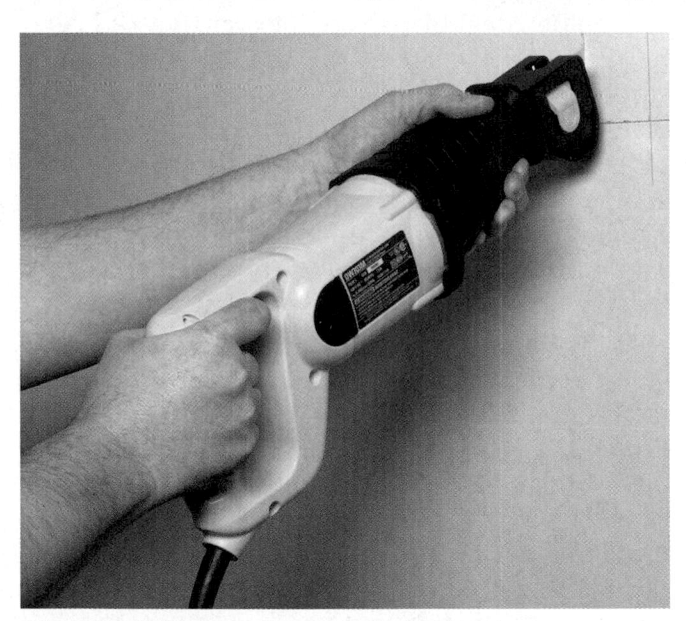

Fig. 7-35. Making a plunge cut with a reciprocating saw.

SECTION 7.5

Check Your Knowledge

1. By what other names is the jigsaw sometimes known, and what is the best use for this tool?
2. How much pressure should you use when cutting with the jigsaw?
3. What other power tool is required before using a jigsaw to make an internal cut?
4. You have finished using a reciprocating saw. What should you do before pulling the blade from the cut and setting the saw down?

On the Job

Using the *Readers' Guide to Periodical Literature* or the Internet, look up buying-guide articles concerning jigsaws. Write a brief report noting the jigsaw features that are most highly recommended. Explain why these features might be important.

SECTION 7.6

Blades for Power Saws

Circular and straight blades are the two basic types used on power saws. The type and size of the blade should be matched to the saw as well as to the material being cut.

CIRCULAR BLADES

Circular blades are used on circular saws, table saws, radial-arm saws, and miter saws. Blades that cut wood, plastic, and metal have teeth formed in the perimeter of the blade. Blades that cut masonry, ceramic tile, and other hard-to-cut materials have a grinding edge that is coated with an abrasive.

Parts of a Circular Blade

The parts of a circular blade can be altered by the manufacturer to cut different materials or to increase the effectiveness of the saw. **Fig. 7-36.** The key parts of a circular blade are the arbor hole, body, teeth or grinding edge, gullet, and shoulder.

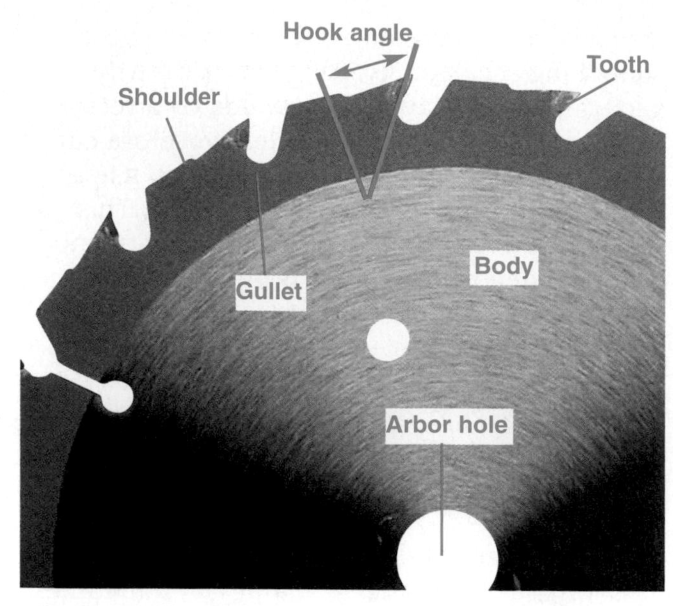

Fig. 7-36. The main parts of a circular blade. This blade has carbide-tipped teeth.

- *Arbor hole.* This is where the blade is mounted on the saw. The hole is round on most power saws used in residential construction and measures ⅝″ in diameter. However, some arbor holes have a diamond shape. Be sure to select a blade with the correct arbor hole for your saw. Never install a blade with an arbor hole that is too large.
- *Body.* This is the flat disk that serves as a base for the teeth. It is also sometimes called the *plate.* Thin, straight slots at the edge of the body prevent the blade from warping as it heats up. Wider, curved slots between the arbor hole and the teeth are called *body vents.* They reduce the noise of the blade and help to cool it.
- *Teeth* or *grinding edge.* Like tiny chisels, teeth slice through the material being cut. Some blades have a grinding edge instead. The edge is coated with an industrial abrasive such as carbide or diamond grit.
- *Gullet.* This pocket in front of each tooth helps remove sawdust during the cut.
- *Shoulder.* The raised portion behind each tooth supports the tooth. A large shoulder is needed where teeth might encounter a nail. Some shoulders are raised to limit the amount of material each tooth can remove. They help prevent kickback.

The cutting surface of the teeth may be steel or carbide. Steel blades are inexpensive and can be sharpened on site by the user. However, most carpenters and builders now use carbide-tipped blades. Each tooth is a chunk of tungsten carbide that has been permanently fastened to a shoulder. *Tungsten carbide* is a metal alloy that maintains a sharp edge much longer than steel. These blades cut a wider variety of materials, but they must be taken to a professional for sharpening.

The angle, shape, size, and number of teeth have a great effect on the blade's cutting ability. **Fig. 7-37.** The number of teeth also affects the blade's cost. More teeth usually means a more expensive blade. Choosing the right blade for a particular use can be difficult. It requires a compromise between cost and various performance features. In general, however:

- More teeth make a smoother but slower cut.
- Fewer teeth make a faster but rougher cut.
- Blades with fewer than forty teeth are good for ripping.

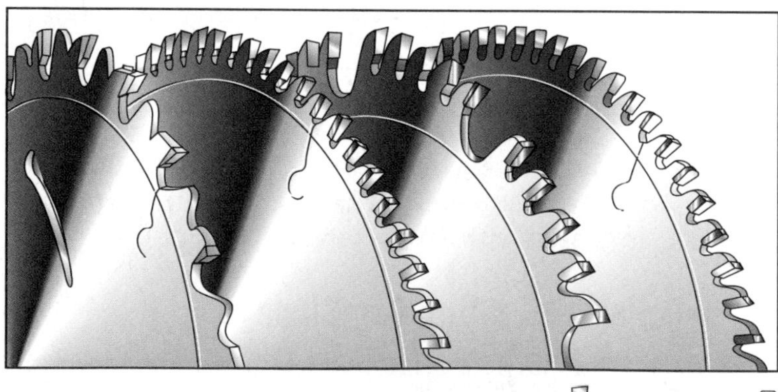

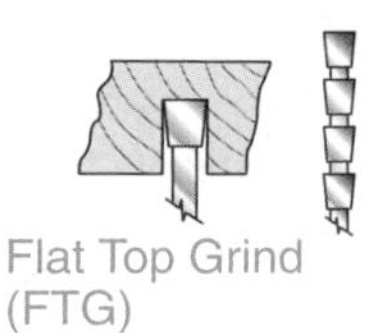

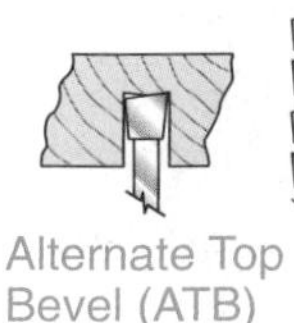

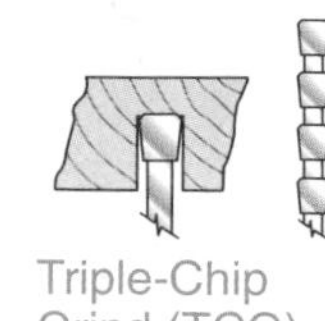

Fig. 7-37. Carbide Tooth Patterns
Flat Top Grind (FTG). These blades are particularly suited to making rip cuts. Each tooth removes a uniform chip of wood.
Alternate Top Bevel (ATB). Pointed surfaces sever wood fibers, which makes this pattern especially suitable for crosscutting.
Alternate Top Bevel with Rakers (ATB w/R). This arrangement combines tooth patterns. STG teeth scrape the bottom of the kerf, while ATB teeth sever the fibers. One set of teeth cuts while the other set cleans up.
Triple-Chip Grind (TCG). This style of blade is similar to an FTG style. The number of teeth that might chip is reduced.

- Blades with fifty teeth or more are good for making smooth crosscuts.
- Teeth with a steep forward angle cut fast but leave a rough edge.
- Teeth with a shallow forward angle make slower, smoother cuts.

Thin-Kerf Blades

The amount of power required to cut through a material depends partly on the thickness of the blade and the width of the cut (*kerf*). A thin-kerf blade has narrower teeth and a narrower body. It requires less power behind it during cutting than a standard-kerf blade. This makes a thin-kerf blade particularly suitable for cordless circular saws that rely on batteries.

Grinding-Edge Blades

Grinding-edge blades can be classified by whether they cut wet or dry. They can also be classified by the type of abrasive that does the grinding: diamond, aluminum oxide, or silicon carbide.

Wet-cutting blades must be sprayed with water during use. Water cools the blade and prevents it from clogging. Wet-cutting blades are also used to reduce the amount of dust caused by abrasive materials.

Dry-cutting blades can be used to cut brick, stone, and cement block. They are used without water, but they create a large amount of fine dust. When using them, wear a dust mask or respirator, depending on the material being cut.

An inexpensive type of dry-cutting blade has a resinlike body made from silicon carbide reinforced with fiberglass. It is used to cut masonry materials such as concrete, brick, and cement block. It can also be used to cut nonferrous metals.

Choosing a Circular Blade

Some common blades used for particular saws are listed here. Note that for carbide blades, the tooth pattern given is for general purposes.

- *Miter-saw blade.* This blade is sometimes referred to as a crosscut blade or cutoff blade. It is used primarily on miter saws and radial-arm saws for trimming stock to length. It provides a good-quality cut across the grain of a board. A 40-tooth blade is a good general purpose miter-saw blade. A blade with 60 teeth or more would be used for fine cuts on expensive molding. The best tooth pattern is ATB or TCG (see Fig. 7-37) with a 0° hook angle. The hook angle is the angle at which the tooth leans forward. This angle is important in determining how quickly and smoothly the blade cuts. Teeth that lean forward the most cut the fastest. Those teeth that lean forward the least cut the smoothest.
- *Circular-saw blade.* Blades for circular saws are designed to withstand rough job-site conditions, such as cutting through green lumber or hitting an occasional nail. They are intended for general-purpose crosscutting and ripping in soft woods and panel products, such as plywood. A 20-tooth blade cuts quickly, yet fairly smoothly. Best tooth pattern: ATB with a positive hook angle.
- *Table-saw blade.* This blade has a combination of ripping and crosscut teeth and is used for a great variety of cutting jobs. Several styles of teeth are available, and each has a particular application. Best tooth pattern: STG for ripping, ATBw/R for general purpose and a positive hook angle.

STRAIGHT BLADES

Straight blades are a straight piece of steel with teeth or abrasive grit on one edge. They are used on jigsaws and reciprocating saws.

Parts of a Straight Blade

The main parts of blades for jigsaws and reciprocating saws are shown in **Fig. 7-38**.

- *Shank.* This is the end of the blade that is inserted into the saw. A shank made for one brand of saw may not fit another. A ¼″ universal shank is the most common for jigsaw blades. The most common for reciprocating-saw blades is a ½″ universal shank.
- *Body.* The body carries the teeth. It is made of various metals or combinations of metals that offer different cutting characteristics.

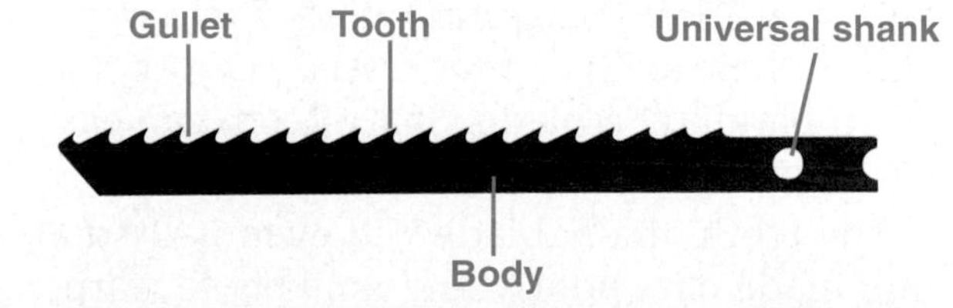

Fig. 7-38. The main parts of the blade for a jigsaw or reciprocating saw. The blade shown fits many types of jigsaws.

- *Gullet.* This is a pocket at the base of each tooth that helps to remove sawdust from the cut.
- *Teeth.* Teeth are made of steel that is sometimes hardened for greater durability. Teeth point upward, toward the saw. This helps to hold the workpiece against the saw's baseplate.

Types of Straight Blades

A blade body made of high-speed steel can cut wood. However, it is best at cutting ferrous metals (such as steel and iron) up to ⅜″ thick and nonferrous metals (brass, copper, and aluminum) up to ¼″ thick. Blade bodies made with carbon steel cut wood, plastics, and plastic laminates.

Bimetal blades are versatile and durable, which makes them very popular in construction. They have flexible spring-steel bodies and hardened tool-steel teeth and are less likely to snap if they hit a nail. Bimetal blades can cut ferrous and nonferrous metals. However, they are also good for cutting wood and plastic. That makes them an especially good choice for reciprocating saw blades used in demolition work.

Jigsaw blades range in length from 2¾″ to 4″. Reciprocating saw blades range in length from 3″ to 12″. **Fig. 7-39.** Blades are also classified by the number of teeth per inch (TPI). Wood-cutting blades usually range between 6 TPI and 12 TPI. Metal-cutting blades range between 12 TPI and 36 TPI. In general, jigsaw and reciprocating saw blades with fewer teeth cut fastest. Those blades with more teeth cut smoothest.

Fig. 7-39. The wide blades are for reciprocating saws. The smaller blades are for jigsaws.

CARE OF SAW BLADES

Any saw blade can be damaged by careless handling. Blades with carbide-tipped teeth are especially vulnerable to damage because carbide is a hard but brittle material. It can be chipped if it comes into contact with another metal, such as a nail embedded in the wood. Chipping might also occur as a blade is being changed.

Whenever you store a blade, be sure to protect its teeth. Do not stack blades in a way that allows their teeth to touch. Also, be very careful when handling a blade. Sharp teeth can easily cut fingers.

The teeth of any blade will eventually dull. A dull blade cuts poorly and is likely to warp. Dulling occurs most quickly when cutting abrasive materials, such as cement board or particleboard. Carbide-tipped blades are also dulled by heat and corrosion.

Always inspect a blade before using it to see if the teeth are sharp. Look closely at teeth at different points along the blade. If they have chipped corners or rounded edges, the blade should be sharpened. A high-quality blade can be sharpened many times, but lesser-quality blades are often considered disposable.

Frequently inspect abrasive blades that have a resinlike body. Never use an abrasive blade that is cracked or damaged. It can shatter in use, spraying pieces away from the saw at high speed. Damaged or worn abrasive blades of this type should be discarded.

Check Your Knowledge

1. Name the five basic parts of a circular-saw blade.
2. What is the purpose of the gullet?
3. What are the advantages and disadvantages of using carbide-tipped teeth on a circular blade?
4. What is the most common type of jigsaw shank?

On the Job

General characteristics of circular blades are listed on pages 149-151. Referring to these characteristics, describe a 7¼″ circular-saw blade that would be good to use if you were going to frame a house. (Hint: Framing requires many crosscuts but few rip cuts.) Explain your answer in a short paragraph.

Chapter 7

Review

Section Summaries

7.1 Circular saws are used for crosscutting. The two basic types are the contractor's saw and the worm-drive saw. Kickback can occur when a spinning blade hits something that stops it while under full power.

7.2 Table saws are used primarily for rip cuts. Tilting-arbor saws are commonly used on construction sites. The feed rate is the speed at which the stock is pushed through the saw blade.

7.3 Radial-arm saws can be used for crosscutting, ripping, dadoing, and combination cuts.

7.4 Miter saws are used for quick crosscuts and accurate cuts on molding and trim. The three basic types include conventional miter saws, compound-miter saws, and sliding compound-miter saws.

7.5 Jigsaws are used for making curved, irregular, and internal cuts. Reciprocating saws are similar to jigsaws.

7.6 Blades should be matched to the saw and the job. Blades may have teeth or a grinding edge. Blades should be treated with care to prevent damage.

Review Questions

1. What should you do to ensure your safety before crosscutting with a radial-arm saw?
2. What are circular saws normally used for?
3. Explain the causes of kickback on circular saws and table saws.
4. Explain how to maintain a circular saw.
5. Describe two methods of making miter cuts with a circular saw.
6. Explain how to maintain a table saw.
7. When is a thin-kerf blade used?
8. In ripping narrow stock on a table saw, what safety device should be used?
9. What is the primary difference between a jigsaw and a circular saw?
10. Describe the tooth pattern of an ATB (alternate top bevel) blade.

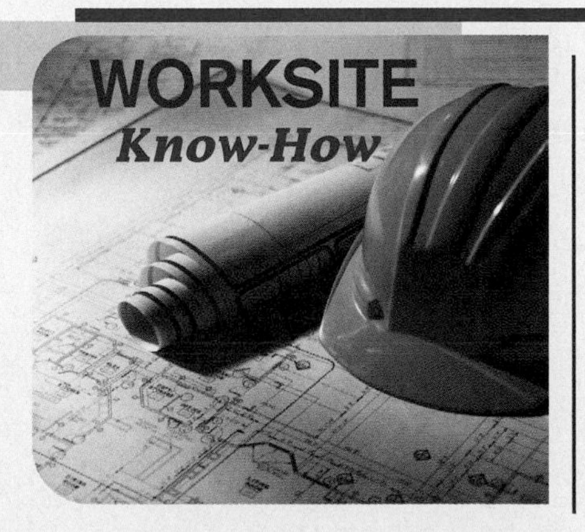

Choosing Circular Saw Blades A blade's diameter determines how deep it can cut. However, always match the size of the blade to the size of your saw. A 7¼″ blade cuts about 3″ deep, and more torque is required to turn it. A 6″ blade cuts about 2½″ deep but needs less torque. The number of teeth is also important. A blade with 24 teeth gives a faster, rougher cut than a blade with 50 teeth. Blades with 60 to 80 teeth produce an even smoother finish cut across the grain. Blades with carbide tips stay sharp longer than ordinary steel blades.

Chapter 8

Electric Drills

Objectives

After reading this chapter, you'll be able to:

- Follow the safety tips for using electric drills.
- Identify the two basic types of electric drills.
- Determine the power rating of an electric drill.
- Tell the uses for different types of drill bits.
- Drill holes in wood and metal.

Terms

amperage
battery pack
countersink
drill index
pilot hole

The portable electric drill is a very versatile power tool. With the right bit it can be used to drill holes in nearly any material. Fitted with various accessories, it can be used to install screws, cut holes, mix paints, and do many other jobs.

A typical builder or contractor will often have several electric drills on the job site. One will usually serve as a general-duty tool for drilling small and medium-size holes. The others might include a heavy-duty model for jobs requiring extra power, a drill/driver for installing screws, and a hammer drill for drilling into masonry. One or more of these drills may be battery powered.

SAFETY FIRST

General Safety

The following are general safety rules for electric drills. We strongly advise you to check the owner's manual for any special safety instructions.

ELECTRIC DRILL SAFETY

- Wear proper eye protection.
- When operating larger drills, use both hands and an auxiliary handle.
- Disconnect the power plug or remove the battery pack before installing or removing drill bits.
- Make certain the drill bit is held securely in the chuck.
- Never use a bit with a square, tapered tang in an electric drill. The drill's chuck will not hold this type of bit securely.
- Be sure the chuck key has been removed before starting the drill.
- Do not force the drill into any material. Use an even, steady pressure.
- Never drill through cloth. It will twist around the bit.
- Always clamp small pieces when drilling them to prevent them from spinning. Do not hold them with your fingers.
- When laying down the drill, always point the drill bit away from you, even when it is coasting to a stop.

SECTION 8.1

Drills, Drill Bits, and Accessories

The major parts of an electric drill are shown in **Fig. 8-1**. The most common sizes of electric drills used in construction are ⅜″ and ½″. These dimensions refer to the diameter of the shank for the largest drill bit that the chuck can hold. The *shank* is the part of the bit that fits into the chuck. The *chuck* is that part of the drill that holds the shank of the drill bit. Many drills, particularly heavy-duty drills, have a key-type chuck. Some drills have a keyless chuck, which can be conveniently tightened by hand. Most drills have a pistol-grip handle.

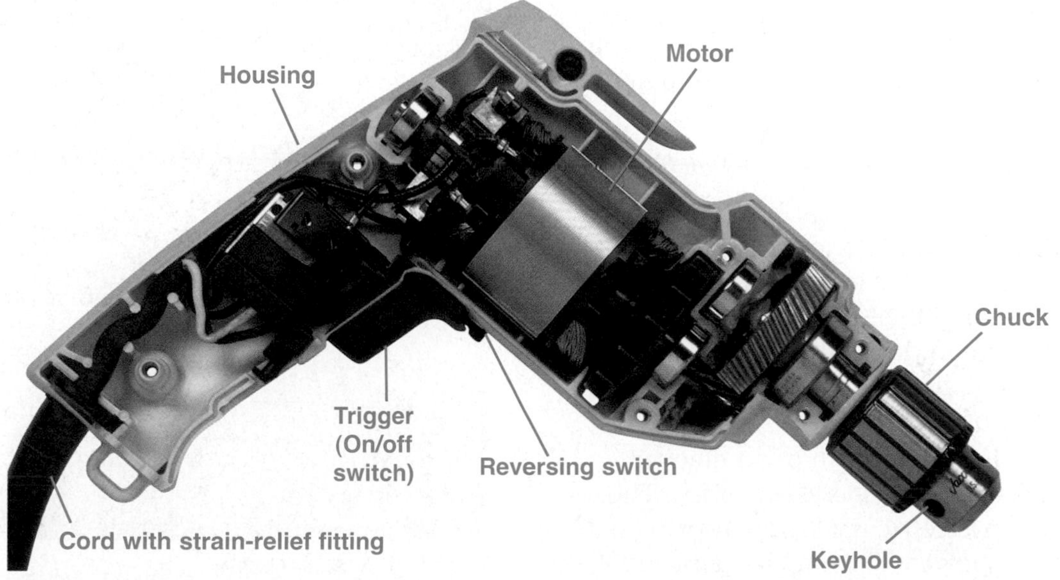

Fig. 8-1. The main parts of an electric drill.

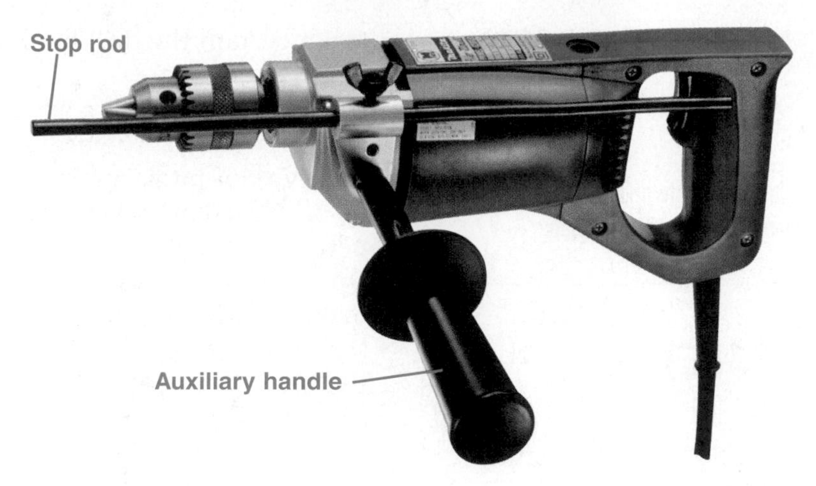

Fig. 8-2. A hammer drill. The auxiliary handle allows better control of the tool. The stop rod limits the depth of the hole.

TYPES OF DRILLS

The two basic types of electric drills are corded drills and cordless drills. Some corded-drill housings are metal. Their power cord is fitted with a three-prong grounding plug to reduce the danger of electrical shock. Drills with a plastic housing have a two-prong plug because the housing itself insulates the operator against shock. Plastic housings are sometimes referred to as *double-insulated* housings.

Most electric drills can be operated at various speeds. Speed control is important when drilling metal and when using the drill to start screws. The speed of a drill is rated in rpm (revolutions per minute). Drill speeds commonly range from 0 to 1200 rpm. Speeds up to 900 rpm usually indicate a heavy-duty drill capable of providing great *torque* (twisting force).

Drills with an adjustable internal clutch are called *drill/drivers.* The clutch allows the tool to drive screws more effectively than standard variable-speed drills.

Corded Drills

A standard corded electric drill should be plugged into a properly grounded electrical outlet. These drills are best for drilling large holes, for drilling through difficult materials such as steel or concrete, and for drilling many holes in a short period of time.

Amperage is the strength of an electric current expressed in *amperes,* or *amps.* The amperage of an electric drill is an approximate measure of its power. The amperage rating is on a small metal specification plate permanently attached to the tool. The amperage of corded drills ranges from 3 to 8 amps. High-amperage drills are used for heavy-duty work.

There are various types of specialized corded drills. *Hammer drills* are used to drill holes in masonry. While the chuck revolves, the drill creates a rapid, hammerlike, reciprocating action. This helps to drive a masonry bit into the material. **Fig. 8-2.** *Right-angle drills* are often used by electricians and plumbers. On such drills, the chuck is at 90° to the drill body. This allows drilling in tight spaces, such as through the sides of studs. **Fig. 8-3.**

Fig. 8-3. A right-angle drill.

Cordless Drills

Cordless electric drills are powered by a rechargeable battery. **Fig. 8-4.** They are especially useful where a long extension cord would be undesirable or where electrical power is not available. The voltage of the battery roughly indicates the tool's power. Batteries typically range from 9.6 to 18 volts. Batteries with a higher voltage can operate longer between charges.

The batteries are sealed within a plastic case inside or at the end of the drill's handle. The case and batteries form a unit called the **battery pack**. To charge the batteries, the battery pack is removed from the drill and placed in a charger. Full battery strength can be restored in one hour or less. Most builders keep two or more battery packs on hand. While one is recharging, the other is in use.

Fig. 8-4. A cordless electric drill with a keyless chuck.

DRILL BITS AND ACCESSORIES

The versatility of an electric drill comes from the great number and variety of bits, cutters, and other accessories that are available. The following are the most common.

Drill Bits

Twist bits and spade bits are used most often on a job site. *Twist bits* with a 118° tip are general utility bits used for drilling holes in wood, metal, and plastic. **Fig. 8-5.** They have a cylindrical shank, spiral flutes (grooves), and a beveled tip. Common diameters range from 1⁄16″ to ½″, in increments of 1⁄64″. Twist bits made from high-speed steel (HSS) are particularly suited to drilling metal. A case that holds a group of twist bits in various sizes is called a **drill index**.

Fig. 8-5. A set of twist bits in a drill index.

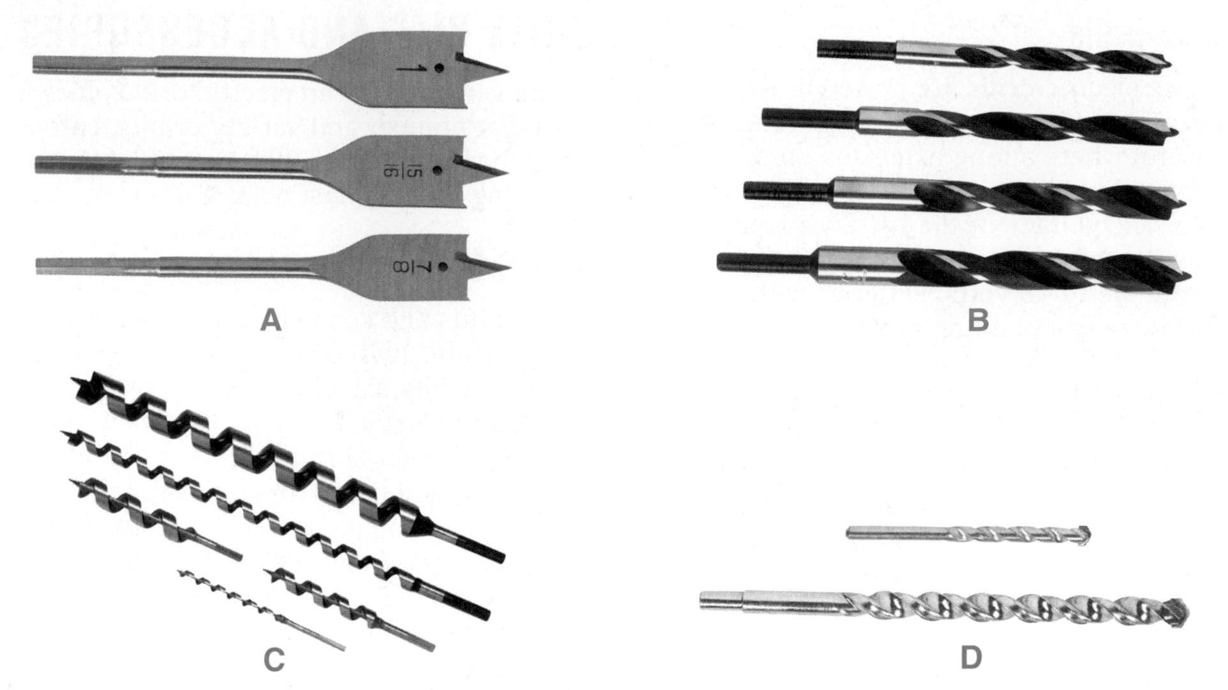

Fig. 8-6. Various types of bits. *A.* Spade bits. *B.* Brad-point bits. *C.* Auger bits (note the wide flutes). *D.* Masonry bits, specially designed with an aggressive cutting angle and a carbide tip.

Spade bits are used to bore holes in wood. **Fig. 8-6A.** The holes range in diameter from ⅜" to 1½". A large point guides the bit. Its horizontal cutting surfaces remove stock. A hexagonal shank reduces slippage.

Brad-point bits have a small center point called a *brad point.* **Fig. 8-6B.** This prevents the bit from wandering as the hole is started. Sharp cutting edges cut very smooth, clean holes in wood.

Auger bits are designed to cut deep holes quickly through wood. **Fig. 8-6C.** A screw point pulls the bit through the stock. Such an auger bit is called a self-feed bit. The wide, deep flutes remove chips efficiently. This bit is often used by electricians.

Masonry bits are for use on brick, concrete, and other masonry materials. **Fig. 8-6D.** They have a beveled carbide tip and wide flutes that carry grit and dust away from the cut. If using a masonry bit in a hammer drill, be sure the bit is designed for use in a hammer drill.

Forstner bits have a brad point and a sharpened rim. They are excellent for boring smooth holes with flat bottoms in wood. Forstner bits can bore through end grain with ease. They are used primarily in cabinetmaking. **Fig. 8-7.**

A **countersink** is a bit with beveled cutting edges. **Fig. 8-8A.** It creates a funnel shape (also called a *countersink*) at the top of a drilled hole.

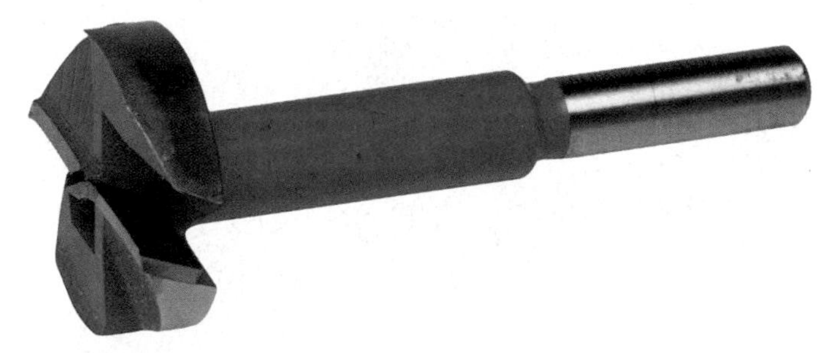

Fig. 8-7. A Forstner bit.

This funnel shape allows the head of a wood screw to be flush with the wood surface. An 82° countersink is suitable for use with wood screws.

A *combination bit* is another convenient tool for use with wood screws. **Fig. 8-8B.** It will drill the pilot hole, shank clearance, and countersink in one operation. A **pilot hole** is a hole drilled in wood to start and guide a screw.

Screw-driving bits enable a variable-speed drill to drive or remove screws. Though bits are available for use with slotted screws, it is much easier to power-drive Phillips-head screws. **Fig. 8-9.**

Drill Accessories

A *hole saw* is a cylindrical metal sleeve having a sawtooth edge. **Fig. 8-10A.** It is commonly used by plumbers to cut holes in wood frame

Fig. 8-8. Countersinks, combination bits, and screwdriving bits. *A.* A countersink is designed to cut a funnel-shaped opening. *B.* Combination bits are available in most of the common wood screw sizes. For example, if a 1″ #8 wood screw is used, a 1″ #8 combination bit should be used.

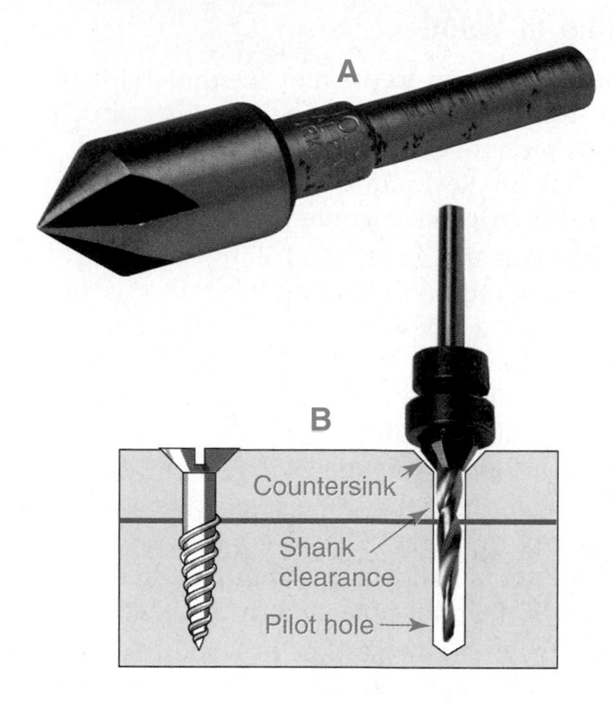

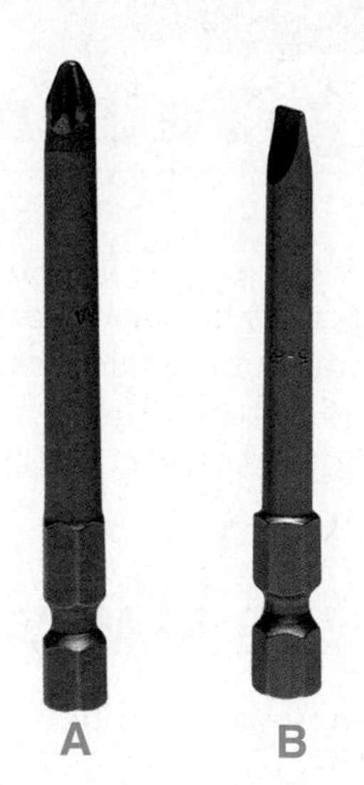

Fig. 8-9. Screwdriving bits. *A.* Phillips tip. *B.* Slotted tip.

members for drain and vent piping. It is also used when installing a door lockset. A twist bit at the center of the hole saw centers the hole. When a hole saw is started, all the teeth should contact the wood at the same time.

A *mixing paddle* is used to stir paint and to mix powdered adhesives, such as thin-set mortar. **Fig. 8-10B.** This work requires a drill capable of high torque. To minimize strain on the drill, the powdered ingredients should be poured into the liquid, not the liquid into the powder.

Check Your Knowledge

1. How can you determine the power of an electric drill?
2. What characteristic of masonry bits serves a similar purpose on auger bits?
3. For what type of drilling is a Forstner bit best suited?
4. What is the purpose of a countersink?

On the Job

Most twist bits have a cylindrical shank. However, you may find twist bits with hexagonal (six-sided) shanks. Based on what you know about other bits that have hexagonal shanks, when would you use a hexagonal-shank twist bit? Explain your answer.

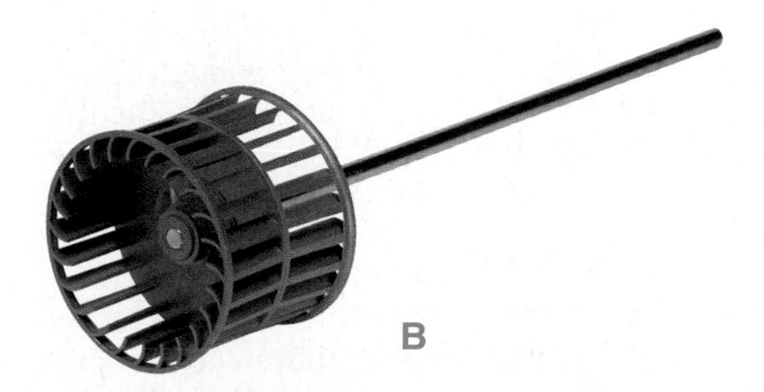

Fig. 8-10. Drill accessories. *A.* Hole saws. The one on the left is mounted on an arbor. *B.* A mixing paddle for use with an electric drill.

SECTION 8.2

Drilling Techniques

The most important factor in correct drilling is to choose a suitable bit or accessory for the material and the job to be done. An unsuitable bit will deliver poor results, could be damaged, and may be unsafe.

INSTALLING AND REMOVING A BIT

To insert or remove a bit, follow this basic procedure:

1. Unplug the drill or remove its battery pack.
2. Determine if the shank of the chosen drill bit will fit into the chuck. (A ⅜″ chuck, for example, will not accept a ½″ shank.)
3. Open the jaws of the chuck by twisting its collar.
4. Insert the shank of the bit as far as possible. Then turn the collar by hand to close the jaws. Check to be sure the shank is centered between the jaws. If not, open the jaws and center it.
5. Tighten the chuck by inserting the chuck key in each of the three keyholes in succession. Remove the chuck key.
6. If the drill has a keyless chuck, twist the two portions of the sleeve in opposite directions until the jaws are tight.
7. The friction of drilling creates heat in a bit. Allow a bit to cool before removing it. To remove a bit, unplug the drill or remove the battery. Then open the chuck. With a keyed chuck, use the chuck key in only one hole.

DRILLING A HOLE

Keep bits sharp. A sharp bit performs much better than a dull one. Apply just enough pressure on the drill to keep the bit cutting. Too little pressure will dull the bit; too much pressure may break it. Hold the tool at a right angle to the work when starting a hole. **Fig. 8-11.** Be sure to clamp down small pieces. Never move the drill from side to side while the bit is in use. When drilling a deep hole, withdraw the bit periodically to clear shavings from the hole. The bit should continue to spin as you withdraw it.

Drilling in Wood

If it is important to prevent the underside of wood from splintering as the bit breaks through, clamp a piece of scrap wood behind the workpiece. Use this technique when drilling through hardwoods or cabinet-grade plywood.

Unless you are using self-drilling screws, a pilot hole is required. Drilling the correct-size pilot hole for a screw is important. If the hole is too small, the screw will be hard to drive and may snap as it is driven. If the hole is too large, the screw will not hold.

When drilling hardwood, it is good practice to bore the pilot hole the same size as the root diameter of the screw. Diameters for common wood screws are shown in **Table 8-A**. In softwood, drill the pilot hole slightly smaller.

When fastening two pieces of wood together, drill the pilot hole through the uppermost piece and into the bottom piece to the desired depth. Then drill a slightly larger hole through the uppermost piece. This hole is for the screw's shank. Countersink the top of the shank hole.

Self-drilling screws, such as drywall screws, do not require a pilot hole when used in softwoods or in panel products such as plywood.

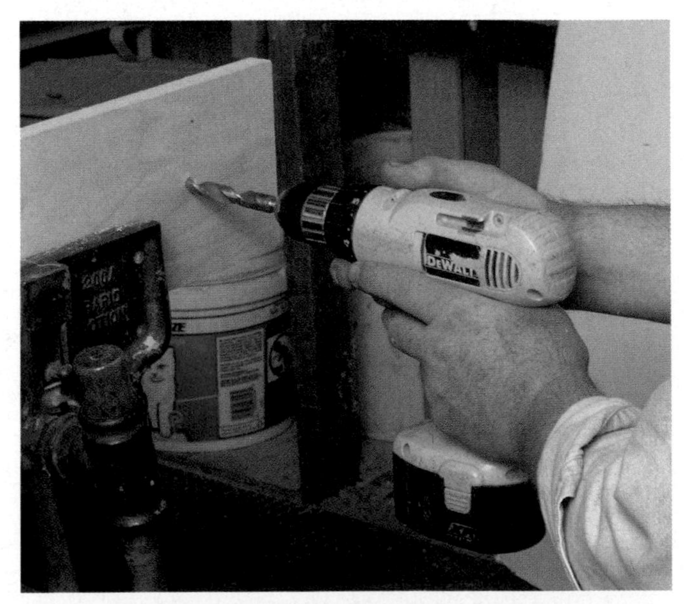

Fig. 8-11. Drilling a hole in flat stock. Be sure to hold the tool at a right angle to the workpiece. Use a clamp to hold the wood steady.

The strength of a connection made with a screw is improved more by increasing the length of the screw than by increasing its diameter.

Fully threaded screws do not require a separate hole for the shank. Size the hole according to the root diameter of the screw.

Drilling in Metal

A twist bit with a 135° split point is best for drilling metals. Drilling into stainless steel, cast iron, and some types of aluminum will quickly dull a twist bit. A cutting lubricant such as light-weight oil will cool the bit and extend its life. When drilling without lubricant, reduce the drill's rpm to prevent the bit from overheating.

Table 8-A. Traditional Wood Screws

Gauge	2	3	4	5	6	7	8	9	10	12	14
Head-bore size	11/64"	13/64"	15/64"	1/4"	9/32"	5/16"	11/32"	23/64"	25/64"	7/16"	1/2"
Shank-hole size	3/32"	3/32"	7/64"	1/8"	9/64"	5/32"	5/32"	11/64"	3/16"	7/32"	1/4"
Pilot-hole size: Hardwood	1/16"	1/16"	5/64"	5/64"	3/32"	7/64"	7/64"	1/8"	1/8"	9/64"	5/32"
Pilot-hole size: Softwood	1/16"	1/16"	1/16"	1/16"	5/64"	3/32"	3/32"	7/64"	7/64"	1/8"	9/64"
Available Lengths (1/4", 3/8", 1/2", 5/8", 3/4", 1", 1 1/8", 1 1/4", 1 3/8", 1 1/2", 1 5/8", 1 3/4", 2", 2 1/4", 2 1/2", 2 3/4", 3", 3 1/4", 3 1/2", 3 3/4", 4")											
Phillips-head point size	#1			#2						#3	
Square-drive bit size	#0			#1			#2			#3	

A twist bit that is bent will cut an irregular hole and may not be safe to use. Check the straightness of the bit by spinning it in the drill briefly before drilling. The tip of a bent bit will wobble noticeably. Always discard even slightly bent drill bits.

Push firmly on the drill as it cuts, but do not force it. Just before the bit emerges from the metal, slow the feed rate to prevent the bit from catching on burrs.

DRIVING SCREWS

A screwdriving bit that is too small or too large for the screw head will spin out when power is applied to the drill. The tip must fit snugly, with no sloppiness in the fit.

Drive screws as follows:

1. Start the screw at a slow speed.
2. Increase speed as the screw moves into the stock.
3. Stop the drill when the screw reaches the correct depth. Some drills have adjustable settings that prevent you from driving the screw too deep. Do not disengage the driving bit while it is spinning.
4. For precise control, drive the screw in partway and then finish with a screwdriver.

SECTION 8.2 Check Your Knowledge

1. What is the most important factor in correct drilling technique?
2. After you have inserted a bit into the drill and tightened the chuck by hand, what should you check for?
3. Why is it important to apply the proper pressure when drilling holes?
4. What is one method for determining if a drill bit is bent?

On the Job

Either by making a visit to your local home center or by consulting a tool catalog or tool Web site, make a list of basic drills and accessories you will need as a carpenter. State why you will need each drill and accessory.

Chapter 8 Review

Section Summaries

8.1 A standard corded electric drill is best for drilling large holes, for drilling through difficult materials such as steel or concrete, and for drilling many holes in a short period of time. Cordless drills are particularly useful where a long extension cord would be undesirable or where electrical power is not available. Twist bits and spade bits are the drill bits most often used on a job site.

8.2 A pilot hole is required for starting screws, except when using self-drilling screws. If the pilot hole for a screw is too small, the screw will be hard to drive and may snap as it is driven. If the hole is too large, the screw will not hold. Apply just enough pressure on the drill to keep the bit cutting. Hold the tool at a right angle to the work when starting a hole.

Review Questions

1. Why should you clamp small pieces of wood or other material when drilling them?
2. Identify the two basic types of electric drills.
3. Why are electric drill housings sometimes made of plastic?
4. What is the amperage range for corded drills?
5. What indicates the length of time a cordless drill can run between rechargings?
6. What is the purpose of the center spur on brad-point and spade bits?
7. What bit would be suitable for drilling a 1″ diameter hole into end grain?
8. When drilling holes for wood screws, what is the advantage of using a combination bit?
9. How can you prevent the underside of wood from splintering as the bit breaks through?
10. When drilling a hole in metal, what can be done to improve the life of the bit?

Specialized Drill Bits Special bits can increase a drill's usefulness. Holes for wood screws can be made with a cone-shaped countersink bit, a combination countersink/pilot bit, or a spring-loaded self-centering bit that is also used with door and window hardware. When installing European-style cup hinges, use a 35-mm hinge-boring bit. Brick, concrete, and other abrasives require masonry bits with thick carbide tips.

Chapter 9

Power Tools for Shaping and Joining

Objectives

After reading this chapter, you'll be able to:

- Follow the safety rules for the use of shaping and joining tools.
- Identify common uses for routers, sanders, planers, and jointers.
- Explain how each tool is classified in terms of its size.

Terms

biscuit
chamfer
collet
cutterhead
dovetail joint
template

Carpenters and builders rely on a variety of power tools for shaping and joining wood. These include routers, sanders, jointers, electric planes, and plate joiners. Some of these tools may also be used to work with other construction materials. Routers, for example, can shape the edges of solid-surface countertops. Sanders can smooth metal surfaces as well as wood surfaces.

These tools operate at high speeds. Be sure to review the general safety precautions as well as safety precautions for individual tools.

General Safety

The following are general safety rules. We strongly advise you to check the manufacturer's manual for any special safety instructions.

GENERAL SAFETY FOR SHAPING AND JOINING TOOLS

- Always wear proper eye protection.
- Wear hearing protection, especially when using routers, belt sanders, electric planes, and planers.
- Avoid wearing loose clothing or jewelry that could get caught in the tool. Tie back long hair.
- Protect yourself from inhaling dust by wearing the proper dust mask or respirator. Make sure the tool's dust bag is properly attached. Connect the tool to a vacuum system if possible.
- Always unplug the tool before changing bits, cutters, or belts.
- Make sure bits and cutters are sharp. Be careful when changing or adjusting them. They can cause serious cuts.
- Clamp the workpiece securely to prevent it from vibrating loose or being forcefully ejected.

SECTION 9.1

Routers

The *router* is a portable electric tool designed to turn a sharpened cutter, called a *bit*, at high speed. The router is used primarily for finishing work, such as for cutting joints and shaping the surfaces and edges of stock. With accessories, a router can also be used to trim plastic laminate and cut openings in panel products. Some builders think that a router is one of the most versatile tools on a job site.

Router Safety

The following are general safety rules. We strongly advise you to check the owner's manual for any special safety instructions.

ROUTER SAFETY

- Always wear proper eye protection.
- Wear hearing protection and a dust mask. Routers generate a lot of noise and sawdust.
- Be certain the power switch is off before plugging the tool into an outlet. Always hold on to the router when turning it on.
- Make certain the fence or guide is securely clamped.
- Make certain the workpiece is securely clamped.
- When using the router, keep a firm grip, using both hands when appropriate.
- Make adjustments only when the bit is at a dead stop. When installing or removing bits, be sure the router is unplugged.
- Feed in the correct direction.
- When putting the router down, point the bit away from you. Be aware of a bit that is still moving.
- When using large bits, remove the stock with two or more passes.
- Never use a dull or damaged bit.
- Bring the router to full speed before cutting. Turn off the router after making the cut.

PARTS OF A ROUTER

There are two basic types of router. The motor and base of a *fixed-base router* always remain stationary during a cut. However, prior

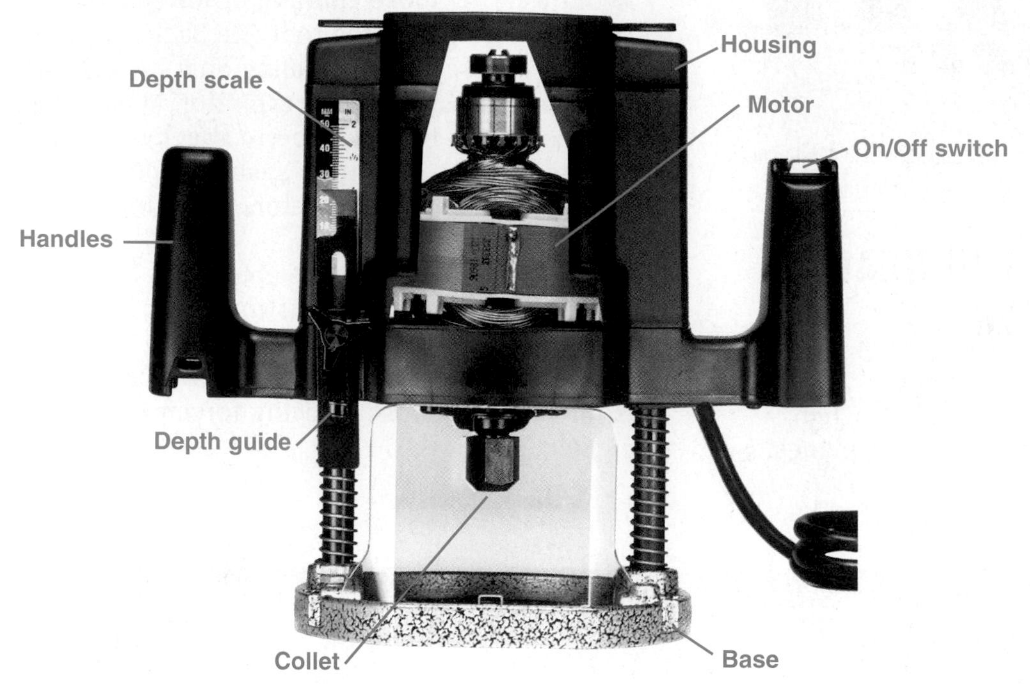

Fig. 9-1. The main parts of a plunge router.

to cutting, the depth of cut can be adjusted by raising or lowering the base. The bit, however, can be raised or lowered. The motor of a *plunge router* is mounted on vertical metal posts. **Fig. 9-1.** The motor assembly slides up and down on the posts. This allows the spinning bit to be "plunged" into the workpiece and lifted away when the work is complete. **Fig. 9-2.**

On some routers, the on/off switch is on the body of the tool. On others it is on the handles. A handle-mounted switch makes it possible to turn off the tool without letting go of the handles. This is a good safety feature.

The **collet** is that part of the router that holds the bit. Routers are often classified by the diameter of their collet. Thus, a ½″ router is a router with a ½″ collet. This determines the size of the bit shank the router will accept.

A router motor is designed to deliver high speed rather than high torque. Speeds range from 10,000 to over 25,000 rpm. (In contrast, an electric drill may have a top speed of only 1,200 rpm.) A variable-speed router allows the user to adjust the speed to suit the material being cut and the size of the bit. Bits over 1″ in diameter should be used at slower speeds.

Fig. 9-2. A plunge router.

Router Bits

The cutting edges of most router bits are on the sides, rather than on the end. One important exception is the plunge-cutting bit. This bit has cutting edges on its sides and on its end. With a plunge-cutting bit in place, a router can drill a pilot hole and then cut or trim material starting from that hole.

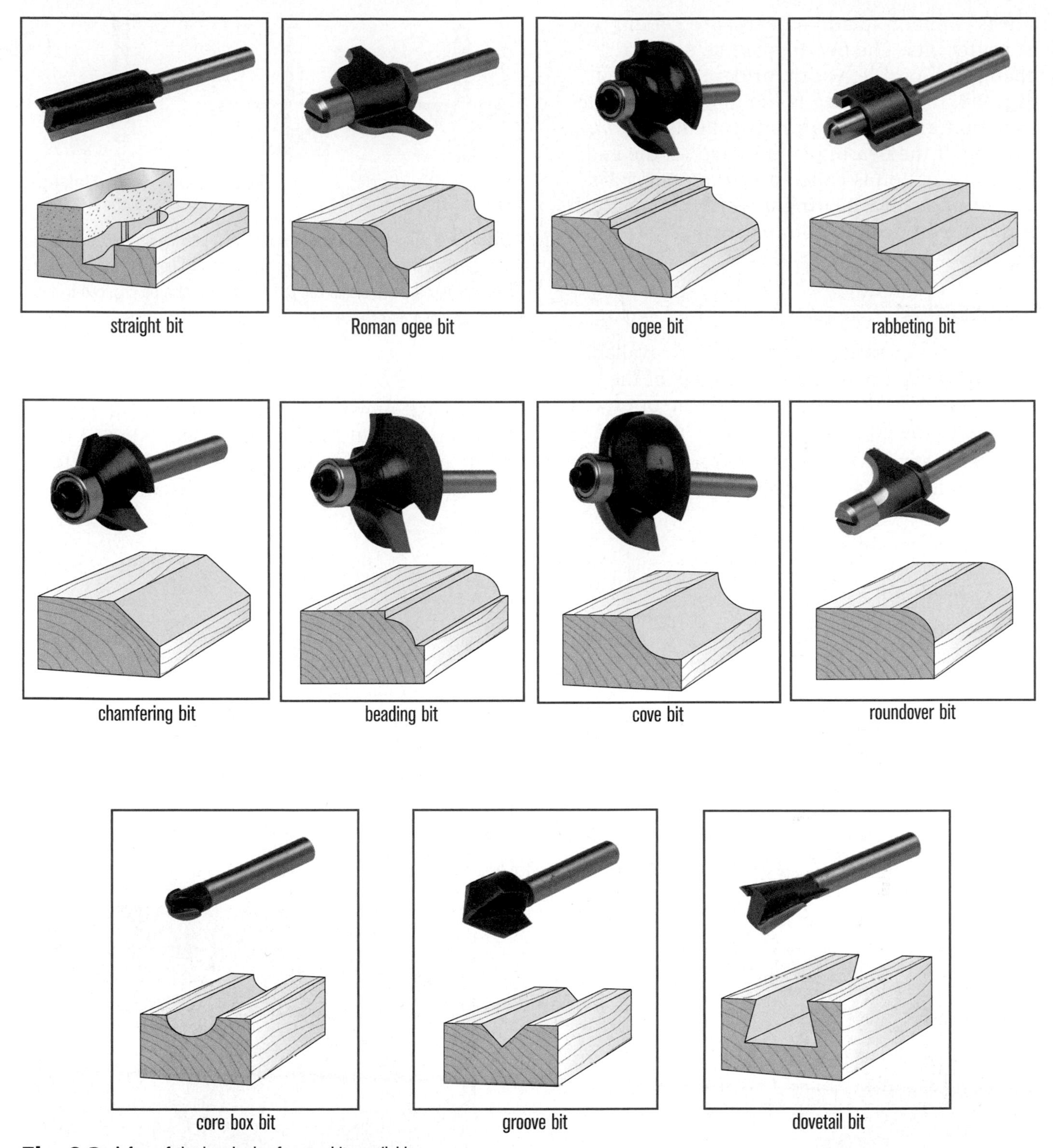

Fig. 9-3. A few of the hundreds of router bits available.

Router bits are available either with high-speed-steel cutting edges or with carbide-tipped edges. Carbide-tipped bits are generally more expensive and fragile. However, the cutting edge remains sharp longer.

Router bits come in many shapes for doing grooved or decorative work on the surface or on the edge of stock. Common bits include straight, rounding-over, beading, cove, and chamfer bits. **Fig. 9-3.** A **chamfer** (CHAM-fur) is a beveled edge. The shank of a router bit commonly has a diameter of ¼″, ⅜″, or ½″.

It is common to add a bearing to certain types of router bits. The bearing can be used to change the profile, width, or depth of the cut. **Fig. 9-4.** If the bearing is mounted on the side of the bit, the combination is called a *bearing-over bit.* If the bearing is mounted on the end, the combination is called a *bearing-under bit.* One example of a bearing-under bit is the flush-trimming bit used to trim plastic laminate. **Fig. 9-5.**

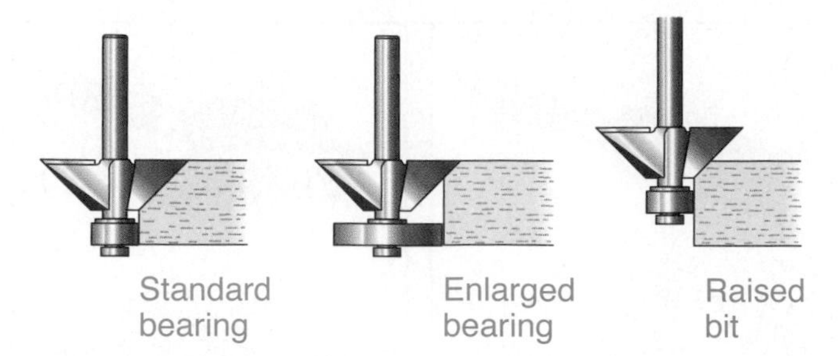

Fig. 9-4. The effects of bearing size. *A.* A bearing controls the depth of cut by holding the bit away from the wood. *B.* Changing the bearing's size changes the size of the cut. *C.* The size can also be changed by raising or lowering the bit.

Accessories

A number of router accessories are available. An *edge guide* rides against the edge of the stock, enabling the router to make a cut exactly parallel to the edge. **Fig. 9-6.**

A **template** is a guide made from metal or thin wood. Templates enable the router to quickly cut mortises for door hinges. Direction and depth of cut can be controlled using a circle guide or a straightedge. **Fig. 9-7.** A dovetail template allows the user to cut a dovetail joint. A

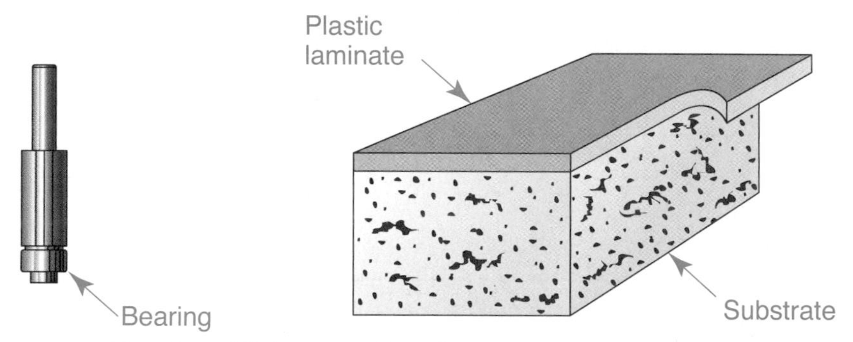

Fig. 9-5. A flush-trimming bit is often used for trimming plastic laminate.

Fig. 9-6. A plunge router with an edge guide.

Fig. 9-7. A wood or metal straightedge clamped to the workpiece can be used to guide a router.

Fig. 9-8. Cutting dovetail joints using a router and a dovetail template. The photograph on the right shows the finished joint.

dovetail joint has interlocking pieces. Dovetail joints are used to assemble the drawers in high-quality cabinetry. **Fig. 9-8.**

Some carpenters mount a router upside-down beneath a sheet of plywood or particleboard. The bit extends through a hole in the board. When a simple fence is added, this device is called a *router table.* In this case, the stock is moved past the cutter, rather than the cutter moved along the stock.

A dust collection hose, connected to a shop vacuum cleaner, removes chips and dust. This allows the operator to see the cut more clearly. It also helps prevent chips from flying at the operator, which increases safety.

Carpenter's Tip

Many router bits used for edging have a pilot tip or roller bearing that rides against the uncut edge of the wood. **Fig. 9-9.** If using a pilot tip, always keep the router moving. Otherwise, the heat generated as the tip spins may scorch the edge of the wood.

Fig. 9-9. Many bits have a bearing or a pilot tip to control the amount of cut.

ROUTING TECHNIQUES

The router bit turns clockwise. Always feed against the direction of bit rotation. **Fig. 9-10.**

The speed at which the best cut is made will depend on the depth and width of the cut and on the hardness of the wood. If you move the router too quickly, the motor will slow down too much, making a poor cut. If you move the router too slowly, the bit may overheat. This can draw the temper from the cutting edge or burn the wood. Don't force the cut. Allow the bit to cut freely. Listen to the motor for an indication of whether it is working at its most efficient speed.

Always make deep cuts in several passes. This is when a plunge router becomes especially useful. It can be quickly reset to several depths.

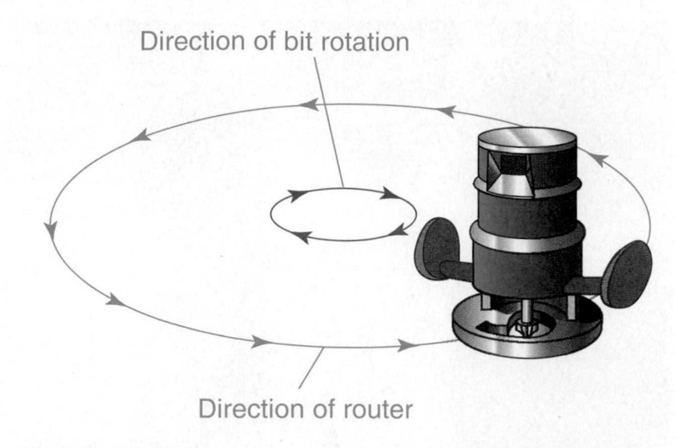

Fig. 9-10. The router bit revolves clockwise. Move the router counterclockwise when cutting outside edges. Move the router clockwise when routing inside edges.

Installing a Bit

The shank of a bit is held by the router collet. When installing a router bit, take care not to cut yourself with its sharp edges.

1. Disconnect the power cord.
2. Turn the router upside down. Depending on the kind of router, either lock the shaft or hold it with a wrench.
3. Slide the bit's shank all the way into the collet. Then back it off slightly and tighten the collet. A bit resting against the bottom of the collet will vibrate and loosen.
4. Tighten the collet firmly with a wrench.

Cutting a Decorative Edge

Different decorative edges can be created using the many different bits. See Fig. 9-3 on page 167.

1. Install the required bit.
2. Adjust the bit to the approximate depth of cut.
3. Plug in the router and turn it on. Resist the starting torque of the motor by holding onto the router with both hands. Otherwise, it can twist out of your grip.
4. Make a test cut in a scrap piece of the same stock.
5. Adjust the depth of cut until the correct profile is obtained.
6. Make the final cut.

SECTION 9.1 **Check Your Knowledge**

1. How is a plunge router different from a fixed-base router?
2. What bit is used to trim plastic laminate to size?
3. What accessory might be used for cutting a groove parallel to the edge of a plywood panel?
4. Why should you hold the router firmly when turning it on?

On the Job

Before electric routers were invented, carpenters used various hand routers to do the same kind of work. Research the history of these tools. Try to find out when the first electric router became available. What are the advantages and disadvantages of hand routers as compared to electric routers? Report your findings in a short paragraph.

SECTION 9.2

Power Sanders

Portable electric sanders are used for tasks ranging from heavy stock removal to delicate finish sanding of woodwork. The most common types are the belt sander and the finishing sander. Random-orbit sanders are gaining in popularity.

Power Sander Safety

The following are general safety rules. We strongly advise you to check the manufacturer's manual for any special safety instructions.

POWER SANDER SAFETY

- Always wear proper eye protection.
- Be sure the sander's abrasive belt, disc, or pad is in good condition and that its grit is correct for the work to be done.
- Be sure there are no nicks or tears in the edge of a disc or belt. An abrasive belt must be installed with the correct tension. Be sure it is tracking (aligned on the rollers) properly.
- Do not let go of the handles until the belt stops moving.
- Avoid nails and screws when sanding.
- Disconnect the power cord when changing abrasives.
- Make certain the tool's switch is in the off position before plugging in the power cord.
- Always wear the proper dust mask or respirator when using sanding equipment.
- Never touch a sanding belt or disc while it is moving.
- Do not use a sander to remove paint containing lead (see Chapter 41, "Exterior and Interior Finishes").

PORTABLE BELT SANDERS

The *portable belt sander* drives a revolving abrasive belt to remove stock quickly. **Fig. 9-11.** The machine is classified by the width and length of its belt. For example, a small machine

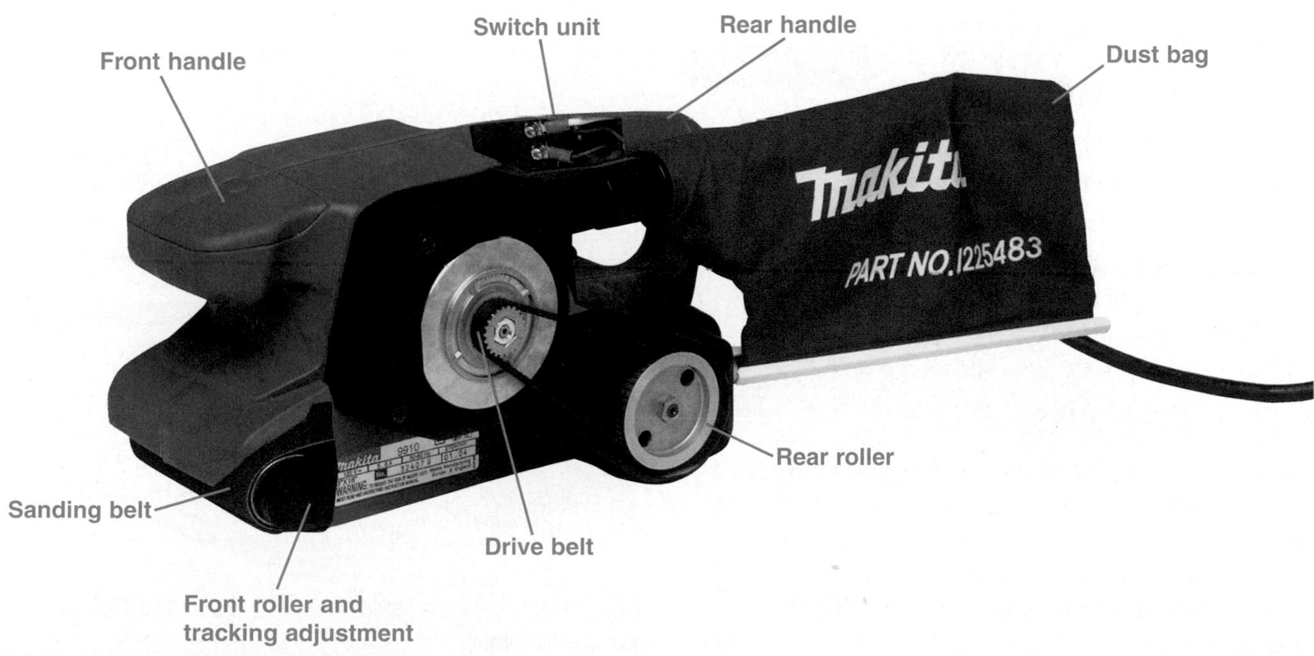

Fig. 9-11. The main parts of a portable belt sander.

with a belt 3″ wide and 18″ in circumference would be referred to as a 3″ × 18″ sander. Other sizes include 3″ × 21″, 3″ × 24″, and 4″ × 24″. Each sander must be fitted with a belt of matching size.

To reduce the amount of dust in the air, most belt sanders have a dust collection bag. The sander can also be connected to a vacuum system.

Installing the Belt

Many sanding belts have a lap seam. If installed improperly, this type of belt can be ripped open during use. There is an arrow on the inside surface of the belt. The belt must be installed so that this arrow points in the same direction as the arrow on the side of the sander. "Seamless" belts are constructed differently. They can be installed in either direction.

To install a new belt:

1. Unplug the sander.
2. Disengage the belt-release lever and remove the old belt.
3. If you are using a lap-seam belt, be sure the new one is turned in the right direction.
4. Slip the new belt onto the rollers and engage the belt-release lever.
5. Plug in the sander and turn it on. If the belt slides to one side or the other, correct this by turning the belt-tracking knob slightly while the sander is running.

Carpenter's Tip

A clogged abrasive belt on a belt sander will not work well. Clean a clogged belt by running it against an inexpensive block of crepe rubber designed for this purpose.

Sanding Techniques

The portable belt sander is the most forceful of all portable sanders and should be used with care. Used carelessly, it can easily gouge the wood. To prevent this, always keep the tool moving when the belt is in contact with the workpiece.

Be sure that the power cord is out of the way before starting the sander. The spinning belt can cut through a cord almost as quickly as a sawblade can.

This tool is generally used to sand in the direction of the wood grain.

1. Hold the sander with both hands and turn it on.
2. Slowly lower the sander onto the wood, letting the heel (rear portion) of the belt touch first.
3. Immediately move the sander either forward and back or from side to side. Never hold it in one place or it will gouge the workpiece. **Fig. 9-12.**

ORBITAL SANDERS

The *orbital sander* uses a sheet of abrasive paper instead of a belt. The paper is held in place by paper-locking levers. **Fig. 9-13.** Some sanders use hook-and-loop or pressure-sensitive adhesive (PSA) systems to hold the sandpaper in place. The sanding pad moves with an orbital (circular) motion. Because orbital sanders are most often used to smooth a surface prior to painting or finishing, they are sometimes called *finishing sanders.* They are also called *pad sanders* because a rubber pad cushions the abrasive paper.

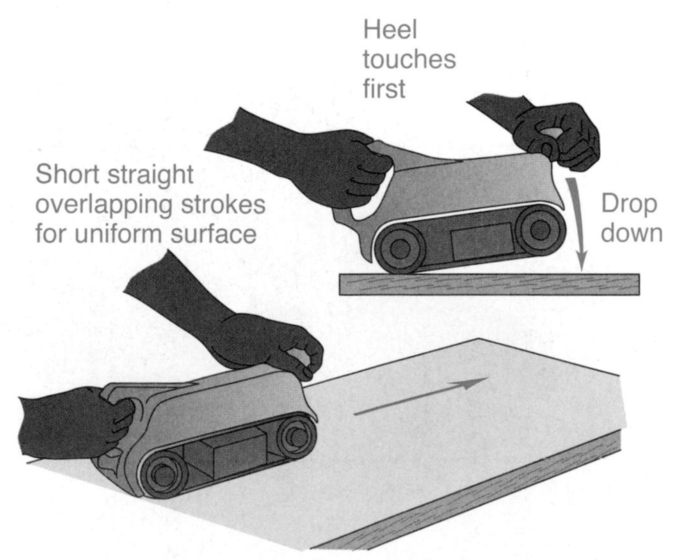

Fig. 9-12. Lower the sander slowly onto the surface. Move the machine immediately.

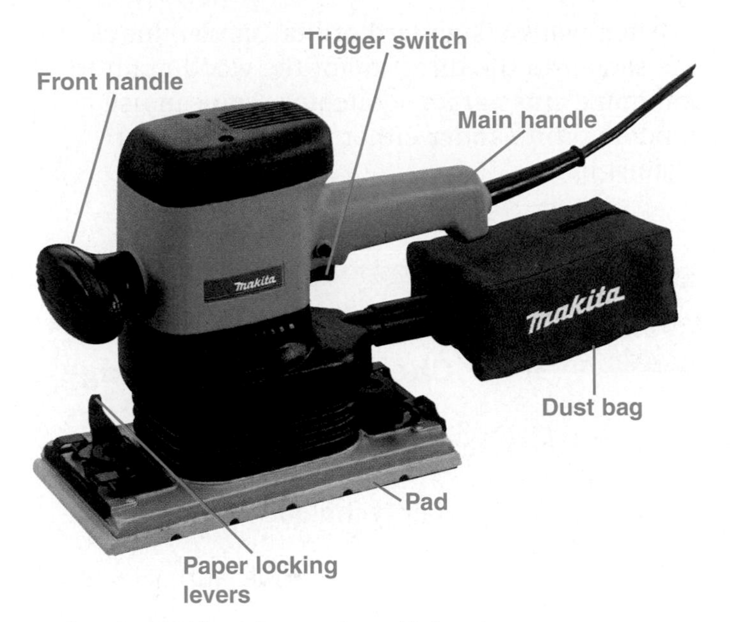

Fig. 9-13. The main parts of an orbital sander.

Fig. 9-14. The small size of this one-quarter-sheet orbital sander allows it to be used to sand trim in place.

Types of Sanders

Orbital sanders are generally classified by the size of the pad, which may be square or rectangular. The pad size is based on standard-size abrasive sheets. Thus, there are *one-quarter-sheet* sanders, *one-third-sheet* sanders, and *one-half-sheet* sanders. **Fig. 9-14.**

One type of orbital sander that has become common is the *random-orbit sander.* **Fig. 9-15.** This versatile tool can be used for fine finishing work as well as forceful stock removal. It usually has a round sanding pad instead of a square one. As the pad moves in a circle, it also moves from side-to-side. The combination of these two motions tends to cut down on swirl marks. The abrasive paper is attached to the pad by a pressure-sensitive adhesive (PSA) backing or a hook-and-loop backing. Holes in the sanding pad and matching holes in the abrasive paper make dust removal easier when the sander is connected to a vacuum system.

Fig. 9-15. A random-orbit sander with sanding discs.

Sanding Techniques

Rest the orbital sander evenly on the stock. Apply moderate pressure and move the sander back and forth, working from one side to the other. **Fig. 9-16.**

Fig. 9-16. A random-orbit sander can be moved in any direction. It does not have to be moved in the direction of the grain.

When using a standard orbital sander, move the sander in the direction of the wood grain to minimize cross-grain scratching. You can use a random-orbit sander either with the grain or against it.

SECTION 9.2

Check Your Knowledge

1. How is the size of a portable belt sander determined?
2. Describe the proper technique for using a portable belt sander.
3. How does a random-orbit sander differ from a standard orbital sander?
4. When using a standard orbital sander, in what direction should you sand?

On the Job

Determine the size of a standard full-size sheet of abrasive paper. Suppose that the pad on your orbital sander measures 4½″ by 4″. How many pad-sized pieces can be cut from one sheet of the paper?

SECTION 9.3

Surfacing Tools

To meet the needs of the construction industry, manufacturers have designed small, portable versions of the surfacing tools common in woodworking shops. These tools, including jointers and planers, are easy to bring to the job site. Also, some builders find that turning rough stock into finished stock on site is less costly than buying finished stock from a lumberyard.

JOINTERS

A *jointer* is a power tool used to remove saw marks from stock and ensure a square edge. A jointer is most likely to be used at late stages of house construction, when cabinets and interior woodwork are being installed. **Fig. 9-17.** The

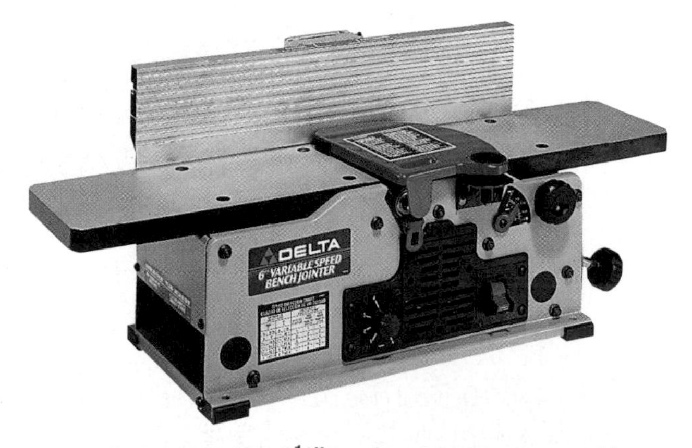

Fig. 9-17. This 6⅛″ benchtop jointer is very portable.

Fig. 9-18. Jointing the edge of a board.

most common use for the jointer on a job site is for jointing an edge. **Fig. 9-18.** An edge is said to be jointed when the edge forms a right angle with the face of the board along its entire length. **Fig. 9-19.** A board is sometimes jointed after being cut to width on a table saw.

The jointer has a **cutterhead**, a solid metal cylinder on which three or four cutting knives are mounted. The cutterhead is mounted below the bed of the machine. As the cutterhead spins, the knives shear off small chips of wood, producing a smooth surface. A guard covers the cutterhead but swings out of the way to enable stock to pass. Basic jointing operations should always be done with the guard in place. A fence guides the stock.

The size of a jointer is indicated by its maximum width of cut. A 6″ or 8″ jointer is common. The length of its bed affects its usefulness. A longer bed provides better support for jointing longer pieces.

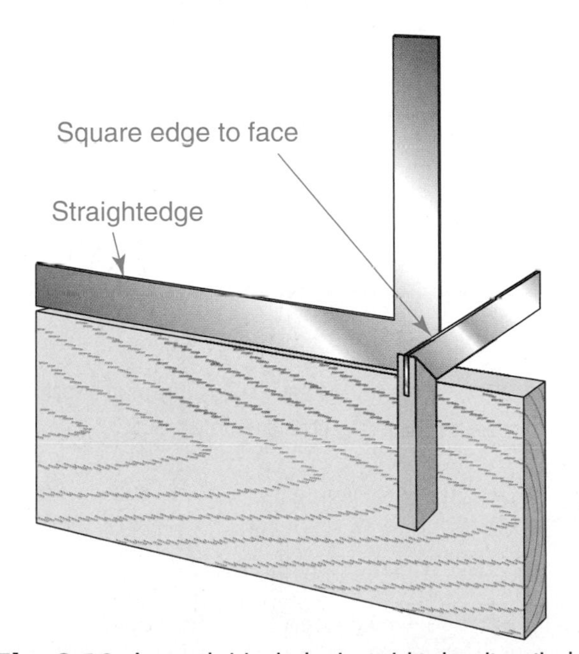

Fig. 9-19. A properly joined edge is straight along its entire length and forms a 90° angle with the board's working face.

Jointer Safety

The following are general safety rules. We strongly advise you to check the manufacturer's manual for any special safety instructions.

JOINTER SAFETY

- Wear proper eye protection.
- Be sure that portable jointers will not tip over during use. They should be secured temporarily to a structure's subfloor or to a workbench.

- Check the stock for knots, splits, and other imperfections before jointing. Defective stock may break up or be thrown from the jointer.
- Always keep the knives of the jointer sharp. Dull knives tend to cause kickback. They also result in a poor cut.
- Never adjust the fence or the depth of cut while the jointer is running.
- Make sure that the guard is in place and operating easily.
- Because of the danger of kickback, always stand to the side of the jointer, never directly behind it.
- Always allow the machine to come to full speed before using it.
- Always cut with the grain. Always use a push stick or push block to move stock past the cutterhead. Do not make cuts too deep.
- Do not joint short pieces of wood.
- Use a brush to remove shavings from the table. Never use your hand.

PLANERS

A *planer* is used to reduce the thickness of a board, smooth its surface, and make one face parallel to another. For example, it might be used to square up stock for stair balusters and other finish work. Portable planers are sometimes used on a construction site, especially when much custom woodworking is required. **Fig. 9-20.**

Like a jointer, a planer has a cylindrical cutterhead fitted with two or more knives. As the cutterhead rotates, the knives make many small cuts in the surface of a board. **Fig. 9-21.** This brings the board to a uniform thickness.

The cutterhead is mounted above the bed of the machine. A powered *infeed roller* moves the stock into the cutterhead. (The *infeed* end of the tool is where stock enters.) Between the infeed roller and the cutterhead is a *chip breaker.* The chip breaker keeps the stock firmly pressed against the bed and prevents tears and splinters. Just beyond the cutterhead is the *pressure bar.* This holds the stock firmly against the bed after the cut is made. An unpowered *outfeed roller* presses against the wood as it exits the machine. (The *outfeed* end of the tool is where stock exits.)

The type and number of controls on a planer vary with its size. All machines, however, have a

Fig. 9-20. This 12″ portable planer can be moved easily around the job site.

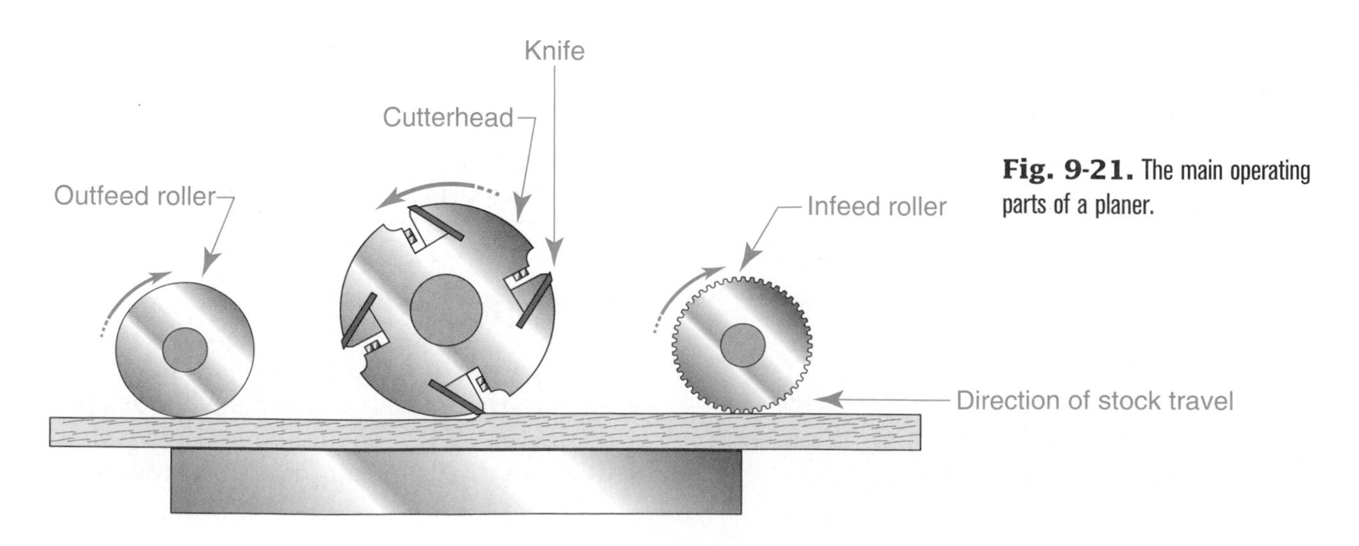

Fig. 9-21. The main operating parts of a planer.

handwheel that moves the bed up and down to control the depth of cut.

The size of a planer indicates the size of its bed and the widest board that it can surface. A 12″ model can handle boards up to 12″ wide.

SAFETY FIRST

Planer Safety

The following are general safety rules. We strongly advise you to check the manufacturer's manual for any special safety instructions.

PLANER SAFETY

- Wear proper eye protection.
- Because of the danger of kickback, always stand to the side of the planer, never directly behind it. Never look into the planer when it is running.
- Check each board for loose or large knots, warped surfaces, and other flaws that might cause a problem.
- Be cautious when running used lumber through the planer. Its blades can be damaged if they hit a nail or staple. Repairs are time consuming and expensive.
- Do not force the stock; let the infeed roller pull the stock through. Do not pull stock out of the planer. Support it on the tips of your fingers or on an outfeed table as it leaves the machine.
- Take a series of shallow cuts rather than one deep cut. This is most important when planing hardwoods. A cut that is too deep can damage the stock and overload the planer.
- To be cut safely, a board must engage both the infeed and the outfeed rollers. Therefore, it must be at least several inches longer than the distance between them.

PORTABLE ELECTRIC PLANE

Sometimes called a *power plane*, the portable electric plane reduces the time and labor needed to plane by hand. It is used to trim or square an edge. **Fig. 9-22.** Because it makes a smooth and accurate cut, it is useful for installing and trimming doors and paneling. **Fig. 9-23.** It can also straighten lumber, trim siding, and surface large timbers.

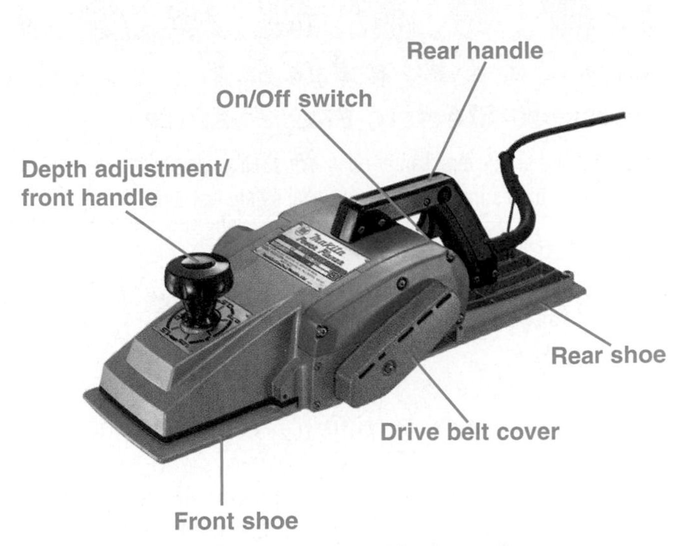

Fig. 9-22. The main parts of a portable electric plane.

The portable electric plane has a cylindrical cutterhead mounted above the fence and protected by a housing. In many cases, the cutterhead is fitted with three straight blades. Some cutterheads, however, have curved blades mounted in a spiral pattern. These are more difficult to sharpen than straight blades, but they make a very smooth cut. In both cases, the cutterhead revolves toward the front of the tool.

Fig. 9-23. Using a portable electric plane to surface the edge of a door.

SAFETY FIRST

Portable Electric Plane Safety

The following are general safety rules. We strongly advise you to check the manufacturer's manual for any special safety instructions.

PORTABLE ELECTRIC PLANE SAFETY

- Wear suitable protection for your eyes and ears.
- Be sure that the blades are sharp. Dull blades result in a poor cut that can be difficult to control.
- Do not allow the workpiece to move or vibrate. Secure it with clamps or in some type of holding device.
- Make adjustments to the plane only when the cord has been disconnected from the power source.
- Use two hands to guide the plane. Stand so you can guide the tool with an uninterrupted cutting motion.
- Do not put an electric plane down until the motor has come to a complete stop.

SECTION 9.3

Check Your Knowledge

1. How is the size of a jointer indicated?
2. Where is the cutterhead mounted on a planer?
3. How does the position of a cutterhead on a planer compare to its position on a jointer?
4. Name three uses for a portable electric plane.

On the Job

Jointers, planers, and electric planes are used by skilled carpenters to surface lumber. Using library or Internet resources, research the history of surfacing tools. What tools did carpenters in America use to surface lumber during the late 1700s? Summarize your findings in a report.

SECTION 9.4

Plate Joiners

A *plate joiner*, or *biscuit joiner*, is a portable power tool that cuts crescent-shaped grooves into the edge of a workpiece. **Fig. 9-24.** A **biscuit**, or plate, is a small flat piece of compressed wood. Biscuits are then glued into the crescent-shaped grooves. **Fig. 9-25.** The workpiece can then form a joint with another workpiece in which matching grooves have been cut. Biscuits strengthen the joint and help to register the pieces accurately.

Trim carpenters use the tool for such tasks as assembling molding and joining shelves to cabinetry. The tool can also be used for butt-joining custom wood flooring that is not end-matched. It can also be used to strengthen the joints in molding or trim. **Fig. 9-26.**

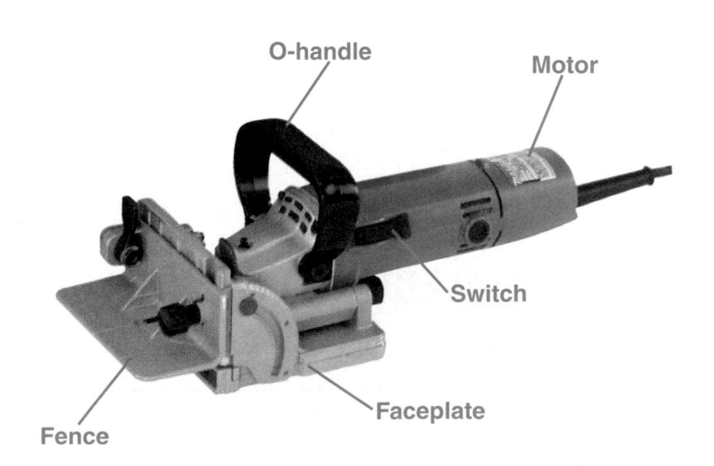

Fig. 9-24. The main parts of a plate joiner.

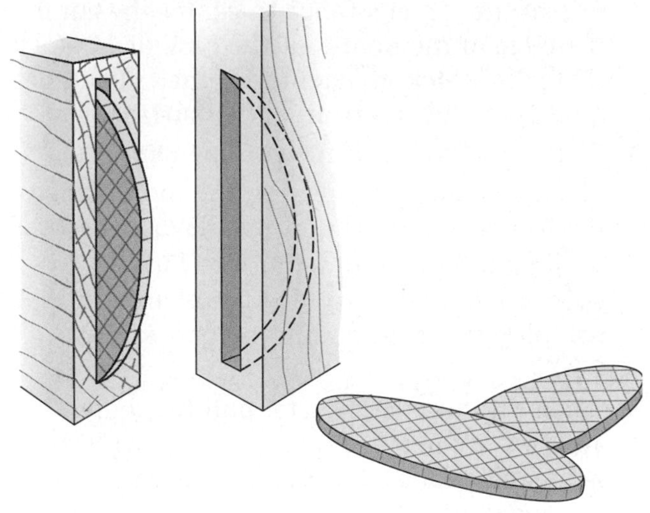

Fig. 9-25. A biscuit joint ready to be assembled.

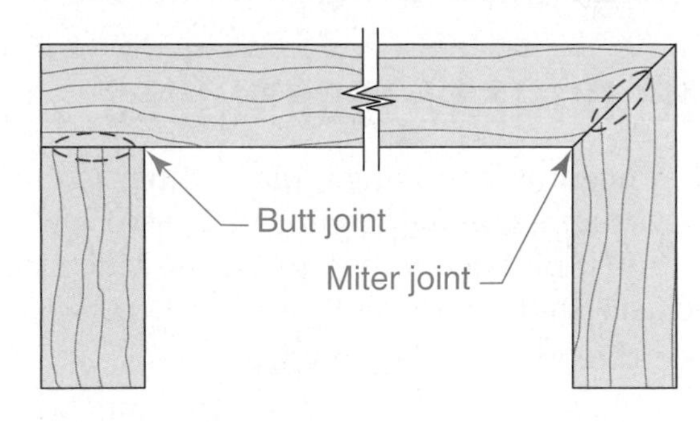

Fig. 9-26. Biscuits can be used to strengthen the joints in molding and trim.

The 4″ diameter blade of a plate joiner has carbide-tipped teeth. It is powered directly by the motor or by a flexible drive belt. At the front of the tool is a metal faceplate. Small metal anti-kickback pins or rubber pads on the lower portion of the faceplate help to keep the tool from sliding during use. An adjustable fence positions the tool against the workpiece. The fence moves up and down and can be angled as well.

SAFETY FIRST

Plate Joiner Safety

The following are general safety rules. We strongly advise you to check the manufacturer's manual for any special safety instructions.

PLATE JOINER SAFETY

- A plate joiner ejects dust and chips at a high rate of speed. Keep your face away from the dust ejection chute. Wear safety glasses at all times.
- Wear ear protection. Most plate joiners are noisy.
- Unplug the power cord when changing blades or performing routine maintenance.
- Any workpiece that is likely to move during the cut should be clamped.
- Be sure that the blades are sharp. Sharp blades improve the cutting action and minimize the possibilities for kickback.
- Check the operation of the guard before using the tool. It should close smoothly over the blade.
- Do not disable the anti-kickback points on the faceplate. Make sure the points engage the workpiece.
- Keep hands away from the blade area when making cuts.
- Never hold a workpiece in your hand while cutting.
- Retract the blade fully after a cut. Failure to retract the blade may allow it to contact the workpiece too soon during the next cut. This can cause kickback.

BISCUITS

The small, thin, oval wood biscuits used in plate joinery are die-cut from beech blanks. The grain of each biscuit runs diagonally to its width. This helps it to resist shear forces across the completed joint.

The biscuits are compressed during manufacture. When one is placed in a glued joint, it absorbs moisture from the glue and expands slightly. This makes it fit the joint tightly as the glue dries. White glue or carpenter's glue may be used.

Biscuits come in three standard sizes:

- #0 (approximately ⅝″ by 1¾″).
- #10 (approximately ¾″ by 2⅛″).
- #20 (approximately 1″ by 2½″).

Plastic biscuits are available for joining synthetic countertop materials such as Corian.

Because plastic biscuits do not absorb moisture from adhesives, they will not expand within the joint. Plastic biscuits are used primarily to speed assembly and to strengthen the joint.

PLATE JOINERY TECHNIQUES

The procedure for using a plate joiner is fairly simple. As an example, suppose that two 1x6 boards must be edge-joined to create wide stock for a closet shelf. You would follow these steps:

1. Place the boards edge to edge.
2. Draw short layout lines across the joint with a pencil. The lines should be 8″ to 10″ on center.
3. Adjust the joiner's depth of cut for the size of biscuit you wish to use.
4. Adjust the joiner's fence to center the cut in the edge of the board. In the case of 1x stock that is ¾″ thick, the center of the cut will be approximately ⅜″ from either surface.
5. Clamp one board to the workbench.
6. Use the centerline guide on the tool to align the faceplate with the board's layout marks.
7. Turn on the plate joiner. Bring it to full speed, and push it toward the board. This will plunge the blade into the stock. **Fig. 9-27.**
8. When the cut is complete, pull the joiner away from the stock and line it up with the next layout mark. Continue to make cuts in this manner.
9. After turning off the tool, clamp the second board in place and repeat Steps 6–8.

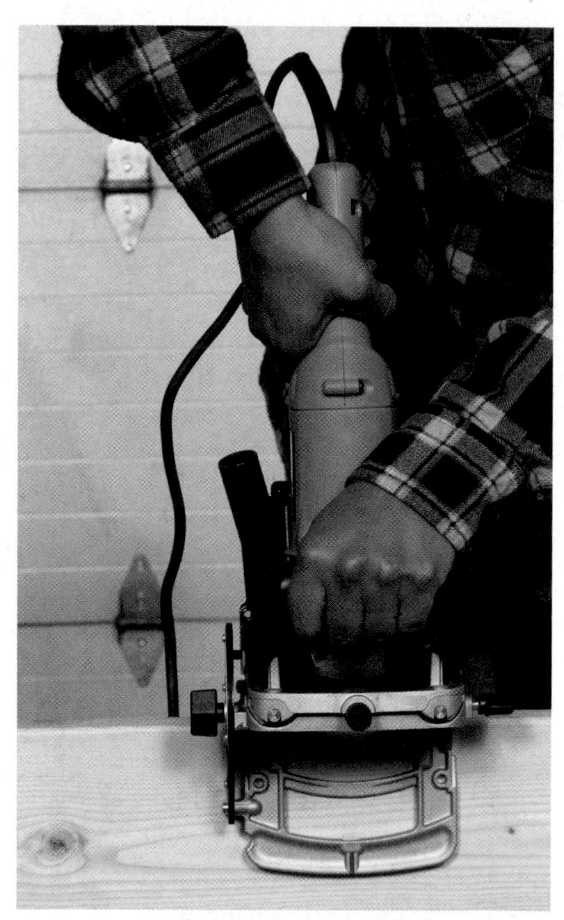

Fig. 9-27. A plate joiner.

To assemble the boards edge to edge, brush glue into the biscuit grooves of one board. Insert the biscuits. Then apply additional glue to the exposed portions of the biscuits and to the edges of both boards. Press the boards together, using the penciled layout lines to ensure precise alignment. Clamp the boards together until the glue dries.

SECTION 9.4 Check Your Knowledge

1. Name two applications for plate joinery in residential construction.
2. What wood is often used to make biscuits?
3. Why does the grain of a biscuit run diagonally to its width?
4. Biscuits come in three standard sizes. What are they?

On the Job

The plate joiner allows two pieces of wood to be joined along the edge. In your view, would a plate shaped like a triangle or a rectangle be as easy to install as one shaped like an oval? Explain your answer in a brief paragraph.

Chapter 9

Review

Section Summaries

9.1 A router is a portable tool that is used primarily for finishing work once a structure is enclosed. It is used for shaping the surfaces and edges of stock and for cutting joints.

9.2 Portable electric sanders are used for tasks ranging from heavy stock removal to delicate finish sanding of woodwork. There are many kinds of sanders, but the most common are the belt sander and the finishing sander.

9.3 Using surfacing tools to convert rough stock into finished stock on site can be less costly than buying finished stock from a lumberyard.

9.4 A plate joiner is used by finish carpenters to strengthen the joints in wood molding, for shelving, and for many other applications.

Review Questions

1. When using a belt sander, when is it safe to let go of the handles?
2. Explain how routers, sanders, and planers are classified in terms of size.
3. What is the purpose of a router?
4. Describe the best uses for each type of power sander.
5. Why would you need to know how a sanding belt was constructed?
6. What does "jointing an edge" mean?
7. What is the purpose of jointing?
8. What is a planer used for?
9. Explain how jointers and planers surface wood.
10. What are plate joiners used for?

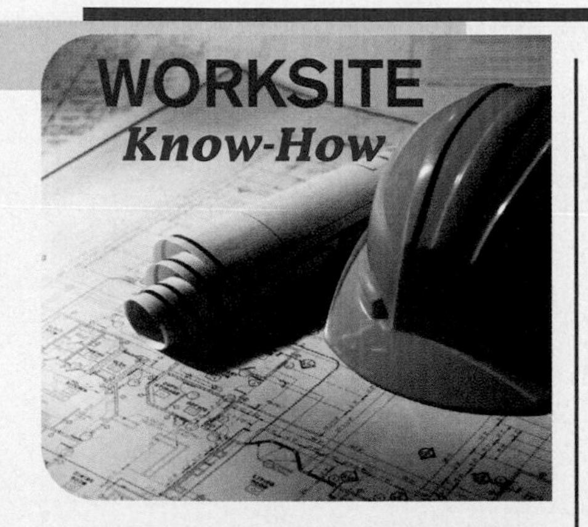

Selecting Abrasives The four major types of abrasives used in home building are aluminum oxide, silicon carbide, ceramics, and garnet. *Aluminum oxide* is the most commonly used for general tasks because it is inexpensive and reasonably durable. As it works, its particles fragment, producing new cutting edges. *Silicon carbide* is harder and sharper than aluminum oxide. It is often used to sand unusually hard materials or materials that are themselves abrasive. *Ceramics* are the hardest and toughest abrasives. They are usually available only in coarse grits for rough sanding. *Garnet* is the only natural mineral still used as an abrasive for wood. It is not very tough and dulls quickly.

Chapter 10

Power Nailers and Staplers

Objectives

After reading this chapter, you'll be able to:

- Follow the safety rules for using nailers and staplers.
- Name the parts of a pneumatic fastening system.
- Tell the main differences between a pneumatic nailer or stapler and a cordless model.
- Identify the two types of fastener magazines.
- Identify fasteners used with power nailers and staplers.

Terms

collated fasteners
gasket
inside diameter
magazine
pneumatic tool
regulator

Power nailers drive many types of fasteners, including framing nails, finish nails, roofing nails, drywall nails, brads, and corrugated fasteners. Power staplers are used primarily for installing sheathing, subflooring, and roofing. However, they can also be used to fasten framing, trim, and wood flooring.

Power nailers and power staplers allow carpenters to install fasteners more quickly and with less fatigue. In addition, they are useful in confined work spaces where it is difficult or impossible to use other tools. Framing carpenters, finish carpenters, and workers in several other trades have come to rely on them. Some local building codes restrict the use of staplers. Check your local code.

SECTION 10.1

Nailing and Stapling Systems

Power nailers and staplers are either pneumatic (new-MAT-ic) or cordless. A **pneumatic tool** is a tool powered by compressed air. The cordless types are driven by an internal combustion engine and compressed gas. In this book, the terms *nailer* and *stapler* refer to both pneumatic and cordless models.

OPERATION

Nailers and staplers operate in the same way, depending on whether they are pneumatic or cordless.

Pneumatic Tools

Compressed air is fed to a pneumatic tool through a high-pressure hose connected to an air compressor. **Fig. 10-1.** The head and sometimes the handle hold the air.

Most nailers and staplers operate on pressures of 60 to 120 psi (pounds per square inch). If the pressure is too low, the fastener may not be driven completely into the workpiece. If the pressure is too high, the fastener may be driven too deep. Excess pressure is also hard on the tool. The operating pressure appropriate for each tool can be found in the owner's manual.

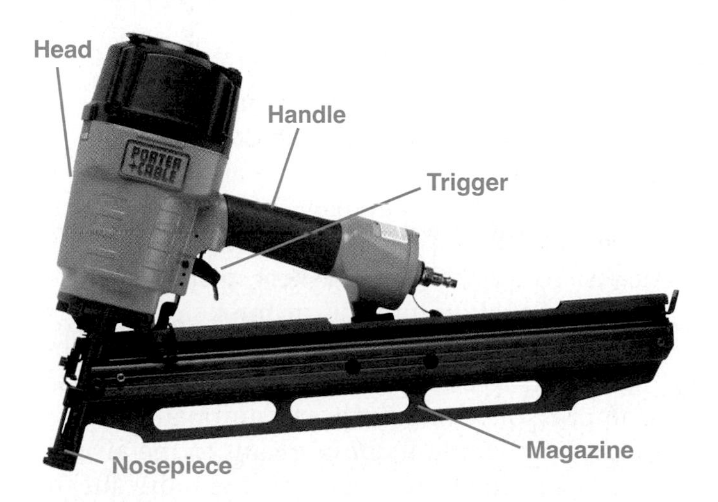

Fig. 10-1. The main parts of a pneumatic strip nailer. This one has an angled magazine.

SAFETY FIRST

Safety with Nailers and Staplers

The following are general safety rules. We strongly advise you to check the manufacturer's manual for any special safety instructions.

General Nailer and Stapler Safety

- Keep bystanders away from the immediate work area. Power-driven fasteners sometimes ricochet (RICK-oh-shay), causing injury.
- Always wear proper eye and hearing protection when using a nailer or stapler.
- Never carry a nailer or stapler while keeping your finger on the trigger. If you were to bring the nosepiece of the tool into contact with a person or object, a fastener could be fired accidentally.
- Never attempt to override the safety mechanism.
- Never use bottled gases to power the tool. The driver blade of a nailer or stapler sometimes makes a spark when it hits the fastener. Thus, running the tool on oxygen, for example, could cause an explosion. Also, carbon dioxide and other gases are bottled at pressures that are unsafe for use by nailers and staplers.
- Never operate a nailer or stapler at a pressure higher than it was designed to handle. Check the pressure gauge of the air compressor periodically.
- If you are using a belt-driven air compressor, make sure that the belts are protected by a cover.
- Before transporting an air compressor, release the pressure in the air-storage tank. Secure the air compressor so it does not roll around in the back of the vehicle.
- Make sure the tool is pointed at the ground when you connect a pressurized air hose to it. The sudden entrance of pressurized air into the tool can cause it to fire.
- Check the hoses connected to a tool to make sure they are in good condition. Never step on a hose. This causes it to wear prematurely.
- Pay particular attention to hoses while using pneumatic tools on a roof. Hoses are easy to trip over. They can also sweep tools off the roof. Secure the hose to a point near the place where you are working. Do not work while moving backwards.
- Never fire the tool until the nosepiece is in contact with the workpiece.
- Never try to clear a jammed tool while it is still connected to an air supply or power source. Disconnect the tool before performing any maintenance on it.

Pulling the trigger on the tool releases the compressed air, which moves a piston in the head of the tool. This piston is attached to a driver blade. When the piston is forced downward, the driver blade strikes a fastener and pushes it into the workpiece at high speed. After the fastener has been driven, the piston retracts, pulling the driver blade with it. When this sequence is complete, another fastener is pushed into place.

All newer nailers and staplers have a two-step firing sequence. This is an important safety feature. The trigger must be pulled and the nosepiece of the tool must be pressed against the workpiece before the tool can be fired. This helps to prevent the tool from being fired accidentally.

Nailers and staplers are available in a variety of sizes that fit a certain type and size of fastener. For example, a nailer designed to drive 16d nails cannot be used to drive brads. When choosing a tool for a particular application, first determine the type and size of fastener needed. Then find a tool that will drive that fastener. If the tool is not cordless, you will need to then find an air compressor that will work with it.

Cordless Tools

A *cordless nailer* or *cordless stapler* resembles a pneumatic model but operates differently. **Fig. 10-2.** Fasteners are driven by a small internal combustion engine in the head of the tool. Fuel for the engine is liquefied gas compressed into disposable canisters. This gas is injected into a chamber above the piston. The gas is then ignited by a spark from a rechargeable battery in the tool's handle.

Cordless tools are self-contained and a hose and an air compressor are not required. This makes them useful in remote locations or where air hoses and an air compressor would be awkward to use. Cordless models are sometimes referred to as *gas*, *hoseless*, or *portable nailers* or *staplers.*

MAINTENANCE

Nailers and staplers are used for high-volume and high-speed installation of fasteners. They must be given regular care. Otherwise, fasteners will become jammed in the tool or be set improperly. Periodic maintenance also makes the tools safer to use.

Fig. 10-2. This cordless nailer is sized to install framing nails. It does not require a compressor or air hose.

Maintaining a Nailer

Proper maintenance of a pneumatic nailer (sometimes called an *air nailer*) is important if it is to operate properly.

- Store the tool at room temperature.
- Lubricate the gaskets on a regular basis in unusually cold weather. A **gasket** is a piece of flexible material that prevents air or liquid from moving between parts of a tool. The various gaskets on a pneumatic tool prevent air leaks. To lubricate the gaskets, place a few drops of tool oil into the air intake of the nailer just before connecting the hose. Another method is to attach a line lubricator to the air compressor. A *line lubricator* automatically adds small amounts of lubricant to the air in the hose, which then conveys the lubricant to the tool. Be sure to check the owner's manual for lubrication requirements.
- Check the *magazine*, which holds the fasteners. It can become clogged by dirt and sawdust. Spray the magazine with a lightweight

lubricant recommended by the manufacturer. Then wipe it clean.

A cordless nailer requires different maintenance. Follow instructions in the owner's manual or have the tool serviced professionally.

General maintenance rules are as follows:

- Charge the battery and replace the fuel cylinders as needed. Be sure to use the correct fuel cylinder.
- If a combustion chamber filter is present, clean it frequently. The filter prevents dust and debris from being drawn into the combustion chamber. Replace the filter if it cannot be cleaned.
- Periodically clean the combustion chamber with an aerosol degreaser.
- Periodically clean the nosepiece. This is important if the tool is used to install roofing, because the asphalt from shingles will foul it. Use a putty knife to remove the asphalt. Although solvents are sometimes used for cleaning, they can damage O-rings in some nailers. Check the owner's manual for instructions. If the nosepiece cannot be cleaned or if it is worn, replace it.

Maintaining a Stapler

The basic mechanism of a pneumatic or cordless stapler is identical to that of a pneumatic or cordless nailer. Follow the maintenance guidelines for nailers. Check the owner's manual.

AIR COMPRESSORS

An *air compressor* squeezes air into an air-storage tank. The air can then be released through a hose to power tools. The main parts of an air compressor include a pump, a motor, an air-storage tank, a tank-pressure gauge, a line-pressure gauge, and a regulator. **Fig. 10-3.** The **regulator** is a valve that controls the air pressure reaching the tool.

Inside the pump, one or more pistons compress the air into a small chamber. Most pumps on portable compressors are single-stage pumps. This means they pump the compressed air directly into the air-storage tank. Portable air compressors are often powered by electric motors. The motor usually drives the air pump by means of a belt connected to a flywheel. The

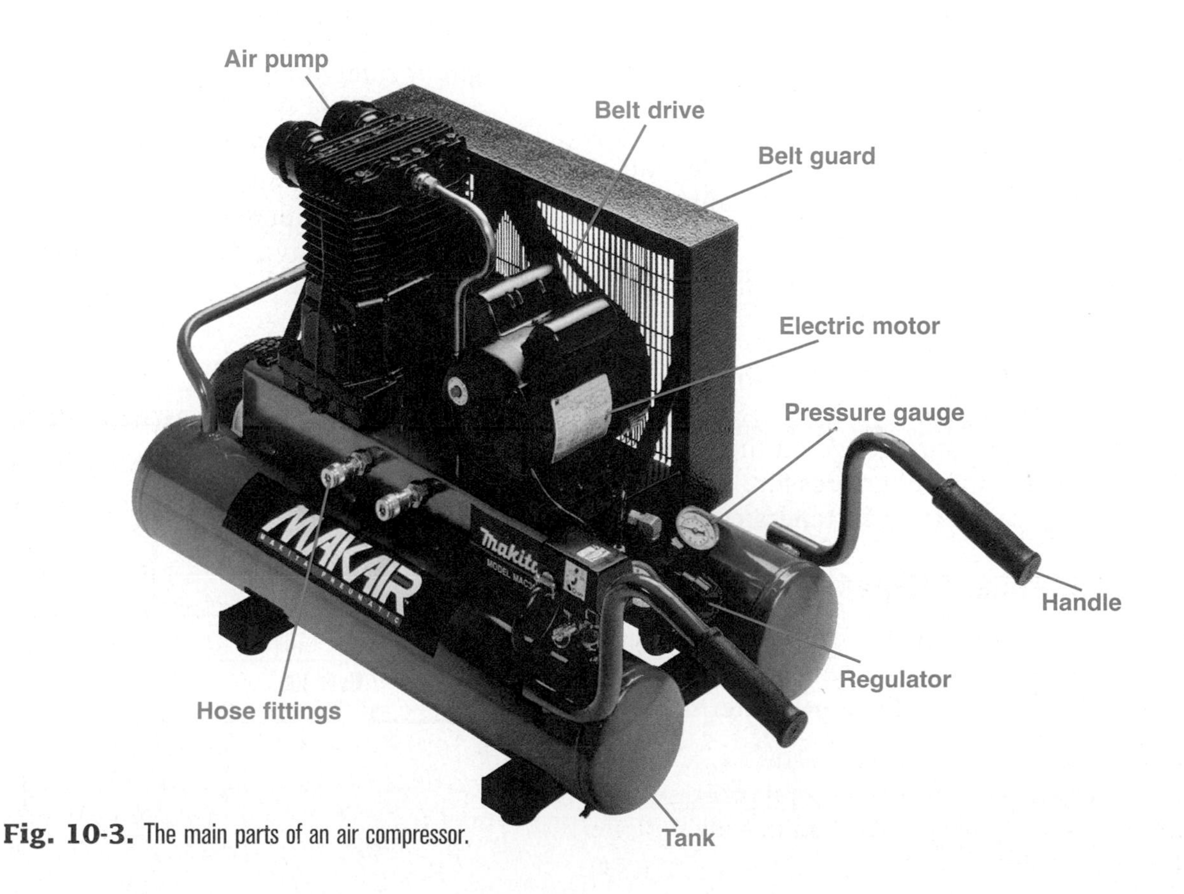

Fig. 10-3. The main parts of an air compressor.

horsepower rating of these electric motors ranges from 0.5 to 2 hp. Large air compressors can be powered by gas engines.

The air-storage tank is usually a cylinder holding 1 to 10 gallons of air. The advantage of a larger tank is that it makes more air available to the tool at any given moment. The disadvantage is that a larger tank makes the air compressor heavier, which makes it harder to move.

A pressure gauge allows the tool user to monitor the pressure within the air-storage tank. The *line-pressure gauge* monitors the pressure in the hose leading to the tool. This is important because the pressure in the air-storage tank may be different from the pressure in the hose.

Air compressors used on job sites are portable. They can easily be moved around the site to be close to the work being done. The smaller, more portable air compressors are not intended for high-volume applications.

Maintenance

Proper maintenance of an air compressor is not complex. The following are general guidelines:

- Maintain the proper oil level in the pump.
- Release the air in the air-storage tank at the end of each workday. This helps to clear any moisture from the tank, which can rust. Removing moisture also keeps the airlines from freezing in cold temperatures.
- Clean the air intake filter on the pump regularly. This filter traps dirt, moisture, and other contaminants. If these contaminants reach the tool, they can cause excessive wear.
- The vibration of an air compressor can loosen fittings over time. Check all the fittings periodically. Tighten them as needed.
- Check the drive belt. Replace the belt if it is worn or damaged.
- Check the pressure gauge on the regulator periodically. Improper pressure will prevent the tool from setting fasteners completely.

Air Compressor Capacity

The amount of air needed by various types and sizes of pneumatic tools varies. The rate and frequency of tool use will determine air consumption. To drive a framing nail, for example, can require fifteen times the air needed to drive a finish nail. Fastening subflooring is repetitive work that calls for many fasteners to be driven quickly. The nailer used requires more air than one used for framing. Generally, pneumatic tools that drive larger fasteners require more air per fastener than those that drive smaller fasteners.

An air compressor must provide a steady air supply. Signs of a low air supply include air leakage from the tool, fasteners that are not set at the proper depth, and skipped shots. The volume of air is measured in cubic feet per minute (cfm) as it is delivered to the tool at a particular pressure. Pressure is measured in pounds per square inch (psi). For example, a framing nailer might operate best at 3 cfm and 90 psi. A brad nailer might require 2 cfm and 70 psi. Some carpenters find that they can fire fasteners faster than an air compressor can supply air. This usually means that the air compressor is undersized.

AIR HOSES

The hose supplying air to a tool should have a minimum working-pressure rating that is 50 percent higher than the maximum pressure delivered by the compressor. This allows a margin of safety in case of malfunctions.

An air hose should have a minimum inside diameter of 5⁄16″. **Table 10-A.** The **inside diameter** of a hose is measured across the widest part of the hose's opening. Hoses from 25′ to 50′ long should have an inside diameter of ½″. Do

Table 10-A. Recommended Inside Diameters for High-Pressure Hoses

Hose Length	Inside Diameter
25′ - 50′	3⁄8″
51′ - 100′	½″
Over 100′	Do not use

not use hoses longer than 100′. The movement of air through a hose is slowed by friction. The longer the hose, the harder the air compressor must work to overcome friction.

Keep the outside of hoses clean. This helps to avoid premature wear. Keep the snap-on fittings at each end of the hose out of the dirt. Dirt and sawdust can clog the fittings, making it difficult to attach them to a nailer or stapler. Dirt-caked fittings can allow dirt into the tool.

SECTION 10.1

Check Your Knowledge

1. What is the firing sequence of a nailer or stapler and how is it related to safety?
2. What is the best way to choose a pneumatic nailer or stapler for a particular application?
3. Name the major parts of a portable air compressor.
4. Why should air hoses longer than 100′ not be used?

On the Job

Use the Internet to locate two manufacturers of pneumatic nailers or staplers. Visit the Web site of each and download information about safety. Print this information and compare the safety recommendations. How do they differ?

SECTION 10.2

Fasteners

Fasteners used in pneumatic or cordless tools are purchased from the manufacturer of the tools. Fasteners made by one manufacturer may not fit another manufacturer's tools. When purchasing a stapler or nailer, be sure that you have access to a steady supply of suitable fasteners.

NAILS

Nailers must be loaded with nails that are collated. **Collated fasteners** are arranged into strips or rolls, with each fastener connected to the fasteners on either side. The nails are joined by plastic or paper strips or by fine wire. This enables nails to be fed through the tool automatically. **Fig. 10-4.** The plastic or wire falls away as the nails are driven.

Collated nails are available in a variety of metals, including galvanized. Nails are classified by the shape of the nail head, the type of shank, and the length.

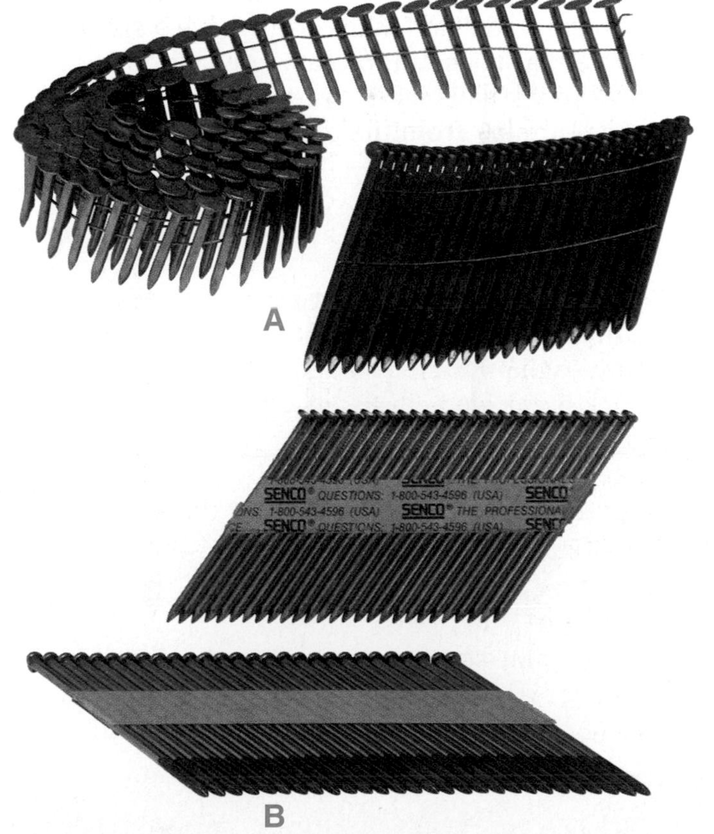

Fig. 10-4. Collated nails. *A.* Nails in coil form and strip form. The nails have a D-head. *B.* Nails collated on paper strips.

Nail Head Shapes

Nails for nailers come with different types of heads. **Fig. 10-5.** The *D-head*, or *clipped head*, nail is used only with nailers. Part of the head has been removed giving it a *D* shape. This allows the nails to be packed closely together. The disadvantage of a D-head nail is that it may not hold as well as a nail with a round head. Do not use D-head nails where building codes restrict their use. Such applications could include fastening shear walls and structures located where severe weather or earthquakes are common.

Nail Shanks

The *shank* of a nail is the portion below the head. The type of shank determines how well the nail will hold in various woods. Nails with several shank designs are available for pneumatic nailers. **Fig. 10-6.** The following are among the more common types:

- Smooth-shank nails are used for general construction. The smooth shank provides good holding power in a variety of woods. Most framing and roofing nails are smooth-shank nails.
- Screw-shank nails have more holding power than smooth-shank nails. They have a spiral shape that is useful for nailing hardwoods.
- Ring-shank nails have a series of ridges or rings running from the point nearly to the head. They are best for applications that require extra holding power, such as for nailing wood that has a high moisture content. Ring-shank nails are sometimes used to nail subfloors because they can reduce the occurrence of squeaks.

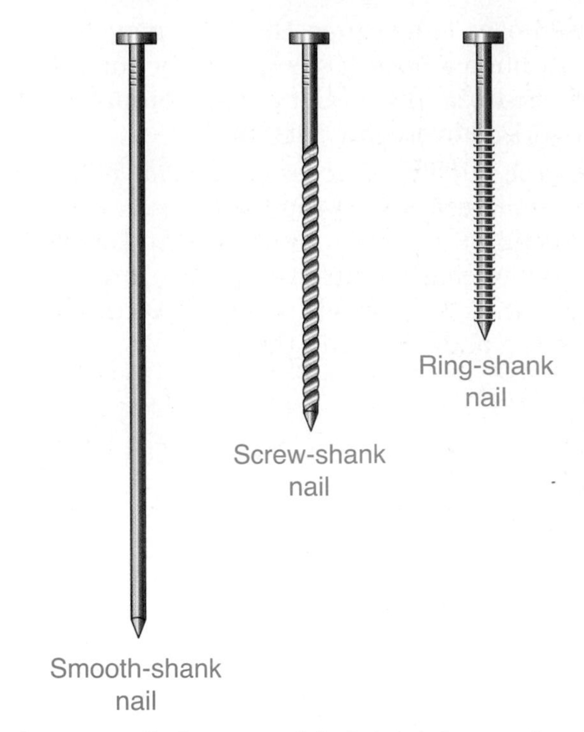

Fig. 10-6. The basic types of shank designs for power fastening.

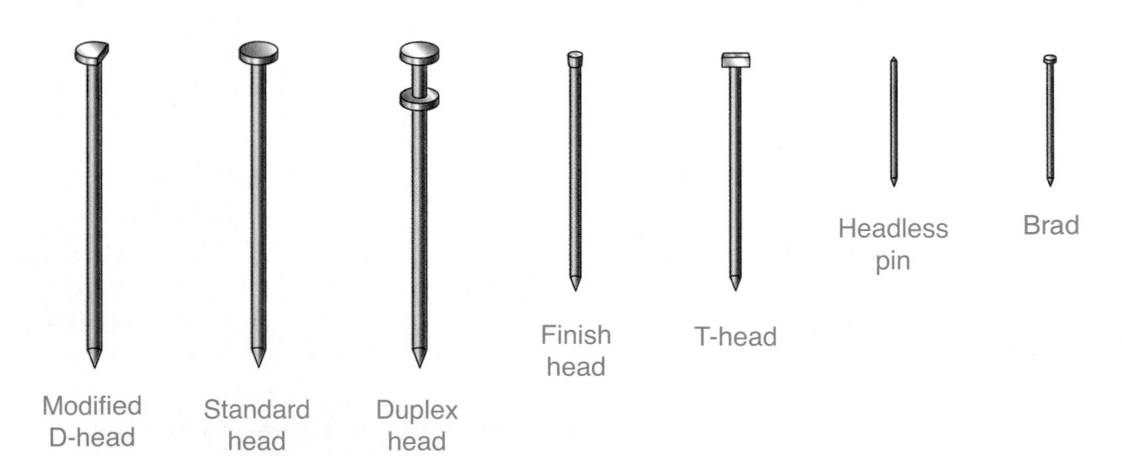

Fig. 10-5. Nail heads for power nailers.

STAPLES

Staples are made of various metals, including steel, galvanized steel, stainless steel, aluminum, and bronze. They are classified by leg length, width of crown, wire size, and type of point. **Fig. 10-7.** Staples are generally available in lengths from ⅛″ to 2½″. The width of the crown is the overall width of the staple, including both legs. Crown width can be narrow, intermediate, or wide. Wire size is either heavy or fine.

Points also vary. **Fig. 10-8.** Chisel-point and blunt-point staples are the most common on job sites because they are suitable for most applications. Their legs penetrate straight into the wood. The legs of divergent-point staples have opposing bevels. When the staple enters the wood, the legs splay out in opposite directions. This offers strong holding power in softwoods.

Choosing the correct staple depends on the work to be done. For example, a fine-wire, narrow-crown staple is used where the staple must not show, as in fastening trim. Heavy-wire, wide-crown staples are used for attaching asphalt roofing and for other applications where extra holding power is needed.

The crown of the staple should be kept perpendicular to the grain of the wood. This "locks" it into the wood fibers. Inspect installed staples periodically to be sure that they are being driven properly.

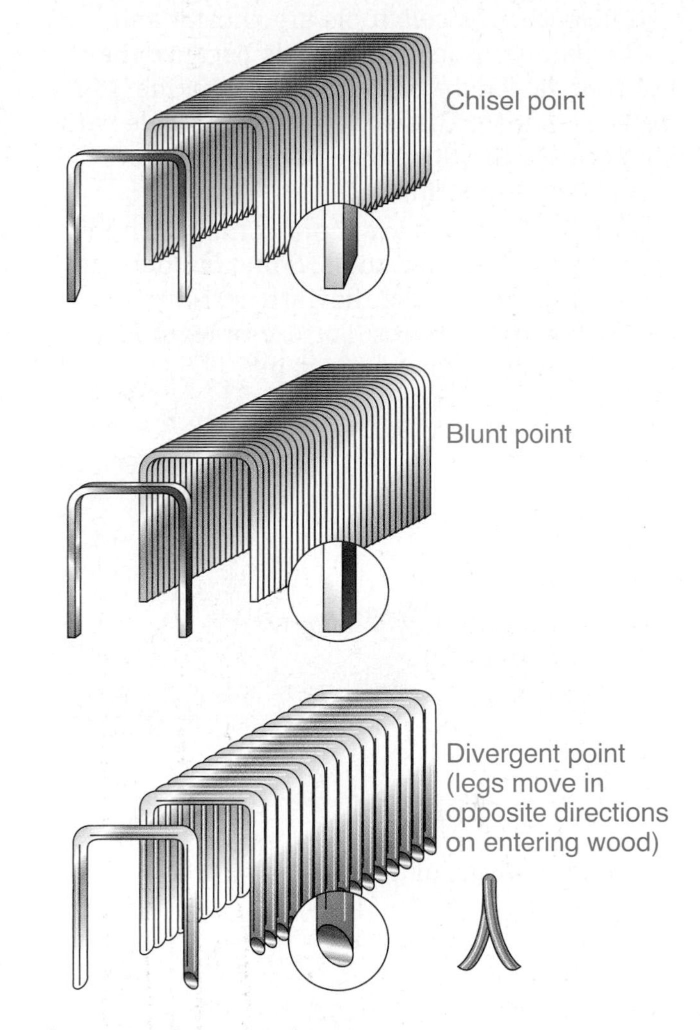

Fig. 10-8. Common staple points.

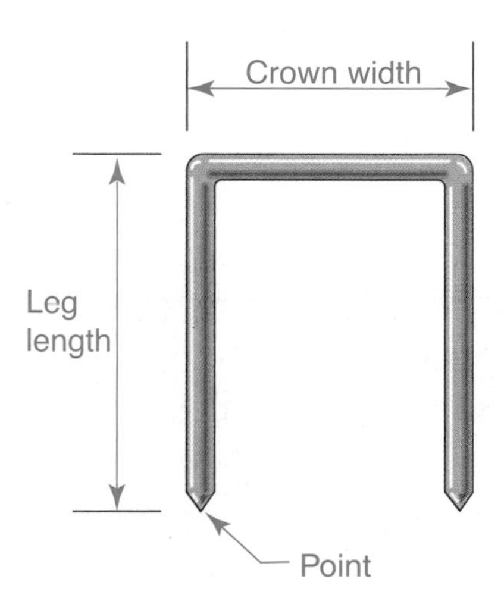

Fig. 10-7. The basic parts of a staple.

FASTENER MAGAZINES

The **magazine** is the container on a tool that holds a ready supply of fasteners. In both pneumatic and cordless nailers and staplers, the fasteners are held in one of two types of magazine.

Strip-loaded, or *strip*, tools hold a straight row of nails or staples in a spring-loaded magazine. The magazine is sometimes angled toward the tool's handle (see Fig. 10-1 on page 183). This helps the tool reach into confined areas. A straight magazine holds fewer fasteners.

Coil-loaded, or *coil,* tools are shorter and wider than strip-loaded models because they hold the fasteners in a circular magazine. **Fig. 10-9.** This magazine style is not available with staplers. Up to 300 nails can be loaded into a coil nailer at one time.

Strip-loaded tools are more common on job sites than coil-loaded tools. Some builders prefer strip tools because they are narrow and can be used in tight spaces. For example, toenailing studs is easier with a strip nailer.

Fig. 10-9. This coil-loaded nailer has a cushioned handle. This arrangement is compact and is suitable for various types of nails.

SECTION 10.2 Check Your Knowledge

1. What are collated fasteners?
2. What is the disadvantage of a D-head nail?
3. How are staples classified?
4. What would be the advantage of using a pneumatic nailer having a coil-loaded magazine?

On the Job

Locate a supplier of nails for any brand of pneumatic nailer. Compare the cost of collated 16d framing nails with the cost of the same quantity of 16d loose nails that are sold by your local building supply. Calculate the cost per nail.

Chapter 10 Review

Section Summaries

10.1 A pneumatic nailer or stapler uses compressed air to drive fasteners. A cordless nailer or stapler uses a small internal combustion engine and special fuel to drive fasteners. All newer nailers and staplers employ a two-step firing sequence. Proper care of a nailer or stapler is important if it is to perform properly. An air compressor must be chosen to suit the type and size of nail being driven. An air compressor must provide a steady supply of compressed air to the tool. The hose supplying air to a pneumatic nailer or stapler should be properly sized for the job, and not longer than necessary.

10.2 Fasteners for nailers and staplers are available in a great variety of shapes and sizes. They are collated to fit the tool. The type of collation can affect the suitability of the fastener. Fastener magazines are either strip-loaded or coil-loaded.

Review Questions

1. Why should a power nailer or stapler be pointed at the ground when you connect a pressurized air hose?
2. Name the three basic parts of a pneumatic fastening system.
3. What problems are associated with too much or too little air pressure in a pneumatic nailer or stapler?
4. What part of a pneumatic tool actually drives the fastener into the wood?
5. How does a pneumatic nailer or stapler differ from a cordless nailer or stapler?
6. How should pneumatic tools be maintained?
7. Within what air pressure range do most nailers and staplers operate?
8. Name the basic types of nail shanks used with nailers, and tell their advantages.
9. Identify the fasteners used with power nailers and staplers.
10. Name the two types of fastener magazines.

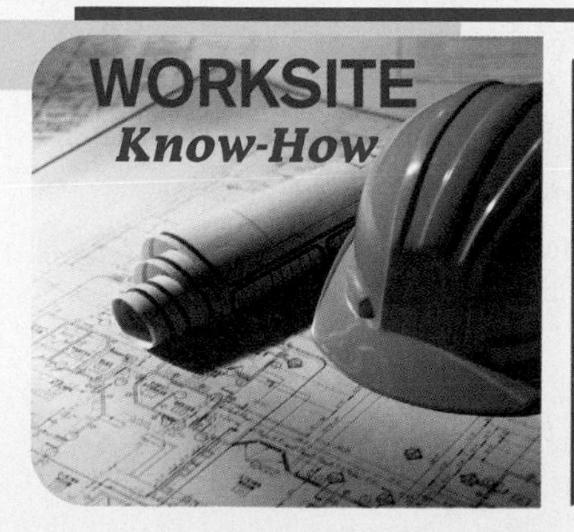

Increasing Nailer Safety Take special care to be sure other workers are not in harm's way when using a nailer. This includes people who may be on the other side of the workpiece. Nailers have been known to send a nail at high speed completely through a material, striking someone unseen. Noise is another factor to consider. Because equipment used to power a nailer can be loud, it should be kept at a distance. Otherwise, workers cannot hear someone approaching and may be startled or may swing the nailer around unexpectedly, causing an accident.

Chapter

Ladders and Scaffolds

Objectives

After reading this chapter, you'll be able to:

- Follow the safety rules for working with ladders.
- Set up a straight ladder and a stepladder safely.
- Compare manufactured metal scaffolding to wood scaffolding.
- Describe brackets, a pump jack, and a lifeline.

Terms

lifeline
pump jack
rails
spreader
trestle

Falls cause the greatest number of deaths in the construction industry. Each year, between 150 and 200 people are killed and more than 100,000 are injured due to falls at construction sites. The proper use of ladders and scaffolds reduces the risk of falling. Also, studies have shown that the use of guardrails and other safety devices can prevent many deaths and injuries from falls.

Before using ladders and scaffolds, it is very important to read and follow the safety guidelines in this chapter. You should also follow the instructions that come with the ladder or scaffold. They may include special safety instructions. Safety information may also be present on stickers attached to equipment.

SECTION 11.1

Ladders and Scaffolds

Because of the size of most structures, carpenters and other tradespeople depend on scaffolds and ladders to work in areas that would otherwise be out of reach. Ladders are fast and easy to set up and take down, but they must be moved frequently. Scaffolding takes longer to set up and take down. It does, however, provide access to a larger area of wall or ceiling before it must be moved.

LADDERS

Ladders come in lengths from 3′ to 50′. The basic parts of a ladder are the rungs, or steps, and the rails. *Rungs* and steps are the horizontal members that a worker climbs on. The **rails** are the vertical supports to which the rungs or steps are attached.

There are two basic types of ladders: folding ladders and straight ladders. **Fig. 11-1.** *Folding ladders* are self-supporting and are used primarily indoors for reaching low and intermediate heights. They are the most portable type of ladder. A *stepladder* is a common type of folding ladder that has flattened steps instead of rungs. A folding *articulated ladder,* also called a *multipurpose ladder,* can be adjusted to fit into such spots as stairwells. **Fig. 11-2.**

Straight ladders are used primarily outdoors where greater heights must be reached. They are not self-supporting. Instead, they must be leaned against a wall or some other object. The ladder's *working length* is the distance from the ground to the top support, measured along the ladder. An *extension ladder* is a common type of straight ladder that can be adjusted to various lengths.

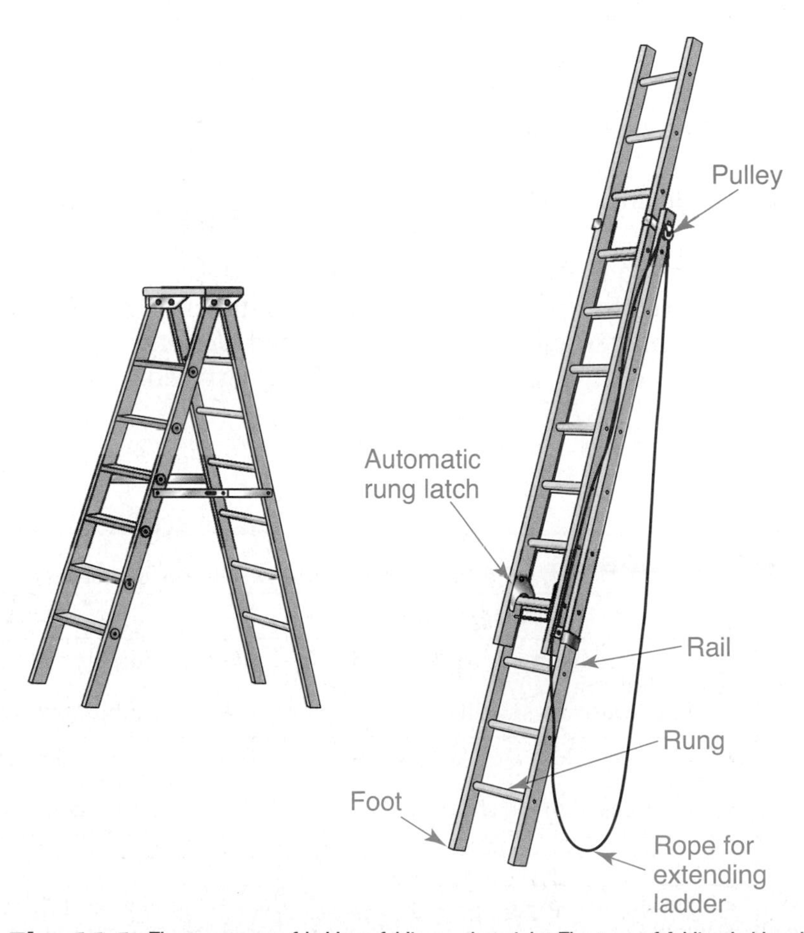

Fig. 11-1. The two types of ladders: folding and straight. The type of folding ladder shown is a stepladder. An extension ladder is a type of straight ladder.

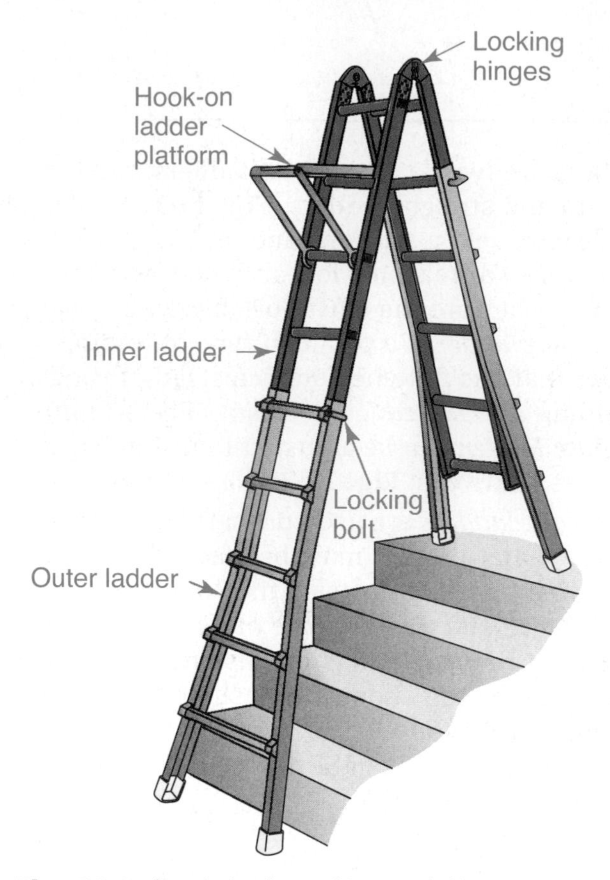

Fig. 11-2. An articulated, or multipurpose, ladder.

Folding ladders and straight ladders are available in various grades or duty ratings. **Table 11-A.** The grade indicates the maximum load the ladder can support.

The materials used most often to make ladders are wood, aluminum, and reinforced fiberglass. **Table 11-B** lists the advantages and disadvantages of each.

Table 11-A. Grades of Ladders

Type	Duty Rating (lbs.)	Typical Uses
Household, Type III	200	Light duty. For household use.
Commercial, Type II	225	Medium duty. For painters and light-construction workers.
Industrial, Type I	250	Heavy duty. For contractors and maintenance workers.
Industrial, Type IA	300	Extra heavy duty. For rugged industrial and construction use.

Note: The user's weight, plus any tools, jacks, planks, and materials, must not exceed the duty rating.

SAFETY FIRST

General Safety

The following are general safety rules. We strongly advise you to check the manufacturer's manual for any special safety instructions. Safety information may also be found on a permanent sticker attached to the ladder.

General Ladder Safety

- Inspect ladders carefully. Keep nuts, bolts, and other fasteners tight. Do not try to repair a damaged ladder. Replace it or have it professionally serviced.

Table 11-B. Ladder Materials

Material	Advantages	Disadvantages
Wood	• Does not conduct electricity when clean and dry • Weight improves stability	• Less durable than other materials • Heavy • Susceptible to weather damage
Fiberglass	• Does not conduct electricity when clean and dry • High strength-to-weight ratio	• Long-term exposure to sunlight can lead to deterioration • Heavier than aluminum • Damage cannot be repaired • Expensive
Aluminum	• Lightweight • Durable • High strength-to-weight ratio • Weather resistant	• Conducts electricity • Damage cannot be repaired

Fig. 11-3. A straight ladder should be stored horizontally on supports to prevent sagging. Never store ladders where they will be exposed to weather or near a source of heat.

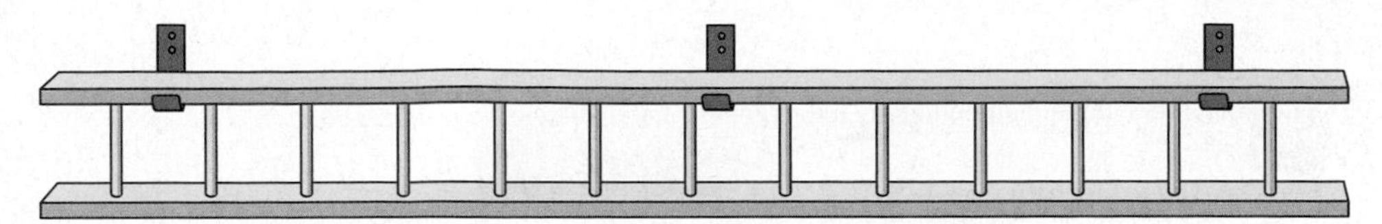

- Keep steps and rungs free of oil, grease, paint, and other slippery substances. Wood ladders should not be coated with any opaque finish. Such a finish will hide cracks.
- Place the ladder on a firm, level surface. Make sure that it has non-slip safety feet.
- Never place a ladder in front of a door or other opening unless the ladder is secured to prevent an accident or a barricade is used to keep traffic away.
- Never use a ladder as a scaffolding plank.
- Never use ladders after they have been soaked in water for a long time or been exposed to fire, chemicals, or fumes that could affect their strength.
- Always place the ladder close enough to the work to avoid a long, dangerous reach.
- Face the ladder when climbing up or down.
- Keep your weight centered between both side rails.
- Do not use metal, metal-reinforced, or wet ladders where direct contact with a live power source is possible. Metal and water conduct electricity.
- Do not overload a ladder. A ladder is designed to carry only one person at a time.

For stepladders

- During use, be sure that stepladders are fully open and the spreader is locked.
- Make sure all locking devices are secure.
- Never step on the stabilizing bars of a stepladder. These are the horizontal bars between the back rails. They are not designed to support a load.
- Never lay tools on the top step.

For straight ladders

- Store straight ladders horizontally in a dry, ventilated place. **Fig. 11-3.**
- Always be sure that the working length of the ladder will reach the height required for support. The ladder should extend at least 3′ above a roof or other elevated platform you wish to reach. Never stand on the top three rungs.
- For safety, the foot of the ladder should be a distance equal to one-fourth its working length from the building or other support. The angle created should be approximately 75°.
- To keep the legs from slipping when outdoors, drive a strong stake into the ground behind the ladder. Then tie the bottom of the ladder to the stake with rope.
- Do not tie or fasten ladders together to create longer sections. Use an extension ladder instead.
- Always make sure that both side rails are fully supported at top and bottom. **Fig. 11-4.**
- To keep a straight ladder from shifting, tie it to an immovable object as close as possible to the upper (top) support point.
- Be sure all locks on extension ladders are securely hooked over rungs before you use them.
- Do not adjust the height of an extension while you are standing on it.

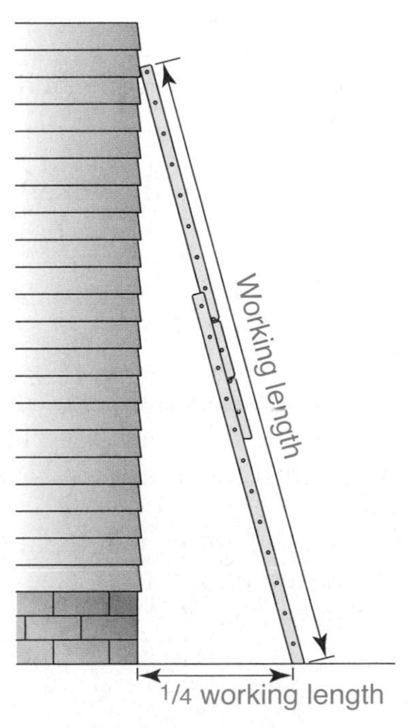

Fig. 11-4. For safety, the pitch, or angle, should be approximately 75°. It should be such that the horizontal distance at the bottom from the ladder to the support is one-fourth the working length of the ladder.

Position yourself at about the center of the ladder before lifting it. **Fig. 11-5.** Never carry a ladder in an upright position. Always carry it in a horizontal position. This will ensure that it does not accidentally bump into power lines and other objects. Also, by carrying a ladder horizontally, you can control it more easily and will be less likely to hurt your back.

Fig. 11-5. Carry a ladder horizontally. Do not let it touch electrical power lines.

STEP BY STEP

Setting Up a Straight Ladder

Set up a straight ladder as follows:

Step 1 Brace the lower end against a step or other object so the ladder cannot slide.

Step 2 Grasp a rung at the upper end with both hands.

Step 3 Raise the top end and walk forward under the ladder, grasping other rungs as you proceed. **Fig. 11-6.**

Step 4 When the ladder is erect, lean it forward into the desired position.

Step 5 Check the angle, height, and stability at top and bottom (see Fig. 11-4 on page 195).

Fig. 11-6. To raise a straight ladder, walk forward under the ladder as shown, moving your hands to grasp other rungs as you proceed.

Using a Ladder

Before using a stepladder, always be certain that the feet are firmly supported and that its spreader is locked into position. The **spreader** holds the ladder open and prevents it from closing accidentally. Never stand on the top step because your weight can easily unbalance the ladder and tip it over. Do not step on the tray on the back of the ladder. It is for holding tools and materials, not people.

When going up or down a straight ladder, grip the ladder firmly and place your feet squarely on the rungs. Make certain your work boots and the rungs are free of mud and grease. When using a ladder to access a roof, make sure the ladder extends above the edge of the roof by at least 3′. **Fig. 11-7.**

Fig. 11-7. The top of the ladder should extend above the edge of the roof at least 3'. If the ladder is used when conditions are slippery, it must be tied off (secured) to the building.

Overlap extension-ladder sections by the following amounts:

- 3′ for total extended lengths up to 32′.
- 4′ for total lengths of 32′ to 35′.
- 5′ for total lengths of 36′ to 47′.

Certain accessories make extension ladders safer to use. A *ladder stabilizer* can be bolted to the top of the ladder. It has arms 4′ apart that steady the top of the ladder and prevent it from slipping. **Fig. 11-8.** *Leg levelers* can be attached to the feet of the ladder. **Fig. 11-9.** They support the ladder on uneven ground.

Fig. 11-8. A ladder stabilizer prevents the ladder from sliding sideways.

Fig. 11-9. Leg levelers adjust to uneven ground.

SCAFFOLDS

A *scaffold* is a raised platform used for working at a height. Scaffolds make it possible to work safely, in a comfortable and convenient position, with both hands free. A scaffold is sometimes built on site from framing lumber and duplex-head nails. A *duplex-head* nail is a nail with a double head. It holds tightly but is easy to pull out again when taking the scaffold apart.

The horizontal parts of a scaffold on which a worker stands are called *scaffold planks.* Because of their quality and extra strength, laminated wood planks made especially for scaffolds are sometimes used. However, some builders prefer aluminum planks to laminated wood planks because they are lighter in weight. Standard construction lumber is not recommended for scaffold planks.

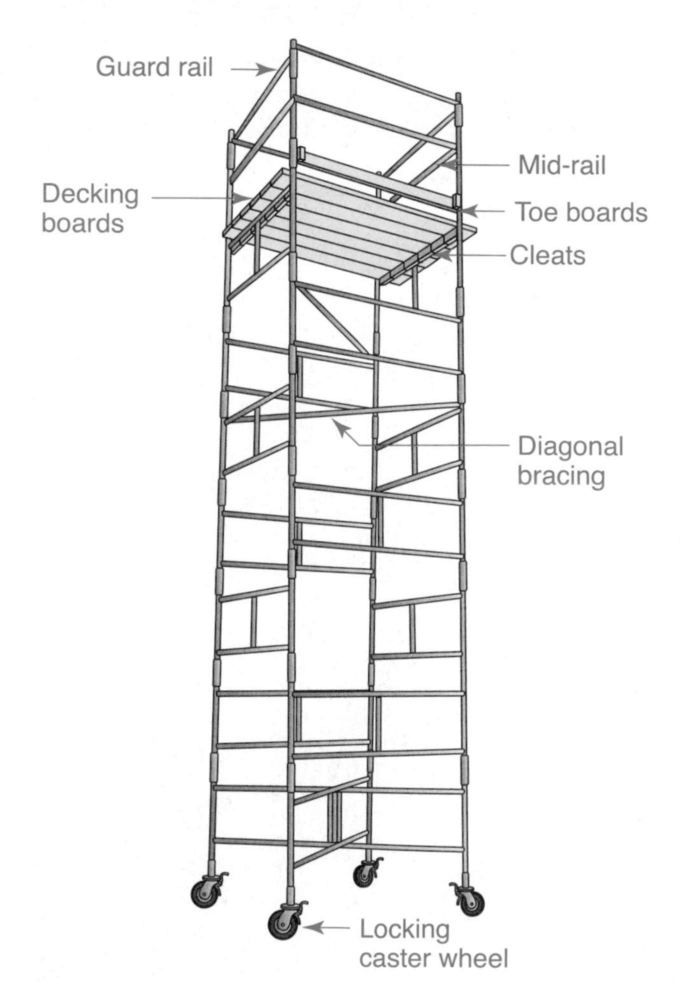

Fig. 11-10. Commercial metal scaffolding assembled for interior use.

Commercial metal scaffolding, sometimes called *pipe scaffolding,* has many advantages over scaffolding made from wood. **Fig. 11-10.** Metal scaffolding is engineered and tested to withstand specific loads. It can be rented as needed, takes up less space than wood scaffolding, and is more weather resistant. It is also easier to assemble and disassemble. The end frames can be put together in a staggered position, making it possible to work from a stairway.

Scaffolds vary in design. For scaffold assembly, the manufacturer's instructions should be carefully followed.

When a metal scaffold is used indoors, it is sometimes equipped with locking caster wheels. With wheels, the scaffold can be rolled from place to place.

Scaffolding should include guardrails to protect workers from falls. For all scaffolding manufactured after January 1, 2000, OSHA requires that a guardrail be placed between 38″ and 45″ above the scaffold planks. A mid-rail should be placed about halfway between the guardrail and the planks.

SAFETY FIRST

General Safety

The following are general safety rules. We strongly advise you to check the manufacturer's manual for any special safety instructions.

Scaffolding Safety

- Check that all scaffolding is plumb and level. Use adjusting screws, not blocks, to compensate for uneven ground.
- Some scaffolds have casters or wheels. Make sure these casters or wheels are locked before using the scaffold.
- Provide adequate support for scaffolds. Use base plates, making sure that they rest firmly

on the ground. Secure freestanding scaffold towers by attaching guy ropes or wires or by other means.

- Fasten all braces securely.
- Do not climb cross braces. Access to scaffolds should be by stairs or fixed ladders only.
- Provide proper guardrails. Add toe boards when required on planks.
- Never use ladders on top of a scaffold.
- Never overload a scaffold. Follow manufacturer's recommendations regarding load limits.
- Inspect the scaffolding regularly and tighten any loose connections.
- Inspect lumber used for scaffold planks. It should be graded for that purpose. Both ends of wood planks should have cleats to prevent the planks from sliding off the supports.

SECTION 11.1

Check Your Knowledge

1. Name and describe the two basic types of ladders.
2. What should you do if you encounter a ladder that is damaged?
3. What two types of planks are most suitable for use as scaffold planks?
4. What are the advantages of metal scaffolding over wood scaffolding?

On the Job

You have been asked to paint an attic vent in the gable of a two-story house. The vent, which is 3′ square, is located 24′ above the ground. Make sketches to show how you would set up an extension ladder to perform this task. Include a side view and a front view. Label the important dimensions.

SECTION 11.2

Other Support Equipment

It is not always possible or desirable to work from scaffolding and ladders. This is often the case in tight spots or when working atop a roof. Other means must then be found for ensuring a safe way to work.

BRACKETS

Special *brackets* are available that can be attached to the frame of a structure. Scaffold planks are then laid on the brackets to form a platform. Some brackets are nailed to side-wall studs while others are bolted to them or hooked around them. **Fig. 11-11.** Nail-attached wall and corner brackets are secured with 20d nails driven into the stud at an angle through the tapered holes in the bracket. The brackets may

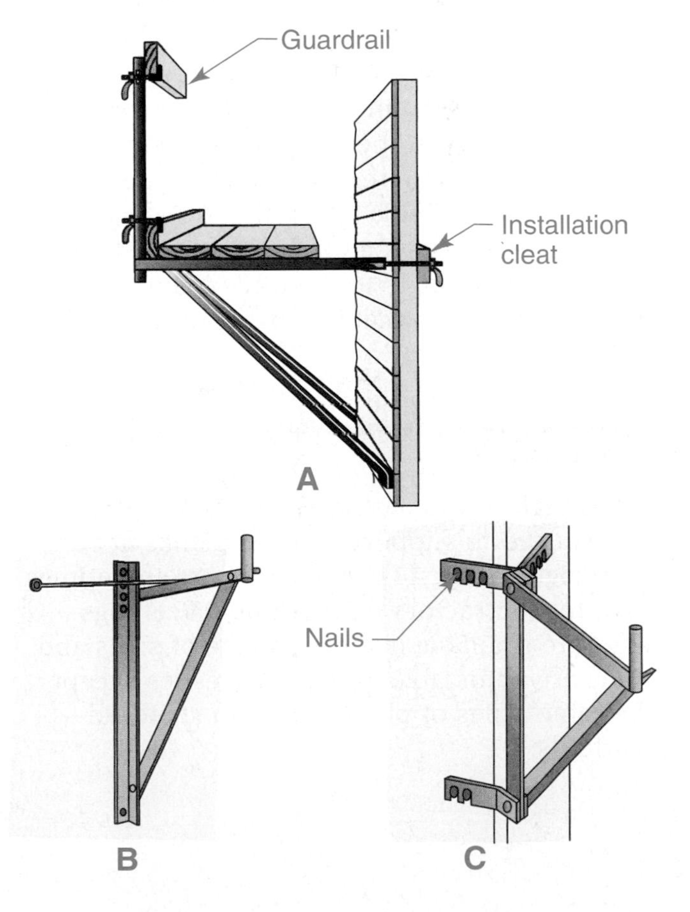

Fig. 11-11. Brackets. *A.* Bolt-attached brackets. Note the guardrail. This rail can also be used with other types of brackets. *B.* A nail-attached wall bracket. *C.* A nail-attached corner bracket.

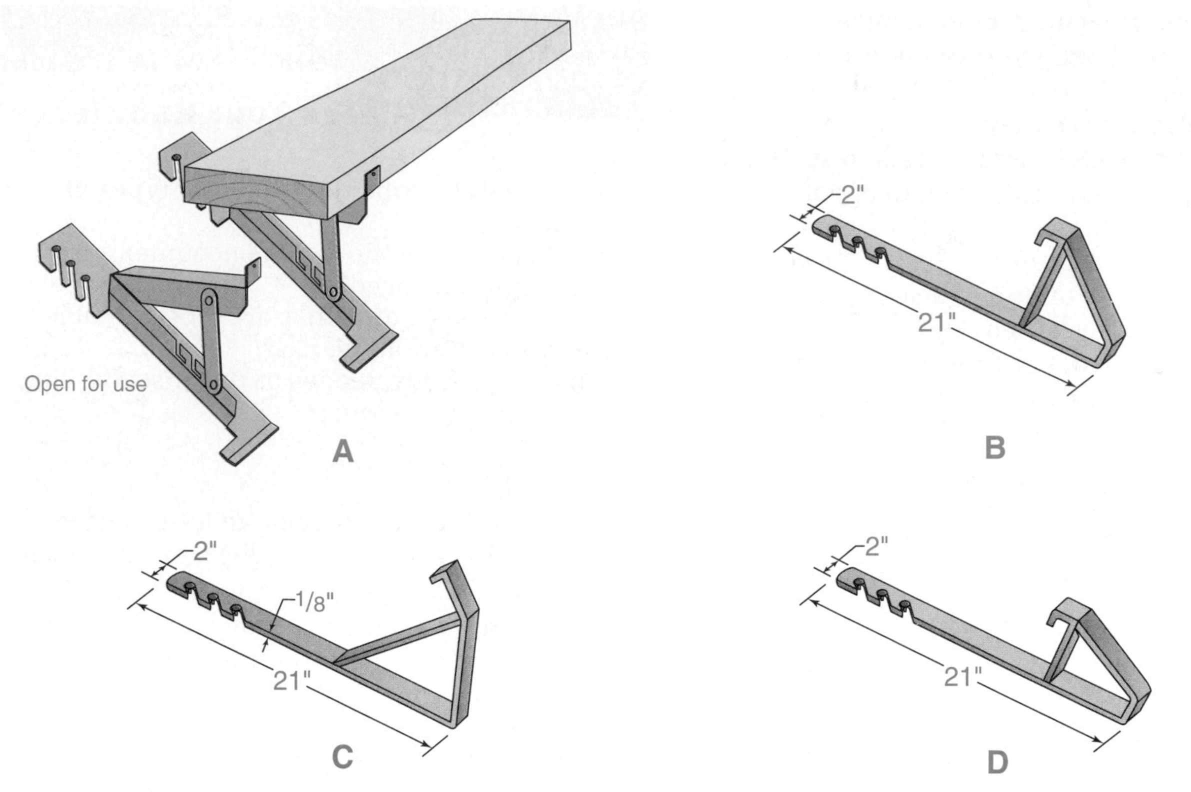

Fig. 11-12. Roofing brackets. *A.* The folding roof bracket adjusts to various roof pitches, from 90° to level. It is ideal for use on steep roofs. *B.* This bracket supports a 2x6 at a right angle to the roof. *C.* This bracket positions a 2x6 to provide a level walkway. *D.* This bracket supports a 2x4 at a right angle to the roof.

be easily removed without pulling the nails. Any nails remaining after the brackets have been removed can be driven flush.

Brackets for working on a roof are attached by nailing through them into the rafters. **Fig. 11-12.** They can be removed without pulling the nails. One style holds a 2x4 or 2x6 flat against the roof. Another type holds a 2x4 or 2x6 on edge at a right angle to the roof. A third type positions a 2x6 so that it provides a level walkway.

TRESTLES

A **trestle** is a portable metal frame with rungs that is used to support scaffold planks at various heights. **Fig. 11-13.** Trestles are sometimes used by contractors for working on ceilings. They are available in a wide range of sizes and some are adjustable in height. Trestles accept the same types of planks used on standard scaffolds.

Fig. 11-13. A folding trestle. It adjusts to hold planks at various heights.

Though a trestle may resemble a sawhorse, it is designed specifically to support scaffolding. Sawhorses are not intended for this purpose and should not be used.

PUMP JACKS

A **pump jack** is a metal device with a foot pedal that a worker pumps to make it slide up and down on a wood or aluminum post. **Fig. 11-14.** Two or more jacks in a row support planks that a worker can use as a scaffold. Pump jacks are commonly used to reach the side walls of a house during siding or painting operations. To lower the jack, the worker turns a hand crank.

The wood posts are often created by two 2x4s. The lumber should be solid, knot-free, and no more than 30′ long. For solid support, each post must rest on a wood or steel pad. It must also be anchored to the structure at least every 10′ by metal stand-offs nailed or screwed into the studs.

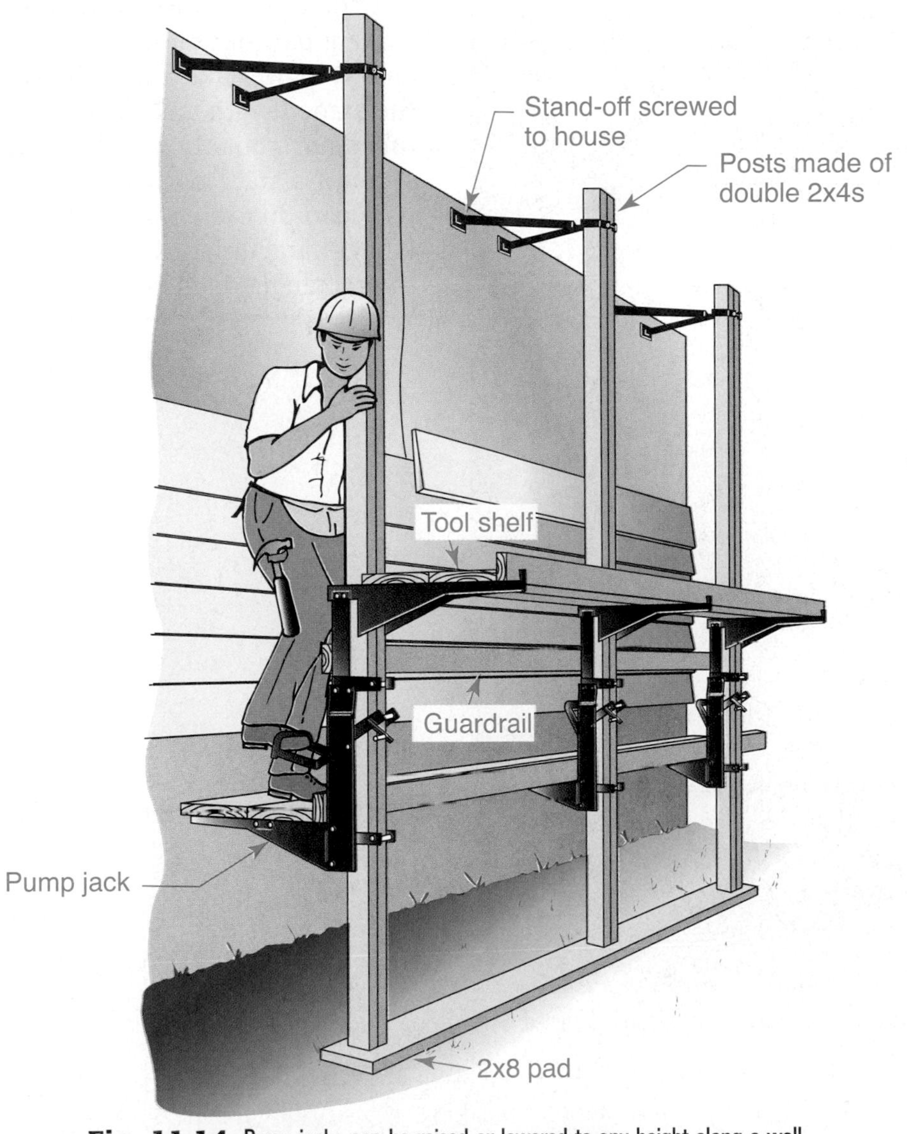

Fig. 11-14. Pump jacks can be raised or lowered to any height along a wall.

LIFELINES

A **lifeline** is a rope intended to prevent a worker from falling more than 6′. The lifeline is fastened at one end to a secure point on the structure and at the other end to a harness worn by the worker. **Fig. 11-15.**

According to OSHA, a lifeline must be secured to a structural member above the worker that is capable of supporting a minimum deadweight of 5,400 lbs. (This accounts for the weight of the worker plus the force of the fall.) Lifelines used where they may be subjected to cutting or abrasion must have a wire core. For all others, manila rope or its equivalent, with a diameter of at least ¾″ and a minimum breaking strength of 5,400 lbs., must be used.

Fig. 11-15. Harnesses and lifelines must be securely fastened.

SECTION 11.2 Check Your Knowledge

1. In what kinds of situations might a worker prefer to set up planks on a bracket or pump jack instead of using standard scaffolding?
2. What might be the advantage of using a pump jack instead of a wall bracket when installing siding?
3. Trestles and sawhorses are similar in appearance. Can they both be used to support scaffolding?
4. What is a lifeline, and what is its purpose?

On the Job

The triangle shape is present in some of the devices noted in this chapter. With a partner, use corrugated cardboard and masking tape to make a pair of hollow triangular tubes 12″ long and 3″ high. Make a pair of rectangular tubes of the same length and height. Place each pair of tubes horizontally on a table and use them to support a stack of books. How many books can you load on each pair before the tubes collapse? What characteristics does the triangle have that the rectangle does not have?

Chapter 11

Review

Section Summaries

11.1 The two types of ladders are folding and straight. They come in many sizes and are commonly made of wood, aluminum, or fiberglass. The proper use of ladders and scaffolds reduces the risk of falling. Before using any ladders or scaffolding, it is extremely important to read and follow the safety rules presented in this chapter. Also, read and follow the instructions in any literature that accompanies the ladder or scaffolding.

11.2 Brackets, trestles, and pump jacks also can be used for support. Brackets are attached to the structure. Trestles and pump jacks are freestanding and support scaffold planks. Lifelines prevent workers from falling more than 6′. They are attached to the structure and to the worker's harness.

Review Questions

1. If you must place a ladder in front of a door or other opening, what should you do to prevent an accident?
2. Tell how to set up a straight ladder and a stepladder safely.
3. What is the proper angle for a straight ladder to form in relation to its support?
4. Why is it important never to stand on the top step of a ladder?
5. What is a scaffold?
6. What is a duplex-head nail?
7. Compare manufactured metal scaffolding with wood scaffolding.
8. List the main types of brackets.
9. What is a pump jack?
10. What size rope should be used as a lifeline in situations where it will not be subjected to cutting or abrasion?

Scaffolding Ropes and Knots Some scaffolding consists of a platform supported by parallel ropes. According to OSHA, ropes used for scaffolding must be capable of supporting, without failure, six times the maximum intended load. The ropes must be securely attached using wire rope clips or various knots. Two types of knots recommended for scaffolding include the *scaffolding hitch* and a properly made *eye splice.* Hitches are used to fasten one rope to another or to a solid object. Splices are made by separating strands of two different ropes and weaving them together. For safety, knots made in scaffolding rope should be made only by someone trained in the technique.

Unit 3

BUILDING FOUNDATIONS

Careers in Construction

Cement Mason

Construction workers can be divided into three types: structural, finishing, and mechanical. Cement masons are structural workers who place concrete. They may also make concrete beams, columns, and panels.

Cement masons set the forms for holding concrete and align them. They direct the placement of the concrete, level it, and smooth the surface. They may also finish the concrete, or concrete finishers may do that job.

Cement masons must know the characteristics of concrete and understand how weather conditions affect the curing process. By using sight and touch, an experienced cement mason can determine what is happening to the concrete and take steps to prevent defects.

Most cement masons receive their training either on the job as helpers or through apprenticeship programs. Many of them start as construction laborers.

For more information, check the *Occupational Outlook Handbook* or look up "cement mason" on the Internet.

Chapter 12

Concrete As a Building Material

Objectives

After reading this chapter, you'll be able to:

- List the characteristics of concrete that make it a useful construction material.
- List the basic ingredients of concrete.
- List the five basic types of cement.
- Mix a small batch of concrete from a pre-mix.

Terms

admixture
aggregate
hydration
Portland cement
slump test

Made with various ingredients, concrete has been used as a building material for thousands of years. For example, the Romans became quite expert at using it for architecture. Concrete has the following characteristics:

- It has tremendous compressive strength.
- It is resistant to chemicals.
- It will not rot or be damaged by insects.
- It hardens even under water.
- When properly cured, it withstands extreme heat and cold.
- It can be formed into almost any shape.
- It is widely available and fairly inexpensive.

In residential construction, concrete is used primarily as a foundation material. **Fig. 12-1.** This takes advantage of its compressive strength. It is also used for walks, driveways, entry steps, floors, and even kitchen countertops.

SECTION 12.1

Concrete Basics

The strength and usefulness of concrete depend on the quality and type of materials used in the mix. It is made by mixing cement, fine aggregate (a granular material, such as sand), coarse aggregate (usually gravel or crushed stone), and water in the proper proportions. **Fig. 12-2.** When these materials are combined, a chemical reaction causes the concrete to harden. This chemical reaction, called **hydration**, generates heat as the concrete cures (hardens). Builders can alter its characteristics by changing the proportion or type of ingredients or by adding other materials. Its strength is also affected by the curing methods and the curing time.

The fine and coarse aggregates in a concrete mix are its *inert* (inactive) ingredients, while cement and water are the *active* ingredients. The material is not concrete unless all four of these ingredients are present. If only the coarse aggregate is missing, the resulting material is called *mortar* or *grout*.

Fig. 12-1. Concrete being placed into footing forms.

Fig. 12-2. The basic ingredients of concrete.

PORTLAND CEMENT

Roman builders obtained natural cement from pumice (PUH-miss), a mineral deposited on the slopes of volcanoes. When mixed with water it formed a hard, durable substance. The cement used in modern concrete is called **Portland cement**. It is a manufactured substance, not a natural one. It got its name from being similar in color to Portland stone, an English limestone used for constructing buildings. Various types of Portland cement have different strength characteristics.

Manufacturing

Portland cement consists of compounds of lime (calcium oxide) mixed with silica (silicon dioxide) and alumina (aluminum oxide). The lime comes from raw materials such as limestone, chalk, and even coral or shell deposits.

To make Portland cement, the raw materials are crushed and then ground to a powder. They are then mixed in various proportions, based on the desired characteristics of the end product. The mixture is heated in a large kiln (oven) to approximately 2,700°F [1,482°C] or more.

Heating changes the chemical composition of the ingredients and they form small lumps called *clinker*. A small amount of gypsum (no more than 5 percent) is added to the clinker. The mixture is then pounded into the fine powder we call cement.

Basic Types of Cement

There are five basic types of Portland cement. They are standardized in the United States by the American Society for Testing and Materials (ASTM). The basic types of Portland cement are shown in **Table 12-A**.

Specialty Cements

In addition to the five basic types of cement, specialty cements are also available. The following are used in new construction or remodeling.

- *Self-leveling cement* flows like thin syrup. It is often poured over a floor to cover tubes used in radiant heating systems.
- *Hydraulic cement* expands when mixed with water and hardens within minutes. It is used to plug holes and cracks in foundations.
- *Anchor cement* is fast-setting. It is used to secure railings and hardware in holes drilled in a concrete surface. It has a higher compressive strength than standard cement.
- *Resurfacing cement* is used to repair damaged concrete surfaces. Its fine aggregate allows it to be spread in thin layers.

Table 12-A. Basic Types of Portland Cement

Type and Use	Characteristics
Type I (standard) Most general construction purposes	Economical, with a long setting time
Type II (modified) Most general construction purposes	Generates less heat during hydration than Type I Resists breaking down when exposed to sulfates
Type III (high-strength) Used where forms must be removed quickly or concrete must be put in service quickly	Gains strength faster than other types of cement
Type IV (low heat) Used only on very large concrete projects, such as dams	Unusually low heat generated by hydration prevents cracking caused by wide ranges of temperature
Type V (sulfate-resistant) Used where concrete will be exposed to highly alkaline conditions and sulfates	Resists alkalines and sulfates

AGGREGATES

Aggregate is granular material, such as sand, gravel, or crushed stone. Fine aggregate consists of washed sand or other suitable materials up to ¼″ in diameter. Coarse aggregate consists of pea gravel, crushed stone, or other suitable material larger than ¼″ (see Fig. 12-2). Large aggregate pieces used in concrete should be solid. Layered material such as shale must be avoided. All aggregates must be clean and free of dirt, clay, or vegetable matter, which reduces the strength of the concrete.

The size of the aggregate varies, depending on the kind of work for which the concrete is to be used. In walls, the largest pieces of aggregate should not be more than one-fifth the thickness of the finished wall section. For slabs, the pieces should not be more than one-third the thickness of the slab. The largest piece of aggregate should never be larger than three-fourths the width of the narrowest space through which the concrete will be required to pass during pouring.

A large percentage of finished concrete consists of aggregate. For this reason, aggregate quality can have a significant impact on the strength of the concrete. Contaminants, such as dirt and organic material, can generally be removed by washing the aggregate with clean water.

WATER

The water used to mix concrete must be clean and free from oil, alkali, or acid. A good rule to follow is that the water used must be suitable for drinking. Other contaminants must be avoided as well. For example, sugar prevents concrete from hardening. Sugar might accidentally be introduced if ingredients are mixed in a container that was once used for food products.

The ratio of water to cement is an extremely important factor in the strength of concrete. As more water is added, compressive and tensile strength decrease.

HYDRATION

The chemical reaction that occurs when cement is mixed with water is called hydration. The key to mixing and using concrete is to understand hydration. The aggregate and other inert ingredients are thoroughly mixed with the cement first. When the water is added, hydration between the water and the cement begins. This reaction causes the concrete to harden. Anything that slows hydration also slows the hardening process.

Notice the difference between the terms *hydration* and *dehydration*. In dehydration a drying out takes place. This is not what happens when concrete hardens. In fact, concrete hardens just as well under water as in air. This shows that hydration is truly a chemical reaction, not just a drying out of the concrete. Concrete must be kept as moist as possible during the early stages of hydration. Premature drying causes the water content to drop below the amount needed for satisfactory results.

After an initial stage, the hydration process comes to a stop. This dormant (inactive) period is what allows cement trucks to carry mixed concrete to the job site. Dormancy can last several hours, after which the concrete begins to harden.

Moist-Curing

Moist-curing improves the strength of concrete. The surface is kept moist for at least several days after placement, if possible. This can be done by delaying the removal of formwork. It can also be done by covering the concrete with a material that retains moisture or by spraying it lightly with water or with chemicals that slow evaporation.

Concrete gains most of its strength in the 28-day period after being placed. However, it continues to gain strength for many years afterward.

ADMIXTURES

Ingredients called admixtures are sometimes added to concrete. An **admixture** is an ingredient other than cement, aggregate, or water that is added to a concrete mix to change its physical or chemical characteristics. For example, they can make it more workable or increase its strength. They can be added before or during the mixing process. The following are common:

- *Air-entraining admixtures* introduce very tiny bubbles into the concrete. **Fig. 12-3.** The bubbles increase its durability when it is exposed to moisture and frequent freeze/thaw cycles. This is why these admixtures are commonly added to concrete used in cold-weather climates. They also improve the material's workability.
- *Retarding admixtures* make the concrete set up at a slower rate. This is useful in hot weather or when it is difficult to finish placement before the concrete normally sets up.
- *Accelerating admixtures* increase the rate at which concrete gains strength. This can be important if the concrete must be put into service quickly. Calcium chloride is one type of accelerator. It is added to the mixing water in liquid, not powdered, form to avoid problems caused by undissolved material.
- *Water-reducing admixtures* make it possible to reduce the amount of mixing water without reducing the workability of the concrete. This makes the concrete stronger.
- *Super-plasticizing admixtures* generally can do one of two things. They can make the concrete flow very easily, or they can significantly increase its strength.

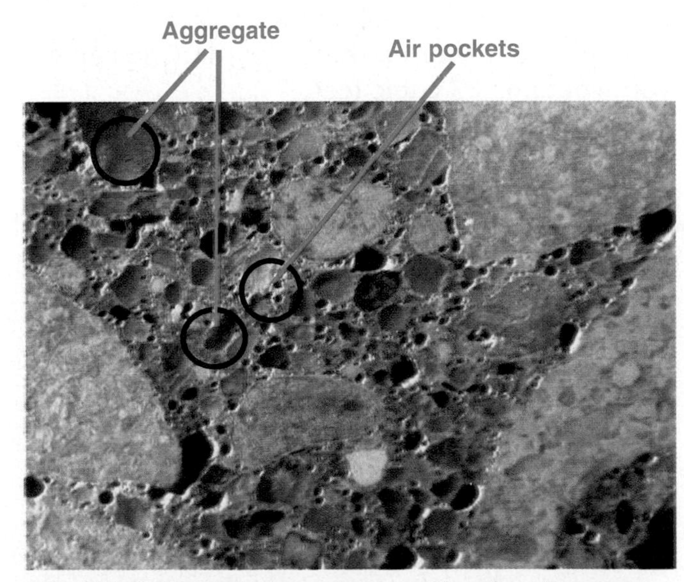

Fig. 12-3. Air-entrained concrete as seen through a microscope.

COLORANTS

Color is sometimes added to concrete that will be used as a finished surface. An alternative method is to place a standard, uncolored layer of concrete and then immediately add a colored layer over it. A third method is to dust powdered colorant over the surface of wet concrete. As the surface is troweled flat and smooth, the colorant is absorbed into the surface.

SECTION 12.1

Check Your Knowledge

1. If a material contains fine aggregate, cement, and water, but not coarse aggregate, what is it called?
2. What is clinker?
3. What is the purpose of using high-strength (Type III) cement?
4. What is an admixture?

On the Job

Use your phone book to locate a local supplier of Portland cement. Contact the company and ask what types of concrete admixtures are most frequently requested in your area. Ask why this might be the case. Present your findings to the class.

SECTION 12.2

Working with Concrete

The word *pour* is often used to describe the process of putting wet concrete into position. However, the term favored by the industry is *place*. For example: "The concrete is *placed* in foundation forms."

Concrete is measured by the cubic yard. Builders often shorten this to "yard." One cubic yard contains 27 cubic feet.

MIXING

Concrete can be mixed on the job from raw materials or bags of pre-mixed dry ingredients. It can also be ordered ready mixed. Strength, durability, watertightness, and wear resistance are controlled by the amount of water in proportion to the amount of cement. The lower the proportion of water, the stronger the cement. However, low levels of water also make the concrete stiffer. This can make it more difficult to place.

Mixing is often done in a wheelbarrow, but any similar container may be used. A *mixing hoe* with holes in the blade is also often used. In general, the dry ingredients are mixed together first. Water is then poured into the dry ingredients to reduce lumps. When mixing concrete by hand, do not add the water all at once, however. Instead, pour in about half and mix it evenly. Then pour in another quarter or so and mix it evenly. Add the remaining water gradually and mix it in. This allows you to judge the consistency of the concrete as you work, reducing the chance that you will add too much water.

Using Pre-Mixed Materials

When small amounts of concrete are needed, the pre-mixed dry ingredients are most often purchased in 60-lb., 80-lb., or 94-lb. sacks. When mixed with water, a 60-lb. sack yields 1 cubic foot of concrete. If the job requires more than

SAFETY FIRST

Protect Your Skin

Because fresh concrete is highly alkaline, it can irritate the skin and eyes. Wear gloves, rubber boots, and eye protection when mixing and placing concrete.

Table 12-B. Proportions for Various Trial Mixes of Concrete

Proportions		Cement Bags(b)	Aggregates Fine (cubic feet)	Aggregates Coarse (cubic feet)
With ¾″ maximum size aggregate	Mixture for 1 bag trial batch(a)	1	2	2¼
	Materials per cu. yd. of concrete	7¾	17 (1,550 lbs.)	19.5 (1,950 lbs.)
With 1″ maximum size aggregate	Mixture for 1 bag trial batch	1	2¼	3
	Materials per cu. yd. of concrete	6¼	15.5 (1,400 lbs.)	21 (2,100 lbs.)
With 1½″ maximum size aggregate (preferred mix)	Mixture for 1 bag trial batch	1	2½	3½
	Materials per cu. yd. of concrete	6	16.5 (1,500 lbs.)	23 (2,300 lbs.)
With 1½″ maximum size aggregate (alternate mix)	Mixture for 1 bag trial batch	1	3	4
	Materials per cu. yd. of concrete	5	16.5 (1,500 lbs.)	22 (2,200 lbs.)

(a) Mix proportions will vary slightly depending on gradation of aggregates. A 10 percent allowance for normal waste has been included in the above figures for fine and coarse aggregate.

(b) One bag of cement equals 1 cu. ft.

twelve sacks of pre-mix, however, it is generally more efficient and less expensive to obtain concrete in other ways.

Because water triggers the hydration process, take care to store sacks of pre-mix under dry conditions. Small amounts of moisture can cause the cement to become lumpy. Lumps that cannot be broken up by squeezing in your hand mean the pre-mix should not be used.

It is best to store the sacks indoors. If this is not possible, they must be covered with a waterproof tarp. Stack the sacks off the ground and arrange them tightly to limit air circulation. Material in sacks that have been stacked for a long time may seem hard. This is called *warehouse pack.* It can be loosened simply by rolling the sack back and forth.

Mixing on Site

It was once common to mix concrete on site, using separate quantities of cement and aggregate. Most builders now rely on ready-mixed concrete, but there are still times when mixing on site is preferable. This might include occasions when sites cannot be reached by a ready-mix truck.

When concrete is mixed on the job site, the quantities of cement and aggregate must be figured separately for each cubic yard needed. **Table 12-B** shows the number of bags of Portland cement and the cubic feet of aggregates required to produce 1 cubic yard (27 cu. ft.) of mixed concrete for several trial mixes. **Tables 12-C** and **12-D** show the amount of water to use in trial mixes.

Table 12-C. Trial Mix Proportions for Sand of Various Moisture Contents

Trial Mix Aggregate Size	Gallons of Water Added to 1-Bag Batch if Sand is: Dry	Damp(a)	Wet(b)	Very Wet(c)	Suggested Mixture for 1-Bag Trial Batches(d): Bags of Cement (cu. ft.)	Aggregates (cu. ft.) Fine	Aggregates (cu. ft.) Coarse
For mild exposure: 1½″ max. size aggregate	7	6¼	5½	4¾	1	3	4
For normal exposure: 1″ max. size aggregate	6	5½	5	4¼	1	2¼	3
For severe exposure: 1″ max. size aggregate	5	4½	4	3½	1	2	2¼

(a) "Damp" describes sand that will fall apart after being squeezed in the palm of the hand.

(b) "Wet" describes sand that will ball in the hand when squeezed but leave no moisture on the palm.

(c) "Very wet" describes sand that has been subjected to a recent rain or been recently pumped.

(d) Mix proportions will vary slightly depending on gradation of aggregates.

Table 12-D. Water Proportions for Mixing Small Batches of Concrete

Size of Batch	Pints of Mixing Water to Add			
	Very wet sand	Wet sand	Damp sand	Dry sand
5 Gal. Water per Whole Sack of Cement				
½ sack	14	16	18	20
¼ sack	7	8	9	10
⅕ sack (18.8 lbs.)	5⅗	6⅖	7⅕	8
⅒ sack (9.4 lbs.)	2⅘	3⅕	3⅗	4
6 Gal. Water per Whole Sack of Cement				
½ sack	17	20	22	24
¼ sack	8½	10	11	12
⅕ sack	6⅘	8	8⅘	9⅗
⅒ sack	3⅖	4	4⅖	4⅘

For accurate proportions, a bottomless *measuring box* may be used. **Fig. 12-4.** This is a frame made of 1″ or 1½″ material with a capacity of 1, 2, 3, or 4 cu. ft. The frame should be marked on the inside to show volume levels, such as 1 cu. ft., 2 cu. ft., or less. Handles on the side of the box make it easier to lift after the material has been measured.

Fig. 12-4. A four-cubic-foot measuring box used for obtaining accurate proportions.

To measure the materials, the box is placed on a mixing platform and filled with the required amount of material. The box is then lifted and the material remains on the platform.

Pails can also be used to proportion materials. For example, a batch of concrete could be measured by using one pail of Portland cement, two pails of sand, and three pails of gravel or crushed stone. (This would be called a *1:2:3 batch.*) Measuring can also be done with shovels or wheelbarrows, depending on the amount required. However, these methods are less precise.

Suggested proportions are shown in Tables 12-B, 12-C, and 12-D. Ingredients should be blended until all materials are uniformly distributed. **Fig. 12-5.**

SAFETY FIRST

Respirator Use

Mixing concrete is a very dusty operation. Be sure to wear a suitable respirator, particularly when mixing the dry ingredients. The respirator should be specifically designed for protection when mixing these ingredients.

Fig. 12-5. A portable drum mixer may be used for mixing concrete on site.

Using Ready-Mix

Most concrete is supplied to job sites by ready-mix plants. Proper amounts of cement and water are poured into the rotating drum of a truck-mounted concrete mixer. The concrete is mixed as the truck travels to the site. At the site, the concrete slides down metal chutes as it is placed into forms. This method is most economical when at least two cubic yards of concrete are ordered. The ready-mix company usually charges a premium for smaller volumes.

Ready-mix concrete is ordered by the number of bags of cement required per cubic yard of concrete. Five-bag mix (that is, five bags per cubic yard) is considered to be the minimum for most work. Where high strength is needed or where steel reinforcement is used, six-bag mix is commonly specified. Another way of ordering ready-mix is by its compressive strength. Building plans often specify compressive strength, such as 2,500 or 3,500 psi. Ingredients are then blended to meet this requirement.

Where concrete will be exposed to moderate or severe weathering, building codes generally require stronger and more durable concrete. Such concrete may be used in sidewalks, exposed basement walls, porch slabs, carport slabs, and garage slabs. Codes may also require that the concrete be air-entrained. This concrete is better able to withstand temperature extremes and the chemicals sometimes used for melting ice and snow.

from Another Angle

In some parts of the country, specialized "short load" concrete companies deliver small loads. Instead of carrying the ingredients already mixed with water, a truck carries the dry ingredients and water in separate tanks. It mixes them in a third tank only after arriving on site.

SLUMP TEST

A **slump test** is a test to measure the consistency of concrete. After the ingredients have been mixed, a slump test can easily be done at the job site or at the ready-mix plant. The test should be done whenever the consistency of the concrete is of critical importance. A slump test is often required in commercial construction and sometimes in residential construction.

In a slump test, concrete straight from the mixer is poured into a small sheet-metal cone of specific dimensions. **Figs. 12-6** and **12-7.** After this concrete has been speared with a rod to remove air pockets, the cone is removed. A measurement is then taken of how much the unsupported mass of concrete slumps, or loses its conical shape. The greater the slump, the wetter the concrete. Concrete used in paving and floor slabs might have a minimum slump of 1″ and a maximum of 4″. Concrete used for columns and walls, on the other hand, might have a slump ranging from 4″ to 8″.

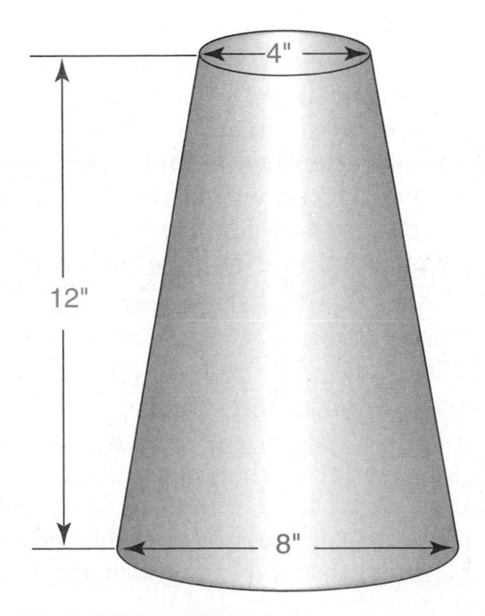

Fig. 12-6. A slump-test cone.

Fig. 12-7. When the cone mold is removed from the concrete, the resulting "slump" can be measured with a ruler.

PLACEMENT

Concrete should be poured continuously whenever possible and kept fairly level throughout the area being poured. To remove air pockets and force the concrete into all parts of the forms, it is vibrated, tamped, or speared with a spade. **Fig. 12-8.**

For concrete to gain full strength, it must cure properly. Rapid drying reduces its strength and may damage the exposed surfaces of sidewalks and drives. If maximum strength is important, the concrete should be covered with a material that will slow its loss of moisture, such as polyethylene sheets, wet burlap, or wet straw.

In hot weather, protect concrete from rapid drying. Keep it moist for several days after pouring. In very cold weather, keep the temperature of the concrete above freezing until it has set. The rate at which concrete sets is affected by temperature, being much slower at 40°F [4°C] and below than at higher temperatures. In cold weather, the use of heated water and heated aggregate during mixing is good practice. In severely cold weather, insulation or heat is necessary until the concrete has set.

Fig. 12-8. Using a vibrator to ensure that air pockets are removed.

Concrete can usually be poured directly from the concrete truck. On a steep or heavily wooded site, however, it is sometimes impossible for the truck to get near enough to deliver the concrete by chute. In such cases, it can be pumped through long, flexible pipes. **Fig. 12-9.** The concrete is poured from the ready-mix truck into the hopper on a pump truck. From there, it is pumped into the forms.

Fig. 12-9. A pump truck can be used to deliver concrete to sites that are difficult to reach.

SECTION 12.2 Check Your Knowledge

1. What four characteristics of concrete are controlled by the amount of water in proportion to the amount of cement?
2. How much concrete does a 60-lb. sack of premix yield when mixed with water?
3. What is the purpose of a slump test?
4. What precaution should be taken when placing concrete in hot weather, and why?

On the Job

For a 1:2:3 batch of concrete, figure:

1. The number of pounds of fine and coarse aggregate needed if there are 300 lbs. of cement.
2. The number of pounds of cement and coarse aggregate needed if there are 400 lbs. of fine aggregate.

SECTION 12.3

Concrete Reinforcement

Both steel and synthetic fibers can be added to concrete to improve its qualities.

REINFORCING STEEL

Concrete has great strength in compression, which means that it can support huge loads placed directly upon it. Steel has excellent *tensile strength*, which is resistance to forces that bend and pull. When steel is embedded in concrete, the resulting material, called *reinforced concrete*, has some characteristics of both materials. Reinforced concrete has excellent compression strength and good tensile strength. Concrete footings, slabs, and walls are nearly always reinforced with steel.

Reinforcing steel can be purchased in the form of bars, called *rebar*, or welded-wire fabric. Rebar has a patterned surface that helps the concrete grip the steel. **Fig. 12-10.** It is used most often in footings and walls, while welded-wire fabric is used mostly in slabs.

Rebar comes in 20′ lengths that can be cut or bent on the job site. A hacksaw or a cutting torch can cut rebar, but a rebar shear makes the job easier. **Fig. 12-11.** The diameter of the rebar needed varies according to the amount of tensile strength needed. **Table 12-E.** Where conditions call for it, corrosion-resistant rebar can be used instead of standard rebar. This might be called for where the concrete would be exposed to salt-spray. This would include sea coast locations.

Fig. 12-11. A rebar shear can be used to cut rebar to length.

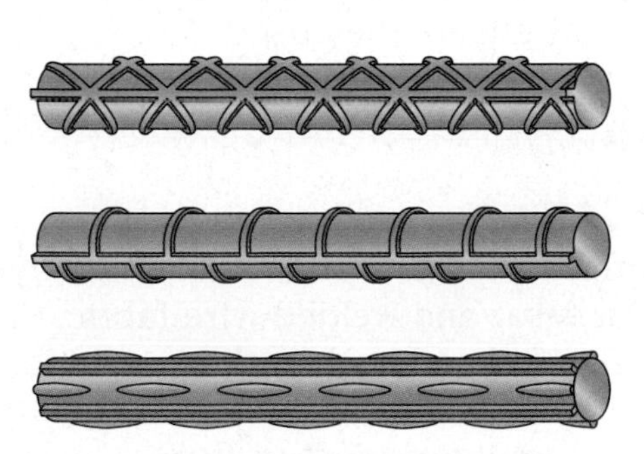

Fig. 12-10. Several types of steel reinforcing bars. The pattern helps the concrete grip the bar.

Table 12-E. Size and Weight of Reinforcing Bars

Bar Number[a]	Bar Diameter (inches)	Approximate Weight of 100 Ft.
2	¼	17
3	⅜	38
4	½	67
5	⅝	104
6	¾	150
7	⅞	204
8	1	267

(a) Bar numbers are multiples of ⅛″.

SAFETY FIRST

Exposed Rebar Ends

In some instances the ends of rebar will protrude from a concrete form. In other instances, rebar will stick out temporarily from an area of concrete that has already been placed. The exposed ends of rebar must always be protected with a cap, shield, or some other device that will prevent accidental impalement injuries.

Welded-wire fabric is really not a fabric. It is an open mesh of wires running perpendicular to each other. **Fig. 12-12.** The most common welded-wire fabric used on a residential job site has wires spaced 6″ apart in two directions. This type is referred to as *6x6 welded-wire reinforcement.* When used to reinforce a slab, the wire is unrolled first. It is then pulled up into the concrete as the slab is being poured. An alternative (and more accurate) technique is to first place the welded-wire fabric on small supports called *wire chairs* that hold it slightly above grade. *Grade* is the height or level of the surrounding soil.

Any steel reinforcement must be covered by enough concrete to be effective. **Table 12-F.** The steel must also be protected from rusting. If the steel reinforcement rusts, the concrete will be damaged.

Table 12-F. Concrete Protection for Reinforcing Steel

Location	Minimum Concrete Protection (inches)
Rebar in footings	3
Rebar in concrete surface exposed to weather	2 for bars larger than No. 5; 1½ for No. 5 bars and smaller
Rebar in slabs and walls	¾
Beams and girders	1½

American Concrete Institute ACI 318, *Building Code Requirements for Reinforced Concrete.*

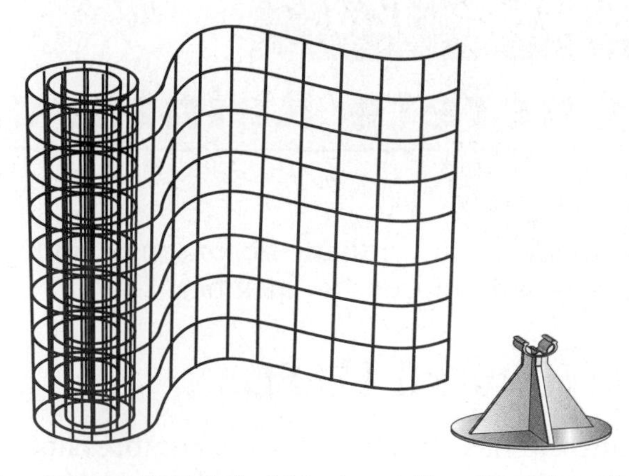

Fig. 12-12. Welded-wire fabric shown with a wire chair used to support such fabric. Such chairs are usually between 2″ and 4″ in height.

FIBER REINFORCEMENT

Short synthetic fibers are sometimes mixed with the concrete to reinforce it. However, the fibers are not a substitute for steel reinforcement. Instead, they help to reduce shrinkage cracking that sometimes occurs as concrete cures. Because fibers also increase concrete's resistance to impact and abrasion, they are most often added to floor slabs.

SECTION 12.3 Check Your Knowledge

1. Why is steel embedded in concrete?
2. What is the purpose of the patterned surface on rebar?
3. Name the two basic types of steel reinforcement. Where are they used?
4. What is the most common size of welded-wire fabric used in residential construction?

On the Job

On the Internet, locate a supplier of equipment used to cut rebar and welded-wire fabric. Can you find any tools other than those mentioned in this section? If so, what type of contractor might find these tools most useful?

Chapter 12

Review

Section Summaries

12.1 One of the most common and important construction materials is concrete. It is made by mixing cement, fine aggregate (usually sand), coarse aggregate (usually gravel or crushed stone), and water in the proper proportions. Concrete hardens through a chemical process called *hydration.*

12.2 The proportion of water to cement in a batch of concrete is extremely important in determining its strength. Concrete can be made on site from pre-mixed dry ingredients or from ingredients bought separately. It can also be ordered ready mixed from a concrete supplier.

12.3 When steel reinforcing is added to concrete, the resulting material combines compressive strength with tensile strength. Reinforcing comes in several forms, including steel rods, welded-wire fabric, and synthetic fibers.

Review Questions

1. List at least four useful characteristics of concrete.
2. What are the four basic ingredients of concrete?
3. What type of cement is most commonly used for concrete in general construction and why?
4. What is hydraulic cement used for?
5. Why is it important for coarse aggregate to be clean?
6. What is hydration?
7. Name three factors that influence the strength of concrete.
8. What safety precautions should be taken when mixing or placing concrete?
9. Name two methods for specifying the strength of ready-mix concrete.
10. What is the purpose of using fiber reinforcement in concrete?

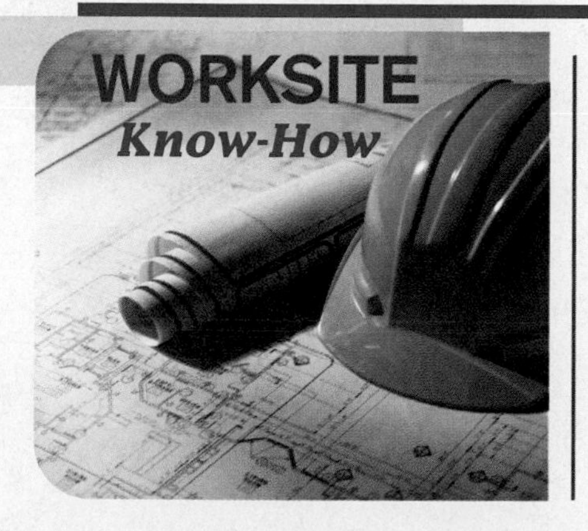

Taking Care of Equipment Responsible employees practice good resource management, such as keeping equipment in good condition. The drivers of concrete delivery trucks sometimes keep bags of sugar on hand. If a truck is prevented from making a delivery, sugar thrown into the mixer prevents the concrete from hardening until the truck can return to its base. The load of concrete is ruined, but at least it doesn't harden inside the mixer and damage it.

Chapter 13

Locating the House on the Building Site

Objectives

After reading this chapter, you'll be able to:

- Establish a simple building layout, working from an existing reference line.
- Identify the basic types of surveying instruments and list their limitations.
- Use a builder's level to lay out a right angle.
- Describe how to set up batter boards.
- Measure a difference in elevation between two points, using a level or transit.
- Estimate the volume of soil excavated for a house foundation.

Terms

batter board
bench mark
plot plan
station mark
theodolite

Before a house can be built, its location on the land must be established with accuracy. The **plot plan** is the part of the house plans that shows the location of the building on the lot, along with related land elevations. The location of the building must then be marked out on the land itself, in a process referred to as *site layout*. This may be done by a surveyor or by a builder familiar with basic surveying methods.

SECTION 13.1

Basic Site Layout

The purpose of site layout is to position the house correctly on the lot. The position of the house on the site must meet local building and zoning codes. Other factors also apply, such as the placement of utilities. The position may have been chosen to take advantage of views, to increase privacy, or to avoid a site feature such as a ledge (area of rock below grade) or a stream. It may also have been chosen to maximize solar heat gain for increased energy efficiency. **Fig. 13-1.**

Two basic methods can accurately determine the location of the proposed building on the property. They include:

- Measuring from an existing reference line.
- Using a surveying instrument such as a level or a transit. **Fig. 13-2.**

Fig. 13-2. Using a transit. Both transits and levels rest on a tripod.

Fig. 13-1. This house uses photovoltaic panels to generate electricity from the sun. The panels are mounted near the ridge of the roof. For them to work efficiently, the house must be placed properly on the lot.

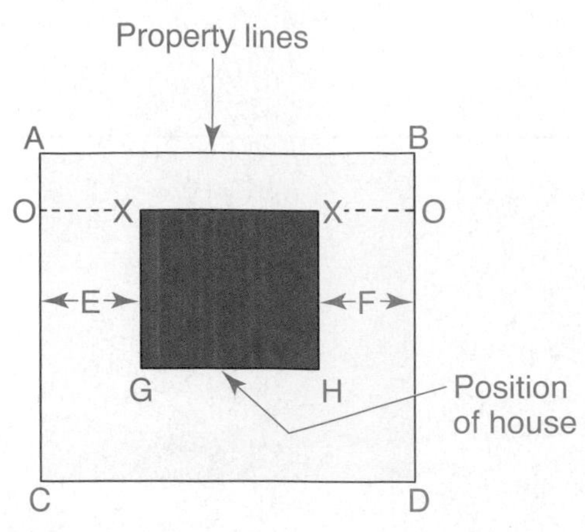

Fig. 13-3. Staking out a rectangular building without the use of a surveying instrument.

MEASURING FROM A REFERENCE LINE

A building or excavation may be planned parallel to an existing line, such as a street or marked property line. Such a line can then be used as a guide, or *reference line.* This makes it possible to stake out the site without using a surveying instrument. When working in this way, it is best to make a drawing of the property first. Such a drawing is shown in **Fig. 13-3.** Rectangle *ABCD* represents the property lines, and boundary *AB* is the reference line.

To stake out the site in the drawing, you would proceed as follows:

1. Check the plot plan to find the setback distance. The *setback distance* is the minimum allowed by local codes between a house and the property lines. Codes also specify setback distances between the house and utility lines, streams, and ponds. Along boundaries *AC* and *BD* measure this distance back from front line *AB.* In the drawing, the setback is shown by segments *AO* and *BO.*
2. Stretch a line tightly between the points marked *O.* The front corners of the building will be located on line *OO.* There are two ways to locate them. You can obtain the measurement from the plot plan to see how far the corners should be from the side boundaries. Then along line *OO* measure the indicated distances in from *AC* and *BD.* Xs represent the front corners of the building in Fig. 13-3. If the building is to be centered between the side boundaries, you need not refer to the plot plan. Instead, subtract the length of the building from the length of *OO.* Then measure half this distance in from each end of *OO.* Measure the distance between the two points marked *X* and check this distance with the plans. The distance *XX* represents the length of the building. It must be accurately measured and match the length on the plans.
3. Check the plans to determine the depth of the building (how far back it will extend from the front corners). Mark off the depth by extending lines back from the two points marked *X.* If the boundary lines of the lot form a 90° angle at the corners, these lines should be parallel to *AC* and *BD.* Note that *E* is the same as *OX,* and *F* is the same as *XO.* Thus *E* and *F* show the distance between sides of the building and the side boundary lines of the lot. Points *G* and *H* represent the rear corners of the building.
4. The boundary lines of the lot may not be at right angles to each other. If this is the case, you will need to first establish the corner of the building that will be closest to a boundary line. Next, make certain that the minimum front and side yard requirements are established from this point. Lay out the building from this point by using the method described on page 223, "Laying Out a Right Angle." Refer also to "Laying Out a Simple Rectangle" on page 224. Establish a line to indicate the rear of the building. This is shown by *GH* in Fig. 13-3.
5. If the building is complicated, divide it into smaller rectangles. Establish more lines such as *OO* to indicate the front of each rectangle. You can get the necessary information from the plans. Then carry out the same steps to establish the rest of each rectangle. The result will be a group of adjoining rectangles that will show the total outline of the building.

USING SURVEYING INSTRUMENTS

When a building cannot be laid out by working from reference lines, the builder or surveyor can use one of several kinds of surveying instruments. These instruments work with either optical or laser technology. Some surveying instruments are based on GPS (global positioning system) technology. Users of *optical instruments* rely on line-of-site observations to determine position. The user must look through the instrument to spot a target or leveling rod held by an assistant. A *leveling rod* is a slender, straight rod marked with graduations in feet and fractions of a foot. It is held in a vertical position during use.

Global positioning system (GPS) instruments are the newest development in surveying systems. The GPS system consists of instruments that receive signals from satellites orbiting the earth. The satellite portion of the system consists of four satellites located in each of six evenly distributed orbits (twenty-four satellites in all). Each satellite transmits unique signals. When a GPS instrument receives several signals, it is able to locate its position on the earth's surface with great accuracy. These systems are much more expensive than optical or laser surveying instruments. They are being used increasingly for construction site layouts.

Laser instruments do not have a telescope. Instead, a highly focused beam of light is aimed at the target. The user does not need to look through the instrument, so an additional person is not required. One person can set up the laser and then move to another portion of the site and determine level by holding an electronic detector against a leveling rod. When the detector senses the reference plane projected by the laser, it signals the user with a light or sound. The disadvantage of a laser instrument is that its light can be difficult to see in bright daylight.

Types of Instruments

The two basic types of surveying instruments commonly used in residential construction are levels and transits. Both sit atop a tripod.

Levels. The telescope of a level is fixed in a horizontal plane. It can be used only for measuring horizontal angles because it cannot be tilted up and down. It can only be turned from side to side. This is sufficient, however, for most building layouts. There are three types of levels.

A *builder's level*, sometimes called a *dumpy level*, is the least expensive surveying instrument. **Fig. 13-4.** It must be set up carefully to ensure accurate results. A good quality model is usually accurate to within ±¼″ at a distance of 75″.

An *automatic level* automatically adjusts for variations in setup. **Fig. 13-5.** It takes less time and effort to set up than a builder's level. It is also more accurate, usually to ±¼″ at 100′. Some are accurate to ±1/16″ at 200′.

A *laser level* does not have a telescope. **Fig. 13-6.** Some use an audible sound to signal a certain level point. It projects its intense beam of light along a horizontal plane. The light shows up as a small red dot at great distances. Some models continually rotate atop the tripod. They project what appears to be a solid, level line around the job site. Other laser levels can be rotated, as needed, using a remote control.

Fig. 13-4. A builder's level.

Fig. 13-5. An automatic level.

Fig. 13-6. A laser level allows measurements to be taken by one person.

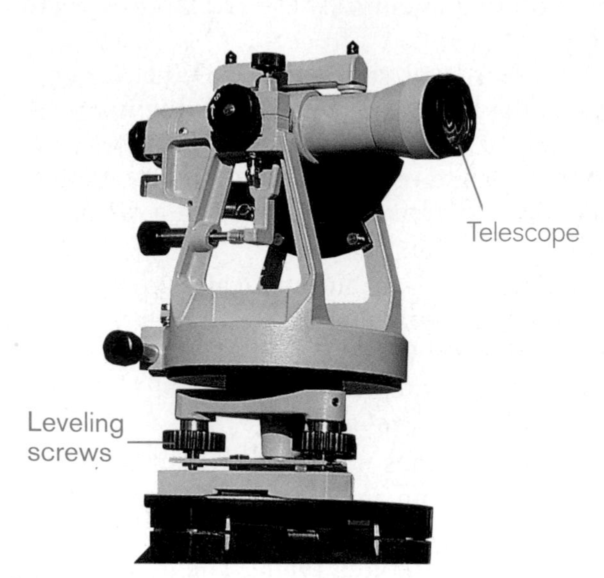

Fig. 13-7. A transit.

Transits. The transit is sometimes called a transit level. Fig. 13-7. Unlike the telescope of a level, the telescope of the transit can be moved up and down as well as from side to side. Because of this, a transit can do everything a level can do, and more. It can measure vertical angles. It can also be used to determine if a post or wall is plumb.

A transit is classified by the smallest increment that can be read on its vernier scale. (A *vernier scale* slides along a longer scale.) The graduations on this vernier scale are in minutes or seconds. A transit may be referred to as a five-minute transit, a one-minute transit, or a twenty-second transit. Measurements made in seconds are more accurate.

A **theodolite** is a transit that reads horizontal and vertical angles electronically. It needs no vernier scale. **Fig. 13-8.** It displays the measurements on an LCD (liquid-crystal display) screen. It is used when extremely accurate measurements are required. A device called an *electronic field book* can be attached to a theodolite to store information. The theodolite is easy to set up.

Basic Layout with a Level or Transit

Most of the basic layouts described on the following pages can be made with a level. All of them can be made using a transit. The same concepts apply to the use of other surveying instruments, although layout methods will differ.

Fig. 13-8. This surveyor is entering information into a theodolite, or electronic transit.

Locating a Bench Mark. To lay out a building using a transit or a level, you must have a basic starting point. This starting point from which measurements can be made is usually called the bench mark, or point of reference (POR).

A bench mark may be a mark on the foundation of a nearby building. More often it is a stone or concrete marker in the ground at a certain location. The location of the bench mark may appear on the architect's drawings. If so, the plans will usually be oriented to that point.

Setting Up a Transit or Level. Set up the transit or level in a position outside the expected flow of activities on a job site. Fig. 13-9. This will prevent it from being accidentally disturbed.

Fig. 13-9. Laying out a building site with a level outside the general work area.

The point over which the level is directly centered is called the **station mark**. The layout is sighted (or shot) from this point. The station mark may be a bench mark or a corner of the lot, but it should be where the area can be conveniently sighted. (If the bench mark and the station mark are not the same, be sure you can sight the bench mark easily.)

A hook is located under the head of the instrument. A plumb bob suspended from this hook is used to center the level or transit directly over the station mark. Adjust the tripod so that it rests firmly on the ground, with the telescope at eye level.

Level the head of the instrument as follows:

1. Refer to **Fig. 13-10**. Loosen the horizontal clamp screw and turn the telescope until the bubble is in line with one set of opposing leveling screws. Grip the screws, one in each hand, using a thumb and forefinger. Loosen one screw as you tighten the other to center the bubble. Keep the screws snug on the foot plate but do not overtighten them. Continue to adjust the screws until the bubble is centered.
2. Rotate the telescope 90° so that it is over the second set of leveling screws and repeat the process in step 1.
3. Return the telescope to the first position. Check the bubble to be sure it is centered, and readjust if necessary. Recheck the second position.
4. Continue to check the bubble in both positions until it is within one graduation on either side of center in the bubble tube.

Once a level or transit has been properly set up, be careful not to move or jar the tripod. If this occurs, the instrument must be readjusted. Some or all of the sightings may have to be redone.

Establishing Points along a Line. To establish points along a line, you must use a transit. Use the plumb bob to center the transit accurately over one point on the line. Then level the instrument. Sight the telescope on the most distant visible point along the same line. Lock the horizontal clamp screw to hold the telescope in position. Then adjust the instrument to place the vertical crosshair exactly over the distant point. Now, by tipping the telescope up or down, you can determine the exact location of any number of points on the line. Fig. 13-11.

Laying Out a Right Angle. Using a plumb bob, set up the level or a transit directly over the point where the right angle is to be located. This is shown as point A in Fig. 13-12. Sight a reference point along a base line and set the 360° scale at zero. In Fig. 13-12 this is point B, and the base line is AB. Turn the telescope until the scale indicates that an arc of 90° has been completed.

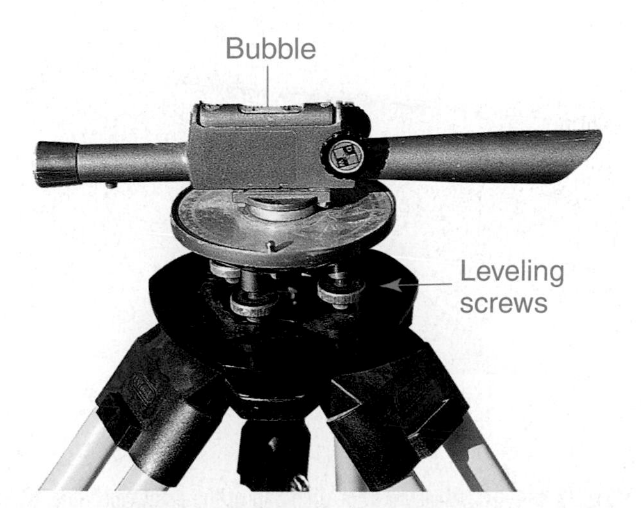

Fig. 13-10. The level of the head of the instrument can be adjusted by using the leveling screws and checking the bubble.

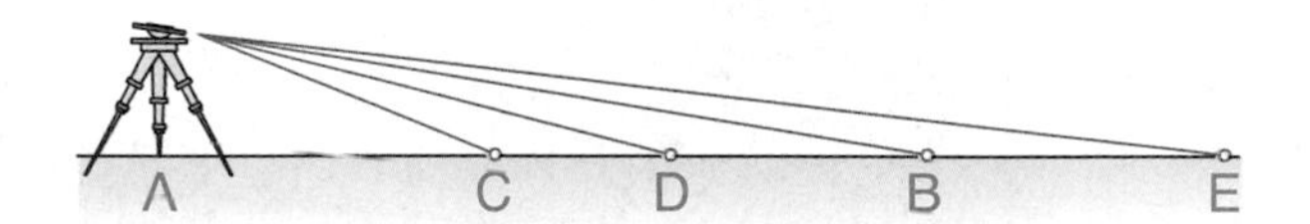

Fig. 13-11. Establishing points on a line with a transit.

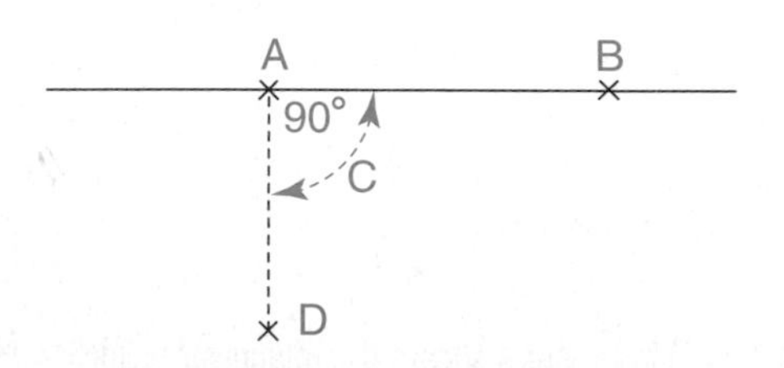

Fig. 13-12. Laying out a right angle with a transit or a level.

Place a leveling rod (**Fig. 13-13**) in a vertical position along this second line at the desired distance. This is shown as point *D* in Fig. 13-12. A line drawn from point *A* to point *D* will be perpendicular to the base line. Thus a right angle is formed where the lines intersect at point *A*.

For accurate work, a *spirit level* (*carpenter's level*) may be attached to the leveling rod to check if the rod is being held plumb. The rod can also be kept plumb by aligning it with the vertical crosshair in the telescope. The person at the telescope can tell the rod holder which way to move the top of the rod. An assistant should hold the leveling rod and move the target on the rod up or down until the crossline on the target aligns with the crosshair sights in the telescope.

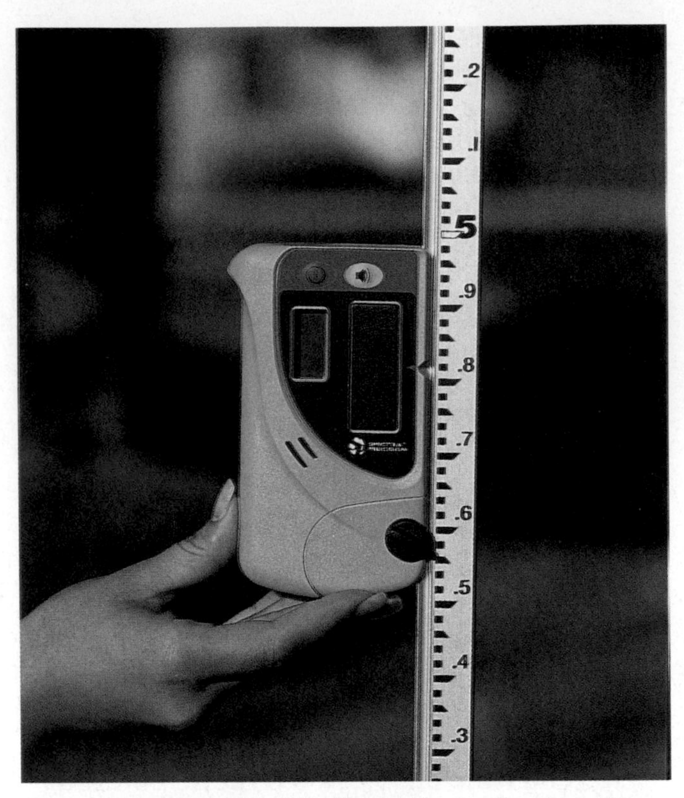

Fig. 13-13. An engineer's leveling rod. The target on the leveling rod can be moved up or down by releasing the clamp on the back of the target. The rod is divided into whole feet, tenths, and hundredths of a foot.

Laying Out a Simple Rectangle. To perform this operation you must work from an existing line such as a road, street, or property line. In Fig. 13-14A, this reference line is shown as AB. Locate the point (C) that represents the side limit for a front corner of the building. Set up the level or transit at point C. Lay out a simple rectangle parallel to the existing line as follows:

1. Set the telescope at point *C* to sight down line *AB*.
2. Measure from point *C* to establish point *D*. This dimension will be found on the building plans. It represents the width of the building.
3. Turn the telescope 90° and establish points *E* and *G* by measurement.
4. Move the level or transit to point *D* and sight through the telescope to point *C*.
5. Turn the telescope 90° and establish points *F* and *H* by measurement.

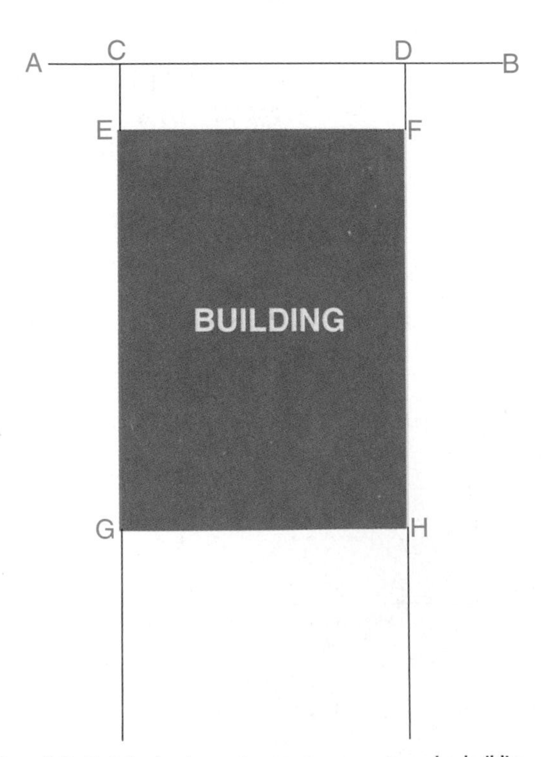

Fig. 13-14A. Laying out a square or rectangular building with a level or transit.

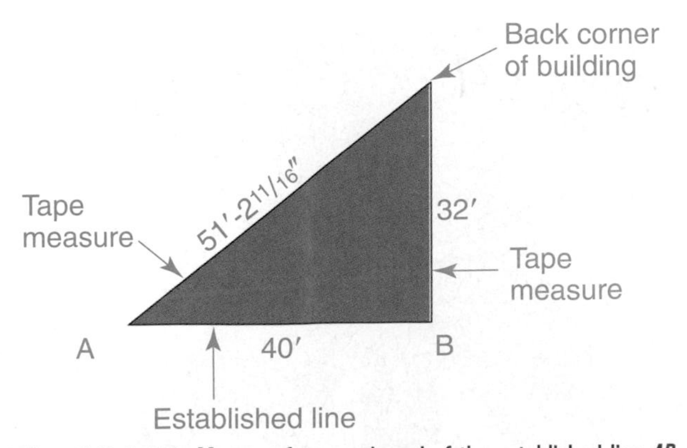

Fig. 13-14B. Measure from each end of the established line *AB*. The back corner will be where the diagonal measurement (51′-2 11/16″) and the end measurement (32′) intersect.

6. Points *E* and *F* represent the front corners of the building. To check your accuracy, measure lines *EF* and *GH*. They should be the same length. Check the layout for square by measuring diagonally from point *E* to point *H*, and from point *F* to point *G*. If these two measurements are identical, the layout is square.

Another method of laying out a rectangular project is to figure the diagonal of the rectangle. **Fig. 13-14B.** After one side of the project is established (*AB*), usually the front setback line, the rectangle can be laid out accurately by using two long tape measures. The side and end measurements are input as rise and run into a construction calculator, and the diagonal of the rectangle is figured automatically. Using one tape measure, simply measure the desired distance from one end of line *AB*. Then, with a second tape measure, measure the diagonal. The lines will intersect precisely at one of the corners. Do this from both ends of the established line and a perfect rectangle is established. The example in Fig. 13-14B shows a house that is 40′ long and 32′ deep. It has a diagonal of 51′-2¹⁄₁₆″.

Laying Out an Irregularly Shaped Building. The outline of the building may be other than a rectangle. However, the process for establishing each point is basically the same. More points must be located, and the final check is more likely to reveal a small error.

When the building is not regular in shape, it is usually best to start by laying out a large rectangle that will take in all or most of the building. This is shown in **Fig. 13-15** as *QHOP*. After the large rectangle is established, the remaining portion of the layout will consist of small rectangles. Each small rectangle can be laid out and proved separately. In Fig. 13-15, these rectangles are shown as *NMLP*, *ABCQ*, *DGFE*, and *JIOK*.

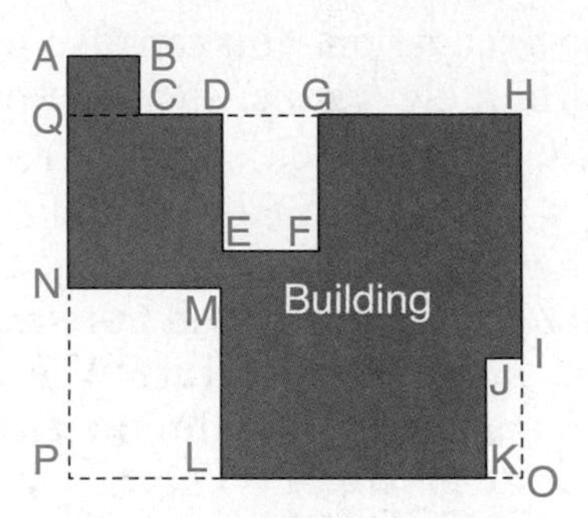

Fig. 13-15. Laying out an irregularly shaped building made of a series of squares and rectangles.

SECTION 13.1

Check Your Knowledge

1. What is a plot plan?
2. Name one advantage and one disadvantage of surveying instruments based on laser technology.
3. What is the difference between a level and a transit?
4. What is the purpose of the hook under a level or transit?

On the Job

Conduct a demonstration for your class on how to lay out a simple rectangle. Use sketches and other tools to illustrate your points.

SECTION 13.2

Establishing Lines and Grades

After its location and alignment have been determined, a rectangle showing the outer dimensions of the structure is staked out. If the building is to form a simple rectangle, the staked-out area will follow the foundation line exactly.

GRADE

The *grade* refers to the level of the ground where it will meet the foundation of the completed building. The grade is found on the building plans. It must be established accurately because it is used for making important measurements. From the grade you can find the depth of the excavation. You can also use it to establish certain elevations, such as floor and foundation levels.

Sometimes the bench mark is used as a reference point for establishing the grade. At other times the grade may be located in relation to the level of an existing street or curb. The grade is indicated on a stake driven into the ground outside the excavation area.

BATTER BOARDS

After the grade and the corners of the house have been established, building lines must be laid out as aids in keeping the work level and true. A **batter board** is a board fastened horizontally to stakes placed to the outside of where the corners of the building will be located. These boards and string tied between them locate and mark the outline of the building. **Fig. 13-16.** The height of the boards is sometimes the height of the foundation wall.

Before setting up batter boards, locate the corners of the building precisely by one of the methods already discussed. Drive nails into the tops of the stakes that indicate the outside edge of the foundation walls.

To be certain that the corners are square, measure the diagonals of the completed layout to see if they are the same length. The corners can also be squared by using the 3-4-5 method. **Fig. 13-17.** This is done by measuring a distance along one side in 3′ increments, such as 6, 9, or 12. Then measure along the adjoining side in the same number of 4′ increments (8, 12, or 16). The diagonal drawn between the end points will then measure in an equal number of 5′ units (10, 15, or 20) when the unit is square.

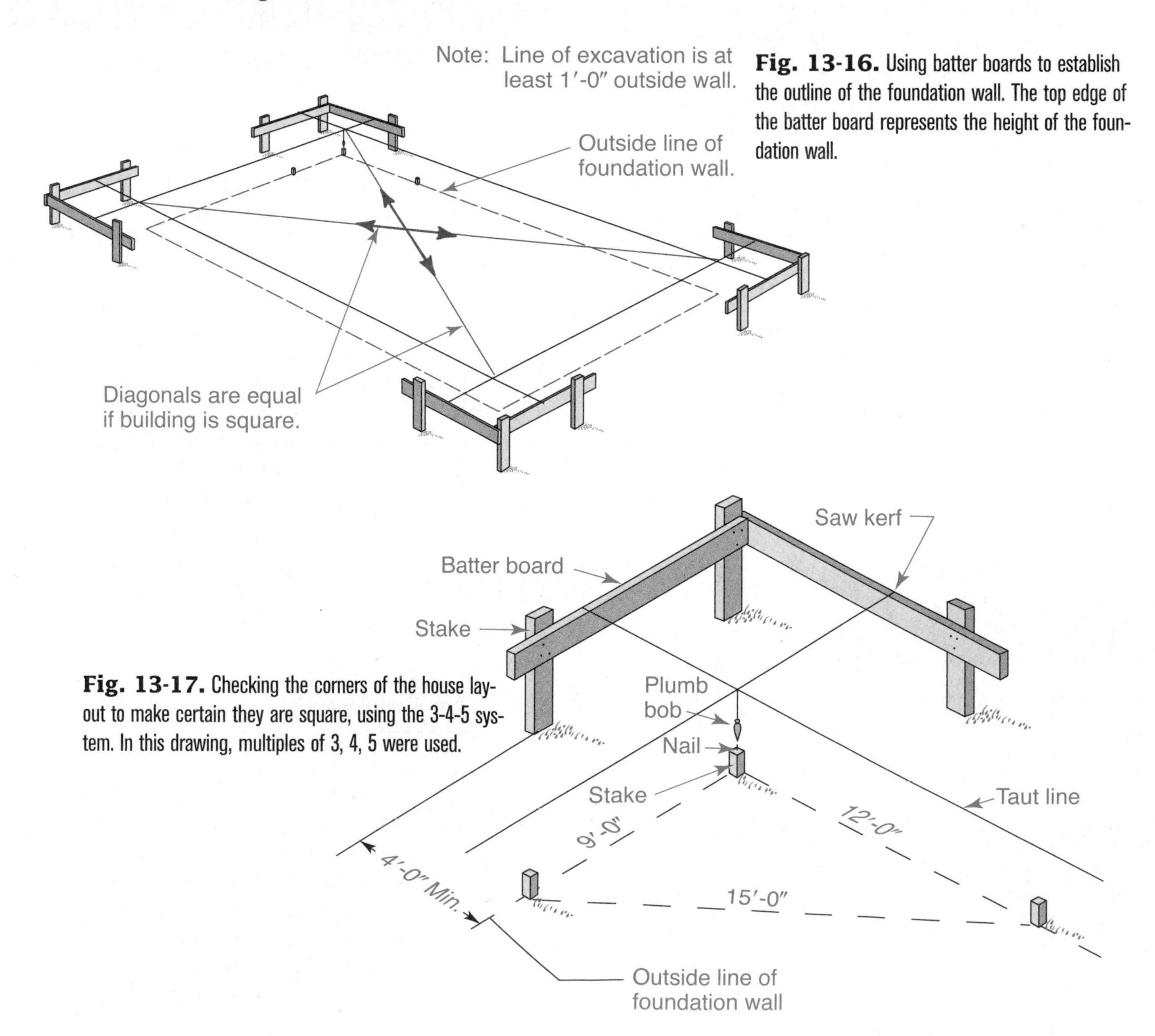

Fig. 13-16. Using batter boards to establish the outline of the foundation wall. The top edge of the batter board represents the height of the foundation wall.

Fig. 13-17. Checking the corners of the house layout to make certain they are square, using the 3-4-5 system. In this drawing, multiples of 3, 4, 5 were used.

Thus a 9′ distance on one side and a 12′ distance on the other should result in a 15′ diagonal measurement if the corner is a true 90°.

Setting up batter boards is explained in the Step-By-Step feature on this page.

LAND ELEVATIONS

Check the architect's plan to see where elevations are to be determined. Set up a level or transit. Be certain that the locations can be seen through the telescope. Place a leveling rod upright on any location to be checked. Then sight through the telescope at the leveling rod. Take a reading of where the horizontal crosshair in the telescope crosses the rod. Then move the rod to the second location to be established. Raise or lower the rod until the reading is the same as for the first point. The bottom of the rod is then at the same elevation as the original point.

Measuring a Difference in Elevation

To learn the difference in elevation between two points, such as *A* and *B* in **Fig. 13-18**, set up a transit or level at an intermediate point. With the measuring rod held at point *A*, note the mark where the horizontal crosshair in the telescope crosses the rod. Then with the rod held at point *B*, sight the rod and note the point where the horizontal crosshair crosses the rod. In our example, the difference between the reading at *A* (5′) and the reading at *B* (5′ 6″) is the differ-

Fig. 13-18. Obtaining the difference in elevation between two points that are visible from an intermediate point.

STEP BY STEP

Setting Up Batter Boards

Refer to Fig. 13-16. After the corners of the building have been located, set up the batter boards as follows:

Step 1 Drive three 2x4 stakes at each corner of the building, at least 4′ beyond the foundation lines.

Step 2 Nail 1x6 or 1x8 boards to the stakes horizontally. The top of each board must be level. All boards must be level with each other. Use a level or transit to locate the height of the boards.

Step 3 Stretch string across the tops of boards at opposite corners and align it exactly over the nails in the corner stakes. A plumb bob is handy for setting the lines.

Step 4 Make a shallow saw kerf where the string overlaps the boards. This will keep the string from sliding. It will also make it easy to reposition the string if it must be temporarily removed to let equipment or machinery pass. Make similar cuts in all eight batter boards.

Step 5 Tie the string to the boards, using the saw kerfs to position it (see Fig. 13-17). This establishes the lines of the house.

Step 6 Check the diagonals again to make sure the corners are square. (The area for an L-shaped building can be divided into rectangles and the diagonal measurement of each rectangle checked.)

ence in elevation between *A* and *B*. Thus the ground at point *B* is 6″ lower than the ground at point *A*.

Sometimes it is not possible to sight two points from a single point between them. A high mound can cause this difficulty. To solve this problem, one or more additional intermediate points, such as *C* and *D* shown in **Fig. 13-19**, must be used for setting up the instrument. The process of determining differences in elevation between points that are remote from each other is called *differential leveling.*

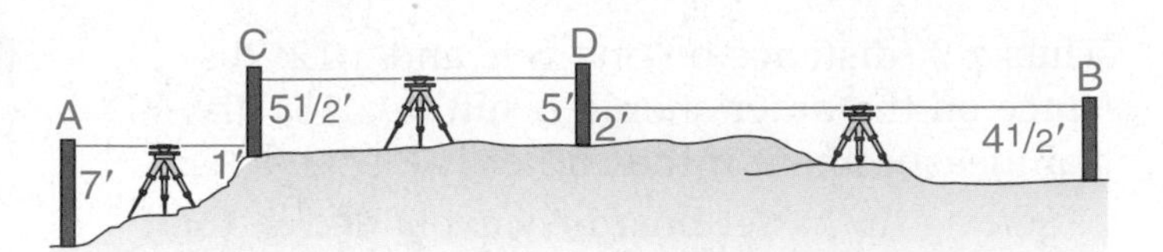

Fig. 13-19. Obtaining the difference in elevation between two points not visible from a single intermediate point.

FOUNDATION WALL HEIGHT

The proposed height of the foundation walls above grade determines how deep the excavation must be. The excavation is dug to a depth that will give the foundation walls the correct height above grade. To determine this depth, it is common practice to use the highest point on the perimeter of the excavation as the reference point. **Fig. 13-20.** This is true for both graded and ungraded sites. Good drainage is ensured if sufficient foundation height is allowed for the sloping of the finished grade. **Fig. 13-21.** *Finished grade* is the level of the ground when grading is completed. Foundation walls at least 7′-4″ high are necessary for full basements, and 8′ walls are common.

The top of the foundation wall must be at or above a minimum height set by code. This distance is often at least 8″ above the finished grade, but this may vary with local code. This allows the siding and framing members to be protected from soil moisture and places them well above the grass line. In termite-infested areas, this also makes it possible to observe signs of any termite activity between the soil and the wood. Protective measures can then be taken before the wood is damaged.

Crawl spaces should have enough height to permit inspections for termites and to allow plastic soil covers to be installed. *Soil covers* reduce the effect of ground moisture on framing members. Ordinarily there should be at least 18″ between the undersides of the joists and the highest point of ground enclosed by the foundation walls.

If the ground beneath the structure is excavated or is otherwise lower than the outside finished grade, measures must be taken to assure good drainage. The finished grade should always slope away from the house. Fig. 13-21. Below-surface drainage systems might also be required.

THE EXCAVATION

Any variation from standard construction practices increases the cost of the foundation and footings. This might influence the design of the house. Before excavating for a new home, subsoil conditions should be determined by test

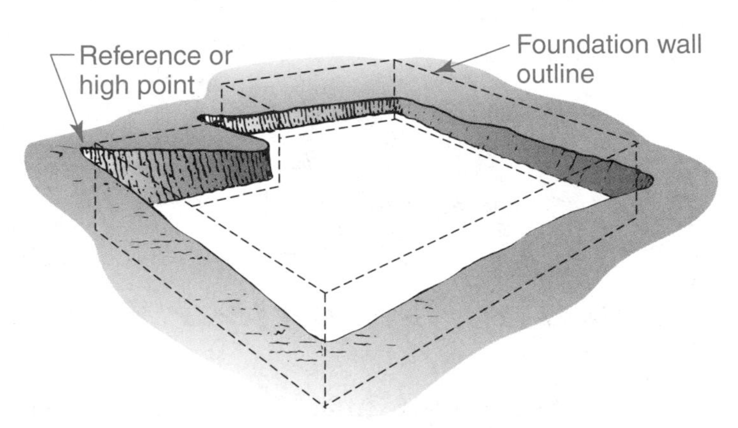

Fig. 13-20. To establish the depth of the excavation, use the highest point around the excavation as the reference point.

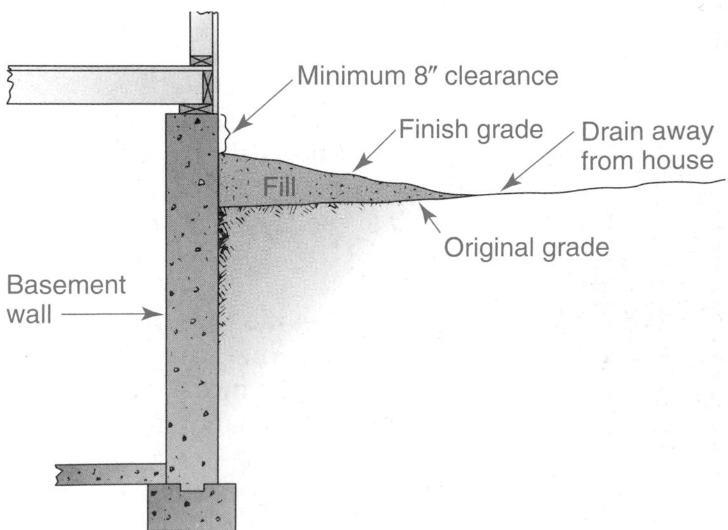

Fig. 13-21. Added fill brings the finish grade above the original grade and ensures drainage away from the house.

borings or by checking foundations used for existing houses near the site. A rock ledge may require costly removal. A high water table may require design changes from a full basement to a crawl space or concrete slab construction. If there has been a previous excavation on the site, the soil may have been disturbed and may not have sufficient bearing strength for footings. (*Footings* are sections of concrete that support a foundation wall.)

Several types of earth-moving equipment, such as a power shovel or backhoe, can be used for basement excavations. Topsoil is often stockpiled by a bulldozer, a front-end loader, or a grader for future use. **Fig. 13-22.** Power trenchers are often used in excavating slab footings or shallow foundation walls.

It is best to excavate only to the top of the footings or the bottom of the basement floor. The soil must be stable enough to prevent cave-ins, and some soil becomes soft upon exposure to air or water. Thus, unless form boards are to be used, it is advisable not to make the final excavation for footings until nearly time to pour the concrete.

The excavation must be wide enough to provide space to work. For example, there must be enough room to install and remove concrete forms, to lay up block, to waterproof the exterior surfaces of the walls, and to install foundation drainage. The steepness of the back slope of the excavation is determined by the type of subsoil. **Fig. 13-24** on page 232. Follow OSHA regulations.

SAFETY FIRST

Utility Lines

Utility lines that are accidentally severed can pose a serious risk to workers. Before excavating, contact the local utility companies for information about the location of sewer, telephone, fuel, electric, water, or cable lines that may cross the area. Locations should then be marked.

Fig. 13-22. A grader being used to strip the topsoil from a building site in preparation for excavating the basement.

Estimating...

Excavation Volume

Excavation costs are based on the total cubic yards of earth to be removed. To determine the volume of material, multiply the length of the excavation times the width times the depth. Calculating is usually done in decimals. **Table 13-A.**

Step 1 For the house shown in **Fig. 13-23**, multiply 7′ (depth of excavation) times 30′ (26′ width of house plus 2′ clearance at each end, between the excavation and the outside of the foundation wall) times 44′ (40′ length of house plus 2′ clearance at each end). The answer is 9,240 cubic feet.

Step 2 There are 27 cubic feet in 1 cubic yard. To convert cubic feet to cubic yards, divide by 27:

$$9{,}240 \div 27 = 342.2$$

Rounded off, approximately 342 cubic yards of material will have to be excavated.

Table 13-A. Converting Inches to Decimal Fractions of a Foot

Inches	Feet
1	0.083
2	0.167
3	0.250
4	0.333
5	0.417
6	0.500
7	0.583
8	0.667
9	0.750
10	0.833
11	0.916
12	1.000

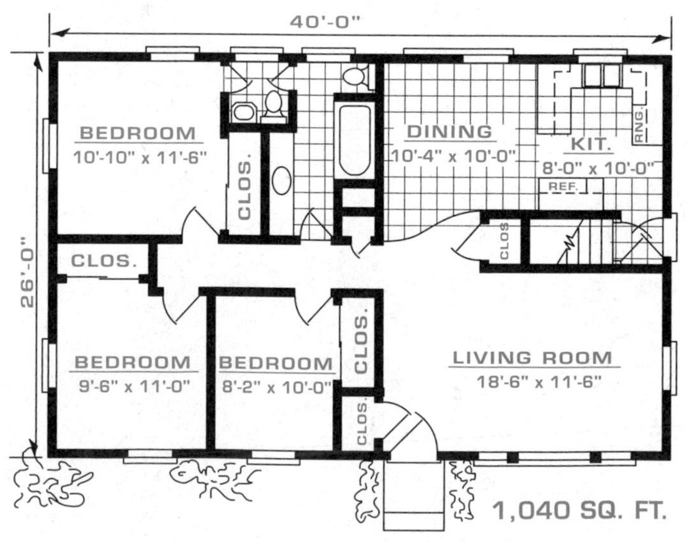

Fig. 13-23. With a 7′ deep excavation, the basement for this house will require the removal of 342 cubic yards of material.

(Continued)

Estimating...

(continued)

Table 13-B provides another way of determining the cubic yards of material to be removed. It can be used if the excavation depth is a standard one shown on the table.

Step 1 Refer again to Fig. 13-23. The excavation needed for this house is 30′ wide, 44′ long, and 7′ deep. Multiply the width by the length to find the area of the excavation, which is 1,320 square feet.

Step 2 Refer to Table 13-B. For an excavation 7′ deep, 0.259 cubic yards of material are removed for each square foot of area. Multiply 1,320 by 0.259 to find that 341.88 cubic yards of material will be removed. This is rounded off to 342 cubic yards.

TRENCHES

The amount of material removed from trenches, such as those that might be dug for utilities, can be figured by using **Table 13-C**. For example, if a trench is to be 42″ deep and 18″ wide, Table 13-C shows that 19.4 cubic yards of material will be removed for every 100 lineal feet. Such a trench might be dug for a house with a 30′ setback. To determine how much material would be removed, multiply 19.4 by 0.30 (because 30′ is about 0.30 of 100′). The answer is that 5.82 cubic yards of material would be removed.

ESTIMATING ON THE JOB

Using Table 13-B, estimate the cubic yards removed from an excavation that measures 33′ wide by 44′ long by 8′-6″ deep. Round off your answer.

Table 13-B. Excavation Factors for Standard Depths

Depth per Square Foot	Cubic Yards Removed	Depth per Square Foot	Cubic Yards Removed
2″	0.006	4′-6″	0.167
4″	0.012	5′-0″	0.185
6″	0.018	5′-6″	0.204
8″	0.025	6′-0″	0.222
10″	0.031	6′-6″	0.241
1′-0″	0.037	7′-0″	0.259
1′-6″	0.056	7′-6″	0.278
2′-0″	0.074	8′-0″	0.298
2′-6″	0.093	8′-6″	0.314
3′-0″	0.111	9′-0″	0.332
3′-6″	0.130	9′-6″	0.350
4′-0″	0.148	10′-0″	0.369

Note: To find the factor, first locate the excavation depth. The factor is in the column to the right.

(Continued)

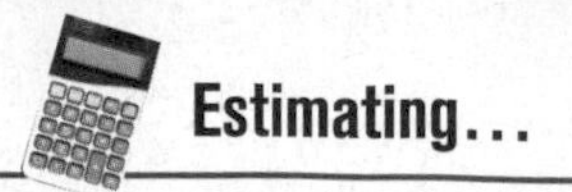

Estimating...

(continued)

Table 13-C. Cubic Yard Content of Trenches per 100 Lineal Feet

Depth in Inches	Trench Width in Inches						
	12	18	24	30	36	42	48
6	1.9	2.8	3.7	4.6	5.6	6.6	7.4
12	3.7	5.6	7.4	9.3	11.1	13.0	14.8
18	5.6	8.3	11.1	13.9	16.7	19.4	22.3
24	7.4	11.1	14.8	18.5	22.2	26.0	29.6
30	9.3	13.8	18.5	23.2	27.8	32.4	37.0
36	11.1	16.6	22.2	27.8	33.3	38.9	44.5
42	13.0	19.4	25.9	32.4	38.9	45.4	52.0
48	14.8	22.2	29.6	37.0	44.5	52.0	59.2
54	16.7	25.0	33.3	41.6	50.0	58.4	66.7
60	18.6	27.8	37.0	46.3	55.5	64.9	74.1

When excavating for basements, some contractors rough-stake only the outline of the building to indicate where earth must be removed. When the proper elevation has been achieved for the basement floor, the footings are laid out and the final excavation dug. After the concrete has been placed and has hardened, the building wall outline is established on the footings and marked to indicate the position of the formwork or concrete block wall.

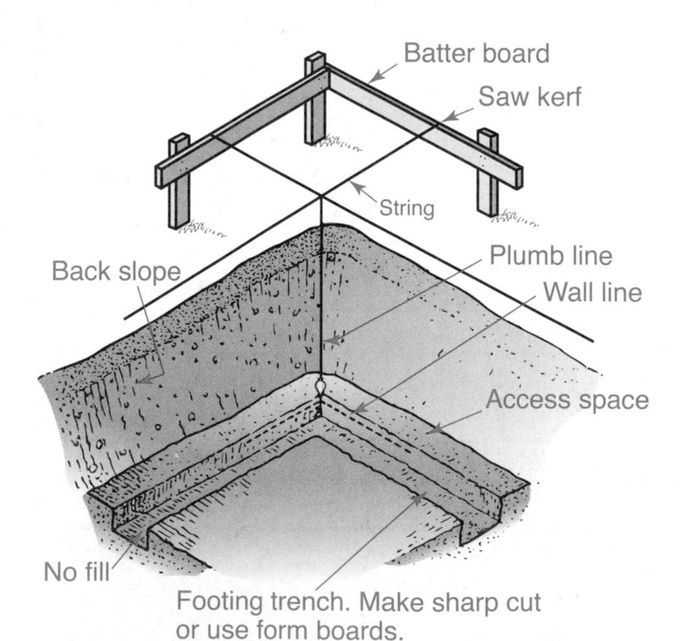

Fig. 13-24. The basement excavation is back-sloped to prevent cave-ins. Note the use of the plumb line for accurately locating the foundation wall line.

SAFETY FIRST

Escape Routes

Any excavation or trench that is more than 4′ deep must be provided with a stairway, ladder, ramp, or other safe means of escape. This includes foundation excavations. The escape devices must be within 25′ of a worker.

SECTION 13.2 Check Your Knowledge

1. Name three possible reference points for establishing a grade.
2. What is a batter board and what is its purpose?
3. Briefly describe the process of identifying two points at the same elevation when using a level or transit.
4. Why is the excavation for a basement somewhat larger than the outside dimensions of the foundation wall?

On the Job

An excavation 5′ deep is needed to build a house that is to be 26′ by 32′.

1. How many cubic yards of material should be removed if a 2′ clearance is needed outside the foundation walls?
2. How much more material must be removed if the builder requires 4′ of clearance?

Chapter 13 Review

Section Summaries

13.1 A house can be positioned on a piece of property either by measuring from an established reference line or by using an instrument such as a level or a transit. Most layouts begin at a bench mark. Surveying instruments include levels and transits. The point at which they are set up is called the station mark.

13.2 String stretched between batter boards is used to establish the outline of a house. Once this has been done, the excavation can proceed. The excavation must be wide enough to provide space to work. Soil taken from an excavation is measured in cubic yards.

Review Questions

1. Name and briefly describe the three basic types of levels.
2. Name three tasks that a transit can perform that a builder's level cannot.
3. What is the difference between a bench mark and a station mark?
4. Briefly describe how to lay out a right angle from a given point, using a level or transit.
5. What is the first thing to be done when laying out from an existing reference line?
6. What device is hung over the point for a right angle?
7. What is the general strategy for laying out an irregularly shaped building?
8. When measuring the difference in elevation between two points, where is the transit or level placed?
9. What must be done before batter boards can be set up?
10. How many cubic yards of soil are in an excavation that measures 23′ x 38′ x 8′ with a 2′ clearance on all sides?

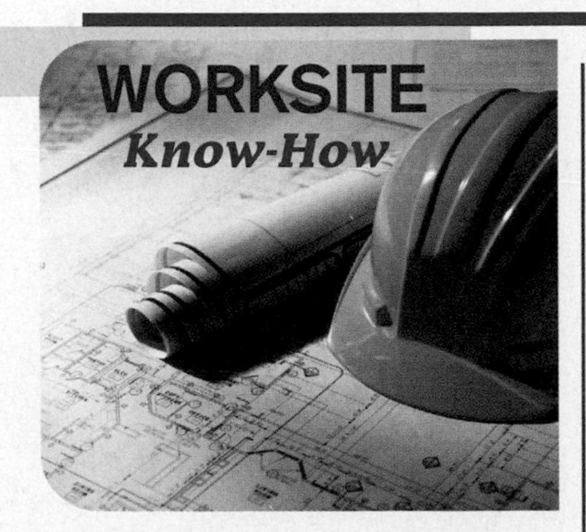

Who Does What? Surveyors, field engineers, and carpenters are all essential to preparation and site layout. Surveyors establish the boundaries for a lot, record their results, and verify the accuracy of the data. They also locate the building on the site, measuring distances, directions, and elevations. Field engineers are present on commercial construction projects to supervise the work. They oversee the connection to water supply and sewage systems, as well as links to roadways. They work with architects to ensure that the building meets code requirements for loads and unusual stresses. Carpenters can then use the site and building plans to lay out and create foundation formwork, as needed.

Chapter

14

Foundation Walls

Objectives

After reading this chapter, you'll be able to:

- Explain the purpose of footings.
- Tell how solid foundation walls are formed and poured.
- Describe the process of laying a concrete block foundation.

Terms

bed joint
cold joint
control joint
footing
form
head joint
parging
radon
story pole
wale

A foundation anchors a house to the earth and provides a solid, level base for the framing. It carries all the loads of the house and transmits them to the ground. Most houses are built either on foundation walls or on a foundation slab.

Most foundation walls are made of concrete or masonry units. However, in some areas foundation walls are made entirely of pressure-treated plywood, pressure-treated lumber, or precast concrete panels.

The overall heights of foundation walls also vary. The top of any foundation wall supporting a house having wood siding must be at least 6″ above finished grade. Walls tall enough to create a basement are referred to as *full-height foundation walls.* In mild climates, it is more common to find shorter walls. These are *crawl-space foundation walls.*

The job of building a foundation is usually subcontracted. Therefore, this chapter will discuss only general procedures and requirements.

SECTION 14.1

Footings

A **footing** is a base that provides a larger bearing surface against the soil for load-bearing parts of the structure. Footings are generally made of concrete that is poured into place. **Fig. 14-1.** In *monolithic construction*, the footing and the foundation are poured as a single unit. This section describes the separate installation of footings.

FOUNDATION-WALL FOOTINGS

Footings, also called *spread footings*, are an important part of the foundation. Particular attention should be paid to their size and shape. Footing details will generally be specified on the architectural plans. The depth and width of a footing are determined by such things as the loads it must bear, the bearing capacity of the soil, and local codes. If the bearing capacity of the soil is in doubt, a laboratory test may have to be done to learn its capacity.

Footings must always rest on undisturbed soil (soil that has not been previously dug up). This reduces the chance for uneven settling of the foundation. This is especially important where the building site has been raised with the addition of compacted fill. If the excavation for a footing has been dug too deep, it should never be brought up to proper height with soil. Instead, it should be filled with additional concrete to prevent settling problems.

Footing Design

Proper footings are important in preventing settling or cracks in a foundation wall. Local codes specify the type and size of footings suitable for soil conditions. Footings should be placed at least 12″ below grade. However, in cold climates the footings should be far enough below finished grade to be protected from frost. Local building codes usually specify the frost penetration depth, which may be 48″ or more in the northern United States. Builders often put footings deeper than code requires in order to create a basement area. The additional expense is small compared to the benefit of getting usable basement space.

The width of a footing depends on the bearing capacity of the soil and is specified by building

Fig. 14-1. Wood or steel forms prevent the concrete from spreading out as it is placed. Forms also ensure footings of a uniform shape and size.

Table 14-A. Minimum Width of Concrete or Masonry Footings in Inches						
Load-Bearing Value of Soil (psf)	1,500	2,000	2,500	3,000	3,500	4,000
Conventional light-frame construction						
1-story	16	12	10	8	7	6
2-stories	19	15	12	10	8	7
4-inch brick veneer over light frame or 8-inch hollow concrete masonry						
1-story	19	15	12	10	8	7
2-stories	25	19	15	13	11	10
8-inch solid or fully grouted masonry						
1-story	22	17	13	11	10	9
2-stories	31	23	19	16	13	12

Reprinted with permission from *2000 International Residential Code.* Copyright 2000 by International Code Council, Inc., Falls Church, Virginia. All rights reserved.

codes. **Table 14-A.** One general guideline for determining size is based on the thickness of the foundation wall. It applies only to footings on standard soils:

- The thickness of the footing should be equal to the thickness of the foundation wall.
- The width of the footing should be twice the thickness of the foundation wall.

Thus the footing projects beyond each side of the foundation wall a distance that is one-half the thickness of the wall. **Fig. 14-2.**

If the soil is of low load-bearing capacity, wider and thicker footings may be required. Also, some local codes set requirements for footings based on danger from earthquakes.

Footing Reinforcement

The strength of a footing is greatly improved when reinforcing bar (rebar) is embedded in it. However, footing rebar is not required by code in every region. Often reinforcement consists of two lengths of ½″ diameter (#4) rebar. The rebar must be positioned at least 3″ above the bottom of the footing.

Footing Forms

The exact location of the footings is determined by plumb bobs hung from the foundation batter boards. The shape of the footing is created either by pouring the concrete into dirt trenches or by pouring it into a form. A **form** is any framework designed to contain wet concrete. Forms can be made of steel, lumber, or a combination of lumber and plywood. A common type of wall footing form is shown in **Fig. 14-3**. The sides are formed by 2x lumber and braced to prevent them from being spread apart by the wet concrete. These boards are sometimes called *haunch boards. Spreaders*, or *form brackets*, are the boards that hold apart the sides of the forms. Lumber formwork is often assembled with duplex head nails to make disassembly easy later on.

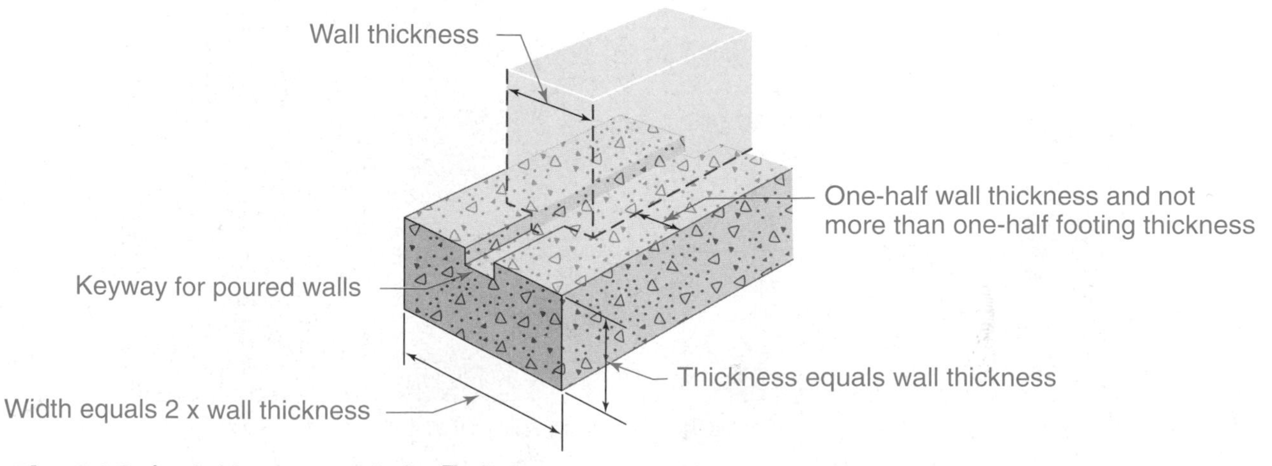

Fig. 14-2. A typical foundation wall footing. The basic proportions noted here are guidelines only.

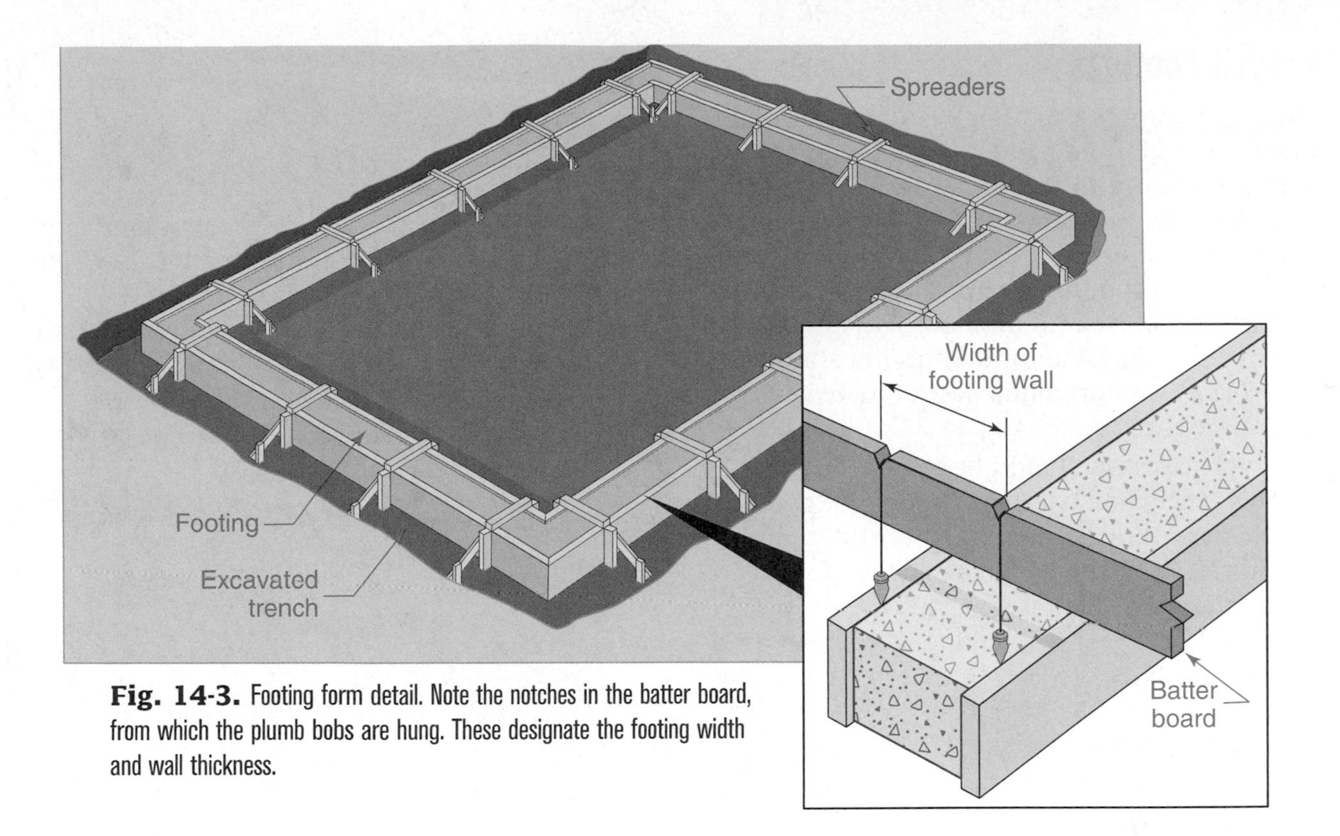

Fig. 14-3. Footing form detail. Note the notches in the batter board, from which the plumb bobs are hung. These designate the footing width and wall thickness.

A keyway should be formed in the top of the footing, as in Fig. 14-2. The keyway locks the foundation walls to the footing. This makes it less likely that moisture will seep through the joint between the wall and the footing. A keyway is usually 3½″ wide and 1½″ deep because a 2x4 is often used to form it. Lengths of 2x4 can be pressed into the footings after the concrete has been poured and removed after it has cured.

After the footings are poured and any rebar has been placed, the top surface of the footing is troweled smooth.

OTHER TYPES OF FOOTINGS

Other load-bearing parts of the structure, such as columns and chimneys, must also be supported by footings. The exact size and location of these footings are specified on the building plans.

Pier and Post Footings

A typical footing for a pier or post is square. A *pier* is a block of concrete that is usually separate from the main foundation. It is often used in girder floor systems or to support decks. To anchor a wood post, a steel pin or a metal bracket is anchored in a pedestal above the footing. **Fig. 14-4.** The pedestal is poured after the footing. The pedestal should be about 3″ above the finished basement floor and 12″ above finished grade in crawl-space foundations. When steel posts are used, they are often set directly on the footing. The concrete floor is then poured around them.

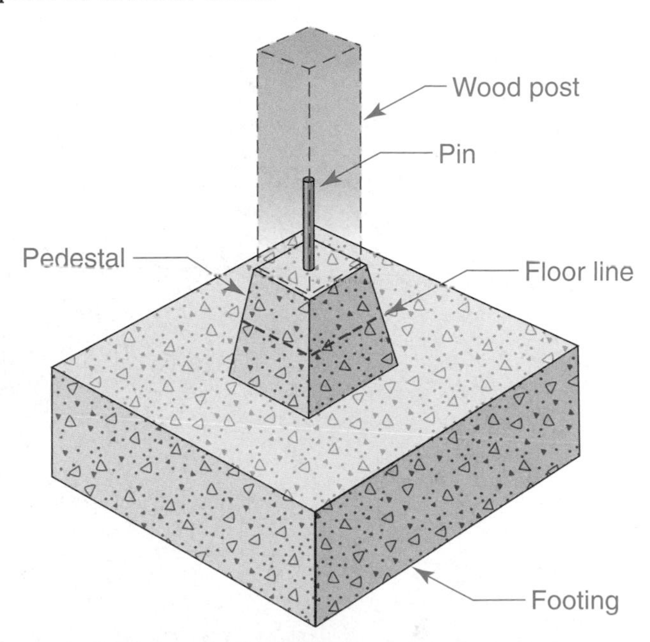

Fig. 14-4. Post footing. This drawing shows a steel pin, although a metal bracket might be used.

Stepped Footings

Stepped footings are often used on a lot that slopes. Instead of being at the same height around the entire foundation, these footings "step" down the sloped site. **Fig. 14-5.** The vertical step should be poured at the same time as the rest of the footing. The bottom of the footing is always placed on undisturbed soil below the frost line. Each run of the footing should be level. A *run* is a horizontal section between two vertical sections.

The vertical step should be at least 6″ thick and be of the same width as the rest of the footing. On steep slopes, more than one step may be required. It is good practice, when possible, to limit the vertical step to 2′ in height. This results in a stronger wall and makes finish grading much easier.

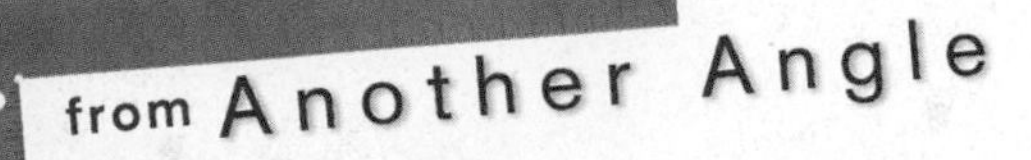

The foundations supporting tall buildings dwarf those used in ordinary residential construction. The world's tallest building, the Petronas Twin Towers in Malaysia (88 stories), is an example. The foundation of each tower consists of a 15′ thick raft containing 466,000 cubic feet of reinforced concrete that weighs about 35,879 tons. It is supported by 104 piles from 196′ to 377′ in length.

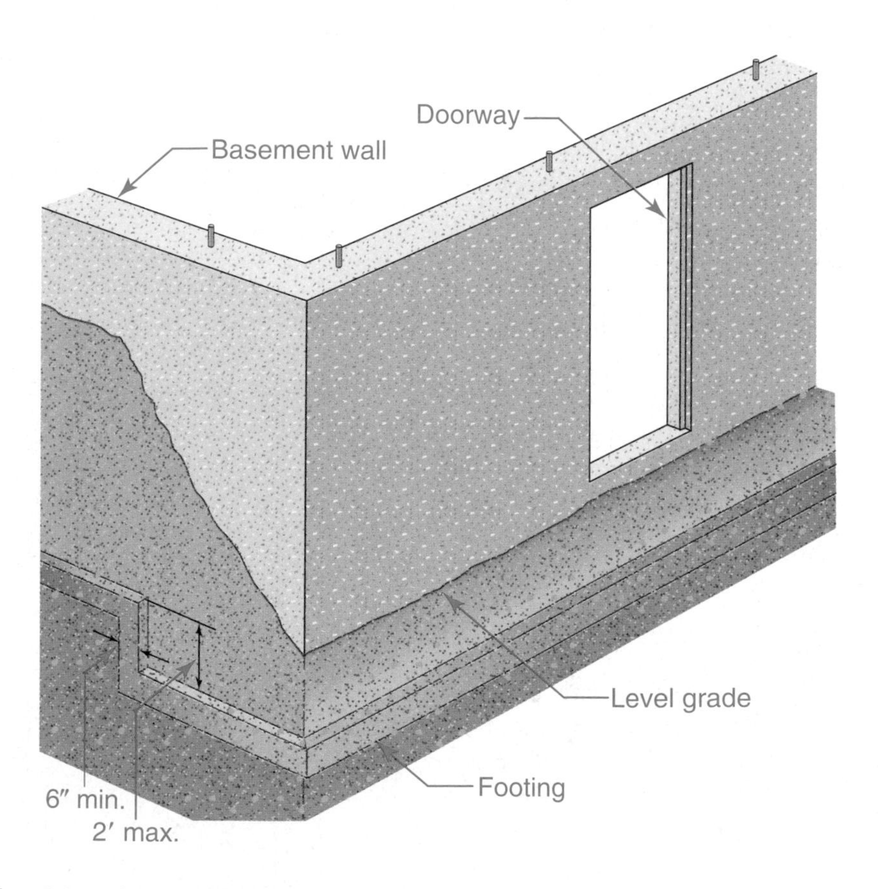

Fig. 14-5. Stepped footing details.

Estimating...

Concrete and Labor for Footings

To determine the amounts of concrete required for footings, determine the total length of the footings and then calculate the volume. Another way to do this is to refer to a volume table such as the one shown in **Table 14-B**. For example, look at the house plan in **Fig. 14-6**.

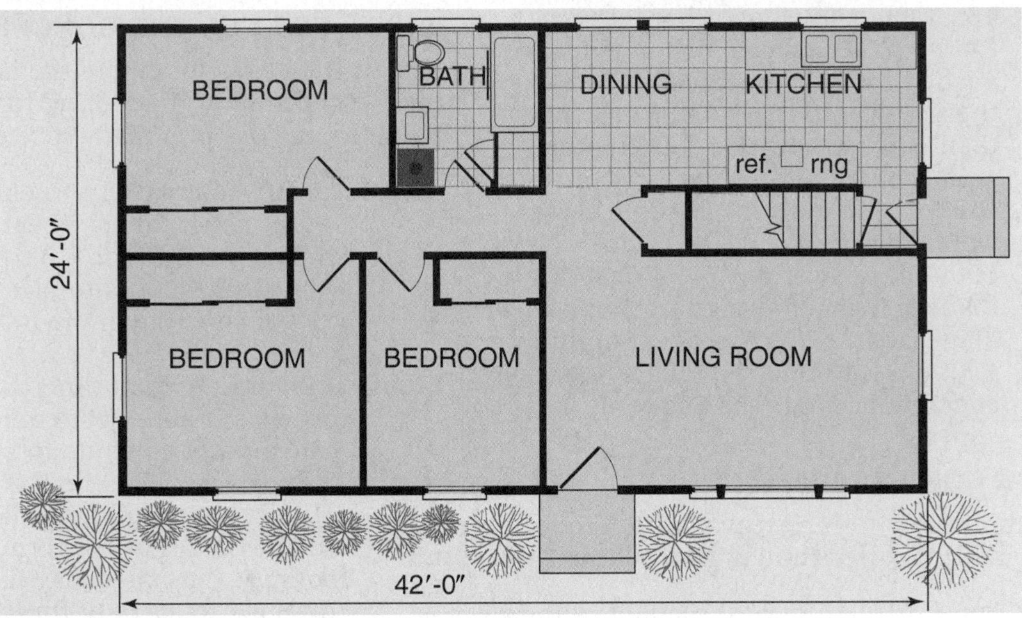

Fig. 14-6. House plan for use in calculating materials and labor for footings.

Table 14-B. Estimating Material and Labor for Footings

Footing Size	Material			Labor	
	Cubic Feet of Concrete Per Lineal Foot	Cubic Feet of Concrete Per 100 Lineal Feet	Cubic Yards of Concrete Per 100 Lineal Feet	Excavation Hours per 100 Lineal Feet[a]	Placement Hours per Cubic Yard[b]
6 x 12	0.50	50.00	1.9	3.8	2.3
8 x 12	0.67	66.67	2.5	5.0	2.3
8 x 16	0.89	88.89	3.3	6.4	2.3
8 x 18	1.00	100.00	3.7	7.2	2.3
10 x 12	0.83	83.33	3.1	6.1	2.0
10 x 16	1.11	111.11	4.1	8.1	2.0
10 x 18	1.25	125.00	4.6	9.1	2.0
12 x 12	1.00	100.00	3.7	7.2	2.0
12 x 16	1.33	133.33	4.9	9.8	2.0
12 x 20	1.67	166.67	6.1	12.1	1.8
12 x 24	2.00	200.00	7.4	15.8	1.8

(a) Reduce hours by ¼ for sand or loam. Increase hours by ¼ for heavy clay soil.

(b) Placement labor based on ready-mixed concrete.

(Continued)

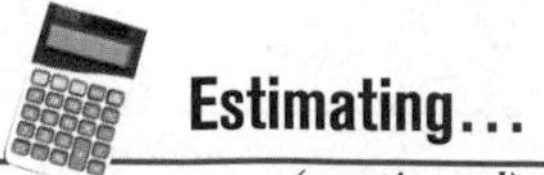

Estimating...

(continued)

Step 1 Note that the foundation measures 42′ by 24′. Thus the perimeter—the total length of the four sides—is lineal 132 feet.

Step 2 Suppose that the footing size is 8″ x 16″. Table 14-B shows that for 8″ x 16″ footings, 3.3 cu. yds. of concrete are needed for 100 lineal feet. However, the footings in the example are longer than 100′, so additional calculations are needed. If 3.3 cu. yds. of concrete will fill 100′, how many cubic yards will be needed for 132′? Divide 132 by 100. The answer is 1.32. This indicates that the house footings are 1.32 times longer than 100′. Therefore, multiply 1.32 × 3.3 to find the total amount of concrete needed. The answer is 4.36 cu. yds.

LABOR FOR EXCAVATION

The labor required for excavation of the footings can also be determined using Table 14-B.

Step 1 For 8″ × 16″ footings, the table shows it will take 6.4 hours to excavate 100 lineal feet. Because the perimeter is 132 lineal feet, allowance must be made for the excess over 100. You again divide 132 by 100 and get 1.32.

Step 2 Multiply 1.32 by 6.4 for an answer of 8.448 hours of labor, rounded off to 8.5. In other words, if it takes 6.4 hours to excavate 100 lineal feet, it will take 8.5 hours to excavate 132 lineal feet.

LABOR FOR PLACING CONCRETE

Table 14-B also helps figure the labor of placing the concrete in the footing forms. This is based on the use of a ready-mixed concrete.

Step 1 The house in Fig. 14-6 required 3.3 cu. yds. of concrete per lineal foot. Table 14-B shows that for 8″ x 16″ footings, it will take 2.3 hours to place one cubic yard of concrete in the forms.

Step 2 To figure the total time, multiply 2.3 (placement hours per cubic yard) by 3.3 (yards of concrete to be placed). The answer is 7.59 hours, rounded off to 7.6 hours of labor. This also includes the time for forming the footings. Estimates may have to be corrected to account for differing soil conditions, as noted at the bottom of the table.

ESTIMATING ON THE JOB

Using Table 14-B, estimate the cubic yards of concrete needed and the hours required for excavation and placement of 10″ × 12″ footings for a foundation that measures 62′ × 38′.

FOOTING DRAINS

If water builds up on one side of a foundation wall, the pressure created forces moisture through the concrete. This is called *hydrostatic pressure. Footing drains*, or *foundation drains*, are generally required for foundations that enclose usable space below grade. **Fig. 14-7.** They are also required where a house is located near the bottom of a long slope with heavy runoff. The drains direct subsurface water away from the foundation. This helps to prevent damp basement walls and wet floors. Many builders install drains even when they are not required by code.

Most new houses have plastic pipes for footing drains. These 4″ diameter pipes are placed alongside the base of the footing. They are usually connected to storm sewers but may run to daylight. The piping can also drain into subsurface drain fields. However, footing drains must not empty into the drain field of a septic system. This is restricted by code because large amounts of water can damage the septic system.

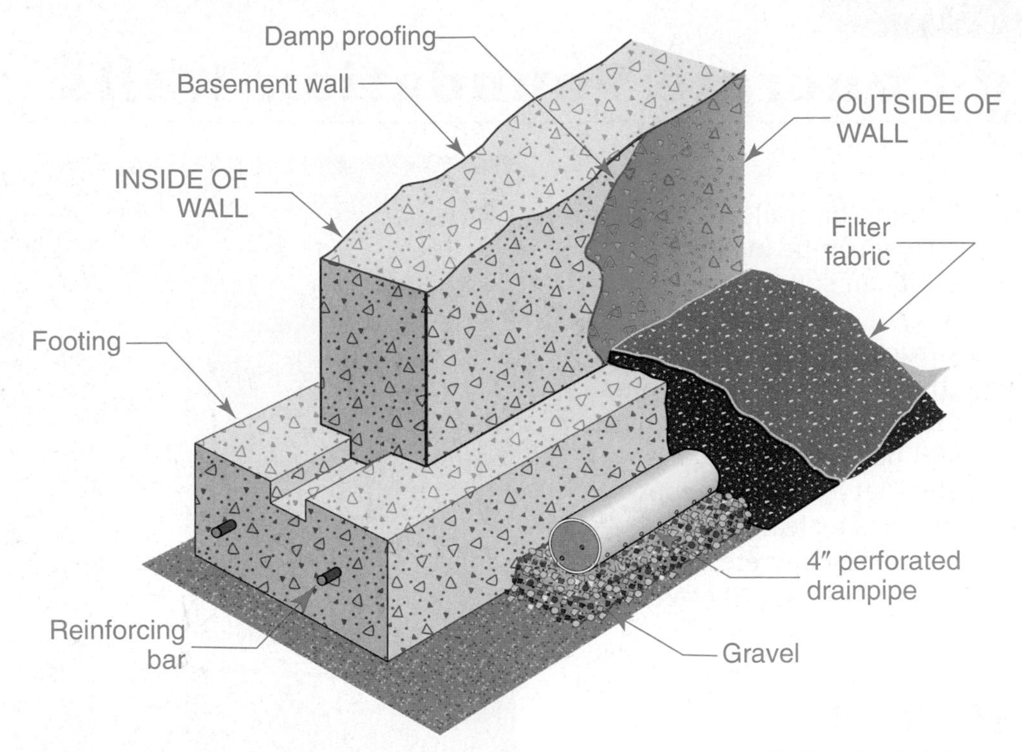

Fig. 14-7. Footing drains prevent water from building up against foundation walls. Note that the holes are along the bottom of the perforated drainpipe.

There are many small holes along the bottom edge of drain pipes. **Fig. 14-8.** When water rises into the pipes, it is carried away from the house. To keep the water moving, the pipes should be sloped toward the drain at least ⅛″ per foot. After the pipes are in place, the drainage area should be covered with *filter fabric* (also called *geotextile* or *landscaping fabric*). This fabric is made of polyester or polypropylene. It allows water to pass through but prevents tiny particles of soil (called *fines*) from getting into the drainage system and clogging it. The filter fabric is backfilled with more gravel. The foundation is then backfilled up to rough grade with dirt.

Fig. 14-8. The holes in perforated drain pipe should face down. Water rising into the pipe from below will be carried away.

SECTION 14.1 Check Your Knowledge

1. What is the purpose of a footing?
2. What type of reinforcement is commonly added to strengthen a footing? How is it placed?
3. When are stepped footings required?
4. What is a footing drain, and why is it important?

On the Job

Manufacturers have developed many products to improve the performance of construction materials or speed their installation. One example is a footing form that stays in place permanently to serve also as a footing drain. Using any resources available to you, locate other manufactured products related to footings and footing drains. Gather this information in a file. Then pick a product that interests you and describe it to your class in an oral report. Be sure to explain why you find the product interesting.

Poured-Concrete Foundation Walls

Poured-concrete foundation walls are durable and water resistant. They can be installed on most building sites and can support any type of house.

In residential construction, solid foundation walls usually range from 8″ to 10″ in thickness. **Fig. 14-9.** The minimum compressive strength for such walls is 2,500 psi. Many foundation contractors pour walls that are 8′ high above the footings. This provides a clearance of 7′-8″ from the top of the finished concrete floor to the bottom of the first-floor joists. Shorter walls enclose crawl space areas.

Fig. 14-9. Poured concrete foundation walls with anchor bolts.

FULL-HEIGHT WALLS

For nearly all poured-concrete foundation walls, formwork must be constructed for each wall face. Reusable forms are the most cost effective when a contractor does this work regularly. The forms must be accurately constructed and properly braced to withstand the forces of the pouring and vibrating operation and the pressure from the fluid concrete. **Fig. 14-10.**

For reusable forms, horizontal bracing members are usually sufficient. Such a horizontal bracing member is called a **wale**.

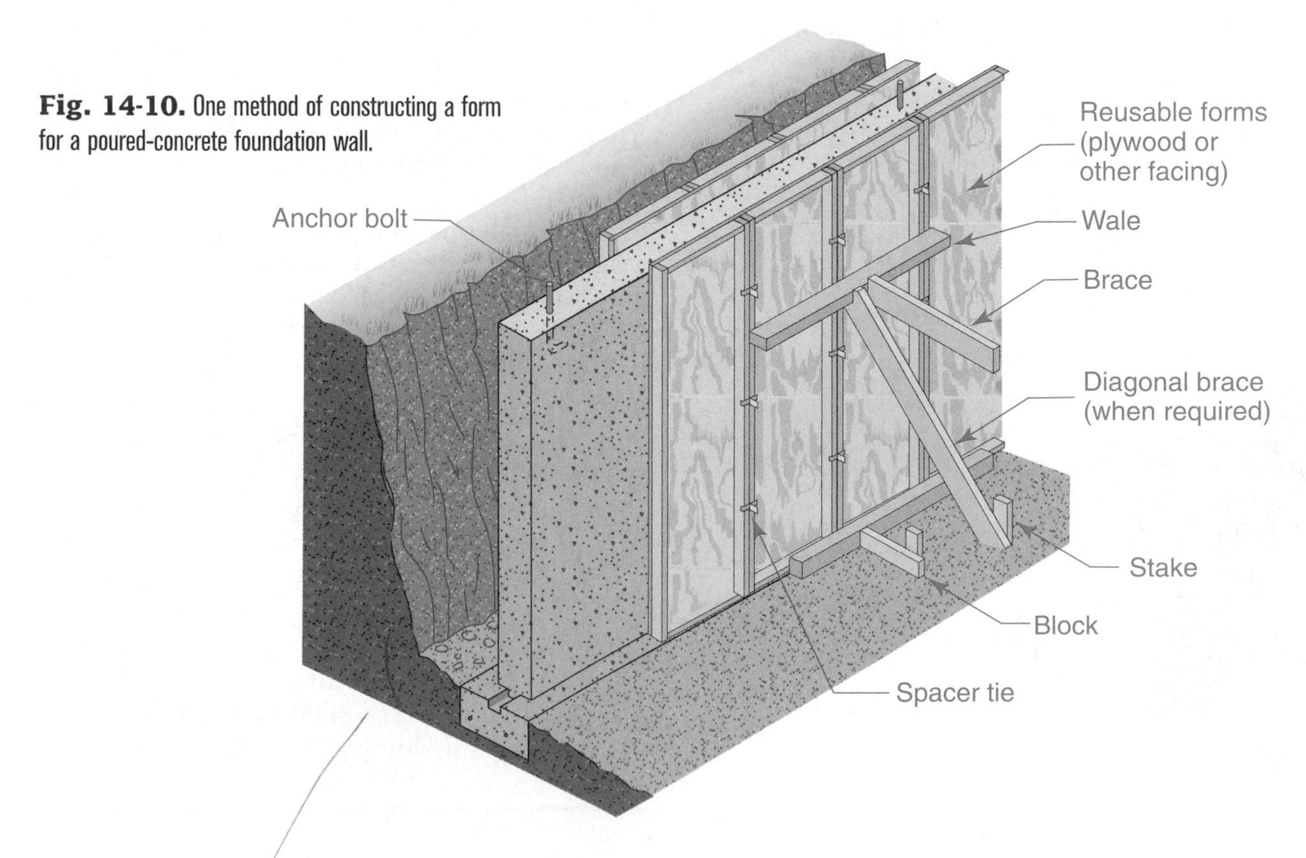

Fig. 14-10. One method of constructing a form for a poured-concrete foundation wall.

Standard Wall Forms

Standard wall forms may be made from wood or metal, depending on how durable they must be. Many are made from plywood and lumber. Though any exterior-grade plywood can be used, special form-grade plywood is available. Form-grade plywood made by member mills of APA—The Engineered Wood Association is referred to as Plyform. An overlaid surface material is bonded to both sides of the plywood under high heat and pressure. Medium-density overlay (MDO) has a smooth surface and can be reused many times. High-density overlay (HDO) offers the smoothest finish and can be reused the most. Mill-oiled plywood, another type, has a sanded veneer surface that is coated with a release agent at the mill. This coating prevents the forms from sticking to the concrete walls. The coating must be reapplied periodically.

Forms may be built on site and then taken apart after the concrete hardens. The lumber can then be reused elsewhere in the project. However, it is generally more cost effective and efficient to use and reuse prefabricated forms.

The two sides of each form are fastened together with clips or other ties. Thin metal rods called *snap-ties* are commonly used. The rods extend through the foundation. Metal brackets attached to the rods prevent the forms from spreading. **Fig. 14-11.** After the concrete is poured and the forms are stripped, the protruding ends of each rod are snapped off. Forms should be left in place for three to seven days before being stripped. This slows the curing process and results in stronger walls.

Fig. 14-11. Snap-ties prevent the two sides of a concrete form from spreading apart when concrete is placed. Note the use of horizontal and vertical reinforcing bar in this wall.

Insulating Wall Forms

A fairly new type of formwork is made of rigid foam insulation, usually expanded or extruded polystyrene. These products are referred to as *insulating concrete forms* (ICFs). Rather than being stripped off after the concrete cures, they are left in place permanently. **Fig. 14-12.** This greatly increases the insulating power of the foundation walls, an advantage when living space is located below grade. The forms can also be used for above-grade walls. ICFs eliminate the need to strip and store the formwork. Because the forms are very light in weight, they are easy to install. However, for the same reason, they must be braced with care. Care must also be taken to ensure that termites and other insects cannot reach the foam. They do not eat rigid foam insulation but tunnel through it to reach wood.

Fig. 14-12. Once insulating wall forms have been plumbed and braced, they are ready to be filled. Concrete is often placed with the aid of a pump truck.

The basic components of an ICF can be planks, sheets, or hollow blocks. In many cases, the two sides of the form are held together with plastic or steel connectors that remain within the finished wall. Depending on the product, the concrete placed for the foundation may take one of two forms:

- Standard wall. The concrete forms a solid wall identical to a wall poured between traditional concrete forms. **Fig. 14-13.**
- Grid wall. The concrete forms a wafflelike grid and varies in thickness at different places. **Fig. 14-14.** This type uses less concrete than other ICF foundations.

ICF foundations should be reinforced with rebar. For reinforcing and other installation details, read instructions supplied by the manufacturer. Also, check to be sure that local codes permit use of the type of ICF you are considering.

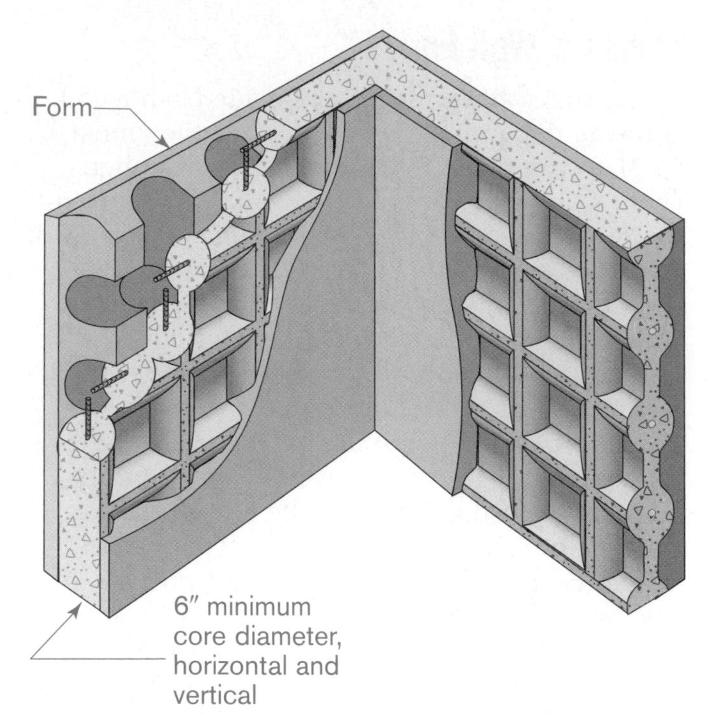

Fig. 14-14. A wafflelike grid wall uses less concrete than other ICF foundations.

SAFETY FIRST

Wear Proper Clothing

When placing or finishing concrete, take care to prevent excessive or prolonged contact of concrete with your skin. It is good practice to wear gloves, long pants, and high rubber boots.

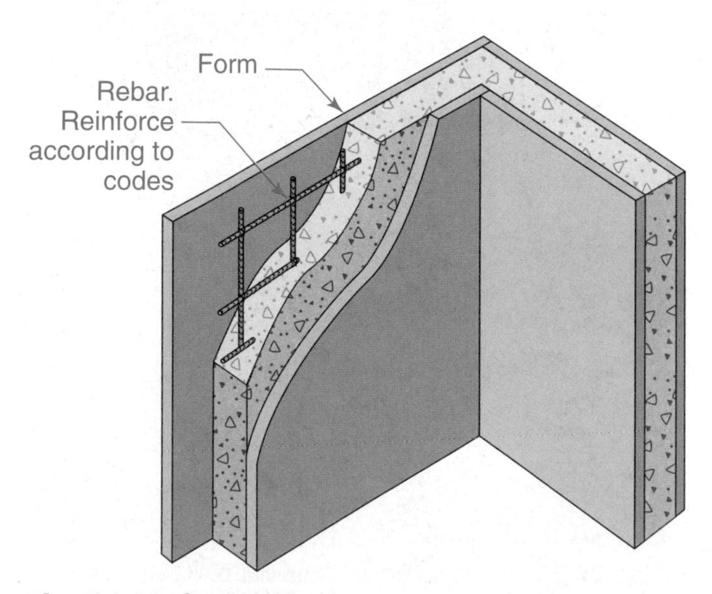

Fig. 14-13. Standard ICF walls create a channel for concrete that is similar to traditional formwork.

Placement

Concrete should be poured continuously, without interruption. This prevents a cold joint. A **cold joint** occurs where fresh concrete is poured on top of or next to concrete that has already begun to cure. A cold joint is more likely to leak and is weaker than the surrounding wall.

The water content of concrete is very important. Though it is tempting to add extra water to make the concrete flow better into the forms, this weakens the finished walls and encourages cracking. Concrete should always be as stiff as it is practical. Because stiff concrete is more difficult to move inside the forms, it should always be placed as close as possible to where it is needed. This reduces the need to push it around with shovels.

Concrete is normally delivered by ready-mix trucks. As it is placed in the forms, it should be worked to remove air pockets and to help it flow. The most basic technique is to jab it repeatedly with a shovel or pipe as it is being poured. This is generally enough for residential foundations. However, a concrete vibrator, sometimes called a stinger, is more effective. It is commonly used in commercial construction.

CRAWL-SPACE WALLS

In some areas, a crawl space is often preferred to a basement or a concrete slab. **Fig. 14-15.** One of the main advantages of the crawl-space house as compared with the full-basement house is reduced cost. Little or no excavation or grading is required except for the footings and walls. For crawl-space foundations:

- Soil beneath the house must be covered with a material to block moisture.
- The crawl space usually must be ventilated. Check local codes.
- The floor framing above the crawl space should be insulated to reduce heat loss.

Poured-concrete or concrete-block piers are often used to support floor girders in crawl-space houses. They should be no closer than 12″ to the ground.

To prevent ground moisture from reaching floor framing, bare dirt should be covered with 6-mil plastic sheeting. Otherwise, the floor framing may absorb enough moisture to encourage fungi. When temperatures favorable for fungus growth are reached, much decay may result. To protect the plastic from damage, some builders cover it with a layer of pea (rounded) gravel.

REINFORCING CONCRETE WALLS

In most areas, standard concrete walls do not need to be reinforced with steel except over window or door openings located below the top of the wall. However, vertical and horizontal rebar are sometimes added for extra strength. This is especially common in earthquake hazard zones. Always check local codes for requirements. The rebar should be centered in the wall. Where openings occur in the foundation, a steel or reinforced-concrete lintel should be installed over the opening. A *lintel* is a horizontal member that supports the weight of the wall above it. A lintel in a masonry wall is like a header in a wood-frame wall. It directs loads around the opening.

Where concrete work includes a connecting porch or garage wall not poured with the main basement wall, rebar ties must be provided. The rebar is placed as the main wall is poured. Keyways may also be used to resist sideways movement by forming a lock between the walls. Connecting walls should extend below the normal frost line and be supported by undisturbed soil.

Fig. 14-15. A crawl space foundation (shown at left) is sometimes combined with a concrete slab (being prepared at right). Circular piers in the crawl space will support the floor framing system. Note the location of foundation vents.

SILL PLATE ANCHORS

In wood-frame construction, the sill plate must be securely fastened to the foundation. Most builders use ½″ diameter L-shaped bolts called *anchor bolts.* These are embedded in the concrete immediately after the top of the foundation walls have been floated smooth. **Fig. 14-16.** They should be spaced no more than 8′ apart and no more than 12″ from the ends of any plate section. In areas exposed to high winds or earthquake hazard, anchorage requirements are more stringent. Bolts or other anchoring devices may have to be placed closer together. Anchor bolts should be set 8″ deep or more in poured concrete walls. A large flat washer should be used at the head end of the bolt.

Another type of anchor is a metal strap that is embedded in the concrete. **Fig. 14-17.** The legs of the strap fit around the plate. Where high winds and earthquakes occur, well-anchored plates are very important. The strap can be anchored to rebar in the foundation.

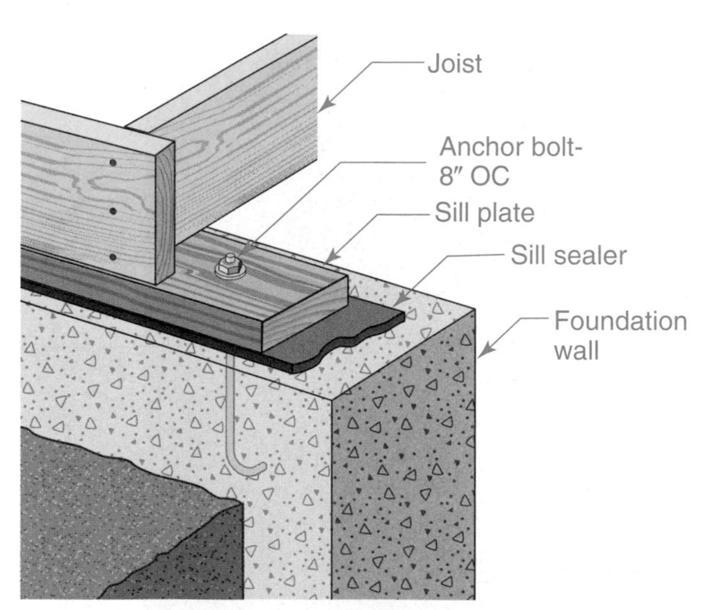

Fig. 14-16. Anchor bolts embedded in the foundation wall are used to secure the floor frame.

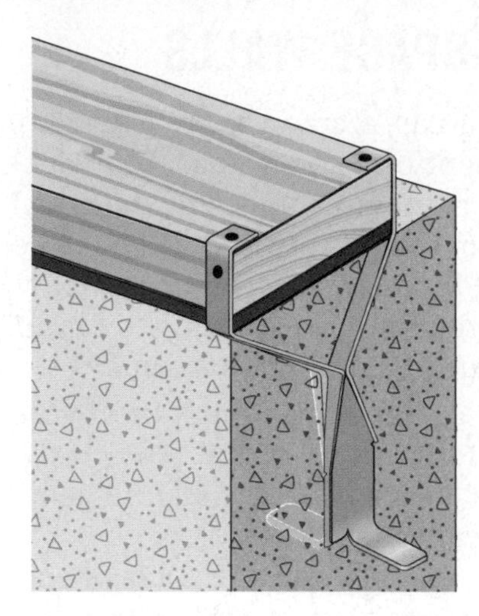

Fig. 14-17. Some builders use metal straps embedded in the concrete.

A sill sealer is often placed under the sill plate on poured walls to smooth any uneven spots that might have occurred during placement. If termite shields are used, they should be installed under the plate and sill sealer.

FOUNDATION WALL DETAILS

A foundation wall must often support special features, such as brick-veneer siding or utility sleeves. These features must be accounted for in the design of the foundation.

Masonry Ledges

If brick or stone veneer is used for the outside finish over wood-frame walls, the foundation must include a supporting ledge or offset about 5″ wide. **Fig. 14-18.** This results in a space of about 1″ between the masonry and the sheathing that is needed for ease in laying the brick. A base flashing is used at the brick layer below the bottom of the sheathing and framing. The flashing should be lapped with sheathing paper. *Weep holes* (to provide drainage) are also located at this course and are formed by omitting the mortar in a vertical joint. (Brick-veneer walls are discussed in Chapter 33, "Brick-Veneer Siding.")

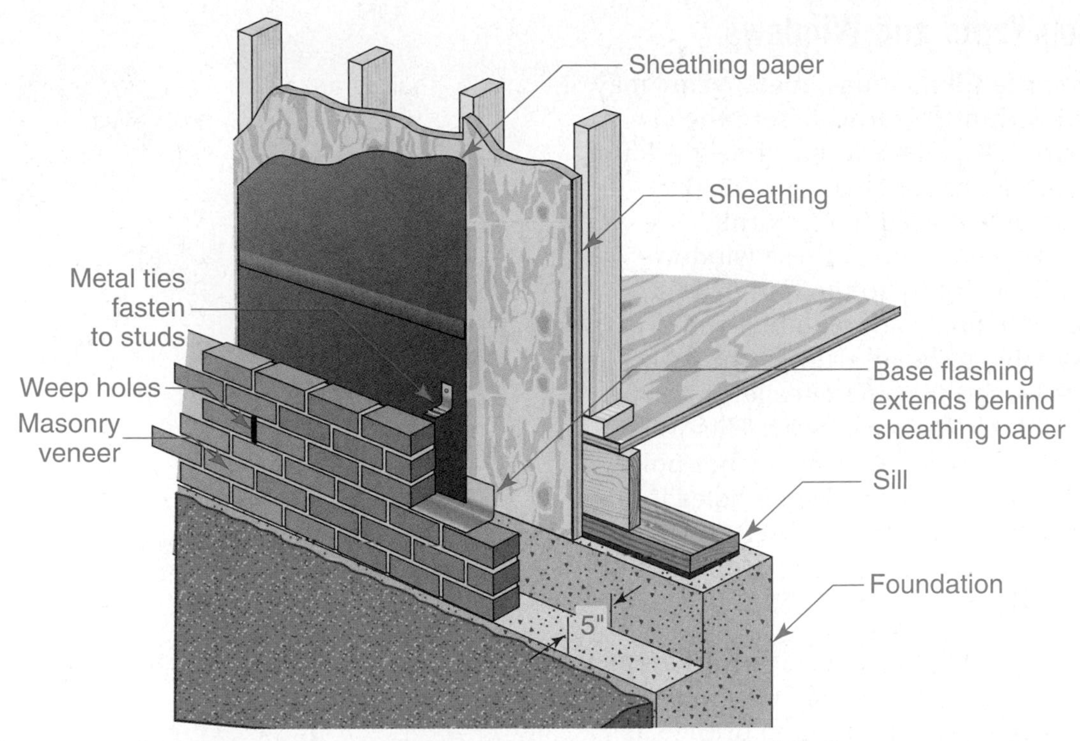

Fig. 14-18. A foundation wall under a wood-frame house must include a supporting ledge if a masonry veneer is to be applied. Note that weep holes in the masonry veneer are located just above the base flashing.

Utility Sleeves

It is often necessary for pipes, such as the main drain to the sewer or septic system, to pass through the foundation. Other examples include water supply pipes and electrical conduits. It is easier to provide for these as the forms are being placed, rather than drill large holes in the foundation later. Where a pass-through is required, a tight-fitting foam block is placed within the formwork and secured with nails. A short length of plastic pipe can also be used. **Fig. 14-19.** These barriers prevent concrete from flowing into these areas, creating a hole in the wall at that point. After the forms have been stripped, the block is removed. Later, pipes can be routed through the hole. Any space around them can be sealed with hydraulic cement and waterproofed.

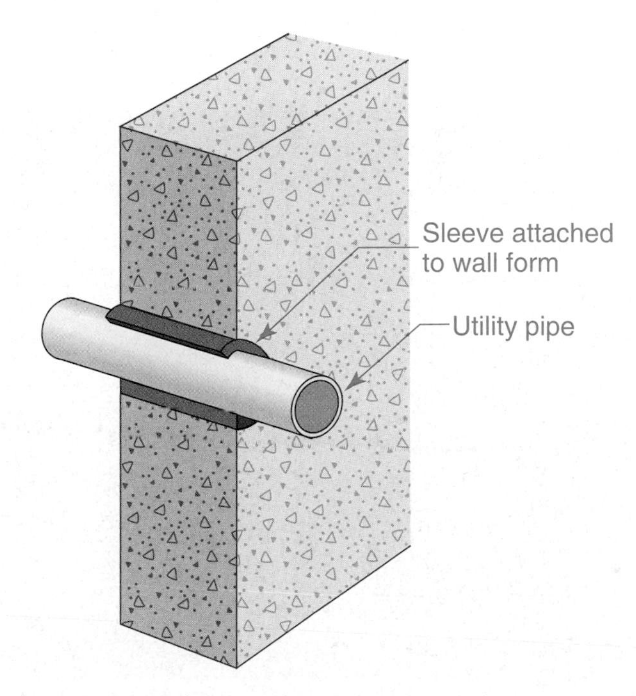

Fig. 14-19. A sleeve provides openings through the basement wall for utilities.

Foundation Vents and Windows

In crawl-space foundations, metal vents may be installed within the forms before the concrete is poured. **Fig. 14-20.** In full-height foundation walls, frames for small, grade-level windows may also be placed in the forms. The rust-resistant steel frame of these windows will then be locked securely to the foundation. Where larger openings are required, wood frames may have to be inserted in the forms. In this case, the wood is sometimes left in place after the forms are stripped away. This wood must be pressure treated. Small anchor bolts should be inserted into pre-drilled holes in the frame before the concrete is poured.

Beam Pockets

A wall notch or pocket is needed for basement beams or girders. The notch allows the top of the girder to be flush with the top of the sill plate. It should be large enough to allow at least ½″ of clearance at sides and ends of the beam for ventilation. **Fig. 14-21.** If wood beams and girders are so tightly set in wall notches that moisture cannot readily escape, they may decay unless treated. A waterproof membrane, such as roll roofing, is applied under the end of the beam to reduce moisture absorption.

Fig. 14-20. Openings such as those for foundation vents can be cast into the concrete when the walls are poured.

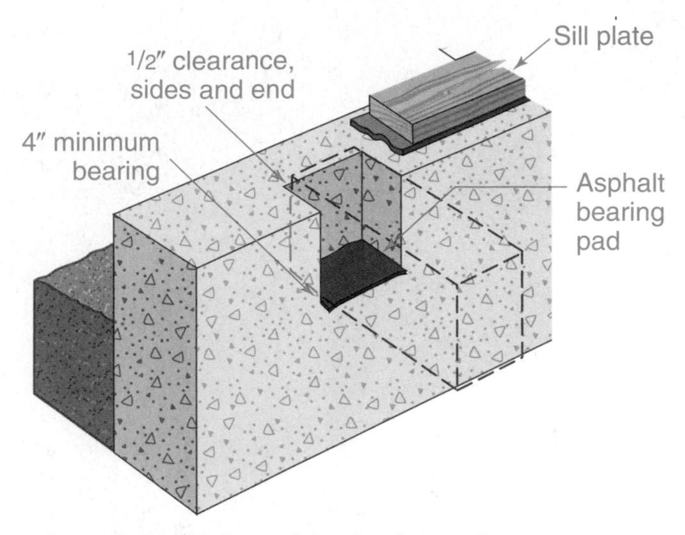

Fig. 14-21. A beam notch in a foundation wall.

STRIPPING AND MAINTAINING FORMS

Forms should not be removed until the concrete has enough strength to support the loads of early construction. Leaving the formwork in place also slows the loss of moisture, which improves the strength of the concrete. At least two days (preferably longer) are required before forms can be stripped in temperatures above freezing. A week may be required when outside temperatures are below freezing.

Metal prybars should not be used when stripping wood forms. They can easily damage the edges and faces of the panels. Instead, use wood wedges to pry panels away from the concrete. As soon as the forms have been removed, they should be cleaned, inspected for damage, and repaired if necessary. Concrete residue and scaling can be removed by scraping the surfaces with a hardwood wedge and brushing them with a stiff bristle brush. Do not use a wire brush, because it can damage the wood surface. Before the forms are used again, they should be recoated with a *form-release agent.* This is a liquid that prevents concrete from sticking to the forms.

MOISTURE PROTECTION

Before concrete foundation walls are backfilled, steps should be taken to protect them from ground moisture. Where walls will be exposed to standard soil conditions and no unusual drainage problems, this may be done with *damp proofing.* The walls are coated with a material that protects against ordinary seepage, such as may occur after a rainstorm. The coating should extend from the top of the footings to the finished grade level. However, it should not be applied until the surface of the concrete has dried enough so it will stick. Various materials can be used. The most common is a bituminous coating that is either sprayed or brushed over the walls. **Fig. 14-22.**

Where the soil drains poorly, where the water table is high, or where living spaces will be located below grade, greater efforts must be made to protect the foundation. They often involve applying a waterproofing membrane to the foundation walls. The membrane should extend from the top of the footings to the finished grade level. All joints in the waterproofing membrane must be overlapped and sealed with an adhesive suitable for the membrane material. Various materials can serve as a waterproofing membrane, including:

- 2-ply hot mopped felts.
- 55-lb. rolled roofing.
- 6-mil plastic sheeting.
- Multilayer combinations of rigid insulation board, drainage media, and spray- or sheet-membranes.

BACKFILLING

Backfilling is the process of filling in the excavated area around a foundation with soil. **Fig. 14-23.** This brings the area up to rough grade around the house. Backfilling should be done as soon as possible for safety. Backfilling also makes it easier to transport materials to and from the house. However, a foundation must not be backfilled too soon. The weight of the earth can damage walls that are not yet strong enough to withstand the pressure.

All foundation drainage, damp proofing and waterproofing must be complete before backfilling begins. Under ideal conditions, the floor framing (or floor slab) is also in place. This braces the tops of the walls. In cases where the wall must be backfilled before floor framing is in place, the walls can be temporarily braced from inside the excavation. This can be done using framing lumber.

Fig. 14-22. A bituminous coating prevents seepage of water through the foundation walls. Plastic pipes direct gutter runoff away from the house.

Fig. 14-23. Only an experienced operator should use heavy equipment to backfill. Care must be taken to avoid damage to the foundation.

Estimating...

Poured Foundation Walls

FORMS

Refer to the house in **Fig. 14-24**, which measures 40′ × 26′.

Step 1 To determine the total foundation wall area, assume that the wall is 8′ high. Multiply 8′ × 132′ (perimeter of the building). The answer is 1,056 sq. ft.

Step 2 Assume the wall thickness is 8″. Refer to **Table 14-C**. Read down the column headed "Wall Thickness" to 8″. Then read across to the column titled "Forming." Remember, the wall is to be 8′ high. The table shows that the wall will require 7.75 hours per 100 sq. ft. of wall area.

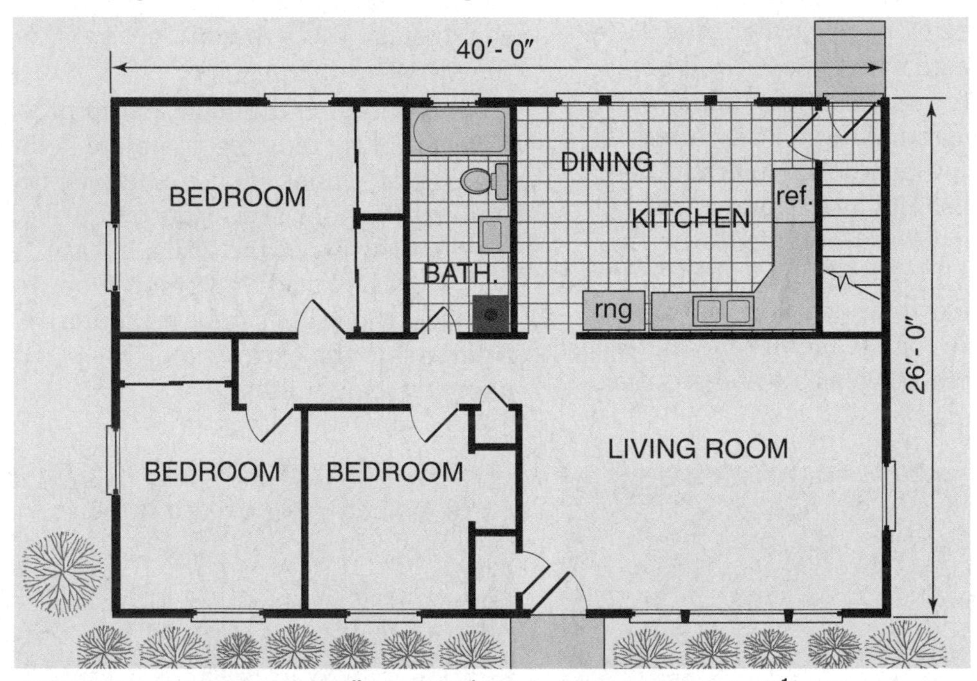

Fig. 14-24. A foundation wall 8″ thick and 8′ high for this home will require 26¼ cubic yards of concrete.

Table 14-C. Estimating Concrete Foundation Walls

Walls	Material		Forming			Concrete Placement
	Per 100 Square Feet of Wall		Hours per 100 Square Feet of Wall			Hours per Cubic Yard
Wall Thickness (inches)	Cubic Feet Required	Cubic Yards Required	Place 0′ to 4′	Place 4′ to 8′	Remove	
4	33.3	1.24	4.7	7.13	2.0	
6	50.0	1.85	4.7	7.75	Varies	Average
8	66.7	2.47	5.0	7.75	As to	3.25
10	83.3	3.09	5.0	7.90	Height	Hours
12	100.0	3.70	5.0	7.90	3.0	

(Continued)

Estimating...

(continued)

Step 3 Next, calculate the total time for installing the forms. Since you know it will take 7.75 hours for each 100 sq. ft., divide the total number of square feet by 100 and multiply by 7.75.

$$1{,}056 \div 100 = 10.56$$
$$10.56 \times 7.75 = 81.84$$

It will take about 82 hours to install the forms.

Step 4 Next, figure the time needed to remove the forms. According to Table 14-C, between 2 and 3 hours are needed to remove forms for 100 sq. ft. of an 8′ wall. Using the larger number:

$$10.56 \times 3 = 31.68$$

It will take about 31⅔ hours total labor time for removing the forms.

CONCRETE

You can also figure the amount of material needed using Table 14-C. In our example, the wall is 8″ thick and has a total area of 1,056 sq. ft.

Step 1 Find the 8″ thickness in the column at left. Reading across, under "Material" you find that 2.47 cu. yds. of concrete are needed for every 100 sq. ft. of wall. Therefore you must again divide the total area by 100 to find how many hundreds of square feet there are.

$$1{,}056 \div 100 = 10.56$$

Step 2 Then multiply by 2.47.

$$10.56 \times 2.47 = 26.08$$

Round your answer to the next larger ¼ cu. yd. Thus a total of 26.25 cu. yds. of concrete are needed.

LABOR

To estimate placement of concrete in the forms for the wall, again use Table 14-C.

Step 1 Under "Concrete Placement," it says that 1 cu. yd. takes an average of 3.25 hours.

Step 2 Multiply the total cubic yards by the time required to pour 1 cu. yd. This will tell you the total time required. In our example, 26.25 cu. yds. of concrete are required. Therefore:

$$26.25 \times 3.25 \text{ (hours)} = 85.31.$$

Rounded off, this comes to 85⅓ hours labor.

ESTIMATING ON THE JOB

Using Table 14-C, estimate the time to install and remove forms, the cubic yards of concrete needed, and the time required to place the concrete for a foundation that measures 43′ x 27′. The wall will be 8′ high and 10″ thick.

Follow the best local building practices when choosing backfill material. Do not use materials such as clay that expand and drain poorly. Layer gravel into the excavation as needed to ensure proper drainage. Backfill 6″ to 8″ at a time and compact the soil to prevent it from settling too much later on. Also, do not allow wood debris, such as lumber scraps and tree limbs, to be included in backfill. This encourages insects.

SAFETY FIRST

Falls and Cave-ins

The area around a new foundation wall is an open excavation. Care must be taken when working around this area to prevent falls. Also, to prevent cave-ins, keep trucks and other equipment well away from the perimeter.

SECTION 14.2 **Check Your Knowledge**

1. What is a wale?
2. Why might ICFs be used to form foundation walls for a house that was designed to include a basement recreation room?
3. Why must concrete always be poured in as stiff a mix as is practical?
4. Name three important aspects of crawl-space foundation construction.

On the Job

The foundations of the Sears Tower in Chicago and the Empire State Building in New York were constructed from poured concrete. Using the Internet or library resources, find out the following about each project:

- The thickness of the foundation walls.
- The height of the foundation walls.
- The volume of concrete, in cubic yards, that was used to build each foundation.

SECTION 14.3

Concrete Block Walls

Concrete block is popular for building foundation walls. **Fig. 14-25.** This is because the walls do not require formwork and the blocks are fairly inexpensive. Also, unlike work on a solid concrete foundation, which must be done all at once, work on a block foundation can start and stop as needed.

Fig. 14-25. Concrete blocks should be stacked near where they will be used.

CONCRETE BLOCK BASICS

Any hollow masonry unit is called a concrete block, or *concrete masonry unit* (CMU). The most common type is made with Portland cement, a fine aggregate, and water. Concrete blocks come in many shapes and sizes for a large variety of applications. **Fig. 14-26.** Those that are most widely used are 8″, 10″, and 12″ wide (nominal dimension). Blocks allow for the thickness and width of a standard ⅜″ mortar joint. Thus they are usually about 7⅝″ high by 15⅝″ long. This

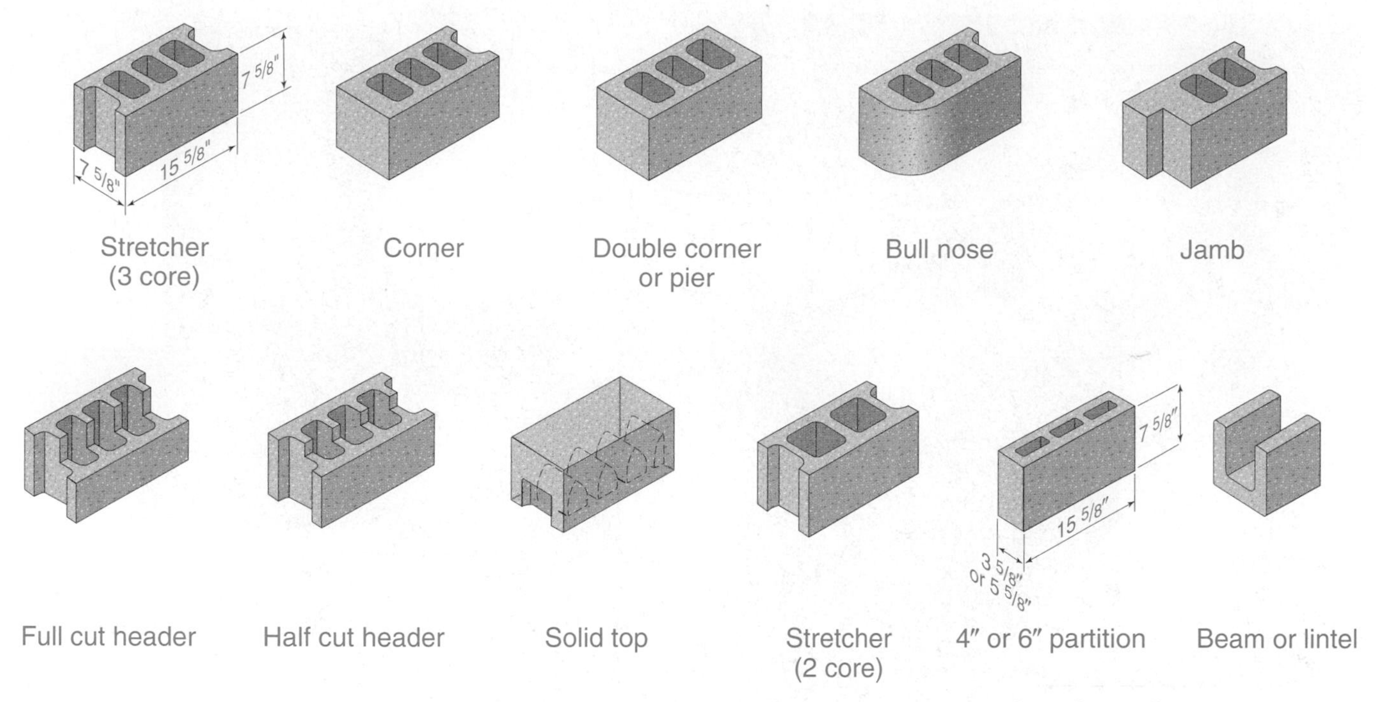

Fig. 14-26. Typical shapes and sizes of concrete masonry units. Actual dimensions are shown. However, a 7⅝″x 7⅝″ x 15⅝″ unit is commonly referred to as an 8″ x 8″ x 16″ block. Half-length sizes are usually available for most of the units shown.

results in assemblies that measure 8″ high and 16″ long from centerline to centerline of the mortar joints. A vertical mortar joint is called a **head joint**. A horizontal joint is called a **bed joint**.

Specialty blocks are made for specific purposes. Split-faced blocks have one rough face that looks something like stone. These are sometimes used for the exposed portions of block foundations. **Fig. 14-27.** Insulated blocks come in various forms, including some that contain inserts of polystyrene. **Fig. 14-28.** Another type of block has one or more glazed surfaces. It can be used as a structural as well as a finish material. **Fig. 14-29.**

In cold climates, block walls are usually constructed of eleven *courses* (layers) above the footings, with a 4″ solid cap block. The cap block seals the cores of the foundation walls. This results in about 7′-4″ between the joists and the basement floor.

Block courses are laid in a *common bond*. This is the overlapping arrangement shown in **Fig. 14-30**. Joints should be tooled smooth to seal them against water seepage. Mortar should be spread fully on all contact surfaces of the block. Such spreading is called a *full bedding*.

Fig. 14-27. Split-faced block is sometimes used for decorative effect in exposed locations.

Fig. 14-28. Heat transfer from one surface to another is reduced when blocks contain rigid insulation.

Fig. 14-29. Glazed-surface blocks can serve both as a structural and as a finish material.

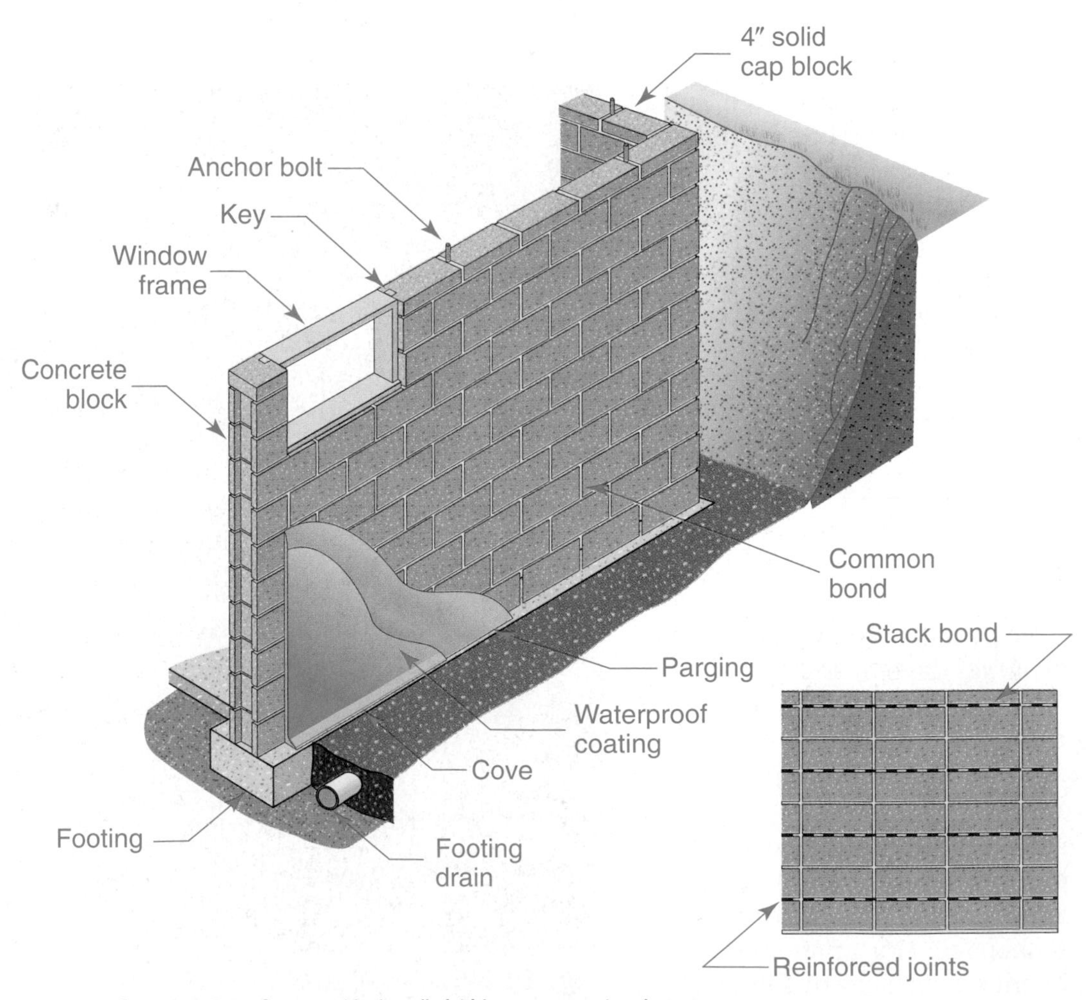

Fig. 14-30. Concrete block walls laid in a common bond.

Pilasters are projections resembling columns that may be used to strengthen a wall under a beam or girder. Some building codes require them. Pilasters are placed on the interior side of the wall and are constructed as high as the bottom of the beam or girder they support. Basement door and window frames should be keyed to the foundation for rigidity and to prevent air leakage. Fig. 14-30.

When exposed block foundation is used as a finished wall for basement rooms, the *stack bond* pattern can give a pleasing effect. Fig. 14-30. This is done by placing blocks directly above one another, resulting in continuous vertical joints. However, it is necessary to add some type of joint reinforcement at every second course. This usually consists of steel rods arranged in a grid pattern.

Freshly laid block walls should be protected in temperatures below 32°F [0°C]. Freezing of the mortar before it has set will often result in low adhesion, low strength, and joint failure. Care must be taken to keep blocks dry on the job. They should be stored on planks or other supports so the edges cannot contact the ground. They should be covered for protection against moisture. Concrete block must not get wet just before or during installation.

Block walls should not be backfilled until they have gained sufficient strength. Follow the precautions noted in Section 14.2 regarding backfilling.

SAFETY FIRST

Silica Dust

Cutting concrete block with a saw produces silica dust. Inhaling this dust is very hazardous.

- When cutting concrete or masonry, use saws that spray water on the blade.
- Use a dust collection system whenever possible.
- Always wear a respirator designed to protect against fine, airborne particles.

Fig. 14-31. For a clean break, score the blocks along both sides with a chisel.

Cutting Block

Blocks are usually available in half-length as well as full-length units. However, it is sometimes necessary to cut a block with a brick hammer and chisel. The block is scored on both sides to make a clean break. **Fig. 14-31.** For fast, neat cutting, portable masonry saws are often used. **Fig. 14-32.**

Fig. 14-32. A masonry saw used for cutting block is fast and accurate.

MORTAR

Good mortar is essential for a strong, solid wall. The strength of the mortar bond depends on:

- The type and quantity of mortar.
- The workability, or *plasticity*, of the mortar.
- The surface texture of the mortar bedding areas.
- The rate at which the masonry units absorb moisture from the mortar.
- The water retention of the mortar.
- The skill of the person laying the block.

Mortar Mixtures

Mortar is a mixture of Portland cement, hydrated lime, sand, and water. Mortar mixes for various purposes are shown in **Table 14-D**. Varying the ingredients yields mortar with different characteristics. A high proportion of Portland cement improves strength. Lime reduces compressive strength but increases flexibility and makes the mortar "stickier." Sand reduces shrinkage as the mortar cures. Mortar can also be made from the following packaged mixes:

- Type N mortar has average strength for most general masonry work above grade. It has only moderate compressive strength.
- Type M mortar has high compressive strength and is particularly durable. This makes it good for heavily loaded or below-grade foundation walls.
- Type S mix has a high tensile strength as well as high compressive strength. This makes it suitable for regions exposed to earthquakes or high winds.
- Type O is a low-compressive-strength mortar used primarily for interior walls.

Masonry walls subject to severe frost or stress require mortars that are stronger and more durable. To ensure that ingredients are well blended, mortar should be mixed in power mixers except for very small jobs, where it may be mixed by hand.

Table 14-D. Proportions of Mortar Ingredients by Volume

Type of Service	Cement	Hydrated Lime	Mortar Sand in Damp, Loose Condition
For ordinary service	1–masonry cement[a] or 1–Portland cement	- 1 to 1¼	2 to 3 4 to 6
Subject to extremely heavy loads, violent winds, earthquakes or severe frost action. Isolated piers.	1–masonry cement[a]) plus 1–Portland cement or 1–Portland cement	- 0 to ¼	4 to 6 2 to 3

[a] ASTM Specification C91, Type II.

Mixing and Placing Mortar

Mortar will stiffen on the mortar board because of either evaporation or hydration. Evaporation occurs when moisture is lost from the mixture. Then water can be added and mixed in to restore its workability. Mortar stiffened by hydration, however, should be thrown away. It is not easy to tell whether evaporation or hydration is the cause. However, a judgment can usually be made on the basis of how much time has passed since initial mixing. Mortar should be used within two-and-a-half hours when the air temperature is 80°F [27°C] or higher, and within three-and-a-half hours when air temperature is below 80°F [27°C]. If more time has passed, assume that any stiffness is caused by hydration.

Mortar must be sticky so that it will cling to the concrete block. When taking mortar from the mortar board, lower the trowel with a quick vertical snap of the wrist to make the mortar stick to the trowel. Shake off the excess.

SAFETY FIRST

Protect against Mortar

To prevent damage to your skin, avoid prolonged contact with wet mortar. Wear protective clothing. Thoroughly wash areas that have been exposed.

LAYING BLOCK FOUNDATION WALLS

Laying block foundation walls is a job for skilled masons. The following section is intended primarily as an overview of the process.

The block and mortar should be placed nearby to reduce your movements. **Fig. 14-33.** Boards, building paper, or tarpaulins should be used to cover the tops of unfinished block walls at the end of the day's work. This prevents water from entering the cores, or *cells*, which are the hollow areas of the block.

Building the Corners

The corners of the wall are built first, usually four or five courses high. After locating the outside corners of the wall, use a chalked line to mark the footing and help align the first block accurately. A full mortar bed should then be spread with a trowel. The corner block should be laid first and carefully positioned.

The first course of the corner should be laid with great care to make sure it is properly aligned, leveled, and plumbed. This helps to build a straight, true wall. After three or four blocks have been laid, use the mason's level as a straightedge to ensure correct alignment. Make blocks plumb by tapping them with the trowel handle.

After the first course is laid, apply mortar to the top of the face shells. A *face shell* is the side wall of a concrete block. **Fig. 14-34.** In some cases, a full mortar bed may be specified. **Fig. 14-35.** Mortar for the vertical joints can be applied to the ends of the next block or to the ends of the block previously laid. Some masons apply mortar to the ends of both blocks. **Fig. 14-36.**

As each course is laid at the corner, check it with a level for alignment, for levelness, **Fig. 14-37**, and for plumb, **Fig. 14-38**. Also, check each block carefully with a level or straightedge to make certain that the faces of the blocks are all in the same plane. Check the horizontal spacing by placing the level diagonally across the corners of the blocks. **Fig. 14-39.** A **story pole**, or *course pole*, is a board with markings 8″ apart. It can be used to gauge the top of the masonry for each course. **Fig. 14-40.**

Fig. 14-33. Distribute the blocks and the mortar to the areas in which they will be used.

Fig. 14-34. Mortar bedding the face shell in preparation for laying up additional courses.

Fig. 14-35. Blocks with a full mortar bed.

Fig. 14-36. Push the block downward into the mortar bed and align it with the previously laid block.

Fig. 14-37. Check the alignment of the blocks frequently.

Fig. 14-38. After the corners have been built up, be sure to check the corner for plumb before continuing.

Fig. 14-39. If the blocks have been stepped back correctly, the alignment can be checked by holding a level or straightedge diagonally across the corners of the block.

Filling in between Corners

When filling in the wall between the corners, a mason's line is stretched from corner to corner for each course. The top, outside edge of each block is laid to this line. **Fig. 14-41.**

The way the block is handled or gripped is important and is learned with practice. Roll the block slightly to a vertical position and shove it against the adjacent block. Final positioning of the block must be done while the mortar is soft and plastic. Any attempt to move or shift the block after the mortar has stiffened will break the mortar bond and allow water to seep in. "Dead" mortar that has been picked up from the scaffold or from the floor should not be used.

Fig. 14-41. After the corners have been built up, stretch a mason's line from corner to corner for each course. Between the corners, set the blocks so their top edges align with the mason's line.

Fig. 14-40. Using a story pole.

To assure a good bond, mortar should not be spread too far ahead of actual laying of the block or it will stiffen. As each block is laid, excess mortar at the joints is cut off with the trowel. Applying mortar to the vertical joints of the block already in the wall and to the block being set means well-filled joints. **Fig. 14-42.**

Fig. 14-42. Well-filled joints will result if mortar has been applied to the vertical joints of the block already in the wall and also to the block being set.

The block that fills the final gap in a course between corners is called the *closure block*. To install this block, spread mortar on all edges of the opening and all four vertical edges of the block itself. The closure block should be carefully lowered into place. **Fig. 14-43.**

Intersections

Bearing walls built of intersecting concrete blocks should not be tied together in a masonry bond, except at the corners. Instead, one wall should end at the face of the other wall, with a control joint at that point. A **control joint** is a joint that controls movement caused by stress in the wall. The joints are built into the wall in a way that permits slight movement without cracking the masonry. They are continuous from the top of the wall to the bottom. They are the same thickness as the other mortar joints.

Control joints should be placed at the junctions of bearing as well as nonbearing walls, at places where walls join columns and pilasters, and in walls weakened by openings.

For sideways support, bearing walls are tied together with a metal tiebar. **Fig. 14-44.** The bends at the ends of the tiebars are embedded in cores filled with mortar or concrete. Pieces of metal lath placed under the cores support the concrete or mortar filling.

Fig. 14-44. Reinforcing bar can be placed in the mortar joint to tie intersecting walls together.

For tying nonbearing block walls to other walls, strips of metal lath or ¼″ mesh galvanized hardware cloth are placed across the joint. **Fig. 14-45.** The metal strips are placed in alternate courses. When one wall is constructed first, the metal strips are built into the first wall and later tied into the mortar joint of the second wall.

Fig. 14-43. The closure block is carefully placed in position.

Fig. 14-45. Metal lath placed across the joint is used to tie a nonbearing intersecting wall to the main wall.

Fig. 14-46. A jointer for concave joints can be made from a piece of ⅝″ round bar.

Tooling the Joints

Weathertight joints and neat block walls depend on proper tooling. This is done after the mortar has become "thumbprint hard" (the thumb makes no indentation). Tooling compacts the mortar and forces it tightly against the masonry on each side of the joint. Proper tooling also produces joints of uniform appearance, with sharp, clean lines. Unless otherwise specified on the plans, all joints should be tooled in either a concave or V-shape.

Tooling of the head joints should be done first, using a small S-shaped jointer. Tooling of the bed joints should follow. The horizontal joint should appear continuous. A jointer for tooling horizontal joints is upturned on one end to prevent gouging the mortar. For concave joints, a tool made from a ⅝″ round bar is fine. **Fig. 14-46.** For V-shaped joints, a tool made from a ½″ square bar is generally used. **Fig. 14-47.** After the joints have been tooled, a trowel or stiff brush is used to trim mortar burrs flush with the wall face.

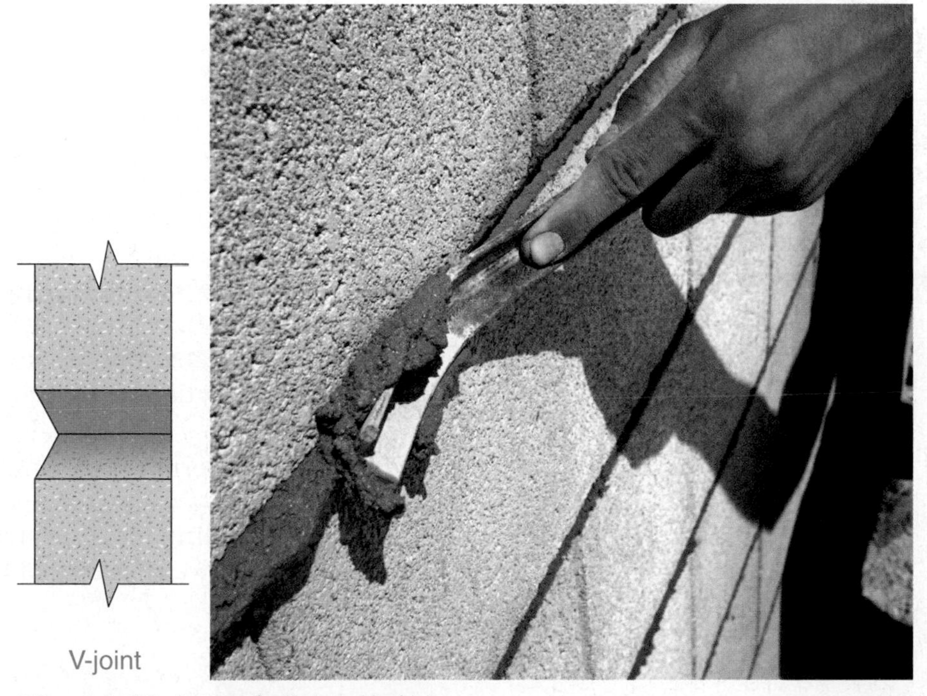

Fig. 14-47. A jointer for V-shaped bed joints.

Fig. 14-48. A solid-top block is often used for the top course.

Fig. 14-49. With metal lath in place, the cores of the top-course blocks can be filled and troweled smooth.

Completing the Walls

Foundation walls of hollow concrete block must be capped with a course of solid masonry to distribute the loads from the floor beams and to act as a termite barrier. *Solid-top blocks*, in which the top 4″ is of solid concrete, are available for this. **Fig. 14-48.** When stretcher blocks are used, a strip of metal lath wide enough to cover the core spaces is placed in the joints under the top course. The cores are then filled with concrete or mortar and troweled smooth. **Fig. 14-49.** Building codes in some parts of the country require that a steel-reinforced bond beam of poured concrete be placed at every fourth course in the wall.

Sometimes a block wall might be strengthened with rebar. If this is called for by the building's designer, #4 to #7 rebar is inserted into the vertical channels created in the wall by successive block cores. Each channel containing rebar is then filled with concrete. This creates a reinforced column within the wall. These columns should be spaced as required by local codes, depending on the height of the wall and the local soil type. Generally, however, columns in a 12″ thick wall should be spaced no more than 72″ OC.

Subterranean termites can crawl up through hidden cracks in a wall to the wood in the building above. Installing metal termite shields on top of the block walls prevents this.

Estimating...

Block Walls

In estimating for block walls, you must consider several items. These include the number of blocks, the amount of mortar, and labor costs.

NUMBER OF BLOCKS

The number of blocks needed for a foundation can be determined by the area of each wall to be built.

Step 1 Nine 8″ × 8″ × 16″ blocks will make 8 square feet of wall area. Therefore, take the total number of square feet in the wall and divide it by eight. Multiply the result by nine. You will then have a good estimate of the number of blocks needed for the wall.

Step 2 For example, consider a house with a 25′ × 40′ foundation that is 7′ high. The simplest way to find the total square footage is to multiply the perimeter times the height. (The perimeter is the lengths of the four walls added together.) In this case 25′ + 25′ + 40′ + 40′ = 130′. Multiply this by 7′ to find the total area of the four basement walls, which is 910 sq. ft. Now apply the formula:

$$910 \div 8 = 113.75$$
$$113.75 \times 9 = 1{,}023.75$$

Rounded off, your answer would be 1,024.

Step 3 Next, because the courses overlap or interlock at the corners, subtract one-half block for each corner of each course. The wall in the example would be 11 blocks high; therefore, subtract 5½ blocks for each corner or 22 blocks all together.

$$1{,}024 - 22 = 1{,}002$$

A total of 1,002 blocks would be needed. This number would be reduced even more to allow for windows or other openings.

The number of concrete blocks necessary for a wall can also be determined by referring to **Table 14-E**. In the left column, find the size of the block used. If you select an 8″ × 8″ × 16″ block, the table indicates 110 concrete blocks for each 100 sq. ft. of wall. The walls in our example have an area of 910 sq. ft. Divide this by 100 to find the number of square feet expressed in hundreds: 910 ÷ 100 = 9.1.

Table 14-E. Estimating Table for Masonry Blocks

Lightweight Block	Material for 100 Sq. Ft. of Wall		Labor
Size	Number of Units	Mortar (cu. ft.)	Blocks per Hour
8x4x12	146	4.0	24
8x4x16	110	3.25	22
12x4x12	100	3.25	30
8x6x16	110	3.25	21
Concrete Block	**Material for 100 Sq. Ft. of Wall**		**Labor**
Size	Number of Units	Mortar (cu. ft.)	Blocks per Hour
8x8x16	110	3.25	18
8x10x16	110	3.25	16
8x12x16	110	3.25	13

Note: Mortar quantities based on ⅜″ mortar joints, plus 25% waste. For ½″ joints add 25%.

(Continued)

Estimating...

(continued)

The table shows that 110 blocks are needed for each 100 sq. ft., so multiply 9.1 times 110 to find the total number of blocks needed: $9.1 \times 110 = 1{,}001$ total blocks.

Some adjustment may still be necessary if there are openings in the wall. However, the table allows for the overlapping of blocks at the corners, so it is not necessary to subtract for this as in the previous example. Note also that the answer is not precisely the same as when calculated by the first method. However, the estimates are very close, and both methods are reliable.

AMOUNT OF MORTAR

The number of cubic feet of mortar needed for a block wall can also be determined from Table 14-E.

Step 1 For the walls in our example, the table shows that 3.25 cu. ft. of mortar would be needed for every 100 sq. ft. of wall area.

Step 2 There are 9.1 hundreds of square feet in the walls. By multiplying 9.1 times 3.25 you find the total amount of mortar needed.

$9.1 \times 3.25 = 29.575$ cu. ft. of mortar, rounded off to 29.6

LABOR COSTS

To determine labor costs, again consult Table 14-E.

Step 1 You will see that 8″ × 8″ × 16″ blocks are laid at a rate of 18 per hour.

Step 2 Using the figure 1,001 for the total number of blocks, divide by 18 to learn the number of hours needed:

$1{,}001 \div 18 = 55.6$

Step 3 Multiply the hours needed by the hourly rate of pay to find the labor cost.

ESTIMATING ON THE JOB

Using Table 14-E, determine the number of blocks, amount of mortar, and labor hours needed to make a 22′ × 38′ foundation that is 7′ high. Concrete blocks that measure 8″ × 8″ × 16″ will be used.

Installing Anchor Bolts

Wood sill plates on which the house framing bears are fastened to the top of the walls. This is done by means of anchor bolts ½″ in diameter and 18″ long, spaced not more than 8′ apart. These anchor bolts are placed at least 16″ deep in the cores of the top two courses of block, and the cores are filled with concrete or mortar. The threaded end of the bolt should extend above the top of the wall. **Fig. 14-50.** Pieces of metal lath are placed in the second horizontal joint from the top of the wall and under the cores to be filled. The lath supports the concrete or mortar filling.

Cleaning Block Walls

Any mortar droppings that stick to the block wall should be allowed to dry slightly before removal with a trowel. The mortar may smear if removed while too soft. When dry and hard, most of the remaining mortar can be removed by rubbing it with a small piece of concrete block and then brushing.

Fig. 14-50. Fill the core with concrete or mortar and insert the bolt so that the threads extend above the top of the wall.

Fig. 14-51. Parging a block wall provides a barrier against water infiltration. It can be applied to above-grade as well as below-grade walls.

MOISTURE PROTECTION

Like solid concrete walls, block walls must either be damp proofed or waterproofed. Block walls are sometimes parged as part of this process. **Parging** is the process of spreading mortar or cement plaster over the block and forming a cove where the wall joins with the footing. The parging should be at least ⅜″ thick. When the parging is dry, a coating of asphalt is applied to the exterior of the wall. **Fig. 14-51.** This, along with a properly designed footing drain, will normally ensure a dry basement.

Sometimes added protection is needed, as when soil is often wet. In such cases, the entire wall should be waterproofed like a solid concrete foundation (see Section 14-2).

SURFACE BONDING

Mortared block walls are the most common type of concrete block foundation wall. However, one technique, called *surface bonding*, or *dry-stacking*, requires no mortar above the first course. The first course is bedded in mortar as usual. However, additional courses are stacked dry, with no mortar between them. **Fig. 14-52.** Fiberglass-reinforced mortar, or *surface-bonding mortar*, is then troweled over both sides of the walls in a layer at least ⅛″ thick. The ½″ long

Fig. 14-52. Using surface-bonding mortar to build a block wall eliminates the need to mortar each course as the wall is built.

fibers improve the tensile strength of the mortar much like steel mesh reinforces concrete.

Because individual joints are not mortared, walls are built more quickly and are easier for unskilled workers to install. Also, the coating of surface-bonding mortar provides water resistance.

RADON

Radon is a colorless and odorless radioactive gas that travels through soil. According to the U.S. Environmental Protection Agency, radon can be extremely toxic to humans if it builds up inside a house. Long-term exposure to radon has been linked to an increased risk of lung cancer. All types of house foundations, including concrete slabs, should be designed to reduce penetration by radon.

Because house foundations are in direct contact with the soil, they are a common entry point for radon. Radon enters through floor and wall cracks, expansion joints, gaps around pipes, and even through the pores in concrete. Because radon is soluble in water, it can also enter a basement through water seepage and through water vapor.

Because radon is nine times heavier than air, it tends to accumulate in basements. However, air circulation and other forces help to distribute radon throughout a house.

Radon-Resistant Construction

Radon affects houses throughout the country. However, its presence is often erratic. Therefore, steps should be taken during the foundation construction of every house to minimize radon problems. The following protective features are common:

- Gas-permeable layer. This is a 4″ thick layer of drainage gravel directly beneath the floor slab. It allows radon to move freely beneath the house. A 4″ thick layer of sand, topped with geotextile fabric, is an alternative.
- Soil-gas retarder. Polyethylene sheeting 6-mil thick is placed on top of the gas-permeable layer. This prevents radon from moving through the slab.
- Sealants. All openings and joints in the foundation floor are sealed to reduce radon entry. Sealant techniques include the use of high-performance caulks as well as plastic covers over sump pits.
- Vent pipe. A 3″ or 4″ diameter PVC pipe is connected to the gas-permeable layer. It leads to the roof. The pipe acts as an exhaust to safely vent radon outside the house.
- Cap course. Concrete block foundation walls must incorporate either a continuous course of solid masonry, a continuous course of concrete, or one course of masonry-grouted solid. This prevents radon from moving through the hollow cores of the block.

Building codes in some parts of the country require the use of radon-resistant foundation techniques. Always check local codes for specific construction requirements.

SECTION 14.3 Check Your Knowledge

1. List three advantages of concrete block foundation walls, as compared to solid concrete walls.
2. Name the type of packaged mortar that is most suitable for regions where earthquakes occur.
3. What is a story pole and how is it used when laying concrete block?
4. What is parging and what is its purpose?

On the Job

Concrete masonry units are the most common type of block used in modern residential construction. However, many other types of blocks have been used to build houses over the centuries. Research this topic to find information on at least five different blocks in addition to standard concrete masonry units. These could be from ancient or modern times. Summarize your findings by listing each block by name along with the following information:

- The method for attaching blocks to each other.
- The material the block was made of.
- The country or region in which the block was used.

Chapter 14 Review

Section Summaries

14.1 Footings provide a base that supports a foundation wall, a pier, or a post. Footings can be reinforced with rebar. Footing drains help prevent damp basements.

14.2 Foundation walls may be full height for basements or shorter for crawl spaces. Poured foundations require forms. Rebar can be added for extra strength. Damp proofing and waterproofing must be done where moisture is a problem.

14.3 Concrete block walls do not require formwork. The blocks are fairly inexpensive. Mortar holds the blocks together. Block walls, too, require protection from moisture.

Review Questions

1. What is the minimum depth required for an exterior-wall footing?
2. Describe the type and position of reinforcement that is commonly added to strengthen a footing.
3. What is a keyway, and how is it formed?
4. Name and describe the three types of plywood that are commonly used in foundation forms.
5. For nearly all poured-concrete foundation walls, formwork must be constructed for each wall face. What holds the formwork together?
6. What is the difference between damp proofing and waterproofing?
7. What creates a cold joint?
8. Why are the joints in a concrete block wall tooled?
9. Describe a stack bond pattern.
10. When using mortar, why is it helpful to know the differences between hydration and evaporation?

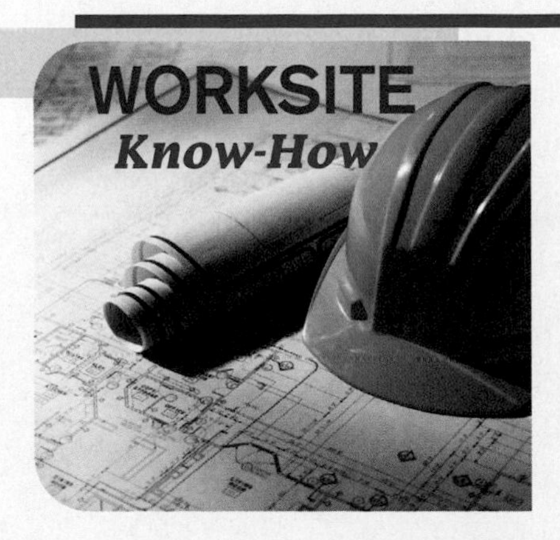

Following Directions Construction work requires cooperation. When you're new at a job, it's easy to find fault with how things are done. A particular method may not seem efficient, or you may know of an easier way to accomplish the same thing. However, there is often a good reason that a job is done a certain way, and your boss may not have the time to explain it to you right away.

If you don't follow directions, you might impact someone else's work. Your mistake might mean the job has to be redone. That's why employers appreciate workers who follow directions.

What about your creativity and problem-solving skills? Do you ever get to use them? Of course you do. After you've been on the job for several months and know something about what needs to be done and why, talk to your boss about trying some of your ideas. You may find him or her glad to listen.

Chapter

Concrete Flatwork

Objectives

After reading this chapter, you'll be able to:

- Identify the two types of foundation slabs.
- Understand foundation slab basics.
- Discuss various types of slab reinforcement.
- List the steps in finishing flatwork.

Terms

chair
fines
independent slab
kneeboards
lift
monolithic slab
screed
subgrade

Concrete flatwork consists of flat, horizontal areas of concrete, usually 5″ or less in thickness. Flatwork is placed either directly on the ground or over compacted gravel or sand. Examples of flatwork include foundation slabs, basement floors, driveways, and sidewalks. Concrete flatwork must be contained by forms until it gains a certain level of strength. Two additional procedures are required. First, the top surface of flatwork must be finished. This means that the surface must be smoothed, textured, or otherwise worked using a combination of hand and power tools. Second, steps must be taken to ensure that the concrete cures properly.

Concrete flatwork is generally installed by subcontractors who specialize in this work. This chapter will provide a general introduction to the topic.

SECTION 15.1

Foundation Slabs

One common use for flatwork in residential construction is in houses built without a basement or a crawl space. In mild or warm climates, a foundation slab has some advantages:

- Because very little earth must be removed, excavation costs are reduced.
- Extensive or complex formwork is not required.
- A concrete slab eliminates the need for a separate subfloor.
- Construction costs are lower.
- The concrete provides a solid base for concrete block walls, which are sometimes used in warm climates as the exterior walls of the house.

A foundation slab also has some disadvantages. The primary one is that utilities must be planned carefully and roughed-in in advance. **Fig. 15-1.** Changes are very difficult once the slab has been placed.

from Another Angle

Where winter temperatures are fairly mild, slab foundations are often more cost-effective than other types of foundations. This is because the amount of excavation required to reach below frostline is minimal in a mild climate. Full basements are not common in mild climates for this reason.

TYPES OF FOUNDATION SLABS

There are two types of foundation slabs: monolithic and independent. The choice to use one or the other depends largely on climate and local custom. In both cases, the minimum thickness required by code is 3½″. A thickness of 4″ is more common.

Fig. 15-1. Floor slabs are common examples of concrete flatwork. This slab shows how pipes for the rough plumbing are cast into the floor as the concrete is placed during pouring.

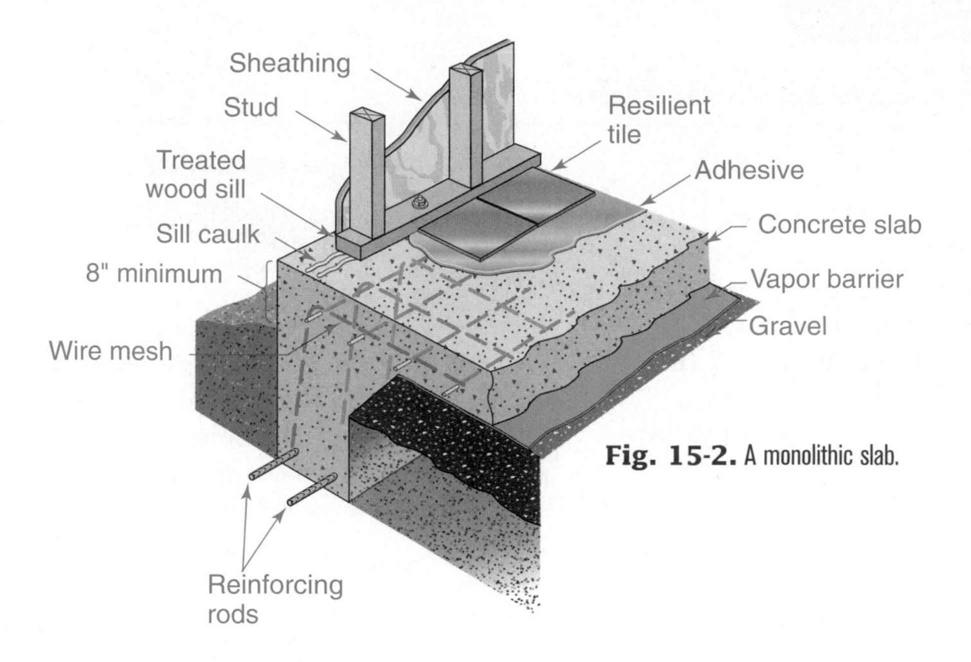

Fig. 15-2. A monolithic slab.

A **monolithic slab** consists of a footing and floor slab that are formed in one continuous pour. It is also referred to as a *unified slab*, a *thickened-edge slab*, or a *slab with a turned-down footing*. **Fig. 15-2.** The perimeter of the slab is thicker than the main area. It is strengthened with rebar at the edges. The bottom of the footing should be at least 1′ below the natural grade line and supported by solid, unfilled, well-drained soil. A monolithic slab is useful in warm climates where frost penetration is not a problem and where soil conditions are favorable. It is also preferred in areas where termite infestations are common.

An **independent slab**, also called a *ground-support slab*, is used in areas where the ground freezes fairly deep during winter. The house is supported by foundation walls and piers that extend to solid bearing below the frostline. The slab is then poured between the foundation walls. (Foundation walls are discussed in Chapter 14, "Foundation Walls.") After the wall formwork has been removed, the slab is poured. Two methods for laying this type of slab are shown in **Figs. 15-3** and **15-4**.

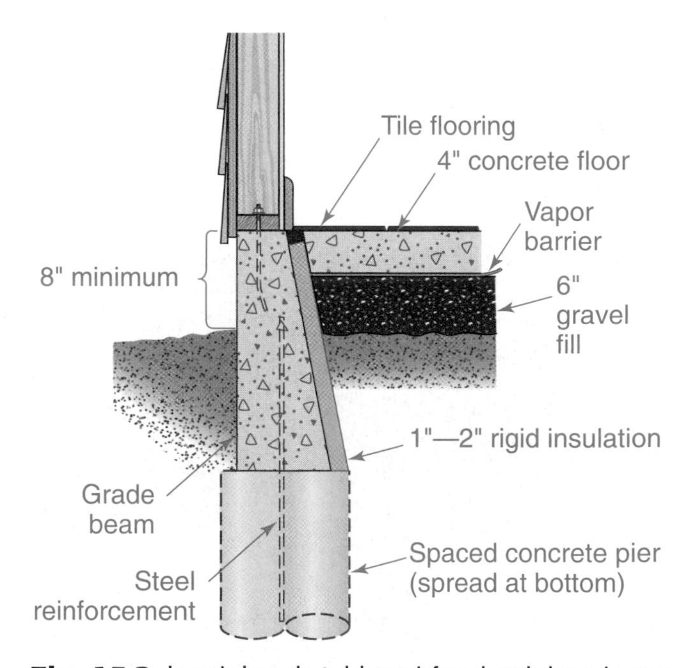

Fig. 15-3. In an independent slab, a reinforced grade beam is sometimes used to support the concrete floor. The grade beam spans the area between the concrete piers located below the frostline.

FOUNDATION SLAB BASICS

Several factors are involved in the construction of a foundation slab.

Support for Bearing Walls

Exterior bearing walls are supported either by the thickened edge of the slab or by foundation walls. Beneath interior bearing walls, the slab may be thickened to provide the necessary support. **Fig. 15-5.** This thickened area is like a footing. It should be strengthened with rebar.

Fig. 15-4. Another type of independent slab. The concrete block foundation wall is supported on a footing that is below the frostline.

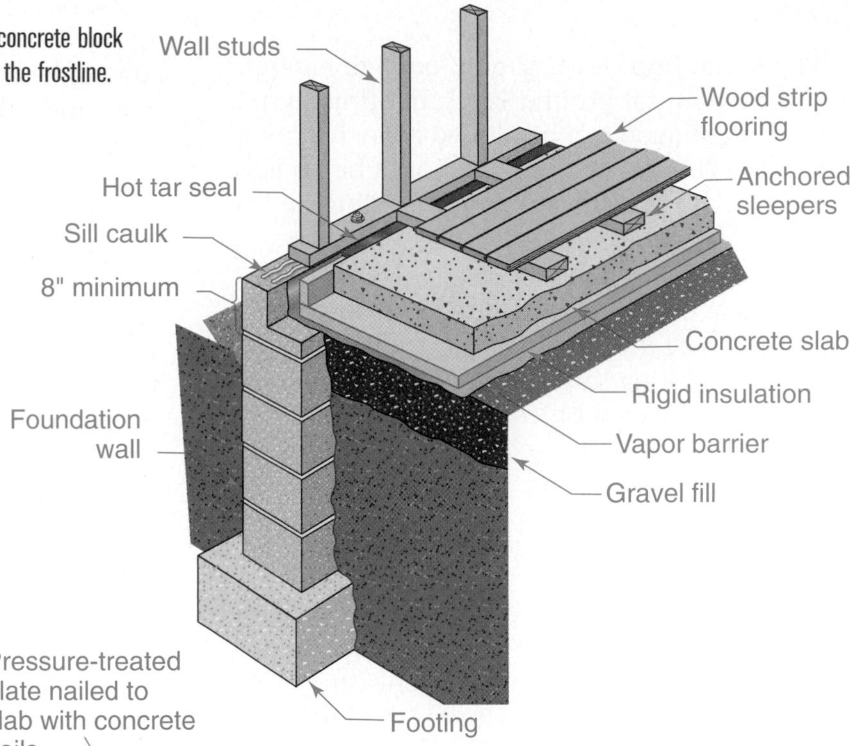

Fig. 15-5. A foundation slab should be thickened beneath bearing walls. This provides additional support for the walls and stiffens the slab to prevent cracking. The thickened area is formed by a trench, not by formwork.

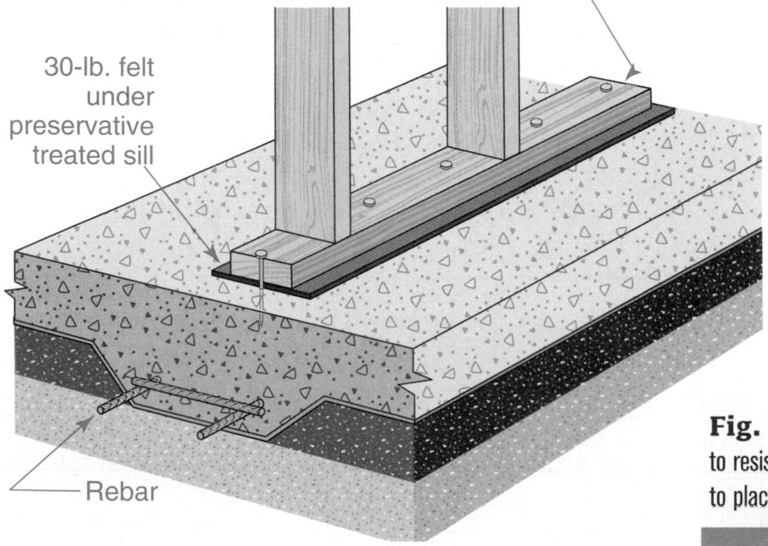

Formwork

A slab foundation does not require much formwork. For a monolithic slab, builders sometimes use lumber or plywood to form the slab edges. Foundation contractors may prefer reusable metal or wood forms. **Fig. 15-6.** In any case, the outer edges of the forms must be braced to resist the pressure of the wet concrete. After the concrete has partially cured, the forms can be removed.

Fig. 15-6. Reusable wood or metal forms must be braced well to resist the weight of the concrete. Note the use of a pump truck to place concrete for this slab.

Drainage

The finish-floor level should be high enough above the natural ground level that finish grade around the house can be sloped away for good drainage. The top of the slab should be no less than 8″ above the ground and the siding no less than 6″.

A perimeter drain should be placed around the outside edge of the exterior wall footings. **Fig. 15-7.** The drain helps keep ground moisture from wicking into the slab. Drain lines are not always required by code where the floor is located on fairly high ground, where subsoil is well drained, or in a very dry climate.

Reinforcement

Metal reinforcement is often placed in a concrete slab to increase its tensile strength and reduce cracking. This reinforcement can consist of either rebar or welded-wire mesh fabric. *Wire fabric* is a grid of horizontal and vertical wires. It comes in rolls and is cut to size at the site. Any reinforcement should be in place before the concrete is poured.

Code requirements for rebar vary, depending on the type of slab and its location. However, with a monolithic slab, either one No. 5 or two No. 4 bars should be located in the middle third of the footing's depth. Vertical lengths of rebar are sometimes added to reinforce the thickened portion of the slab. In earthquake areas, reinforcement is important. Local codes should be followed carefully.

Wire fabric should be placed near the center of the slab thickness. Contractors sometimes roll out the fabric over the excavation. They then use a rake or hook to pull it up into the concrete during the pour. This method, however, makes it difficult to tell the exact position of the reinforcement. A more precise method is to support it on chairs. **Fig. 15-8.** A **chair** is a small device that supports the wire fabric at a particular height. Chairs are left in place as the concrete is poured.

Insulation

In cold climates, a foundation slab can feel uncomfortably cold if it is not insulated. The best insulation for slabs is rigid, nonabsorbent boards or sheets, such as extruded or expanded polystyrene. Fig. 15-4. It can be placed around the perimeter of a monolithic slab, where the concrete is exposed to colder temperatures. For independent slabs, rigid insulation can be placed between the foundation walls and the

Fig. 15-7. Plastic drainage pipe is perforated. The holes allow water into the pipe so it can be drained away.

Fig. 15-8. Any reinforcement within the slab should be supported by chairs. It should not be supported on bricks or pieces of brick.

edge of the floor slab. Studies have shown that this edge insulation is important in reducing the amount of heat lost by conduction. Insulation may also be placed below the slab. This is important when radiant heating tubes are built into the slab (see Chapter 38, "Mechanicals").

Termite Protection

Some areas of the United States have problems with termites. (See Fig. 16-12, page 299.) In these areas, special care must be taken to prevent termites from getting into the wood framing above the concrete. One method is to chemically treat the soil before placing a slab. The chemicals, their strength, and the application methods are determined by local and state building officials. Their guidelines should be followed carefully.

Physical barriers, such as metal termite shields, should also be included (see Chapter 16, "Wood As a Building Material"). On monolithic slabs, shields should be located between the slab and the wall plate. For independent slabs, this barrier is continued to cover the gap between the slab and the foundation wall.

Where the chance of termite infestation is very high, a slab should not be insulated. In fact, building codes limit or prohibit the use of foam plastic insulation on the outside of foundation walls and beneath slabs below grade. Insects do not use this insulation as food, but they will tunnel through it to reach wood framing.

PREPARING FOR A CONCRETE SLAB*

A foundation slab is installed by foundation subcontractors. These specialists are experienced at solving the problems that can occur and they have the right tools. The following discussion outlines the basic steps they use.

Preparing the Subgrade

The **subgrade** is the earth below the slab. The subgrade must be well and uniformly compacted to prevent any uneven settlement of the floor slab. Uneven settlement is a common cause of cracks in concrete.

All organic matter, such as sod and roots, should first be removed and the ground leveled off slightly. Any holes or cracks in the subgrade should be filled and compacted (pressed down). Material for fill should be uniform. It should not contain large lumps, stones, or material that will rot. Any fill should be compacted in layers, or lifts, no more than 6″ deep. (A **lift** is a uniform and fairly shallow layer of material.) If fill is compacted in thicker layers, it may appear to be firm on the surface but it will not be uniformly firm. A *power tamper*, or *plate tamper*, is often used to compact fill. **Fig. 15-9.** This tool is powered by a gasoline engine and guided by hand over the area.

After any holes are filled, the entire subgrade should be thoroughly compacted by tamping or rolling. The finished subgrade should then be carefully checked for height and levelness. Any variations can create a slab of uneven thickness. When this occurs, the slab may not cure evenly, which is another common cause of cracking.

Fig. 15-9. A power tamper can be used to compact the subgrade.

* Adapted from material provided by the Portland Cement Association.

Soil cannot be properly compacted if it is too wet or too dry. You can get a rough idea of the proper moisture content of ordinary soils, except very sandy ones, by squeezing some in your hand. With proper moisture content, the soil will cling together but will not be plastic or muddy. If the soil is too dry, it should be sprinkled with water before compacting. If the soil is too wet, it must be allowed to dry.

Providing for Other Trades

Electrical conduit, ducts for heating systems, and plumbing supply and waste lines can be placed in trenches cut in the subgrade. Care should be taken to protect water supply lines from freezing if the building will not be occupied during cold weather. Careful planning ensures that connections to these utilities can be made where specified on the building plans.

After a monolithic slab has been poured and partially finished, anchor bolts are inserted around the perimeter. Carpenters will use these to secure wall framing to the slab.

Fig. 15-10. Compacting coarse granular fill with a hand tamper.

Preparing the Subbase

Coarse fill should be placed over the compacted subgrade to form the *subbase*, or *base course*. This fill should consist of coarse slag, gravel, or crushed stone no more than 2″ in diameter. The fill particles should be of uniform size to prevent them from packing together tightly. If necessary, the material should be sifted through a screen to remove any fines. **Fines** are finely crushed or powdered materials. The subbase, along with drainage pipes at the perimeter of the foundation, helps to drain water that might collect under the slab. When the slab is below grade, the subbase must be at least 4″ thick.

The fill should be brought to the desired grade and then thoroughly compacted. A power tamper can be used to compact most areas. Areas that are difficult to reach with this equipment can be compacted by hand. **Fig. 15-10.**

Installing Vapor Barriers

Water will not penetrate good quality concrete unless the water is driven by pressure (see Chapter 14, "Foundation Walls"). A properly constructed drainage system will prevent pressures from building up beneath a foundation slab. However, concrete can be penetrated by water vapor. If vapor passes through a slab, moisture can cause problems inside the house. For example, flooring surfaces glued to the slab may loosen. To prevent this, a polyethylene vapor barrier with joints lapped at least 6″ must be placed between the slab and the subbase. Wide sheets of standard 6-mil polyethylene may be used. However, cross-laminated polyethylene is more durable. In either case, workers should be warned not to puncture the membrane when placing the concrete.

One disadvantage of a vapor barrier is that it forces moisture in the fresh concrete to escape through the exposed top surface. This can cause shrinkage cracks in the slab surface, as well as other problems. For this reason, it is sometimes recommended that concrete not be placed directly on the vapor barrier. Instead, a 3″ thick layer of sand can be spread over the vapor barrier and compacted. The concrete can then be placed over the sand.

Radon Control

Radon is a colorless, odorless radioactive gas given off by some soils and rocks. In some parts of the United States, the seepage of radon into houses poses a health threat. Environmental protection agencies have developed a map of counties in the United States. Counties are placed in one of three zones, based on the degree to which radon might be a problem. This map is included in the building codes.

Houses built in areas with much radon seepage must be built to resist radon entry. In some houses, the combination of a granular subbase and a carefully installed vapor barrier may be enough. However, where concentrations are very high, stronger methods may be needed. These may include a sub-slab ventilation system. **Fig. 15-11.**

PLACING THE CONCRETE

Concrete for the floor slab and bearing-wall footings should be made with durable, well-graded aggregate. It must have a compressive strength of at least 2,500 psi.

The concrete should be workable so it can be placed without developing large air pockets (honeycombing) or excess water on the surface.

SAFETY FIRST

Pouring Safely

When placing concrete, always be sure that the operator of the concrete truck or the concrete pumper can communicate clearly with other workers. The operator should be able to see where the concrete is being placed. Proper use of hand signals will ensure that the flow of concrete can be stopped quickly when necessary.

However, too much water should not be added to the concrete just to make it easier to place. This reduces its strength. If necessary, the proportion of fine and coarse aggregate should be adjusted to obtain a more workable mix. Another way to increase workability is to add an admixture to the concrete (see Chapter 12, "Concrete As a Building Material").

Concrete should not drop more than approximately 4′ to the ground as it is poured by the ready-mix truck. **Fig. 15-12.** A greater drop can cause large aggregate to settle unevenly. Extension chutes, temporary ramps, or methods such as pumping prevent this problem.

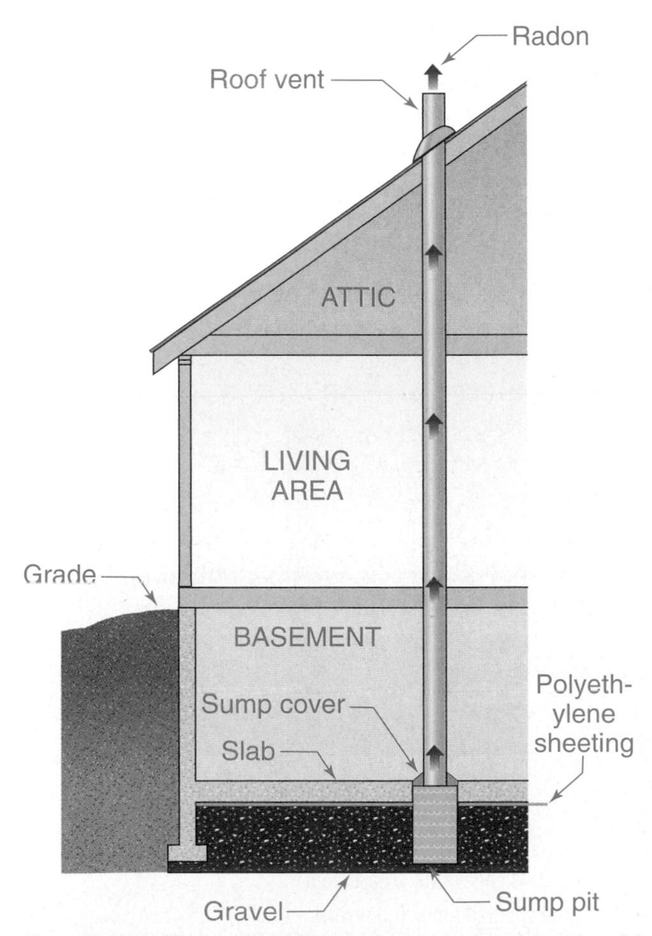

Fig. 15-11. One method of venting radon gas from beneath a slab. This method is called *passive venting* because no fans are involved. Active venting uses one or more fans to move the air.

Fig. 15-12. The end of the chute delivering concrete from a truck should be within approximately 4′ of ground level to prevent the aggregate from settling unevenly.

After placing, the concrete should be made to settle by vibrating, tamping, or spading. Then it should be finished. The steps in finishing the surface will depend upon the floor finish specified (see Section 15-2).

OTHER TYPES OF FLATWORK

Basements are normally finished with concrete floors. These floors are poured after all improvements, such as sewer and water lines, have been connected. Concrete is also often used for walks and driveways, especially where snow removal is important.

Basement Floors

Basement floor slabs should be no less than 3½″ thick and should slope toward a floor drain. There should be at least one drain in a basement floor. For large floors two drains are better.

When concrete is poured in an enclosed area, such as a basement, the foundation walls serve as forms. However, the concrete still must be leveled to the correct thickness. This is done by means of rail-like devices on which a screed rides. **Fig. 15-13.** A **screed** is a long, straight length of metal or wood that is used to "strike off" (level) the concrete. The screed is pulled by hand across the top of the rails. The rails are made of sections of l″ pipe set on stakes driven into the subgrade. The pipes used as rails are called *screed strips.* The stakes are driven deep enough so that when the pipes are set on them, the tops of the pipes will be at the level desired for the surface of the slab. After screeding, the pipes and stakes are removed. A float (see Section 15.2) is then used to pack concrete into any gaps.

Driveways

The grade, width, and radius of curves in a driveway are important when establishing a safe entry to the garage. Driveways that have a grade of more than 7 percent (7′ rise in 100 lineal feet) should not be covered with gravel because the gravel will gradually wash away. Concrete is often used instead.

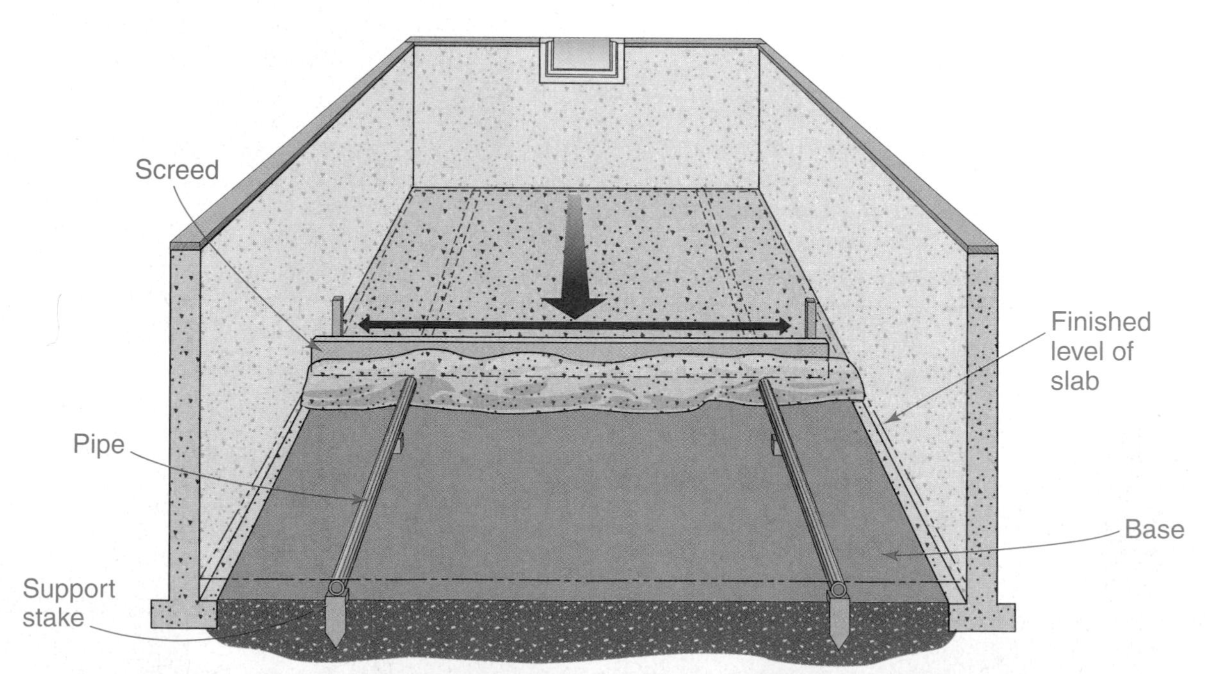

Fig. 15-13. A pipe screed used as a guide for the straightedge when leveling a basement floor. Workers pull the screed toward them by the handles shown at right and left. The arrows indicate the movement of the board. Note that it moves from side to side as well as toward the workers.

Estimating...

Concrete for Flatwork

The volume of concrete needed for flatwork is based on the size of the area covered and the thickness of the slab. The result is expressed in cubic yards.

Step 1 To calculate the amount of material required for the basement floor for the home shown in **Fig. 15-14**, first figure the area of the slab. The house measures 26′ × 40′, so the total area of the basement slab will be 1,040 square feet.

Step 2 The floor will be 4″ thick. **Table 15-A** shows that at a thickness of 4″, one cubic yard of concrete covers 81 sq. ft. To calculate the total amount of concrete required, divide the total slab area (1,040 sq. ft.) by the number of square feet covered by one cubic yard (81):

$$1{,}040 \div 81 = 12.39$$

If you round this off, you will need 13 cu. yds. of concrete. When estimating, you should always round up.

Another way to calculate the volume of concrete is to use the following formula:

length in feet × width in feet × thickness in feet ÷ 27 = cubic yards

To use the formula, each dimension must be in the same unit. For example, if you calculate the volume of concrete for a slab that is 20′-6″ long, 10′ wide, and 4″ thick, convert all dimensions to feet, using decimal equivalents:

$$20.5' \times 10' \times 0.33' = 67.65 \text{ cu. ft.}$$

Then divide by 27 to obtain cubic yards:

$$67.65 \div 27 = 2.50 \text{ cu. yds., or } 2\tfrac{1}{2} \text{ cu. yds.}$$

ESTIMATING ON THE JOB

Using **Table 15-A**, estimate the number of cubic yards of concrete needed for a basement floor that measures 20′ by 30′ and is 4″ thick. Assume that 1 cubic yard of concrete can be placed in .43 hours. Estimate the time it would take to place the concrete.

Table 15-A. Estimating Materials for Concrete Slab

Material	
Thickness (inches)	Square Feet from One Cubic Yard
2	162
3	108
4	81
5	65
6	54

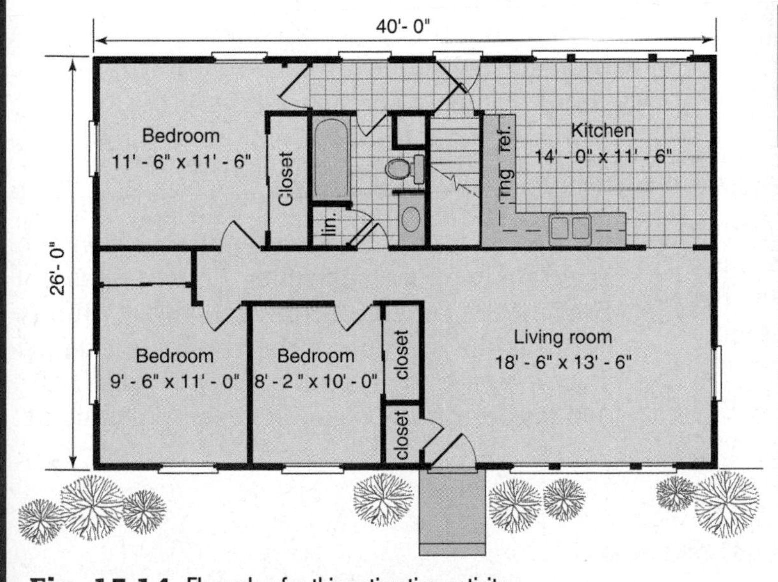

Fig. 15-14. Floor plan for this estimating activity.

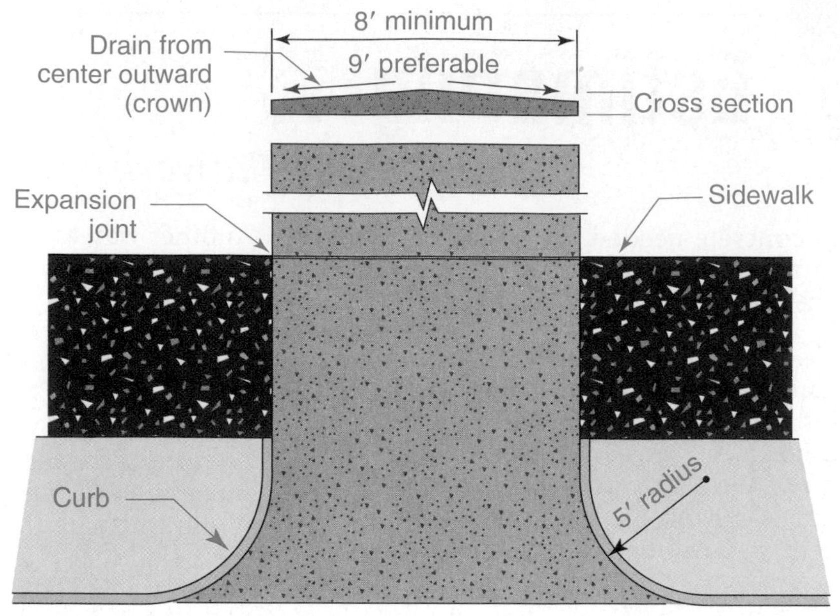

Fig. 15-15. Single-slab driveway details. A concrete slab should drain from the center outward.

A common type of concrete driveway is the full-width slab. **Fig. 15-15.** The concrete should be given a broom finish to prevent both cars and people from slipping.

A gravel base is not ordinarily required on sandy, undisturbed soil. If the area has been recently filled, the fill, preferably gravel, should settle first and be well tamped. A gravel base should be used on all other soils. The concrete should be about 5″ thick, and a vapor barrier is not required. Side forms are often built of 2x6 boards. These members establish the elevation and alignment of the driveway. They are also used to support the board used to strike off the concrete.

Though not required, the addition of 6x6 wire fabric reinforcing reduces cracking. Expansion joints with asphalt-saturated felt strips inserted should be used where the driveway joins the public walk or curb and at the garage slab. They should also be used about every 40′ on long driveways. Concrete containing an air-entraining agent should be used in areas having severe winter climates. Air-entraining produces tiny air bubbles that help the concrete resist damage during freeze/thaw cycles.

Sidewalks

Concrete sidewalks are constructed much the same as concrete driveways. They should not be poured over filled areas unless the fill has settled and is well tamped. This is especially true of areas near the house after basement excavation backfill has been completed.

Minimum thickness of concrete over normal undisturbed soil is usually 4″. Control joints should be used and spaced on 4′ centers. A *control joint* is a joint that helps to minimize random cracks in a concrete slab. By creating a slightly weakened area, it encourages a crack to form in a straight line, rather than across the concrete in an irregular line. Thus it does not prevent the concrete from cracking. It simply controls the location of the crack. An *expansion joint* may also be required for sidewalks. An expansion joint is a gap between portions of concrete that is filled with a flexible material. The concrete is thus able to expand and contract without damage to itself or to adjacent surfaces.

When slopes to the house are greater than 5 percent, steps should be used. **Fig. 15-16.**

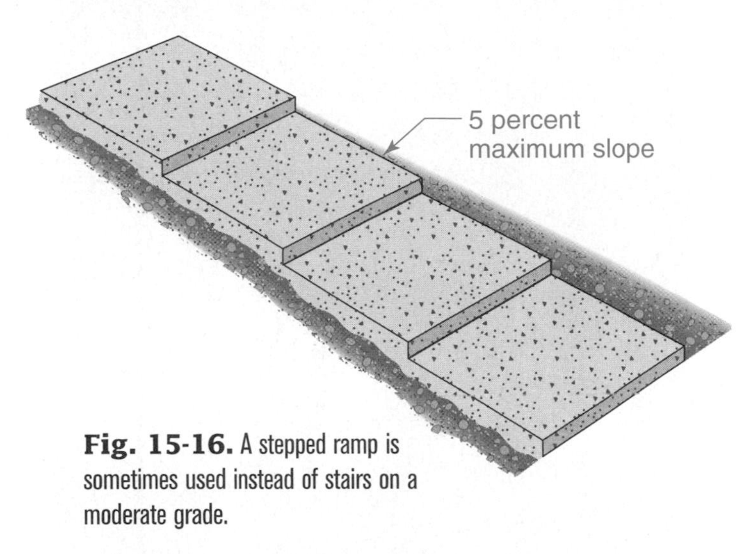

Fig. 15-16. A stepped ramp is sometimes used instead of stairs on a moderate grade.

SECTION 15.1

Check Your Knowledge

1. What is concrete flatwork?
2. Why is it important to compact the subgrade in lifts?
3. What is the purpose of the subbase?
4. What is the formula for figuring cubic yards of concrete?

On the Job

Suppose you are the leader of a team of workers who do not share the same culture or language. You have to communicate to them the amount of concrete needed for a driveway that is 36½′ long, 12′ wide, and 5″ thick. How will you do it? Write the steps you will take and include any sketches. Then present your method to the class.

SECTION 15.2

Finishing Flatwork

A flatwork surface, such as a floor, driveway, or sidewalk, must be finished. Finishing is a multiple-step process that levels the concrete and gives it a surface that will suit the intended use. **Fig. 15-17.** A basement or foundation slab, for example, is given a very smooth finish. This makes the concrete easy to clean and allows finished floors to be attached directly to the surface. A brushed, non-slippery finish is best for sidewalks, while a somewhat coarser surface suits driveways. Various decorative finishes are also available.

STEPS IN FINISHING

Finishing includes screeding, bullfloating, edging, jointing, floating, and troweling.

Fig. 15-17. After a slab is poured, it is finished using a combination of hand and mechanical methods.

Screeding

The first step in finishing any flatwork is *screeding*. A hand-operated screed and the method of using it are shown in **Fig. 15-18**. The concrete is struck off just after it is placed in the forms. The screed rides on the edges of the side forms or on wood or metal strips set up for the purpose. Two people move the screed along the slab, using a sawing motion. Screeding may also be done with mechanical equipment. **Fig. 15-19.** It leaves a level surface with a coarse finish.

Bullfloating

Bullfloating makes the concrete surface more even with no high or low spots. A *bull float* is a wide, flat metal or wood pad that is pushed back and forth over the concrete. A long handle enables the worker to reach every area of the slab. **Fig. 15-20.** A similar tool, called a *darby*, has a shorter handle.

Bullfloating is done shortly after screeding, while the concrete is still plastic enough to allow a slight paste of mortar to be brought to the surface. However, there must be no water visible on the concrete. Otherwise, an excess

Fig. 15-19. A power screed.

Fig. 15-18. Screeding a concrete slab.

Fig. 15-20. Bullfloating a concrete slab.

amount of fines and moisture will also come to the surface. This is one of the principal causes of defects. Among other problems, it causes fine hairline cracks (crazing) or a powdery material (dusting) on the surface. Only enough bullfloating should be done to remove defects and to bring enough mortar to the surface of the slab to produce the desired finish.

Edging and Jointing

When the sheen has left the surface and the concrete has started to stiffen, other finishing operations can be done. *Edging* produces a rounded edge on the slab to prevent chipping or damage. **Fig. 15-21.** The edger is run back and forth and all coarse aggregate particles are covered.

Immediately following edging, larger slabs are *jointed*, or *grooved*. Sometimes shrinkage stresses are present in the slab as a result of temperature changes or dryness. These stresses can cause the concrete to crack. Joints reduce the thickness of the slab and cracks are then likely to occur only at these weakened points. When the concrete shrinks, these joints open slightly, preventing other uneven and unsightly cracks. A jointing tool is used to cut the control joints about ¾″ deep in the slab. The joints should be perpendicular to the slab's edge. To ensure straight joints, it is good practice to guide the jointer with a straight lx8 or 1x10 board. **Fig. 15-22.** A crooked joint detracts from the appearance of the finished slab.

Floating

In some cases, an additional floating step is done, using wood or metal floating trowels, or *floats*. Aluminum or magnesium floats must be used when hand floating air-entrained concrete because wood floats stick to the concrete surface. Hand floating further evens the surface of the concrete. It also compacts the surface

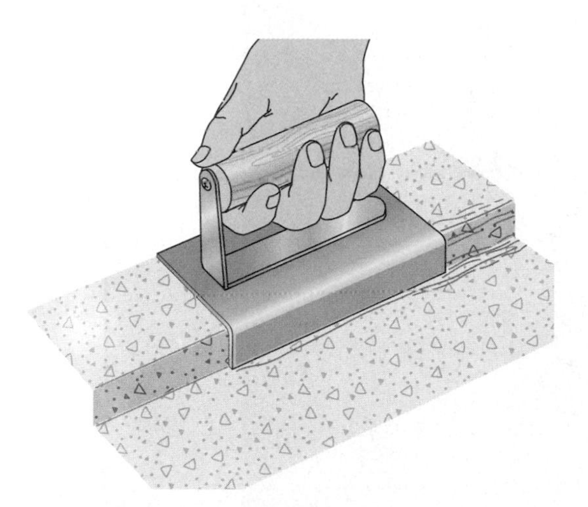

Fig. 15-21. An edger.

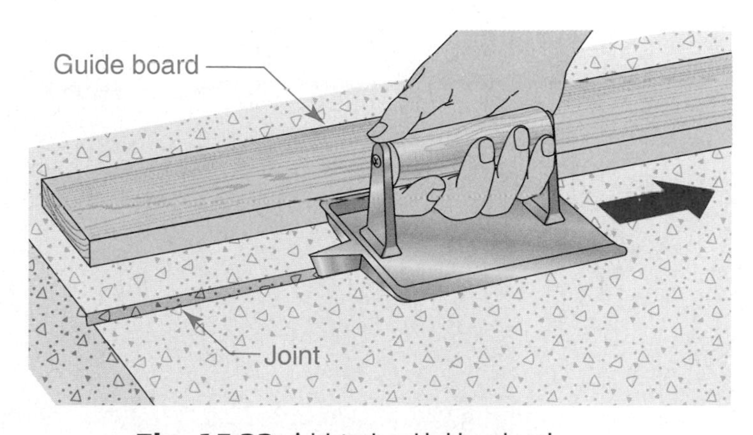

Fig. 15-22. A jointer is guided by a board.

mortar in preparation for the next finishing steps. It produces a very even surface with a light texture. Hand floating also removes any ridges left by jointing tools.

If floating is the last step in finishing, it may be necessary to float the surface a second time after the concrete has hardened slightly.

Troweling

For a dense, smooth finish, floating is followed by *troweling* with a steel trowel. **Fig. 15-23.** For large areas, a power trowel is used instead of a hand trowel. **Fig. 15-24.** Troweling cannot be started until the concrete has hardened enough to prevent fine material and water from working to the surface. In fact, troweling should be planned carefully. A surface that is troweled too early is not durable. A surface that is troweled too late is difficult to finish properly.

Fig. 15-23. Hand troweling a concrete slab.

Fig. 15-24. Power troweling a concrete slab.

Carpenter's Tip

When hand-troweling or floating a large surface, kneeboards (or kneeling boards) may be used. **Fig. 15-25. Kneeboards** measure about 12″ by 24″ and are placed on the concrete to support the weight of the finisher. The kneeboard supports the knees, while a second board goes under the feet. When moving from one area to another, the finisher stands on the foot board, places the kneeboard, then steps onto the kneeboard and places the foot board. The finisher is now in position to continue without having stepped onto the fresh concrete itself.

Fig. 15-25. Using a kneeboard to support the weight of the concrete finisher. This kneeboard includes a toeboard.

Troweling should leave the surface smooth, even, and free of marks and ripples. For a fine-textured surface, the first troweling is immediately followed with a second. In this second operation the trowel, held flat, is passed lightly over the concrete with a circular motion.

For a hard steel-troweled finish, the second troweling should be delayed until the concrete has become hard enough to make a ringing sound under the trowel. In hard steel-troweling, the trowel is tilted slightly. Heavy pressure is applied to compact the surface.

Special Finishes

Concrete can be given a color, a pattern, or a texture. This is done after the concrete has been placed but before it has cured. Patterns come from metal stamps that are pressed into the wet concrete. **Fig. 15-26.** Colors come from various types of masonry dyes. In some cases, small, smooth pebbles can be scattered into the fresh concrete after bullfloating. They are pressed into place during later finishing operations.

Fig. 15-26. This concrete driveway was colored and stamped with a pattern shortly after it was placed. This made the concrete look like another material.

CURING FLATWORK

After finishing, the concrete should be kept moist for at least two days. This ensures that hydration will continue. It also improves the concrete's strength. When the finished floor is to be exposed concrete, at least five days of moist curing are required. Burlap or canvas or a waterproof concrete curing paper may be used to cover the floor slab during this period. If burlap or canvas is used, it should be kept wet by sprinkling it with water. Curing should begin as soon as the concrete is hard enough to make damage unlikely. Chemicals can also be used to coat concrete for curing. By slowing the rate at which moisture leaves the concrete, they help to increase its strength.

When the concrete has cured enough to withstand foot traffic, wall plates can be laid out and construction can continue.

Temperature Extremes

Problems can be caused in concrete by temperature extremes. This is because so much surface area is exposed.

Placing concrete in unusually hot weather can reduce its strength. Hot conditions also encourage workers to add more water to the mix, which further reduces its strength. In hot weather, the water and aggregates should be kept as cool as possible before being mixed with the cement. Forms, rebar, and the subgrade should be cooled by sprinkling them with water just before the concrete is placed. In some cases, it may be wise to place the concrete early in the morning, or even at night, to avoid very hot temperatures. Moist curing is particularly important under these conditions and should be started as soon as possible.

In moderately cold weather, the heat of hydration is usually enough to prevent damage. Concrete placed in temperatures below freezing, however, can suffer a loss of strength unless protected. In fact, if concrete is frozen shortly after being placed, it can lose up to 50 percent of its strength. Concrete can be protected by placing it in insulated forms or by covering it temporarily with insulation. High-early strength, air-entrained, and low-slump concrete can also be used to counteract such conditions.

SECTION 15.2 Check Your Knowledge

1. What is the purpose of a bull float?
2. What defects can be caused by bullfloating too soon?
3. When is a concrete slab ready for jointing and edging?
4. What are kneeboards used for?

On the Job

Suppose you supervise a team of three finishers: Jose, Mike, and Sita. Create a flow chart showing the steps they must follow when finishing a basement floor with a fine-textured surface. Assign each worker specific tasks.

Chapter 15 Review

Section Summaries

15.1 Concrete foundation slabs are often used in warm or mild climates to provide a foundation and a subfloor for houses. Proper preparation of the subgrade and subbase are important to a high-quality job. Slabs are more prone than foundation walls to being damaged by temperature extremes.

15.2 Finishing a slab is a process of preparing the surface for various end uses. After the concrete is placed, the excess is screeded off the slab. After any water has disappeared, bullfloating, edging, jointing, floating, and troweling can take place.

Review Questions

1. Describe the two basic types of foundation slabs.
2. What is the best way to ensure that welded-wire reinforcement will be positioned in the middle of the slab?
3. Explain the disadvantage of placing concrete directly over a vapor barrier.
4. What is radon?
5. What is a screed?
6. List the steps in finishing flatwork.
7. When putting a hard steel-troweled finish on a slab, what determines when the second troweling can begin?
8. What ensures that hydration will continue in the days following concrete placement?
9. List at least three methods that can be used to protect fresh concrete in hot weather.
10. List at least two methods that can be used to protect fresh concrete in cold weather.

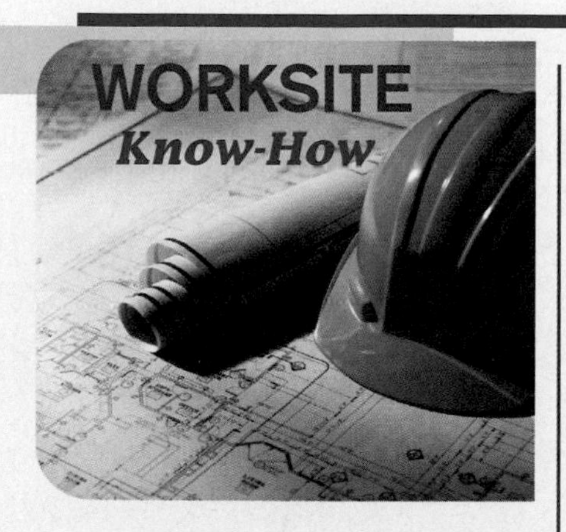

Why Protecting Your Health Matters In addition to the personal cost and suffering that poor health can cause the individual, it also impacts employers. Companies help pay for employee insurance. They also bear the cost in lost productivity when employees miss work. On average, 17,000 workers are injured each day in accidents. The cost to U.S. companies: $121 billion a year. Skin diseases caused by chemicals and other irritants, such as concrete mixtures, cost $1 billion per year. Occupational asthma caused by workplace substances, such as sawdust and concrete dust, cost $400 million annually. You can do your part to help keep these costs down by following safety rules and wearing personal protective gear, such as dust masks.

Unit 4

WOOD FRAME CARPENTRY

Careers in Construction

Framing Carpenter

Framing carpenters are another type of structural worker. Framing carpenters are also called rough carpenters because they "rough out" or assemble basic structural units that are later "trimmed out" or finished by other specialty carpenters.

Framing carpenters construct and install wooden structures. In building construction, framing carpenters construct the frame of the building. They install the subflooring, wall sheathing, and prefabricated panels and windows. Framing carpenters also build scaffolds on which other workers can stand. They construct the chutes that are used to direct the flow of wet concrete and build the forms for concrete foundations and the support systems for machinery installed in buildings.

Most framing carpenters learn their trade on the job by working under the supervision of experienced carpenters. Others acquire their skills through vocational/technical education, employer training programs, or apprenticeships.

For more information, check the *Occupational Outlook Handbook* or look up "framing carpenter" on the Internet.

Chapter 16

Wood As a Building Material

Objectives

After reading this chapter, you'll be able to:

- Identify flat-sawn and quarter-sawn boards.
- Explain how the moisture content of wood is controlled.
- Identify common defects in lumber.
- Recognize conditions that lead to lumber decay.
- Identify insects that can infest lumber.

Terms

cambium
coniferous tree
deciduous tree
fiber-saturation point
grade stamp
kiln
seasoning

Wood is used more than any other material in the construction of a house. It can be used to form most of the structure's frame and many of the interior and exterior surfaces. It is also a key element in the construction of doors, windows, cabinetry, stairs, and other features. This is because wood is versatile and readily available. It can be cut to different sizes and formed into many different shapes.

Because wood has been used for centuries, carpenters, builders, architects, and others know a great deal about how it performs. Even so, new types of wood and wood-based materials are being developed all the time. For more on these materials, see Chapter 17, "Engineered Lumber," and Chapter 18, "Engineered Panel Products." This chapter will focus on solid wood.

SECTION 16.1

Wood Basics

For all-around utility, wood has few, if any, equals as a building material. It is preferred for many types of construction for several reasons:

- Wood is strong. Certain common framing woods are as strong and rigid as some types of steel.
- Wood is easily fastened with nails, staples, bolts, connectors, screws, or glue.
- Wooden buildings are easily altered or repaired. Openings can be cut and additions made without difficulty.
- Wood has low heat conductivity, which helps keep wood buildings warm.
- Wood accepts decorative coatings such as paint and stains.
- Wood resists acids, saltwater, and other corrosive agents better than many other structural materials.
- Wood is a renewable resource.

OUR FOREST RESOURCES

Most of the wood used in the United States is harvested from millions of acres of forestland spread across North America. Many years ago, trees were cut without regard for the effect cutting would have on the forest itself and the surrounding areas. However, many people now understand that we must take greater care of our forests. The benefits include:

- Continued ability to harvest lumber.
- Preservation of wildlife habitats and endangered species.
- Protection of important water resources.
- Soil conservation.
- Maintenance of scenic areas.

Because forests are renewable, we won't run out of them as long as we manage them properly.

How Trees Grow

The growing, "working" parts of a tree are the tips of its roots, the buds, the leaves, and a thin layer of cells just inside the bark called the cambium. **Fig. 16-1.** The **cambium** is a layer of living tissue that produces new wood, called *sapwood*, along its inner surface. New bark is

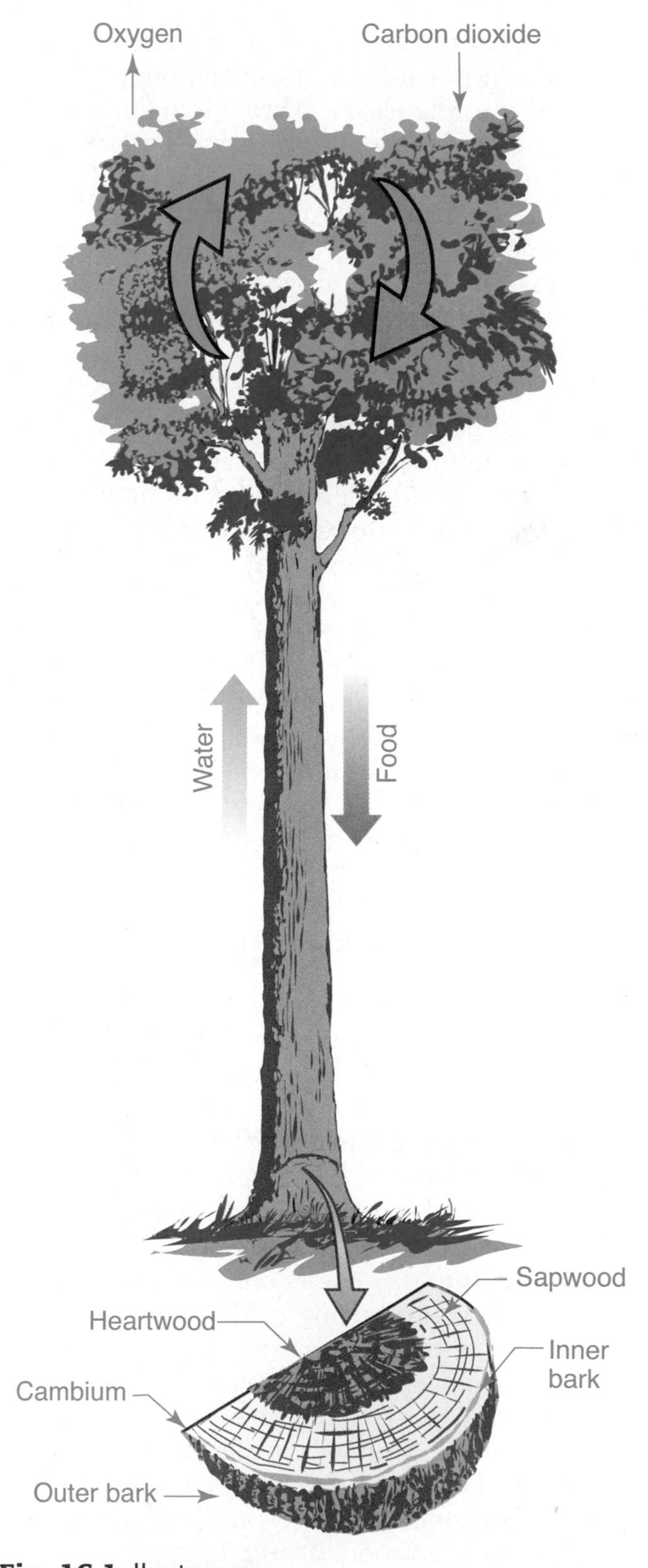

Fig. 16-1. How trees grow.

created along its outer surface. Sapwood carries water and nutrients from the tree's roots to its leaves. As successive layers of sapwood build up around the tree, the layers nearest the center gradually turn into a nonliving material called *heartwood.* Heartwood does not contribute to growth, but it gives strength and rigidity to the tree.

Water from the soil enters a tree through its roots. The water travels upward through the sapwood into the leaves. Through the process of *photosynthesis*, carbon dioxide and water are combined in the presence of chlorophyll and sunlight. This provides food to nourish the whole tree. This food is carried from the leaves to the rest of the tree through the inner bark. Oxygen is released through the leaves as a byproduct of photosynthesis.

After a tree has been harvested, its life story can be read in the *annual rings* (growth rings) of the stump. In temperate climates, the tree adds one annual ring during each year of growth. Most annual rings consist of a light band formed in the spring (early wood) and a dark band formed in the summer (late wood). When growth conditions are good and food and water abundant, the rings are wide. When long dry spells or other adverse conditions occur, growth slows and the rings are narrow. Annual rings are visible in the end grain of lumber. **Fig. 16-2.** Experienced builders sometimes study these rings to determine the suitability of the lumber for various uses.

Fig. 16-2. Growth rings are evident in the end grain of lumber.

Traditionally, wood for construction has been used in the general region in which the logs were harvested. However, the global economy and improvements in shipping have made wood products from one region available in other regions. For example, tropical hardwoods from Central and South America are found increasingly in North American markets. Only those tropical woods purposely grown on tree plantations (farms), however, can be considered renewable resources.

Hardwoods and Softwoods

The terms *hardwood* and *softwood* identify woods based on the two main types of trees. The terms do not indicate actual softness or hardness of the wood. In fact, some hardwoods, such as balsa wood, are softer and less dense than some softwoods. Some softwoods, such as yew, are harder than some hardwoods. Hardwoods are cut from broad-leaved, deciduous trees. A **deciduous tree** is one that sheds its leaves annually, during cold or very dry seasons. Some common hardwoods are walnut, mahogany, maple, birch, cherry, oak, and ash. Softwoods are those that come from a **coniferous tree**, which produces seeds in cones and has needlelike or scalelike leaves. Common examples of coniferous trees are pine, hemlock, fir, cedar, and redwood. **Table 16-A.**

from Another Angle

In the United States and other countries with temperate climates, most broad-leaved trees are deciduous and lose their leaves in the fall. However, some broad-leaved trees that live where winters are mild but wet and summers are hot and dry keep their leaves for several years. They are not conifers, because they do not produce their seeds in cones. Like conifers, however, they produce smaller leaves, which helps them conserve moisture. Examples of broad-leaved evergreens include the olive tree, which grows in the Mediterranean region, and the canyon live oak of California.

Table 16-A. Principal Commercial Softwoods	
Common Commercial Names	**Alternate Names**
Cedar	
Alaska cedar Eastern red cedar Incense cedar Northern white cedar Port Orford cedar Southern white cedar Western red cedar	Southern red cedar Atlantic white cedar
Cypress	
Cypress	Bald cypress Pond cypress
Fir	
Balsam fir Douglas fir Noble fir White fir	Fraser fir Subalpine fir California red fir Grand fir Pacific silver fir
Hemlock	
Eastern hemlock Mountain hemlock West Coast hemlock	Carolina hemlock Western hemlock
Juniper	
Western juniper	Alligator juniper Rocky Mountain juniper Utah juniper
Larch	
Western larch	
Pine	
Jack pine Lodgepole pine Norway pine Ponderosa pine Sugar pine Idaho white pine Northern white pine Longleaf yellow pine Southern yellow pine	Red pine Western white pine Eastern white pine Longleaf pine Slash pine Loblolly pine Longleaf pine Pitch pine Shortleaf pine
Redwood	
Spruce	
Eastern spruce Engelmann spruce Sitka spruce	Black spruce Red spruce White spruce Blue spruce
Tamarack	
Yew	
Pacific yew	

PROCESSING LUMBER

Wood is the raw material that grows in the forest. When the tree has been cut down and its limbs have been removed, the result is called a log. Logs are sawn lengthwise into smaller pieces at a mill. These pieces of wood have a uniform thickness and width and are referred to as *lumber*.

Cutting Boards from Logs

The way in which a board is cut from the log can affect its appearance and performance. Two methods are commonly used: flat-sawing and quarter-sawing.

Flat-Sawn Lumber. Most construction lumber is flat sawn. At the mill, a log is squared up lengthwise, and then sawn into boards. **Fig. 16-3.** Looking at the end grain of a flat-sawn board, you can see that the growth rings run across the board's width. Looking at the face, you can see a distinctive archlike pattern. Flat-sawn lumber is relatively inexpensive. Flat sawing produces boards of greater width than other cutting methods. However, such boards are more likely to shrink and warp.

Quarter-Sawn Lumber. Quarter-sawn lumber is a premium wood. At the mill, a log is first sawn lengthwise into quarters. Boards are then cut from the faces of each quarter. **Fig. 16-4.** Looking at the end grain of a quarter-sawn board, you can see that the growth rings run across the thickness of the board. These growth rings generally form angles of 60° to 90° to the board's surface. Quarter-sawn boards with end grain at angles between 30° and 60° are referred to as rift-sawn boards.

Quarter-sawn boards have a low tendency to warp, shrink, or swell. They also provide a more durable surface than flat-sawn lumber. They do not tend to twist or cup. They hold paints and finishes better. However, quarter-sawn lumber is more expensive and less plentiful than flat-sawn lumber.

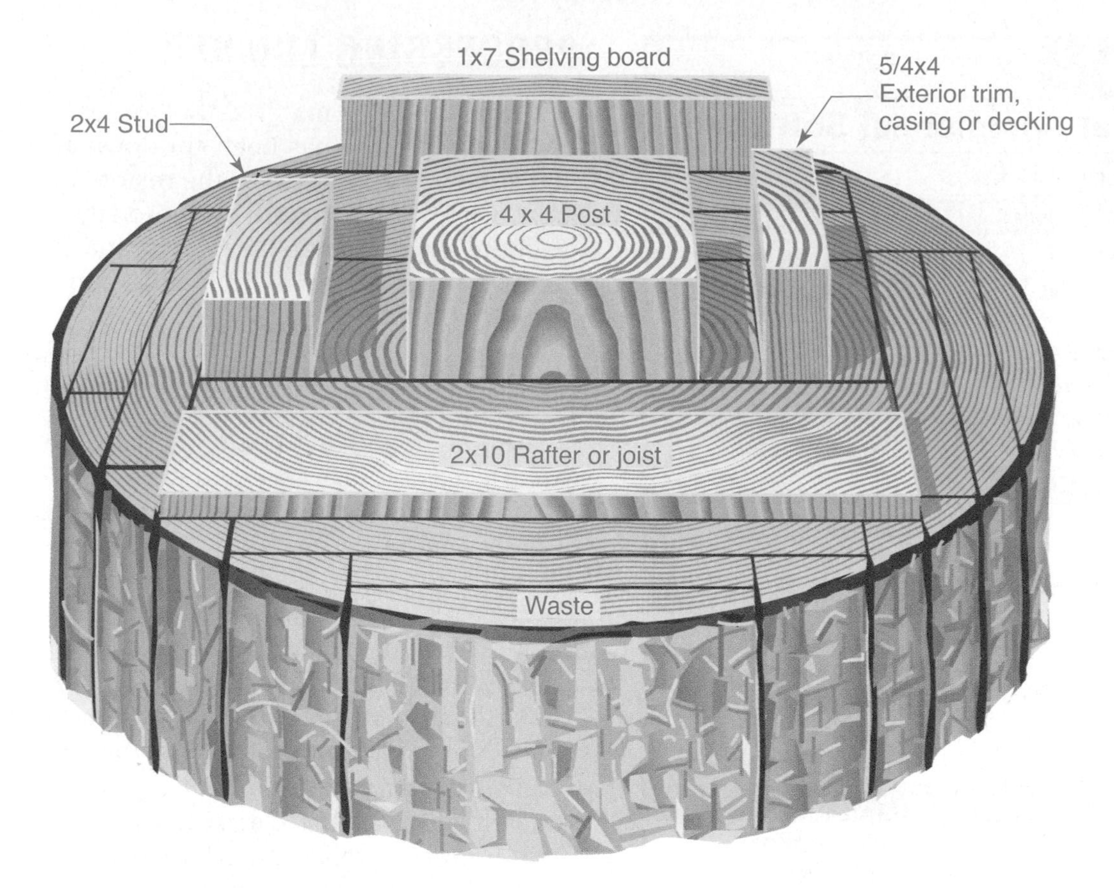

Fig. 16-3. Flat-sawn lumber. Notice the orientation of growth rings on the ends.

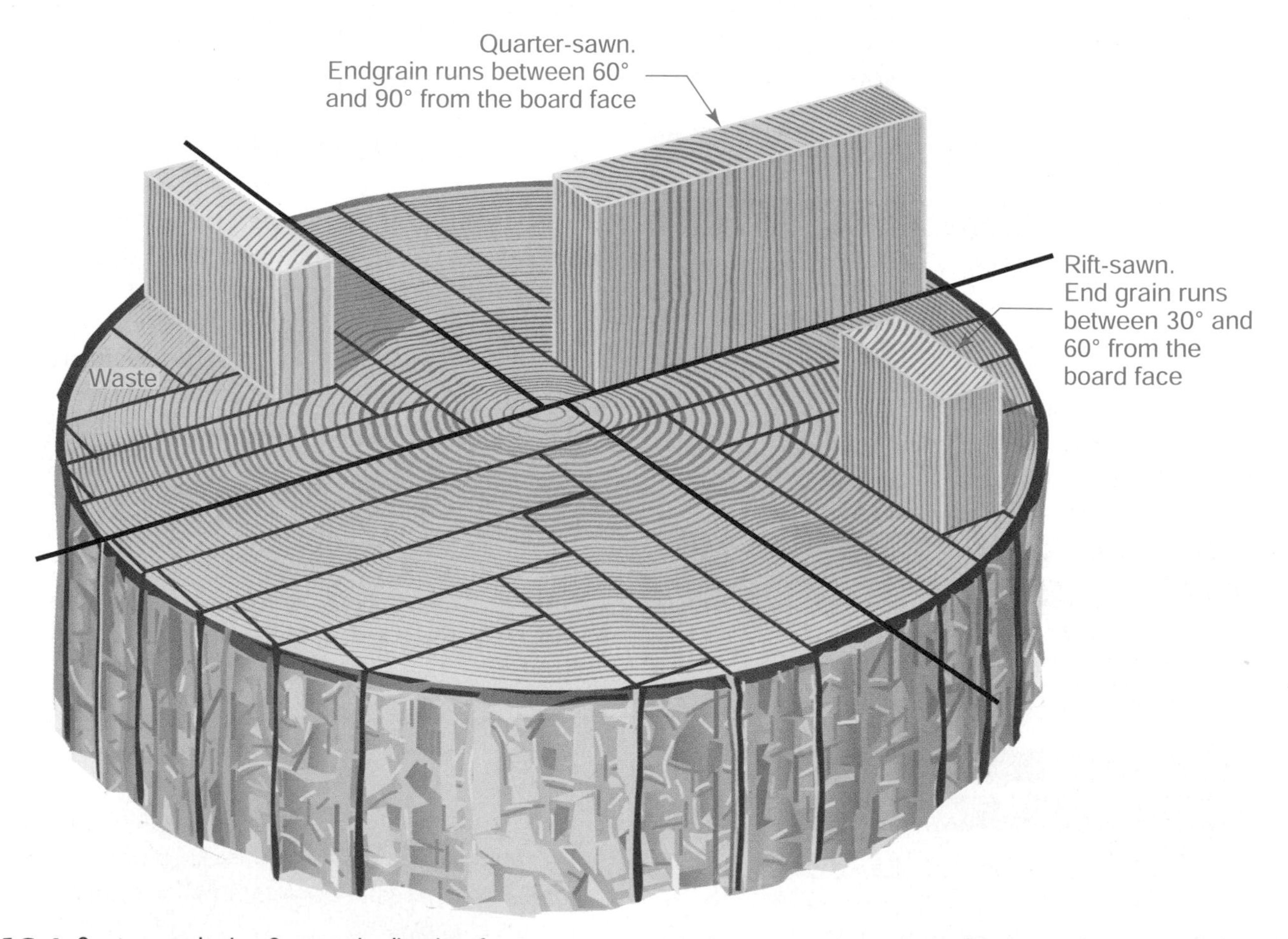

Fig. 16-4. Quarter-sawn lumber. Compare the direction of grain on the ends of the boards shown here with the directions on those in Fig. 16-3.

Controlling Moisture Content

The amount of water wood contains is referred to as its *moisture content* (MC). It is expressed as a percentage of what the wood would weigh if it were completely dry. For example, assume that a block of wood that has just been cut from a tree weighs 60 lbs. After being dried in an oven, it weighs only 50 lbs. Thus the original piece contained 10 lbs. of water. That is 20 percent of the wood's dry weight ($10 \div 50 = .20$). The lower the percentage, the drier the wood.

Fiber-Saturation Point. A living tree takes in a great deal of water. The tree stores water first in the cell walls. When the cell walls have absorbed all the water they can hold, the wood is at the **fiber-saturation point.** Though it can vary, for most woods the fiber-saturation point occurs when the wood contains about 28 percent moisture. If the tree takes in additional water, it stores that water in the cambium cell cavities.

Removal of water from the cell cavities of harvested wood has no apparent effect upon its properties except to reduce its weight. For this reason, drying the wood until its moisture content is roughly 28 percent does not result in shrinkage. However, reducing moisture to less than 28 percent will remove water from the cell walls, causing the wood to shrink in all directions.

Seasoning. The process of drying wood is called **seasoning**. There are two methods of seasoning wood: air drying and kiln drying.

In *air drying*, the rough lumber is stacked outdoors in layers separated by thin wooden crosspieces called *stickers.* The lumber remains stacked from one to three months or longer. After air drying, the lumber has an average moisture content of 19 percent or less.

In *kiln drying*, the lumber is also stacked in layers with stickers between. It is then placed in a kiln. **Fig. 16-5.** A **kiln** is an oven in which moisture, airflow, and temperature are carefully controlled. Heat in the oven removes moisture from the wood. Properly kiln-dried (KD) lumber has less than 10 percent moisture content. In a kiln, drying may take less than four days.

Even though lumber is dried to a certain moisture content, it continues to absorb or give off water, depending on the humidity of the surrounding air. If the air is damp, dry wood absorbs moisture and swells. If the air is very dry, the wood shrinks. If the air alternates between moist in the summer and dry in the winter, as it does in many parts of North America, wood expands and contracts. This is sometimes referred to as *seasonal expansion.*

Fig. 16-5. When the doors of this kiln slide open, the stacked lumber will be moved inside for drying.

Lumber shrinks in both width and length. However, shrinkage in length is usually so small it is not considered a problem. Shrinkage across the width of the board, however, can be more troublesome. The shrinkage of studs, for example, can cause drywall nails to pop. The shrinkage of hardwood floorboards can cause gaps to appear in the flooring. **Fig. 16-6.**

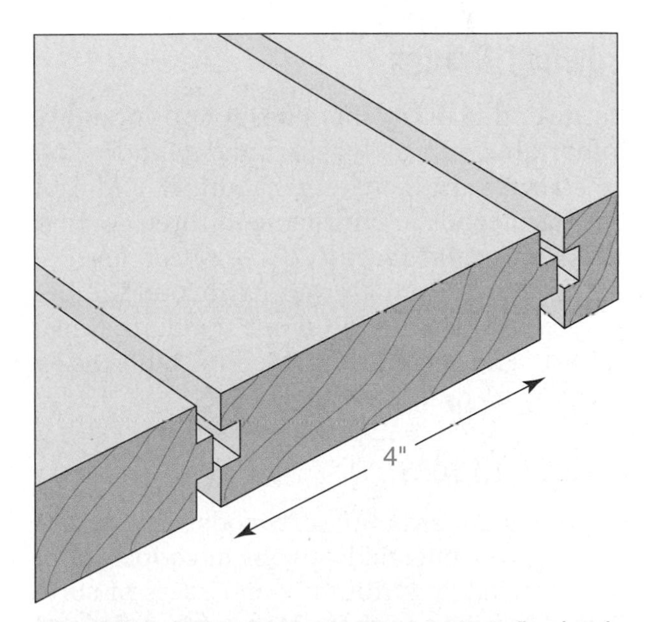

Fig. 16-6. If the moisture content is excessive in floor boards, gaps will appear between the boards as the wood dries. In wood maintained at a consistent moisture content, swelling and shrinkage are kept to a minimum.

The size of a board will vary about 1 percent for each 4 percent change in moisture content. When the moisture content of the wood is in balance with the humidity of the surrounding air, it neither gains nor loses moisture. At that point, the moisture content is said to have reached *equilibrium.* A portable moisture meter is the most common instrument for checking the moisture content of wood. **Fig. 16-7.**

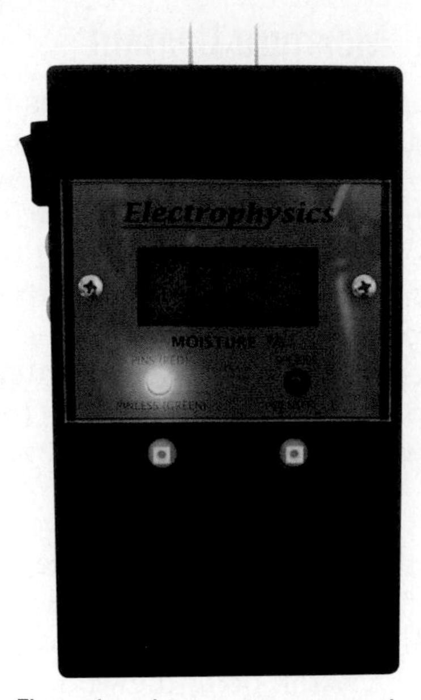

Fig. 16-7. Electronic moisture meters measure the wood's moisture content.

On-Site Storage. Lumber kept outside at the job site should be stored carefully to prevent it from shrinking or swelling. It should be supported off the ground and stacked with stickers (thin pieces of wood) between layers. It should be covered with waterproof material until used.

Lumber kept indoors will absorb or lose moisture until it reaches a balance with the moisture of the air in the room. Flooring and wood paneling should be delivered at least several days in advance of installation to allow the wood to reach equilibrium. Delivery one week in advance is even better. Storing the materials in the room prior to installation is called *conditioning.*

GRADING LUMBER

Lumber is graded according to various characteristics of the wood. *Grade* is a general indication of the quality of a piece of lumber. Being able to identify grades is an important skill for carpenters and other building professionals.

Hardwood Grades

Hardwood is used where beauty or durability is important, such as for door and window casings, stair treads, balusters, handrails, and cabinetry. Hardwoods are available in three common grades, *firsts and seconds (FAS), select,* and *No. 1 common.* Each kind of hardwood lumber is graded by a slightly different standard. Generally, firsts and seconds are used for built-ins, fine casework, and paneling.

Softwood Grades

Grading standards for softwoods were developed by governmental agencies in cooperation with producers, distributors, and users of softwoods. According to these standards, softwood lumber is divided into two basic groups:

- Green (unseasoned) lumber with a moisture content of more than 19 percent.
- Dry (seasoned) lumber with a moisture content of 19 percent or less.

Starting with these groups, each major lumber association has developed a complete set of grading standards. These rules are extensive and vary somewhat for each association. The builder who uses lumber primarily from one section of the country should understand the grading used in that area. For example, if most of the lumber used comes from the western states, then the standards published by the Western Wood Products Association might be most appropriate. If the lumber comes from southern states, standards set by the Southern Forest Products Association would apply. Familiarity with common lumber abbreviations will simplify the selection and specifications of softwood lumber. For information, refer to the Ready Reference Appendix table "Lumber Abbreviations."

After a softwood board has been graded, it is marked with a stamp. **Fig. 16-8.** A **grade stamp** is a permanent mark that identifies the board's species, quality, mill source, and a general indication of strength. The grade stamps enable carpenters and others to identify the most appropriate grade for a given use. Grade stamps let building inspectors know if a house is being built with lumber of suitable quality.

Information on the specific grades of framing lumber used in residential construction can be found in Chapter 19, "Framing Methods."

(A) WWPA Certification Mark: Certifies Association quality supervision. Ⓦ is a registered trademark.

(B) Grade Designation: Grade name, number, or abbreviation.

(C) Species Identification: Indicates species by individual species or species combination.

(D) Mill Identification: Firm name, brand, or assigned mill number. WWPA can be contacted to identify an individual mill whenever necessary.

(E) Condition of Seasoning: Indicates condition of seasoning at the time of surfacing.
S-GRN. Over 19 percent moisture content (unseasoned).
MC15 or KD15. 15 percent maximum moisture content. □
S-DRY or KD. 19 percent maximum moisture content.

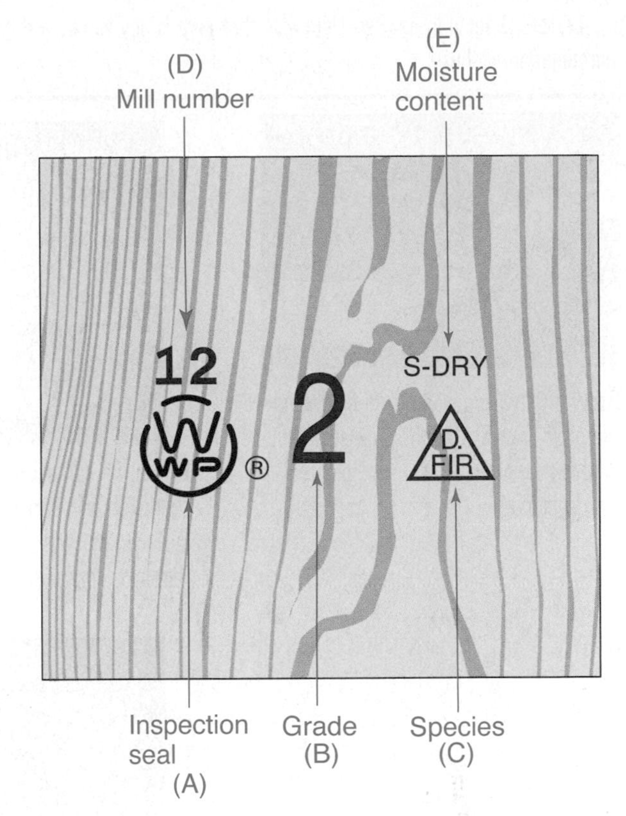

Fig. 16-8. Most grade stamps contain information similar to the information in this stamp from the Western Wood Products Association.

Lumber Defects

Defects in lumber are flaws that detract from the quality of the wood, either in appearance or usefulness. About twenty-five characteristics and conditions are considered when wood is graded. They are described in any set of grading rules. Some of the more common defects are shown and described in **Fig. 16-9** (see page 296).

When selecting lumber, the carpenter must examine each board for defects. Boards do not always have to be perfect, however. It is important to consider the exact use required of the wood. For example, a minor defect along one edge of a board would not be a problem if the board was to be ripped to a slightly narrower width. Likewise, a large knot near the end of a 12′ board would not be a problem unless the carpenter needed the full length of the board. A flawed board should be set aside for cutting into shorter lengths. A more suitable board should then be selected.

SIZING LUMBER

The width and thickness of lumber are given by two types of measurements: nominal and actual. The *nominal dimension,* such as 2″ x 4″, is the size of the board, in inches, as originally cut. Nominal dimensions, or nominal sizes, refer to rough-sawn lumber.

After the board has been surfaced and seasoned at the mill, its *actual dimension* becomes less than its nominal dimension. *Dressed sizes* apply after the wood has shrunk and been surfaced with a planing machine. The width and thickness of dressed lumber are considerably less than its nominal width and thickness. For example, a 2x4 stud actually measures 1½″ x 3½″. For the differences between nominal and actual sizes, see the Ready Reference Appendix table "Standard Sizes for Framing Lumber, Nominal and Dressed."

Sizes of lumber used in building construction have been standardized for convenience in ordering and handling. Common materials run 8′, 10′, 12′, 14′, and 16′ in length; 2″, 4″, 6″, 8″, 10″, and 12″ in width; and 1″, 2″, and 4″ in thickness.

Hardwoods are not standardized for length or width. They run ¼″, ½″, 1″, 1¼″, 1½″, 2″, 2½″, 3″, and 4″ in thickness.

Fig. 16-9. Defects in lumber. Note also that *warp* is any variation from a true (plane) surface. It includes bow, crook, and cup, or any combination of these.

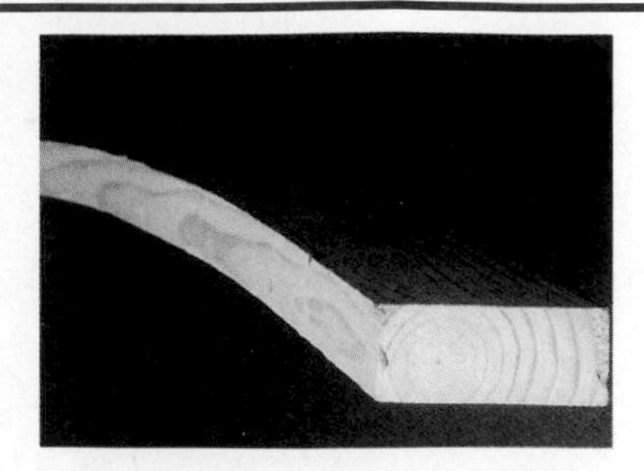

Bow. A flatwise deviation (bend) along the grain from a straight, true surface. Bow is measured at the point of greatest deviation.

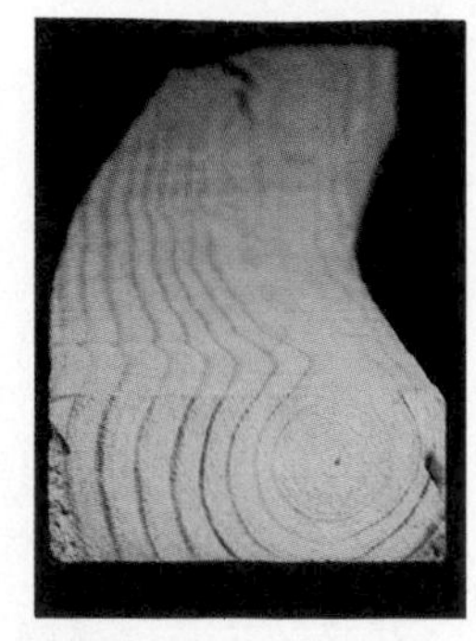

Crook. An edgewise deviation (bend) from a straight, true surface. Check is measured at the point of greatest deviation.

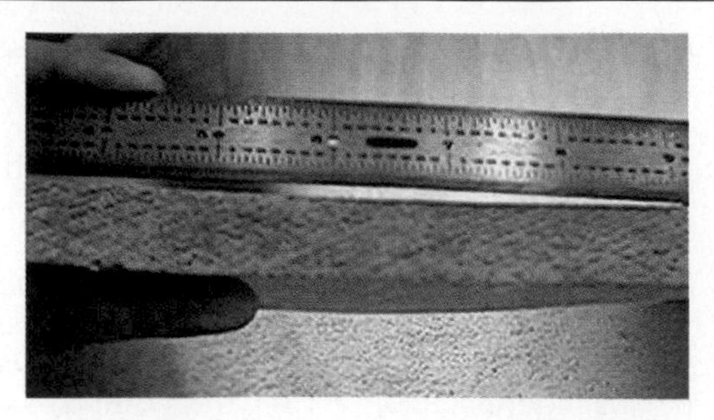

Cup. A flatwise deviation (bend) across the grain from a straight, true surface. Cup is measured at the point of greatest deviation.

Check. A small crack that runs across the growth rings, parallel with the grain. Check usually occurs as a result of seasoning.

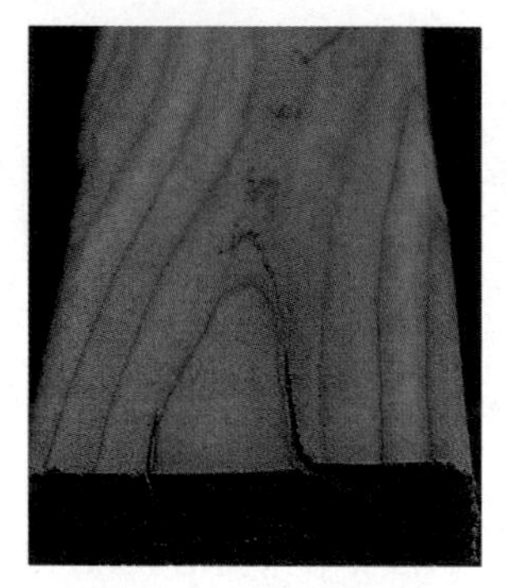

Shake. A lengthwise grain separation between or through the growth rings. It may be further classified as *ring shake* or *pitch shake.*

Split. A lengthwise separation extending from one surface through the piece of lumber to the opposite side or an adjoining surface.

Decay. Disintegration of wood due to the action of wood-destroying fungi. It also may be called *dote, rot,* or *unsound wood.*

Knot. Place where a branch once grew. Knots are classified according to size, quality, and occurrence. To determine the size of a knot, average the maximum length and maximum width, unless otherwise specified. A sound, encased knot and a sound intergrown knot are shown above.

(Continued)

Fig. 16-9. Defects in lumber. *(continued)*

Knothole. Hole left by the removal of an embedded knot.

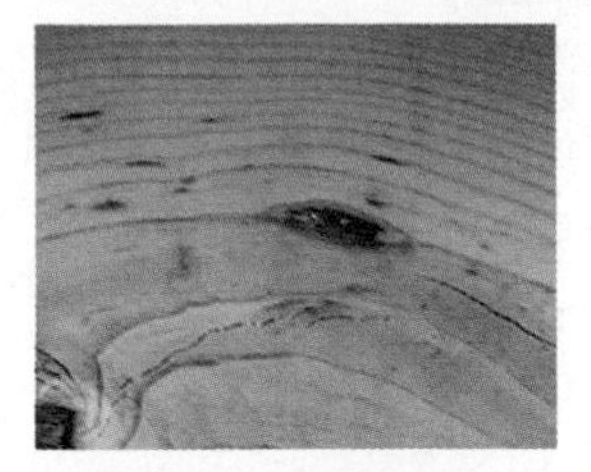

Pitch. Accumulation of resin in the wood cells in a more or less irregular patch.

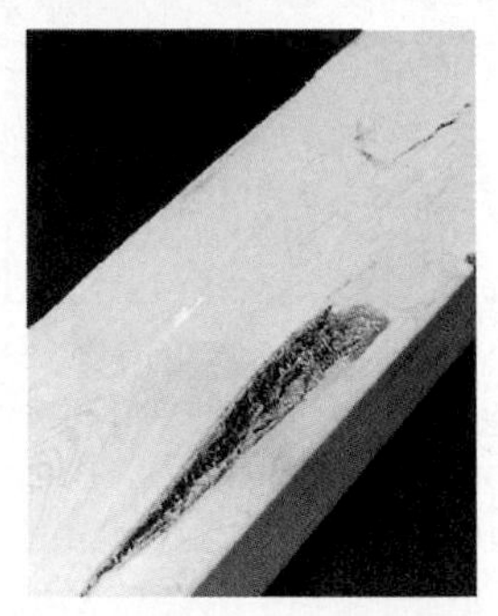

Pitch-pocket. An opening between growth rings that usually contains or has contained resin, bark, or both.

Stain. Discoloration on or in lumber other than its natural color.

Torn grain. Torn spot created as the board is machined to size.

Wane. Presence of bark or lack of wood on the edge or corner.

Metric Sizes

The United States is the only major lumber-producing country that does not use the metric system of measurement exclusively. Wood intended for export to other countries may be sized to metric measurements. Also, wood produced in other countries and imported to the U.S. for certain uses may be sized to metric measurements. Thickness and width are given in millimeters (mm). Length is given in meters (m).

Common sizes are almost identical in both the customary and metric systems. For example, the basic thicknesses are 25 mm and 1″, and the basic widths are 100 mm and 4″. Metric lengths range from 1.8 m (about 6′) to 6.3 m in increments of 300 mm. Note that 300 mm is close to, but slightly shorter than, 1′.

SECTION 16.1 Check Your Knowledge

1. What is the difference between hardwoods and softwoods?
2. Name the advantages of quarter-sawn lumber compared with flat-sawn lumber.
3. What is KD lumber?
4. What causes the moisture content of lumber to reach a point of equilibrium?

On the Job

Identify the trade association that is responsible for grading most of the softwood lumber used where you live. Contact that association to obtain a specifications list. Identify the grading specifications used by this association.

SECTION 16.2

Protecting Wood

Wood must be protected from decay and from certain insects. Both problems are more likely to occur when wood becomes wet.

Moisture can be introduced to wood in a variety of ways. Rain is the most obvious source. A house must be designed to encourage rainwater to drain freely away. Water vapor is another source. Water vapor is given off during cooking, washing, and other household activities. This vapor can pass through walls and ceilings. When it reaches a cold surface, such as sheathing or studs in the winter, it condenses into water droplets. Leaking pipes are a third source of moisture. They should be fixed immediately to prevent damage to the house. Gaps around exterior wood trim or between a chimney and the siding can allow water to seep into walls. Such problems should be eliminated with regular maintenance, such as caulking all gaps.

DECAY

Wood used where it will always be dry, or even where it may be wetted briefly and promptly dried, will not decay. However, wood will decay if kept wet for long periods at temperatures favorable to the growth of decay organisms. Wood decay, or rot, is caused by certain *fungi* (such as mildew and mold) that use wood for food. These fungi, like the higher plants, require air, warmth, food, and moisture for growth. Damp wood provides an ideal environment for them.

In early stages, decay caused by fungi may show up as a discoloration of the wood. Paint also may become discolored where the underlying wood is rotting. Advanced surface decay is more easily recognized. Generally, the affected wood is brown and crumbly. Brown, crumbly decay is sometimes called *dry rot.* This is a misnomer because wood must be damp for rotting to occur. At other times the wood may be rather white and spongy. Decay inside the wood is often indicated by sunken areas on the surface or by a hollow sound when the wood is tapped with a hammer. Where the surrounding air is very damp, the decay fungus may grow out on the surface, appearing as white or brownish growths in patches or strands or, in special cases, as vinelike structures. **Fig. 16-10.**

The presence of fungus stains or mold is a warning that conditions are or have been suitable for decay. Affected lumber should always be examined for decay damage before installation.

Preventing Decay

Fungi grow most rapidly at temperatures between 70°F and 85°F [21°C and 29°C]. High temperatures, such as those used in kiln-drying of lumber, kill fungi. Low temperatures, even far below 0°F [-18°C], merely cause them to become dormant. The best preventative is to keep wood dry. Wood-destroying fungi cannot grow in dry wood. A moisture content of 20 percent or less is generally dry enough to prevent or stop growth.

Construction lumber that is improperly seasoned may be infected with one or more fungi and should be avoided. Such wood may contribute to serious decay in both the structure and exterior parts of buildings. You may see signs of infection in wood that is improperly seasoned. You can also test such wood with an electronic moisture meter.

Fig. 16-10. Dampness is essential for the growth of fungi on wood.

Decay-Resistant Woods

When untreated, the sapwood of all common native woods has low resistance to decay. This gives it a short life under decay-producing conditions. The natural decay resistance of native woods lies in the heartwood. Of the species commonly used in house construction, the heartwood of bald cypress, redwood, and various cedars is highest in decay resistance. However, lumber made from all heartwood is becoming more and more difficult to obtain. This is because increasing amounts of timber are cut from the smaller trees of second-growth stands in which little heartwood has developed. In general, when decay resistance is needed in load-bearing members that would be difficult or expensive to replace, preservative-treated wood is used.

INSECTS

Under certain conditions, wood can be damaged by insects such as termites, carpenter ants, and beetles. Some of the conditions that encourage fungi, such as too much moisture, can also encourage wood-infesting insects.

Termites

Termites are the most destructive of the insects that infest wood. **Fig. 16-11.** The best time to protect against them is during the planning and construction of the building. Remove all woody debris, such as stumps and lumber scraps, from the soil at the building site before and after construction. No wood member of the structure should be in contact with the soil.

Fig. 16-11. Termites are the most destructive insect pests in the United States.

Termites can be grouped into two main classes: subterranean and dry-wood. *Subterranean termites* account for about 95 percent of all termite damage. They eat the interior of the wood and can cause much damage before they are discovered. They honeycomb the wood with tunnels separated by thin layers of sound wood. They are common throughout Hawaii and the southern two-thirds of the United States, except in mountainous and extremely dry areas. **Fig. 16-12.**

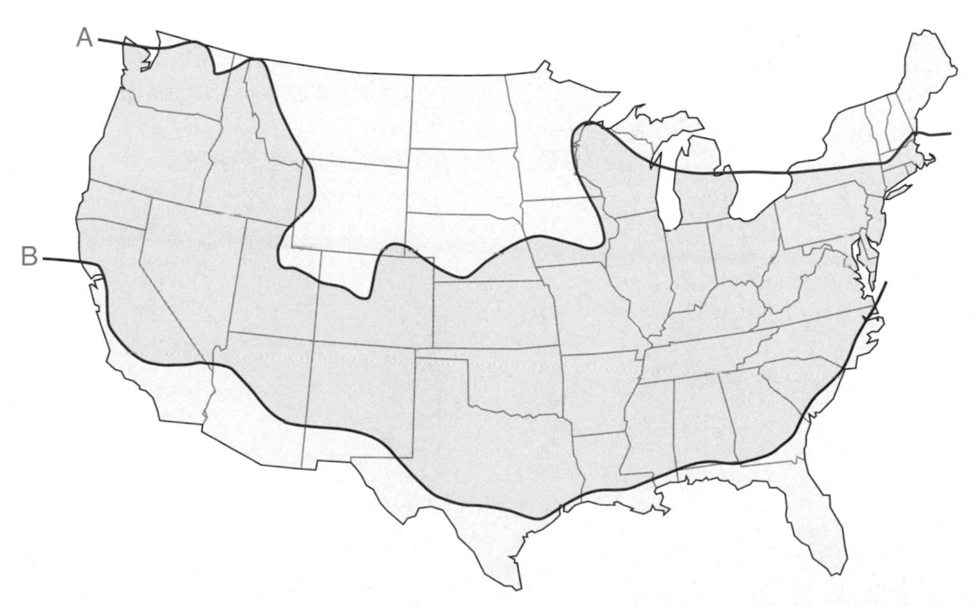

Fig. 16-12. The red line *(A)* marks the northern limit of damage by subterranean termites. The black line *(B)* marks the northern limit of damage by dry-wood termites.

Subterranean termites thrive in moist, warm soil containing a large supply of food in the form of wood or other material containing cellulose (plant fibers). In their search for additional food, they build shelter tubes over foundation walls, in cracks, or on pipes or supports leading from the soil into the house. These flattened tubes, from ¼″ to ½″ or more in width, protect the termites in their travels. Metal or masonry barriers should be installed in areas where these termites are common. **Fig. 16-13.**

An especially destructive type of subterranean termite is the *Formosan termite.* This termite was introduced into the United States after World War II, and it is now found in most of the southern states as well as California and Hawaii. Native species feed on dead trees and processed wood. Formosan termites will eat these plus anything else that contains wood fiber, including live trees and many plants. Because they are aggressive, live in very large colonies, and can survive on many different food sources, Formosan termites are more destructive than native species.

Dry-wood termites fly directly to the wood instead of building tunnels from the ground. They chew across the grain of the wood, creating broad pockets, or chambers. These chambers are connected by narrow tunnels. The termites remain hidden in the wood and are seldom seen, except when they take flight. They are more difficult to control, but the damage is less serious than that caused by subterranean termites.

Dry-wood termites are common in the tropics. They have also been found in the United States along the Atlantic Coast from Virginia to the Florida Keys, westward along the coast of the Gulf of Mexico, and up the Pacific Coast as far as northern California.

Carpenter Ants

Carpenter ants are a problem primarily in the Northeast, Midwest, and Northwest, though they can be found throughout the United States. **Fig. 16-14.** They nest in the ground as well as in dead trees, firewood, and houses. They do not, however, eat the wood. Instead, they eat plant juices, other insects, honey, and food particles found inside a house. Small sawdust piles may indicate the presence of carpenter ants. The damage they cause comes from the irregular tunnels they create in wood for their nests.

Controlling carpenter ants can be difficult. To be most effective, chemical treatments must be applied to the nest itself.

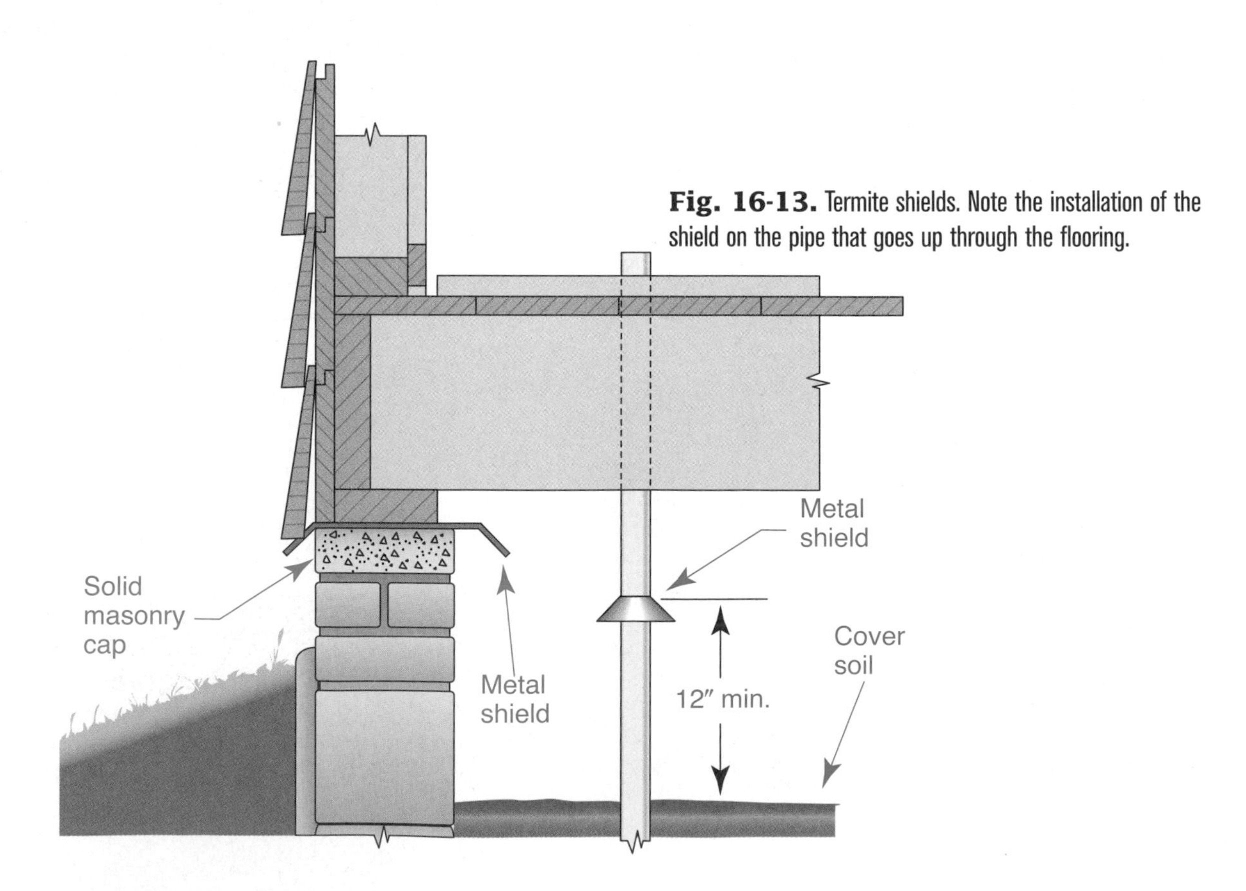

Fig. 16-13. Termite shields. Note the installation of the shield on the pipe that goes up through the flooring.

Fig. 16-14. Carpenter ants do not eat wood, but they do burrow into it to create nests.

Fig. 16-15. Powderpost beetle.

Beetles

Two types of beetles commonly infest wood: the powderpost beetle and the deathwatch beetle.

The *powderpost beetle* is the more common. It is second only to the termite in the amount of damage it causes. **Fig. 16-15.** Powderpost beetles commonly enter the house via already infested wood. This can include firewood, rough-sawn timbers, and barn wood. They attack hardwoods only, preferring ash, oak, mahogany, hickory, maple, and walnut. Most of the infestation occurs in sapwood that has a moisture content between 10 and 20 percent.

One common sign of a powderpost beetle infestation is a tiny pile of fine, flourlike powder. This material is pushed out of the wood as the beetles emerge. Infested wood should either be removed or professionally treated. Treating only the surface of the infested wood with an insecticide will not kill beetles deep within the wood.

Deathwatch beetles are larger than powderpost beetles. **Fig. 16-16.** They infest the sapwood of both hardwoods and softwoods. They are most likely to be found in wood with a high moisture content, such as that used in unheated housing and damp crawl spaces. Treatment is similar to that required for powderpost beetles. In addition, it is very important to cut off the supply of moisture.

Fig.16-16. Deathwatch beetle.

Fig. 16-17. Carpenter bee.

Carpenter Bees

Carpenter bees resemble bumblebees in shape. The bee has a metallic blue-black body covered with yellow or orange hairs. **Fig. 16-17.** They cut a ½″ circular hole in bare or untreated wood. They then build their nests by boring a tunnel parallel to the surface of the wood. Sawdust will reveal their presence. New generations of bees will return to the nest annually. Carpenter bees can be controlled with insecticides.

SAFETY FIRST

Treated Woods

The chemicals used can be toxic, so it is important to handle treated wood properly. It should never be burned because toxic fumes may be produced. When loading or unloading it at the job site, wear gloves to protect your hands. When sawing or machining treated wood, wear a dust mask to avoid breathing the sawdust. Whenever possible, cut preservative-treated lumber outdoors to avoid indoor accumulations of airborne sawdust. Be sure to wear eye protection. After handling the wood, wash your hands thoroughly, particularly before eating.

Fig. 16-18. Chemically-treated wood is used outdoors for a wide variety of purposes, including decks, stairs, railings, and retaining walls.

PRESERVATIVE TREATMENTS

To increase the ability of lumber to resist decay and insect attack, it can be treated, with liquid preservatives soon after being milled. Various woods can be successfully treated, but fir, spruce, and pine are the most common. Preservative-treated wood is generally used outdoors or where it is in contact with concrete or masonry.

In one treatment process, the wood is dipped into vats of chemicals. It is then allowed to air-dry. In another process, the chemicals are forced deep into the wood under pressure. In a third process, the chemicals are injected into the wood. Depending on the process and the chemicals used, treated wood will be various shades of green or brown. Some treated wood can be painted or stained.

The amount of preservative used can be adjusted to provide different levels of protection. Wood that will be in direct contact with the ground (fence posts, for example) should receive the highest level available. Preservative-treated lumber is graded and stamped to indicate its suitability for various uses. **Fig. 16-18.**

SECTION 16.2 Check Your Knowledge

1. Decay fungi grow best within what temperature range?
2. What condition creates the best environment for decay?
3. Wood from what part of the tree is most decay resistant?
4. Explain the differences between the two basic types of termites.

On the Job

Consult the map showing areas most affected by termites (Fig. 16-12). Identify the state that is entirely within the dry-wood termite zone. Using the library or the Internet, locate information about what homeowners in that state can do to guard against termite damage. Are any special building materials used that can help prevent decay? Summarize your findings in a short report.

16 Review

Section Summaries

16.1 The suitability of lumber for construction depends on the species of wood, how the lumber is manufactured, and on various measurements of its strength and stiffness. Wood may be either hardwood or softwood. Softwoods are more common in construction. Defects can reduce the utility of lumber. Grading standards take defects and other characteristics of wood into account.

16.2 Wood can be damaged by decay and by wood-infesting insects, such as termites and beetles. This damage can be prevented by reducing the moisture content of lumber and ensuring that wood is not allowed to remain wet. Decay-resistant or preservative-treated woods can prevent problems.

Review Questions

1. List five advantages of wood as a building material.
2. Describe the difference in appearance between early wood and late wood.
3. Describe the two common methods of cutting boards from a log.
4. What is the fiber-saturation point?
5. How is the measure of the moisture content of wood expressed?
6. Describe the two methods of drying lumber.
7. Tell how lumber should be stored outside at the job site.
8. Describe these three closely related lumber defects: bow, crook, and cup.
9. Name the two types of beetle that commonly infest wood.
10. In what locations is it most important to use preservative-treated lumber?

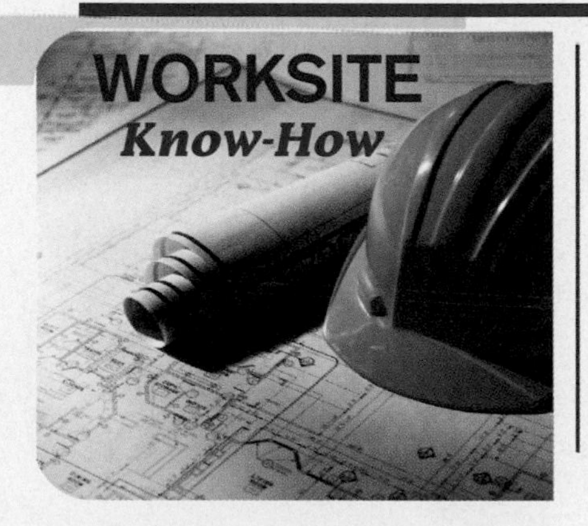

Resources Several organizations publish or distribute information about design values, spans, standard sizes, grades, and properties of wood. Some examples are the American Wood Council, American Forest and Paper Association, Canadian Wood Council, Construction Specifications Institute, Southern Forest Products Association, and Western Wood Products Association. You can find out more about these organizations by visiting their Web sites.

Chapter

Engineered Lumber

Objectives

After reading this chapter, you'll be able to:

- Explain how the use of engineered lumber helps conserve wood resources.
- Tell how to store, handle, and install LVL I-joists.
- Tell the differences among various types of engineered lumber.
- Recognize the connectors most often used with engineered lumber.

Terms

camber
engineered lumber
finger joint
framing connector
glulam
laminated-veneer lumber
rim board

Builders are often slow to accept new materials and methods. This is because it takes considerable time and money to build a house, and mistakes can be costly. The industry has, however, accepted many new materials and products in recent years. In particular, there are many new structural and trim products made from various combinations of wood, wood veneer, wood pieces, and wood fibers.

The wood ingredients are bonded together with adhesives to form products that are stiff, strong, dependable, and versatile. They are increasingly popular as substitutes for solid lumber. Such products include:

- Laminated-veneer headers and I-joists.
- Glue-laminated beams.
- Finger-jointed studs.
- Laminated-strand lumber posts.

Engineered lumber is any manufactured product made of solid wood, wood veneer, wood pieces, or wood fibers in which the components have been bonded together with adhesives. Plywood and other panel products are discussed in Chapter 18, "Engineered Panel Products."

Engineered products are often used in combination with conventional materials. For example, a house might be built with engineered lumber floor joists, but with solid lumber rafters and studs. Engineered lumber has the following advantages:

- It uses wood that might otherwise be wasted.
- Its performance is highly predictable.
- It is available in a wide variety of dimensions and in unusually long lengths to solve nearly any structural problem.
- It is free of defects often found in solid lumber.

Engineered lumber products can be substituted for solid lumber in nearly every case. Commonly used forms include laminated-veneer lumber, glue-laminated lumber, finger-jointed lumber, and laminated-strand lumber.

Engineered lumber is made in different ways by various manufacturers. Always consult the manufacturer's instructions for handling, care, and usage information.

SECTION 17.1

Laminated-Veneer Lumber

Laminated-veneer lumber (LVL) is a family of products made with wood veneer as the basic element. Layers of veneer are glued together to form LVL. LVL products are used for beams, headers, joists, and rafters in both residential and commercial construction. **Fig. 17-1.**

Fig. 17-1. Laminated-veneer products include I-joists (left) and headers (right).

LVL BASICS

Laminated-veneer lumber is lightweight, rigid, cost effective, and available in lengths up to 60′. **Fig. 17-2.** It also shrinks and swells less than solid lumber.

Manufacturing Methods

Laminated-veneer lumber products are made in plants in the United States and Canada. Any species of wood may be used, depending on availability and the manufacturer's preference. The sheets of veneer are moved through large, open-ended drying ovens. They are dried until they have the same moisture content, which is usually 8 percent. As each sheet leaves the drying oven, it is checked for quality and graded. **Fig. 17-3.**

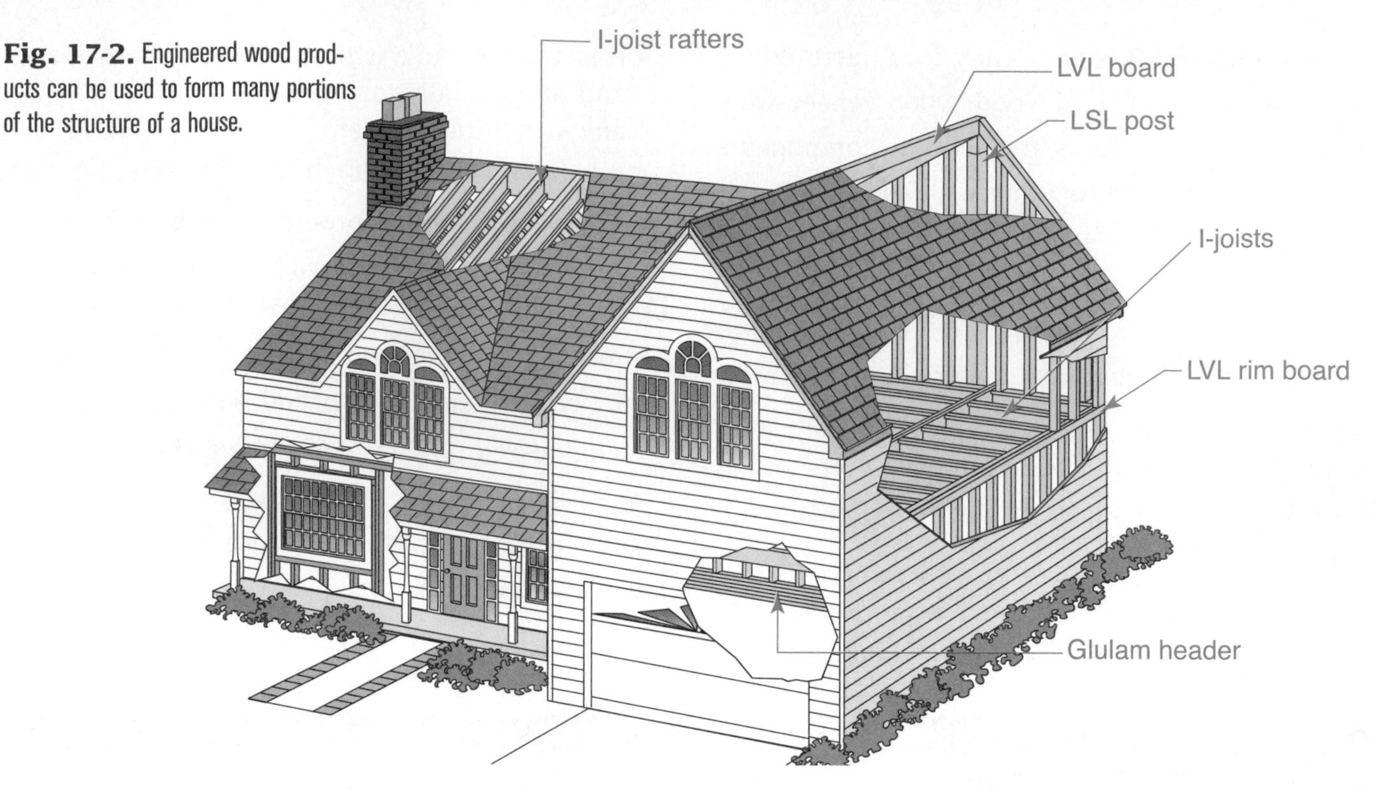

Fig. 17-2. Engineered wood products can be used to form many portions of the structure of a house.

The veneer is then fed into an automatic glue-spreader. The spreader coats the top of each sheet with adhesive. The adhesive used is often phenol resorcinol formaldehyde. It is waterproof, resistant to heat, and very strong. As the glued sheets are assembled, the highest-grade veneers are placed at the top and bottom of the stack. This increases the overall strength of the finished product. The sheets are then fed into a machine that uses heat and pressure to cure the adhesive. The resulting material, called a *billet*, may be as much as 80′ long. Billets are then cut into stock shapes and sizes for headers, beams, or portions of wood I-joists.

Finished LVL products are shipped to materials dealers in 60′ lengths. When a builder orders LVL products, the dealer cuts them to common lengths in increments of 2′ and delivers them to the job site. The builder then cuts them to the lengths needed for the job.

Performance

A cross section of laminated-veneer lumber looks similar to a cross section of plywood. **Fig. 17-4.** However, there is an important difference. Plywood is cross laminated. This means that the grain of each layer runs perpendicular to the

Fig. 17-3. Bundles of veneer waiting to be made into LVL products.

Fig. 17-4. A cross-section of LVL stock.

grain of adjoining layers. In contrast, the grain of every layer in LVL runs in the same direction. This is called *parallel lamination*, and it produces a material that is more uniform. It also means that the end grain of each veneer layer is exposed only at the ends of the product.

Pieces of solid lumber may shrink or swell in slightly different degrees after leaving the mill. However, the qualities of each piece of LVL stock can be controlled. This means that LVL products are very predictable in their performance. Each piece of LVL behaves exactly like the other pieces in a load. If there is any swelling, for example, all the pieces will swell by the same percentage. As a result, architects and engineers can better control the structural soundness of buildings.

Care and Handling

Laminated-veneer products are produced using waterproof adhesives. They can withstand normal exposure to moisture. As with other manufactured wood products, however, they should not be exposed needlessly to moisture. Most LVL products are wrapped in protective material for transport to the job site. Do not remove this wrapping until you are ready to install the materials.

Do not store LVL products in direct contact with the ground. Rest the bundles on stickers to encourage air circulation and to prevent contact with ground moisture. **Fig. 17-5.**

LVL I-JOISTS

One of the most common laminated veneer lumber products is the *I-joist*. **Fig. 17-6.** Seen on end, an I-joist is shaped like the letter *I*. Its vertical member is called the *web*. The two horizontal members are called *flanges*. I-joists are most often used in floor construction to support subflooring. They can also be used in place of rafters in roof construction. **Fig. 17-7.**

Fig. 17-5. Protect bundles of I-joists by storing them as shown.

Fig. 17-6. I-joist floor framing supported by an engineered-wood beam.

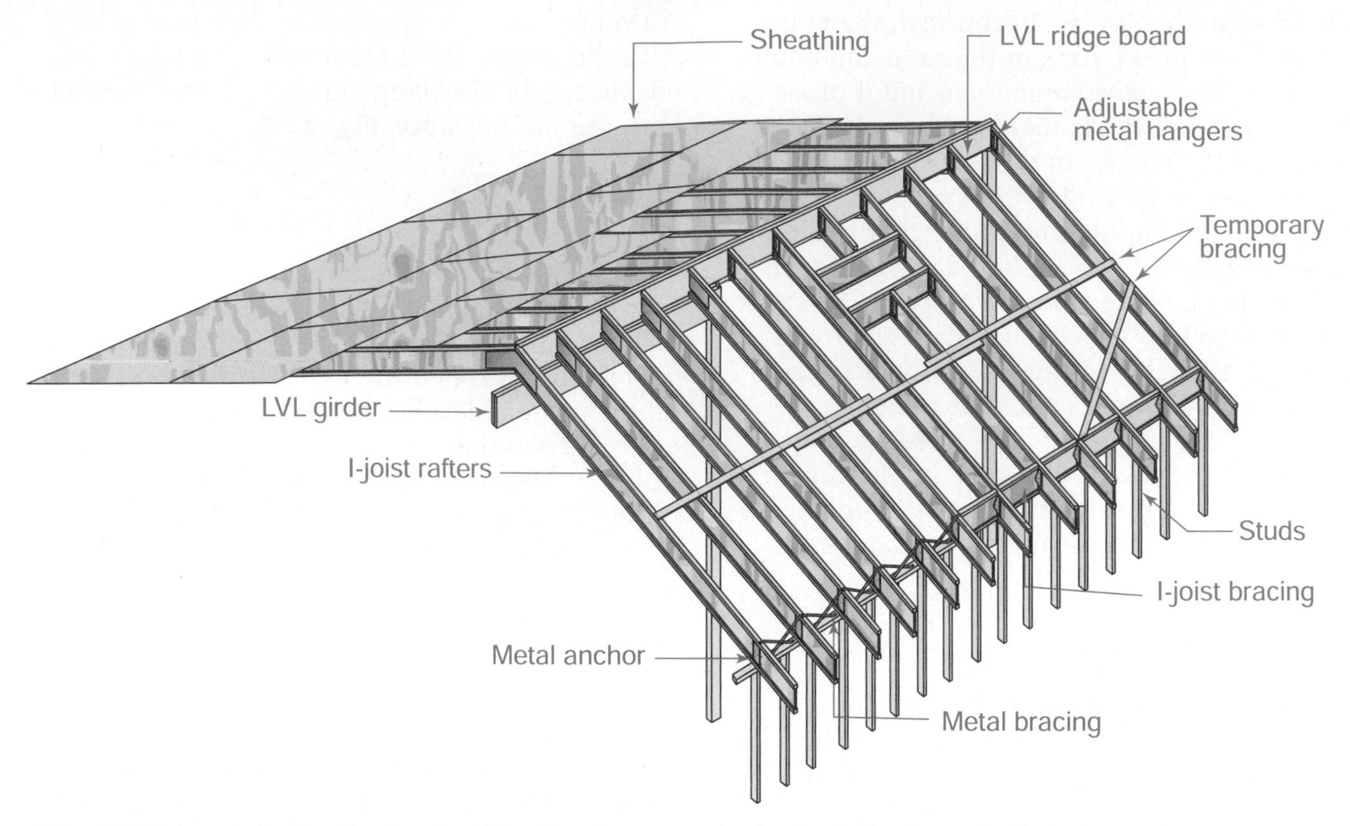

Fig. 17-7. An example of roof framing using I-joists. Note the temporary bracing details. Floor I-joists should also be braced.

The construction of an I-joist varies according to manufacturer. The top and bottom flanges may be made of solid lumber or laminated-veneer lumber. I-joist flanges range from 1½″ to 3½″ in width. The web may be made from sections of structural ⅜″ plywood or oriented-strand board (OSB). Waterproof adhesive is used to attach webs to flanges. No nails or staples are used. LVL I-joists are available in depths ranging from 9½″ to 20″.

I-joists have several advantages over solid lumber joists. Because they are available in lengths up to 60′, a single I-joist can run the entire width of a house. This removes the need to overlap joists at the center of the house. It also reduces the number of separate pieces that must be handled. The flooring system can be installed faster. An I-joist is lighter in weight than an equal length of solid lumber. This makes it easier to carry. For example, an I-joist 26′ long and 9½″ deep weighs about 50 lbs. A piece of 2x10 solid lumber of the same length weighs about 96 lbs.

Installation

Engineered-wood I-joists are made by a number of manufacturers. Each manufacturer provides span tables and recommended installation details. Be sure to obtain them for the specific product you intend to use. The methods described here are typical.

The web of an I-joist is not in the same plane as its flanges, so take care when cutting the product. For crosscutting, the easiest method is to use a radial-arm saw. To cut safely with a circular saw, you must prevent the shoe of the saw from lodging against a flange during the cut. You can do this by placing a wood block against the web and between the flanges. You can then cut the I-joist with ease. **Fig. 17-8.**

Brace and nail each I-joist as it is installed (see Fig. 17-7). Permanent bracing is provided by the sheathing, by the rim board, and by cross-bracing. If temporary bracing is required before the sheathing is in place, install it as follows:

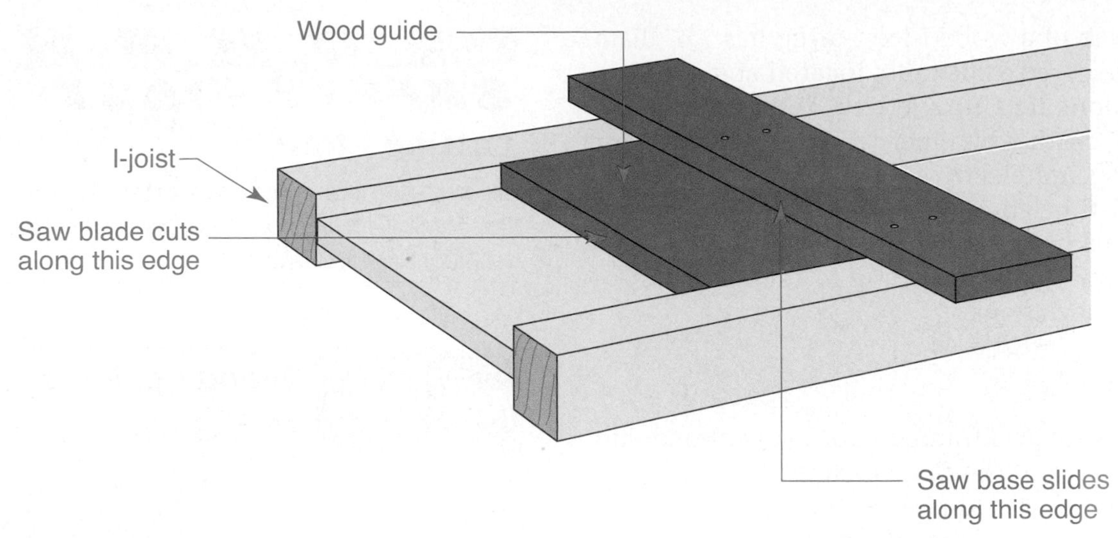

Fig. 17-8. A wood block will prevent the shoe of the saw from lodging against a flange. The manufacturer may supply a cutting guide.

1. Use stock at least 1x4 in size.
2. Braces should be at least 8′ long. Space them no more than 8′ on center.
3. Secure each brace into the top of each I-joist using two 8d nails.
4. Nail the bracing to a lateral restraint, such as an existing subfloor or a braced end wall, at the end of each bay.
5. Lap the ends of adjoining bracing over at least two I-joists.

I-joists used in floor construction are installed in a way similar to solid lumber joists. They can be nailed to the plate by toenailing through the lower flange or secured by metal joist hangers. They can be braced with solid blocking, I-joist blocking, or metal cross-bracing (see Fig. 17-7).

When using joist hangers, keep several factors in mind (see also pages 318-320). Joist hangers are generally nailed to the I-joist with 10d common nails. Never drive nails sideways (parallel to the layers) into an I-joist flange. This tends to split the layers, reducing the strength of the joist. Instead, drive nails into the flange at a 45° angle. **Fig. 17-9.** In some cases, you must permanently install thin blocks of wood against either side of the web. These are called *web stiffeners*, *bearing blocks*, or *squash blocks*. They help prevent cross-grain bending. They also prevent the web from buckling at points of high stress. They should be placed where an I-joist crosses a mid-span support, such as a floor girder. **Fig. 17-10.**

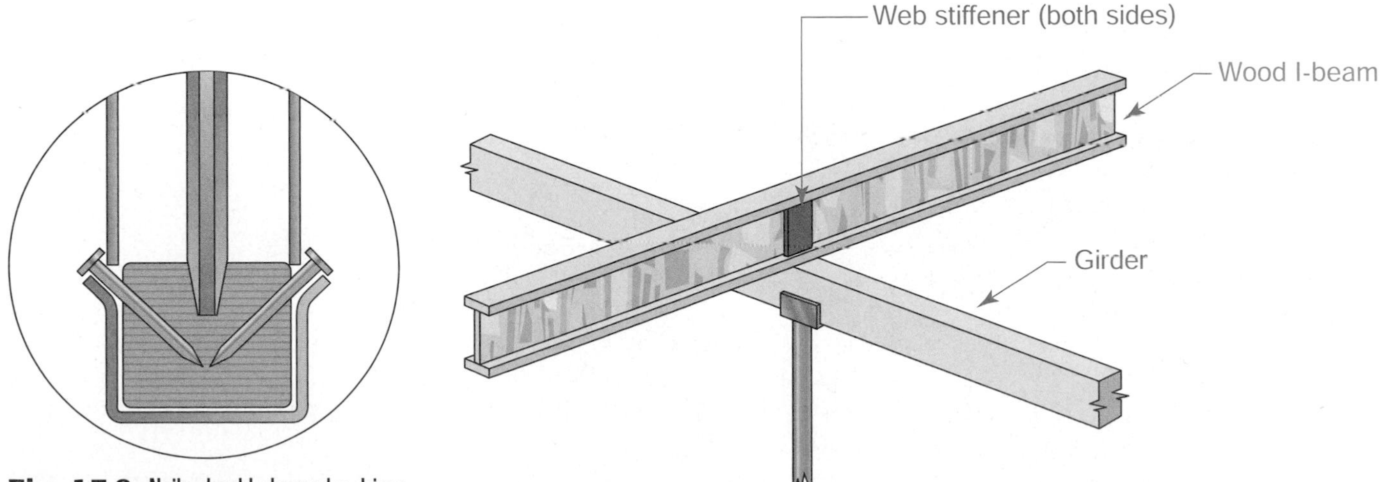

Fig. 17-9. Nails should always be driven through an I-joist flange at a 45° angle to avoid splitting the stock.

Fig. 17-10. Web stiffeners should be installed on both sides of the web where the I-joist crosses a support.

The web of a wood I-joist often has 1½″ diameter pre-scored knockouts located about 12″ on center along its entire length. You can punch these out with a hammer to create passages for plumbing and electrical lines. This removes the need for time-consuming drilling or notching. Additional holes can be cut along the length of the web, but only according to the manufacturer's instructions.

Rim Boards

When a floor is framed with conventional lumber, the ends of the floor joists can be connected with solid lumber of the same size. This lumber is called a *rim joist*. Solid-lumber rim joists do not work with flooring systems framed with I-joists. This is because the two products expand or shrink differently. A rim board is used instead. A **rim board** is a length of engineered stock that has the same depth as the I-joists. **Fig. 17-11.**

Rim boards come in various sizes. **Table 17-A.** Stock intended for rim boards is often made from laminated-veneer lumber. It may also be made from plywood, OSB, or laminated-strand lumber (page 316).

SAFETY FIRST

Cutting I-Joists

The only cutting done to the flange of an LVL I-joist should be for length. Never notch or drill the top and bottom flanges. This could weaken the product to the point of failure.

Table 17-A. Standard Sizes for Rim Boards [a]

Thickness (inches)	1[b], 1⅛[b], 1¼, and 1½
Depth (inches)	9½, 11⅞, 14, 16, 18, 20, 22, 24
Length (feet)	8 to 24

[a] All sizes may not be available. Check suppliers for availability.

[b] Predominant thicknesses manufactured by APA members.

Care and Handling

It is important to store and carry I-joists on edge because they are fairly weak in lateral strength. **Fig. 17-12.** Storing or carrying an

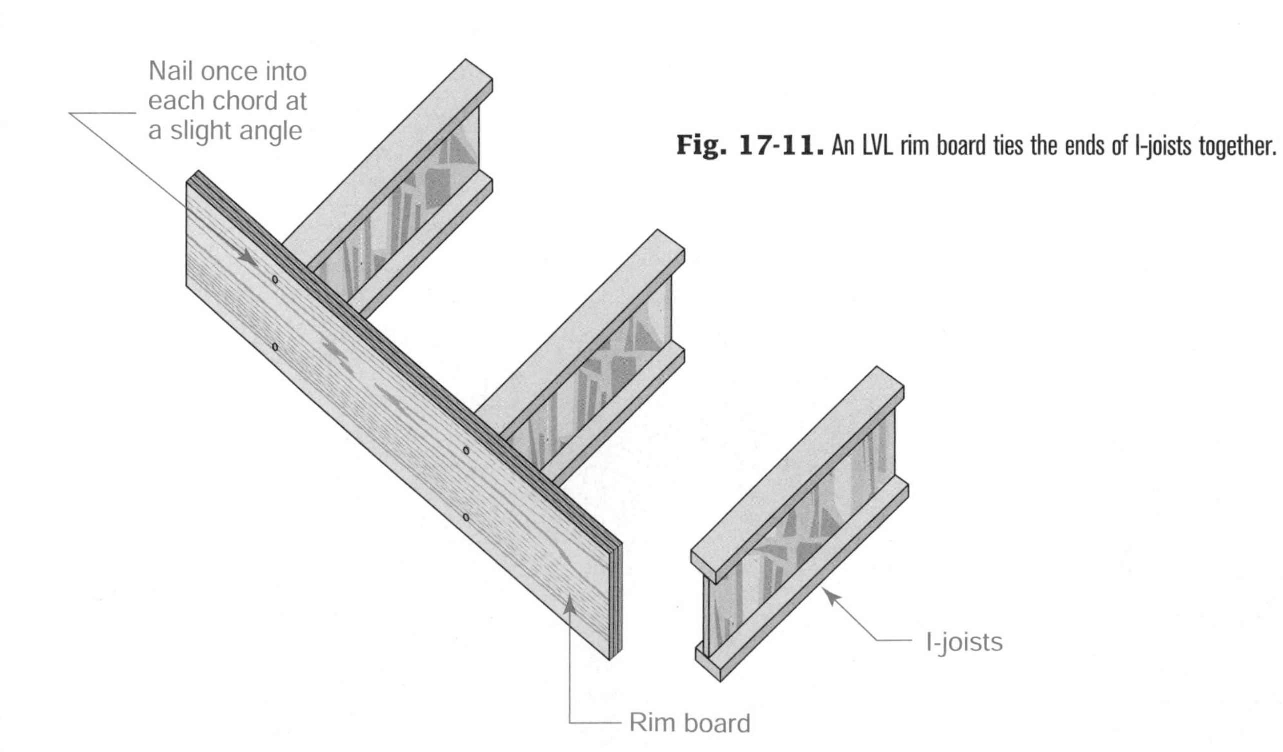

Fig. 17-11. An LVL rim board ties the ends of I-joists together.

Fig. 17-12. One advantage of LVL I-joists is that they are light in weight. Care should be taken, however, not to let them flex back and forth too much.

I-joist on its side or allowing it to flex back and forth could break the glued butt joints that join individual sections of web. This would severely weaken the product. Never install a damaged I-joist.

When I-joists are first delivered to the job site, do not open the protective covering around each bundle. Open or remove it shortly before the I-joists are used. The covering protects them from weather and reduces the chances of damage. If bundles are stacked, separate them with stickers. Before installing an I-joist, inspect it to make sure it has not been damaged during storage.

SAFETY FIRST

I-Joist Floors

Until an I-joist floor has been sheathed, the I-joists will not support the weight of workers. Plan the work so that no one will need to walk atop I-joists until the sheathing is in place.

I-Joist Performance Ratings

Because I-joists are a manufactured product, they are not graded in the same way as solid lumber. Each solid-lumber 2x10, for example, is similar in size to other solid 2x10s but may be any of several different wood species. Each board has characteristics and defects that make it unique. By contrast, each I-joist is made to fit a specific performance standard. In construction, a *performance standard* is a standard that defines the required performance of a specified building component. Each I-joist is nearly identical to every other I-joist.

The information stamped on each piece of engineered lumber identifies the performance standard it meets. The position of this stamp may vary by manufacturer. On I-joists, it is often located on the flange. **Fig. 17-13.**

Fig. 17-13. A typical I-joist, showing grade specifications along the upper flange.

Fig. 17-14. Metal hangers should be used to connect lengths of engineered lumber to each other.

LVL HEADERS AND BEAMS

Laminated-veneer headers and beams can be used in place of solid-wood or built-up-wood headers. **Fig. 17-14.** LVL header and beam stock comes in various thicknesses. Stock with a thickness of 1¾″ is most common in residential work. When two pieces are combined, they are the thickness of a standard 2x4 wall. LVL headers and beams range in depth from 5½″ to 18″. **Table 17-B.**

Cutting and nailing requires the same tools as those used with solid lumber. When nailing LVL headers face to face, use three rows of 16d nails spaced 12″ on center. Some builders have found that the nail-holding ability of LVL headers and beams is greater than that of solid lumber.

Table 17-B. Common LVL Headers and Beams

Depth (inches)	Thickness (inches)
5½, 7¼, 9¼, 9½, 11¼, 11⅞, 14, 16[a], 18[a]	1¾, 3½
9½, 11⅞, 14, 16[a], 18[a]	5¼

[a] 16″ and 18″ beams should be used only in multiple thicknesses.

LVL headers can be cut to length on site, using carbide-tipped blades. However, holes must never be cut in LVL headers or beams.

SECTION 17.1

Check Your Knowledge

1. What are the differences between plywood and LVL?
2. Describe two methods for cutting I-joists to length.
3. When is it all right to cut into the flange of an I-joist?
4. What is the correct term for the LVL product that is used to connect the ends of I-joists in a floor system?

On the Job

One of the advantages of LVL lumber is that wood is used very efficiently. Contact a trade association that represents the engineered-wood products industry. Find out exactly how much less wood an I-joist contains as compared with solid lumber of the same size.

SECTION 17.2

Glue-Laminated Lumber

When layers of lumber are glued together, their strength and stiffness are greater than that of solid lumber of equal size. This is the principle behind the glue-laminated beam called a **glulam**. In fact, pound for pound, a glulam is stronger than a steel beam. Glulams can take various forms and span great distances. **Fig. 17-15.** These characteristics make them increasingly useful in both residential and commercial

Fig. 17-15. This roof is supported by curved glulam arches.

Lifting Glulams

Glulam beams are commonly loaded and unloaded with a fork lift. For greater stability, the sides of the beams, rather than the narrower edges, should rest on the forks.

construction. **Fig. 17-16.** They are used for garage door headers, patio door headers, carrying beams, window headers, and even exposed stair stringers. Glulam posts are also available. Glulams are very fire resistant and do not ignite easily. If they do catch fire, they burn slowly. In some fires where an unprotected steel beam fails completely, a glulam will retain much of its strength.

Fig. 17-16. This glulam beam supports second-story floor framing.

MANUFACTURING METHODS

Glulams are made by gluing lengths of dimension lumber together. The individual layers are adhered face to face, clamped together, and allowed to cure at room temperature. The grain of all layers is parallel along the length of the beam. Each layer is generally no more than 1½" thick. The woods most commonly used for glulams are southern yellow pine and Douglas fir.

The best-quality material is used in the top and bottom layers. This improves the strength of a glulam by nearly 100 percent as compared to random layering. When a one-hour fire rating is required, additional layers of high-quality lumber are placed on the bottom of the beam. **Fig. 17-17.**

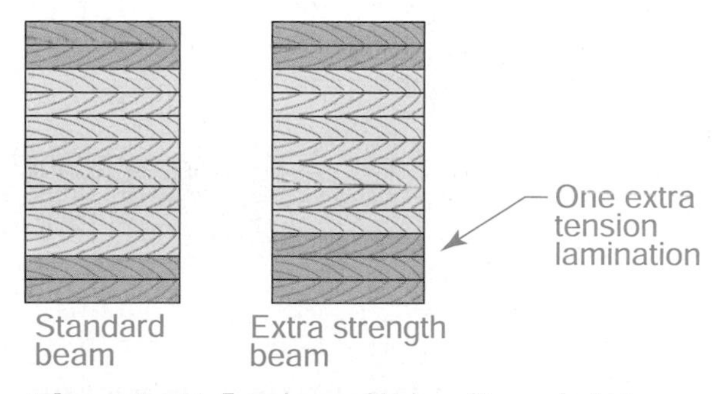

Fig. 17-17. Extra layers of high-quality wood add to a glulam's fire resistance.

Glulams are sometimes manufactured with a slight upward curve, called **camber**. The beam is installed with the curve oriented up. **Fig. 17-18.** When the beam is in place and fully loaded, the curve straightens out. The amount of camber in any glulam varies according to its length. Camber is measured in the following two ways:

- *Inches of camber.* The actual amount of camber is measured in inches at the center of the beam. It is the amount the beam curves above a flat surface.
- *Radius of curvature.* The camber of a glulam represents a segment of a huge circle. Stock beams used in residential construction are cambered based on a radius of 3,500′. In commercial construction, this radius may be only 1,600′ or 2,000′.

GRADES

Four grades of glulams are available. The differences among the grades are based on appearance. There are no differences in strength. As the appearance of the beam becomes more important, its cost increases.

- *Framing grade glulams* are intended for use where they will not be seen. They are available in widths that fit flush with 2×4 or 2×6 framing.
- *Industrial grade glulams* are for areas in which appearance is not of much importance. Voids (gaps) may appear on exposed edges. Beams are surfaced only on the sides.
- *Architectural grade glulams* are used where appearance is more important. Some voids are permitted, but any over ¾″ in diameter will be filled. All exposed faces are surfaced, and the exposed edges are eased (slightly rounded over).
- *Premium grade glulams* are available only as a custom order. They are used where appearance is very important. All knotholes and voids are filled. All exposed faces are surfaced, and the exposed edges are eased.

Specifying Glulams

When glulams are specified or ordered, width and depth are the most important factors. Stock beams are manufactured in widths of 3⅛″, 3½″, 5⅛″, 5½″, and 6¾″. Depths range from 9″ to 36″. It is also important to specify whether any camber is necessary or whether the glulam should instead be flat. Custom glulams can be ordered if an unusual strength, length, shape, or degree of camber is required.

Excessive exposure to direct sunlight can cause the wood in a glulam beam to fade in color. If the beam will be exposed in the completed structure, take care to wrap it in an opaque covering prior to installation.

STORAGE AND INSTALLATION

Glulams generally leave the mill with a moisture content of 12 percent. Before shipping, they are sealed, primed, or wrapped in water-

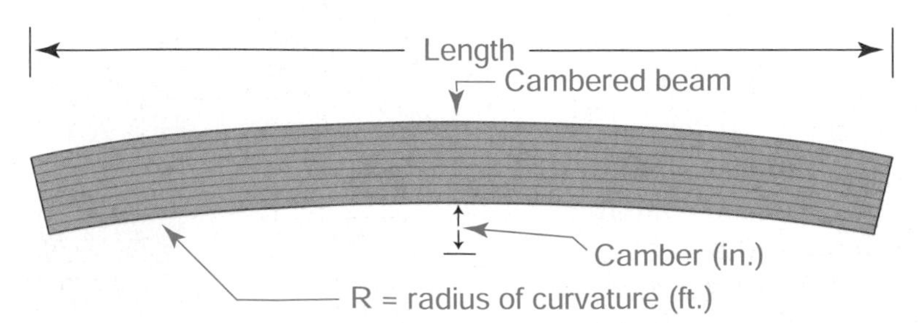

Fig. 17-18. Camber in a glulam beam. In this drawing, the curve of the beam has been exaggerated.

resistant paper. The ends are sealed to limit moisture penetration. When a beam must be stored on site before installation, take care to protect it. Support it off the ground. It can be stored on edge, but laying it flat reduces the chance that it will tip over accidentally. If the beam is wrapped in protective paper, make a small slit in the underside to allow moisture to drain and to encourage air circulation.

Take care to install glulams properly. They must not be notched or drilled in any way unless this has been accounted for in their design. If a beam must be cut to length on site, the cut ends should be sealed according to the maker's specifications. Heavy-gauge metal framing connectors are often used to support glulams.

SECTION 17.2

Check Your Knowledge

1. How does a glulam behave in a fire?
2. What parts of a glulam contain the best-quality wood?
3. When is it all right to drill or notch a glulam beam?
4. What is a common method for attaching glulams to a structure?

On the Job

Locate two manufacturers of glulams and ask about recommended methods for fastening them to a structure. Compare installation methods. Keep this information in a file for future use.

SECTION 17.3

Other Engineered Lumber

Other engineered structural products are also available. They include finger-jointed lumber, laminated-strand lumber, and parallel-strand lumber. For installation, review the product literature provided by each manufacturer. Also, be sure to find out if the products are covered by the building codes adopted by your area.

FINGER-JOINTED LUMBER

It is increasingly difficult to find framing lumber of the consistent quality once available. This is partly because of the heavy demand for wood products. To help meet demand, *finger-jointed lumber*, sometimes referred to as *structural end-jointed lumber*, has been developed. Lengths of solid wood are joined end to end.

A **finger joint** is a closely spaced series of wedge-shaped cuts made in the mating surfaces. These cuts create a large surface area that improves the glue bond between the two parts. **Fig. 17-19.**

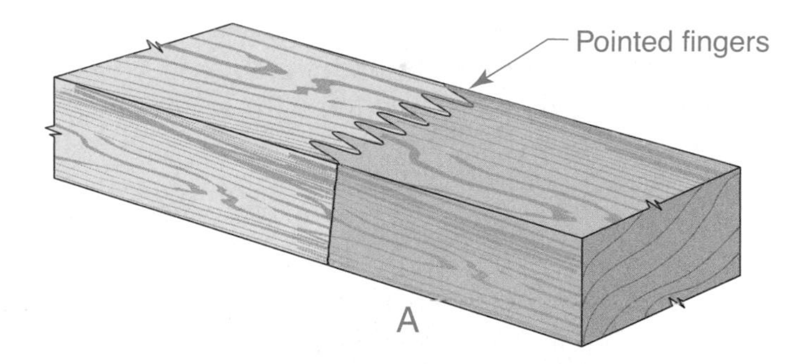

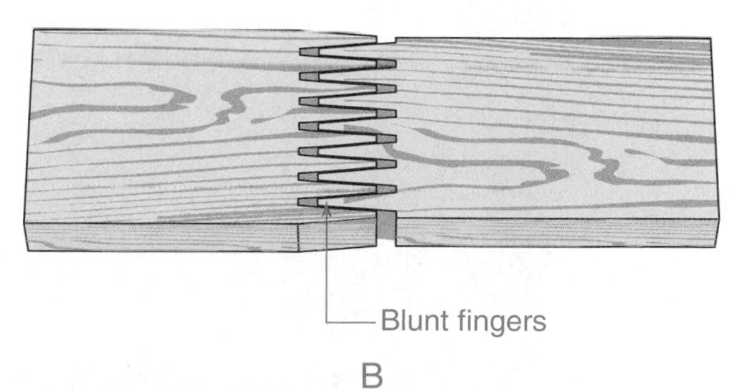

Fig. 17-19. Finger-jointed lumber. *A.* The fingers of lumber used in certified exterior joints are pointed and approximately 7/8″ to 1 1/8″ long. *B.* The fingers of joints for interior use only are blunt and 3/8″ to 5/8″ long.

Finger-jointed lumber has several important characteristics:

- It is always straight.
- It can be sawed and nailed exactly like solid lumber.
- It makes use of short pieces of wood that would be wasted otherwise.
- It is available in longer lengths than standard lumber.

Finger-jointed products are available for use as wall framing lumber, paint-grade interior molding, and exterior trim.

Finger-Jointed Studs

The grading agencies that supervise the manufacture of standard lumber also supervise finger-jointed lumber. Each piece of finger-jointed lumber should be stamped with a grade mark. **Fig. 17-20.** The type of finger joint and the adhesives used determine what the material is used for. Building codes generally treat lumber with *certified exterior joints* as if it were standard lumber. It can be used interchangeably with standard lumber of the same size, species, and grade. Lumber with *certified glued joints* is suited to vertical use only. It should not be used in floor, ceiling, or rafter framing. For framing, finger-jointed lumber is available as precut studs in lengths up to 32′.

Some finger-jointed lumber, such as *vertical-use-only grades*, is assembled with water-resistant adhesives. You should never store such lumber where water might collect in the stack for prolonged periods. Store this product indoors or under cover until you are ready to use it.

LAMINATED-STRAND LUMBER

Laminated-strand lumber (LSL) is made of wood strands glued together and cut to uniform dimensions. Its performance is predictable. It can be used for rim boards, studs, plates, headers, beams, and columns. **Fig. 17-21.**

An LSL product is made from fast-growing aspen or yellow poplar, though small amounts of other hardwoods may be included. After debarking, logs are processed into wood strands from 0.03″ to 0.05″ thick, 1″ wide, and about 12″ long. The strands are dried and sorted to remove waste and pieces that are too short. The dried strands are coated with a blend of polymeric diphenylmethane diisocyanate adhesive and wax. The coated strands are then formed into a thick mat. The mat is cut to a 35′ or 48′ length and formed under heat and pressure into a billet of the desired dimensions. When cooled, the billet is sanded and cut to lengths up to 22′. The finished LSL lumber is then marked with a grade stamp.

Fig. 17-20. Sample grade markings for finger-jointed lumber.

Fig. 17-21. Laminated-strand lumber products.

PARALLEL-STRAND LUMBER

Another product that can be used for such things as columns and studs is *parallel-strand lumber* (PSL). Like laminated-veneer lumber, PSL is made with veneers that are glued together. **Fig. 17-22.**

The wood comes from Douglas fir, western hemlock, southern pine, or yellow poplar logs. The logs are cut in 8′ lengths, then rotary-peeled into veneer with a thickness of 1/10″ or 1/8″. The veneers are cut into large pieces, dried, and cut into ribbons (called *strands*) about 1″ wide and up to 8′ long. Unwanted short strands and other waste are removed.

The strands are then coated with a phenol formaldehyde adhesive mixed with a small amount of wax. The wax helps to keep out moisture. Strands are laid parallel and built up into a mat. The mat is then compressed and the adhesive is cured using microwave energy. The resulting billet may be as much as 11″ thick. When cool, it is cut to size and sanded. The pieces are grade stamped and coated with a sealant to further slow moisture intake.

Fig. 17-22. Parallel-strand lumber.

SECTION 17.3 Check Your Knowledge

1. What is a finger joint?
2. Name four important characteristics of finger-jointed lumber.
3. What are the two basic types of finger-jointed lumber?
4. What is the difference between laminated-strand lumber (LSL) and parallel-strand lumber (PSL)?

On the Job

Research your local building codes to find out if finger-jointed studs are approved for use in your area. Make note of any restrictions. Present your findings to the class.

SECTION 17.4

Metal Framing Connectors

At one time, all wood-to-wood connections were secured only with nails. Because of differences in nailing technique, the strength of the connections varied. A metal **framing connector** is often used to support and connect standard framing lumber. Such connectors consist of a formed metal bracket. They speed framing and improve the uniformity of connections. They are even more important when the framing is made of engineered lumber. Some engineered products, such as I-joists, are difficult or impossible to secure without the use of metal framing connectors.

A metal framing connector makes not only wood-to-wood, but also wood-to-masonry or wood-to-concrete connections stronger. Some ornamental connectors are meant to be exposed. However, most will never be seen after the building is completed. These are made from various gauges of galvanized steel. **Table 17-C.**

Metal connectors are galvanized after they have been formed into a specific shape. Galvanizing deposits a layer of zinc on all sides. This protects the metal by slowing corrosion (the formation of rust). The thickness of the zinc coating is indicated by a code. The standard zinc coating is G 60. This means that the zinc is 0.005″ thick on each side of the steel. A connector with a G 90 coating would have a layer of zinc one-and-one-half times as thick as one with a G 60 coating. Some connectors have a G 185 coating. If even greater corrosion resistance is required, stainless steel connectors should be considered. They must be installed using stainless steel nails because other nails would rust.

from Another Angle

Salt spray from the ocean increases the speed of corrosion. The amount of salt spray in the air declines rapidly in the first 300′ to 3,000′ inland. When constructing a house within this "corrosion zone," builders should use metal connectors that have extra corrosion resistance.

Table 17-C. Thickness of Galvanized Steel Used for Framing Connectors

Gauge	In Decimal Inches	In Millimeters	In Approximate Fractions of an Inch
7	0.186	4.8	3/16
10	0.138	3.5	1/8
11	0.123	3.1	1/8
12	0.108	2.7	3/32
14	0.078	2.0	3/32
16	0.063	1.6	1/16
18	0.052	1.3	1/16
20	0.040	1.0	1/32
22	0.034	0.8	1/32

Note: Actual steel dimensions will vary from nominal dimensions according to industry tolerances.

TYPES OF CONNECTORS

A wide variety of connectors is available. The best source of information about a connector is the manufacturer. Framing connectors are widely accepted by building codes. However, you should always make sure that the use you have in mind is approved by the manufacturer and by local codes.

Joist Hangers

Perhaps the most common metal connector is the *joist hanger*. **Fig. 17-23.** These sturdy brackets are used where floor or ceiling joists meet another framing member, such as a beam. Standard hangers are made from 18-gauge galvanized metal. They are typically installed with 10d common nails. However, always follow the manufacturer's recommendations for the type and size of nail. Special *joist-hanger nails* may also be supplied by the manufacturer. They are the same diameter as a 10d nail but shorter.

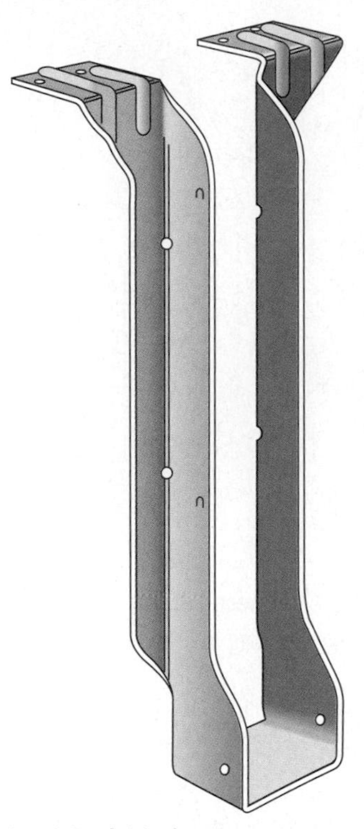

Fig. 17-23. A joist hanger.

Fig. 17-24. These joist hangers are aligned with the bottom of an intersecting beam.

The most common mistake made when installing joist hangers is to use too few nails. The connection depends on nails for shear strength. Undernailing can cause the connection to fail when loads are placed on it. Check the manufacturer's instructions carefully. Use all the nails recommended.

Joist hangers are available in sizes to fit most common framing situations. Headers, for example, may be hung from a pair of joist hangers. Even large glulam beams and solid timbers may be secured with joist hangers. They can be used when the top edge of the joists must be at the same level as the top edge of the intersecting beam. They are also used when the bottom edges of the intersecting members must be flush. **Fig. 17-24.**

Installing a joist hanger is simple. The hanger is first nailed to the beam. Then the joist is slipped into the hanger. Finally, nails are hammered through holes in the hanger and into the joist.

Proper installation is important. If the sides of the hanger are spread too wide, the joist will be raised slightly. **Fig. 17-25.** This can cause a lump in the floor sheathing. If the seat of the hanger is "kicked out" from the beam, settling later on may cause the floor to squeak.

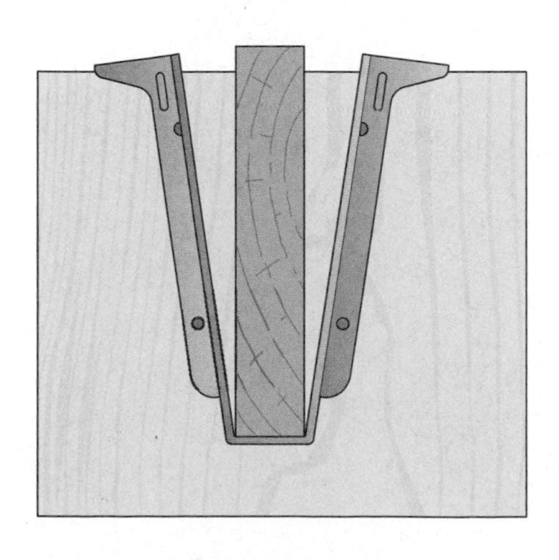

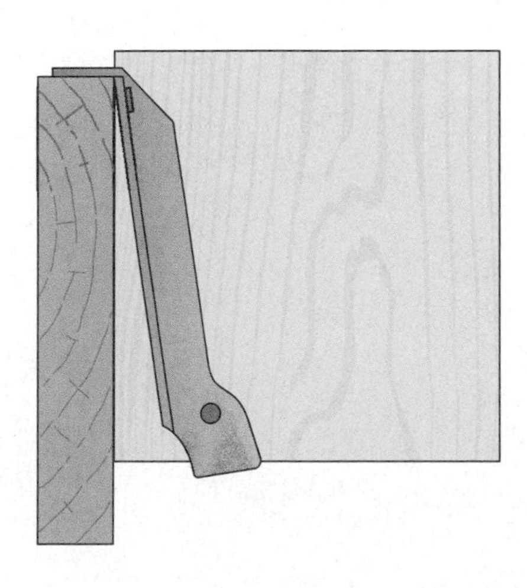

Fig. 17-25. An overspread hanger raises the height of the joist (left). If the hanger is "kicked out" from the header (right), the floor may squeak later.

To ensure that the tops of all joists are in exactly the same plane, a joist hanger can be nailed to the end of the joist first. As the joist is held in position, the hanger can then be secured to the beam.

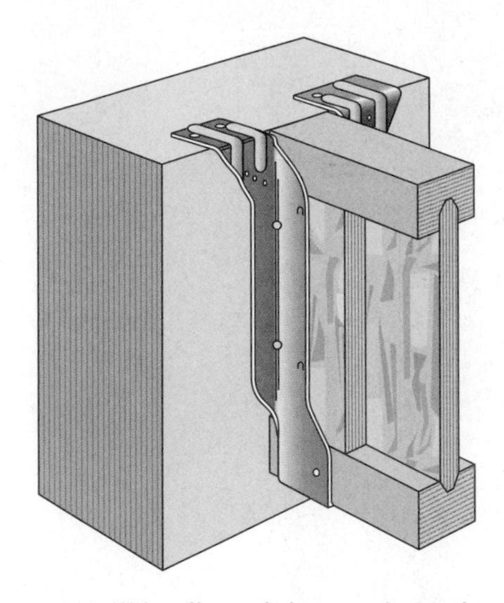

Fig. 17-26. Web stiffeners fit between the joist hanger and the I-joist. They prevent the web from buckling at stress points.

I-Joist Hangers

Because the shape of I-joists might allow them to tip from side to side in a standard joist hanger, choose hangers with care. If the sides of the hanger do not extend at least ⅜″ up the sides of the I-joist's top flange, install a web stiffener. This will prevent the I-joist from tipping from side to side. **Fig. 17-26.** Some hangers are designed specifically for use with I-joists, and web stiffeners may not be needed.

When I-joists are attached to an intersecting I-joist, the joist hangers should be "backed." This means placing backer blocks against the web, between the flanges of the supporting I-joist. Nails are driven into the blocks for extra support.

Ties and Straps

Metal framing ties are also used to hold pieces of wood together or to reinforce a joint. The most common form of tie is a flat strap. **Fig. 17-27.** The straps are perforated so that they can be nailed in place without pre-drilling. They may also be bent to fit various angles.

A tie in an angular shape can be used to join wood members at right angles. Such ties do not carry structural loads. They simply hold the pieces of wood together. An example is the tie that connects deck railings to deck posts. **Fig. 17-28.** The post holds the railing up. The tie simply holds them together. An advantage of this connection is that it removes the need for surface-nailing. It also reduces the chance that water will penetrate the area around the nails.

Other Metal Connectors

The wide variety of metal connectors makes them useful from foundation to roof. Metal post bases can be embedded in concrete slabs or piers. The base holds the wood post slightly above the level of the concrete. This reduces the possibility of rot. When the post is bolted to the post base, it is securely tied to its foundation. **Fig. 17-29.**

Fig. 17-27. Metal ties are being used here to connect various parts of a truss.

Fig. 17-28. Railing ties are first connected to the post. Galvanized screws may be used because the connection is not load bearing.

Fig. 17-29. A post base holds the wood slightly above the top of the pier to reduce rot.

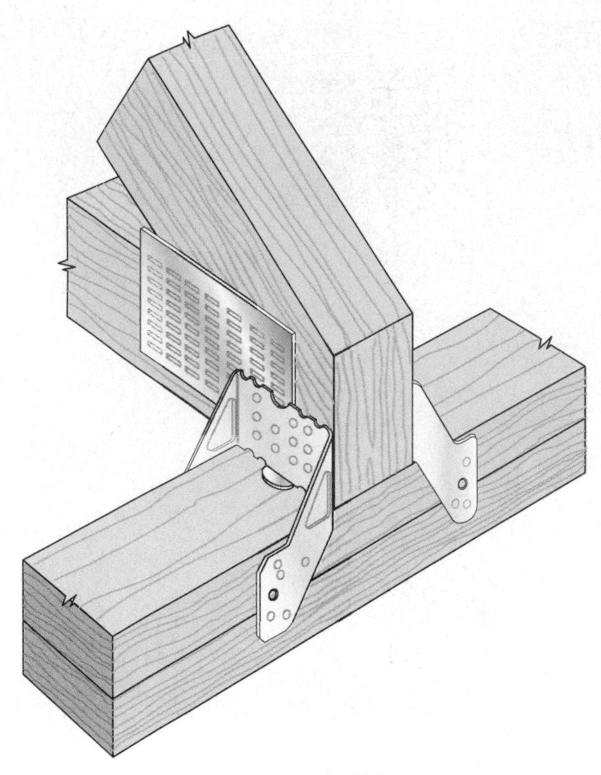

Fig. 17-30. These metal connectors are being used to improve the connection between a truss and a double top plate.

Rafters and trusses can be tied securely to the top plate with various types of metal clips and brackets. **Fig. 17-30.** In areas affected by earthquakes or fierce weather, metal connectors are sometimes required in residential construction. For example, metal hurricane clips connecting top plates to rafters prevent a roof from lifting off in high winds.

FASTENERS FOR METAL CONNECTORS

Most structural framing connectors are used where the nails that fasten them are exposed to shear stresses. In other words, the nail is loaded perpendicular to its length. It is very important that the fasteners used are able to withstand shear stress. Otherwise, the connection may fail. For this reason, drywall screws should never be used because they do not have the necessary shear strength.

Only nails should be used with most framing connectors. In some instances, bolts are also appropriate. The length of nail varies with the type of connection. The manufacturer's instructions include nail schedules. However, when 16d nails are specified, this generally refers to common nails, not 16d sinkers. (*Sinkers* are nails that are slightly thinner and shorter than commons.) Some manufacturers provide special nails, sometimes called joist-hanger nails, for use with their connectors. Their larger diameter, as compared with standard nails of similar length, improves their shear strength.

Pneumatic nailers can be used to fasten metal connectors into place. However, you must be careful to place the nail through existing holes in the connector. A nail that pierces the metal elsewhere reduces the connector's strength. Some connectors have angled holes for nails, which increases the strength of the connection. However, they must be installed by driving the nails with a hammer, not a pneumatic nailer.

SECTION 17.4 Check Your Knowledge

1. What is a joist hanger?
2. What sizes of nails are most commonly used to install framing connectors?
3. What is the correct method to use when an I-joist must be attached to another I-joist using a metal connector?
4. What does the code *G 60* mean?

On the Job

Suppose that the plans for the house you are about to build show that the floors should be framed with I-joists. You notice that in one location, I-joists will be doubled to create a beam. Locate a manufacturer of metal joist hangers. Obtain the product number for a hanger that could be used for doubled I-joists.

Chapter 17

Review

Section Summaries

17.1 Engineered-lumber products are often used in combination with conventional materials. "Laminated-veneer lumber" (LVL) is a family of engineered products made with wood veneer as the basic element. One common laminated-veneer lumber product is the I-joist. It is used in floor and roof framing.

17.2 Glulam beams are made of layers of lumber glued together. There are four glulam grades. Glulams are fire resistant. Some are made with a curve called camber.

17.3 A finger-joint is a way of joining solid wood end to end. Finger-jointed lumber is consistently straight, can be sawed and nailed like solid lumber, and is available in longer lengths than standard lumber. Laminated-strand lumber (LSL) is made from strands of wood glued together. Parallel-strand lumber (PSL) is made from ribbons of wood veneer glued together.

17.4 Metal framing connectors improve the strength of joints. Types include joist hangers, I-joist hangers, and ties and straps. Using the correct nail is extremely important.

Review Questions

1. What is engineered lumber and how does it help conserve wood resources?
2. List four advantages of engineered lumber.
3. What are the key ingredients of LVL lumber?
4. At what moisture content does laminated-veneer lumber leave the mill?
5. What is the proper method for driving nails into the side of an I-joist flange?
6. How can an I-joist be damaged when it is being stored or carried?
7. In residential construction, what are glulams used for?
8. What is camber?
9. What is a joist-hanger nail?
10. What is the most common mistake made when installing joist hangers?

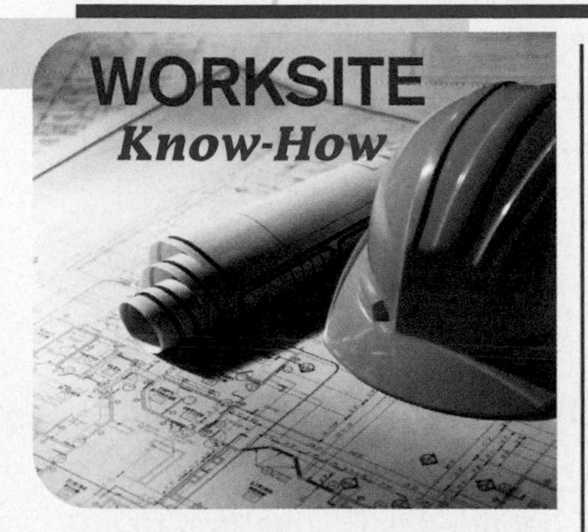

The Problem-Solving Process The problem-solving method is common to all technologies. It's a method you yourself can use. *First, state the problem clearly.* This helps define what needs to be done. *Second, collect information.* What's causing the problem? What resources are available? *Third, develop possible solutions.* Consider several ideas. *Fourth, select the best solution.* Look at the advantages and disadvantages of each. *Fifth, test what appears to be the best solution.* This will reveal its strengths and weaknesses. *Last, evaluate the solution.* Is it effective? If not, select another possibility and test that one until you find one that works.

Chapter 18

Engineered Panel Products

Objectives

After reading this chapter, you'll be able to:

- Identify the various types of engineered panels and their uses.
- Follow safety rules when handling or machining engineered panels.
- Explain the grading system for plywood.

Terms

composite panel product
engineered panel
glue-nailing
medium-density fiberboard (MDF)
oriented-strand board (OSB)
particleboard
plies
veneer match
wood veneer

For many years, solid wood was the only wood product used in residential construction. In various forms, it had many structural and decorative uses. The introduction of plywood changed residential construction techniques. Unlike solid lumber, plywood comes in large sheets, called *panels*, that can be installed quickly.

Several other panel products are now common on residential, as well as commercial, job sites. Some are made of wood flakes, wood dust, or wood fibers mixed with adhesives. Others are made of wood fiber mixed with Portland cement. All of these manufactured panels, including plywood, share the following characteristics:

- They are engineered for the efficient use of wood resources. Often they are made of wood that would otherwise be unused or wasted.
- They are manufactured using various natural or synthetic adhesives.
- Their performance is highly predictable.

In this book, the term **engineered panel** refers to any manufactured sheet product, including plywood, that is made of wood or wood pieces bonded with a natural or synthetic adhesive.

SECTION 18.1

Plywood

Plywood is a versatile building material. **Fig. 18-1.** It is important at almost every stage of home building. For example:

- Plywood made into foundation forms provides a stiff, uniform surface for forming concrete.
- Plywood floor, wall, and roof sheathing stiffens and strengthens the structure of the house.
- Plywood used for soffits provides a smooth, easy-to-paint surface.
- As underlayment, plywood makes a smooth substrate for finish flooring.
- When used in cabinets and built-ins, plywood is relatively light but very strong. It holds fasteners well, and can accommodate various types of joinery.

PLYWOOD BASICS

Plywood panels have traditionally been divided into two categories: softwood plywood (now called *construction and industrial plywood*) and hardwood plywood. Hardwood plywoods are used for paneling, cabinets, built-ins, and other interior features. This chapter deals primarily with construction and industrial plywood because that is the type most widely used in building construction.

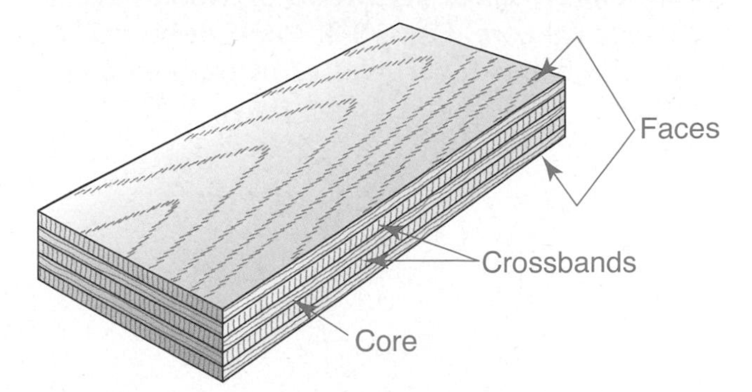

Fig. 18-2. Cutaway view of five-ply plywood with a veneer core.

The Structure of Plywood

Plywood consists of layers of wood veneer that have been glued together. A **wood veneer** is a very thin, pliable sheet of wood that has been sawed, peeled, or sliced from a log. When used in plywood, these thin sheets are called **plies**. Plywood is manufactured with an odd number of layers of these veneers. The grain of each layer runs at a right angle to that of the adjacent layers. Construction and industrial plywoods may have three, five, or seven layers.

The grain of the outermost plies always runs in the same direction. This is usually along the length of the panel. The outermost plies are called *face plies*. The face ply of best quality is called the *front face*, or *face*. The other is called the *back face*, or *back*. The plies between the two face plies make up what is called the core. Plies that are arranged at a 90° angle to the face plies are called *crossbands*. **Fig. 18-2.**

Fig. 18-1. Plywood is a versatile building material. Here it is being used for roof sheathing.

Hardwood plywoods may be made entirely of veneers or of veneers bonded to a core of glued-up lumber. The latter is called *lumber-core plywood.* Some types of hardwood plywood have a particleboard core. **Fig. 18-3. Particleboard** is made of very small particles of wood bonded together.

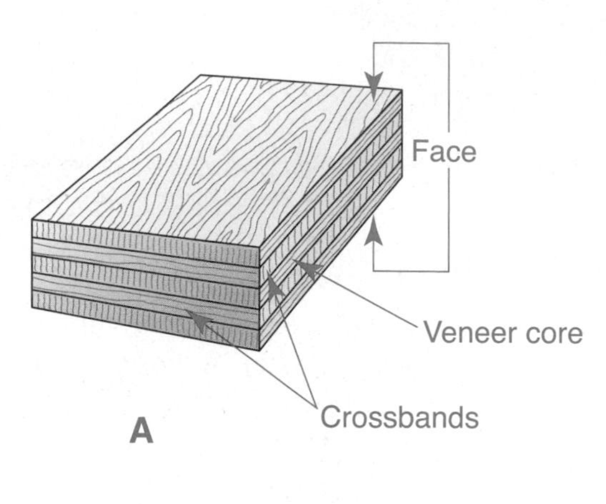

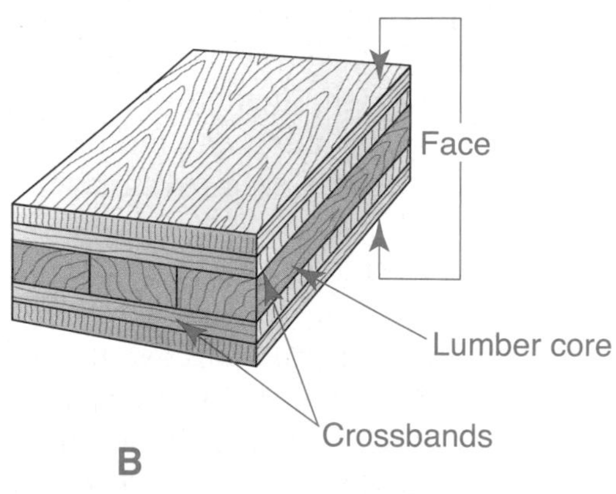

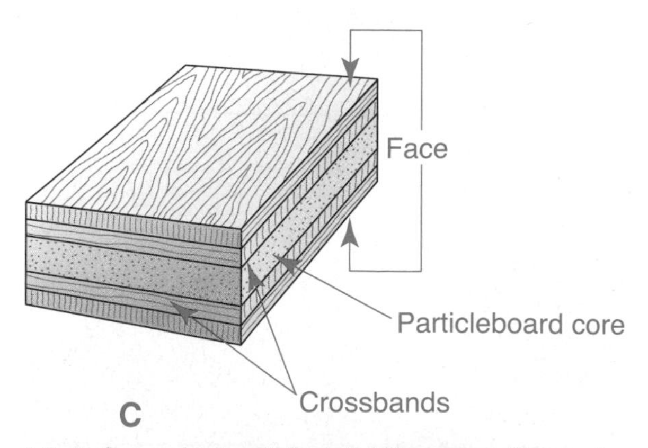

Fig. 18-3. Cores in hardwood plywood. *A.* Veneer core. The core is made of thick wood veneer. *B.* Lumber core. The core consists of strips of lumber bonded together. *C.* Particleboard core. The core of this five-ply plywood is made of particleboard. It is commonly used for cabinet doors because it is very stable.

Plywood Manufacturing

After a tree is cut and the log is trucked to a plywood mill, it goes into a pond for storage. Only select logs qualify as plywood *peeler* logs, from which veneers will be cut. Eventually a chosen log is lifted from the pond and cut to length. As it moves into the mill, it passes through a debarker that uses high-pressure jets of water to blast off the bark. The following describes the general process for manufacturing construction-grade plywood.

With huge tongs, an overhead crane lifts the stripped log into a lathe. Metal chucks grip both ends. The log is then spun against a long, razor-sharp steel blade. This blade slices a continuous strip of thin wood veneer from the log, like paper towels being unwound from a roll. **Fig. 18-4.**

Veneers are generally cut from the lower, larger portion of the trunk where the wood is mature and strong and has the clearest grain. As the veneer is sliced from the log, it moves over conveyors to the clipping machine, where giant knives cut it to a specific width. Then the veneer sheets pass into the dryers. There the moisture content of the wood is reduced to provide for the greatest panel stability and the best glue bond.

Fig. 18-4. Each sheet of veneer has a uniform thickness.

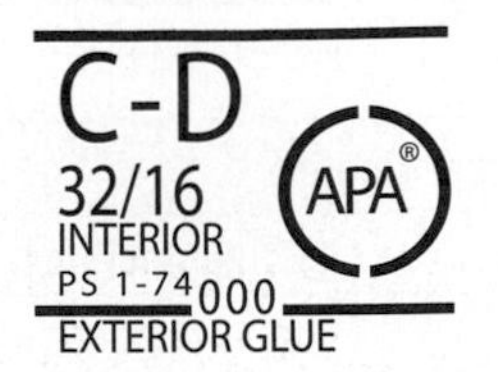

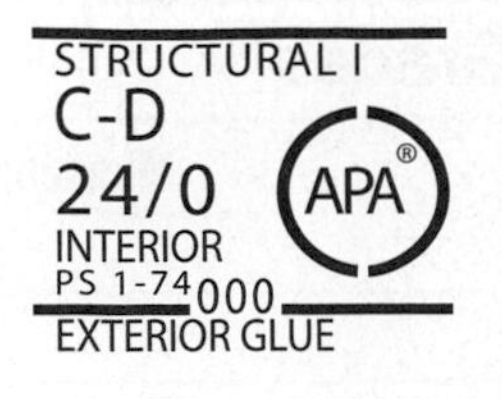

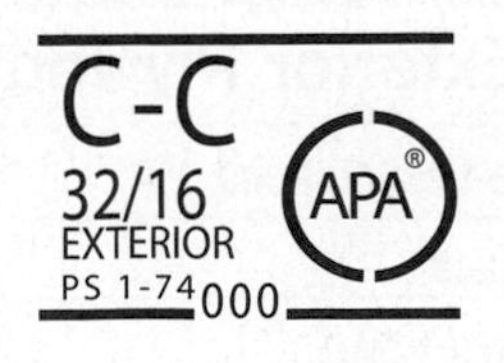

Fig. 18-5. Grade marks on sheathing panels.

Next, natural defects in the veneer sheets are cut out. The resulting holes are patched with solid wood or synthetic patching material. Some of the sheets then go through the glue spreader, where large rollers cover both sides with adhesive. These glue-covered sheets are stacked alternately with unglued sheets to make up panels of the desired thickness. This is called the *lay-up process.*

After lay-up, panels go into presses where the wood and glue are bonded together using pressure and, in some cases, heat. The result is a highly durable bond. This creates a product that is strong, rigid, dimensionally stable, and able to resist great impact.

Next, the panels are trimmed to exact length and width. Then they are sanded slightly to final thickness and inspected. Blemishes in the face plies are repaired. The panels are then graded and bundled.

CLASSIFYING PLYWOODS

Construction plywoods are graded. Hardwood plywoods are classified according to face-ply arrangements.

Construction Plywood Grades

Grade marks are stamped on the face of all plywood that meets APA–The Engineered Wood Association's standards. Typical grade marks are shown in **Figs. 18-5** and **18-6**. The purpose of a grade mark is to identify all the features of a panel. This enables builders to select the right panel for the job. The grade mark also enables

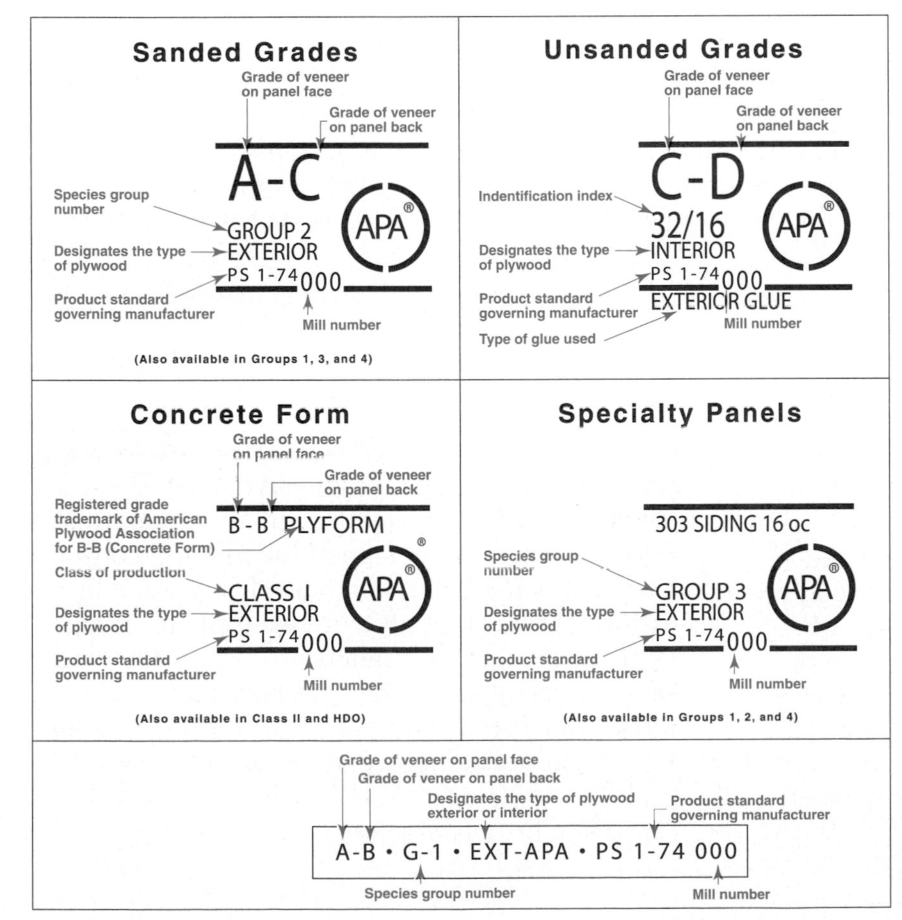

Fig. 18-6. The top four grade marks are back stamps and the lower one is an edge mark.

Table 18-A. Exterior Plywood Grades [a]				
Panel Grade Designations	Minimum Veneer Quality			Surface
Face		Back	Inner Plies	
Marine, A-A, A-B, B-B, HDO, MDO [b]				Sanded 2 sides
Special exterior, A-A, A-B, B-B, HDO, MDO [c]				Sanded 2 sides
A-A	A	A	C	Sanded 2 sides
A-B	A	B	C	Sanded 2 sides
A-C	A	C	C	Sanded 2 sides
B-B (concrete form) [d]				
B-B	B	B	C	Sanded 2 sides
B-C	B	C	C	Sanded 2 sides
C-C Plugged	C Plugged	C	C	Touch-sanded
C-C	C	C	C	Unsanded [e]
A-A High-density overlay	A	A	C Plugged	-
B-B High-density overlay	B	B	C Plugged	-
B-B High-density concrete form overlay	B	B	C Plugged	-
B-B Medium-density overlay	B	B	C	-
Special overlays	C	C	C	-

National Institute of Standards and Technology

(a) Available also in Structural I and Structural II classifications.

(b) Marine grades shall meet the requirements of exterior type and shall be of one of the following grades: A-A, A-B, B-B, high-density overlay, or medium-density overlay.

(c) Special exterior–An exterior type panel that may be produced of any species covered by this Standard. Except in regard to species, it shall meet all of the requirements for marine panels (see b) and be produced in one of the following grades: A-A, A-B, B-B, high-density, or medium-density overlay.

(d) B-B concrete form panels–Face veneers shall be not less than B grade and shall always be from the same species group. Inner plies shall be not less than C grade. This grade of plywood is produced in two classes, and panels of each class shall be identified accordingly. Panels shall be sanded two sides and mill-oiled unless otherwise agreed upon.

(e) Except for decorative grades, panels shall not be sanded, touch-sanded, surface textured, or thickness sized by any mechanical means.

building inspectors to verify that the correct materials have been used.

The grades of exterior plywood are listed in **Table 18-A**. The grades of interior plywood are listed in **Table 18-B**. The characteristics of plywood that affect its grade include type of adhesives used, veneer quality, wood species, construction, size, performance, and special characteristics.

Adhesives. The type of adhesive used affects a panel's resistance to weathering and moisture. Exterior panels are designed for full and continuous exposure to the weather. They are made with water-resistant glue. An example is siding plywood. Exposure-1 panels are also made with water-resistant glue. They are suitable for areas where moisture content is high, but they are not as weather resistant as exterior panels. They

Table 18-B. Interior Plywoods Grade

Panel Grade Designations	Minimum Veneer Quality			Surface
	Face	Back	Inner Plies	
N-N	N	N	C	Sanded 2 sides
N-A	N	A	C	Sanded 2 sides
N-B	N	B	C	Sanded 2 sides
N-D	N	D	D	Sanded 2 sides
A-A	A	A	D	Sanded 2 sides
A-B	A	B	D	Sanded 2 sides
A-D	A	D	D	Sanded 2 sides
B-B	B	B	D	Sanded 2 sides
B-D	B	D	D	Sanded 2 sides
Underlayment	C plugged	D	C & D	Touch-sanded
C-D plugged	C plugged	D	D	Touch-sanded
Structural I C-D[a]				Unsanded[b]
Structural I C-D plugged, underlayment[a]				Touch-sanded
Structural II C-D[a]				Unsanded[b]
Structural II C-D plugged, underlayment[a]				Touch-sanded
C-D	C	D	D	Unsanded[b]
C-D with exterior glue	C	D	D	Unsanded[b]

National Institute of Standards and Technology

(a) Structural panels–These panels are especially designed for engineered applications such as structural components where design properties, including tension, compression, shear, crosspanel flexural properties and nail bearing, may be of significance.

(b) Except for decorative grades, panels shall not be sanded, touch-sanded, surface textured, or thickness sized by any mechanical means.

could, for example, be used for soffits but not for siding. Exposure-2 panels are made with water-resistant glue. They are appropriate for brief, non-continuous exposure to the weather. Sheathing plywood fits into this category. The grade marking for a panel coated with water-resistant adhesive is followed by an *X* (for example, CDX). Interior panels are made with glues that are not necessarily water resistant. They should be used indoors only.

Veneer Quality. The quality of the veneer is specified by a letter designation, ranging from A (highest) to D (lowest). Plywood often has faces of differing quality. For example, cabinet plywood labeled A-C would have one face of high-quality veneer and one of lesser-quality veneer. A roof sheathing plywood might be classified as C-D. The C surface provides a smooth substrate for shingles. Smoothness is not as important on the side installed against the framing. Veneer

Table 18-C.	Veneer Quality
N	Intended for natural finish. Selected all heartwood or all sapwood. Free of open defects. Allows some repairs.
A	Smooth and paintable. Neatly made repairs permissible. Also used for natural finish in less demanding applications.
B	Solid surface veneer. Repair plugs and tight knots permitted. Can be painted.
C	Sanding defects permitted that will not impair the strength or serviceability of the panel. Knotholes to 1½″ and splits to ½″ permitted under certain conditions.
C plugged	Improved C veneer with closer limits on knotholes and splits. C-plugged veneers are fully sanded.
D	Used only in interior type for inner plies and backs. Permits knots and knotholes to 2½″ maximum dimension and ½″ larger under certain specified limits. Limited splits permitted.

quality grades are listed in **Table 18-C**. By mixing veneers, mills can conserve quality woods and produce panels more cost effectively.

Wood Species. Most construction plywood is made of softwoods such as Douglas fir. On the basis of stiffness and other factors, these species are divided into five groups. The strongest woods are found in Group 1. **Table 18-D.**

Table 18-D. Wood Species Used for Plywood

Group 1	Group 2	
Apitong [a] [b]	Cedar, Port Orford	Maple, black
Beech, American	Cypress	Mengkulang [a]
Birch	Douglas fir 2 [c]	Meranti, red [a] [d]
Sweet	Fir	Mersawa [a]
Yellow	California red	Pine
Douglas fir 1 [c]	Grand	Pond
Kapur [a]	Noble	Red
Keruing [a] [b]	Pacific silver	Virginia
Larch, western	White	Western white
Maple, sugar	Hemlock, western	Spruce
Pine	Lauan	Red
Caribbean	Almon	Sitka
Ocote	Bagtikan	Sweetgum
Pine, southern	Mayapis	Tamarack
Loblolly	Red lauan	Yellow poplar
Longleaf	Tangile	
Shortleaf	White lauan	
Slash		
Tanoak		
Group 3	**Group 4**	**Group 5**
Alder, red	Aspen	Basswood
Birch, paper	Bigtooth	Fir, balsam
Cedar, Alaska	Quaking	Poplar, balsam
Fir, subalpine	Cativo	
Hemlock, eastern	Cedar	
Maple, bigleaf	Incense	
Pine	Western red	
Jack	Cottonwood	
Lodgepole	Eastern	
Ponderosa	Black (western poplar)	
Spruce		
Redwood	Pine	
Spruce	Eastern white	
Black	Sugar	
Engelmann	White	
White		

(a) Each of these names represents a trade group of woods consisting of a number of closely related species.

(b) Species from the genus Dipterocarpus are marketed collectively: apitong if originating in the Philippines; keruing if originating in Malaysia or Indonesia.

(c) Douglas fir from trees grown in the states of Washington, Oregon, California, Idaho, Montana, Wyoming, and the Canadian Provinces of Alberta and British Columbia shall be classed as Douglas fir No. 1. Douglas fir from trees grown in the states of Nevada, Utah, Colorado, Arizona, and New Mexico shall be classed as Douglas fir No. 2.

(d) Red meranti shall be limited to species having a specific gravity of 0.41 or more based on green volume and oven dry weight.

Table 18-E. Plies and Layers

Panel Grades	Finished Panel Nominal Thickness Range (inch)	Minimum Number of Plies	Minimum Number of Layers
Exterior			
Marine Special exterior B-B concrete form High-density overlay High-density concrete form overlay	Through ⅜ Over ⅜, through ¾ Over ¾	3 5 7	3 5 7
Interior			
N-N, N-A, N-B, N-D, A-A, A-B, A-D, B-B, B-D Structural I (C-D, C-D Plugged and underlayment) Structural II (C-D, C-D Plugged and underlayment)	Through ⅜ Over ⅜, through ½ Over ½, through ⅞ Over ⅞	3 4 5 6	3 3 5 5
Exterior			
Structural I and Structural II A-A, A-B, A-C, B-B, B-C Medium-density and special overlays			
Interior (including grades with exterior glue)			
Underlayment	Through ½ Over ½, through ¾ Over ¾	3 4 5	3 3 5
Exterior			
C-C plugged			
Interior (including grades with exterior glue)			
C-D C-D plugged	Through ⅝ Over ⅝, through ¾ Over ¾	3 4 5	3 3 5
Exterior			
C-C			

Note: The proportion of wood based on nominal finished panel thickness and dry veneer thickness before layup, as used, with grain running perpendicular to the panel face grain shall fall within the range of 33 to 70 percent. The combined thickness of all inner layers shall be not less than one-half of panel thickness based on nominal finished panel thickness and dry veneer thickness before layup, as used, for panels with 4 or more plies.

Construction. The number of layers in a plywood panel usually corresponds to the number of plies. **Table 18-E.** In some cases, two of the inner plies may be glued together with their grain running parallel, forming a single inner layer. **Fig. 18-7.**

Size. The thickness of standard plywood ranges from ¼″ to 1¼″ or more. Plywood is most commonly available in panels that are 4′ wide and from 8′ to 12′ long. The most common sheet size used in residential construction is 4′×8′ . When referring to the size of panel products, remember that the width is always given

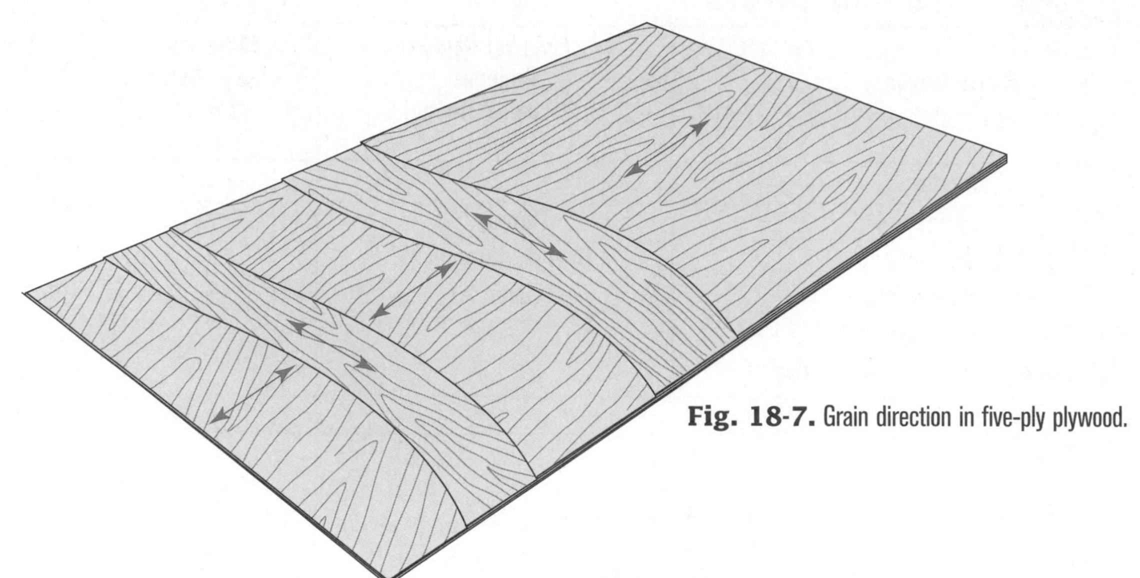

Fig. 18-7. Grain direction in five-ply plywood.

first. Thus a 4′ × 10′ sheet is 4′ wide and 10′ long. The grain of the face plies usually runs along the length.

Performance. Some panels are designed for special engineering uses where strength and stiffness are of maximum importance. Grades of these structural panels are listed in **Table 18-F**. Certain grades are used for subflooring, interior and exterior wall sheathing, and roof decking. These include grades marked *C-C*, *C-D*, structural *C-C*, and structural *C-D*. It is important to select the correct sheathing for each construction need.

Special characteristics. Plywoods are often adapted for special uses. For example, foundation-grade plywood includes panels that have been treated with preservative chemicals. These are used where the wood will be permanently installed in contact with the earth. Tongue-and-groove plywood is used in the construction of single-layer flooring systems.

Hardwood Plywood

Hardwood plywood is more expensive than construction plywood of a like thickness and size. Hardwood plywoods are commonly found in 4′ x 8′ x ¾″ sheets, but other sizes are available. Birch, maple, and oak are frequently used for the face plies. However, panels made from other domestic and exotic woods can be obtained from specialty supply sources.

The appearance of a hardwood plywood panel depends upon the species of wood used and the way the face plies are milled and applied. Hardwood plywood is used for finish work in which appearance is very important. Mills

Table 18-F. Structural Panels

Grade	Glue Bond	Species
Structural I C-D [(a)] C-D plugged [(a)] Underlayment [(a)]	Exterior	Face, back, and all inner plies limited to Group 1 species
Structural II C-D [(a)] C-D plugged [(a)] Underlayment [(a)]	Exterior	Face, back, and all inner plies may be of any Group-1, -2, or -3 species
Structural I All exterior grades	Exterior	Face, back, and all inner plies limited to Group 1 species
Structural II All exterior grades	Exterior	Face, back, and all inner plies, may be any Group-1, -2, or -3 species

(a) Special limitations applying to structural (C-D, C-D plugged, underlayment) grade panels are:

–In D grade veneers white pocket in any area larger than the size of the largest knothole, pitchpocket or split specifically permitted in D grade shall not be permitted in any ply.

–Sound-tight knots in D grade shall not exceed 2½″ measured across the grain.

–Plugs, including multiple repairs, shall not exceed 4″ in width.

provide many options for the manufacture and arrangement of face plies. There are four basic milling methods, called *cuts*. **Fig. 18-8.** Face plies are then applied to the panels using one of five basic arrangements. The arrangement of pieces of veneer is called a **veneer match**. **Fig. 18-9.** This creates different patterns and effects. An unusual combination of cut and veneer match may have to be special-ordered from the plywood supplier.

Fig. 18-8. The manner in which veneers are cut is an important factor in producing various effects. Two logs of the same species, with their veneers cut differently, will have an entirely different appearance even though their colors are similar.

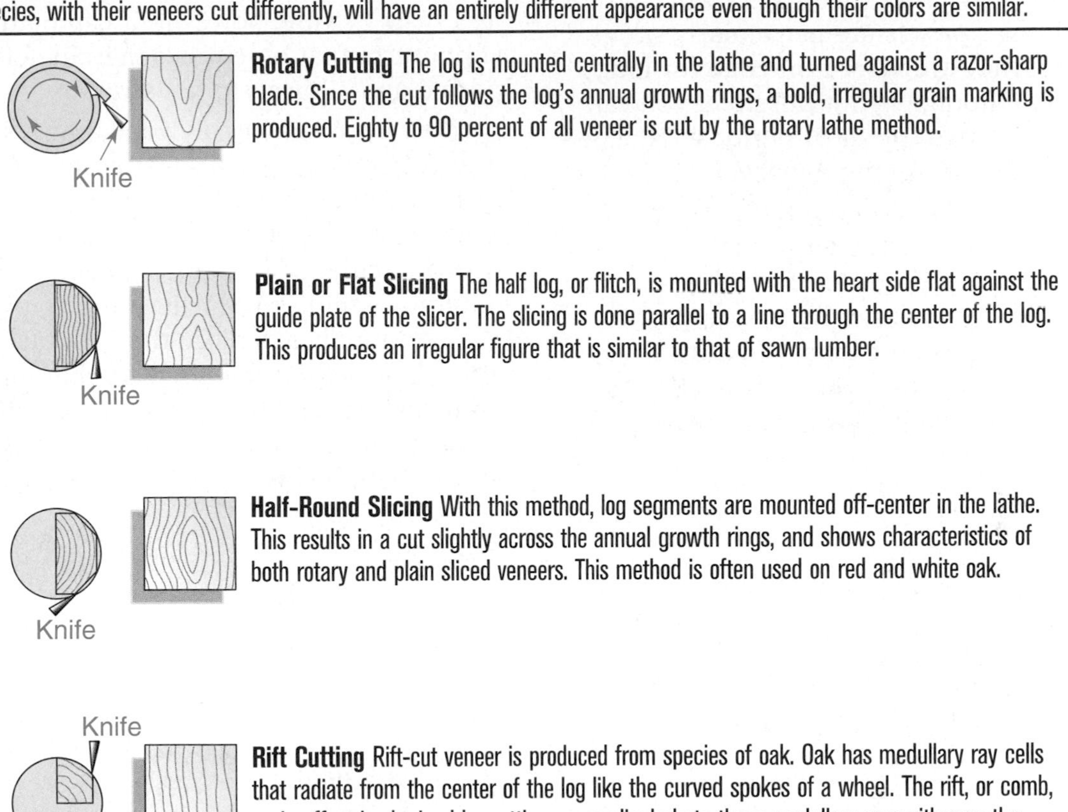

Fig. 18-9. Veneer matching refers to the alignment of veneer strips on a panel. Hardwood plywood panels are precision matched and available in a variety of veneer types.

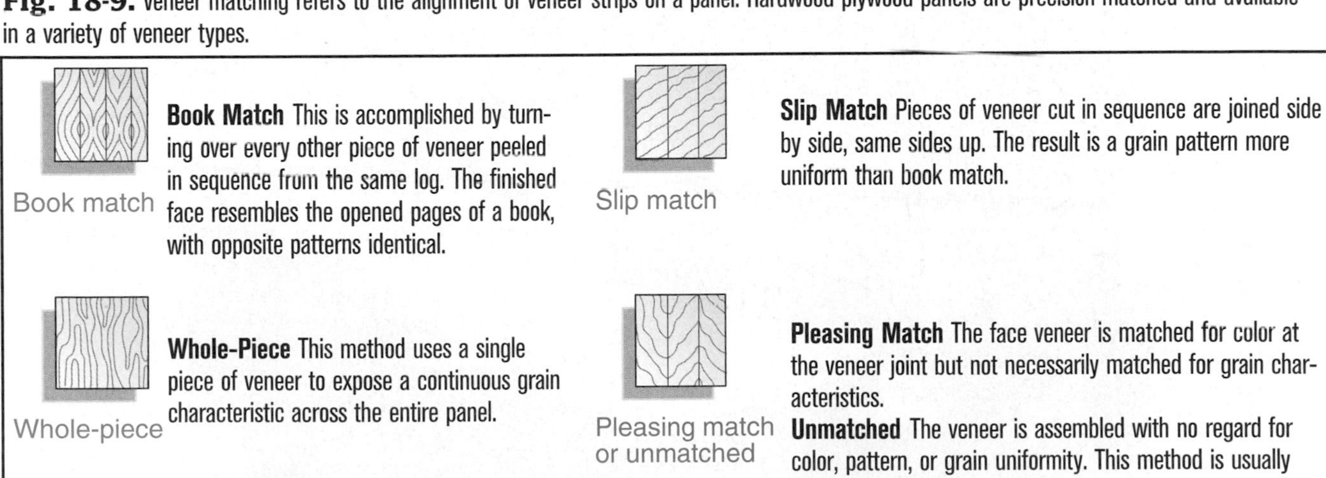

WORKING WITH PLYWOOD

Working with plywood involves knowing how to store, cut, shape, and fasten it.

Storage

Store plywood sheets flat whenever possible. This reduces the chance that sheets will warp or tip over. Thinner panels are particularly prone to warping if they are stored on edge for long periods. If flat storage is not possible, you can store sheets on edge for short periods. Take precautions to prevent tipping, however.

Plywood should be stored indoors until it is ready for use and is delivered to the job site. There it can be stored outdoors as long as it is protected from the weather by a waterproof tarp. The sheets should be stacked atop wood spacers that support the pile at least 1½″ above the ground. Use enough spacers to prevent the sheets from bowing.

Cutting

Like any panel product, plywood must always be supported firmly as it is cut. **Fig. 18-10.** This prevents dangerous kickback when using power saws (see "Preventing Kickback" on page 129). It also prevents binding when using a handsaw. Sawhorses are often used. Sheets of plywood should be supported between the sawhorses to avoid kickback. Some builders make a simple cutting table (see Fig. 7-4) to improve safety and convenience.

Plywood should be supported on each side of the cut line, as well as at each end of the piece to be kept and the offcut. When the offcut is less than 1′ wide, however, it can be difficult to support. In that case it is generally left unsupported and allowed to fall away.

When hand sawing plywood, always place the best face up and use a saw that has at least 10 to 15 points to the inch. Hold the saw at a low angle. If you must cut cabinet-quality plywood with a circular saw, place the best face down to minimize splintering. When cutting plywood on a table saw, always place the best face up. With either saw, adjust the blade so that its teeth just clear the top of the plywood. This reduces blade exposure and increases safety. Scoring the veneer before cutting helps reduce splintering.

Shaping

Plywood can be shaped with various tools. A belt sander, for example, can be used to round off corners or shape edges to fit an irregular surface. Large holes can be made in plywood using a jigsaw or a large-diameter, toothed drill bit called a *hole saw*.

Fig. 18-10. When cutting plywood or any other sheet product, always support it on each side of the cut line. This will prevent it from binding on the saw blade.

When you are drilling through plywood, the panel may splinter on the back where the bit emerges. To prevent this, clamp a scrap piece of plywood beneath the area to be drilled. Then drill through the top piece and into the scrap. The scrap minimizes splintering by supporting the edges of the hole.

Fastening

Plywood can be fastened to other materials using wood adhesives, nails, and screws. However, no fastener works as well on the edges of plywood as it does on the face plies. It is important to remember this, especially when attaching hinges.

Pre-drilling a hole is generally necessary when starting screws into plywood by hand. Also, holes should be pre-drilled when driving screws close to the edge of a sheet. This prevents the edge from splitting. However, screws with sharp points, such as drywall and decking screws, can be driven directly into plywood with a screw-gun or an electric drill fitted with a screwdriving tip. (A *screw-gun* is an electric drill adapted to drive screws exclusively.)

When nails or screws are not enough to hold plywood in place, adhesives should also be used. The combination, called **glue-nailing**, produces a particularly strong bond. For example, many builders glue and nail sheathing plywood to the floor framing to produce an extra stiff floor. **Fig. 18-11.**

Where finish nails are used, conceal the nail holes with wood putty. Press the putty into the hole, level it off with a putty knife, and then sand the putty after it is dry. When using screws to fasten plywood, set the heads flush with the plywood.

Fig. 18-11. The combination of nailing and applying adhesive will produce a floor that minimizes squeaks.

SECTION 18.1 Check Your Knowledge

1. Name at least three general uses for plywood in residential building construction.
2. Describe the arrangement of plies in a typical sheet of plywood.
3. What is the purpose of veneer matching of hardwood plywood?
4. Describe the technique used to minimize splintering when drilling through plywood.

On the Job

Like any wood product, plywood is affected by moisture. Obtain a scrap piece of plywood and a scrap piece of solid softwood in the same size. Scraps 3½″ wide and 4″ to 5″ long would be ideal. Both scraps should be the same thickness (½″ to ¾″). Measure their exact width, length, and thickness. Submerge both pieces in water for 24 hours, then compare them. How have the dimensions changed? Let the two pieces dry for 24 hours. Then use a metal straightedge to check for signs of warping. What do you notice? Let the pieces dry for six more days and measure again. Which piece shows the most change?

Composite Panel Products

Unlike plywood, which is made from layers of wood veneer, a **composite panel product** is made from pieces of wood mixed with adhesive. These panel products often share many of the same characteristics as plywood. They are used for sheathing, subflooring, cabinetry, and paneling. The most common types of composite panels are oriented-strand board (OSB), hardboard, medium-density fiberboard (MDF), and particleboard. **Fig. 18-12.** Various other names are often used to describe certain engineered panels. *Chipboard*, *waferboard*, and *flakeboard* are all names for panels that are essentially the same or similar to oriented-strand board. The popularity of these names varies from region to region.

COMPOSITE PANEL BASICS

Composite panels are often made from wood that would otherwise be unused or wasted. This includes:

- Trees not appropriate for veneers.
- Trees that are too small for lumber production.
- Trees that grow too quickly to produce sound lumber.
- Portions of trees that would otherwise go unused, such as stumps and limbs.

The Structure of Composites

The wood pieces used in composite panels range in size from small fibers to large flakes. **Fig. 18-13.** Two strong influences on the properties of composite panels are:

- The size and shape of individual flakes and particles.
- The ratio of adhesive to particles.

Particle shape and adhesive content can be controlled to create a given set of physical properties. The size, type, and position of the particles also will affect a panel's surface smoothness.

Adhesives. A critical ingredient of a composite panel is the adhesive used to bond the wood pieces or particles. *Phenol-formaldehyde adhesives* are used for exterior structural panels, such as sheathing. These panels must withstand some exposure to water. *Urea-formaldehyde*

Fig. 18-12. Composition panels. From left to right: oriented-strand board (OSB), particleboard, medium-density fiberboard, hardboard, and tongue-and-groove oriented-strand board. Panels most often come in 4′ × 8′ sheets.

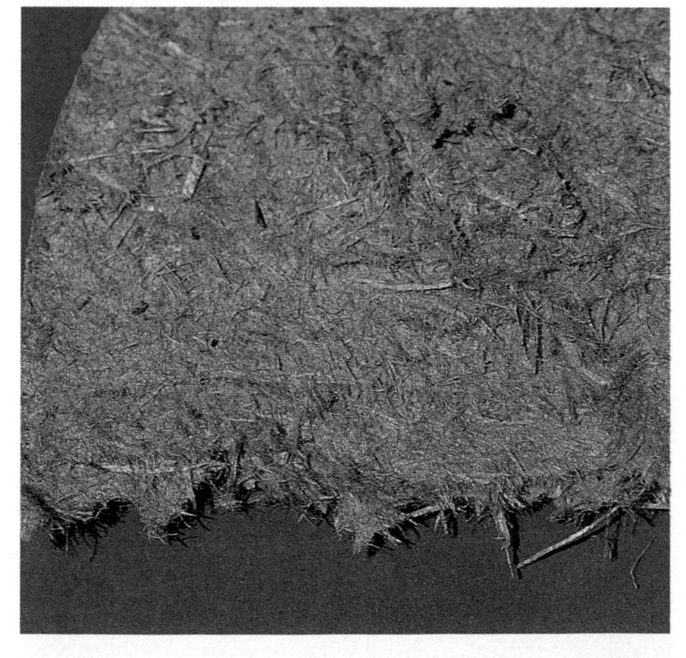

Fig. 18-13. These fibers are typical of those used in manufacturing fiberboard.

adhesives are more suited for panels used indoors. Another characteristic of panels made with this adhesive is that they have an exceptionally smooth surface. Particleboard and MDF are examples. Other adhesives can be used in composition panels, but these two are common.

Some people are very sensitive to formaldehyde vapors. The chemical can cause eyes to water or lead to breathing problems. When products containing formaldehyde are used in tightly-sealed structures, vapors can accumulate to unhealthy levels. Urea-formaldehyde resins are a particular problem in this regard. Urea resins release more formaldehyde vapors than phenolic resins do. Because of health concerns, various panel products are now available in which the amount of formaldehyde has been reduced significantly.

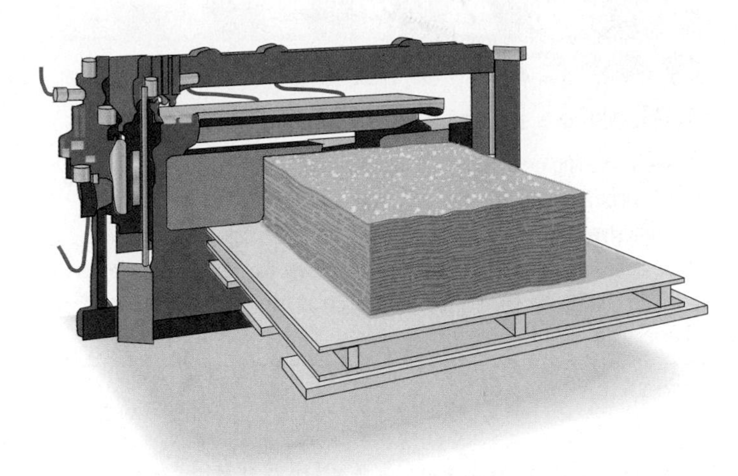

Fig. 18-14. A mat about to enter a laboratory press. It will be compressed into a panel approximately 0.12″ thick.

Additives. Other ingredients may be added to the mix of adhesives and wood to change panel characteristics. Small amounts of wax (0.5 percent to 1 percent) reduce a panel's tendency to absorb moisture and make it more suitable for such uses as sheathing. Fire-retardant chemicals can be added to make the panel more suited to areas where wildfires occur. Preservatives can be added to make the panel last longer.

Composite Panel Manufacturing

The difference in manufacturing between plywood panels and composite panels rests in the way the wood is processed. In composite products, logs or wood scraps are processed mechanically to create fairly small, uniform pieces. In some cases, the pieces are chemically treated to make them even smaller. The pieces are mixed with adhesives and other additives. The mixture is then formed into a thick layer called a *mat*. The mat is squeezed under heat and pressure into sheets of a specified thickness. The heat and pressure are released when the adhesive has cured. **Fig. 18-14.**

Composite panels can be given special finishes or treatments at the mill. Surfaces may be filled or primed for easy painting, embossed or textured for a decorative surface, or covered with a vinyl overlay. The edges of panels may be banded with lumber, machined for tongue-and-groove joints, or given special sanding or overlays. Panels can be laminated together to make unusually thick panels. They also can be glued edge to edge to create unusually large panels. The most common panel size is 4′×8′, but panels up to 8′×16′ are available.

The Future of Composites

As our forests are managed with ever more care, scientists and wood technologists continue to develop new composite products. The goal is to make the most efficient use of our forest resources. Various materials are being studied in addition to those noted in this chapter. They include recycled wood products, compressed natural grasses, and wood fiber mixed with thermoplastics.

Each new product must be thoroughly tested before it is approved for construction use. Many composite products incorporate chemicals and other additives that are not in solid wood. Therefore it is always important to learn as much as you can about a new product before using it. This would include gathering information about its long-term structural performance as well as its impact on the environment and human health. Always review the material safety data sheet for any composite product you are not familiar with. The *material safety data sheet (MSDS)* identifies potential health and safety hazards associated with handling or machining a material. It will suggest suitable precautions.

SAFETY FIRST

Adhesive Dust

When machining or sanding a composite product or the edges of plywood, wear a dust mask. This will prevent you from inhaling dust from the adhesives used in the panel's manufacture. Excessive exposure to these adhesives is a health hazard. This is especially important with products that generate very fine dust, such as particleboard, MDF, and fiber-cement board.

WORKING WITH COMPOSITES

Composite panels are free from cracks and other imperfections commonly found in solid and veneered wood. They present none of the problems related to grain in wood. Generally, they can be worked with standard woodworking tools. Because composite panels are made to exact thicknesses at the mill, there is little need for further surface preparation, such as sanding. They can be sawed, routed, shaped, and drilled cleanly, with good edges and corners. **Fig. 18-15.**

All types of joints for casework or architectural assemblies are readily made with composites. Architectural panels may be butted or splined. In cabinetry, miter, lock-miter, doweled, mortise-and-tenon, and tongue-and-groove joints are common.

The absence of voids gives these products a full, uniform contact surface for gluing. This means strong butt joints. Short lengths can be glued into longer sections for a minimum of waste. Check the manufacturer's literature for advice on the best adhesives to use.

ORIENTED-STRAND BOARD

Oriented-strand board (OSB) is made from wood strands bonded with adhesive under heat and pressure. It has been available since the early 1980s. It is now considered similar to plywood in strength and usefulness, especially for sheathing and subflooring.

Though a variety of wood species can be used, most OSB is made from aspen, southern pine, and various medium-density hardwoods. The strands in each layer of an OSB panel are oriented (positioned) so they run in one direction. Then the layers are placed perpendicular to each other. **Fig. 18-16.** Panels usually have three or five layers. The most common adhesive used is phenolformaldehyde.

OSB is available with square or tongue-and-groove edges. Thicknesses range from ⅜″ to 1⅛″. Though OSB is generally made with a waterproof adhesive, the panels are not suited to long-term exposure to the weather. OSB sheathing should be covered as soon as is practical. To increase its moisture resistance, the edges are often coated at the factory with a sealant.

Fig. 18-15. There is no chipping or splintering when composite panels are cut.

Fig. 18-16. The strands are directionally oriented in OSB.

Like most wood products, OSB will shrink or swell slightly with changes in humidity. It is more likely to change in thickness than plywood. Sheathing and subflooring should be installed with a ⅛″ gap between the ends of adjacent panels and ¼″ at the sides. If the edge seal is damaged during storage or installation, moisture can wick into the panel and swell its edges.

Panels at a job site should not be stored directly on the ground. Instead, they should be stacked on a level platform supported by 4x4 stringers or other blocking. They should be covered loosely with a waterproof tarp as soon as possible. The tarp should be arranged so as not to trap ground moisture beneath it. The steel banding that secures the panels during delivery should be cut right away to prevent the edges from being damaged if swelling occurs.

FIBERBOARD

The term *fiberboard* generally includes panel products such as *hardboard* and *medium-density fiberboard.* To make fiberboard, logs are chipped into small pieces of wood that are then reduced to fibers by steam or mechanical processes. These fibers are refined and mixed with an adhesive. They are then compressed under heat and pressure to produce panels. A fiberboard product will not split, crack, or splinter. It is dense, with extremely smooth front and back surfaces, and has superior wear resistance.

Hardboard

Hardboard is a high density fiberboard that is often used for such things as interior paneling, flooring underlayment, and cabinet back panels. **Fig. 18-17.** The manufacturing process is similar to that used for paper. A slurry (a mixture of fibers and water) is formed into a mat. The mat is then compressed in several stages under pressure and steam heat until the final panel is formed. In some cases, binders or adhesives do not have to be added to the mat. The lignin in the wood fiber, when heated and pressed, serves as a natural adhesive.

Fig. 18-17. A major advantage of using panel stock such as this hardboard is uniformity of size and shape.

Hardboard is generally available in standard and tempered grades. *Standard hardboard* is given no additional treatment after manufacture. It has high strength and good water resistance. It is commonly used in cabinetwork because it has a very smooth surface. *Tempered hardboard* is standard hardboard to which linseed oil or tung oil has been added prior to pressing. This process improves stiffness as well as scratch and water resistance.

Hardboard is manufactured with one or both sides smooth. Hardboard with one side smooth is known as *S1S.* Hardboard with two sides smooth is *S2S.* It is available in thicknesses from ⅛″ to ⅜″. The standard panel size is 4′ × 8′, but widths up to 6′ and lengths to 16′ are also available. *Perforated hardboard* has very closely spaced holes punched or drilled into it. The holes can be fitted with metal hooks, holders, supports, or similar fittings. **Fig. 18-18.**

Fig. 18-18. Perforated hardboard can be useful in storage areas.

Wood-grain hardboard is printed to match the color and texture of oak, walnut, mahogany, and many other woods. It is popular for interior paneling.

Medium-Density Fiberboard (MDF)

Medium-density fiberboard is made of compressed wood fibers mixed with urea-formaldehyde adhesive. Because of the uniformity of the fibers used in the manufacturing process, MDF panels have a uniform thickness and an extremely smooth surface. This makes them ideal for use where the end product will be painted, such as door panels and cabinetry. Painted cabinet doors that appear to be frame-and-panel doors are often made of MDF, for example. Though considered a type of fiberboard, MDF is manufactured in a way similar to that used for particleboard.

SAFETY FIRST

Working with MDF

MDF can be worked with standard cutting tools, but carbide-tipped saw blades give the best results. Because the sawdust is extremely fine, it is important to wear appropriate dust protection when cutting or sanding. Also, MDF is quite dense. A ¾″ thick, 4′ × 8′ panel can be awkward to lift or transport. Take precautions to avoid backstrain when lifting this product.

PARTICLEBOARD

Particleboard is used indoors wherever a smooth and relatively inexpensive surface is required. It is rarely used as a finish surface, however, except for utility shelving. It is more commonly used as a cabinet carcase material and as a substrate to which other materials are applied. For example, it may be the chosen substrate for plastic laminate countertops because of its unusually smooth, grain-free surface. **Fig. 18-19.** Another use is as floor underlayment because it provides a smooth, stable base for resilient tile or carpeting. **Table 18-G.**

Construction particleboard is made by combining wood particles or flakes with adhesives and hot-pressing them into panels. The particles near the top and bottom surfaces are relatively fine. Somewhat coarser particles are located at the core. This construction is not obvious, however.

Because the particles don't interlock in the way fibers do, particleboard is not as strong as MDF and OSB. When stressed beyond certain limits, fasteners may pull out of the material. As with OSB, small amounts of wax may be added to the material during manufacture to improve its water resistance.

Panels range from ¼″ to 1½″ thick, from 3′ to 8′ wide, and up to 24′ in length. They come in ten different grades and three different densities (high, medium, and low).

Table 18-G. Plywood Wall Sheathing Application Details		
Type	Composition	Uses
Corestock	Flakes or particles bonded with urea-formaldehyde or phenolic resins; has various densities and related properties	Furniture, casework, architectural paneling, doors, and laminated components
Wood-veneered particleboard	Corestock overlaid at the mill with various wood veneers	Furniture, panels, wainscots, dividers, cabinets, etc.
Overlaid particleboard	Particleboard faced with impregnated fiber sheets, hardboard, or decorative plastic sheets	Furniture doors, wall paneling, sink tops, cabinetry, and store fixtures
Embossed particleboard	Surfaces are heavily textured in decorative patterns by branding with a heated roller	Doors, architectural paneling, wainscots, display units, and cabinet panels
Filled particleboard	Particleboard surface-filled and sanded; ready for painting	Painted end-products requiring firm, flat, true surfaces
Primed or undercoated particleboard	Factory-painted base coat on either filled or regular board; exterior or interior	Any painted products
Floor underlayment	Panels specifically engineered for floor underlayment	Underlay for carpets or resilient floor coverings

Fig. 18-19. Applying plastic laminate to a particleboard core for countertops.

During manufacturing, density, adhesives, and moisture content can be controlled to produce a variety of products. Stock panels range in density from 24 to 62 pounds per cubic foot. Ordinarily, a high-density panel will also have greater strength and a smoother, tighter edge than a low-density panel.

Two types of adhesives, urea-formaldehyde and phenol-formaldehyde, are used in the manufacture of particleboard. Urea-formaldehyde is suitable for interior use. Phenol-formaldehyde is used for panels that may be subjected to unusual heat or humidity.

It is especially important to control the moisture content of particleboard panels that will serve as a substrate. This is because the core material and the overlay material must have nearly equal moisture content. Panels normally are shipped from the mill with a moisture content of 7 to 9 percent, unless otherwise specified.

FIBER-CEMENT BOARD

Fiber-cement board differs from other engineered panel products. Instead of formaldehyde-based adhesives, its cellulose fibers are bound together with a mixture of Portland cement, ground sand, additives, and water. However, the panels are as efficient, uniform, and predictable as the other panel products discussed in this chapter. They are considered noncombustible and rot proof.

The standard fiber-cement panel is 5⁄16″ thick and very dense. It comes in sheets 4′ wide, and 8′, 9′, 10′, or 12′ long. One side is typically very smooth, while the other is rougher. However, finishes of various textures are available. Its smooth finish, along with its stability, make fiber-cement board desirable for use as siding. It is available as lap siding as well as in shingle siding patterns.

Handling and Cutting

Fiber-cement panels should be stored under cover on a dry, level surface. Steps should be taken to protect the edges and corners, as they can be damaged if struck. The panels can be awkward to transport because they are thin, somewhat flexible, and quite heavy. For comfort and safety, each panel should be carried on edge by two people.

Panels can be cut with special shears, but carbide-tipped circular saw blades are more often used. However, cutting with a blade generates a great deal of very fine dust that cannot be contained by standard dust bags. Fiber cement contains silica. Breathing excessive amounts of silica dust can lead to an illness called *silicosis*.

SAFETY FIRST

Dust Masks

Always wear a dust mask when cutting fiber-cement products. If large quantities of dust are generated, a respirator may be necessary. Special dust collection accessories are available for circular saws. For safety precautions, refer to Chapter 5, "Construction Safety and Health."

SECTION 18.2 Check Your Knowledge

1. How does a composite panel differ from a plywood panel?
2. What is the purpose of adding wax to a composite panel during manufacture?
3. Name the two types of fiberboard.
4. Where is fiber-cement board used?

On the Job

Particleboard is manufactured in a range of densities. Suppose you have decided to use 3⁄4″ particleboard as underlayment for flooring. You can choose board with a density of either 24 lbs. per cubic foot or 40 lbs. per cubic foot. If you have 1,800 square feet to cover, what would the difference in weight be for these two different densities? Why might the weight difference be important?

Chapter 18 Review

Section Summaries

18.1 Plywood may be made from either softwood or hardwood. Plywood is made from layers of wood veneer called plies. The plies are glued together with adhesives, some of which are water resistant. The plies are then joined under heat and pressure. Construction plywood grades are based on type of adhesives, veneer quality, wood species, construction, size, performance, and special characteristics.

18.2 Composite panels are made from pieces of wood mixed with adhesives and joined under heat and pressure. Composites include oriented-strand board, fiberboard, particleboard, and fiber-cement board. Some panels are given special finishes. Precautions should be taken when cutting fiber-cement board. A dust mask or respirator should be used.

Review Questions

1. What are the three characteristics that all engineered panel products share?
2. What does the term *face plies* refer to?
3. What is a veneer?
4. Name at least four features of plywood that are used to identify its grade.
5. When and why is it advisable to pre-drill screw holes when fastening plywood?
6. What is glue nailing?
7. Why is an MSDS important in regard to composite panels?
8. Describe OSB.
9. Identify the various types of engineered panels and list several uses.
10. What precautions should be taken when cutting fiber-cement board and why?

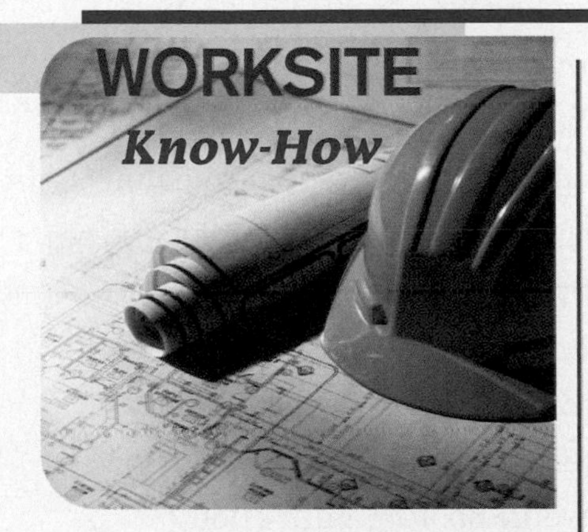

Learning from Trade Associations Industry trade associations are often a very good source of information about construction materials and techniques. APA–The Engineered Wood Association is a good example of such a resource. Members of the association are companies whose mills produce most of the structural wood panel products in North America. They also produce other engineered wood products such as laminated-veneer lumber and glulams. The association conducts research on how to maintain product quality. It also establishes installation techniques that make houses stronger and safer. This information is made available to builders and architects in hundreds of print and online products such as specifications and span tables. The APA also employs field representatives in major cities in the United States and Canada. Often, they can visit a job site to provide specific advice about the use of engineered wood products.

Chapter 19

Framing Methods

Objectives

After reading this chapter, you'll be able to:

- Name the stresses that structural wood must resist.
- Explain the difference between a live load and a dead load.
- Read a span table.
- Tell the differences between platform-frame construction and balloon-frame construction.
- List the advantages of structural insulated panels.

Terms

balloon-frame construction
dead load
design value
live load
load
on center (OC)
platform-frame construction
shear wall
span table
structural insulated panel

Most homes in the United States and Canada have a structural frame made of wood or wood products. Wood-frame houses have several important advantages. They often cost less than houses built using other structural systems. They are easily insulated, which reduces heating and air-conditioning costs. They can support a wide variety of exteriors. This flexibility allows architects and builders to produce nearly any architectural style. Also, a well-built and properly maintained wood-frame home is very durable. One of the oldest wood buildings in North America is Paul Revere's house in Boston, built about 1680. (See photo on page 348.)

Each method for building a wood-frame house has its advantages, which will be discussed in this chapter. Metal-frame houses are structurally similar. They are discussed in detail in Unit 5, "Steel Frame Construction."

SECTION 19.1

Stresses on Framing

When a load is placed on lumber, stresses are created inside the wood. A **load** is a force that creates stresses on a structure. Weight is one type of load. Wind is another. Wind creates stress when it pushes against the walls. The size and spacing of joists, studs, and rafters are based on the way wood responds under stress.

Table 19-A. Design Values for Beams and Stringers[a]

5″ and thicker, width more than 2″ greater than thickness[b] — Grades described in sections 53.00 and 70.00 of *Western Lumber Grading Rules*

Species or Group	Grade	Extreme Fiber Stress in Bending — Single Member F_b	Tension Parallel to Grain F_t	Horizontal Shear[c] F_v	Compression Perpendicular F_c	Compression Parallel to Grain F_c	Modulus of Elasticity E
Douglas fir-Larch	Dense Select Structural	1900	1100	170	730	1300	1,700,000
	Dense No. 1	1550	775	170	730	1100	1,700,000
	Dense No. 2	1000	500	170	730	700	1,400,000
	Select Structural	1600	950	170	625	1100	1,600,000
	No. 1	1350	675	170	625	925	1,600,000
	No. 2	875	425	170	625	600	1,300,000
Douglas fir-South	Select Structural	1550	900	165	520	1000	1,200,000
	No. 1	1300	625	165	520	850	1,200,000
	No. 2	825	425	165	520	550	1,000,000
Hemlock-Fir	Select Structural	1300	750	140	405	925	1,300,000
	No. 1	1050	525	140	405	750	1,300,000
	No. 2	675	350	140	405	500	1,100,000
Mountain Hemlock	Select Structural	1350	775	170	570	875	1,100,000
	No. 1	1100	550	170	570	725	1,100,000
	No. 2	725	375	170	570	475	900,000
Sitka Spruce	Select Structural	1200	675	140	435	825	1,300,000
	No. 1	1000	500	140	435	675	1,300,000
	No. 2	650	325	140	435	450	1,100,000
Spruce-Pine-Fir (South)	Select Structural	1050	625	65	335	675	1,200,000
	No. 1	900	450	65	335	575	1,200,000
	No. 2	575	300	65	335	350	1,000,000
Western Cedars	Select Structural	1150	700	70	425	875	1,000,000
	No. 1	975	475	70	425	725	1,000,000
	No. 2	625	325	70	425	475	800,000
Western Hemlock	Select Structural	1400	825	170	410	1000	1,400,000
	No. 1	1150	575	170	410	850	1,400,000
	No. 2	750	375	170	410	550	1,100,000
Western Woods (and White Woods)	Select Structural	1050	625	65	335	675	1,100,000
	No. 1	900	450	65	335	575	1,100,000
	No. 2	575	300	65	335	350	900,000

(a) Design Values in pounds per square inch. See Sections 100.00 through 180.00 in the *Western Lumber Grading Rules* for additional information on these values.

(b) When the depth of a sawn lumber member exceeds 12″, the design value for extreme fiber stress in bending (F_b) shall be multiplied by a size factor in Table J.

(c) All horizontal shear values are assigned in accordance with ASTM standards, which include a reduction to compensate for any degree of shake, check, or split that might develop in a piece.

Reprinted From *Western Lumber Product Use Manual* published May 2001 by Western Wood Products Association. © WWPA-2001. All Rights Reserved.

DESIGN VALUES

How wood will behave can be calculated once its species and grade are known. The results of laboratory stress tests on wood are summarized in tables of design values. A **design value** is a number assigned to how well each wood resisted stresses. Part of a design value table is shown in **Table 19-A**. This is shown only as an example. *Always read the footnotes that accompany the table.*

Carpenters and builders should have a basic understanding of design values. Design values are based on the following stress factors:

- *Extreme fiber stress in bending.* When a load is applied to a joist, header, or beam, it bends. This produces tension stresses in the wood farthest from the load and compression stresses closest to the load. **Fig. 19-1A.**
- *Tension parallel to grain.* When the ends of a piece of wood are pulled in opposite directions, tension along the grain results. **Fig. 19-1B.** This might occur in a floor joist attached to two walls that are bowing outward.
- *Horizontal shear.* Shear stresses occur where two portions of the wood are trying to slide past each other in opposite directions. **Fig. 19-1C.** A deep, heavily loaded beam might experience shear stresses near the centerline of the wood.
- *Compression.* When the wood rests on supports, c*ompression perpendicular to the grain occurs.* An example would be a joist. **Fig. 19-1D.** Any load on the wood tends to crush wood fibers at the bearing points. This problem can be reduced by increasing the bearing area. *Compression parallel to the grain* occurs when loads are supported on the ends of the wood. **Fig. 19-1E.** This is

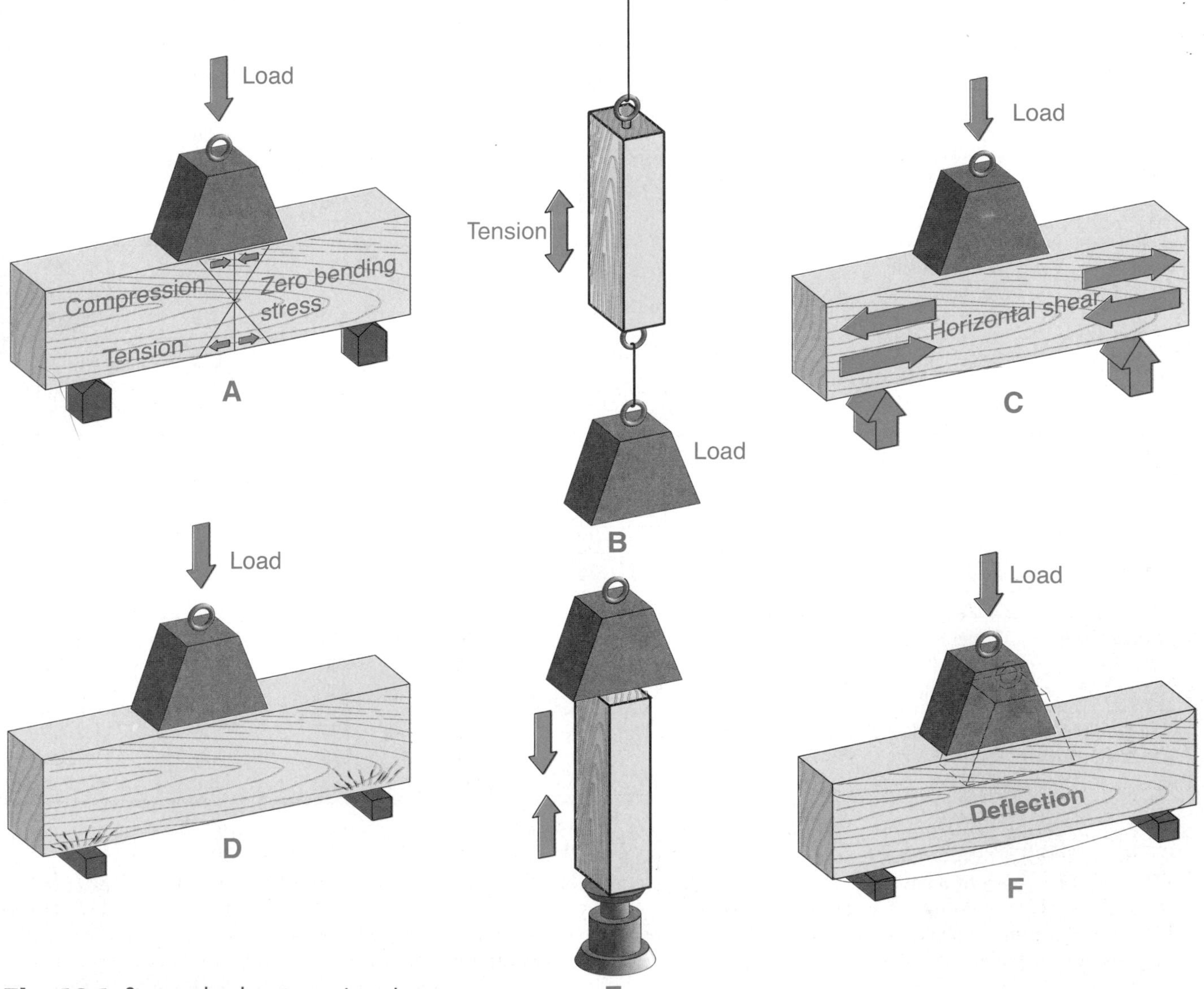

Fig. 19-1. Stresses placed on structural members.

typical of studs, posts, and columns. The resulting stresses affect the wood fibers uniformly along the full length of the wood.

- *Modulus of elasticity* is the ratio showing the amount that wood will bend in proportion to its load. The actual amount of bending is called *deflection.* An example would be how "springy" a floor is when walked on. **Fig. 19-1F.**

SPAN TABLES

Carpenters do not need to figure out how a certain wood will behave in a floor or ceiling. Instead, they can refer to a span table. **Table 19-B** shows part of a sample span table for floor joists. A **span table** lists the maximum spacing allowed between different sizes of joists or rafters. This spacing is referred to as **on center (OC)** spacing. It is the distance from the centerline of one structural member to the centerline of the next closest member. Using span tables, a carpenter can quickly find the right spacing for the species, grade, and dimensions of wood being used. Span tables are included in building code books and in literature from the major lumber trade associations. More complete examples of span tables are shown in the Ready Reference Appendix. Steps in reading a span table are given on page 348.

To simplify span tables, loads on a structure are divided into two types. A **dead load** is the total weight of the building. This includes the structural frame and anything permanently attached, such as wall coverings. A **live load** is weight that is not permanently attached. Examples of live loads include furniture and people. Live loads are related to the use of the building.

Table 19-B. Floor Joist Spans

40 lbs. LIVE LOAD. 10 lbs. DEAD LOAD. L/360

Design Criteria: *Strength*—10 lbs. per sq. ft. dead load plus 40 lbs. per sq. ft. live load.
Deflection—Limited in span in inches divided by 360 for live load only.

Species or Group	Grade	2x8				2x10				2x12				2x14			
		12″	16″	19.2″	24″	12″	16″	19.2″	24″	12″	16″	19.2″	24″	12″	16″	19.2″	24″
Douglas Fir-Larch	Sel. Struc.	15-0	13-7	12-10	11-11	19-1	17-4	16-4	15-2	23-3	21-1	19-10	18-5	27-4	24-10	23-5	21-4
	1 & Btr.	14-8	13-4	12-7	11-8	18-9	17-0	16-0	14-9	22-10	20-9	19-1	17-1	26-10	23-4	21-4	19-1
	No. 1	14-5	13-1	12-4	11-0	18-5	16-5	15-0	13-5	22-0	19-1	17-5	15-7	24-7	21-4	19-5	17-5
	No. 2	14-2	12-9	11-8	10-5	18-0	15-7	14-3	12-9	20-11	18-1	16-6	14-9	23-4	20-3	18-5	16-6
	No. 3	11-3	9-9	8-11	8-0	13-9	11-11	10-11	9-9	16-0	13-10	12-7	11-3	17-10	15-5	14-1	12-7
Douglas Fir-South	Sel. Struc.	13-6	12-3	11-7	10-9	17-3	15-8	14-9	13-8	21-0	19-1	17-11	16-8	24-8	22-5	21-1	19-7
	No. 1	13-2	12-0	11-3	10-6	16-10	15-3	14-5	12-11	20-6	18-4	16-9	15-0	23-8	20-6	18-9	16-9
	No. 2	12-10	11-8	11-0	10-2	16-5	14-11	13-10	12-5	19-11	17-7	16-1	14-4	22-8	19-8	17-11	16-1
	No. 3	11-0	9-6	8-8	7-9	13-5	11-8	10-7	9-6	15-7	13-6	12-4	11-0	17-5	15-1	13-9	12-4
Hemlock-Fir	Sel. Struc.	14-2	12-10	12-1	11-3	18-0	16-5	15-5	14-4	21-11	19-11	18-9	17-5	25-10	23-6	22-1	20-6
	1 & Btr.	13-10	12-7	11-10	11-0	17-8	16-0	15-1	14-0	21-6	19-6	18-3	16-4	25-3	22-4	20-5	18-3
	No. 1	13-10	12-7	11-10	10-10	17-8	16-0	14-10	13-3	21-6	18-10	17-2	15-5	24-4	21-1	19-3	17-2
	No. 2	13-2	12-0	11-3	10-2	16-10	15-2	13-10	12-5	20-4	17-7	16-1	14-4	22-8	19-8	17-11	16-1
	No. 3	11-0	9-6	8-8	7-9	13-5	11-8	10-7	9-6	15-7	13-6	12-4	11-0	17-5	15-1	13-9	12-4
Spruce-Pine-Fir (South)	Sel. Struc.	13-2	12-0	11-3	10-6	16-10	15-3	14-5	13-4	20-6	18-7	17-6	16-3	24-1	21-11	20-7	19-2
	No. 1	12-10	11-8	11-0	10-2	16-5	14-11	14-0	12-7	19-11	17-10	16-3	14-7	23-0	19-11	18-2	16-3
	No. 2	12-6	11-4	10-8	9-8	15-11	14-6	13-3	11-10	19-4	16-10	15-4	13-9	21-8	18-9	17-2	15-4
	No. 3	10-5	9-0	8-3	7-5	12-9	11-0	10-1	9-0	14-9	12-10	11-8	10-5	16-6	14-4	13-1	11-8
Western Woods	Sel. Struc.	12-10	11-8	11-0	10-2	16-5	14-11	14-0	12-9	19-11	18-1	16-6	14-9	23-4	20-3	18-5	16-6
	No. 1	12-6	11-1	10-1	9-0	15-7	13-6	12-4	11-0	18-1	15-8	14-4	12-10	20-3	17-6	16-0	14-4
	No. 2	12-1	11-0	10-1	9-0	15-5	13-6	12-4	11-0	18-1	15-8	14-4	12-10	20-3	17-6	16-0	14-4
	No. 3	9-6	8-3	7-6	6-9	11-8	10-1	9-2	8-3	13-6	11-8	10-8	9-6	15-1	13-1	11-11	10-8

Span (ft. and in.); Spacing on Center.

Reprinted From *Western Lumber Product Use Manual* published May 2001 by Western Wood Products Association. © WWPA-2001. All Rights Reserved.

STEP BY STEP

Reading a Span Table

Suppose that you need to determine what dimension of floor joist is suitable for use over a span of 18′. To use a span table:

Step 1 Determine the live load category of the building (30 or 40 lbs. per square foot). The designer determines the live load based on the usage of the building. For example, refer to Table 19-B, which deals with structures with a live load of 40 psf (pounds per square foot).

Step 2 Locate the "Species or Group" column. Identify the species of wood being considered.

Step 3 Refer to the "Grade" column. Identify the wood grade.

Step 4 Follow the row to the right until you find 18-0 or greater. This is the span you are looking for, in feet and inches.

Step 5 Now follow the column directly upward to the "Spacing on Center" row. The numbers there will tell you how far apart the joists must be spaced.

Step 6 In the row above that are the lumber dimensions.

For example, Hem-Fir (hemlock-fir) joists graded No. 1 would have to be 2x12s in order to span 18′. They could be spaced either 12″ or 16″ on center (OC), but no farther apart.

Fig. 19-2. Built of wood, the Paul Revere House in Boston is over 300 years old. It is proof of wood's strength and durability. Revere left from here on his historic ride to Lexington in 1775. The house is open to the public as a museum.

Though it was built before span tables were available, the Paul Revere House demonstrates the durability of quality construction. **Fig. 19-2.**

SECTION 19.1 Check Your Knowledge

1. What do design value tables show and what are they used for?
2. What is the modulus of elasticity?
3. Where can span tables be obtained?
4. Define *live load.*

On the Job

The Western Wood Products Association and the Southern Forest Products Association represent most of the softwood lumber producers in the United States. Contact one of them to obtain span tables for joists and rafters. If possible, obtain the tables online. Keep the tables in a file for future reference.

Conventional Framing

Conventional wood framing consists of many individual pieces. The main pieces are joists, studs, beams, and rafters. **Fig. 19-3.** These pieces are spaced at regular intervals. They are fastened together in a way that enables them to support and strengthen a part of the house. In that way, every piece supports part of the load.

Wood panels, called *sheathing*, are fastened to wood framing to give it more strength and stiffness (see Chapter 18, "Engineered Panel Products"). Together, the framing and sheathing form the basic structure of a house. The two main types of conventional framing are balloon-frame construction and platform-frame construction.

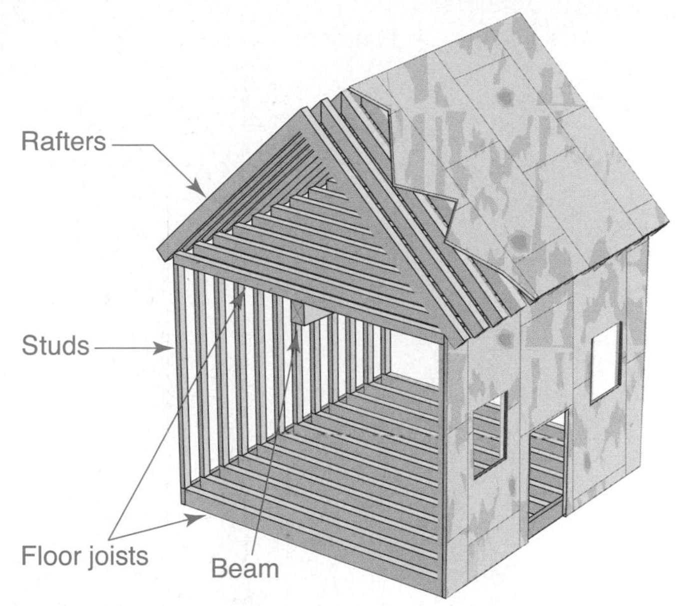

Fig. 19-3. The major framing members are joists, studs, beams, and rafters.

BALLOON-FRAME CONSTRUCTION

In **balloon-frame construction**, also called *balloon framing*, the studs run from the sill attached to the foundation to the top plate of the second floor. **Fig. 19-4.** The first-floor joists also rest on this sill. The second-floor joists bear on 1x4 ribbons cut into the inside edges of the studs. Wood expands and contracts *across* the grain but is relatively stable *with* the grain. Because less cross-grain framing is used, balloon-frame construction is less affected by expansion and contraction.

PLATFORM-FRAME CONSTRUCTION

In **platform-frame construction**, also called *platform framing*, each level of the house is constructed separately. The floor is a platform built independently of the walls. The top surface of this platform is called the *subfloor*. It extends to the outside edges of the building. **Fig. 19-5.** Each wall is usually assembled flat on its subfloor and then tilted into place.

Because the floors, walls, and roof are all separate parts, the connections between them can fail if not made properly. This is particularly true in areas affected by severe weather or earthquakes. However, if its parts are securely connected, a platform frame will be strong and rigid.

Platform-frame construction is easily adapted to prefabrication. Walls can be built elsewhere and then lifted into place on the subfloor. Another advantage of platform-frame construction is that it does not require unusually long lengths of lumber.

Building techniques in most parts of the United States have developed almost entirely around platform-frame construction. It is the most common method used for one- and two-story houses. Therefore, this book will focus on its techniques.

Spacing Variations

In standard platform-frame construction, wall studs are commonly spaced 16″ OC. However, floor joists might be spaced at intervals of 12″, 16″, 19.2″, or 24″ OC. The result is that structural loads are not passed directly from one framing member to another. This is not a problem because wall plates distribute the loads.

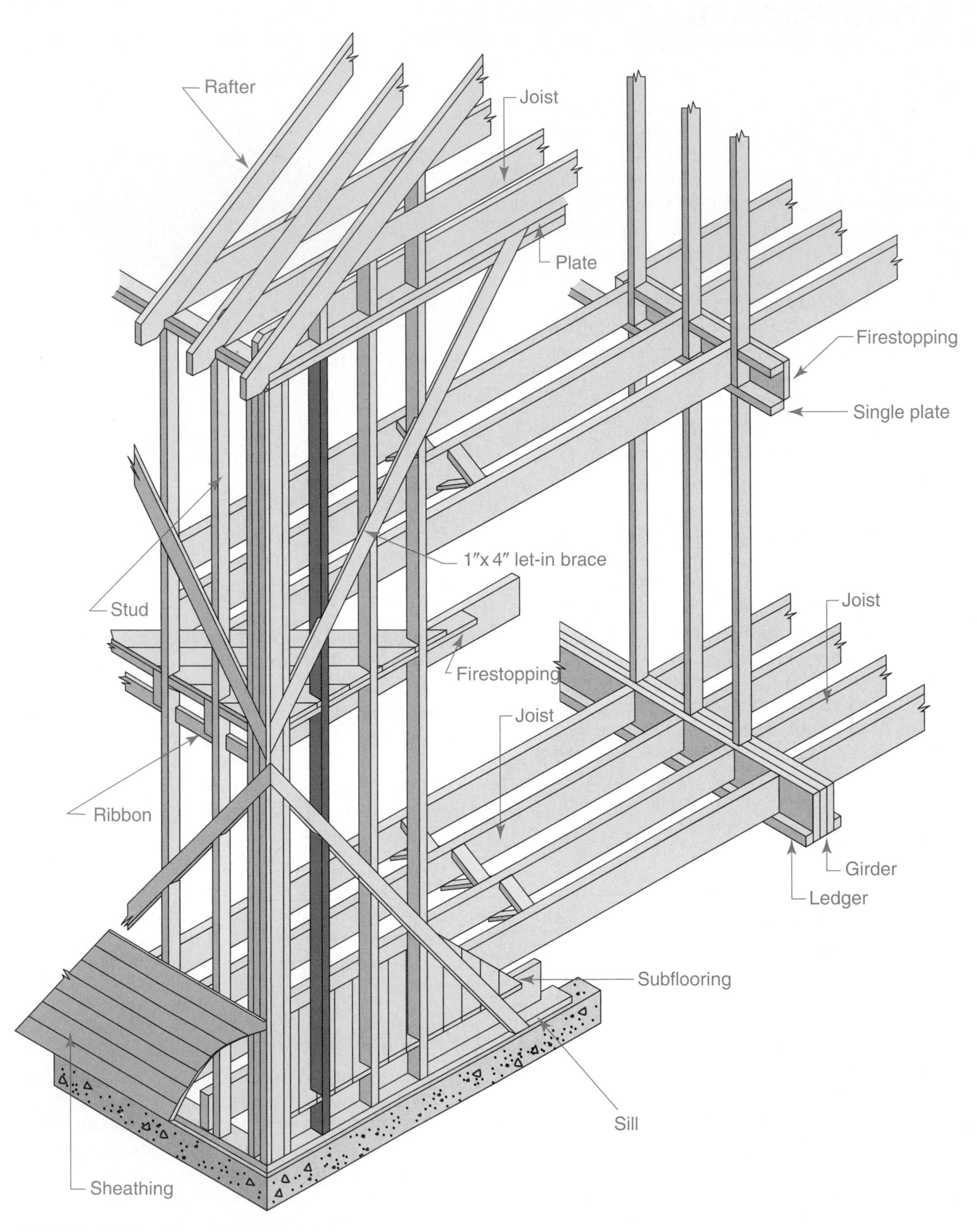

Fig. 19-4. Balloon-frame construction.

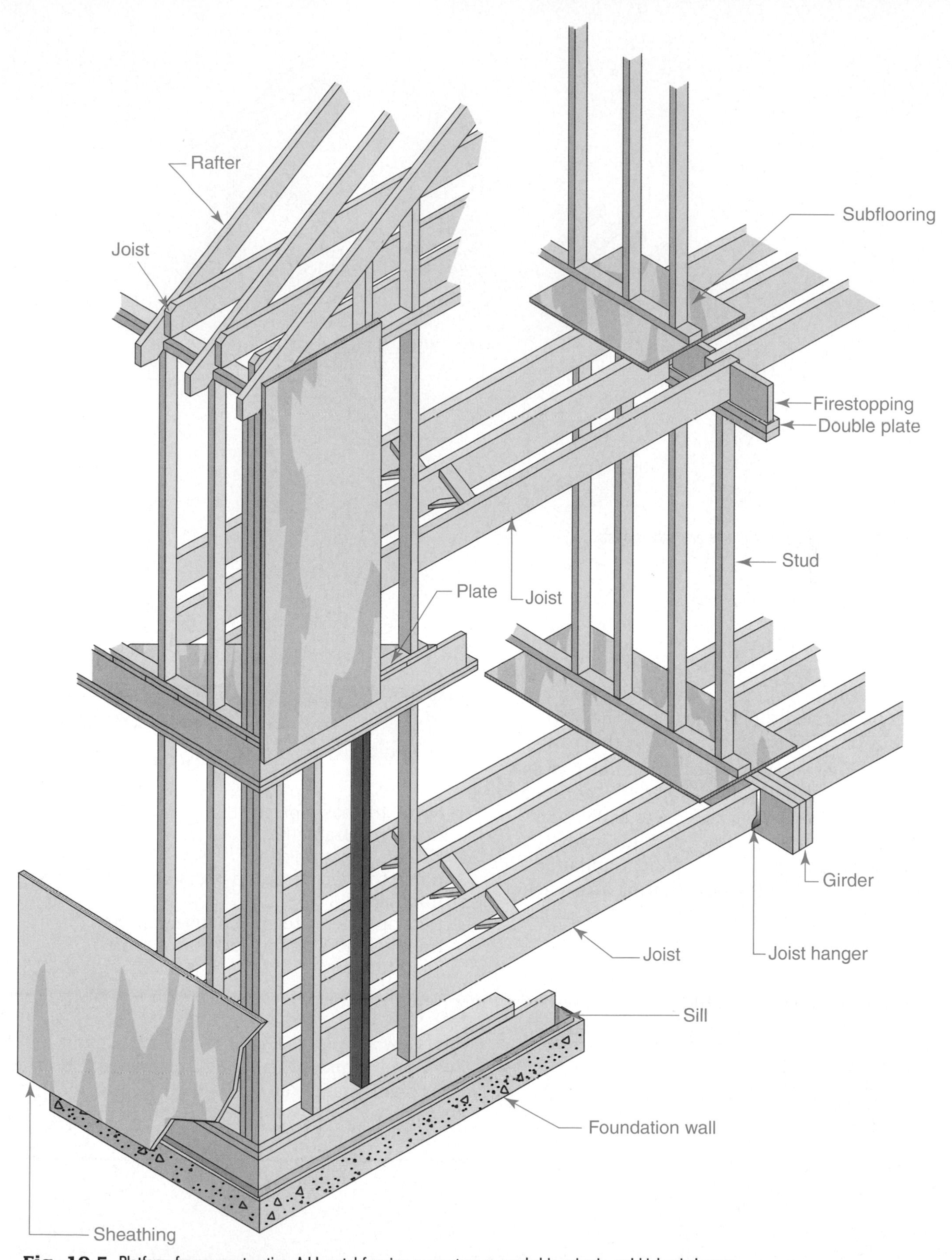

Fig. 19-5. Platform-frame construction. Add metal framing connectors as needed in seismic and high-wind zones.

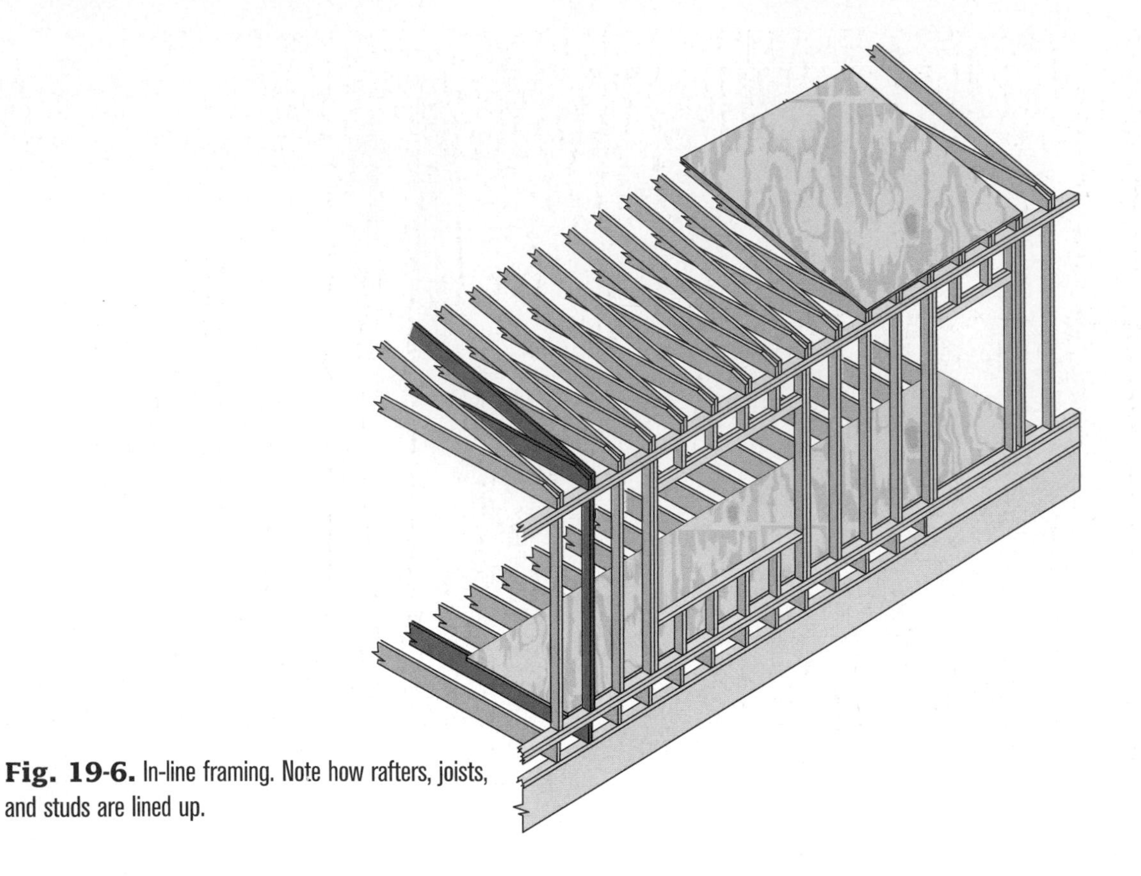

Fig. 19-6. In-line framing. Note how rafters, joists, and studs are lined up.

Also, the number of studs in a typical wall makes up for slight irregularities in the load distribution. This helps to even out the load.

One spacing variation is called *in-line framing.* All joists, studs, and rafters are given the same spacing. **Fig. 19-6.** This spacing is usually 16″ or 24″ OC. It creates a direct path for loads, from the rafters right down to the foundation wall. This increases the load-bearing efficiency of the frame and reduces the amount of lumber needed for a house.

SECTION 19.2 Check Your Knowledge

1. Name the basic pieces that form the structure of a wood-frame house.
2. What is sheathing?
3. Name the two basic types of conventional framing.
4. Describe the difference between in-line framing and standard platform-frame construction.

On the Job

Interview a builder in your community about in-line framing and/or balloon-frame construction. Does he or she use either method frequently? Why or why not? Report your findings to the class.

SECTION 19.3

Other Framing Methods

Other framing methods can be used to build a house. Some, such as structural insulated panels, are fairly new. Others, such as timber framing, are time-honored systems.

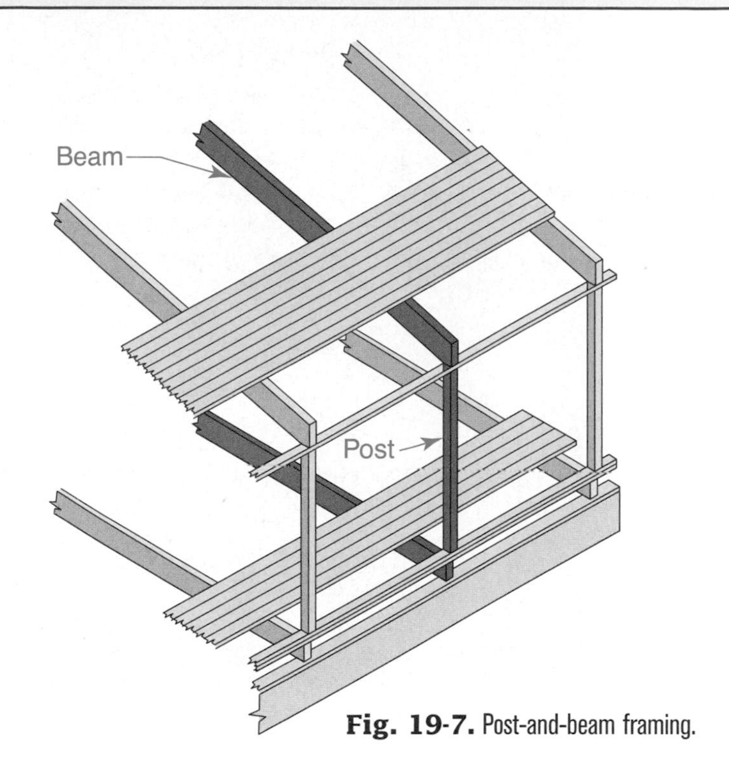

Fig. 19-7. Post-and-beam framing.

POST-AND-BEAM FRAMING

Post-and-beam framing calls for fewer but larger pieces of wood spaced farther apart than those used in conventional framing. **Fig. 19-7.** Subfloors and roofs are supported by a series of beams spaced up to 8′ apart. The ends of the beams are supported by structural timber posts. (*Structural timber* is lumber that is 5x5 or larger. It is used mainly for posts and columns.) The roof sheathing and the subfloor may consist of planks, usually with a 2″ nominal thickness, or structural tongue-and-groove (T&G) plywood that is 1⅛″ thick. Spaces between posts are framed as needed for attaching exterior and interior finish.

One advantage of post-and-beam framing is the architectural effect provided by the exposed ceiling. Added height is given to the living area at no additional cost. Roof planking serves as the finished ceiling. Generally, the planks are selected for appearance. No further ceiling treatment is required.

Timber Framing

A *timber frame* is a freestanding type of post-and-beam frame that rests on a foundation. The supporting members are fairly far apart. Made from either hardwood or softwood, the timbers are surfaced and connected with interlocking joinery. The joints are secured with wooden pegs. This requires a high degree of woodworking craftsmanship. Some joints are quite complex, but most are a variation of the mortise and tenon.

The use of timbers to frame buildings is a technique with a very long history. There has been a revival of interest in timber framing, particularly where nearby forests can provide the timber stock of suitable dimensions. **Figs. 19-8** and **19-9.**

Fig. 19-8. The individual pieces of a timber frame are fastened with interlocking wood joinery.

Fig. 19-9. The structure is often exposed in the interior of the timber-frame house.

STRUCTURAL INSULATED PANELS

Structural insulated panels (SIPs) are used with increasing frequency to form the shell of a house. **Fig. 19-10.** A **structural insulated panel** consists of 3½″ thick expanded polystyrene (EPS) foam insulation between sheets of exterior plywood or oriented-strand board (OSB). Because their interiors are made of foam insulation, SIPs are sometimes referred to as *foam-core panels*.

Panels usually range in size from 4′ x 8′ to 8′ x 28′. Larger panels are also available. These load-bearing panels are built in a factory and

Fig. 19-10. The use of structural insulated panels speeds the construction process.

delivered to the job site. There they are fastened together using a system of 2x4 or 2x6 splines. **Fig. 19-11.** A *spline* is a thin strip of wood used to reinforce a joint.

Building a house with structural insulated panels has several advantages. First, the shell of the house can be erected very quickly. The house is very strong because there is wood sheathing on the inside as well as on the outside. Some panels also come with an inside skin of drywall. This saves time and work in completing the interior of the house. The panels are energy efficient because they allow very little cold air to leak into the house. **Table 19-C.** On the other hand, it can be difficult to run wiring through the panels. Plumbing and wiring plans should be developed with this in mind. Also, a crane is required to lift heavier panels into place.

Table 19-C. R-Values of Structural Insulated Panels

R-Value[a]	Panel Thickness (inches)
16.87	4½
25.60	6½
33.20	8¼
41.90	10¼
50.60	12¼

Precision Panel Corporation

(a) R-values are discussed in detail in Chapter 39, "Thermal and Acoustical Insulation."

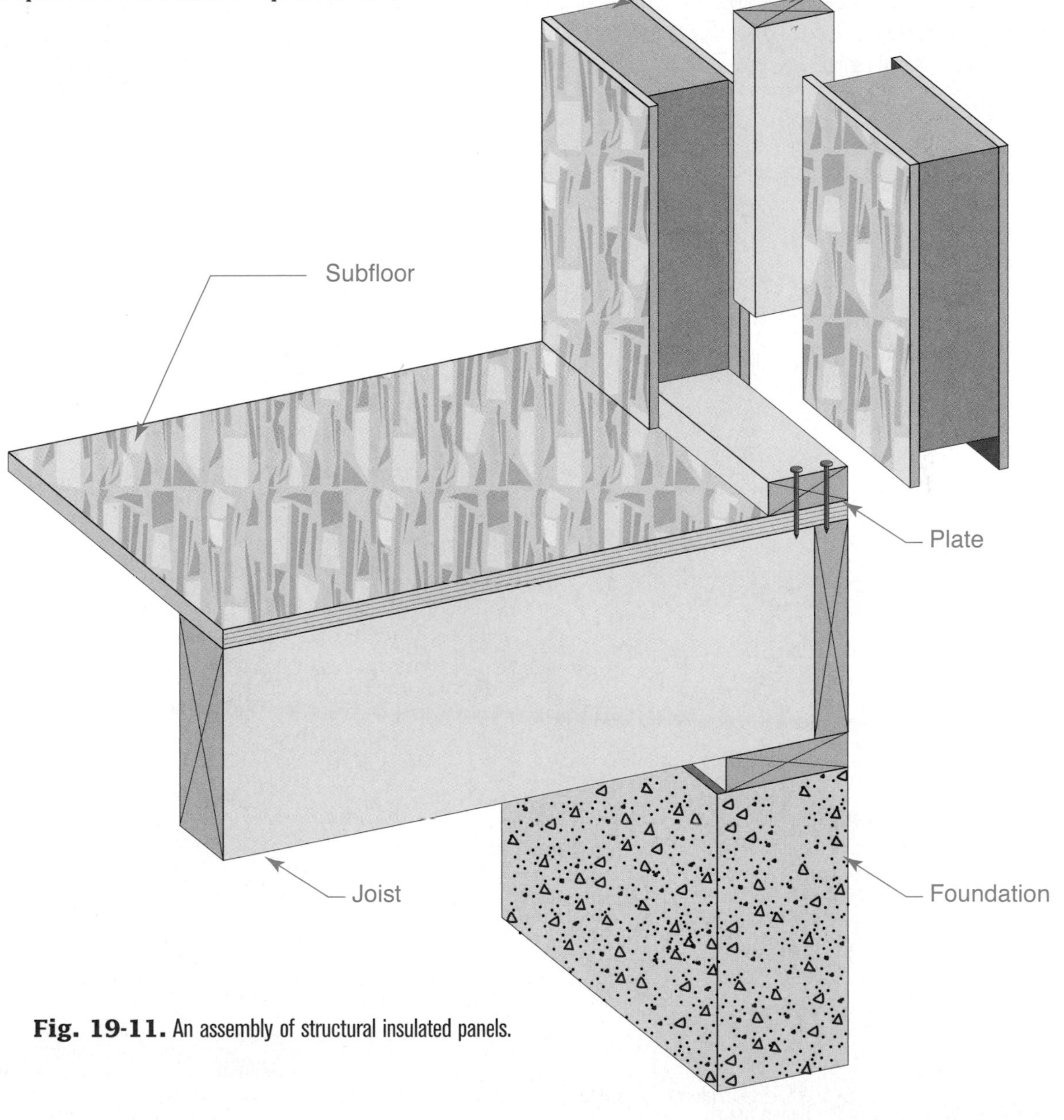

Fig. 19-11. An assembly of structural insulated panels.

Structural insulated panels are sometimes used along with conventional framing. For example, a house may have a conventionally framed roof and floor system but SIP exterior walls. However, some builders use SIPs for floor and roof systems as well, although conventional framing is used for interior partitions. SIPs are frequently used in the construction of timber-frame houses. In this case, the panels completely enclose the timber framing.

Lifting with a Crane

Some building components, such as wood timbers and SIPs, are sometimes too heavy or large to lift into place by hand. Small cranes may be used instead. Take care to ensure that any object being lifted by crane is properly balanced and secured. Attach a guide rope to the object to prevent it from swinging out of control.

FRAMING FOR NATURAL HAZARDS

Many regions of the United States are affected by severe weather, including hurricanes and tornadoes. Other regions are affected by earthquakes. Wherever these hazards exist, building codes are stricter than in other areas. Carpenters and builders must take extra steps to strengthen house framing.

Wind Resistance

Hurricanes repeatedly strike the Gulf Coast of Florida. After one major hurricane, researchers studied houses that had received the most damage. They found many in which floor framing had failed. Failures of joist-to-beam and beam-to-beam connections were also common.

Many other areas of the United States are also exposed to high winds. **Fig. 19-12.** In these areas, building codes require using special

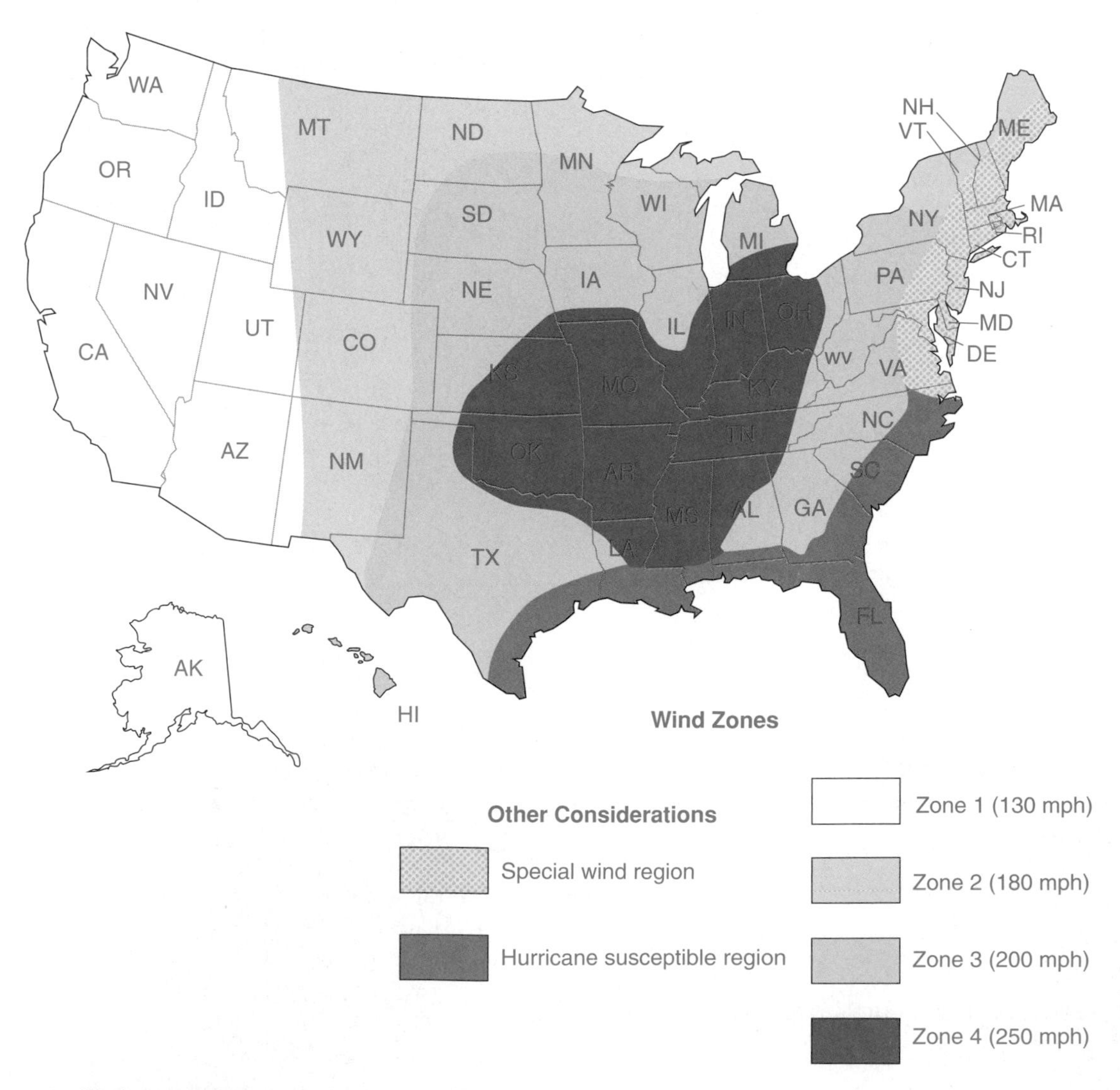

Fig. 19-12. Wind zones in the United States.

techniques, such as securing the roof framing to the wall framing with metal straps. **Fig. 19-13.** Gable roofs are more easily damaged by high winds than hip roofs or flat roofs. Strengthening a gable end may require special structural bracing. Follow local building codes carefully when building in a region subject to high winds.

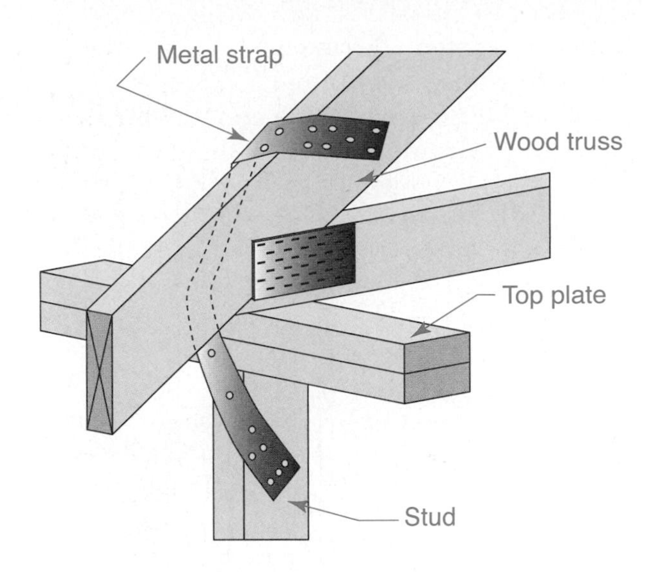

Fig. 19-13. Metal straps reinforce the connection between roof and wall members. These straps are available in a variety of types.

Earthquake Resistance

The ground moves violently during an earthquake. This may deform the structure of a house or even push it off its foundation. After the ground stops moving, the house will continue to move for a short time. This movement puts great strain on structural materials and connections. In earthquake areas (seismic zones), building codes require additional construction features. These are designed to make the structure more rigid and to hold it securely to the foundation.

Metal brackets, anchors, and straps increase a structure's ability to resist severe weather and earthquakes. However, to be effective these seismic connectors must be installed exactly according to the manufacturer's specifications. It is particularly important to use the correct number and size of fasteners. This information may be found on building plans, in the manufacturer's product catalog, or in literature supplied with the products.

Using sheathing to create shear walls is one of the easiest ways to stiffen a wood-frame house. A **shear wall** is designed to resist lateral (sideways) forces. Most exterior walls of a house can be designed as shear walls. However, it is most important to provide shear strength at the corners of a house. **Fig. 19-14.**

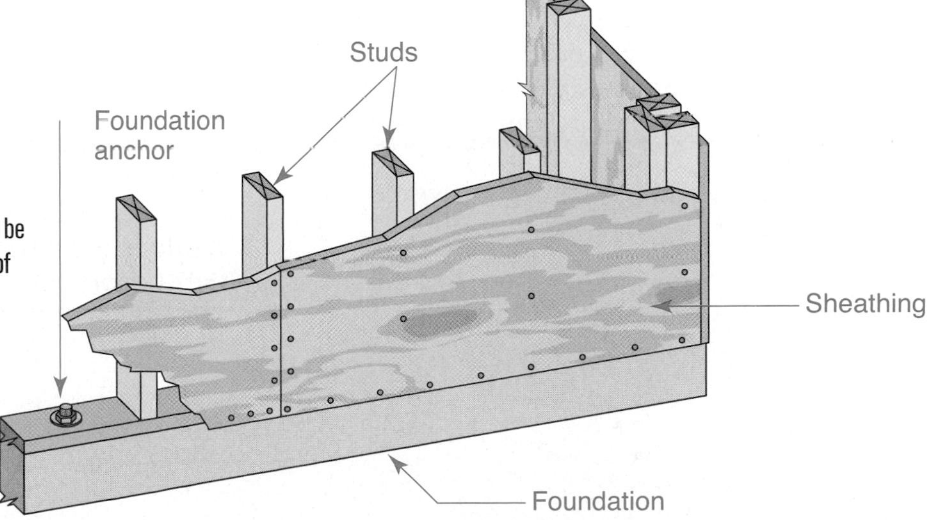

Fig. 19-14. The corners of a house must be reinforced to resist shear forces. The addition of metal framing anchors is optional.

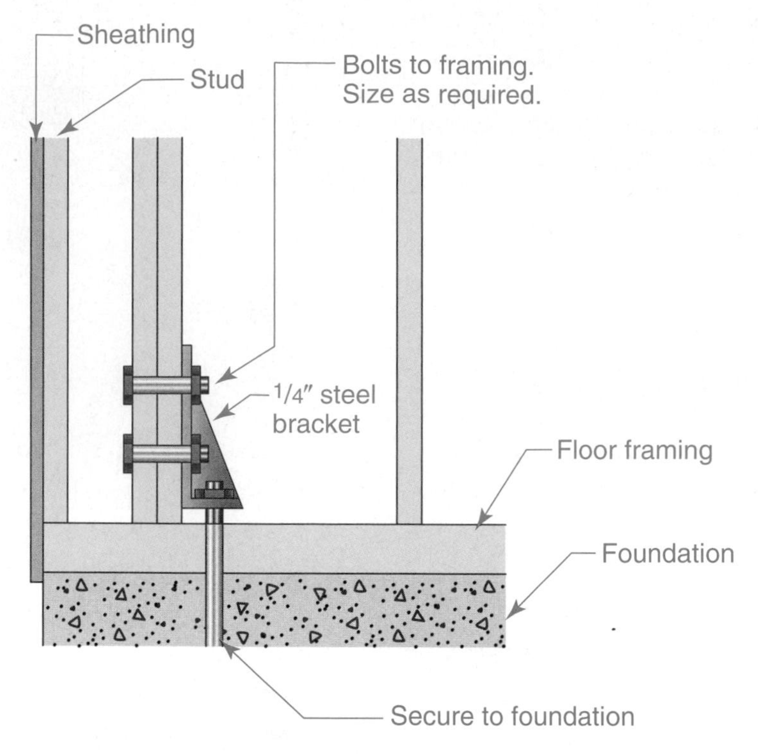

Fig. 19-15. Hold-down anchors are steel brackets that prevent walls from toppling.

The top of a shear wall must be fastened to the second-floor framing. The bottom of the wall must be fastened to the sill plate. The sill plate must be bolted securely to the foundation. A sheathing panel should be set in place vertically in order to be able to make these connections. If a 4x8 panel won't reach, a 4x9 or 4x10 panel or solid blocking at joints may be required. The panel must be nailed to the framing according to local codes.

To provide added security, seismic connectors called *hold-down anchors* can be installed at each corner of the house, or as required by local codes. **Fig. 19-15.** These steel brackets prevent walls from tipping over. They are attached to the foundation with anchor bolts. They are attached to the framing with lag screws or machine bolts.

SECTION 19.3 Check Your Knowledge

1. What is a timber frame?
2. What type of roof is most easily damaged by high winds?
3. Where is it most important to provide shear walls in a house?
4. Where should hold-down anchors be located?

On the Job

Obtain a copy of the building code for your area. The reference section of your local library may have a copy. Locate references to the fire safety of foam plastic insulation, such as that used in structural insulated panels. What precautions must be taken when using this material? Report your findings to the class.

Chapter 19

Review

Section Summaries

19.1 The design of wood framing is based on laboratory tests of wood samples. The wood is given a rating based on its resistance to stresses. Test results are summarized in tables of design values.

19.2 Balloon-frame and platform-frame construction make use of many individual pieces of wood. Platform-frame construction is the most common system used to build houses.

19.3 Other framing methods include post-and-beam, timber framing, and structural insulated panels. Framing can be strengthened and stiffened to minimize damage during high winds or earthquakes.

Review Questions

1. Name four advantages of wood frame construction.
2. What sheer stress occurs where two portions of the wood are trying to slide past each other in opposite directions?
3. What can be done to reduce compression perpendicular to the grain of a joist or beam?
4. What is deflection?
5. What is a span table?
6. What is the difference between a dead load and a live load?
7. What are the basic differences between platform-frame construction and balloon-frame construction?
8. How does post-and-beam framing differ from conventional framing?
9. What is an SIP? List the advantages in using SIPs.
10. What is the purpose of a shear wall?

Fit Workers Are Better Workers Carpentry can be demanding work, mentally as well as physically. Studies have shown that your level of physical fitness can affect not only how strong you are but also how well you can think. Immunity from illness is another benefit. People who exercise regularly have immune cells that are 85 percent more active than those who don't exercise.

Employers are paying attention to such findings. They now know that physically fit workers do work of higher quality, lose less time due to illness, and are less likely to be injured in accidents. This means higher productivity, fewer health insurance claims, and lower insurance premiums.

Chapter

20

Floor Framing

Objectives

After reading this chapter, you'll be able to:

- Identify the basic floor-framing components and explain the purpose of each.
- Install posts and girders.
- Install sill plates and lay out basic joist spacing.
- Recognize cases where special framing details may be required, such as beneath a bearing wall.
- Lay a panel subfloor.
- Recognize other types of framing systems and products, such as those using trusses and girders.

Terms

bearing wall
box sill
bridging
cantilever
crown
girder
header
subflooring
tail joist
trimmer joist

Floor framing consists of posts, girders, sill plates, joists or trusses, and subflooring. These framing members are fastened together to form a strong platform that supports the house. In first-floor framing, joists rest on the sill plate. They may also rest on girders or be attached to them. In second-floor framing, they rest on a double top plate. The floor joists distribute loads to the foundation walls. They also provide the nailing surface when floor sheathing is attached.

Nominal 2″ lumber or LVL (laminated-veneer lumber) I-joists are generally used for floor framing. Trusses may also be used, and finger-jointed lumber is acceptable under some circumstances. Engineered materials offer the advantages of light weight, consistent strength, and long spans (see Chapter 17, "Engineered Lumber"). This chapter describes floor framing using conventional lumber. However, framing with LVL I-joists is similar. Where it differs, the differences will be noted.

SECTION 20.1

Posts and Girders

In the average house, the distance between opposite foundation walls is too great for a single floor joist to span. A *floor joist* is any light beam that supports a floor. Pairs of joists are often used instead. The outer ends of the paired joists are supported by the foundation walls, while the inner ends are supported by a girder. A **girder** is a large principal horizontal member used to support the floor joists. The ends of a girder are supported by the foundation walls. A *post* is a wood or steel vertical member that provides intermediate support for a girder.

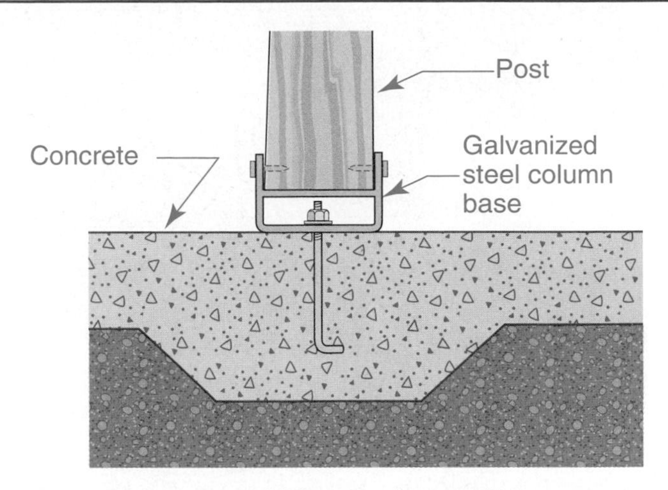

Fig. 20-1. A concrete slab floor must be made thicker to support the load from a post. This must be done when the slab is poured. The thickened portion is called a footing.

POSTS

Posts are often used in basements beneath the main girder. They may also be used in a garage to support ceiling girders. They are generally spaced 8′ to 10′ on center. The exact spacing depends on the size of the load.

A wood post must be solid and not less than a 4x4. It is often a 6x6. Its ends must be flat and securely fastened. The loads it carries are transferred to a fairly small area of the foundation. Because of this, a portion of the concrete slab directly below a post is made thicker to provide greater bearing capacity. **Fig. 20-1.** In some cases, a wood post is supported by a heavy-gauge metal bracket that lifts it clear of any moisture that might cause rot.

Steel posts, sometimes called *Lally columns*, are often preferred in residential construction. **Fig. 20-2.** They are strong, easy to handle, and take less space than solid wood posts. They must be at least 3″ in diameter and protected against rust, such as with rust-resistant paint. Steel posts have steel bearing plates at each end. Some posts are adjustable to various lengths. They are sometimes filled with concrete for extra strength.

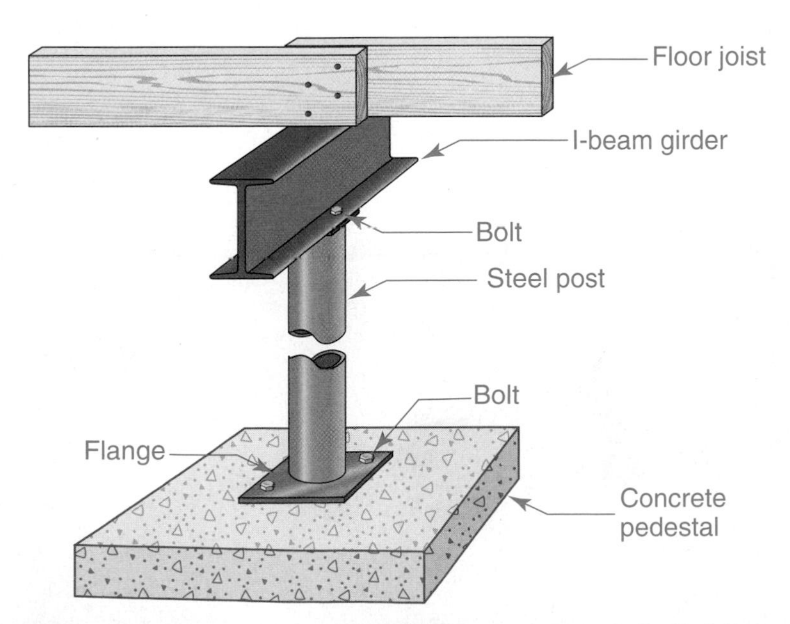

Fig. 20-2. A steel post used with a steel I-beam girder. The flanges welded onto each end of the post are used for fastening it to the girder and to the slab. In some cases the top flange has metal straps that secure it to a steel girder.

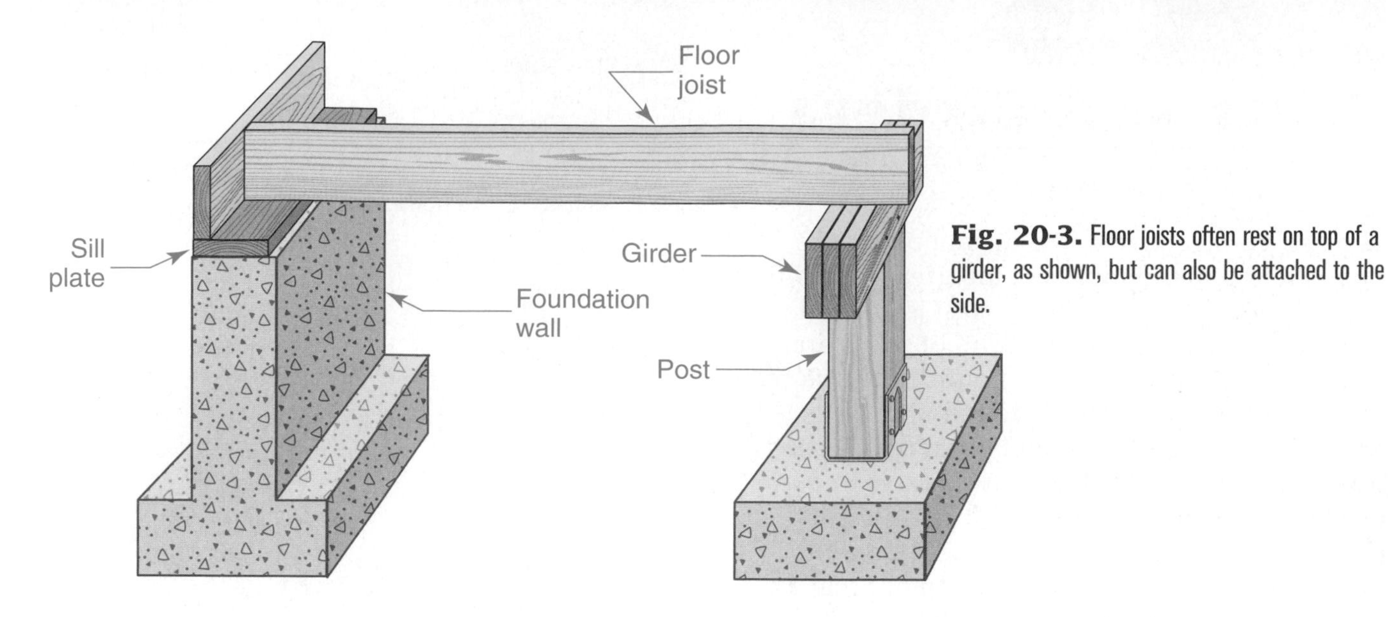

Fig. 20-3. Floor joists often rest on top of a girder, as shown, but can also be attached to the side.

GIRDERS

Girders are generally placed halfway between the longest foundation walls and parallel to them. They may be made of wood or steel. Steel does not shrink as solid wood does. However, wood girders are lighter and therefore easier to install. Also, connections are easier to make.

In one framing method, the floor joists rest on top of the girder. **Fig. 20-3.** However, the top of the girder must be at the same level as the top of the sill plate. (The *sill plate* is the horizontal framing member anchored to the foundation wall.) If more clearance is needed, the girder can be installed so that its top surface is level with the top of the floor joists. **Fig. 20-4.** In this case, metal framing connectors attached to the girder support the ends of the joists.

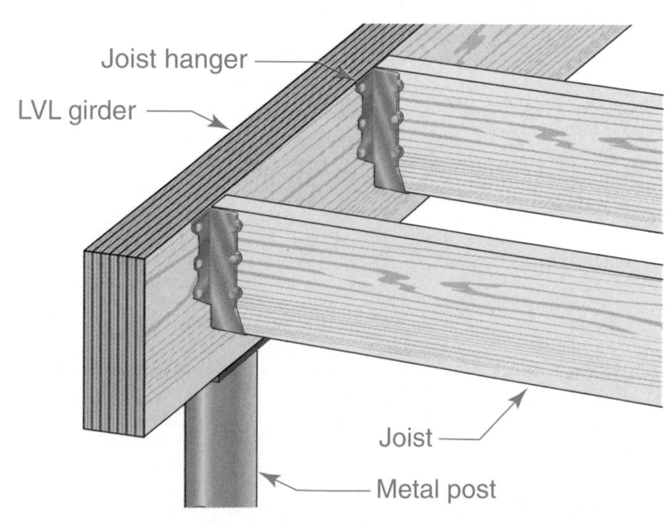

Fig. 20-4. Joists supported by joist hangers nailed to the side of the girder.

Throughout this book, many references will be made to face-nailing and toenailing. These terms refer to the two basic types of nailed connections. In *face-nailing*, a nail is driven straight through the thickness of the lumber and into another piece. In *toenailing*, a nail is driven at an angle from the face through the edge of the lumber and into another piece. In general, toenailing calls for smaller nails than face-nailing. This reduces the risk of splitting the wood. Both types of connections can be made using a hammer or a pneumatic nailer.

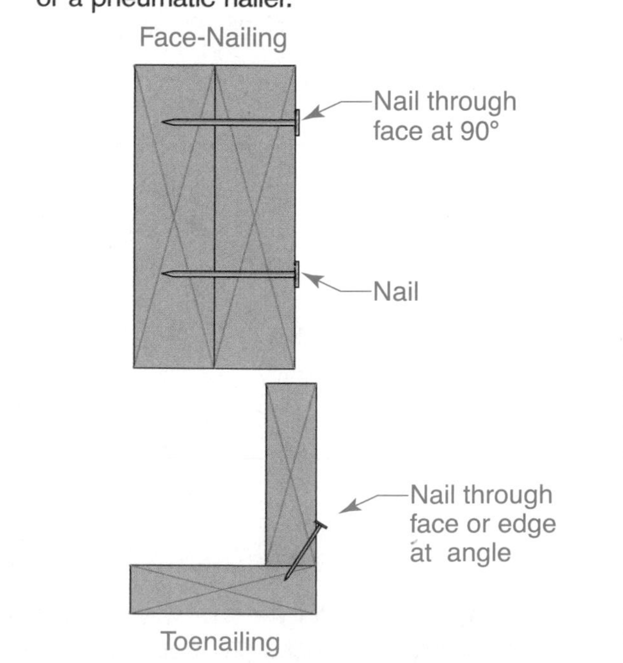

Wood Girders

Wood girders are available in several forms. Solid wood girders were once common, but solid wood of suitable size and quality is no longer readily available. Built-up wood girders that consist of three or four boards nailed face to face may be used. **Fig. 20-5.** To determine material requirements, refer to **Table 20-A**.

To make a built-up girder, face-nail each layer with 10d nails as follows:

- Stagger the nails 32″ OC at top and bottom.
- Nail two or three times at the end of every board (depending on size), including splices.
- Stagger the joints.

Glue-laminated beams and laminated-veneer lumber can also be used as girders. They offer the dimensional stability of steel and the easy installation of wood.

Table 20-A. Materials for Built-Up Girders[a]

Size of Girder	Board Feet per Lineal Foot	Nails per 1,000 Board Feet
4x6	2.15	53
4x8	2.85	40
4x10	3.58	32
4x12	4.28	26
6x6	3.21	43
6x8	4.28	32
6x10	5.35	26
6x12	6.42	22
8x8	5.71	30
8x10	7.13	24
8x12	8.56	20

[a] A 4x6 girder 20′ long contains 43 board feet of lumber (20 × 2.15 = 43).

Steel Girders

A steel beam has great strength and can span long distances. If it is to be used as a girder, secure a wood bearing plate to the top of the beam. The plate will enable you to toenail floor joists to the beam. **Fig. 20-6.**

Wood bearing plates can be fastened to steel with steel pins. The pins are driven with a powder-actuated fastening tool. An explosive gunpowder charge, called a *load*, drives the hardened steel pins into steel or concrete. Attaching the plate to a girder with pins may be easier to do before the girder is lifted into place. As an alternative, the steel fabricator can weld

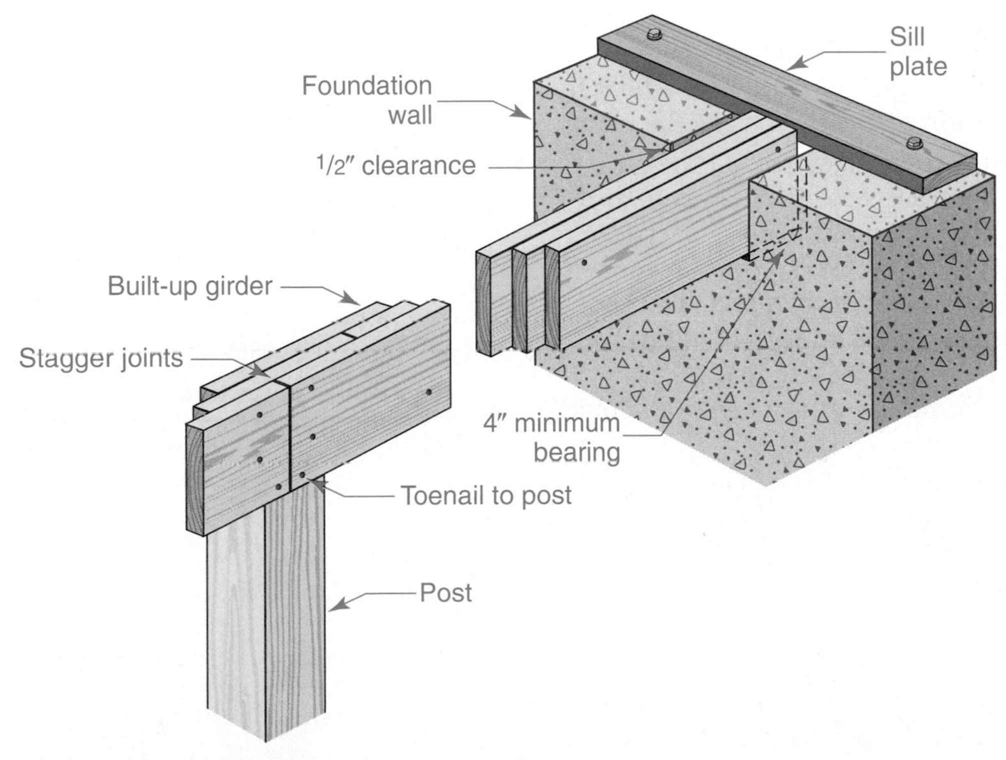

Fig. 20-5. A built-up girder set into a masonry pocket.

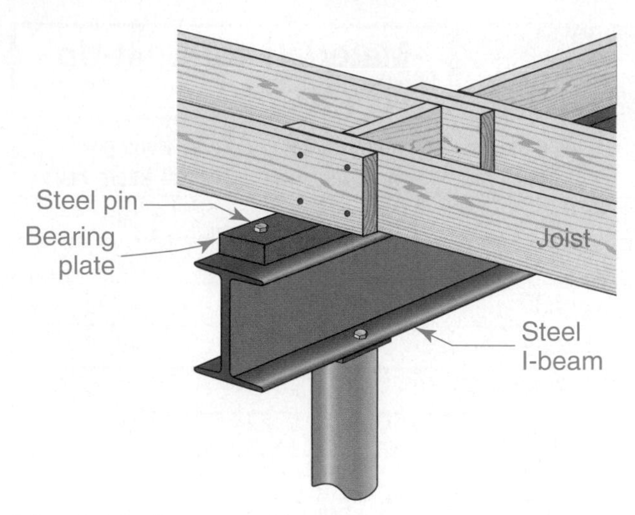

Fig. 20-6. Fasten a wood bearing plate to a steel beam so that joists can be nailed to the plate.

short lengths of threaded steel rod to the top of the girder. The wood plate can then be drilled to match and secured with nuts and washers.

INSTALLING POSTS AND GIRDERS

Posts and girders are installed after the foundation walls are complete and the forms have been stripped. In houses that will have a basement, the basement floor slab may also be in place. Posts should be located only where the slab has been made thicker to distribute the expected loads. Metal anchors are sometimes placed when the slab is poured. The posts can then be plumbed, braced temporarily, and bolted to the anchors. If there are no anchors to indicate the location of posts, consult the plans.

After the posts are in place, install the girder and brace it if necessary. Steel and glulam girders are placed by a small crane or a special forklift. Solid wood and built-up girders can sometimes be lifted into position by hand. The ends of wood girders should bear at least 4″ on masonry walls. This will reduce the risk of crushing the wood fibers. A ½″ clearance should be provided at each end and at each side of a wood girder framed into the masonry (see Fig. 20-5 on page 363). This will prevent the wood from absorbing moisture from the masonry. The bearing details for a steel girder are specified on the plans.

To determine the height of a post, stretch a string line tightly across the foundation. Measure from the floor to the line. Then calculate the length of the post based on the height and other dimensions of the girder. The post should be centered on the girder's width.

SAFETY FIRST

Powder-Actuated Tools

Because a powder-actuated fastening tool can be dangerous if used improperly, special training is required. Only qualified users should operate this tool. It is also essential that the user wear hearing and eye protection. Others in the area should be warned when the tool is to be used.

SECTION 20.1 Check Your Knowledge

1. What is a girder, and what supports it?
2. What is a Lally column?
3. How is a built-up wood girder constructed?
4. What must be done to a steel beam before it is ready to use as a girder to support joists, and why?

On the Job

Review a set of plans for the construction of a house. Find the drawing on which girders and posts are identified. What information is given about how these elements will be connected to the structure? Report your findings to the class.

Floor Framing with Joists

For many years, solid lumber was the only material used for floor joists. Builders can now use laminated-veneer lumber (LVL) instead. The most common LVL product used in floor framing is the I-joist. **Fig. 20-7.** The information that follows relates to solid lumber as well as to LVL floor framing. Any differences between the two will be noted.

A **box sill** is used for framing floors in platform construction. **Fig. 20-8.** A box sill consists of a sill plate (also called a *mudsill*, or just the *sill*) that is anchored to the foundation wall, floor joists and rim (or *band*) joist, and subflooring. **Subflooring** consists of engineered wood sheets or construction grade lumber.

INSTALLING THE SILL PLATE

The sill plate is the lowest member of the wood frame and supports the rest. It rests on the foundation wall and is bolted to it. The sill plate is made of 2x4 or 2x6 preservative-treated lumber. Preservatives protect it against moisture damage and insect attack. The sill plate provides a smooth bearing surface for the floor joists. It also serves as a connection between the foundation wall and the floor system. Joists are toenailed to the plate or secured with metal framing anchors.

Sill plates should be anchored to the foundation with at least two ½″ bolts in each plate. (For more information on how this is done, see Chapter 14, "Foundation Walls.") Sill plates establish the quality of all the framing that will follow. If they are not level, the entire floor system will not be level. If they are poorly secured to the foundation, the house may not survive very severe weather or an earthquake. Local building codes should be followed carefully.

To prevent cold air from leaking into the house, the plate should be set on top of a foam or fiberglass *sill sealer*. This product comes in a roll approximately 6″ wide. It fills any gaps between the irregular surface of the concrete and the smooth surface of the sill plate.

Steps for installing sill plates are given on page 366.

Fig. 20-7. A typical I-joist. The web and flanges can be made from various materials.

INSTALLING FLOOR JOISTS

Joists are usually placed perpendicular to the girders on 16″ or 24″ centers. However, check the house plans for the exact size, spacing, and direction of the joists. If the sizes for joists are not specified, refer to **Table 20-B**.

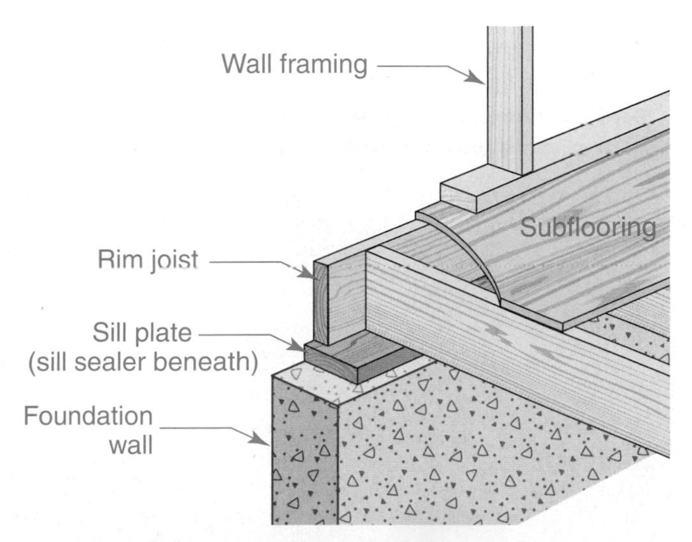

Fig. 20-8. First-floor framing at the exterior wall in platform-frame construction. A box sill assembly has been used.

STEP BY STEP

Installing Sill Plates

Sill plates on opposite walls must be parallel to each other if the foundation walls are parallel.

Step 1 Check to see that the foundation is level and square. To check a simple rectangular foundation, measure diagonally from corner to corner. To check a more complex foundation, use the 3-4-5 method for squaring walls (see Chapter 21, "Wall Framing and Sheathing"). If minor irregularities are discovered, adjust the plates as needed so they will be square.

Step 2 Establish the location of the sill plate. From the outside edge of the foundation wall, measure back a distance equal to the width of the sill plate. If the outside of the wall sheathing will be flush with the outside edge of the foundation wall, measure back the width of the sill plate *plus* the thickness of the sheathing.

Step 3 Place sill plate stock around the foundation. Use only straight, flat lumber. Place the edge of each piece against the foundation anchor bolts and mark the centerline of the bolts on the plate. Using a square, extend these marks across the width of the sill plate. **Fig. 20-9.**

Step 4 Measure from the center of each bolt to the chalk line on the foundation. Measure the same distance on the plate, starting from the edge that is resting against the bolt. Mark the bolt centerline at this point.

Step 5 Using a ⅝″ spade bit, bore holes through the plate at each marked point. (If termite shields will be used, bore holes at the same locations in them, using a suitable drill bit.)

Step 6 Roll out sill sealer over the top of the foundation walls and press it into place. **Fig. 20-10.** The weight of the building presses the sill sealer against the foundation wall to stop drafts.

Step 7 Slip the sill plate over the anchor bolts. Start at the high point of the foundation wall and check to see that the sill plate is level, using a builder's level. Shim the sill plate with grout or with preservative-treated wood shims, as needed, to make it level.

Step 8 Place a flat washer and a nut on each foundation bolt. Use a wrench to tighten each nut securely.

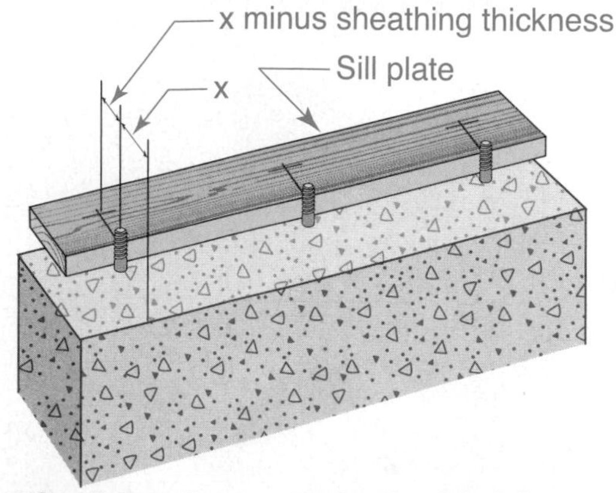

Fig. 20-9. Laying out the location of the bolt holes on the sill plate.

Fig. 20-10. Roll out a strip of sill sealer on the foundation wall just before laying the sill plate. Sill sealer fills irregularities and helps keep out dirt. It also keeps out drafts and reduces heat loss.

Table 20-B. Floor Joist Spans for Common Lumber Species

			Dead Load = 10 psf				Dead Load = 20 psf			
			2x6	2x8	2x10	2x12	2x6	2x8	2x10	2x12
			Maximum floor joist spans							
Joist Spacing (inches)	Specie and Grade		(ft.-in.)	(ft.-in.)	(ft.-in.)	(ft.-in.)	(ft.-in.)	(ft.-in.)	(ft.-in.)	(ft.-in.)
16	Douglas fir-larch	SS	11-4	15-0	19-1	23-3	11-4	15-0	19-1	23-0
	Douglas fir-larch	#1	10-11	14-5	18-5	21-4	10-8	13-6	16-5	19-1
	Douglas fir-larch	#2	10-9	14-1	17-2	19-11	9-11	12-7	15-5	17-10
	Douglas fir-larch	#3	8-5	10-8	13-0	15-1	7-6	9-6	11-8	13-6
	Hemlock-fir	SS	10-9	14-2	18-0	21-11	10-9	14-2	18-0	21-11
	Hemlock-fir	#1	10-6	13-10	17-8	20-9	10-4	13-1	16-0	18-7
	Hemlock-fir	#2	10-0	13-2	16-10	19-8	9-10	12-5	15-2	17-7
	Hemlock-fir	#3	8-5	10-8	13-0	15-1	7-6	9-6	11-8	13-6
	Southern pine	SS	11-2	14-8	18-9	22-10	11-2	14-8	18-9	22-10
	Southern pine	#1	10-11	14-5	18-5	22-5	10-11	14-5	17-11	21-4
	Southern pine	#2	10-9	14-2	18-0	21-1	10-5	13-6	16-1	18-10
	Southern pine	#3	9-0	11-6	13-7	16-2	8-1	10-3	12-2	14-6
	Spruce-pine-fir	SS	10-6	13-10	17-8	21-6	10-6	13-10	17-8	21-4
	Spruce-pine-fir	#1	10-3	13-6	17-2	19-11	9-11	12-7	15-5	17-10
	Spruce-pine-fir	#2	10-3	13-6	17-2	19-11	9-11	12-7	15-5	17-10
	Spruce-pine-fir	#3	8-5	10-8	13-0	15-1	7-6	9-6	11-8	13-6
24	Douglas fir-larch	SS	9-11	13-1	16-8	20-3	9-11	13-1	16-2	18-9
	Douglas fir-larch	#1	9-7	12-4	15-0	17-5	8-8	11-0	13-5	15-7
	Douglas fir-larch	#2	9-1	11-6	14-1	16-3	8-1	10-3	12-7	14-7
	Douglas fir-larch	#3	6-10	8-8	10-7	12-4	6-2	7-9	9-6	11-0
	Hemlock-fir	SS	9-4	12-4	15-9	19-2	9-4	12-4	15-9	18-5
	Hemlock-fir	#1	9-2	12-0	14-8	17-0	8-6	10-9	13-1	15-2
	Hemlock-fir	#2	8-9	11-4	13-10	16-1	8-0	10-2	12-5	14-4
	Hemlock-fir	#3	6-10	8-8	10-7	12-4	6-2	7-9	9-6	11-0
	Southern pine	SS	9-9	12-10	16-5	19-11	9-9	12-10	16-5	19-11
	Southern pine	#1	9-7	12-7	16-1	19-6	9-7	12-4	14-7	17-5
	Southern pine	#2	9-4	12-4	14-8	17-2	8-6	11-0	13-1	15-5
	Southern pine	#3	7-4	9-5	11-1	13-2	6-7	8-5	9-11	11-10
	Spruce-pine-fir	SS	9-2	12-1	15-5	18-9	9-2	12-1	15-0	17-5
	Spruce-pine-fir	#1	8-11	11-6	14-1	16-3	8-1	10-3	12-7	14-7
	Spruce-pine-fir	#2	8-11	11-6	14-1	16-3	8-1	10-3	12-7	14-7
	Spruce-pine-fir	#3	6-10	8-8	10-7	12-4	6-2	7-9	9-6	11-0

Copyright 2000, International Code Council, Inc., Falls Church, Virginia. 2000 International Residential Code. Reprinted with permission of the author. All rights reserved.

from Another Angle

Where termites are a significant problem, a metal termite shield should be installed beneath the sill plate. This shield makes it difficult for termites to reach wood members directly from the foundation walls without being noticed.

Plans will also specify a lumber grade. The Ready Reference Appendix table "Nonstress-Graded Lumber" provides information about grades.

Joists are often nailed into place. However, metal connectors can be used to replace many of the nailed connections described in this chapter. The most common metal connector used in floor framing is the joist hanger. **Fig. 20-11.**

Joist Layout

Joists are spaced evenly from one end of the house to the other. However, certain needs may interrupt this spacing, such as for a stairwell opening or extra room for plumbing drain lines. Always consult the plans to identify these needs before you begin the joist layout.

Use a tape measure to lay out the desired joist spacing on the sill or wall plate. Begin the layout by measuring from the corner of the sill plate. Make a mark 15¼″ from the outside edge of the sill plate. This will be the location to the edge of the first joist. Mark an *X* on the side of the line where the joist will be. That will ensure that the joist will not be placed on the wrong side of the layout line. **Fig. 20-12.** From that point on, mark every 16″ to indicate the positions of all the joists on that plate. **Fig. 20-13.**

Fig. 20-11. Metal framing connectors, such as the joist hangers shown here, are frequently used to support solid-lumber joists or I-joists.

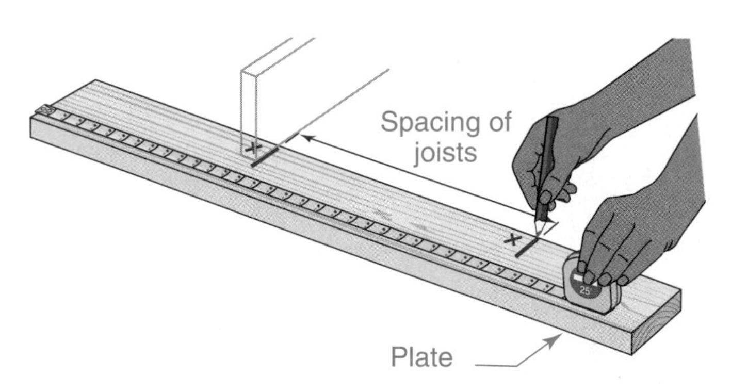

Fig. 20-12. The *X* next to each layout mark indicates which side of the line the joist will be on.

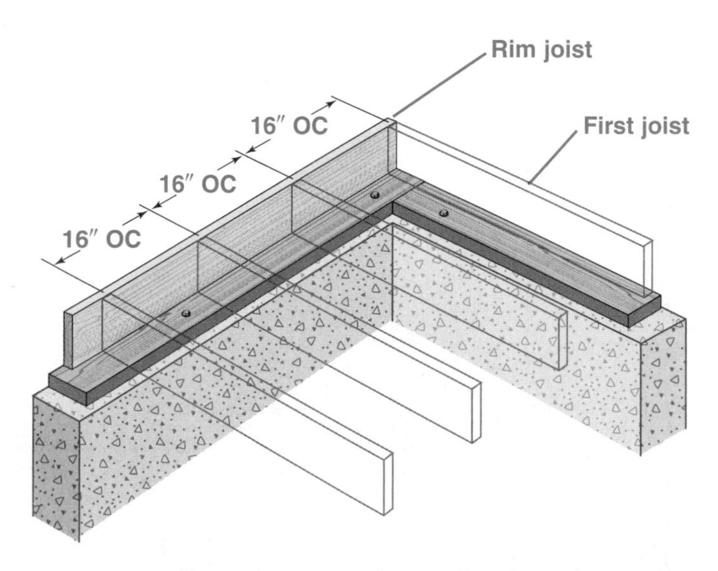

Fig. 20-13. Notice that the edge of the first joist will be 15¼″ from the outside edge of the sill plate.

When you have marked the position of all the joists, double-check to be sure that a joist is centered every 4′. When joists are laid out correctly, the edges of the floor sheathing panels will always fall along the centerline of a joist.

If the joists span the distance from one foundation wall to the opposite wall, as I-joists often do, the layout on both sill plates will be identical. When joists will be overlapped at a girder, however, the layouts will differ. **Fig. 20-14.** In this case, first mark the layout on one sill plate. Make the same layout on the girder. On the opposite wall, offset the position of joists by 1½″ (the thickness of a joist) to ensure that the joists overlap at least 3″. In this case, the floor sheathing panels will slightly overhang the offset joists.

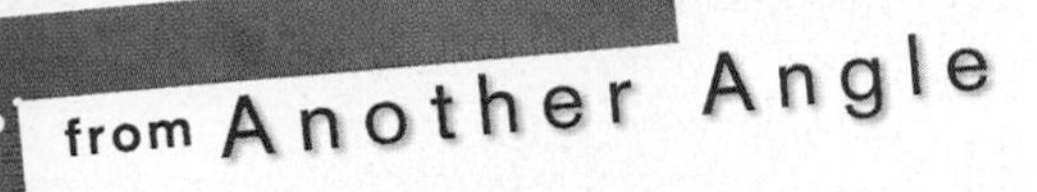

Some carpenters lay out the spacing of the floor joists by marking the sill plates. Others prefer to mark their layout on the top edge of the rim joists. This is done after the rim joist has been toenailed to the plate.

Steps for installing joists over a girder are given below.

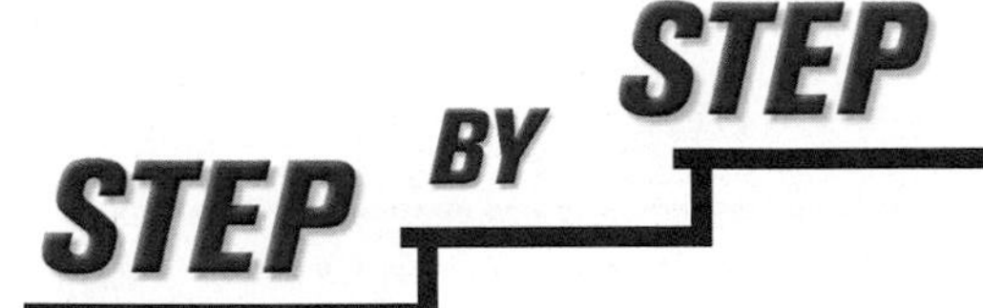

Installing Solid-Wood Joists over a Girder

Select floor joist lumber carefully so the floor will be flat and strong. Any joists having a slight edgewise bow should always be placed with the crown on top. The **crown** is the outermost curve of the bow. Mark the joist with an arrow pointing to the crown. A crowned joist will tend to straighten out when subfloor and normal floor loads are placed on it.

Also, be sure that knots in the joist are on its compression (top) side. They are less likely to cause failure in this location. A large knot on the tension side of a joist can be pulled apart, weakening the joist. **Fig. 20-15.**

Step 1 Inspect each piece for usability before carrying it to the foundation. Set aside unusable lumber to cut up later for blocking.

Step 2 Toenail the rim joists to the sill plates, using 16d nails every 16″ OC. Be sure that the outside face of the joist is in the same plane as the outside edge of the sill plate.

Step 3 Place the joists over the layout marks, laying them flat for now. Add extra joists or leave out joists where large openings will be located.

Step 4 Tip the outermost joist up on edge and align one end with the end of a rim joist. Nail through the rim joist and into this joist with two 16d nails. **Fig. 20-16.** Toenail this joist to the plate with 16d nails spaced 16″ OC.

Step 5 Proceeding from one end of the house to the other, tip each joist on edge, crown up, and align it with the layout marks. This process is sometimes called *rolling* the joists. Nail through the rim joist and into each floor joist with two 16d nails. Toenail each joist to the sill plate with three 8d nails.

Step 6 Toenail each joist to the girder with 8d nails.

Step 7 Face-nail overlapping joists to each other with at least three 10d nails.

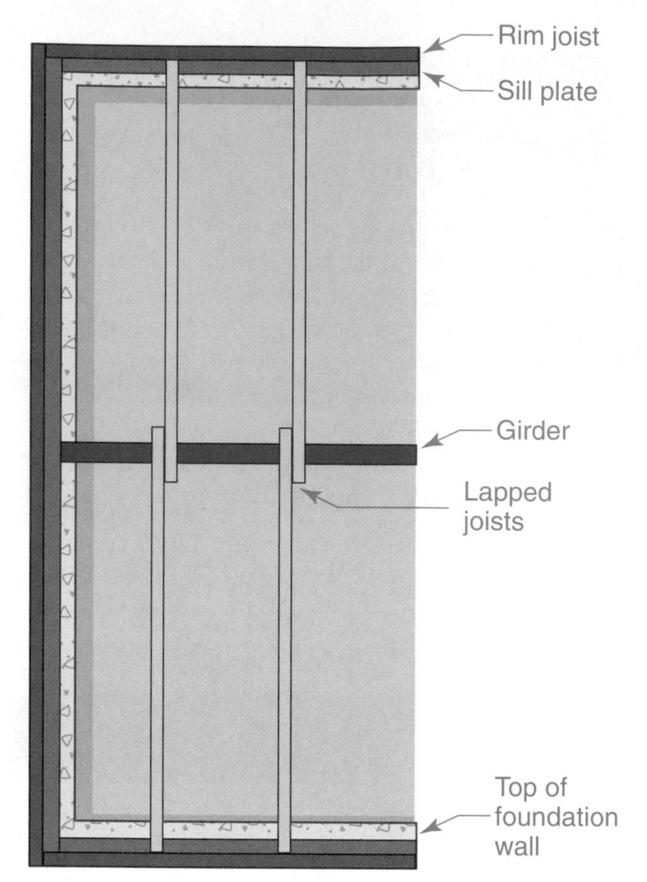

Fig. 20-14. Lapped joists mean different layouts on opposite plates.

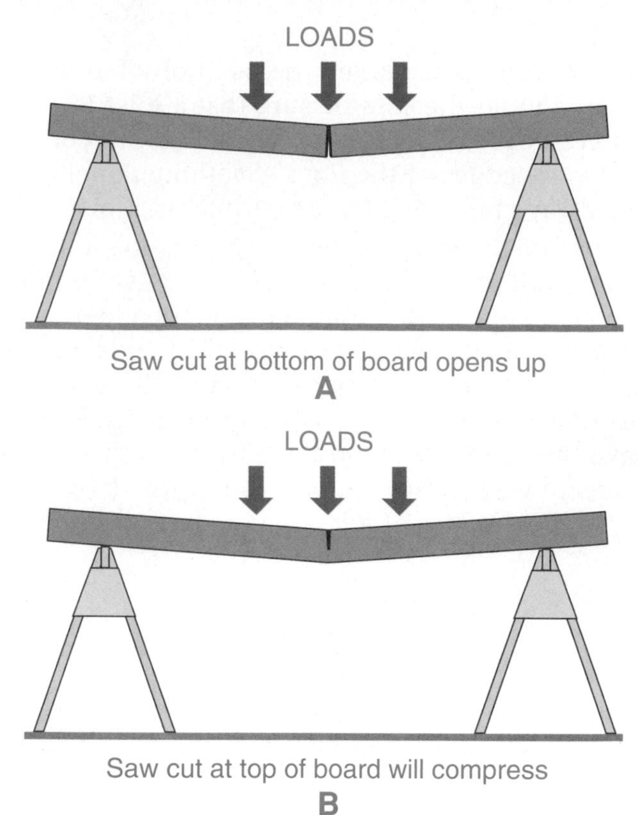

Fig. 20-15. The effect of defects on lumber strength. *A.* With a saw cut placed at the bottom, the board opens up and breaks. A knot or other defect will produce the same effect. *B.* A saw cut at the top of the board closes up (compresses). The board in *B* retains more strength than the board shown in *A.*

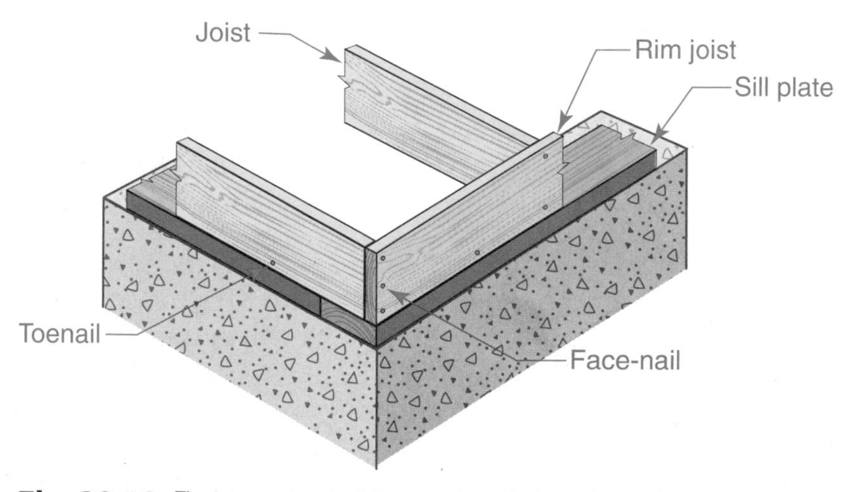

Fig. 20-16. The intersecting rim joists must be nailed together at the corners.

Special Methods for I-Joists

As with most products, the characteristics of I-joists vary with the manufacturer. Always read the instructions for the specific I-joist you plan to use. You must also check the span tables for that product. Do not assume that the span listed for one line of products will be the same as the span for another line. The following methods are generally used for I-joists. **Fig. 20-17.**

Backing and Blocking. I-joists are nearly always supported by metal joist hangers. The width of the hanger should match the width of the I-joist. A backing block can be nailed to both sides of the I-joist to improve the fit. **Fig. 20-18.**

Fig. 20-17. A typical I-joist floor system.

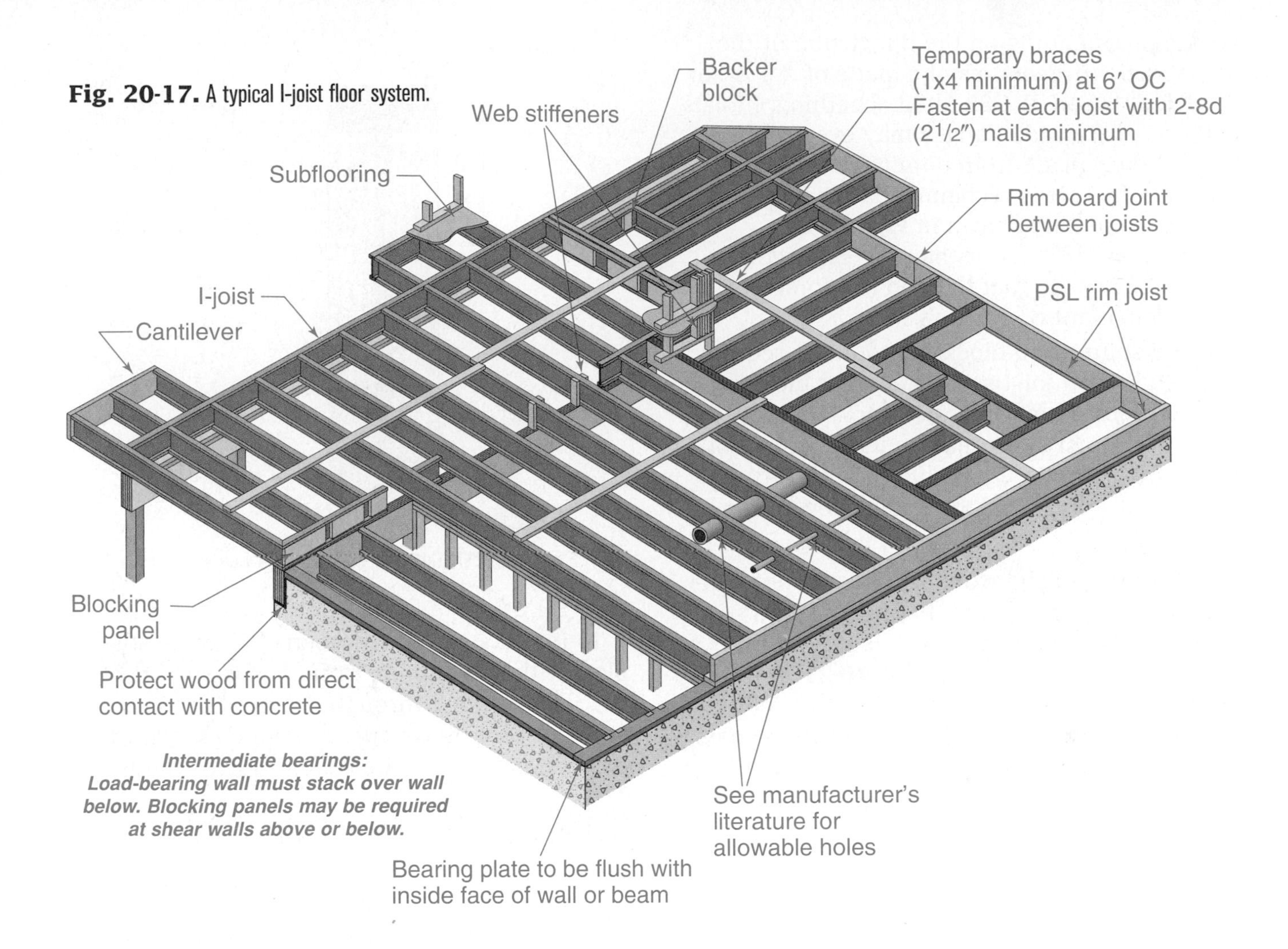

Where a wood I-joist runs continuously over a support (a girder, for example), web stiffeners should be nailed to both sides of the web. Fig. 20-19. They will improve load-bearing characteristics. The stiffeners can also provide additional bearing surface for lumber or I-joist

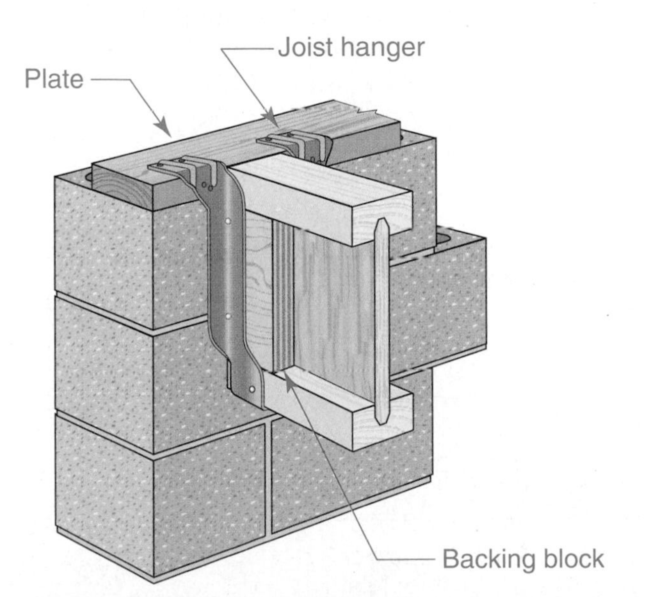

Fig. 20-18. A metal joist hanger for wood I-joists. A backing block is fastened to each side of the I-joist. To prevent sideways movement, the joist hanger is nailed to the backing block.

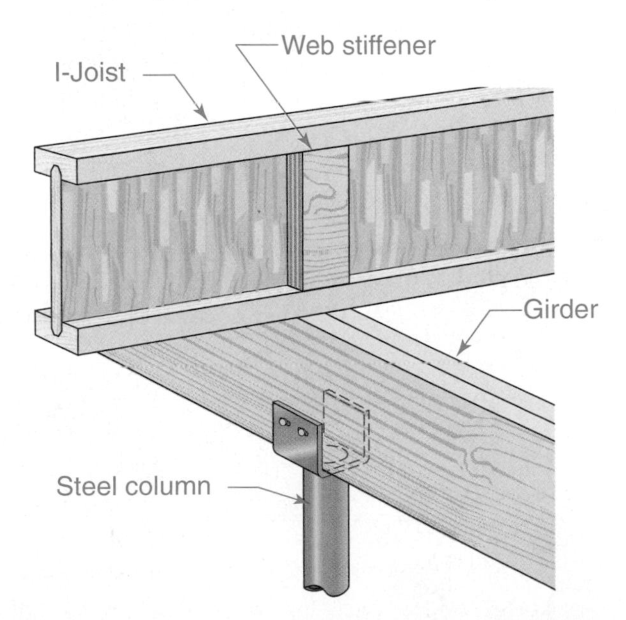

Fig. 20-19. Web stiffeners should be installed on both sides of an I-joist where it crosses a support.

blocking. Depending on the dimension of the I-joist, web stiffeners may be made of ½″, ⅝″, or 1″ thick plywood or OSB-rated sheathing. I-joists with unusually wide flanges may even require a web stiffener made from nominal 2″ lumber. One manufacturer's recommendations for using a web stiffener are shown in **Fig. 20-20**. Stiffeners are ⅛″ shorter than the exposed portion of the web so that they do not force the upper flange out of position.

Where solid-wood blocking would be required on a solid-wood joist system, similar blocking may be required for an I-joist floor. Short lengths of I-joist stock may be used instead of solid lumber. Where I-joist blocks intersect I-joists, a backing block or web stiffener may be required.

Rim Boards. A solid-wood rim joist is not suitable for use with an I-joist floor. Instead, a length of plywood, OSB, or LVL is used. This piece is called a *rim board*. **Fig. 20-21.** It may be up to 1⅛″ thick and must be as deep as the I-joists. A rim board ties the ends of the I-joists together. It does not shrink as much as solid lumber and comes in lengths of up to 24′.

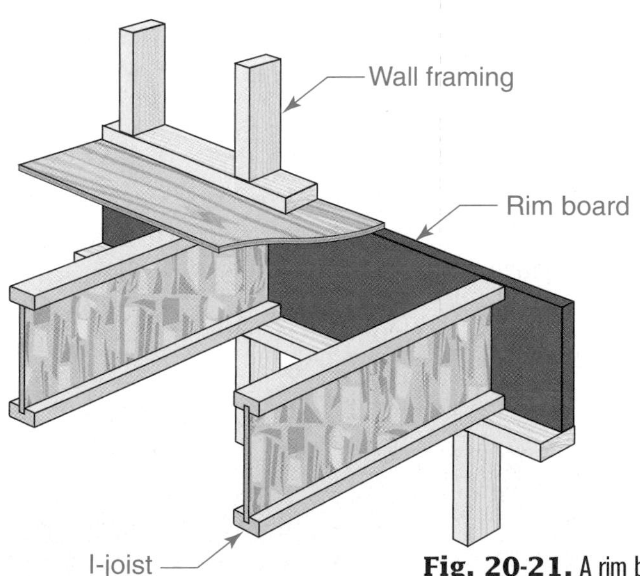

Fig. 20-21. A rim board ties the ends of I-joists together. Here it is shown on second-story floor framing.

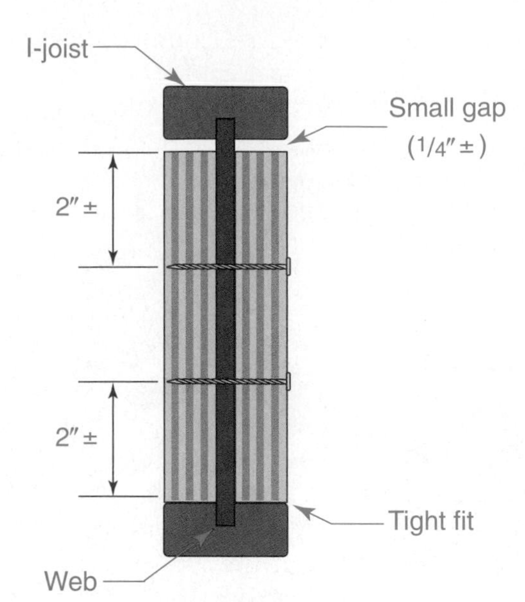

Fig. 20-20. Correct installation of a web stiffener.

To install a rim board, toenail it to the sill plate with 8d common or box nails spaced 6″ OC. When nailing through the rim board and into an I-joist, make sure one 8d common or box nail penetrates the center of each flange.

Cutting and Notching Floor Joists

During installation of ducts, plumbing pipes, or wiring, solid-wood floor joists must sometimes be notched or drilled. A *notch* is a saw cut made in the end or edge of lumber. Careless notching or drilling can reduce the joist's strength. For this reason, building codes restrict notching. **Fig. 20-22.** For example, joists must never be notched in the middle one-third of their span or on the bottom edge. Codes also restrict the size and position of holes.

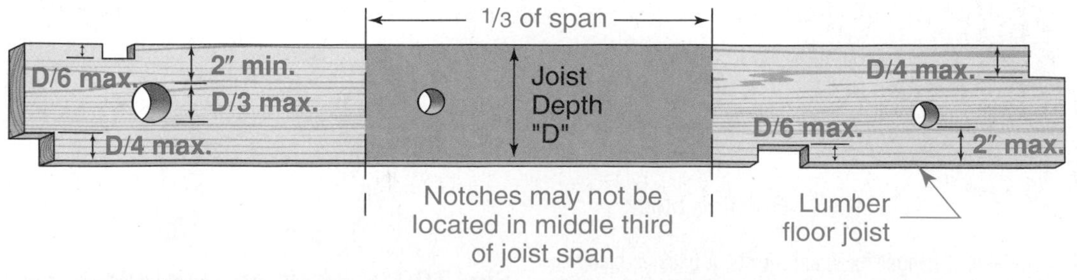

Fig. 20-22. The location and size of notches that are permitted in a solid-wood floor joist are based partly on the depth (D) of the floor joist.

The situation with I-joists is more straightfor ward. Except when cutting an I-joist to length, the flanges must never be cut, drilled, or notched. The existing knockouts in the web of the I-joist are used for utility access. If holes of any other size are needed, consult the manufacturer's literature.

Pneumatic Nailer Safety

Many carpenters use a pneumatic nailer to install floor joists. When nailing through the rim joist and into the ends of a joist, always place the bottom nail first. This holds the two pieces together so you can move your hand out of harm's way as you fire the upper nail into place. Don't forget to wear eye protection.

Bridging

Long joists should be stiffened with bridging. **Bridging** is a method of bracing between joists. It is done to distribute loads, prevent the joists from twisting, and add stability and stiffness.

Bridging is of two kinds. *Solid bridging* is similar to blocking. **Fig. 20-23A.** *Cross bridging* (also called *diagonal bridging*) is more common because it is very effective and requires less material. Precut lx3 or 2x2 lumber is sometimes used for cross bridging. **Fig. 20-23B.** Metal-strap cross bridging with nailing flanges may also be used. **Fig. 20-23C.** If the joists are over 8′ long, install one row of bridging at the center of the joist span. For joists 16′ and longer, install two rows of bridging equally spaced on the joist span.

Bridging is not generally required by code unless joists exceed 2x12. However, bridging is a cost-effective and efficient way to stiffen a floor. Many builders add it even though it is not required.

Before installing bridging, snap a chalk line across the tops of the joists as a guide. When installing solid-wood cross bridging, leave the bottom ends loose until the subfloor has been laid. This permits the joists to adjust themselves to their final positions. Then complete the nailing.

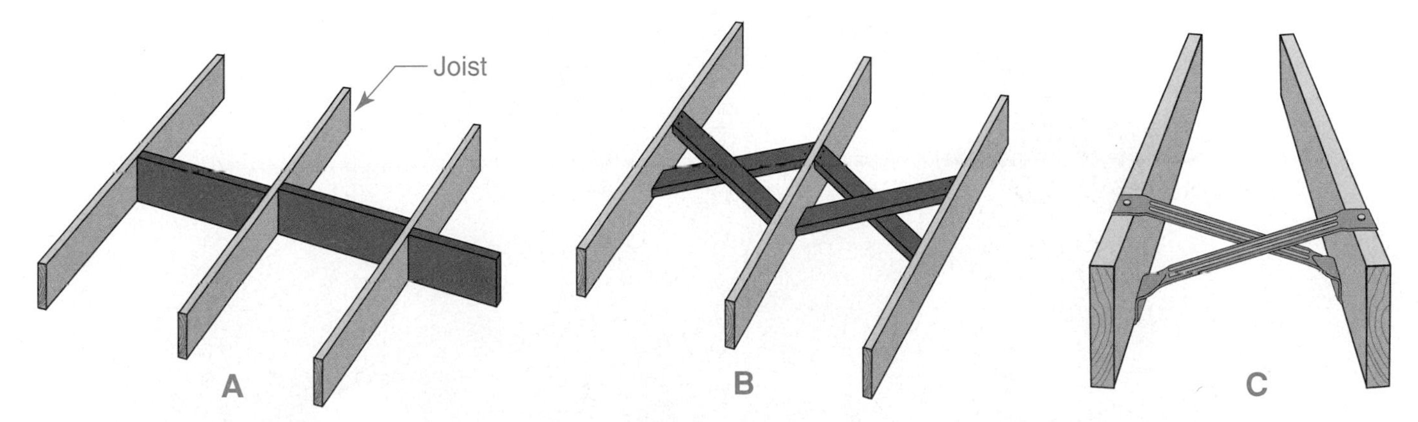

Fig. 20-23. The three types of bridging. *A.* Solid bridging. Offsetting the blocks allows them to be end nailed. *B.* Cross bridging. *C.* Metal-strap cross bridging.

SPECIAL FLOOR FRAMING CONDITIONS

Often a carpenter must adjust the layout of a floor system to accommodate special conditions. These conditions should be identified before the joist layout begins.

Framing under Bearing Walls

Joists should be doubled under each load-bearing wall that is parallel to the joists. If needed, a double joist hanger or two joist hangers could be used. **Fig. 20-24.** A **bearing wall** is a wall that supports loads in addition to its own weight. If the wall will contain plumbing pipes or heating ducts, the joists can be separated by blocking. The blocking must be cut from the same size stock as the floor joists. **Fig. 20-25.** Blocking should be spaced not more than 4′ OC.

Framing Large Openings

It is often necessary to create large openings in the floor system, such as for stairwells and chimneys. In these cases, the joists framing the opening should be doubled, and the interrupted joists must be supported by headers. **Fig. 20-26.** A **header** is a horizontal member that carries loads from other members and directs them around an opening. In a floor system, a

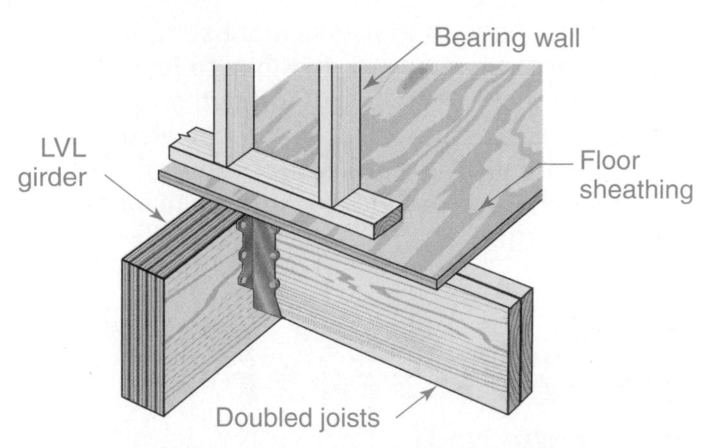

Fig. 20-24. Floor joists are doubled under bearing walls.

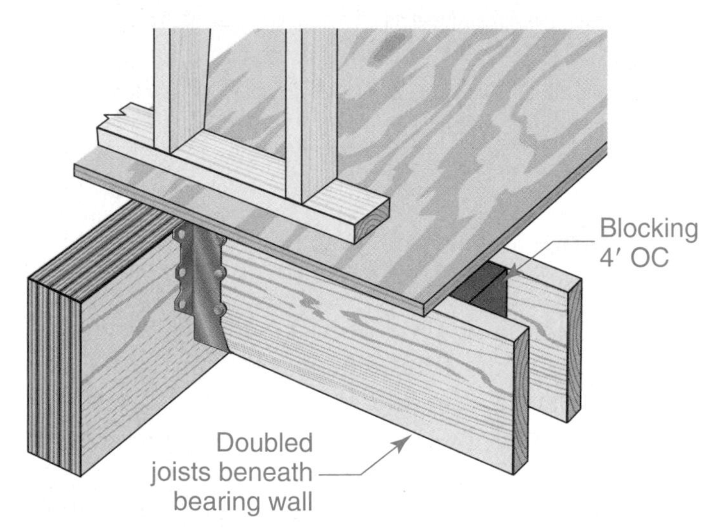

Fig. 20-25. Doubled joists can be spaced as shown to create room for plumbing drains.

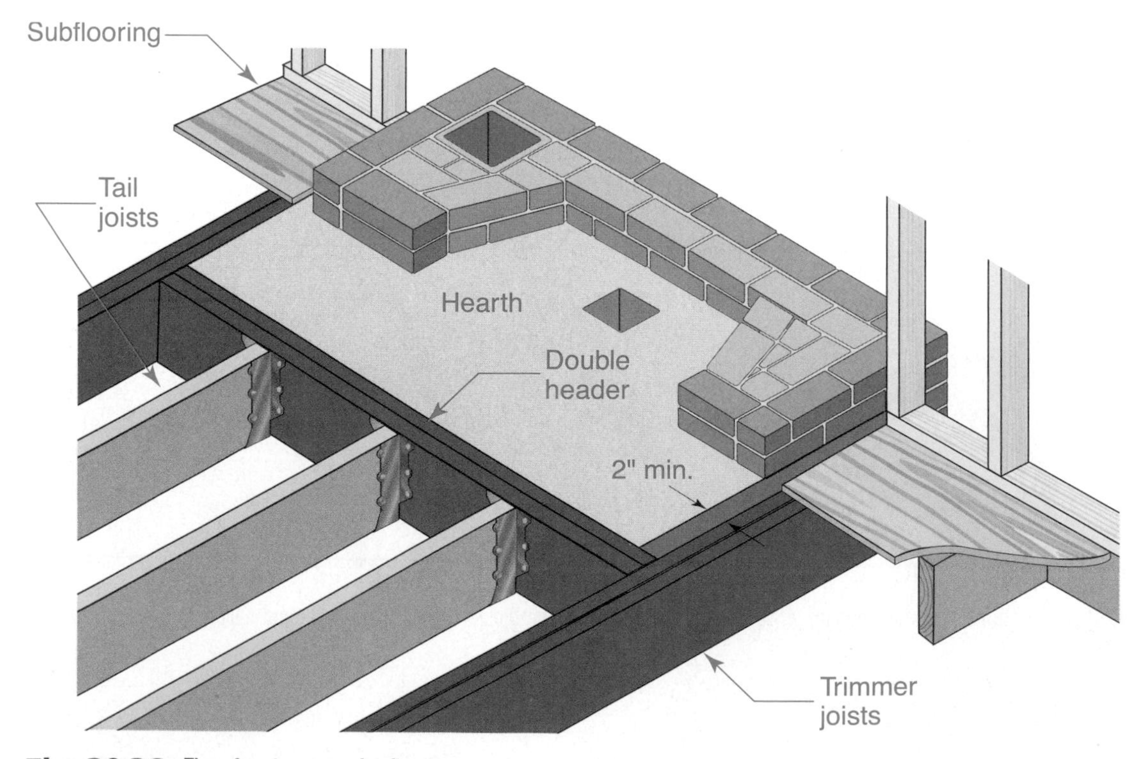

Fig. 20-26. Floor framing around a fireplace.

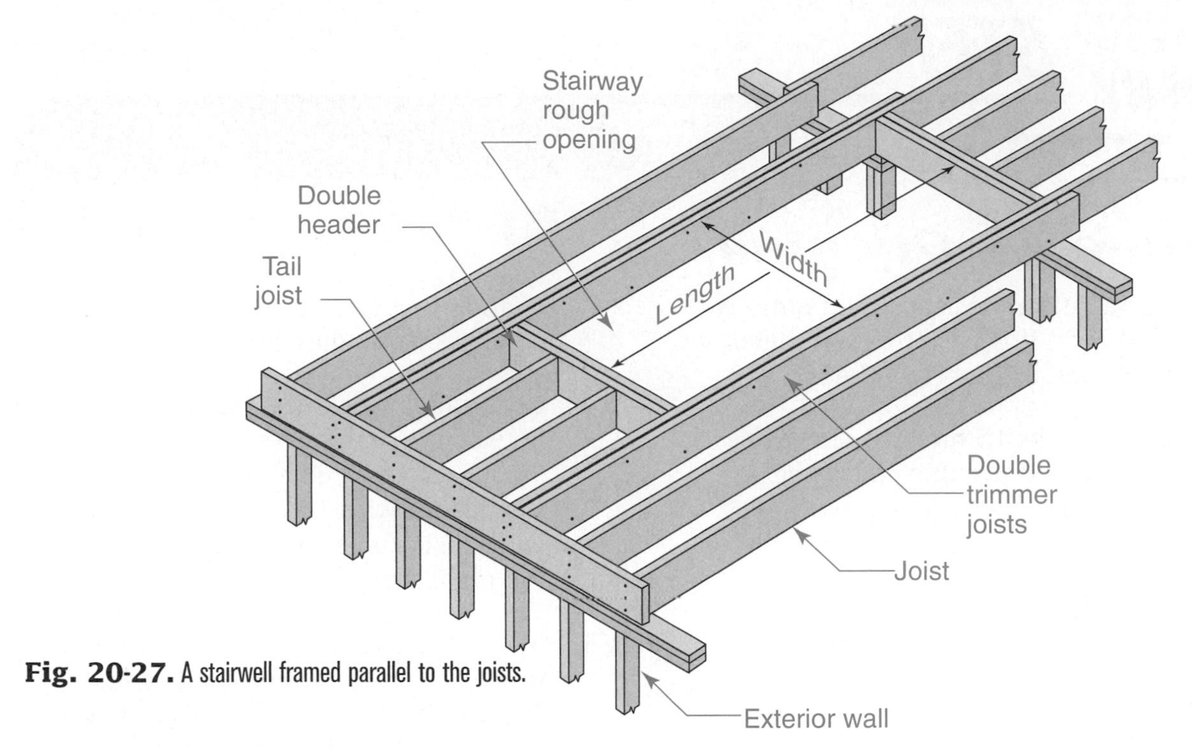

Fig. 20-27. A stairwell framed parallel to the joists.

header is supported by trimmer joists. A **trimmer joist** is used to form the sides of a large opening.

The exact layout of headers is based on the flooring loads, as well as the size and shape of the opening. However, doubled lengths of joist stock are generally used when the header must span more than 4′. In the case of an I-joist floor, an LVL header is often used. Consult the plans for framing details as well as for rough opening sizes.

The difficulty of framing a stairwell depends on whether the opening runs parallel to the floor joists, as in **Fig. 20-27**, or perpendicular to them, as in **Fig. 20-28**. A parallel opening is easier to frame. In either case, the rough opening must be at least 37″ wide. If ½″ drywall will be used to cover the walls of the stairwell, this will leave a finished opening of 36″, as required by code. The length of a stairwell opening is specified on the plans. (For further information about stairwells, see Chapter 34, "Stairways.")

Steps in framing an opening are given on page 376.

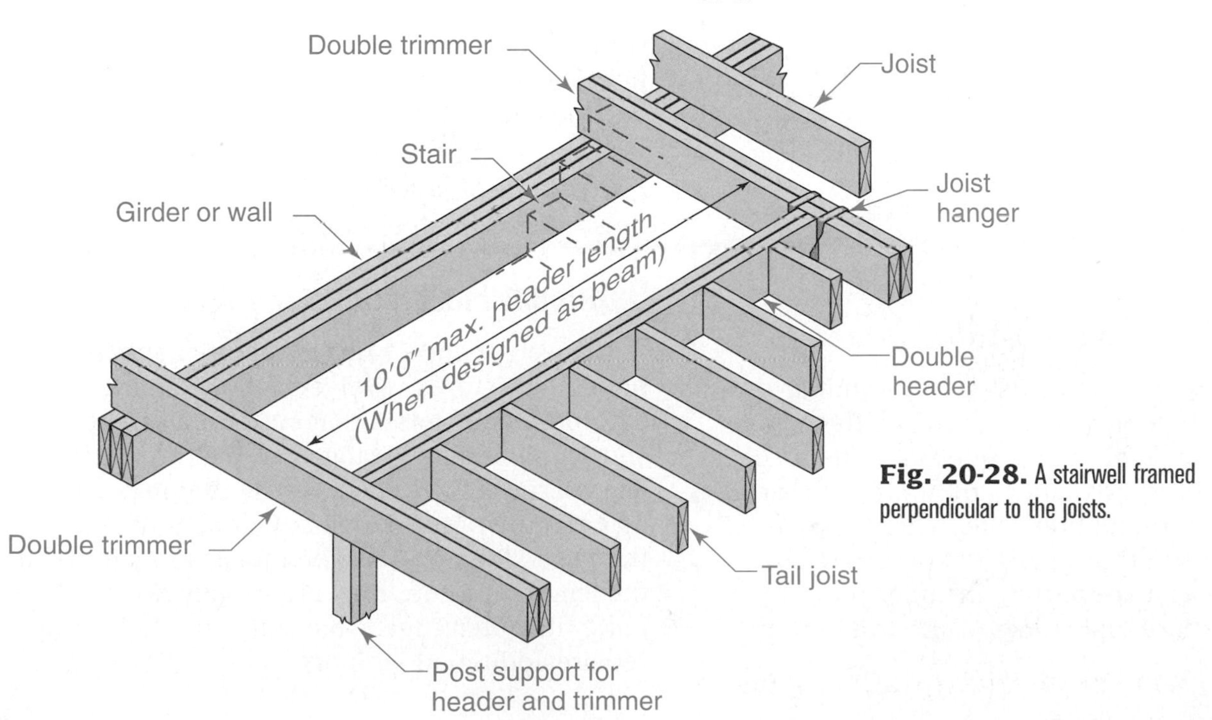

Fig. 20-28. A stairwell framed perpendicular to the joists.

STEP BY STEP

Framing an Opening

The opening frame can be assembled entirely with nails. However, it is easier to use metal framing connectors, as described here.

Step 1 Make sure the trimmer joists have been doubled. Double-check the width of the opening against the plans.

Step 2 Use a square to lay out the position of both headers. The dimensions of the rough opening will be noted on the plans.

Step 3 Attach framing connectors to the sides of the trimmer joists (see Fig. 20-11 on p. 368). Framing connectors are required by code if the header spans more than 6′. Nail with 16d common nails or as specified by the connector's manufacturer.

Step 4 Cut header stock to fit snugly between the trimmers. Insert the stock into the connectors. Nail into the header with 10d common nails or with joist-hanger nails supplied by the manufacturer.

Step 5 Install the tail joists. A **tail joist** is a floor joist interrupted by a header. **Fig. 20-29.** Support the tail joists on joist hangers nailed as in Step 4. According to the building code, tail joists over 12′ long must be supported by framing connectors or on 2″ square (or larger) ledger strips.

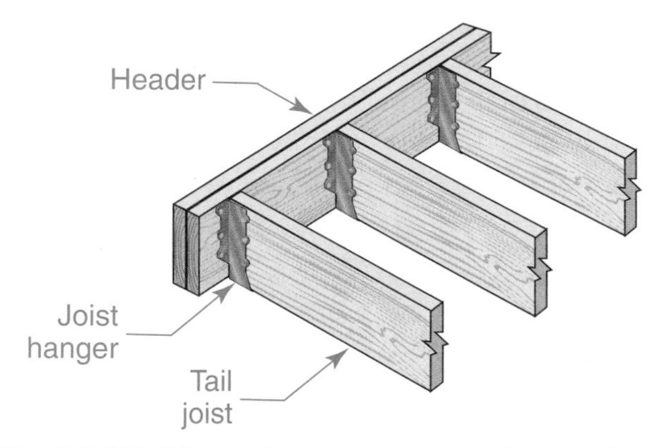

Fig. 20-29. Using joist hangers to secure the tail joists to the header.

Cantilevered Floor Framing

The framing for a bay window or similar projection is often arranged so that the floor joists extend beyond the foundation wall. The joists carry the necessary loads, and there is no need for separate foundation walls. This cantilevered extension should normally not exceed 2′. (A **cantilever** is a supporting member that projects into space and is itself supported at only one end.)

The joists forming each side of the bay, as well as the header, should be doubled. How this is done depends on whether the floor joists run parallel to the cantilevered section (**Fig. 20-30**) or not (**Fig. 20-31**). Nailing, in general, should conform to that for floor openings. The subflooring is extended to the outer framing member and sawed flush with that member.

Check local building codes for other rules related to cantilevered framing. For example, preservative-treated lumber may be required.

Bathroom Floor Framing

The weight and drainage requirements of plumbing fixtures involve special framing. Bathroom floor joists that support a tub or shower should be arranged so that no cutting is necessary when connecting the drainpipe. This may require only a small adjustment in spacing the joists. **Fig. 20-32.** When joists are parallel to the length of a tub, they are usually doubled under its outer edge. Unusually large tubs may require additional support.

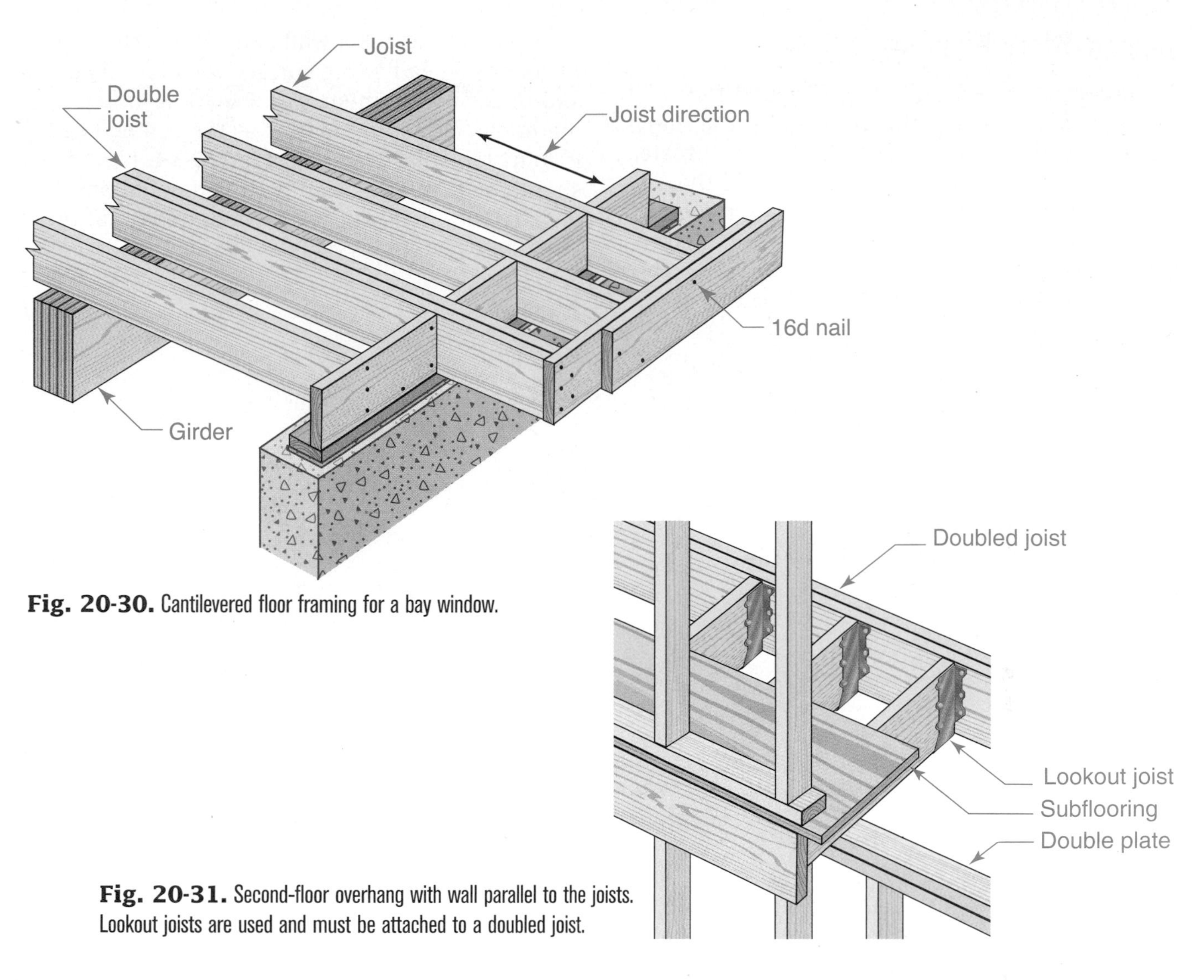

Fig. 20-30. Cantilevered floor framing for a bay window.

Fig. 20-31. Second-floor overhang with wall parallel to the joists. Lookout joists are used and must be attached to a doubled joist.

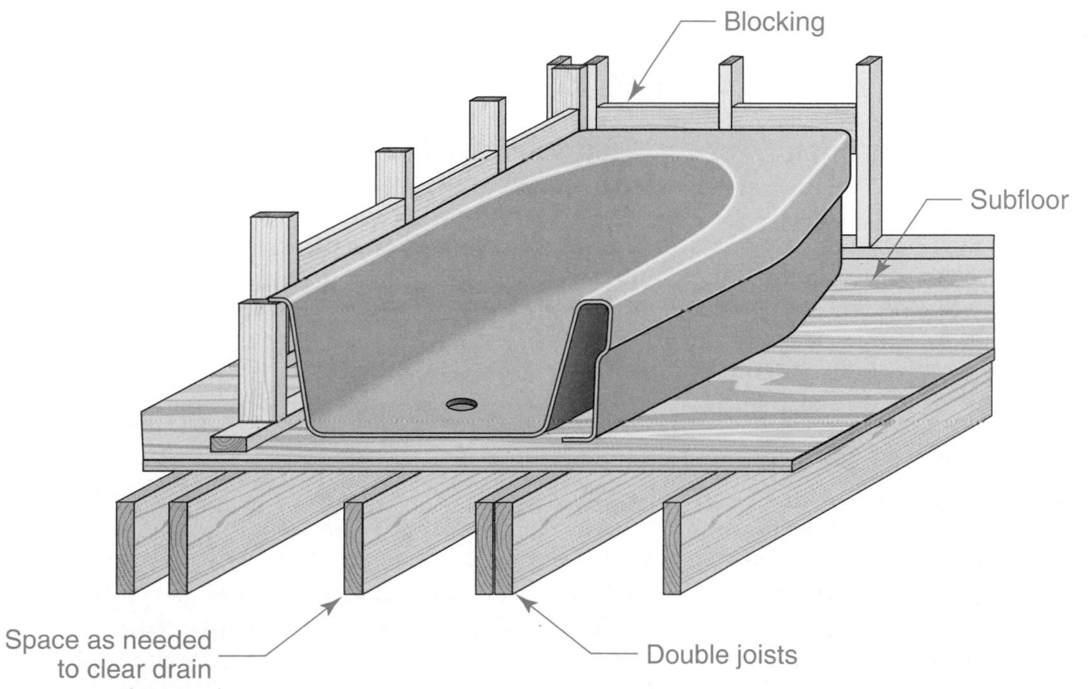

Fig. 20-32. Framing for a bathtub. The joists under the bathtub are placed 12″ OC. For a cast-iron bathtub, a double joist may be needed.

Second-Story Framing

The layout and installation of second-story floor joists is basically the same as for the first story. However, instead of resting on a sill plate, the joists rest on the double top plate of the first-story walls. It is also important to remember that finish ceiling materials will be nailed to the underside of the second-story floor joists. This calls for some special framing details.

At the junction of a wall and ceiling, doubled joists provide a nailing surface for the ceiling and interior wall finish. **Fig. 20-33.** Another method of providing nailing at the ceiling line is to install solid blocking. **Fig. 20-34.** Blocks should be firmly secured with 16d common nails so that they will not be hammered out of position when the drywall is installed.

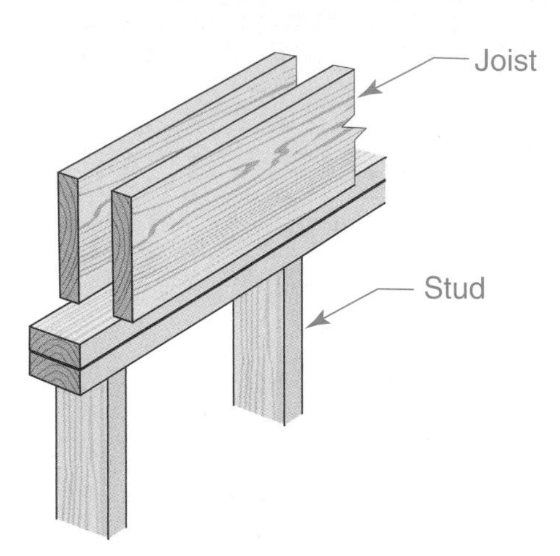

Fig. 20-33. Joists can be added or spaced differently to provide a nailing surface for interior wall finish or ceilings.

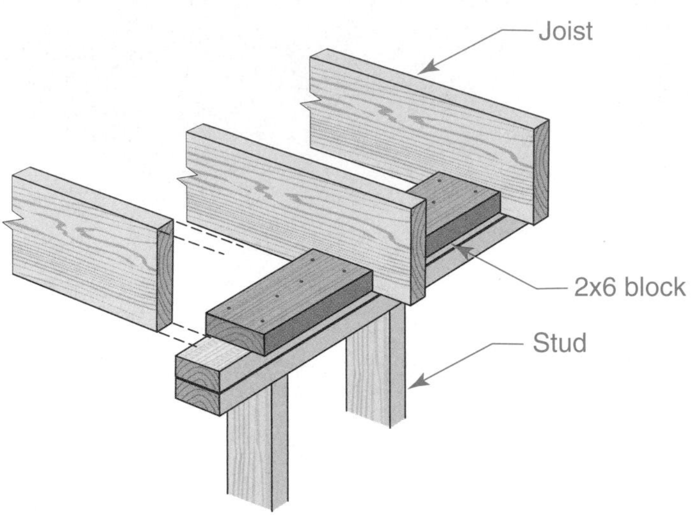

Fig. 20-34. Horizontal blocks can be installed as needed to support the edges of ceiling finishes. This may be required where a wall runs perpendicular to the floor joists. If 2x6 blocks are centered over a 2x4 partition wall, they will provide a nailing surface of approximately 1″ on each side of the wall.

Estimating...

Floor Framing

Estimating methods are similar for both solid-lumber and I-joists.

NUMBER OF JOISTS

Step 1 To find the number of joists needed for a house, first divide the length of the floor (in feet) by the joist spacing (in feet). Conventional joist spacing is 16″ (1.33′) on center. Dividing by 1.33 is the same as multiplying by 0.75. Therefore, for joists 16″ on center, simply take three-fourths of the length of the building and add 1. For example, for a building that is 40′ long, multiply 0.75 by 40. The answer is 30.

Step 2 Add 1 for the end joist, which gives a total of 31 joists.

Step 3 I-joists may extend from wall to wall, but solid lumber joists usually do not. More are needed. Suppose that the building in the previous example is 20′ wide and that you are using 10′ joists. The joists will extend only from one wall to a center girder. Another 31 joists will be needed to cover the span from the girder to the opposite wall, for a total of 62 joists.

Step 4 Add one extra joist for each wall for which double joists are specified.

Step 5 To determine the number of joists, you can also refer to **Table 20-C**. In the column headed "Length of Span," find the length of the building

(Continued)

Estimating...

(continued)

Table 20-C. Number of Solid-Wood Joists Required

Length of Span (feet)	Spacing of Joists (inches)									
	12	16	20	24	30	36	42	48	54	60
6	7	6	5	4	3	3	3	3	2	2
7	8	6	5	5	4	4	3	3	3	2
8	9	7	6	5	4	4	3	3	3	3
9	10	8	6	6	5	4	4	3	3	3
10	11	9	7	6	5	4	4	4	3	3
11	12	9	8	7	5	5	4	4	3	3
12	13	10	8	7	6	5	4	4	4	3
13	14	11	9	8	6	5	5	4	4	4
14	15	12	9	8	7	6	5	5	4	4
15	16	12	10	9	7	6	5	5	4	4
16	17	13	11	9	7	6	6	5	5	4
17	18	14	11	10	8	7	6	5	5	4
18	19	15	12	10	8	7	6	6	5	4
19	20	15	12	11	9	7	6	6	5	5
20	21	16	13	11	9	8	7	6	5	5
21	22	17	14	12	9	8	7	6	6	5
22	23	18	14	12	10	8	7	7	6	5
23	24	18	15	13	10	9	8	7	6	6
24	25	19	15	13	11	9	8	7	6	6
25	26	20	16	14	11	9	8	7	7	6
26	27	21	17	14	11	10	8	8	7	6
27	28	21	17	15	12	10	9	8	7	6
28	29	22	18	15	12	10	9	8	7	7
29	30	23	18	16	13	11	9	8	7	7
30	31	24	19	16	13	11	10	9	8	7
31	32	24	20	17	13	11	10	9	8	7
32	33	25	20	17	14	12	10	9	8	7
33	34	26	21	18	14	12	10	9	8	8
34	35	27	21	18	15	12	11	10	9	8
35	36	27	22	19	15	13	11	10	9	8
36	37	28	23	19	15	13	11	10	9	8
37	38	29	23	20	16	13	12	10	9	8
38	39	30	24	20	16	14	12	11	9	9
39	40	30	24	21	17	14	12	11	10	9
40	41	31	25	21	17	14	12	11	10	9

Note: One joist has been added to take care of extra joist required at end of span. Add as needed for doubling joists under all partitions.

(Continued)

(40′ in our example). Read across to the spacing of the joists (in the example 16″) to find the number of joists required (31). Again, this number will have to be doubled if the joists extend only to a center girder. Extra joists must also be added for any that must be doubled.

MATERIAL COSTS

An accurate cost estimate of materials is made by multiplying the number of joists required by the cost per joist. A rough estimate can be made without knowing the exact number of pieces needed.

Step 1 Find the area of the floor by multiplying the length times the width for each level. For example, a one-story building 20′ wide and 40′ long has a floor area of 800 sq. ft. ($20 \times 40 = 800$).

Step 2 The number of board feet required for joists can be found by referring to **Table 20-D**. According to the table, using 2x6 joists placed 16″ OC, 102 board feet of lumber are needed for each 100 sq. ft. of floor surface area.

Step 3 Divide the total floor area by 100, and multiply by the number of board feet that you obtained from the table. The answer to the example problem is 816 board feet ($800 \div 100 = 8$, and $8 \times 102 = 816$).

Step 4 By multiplying the cost per board foot of lumber by the number of board feet required, you can obtain a rough cost estimate.

Step 5 Table 20-D also helps determine the number of nails needed. For 2x6 joists, 10 lbs. of nails are needed for each 1,000 board feet. Since our floor has only 800 board feet, it will require about 8 lbs. of nails.

Step 6 Multiply the number of pounds needed by the cost per pound to find the total cost of the nails.

LABOR COSTS

To determine the labor cost for framing a floor, you must know the joist size.

Step 1 In our example, the joists are 2″ x 6″ x 10′. Refer to **Table 20-E**, which shows that 2″ x 6″ x 10′ boards contain 10 board feet. For a building with 62 joists, as in our example, there would be a total of 620 board feet of joists ($10 \times 62 = 620$).

Step 2 Refer to Table 20-D to find the labor rate. One worker in one hour can frame 65 board feet of 2x6 joist material.

(Continued)

Table 20-D. Estimating Board Feet, Nails, and Labor

	Joists				Nails	Labor
	Board Feet Required for 100 Sq. Ft. of Surface Area				Per 1,000 Bd. Ft. (pounds)	Bd. Ft. (per Hour)
Size of Joist	12″ OC	16″ OC	20″ OC	24″ OC		
2x6	128	102	88	78	10	65
2x8	171	136	117	103	8	65
2x10	214	171	148	130	6	70
2x12	256	205	177	156	5	70

Table 20-E. Board Feet in Standard Lumber

Width and Depth (inches)	Length (feet)							
	10	12	14	16	18	20	22	24
1x2	1⅔	2	2⅓	2⅔	3	3⅓	3⅔	4
1x3	2½	3	3½	4	4½	5	5½	6
1x4	3⅓	4	4⅔	5⅓	6	6⅔	7⅓	8
1x5	4⅙	5	5⅚	6⅔	7½	8⅓	9⅙	10
1x6	5	6	7	8	9	10	11	12
1x8	6⅔	8	9⅓	10⅔	12	13⅓	14⅔	16
1x10	8⅓	10	11⅔	13⅓	15	16⅔	18⅓	20
1x12	10	12	14	16	18	20	22	24
1x14	11⅔	14	16⅓	18⅔	21	23⅓	25⅔	28
1x16	13⅓	16	18⅔	21⅓	24	26⅔	29⅓	32
1x20	16⅔	20	23⅓	26⅔	30	33⅓	36⅔	40
1¼x4	4⅙	5	5⅚	6⅔	7½	8⅓	9⅙	10
1¼x6	6¼	7½	8¾	10	11¼	12½	13¾	15
1¼x8	8⅓	10	11⅔	13⅓	15	16⅔	18⅓	20
1¼x10	10⅓	12½	14½	16⅔	18⅔	20⅚	22⅚	25
1¼x12	12½	15	17½	20	22½	25	27½	30
1½x4	5	6	7	8	9	10	11	12
1½x6	7½	9	10½	12	13½	15	16½	18
1½x8	10	12	14	16	18	20	22	24
1½x10	12½	15	17½	20	22½	25	27½	30
1½x12	15	18	21	24	27	30	33	36
2x4	6⅔	8	9⅓	10⅔	12	13⅓	14⅔	16
2x6	10	12	14	16	18	20	22	24
2x8	13⅓	16	18⅔	21⅓	24	26⅔	29⅓	32
2x10	16⅔	20	23⅓	26⅔	30	33⅓	36⅔	40
2x12	20	24	28	32	36	40	44	48
2x14	23⅓	28	32⅔	37⅓	42	46⅔	51⅓	56
2x16	26⅔	32	37½	42⅔	48	53⅓	58⅔	64
2½x12	25	30	35	40	45	50	55	60
2½x14	19⅙	35	40⅚	46⅔	52½	58⅓	64⅙	70
2½x16	33⅓	40	46⅔	53⅓	60	66⅔	73⅓	80
3x6	15	18	21	24	27	30	33	36
3x8	20	24	28	32	36	40	44	48
3x10	25	30	35	40	45	50	55	60
3x12	30	36	42	48	54	60	66	72
3x14	35	42	49	56	63	70	77	84
3x16	40	48	56	64	72	80	88	96
4x4	13⅓	16	18⅔	21⅓	24	26⅔	29⅓	32
4x6	20	24	28	32	36	40	44	48
4x8	26⅔	32	17⅓	42⅔	48	53⅓	58⅔	64
4x10	33⅓	40	46⅔	53⅓	60	66⅔	73⅓	80
4x12	40	48	56	64	72	80	88	96
4x14	46⅓	56	65⅓	74⅔	84	93⅓	102½	112

(Continued)

Estimating...
(continued)

Step 3 To find the total hours needed, divide the total board feet by the number of board feet framed in one hour. The answer is 9.5 hours (620 ÷ 65 = 9.5).

Step 4 Multiply the number of hours by the hourly rate.

ESTIMATING ON THE JOB

A two-story house measures 48′ by 22′. The floor joists will be solid lumber 2x10s that are 12′ long. They will be placed 16″ OC. How many lineal feet of 2x10 lumber are required?

SECTION 20.2 **Check Your Knowledge**

1. What is the purpose of the sill plate?
2. What size and type of bit should be used when boring holes in the sill plate for foundation anchor bolts that are ½″ in diameter?
3. What does the term crown refer to and why is it important?
4. What is a web stiffener and what is its purpose?

On the Job

In platform-frame construction, the construction of the floor system can affect the work of tradespeople who follow. Examine the floor system at your house or the house of a friend. This would be easiest in the basement. Can you determine which trades might be affected by the work of the floor-framing carpenter? Discuss this with a classmate. See if the two of you can identify other parts of the house that could be affected by the quality of the floor framing. As a team, present your findings to the class.

SECTION 20.3

The Subfloor

The layer of material over the floor joists is called *floor sheathing*. It forms what is called the *subfloor*. Sheathing serves several important purposes. It lends bracing strength to the building. It provides a solid base for the finish floor. By acting as a barrier to cold and dampness, it helps keep the building warmer and drier in winter. In addition, it provides a safe working surface for building the house.

Many years ago, floor sheathing was made of solid 1x boards, which were nailed diagonally across the floor joists. Today, the boards have been replaced by 4′ x 8′ engineered panel products such as plywood and OSB. These panels are easier to install and create a stiffer subfloor that is less likely to squeak. Panel subfloors are of two types: single-layer and double-layer. They will be discussed in this section.

Steps for installing a panel subfloor are given on page 386.

FASTENING THE SUBFLOOR

Common nails are often used to install floor sheathing. However, some panel manufacturers recommend the use of ring-shank or screw-shank nails. They are no more difficult to install but hold much better. Some builders use them exclusively for floor sheathing. For an even better connection and fewer squeaks, the subfloor may be screwed to the joists.

Nailing Techniques

Hand nailing a subfloor is time consuming and physically difficult. Using pneumatic tools is much more efficient. This has become the standard method.

For builders who prefer to screw the sheathing to the joists, special attachments enable electric drills to drive a great number of screws quickly. These attachments use coils of screws, automatically feeding each one to the tip of the drill. **Fig. 20-35.** Some models are fitted with a long extension. The carpenter does not have to lean over during installation.

Many builders use a technique called glue-nailing. In *glue-nailing*, a bead of adhesive is applied to the tops of joists before the panels are nailed in place. This is not required by building codes, but it results in a stiffer floor. Also, the floor is less likely to squeak later on.

Construction adhesive is thick, like a mastic, and is packaged in caulking tubes. A standard caulking gun is used to apply a single bead to the joists just before a panel is placed. The adhesive should be placed as each sheet of subflooring is installed. If the adhesive is applied too long in advance, it will dry out or harden and will not hold.

Blocking

The edges of square-edged sheathing panels should be supported. They must rest either on a joist or on blocking laid between the joists. This blocking is cut from nominal 2″ lumber.

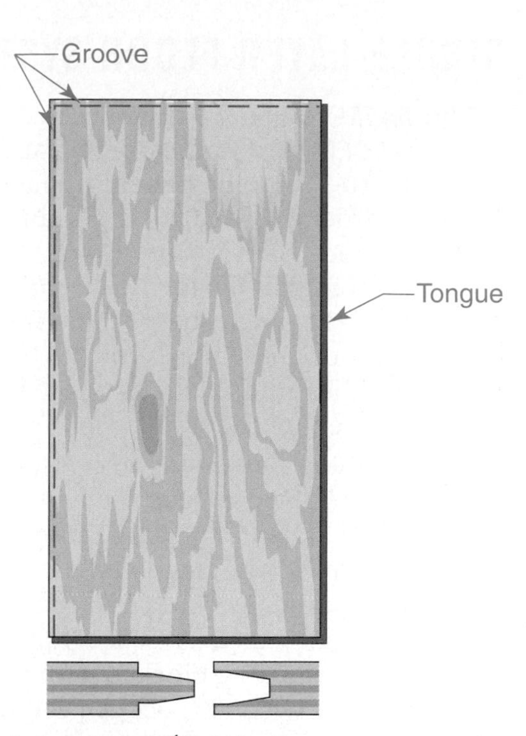

Fig. 20-36. A plywood panel 1⅛″ thick with a groove on one end and one edge and a tongue on the other end and edge. The surface is a full 4′ x 8′ with an allowance for the tongue.

Sheathing with a tongue-and-groove (T&G) edge does not need to be blocked between supports. **Fig. 20-36.** Tongue-and-groove subflooring should be started with the tongue toward the outside of the building. Any pounding required to close the joints between the panels can then be done on a scrap block held against the groove.

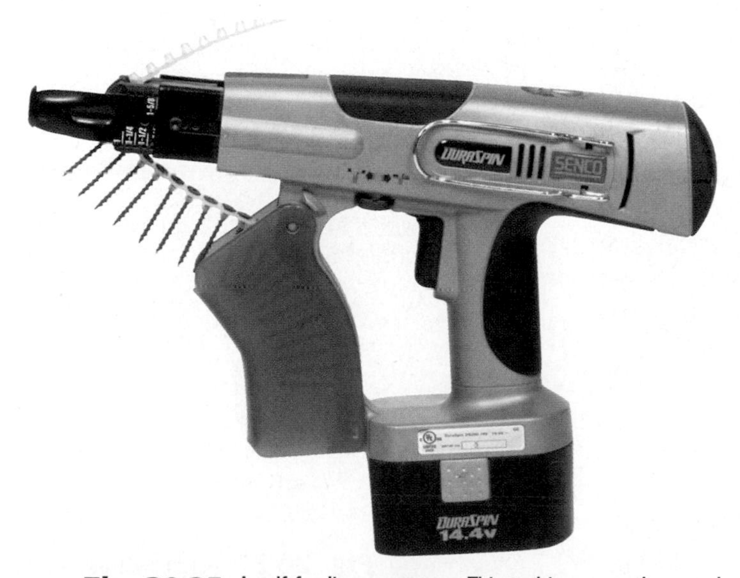

Fig. 20-35. A self-feeding screw gun. This tool increases the speed at which screws can be installed in a subfloor.

SINGLE-LAYER FLOOR SYSTEMS

The *single-layer floor system* was designed for use beneath wall-to-wall carpeting and carpet pad. **Fig. 20-37.** Single panels are fastened to joists or girders. The carpeting and pad are laid on this surface later. A single-layer floor has only one structural layer. (The carpeting is non-structural.) The single layer is, in effect, a combined subfloor and underlayment. The panels used should be rated for this purpose. The rating is stamped on the back.

The advantages of a single-layer floor system are that it is inexpensive and quick to install. For fastening details, refer to **Table 20-F**. Note that when panels are glued and nailed, fewer nails are required, as compared to nailing only. If square-edged panels are used, any unsupported edges must be blocked with nominal 2″ lumber. Panels with T&G edges need not be blocked.

DOUBLE-LAYER FLOOR SYSTEMS

A *double-layer floor system* has a separate subfloor and underlayment. **Fig. 20-38.** It is used beneath such finish floors as sheet vinyl. The subfloor panel is first fastened to the joists. The plywood underlayment panel goes on top of the subfloor. The underlayment covers any minor construction damage to the subfloor and provides a smooth substrate for the finish flooring. For fastening details refer to **Table 20-G** on page 386.

Underlayment plywood has a *touch-sanded surface*. This means that it is sanded at the mill just enough to ensure uniform thickness. The inner plies resist dents and punctures from heavy loads, such as furniture. To improve the stiffness of the floor, the face grain of the underlayment should be placed perpendicular to supports. The edges should be offset at least 2″ from the edges of the subfloor panels. This is usually done automatically because the subfloor extends beneath the wall plates, while the underlayment does not (see Fig. 20-38).

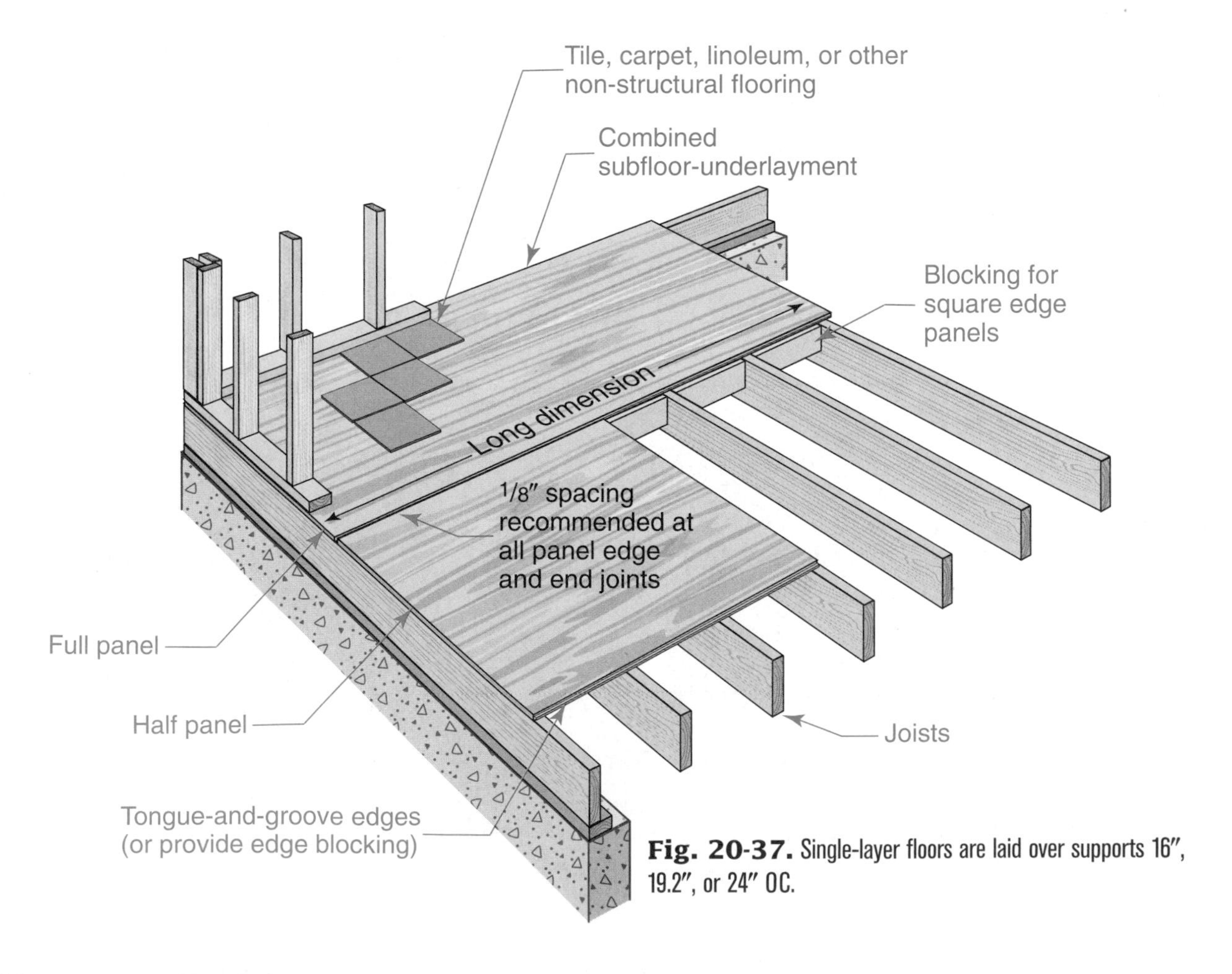

Fig. 20-37. Single-layer floors are laid over supports 16″, 19.2″, or 24″ OC.

Table 20-F. Single-Layer Floors[a]

Span Rating (Maximum Joist Spacing) (inches)	Panel Thickness (inches)[b]	Fastening: Glue-Nailed[c]			Fastening: Nailed Only		
		Nail Size and Type	Spacing (inches)		Nail Size and Type	Spacing (inches)	
			Supported Panel Edges	Intermediate Supports		Supported Panel Edges	Intermediate Supports
16	19/32, 5/8, 21/32	6d ring- or screw-shank[d]	12	12	6d ring- or screw-shank	6	12
20	19/32, 5/8, 23/32, 3/4	6d ring- or screw-shank[d]	12	12	6d ring- or screw-shank	6	12
24	11/16, 23/32, 3/4	6d ring- or screw-shank[d]	12	12	6d ring- or screw-shank	6	12
24	7/8, 1	8d ring- or screw-shank[d]	6	12	8d ring- or screw-shank	6	12
32	7/8, 1	8d ring- or screw-shank[d]	6	12	8d ring- or screw-shank	6	12
48	1⅛	8d ring- or screw-shank[e]	6	(f)	8d ring- or screw-shank	6	(f)

(a) APA Rated Sturd-I-Floor. Special conditions may impose heavy traffic and concentrated loads that require construction in excess of the minimums shown.

(b) Panels in a given thickness may be manufactured in more than one span rating. Panels with a span rating greater than the actual joist spacing may be substituted for panels of the same thickness with a span rating matching the actual joist spacing.

(c) Use only adhesives conforming to APA Specification AFG-01, applied in accordance with the manufacturer's recommendations. If non-veneered panels with sealed surfaces and edges are to be used, use only solvent-backed glues; check with panel manufacturer.

(d) 8d common nails may be substituted if ring- or screw-shank nails are not available.

(e) 10d common nails may be substituted with 1⅛″ panels if supports are well seasoned.

(f) Space nails 6″ for 48″ spans and 12″ for 32″ spans.

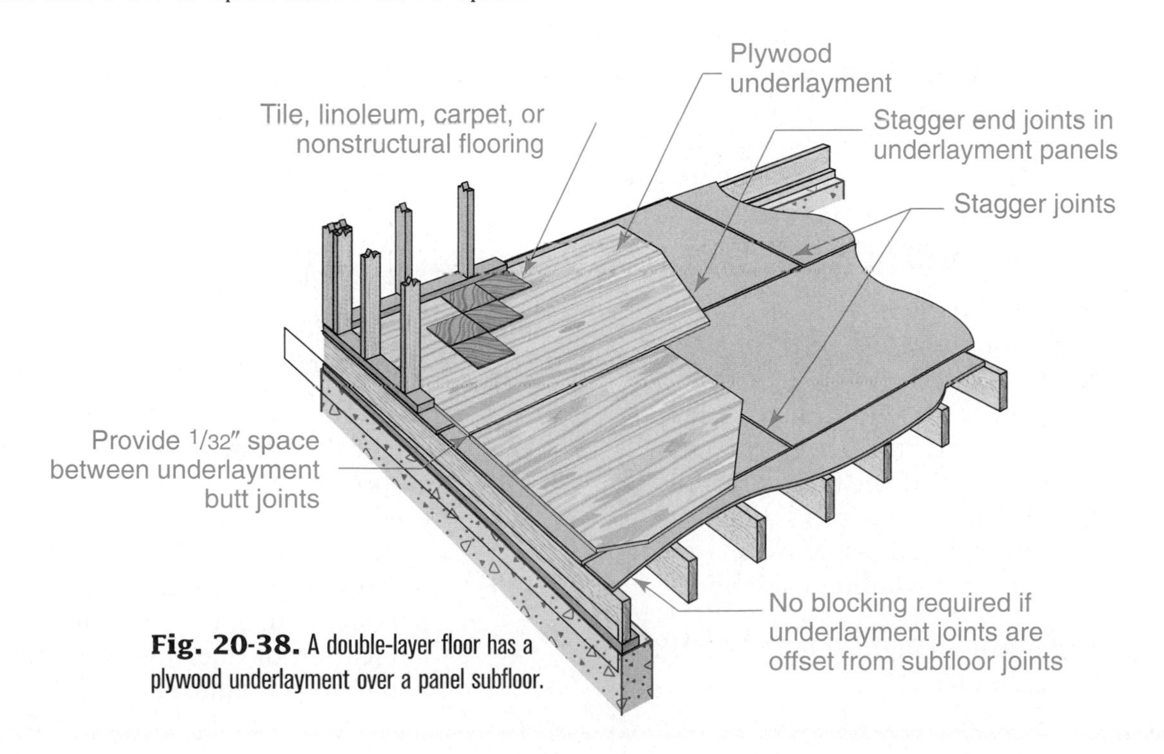

Fig. 20-38. A double-layer floor has a plywood underlayment over a panel subfloor.

Table 20-G. APA Plywood Underlayment[a]

Plywood Grades[a]	Application	Minimum Plywood Thickness (inches)	Fastener Size and Type[b]	Fastener Spacing (inches)[c]	
				Panel Edges	Intermediate
APA UNDERLAYMENT	Over smooth subfloor	¼	3d ring-shank nails[d]	3	6 each way
APA C-C Plugged EXT APA RATED STURD-I-FLOOR (19/32″ or thicker)	Over lumber subfloor or other uneven surfaces	11/32	3d ring-shank nails[d]	6	8 each way
Same grades as above but species Group 1 only	Over lumber floor up to 4″ wide; face grain must be perpendicular to boards	¼	3d ring-shank nails[d]	3	6 each way

(a) In areas to be finished with thin floor coverings such as tile or sheet vinyl, specify Underlayment C-C Plugged or STURD-I-FLOOR with "sanded face." Underlayment A-C, Underlayment B-C, Marine EXT, or sanded plywood grades marked "Plugged Crossbands Under Face," "Plugged Crossbands (or Core)," "Plugged Inner Plies," or "Meets Underlayment Requirements" may also be used under thin floor coverings.

(b) Other code-approved fasteners may be used.

(c) Space fasteners so they do not penetrate framing.

(d) Use 3d ring-shank nails for ½″ panels and 4d ring-shank nails for ⅝″ or ¾″ panels.

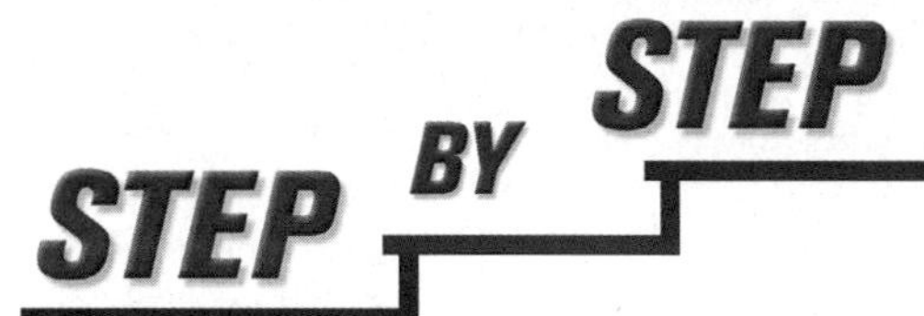

Laying a Panel Subfloor

The general method for installing a subfloor is the same for plywood and OSB panels. However, always consult the manufacturer's instructions.

Step 1 Measure 48″ along the side of the foundation from the starting corner and mark this point. Repeat the process on the opposite side of the foundation. Snap a chalk line between these points. This serves as an alignment guide for the sheathing.

Step 2 Place a full panel even with one of the outside corners of the floor joists. Align the edge with the chalk line. The grain of the plywood should run at right angles to the joists. If the subfloor will be glue-nailed, spread a bead of construction adhesive on the joists just before installing each sheet.

Step 3 Drive just enough nails to hold the panel in place.

Step 4 Place the next full panel in position at the end of the first panel. Be sure the joint is centered over the joist, and leave about ⅛″ space between panels. Install it as in Step 2.

Step 5 Begin the second row of panels at the end of the building, alongside the first panel laid. Cut a panel in half, lay the end flush with the outside of the floor framing, and nail the half panel to the joists, as in Fig. 20-37. Continue to lay and nail full panels in this row.

Step 6 Start the next (third) row with a full panel. This alternating method will stagger the joints used for support and provide the strongest floor. Continue to lay panels, driving just enough nails in each to hold it in position until all panels are laid. Then snap chalk lines to indicate the location of floor joists. Complete the nailing as required.

Estimating...

Subflooring

Use this method to estimate the number of plywood sheets needed for subflooring.

Step 1 Figure the square footage of floor area in the building. For example, a one-story, 28′ by 50′ building has 1,400 sq. ft. (28 × 50 = 1,400).

Step 2 Figure the number of square feet in 1 sheet of plywood. A 4x8 sheet of plywood contains 32 sq. ft. (4 × 8 = 32).

Step 3 Divide the square footage of floor area by the square feet in 1 sheet of plywood. For our example, 1,400 divided by 32 is 43.75. The floor area will require 43.75 sheets of plywood. This would be rounded off to 44 sheets.

ESTIMATING ON THE JOB

Estimate the number of 4x8 floor sheathing panels that will be required for a two-story house that measures 48′ long by 22′ wide.

Carpenter's Tip

Floor sheathing panels are often installed with a ⅛″ gap between them to allow for expansion. Rather than measure this gap, use a 10d box nail as a spacer. It is approximately ⅛″ in diameter.

SECTION 20.3 Check Your Knowledge

1. When glue-nailing a subfloor, when should adhesive be applied to the joists?
2. List four fasteners used to attach sheathing to the floor joists.
3. What is underlayment and why is it used?
4. What can be used to gauge the required ⅛″ separation between subflooring panels?

On the Job

Construction adhesives can dramatically improve the performance of a subfloor system. However, improvements in adhesive technology are expected in coming years. Using the most current sources of information available, locate at least three manufacturers of adhesives that are suitable for subfloors. Are any of their products suitable for use on wet lumber? Are any suitable for use on preservative-treated lumber? What features of these products do you think carpenters would find most important? Summarize your results in a short report.

Other Floor Framing Systems

The floor of most houses is built with solid lumber or laminated-veneer lumber. However, there are other ways to build floor systems. Floor trusses are sometimes used when a floor must withstand heavy loads or when unusually long spans are required. Girder floor framing is common in mild climates.

FLOOR TRUSSES

Special floor trusses can be used in place of lumber joists where long spans are required. **Fig. 20-39.** These trusses are made in a factory to the specifications of the job.

A floor truss has only three basic parts: chords, webs, and connector plates. The open webs allow heating ducts, water lines, drain lines, and other items to be passed through with ease.

The most common type of floor truss in residential construction is the *parallel-chord floor truss.* The top and bottom chords are parallel to each other over the length of the truss.

It is important to brace floor trusses as they are being installed (see Fig. 20-39). This increases the safety of workers installing the subfloor. It also prevents the trusses from being damaged by sideways movement before the subfloor is laid. The truss fabricator can provide detailed bracing instructions.

GIRDER FLOOR FRAMING

The girder method of floor framing is sometimes used where homes are built over a crawl space instead of a basement. A system of posts and girders, instead of joists, supports the subfloor. Frequently, 4x6 girders are used and spaced 4′ OC. They are supported by 4x6 posts spaced no more than 5′ OC. Sometimes girders are combined with box-sill framing. **Fig. 20-40.** In other cases, the box sill is replaced by a plate.

Installation

After the foundation walls are in place, locations for concrete piers are laid out and holes can be dug for the pier footings. The piers should be set in a reasonably straight line. Their height is not critical because the posts will be cut to the correct length. The sill is then cut to size and bolted in place.

The bearing posts must be cut to length accurately to provide a level floor. A string is pulled

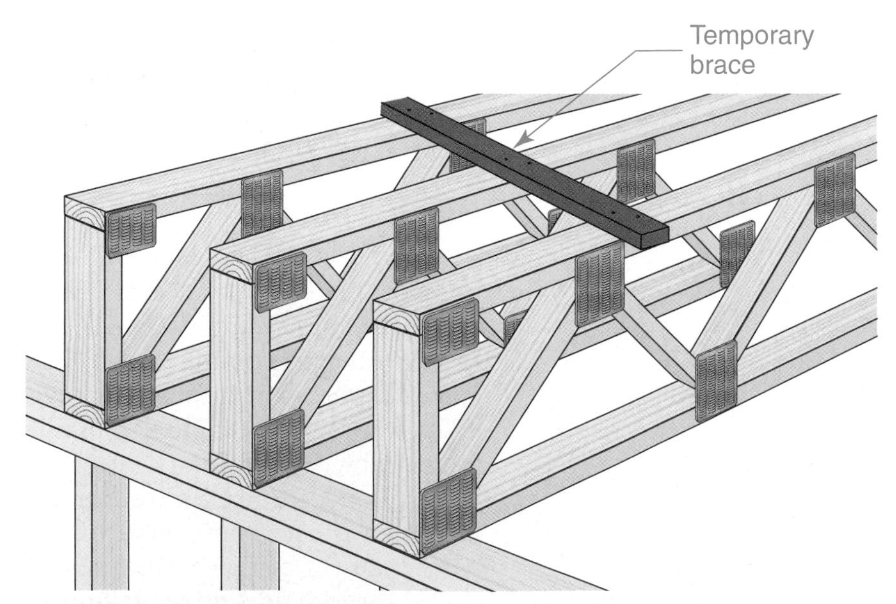

Fig. 20-39. This type of truss is called a parallel-chord truss. Floor trusses are braced temporarily with 2x4 stock. In some areas, floor trusses must be secured to plates with metal brackets. This improves structural performance during an earthquake or severe weather.

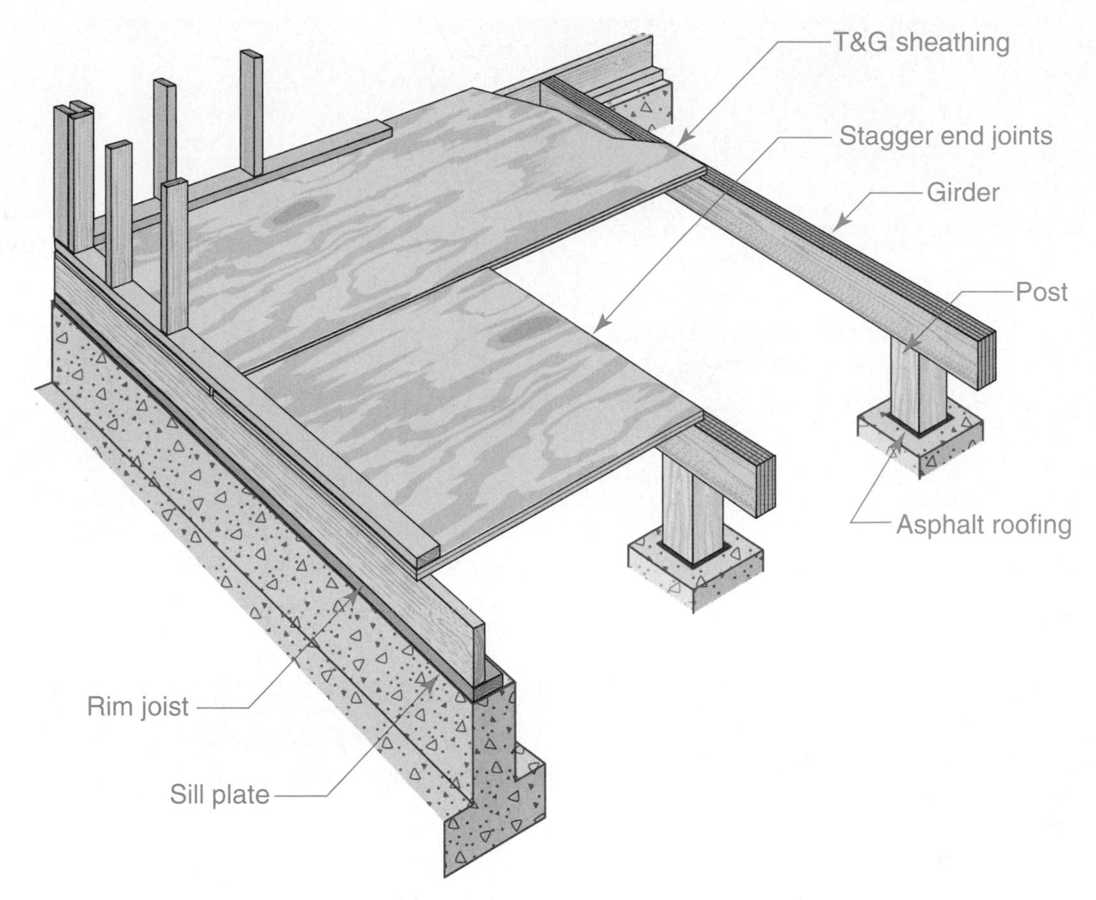

Fig. 20-40. Girder construction with box-sill framing. The asphalt roofing material keeps the wood from contacting the pier. If square-edge panels are used, blocking is required at unsupported edges.

tight from opposite sill plates over the piers. Then the distance is measured from the line to the top of each pier and recorded. This process is repeated for each line of piers until the height of each bearing post has been determined and recorded. Posts can be cut to length with a circular saw or radial-arm saw.

Each post is toenailed to a wood cap on the pier. **Fig. 20-41.** Then the girders are cut to length and toenailed to the posts. If a low house profile is desired or if the finished floor is to have a step-down area, the tops of the girders in the step-down area are set flush with the top of the sill. A special metal hanger is used to support the girder.

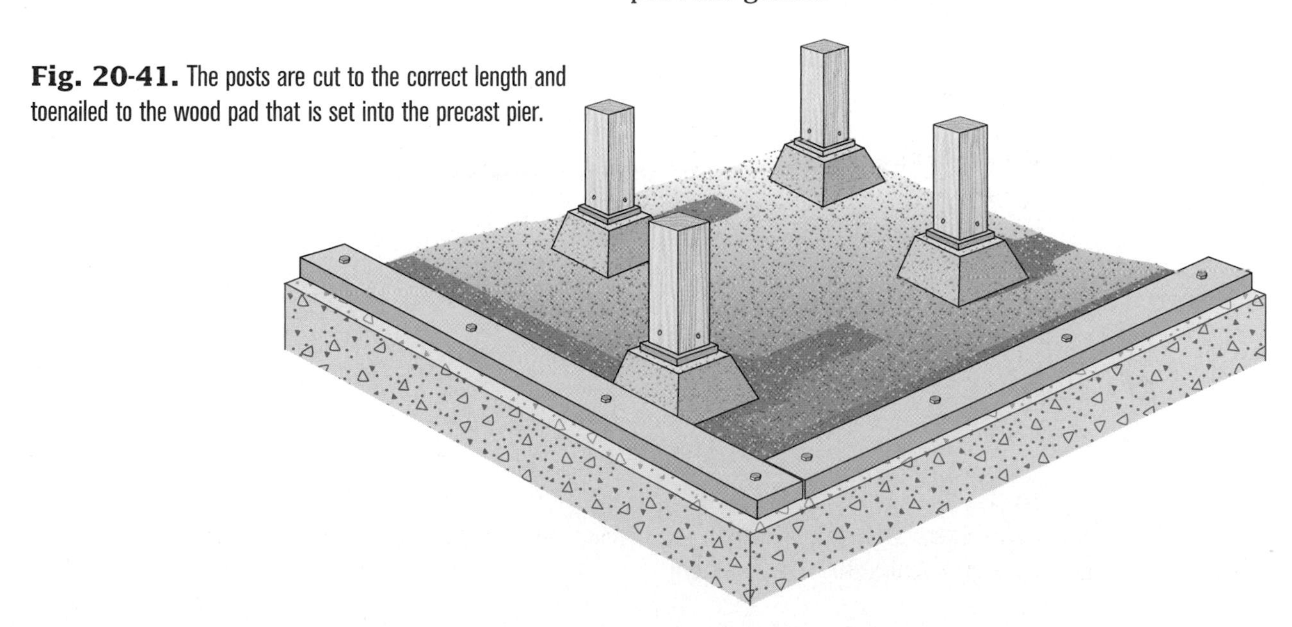

Fig. 20-41. The posts are cut to the correct length and toenailed to the wood pad that is set into the precast pier.

Fig. 20-42. Girder construction with 2x6 tongue-and-groove subflooring.

Because working space under the girders is limited, plumbing and heating lines are roughed in before the subfloor is laid. The subfloor is then cut and nailed in place.

Laying the Subfloor

The subfloor is usually of 1⅛″ or thicker tongue-and-groove plywood. Some local building codes permit the use of 2x6 tongue-and-groove subflooring over girder floor framing. The subflooring is cut even with the outside of the framing and nailed to the top of the girders. **Fig. 20-42.** 16d nails are used to toenail at the tongue and to face-nail at a joint on all girders. After the subfloor has been cut and nailed in place, the surface is ready for the layout and erection of the walls.

SECTION 20.4 Check Your Knowledge

1. Name the three basic parts of a floor truss.
2. What supports the posts in girder floor framing?
3. What determines how level a girder floor is?
4. When are plumbing and heating lines roughed in for a girder system?

On the Job

Conduct a search on the Internet to obtain more information about girder floor framing. Determine what construction details are used for multilevel floors.

Chapter 20 Review

Section Summaries

20.1 Girders, supported by wood or metal posts, are often used to support floor joists.

20.2 Floor joists are commonly made of solid or LVL lumber. Special framing techniques can be used for large openings. Rim boards should be used instead of rim joists when the floor is assembled with I-joists. Cross bridging improves the stiffness of joists.

20.3 The single-layer floor system is used beneath carpeting. The double-layer floor system includes an underlayment in addition to the subfloor.

20.4 Floor trusses can be used instead of joists when long spans are required. Girder floor framing is used over a crawl-space foundation.

Review Questions

1. Name the basic components used in floor framing.
2. Where is a girder placed?
3. What is the first step in installing a sill plate?
4. Where must the edges of floor sheathing panels fall during installation?
5. What is the purpose of joist bridging?
6. What adjustments to the floor framing must be made beneath bearing walls?
7. What is a tail joist and what supports it?
8. What is the purpose of doubled joists at the junction of a wall and ceiling?
9. What is the purpose of floor sheathing?
10. What supports the posts in girder floor framing?

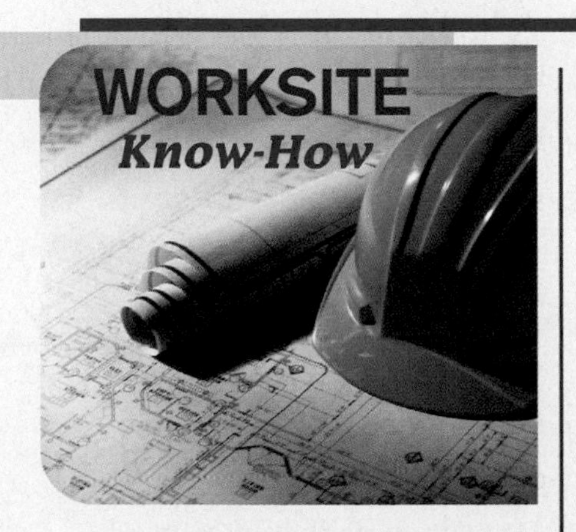

Working with Fractions Making calculations in carpentry often involves fractions. Fractions are easy to add or subtract when their denominators (the lower parts) are the same, but what if they are different? You must then convert the fractions.

First, find a common denominator. For example, to add $3/8$ + $5/16$, you would use 16 as the common denominator because 16 can be divided evenly by 8. (If the common denominator is not easily discovered, you can multiply the two denominators. For example, to add $2/3$ + $4/5$, you would multiply 3×5 to obtain a common denominator of 15.)

Next, convert the numerators (the upper parts). To convert $3/8$, figure how many times 8 goes into 16. The answer is 2. Then multiply the original numerator (3) times 2 to get a new numerator of 6. The new fraction equivalent to $3/8$ is $6/16$. Adding $6/16$ + $5/16$ is now easy. The answer is $11/16$.

Chapter 21

Wall Framing and Sheathing

Objectives

After reading this chapter, you'll be able to:

- Identify wall-framing members.
- Lay out a wall.
- Assemble and erect a wall.
- Identify situations that require special framing.
- Apply sheathing.
- Estimate materials for wall framing and sheathing.

Terms

corner post
cripple stud
plate
rough opening (RO)
rough sill
sheathing
stud
temporary bracing
trimmer stud

The framing and sheathing for the first floor create a flat and level platform on which to build the walls. The same carpenters who framed the floor system also lay out, assemble, and erect the walls. This work must be done with great care. Mistakes or poor work practices at this stage will make it more difficult to complete the rest of the house. Cabinets, for example, will not fit well if walls are not straight.

After the walls are framed, sheathing may be attached to them. **Sheathing** consists of rigid 4x8 or larger panels that are attached to the outside surface of the exterior wall framing. Sheathing adds great stiffness and strength to the walls.

Wall-Framing Materials

The walls of a house serve as a framework for attaching interior and exterior coverings. A wall that also supports weight from portions of the house above, such as the roof, is called a *load-bearing wall*, or simply a *bearing wall*. Exterior walls are nearly always load-bearing walls. Interior walls, also called *partition walls* or *partitions*, are sometimes load-bearing walls. If they carry only their own weight and the weight of wall coverings, they are not considered to be load-bearing walls.

When roof trusses span the width of the house, the exterior walls carry both the roof and ceiling loads. Interior walls then serve mainly as room dividers. When ceiling joists are used, interior walls usually carry some of the ceiling load. **Fig. 21-1.**

Platform-frame construction simplifies the framing of multilevel structures. Walls on the second level of a two-story house are framed like those on the first level.

The standards and specifications in this chapter are based on the 2000 *International Residential Code for One- and Two-Family Dwellings* (IRC). Be sure to check local codes, which may differ.

LUMBER CHARACTERISTICS

Wall-framing lumber should be stiff and free from warpage and twist, have good nail-holding capability, and be easily worked. Bottom plates should be of treated lumber when installed on a concrete slab. The woods used for wall-framing members are, in general, the same species as those used for floor framing. Common species include Douglas fir and southern yellow pine.

Some building codes consider end-jointed lumber to be no different than solid-sawn lumber of the same species and grade. Wall studs (vertical members) should be at least No. 3, standard, or stud-grade lumber. Lumber used for wall plates is sometimes a higher grade or different species than that used for studs due to the need for long, straight lengths. Wall plates must be straight if the wall is to be straight. High-quality construction may require kiln-dried (KD) lumber to minimize problems associated with shrinkage.

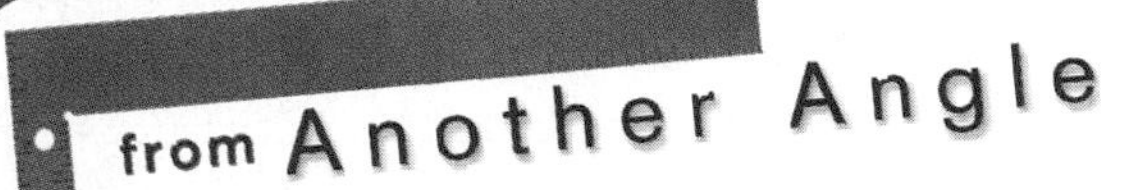

Precut studs are supplied by local lumberyards. Standard lengths vary in different parts of the United States. In some regions, precut studs are $92\frac{1}{4}''$ or $93''$ long. There is no particular reason for this other than local preferences.

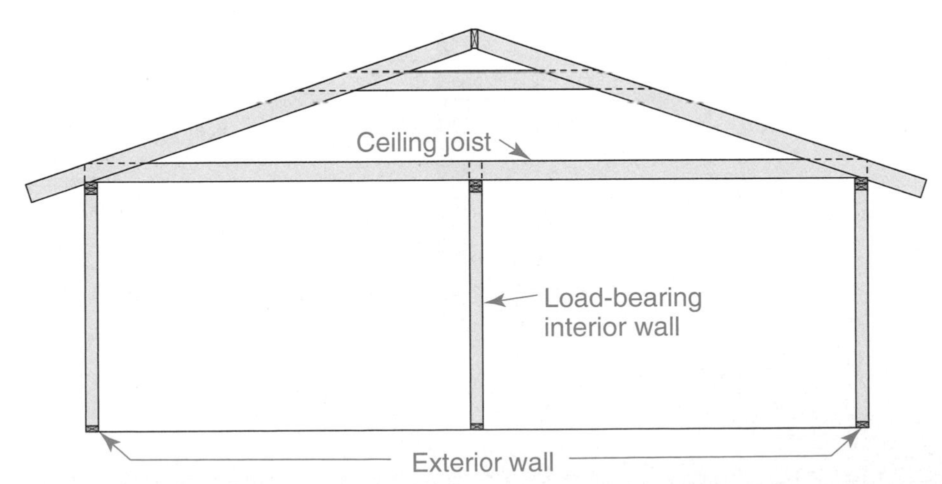

Fig. 21-1. In some structures, ceiling joists span one-half the width of the house. This requires an interior wall to support part of the ceiling load.

Lengths of general framing lumber are available in increments of 2′. However, studs are usually precut to a particular length. Standard precut studs are usually 92⅝″ long for an 8′ wall. **Fig. 21-2.**

WALL-FRAMING MEMBERS

The primary framing members for walls are studs and plates. Other framing members, including headers, sills, cripple studs, and trimmer studs, are connected to these two. The Step-by-Step feature on page 395 shows framing members and summarizes the steps for framing a wall.

Studs

A **stud** is a vertical framing member. Conventional construction commonly uses 2x4 studs spaced 16″ on center (OC). The full-length stud on either side of an opening is sometimes referred to as a *king stud.*

Use of 2x6 studs for exterior walls is increasingly popular. The extra thickness of the resulting walls allows space for additional insulation. These 2x6 studs may be placed 16″ or 24″ OC. Some interior walls are also framed with 2x6 or larger studs, particularly those that will contain the main drainpipes for plumbing fixtures. However, most interior walls are framed with 2x4 lumber, and building codes sometimes allow 2x3 lumber. Spacing for interior-wall studs is normally 16″ OC.

The ends of studs must be cut square so they bear evenly on the plates. Cutting may be done with a circular saw, power miter saw, or radial-arm saw.

Plates

A **plate** is a horizontal framing member used to tie together interior and exterior wall framing. The width of the plates corresponds to the thickness of the wall. In a 2x6 wall, for example,

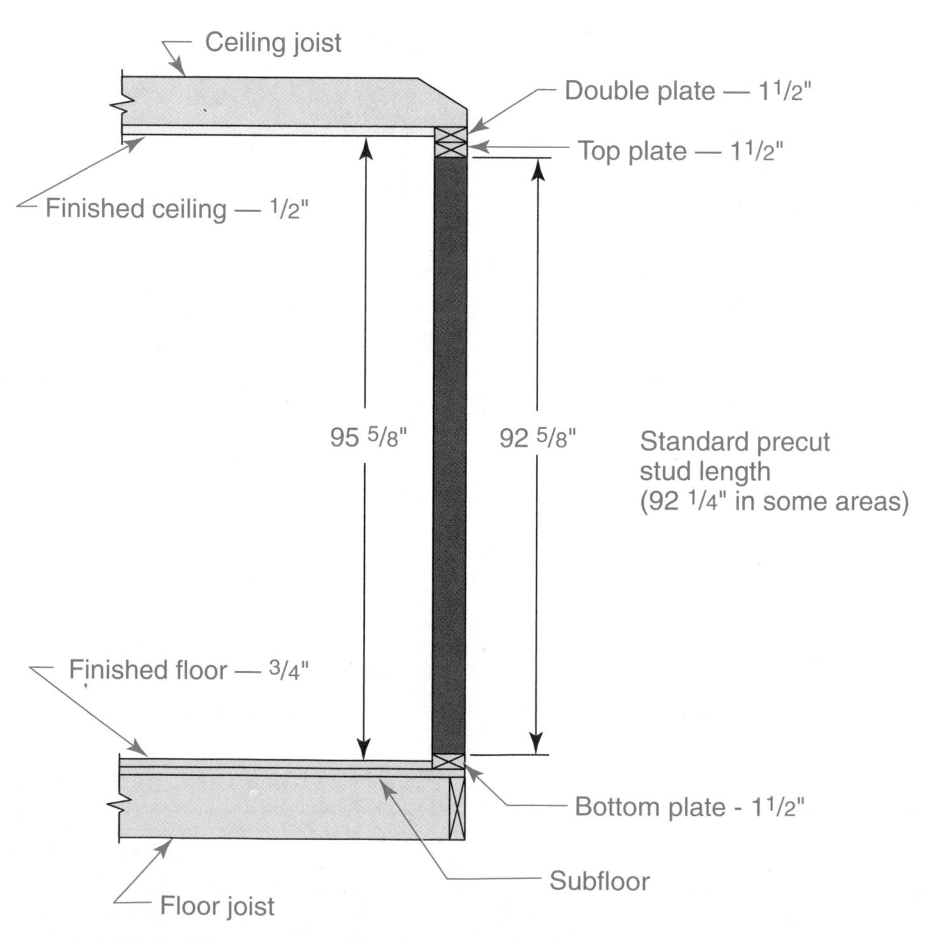

Fig. 21-2. A standard precut stud is 92⅝″ long (92¼″ in some parts of the United States). Some studs may be cut 93″ long for a 96″ (8′) ceiling.

STEP BY STEP

Framing a Wall

Step 1 Cut the bottom plate and top plate to length. If the plates will require more than one piece, make sure that the break falls 16″ OC.

Step 2 Align the bottom plate with the top plate. Tack them together temporarily.

Step 3 Lay out the location of the windows, partitions, studs, and other components on the edges of both plates simultaneously.

Step 4 Spread the top and bottom plates apart.

Step 5 Place the required number of precut studs between the plates.

Step 6 Install cripple studs, headers, and other parts of the framing. Nail the bottom and top plates to the studs by driving nails through the plates and into the end of each stud.

Step 7 Square the wall and brace the corners.

Step 8 Install panel sheathing (plywood or oriented-strand board).

Step 9 Tilt the wall into place.

Step 10 Install temporary braces to keep the wall in place.

Step 11 Repeat the process for adjacent walls.

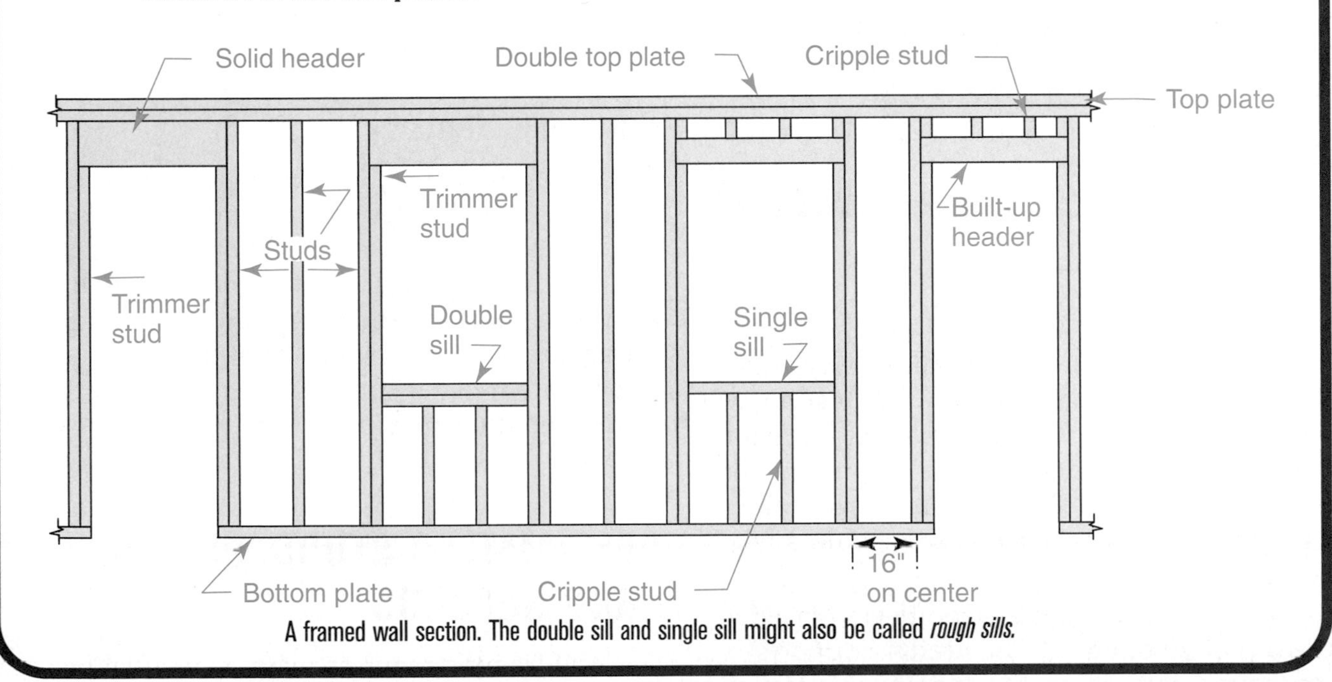

A framed wall section. The double sill and single sill might also be called *rough sills.*

the plates would be made from 2x6 lumber. Each wall has three plates: a bottom plate and two top plates.

The *bottom plate*, also called the *sole plate*, ties the bottom ends of the studs together. It also provides a nailing surface for the bottom edge of wall coverings and wall sheathing. The bottom plate is secured to the bottom of the studs with nails. It is also nailed to the subfloor.

The *top plate* is nailed to the top ends of the studs and ties them together. It also provides a nailing surface for wall coverings and sheathing. The top plate has the same dimensions as the bottom plate.

A second top plate, called the *double plate*, is nailed to the first top plate after the walls have been erected. The second top plate has four purposes:

- It adds strength and rigidity to the top of the wall.
- It supports the ends of joists and the bottom ends of rafters.
- It helps distribute structural loads that do not fall directly over studs.
- It ties intersecting walls together.

The double plate can be omitted in some cases, such as when an in-line framing system is used. If the double plate is omitted, intersecting walls must be tied together with a steel plate (see Chapter 19, "Framing Methods").

from Another Angle

There are two plates at the top of a load-bearing wall. However, terms for these plates differ from region to region. The terms can be confusing, partly because the lower plate is usually called the *top plate*. The plate above the top plate may be called a *double plate*, a *doubled top plate*, a *doubler*, or a *rafter plate*. Together, the two plates are sometimes called a *double plate* or *doubled plate*.

Headers

Wherever an opening in a wall is wider than the stud spacing, parts or all of some studs will have to be left out. This occurs most frequently with windows and doors. It is also present with fireplaces and pass-throughs. To prevent the wall from being weakened at this point, a header is installed.

A *header*, or *lintel*, is a wood beam placed at the top of an opening. The header supports structural loads above the opening and transfers them to framing on each side of the opening. Headers are sometimes made of solid lumber. They are also built up from two or more pieces of 2x lumber laid on edge with spacer blocks to match the thickness of the wall. They are also made from engineered lumber, such as laminated-veneer lumber (LVL).

Rough Sill

A **rough sill** is a horizontal member placed at the bottom of a window opening to support the window. It connects the upper ends of the cripple studs that are below the window. The rough sill does not need the same strength as a header because it supports only the window, not structural loads. It is made from lumber having the same dimensions as the studs. It may be a single piece of lumber (single sill) or two pieces (double sill) if extra strength is required. Note that a *rough sill* is a framing member, while a *windowsill* is a part of the window itself.

Cripple Studs

A **cripple stud**, or *cripple*, is a stud that does not extend all the way from the bottom plate to the top plate. It does not extend because there is an opening in the wall. Cripple studs are installed above headers and below rough sills. They are located where a full-length precut stud would be placed if there were no opening.

Cripple studs provide a nailing surface for the sheathing (outside) and for wall covering (inside). To conserve lumber, they are often cut from stock that is too short for other purposes.

Trimmer Studs

A **trimmer stud**, or *trimmer* or *jack stud*, supports the header over a window or door opening. A trimmer stud is shorter than a standard stud but longer than a cripple stud. It is cut to fit beneath the header. A trimmer stud transfers structural loads from the header to the bottom plate. For wide openings, additional trimmer studs may be needed. Check your local code.

ESTIMATING STUDS, PLATES, AND HEADERS

Wall framing requires many individual pieces of lumber. At the design and planning stages, you may need to know only the approximate number of pieces. Later, you will need a more accurate calculation.

You can estimate the number of 16″ OC studs required for exterior walls by figuring one stud for each lineal foot of wall. This allows for the extra framing required around openings and at corner posts. To determine the number of studs needed for a partition, refer to the table "Partition Studs Needed" in the Ready Reference Appendix.

To determine the number of lineal feet of top and bottom plates for walls having double top plates, multiply the length of the wall by three. Add materials for such items as gable-end studs, corner braces, fireblocking, and wall blocking.

The dimensions of each header will sometimes be found on the building plan. The length of a header is generally 3″ longer than the rough opening width (for more on rough openings, see Chapter 28). This assumes that the header will be supported by one trimmer stud on each end. This is generally the case with openings less than 6′ wide. However, headers over larger openings should be supported by two trimmers at each end. In that case, the length of the header will be 6″ greater than the rough opening width. Make a list of headers and their dimensions for use as a cutting list during construction.

Review the plans to identify any areas requiring special framing. Add this material to the estimate.

Framing lumber is usually sold by the lineal foot. To estimate total cost, multiply the number of lineal feet by the cost per lineal foot. Add to that the cost of the precut studs.

Another method would be to determine the total cost by multiplying the total number of board feet by the cost of one board foot of lumber.

SECTION 21.1

Check Your Knowledge

1. What stud spacing is commonly used in conventional construction?
2. Name another term sometimes used to refer to the bottom plate.
3. What is the purpose of a header?
4. What problems might occur if a carpenter did not install cripple studs beneath a window?

On the Job

Suppose you are constructing a small building that will be 18′ long and 13′ wide. Before you place the lumber order, you must estimate the number of studs needed for the exterior walls. You will be placing the studs 16″ OC. How many studs will you order?

SECTION 21.2

Wall Layout

The most experienced carpenter, also called the *lead carpenter*, is entrusted with reading the plans and translating them into a series of lines and symbols on the structure. These marks are called a *layout*. The layout shows other carpenters exactly where to build the walls. During this process the lead carpenter refers to the plans to "take off" dimensions. Wall layout involves two main steps:

- Marking the location of walls on the subfloor.
- Marking the location of studs, windows, and doors on the wall plates.

Layout is a very important job. Accuracy is more important than speed. The lead carpenter must be aware of special framing requirements for work to be done by other skilled workers, such as plumbers and electricians. The carpenter must have a thorough understanding of the building plans before layout begins.

Before the layout is started, the subfloor must be swept clean. This makes it easier to snap chalk lines on the subfloor. All objects that might be in the way, such as sawhorses, must be removed.

The layout can be done by one person. However, it is often done by a carpenter and an apprentice. The carpenter is responsible for measuring and marking. The apprentice observes and learns while holding one end of a chalk line or tape measure. A carpenter doing the layout alone might use a small nail or an awl to hold the end of the tape or chalk line.

from Another Angle

In some parts of the country, it is common to build houses on a concrete slab foundation instead of on concrete or block foundation walls. The wood-framed walls of such a house must be bolted directly to the foundation. The principles for laying out and assembling walls atop a slab foundation are essentially the same as those for walls atop a concrete or block foundation.

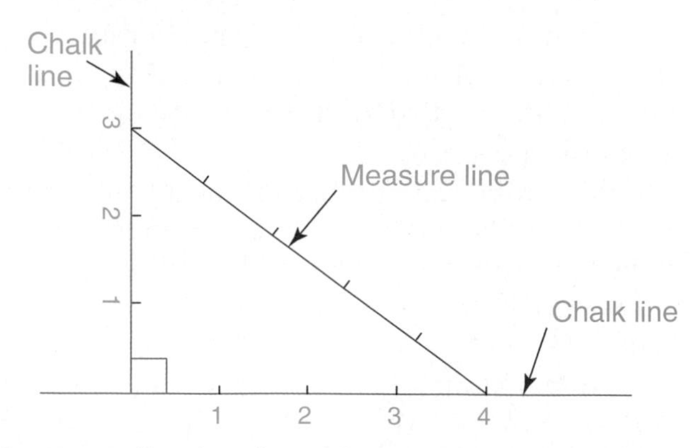

Fig. 21-3. If two legs of a triangle measure 3′ and 4′, they form a 90° angle if the diagonal between the ends of the legs measures exactly 5′.

LAYING OUT WALL LOCATIONS

The first step in wall framing is to lay out the location of two intersecting exterior walls. Carpenters usually start with two long walls that meet at a corner. Measurements taken from these two walls can then be used to locate other walls. Once the exterior walls have been located, layout proceeds to the interior walls.

Exterior Walls

The outside edge of the exterior wall plate should be flush with the outside edge of the subfloor. To begin layout, measure 3½″ in from the edge of the sheathing (or 5½″ for a 2x6 wall) and snap a chalk line parallel to the edge. Repeat the process for the intersecting wall.

Check the two chalk lines to make sure they form a 90° angle. Good carpenters never assume that the floor framing is perfectly square. To check for squareness, measure exactly 3′ along one line and 4′ along the other. If the diagonal measurement between these two points is exactly 5′, the corner is square. This is an example of the *3-4-5 rule.* Any multiples of these numbers that preserve the same ratio, such as 9, 12, and 15, will work in the equation. **Fig. 21-3.**

If the corner is not square, adjust one of the layout lines until it is. After the first two layout lines are correct, locate and mark the position of the remaining exterior walls.

Carpenter's Tip

You can use a construction calculator to determine whether intersecting lines are square. Using the calculator's roof-framing setting, enter one line length as the Rise. Enter the other line length as the Run. The answer will be the length of the diagonal line connecting the two end points.

from Another Angle

In mild or warm climates, houses are often built on concrete slabs. Wall layout is marked directly on the slab instead of on a subfloor. Layout on a slab may be slightly more difficult because of the rough plumbing drains and electrical conduits that protrude through the slab. The layout may have to be adjusted if pipes are slightly out of position.

Interior Walls

Consulting the plans, locate the position of interior walls by measuring from the chalk lines that indicate exterior walls. Pull a chalk line taut and snap it to indicate the exact location of one edge of each partition's bottom plate. To prevent confusion, mark an *X* on the subfloor to show the side of the line on which the plate will be located. This is where new carpenters often make a mistake. If the *X* is marked on the wrong side of the layout line, the wall will be built 3½″ from its correct position. Check partition walls during layout to ensure that they are square with intersecting walls.

It is important to identify special partitions as layout proceeds. Special partitions will contain plumbing drains or other features. They may have to be thicker than standard walls. This should be noted on the subfloor.

CUTTING THE PLATES

After the layout for the exterior and interior walls has been snapped out on the subfloor or the slab, cut the top and bottom plates to fit the layout. Some carpenters use a tape measure to measure the length of plates. Others cut plates using the subfloor layout marks as a guide.

Plates for the exterior walls are cut first. Before cutting, you must decide which exterior walls are by-walls and which are butt-walls. A *by-wall* runs from the outside edge of the subfloor at one end of the building to the outside edge of the subfloor at the opposite end. **Fig. 21-4.** By-walls are framed first and tipped into position. A *butt-wall* fits between the by-walls. Butt-walls are framed after by-walls. The double plate (rafter plate) will later tie butt-walls and by-walls together.

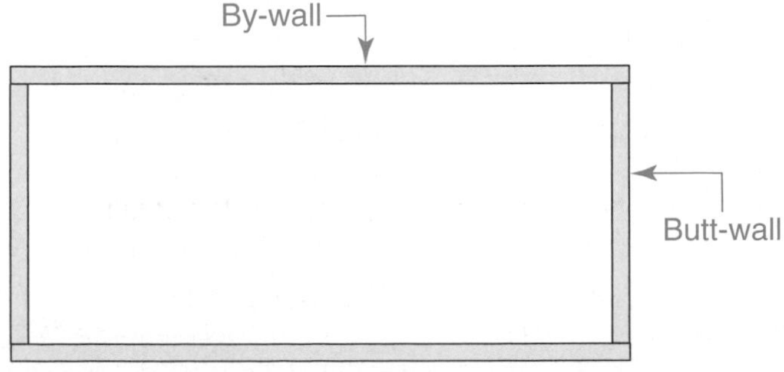

Fig. 21-4. To begin layout of the plates, decide which walls will be by-walls and which will be butt-walls. The top and bottom plates of a given wall will be the same length.

Cut the exterior plates to length, making sure that the ends of the plates for long walls break on 16″ marks. Then place the plates on the subfloor and align them with the chalk lines. **Fig. 21-5.** After you have cut the exterior wall plates, cut the interior wall plates. Place these plates on the X side of the chalk lines.

Fig. 21-5. After cutting the plates, place them on the subfloor.

from Another Angle

When walls will be installed on a slab foundation, the bottom plates should be made from preservative-treated lumber. In climates where termites pose an extreme risk, entire wall frames are sometimes made of preservative-treated lumber. For more information about protecting wood from insects, refer to Chapter 16, "Wood As a Building Material."

LAYING OUT THE PLATES

Plate layout identifies the location of each stud in a wall, as well as the location of doors and windows. These locations are marked on the edges or the sides of the plates using a carpenter's pencil. Start by tacking the top and bottom plates together with two or three 8d nails. This prevents them from shifting during layout. If the edges of the plates are marked, then the edges should face up. **Fig. 21-6.** If the sides of the plates are marked, then the sides should face up.

The procedure for laying out the plates depends partly on how walls, windows, and doors are dimensioned on the plans. If they are dimensioned in reference to centerlines, use the procedure described under "Openings." If another dimensioning system is used, adapt the technique in some way. For example, you might measure between the faces of the plates, instead of to the centerlines of the plates.

Openings

Refer to the building plans to find the distance from one corner of the building to the center of the first opening. Measure this distance and square a line across both plates at this point. Mark the line with a centerline symbol and an identification letter or number. This can be used for reference when cutting other parts for this opening.

Continue to lay out and mark openings on the remaining exterior wall plates. Use a letter or symbol to distinguish between door and window centerlines. When laying out plates on a slab foundation, pay attention to the location of foundation anchor bolts during the layout process. There should be an anchor bolt within 12″ of the end of each section of plate.

As they mark centerlines, many carpenters also "detail" the openings, marking the rough opening as well as the location of trimmer and king studs. The **rough opening (RO)** is the space into which a door or window will fit. **Fig. 21-7.** It allows room for the door or window and its frame. It also provides space for leveling and plumbing the frame.

Building plans include window and door *schedules,* charts that provide rough-opening sizes. Maximum spans for headers and estimates of material needed for studs are listed in the Ready Reference Appendix. Refer to the tables titled "Maximum Spans for Headers," "Exterior Wall Studs, Including Corner Bracing," and "Partition Studs, Including Top and Bottom Plates."

When the rough opening size is not provided, it can be obtained from the window manufacturer's catalog (see Fig. 28-19). The rough opening sizes vary somewhat among manufacturers.

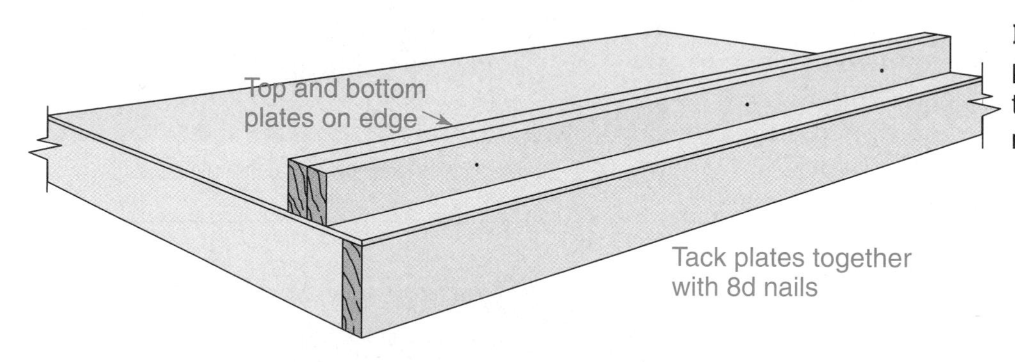

Fig. 21-6. Place top and bottom plates together on edge and tack them together. In this case, the layout will be marked on the edges.

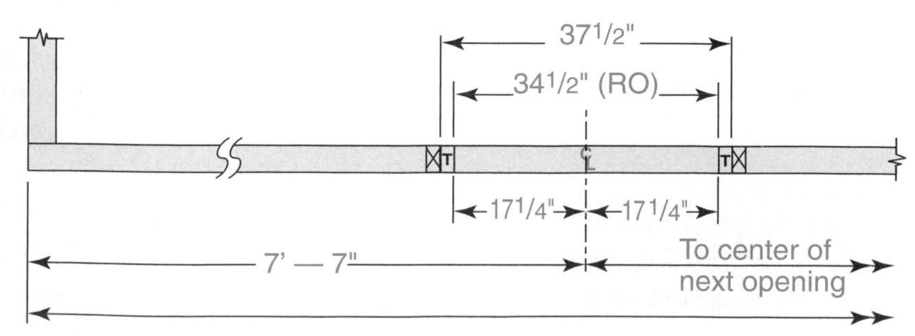

Fig. 21-7. Here, the centerline of a door opening has been marked 7′-7″ from the outside corner. The rough opening (RO) measures 34½″. One-half the RO (17¼″) is laid out on each side of the centerline. The thickness of the trimmer stud is laid out on each side of this. The header (37½″ long) will rest on top of the trimmer studs and between the king studs (marked with an *X*).

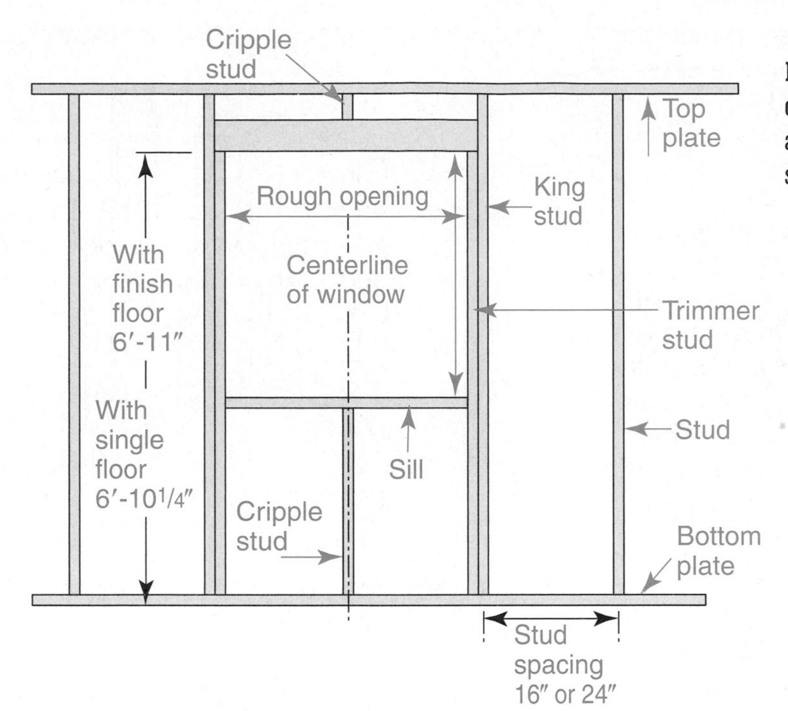

Fig. 21-8. Framing for a rough opening for a window. Some carpenters add cripple studs under the ends of the sill for increased strength.

Each catalog typically contains tables showing four width and height measurements for each window: masonry openings, rough openings, frame size, and glass size. Some may also list the sash size.

After you mark a window or door centerline on the plates, measure from each side of the centerline a distance equal to one-half the rough opening. **Fig. 21-8.** Square a line at this point. This line represents the inside face of the trimmer stud. Now mark the plate to locate the position of each king stud. The face of the king stud is 1½″ away from the inside face of the trimmer stud.

Wall Intersections

Mark the exterior plates to indicate the centerlines of all intersecting interior walls. Again, start from one corner of the building. Mark the interior wall centerlines with a *P.* **Fig. 21-9.**

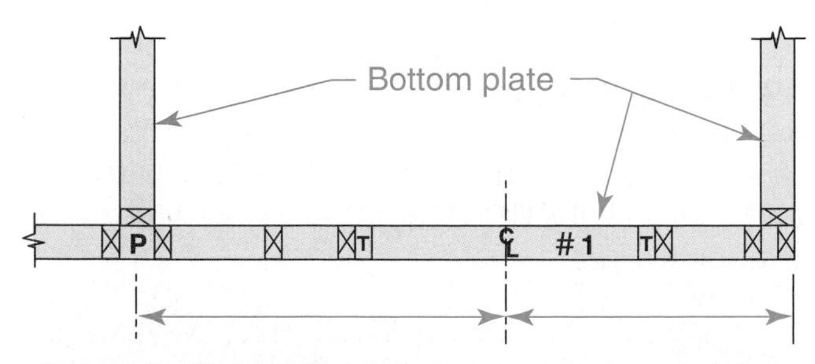

Fig. 21-9. The centerline of the interior wall has been marked with a *P.* Start the layout from a corner.

Exterior Corner Posts

A **corner post** is an assembly of full-length studs at the corner of a building. An *exterior corner post* is a corner post that forms an inside corner and an outside corner. The inside corner provides nailing surfaces for interior wall coverings. The outside corner provides nailing surfaces for sheathing. (Sheathing is discussed in Section 21.5.)

Corner posts are usually built from three or more studs to provide greater strength. They may be made in several ways. Two of the more common methods are shown in **Figs. 21-10** and

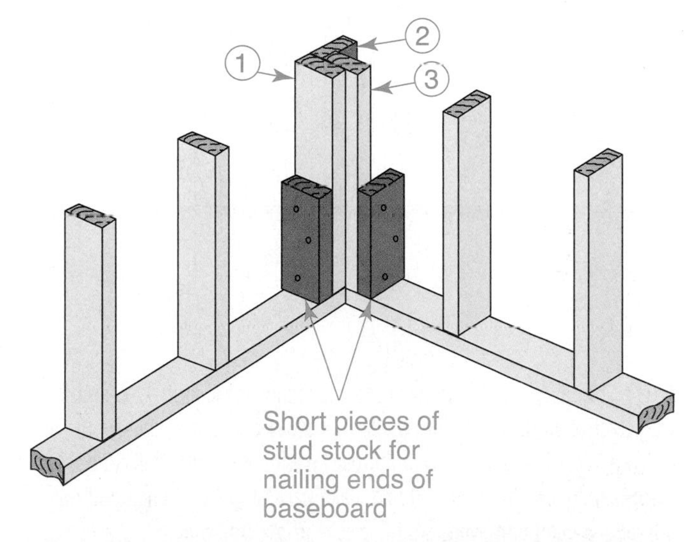

Fig. 21-10. The simplest type of corner post. The studs numbered 1, 2, and 3 are selected straight standard studs. This is an energy-efficient post because it allows insulation to reach the outer edge of the building.

21-11. Whatever method you choose, remember to mark the arrangement of studs on the exterior wall plates.

Partition Corner Posts

A partition corner post is needed where a partition meets another wall. A partition corner post is sometimes called a *channel*, a *partition-T*, or a *T-post.* In the type shown in **Fig. 21-12**, the regular spacing of the outside wall studs is interrupted by double studs where the partition ties in. The double studs are set 3″ apart. This interval allows the partition's end stud to lap the others just enough to permit nailing. It leaves most of the inner edges of the other studs clear to serve as nailing bases for inside wall covering. The variation in **Fig. 21-13** gives more nailing surface for the inside wall covering.

Many carpenters detail the arrangement of partition corner posts as they locate partition centerlines. This is sometimes done with the aid of a site-built jig made of two blocks of framing lumber nailed together.

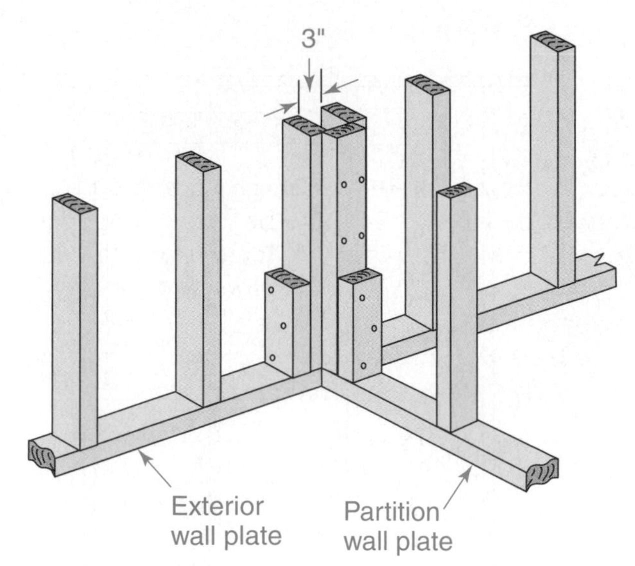

Fig. 21-12. Double-stud partition corner assembly.

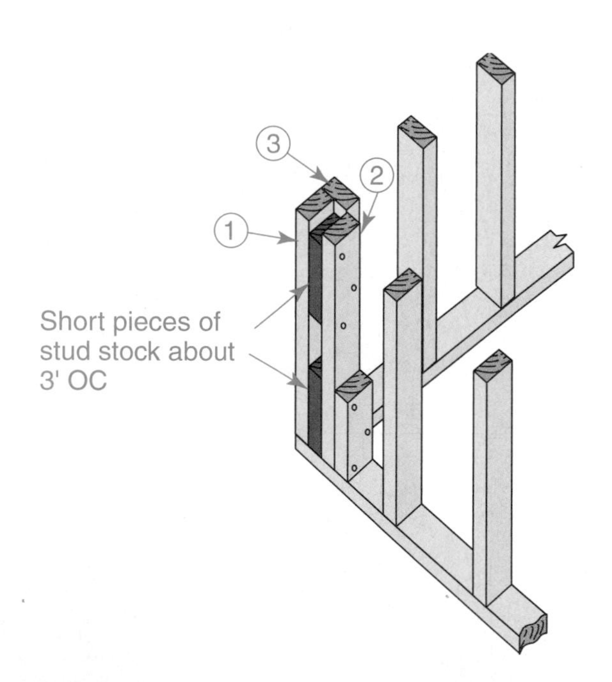

Fig. 21-11. In this corner post, the pieces numbered 1, 2, and 3 are selected straight standard studs. The short blocks are usually 10″ or 12″ long. Nail Studs 1 and 2 to the blocks with 10d nails. Nail Stud 3 to the assembly of Stud 1 and Stud 2. Take care to keep all ends and outside edges flush and even. Stud 3 is part of the butt-wall.

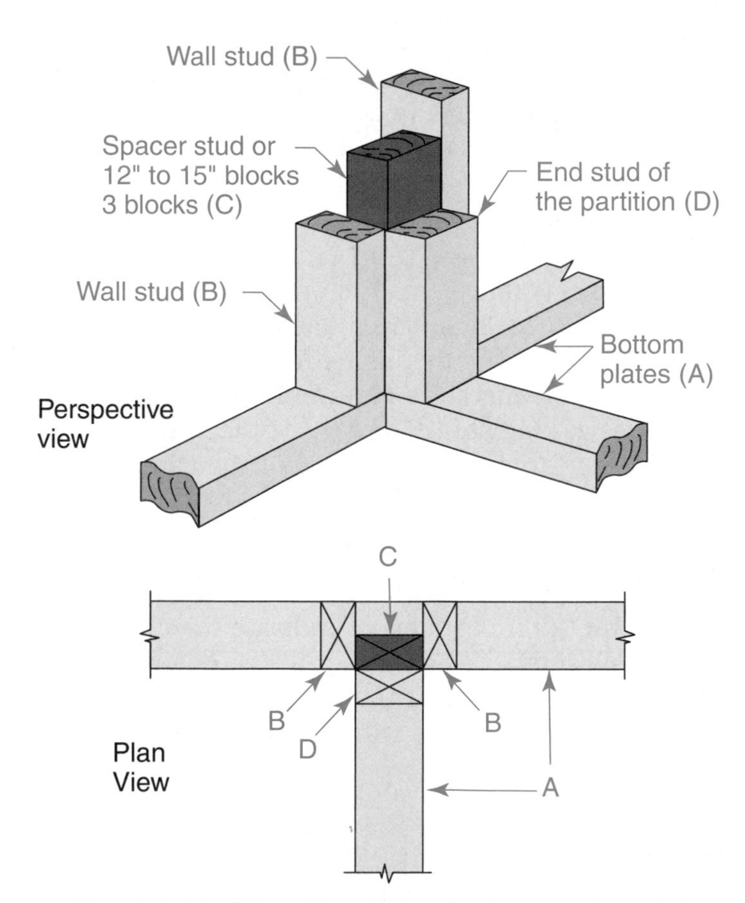

Fig. 21-13. This partition corner post is the one most commonly used. It allows more nailing space on the inside corners than the corner post shown in Fig. 21-12. Nail the two wall studs to the spacer with 10d nails. Nail the end stud of the partition to these studs and spacers when the partition is erected.

Stud Locations

Mark all the exterior plates and all the partition plates for the location of wall studs and cripple studs. There are various ways to do this. Tape measures marked with special symbols at intervals of 16″ and 24″ may be used. Some carpenters find it faster and easier to use a layout template. A *layout template*, or *layout stick*, is a metal bar with 1½″ wide "fingers" that correspond to the particular stud spacing being used. **Fig. 21-14.**

At this stage, you should be thinking ahead. Remember that sheathing and wallboard come in standard 4′ widths. There must always be a stud where two panels will meet in a vertical joint. The panels are fastened to the studs at these joints.

Begin the layout on the plates by measuring from the corner of a by-wall. Make a mark 15¼″ from the end of the plate. This will be the location to the edge of the first stud. Mark an *X* on the side of the line where the stud will be. That will ensure that the stud will not be placed on the wrong side of the layout line. From that point on, mark every 16″ to indicate the positions of all the studs on that wall. **Fig. 21-15.**

Double-check the layout by measuring along the plate to see that a stud will always be located where there will be a vertical joint between 4′ wide sheathing panels.

Before laying out the studs on a butt-wall, check the plans to determine the thickness of the wall sheathing. The spacing of the butt-wall studs must account for the thickness of the intersecting by-wall and its sheathing. This is needed because the butt-wall sheathing will overlap the by-wall and its sheathing. Measure 15¼″ in from the outside edge of the sheathing. **Fig. 21-16.** This ensures that the edges of the sheathing on the butt-wall will be properly supported at 4′ intervals.

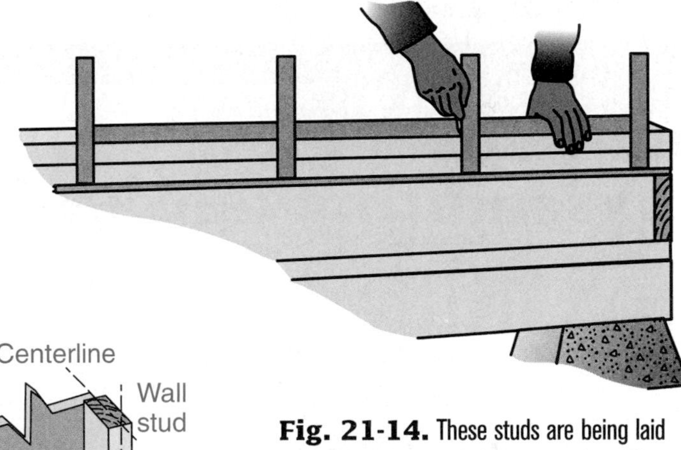

Fig. 21-14. These studs are being laid out with a homemade layout template. This template is 4′ long, the standard width of wall sheathing. The template has four fingers, 1½″ wide and 16″ OC, representing four stud markings. The fingers are attached to a piece of aluminum angle stock.

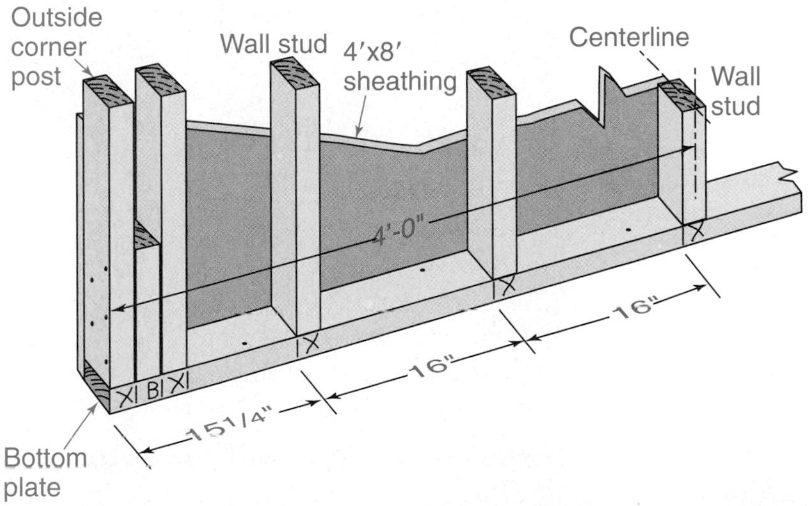

Fig. 21-15. Laying out a by-wall.

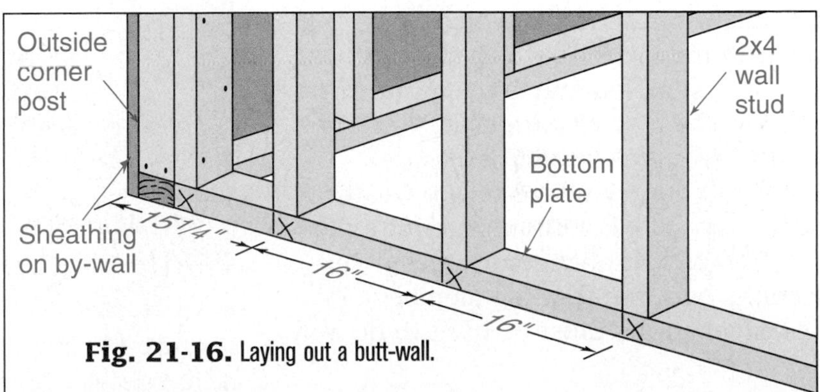

Fig. 21-16. Laying out a butt-wall.

Where the stud layout is interrupted by a window or door opening, lay out cripple studs above and below the opening. Maintain the 16″ or 24″ OC spacing that you used for the full-length studs. The position of each cripple stud is marked on the plates. The position of a cripple stud is usually marked with a *C*, rather than an *X*.

SECTION 21.2

Check Your Knowledge

1. What is the 3-4-5 rule used for?
2. What is meant by plate layout?
3. Explain the difference between a by-wall and a butt-wall.
4. What is a rough opening?

On the Job

The measurement of diagonals is used to check for squareness. With a partner, use a 25′ tape measure to measure the diagonals of at least four large rectangles to see whether they are square. You might, for example, measure the floor or walls of a room.

SECTION 21.3

Assembling and Erecting Walls

When plate layout is complete, the various parts of the wall framing can be cut to length, assembled on the subfloor, nailed together, and lifted into place. **Fig. 21-17.** Several procedures can be used to assemble walls. Some carpenters prefer to tip framed walls into place and sheathe them later. Other carpenters install sheathing, windows, and sometimes siding on exterior walls before lifting them into place. In either case, the walls should be squared. A common technique is to sheathe the walls on the floor deck but install windows and siding after the walls have been erected.

The method chosen depends in part on the length and weight of the walls. Whichever method is used, the order in which the exterior walls are to be assembled and erected must first be determined. The by-walls are usually erected first. The butt-walls are erected next.

In areas of the country where severe weather or earthquakes are a risk, buildings require the use of metal straps and anchors to strengthen the connections between framing members. In some cases, steel straps must be used to tie wall

Fig. 21-17. Tilting up a tall stud wall. In this case, the sheathing will be applied after the wall is in place.

framing to the roof framing. Be sure to follow local codes in this regard. (This topic is covered further in Chapter 17, "Engineered Lumber.")

CUTTING COMPONENTS TO LENGTH

In the most common method of assembling walls, the cripple studs, trimmer studs, and headers are precut to length on the job site. Then they are distributed to the area on the subfloor where they will be assembled. Cutting is usually done with a circular saw. However, a radial-arm saw or power miter saw ensures square cuts. Such a saw is often easier to use when making repetitive cuts to a standard length.

Power Saw Safety

In using any power saw, be sure to follow all safety practices. Wear approved eye protection. Be sure all guards are in place.

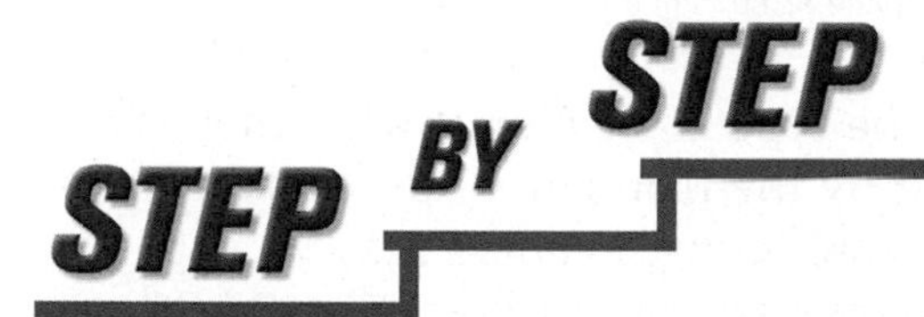

Making a Story Pole

The length of each wall component can be determined from the plans. Because the height of wall openings is standardized, carpenters often lay out a story pole. A *story pole* is a piece of framing lumber that represents the wall from the top of the subfloor to the bottom of a ceiling joist. It includes information about the location and size of the window headers, sills, and door headers. It also includes the heights of various openings above the subfloor. If there are several different heights to mark off above the subfloor, you may need to make additional story poles. These should be labeled for the various rooms or areas.

To make a story pole:

Step 1 Select a straight length of framing lumber.

Step 2 Nail a 2x4 block to the bottom of the stud. This block represents the bottom plate of a wall.

Step 3 Examine the plans for standard window- and door-opening dimensions.

Step 4 Transfer these dimensions to the pattern.

You can now use the story pole as a reference for cutting cripple studs and trimmer studs.

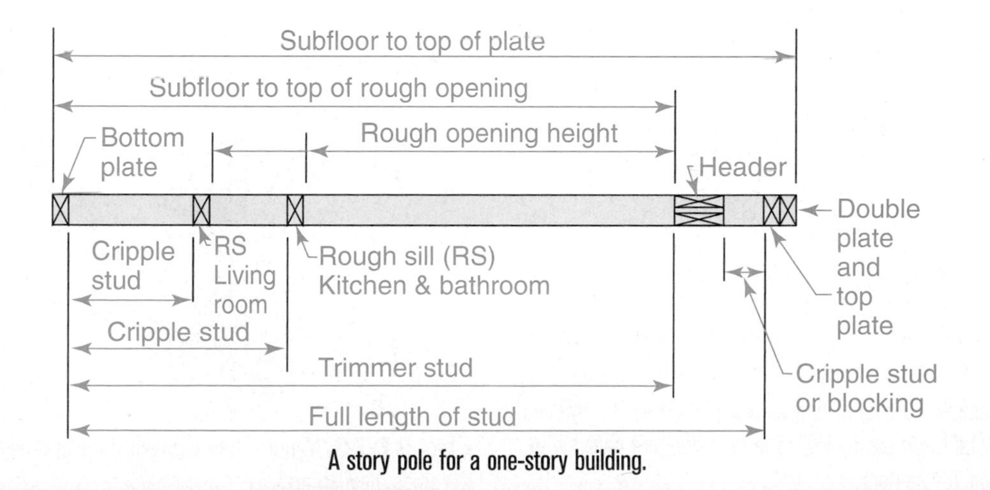

A story pole for a one-story building.

Trimmer Studs and Cripple Studs

Trimmer studs should be cut to fit snugly under the header so they will support it properly. If a header settles, cracks in the plaster or drywall may develop and doors and windows may fit improperly. The trimmer studs also reinforce the door and window openings.

Determine the lengths of the cripple studs by referring to the story pole. To determine how many are required, count the cripple-stud layout marks on the wall plates. (Step-by-step procedures for making a story pole are on page 405.)

Headers

The depth of a header (lintel) is determined by the length of the opening it must span. Longer openings require stronger, deeper headers. This information will be found in the building plans or local code requirements. Make sure that the header is long enough to bear on all of the trimmer studs.

Header lengths are obtained by measuring the top plate between layout marks for the king studs. In the case of the door opening shown in Fig. 21-7, the header length would be 37½″. Window and door headers are sometimes cut from solid pieces of 4x6 or larger stock. Commonly, however, the header is built up from 2x6 or wider framing stock. Two 2x members are only 3″ thick. A ½″ plywood spacer must be sandwiched between the two pieces to give the header the full 3½″ thickness of the wall.

Various other types of headers can be assembled. **Figs. 21-18** and **21-19.** Many builders today use engineered lumber, such as microlam LVL, as header material. This product is generally stronger and saves time because it does not need to be assembled.

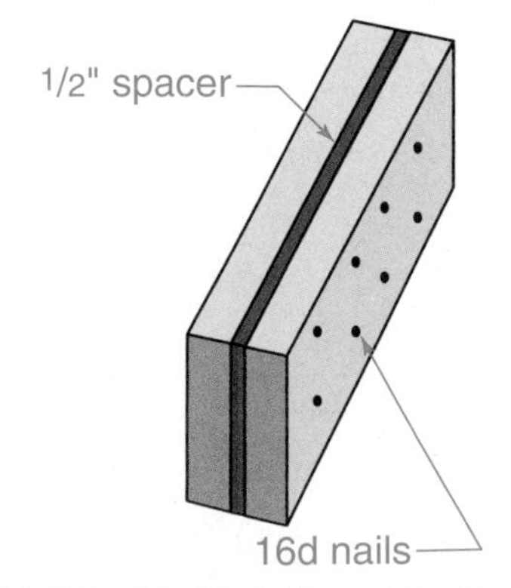

Fig. 21-18. A header built up of two 2x members with ½″ plywood spacer to bring the total thickness to 3½″. The members are nailed with 16d nails staggered on 16″ centers.

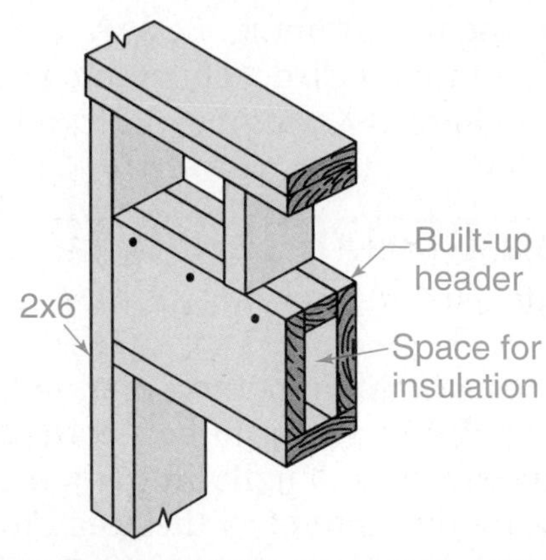

Fig. 21-19. This type of header is sometimes used because it allows insulation above openings. The insulation must be installed before the header is nailed into place.

Whatever the type of header, it will normally be supported by the trimmer studs. In some cases, as in remodeling, headers may be supported by metal framing brackets. **Fig. 21-20.** In states where hurricanes are a threat, it is required that metal straps be used to connect headers/plates and studs.

Number the openings (such as windows, doors, and fireplaces) for identification. Then make a cutting schedule for all headers. One person can cut these to length as another assembles them. Use 16d nails, two near each end. Stagger the others 16″ apart along the length of the header. Do not forget to use ½″ spacers between the 2x members. Place assembled headers at their locations on the subfloor in readiness for the assembly of the wall sections.

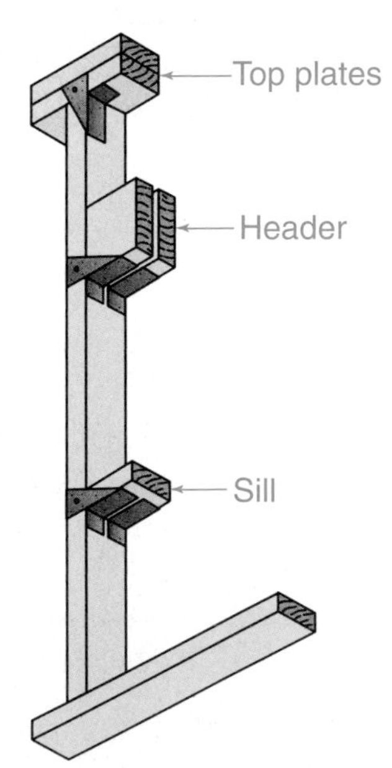

Fig. 21-20. Window framing with framing brackets used to support the studs, header, and sill.

Corner Posts

Because corner posts are made from precut studs, cutting is not required. Corner posts are nailed together with 10d and 16d nails. They are then taken to the place on the subfloor where they will be used for assembly of the wall sections. The short pieces of 2x4s at the base of the corner posts in Figs. 21-10 and 21-11 are installed after the walls have been raised. They provide places for nailing the ends of the baseboard. In areas where energy efficiency is especially important, other corner-post assemblies are used.

ASSEMBLING AND ERECTING EXTERIOR WALLS

Each wall section is assembled on the subfloor. Begin the assembly by separating the plates that were tacked together for layout. Lay the top plate on edge on the subfloor about 8′ from the bottom plate. Do not flip the top plate end-for-end as you move it. If the plate is flipped, the layout marks will not match those on the bottom plate. This is a common mistake.

Lay a stud at each mark. Place the header so that the rough sill, cripple studs, and trimmer studs are in position. Place the preassembled exterior corners and partition corners at the marked locations.

You can now nail the components together. The order of assembly depends on the preference of the carpenter. The following is one approach.

Beginning at one end of the top plate, drive two 16d nails through the plate into each stud at the correct location. Secure the bottom plate in the same way. Then nail all the remaining components into place as described below and shown in **Figs. 21-21** and **21-22**. Be careful to keep the edges of the framing members flush with each other. This is essential if sheathing is to fit correctly.

SAFETY FIRST

Using Power Nailers and Staplers

Using power fastening tools saves time. These tools also ensure that each fastener is applied with the same amount of force. This helps maintain quality. Such tools, however, present safety hazards if used improperly. Be sure to follow all safety rules. Wear proper personal protective equipment, including eye protection. Check the manufacturer's manual for any safety rules that may apply to the specific tool you are using.

Fig. 21-21 Framing a Window Opening

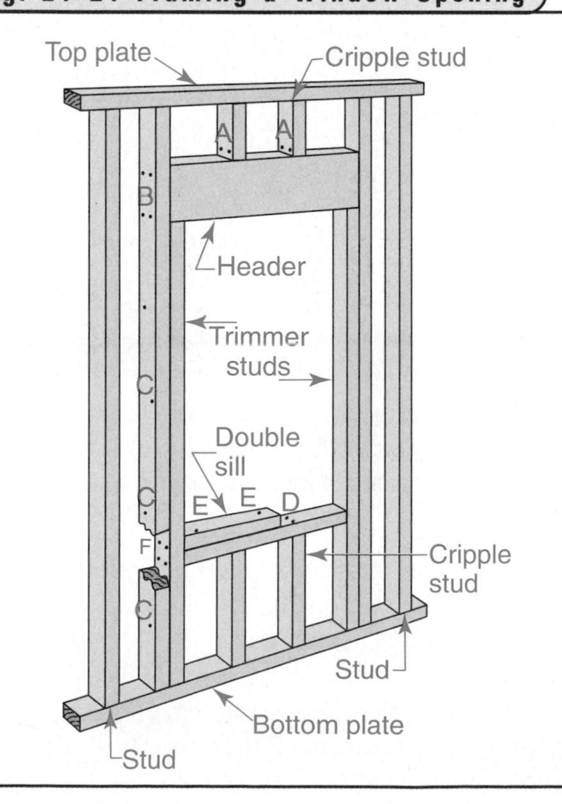

- The cripple studs at *A* are toenailed with four 8d nails, two on each side.
- The full stud is nailed to the header at *B* with four 16d nails and to the trimmer at *C* with 10d nails 16″ OC.
- The full studs are toenailed to the bottom plate or nailed through the bottom plate.
- The lower part of the double sill is nailed with two 10d nails into the ends of the cripples at *D*.
- The upper part of the sill *(E)* is nailed to the lower with 10d nails 8″ OC and staggered.
- The ends of the sills are nailed through the trimmer studs with two 16d nails at each end *(F)*.

Fig. 21-22 Framing a Door Opening

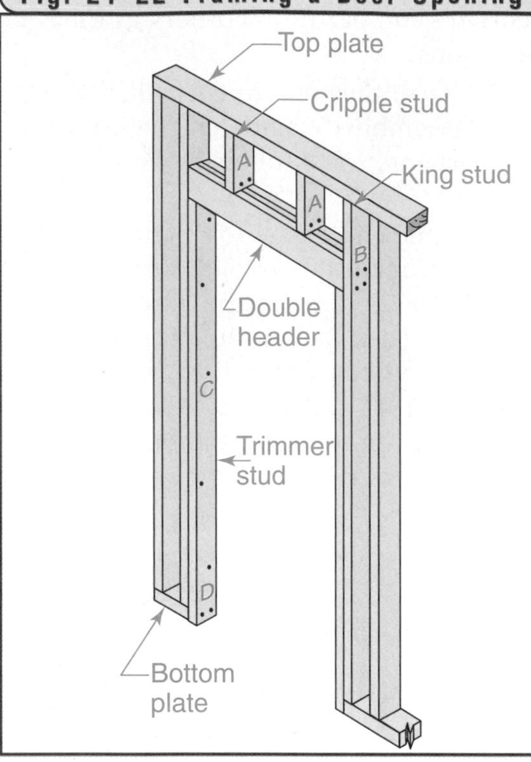

- The cripple studs *(A)* are toenailed with four 8d nails, two on each side.
- The full studs *(B)* are nailed to the header with four 16d nails on each side and toenailed to the bottom plate with two 8d nails. The full stud *(B)* could be nailed from the bottom up through the plate, with two 16d nails, if the plate is attached before the wall is erected.
- The trimmer *(C)* is nailed with 16d nails staggered 16″ OC.
- Two 10d nails are driven into the end of the bottom plate at *D*.

To keep the edges of studs and plates perfectly aligned during nailing, carpenters step on the intersection as they nail through the plate. This also keeps the wall from sliding if it is being hand nailed. This problem is eliminated with pneumatic nailing.

Trimmer studs fit under a window or door header. They are nailed to a king stud with 16d nails, spaced 16″ apart and staggered. Notice that the trimmer stud for a door may extend from the header to the bottom plate. This portion of the bottom plate will be cut out after the wall is erected.

Nail through the king studs and into the header with 16d nails. Once the header is secure, insert the cripple studs above it. Nail their tops as if they were studs. Toenail the bottom end of each cripple to the header with two 8d nails on each side.

When you have fully assembled the wall on the subfloor, square it. Do this by running a tape measure across diagonally opposite corners. If the diagonal measurements between all corners are the same, the wall is square. If the wall is not square, push the plates in opposite directions until it is.

Fig. 21-23. Checking a wall for square must be done before it is sheathed. This may occur before or after it is tipped up. Measure diagonally across the corners. If both measurements are equal, the wall is square.

As mentioned earlier, some carpenters apply sheathing at this point. Others apply it after the wall has been erected. **Fig. 21-23.**

When securing the studs at the ends of a wall, slightly blunt each nail by tapping its point with a hammer. The nail will then be less likely to split the plate. You can use this technique whenever you nail close to the end of a board.

Temporary Bracing

Temporary bracing is bracing that has the following two purposes:

- It prevents the walls from tipping as they are being erected.
- It holds them in position after they have been plumbed and straightened.

Temporary bracing may consist of 2x4 or 2x6 members nailed to one face of a stud and to a 2x4 block nailed to the subfloor. **Fig. 21-24.** The wall braces may also be nailed to wood stakes driven into the ground outside the perimeter of the foundation.

Take care not to let the ends of the temporary braces project above the top plate. Otherwise, the braces could interfere with ceiling and roof framing and would have to be removed. This would disturb the plumbed and straightened walls.

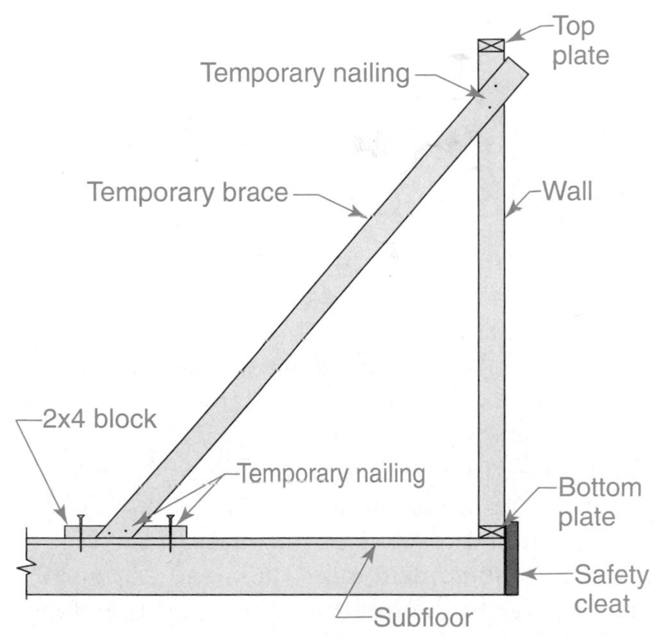

Fig. 21-24. A raised wall. The temporary brace shown here pivoted on the nail that attached it to the stud as the wall was erected. The block nailed on the subfloor holds it in place. A safety cleat keeps the wall from slipping.

Use enough nails to brace the wall securely, but do not drive the nails in all the way. Each nail head should still project enough to allow easy withdrawal. Leave the temporary bracing in place until the ceiling and the roof framing have been completed and sheathing has been applied to the outside walls.

Erecting the Wall

As a wall is lifted into position, align the bottom plate with the chalk lines made earlier. This is a job for several carpenters. One carpenter is needed at each end of the wall. One or more may be needed in between, depending on the length of the wall. Have temporary bracing ready for use as soon as the wall is partially upright. As an extra measure of safety, nail 2x4 cleats to the outside of the rim joist to prevent an exterior wall from slipping off the subfloor as it is lifted. (A *rim joist* is a joist at the edge of the floor system.) In some cases, hand-cranked lifts are used to tilt a heavy wall into position.

When the wall is upright, fasten the bottom plate to the floor framing with 16d nails spaced 16″ apart and staggered when practical. You can now plumb and brace the wall.

Plumbing the Wall

To *plumb* a wall means to make sure it is perpendicular to the subfloor. Either a carpenter's level or a plumb bob may be used to plumb wall sections.

As noted earlier, framed exterior walls may be raised into position with or without sheathing already applied. In either case, the walls must be plumbed and straightened. This is done after all the framed walls are in position and tem porarily braced.

Raising Walls

A wall that is being raised must be braced quickly to lessen the chance that it will topple. Carpenters often secure the tops of the braces to the studs before erecting the wall. A single nail at this point allows the brace to swing into position as the wall is being raised.

Using a Plumb Bob. To plumb a corner post with a plumb bob, attach the plumb line (string) securely to the top of the post. **Fig. 21-25.** Make sure that the line is long enough to allow the plumb bob to hang near the bottom of the post. Use two blocks of wood identical in thickness as gauge blocks. Tack one block near the top of the post between the plumb line and the post. Insert the second block between the plumb line and the bottom of the post. If the entire face of the second block makes contact with the line, the post is plumb.

Using a Carpenter's Level. To plumb a corner with a carpenter's level, do not place the level directly against a stud. The face or edge of the stud may be irregular in shape. Instead, place an 8′ level against the top and bottom plates. To increase accuracy when plumbing the corner, hold the level so that you can look straight in at the bubble. If a long level is not available, place a shorter level against a straightedge. **Fig. 21-26.** While one carpenter reads the level, another should be ready to move the braces as needed and secure them as soon as the correct position is found.

Plumb and brace outside corners both inside and outside and from side to side. After you have plumbed and braced all exterior walls, plumb and brace the intersecting interior walls. This will also plumb the exterior wall at the point of intersection.

Straightening Walls

To straighten walls, fasten a string line to the outside top of one of the corner posts. Stretch the line to the outside top of the corner post at the opposite end of the building. Fasten the line to this post in the same manner as for the first post. Place a ¾″ thick wood block under each end of the line to give clearance. **Fig. 21-27.**

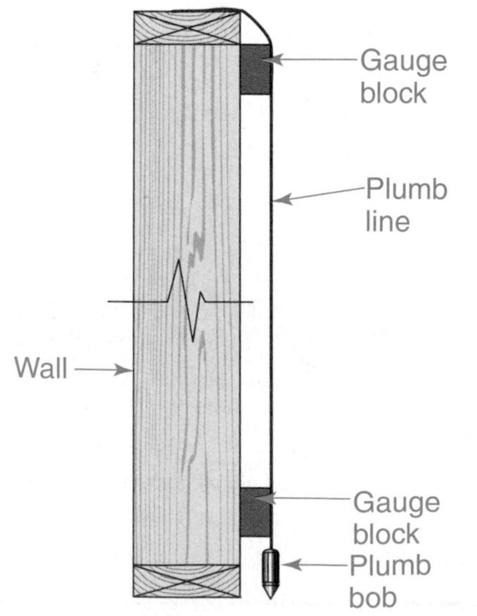

Fig. 21-25. Plumbing a wall using a plumb line and plumb bob.

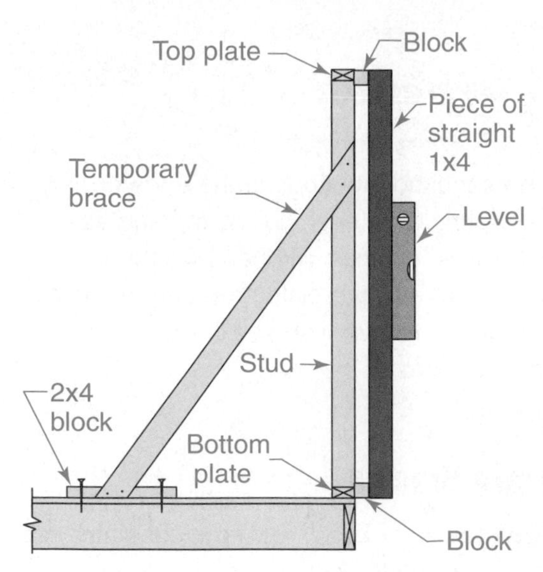

Fig. 21-26. The straightedge can simply be a piece of 1x4 stock. Make sure the edge on which the level is placed is parallel to a line drawn between the two blocks nailed on the ends.

Place additional temporary braces at intervals close enough to hold the wall straight. When the wall is far enough away from the line to permit a ¾″ block to slide between the line and the plate, nail the braces. This straightening procedure is sometimes called *lining the walls.* It is carried out for the entire perimeter of the building. Later, you should also straighten any long partitions in the same manner.

ASSEMBLING AND ERECTING INTERIOR WALLS

After all the exterior walls are set up, plumbed, and braced and the bottom plate securely nailed, assemble and erect the interior walls. Interior walls are easier to assemble than exterior walls because they usually do not require framing for windows. They do, however, require framing for doors. Otherwise, they are assembled in the same manner as exterior walls. To determine the sizes of the various parts (such as headers, trimmer studs, and cripple studs), refer to the building plans and the story pole.

Careful planning of the order in which the interior walls are assembled and erected is very important. See the Step-by-Step procedure on page 411.

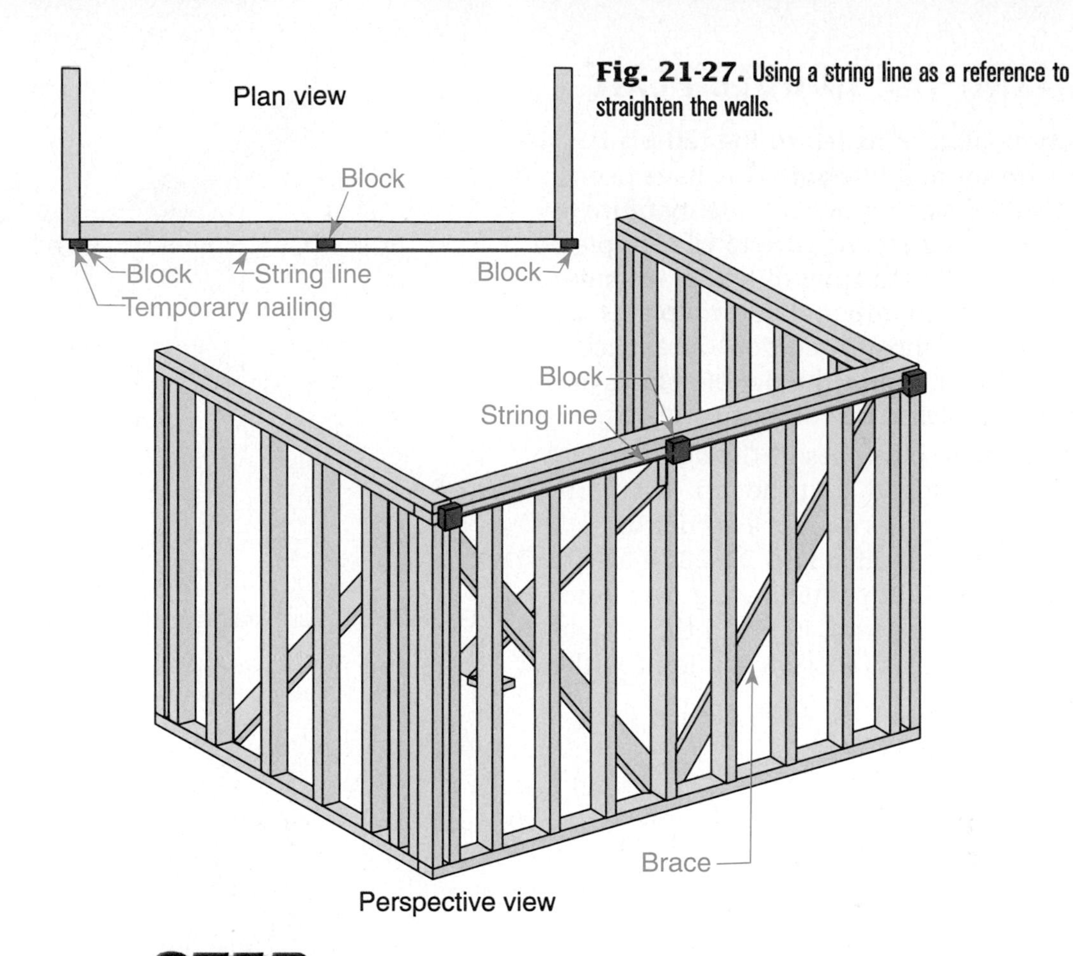

Fig. 21-27. Using a string line as a reference to straighten the walls.

STEP BY STEP

Assembly and Erection of Interior Walls

Step 1 Raise, fasten, and temporarily brace the longest center partition (1). Work should then proceed from one end of the building to the other and from the center wall out to the exterior walls. Complete operations in one area before moving to the next area.

Step 2 Note that the partitions are numbered 1 through 16. Partition 1, though interrupted by openings, is considered to be one piece. Note that Partition 2 helps support the center partition and connects it to the previously plumbed exterior wall. Partition 4 is at a right angle to Partition 3.

Step 3 Continue working in this pattern to the back of the building. This sequence is better than erecting two parallel partitions (such as 2 and 4) and then working in a confined area to erect the connecting partition (3).

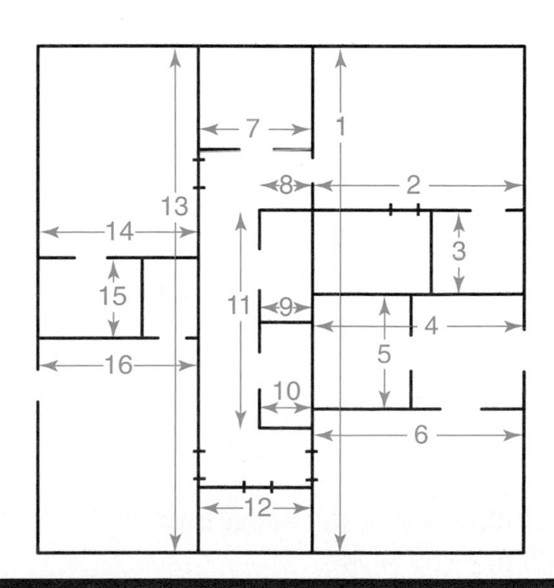

INSTALLING THE DOUBLE PLATE

The double plate is nailed to the top plate after the exterior and interior walls have been erected. Use the same type and quality of material as for the top plate. Be sure to cut the pieces accurately to length. Cutting to length is sometimes done when the top and bottom plates are cut. However, it is most often done after the walls are erected because the double plates are a different length than the other two plates.

One of the main purposes of the double plate is to tie the walls together at the top. Therefore, it laps over the joint formed at a corner of intersecting exterior walls. **Fig. 21-28.** It also laps the joint formed by intersecting partitions. **Fig. 21-29.** On a long wall, joints in the double plate should be at least 4′ from any joint in the top plate.

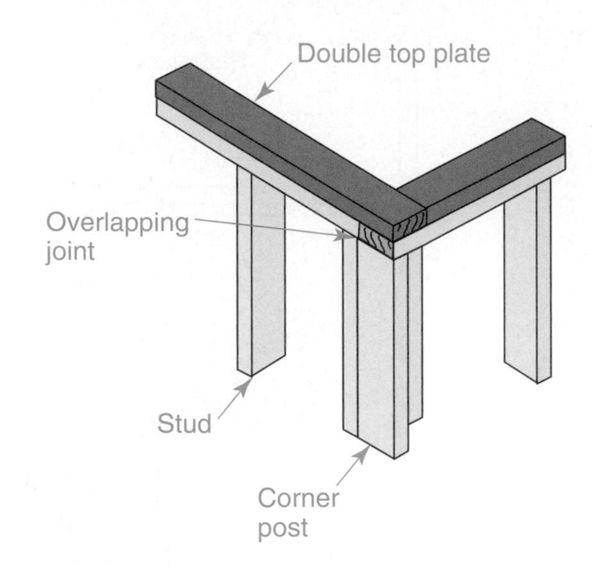

Fig. 21-28. Double plates are joined by a lap joint.

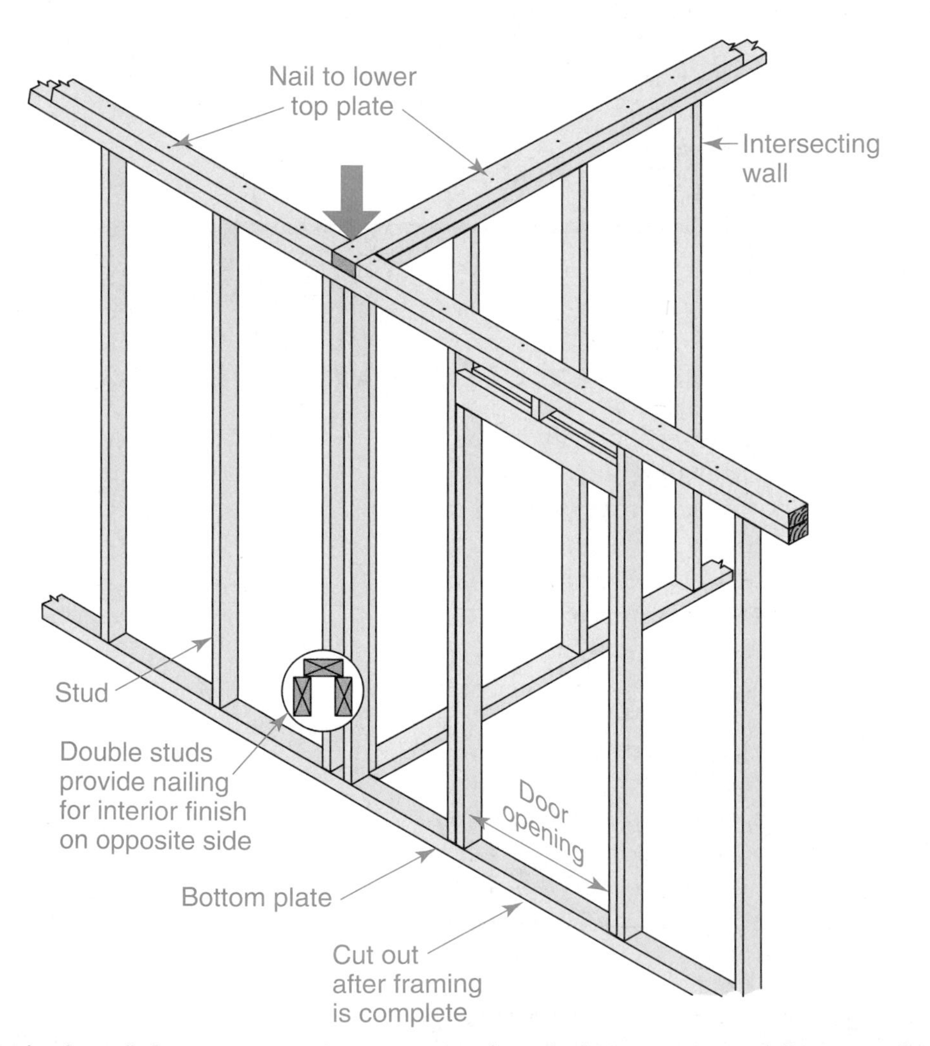

Fig. 21-29. The double plate is usually fastened in place after the walls have been plumbed and straightened. Ten-penny nails are used to attach the double plate to the top plate.

Fasten the double plate with 10d nails spaced 16″ OC. Nail end laps between adjoining plates with two 16d nails on each lap. (See arrow, Fig. 21-29.)

SECTION 21.3
Check Your Knowledge

1. What is the purpose of a story pole?
2. What may happen if a trimmer stud does not properly support a header?
3. What determines the depth of a header?
4. What size nail is used to nail through the top and bottom plates and into the studs? How many nails are used?

On the Job

Suppose that a 2′ carpenter's level is accurate enough to measure only within 1⁄16″ of true level over 2′. If it is used to plumb an 8′ wall, how much might the top of the wall vary from true plumb?

SECTION 21.4
Special Framing

Special framing is needed:

- For unusual architectural features.
- To provide openings for plumbing vents and fixtures.
- To provide openings for heating ducts.
- To add support for heavy items.
- To add blocking that supports the edges of interior wall coverings.
- To provide extra strength to houses built in earthquake or hurricane zones.
- In some cases, for fire safety.

Special framing adds strength and quality to the construction. Its requirements are not always noted on the building plans. However, the carpenter should be familiar with them.

A building must be enclosed quickly to protect it from the weather. However, special framing can be time consuming. Therefore, it may not always be installed as the walls are being framed and erected. Instead, a builder may concentrate on sheathing the walls first. The builder may then install special framing as fill-in work during slack periods in later construction stages.

SPECIAL WALLS

Most walls can be framed using standard precut studs, along with the other components noted earlier. In some situations, however, wall framing must be handled differently.

Gable Walls

Walls that angle upward to meet the underside of the roof framing are called *gable walls* or *rake walls*. The spacing of the studs is the same as for surrounding walls, but precut studs cannot be used. Instead, each stud in the gable wall must be cut to a specific length. Its top end must be cut at an angle that matches the roof pitch (slope). The bottom plate of a gable wall is similar to that in a standard wall. The top plate slopes to follow the roof angle.

Gable walls are sometimes built and erected along with the rest of the wall framing. In other cases, the roof framing is installed first and the gable-wall framing is added afterwards. If the roof framing consists of trusses, the truss manufacturer supplies the gable-wall framing.

The cuts involved in building a gable wall are directly related to the slope of the roof. For this reason, gable-wall construction is discussed in Chapter 23, "Hip, Valley, and Jack Rafters."

Bay Windows

Bay windows have special framing requirements. **Fig. 21-30.** The floor framing is provided during an earlier stage. The projecting walls of the bay may be framed and erected as if they were standard walls. Sometimes, however, an angled bay may call for framing that has been beveled with a circular saw or table saw. Note also that a bay window may require two headers. One header is over the opening in the main wall and one is over the window itself.

Shear Walls

A *shear wall* has been engineered to withstand unusual stresses. Shear walls are often used in areas where earthquakes and severe storms are common. Such a wall may also be a feature of houses with unusual designs. Constructed much more carefully than standard walls, shear walls require extra nailing.

They may require hold-downs and/or special anchor bolts. Wider studs may be needed to accommodate close nailing patterns. Shear walls may also require the use of construction adhesives and/or sheathing on both sides of the wall. The requirements for a shear wall are specified by an architect or engineer and detailed on the plans. The carpenter must not deviate from those specifications.

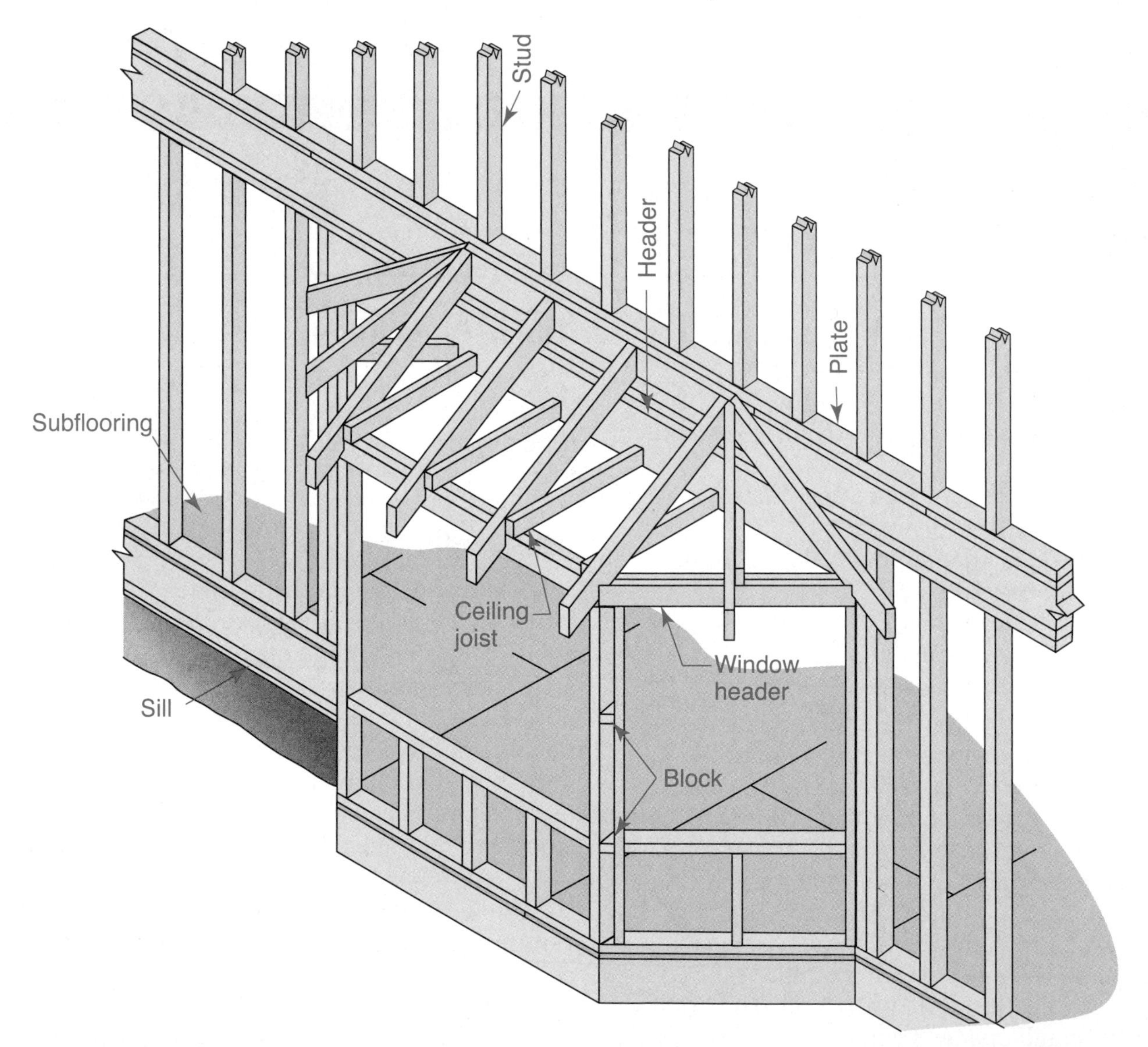

Fig. 21-30. Framing a bay window. The ceiling joists in the framing of this bay are set on top of the window headers. The top of a bay window should be kept in line with the other windows and doors in the room. Therefore, the wall header will not be a standard header height. It will have to be raised so that its bottom is in line with the bottom of the bay ceiling joists.

Fig. 21-31. A piece of material somewhat larger than a 2x4 is used for a bottom plate to provide room for a 4″ soil stack. The 2x4 studs are then installed flatwise *(A)*, or 2x6 studs are installed in the normal way *(B)*.

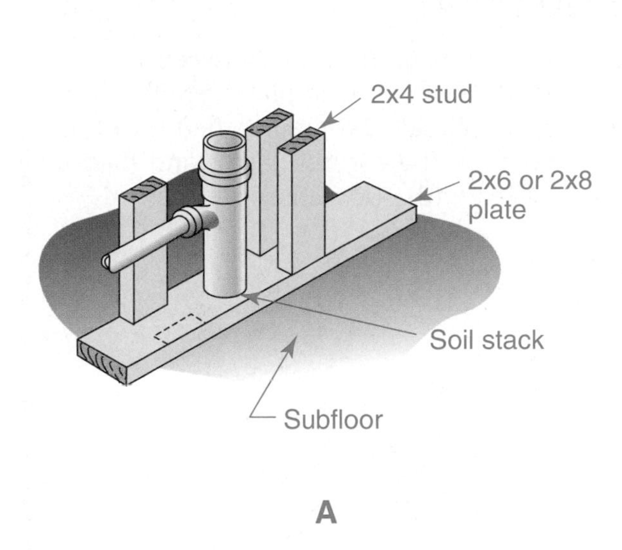

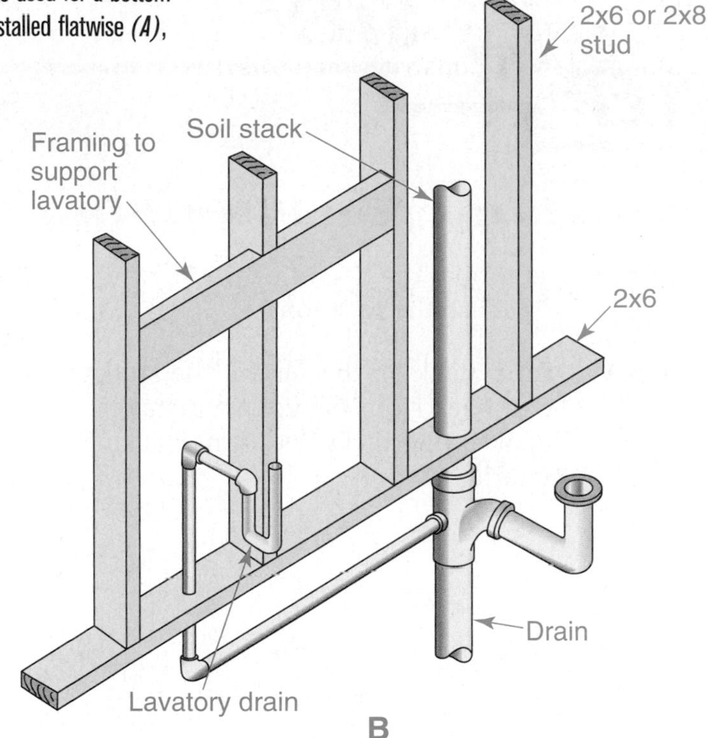

Radius Walls

Some modern architectural designs include curved walls, called *radius walls*. The dimensions of the curve are detailed on the plans. The studs may be the same dimensions as in surrounding walls. However, the curved plates are cut from plywood instead of lumber. The ends of blocking must be cut to an angle. The ability to build such unusual walls is the mark of an experienced framing carpenter.

PLUMBING NEEDS

Plumbing vents are usually installed in a 2x6 wall, with 2x6 studs or 2x4 studs flatwise at each side. **Fig. 21-31.** This provides the needed wall thickness for the bell (large end) of a 4″ cast-iron soil pipe, which is larger than the thickness of a 2x4 stud wall.

In some cases, builders stagger wall studs in a way that reduces sound transmission through the wall. Fiberglass batt insulation is then added to form a continuous, unbroken layer. This type of construction is sometimes called a *sound wall*. It helps to muffle the sound of water rushing through drain pipes. **Fig. 21-32.**

Some plumbing fixtures may require extra backing prior to installation. This framing is sometimes noted on the plans and installed by the carpenter. (See the Step-by-Step procedure on page 416.) The framing may also be installed by the plumber. For example, where a bathtub is enclosed by walls, support for its edges must be provided. (See Fig. 20-32.) Blocking must also be provided for the shower-arm fitting and for any grab rails that will be installed in the tub area.

Sometimes a hatch will be built on the back of the shower wall. This provides access to the tub drain and overflow riser. Suitable blocking should be installed to support the edges of the hatch. Wall-mounted sinks and toilets require special blocking to ensure a secure attachment to the wall.

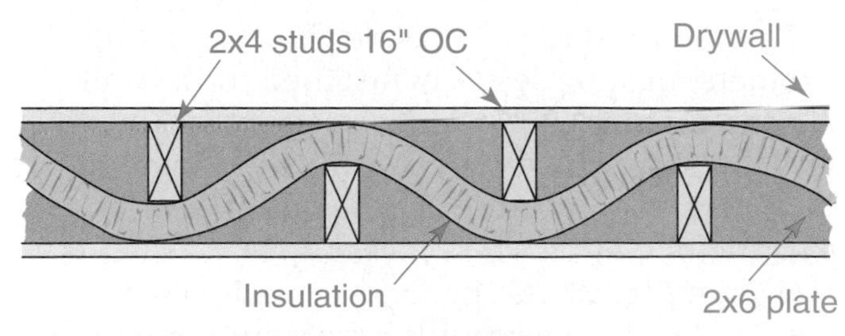

Fig. 21-32. Construction of a sound wall.

STEP BY STEP

Blocking for Plumbing Fixtures

Step 1 Determine the height of the fixture and mark the location.

Step 2 Nail a block on the side of the stud. Set it back from the edge a distance equal to the thickness of the backing material.

Step 3 Cut the backing to fit between the studs and nail it in place. The backing material can also be notched into the studs at the correct height and face-nailed with 10d nails.

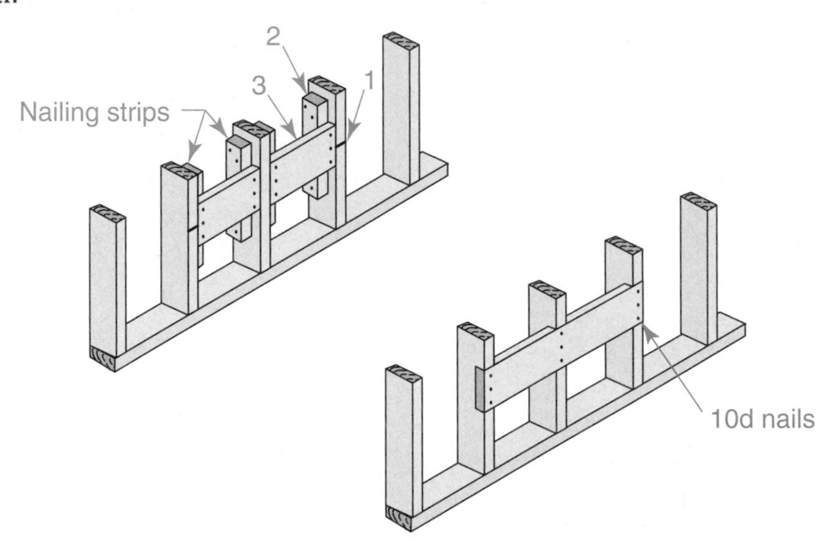

CABINETS AND UTILITY BOXES

Special support and blocking must be provided for inset cabinets that are to fit between studs and be flush with the wall covering. These cabinets are usually designed to be fastened directly to faces of the studs or to blocking. Backing for nailing the wall covering must be provided at the top and bottom of the cabinets.

Bathroom vanities, kitchen cabinets, and other cabinets must be securely fastened to the wall. A good framing job includes special blocking for this purpose. The location of the blocking can be determined by studying the building plans. One method of blocking for an upper cabinet is shown in **Fig. 21-33**. In some cases it is advisable to install an extra full-length stud or even a 2x6 flat in the wall. This is especially true in kitchens where upper and lower cabinets will be installed.

TRIM BLOCKING

The installation of baseboard, chair rail, crown, and other moldings is made easier if blocking is provided for nailing at the ends. Without it, the nails must be driven very near the ends of the molding and usually at a slight angle to reach the corner posts. This often results in splitting the ends of the molding. Blocking such as that shown in Fig. 21-10 on p. 401 will minimize this problem. These small blocks are made from scrap framing stock that would otherwise be discarded. Trim carpenters appreciate this detail but do not often encounter it. Trim backing is often left out at the framing stage unless specifically noted on the plans.

Fig. 21-33 Blocking for a Hanging Cabinet

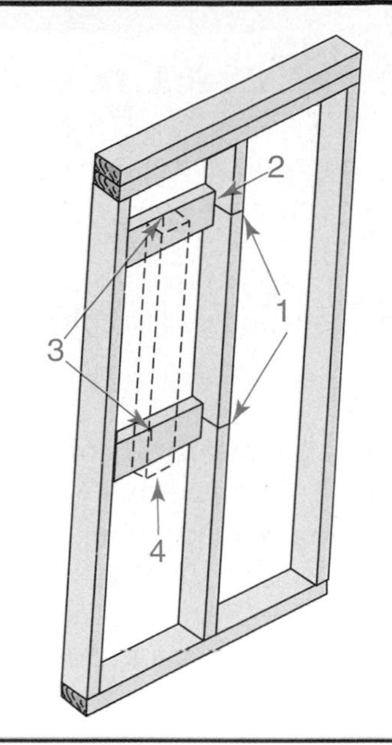

- The top and bottom of the cabinets are marked on the studs (1).
- Blocks for attaching the cabinet backing are fastened between the studs (2). These blocks must be back from the edge of the studs a distance equal to the thickness of the cabinet backing.
- The position of the cabinet backing is marked on the blocks (3).
- The cabinet backing is fastened to the blocks on the location marks (4).

HEATING DUCTS

Heating ducts require openings in the ceiling, floor, or wall. **Fig. 21-34.** Backing must therefore be provided for fastening the covering material. An opening in the wall larger than the distance between the studs requires cutting off one or more studs. It also requires a header to support the shortened stud, which serves as a nailing surface for the wall covering.

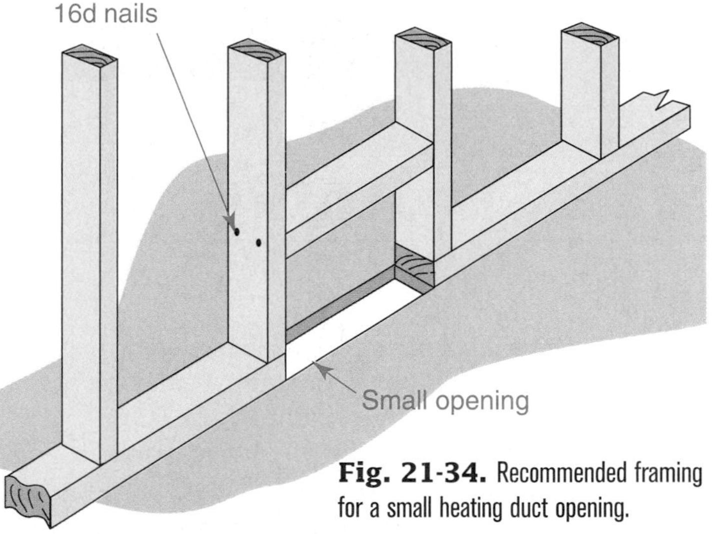

Fig. 21-34. Recommended framing for a small heating duct opening.

CABINET SOFFITS

The *cabinet soffit* is commonly used where prefabricated upper cabinets do not extend to the ceiling. **Fig. 21-35.** It is usually 2″ deeper than the cabinets so that molding may be installed at the cabinet top. Some carpenters will assemble a soffit from framing lumber and lift it into place as a unit. Others may install it in place. Whatever the method, the soffit must be level and securely attached to the surrounding framing. This makes cabinet installation easier.

The bottom of the soffit is usually about 84″ from the finished floor. It is assembled from 2x2 and 2x4 lumber nailed together with 16d and 10d nails. It should be fastened directly to the wall and ceiling framing. After the wall covering has been applied and painted, the cabinets are attached to the wall and to the bottom of the soffit. A piece of cove or quarter-round molding may be used to close the joint between the cabinet and the soffit.

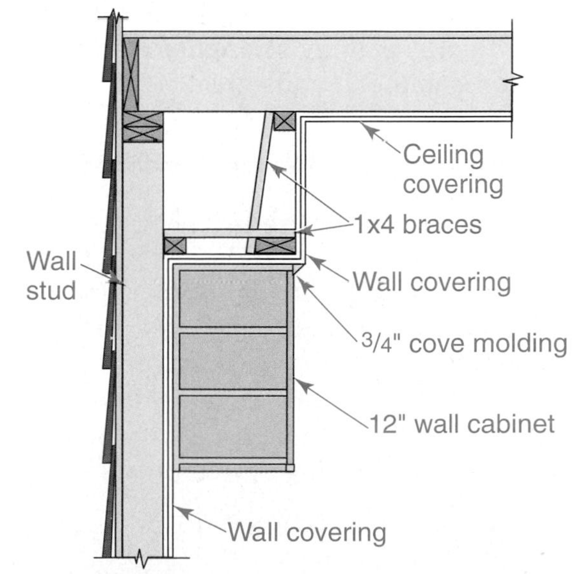

Fig. 21-35. One method for constructing a cabinet soffit.

FIREBLOCKING

Building codes may require *fireblocking* in walls that are over 10′ high. Fireblocking is meant to slow the passage of flames through wall cavities. It also strengthens the walls. It is made from short lengths of 2x framing lumber installed crosswise between studs. The blocking must be the same width as the surrounding framing and should fit snugly. The blocking can be staggered to make end nailing easier. In standard-height walls, the top and bottom plates are considered sufficient fireblocking.

SECTION 21.4

Check Your Knowledge

1. What is a shear wall? When might it be used?
2. Name three types of special framing that might be required in a bathroom.
3. What is the purpose of a cabinet soffit?
4. What is the purpose of fireblocking?

On the Job

Imagine that you work for a construction company that builds twenty houses each year. The president of the company has asked you to join a team responsible for quality control. Create a checklist that will remind the carpenters to review the plans for special framing requirements. How will you ensure that they use the checklist?

SECTION 21.5

Wall Sheathing

Wall sheathing is a panel product nailed to the outside surface of exterior walls. It may be applied vertically or horizontally. **Fig. 21-36.** If the wall is to be finished with stucco, wall sheathing may not be required.

Wall sheathing has several functions:

- It strengthens and braces the wall framing, just as floor sheathing strengthens and braces the floor framing. It adds great rigidity to the house.
- Sheathing forms a solid nailing base for the siding.
- It helps to seal the house by reducing air infiltration.
- Sheathing ties wall framing to floor framing. A solid connection here is especially important in areas prone to high winds and earthquakes.

The use of diagonal bracing is another way to strengthen a wall. It can be used with or without sheathing. In one bracing system, the studs are notched to receive 1x4 pieces that are let into the notches. This is known as let-in bracing. Another system uses metal-angle strips.

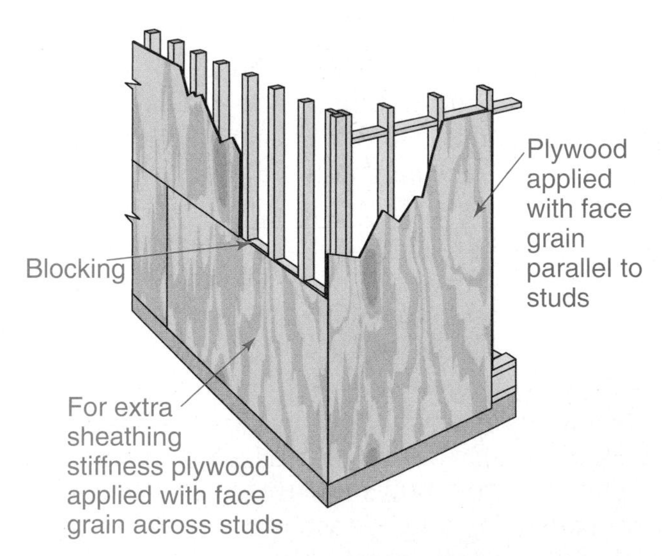

Fig. 21-36. Plywood sheathing may be applied horizontally or vertically. If applying it horizontally, include additional blocking at the horizontal joint between the studs as a base for nailing.

Estimating...

Number of Sheets Needed for Sheathing

A one-story vacation house has four walls and a gable roof. Two of the walls are 8′ high and 28′ long. The other two walls are 8′ x 36′.

Step 1 Multiply the height of each wall by its width to determine the total area of each wall.

89 × 289 = 224 sq. ft.
224 sq. ft. × 2 = 448 sq. ft.
8′ × 36′ = 288 sq. ft.
288 sq. ft. × 2 = 576 sq. ft.

Step 2 For a house with a gable roof, find the area of one gable. (A *gable* is the triangle formed in a wall by the sloping ends of a roof.) To find the area of a gable, multiply the height of the gable by one-half its width at the bottom. Multiply the result by the number of gables to determine the total gable area. (For ease in calculating this example, change 4′ 8″ to a decimal, or 4.66′.)

4.66′ × 14′ = 65.24 sq. ft.
65.24 sq. ft. × 2 = 130.48 sq. ft.

Step 3 Add the total area of each wall and the gables to determine the total wall area of the house.

448 + 576 + 130.48 = 1,154.48 sq. ft.

Step 4 There are 32 square feet in a 4x8 sheet of plywood. Divide the total wall area by 32 and round off the result. This will give the number of plywood sheets required to sheathe the house.

1,154.48 ÷ 32 = 36.08
37 sheets would be needed.

ESTIMATING ON THE JOB

A one-story house has four walls and two gables. Two of the walls are 36′ long. The other two walls are 48′ long. The walls are 9′ high. Each gable has a height of 10′. The gables are on the shorter walls. How many sheets will be needed?

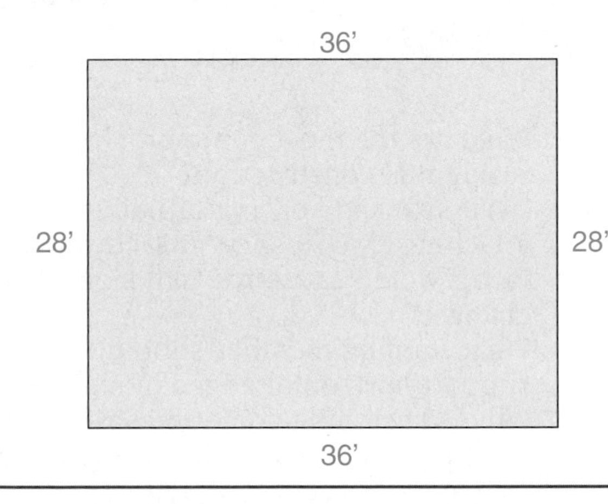

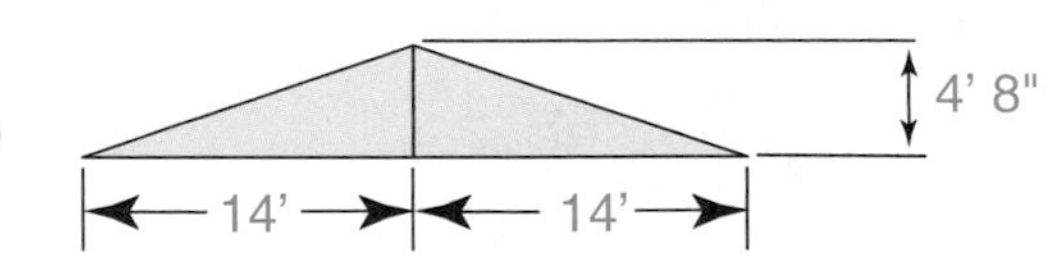

SHEATHING MATERIALS

The most common sheathings used in residential construction are square-edged 4x8 panels made of plywood or oriented-strand board (OSB). Panel thickness ranges from 5/16″ to 1″. Walls with stud spacing 16″ OC must have sheathing that is at least 5/16″ thick, although 1/2″ is more common. When finish siding requires nailing between studs (as with wood shingles), the sheathing should be at least 3/8″ thick.

Though OSB is different from plywood in terms of manufacture, it is generally used as a direct replacement for plywood sheathing. Nailing and installation details for OSB sheathing are similar to those for plywood.

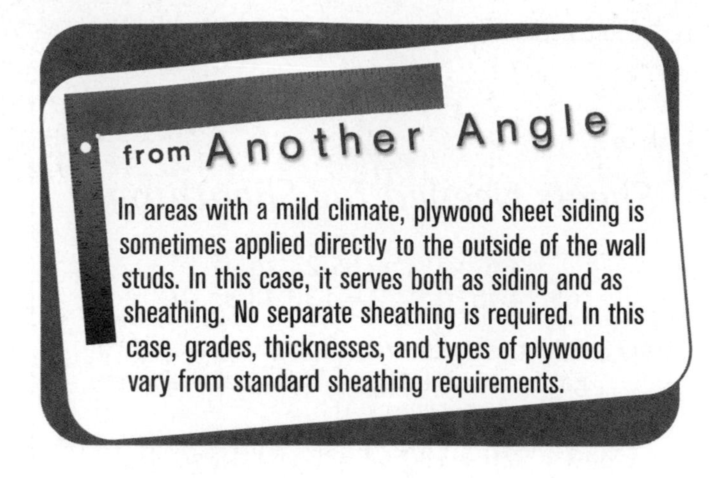

SHEATHING APPLICATION

Walls that have been covered with sheathing provide a more solid support for the ceiling and roof members. That is why most carpenters apply the sheathing as soon as possible. However, it may be applied at either of the following stages:

- Sheathing may be applied when the wall frame is lying on the subfloor, completely framed and squared. The advantage in applying the sheathing at this time is that it can be nailed in place while the wall sections are lying flat. This eliminates the need for ladders or scaffolding. The disadvantage is the added weight that must be lifted when erecting the walls.
- Sheathing can also be added after the wall frame has been erected, plumbed, and braced and the ceiling joists have been installed.

Orientation and Fastening

Sheathing is usually applied vertically, using perimeter nailing with no additional blocking. If a panel does not extend to the top of the wall, its top edge should be nailed to blocking. **Fig. 21-37.** An alternative would be to use longer sheathing panels. Local building codes may require that sheathing be applied only vertically near the corners of a building. This provides additional rigidity to the structure. Plywood can also be applied horizontally, although the horizontal joints between panels should be supported by solid blocking as a base for nailing.

Building codes sometimes allow sheathing to be fastened by stapling. However, nailing is more common. The spacing and gauge of fasteners is important in creating a solid connection between sheathing and framing. Nailing and stapling requirements for plywood sheathing are listed in the Ready Reference Appendix. See the tables titled "Stapling Schedule" and "Plywood Wall Sheathing Application Details."

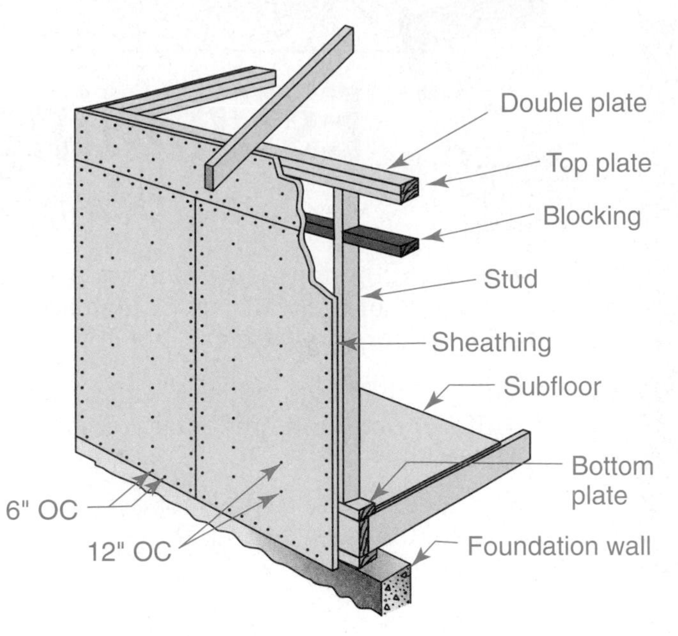

Fig. 21-37. Plywood sheathing started at the foundation wall will require blocking along the top joint. Be sure to check local codes for nail spacing and blocking.

SECTION 21.5

Check Your Knowledge

1. What are the most common sheathings for residential construction?
2. What size and spacing of nail is required for attaching ½″ OSB sheathing to walls? What factor would cause the nail size to be changed?
3. What framing member should be installed to support horizontal edges of sheathing?
4. Why is sheathing sometimes required to be installed vertically at the corners of a house?

On the Job

How many 4x8 sheets will be required to sheathe a 26′ x 42′ one-story house with 8′ walls and studs placed 16″ OC? Call a local building supplier to find out the price of one sheet of ½″ sheathing plywood. Multiply this number by the number of sheets in your estimate. How much will the wall sheathing cost for this house? (Note: Builders may be offered a lower price per panel because they usually order in large quantities.)

Chapter 21

Review

Section Summaries

21.1 Exterior walls are nearly always load-bearing walls. Wall framing members include studs, plates, headers, cripple studs, sills, and trimmer studs.

21.2 Wall framing begins with laying out the location of two intersecting exterior walls. Plate layout identifies the location of each stud in a wall, as well as the location of doors and windows.

21.3 A story pole is useful as a quick layout reference. Exterior walls are set up, plumbed, and braced before interior walls.

21.4 Special framing adds strength and quality to a structure. Special framing is often done after the building is enclosed.

21.5 Sheathing may be applied before or after a wall is raised. The spacing and gauge of sheathing fasteners is important for establishing a solid connection.

Review Questions

1. What is the difference between a bearing and a nonbearing wall?
2. What are the requirements for wall-framing lumber?
3. Name the primary wall-framing members and the members that connect to them.
4. Name the three types of plates.
5. What are the two main steps in wall layout?
6. When assembling a wall, why is it important to keep the edges of framing members flush with each other?
7. Name three situations that require special framing.
8. Name four functions of wall sheathing.
9. What is a quick way to determine the number of studs needed for an exterior wall?
10. How is the area of a wall calculated?

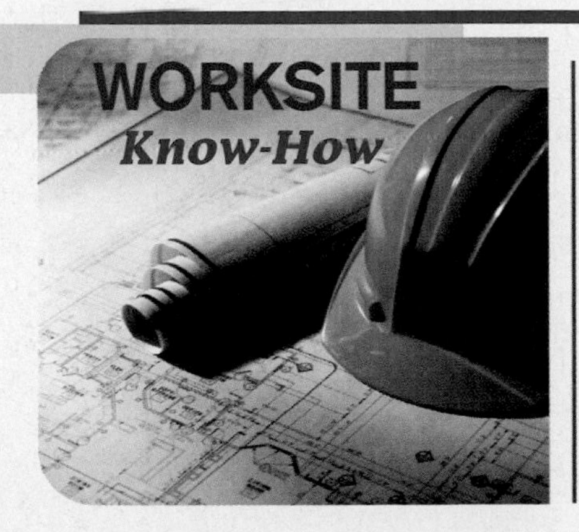

Raising Walls Carpenters often frame and sheathe walls flat on the subfloor. However, raising the completed wall can be awkward because the sheathing makes it hard to get a good grip on the wall.

To make walls easier to raise, use a prybar to lift the top end of the wall off the deck. Slip in scrap 2x4 blocks at numerous locations beneath this. When the crew is ready to raise the wall, they will find it easier to get a solid grip.

Chapter 22

Basic Roof Framing

Objectives

After reading this chapter, you'll be able to:

- **Identify the basic roof styles.**
- **Understand the basic terms relating to roof-frame carpentry.**
- **Develop framing plans for a gable roof, hip roof, and variations that include valleys.**
- **Lay out a common rafter, using at least one of the four basic methods.**
- **Lay out ceiling joists.**
- **Recognize when special ceiling framing may be required.**

Terms

bird's mouth
pitch
rafter
ridge board
slope
span
tail
total rise
total run
unit rise
unit run

In this chapter, you will be introduced to common types of roofs, the basics of roof framing, and the skills of laying out and cutting a rafter. In following chapters, you will learn more about advanced roof framing, roof sheathing, and roof assembly.

Roof framing begins after the house walls have been framed. In most cases, the walls have also been sheathed to increase their strength and stiffness. For information on additional roof framing options, refer to Chapter 31, "Roof Edge Details." Nominal 2″ lumber is generally used for roof framing. It should normally not exceed 19 percent moisture content. Some builders use engineered lumber instead, such as I-joists (see Chapter 17, "Engineered Lumber"). This and following chapters describe roof framing using conventional lumber. Using I-joists requires the same basic understanding of rafter layout and roof design. Installation details for I-joists are given in Section 22.2.

SECTION 22.1

Planning a Roof

Roof framing is considered the most complicated frame carpentry in a house because of all the angles involved. It may also seem difficult to learn because of the special terms. However, it is important to understand that even the most complex roofs are based on a few standard designs.

ROOF STYLES

The main purpose of a roof is to protect the house in all types of weather with a minimum of maintenance. A roof must be strong to withstand snow and wind loads. The parts must be securely fastened to each other.

Another consideration is appearance. A roof should add to the attractiveness of the home. Roof styles are used to create different architectural effects. A carpenter must understand and be able to frame roofs in various styles. **Fig. 22-1.**

The basic roof styles used for homes and small buildings are gable, hip, flat, and shed. **Fig. 22-2.** Variations are associated with architectural styles of different regions or countries. Some of these include the gambrel roof, the mansard roof, and the Dutch hip roof.

Gable Roof

The *gable roof* has two sloping sides that meet at the top to form a gable at each end. (A *gable* is the triangular wall enclosed by the sloping ends of the roof.) A gable roof may include *dormers* (upright window projections) that add light and ventilation to second-floor rooms or the attic. The gable roof is the most common type of roof.

Hip Roof

A *hip roof* slopes at the ends of the building as well as at the two sides. The slope on all sides results in an even overhang all around the building and gives a low appearance. Because there is no siding above the overhang, maintenance needs are reduced. The hip is also a very strong roof and is often found in regions where severe storms are common. All of these factors make it a popular choice.

A

B

Fig. 22-1. The gable roof compared with the hip roof. *A.* The gable roof is a common roof style in homebuilding. This one includes gabled dormers. *B.* The hip roof presents a slope on all sides.

Low-Slope Roof

Sometimes called a *flat roof*, a *low-slope roof* is not perfectly flat. Instead, the *rafters* (inclined members supporting the roof) are laid at a slight angle to encourage water to drain. Sheathing and roofing are applied to the top of the rafters.

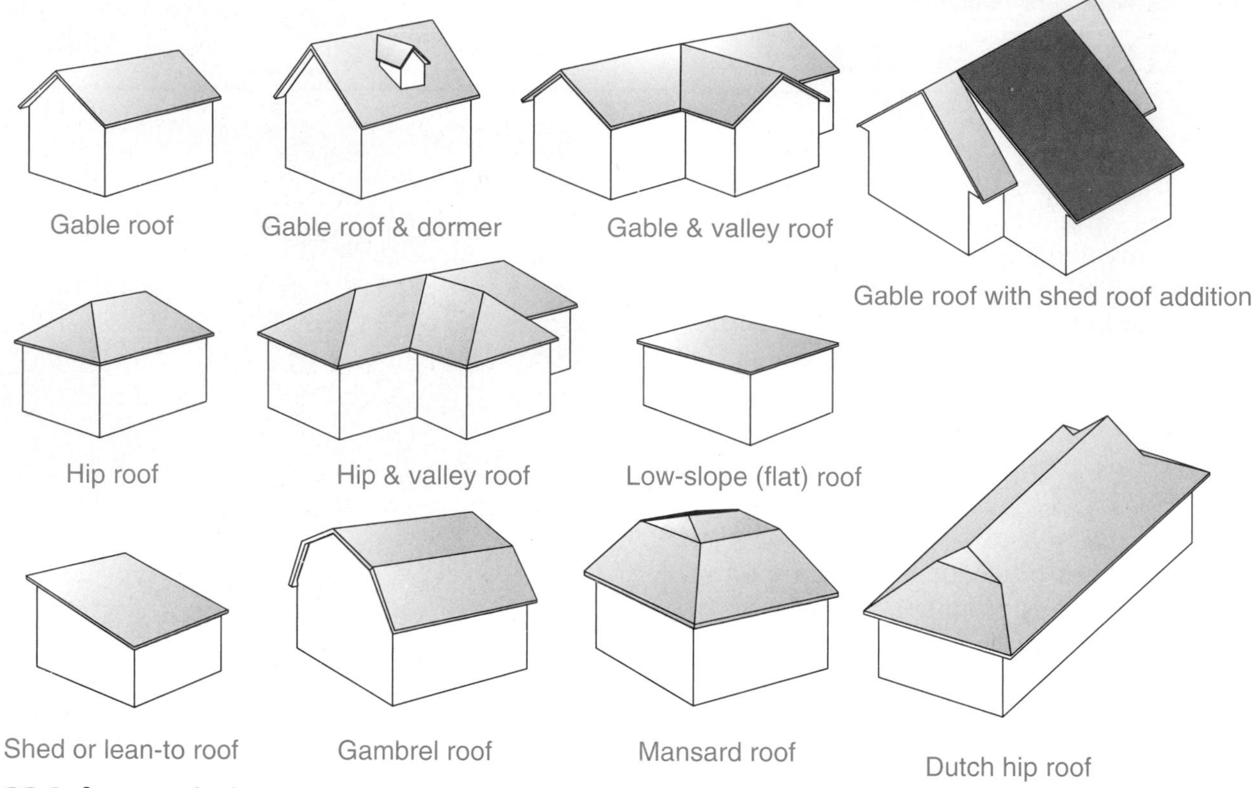

Fig. 22-2. Common roof styles.

The ceiling material is applied to the underside of the rafters. Because a flat roof can be difficult to waterproof, it is found most often in dry climates.

Shed Roof

Sometimes called a *lean-to roof*, the *shed roof* slopes in one direction only. A shed roof is often used for an addition to an existing structure. In this case, the roof may be attached to the side of the structure or to the roof.

Gambrel Roof

The *gambrel roof* is a variation of the gable roof. It has a steep slope on two sides. A second slope begins partway up and continues to the top. This roof style was brought to North America by German immigrants who settled in New York and Pennsylvania. It is commonly used on barns.

Mansard Roof

The *mansard roof* is a variation of the hip roof. It has steep slopes on all four sides. Partway up, a shallow second slope is developed and continues to the top where it meets the slopes from the other sides. The mansard roof style was brought to North America by the French who settled in Quebec, Canada.

Dutch Hip Roof

A *Dutch hip roof* is related to both the gable roof and the hip roof. Basically, it is a hip roof with a small gable at each end near the top. Like a hip roof, it has an even overhang around the entire building. This protects the walls from rain. Like a gable roof, portions of a Dutch hip roof are formed by two slopes that meet at the top. A Dutch hip roof is more common on single-story houses than on two-story houses.

ROOF FRAMING BASICS

Mastering the special terms used in roof framing will make it easier for you to understand roofing concepts. Also, become familiar with the *framing square*, which you will be using. Its short leg is called the *tongue*. Its long leg is called the *blade*, or *body*.

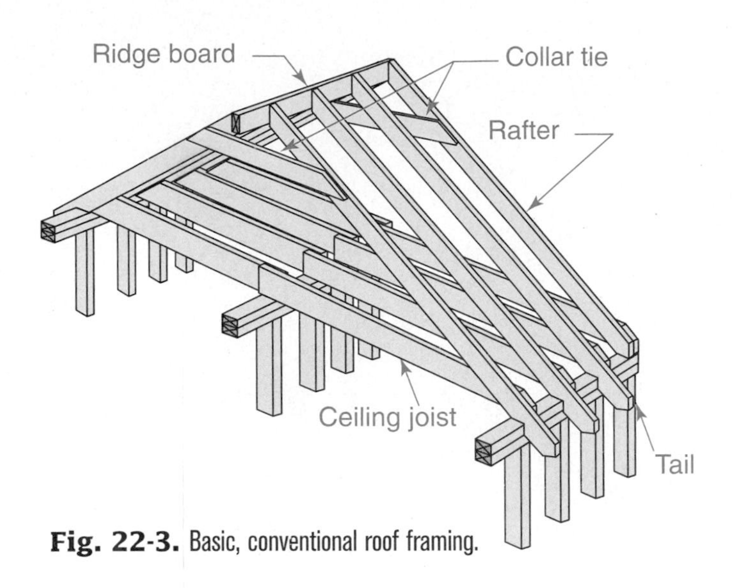

Fig. 22-3. Basic, conventional roof framing.

Parts of a Roof

A basic, conventional roof consists of rafters, collar ties, ceiling joists, and a ridge board. **Fig. 22-3.** More complex roofs include valley rafters and jack rafters (see also Chapter 23, "Hip, Valley, and Jack Rafters").

A **rafter** is an inclined member of the roof framework. Rafters serve the same purpose in the roof as joists in the floor or studs in the wall. They are usually spaced 16″ or 24″ apart. Rafters vary in depth depending on their length, the distance they are spaced apart, their slope, and the kind of roof covering to be used. A *collar tie* is a horizontal tie that connects opposite pairs of rafters to help stiffen the roof. The **ridge board**, or *ridge*, is the horizontal piece that connects the upper ends of the rafters.

Rafters often extend beyond the exterior walls to form *eaves* (also called *overhangs*) that protect the sides of the house. The **tail** is the portion of the rafter that extends beyond the wall of the building to form the eave.

The following rafters are needed for framing the different roof styles (**Fig. 22-4**):

- *Common rafters* extend from the top plate to the ridge board at 90° to both.
- *Hip rafters* extend diagonally from the corners formed by the top plates to the ridge board.
- *Valley rafters* extend diagonally from the top plates to the ridge board along the lines where two roofs intersect.
- *Jack rafters*, also called *jacks*, never extend the full distance from the top plate to the ridge board. There are three kinds of jack rafters. *Hip jack rafters* extend from the top plate to a hip rafter. *Valley jack rafters* extend from the ridge board to a valley rafter. *Cripple jack rafters* extend between a hip rafter and a valley rafter or between two valley rafters.

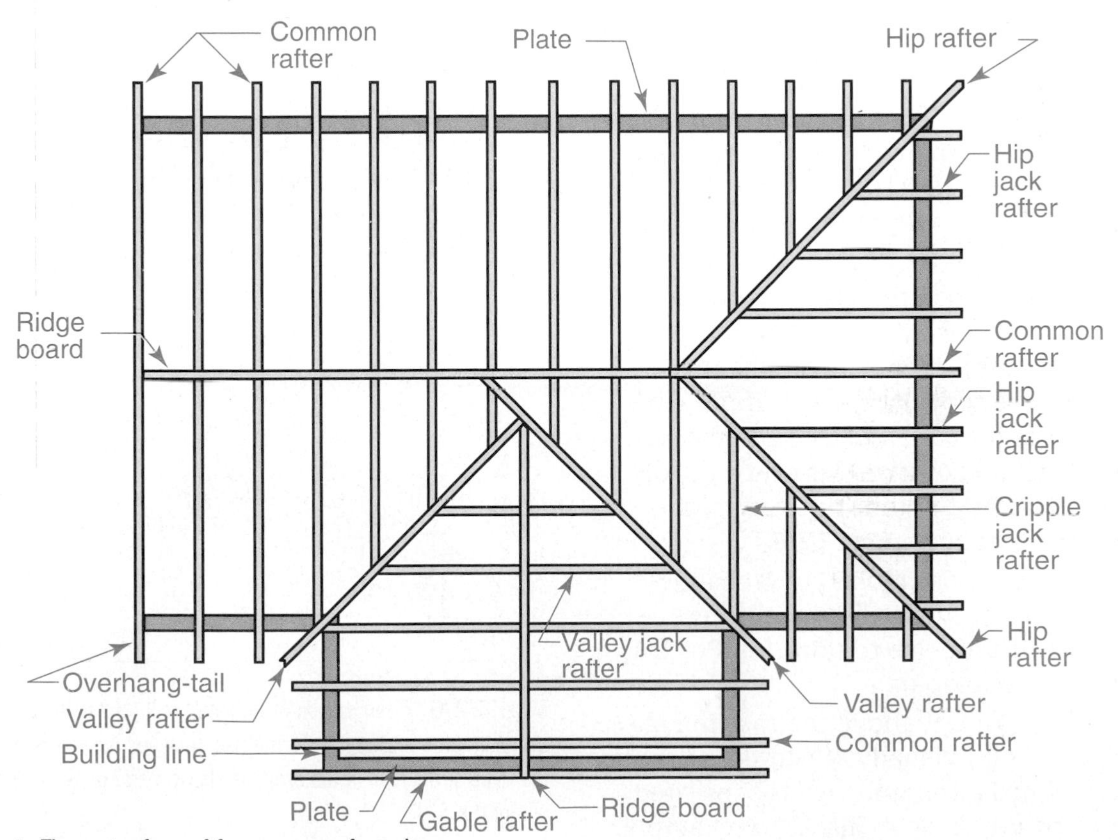

Fig. 22-4. The parts of a roof frame as seen from above.

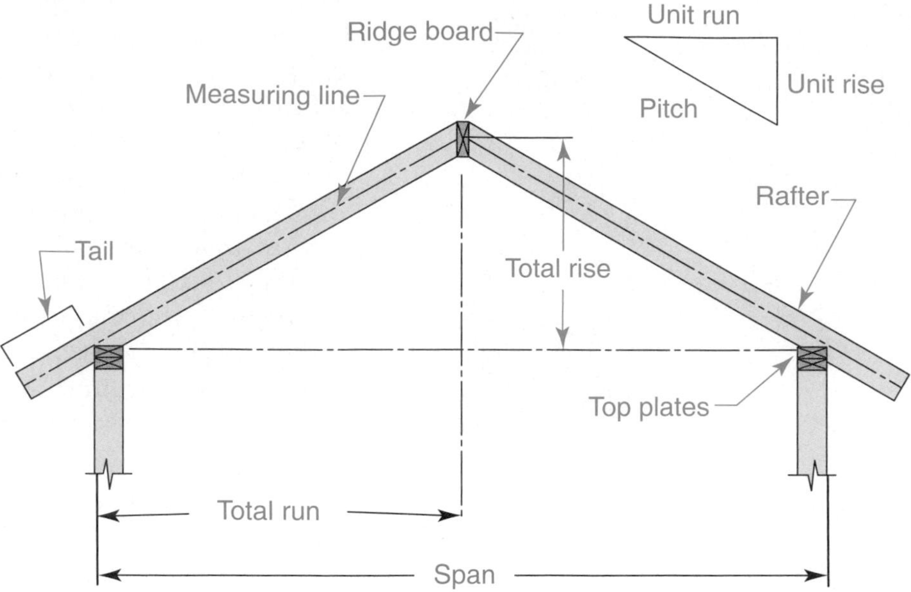

Fig. 22-5. Terms used in roof framing.

Calculating Roof Slope

The slope of a roof must be calculated before construction can begin. It depends upon several factors, including the roof's span, run, and rise.

The distance between the outer edges of the top plates is the **span**. **Fig. 22-5.** It is measured at right angles to the ridge board.

The **total run** is one-half the span (except when the slope of the roof is irregular). The **unit run**, or *unit of run*, is a set length that is used to figure the slope of rafters. The unit run for a rafter that is at a 90° angle to the ridge (a common rafter) is always 12″. The unit run for a rafter that is at a 45° angle to the ridge is 17″. Refer to Fig. 22-4.

The *measuring line* is an imaginary line running from the outside wall to the top of the ridge. The **total rise** is the vertical distance from the top of the top plate to the upper end of the measuring line. The **unit rise** is the number of inches that a roof rises for every 12″ of run (the unit run). As the unit rise varies, the slope of the roof changes. **Fig. 22-6.**

Slope and *pitch* are often used interchangeably, but they do not mean the same thing. **Slope** is a ratio of unit rise to unit run. **Pitch** is a ratio of total rise to span.

The triangular symbol above the roof in Fig. 22-6 shows the slope visually. When the slope is written out in words, the unit rise is separated from the unit run by a slash mark. For example,

Many carpenters use the terms *slope* and *pitch* as if they mean the same thing. Some construction dictionaries also consider these two terms to be synonymous. However, this is not precisely correct. Slope refers to a ratio of rise to run. Pitch refers to a ratio of rise to span. Either term can be used to describe the inclination (slant) of roofs and rafters, but *slope* is the term most suited to roof framing.

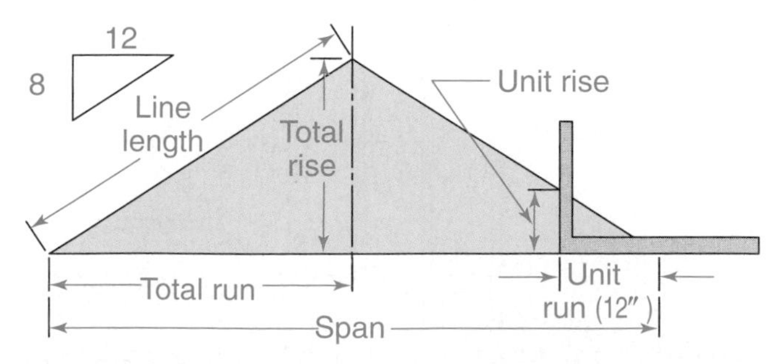

Fig. 22-6. A comparison of total and unit terms. The unit run of a common rafter is always 12″. The rise in inches is variable, depending on the slope of the roof. In the example shown here, there are 8″ of rise per unit of run.

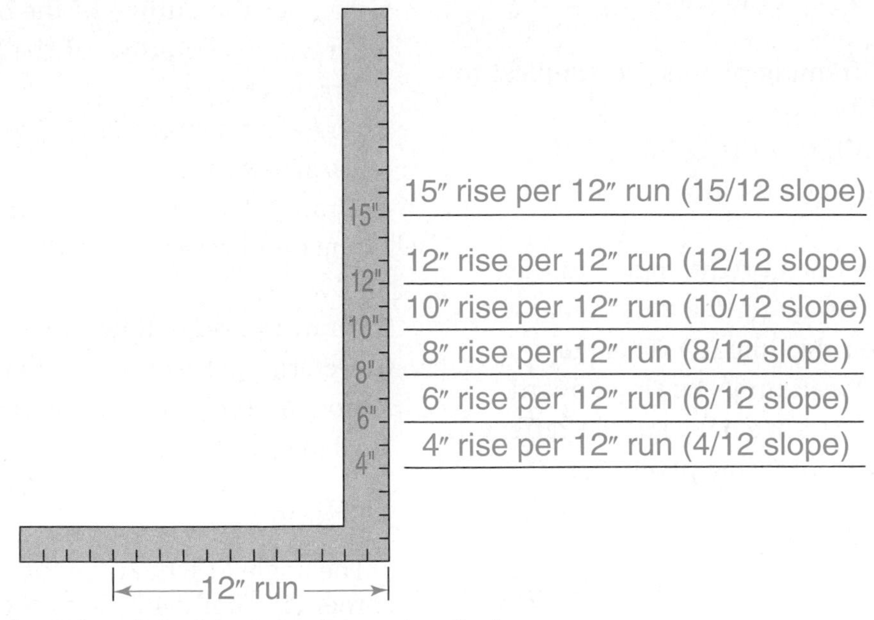

Fig. 22-7. A visual description of slope using a framing square.

a roof may have a unit rise of 6″ and a unit run of 12″. The information would be written "6/12 slope" and pronounced "six twelve slope" or sometimes "six in twelve slope." **Fig. 22-7.** The slope of a roof can also be given in degrees. For example, a roof with a 12/12 slope forms a 45° angle. **Fig. 22-8.** However, referring to degrees is not a common practice.

Plumb lines and level lines refer to the direction of a line on a rafter, not to any particular rafter cut. Any line that is vertical when the rafter is in its proper position is called a *plumb line.* Any line that is horizontal when the rafter is in its proper position is called a *level line.* **Fig. 22-9.**

LAYING OUT A ROOF FRAMING PLAN

Before cutting rafters, the carpenter must determine what kinds are needed to frame the roof. A roof framing plan may be included in the set of building plans. If it is not included, you must lay one out for yourself.

If the plan is drawn to scale, the exact number of each kind of rafter can also be determined. However, the actual rafter length should be figured based on dimensions taken directly from the building.

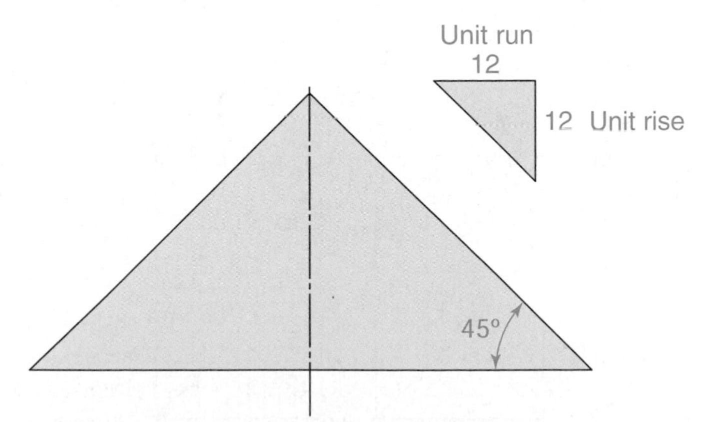

Fig. 22-8. A roof with a 12/12 slope is angled at 45° and has a 1/2 pitch.

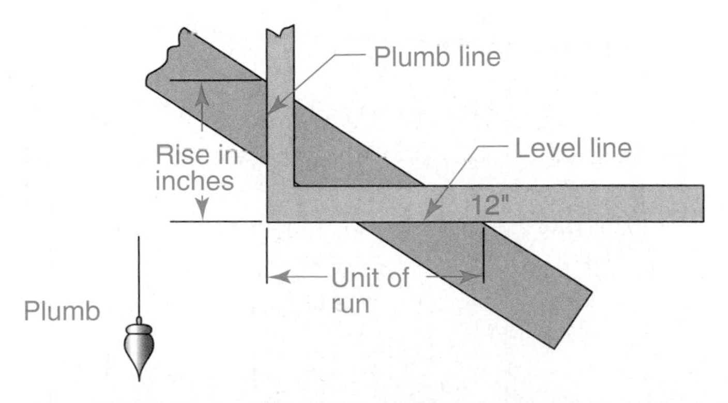

Fig. 22-9. The framing square is used to lay out the plumb and level lines on a rafter. The plumb line is drawn along the tongue of the square. The level line is drawn along the body, or blade.

Gable Roof

The gable roof framing plan is the simplest to develop. **Fig. 22-10.**

1. Lay out the outline of the building (*A*).
2. Determine the direction in which the rafters will run.
3. Draw the centerline at right angles to this direction (*B*). The centerline determines the location of the ridge line (*C*). This corresponds to the location of the ridge board.
4. Determine the distance between the rafters and lay out the roof frame plan (*D*).

Gable and Valley Roof

A gable and valley roof is simply two gable roofs that intersect. In the majority of cases they intersect at a 90° angle. The intersection creates two valleys. **Fig. 22-11.**

1. Lay out the outline of the building (*A*).
2. Draw the centerline of the larger rectangle (*B*, arrow 1).
3. Draw the centerline of the smaller rectangle (*B*, arrow 2).
4. Draw 45° lines from the interior corners of the building to where the centerlines intersect (*C*).
5. Draw the ridge lines (*D*).
6. Determine the distance between the rafters and lay them out on the roof framing plan (*E*).

Hip Roof

The angle at which the hip extends from each corner is usually 45°, but other angles are possible. **Fig. 22-12.**

1. Lay out the outline of the building (*A*).

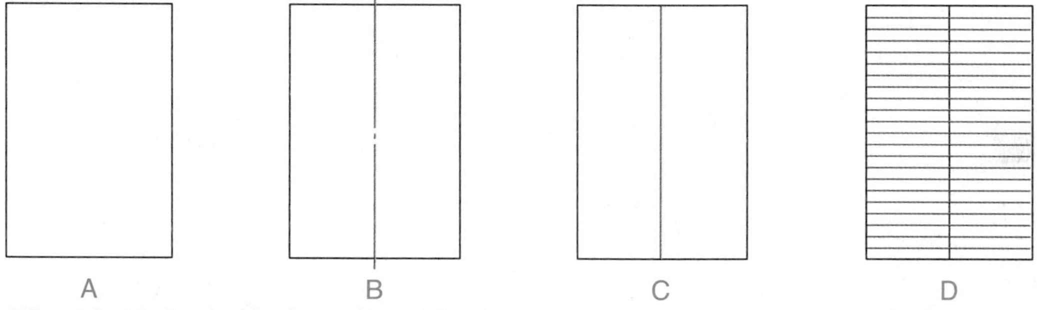

Fig. 22-10. Framing plan for a gable roof. The frame plan for a shed roof would be one-half of this.

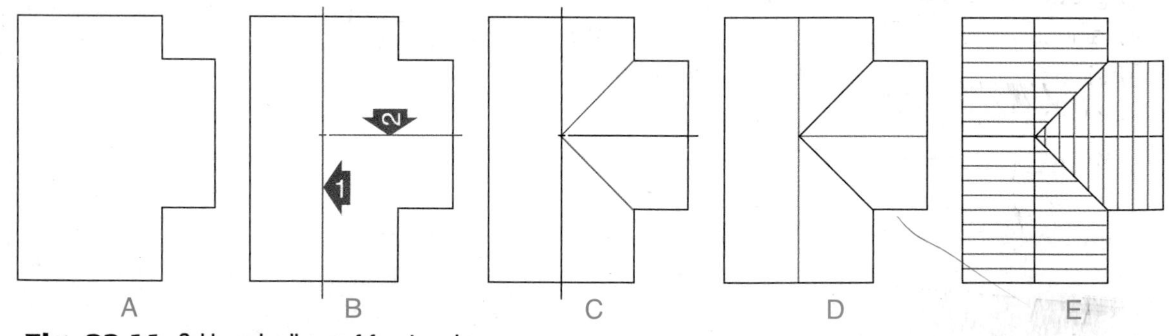

Fig. 22-11. Gable and valley roof framing plan.

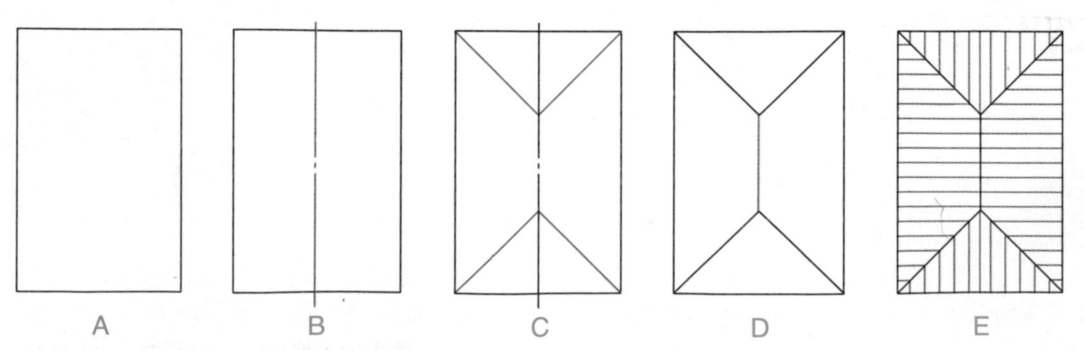

Fig. 22-12. Framing plan for a hip roof.

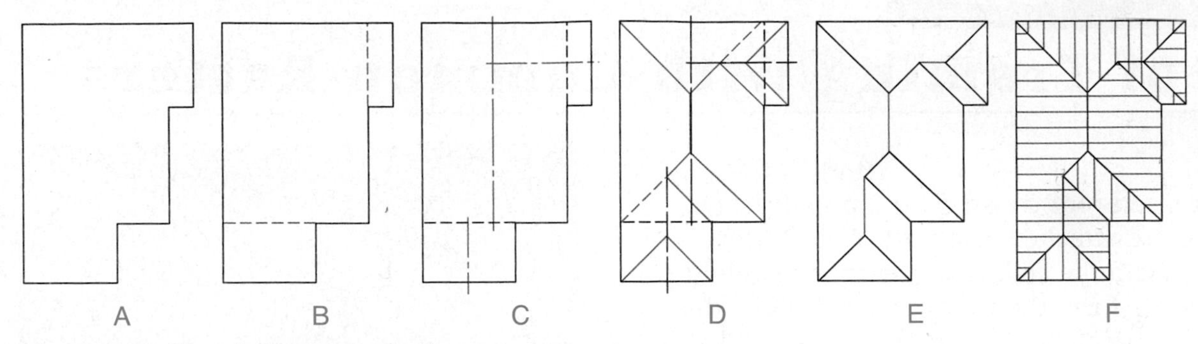

Fig. 22-13. Hip and valley roof framing plan.

2. Locate and draw a centerline (*B*).
3. Starting at each corner, draw a 45° line from the corner to the centerline (*C*). This establishes the location of the hip rafters.
4. Draw the ridge line between the intersecting points of the hip rafters (*D*).
5. Determine the distance between the rafters and lay them out on the roof framing plan (*E*).

Hip and Valley Roof

A hip and valley roof can be quite complex. It is created when one or more hip roofs intersect at 90° angles. **Fig. 22-13.**

1. Lay out the outline of the building (*A*).
2. Outline the largest rectangle inside the building outline (*B*).
3. Draw centerlines for every rectangle formed inside the building outline (*C*).
4. Draw a 45° line from each inside and outside corner. Extend these lines to intersect with the centerlines (*D*). The lines indicate the location of the hip rafters on outside corners and valley rafters on inside corners.
5. The centerlines drawn in (*C*) connect the hip and valley rafters. Draw these as solid lines where the ridges will be located (*E*).
6. Figure the distance between the rafters and lay them out on the roof framing plan (*F*).

SECTION 22.1

Check Your Knowledge

1. Name the four basic roof styles used for homes.
2. The gambrel roof is a variation of which basic roof style?
3. Explain the difference between a plumb line and a level line.
4. What is the purpose of a roof framing plan?

On the Job

Draw a roof framing plan for a house with the following characteristics:

- It will be the same width as the house shown in Fig. 22-10, but twice its length.
- The main roof will be a gable. Two other gable roofs will intersect with it, one on each long side of the house.
- The ridges of the intersecting gable roofs should meet the main ridge one-third of the distance from the end of the house.
- The side walls of one intersecting roof should be twice as long as the walls of the other.

SECTION 22.2

Roof Framing with Common Rafters

In trussed-roof construction, prefabricated trusses are attached as a unit. Their lower chords form the ceiling of the room, while the top chords form the roof. Trusses will be discussed separately in Chapter 25, "Roof Trusses."

In conventional roof construction, carpenters assemble the roof from individual ceiling joists and rafters. **Fig. 22-14.** The rafters should not be erected until the ceiling joists have been fastened in place (see Section 22.3). The ceiling joists act as a tie to prevent the rafters from pushing the exterior walls outward.

The following methods are used for a gable roof. Variations apply to gambrel, shed, and flat roofs.

Fig. 22-14. A conventionally framed roof is installed piece by piece.

LAYING OUT COMMON RAFTERS

The rafters form the skeleton of the roof. They must be carefully made and fitted if they are to support the roof's weight. The top of the rafter rests against the ridge board. The cut made in the rafter so it fits against the ridge is called a *plumb cut*. The bottom of the rafter rests on the plate. The cut made here is called a *level cut*, or *seat cut*. **Fig. 22-15.**

A line for the plumb cut is drawn using a framing square as a guide. **Fig. 22-16.** The unit run (12″ mark) on the blade of the square is aligned with the edge of the rafter. The unit rise on the tongue of the square will correspond to the pitch of the roof. The unit rise is aligned on the same edge of the rafter. The line for the plumb cut is then drawn along the edge of the tongue.

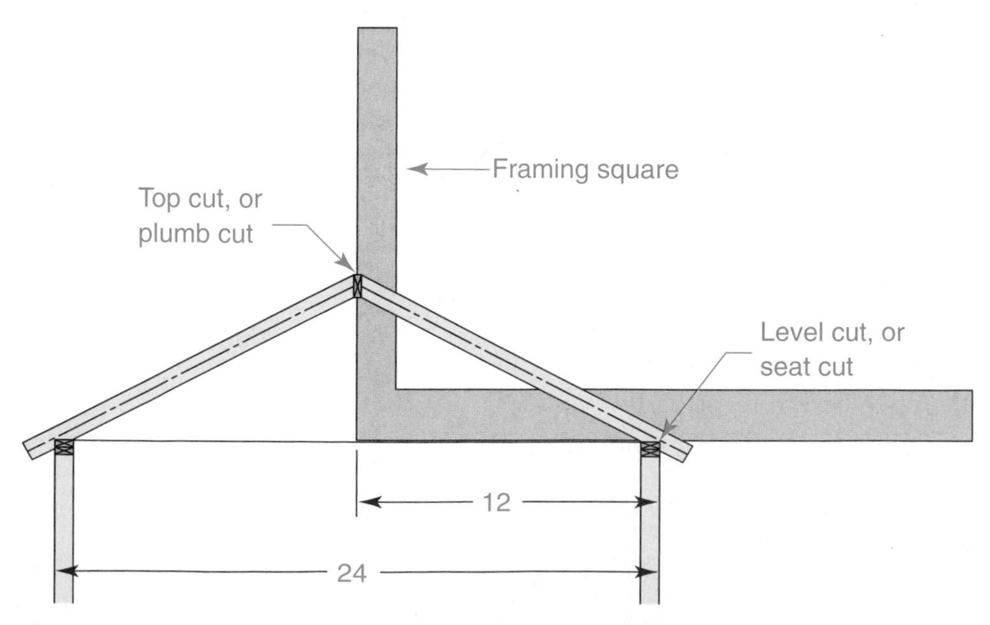

Fig. 22-15. The framing square was enlarged to show its relationship to the roof and to the top and bottom cuts.

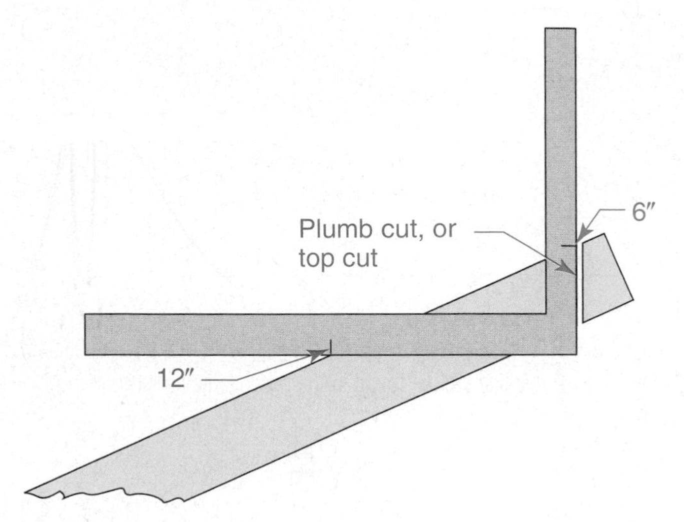

Fig. 22-16. A plumb line has been drawn for the plumb (top) cut on a roof with a 6″ unit rise (1/4 pitch).

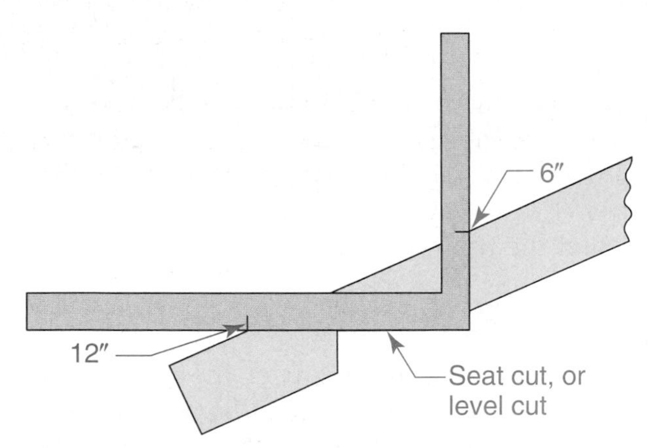

Fig. 22-17. A level line drawn for the seat cut. This cut is made for a roof with a 6″ unit rise.

A line for the seat cut is drawn with the square in the same position on the rafter. A level line is drawn for the same roof pitch, except that the line is drawn along the body of the framing square. **Fig. 22-17.**

Look at **Figs. 22-18** and **22-19**. The *theoretical length* of a common rafter is the shortest distance between the outer edge of the plate (*A*) and a point where the measuring line of the rafter meets the ridge line (*B*). This length is found along the measuring line. It may be calculated in the following ways:

- By using the Pythagorean theorem.
- By using the unit length obtained from the rafter table on the framing square.

Instead of using a standard framing square for laying out roof framing, many carpenters use a triangular framing square. Smaller and more durable than a framing square, this tool can be used for the same purposes. It has a thickened lip along one side. This enables the carpenter to hold the tool against lumber and use it as a guide for a circular saw.

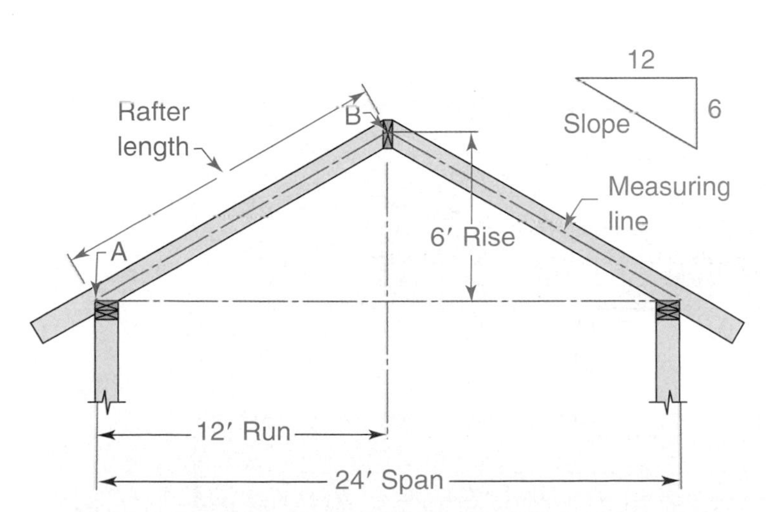

Fig. 22-18. The theoretical rafter length is measured from point *A* to point *B*.

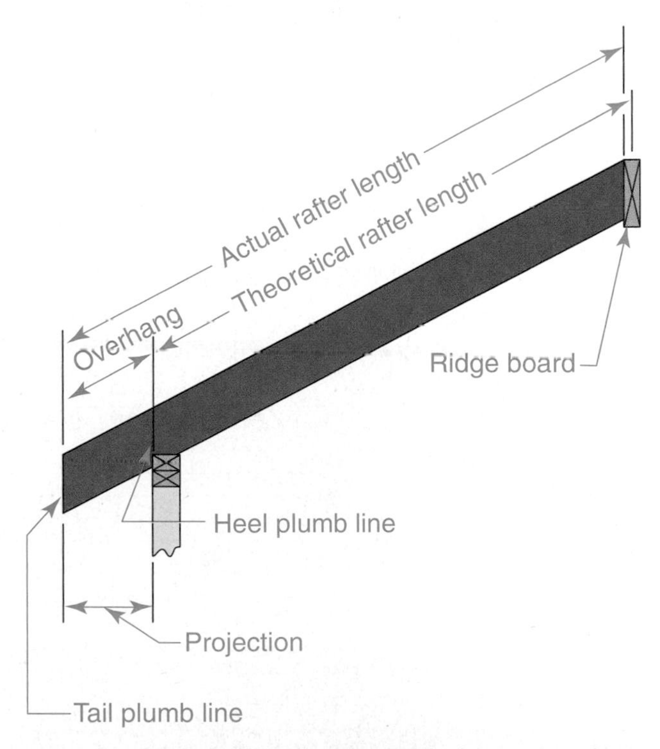

Fig. 22-19. Actual and theoretical length of a common rafter.

SAFETY FIRST

Lifting Rafters

During the layout and assembly of a roof frame, a great volume of lumber must be handled. Rafters are much heavier than wall studs and far more unwieldy. Organize the work to minimize back strain. For example, have lumber delivered close to where it will be cut. Work with a helper to lift rafters into position.

- By stepping off the length with the framing square.
- By entering the rise and run into a calculator designed for solving construction problems.

Pythagorean-Theorem Method

The Pythagorean theorem states that the square of the hypotenuse of a right triangle is equal to the sum of the squares of the other two sides (**Fig. 22-20**):

$$C^2 = A^2 + B^2$$

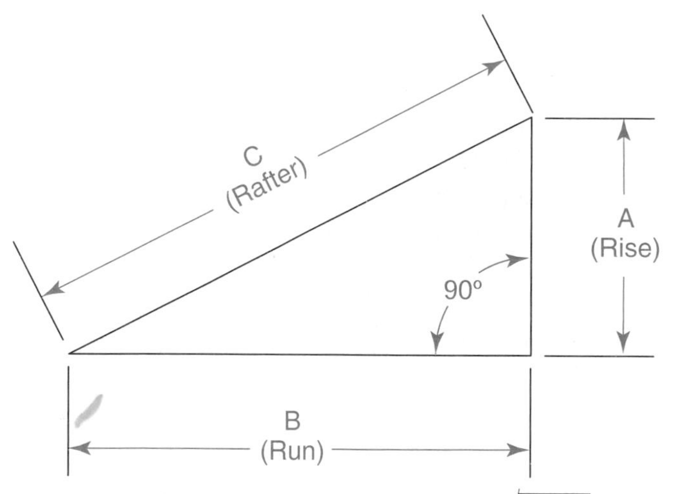

Fig. 22-20. The length of the rafter (*C*) is equal to $\sqrt{A^2 + B^2}$.

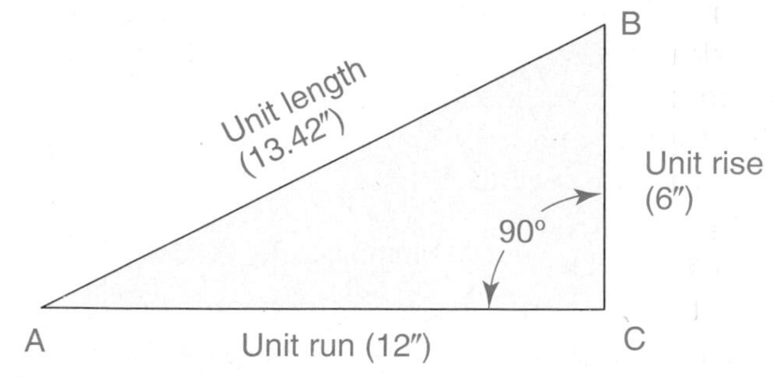

Fig. 22-21A. Unit length of the rafter is represented by the line *AB*. The length of this line can be found in the rafter table on the framing square.

The length of the hypotenuse *(C)* will be the square root of the sum of the square of the other two sides.

$$C = \sqrt{A^2 + B^2}$$

The rise, the run, and the rafter of a roof form a right triangle. The measuring line representing the rafter is the hypotenuse. The length of the rafter *(C)* can thus be calculated from the rise *(A)* and the run *(B)*.

Unit-Length Method

The unit-length method uses the rafter table on a framing square. *Unit length* is the length of a rafter per foot of run. It can be expressed as the hypotenuse of a right triangle. The unit run (12") is the base, and the unit rise (in inches per foot of run) is the altitude. **Fig. 22-21A.** Look at the rafter table on the framing square. **Fig. 22-21B.** The top line of the table reads: "Length

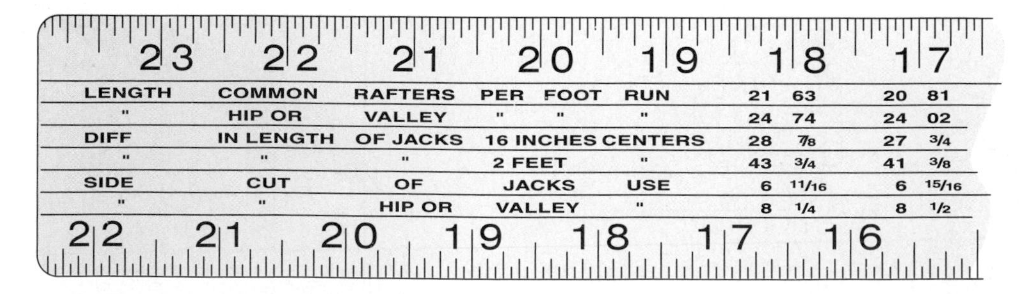

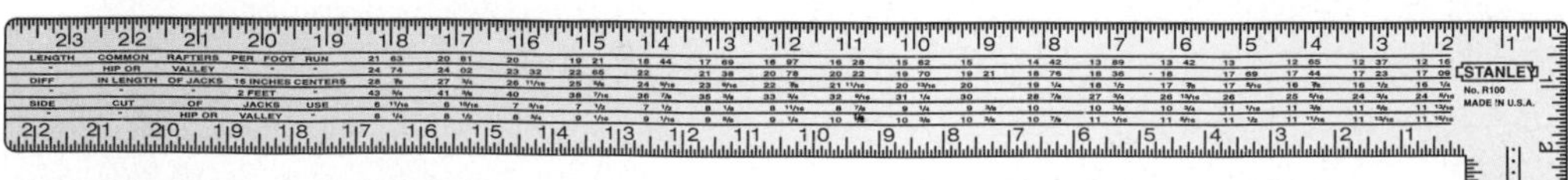

Fig. 22-21B. To find the unit length of common rafters, check the rafter table on the face of the framing square. An enlarged portion is shown above.

Common Rafters per Foot Run." The inch markings along the top represent unit rise. For example, if you follow across the top line to the figure under 6 (for a unit rise of 6″), you will find the number 13.42. This is the unit length for a roof triangle with a unit run of 12″ and a unit rise of 6″.

Let's figure the total length of a rafter for a small building with a unit rise of 5″, a span of 6′, and a run of 3′. Look at the rafter table to obtain the unit length. For a unit rise of 5″, the unit length is 13″ per unit run. The total length is the unit length times the total run. The total run of the building in this example is 3′. Therefore the total length of the common rafters is 39″. **Fig. 22-22.**

Step-Off Method

A third method for finding the theoretical rafter length is by using the framing square to "step off" the length. **Fig. 22-23.** Place the square on the rafter with the tongue along the plumb cut. Step off the length of the unit run on the rafter stock as many times as there are feet in the total run. In this case, it would be three times.

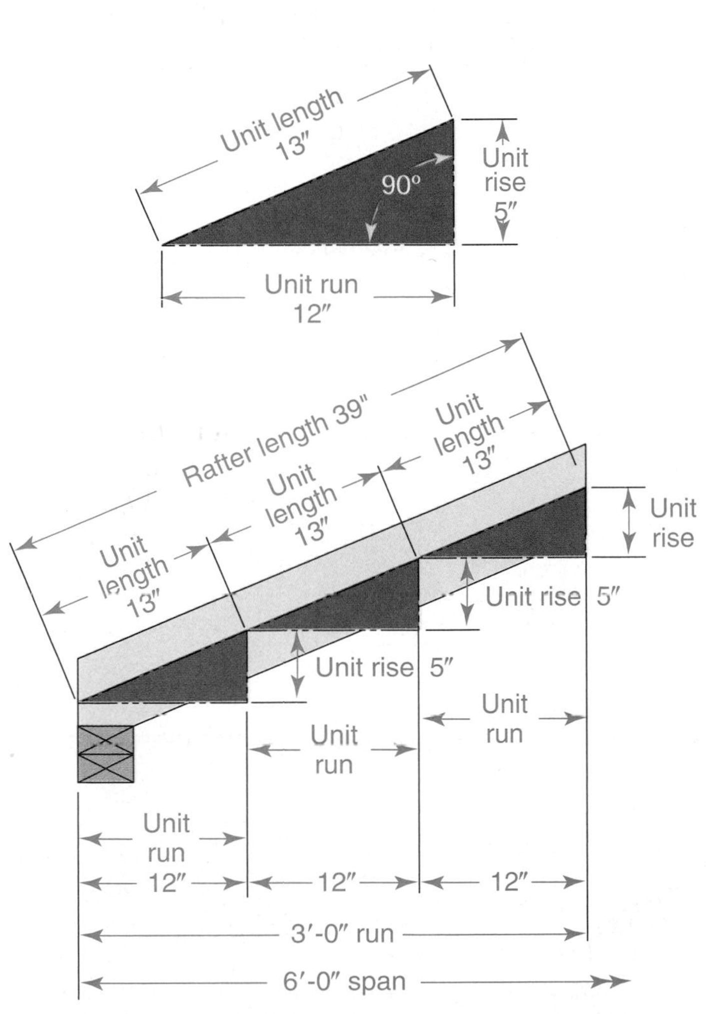

Fig. 22-22. The total theoretical length of a rafter is the total run times the unit length. In this example, the total run is 3′ and the unit length is 13″. Therefore, the length of the rafter is 39″.

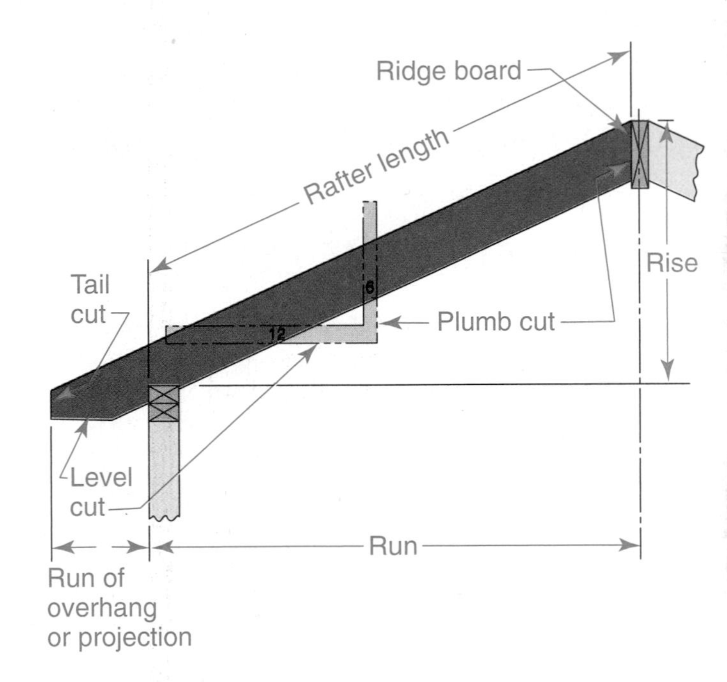

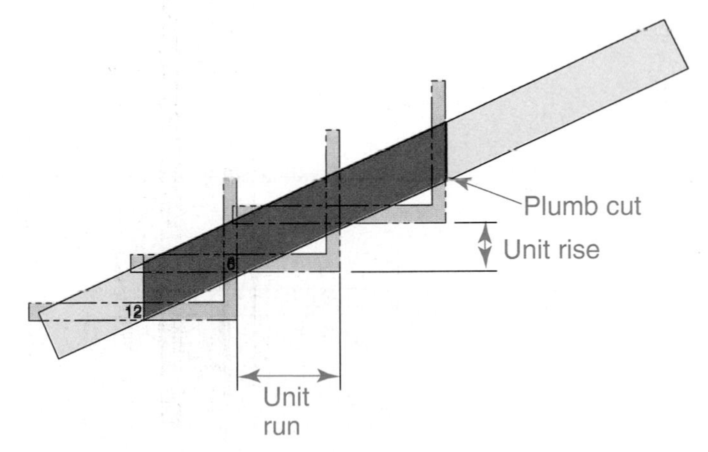

Fig. 22-23. Stepping off the length of a common rafter.

Often the total run of a building will not come out in even feet. For example, the run might be 3′-4″. With the square at the first position, draw a line along the edge of the tongue to represent the plumb cut at the ridge board. **Fig. 22-24.** At the 4″ mark on the blade, make a mark on the rafter along the level line—not along the edge. Then, starting at this mark, step off the unit run three times, for a total run of 3′-4″. This is the theoretical length of the rafter.

Calculator Method

Small, easy-to-use construction calculators are now common on job sites. **Fig. 22-25.** Measurements can be entered into the calculator in feet and inches, including fractions. If you know the rise and the run, you can easily determine the length of a common rafter by entering these figures into the calculator. You can also use the tool to calculate cuts for hip rafters and valley rafters.

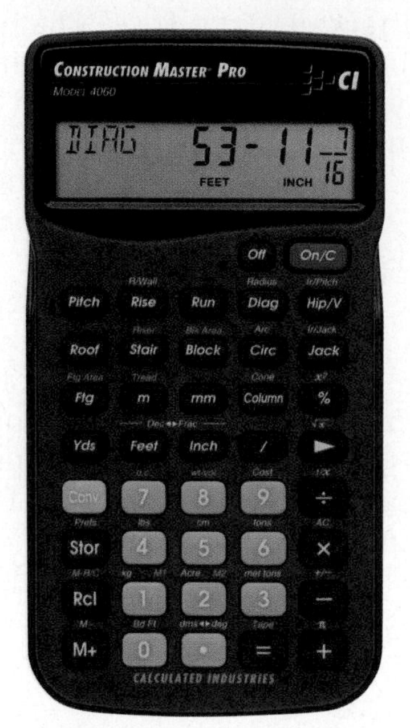

Fig. 22-25. A construction calculator is often used to solve roof framing problems. Dimensions can be entered in feet, inches, and fractions of an inch.

COMPLETING THE LAYOUT

After the basic rafter layout is complete, additional work is required. The ridge allowance, rafter overhang, and bird's mouth must be considered. Layout of the ridge board will be discussed in Chapter 24, "Roof Assembly and Sheathing."

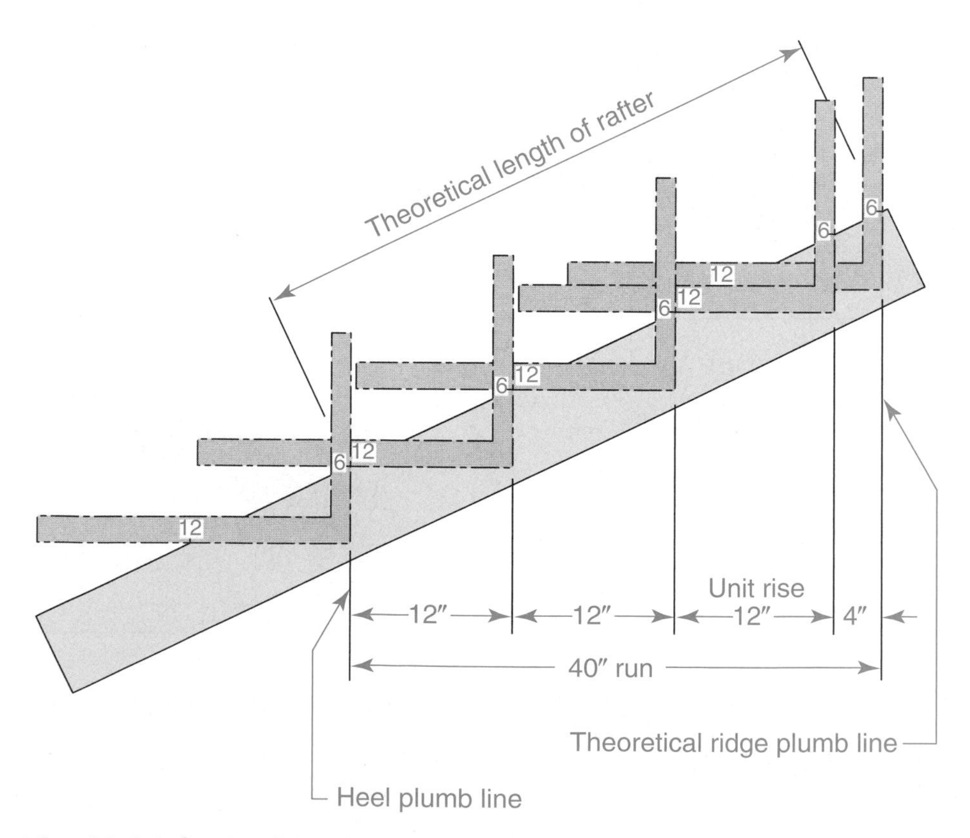

Fig. 22-24. Stepping off the rafter when the total run is not an even number of feet.

Common Rafter Ridge Allowance

The theoretical rafter length does not take into account the thickness of the ridge board or the length of the overhang, if there is one. To cut a rafter without an overhang to its actual length, you must deduct one-half the thickness of the ridge board from the ridge end. **Fig. 22-26.** For example, if 2″ material is used for the ridge board, its actual thickness is 1½″. One-half of this is ¾″. The ¾″ is indicated along the level line, and the line for the actual ridge plumb cut is drawn. **Fig. 22-27.**

Common Rafter Overhang

A roof may or may not have an overhang, or eave. If not, the rafter must be cut so that its lower end is even with the outside of the exterior wall. If the end is cut parallel to the ridge plumb cut, it is said to have a *heel.* **Fig. 22-28.** The portion of the rafter that rests on the plate is called the *seat.* To lay out the seat, place the tongue of the framing square on the heel plumb line. The rafter edge will intersect the correct seat width on the blade. **Fig. 22-29.** Indicate the seat by drawing a line from the heel plumb line along the blade.

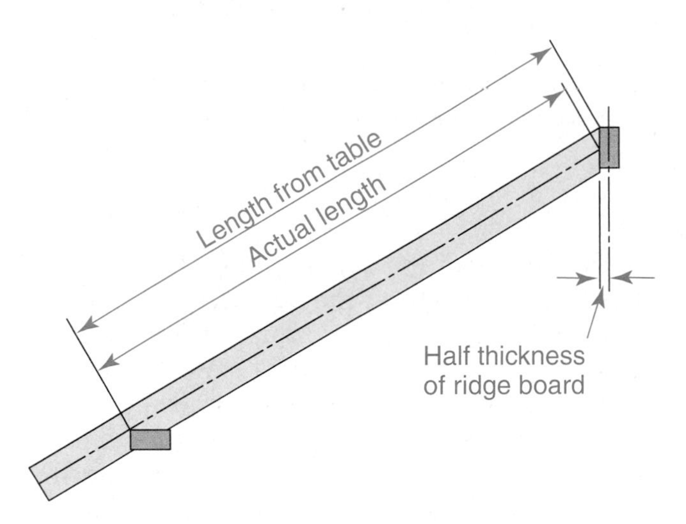

Fig. 22-26. Subtract one-half the actual thickness of the ridge board from the theoretical length of the rafter to obtain the rafter's actual length. If there is to be an overhang, this will be added later.

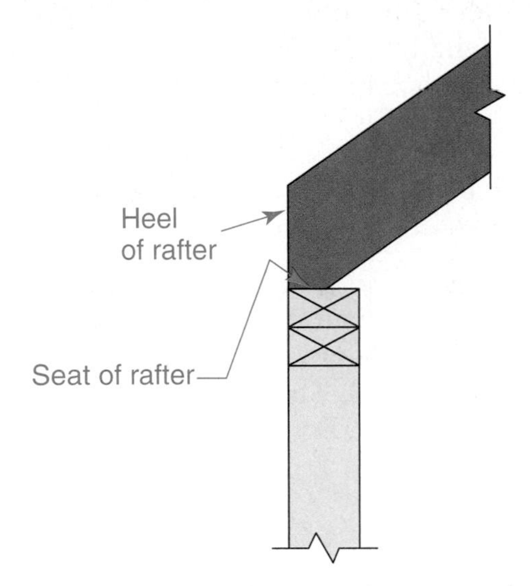

Fig. 22-28. A rafter without an overhang rests on the exterior wall plate.

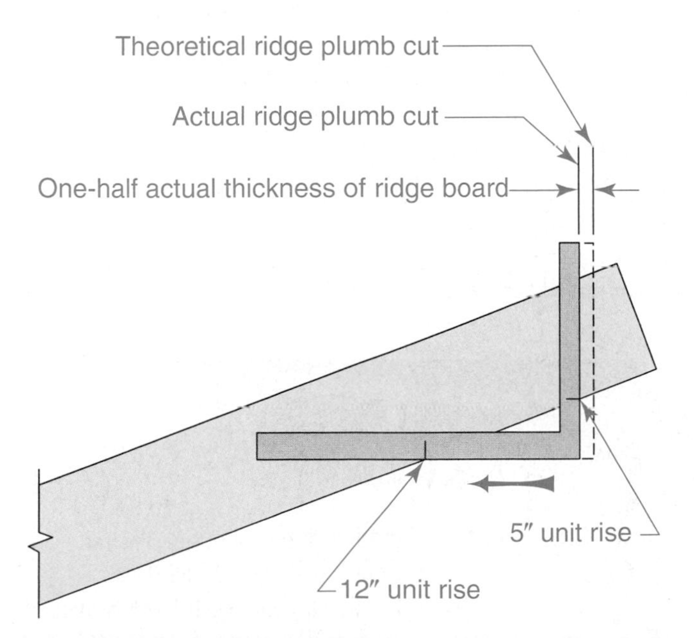

Fig. 22-27. Lay off one-half the thickness of the ridge board along the level line. Do not lay it off along the edge of the rafter.

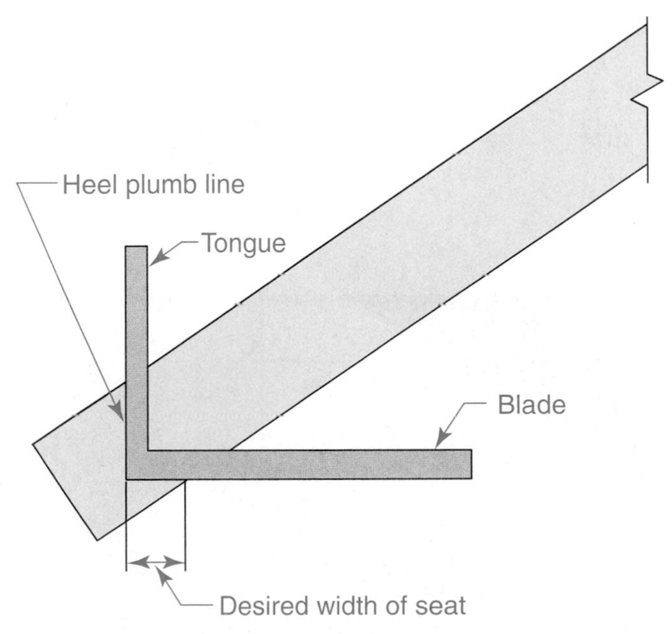

Fig. 22-29. Laying out the rafter seat.

A roof with wide overhangs provides protection for side walls and end walls. Though it adds slightly to the initial cost, this type of roof extension saves on maintenance later.

If the roof does have an overhang, the overhanging part of the rafter is the tail. Its length must be added to the length of the rafter. The length of the tail may be calculated as if it were a separate short rafter. Any of the methods used for finding rafter length may be used to find the length of the tail. For example, suppose the run of the overhang is 24″ and the unit rise of the roof is 8″. **Fig. 22-30.** Look at the rafter table on the framing square to find the unit length for a common rafter with a unit rise of 8″. You will see the unit length is 14.42″. Since the total run of the overhang is 24″, the total length is 28.84″, or 28 27⁄32″.

14.42 (inches per unit run) × 2 (units of run) = 28.84″

Another way to lay out the overhang is with the framing square. Suppose the run of the overhang is 10″. **Fig. 22-31.** Start the layout by placing the tongue of the square along the heel plumb line and setting the square to the pitch of the roof. In Fig. 22-31, the square is set to a unit rise of 8″ and a unit run of 12″. Move the square in the direction of the arrow, as shown, until the 10″ mark of the blade is on the heel plumb line. Draw a line along the tongue. This will mark the tail cut. If fascia or soffits are to be added later, be sure to allow for them in figuring the length of the rafter tail.

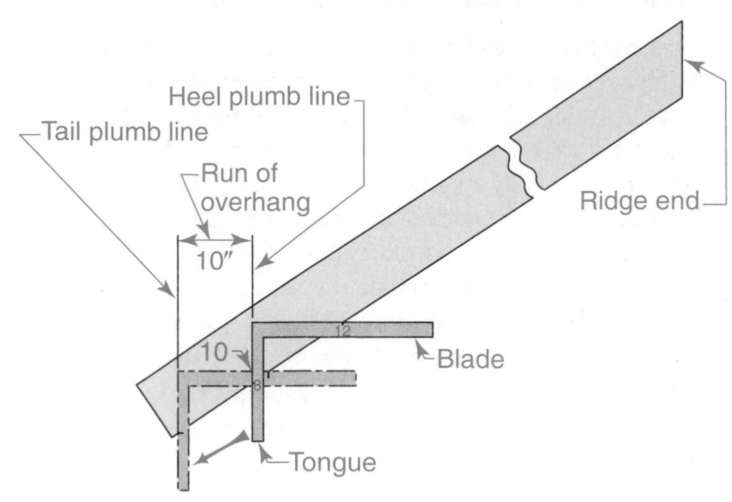

Fig. 22-31. Laying out the run of the overhang directly on the rafter using the framing square.

Many carpenters do not cut the tail to the finished length until after the rafters have been fastened in place. Instead, a sufficient amount of material is allowed for the overhang. After the rafters are fastened in place, a chalk line is snapped on the top edge of all the rafters. A tail plumb line is then drawn down from this chalk line on each rafter and the tail is cut along the line.

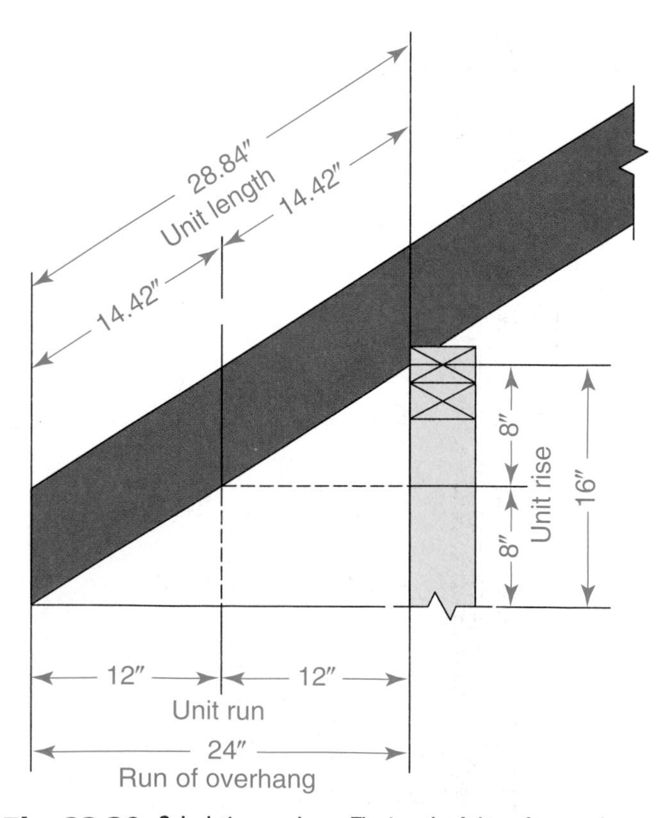

Fig. 22-30. Calculating overhang. The length of the rafter overhang may be found by using the rafter table on the framing square.

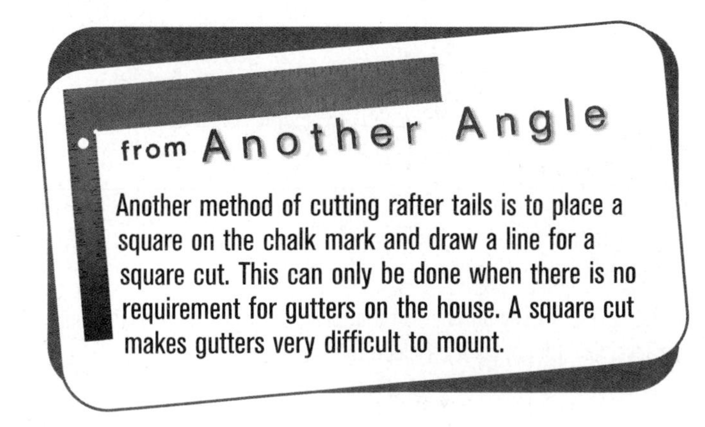

from Another Angle

Another method of cutting rafter tails is to place a square on the chalk mark and draw a line for a square cut. This can only be done when there is no requirement for gutters on the house. A square cut makes gutters very difficult to mount.

Laying Out a Bird's Mouth

A **bird's mouth** is a notch made in a rafter with an overhang so that the rafter will fit against a plate. **Fig. 22-32.** The plumb cut for the bird's mouth, which bears against the side of the plate, is called the *heel cut.* The level cut, which bears on the top of the plate, is called the *seat cut.*

The size of the bird's mouth for a common rafter is usually stated in terms of the depth of the heel cut rather than the width of the seat cut. The bird's mouth is laid out much the same way as the seat cut for a rafter without an overhang. Measure off the depth of the heel on the heel plumb line, set the square, and draw the seat line along the blade. **Fig. 22-33.**

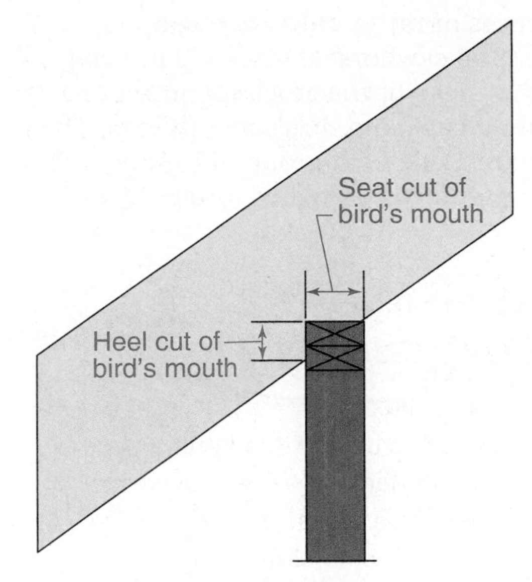

Fig. 22-32. The bird's mouth on a rafter with an overhang.

CUTTING RAFTERS

To cut common rafters, the actual length of one rafter is laid out on a piece of stock. The crown of the rafter should be on the top edge. After the first rafter is cut, it is used as a pattern for cutting a second.

The two rafters are then tested on the building using the ridge board or a scrap piece of the same size material to see how the heel cut and the top cut fit. If they fit properly, one of these rafters can be used as a pattern to cut all the others needed.

Cut rafters should be distributed to their locations along the building. The rafters are usually leaned against the building with the ridge cut up. The workers on the building can then pull them up as needed and fasten them in position.

In large developments, houses must be built quickly. Carpenters using conventional roof framing methods instead of trusses, which are faster, must develop efficient work habits. One way in which they can speed their work without sacrificing quality is to gang-cut rafters. After the master rafter pattern has been established,

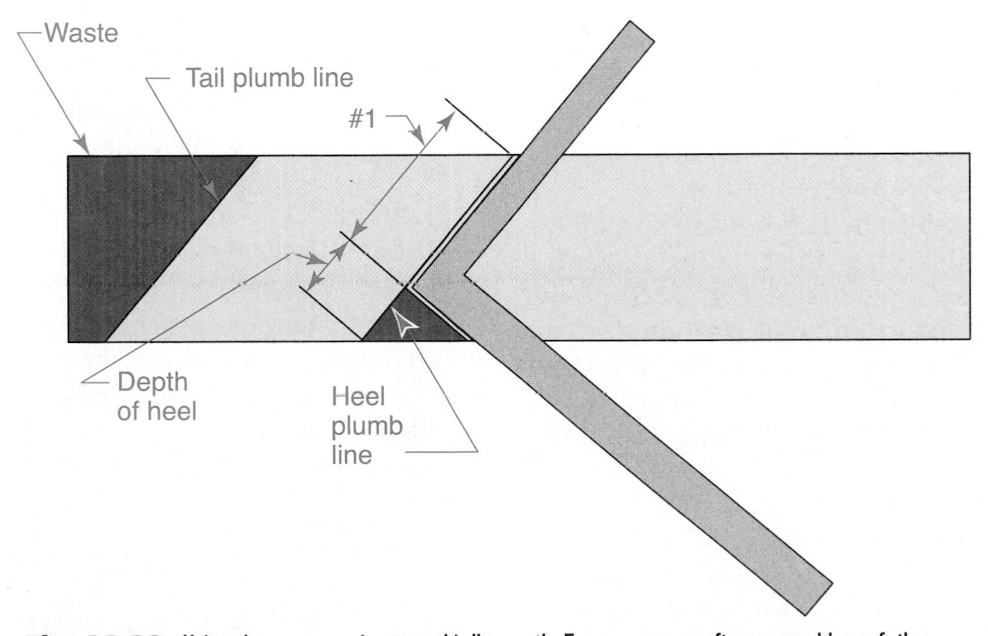

Fig. 22-33. Using the square to lay out a bird's mouth. For a common rafter on a gable roof, the depth of the heel cut is laid out along the heel plumb line. The length of the line at arrow #1 is the important dimension when laying out the bird's mouth for a hip and valley rafter, discussed later.

many pieces of rafter stock are clamped together atop sawhorses. Lines are marked across the edges of the stock to indicate heel cuts, plumb cuts, and bird's-mouth cuts. Then the cuts are made on a group of rafters at the same time, sometimes using special saws.

Carpenter's Tip

Rafter cutting is usually done with a circular saw. It is important not to overcut when making the bird's mouth. This will weaken the rafter. It is best to stop the heel cut and the seat cut short of each intersecting layout line. In other words, make partial cuts. Then finish the cut with a handsaw or jigsaw.

GAMBREL, SHED, AND LOW-SLOPE ROOFS

Other kinds of roofs are framed using variations of the same basic techniques used to build a gable roof. These roofs include gambrel roofs, shed roofs, and flat, or low-slope, roofs.

Framing a Gambrel Roof

The framing for a gambrel roof combines primary and secondary rafters. The lower (primary) rafter has a steep pitch, and the upper (secondary) rafter has a low pitch. If the pitches are known, the rafters may be laid out in the same manner as any common rafter.

The roof may also be laid out full size on the subfloor. Use the run of the building (*AB*) as a radius and draw a semicircle. **Fig. 22-34.** Draw a perpendicular line from point *A* to intersect the semicircle at *E*. This locates the ridge line. Find the height of the walls from the plans. Draw a perpendicular line (*CD*) to this length between the plate and the semicircle. Connect points *B* and *D* and points *D* and *E*. This gives the location and pitch of primary rafter *BD* and secondary rafter *DE*. From this layout the rafter patterns can be made and cut for test fitting on the building.

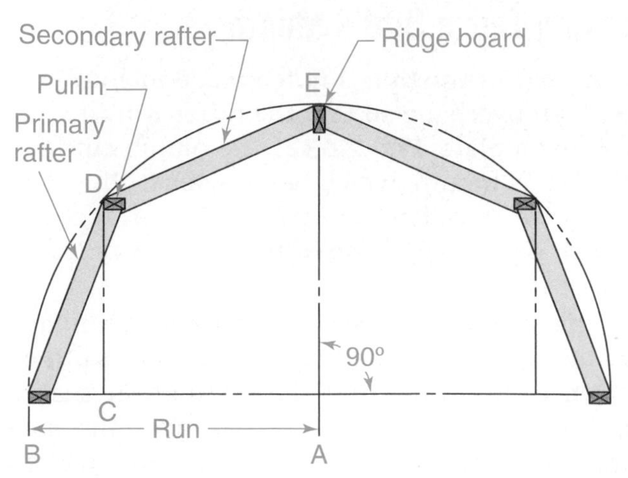

Fig. 22-34. The patterns for the rafters in the gambrel roof may be made by laying out the full-size roof on the subfloor.

Framing a Shed Roof

A shed roof is basically one-half of a gable roof. The full-length rafters in a shed roof are common rafters. The total rise is the difference in height between the walls on which the rafter will bear. The total run is equal to the span of the building minus the width of the top plate on the higher wall. **Fig. 22-35.** Also, the run of the overhang on the higher wall is measured from the inner edge of the top plate. With these exceptions, shed roof common rafters are laid out like gable roof common rafters. A shed roof common rafter has two bird's mouths. They are laid out just like the bird's mouth on a gable roof common rafter.

Framing a Low-Slope Roof

A low-slope roof has a slope of 3/12 or less. This includes so-called "flat" roofs, which actually have a slight slope to encourage water to drain off. A low-slope roof can be framed in the post-and-beam style (see Chapter 19, "Framing Methods") or with nominal 2″ joists.

Low-slope roofs generally require larger rafters than roofs with steeper slopes, but the total amount of framing lumber is usually less. Where rafters also serve as ceiling joists, their size is based on both roof and ceiling loads. The size is given on the plans or determined from rafter span tables.

When there is an overhang on all sides of the house, lookout rafters are ordinarily used. **Fig. 22-36.** *Lookout rafters* project beyond the walls

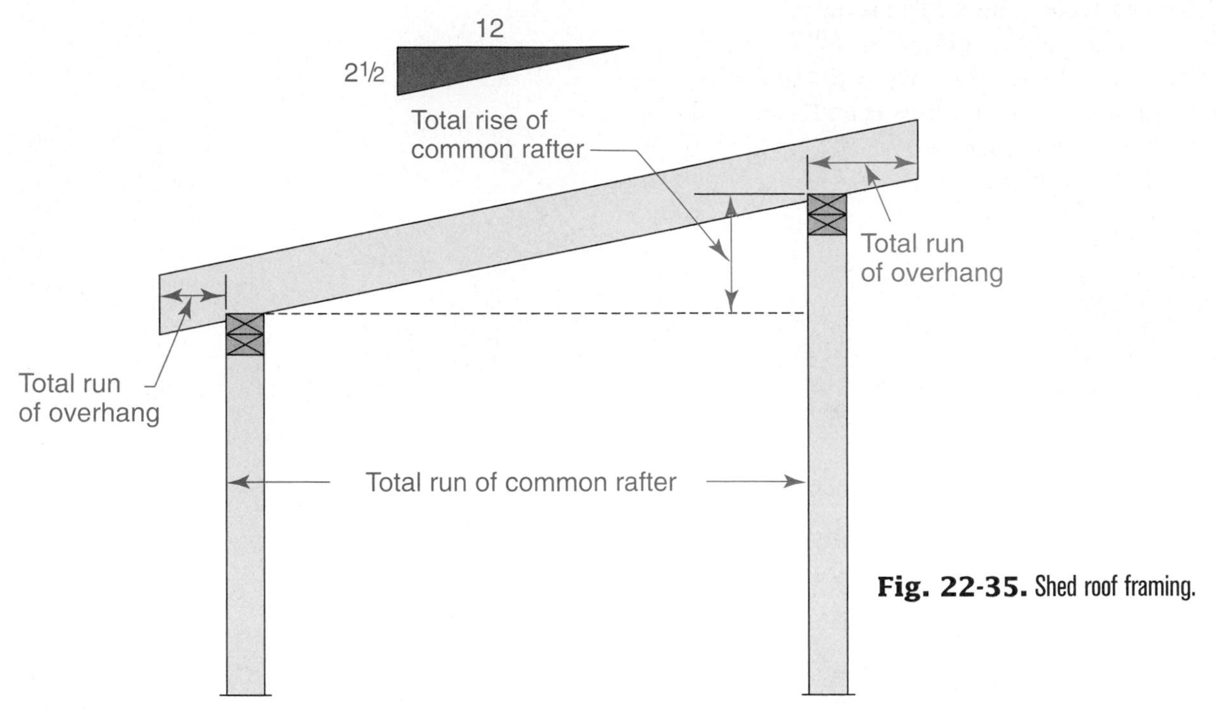

Fig. 22-35. Shed roof framing.

of the house, usually at 90° to the common rafters. Where they run perpendicular to common rafters, they are nailed to a double header and toenailed to the wall plate. The distance from the double header to the wall line is usually twice the overhang. Rafter ends may be capped with a header, which will serve as a nailing surface for trim.

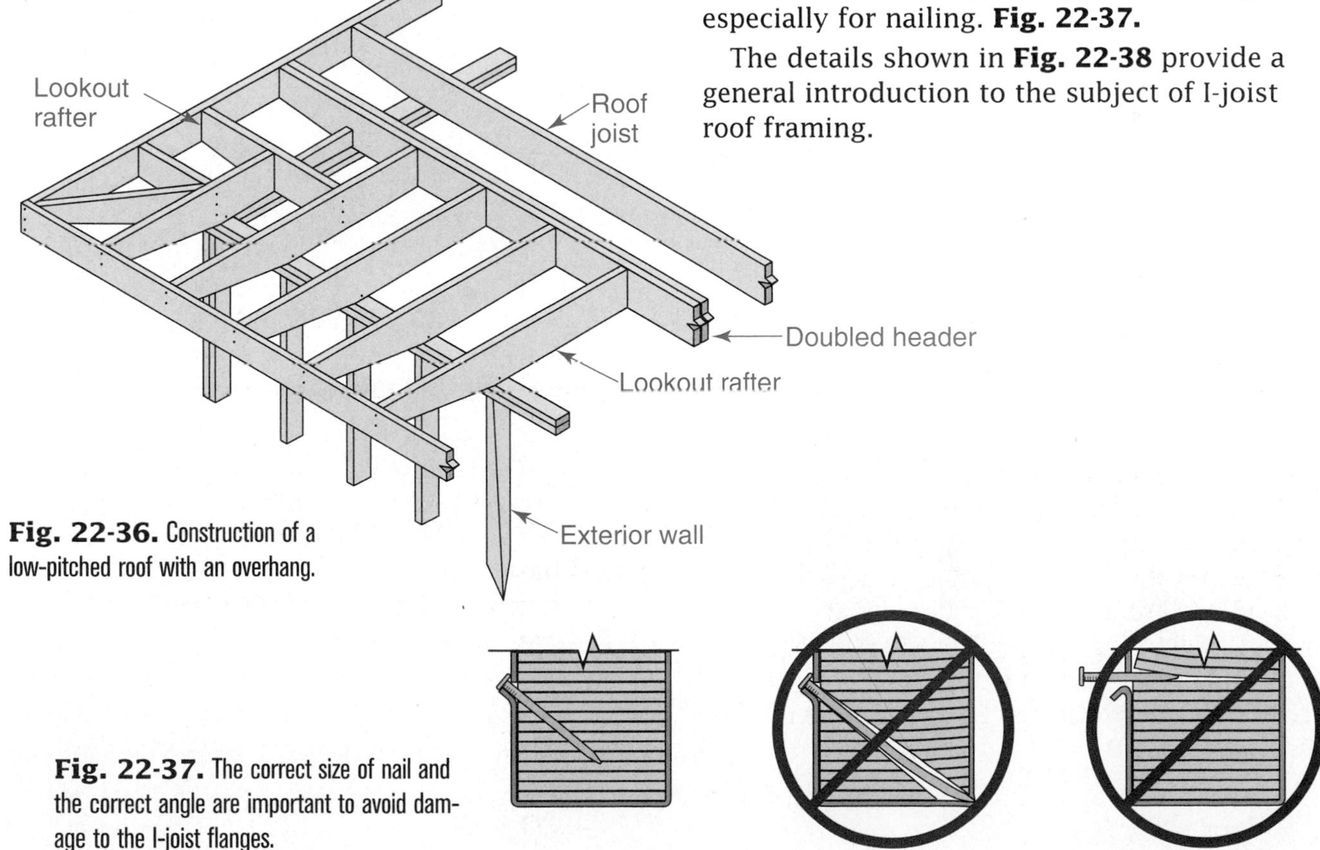

Fig. 22-36. Construction of a low-pitched roof with an overhang.

Fig. 22-37. The correct size of nail and the correct angle are important to avoid damage to the I-joist flanges.

USING I-JOIST RAFTERS

Laminated-veneer lumber can be used to build many portions of the house frame, including the roof. LVL lumber is also used in commercial wood framing. LVL I-joists can be used in place of lumber rafters. Various companies make I-joists. You must follow the manufacturer's instructions for the product you are using, especially for nailing. **Fig. 22-37.**

The details shown in **Fig. 22-38** provide a general introduction to the subject of I-joist roof framing.

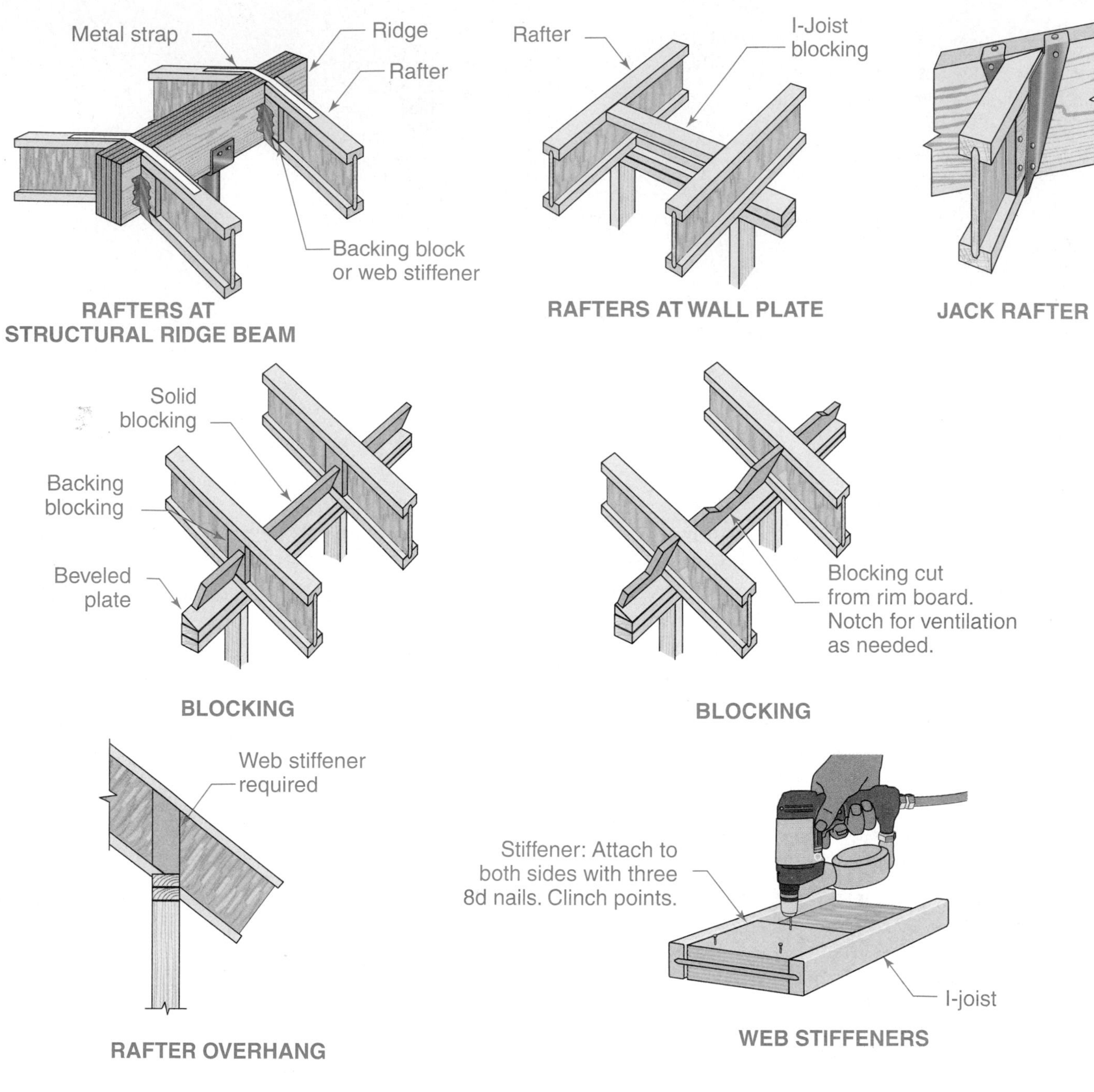

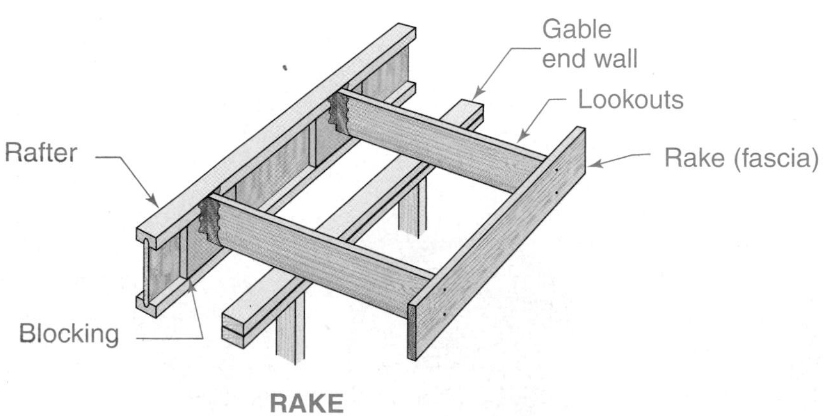

Fig. 22-38. Details for I-joist rafters. These are suggestions only. Always consult the manufacturer's instructions before installation.

SAFETY FIRST

Nailing Safety

Nailing rafters into place is often done under conditions that increase the possibility of injury. Be sure you have solid footing when nailing. Keep your hands safely away from the action. This caution applies both to hand nailing and power nailing.

SECTION 22.2

Check Your Knowledge

1. What prevents rafters from spreading and pushing out on the exterior walls?
2. State the Pythagorean theorem.
3. Name the parts of a bird's mouth and tell where they bear.
4. When making cuts for a bird's mouth, what mistake should you avoid?

On the Job

Find the theoretical rafter length for a common rafter used in a roof with a 7/12 pitch and a span of 23′-6″.

SECTION 22.3

Ceiling Framing

Ceiling joists are the parallel members that support ceiling loads. In the first story of a two-story house, the same framing serves as both ceiling and floor. **Fig. 22-39.** In other words, if you stood downstairs and looked up, you'd refer to it as the ceiling framing. However, if you stood upstairs and looked down, you'd call it the floor framing. The floor framing for the first story of a house is covered in Chapter 20, "Floor Framing."

The ceiling framing discussed in this chapter is directly related to the roof framing. It prevents walls from bowing outward by tying the lower ends of the rafters together. At the same time, it ties the walls of the house together and forms the floor of the attic.

CEILING JOISTS

Ceiling framing for the top level of a house usually proceeds at the same time as roof framing. While the rafters are being laid out and cut, other carpenters cut and install the ceiling joists. Like floor joists, ceiling joists may be supported by girders or by bearing walls.

Fig. 22-39. Ceiling framing often supports a second floor.

Sizing Ceiling Joists

The size of the ceiling joists is determined by the distance they must span and the load they must carry. **Table 22-A.** The species and grade of wood must also be considered. The correct size for the joists will be found on the building plans. Spacing and span limitations must comply with local building codes.

Layout

The layout for ceiling joists is determined as one lays out the rafters. Rafter spacing and placement are determined first. Ceiling joist spacing and placement are determined second.

Ceiling joists are usually placed across the width of the building and parallel to the rafters. The ends of the joists that rest on the exterior wall plates next to the rafters will usually project above the top edge of the rafter. **Fig. 22-40.** These ends must be cut off at an angle to match the angle of the rafters. This is best done before the joists are installed.

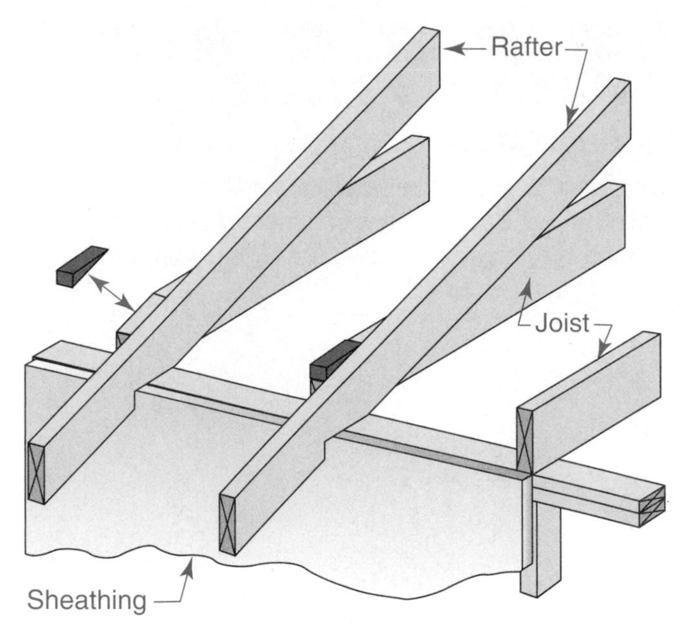

Fig. 22-40. The upper corners of the ceiling joists must be cut off at an angle to match the angle of the rafters. (This angle is the same as the pitch of the roof.) The joists should be cut off about ⅛″ below the rafter's top edge.

Installation begins at one end of the house and continues to the other end. The spacing of the joists is usually 16″ or 24″ OC. Extra joists are placed, as needed, without altering the spacing. For example, a ceiling joist will be needed at the inside edge of the plate on an end wall. This provides an edge nailing surface for the ceiling finish. **Fig. 22-41.** A second joist is usually located over the studs in the side wall. The distance between the first two joists at this location will then be less than the normal OC spacing. **Fig. 22-42.** Each succeeding joist is spaced 16″ or 24″ on center.

Ceiling joists meet other ceiling joists from the opposite side of the building. The joists are offset 1½″ on the two outside walls so that they lap each other when they meet over the bearing

Table 22-A. Allowable Spans for Ceiling Joists Using Nonstress-Graded Lumber

Size of Ceiling Joists (inches)	Spacing of Ceiling Joists (inches)	Maximum Allowable Span (feet and inches)			
		Group I	Group II	Group III	Group IV
2x4	12 16	11-16 10-6	11-0 10-0	9-6 8-6	5-6 5-0
2x6	12 16	18-0 16-0	16-6 15-0	15-6 14-6	12-6 11-0
2x8	12 16	24-0 21-6	22-6 20-6	21-0 19-0	19-0 16-6

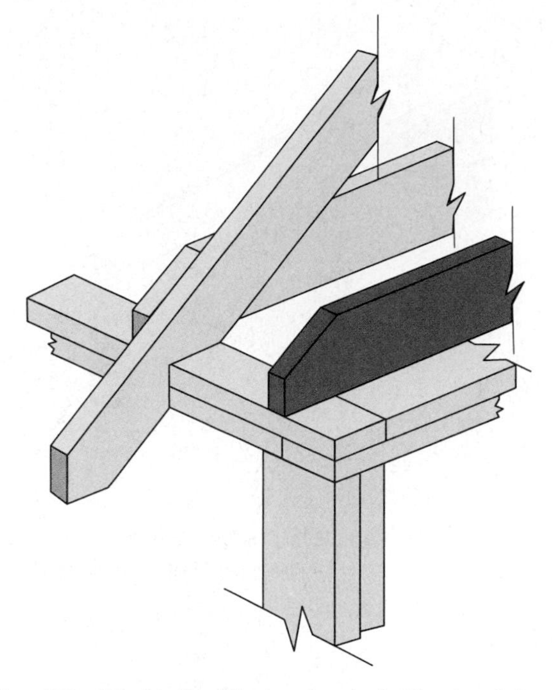

Fig. 22-41. A ceiling joist is set on the inside edge of the end wall to permit nailing of the material for the ceiling surface.

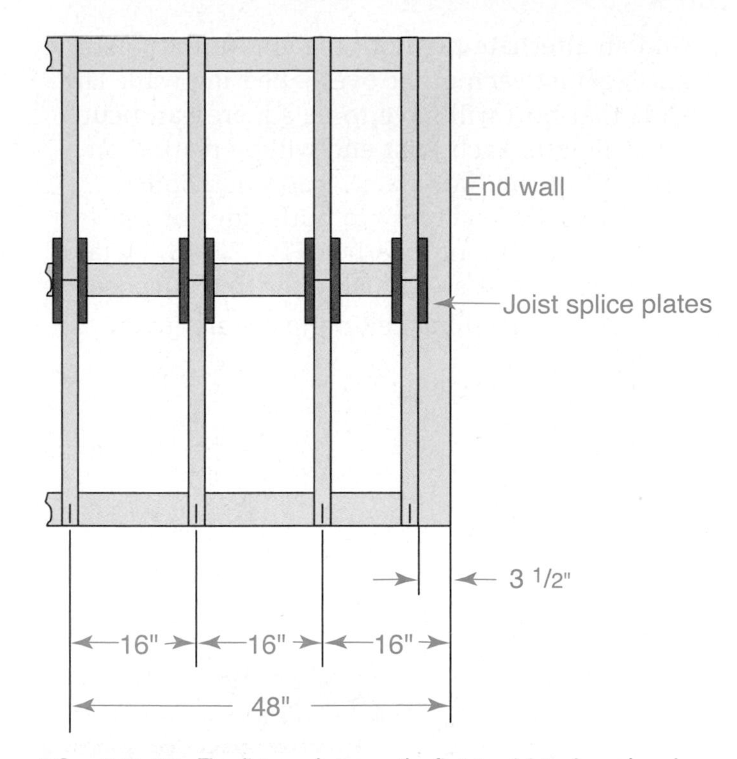

Fig. 22-42. The distance between the first two joists shown here is less than 16″. The joists are butted end to end on the bearing wall. The butt joint must be reinforced.

partition wall. **Fig. 22-43.** This lap is face-nailed with three 16d nails. The joists are toenailed to the bearing wall plate with two 10d nails. Nonbearing partitions that run parallel to the ceiling joists are nailed to blocks installed between the joists. **Fig. 22-44.**

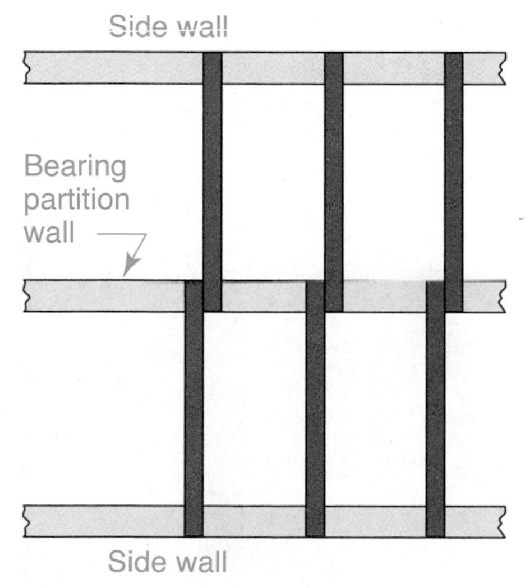

Fig. 22-43. Ceiling joists lapped on the bearing wall.

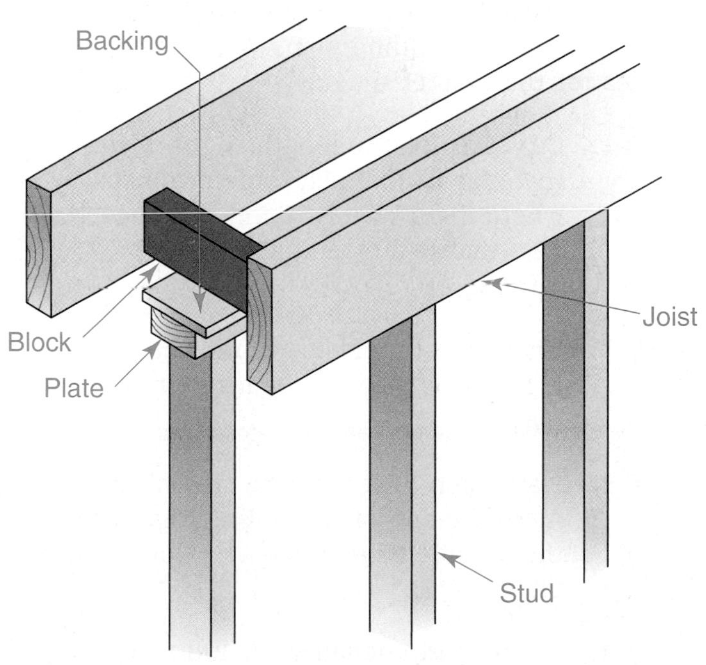

Fig. 22-44. A nonbearing wall is fastened to a block that has been nailed between the joists. Notice the 1x backing that has been attached to the top of the wall for nailing the ceiling material.

In an alternate method, the end of the joists butt against each other over a bearing wall. The ends that butt will have to be squared and cut off to length. Each joist end will be resting on just half of the wall plate. A plywood splice must be nailed securely to both sides of the joists to hold them together. **Fig. 22-45.** Metal connectors are also available for this purpose.

Steps for installing ceiling joists are given below.

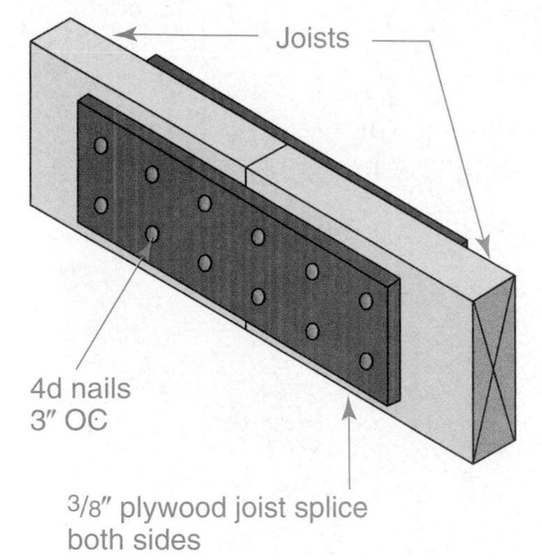

Fig. 22-45. Ceiling joists butted end to end must be spliced together for strength. When solid lumber is used instead of plywood for a splice, it must be ¾″ thick and at least 24″ long.

STEP BY STEP

Installing Ceiling Joists

The locations for ceiling joists are laid out like the locations for floor joists (see Chapter 20, "Floor Framing"). The spacing of the joists will be found on the building plans. Mark the plates for the correct spacing.

Step 1 Cut each joist to length. Sight down the edge of the joist to determine where the crown is. Trim off the corners that will extend above the rafters.

Step 2 Distribute the joists around the building so that they can be lifted into place.

Step 3 Place each joist with the crown up. Align the end of the ceiling joist with the outside edge of the exterior wall plate.

Step 4 At one end, toenail three l0d nails through the joist and into the plate or use a metal framing connector. **Fig. 22-46.**

Step 5 Toenail the other end of the joist to a girder or bearing wall.

Step 6 Nail lapped joists to each other with three 10d nails.

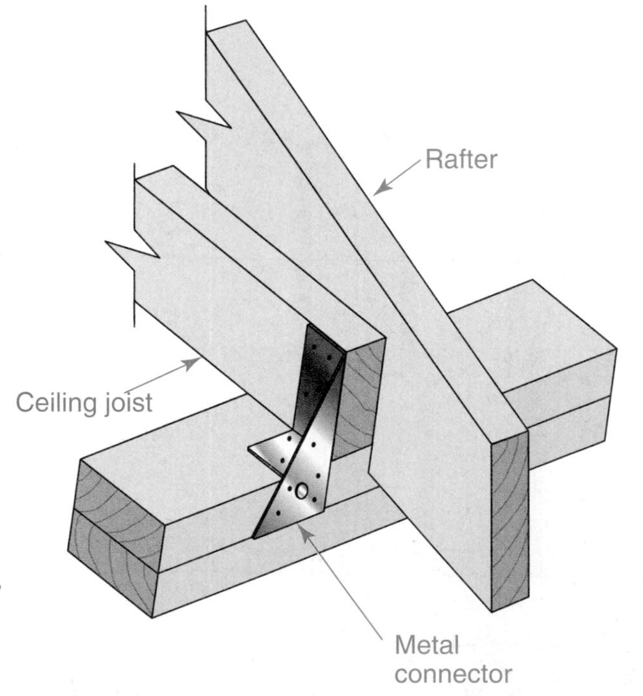

Fig. 22-46. A metal connector can be used to fasten the ceiling joist to the plate.

SPECIAL CEILING FRAMING

Ceiling framing must often accommodate interruptions in the regular spacing of joists. Before beginning layout and installation, the carpenter should check the plans to identify these special situations.

Hip Roofs

In the framing for a hip roof with a shallow slope, the first ceiling joist will interfere with the bottom edge of the rafters. *Stub joists* (short joists) installed at right angles to the regular joists will correct this situation. **Fig. 22-47.** Space the stubs 16″ on center for attaching the finished ceiling. Locate them so that the rafters, when installed, may be nailed directly to their sides.

Ceiling Openings

Openings in the ceiling may be required for a chimney or for access to the attic. These openings are often larger than the spacing between the joists and will require the cutting of one or more joists. Such joists must be supported and framed as described in the section titled, "Framing Large Openings," in Chapter 20.

Building codes require that any framing, including ceiling framing, be kept at least 2″ from the front and sides of masonry fireplaces, and at least 4″ from the back.

Framing Flush Ceilings

In the past, homes usually had many small rooms. Today, however, homeowners often prefer larger and more open living spaces. A combined kitchen and family room is common, for example. To visually tie the rooms together, *flush ceilings* are desirable. (The two ceilings flow together as one.) Because there is no partition, a girder is often needed to support the interior ends of the ceiling joists.

This support can be provided by a *flush girder*. A flush girder is usually built up from the same stock used to frame the rest of the ceiling. It can also be a glulam or LVL beam. Instead of resting on top of the girder, ceiling joists are fastened to the side with joist hangers.

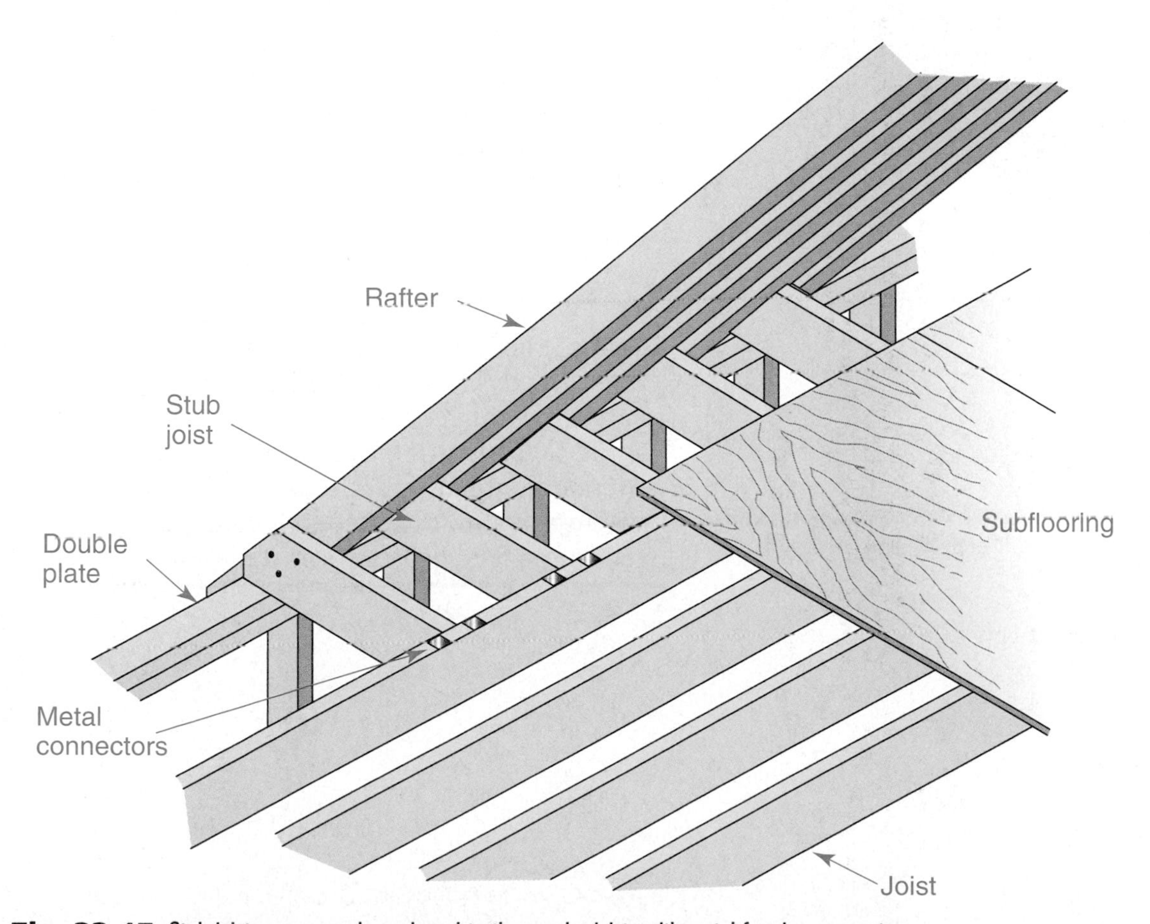

Fig. 22-47. Stub joists are securely anchored to the regular joists with metal framing connectors.

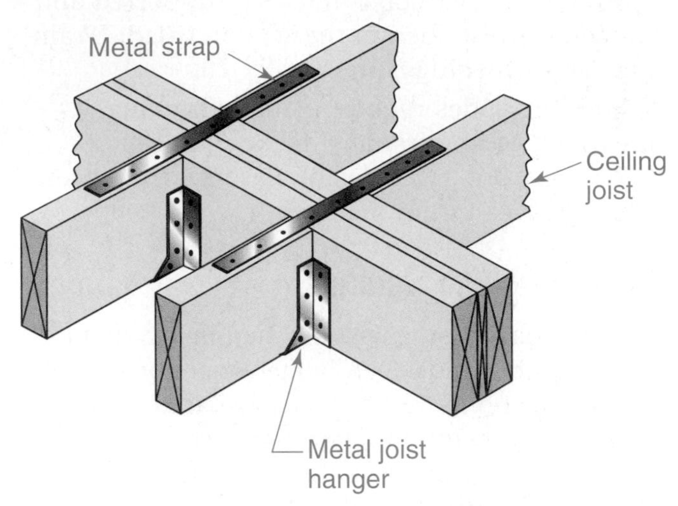

Fig. 22-48. Ceiling joists are fastened to a flush girder with joist hangers. The joints can be reinforced with metal straps.

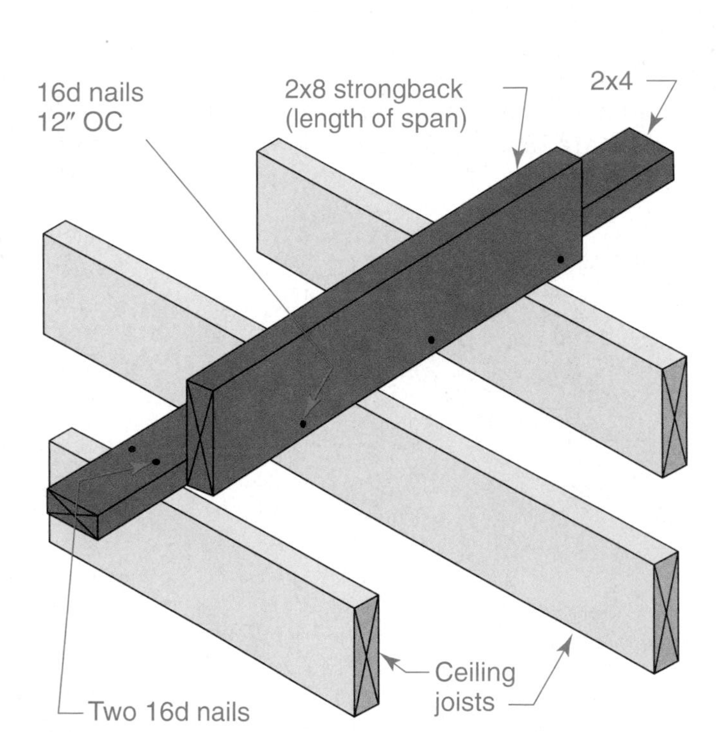

Fig. 22-49. A strongback is used to give long joists additional support.

Fig. 22-48. Joist hangers are nailed to the girder with 10d or larger nails and to the joist with joist hanger nails. It is often easiest to fasten the hangers to the ends of the joists before raising the joists into place.

Another approach that can sometimes be used with shorter spans is to stiffen the ceiling joists with a member called a *strongback*. **Fig. 22-49.** The strongback should be nailed to the tops of the ceiling joists. However, this method will not eliminate the need for some kind of header.

ESTIMATING

The methods for estimating the number of ceiling joists, as well as the material cost, are the same as for estimating floor joists. Refer to Chapter 20, "Floor Framing."

SECTION 22.3 Check Your Knowledge

1. What factors determine the size of ceiling joists?
2. How are ceiling joists arranged in relation to the building and rafters?
3. How much space must be left between ceiling joists and the front and sides of a masonry chimney?
4. How are joists attached to a flush girder?

On the Job

Because roof trusses are prefabricated, it might be assumed that using them is less expensive than using conventional rafters. Find out if this is true by consulting a local builder or by calling a lumber company that sells roof trusses. Be sure to ask about the relative material costs as well as the labor costs for installation.

Chapter 22 Review

Section Summaries

22.1 Planning a roof calls for an understanding of architectural styles, as well as how the individual pieces are assembled. A roof plan must be developed before any framing can begin.

22.2 There are four basic methods for laying out the cuts required for a common rafter. They include the Pythagorean theorem method, the unit length method, the step-off method, and the calculator method.

22.3 Ceiling framing is much like floor framing. However, it is often considered to be a part of roof framing.

Review Questions

1. To what basic roof type is a mansard roof most similar?
2. Name the parts of a simple, conventional roof.
3. Name the four basic types of rafters.
4. What is the span of a roof?
5. Describe the process for laying out a plumb cut line on a rafter.
6. Where is the unit length found for a particular rafter?
7. Name the four methods for calculating the length of a common rafter.
8. What technique can carpenters use to speed up conventional roof construction without sacrificing quality?
9. Why must the upper corners of ceiling joists be cut off when they rest next to rafters?
10. When might openings in the ceiling framing be required?

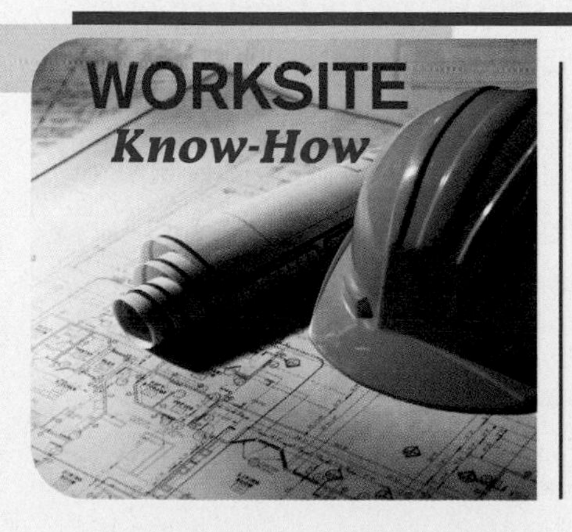

Protecting Other Workers from Ladders When you're carrying a ladder, always be aware of where it is in relation to the people and objects around you. Passageways and doorways are especially dangerous because you don't know what might be on the other side. Be sure to proceed slowly. As you know, long ladders should always be carried horizontally. However, the front end should be high enough to clear the top of a person's head. The back should be kept closer to the ground.

Chapter 23 Hip, Valley, and Jack Rafters

Objectives

After reading this chapter, you'll be able to:

- Lay out a hip rafter for a given roof.
- Lay out a valley rafter for a given roof.
- Lay out a jack rafter for a given roof.
- Explain why the intersection of two roofs makes framing more complex.

Terms

backing the hip
doghouse dormer
dropping the hip
hip rafter
jack rafter
side cut
valley rafter

A simple gable roof can be built entirely with common rafters. However, a carpenter must also know how to lay out and cut hip, valley, and jack rafters. **Fig. 23-1.** These rafters are required when framing complex roofs, such as hip roofs and intersecting gable roofs. A **hip rafter** forms a raised area, or "hip," usually extending from the corner of the building diagonally to the ridge board. A **valley rafter** forms a depression in the roof instead of a hip. Like the hip rafter, it extends diagonally from plate to ridge board. A hip rafter is called for only when framing a hip roof, but a valley rafter is needed on both hip and gable roofs whenever roof planes intersect. A **jack rafter** is a shortened common rafter that may be framed to a hip rafter, a valley rafter, or both. Thus, there are hip jack rafters and valley jack rafters.

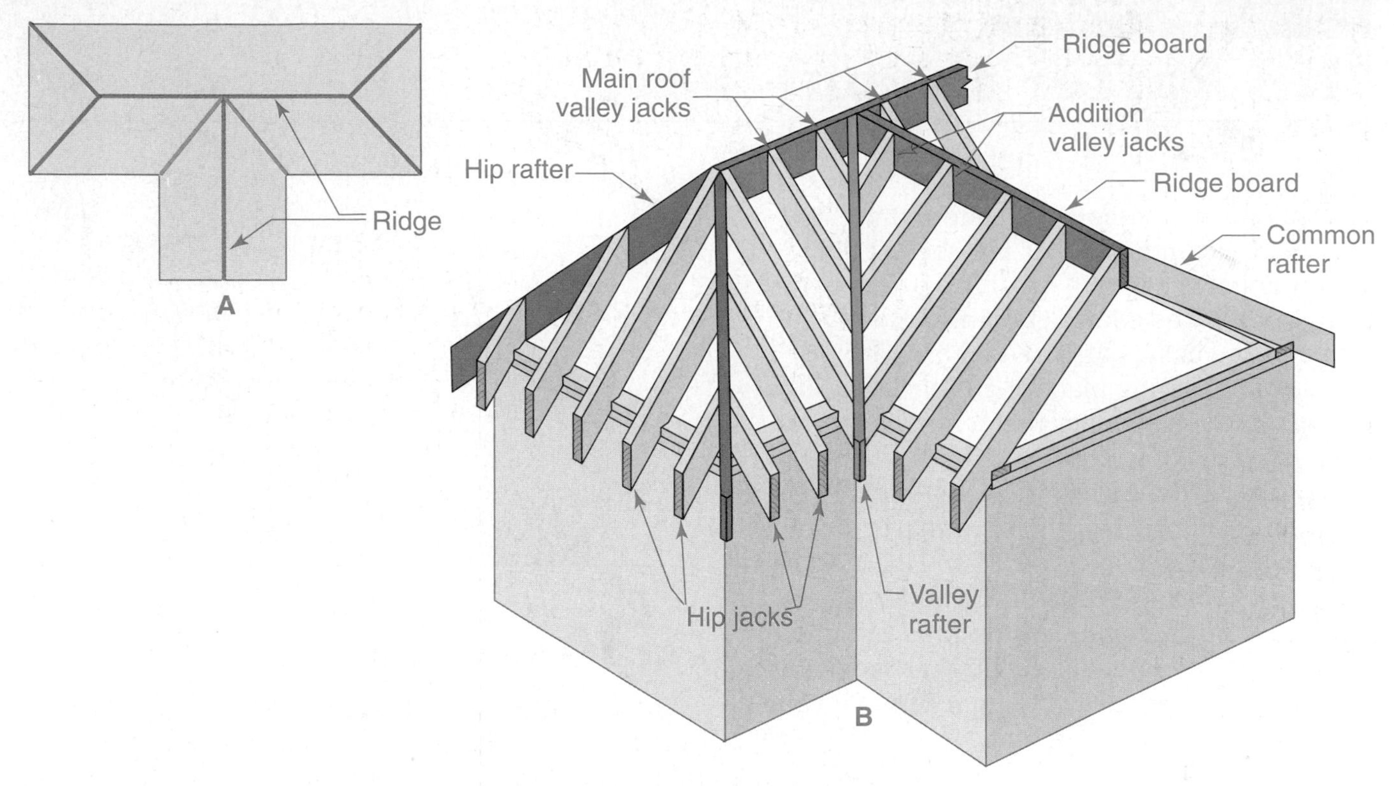

Fig. 23-1. Roof framing. *A.* Roof framing plan. *B.* Roof frame with hip, valley, and jack rafters.

The total rise of hip and valley rafters is the same as that of common rafters. They are also the same thickness as common rafters. However, they should be nominally 2″ wider. For example, if you use 2x6 common rafters, use 2x8 hip rafters when providing full bearing for the end of intersecting jack rafters. **Fig. 23-2.**

Roof framing with hip, valley, and jack rafters is more complex than framing entirely with common rafters. A mastery of this subject is what distinguishes the true professional from the casual carpenter. This chapter describes how to figure rafter layouts manually. On the job, construction calculators and triangular framing squares are often used for this purpose.

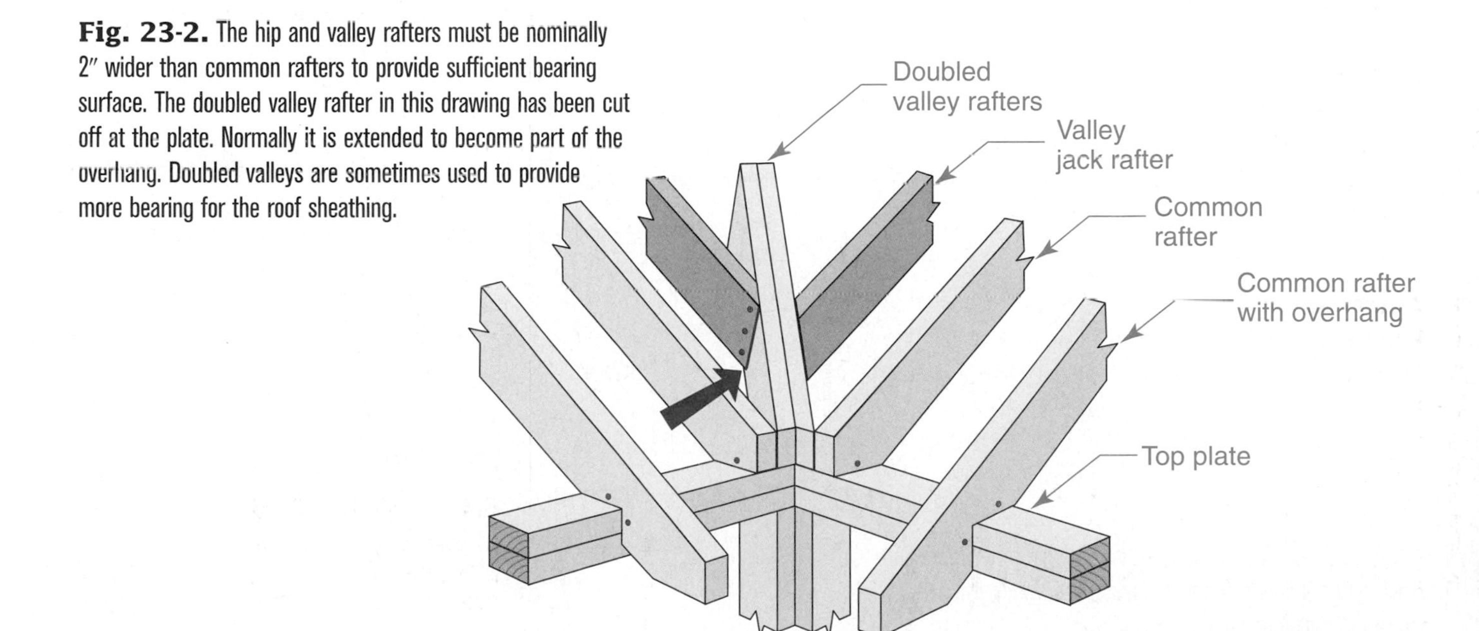

Fig. 23-2. The hip and valley rafters must be nominally 2″ wider than common rafters to provide sufficient bearing surface. The doubled valley rafter in this drawing has been cut off at the plate. Normally it is extended to become part of the overhang. Doubled valleys are sometimes used to provide more bearing for the roof sheathing.

SECTION 23.1

Hip Rafter Layout

Any of the methods for determining the length of a common rafter may be used for determining the length of a hip rafter (see Chapter 22, "Basic Roof Framing"). However, some of the basic data used is different.

Part of a framing plan for a hip roof is shown in **Fig. 23-3**. Remember that a line on the framing plan indicating a rafter represents the total run of the rafter, but not its actual length. On a hip roof framing plan, the lines that indicate the hip rafters (*EC*, *AC*, *KG*, and *IG* in Fig. 23-3) form 45° angles with the edge of the building. You can see from the plan that the total run of a hip rafter is the hypotenuse of a right triangle. Each shorter side is equal to the total run of a common rafter. In **Fig. 23-4**, one corner of the roof framing plan (*ABCF* in Fig. 23-3) has been drawn in perspective. This shows the relative position of the hip rafter to the common rafter.

The unit run of a hip rafter is the hypotenuse of a right triangle with the shorter sides each equal to the unit run of a common rafter. **Fig. 23-5.** The unit run of a common rafter is 12″. Using the Pythagorean theorem, the unit run of a hip rafter is the square root of 122 + 122, which is 16.97″ (rounded up to 17″). **Fig. 23-6A.**

Like the unit length of a common rafter, the unit length of a hip rafter may be obtained from the rafter table on the framing square. In **Fig. 23-6B**, the second line in the table is headed "Length Hip or Valley per Foot Run." This means "for every 12″ of a common rafter in the same roof." Another way to state this would be "per 16.97″ run of hip or valley rafter." For example, the unit length for a unit rise of 8″ is 18.76″. To calculate the length of a hip rafter, multiply the unit length by the number of feet in the total run of a common rafter.

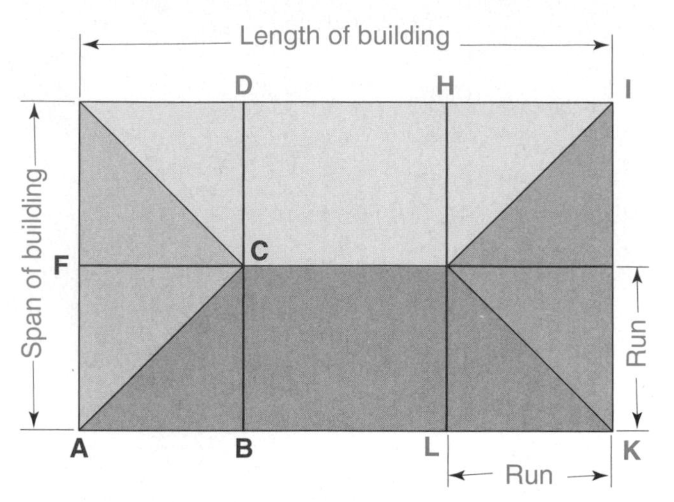

Fig. 23-3. Hip roof framing plan for a small building.

Look again at Fig. 23-5, which shows the corner of the building shown in Fig. 23-3. In this example the total run of a common rafter is 5′. The unit rise is 8″ and the unit length of the hip rafter for this unit rise is 18.76″. The unit length multiplied by the total run in feet is the length of the hip rafter in inches ($18.76'' \times 5 = 93.8''$, or 7′-9$\frac{13}{16}$″). As in the case of common rafters, this is the theoretical length. To obtain the actual length, the ridge board shortening allowance and the rafter tail length will have to be calculated and laid out.

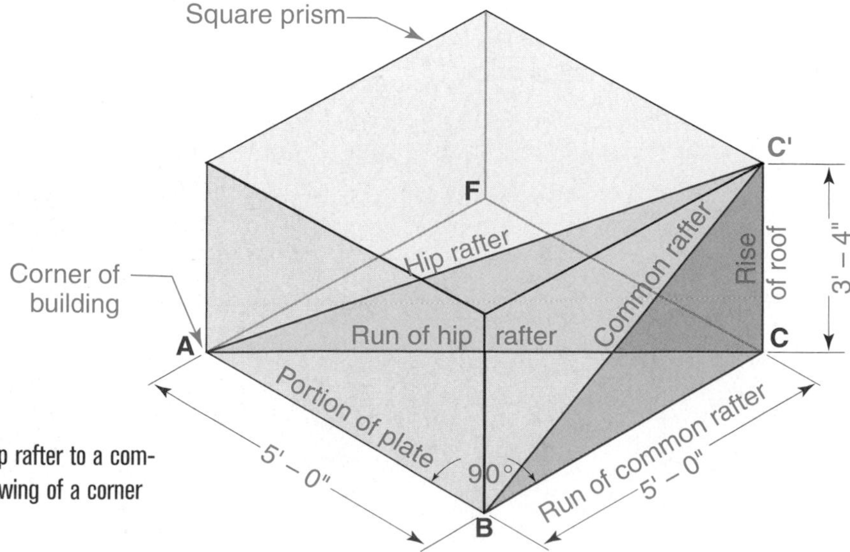

Fig. 23-4. The relative position of a hip rafter to a common rafter is shown in this perspective drawing of a corner from the roof framing plan in Fig. 23-3.

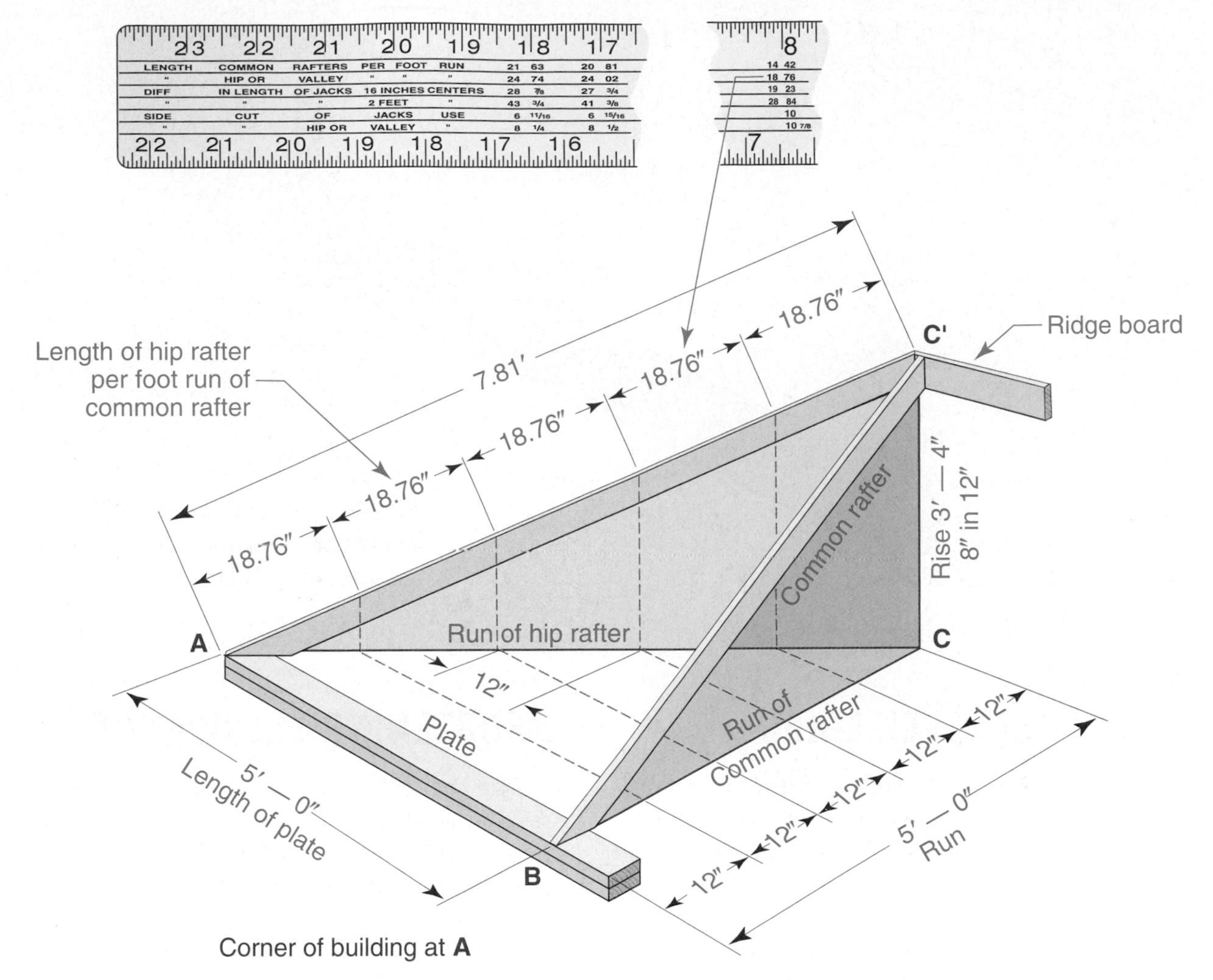

Fig. 23-5. The relationship between the unit run of a hip rafter and the unit run of a common rafter.

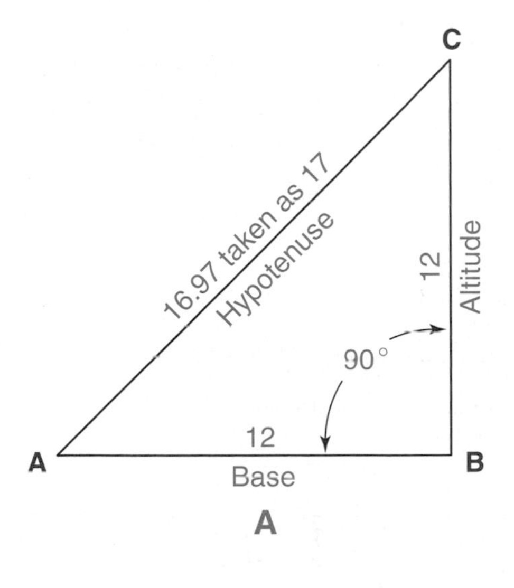

Fig. 23-6. Finding unit run and unit length. *A.* The hypotenuse of a right triangle, the shorter sides of which each equal 12″, is 16.97″. This can be rounded off to 17″. *B.* Unit length can be obtained from the framing square.

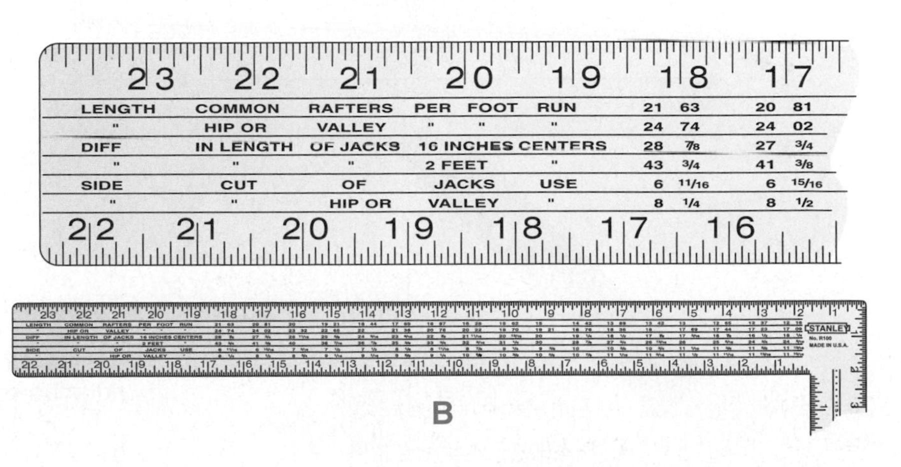

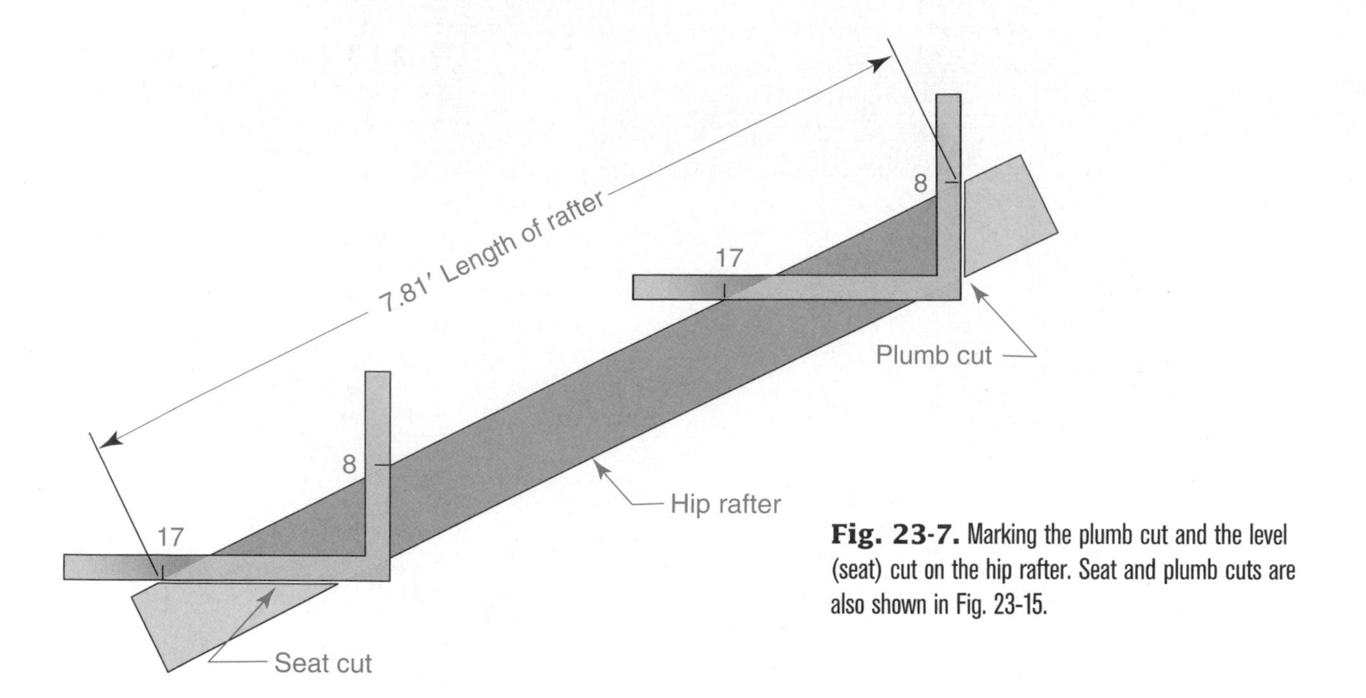

Fig. 23-7. Marking the plumb cut and the level (seat) cut on the hip rafter. Seat and plumb cuts are also shown in Fig. 23-15.

PLUMB AND LEVEL LINES

Cuts made in a hip or valley rafter are made either along plumb lines (plumb cuts) or along level lines (level cuts). To lay out the plumb and level cuts of the hip or valley rafters, set off 17″ on the blade of the framing square. On the tongue set off the rise per foot of common rafter run. A line drawn along the tongue then indicates the plumb cut. A line drawn along the blade indicates the level cut. When the completed rafter is to rest on its level cut, the level cut is sometimes referred to as the *seat cut.* **Fig. 23-7.**

SHORTENING ALLOWANCE

The theoretical length of a hip rafter does not take into account the thickness of the ridge board. This must be allowed for by deducting the shortening allowance. The shortening allowance for a hip rafter depends on the way the rafter is cut to fit against the other structural members. Some carpenters make a single side cut, as in **Fig. 23-8**. Other carpenters prefer a double side cut, as in **Fig. 23-9**.

Sometimes the ridge board is a different thickness than the rafters. The shortening allowance must take this into account. If the hip rafter is

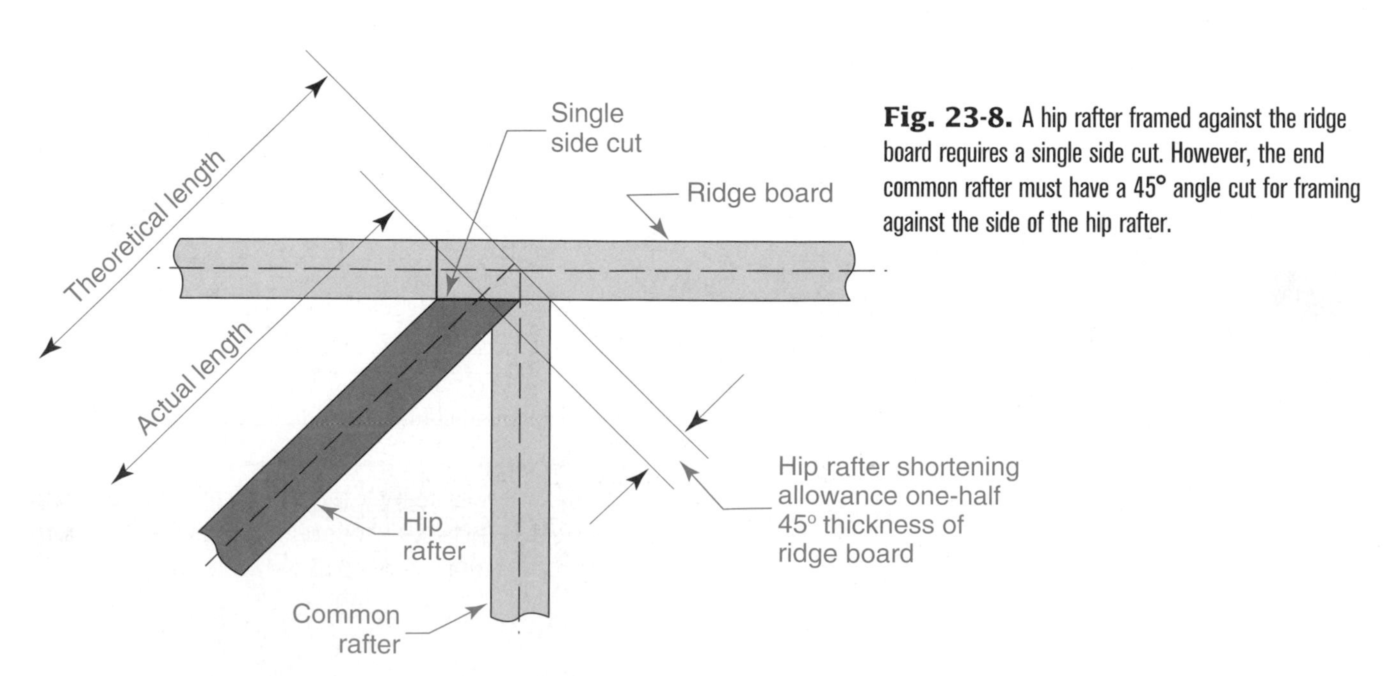

Fig. 23-8. A hip rafter framed against the ridge board requires a single side cut. However, the end common rafter must have a 45° angle cut for framing against the side of the hip rafter.

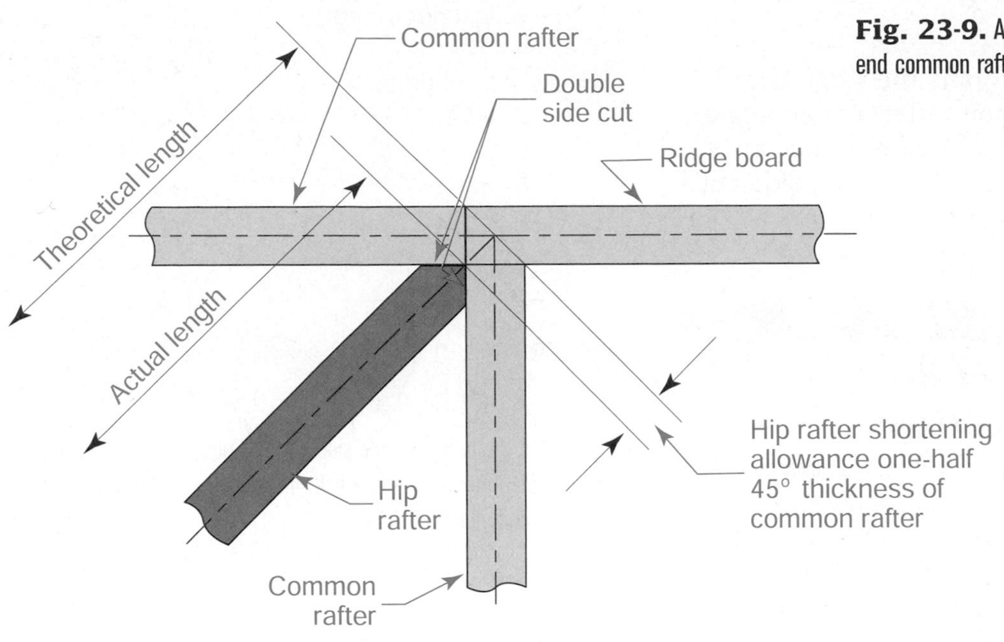

Fig. 23-9. A hip rafter framed against the ridge-end common rafters requires a double side cut.

framed against the ridge board, using a single side cut, the shortening allowance is one-half the 45° thickness of the ridge board. (The 45° thickness is the length of a line laid at 45° across the thickness of the board.) However, if the hip rafter is framed against the common rafters, using a double side cut, the shortening allowance is one-half the 45° thickness of a common rafter.

To lay out the shortening allowance, set the tongue of the framing square along the rafter's plumb line. Measure the shortening allowance along the blade and mark this point. **Fig. 23-10.** Then slide the square sideways until the tongue is lined up with the mark and draw another plumb line. **Fig. 23-11.** This line marks the actual plumb cut for the rafter.

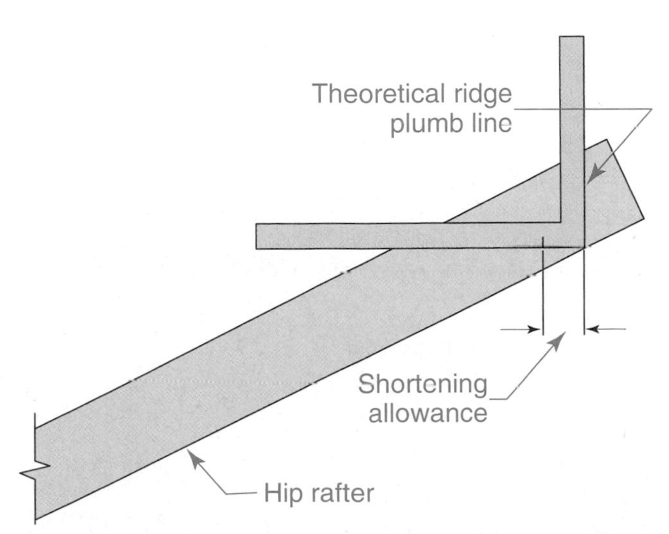

Fig. 23-10. To lay out the shortening allowance, place the tongue of the square along the plumb line and measure the shortening allowance along the blade of the square (level line).

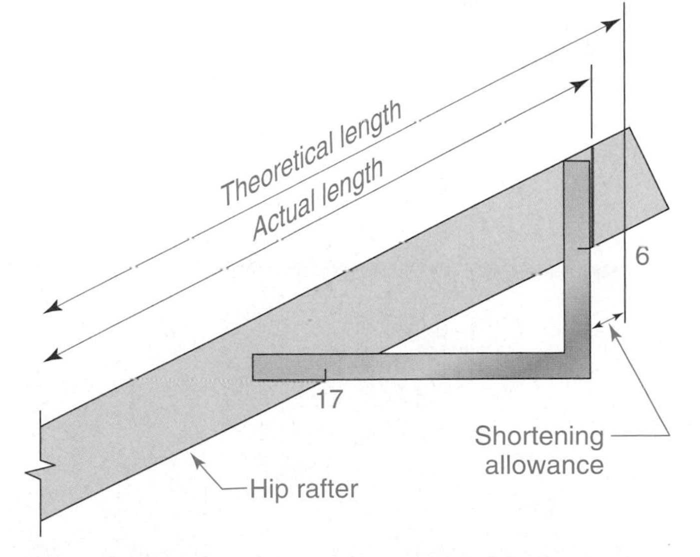

Fig. 23-11. Set the square to the cut of the roof (8″ unit rise for this example) with the tongue on the shortening allowance mark. Draw the actual ridge plumb line along the edge of the tongue.

SIDE CUTS

The end of a hip rafter joins the ridge board (or the ends of the common rafters) at an angle. The cut is called a **side cut** or sometimes a *cheek cut* (see Figs. 23-8 and 23-9). The side cut may be laid out in one of two ways.

SAFETY FIRST

Cutting Compound Angles

The cuts made on hip jack and valley jack rafters are typically made at compound angles. To make such cuts, tilt a portable saw at a bevel angle. Then guide it across the rafter stock at a miter angle. Secure the stock so it will not move during the cut. To prevent the blade guard from binding, retract it to get the cut started. Then release it to complete the cut. Never disable or remove the guard to make a compound-angle cut.

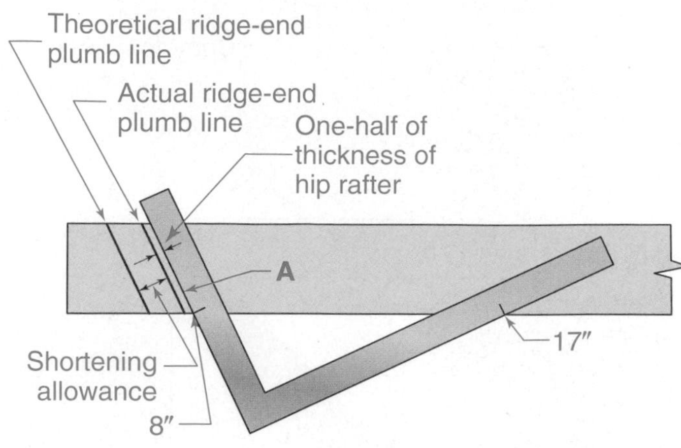

Fig. 23-12. To lay out the side cut at a right angle to the ridge plumb cut line, measure off one-half the thickness of the hip rafter from the actual ridge plumb cut line.

Method 1

1. Place the tongue of the framing square along the actual ridge board plumb cut line. **Fig. 23-12.** Measure one-half the thickness of the hip rafter along the blade (level line).
2. Shift the tongue to the mark, set the square to the cut of the rafter (17″ and 8″ in this example), and draw a plumb line (*A*).
3. Turn the rafter up and draw a centerline along its edge. Then draw the side cut. **Fig. 23-13.** A hip rafter that will be framed against the ridge board has only a single side cut (Fig. 23-8). A hip rafter framed against the ends of the common rafters requires a double side cut (Fig. 23-9). In either case, the tail of the rafter must have a double side cut at the same angle, but in the reverse direction, to allow attachment of the fascia board. **Fig. 23-14.**

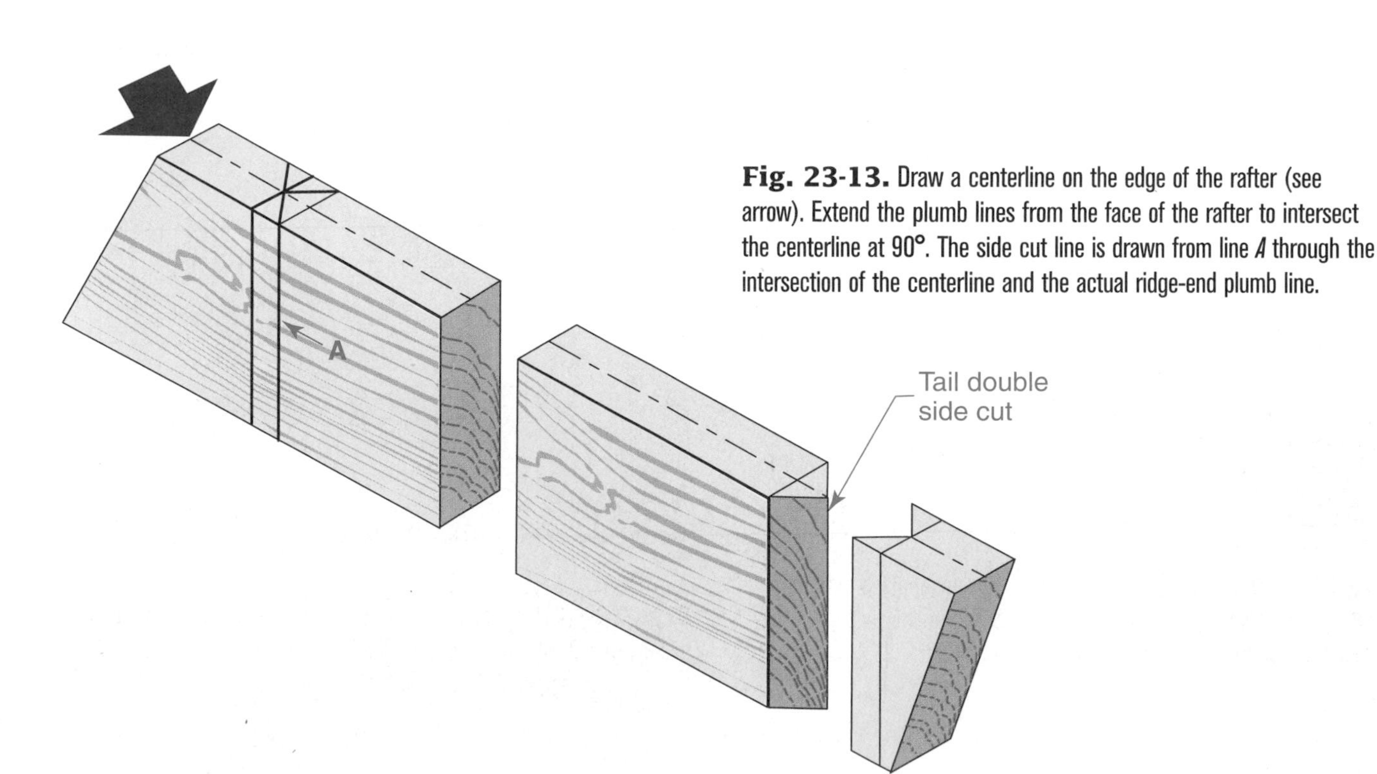

Fig. 23-13. Draw a centerline on the edge of the rafter (see arrow). Extend the plumb lines from the face of the rafter to intersect the centerline at 90°. The side cut line is drawn from line *A* through the intersection of the centerline and the actual ridge-end plumb line.

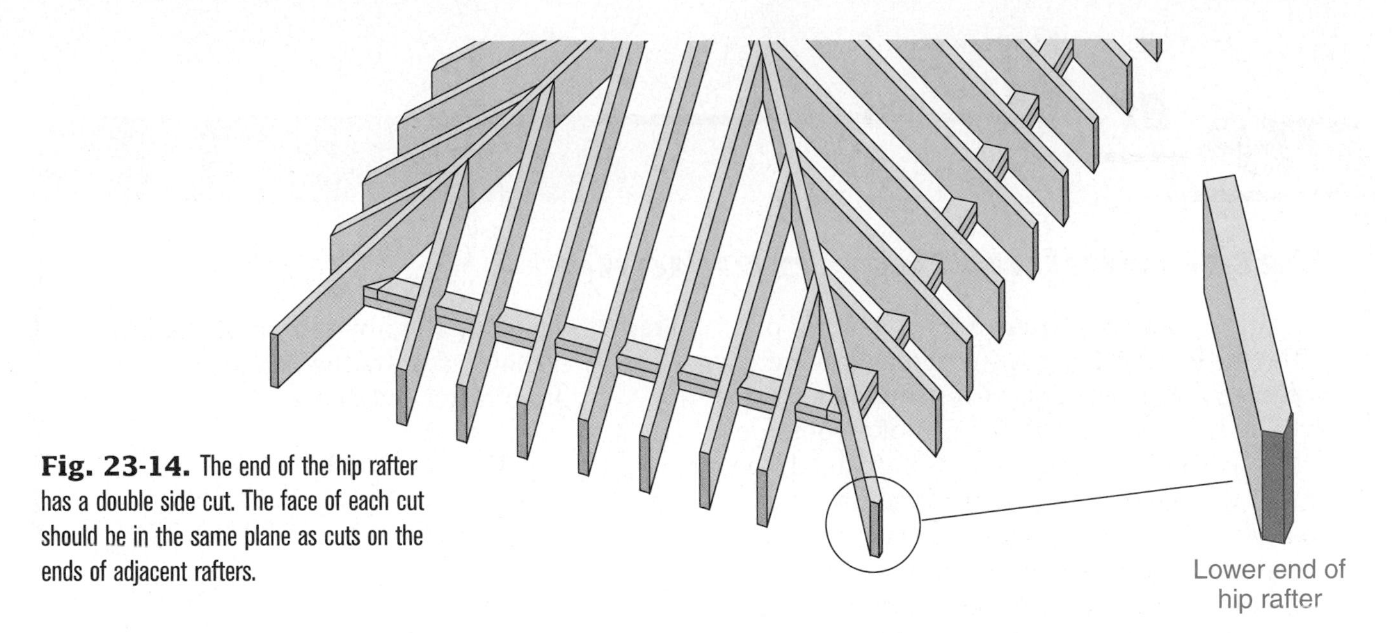

Fig. 23-14. The end of the hip rafter has a double side cut. The face of each cut should be in the same plane as cuts on the ends of adjacent rafters.

Method 2

For this method, refer to the rafter table on the framing square.

1. On the framing square, the bottom line of the table is headed "Side Cut Hip or Valley Use" (see Fig. 23-6B on p. 451). Follow this line over to the column under the number 8 (for a unit rise of 8″). The number shown is 10⅞.
2. Place the framing square face up on the rafter edge, with the tongue on the ridge-end plumb cut line (see line *A* in Fig. 23-13).
3. Set the square to a cut of 10⅞″ on the blade and 12″ on the tongue. **Fig. 23-15.** Draw the side cut angle along the tongue.

For determining the overhang, see the Step-by-Step feature on page 456.

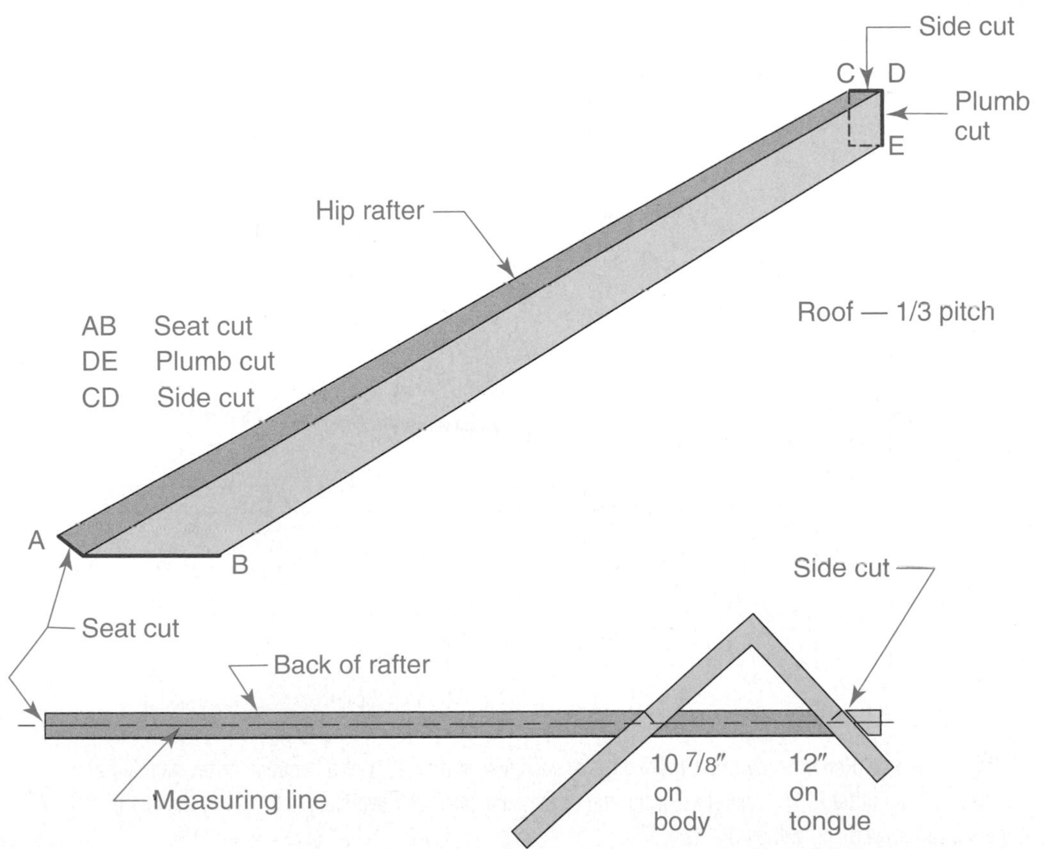

Fig. 23-15. The framing square is in position on the back edge of the hip rafter for a unit rise of 8″. A single side cut will be made for framing against the ridge board.

STEP BY STEP

Determining the Overhang

As with a common rafter overhang, a hip or valley rafter overhang is figured as if it were a separate rafter. The run of this overhang, however, is not the same as the run of a common rafter overhang in the same roof. Instead, the run of the overhang is the hypotenuse of a right triangle whose shorter sides are each equal to the run of a common rafter overhang. **Fig. 23-16.** If the run of the common rafter overhang is 2′ for a roof with an 8″ unit rise, the length of the hip or valley rafter tail is figured as follows.

Step 1 Find the unit length of the hip or valley rafter on the framing square (see Fig. 23-6B). For this roof it is 18.76″.

Step 2 Multiply the unit length of the hip or valley rafter by the run of the common rafter overhang:

18.76″ (unit length of hip or valley rafter) × 2 (feet of run in common rafter overhang) = 37.52″, or 37½″

Step 3 Add this product to the theoretical rafter length.

The overhang may also be stepped off as described in Chapter 22 for a common rafter. When stepping off the length of the overhang, set the 170 mark on the blade even with the edge of the rafter. Set the unit rise, whatever it might be, on the tongue, even with the same rafter edge.

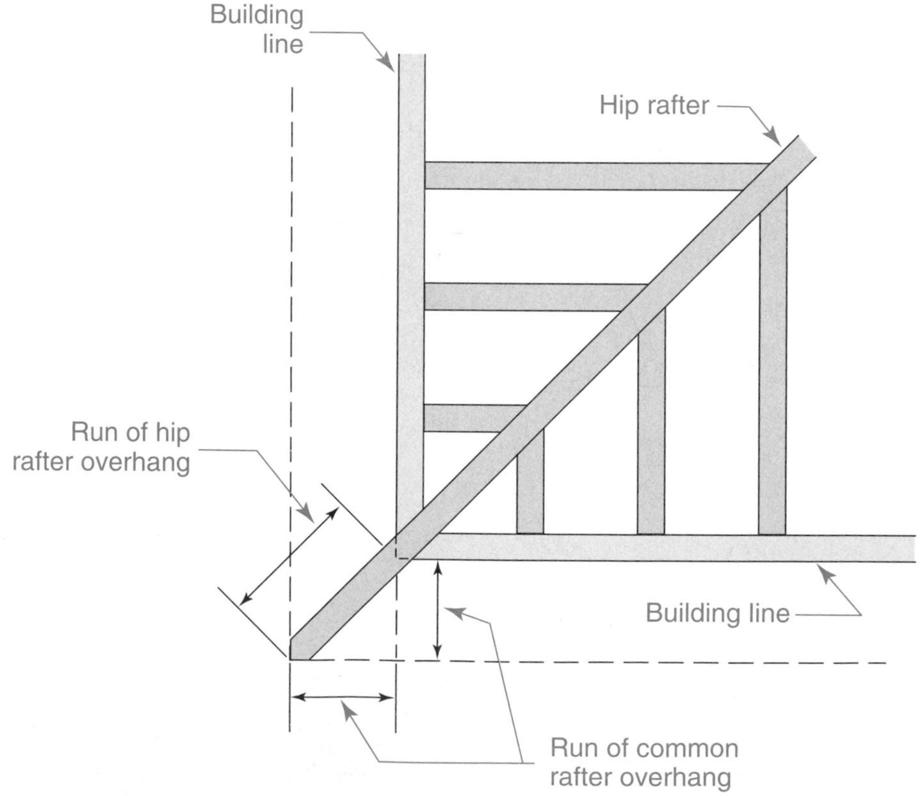

Fig. 23-16. Run of a hip rafter overhang. For each unit of run (12″) of a common rafter, the unit of run for the hip rafter is 17″. Therefore, if the run of the common rafter overhang is 2′ (24″), the run of the hip rafter overhang will be 34″ (2 x 17″).

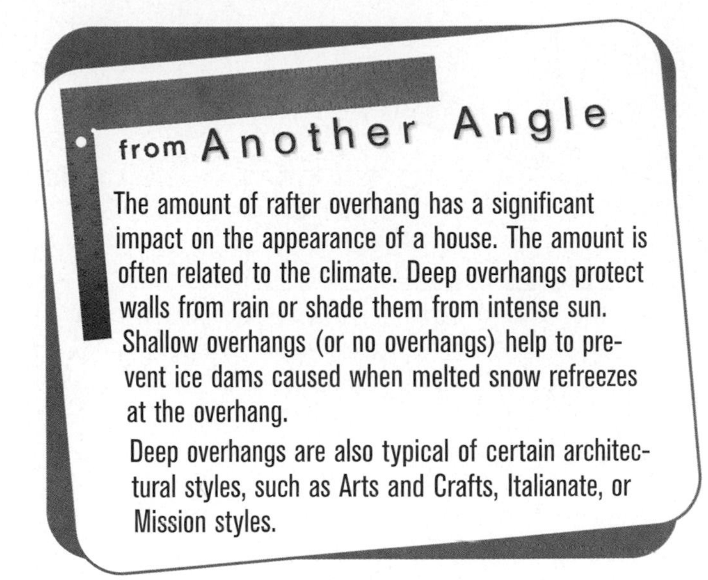

from Another Angle

The amount of rafter overhang has a significant impact on the appearance of a house. The amount is often related to the climate. Deep overhangs protect walls from rain or shade them from intense sun. Shallow overhangs (or no overhangs) help to prevent ice dams caused when melted snow refreezes at the overhang.

Deep overhangs are also typical of certain architectural styles, such as Arts and Crafts, Italianate, or Mission styles.

BIRD'S MOUTH

Laying out the bird's mouth for a hip rafter is much the same as for a common rafter. However, there are a couple of things to remember. When you lay out the plumb (heel cut) and level (seat cut) lines on a hip rafter, set the body of the square at 17″ and the tongue to the unit rise (depending on the roof pitch; see Fig. 23-7 on p. 452). When laying out the depth of the heel, measure along the heel plumb line down from the top edge of the rafter. **Fig. 23-17.** This must be done because the hip rafters are usually wider than common rafters, and the distance should be the same on both. An additional step must also be taken to ensure that the top edge of a hip rafter will be in alignment with jack rafters. In this step, the hip rafter must either be backed or dropped.

Backing or Dropping a Hip Rafter

If the top edge of the hip rafter extends slightly above the upper ends of the jack rafters, it will interfere with the sheathing. **Fig. 23-18A.** **Backing the hip** means to bevel the upper edge of the hip rafter. This allows the roof sheathing to be installed without hitting the corners of the hip rafter. **Fig. 23-18B.** **Dropping the hip** means to deepen the bird's mouth so as to bring the top edge of the hip rafter in line with the upper ends of the jacks. **Fig. 23-18C.**

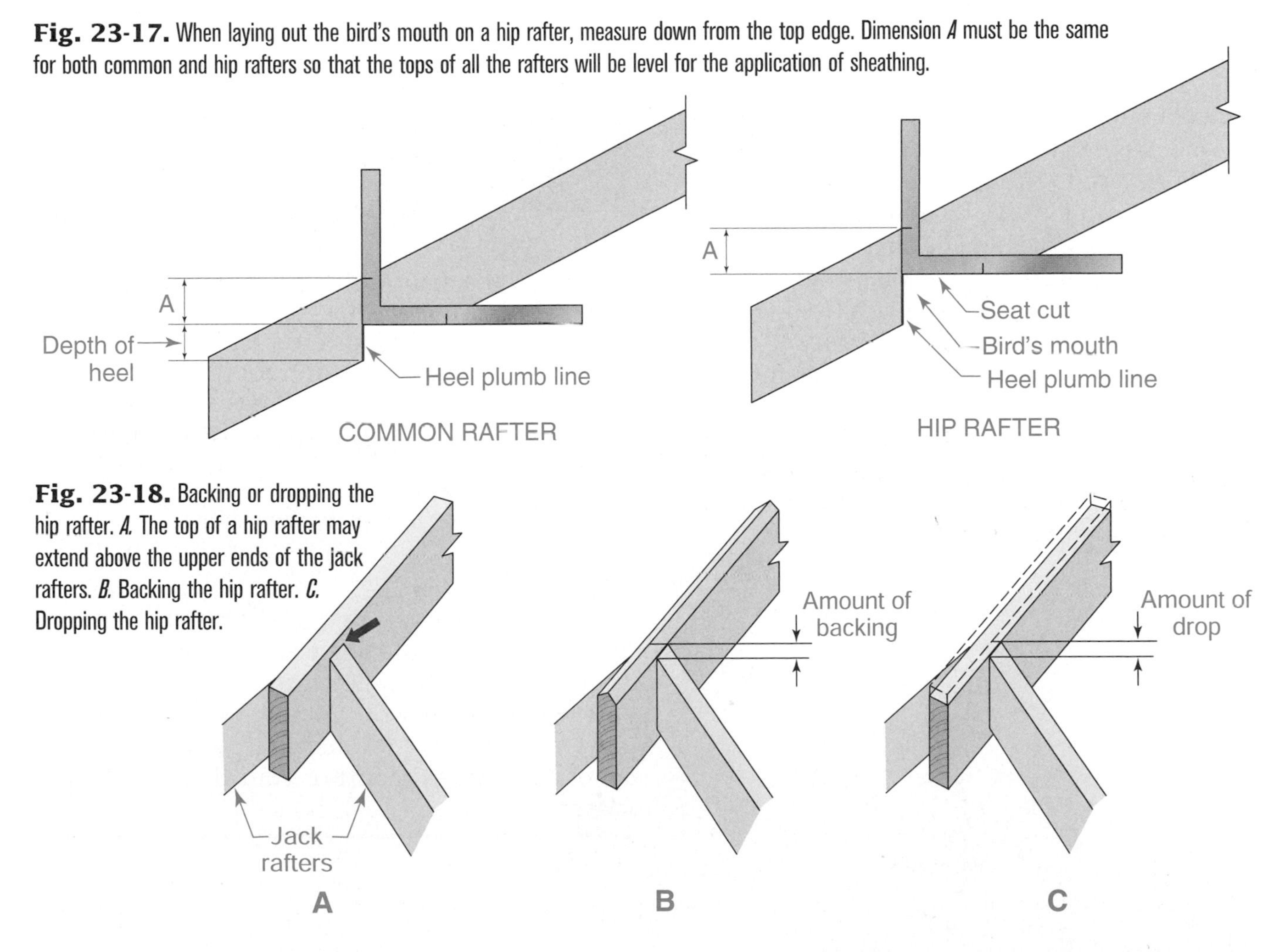

Fig. 23-17. When laying out the bird's mouth on a hip rafter, measure down from the top edge. Dimension *A* must be the same for both common and hip rafters so that the tops of all the rafters will be level for the application of sheathing.

Fig. 23-18. Backing or dropping the hip rafter. *A.* The top of a hip rafter may extend above the upper ends of the jack rafters. *B.* Backing the hip rafter. *C.* Dropping the hip rafter.

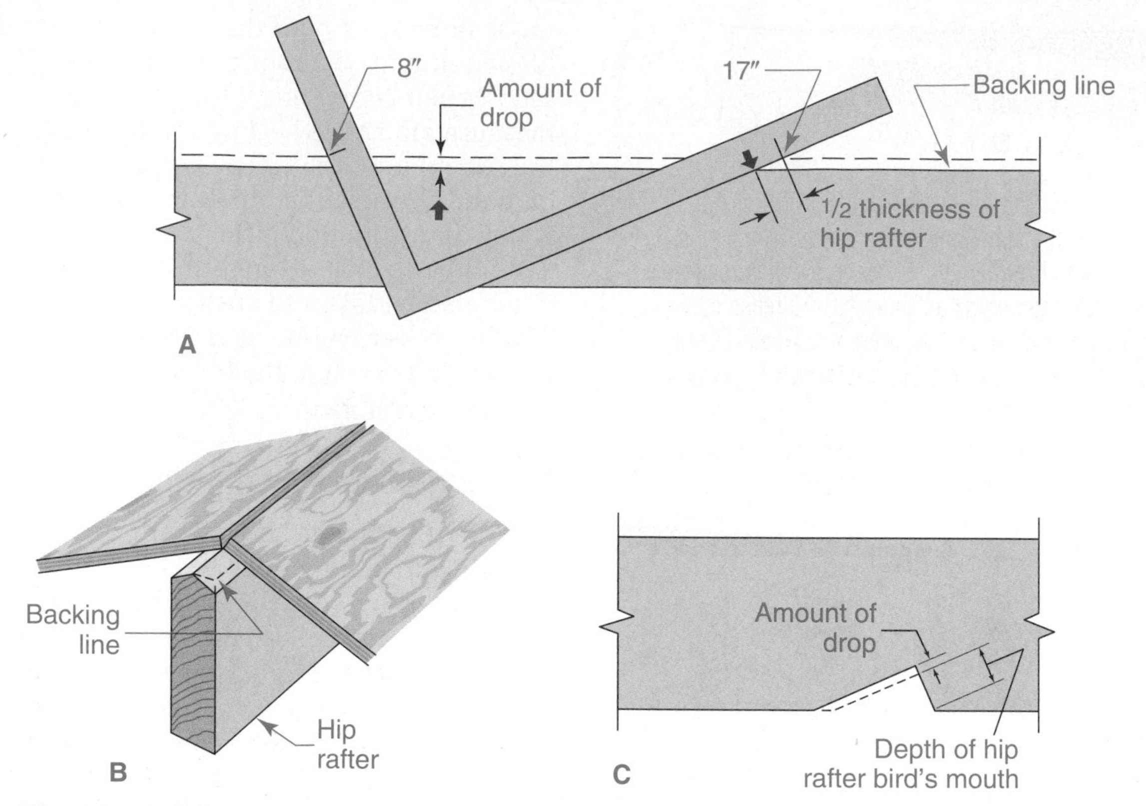

Fig. 23-19. Backing or dropping a hip rafter. *A.* Determining amount of backing or drop. *B.* Bevel angle for backing the rafter. *C.* Deepening the bird's mouth for dropping the rafter.

The amount of backing or drop required is calculated as shown in **Fig. 23-19A**. Set the framing square to the cut of the rafter (8″ and 17″ in this example) on the upper edge. Measure off one-half the thickness of the rafter from the edge along the blade. For backing, a line drawn through this mark and parallel to the edge will indicate the bevel angle. **Fig. 23-19B.** For dropping, the perpendicular distance between the line and the edge of the rafter will be the amount of drop. Fig. 23-19A. This is the amount by which the depth of the hip rafter bird's mouth should exceed the depth of the common rafter bird's mouth. **Fig. 23-19C.**

SECTION 23.1

Check Your Knowledge

1. What is the main difference between a hip rafter and valley rafter?
2. The unit run of a hip rafter is 17″ and the unit run of a common rafter is 12″. Explain how the hip rafter's unit run is calculated.
3. What is the shortening allowance for a hip rafter when the ridge end is framed against the ridge board?
4. What does *dropping the hip* refer to?

On the Job

Interview three carpenters. Ask them to recount their experiences as they were learning to frame roofs with hip and valley rafters. Ask how they learned to do this work accurately and about how much practice it took. Take notes and make an oral or written report of your findings to the class.

SECTION 23.2

Valley Rafter Layout

A valley rafter is necessary where two roofs intersect. It is also needed at the intersection of a dormer roof with the main roof. Most intersecting roofs that contain valley rafters have the same pitch. The valley rafters always run at a 45° angle to the building perimeter and the ridge boards.

EQUAL AND UNEQUAL SPANS

A roof that intersects the main roof is sometimes referred to as an *addition*. This is because the main roof is generally framed first, and the intersecting roof is then added. Another reason is that a common method for expanding an existing house is to build an addition that intersects the main house.

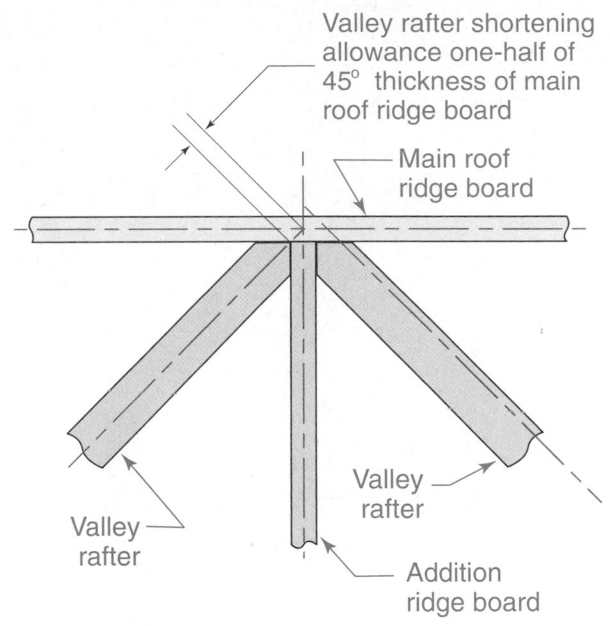

Fig. 23-21. Ridge-end shortening allowance for an equal-span addition valley.

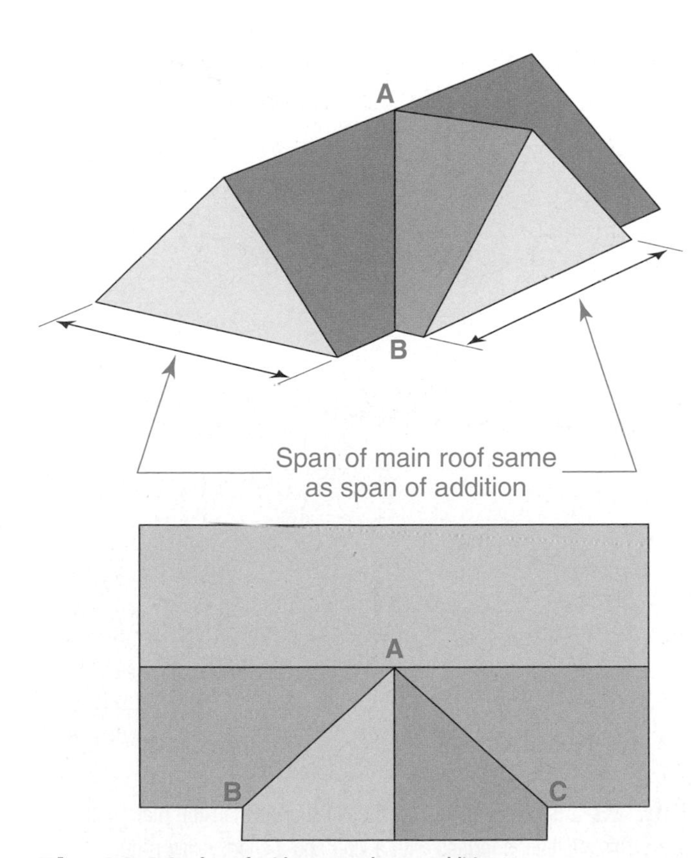

Fig. 23-20. A roof with an equal-span addition.

Equal-Span Roof

In equal-span framing, the span of the addition is the same as the span of the main roof. **Fig. 23-20.** When the pitch of the addition's roof is the same as the pitch of the main roof, the ridges of both roofs are at the same height.

The total run of a valley rafter (indicated by *AB* and *AC* in Fig. 23-20) is the hypotenuse of a right triangle. Each shorter side of the triangle is equal to the total run of a common rafter in the main roof. The unit run of a valley rafter is therefore 16.97", the same as the unit run for a hip rafter. Figuring the length of an equal-span valley rafter is thus the same as figuring the length of a hip rafter.

The shortening allowance for an equal-span addition valley rafter is one-half the 45° thickness of the ridge board. **Fig. 23-21.** Side cuts are laid out as they are for a hip rafter. The valley rafter tail has a double side cut, like the hip rafter tail, but running in the opposite direction. This is because the tail cut must form an inside rather than an outside corner. **Fig. 23-22.** The bird's mouth and the overhang, if any, are figured just as they are for a hip rafter.

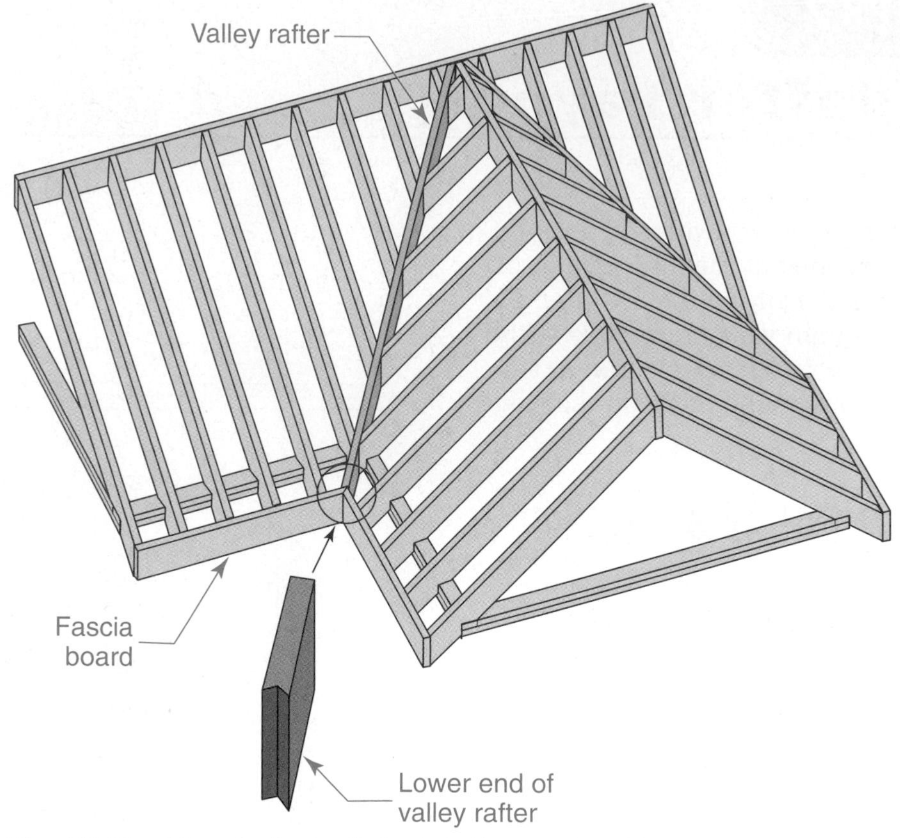

Fig. 23-22. Valley rafter framing. Notice the inside corner formed by the fascia boards.

Unequal-Span Roof

Sometimes the span of the roof addition is shorter than the span of the main roof. **Fig. 23-23.** In this case, when the pitch of the addition roof is the same as the pitch of the main roof, the addition ridge board will be at a lower level than the main roof ridge board.

A single full-length valley rafter (*AD* in Fig. 23-23) is framed between the top plate and the ridge board. A shorter valley rafter (*BC* in Fig. 23-23) is then framed to the longer one at a 90° angle. The total run of the longer valley rafter is the hypotenuse of a right triangle, the shorter sides of which are each equal to the total run of a common rafter in the main roof. The total run of the shorter valley rafter is the hypotenuse of a right triangle with shorter sides each equal to the total run of a common rafter in the addition. The total run of a common rafter in the main roof is equal to one-half the span of the main roof. The total run of a common rafter in the addition is equal to one-half the span of the addition.

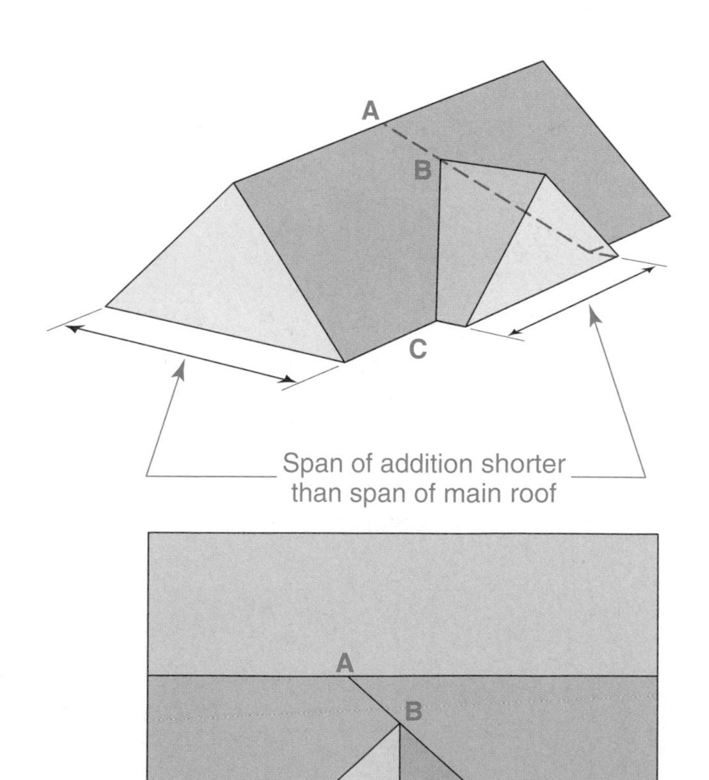

Fig. 23-23. An addition with a span shorter than the main roof span. This addition is formed with a long and a short valley rafter.

DETERMINING THE LENGTH OF A VALLEY RAFTER

When the total run of any rafter is known, the theoretical length can be found by multiplying the total run by the unit length. Suppose, for example, that the addition shown in Fig. 23-23 has a span of 30° and that the unit rise of a common rafter in the addition is 9″. The rafter table in Fig. 23-6B shows that the unit length for a valley rafter in a roof with a common rafter unit rise of 9″ is 19.21″. To find the theoretical length of the valley rafter, multiply its unit length by the total run of a common rafter in the roof to which it belongs. (The total run of a common rafter is equal to one-half the span.) Therefore, the length of the longer valley rafter in Fig. 23-23 would be 19.21″ times one-half the span of the main roof. The length of the shorter valley rafter would be 19.21″ times one-half the span of the addition. Because one-half the span of the addition is 15′, the length of the shorter valley rafter is 19.21″ × 15, or 288.15″. Converted to feet, this is 24.01′.

The shortening allowances for the long and short valley rafters are shown in **Fig. 23-24**. Note that the long valley rafter has a single side cut for framing to the main roof ridge board. The short valley rafter is cut square for framing to the long valley rafter.

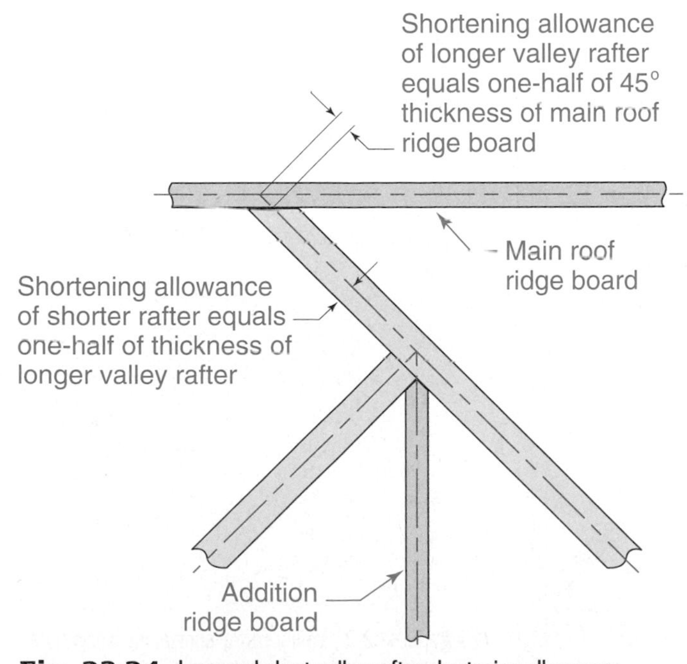

Fig. 23-24. Long and short valley rafter shortening allowances.

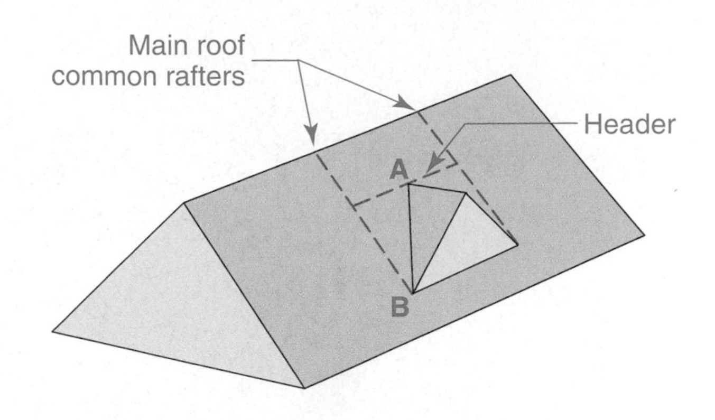

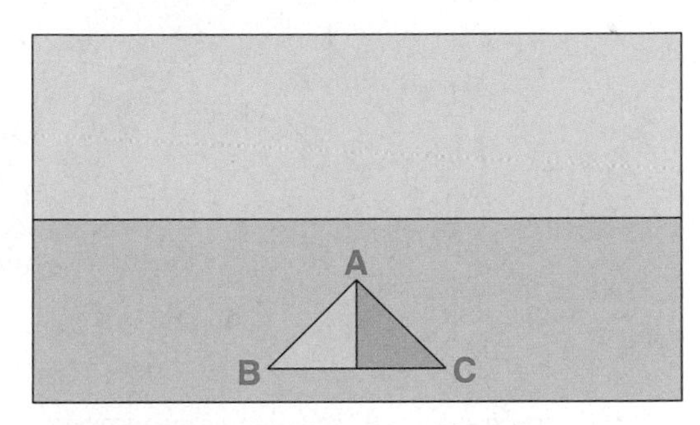

Fig. 23-25. Framing a dormer without side walls.

FRAMING DORMERS

Dormers are often added to a roof. They add architectural interest, allow natural light to reach the top floor, and provide more headroom beneath steep slopes. In many respects, framing a dormer is like framing a small house with a small roof.

Dormers without Side Walls

When constructing a gable dormer without side walls, the dormer ridge board is fastened to a header. The header is supported on each end by doubled common rafters in the main roof. **Fig. 23-25.** The valley rafters are framed between this header and a lower header. The total run of a valley rafter is the hypotenuse of a right triangle, the shorter sides of which are each equal to the total run of a common rafter in the dormer.

The arrangement and names of framing members in this type of dormer framing are shown in **Fig. 23-26**. Note that the upper edges of the headers must be beveled to the pitch of the main roof.

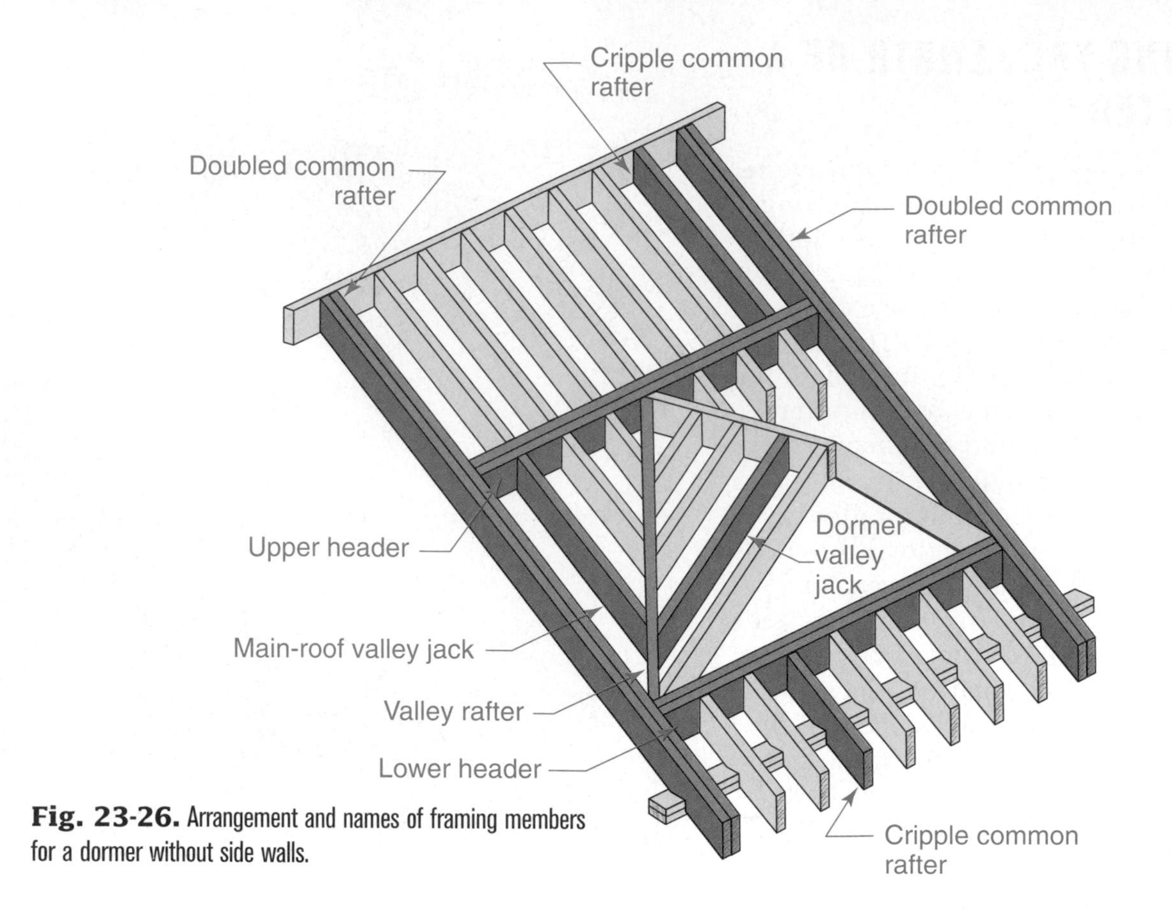

Fig. 23-26. Arrangement and names of framing members for a dormer without side walls.

In this method, the shortening allowance for the upper end of a valley rafter is one-half the 45° thickness of the inside member in the doubled upper header. **Fig. 23-27.** The shortening allowance for the lower end is one-half the 45° thickness of the inside member in the doubled common rafter. Each valley rafter has a double side cut at the upper and lower ends.

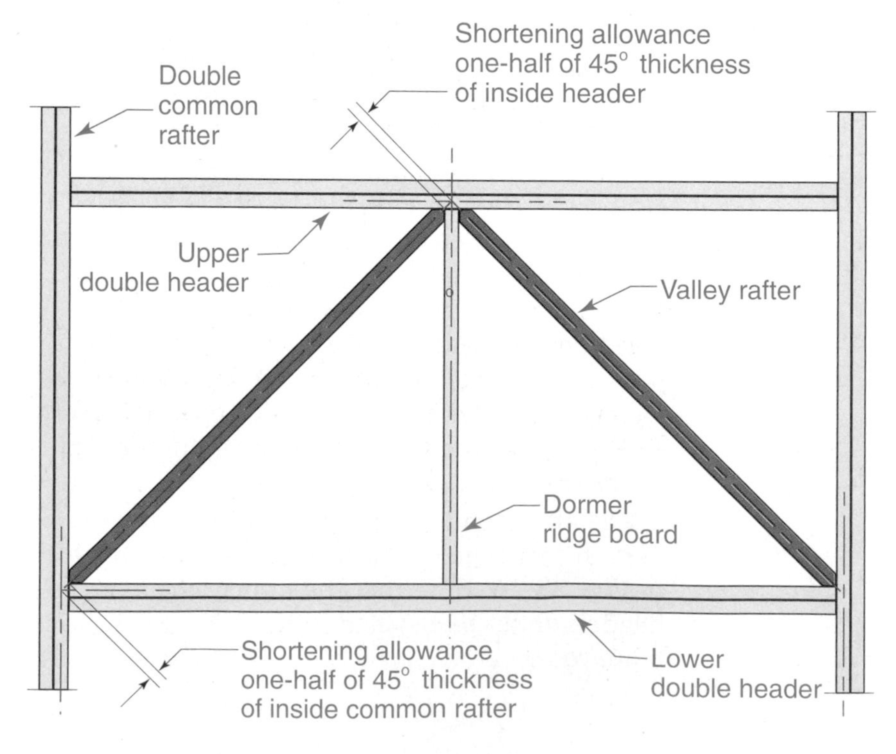

Fig. 23-27. Valley rafter shortening allowances for a dormer without side walls.

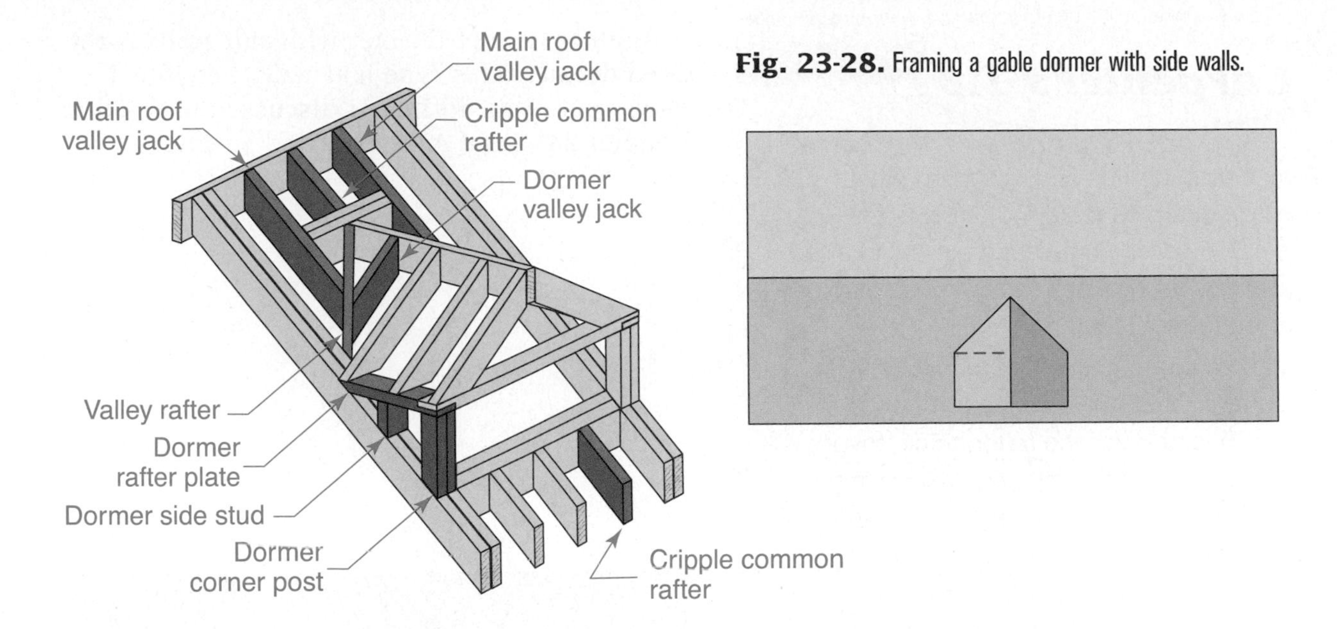

Fig. 23-28. Framing a gable dormer with side walls.

Dormers with Side Walls

A method of framing a gable dormer with side walls is shown in **Fig. 23-28**. This type of dormer is sometimes referred to as a **doghouse dormer** because of its shape. The total run of the valley rafter is the hypotenuse of a right triangle, the shorter sides of which are each equal to the run of a common rafter in the dormer.

Figure the lengths of the dormer corner posts and side studs just as you would the lengths of gable-end studs (see Chapter 24, "Roof Assembly and Sheathing"). Lay out the lower-end cutoff angle by setting the square to the pitch of the main roof. The valley rafter shortening allowances for this method of framing are shown in **Fig. 23-29**.

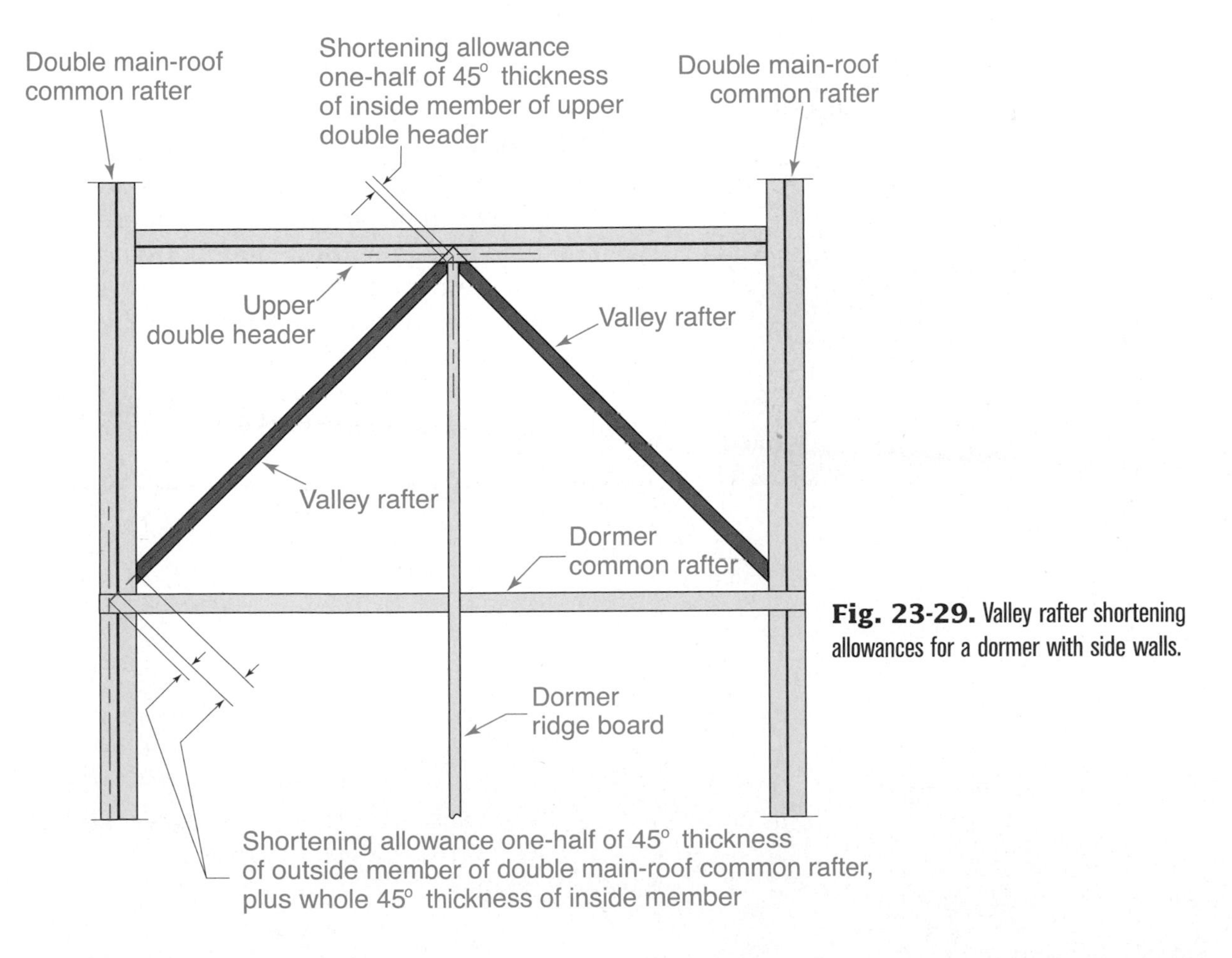

Fig. 23-29. Valley rafter shortening allowances for a dormer with side walls.

Many carpenters use the standard steel framing square when laying out cuts for rafters. However, some carpenters find a triangular framing square easier to use and more convenient to carry.

To make a plumb cut with a triangular framing square, hold the square's pivot point against one edge of the rafter stock. Pivot the square until the appropriate rise number on the "common" scale of the square lines up with the same rafter edge. As shown here, the rise is 6-in-12. Mark the rafter from the pivot point along the top edge of the square. This is the plumb line.

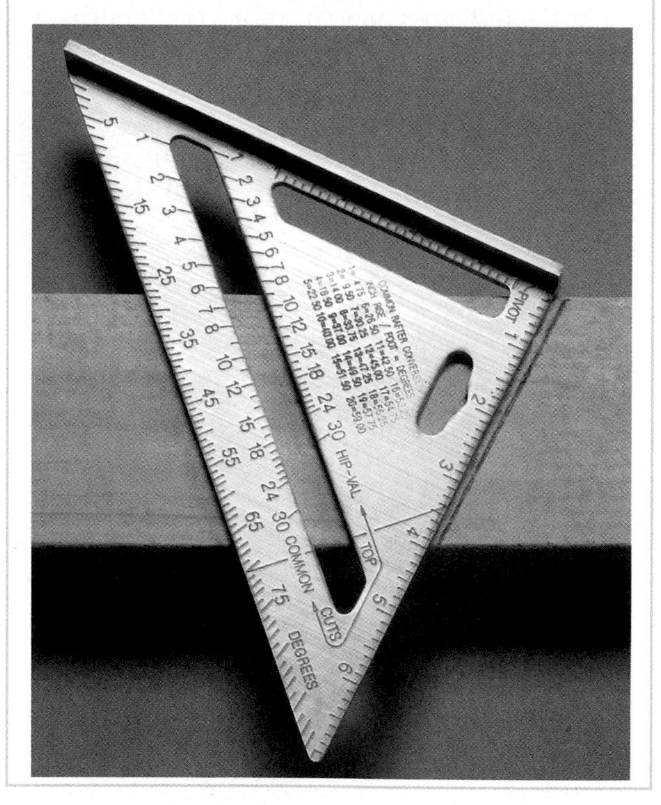

Another type of dormer with side walls is the shed dormer. This type is usually tied into a gable roof. This dormer is discussed in detail in Chapter 24, "Roof Assembly and Sheathing."

SECTION 23.2 Check Your Knowledge

1. Describe an equal-span roof.
2. When the pitch and the span of an addition roof are the same as the pitch and span of the main roof, how are the ridge boards positioned in relation to each other?
3. When framing a gable dormer without side walls, what is the dormer's ridge board attached to?
4. When framing a doghouse dormer, how is the run of a valley rafter determined?

On the Job

Along with three classmates, take photographs of at least sixteen different roofs on houses in your community. Take these photos from the sidewalk or from some other public vantage point. Do not trespass on private property. Organize your photos into the following categories: gable roofs, hip roofs, and intersecting roofs (including dormers). Make a presentation to your class.

Jack Rafter Layout

A jack rafter is a shortened common rafter that may be framed to a hip rafter, a valley rafter, or both. This means that in an equal-span framing situation, the unit rise of a jack rafter is always the same as the unit rise of a common rafter.

There are several types of jack rafters. A hip jack rafter extends from a hip rafter to a rafter plate. A valley jack rafter extends from a valley rafter to a ridge board. **Fig. 23-30.** A cripple jack rafter does not contact either a plate or a ridge board. There are two kinds of cripple jack rafters. The valley cripple jack extends between two valley rafters in the long-and-short-valley-rafter method of addition framing. The hip-valley cripple jack extends from a hip rafter to a valley rafter. **Fig. 23-31.**

A Step-by-Step feature on cutting a jack rafter pattern appears on page 467.

LENGTHS OF HIP JACK RAFTERS

A roof framing plan for a series of hip jack rafters is shown in **Fig. 23-32**. The jacks are always on the same spacing as the common rafters. The spacing in this instance is 16″ on center. You can see in the lower-right part of the plan that the total run of the shortest jack is also 16″.

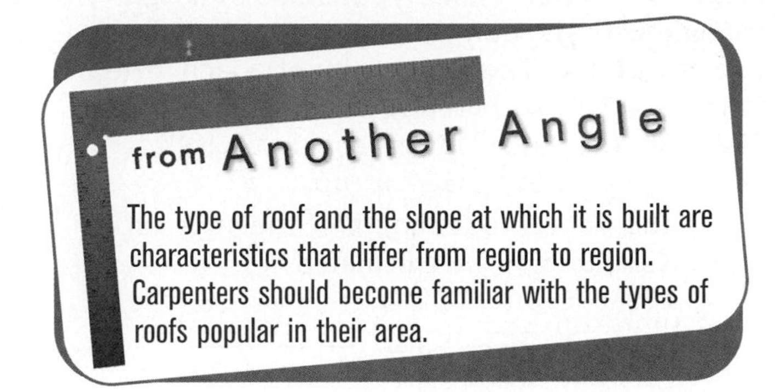
from Another Angle

The type of roof and the slope at which it is built are characteristics that differ from region to region. Carpenters should become familiar with the types of roofs popular in their area.

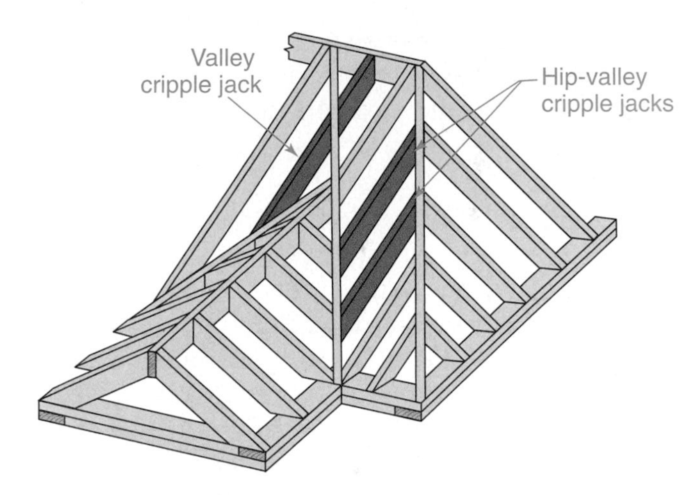

Fig. 23-31. Valley cripple jack and hip-valley cripple jacks.

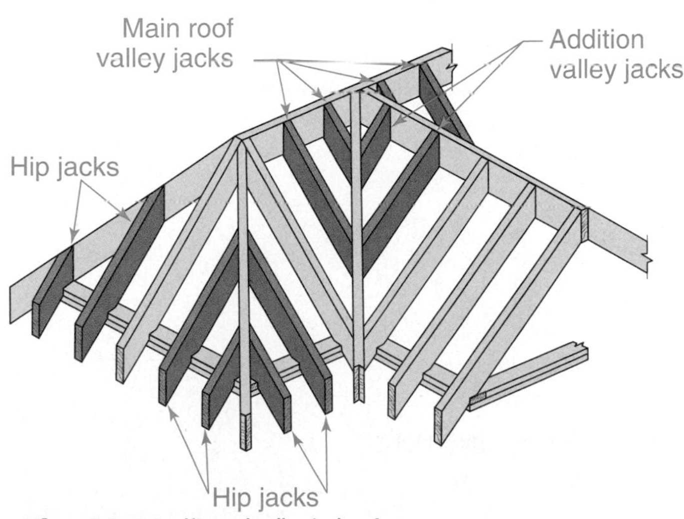

Fig. 23-30. Hip and valley jack rafters.

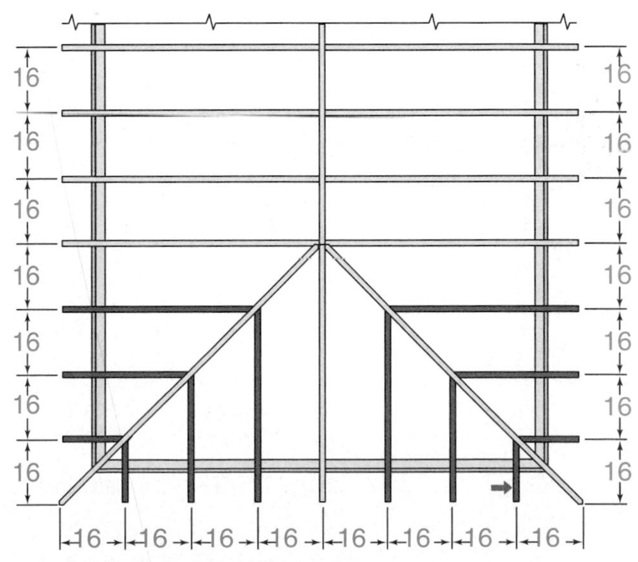

Fig. 23-32. Hip jack framing plan.

Suppose the unit rise of a common rafter in this roof is 8″ per 12″ of run. The jacks have the same unit rise as a common rafter. The unit length of a rafter is the hypotenuse of a right triangle with the unit run as base and the unit rise as altitude. The unit length of a jack rafter in the example is therefore the square root of 122 + 82, or 14.42. This means that a jack is 14.42″ long for every 12″ of run.

The theoretical total length of the shortest jack rafter can now be calculated:

$$\frac{12'' \text{ (unit run)}}{14.42'' \text{ (unit length)}} = \frac{16'' \text{ (total run)}}{X \text{ (total length)}}$$

$$X = 19.23''$$

This is the length of the shortest hip jack when the jacks are spaced 16″ on center and the unit rise is 8″. It is also the *common difference* in length between one jack and the next. This means that the next hip jack will be 2 × 19.23″ long, the one after that 3 × 19.23″ long, and so on.

The common difference for hip jacks spaced 16″ on center and for hip jacks spaced 24″ on center can also be found in the rafter table on the framing square (see Fig. 23-6B). For example, the third line of the table reads "Difference in Length of Jacks 16 Inches Centers." Follow this line to the column headed 8 (for a unit rise of 8″) to find the length of the first jack rafter and the common difference, which is 19¼″.

LENGTHS OF VALLEY JACKS AND CRIPPLE JACKS

The best way to figure the total lengths of valley jacks and cripple jacks is to lay out a roof framing plan. Part of a framing plan for a main hip roof with a long-and-short-valley-rafter gable addition is shown in **Fig. 23-33**. By studying the plan you can figure the total lengths of the valley jacks and cripple jacks as follows:

- The run of valley jack No. 1 is the same as the run of hip jack No. 8, which is the shortest hip jack. The length of valley jack No. 1 is therefore equal to the common difference between jacks.
- The run of valley jack No. 2 is the same as the run of hip jack No. 7. The length is therefore twice the common difference between jacks.
- The run of valley jack No. 3 is the same as the run of hip jack No. 6. The length is therefore three times the common difference between jacks. The run of hip-valley cripples No. 4 and 5 is the same as the run of valley jack No. 3. The length of these rafters is thus the same as the length of No. 3.
- The run of valley jacks No. 9 and 10 is equal to the spacing of jacks on center. Therefore the length of each of these jacks is equal to the common difference between jacks. The run of valley jacks No. 11 and 12 is twice the run of valley jacks No. 9 and 10. The length of each of these jacks is therefore twice the common difference between jacks.

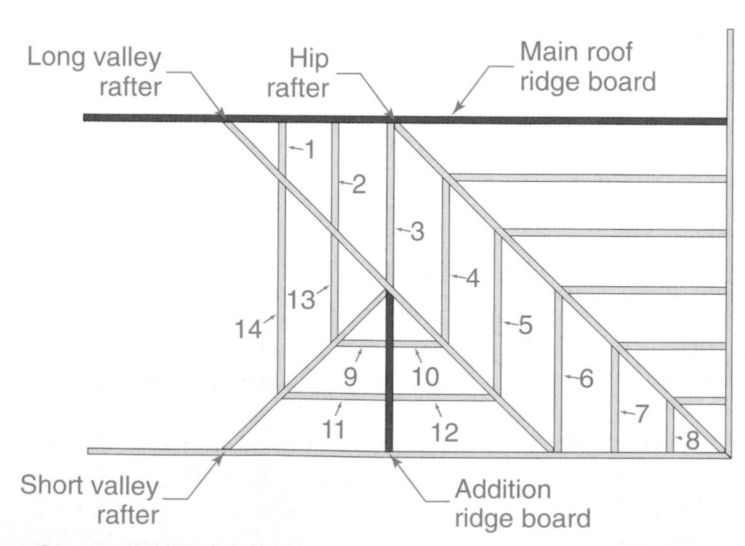

Fig. 23-33. Jack rafter framing plan for a hip roof with a gable addition.

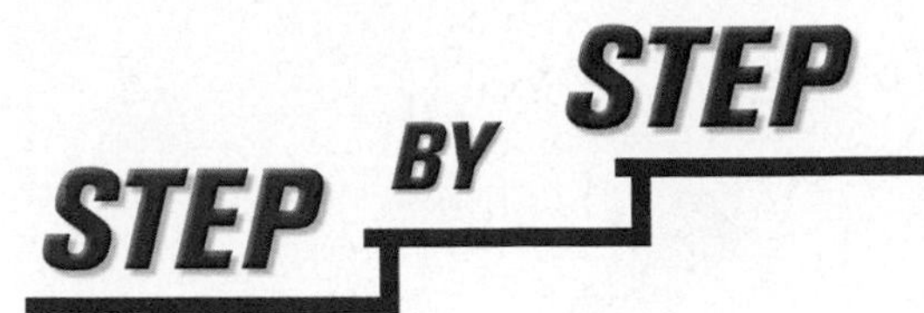

Cutting a Jack Rafter Pattern

Rather than lay out and mark each jack rafter individually, a pattern is used to save time. When all the rafters have been cut, the rafter used as a pattern becomes part of the roof frame.

Step 1 Lay out and cut the longest jack rafter first. Be careful to calculate and make all necessary allowances to determine the actual length.

Step 2 Set the rafter in place on the building and check the fit of all the cuts. See that the spacing between the centers of the rafters is correct.

Step 3 When everything is correct, use this rafter as a pattern. On the top edge of the rafter, measure down the center line from the ridge end a distance equal to the common difference measurement (found on the framing square rafter table). This is the length of the second-longest jack rafter.

Step 4 Continue to mark the common difference measurements along the top edge until the lengths of all the jacks have been laid out. **Fig. 23-35.**

Step 5 Using the pattern, lay out all the jack rafters.

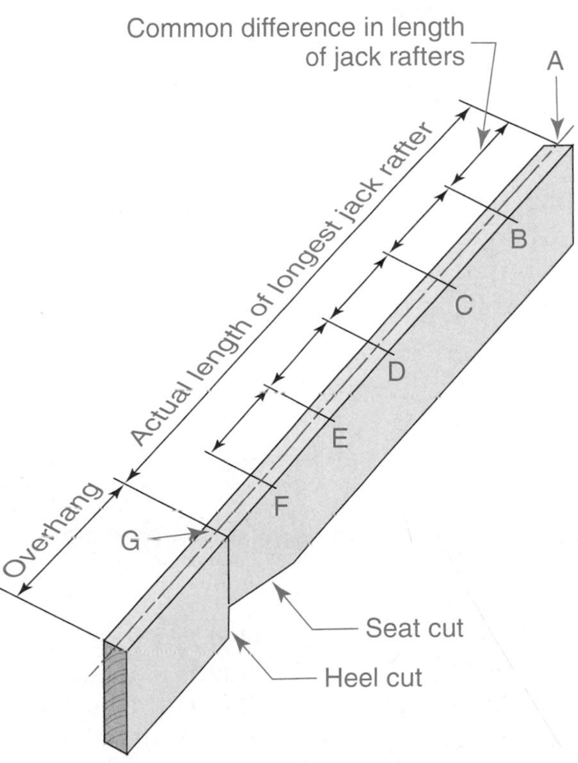

Fig. 23-35. Use the longest jack rafter (*AG*) as a pattern. The second jack rafter is *BG*, the third jack rafter is *CG*, and so on.

- The run of valley cripple No. 13 is twice the spacing of jacks on center, and the length is therefore twice the common difference between jacks. The run of valley cripple No. 14 is twice the run of valley cripple No. 13, and the length is therefore twice the common difference between jacks.

SHORTENING ALLOWANCES

A hip jack rafter has a shortening allowance at the upper end equal to one-half the 45° thickness of the hip rafter. **Fig. 23-34.** A valley jack rafter has a shortening allowance at the upper end equal to one-half the thickness of the ridge board. It also has a shortening allowance at the lower end equal to one-half the 45° thickness of the valley rafter. A hip-valley cripple has a shortening allowance at the upper end equal to one-half the 45° thickness of the hip rafter, and another at the lower end equal to one-half the 45° thickness of the valley rafter. A valley cripple has a shortening allowance at the upper end equal to one-half the 45° thickness of the long valley rafter. At the lower end, the allowance is equal to one-half the 45° thickness of the short valley rafter.

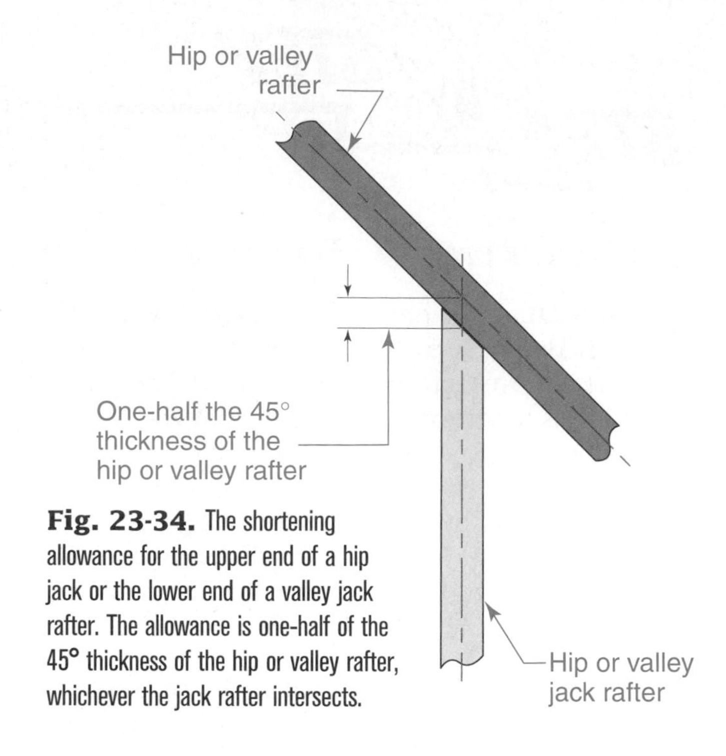

Fig. 23-34. The shortening allowance for the upper end of a hip jack or the lower end of a valley jack rafter. The allowance is one-half of the 45° thickness of the hip or valley rafter, whichever the jack rafter intersects.

SIDE CUTS

The side cut on a jack rafter can be laid out by the method shown in Figs. 23-12 and 23-13 for laying out the side cut on a hip rafter. Another method is to use the rafter table on the framing square (see Fig. 23-6B). Find the line headed "Side Cut of Jacks Use" and read across to the figure under the unit rise. For a unit rise of 8″, the figure given is 10. To lay out the side cut on a jack with this unit rise, set the square face-up on the edge of the rafter to 12″ (the unit run) on the tongue and 10″ on the blade. Draw the side cut line along the tongue (see Fig. 23-15).

BIRD'S MOUTH AND OVERHANG

A jack rafter is a shortened common rafter. Consequently, the bird's mouth and overhang are laid out just as they are on a common rafter (see Chapter 22, "Basic Roof Framing").

When making repetitive angled cuts on roof framing lumber, a radial-arm saw or compound-miter saw can improve the speed and accuracy of your work. Once you have determined the proper angle, set a stop at one end of the saw's outfeed table. All stock resting against this stop will then be cut to the exact same length. Do not let sawdust collect around the stop. It will affect the cut length.

SECTION 23.3 Check Your Knowledge

1. What is a jack rafter?
2. What is a valley jack rafter?
3. What is the best way to figure the total lengths of valley jacks and cripple jacks?
4. What is the purpose of a jack rafter pattern?

On the Job

For a house with a hip roof, the run of a common rafter is 14′, the pitch is 6/12, there is a 2′ overhang, and the rafters are 16″ OC. Figure the length of the two shortest hip jack rafters.

Chapter 23

Review

Section Summaries

23.1 The length of a hip rafter is calculated on the basis of the unit run and unit rise and/or the total run and total rise. Any of the methods previously described for determining the length of a common rafter may be used. However, some of the basic data for hip and valley rafters is different.

23.2 The span of an addition roof may be equal or unequal to that of the main roof. Dormers are framed either with or without side walls. Those with side walls are called *doghouse dormers.*

23.3 Jack rafters are shortened common rafters framed to a hip rafter, valley rafter, or both. The best way to figure the total lengths of valley jacks and cripple jacks is to lay out a framing plan.

Review Questions

1. What is a hip rafter?
2. What is a valley rafter?
3. What type of roof calls for both hip and valley rafters?
4. What is a side cut?
5. How is the total run of a hip rafter overhang determined?
6. What does the term *backing the hip* refer to?
7. In an unequal-span roof, in which the addition span is shorter than the main span, where is the addition ridge board in relation to the main ridge board if the pitch of both roofs is the same?
8. In a dormer without side walls, how is the shortening allowance figured?
9. Describe a hip jack rafter.
10. What complications are introduced to roof framing when an addition roof intersects the main roof?

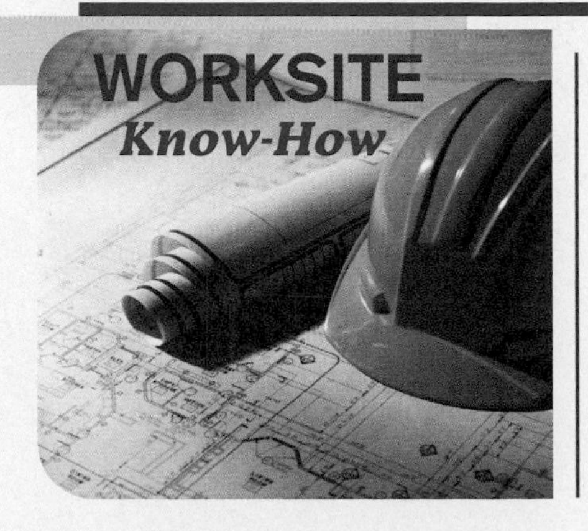

Making Precise Calculations One tool that has made roof framing much easier is the construction calculator. It is different from standard calculators because dimensions can be entered directly in feet, inches, and fractions of an inch. Answers are displayed in the same way, making it unnecessary to convert them from decimal figures. The calculator works quickly and with great precision. This makes it invaluable when laying out hip, valley, and jack rafters. Most construction calculators have built-in functions to make roof calculations even easier.

Chapter

24

Roof Assembly and Sheathing

Objectives

After reading this chapter, you'll be able to:

- Identify the two basic types of ridges.
- Calculate ridge length.
- Create the ridge layout for gable roofs, hip roofs, addition roofs, and dormers.
- Lay out the locations of common rafters on a gable or hip roof.
- Identify where special framing details are required.
- Understand the basic requirements for the placement and nailing of panel roof sheathing.

Terms

brace
collar tie
common difference
purlin
ridge beam

After the ceiling joists and interior walls are in place and properly braced, a structure is ready for roof framing. This is generally a job for two or more carpenters and at least one helper. The order of steps may vary, depending on the type and complexity of the roof. However, work generally proceeds in this order:

1. Install the common rafters and ridge boards.
2. Install hip and valley rafters, if any.
3. Install jack rafters, if any.
4. Frame special items such as gable ends and roof openings.
5. Install roof sheathing.

SECTION 24.1

Ridges

A *ridge* is a roof framing member placed at the intersection of two upward-sloping surfaces. Carpenters may install a ridge in various ways. In most cases, however, they will cut the rafters first. Laying out and cutting common rafters is discussed in Chapter 22, "Basic Roof Framing."

TYPES OF RIDGES

There are two basic types of ridges: nonstructural and structural. The type of ridge is indicated on the building plans.

If the ridge is *nonstructural*, it is called a *ridge board*. It serves as a bearing surface for opposing pairs of rafters. The rafters hold the ridge board in place. This type of ridge is the most common. It is made of nominal 2″ lumber that is slightly wider than the rafter stock. For example, the ridge board for a roof framed with 2×8 rafters would be a 2x10. The extra width ensures that angled cuts at the ends of the rafters will bear fully on the ridge board. **Fig. 24-1.** The ridge board can also be made from a continuous length of LVL stock. The thickness of the ridge stock must be accounted for when calculating the actual length of the rafters.

A *structural ridge* is called a ridge beam. A **ridge beam** is made from LVL, glue-laminated, or nominal 4″ lumber. The rafters rest on top of the ridge beam or are supported by metal brackets nailed to its side. **Fig. 24-2.** The ends of the ridge beam are supported by posts or bearing walls. Intermediate support posts may also be needed. A structural ridge is commonly used when framing low-pitched roofs or when the house is framed using posts and beams (see Chapter 19, "Framing Methods").

Whether installing a structural or nonstructural ridge, the stock should be as long and straight as possible. When a lumber ridge board is used, it can be the same grade of lumber as the rafters. An LVL ridge board is used when the roof is framed with engineered lumber. Seams between lengths of ridge board should occur only between rafter pairs. Seams between lengths of ridge beam should occur only over support posts.

CALCULATING RIDGE LENGTH

The following text refers to solid-lumber ridge boards. However, the information also applies to engineered-lumber ridge boards and ridge beams.

Gable Roofs

Calculating the length of the ridge board for a gable main roof presents no problem. The theoretical length of the ridge board (or ridge beam) is equal to the length of the building, measured to the outside edge of the wall framing. The actual length of the ridge board includes any overhang.

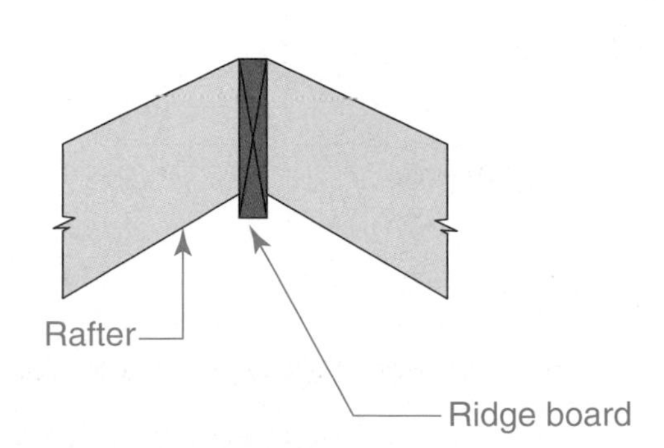

Fig. 24-1. A ridge board.

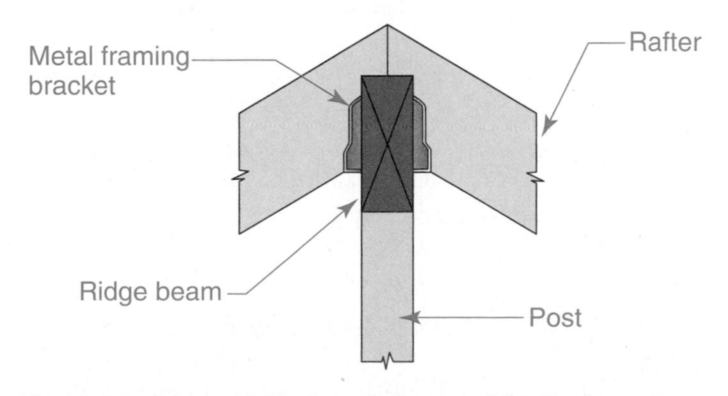

Fig. 24-2. A structural ridge beam. In the case of the ridge beam, the rafters are sometimes notched.

The length of the ridge board or ridge beam can be taken from the building plans. However, a carpenter should always confirm this dimension by measuring the actual framing. This will account for any minor differences between the house as planned and the house as built.

Hip Roofs

For a main hip roof, the ridge board layout requires calculations. In an equal-pitch hip roof, the theoretical length of the ridge board amounts to the length of the building minus twice the total run of a main roof common rafter. The actual length, however, depends upon the way in which the hip rafters are framed to the ridge.

The theoretical ends of the ridge board are at the points where the ridge centerline and the hip rafter centerline cross. If the hip rafter is framed against the ridge board, the actual length of the ridge board exceeds the theoretical length, at each end, by one-half the thickness of the ridge board plus one-half the 45° thickness of the hip rafter. **Fig. 24-3A.** If the hip rafter is framed between the common rafters, the actual length of the ridge board exceeds the theoretical length, at each end, by one-half the thickness of a common rafter. **Fig. 24-3B.**

Equal-Span Additions

For an equal-span addition, the length of the ridge board is equal to the distance that the addition projects beyond the building, plus one-half the span of the building, minus the shortening allowance at the main-roof ridge. **Fig. 24-4.** The *shortening allowance* accounts for the thickness of the main-roof ridge board when determining the length of an intersecting ridge. It is different for different framing situations. For an equal-span addition, it equals one-half the thickness of the main-roof ridge board.

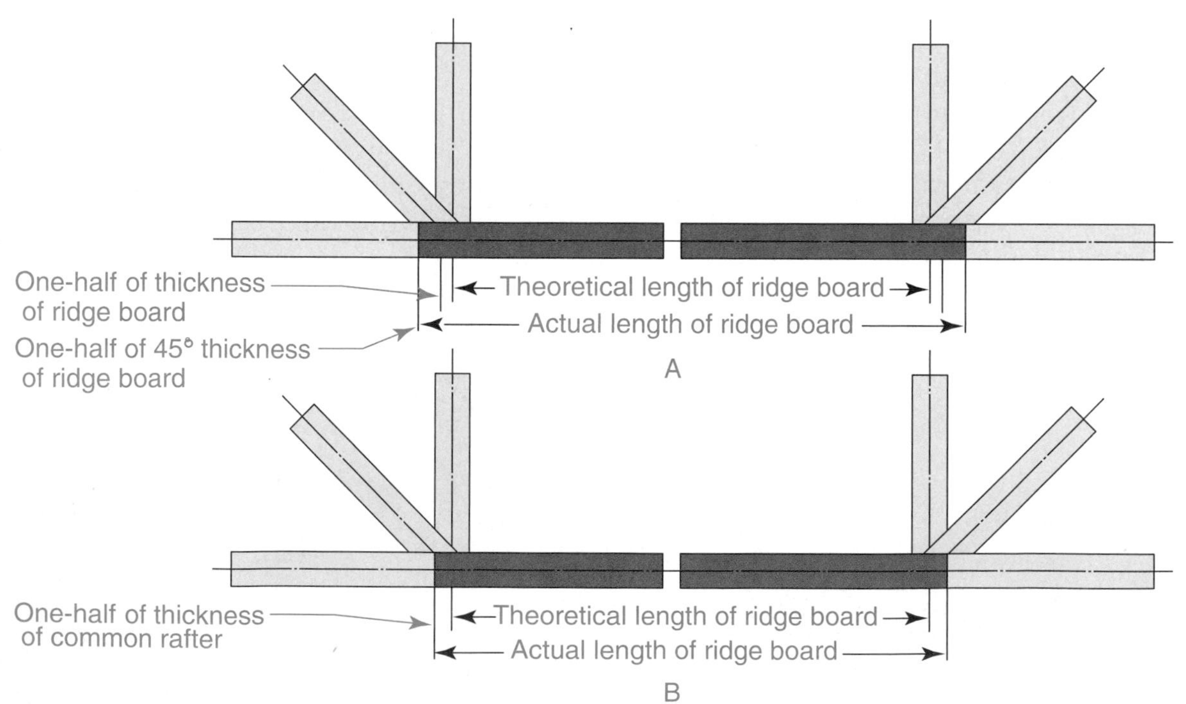

Fig. 24-3. Theoretical and actual lengths of hip roof ridge boards. *A.* Hip rafter framed against the ridge board. *B.* Hip rafter framed between common rafters.

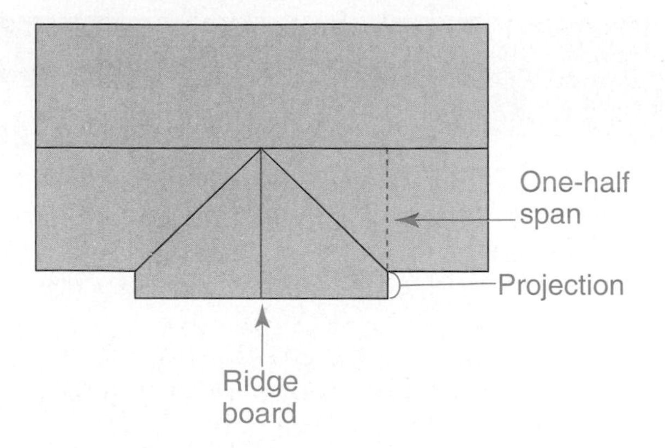

Fig. 24-4. Determining the length of a ridge board for an equal-span addition.

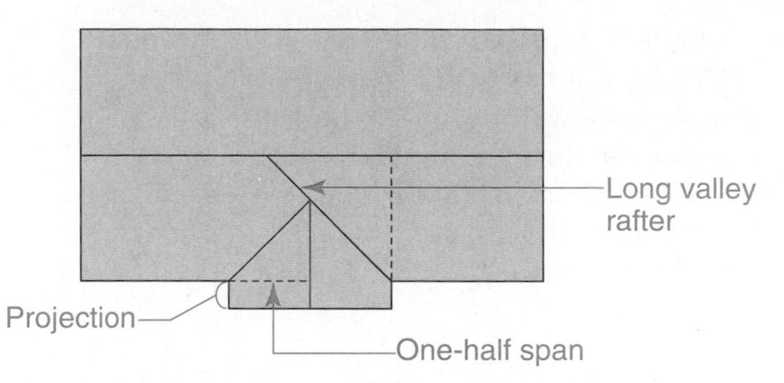

Fig. 24-5. Determining the length of a ridge board for an unequal-span addition.

Unequal-Span Additions

When the width of an addition is less than the width of the main portion of the house, their roof spans are unequal. The length of the ridge board for an unequal-span addition varies with the method of framing the ridge board. If the addition ridge board is suspended from the main roof ridge board, the length is equal to the distance the addition projects beyond the building, plus one-half the span of the main roof.

If the addition ridge board is framed by the long-and-short-valley-rafter method (see p. 477), its length is equal to the distance the addition projects beyond the building, plus one-half the span of the addition, minus a shortening allowance. **Fig. 24-5.** In this case, the shortening allowance is one-half the 45° thickness of the long valley rafter.

If the addition ridge board is framed to a double header set between a pair of doubled main-roof common rafters, the length of the ridge board is equal to the distance the addition projects beyond the building, plus one-half the span of the addition, minus a shortening allowance. This shortening allowance is one-half the thickness of the inner member of the double header.

Dormers

The length of the ridge board on a dormer *without* side walls is equal to one-half the span of the dormer, minus a shortening allowance. The shortening allowance is one-half the thickness of the inner member of the upper double header. **Fig. 24-6.**

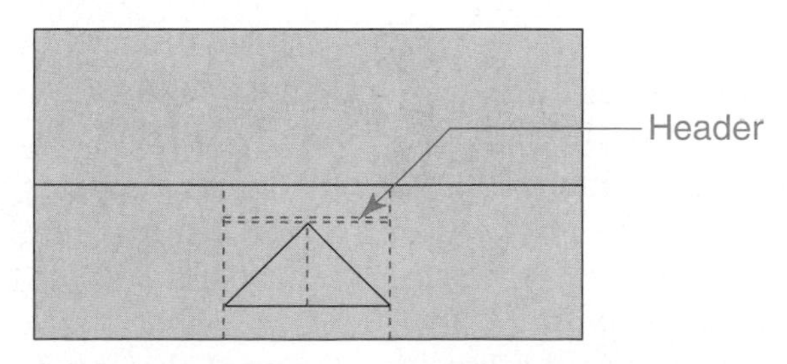

Fig. 24-6. Determining the length of a ridge board on a dormer without side walls.

The length of the ridge board on a dormer *with* side walls is equal to the length of the dormer side-wall top plate, plus one-half the span of the dormer, minus a shortening allowance. The shortening allowance is one-half the thickness of the inner member of the upper double header. **Fig. 24-7.**

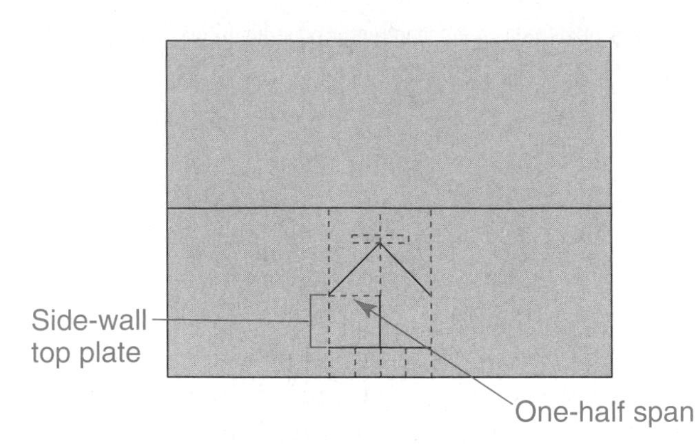

Fig. 24-7. Determining the length of the ridge board on a dormer with side walls.

SECTION 24.1

Check Your Knowledge

1. What is the difference between a ridge board and a ridge beam?
2. Why must a ridge board be wider than the rafters?
3. Based on what you have read, why is the ridge board for a hip roof shorter in length than the ridge board for a gable roof?
4. How do you calculate the length of the ridge board for an equal-span addition?

On the Job

Laminated-veneer lumber has become a common material for the construction of houses. However, it is not used for roof framing as often as it is for floor framing. Determine the reason for this by contacting at least two builders in your area and asking them about their use of LVL lumber. Report your findings to the class.

SECTION 24.2

Roof Assembly

Roof assembly includes laying out the rafters, erecting the ridge board, and erecting the rafters.

LAYING OUT RAFTER LOCATIONS

Laying out the locations of common rafters is much like laying out the locations of floor joists. However, other roof members may make the layout more complex.

The rafter spacing on the wall plates and ridge board is found on either the building plans or the roof framing plan (see Chapter 22, "Basic Roof Framing"). Rafter locations are laid out on plates, ridge board, and other rafters with the same lines and Xs used to lay out stud and joist locations (see Chapter 21, "Wall Framing and Sheathing").

In some cases all the rafters are located next to the ceiling joists. The rafters can then be fastened to the side of the joists as well as to the plate in order to tie the building together. In most cases, however, some rafters will be next to joists and others will rest between the joists. This is because the on-center spacing of the joists is often different from the on-center spacing of the rafters.

Gable Roofs

For a gable roof, lay out the rafter locations on the top plates first. Transfer the locations to the ridge board by laying the ridge board on edge against a top plate and matching the marks. **Fig. 24-8.**

The first rafters on each end are usually set even with the outside wall to provide a smooth, unbroken surface for the wall sheathing. Because the first ceiling joist is along the inside edge of the exterior wall, place a spacer block between the first rafter and the first ceiling joist. **Fig. 24-9.** Fasten the other rafters to the side of the joists along the length of the building.

If the rafters are on 24″ centers and the ceiling joists are on 16″ centers, place the first rafter as shown in Fig. 24-9. The second rafter will rest on the plate between the second and third joists. Nail the third rafter to the side of the fourth joist. The rafters will continue to alternate in this fashion along the length of the building. **Fig. 24-10.**

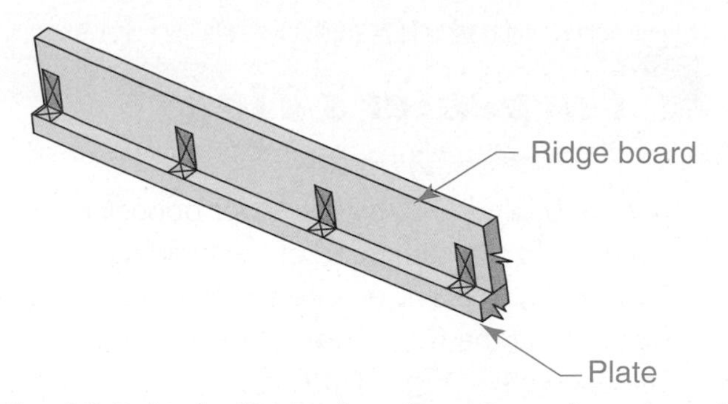

Fig. 24-8. Lay the ridge board on edge on the top plate and extend the layout lines from the plate onto the ridge board.

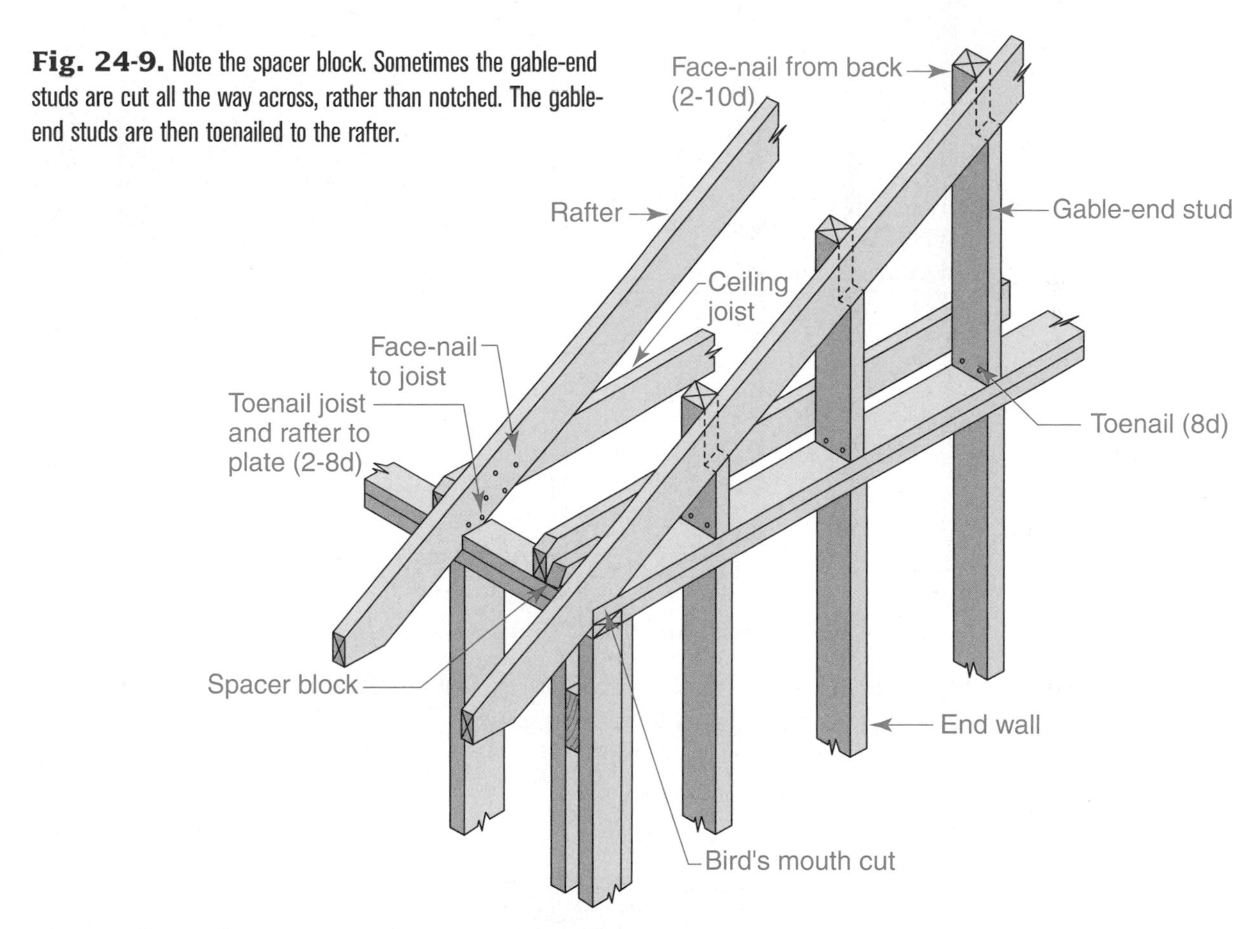

Fig. 24-9. Note the spacer block. Sometimes the gable-end studs are cut all the way across, rather than notched. The gable-end studs are then toenailed to the rafter.

Fig. 24-10. Layout of a building with the rafters on 24″ centers and the ceiling joists on 16″ centers.

Always begin the rafter layout for opposing plates from the same end of the building. **Fig. 24-11.** This will ensure that the rafters butt against the ridge board directly opposite each other. **Fig. 24-12.**

Hip Roofs

The ridge-end common rafters in an equal-pitch hip roof are located in from the building corners a distance equal to one-half the span (or the run of a main-roof common rafter). **Fig. 24-13.** The locations of these ridge-end rafters and the common rafters lying between them can be transferred to the ridge board by matching the ridge board against the top plates.

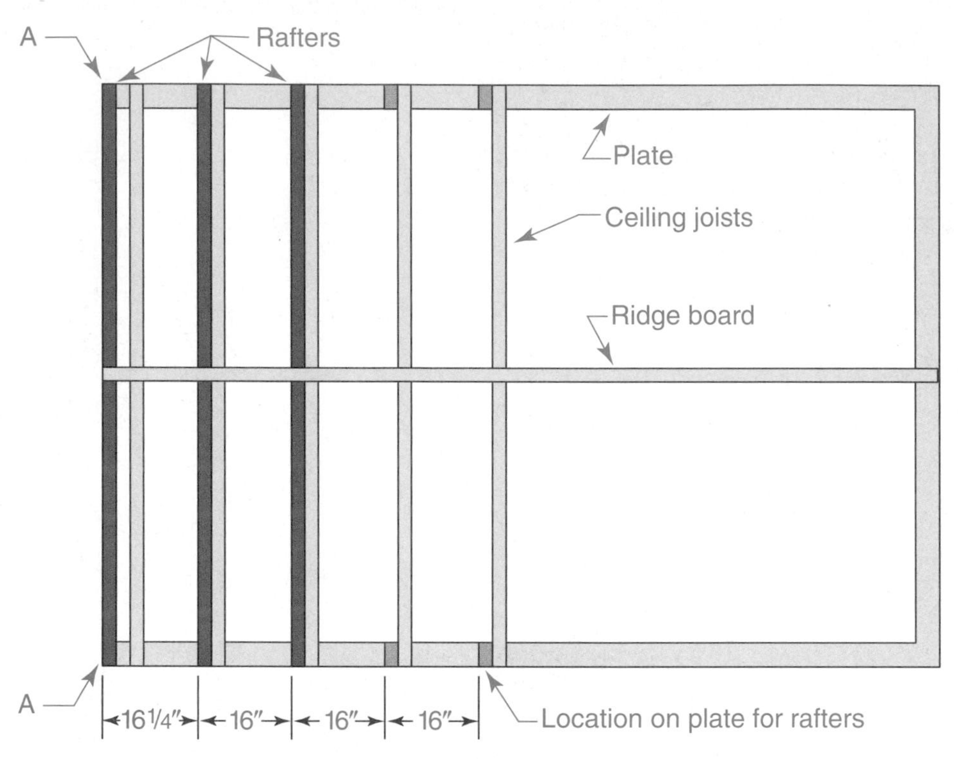

Fig. 24-11. Begin the layout of opposing rafters from the same end of the building. In this drawing, the layout for each phase began at arrow *A* on the same side wall.

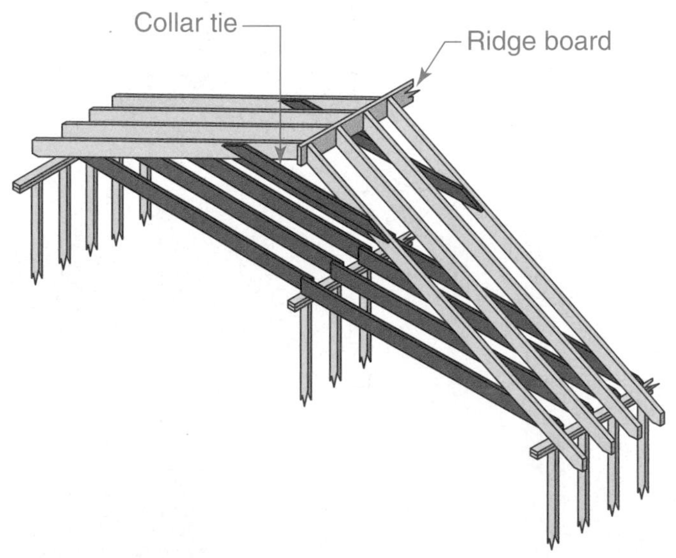

Fig. 24-12. The rafters butt directly opposite each other on the ridge board.

Fig. 24-13. The locations of the rafters in area *A* are transferred to the ridge board from the top plate.

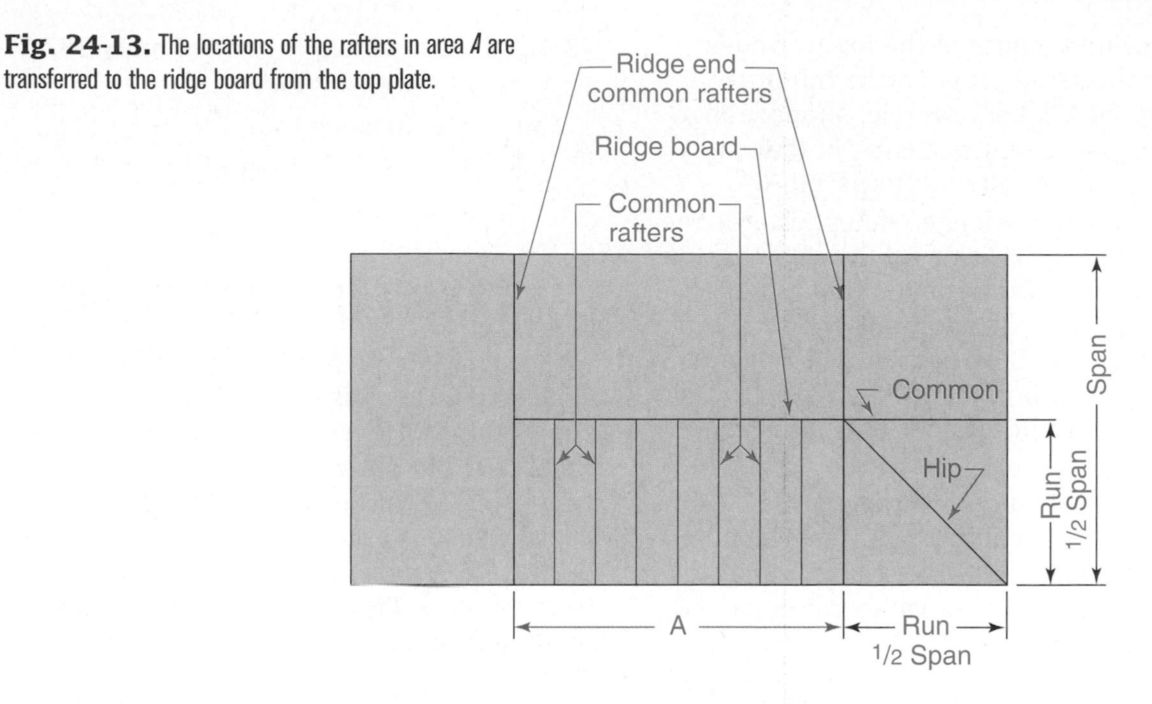

Addition Roofs

An addition complicates the process of laying out the locations of the rafters and ridges. Study the drawings carefully.

Equal Spans. For an equal-span addition, mark the main ridge board to indicate where it will be intersected by the addition ridge board. The top ends of the addition's valley rafters will rest on either side of this location. In **Fig. 24-14**, the distance between the end of the main-roof ridge board and the point where it intersects the addition ridge board is equal to distance *A* plus distance *B*. (Distance *B* equals one-half the span of the addition.) In **Fig. 24-15**, the distance between the *theoretical end* of the main-roof ridge board and the point where it intersects the addition ridge board is the same as distance *A*.

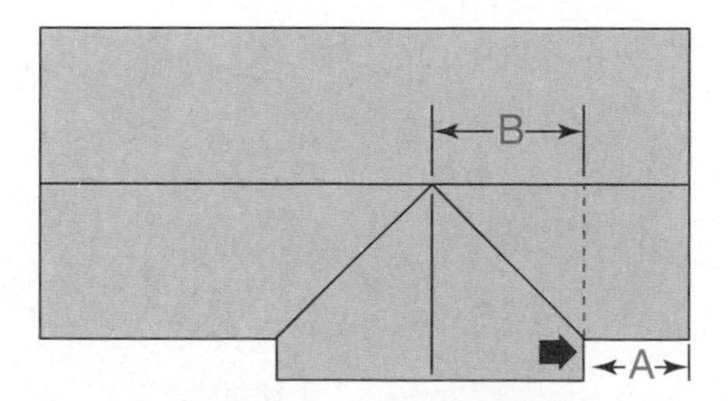

Fig. 24-14. Ridge board location for an equal-span addition on a gable roof.

Unequal Spans. If framing is by the long-and-short-valley-rafter method, the distance from the end of the main-roof ridge board to the upper end of the longer valley rafter is equal to distance *A* plus distance *B*. (Distance *B* is one-half the span of the main roof.) **Fig. 24-16.** The intersection of the shorter valley rafter and the longer valley rafter can be located in the following way.

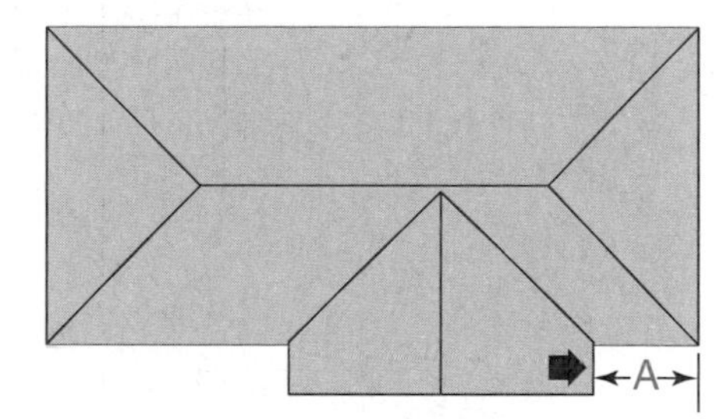

Fig. 24-15. Ridge board location for an equal-span addition on a hip roof.

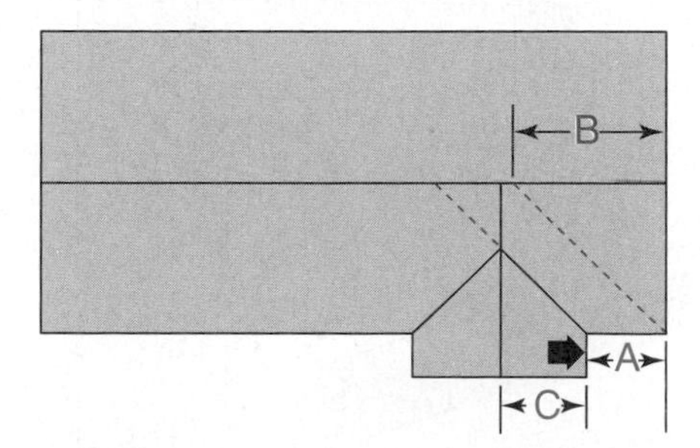

Fig. 24-16. Ridge board and valley rafter locations for an unequal-span addition.

Obtain the unit length of the longer valley rafter from the rafter table on the framing square. **Fig. 24-17.** For example, suppose that the common rafter unit rise is 8″. In that case, the unit length of a valley rafter is 18.76″.

The total run of the longer valley rafter is the hypotenuse of a right triangle. The shorter sides of this triangle are each equal to the total run of a common rafter in the addition. The total run of a common rafter in the addition is one-half the span. If the addition is 20′ wide, the run of a common rafter would be 10′. Refer to distance *C* in Fig. 24-16.

The valley rafter in our example is 18.76″ long for every foot of common rafter run. The point where the inboard end of the shorter valley rafter intersects the longer valley rafter can be calculated as follows:

18.76 (in. per ft. of run) × 10 (ft. of run) = 187.6″

187.6″ = 15.63′ (15′-7 9/16″)

This is the distance from the heel plumb cut line of the longer valley rafter to the intersecting point.

ERECTING THE RIDGE BOARD

Many carpenters raise the ridge board and the gable-end rafters all at one time. The members support one another. Others prefer to put the ridge board in place before raising any rafters, supporting it with temporary framing. **Fig. 24-18.** This also requires that the ridge board be braced along its length to prevent the roof from swaying. **Fig. 24-19.** This is particularly important on a gable roof.

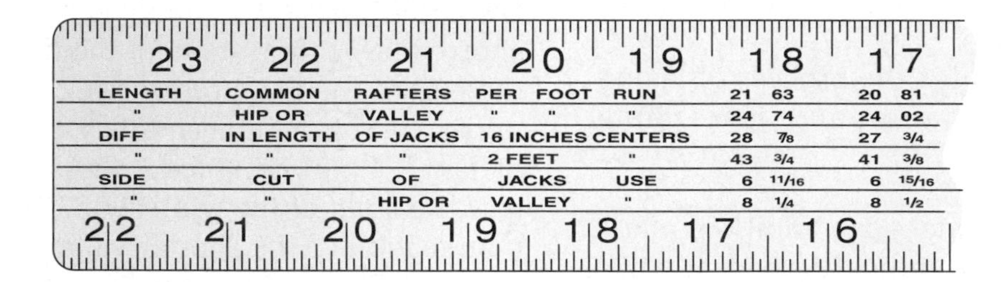

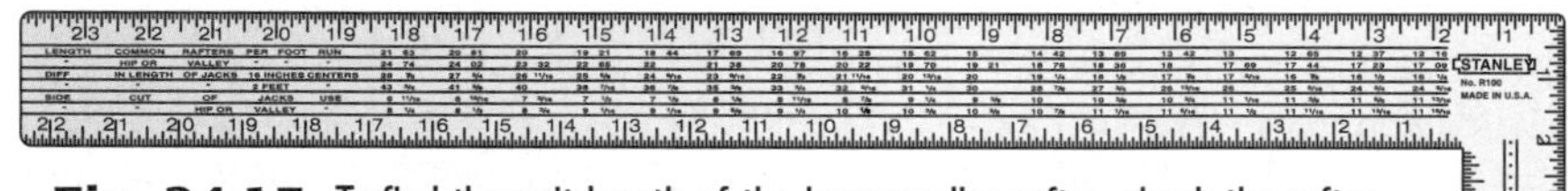

Fig. 24-17. To find the unit length of the longer valley rafter, check the rafter table on the face of the framing square.

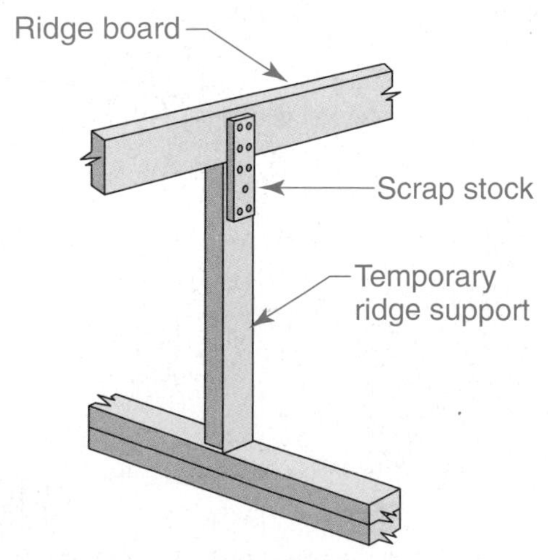

Fig. 24-18. An upright (leg) supports the ridge board in position for erecting the rafters.

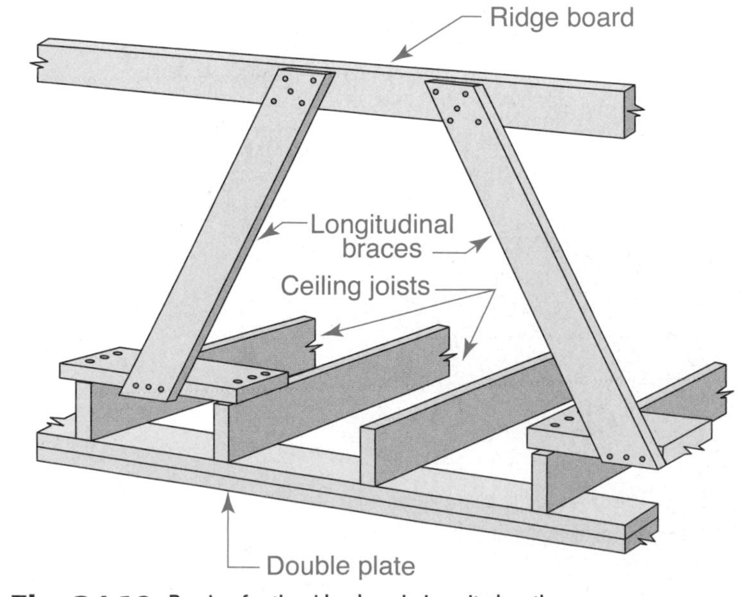

Fig. 24-19. Bracing for the ridge board along its length.

ERECTING THE RAFTERS

Depending on the type and height of the roof, you may have to install the rafters while working from scaffolding. The scaffold planking should not be less than 4′ below the level of the ridge board. In some cases, it may be possible to work from ladders instead.

If the building has an addition, frame as much of the main roof as possible before starting the addition framing. All types of jack rafters are usually left until after the headers, hip rafters, valley rafters, and ridges to which they will be attached have been installed.

The following text describes standard assembly techniques. Other techniques may be required in areas of the country exposed to unusually high winds and seismic activity. In these areas, local building codes may require the addition of special metal anchors or straps to connect the roof framing to wall framing. These anchors must be installed with care. Follow all code requirements regarding the type, spacing, and number of nails used to secure these devices.

Gable Roofs

For a gable roof the two pairs of gable-end rafters and the ridge board are usually erected first. Two people, one at each end of the scaffold, hold the ridge board in position. Meanwhile, a third person sets the gable-end rafters in place and toenails them at the top plate with 8d nails, two on one side and one on the other side. Nailing at the plate first prevents the rafter from slipping out of position as the ridge is being installed. Make certain the heel (plumb) cut of the bird's mouth is tight against the side of the building when the rafter is nailed at the plate. Otherwise, the ridge will not be set at the correct height.

Each worker on the scaffold then end-nails the ridge board to one of the rafters with three 16d nails driven through the ridge board and into the end of the rafter. The opposing rafter is toenailed to the ridge board and to the first rafter with four 16d nails, two on each side of the rafter. **Figs. 24-20** and **24-21.**

If the ridge board has not been previously erected and braced, temporary braces like those for a wall should be installed at the ridge ends.

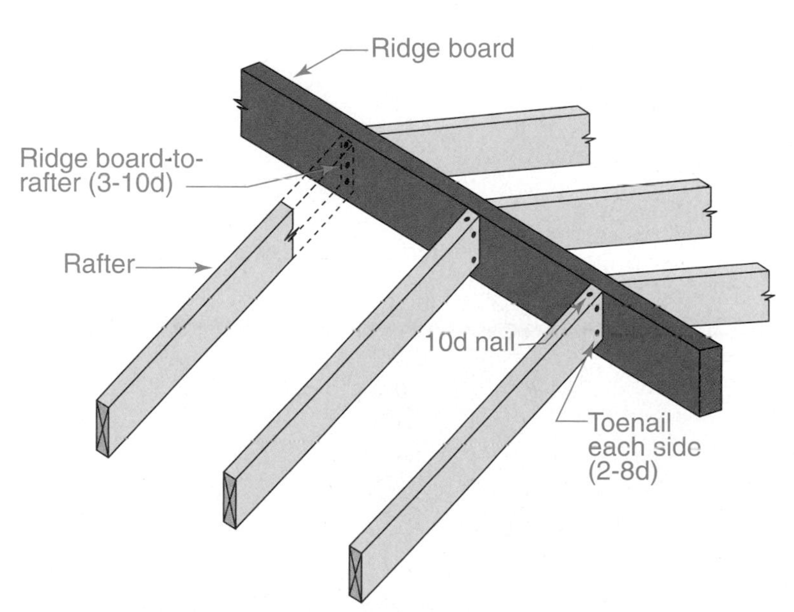

Fig. 24-20. Nailing rafters at the ridge board.

Fig. 24-21. Rafters are often toenailed to the ridge board. However, they may also be attached using metal framing connectors, as shown here.

These will prevent the rafters from tipping from side to side.

Ceiling-joist ends are nailed to adjacent rafters with three 10d nails, two to each side.

Hip Roofs

On a hip roof, first install the ridge board and the common rafters extending from the ridge ends to the side walls. This is done in about the same manner as for a gable roof. Then fill in the intermediate common rafters. Next, install each common rafter that extends from the ridge end to the mid-point on the end wall. Do this for both end walls. These rafters are sometimes referred to as *end rafters.* Finally, install the hip rafters and hip jacks.

The common rafters in a hip roof do not have to be plumbed. If the hip rafters are correctly cut, installing the hip rafters and the common rafter that projects from the end of the ridge board to the end wall will make the common rafters plumb.

Toenail hip rafters to the plate with 10d nails, two to each side. At the ridge board, toenail hip rafters with four 8d nails. After the hip rafters are fastened in place, drive a nail partway into the top edge of the hip rafter at the ridge end and at the plate end. Pull a string taut between the nails as the hip jacks are nailed to the hip rafter. Keep it centered on the top edge of the hip rafter. This allows you to see if the hip rafter is being pushed out of alignment by the jacks and ensures a straight hip line.

The hip jacks should be nailed in pairs, one opposite the other. Do not nail *all* the jacks on one side of the hip first. This would push the hip out of alignment and cause it to bow. Toenail hip jacks to hip rafters with l0d nails, three to each jack, and to the plate with 10d nails, two to each side.

Additions and Dormers

When there is an addition or dormer, the valley rafters are usually erected first. Toenail them to ridge boards and headers with three 10d nails. Install the ridge boards and ridge-end common rafters next. Then install the other addition common rafters and, last, the valley and cripple jacks. As with hip rafters, pull a string along the top edge of the valley rafter and nail the jacks in pairs. A valley jack should be held in position for nailing as shown in **Fig. 24-22**. When the jack has been properly nailed, the end of a straightedge laid along its top edge should contact the centerline of the valley rafter as shown.

USING ROOF FRAMING BRACKETS

Metal brackets may be used to attach common rafters to the plate. **Fig. 24-23.** This is good practice in parts of the country exposed regularly to high winds. The brackets strengthen the connection between the roof system and the walls.

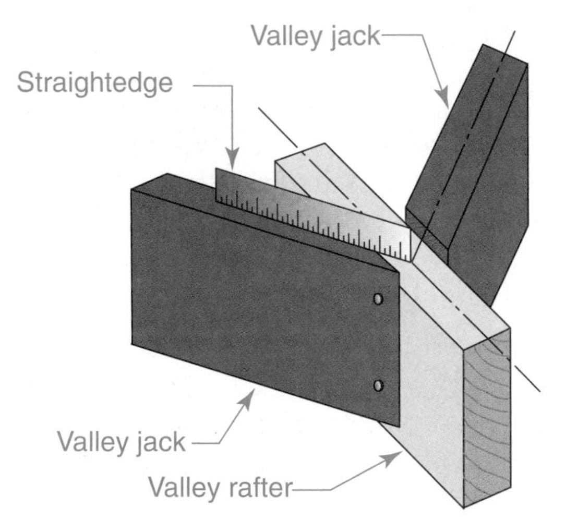

Fig. 24-22. Correct position for nailing a valley jack rafter.

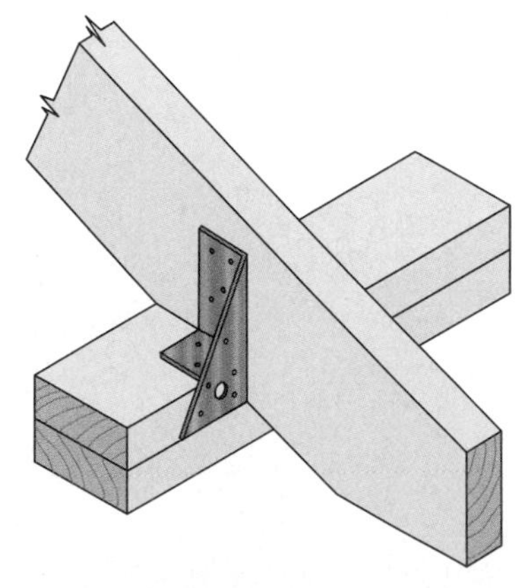

Fig. 24-23. Metal brackets are sometimes used to fasten the rafter to the plate. These brackets are available in a variety of styles.

Estimating...

Roofing Materials

Estimating lumber and nails for a roof can be done in several ways.

METHOD 1

The number of rafters needed may be counted directly from the roof framing plan. For a gable roof, the number may also be estimated as follows:

Step 1 For rafters on 16″ centers, take three-fourths of the building's length in feet, add one for the end rafter, and then double this figure. For example, if a rectangular building is 40′ long, 31 rafters will be required for each of the longer sides.

$$\frac{3}{4} \times 40 = 30$$
$$30 + 1 = 31$$
$$31 \times 2 = 62$$

A total of 62 rafters would thus be needed.

Step 2 Add to this amount extra rafters for the required trimmers and any other special framing. An accurate cost estimate can then be figured by multiplying the number of rafters required by the cost per rafter.

METHOD 2

Sometimes a builder does not make up a complete bill of materials and needs only a rough cost estimate.

Step 1 Find the area of the roof. The area is the length of the building times the width times the factor from **Table 24-A**. For example, a building 20′ wide and 40′ long with no overhang will have an area of 800 sq. ft. (20′ × 40′ = 800).

Step 2 For a roof with a unit rise of 5″, the factor is 1.083. The area of the roof, then,

Table 24-A. Estimating Roof Sheathing from Plans

Rise (inches)	Factor	Rise (inches)	Factor
3	1.031	8	1.202
3½	1.042	8½	1.225
4	1.054	9	1.250
4½	1.068	9½	1.275
5	1.083	10	1.302
5½	1.100	10½	1.329
6	1.118	11	1.357
6½	1.137	11½	1.385
7	1.158	12	1.414

Note: When a roof has to be figured from a plan only, and the roof pitch is known, the roof area may be fairly accurately computed from this table. The horizontal or plan area (including overhangs) should be multiplied by the factor shown opposite the rise, which is given in inches per horizontal foot. The result will be the roof area.

(Continued)

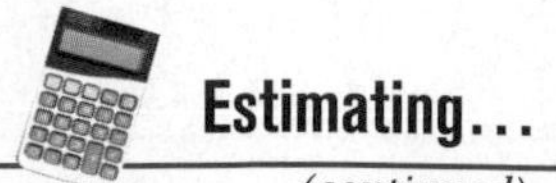

Estimating...

(continued)

Table 24-B. Estimating Materials and Labor for Roof Framing

Rafters	MATERIALS: Board Feet Required for 100 Square Feet of Surface Area — 12″ OC	16″ OC	24″ OC	Nails Per 1,000 Board Feet	LABOR: Board Feet per Hour
2x4	89	71	53	17	Common-35
2x6	129	102	75	12	Hip-35
2x8	171	134	112	9	Jack-25
2x10	212	197	121	7	Valley-35
2x12	252	197	143	6	Ridge-35
					Collar-65

Note: Includes common rafters, hip and valley rafters, ridge boards, and collar ties.

is 800 × 1.083 = 866.4, which is rounded off to 867 sq. ft.

Step 3 To determine the number of board feet needed for rafters, ridge board, and collar ties, refer to **Table 24-B**. For example, if the rafters are 2×6 and 16″ on center, 102 bd. ft. of lumber are needed for each 100 sq. ft. of roof surface area.

Step 4 Divide the total roof area by 100 and multiply by the factor in the table. For our example:

$$867 \div 100 = 8.67$$
$$8.67 \times 102 = 884.3 \text{ bd. ft.}$$

Step 5 Multiply this figure by the cost per board foot to find the total cost of lumber for the roof.

Step 6 Table 24-B also has information for determining the number of nails needed. For the roof in the example, 12 lbs. of nails are needed for each 1,000 bd. ft. Since the roof in the example has only about 884 bd. ft., it will require about 10½ lbs. of nails:

$$884 \div 1{,}000 = 0.884$$
$$0.884 \times 12 = 10.6 \text{ or } 10\tfrac{1}{2} \text{ lbs. of nails}$$

Step 7 The cost of nails for roof framing is determined by multiplying the number of pounds needed by the cost per pound.

ESTIMATING ON THE JOB

Using Method 2, estimate the board feet and pounds of nails needed for a roof that measures 22′ wide and 37′ long and has a rise of 6″. There is no overhang, and 2×8 rafters placed 16″ OC will be used.

Instead of being nailed directly to the ridge, hip and jack rafters may also be connected by using metal brackets. One type of bracket will adjust to any roof pitch. **Fig. 24-24.** The plate end of hip and jack rafters can also be anchored with metal brackets. **Fig. 24-25.**

When using certain types of roof framing brackets, it is sometimes helpful to install them on the ridge board before it is lifted into place.

This technique is also suitable when a ridge beam is being used. Brackets may be attached to the wall plates as well before the rafters are lifted into place. However, care must be taken not to bend or otherwise damage the brackets. Also, protect your hands. The edges of metal brackets are sometimes sharp.

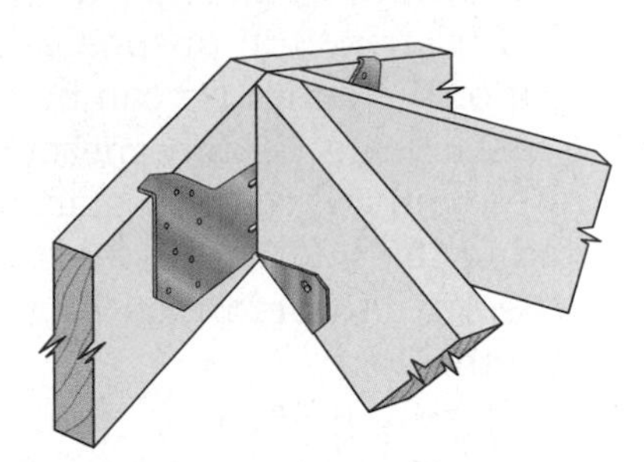

Fig. 24-24. An adjustable-pitch roof bracket.

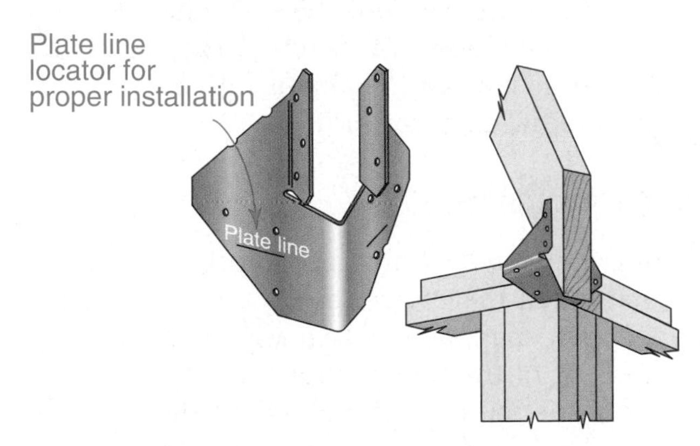

Fig. 24-25. A steel roof bracket can also be used to anchor the lower end of hip and jack rafters.

SECTION 24.2

Check Your Knowledge

1. Describe the procedure for laying out rafter locations for a gable roof.
2. When nailing common rafters in place in a gable roof, why must the rafter be nailed at the plate first?
3. How should the ends of the ceiling joists be connected to the rafters in a gable roof?
4. Why must hip jack rafters be installed in pairs?

On the Job

Using the Internet, locate a manufacturer of metal brackets used for roof framing. Obtain the most recent catalog of residential products. Study the brackets used to hold roof framing in place where high winds can be expected. What features make the brackets suitable for this use? Describe your findings in a paragraph. If necessary, sketch the brackets to explain your findings.

SECTION 24.3

Special Framing Details

A roof is more than just a collection of rafters. Collar ties and purlins and braces may be required for structural reasons. Framing must also be done for such features as gable ends, shed dormers, skylights, and chimneys.

COLLAR TIES

Gable rafters are sometimes reinforced by collar ties. A **collar tie** is a horizontal framing member that prevents opposing rafter pairs from spreading apart. It also prevents the rafters from bowing inward when weight is placed upon them. In a finished attic, collar ties may also support the ceiling surfaces where the ceiling joists have been omitted, or where ceiling joists run perpendicular to the rafters. When ceiling joists tie opposite walls together, collar ties may not be required.

If the collar ties will support a ceiling, they should be installed at every rafter pair. Otherwise, attach a collar tie to every fourth rafter pair if the spacing is 16″ OC and every third rafter pair if the spacing is 24″ OC. Local codes may require a closer spacing.

Collar-Tie Length

A collar tie may be made of nominal 1″ or 2″ thick lumber. Check the building plans for the specified dimensions. The length of a collar tie can be found either by calculation or by measurement.

Calculation Method. This method is used when ceiling framing must be done at a precise height. The length of a collar tie can be calculated based on its distance above the level of the side-wall top plates. **Fig. 24-26.** The theoretical length of a tie in feet is found by dividing this distance in inches by the unit rise of a common rafter and subtracting twice the result from the span of the building. For example, in the roof shown in Fig. 24-26, the collar tie is 3′-6″ (42″) above the top plate. The unit rise of a common rafter in the roof is 10″. Forty-two divided by 10 is 4.2, and twice 4.2 is 8.4. This number is subtracted from the span of the building:

16 – 8.4 = 7.6′, or about 7′-7³⁄₁₆″. This is the theoretical length of the tie.

To bring the ends of the collar tie flush with the upper edges of the common rafters, you must add to the theoretical length of the tie, at each end, an amount equal to the level width of a rafter minus the width of the rafter seat cut. One way to obtain the level width is to set a framing square on the rafter to the pitch of the roof. You then draw a level line from edge to edge and measure the line's length.

Measurement Method. Collar ties are sometimes used only for structural purposes. In such cases, the length of the collar tie can be easily determined by measuring. Simply measure between the rafters on a level line, starting from the height noted in the building plans. Cut one collar tie and check its fit before cutting all the collar ties to length.

After the overall length of a collar tie is determined, the ends must be cut to the pitch of the roof to prevent the tie from getting in the way of roof sheathing. Lay out the end cuts with a framing square set to the pitch of the roof. **Fig. 24-27.** These cuts can be made with a circular saw or a radial-arm saw.

Installing Collar Ties

Collar ties must be aligned during installation to ensure that their lower edges are in the same plane. First, snap a chalk line across the rafters on one side of the house, indicating the desired height of the top or bottom edge of the collar

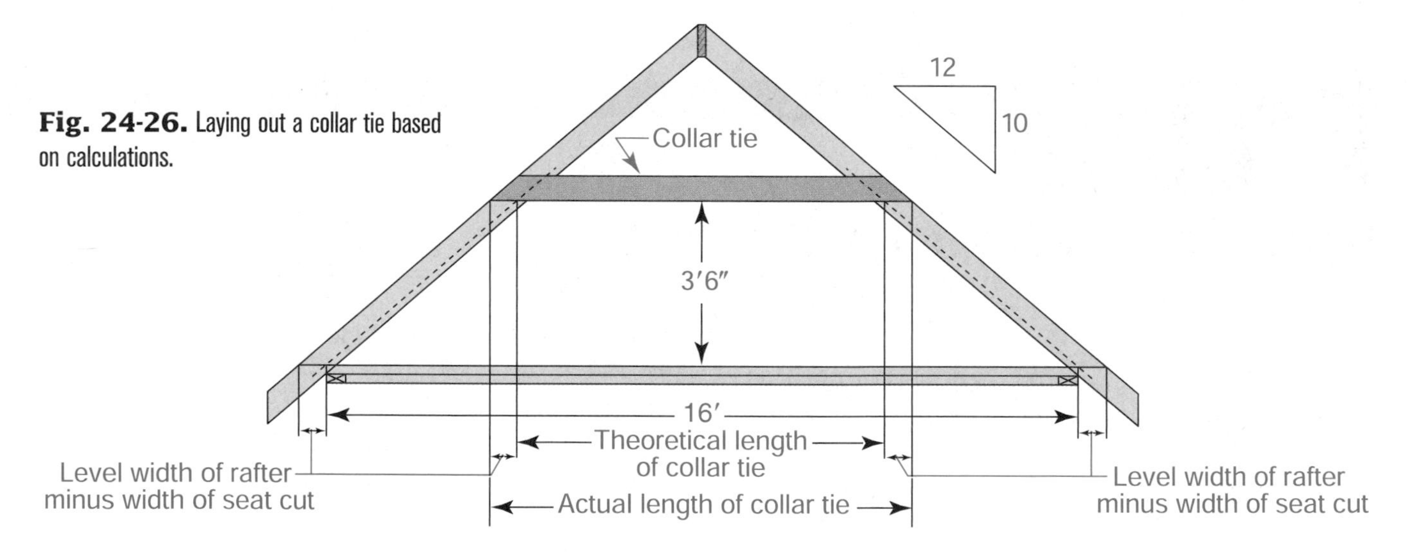

Fig. 24-26. Laying out a collar tie based on calculations.

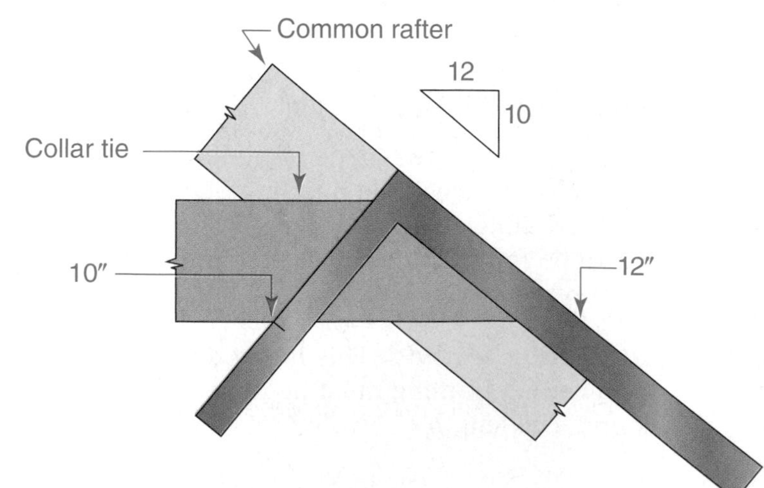

Fig. 24-27. Laying out the end cut on a collar tie for a roof with a unit rise of 10″.

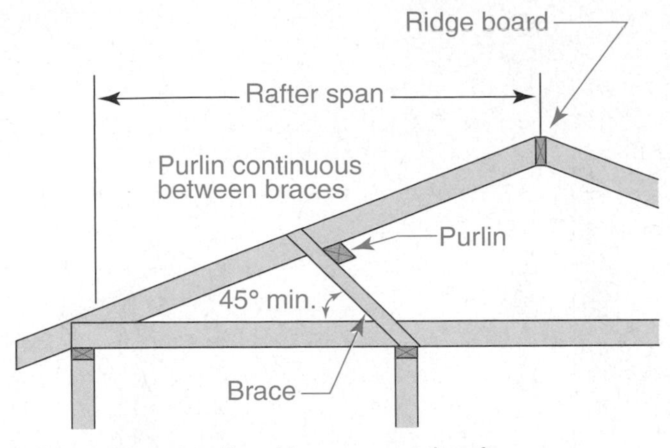

Fig. 24-28. A purlin and braces support the rafters.

tie. Then install one tie at each end of the house by aligning one end to the chalk line and using a level to align the other end. Nail the ties into place. Now stretch a string tightly between the ties. Align the remaining ties to the chalked line and to the string.

Nail nominal 1″ collar ties to the common rafters with four 8d nails in each end. Nail nominal 2″ collar ties with three 16d nails at each end.

PURLINS AND BRACES

To span a greater distance, a rafter must have a greater depth. However, deeper rafters are not always desirable or available. A system of purlins and braces can be used instead. **Fig. 24-28.** A **purlin** is a horizontal structural member that supports roof loads and transfers them to roof beams. A **brace** is a member used to stiffen or support a structure.

Purlins should be no smaller than the rafters they support. They must be continuous between braces. Braces should connect to bearing walls at no less than a 45° angle. They should be no longer than 8′ and be spaced not more than 4′ OC.

GABLE ENDS

Wall studs must be installed at each end of a gable to support sheathing. These gable-end studs rest on the top plate and extend to the rafter line. **Figs. 24-29** and **24-30.** They may be installed facing sideways with a miter at the top that fits the slope of the rafters. However, the

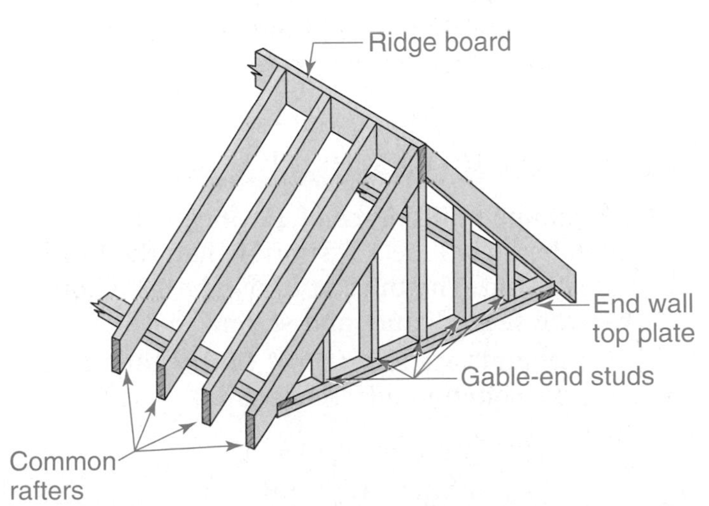

Fig. 24-29. Gable-end framing. There will be no overhang at the end of this roof.

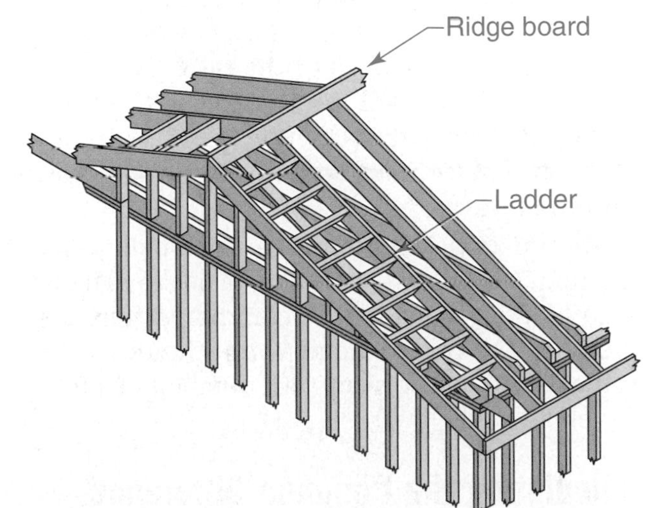

Fig. 24-30. Roof framing for the overhang at a gable end.

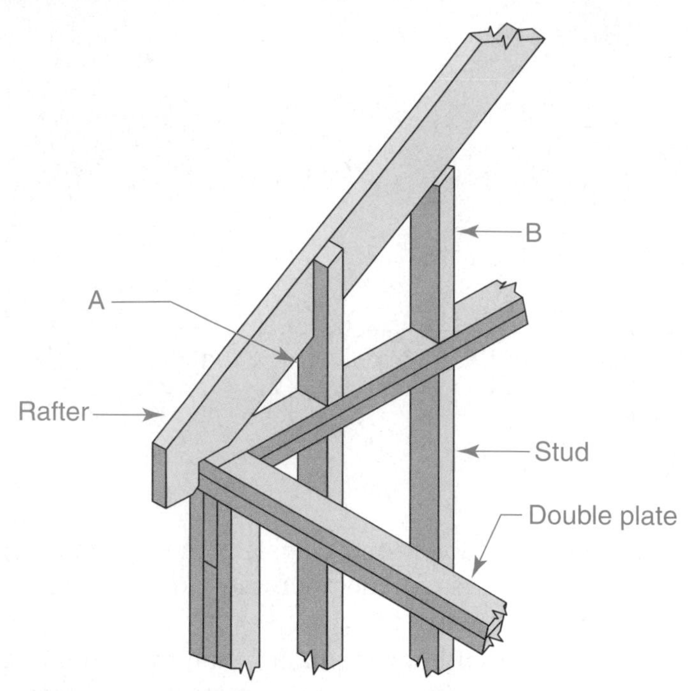

Fig. 24-31. Installing gable-end studs. *A.* Some carpenters notch the studs to fit over the rafter. *B.* Others simply bevel the end.

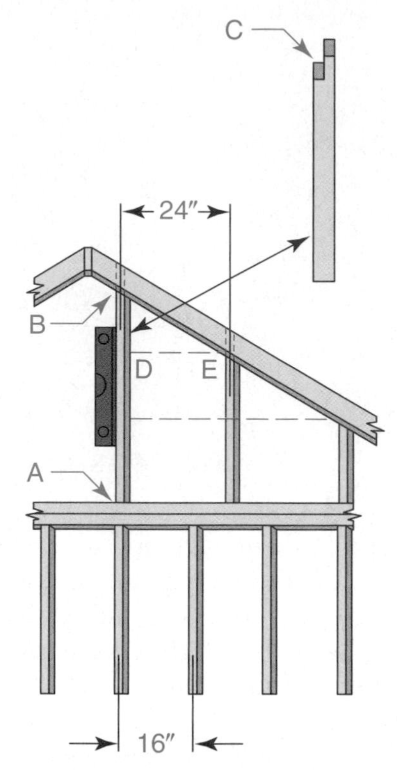

Fig. 24-32. Locating the gable-end studs and determining the common difference in length.

preferred method is to install them like standard wall studs, with one edge flush with the outside wall. The top end may be notched or it may be beveled to fit the slope of the rafters. **Fig. 24-31.**

Locate the first gable-end stud by making a mark on the double plate directly above the wall stud nearest the ridge line. See arrow *A*, **Fig. 24-32**. Plumb the gable-end stud on this mark. Mark the pitch of the roof across the edge of the stud. See arrow *B*, Fig. 24-32.

Now determine the length of the stud. (It must not extend above the top edge of the rafter.) Cut the stud to length and notch it to a depth matching the thickness of the rafter. See arrow *C*, Fig. 24-32. Toenail it into place with three 8d or two 16d nails at each end. As you nail the studs into place, take care not to force a crown into the rafter.

All remaining studs can be sized using this method. However, it is much easier to calculate stud lengths by using the common difference method. The basic calculation technique is the same, whether the studs are notched or just bevel cut.

Calculating the Common Difference

Gable-end studs have the same on-center spacing as standard wall studs. However, each stud is a different length than the studs on either side. Their differences in length are based on a single figure that depends on the pitch of the roof. This figure is called the **common difference**. After you have determined the length of the tallest gable-end stud, you can subtract the common difference to find the length of all the shorter gable-end studs. This is faster than making individual measurements for each stud.

The common difference is calculated using the unit run and unit rise. For example, to find the common difference in the length of gable-end studs placed 24″ OC:

$$24'' \div 12'' \text{ (unit run)} = 2''$$
$$2'' \times 6'' \text{ (unit rise)} = 12''$$

A common difference of 12″ means that the second stud will be 12″ shorter than the first (tallest) stud. The third stud will be 12″ shorter than the second stud, and so on.

If the studs are spaced 16″ OC for the same roof, the common difference is 8″:

$$16'' \div 12'' \text{ (unit run)} = \tfrac{4}{3}''$$
$$\tfrac{4}{3}'' \times \tfrac{6}{1}'' \text{ (unit rise)} = 8''$$

Steps for finding the common difference using a framing square are given on page 487.

STEP BY STEP

Figuring the Common Difference Using a Framing Square

The common difference in the length of the gable-end studs may also be figured directly with the framing square.

Step 1 Place the framing square on the stud and set it to the unit rise and unit run of the roof (6 and 12 for this example). Draw a line along the blade at *A*, as shown in **Fig. 24-33**.

Step 2 Slide the blade along this line in the direction of the arrow at *B* until the spacing between the studs (16 for this example) is at the intersection (*C*) of the line drawn at *A* and the edge of the stud.

Step 3 Read the dimension on the tongue where it meets the same edge of the stud. This is the common difference (8″ for this example) for the gable-end studs.

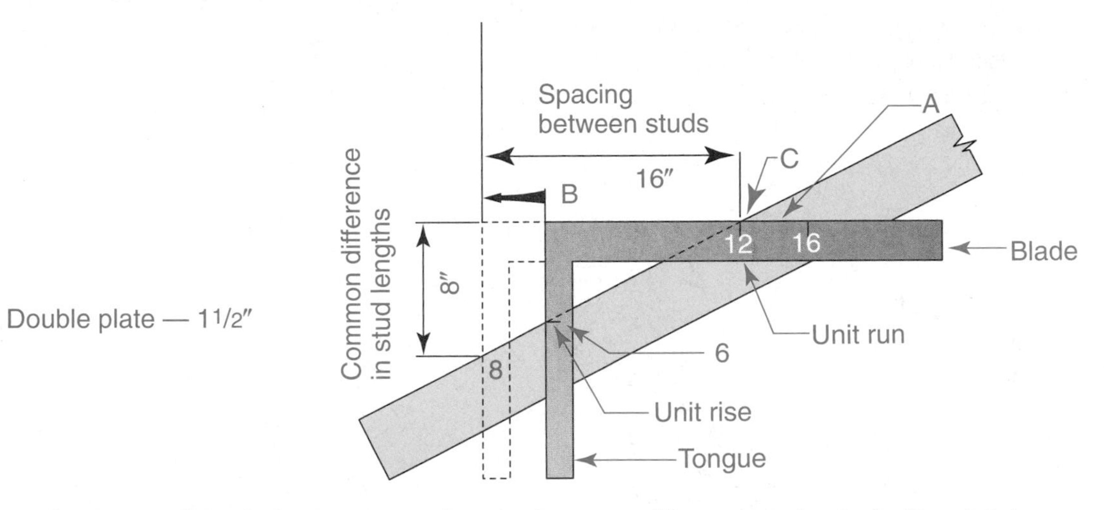

Fig. 24-33. Using the framing square to determine the common difference in the length of gable-end studs.

ROOF OPENINGS

Roof openings require interruption of the normal run of rafters or other roof framing. Openings may be required for a dormer, chimney, or skylight.

Roof openings, like floor openings, are framed by headers and trimmers. **Fig. 24-34.** Single or double headers are used at right angles to the rafters. The rafters are set into the headers in the same manner as joists around a floor opening. Just as trimmers are double joists in floor construction, they are double rafters in roof openings.

There are two ways to frame roof openings. The headers may be plumb, as shown in part **A** of **Fig. 24-35**. This method is used to accommodate vertical objects that must pass through the

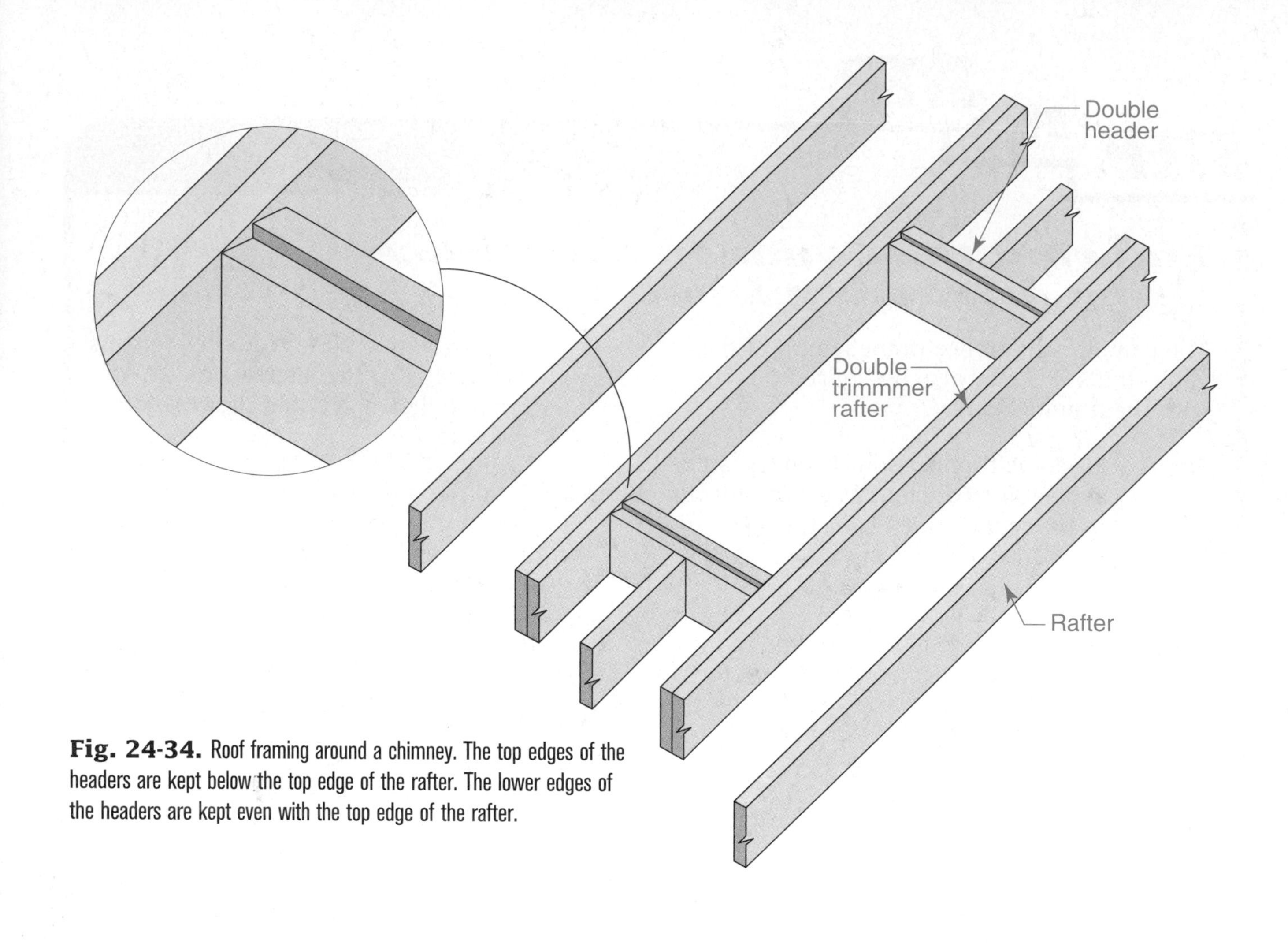

Fig. 24-34. Roof framing around a chimney. The top edges of the headers are kept below the top edge of the rafter. The lower edges of the headers are kept even with the top edge of the rafter.

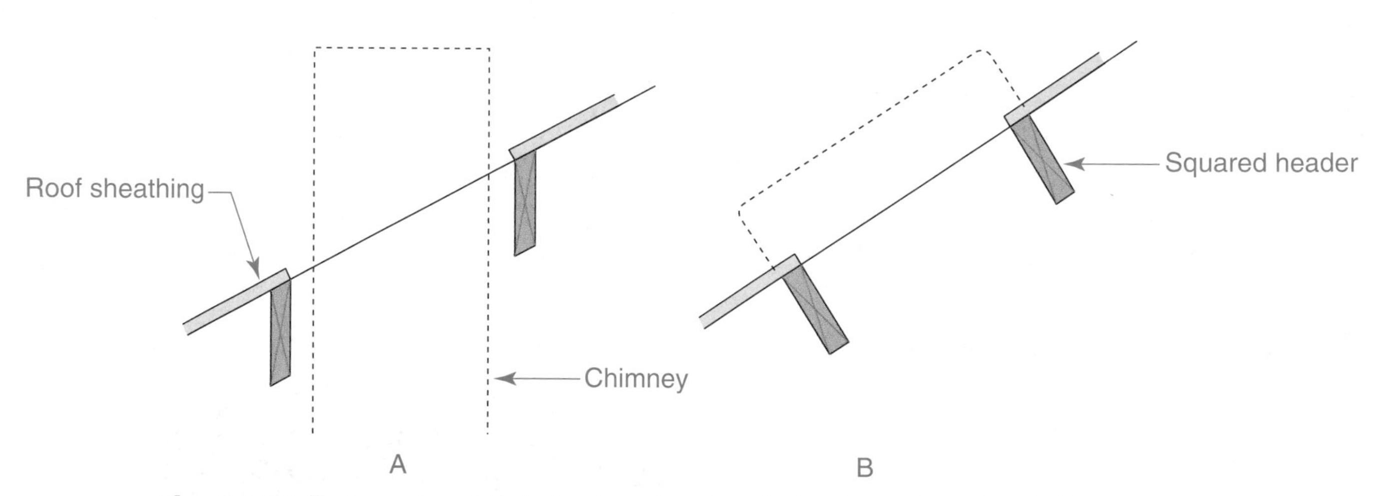

Fig. 24-35. The two basic methods for framing roof openings. The headers may be single or double, as needed.

framing, such as chimneys. In this method, the end of an intersecting rafter must be cut at an angle to fit against the header.

A second method is to keep the headers in the same plane as the surrounding roof framing as shown in part **B** of **Fig. 24-35**. Such an opening is easier to install and is sometimes used for skylights. In this case, the end of an intersecting rafter must be cut square to fit against the header.

SHED DORMERS

Dormers are framed after all of the common rafters are in place and a roof opening has been created. The framing of a gable dormer was discussed in Chapter 23, "Hip, Valley, and Jack Rafters." Shed dormers (**Fig. 24-36**) will be discussed here.

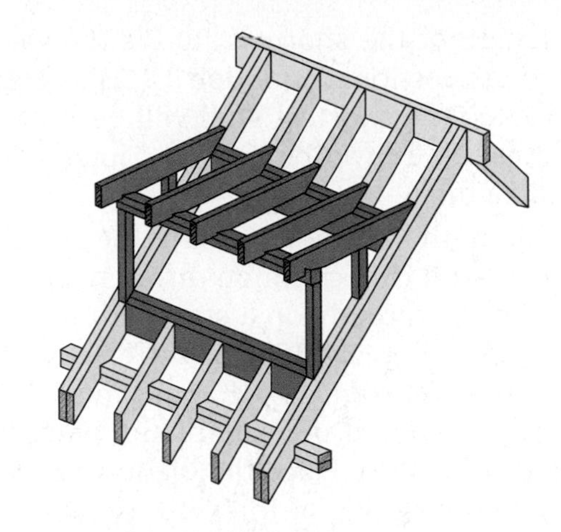

Fig. 24-36. Framing a shed dormer.

Laying Out the Rafters

To determine the total run of a shed-dormer rafter, divide the height of the dormer end wall by the difference in inches between the unit rise of the dormer roof and the unit rise of the main roof. For example, suppose the height of the dormer end wall is 9′, or 108″. **Fig. 24-37A.** The unit rise of the main roof is 8″; the unit rise of the dormer roof is 2½″ The difference between them is 5½″. The total run of a dormer rafter is therefore 108″ divided by 5½″, which is 19.63″. Knowing the total run and the unit rise, you can figure the length of a dormer rafter by any of the methods already described.

The inboard ends of dormer rafters must be cut to fit the slope of the main roof. **Fig. 24-37B.** To get the angle of this cut, set a framing square on the rafter to the pitch of the main roof. **Fig. 24-37C.** Measure off the unit rise of the dormer roof along the tongue, starting at the heel. Make a mark at this point and draw the cut-off line through this mark starting at the 12″ mark on the blade.

Finding the Length of Side-Wall Studs

To frame a shed dormer, you must find the lengths of the side-wall studs. Suppose a dormer rafter rises 2½″ for every 12″ of run, and a main-roof common rafter rises 8″ for every 12″ of run. Fig. 24-37A. If the studs are spaced 12″ OC, the length of the shortest stud is the difference between 8″ and 2½″, which is 5½″. (This is also the common difference.) If the stud spacing is

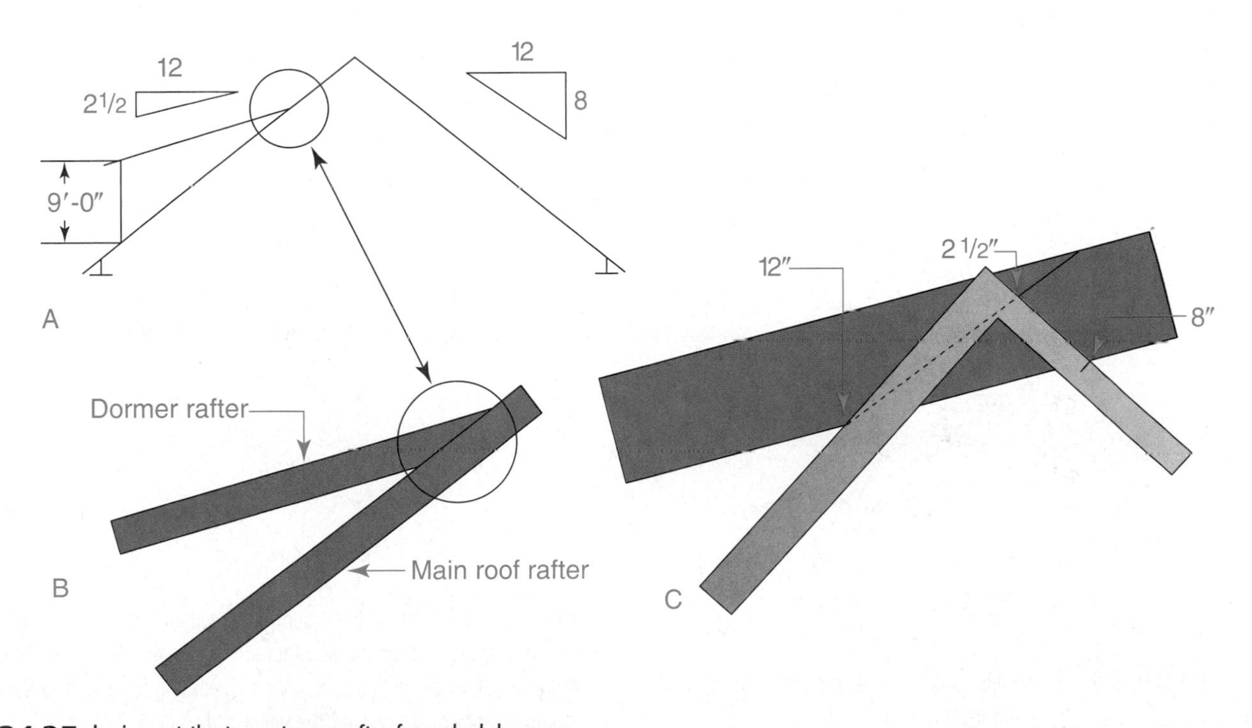

Fig. 24-37. Laying out the top cut on a rafter for a shed dormer.

16″, the length of the shortest stud is the value of x in the proportional equation 12:5½ :: 16:x. Thus $x = 7\frac{5}{16}$. The shortest stud will be 7⁵⁄₁₆″ long. The next stud will be 2 × 7⁵⁄₁₆″ long, or 14⅝″, and so on.

A second method of determining the length of the shortest stud (the common difference) is to make the layout directly on a stud with the framing square. **Fig. 24-38.** The difference in the rise of the two roofs is 5½″. Find the 5½″ mark on the tongue of the square and place it on the edge of a stud. Place the blade's 12″ mark on the same edge of the stud. Draw a line on the stud along the blade. Slide the square along this line until the blade's 16″ mark (the on-center spacing between the studs) is over where the 12″ mark had been. Draw a line along the tongue of the square. This completes the layout for the shortest stud. The second stud will be longer by this measure (the common difference), and so on.

To get the lower-end cut-off angle for studs, set the square on the stud to the pitch of the main roof. To get the upper-end cut-off angle, set the square to the pitch of the dormer roof.

CHIMNEY SADDLES

The *chimney saddle*, or *cricket*, diverts water around a chimney and prevents ice from building up on the roof behind it. The saddle may be constructed while carpenters are on the roof. However, if the chimney span and roof pitch are known, it can also be fabricated on the ground. The completed assembly can then be lifted into position and nailed to the roof framing. There are various methods for building chimney saddles. One method is shown here.

Valley strips for the saddle are 1x4 or 1x6 stock. **Fig. 24-39.** The distance across the widest part of the valley strips must be slightly less than the width of the chimney. This accounts for the distance that the saddle sheathing will project beyond the strips (see *B*, Fig. 24-39). This distance should be estimated by the carpenter. It varies, depending on the slope of the saddle. The length is determined in the same way as for a valley rafter. Use the framing square. Lay out the top and bottom cuts along the tongue of the square. For the length of the strip, use the unit length of a common rafter from the roof on which the saddle is to be framed.

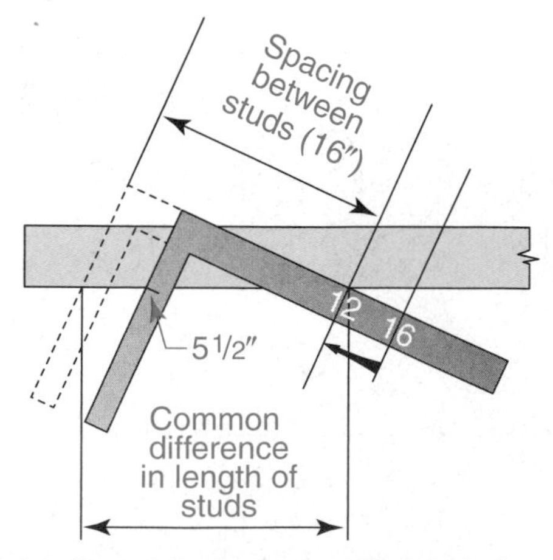

Fig. 24-38. Determining the common difference in the length of dormer side-wall studs by direct layout.

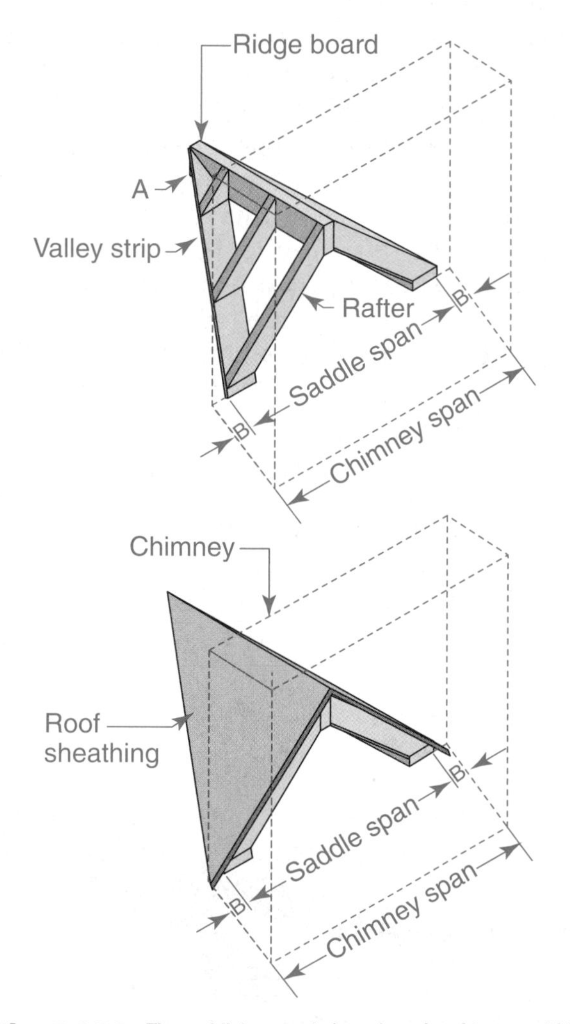

Fig. 24-39. The saddle's span is less than the chimney width, as shown. Distance *B* must be subtracted from each side of the chimney width to obtain the actual span. When sheathing is applied to the saddle rafters, it will project beyond the valley strip.

For example, suppose a roof with a unit rise of 5″ has a unit length of 13″. To lay out the valley strip, position the square with the tongue's 13″ mark and the blade's 12″ mark on the edge of the strip. Draw a line along the tongue for the top cut. Measure and lay out the length of the valley strip. With the square set the same as for the top cut, place the edge of the blade on the length mark and draw a line along the blade for the bottom cut.

The end of the saddle's ridge board rests on the valley strips, as shown at *A* in Fig. 24-39. This cut is the same as the seat cut for a common rafter in the main roof. Place the square on the ridge board for the pitch of the roof (in our example, 5″ on the tongue and 12″ on the blade) and draw a line along the blade. The length of the ridge is equal to the run of the common rafter in the saddle's span minus the allowance for the drop of the ridge, which is approximately ¾″.

To determine the theoretical length of the longest rafter, multiply the saddle's run (half the saddle's span) by the unit length of a common rafter. Deduct the ridge shortening allowance to obtain the actual length. The top and bottom cuts are the same as for a common rafter in the main roof. However, there is a side cut on the bottom where the rafter rests on the valley strip. This cut is the same as for regular valley jacks. On the framing square's rafter table, the side cut figure for a valley jack in a roof with a 5″ unit rise is 11½″. Lay out and make the cut as described on page 469 for jack rafters.

The cuts are the same for all the rafters in the chimney saddle. However, the rafter lengths differ. The difference in the length of the rafters can be found on the framing square's rafter table under "Difference in Length of Jacks." For rafters 16″ on center in a roof with a unit rise of 5″, the second rafter will be 17⁵⁄₁₆″ shorter than the first rafter. The third rafter will be 34⅝″ (2 × 17⁵⁄₁₆) shorter than the first rafter, and so on. When the saddle framing is complete, nail the roof sheathing to it.

from Another Angle

Some builders install the same roofing on the saddle as they do on the rest of the roof. This makes the saddle less noticeable. If this method is chosen, flexible asphaltic flashing sheets should be placed over the sheathing before the saddle shingles are installed. Flashing is a thin sheet of material that prevents water from reaching wood framing. Other builders prefer to cover the saddle with sheets of copper flashing. This material is more durable than shingles, but also more expensive.

SECTION 24.3 Check Your Knowledge

1. What is a collar tie and what is its purpose?
2. What is the purpose of purlins and braces?
3. In gable-end framing, what is meant by "common difference"?
4. At what point in roof construction are dormers framed?

On the Job

A lack of headroom often prevents attics from being converted to living space. One solution is to build a long shed dormer on one or both sides of a house. A back-to-back pair of long shed dormers are sometimes called *saddlebag dormers*. They increase the amount of usable attic floor space. Using library or Internet resources, locate examples of saddlebag dormers. Be sure to check sources of stock building plans. When you find at least one example, make a cross-section sketch of the house with and without the dormer. See if you can determine approximately how much usable floor space, in square feet, is lost if the dormer is removed.

SECTION 24.4

Roof Sheathing

Sheathing provides a nailing base for the finish roof covering and gives rigidity and strength to the roof framing. Spaced boards are sometimes used to sheath roofs that will be covered with wood shingles or shakes (see Chapter 30, "Roof Coverings"). Most roofs, however, are sheathed with panel products. The top surface of a sheathed roof is sometimes referred to as the *roof deck.*

PANEL SHEATHING

Plywood and OSB are the panel products used most often for roof sheathing. Though they are manufactured in different ways, they have about the same capabilities when used as roof sheathing.

Plywood and OSB can be installed quickly over large areas. They provide a smooth, solid base with a minimum of joints. **Fig. 24-40.** They can be used under almost any type of shingle or built-up roofing. Waste is minimal, which helps keep costs low.

Spanning Distance

Depending upon its thickness, panel roof sheathing can be used to span various distances. **Table 24-C** shows the most common combinations used.

Most panels are performance rated. That means they are stamped to indicate their suitability for particular spans. The stamp consists of a pair of numbers separated by a slash mark, such as 32/16 or 12/0. The number in front of the slash indicates the maximum spacing (in inches) of supports when the panel is used for roof sheathing. The number following the slash refers to the maximum spacing (in inches) of supports beneath panels used for subflooring. When one of the numbers is zero, the panel is unsuitable for that particular use. It is assumed that the long dimension of the panel will span at least three supports. Note that greater spans are generally allowed for roof sheathing than for floor sheathing.

SAFETY FIRST

Roofing Hazards

Installing roof sheathing can be dangerous, particularly on steep roofs. Always wear skid-resistant work boots. Many sheathing panels have one surface that is lightly textured or coated to make it skid-resistant. Always place this surface facing up. Remember that wet surfaces are more slippery than dry ones, so be cautious when rain or morning dew has wetted the sheathing.

Fig. 24-40. The roof of this large home is sheathed with plywood.

Table 24-C. Recommended Live Loads for APA Panel Sheathing[a]

Panel Span Rating	Panel Thickness (inches)	Maximum Span (inches)		Allowable Live Loads (psf)[d] Spacing of Supports Center-to-Center (inches)							
		With Edge Support[b]	Without Edge Support	12	16	20	24	32	40	148	60
12/0	5/16	12	12	30							
16/0	5/16, 3/8	16	16	55	30						
20/0	5/16, 3/8	20	20	70	50	30					
24/0	3/8, 7/16, 1/2	24	20[c]	90	65	55	30				
24/16	7/16, 1/2	24	24	135	100	75	40				
32/16	15/32, 1/2, 5/8	32	28	135	100	75	55	30			
40/20	9/16, 19/32, 5/8										
3/4, 7/8	40	32	165	120	100	75	55	30			
48/24	23/32, 3/4, 7/8	48	36	210	155	130	100	65	50	35	
48 OC[e]	1 1/8	60	48				375	205	100	65	40

Note: APA Rated Sheathing and APA Structural I Rated Sheathing.

(a) When roofing is to be guaranteed by a performance bond, check with roofing manufacturer for minimum thickness, span, and edge support requirements.

(b) Tongue-and-groove edges, panel edge clips (one between each support, except two between supports 48 inches on center), lumber blocking, or other.

(c) 24 inches for ½-inch panels.

(d) 10 psf dead load assumed.

(e) Span Rating applied to APA RATED STURD-I-FLOOR "2-4-1."

Installation

Panel roof sheathing should be laid with the grain (the long dimension) perpendicular to the rafters. **Fig. 24-41.** End joints should occur over rafters. The end joints of adjacent rows of panels should be staggered by using half-sheets. Unsupported edge joints can be strengthened with metal panel clips that tie them together. **Fig. 24-42.** These joints could also be supported by wood blocks, but blocks are more time-consuming to install and can limit ventilation beneath the roof.

Panels shrink or swell slightly as their moisture content changes. If panels are butted tightly during installation, they may buckle as they expand. To prevent buckling, allow ⅛″ between panels (the width of a 10d box nail) or as recommended by the manufacturer. This

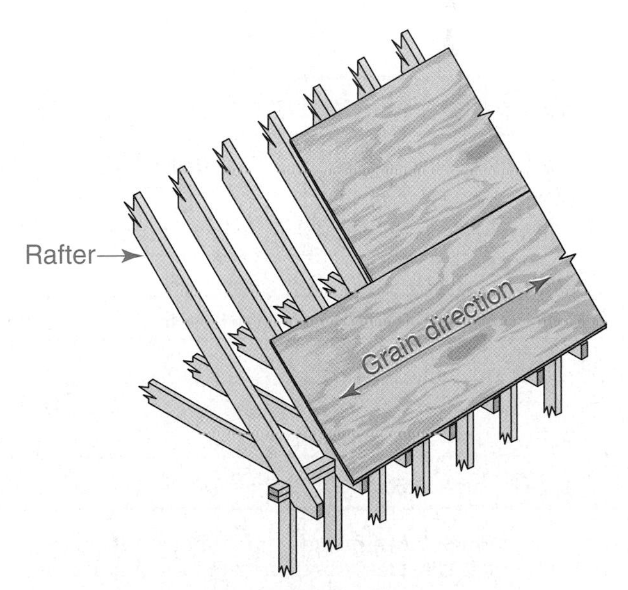

Fig. 24-41. The grain of plywood sheathing should be at right angles to the supporting members.

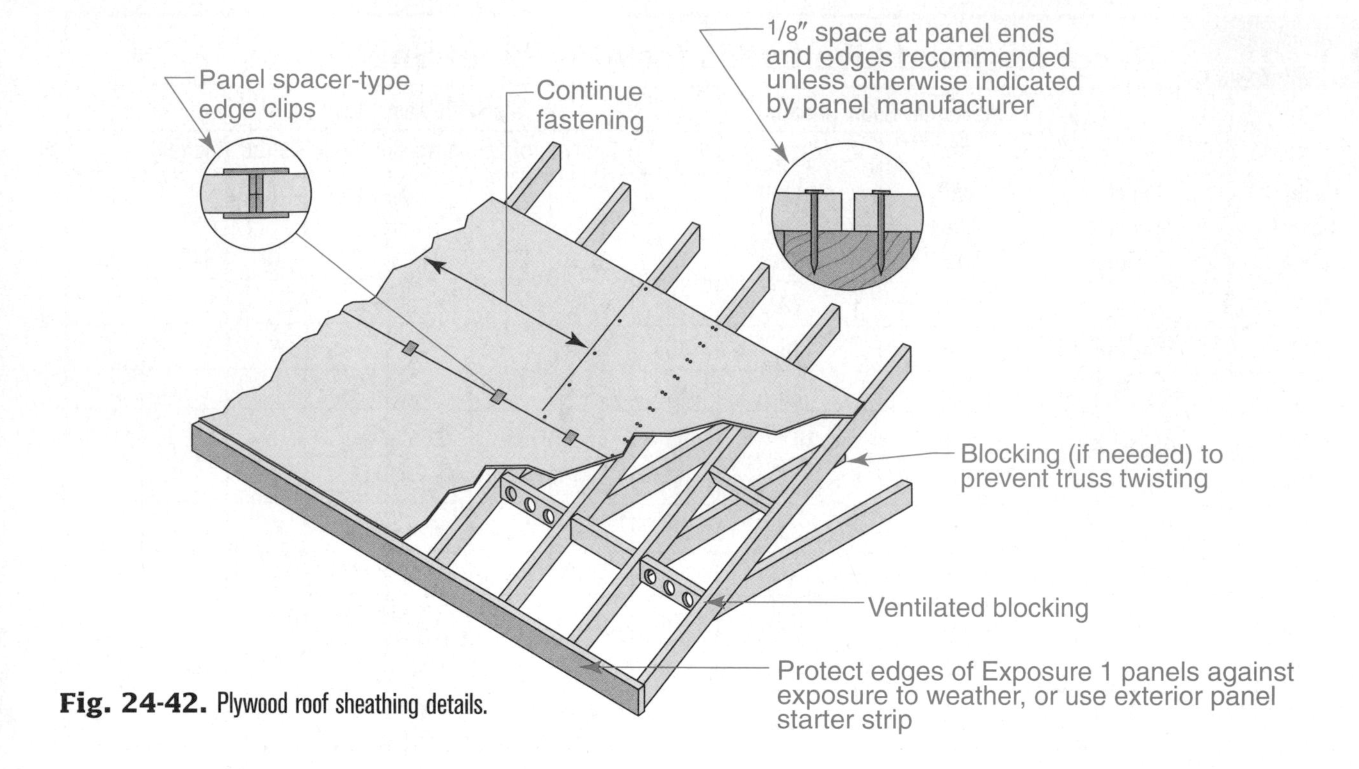

Fig. 24-42. Plywood roof sheathing details.

spacing should be used at all edge joints and end joints. Some panel clips are constructed to automatically space panels the proper distance apart. No surface or edge should be directly exposed to the weather.

Space nails no more than 6″ OC at supported panel ends and edges (perimeter) and 12″ apart at intermediate supports (field). Check local codes. **Table 24-D.** Use 6d common, ring-shank, or spiral-thread nails for plywood ½″ thick or less. For plywood more than ½″ thick, use 8d common nails. For additional holding power, use ring-shank or spiral-thread nails, or glue-nail the sheathing. Place nails approximately ⅜″ in from panel ends and edges.

Steps for installing panel sheathing are given on page 495.

Table 24-D. Minimum Fastening Schedule for APA Panel Roof Sheathing

Panel Thickness (inches)	Size	Nailing[a] Spacing (inches)		Leg Length (inches)	Stapling[b] [c] Spacing (inches)	
		Panel Edges	Intermediate		Panel Edges	Intermediate
5⁄16	6d	6	12	1¼	4	8
⅜	6d	6	12	1⅜	4	8
7⁄16, 15⁄32, ½	6d	6	12	1½	4	8
19⁄32, ⅝, 23⁄32, ¾, ⅞	8d	6	12[d]	–	–	–
1⅛, 1¼	8d or 10d	6	12[d]	–	–	–

[a] Use common smooth or deformed shank nails with panels to 1″ thick. For 1⅛″ and 1¼″ panels, use 8d ring- or screw-shank or 10d common smooth-shank nails.

[b] Values are for 16-gal. galvanized wire staples with a minimum crown width of ⅜″.

[c] For stapling asphalt shingles to 5⁄16″ and thicker panels, use staples with a ¾″ minimum crown width and a ¾″ leg length. Space according to shingle manufacturer's recommendations.

[d] For spans 48″ or greater, space nails 6″ at all supports.

STEP BY STEP

Installing Panel Sheathing

Always use caution when installing roof sheathing. If conditions are wet or windy, postpone installation until conditions improve. Never work on top of a panel that is not nailed securely to the rafters.

To install panel sheathing:

Step 1 Position the panel on the rafters. If necessary, tack it (nail it temporarily) to the rafters to prevent it from shifting.

Step 2 Nail one end of the panel. Drive nails flush with the panel surface. Remove any temporary nails.

Step 3 Snap a chalk line across the panel to indicate the centerline of each rafter. Nail the panel across its width, starting at one end and working toward the other.

Step 4 Once the panel is secure, stand on it over the framing as you nail it. This ensures full contact between sheathing and rafter.

Step 5 When installing the next panel, allow a ⅛″ space between panels, or as recommended by the manufacturer. You can use a 10d box nail to gauge this spacing. Install edge clips as required by local building codes.

Step 6 Cover the sheathing with roof felt as soon as possible to minimize exposure to the weather (see Chapter 30, "Roof Coverings").

LUMBER SHEATHING

The two types of lumber sheathing include open sheathing and plank sheathing. *Open sheathing* consists of 1x4 strips and is common in regions where wood shingles and shakes are popular. *Plank sheathing* is common where post-and-beam framing techniques are used.

Another type, called *closed sheathing*, was common before it was replaced by panel sheathing. Nominal 1″ boards with T&G or overlapping edges were installed over the entire roof surface. Sometimes closed sheathing was combined with open sheathing. **Fig. 24-43.** This was done to improve the leak resistance of the lower roof in climates where ice-damming was a common problem. Closed sheathing may be encountered during remodeling work.

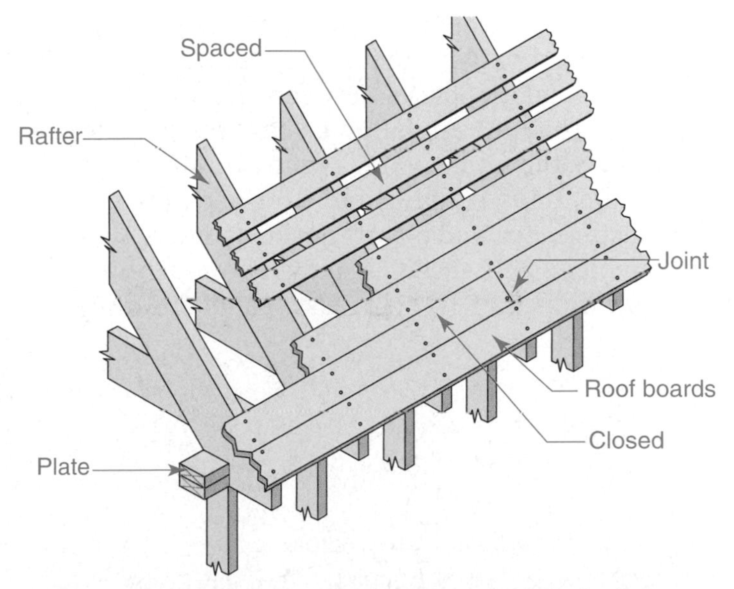

Fig. 24-43. Installation of lumber roof sheathing, showing both closed and open types.

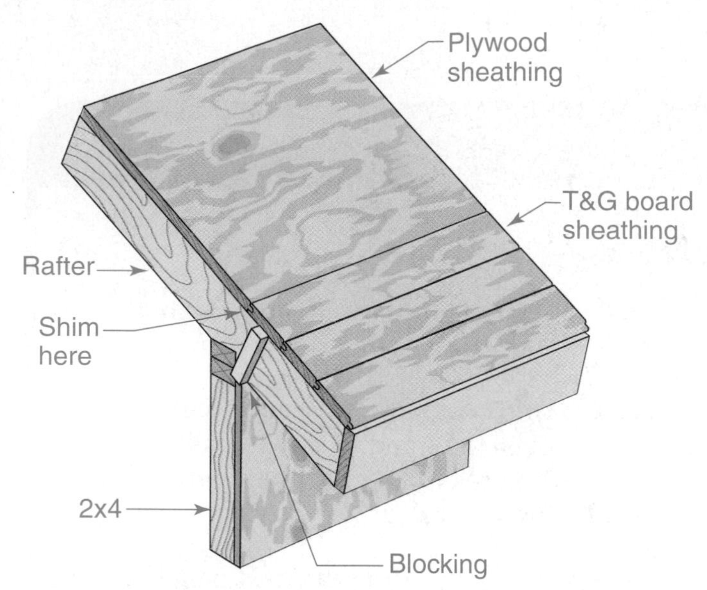

Fig. 24-44. Lumber sheathing is sometimes used where the underside of the roof sheathing will be exposed, as at open soffits. When the plywood sheathing meets the lumber sheathing, the edge of the plywood can be shimmed to match the thickness of the boards.

Open soffits expose the underside of roof sheathing at the eaves. Thus some builders install closed sheathing (T&G boards) in these areas for a decorative effect. The rest of the roof is then sheathed with plywood or OSB. **Fig. 24-44.**

Open Sheathing

Open sheathing (also called *skip sheathing* or *spaced sheathing*) is common under wood shingles and shakes. Spaces between sheathing boards promote ventilation around the shingles and allow them to dry out evenly. However, open sheathing is not suitable for use in regions that experience much earthquake activity. Also, in regions where the average daily temperature in January is 25°F [-4°C] or less, panel sheathing is required on portions of the roof that require an ice barrier. This area generally runs from the edge of the eaves to a point at least 24″ inside the building line. Consult local building codes for specific requirements.

The 1x4 boards of open sheathing are laid with on-center spacing equal to the amount of shingle exposed to the weather but not over 10″. (A 10″ shingle that is lapped 4″ by the shingle above it is said to be "laid 6″ to the weather.") Open sheathing is laid perpendicular to the rafters. In areas where wind-driven snow conditions prevail, panel sheathing is recommended instead.

Open sheathing is nailed to each rafter with two 8d nails. Joints must be made on the rafters. Each board should bear on at least two rafters.

Plank Sheathing

Plank sheathing (also called *roof decking*) provides a solid roof deck and an attractive ready-to-finish interior ceiling. Plank sheathing with double tongue-and-groove edges is available in several patterns. Some of the more common are the regular V-joint, grooved, striated, and eased joint (bullnosed) patterns. Single tongue-and-groove plank sheathing in nominal 2x6 and 2x8 sizes is available with the V-joint pattern only. **Fig. 24-45.**

Planks come in nominal widths of 4″ to 12″ and in nominal thicknesses of 2″ to 4″. The 3″ and 4″ roof decking is available in random lengths of 6′ to 20′ or longer.

Plank sheathing is also manufactured as a glue-laminated product. It comes in several softwood species: Idaho white pine, inland red cedar, Idaho white fir, ponderosa pine, Douglas fir, larch, and southern pine. One wood species may be used on the face while the back and interior laminations consist of different woods.

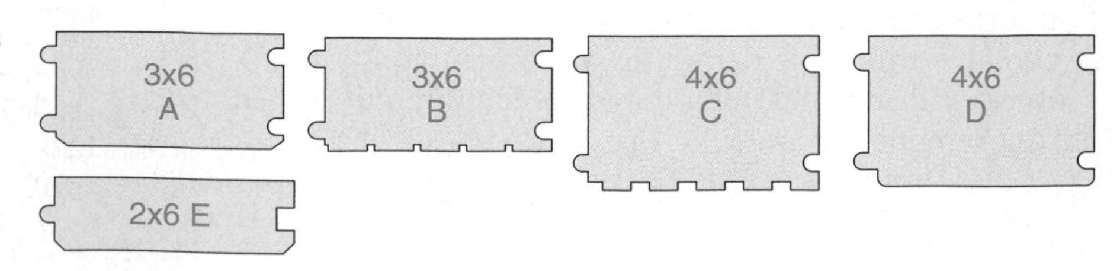

Fig. 24-45. Lumber roof decking patterns and sizes. *A.* Regular V-jointed. *B.* Striated. *C.* Grooved. *D.* Eased joint (bullnosed). *E.* Single tongue-and-groove V-joint.

Estimating...

Sheathing

To figure the area to be sheathed without actually getting on the roof and measuring, find the dimensions on the plans.

Step 1 Multiply the length of the roof times the width and include the overhang. For example, suppose that a home is 70′ long and 30′ wide, including the overhang. The roof has a rise of 5½″.

70′ × 30′ = 2,100 sq. ft.

Step 2 Multiply by the factor shown opposite the rise of the roof in Table 24-A on page 481. The result will be the roof area. For a rise of 5½″, the factor on the table is 1.100.

2,100 sq. ft. × 1.100 = 2,310 sq. ft.

PANEL SHEATHING

Step 1 To estimate the number of sheathing panels required, divide the roof area by 32 (the number of square feet in one 4′×8′ sheet). For example, 2310 ÷ 32 = 72.19.

Step 2 Add 5 percent for a trim and waste allowance:

72.19 × .05 = 3.6
72.19 + 3.6 = 75.79

It is also useful to draw a *roof sheathing plan.* This is a scale diagram of the roof that shows where individual plywood or OSB panels will be installed. **Fig. 24-46.** A plan is especially useful when the roof requires the use of more than one kind of panel. For example, a house may have open soffits where decorative plywood will be used. The exact number of each panel type can be shown on the plan.

DECKING AND PLANKING

Step 1 Determine the area to be covered.

Step 2 Refer to **Table 24-E** to obtain the needed factor. The left column shows the size of planking to be applied. For example, if 2x6 material is selected, the factor given is 2.40.

Step 3 Multiply the area to be covered by this factor. For example, if a deck measures 8′ x 10′:

8 × 2.40 = 192 sq. ft.

Step 4 Add a 5 percent trim and waste allowance to arrive at the amount of material needed:

192 × .05 = 9.6
192 + 9.6 = 201.6

ESTIMATING ON THE JOB

How many sheets of panel sheathing would be required for a roof that measured 50′ long and 27′ wide, including the overhang, and that had a 4″ rise?

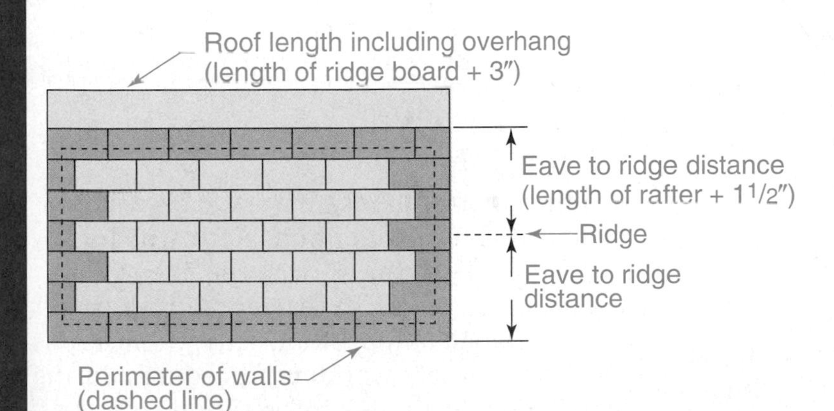

Fig. 24-46. A roof sheathing plan.

Table 24-E. Area Factors for Estimating Decking

Size (inches)	Area Factor
2 x 6	2.40
2 x 8	2.29
3 x 6	3.43
4 x 6	4.57

Note: Waste allowance not included in above factors.

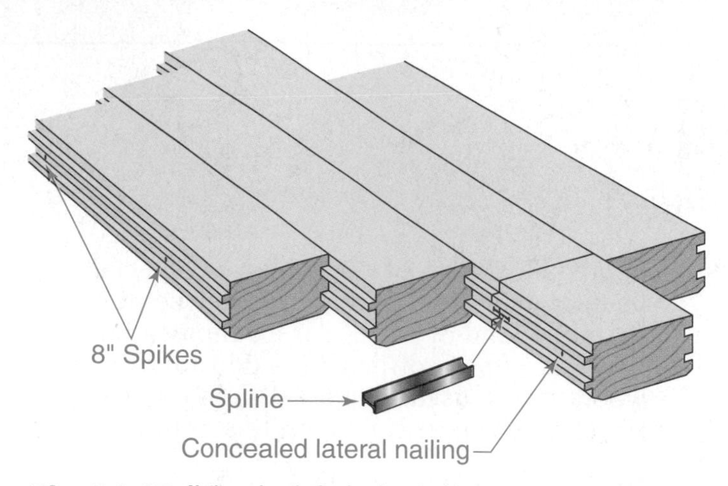

Fig. 24-47. Nailing details for lumber decking.

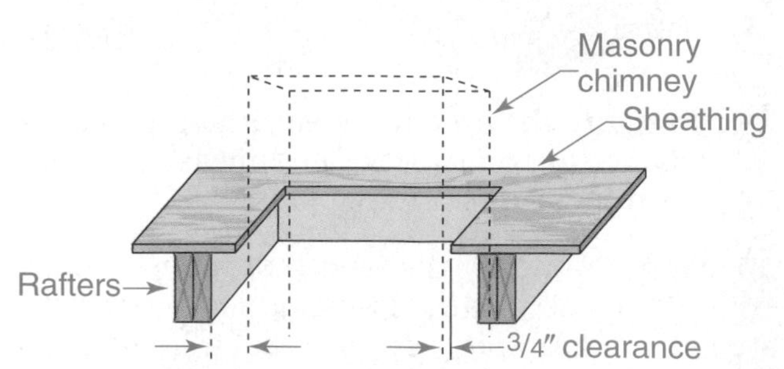

Fig. 24-48. Sheathing details at the chimney opening.

Plank sheathing that is being applied to a sloped roof should be installed with the tongue up. Fasten the planks with common nails twice as long as the nominal plank thickness. For widths 6″ or less, toenail once and face-nail once at each support. For widths over 6″, toenail once and face-nail twice.

Decking 3″ and 4″ thick must be pre-drilled and toenailed with 8″ spikes. **Fig. 24-47.** Some 3″ and 4″ thick roof decking comes with pre-drilled nail holes on 30″ centers. Bright common nails may be used, but dipped, galvanized common nails have more holding power and reduce the possibility of rust streaks. End joints not over a support should be side-nailed within 10″ of each plank end. Metal splines are recommended on end joints of 3″ and 4″ material for better alignment, appearance, and strength.

Sheathing Details

Where gable ends have little or no extension other than the molding and trim, the roof sheathing is usually sawed flush with the outer face of the side-wall sheathing. Cuts should be even so that the trim and molding can be properly installed.

Roof sheathing should have a ¾″ clearance from the finished masonry on all sides of a chimney opening. **Fig. 24-48.** This gap is covered by flashing. Framing members should have a 2″ clearance for fire protection. The sheathing should be securely nailed to the rafters and to the headers around the opening.

The sheathing at the valleys and hips should be fitted to give a tight joint. It should be securely nailed to the valley or the hip rafter. This will give a solid and smooth base for the flashing.

SECTION 24.4

Check Your Knowledge

1. A performance-rated panel is stamped 32/16. What does the number 32 represent?
2. What is the correct spacing for nails when installing roof sheathing panels?
3. What is the advantage of using open sheathing beneath wood shingles?
4. What clearance is recommended between roof sheathing and the finished masonry for a chimney?

On the Job

Use the Internet to locate a trade association responsible for maintaining standards for plywood roof sheathing. Search the site to find publications related to residential roof sheathing. Download and print out any publications that relate to safe working procedures during installation. Share this information with the class.

Chapter 24

Review

Section Summaries

24.1 Ridges can be structural or nonstructural. Calculating the length of a ridge requires actual measurements taken from the framed building. The ridges for dormers and additions can be calculated with the assistance of a sketch of the roof plan.

24.2 A careful rafter layout is important so that rafters will bear properly on the ridge board or ridge beam. Common rafters are generally installed first, then hip and valley rafters. Jack and hip jack rafters are installed last.

24.3 Special framing details include collar ties, purlins and braces, gable ends, roof openings, shed dormers, and chimney saddles.

24.4 Roofs may be sheathed with panels or lumber. Lumber sheathing includes open and plank sheathing.

Review Questions

1. Name the two basic types of ridges.
2. For a gable roof, what is the difference between the theoretical length of a ridge board or ridge beam and its actual length?
3. What is the shortening allowance?
4. Why is it important to begin the rafter layout on opposing plates from the same end of the building?
5. Describe two methods for estimating the number of rafters required for a gable roof with rafters spaced 16″ OC.
6. Identify at least five instances in roof framing where special framing details are required after the rafters have been installed.
7. Why must the ends of a collar tie be cut at an angle, and how is the angle calculated?
8. For a roof with a unit run of 12″ and a unit rise of 6″, what is the common difference of gable-end studs spaced 16″ OC?
9. How can the unsupported edge joints of panel roof sheathing be supported?
10. What should be the width of the spacing between adjacent roof sheathing panels, and why is this necessary?

Getting Sheathing onto the Roof Not only are large sheets of plywood unwieldy to carry, but they also can catch the wind and throw you off balance. The easiest way to get them to the roof of a one-story house is to slide them up a simple framework made from 2×4 lumber. It will be easy for a carpenter on the roof to reach over and pull panels up. For two-story houses, carry the plywood to the second floor. Then hand the sheets up from between the rafters.

Chapter 25

Roof Trusses

Objectives

After reading this chapter, you'll be able to:

- Name the three basic parts of a roof truss.
- Handle roof trusses properly.
- Properly store roof trusses on the job site.
- Install roof trusses.

Terms

chord
connector plate
gable-end truss
machine stress-rated lumber
nominal span
split-ring connector
web

The simple roof truss is an assembly of members forming a rigid framework of triangular shapes. It can support loads over long spans. Many residential and commercial buildings are framed with roof trusses. Trusses are made in factories and delivered to the job site by truck.

Trusses save money on materials and on-site labor. The double top plate on interior partition walls and the double floor joists under interior bearing partitions are not necessary. Because roof trusses are self-supporting, there is often no need for interior bearing partitions for the trusses. Materials may cost about 30 percent less than those used for traditional roof framing.

SECTION 25.1

Roof Truss Basics

The basic parts of a roof truss are shown in **Fig. 25-1**. A **chord** is the top or bottom outer member of the truss. The **web** is between the chords. It creates a rigid assembly. Chords and webs are connected at the joints by rectangular connector plates. A **connector plate** is a pre-punched metal plate with many stamped teeth. **Fig. 25-2.** Plates are pressed into the wood under hydraulic pressure to splice the joint on each side. Some heavy trusses are assembled with split-ring connectors. **Fig. 25-3.** A **split-ring connector** allows truss stock to be built up into layers. Most trusses are built from 2x4 stock. They may also be built of other materials, including metal and timber. **Fig. 25-4.**

Trusses can be erected quickly. Therefore, a house can be enclosed in a short time. They are usually designed to span from one exterior wall to the other with lengths of 20′ to 32′ or more. Because no interior bearing walls are required, interior design can be more flexible. Partitions can be placed without regard to structural requirements. **Fig. 25-5.**

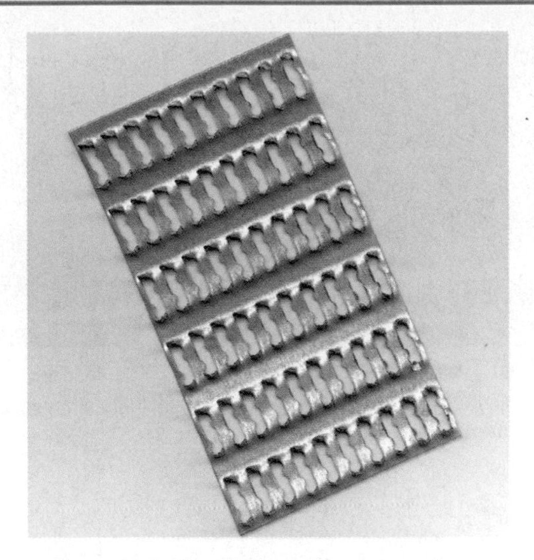

Fig. 25-2. A toothed metal connector plate, also called a gusset plate.

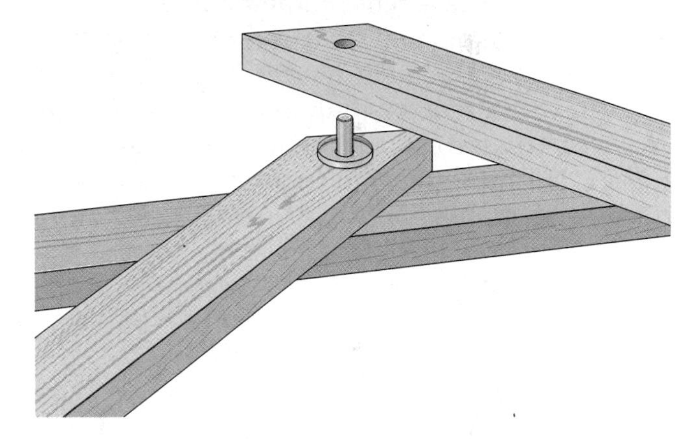

Fig. 25-3. Assembling a truss using split-ring connectors.

TYPES OF ROOF TRUSSES

Though most common trusses are triangular, trusses come in a wide variety of shapes to solve nearly any problem. Span and load

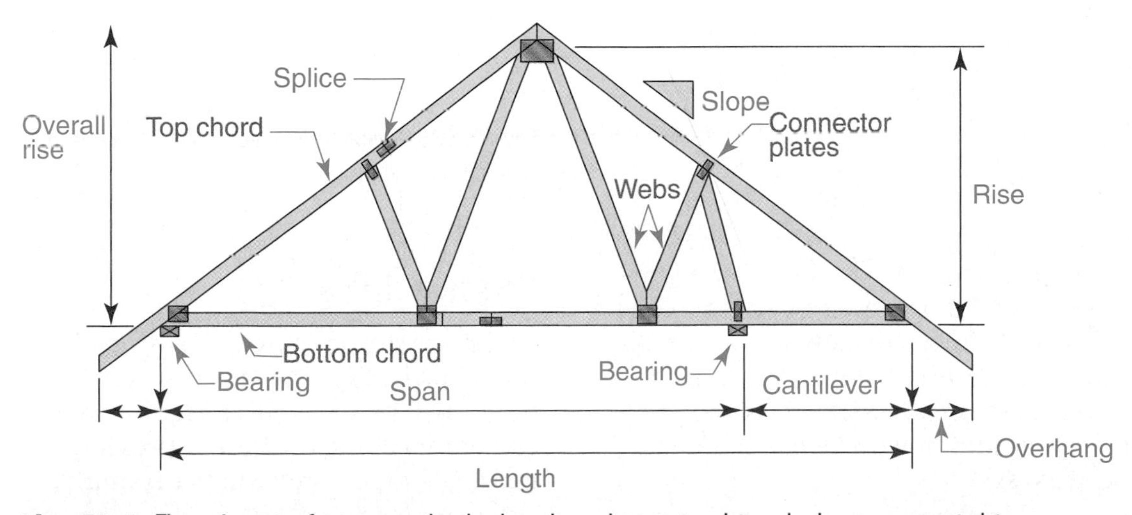

Fig. 25-1. The main parts of a truss are the chords, webs, and connector plates, also known as gusset plates.

Fig. 25-4. These trusses have lumber chords and a tubular steel web. This is a combination frequently found in light commercial construction.

Fig. 25-5. Because these trusses would be exposed to the living space, the truss builder took extra care to make them visually appealing. The absence of interior bearing walls adds to the openness.

requirements (for snow, wind, etc.) govern the type of truss to be used. King-post, Fink, and scissors trusses are most commonly used for houses. These and similar trusses are most adaptable to rectangular houses because the uniform width requires only one type of truss. However, trusses can also be used for L-shaped houses. For hip roofs, hip trusses can be provided for each hip and valley area. **Fig. 25-6.**

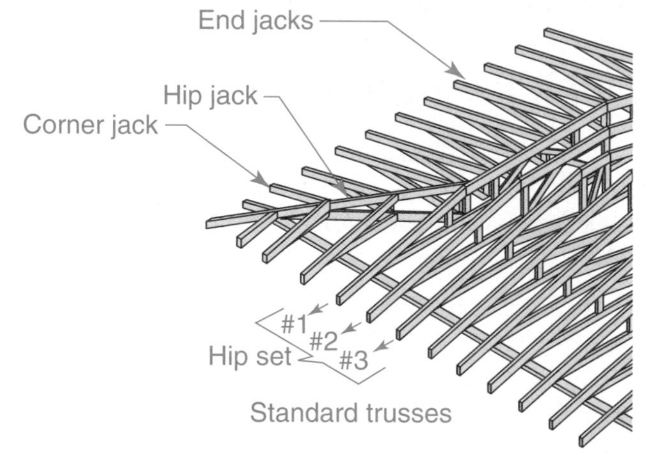

Fig. 25-6. Special trusses are available for nearly every application, including hips and valleys.

King-Post Truss

The *king-post truss* has upper and lower chords and a single vertical post in the center. **Fig. 25-7A.** This vertical post is sometimes called a *strut*. It is the simplest form of truss used for houses. For short and medium spans, the king-post truss is probably more economical than other types. It has fewer pieces and can be fabricated faster. However, because so much of the upper chord is unsupported, allowable spans are somewhat shorter than for the Fink truss when the same size members are used.

Fink Truss

The *Fink truss*, also called a *W-truss*, uses three more supporting members than the king-post truss. **Fig. 25-7B.** Distances between connections are shorter. This usually allows the use of lower grade lumber and somewhat longer spans for the same member size. It is perhaps the most popular and most widely used of the light-wood trusses.

Scissors Truss

The *scissors truss* features sloped top and bottom chords. **Fig. 25-7C.** It is more complicated than the Fink truss. It is used for houses having cathedral ceilings, where it provides a savings in materials over conventional framing.

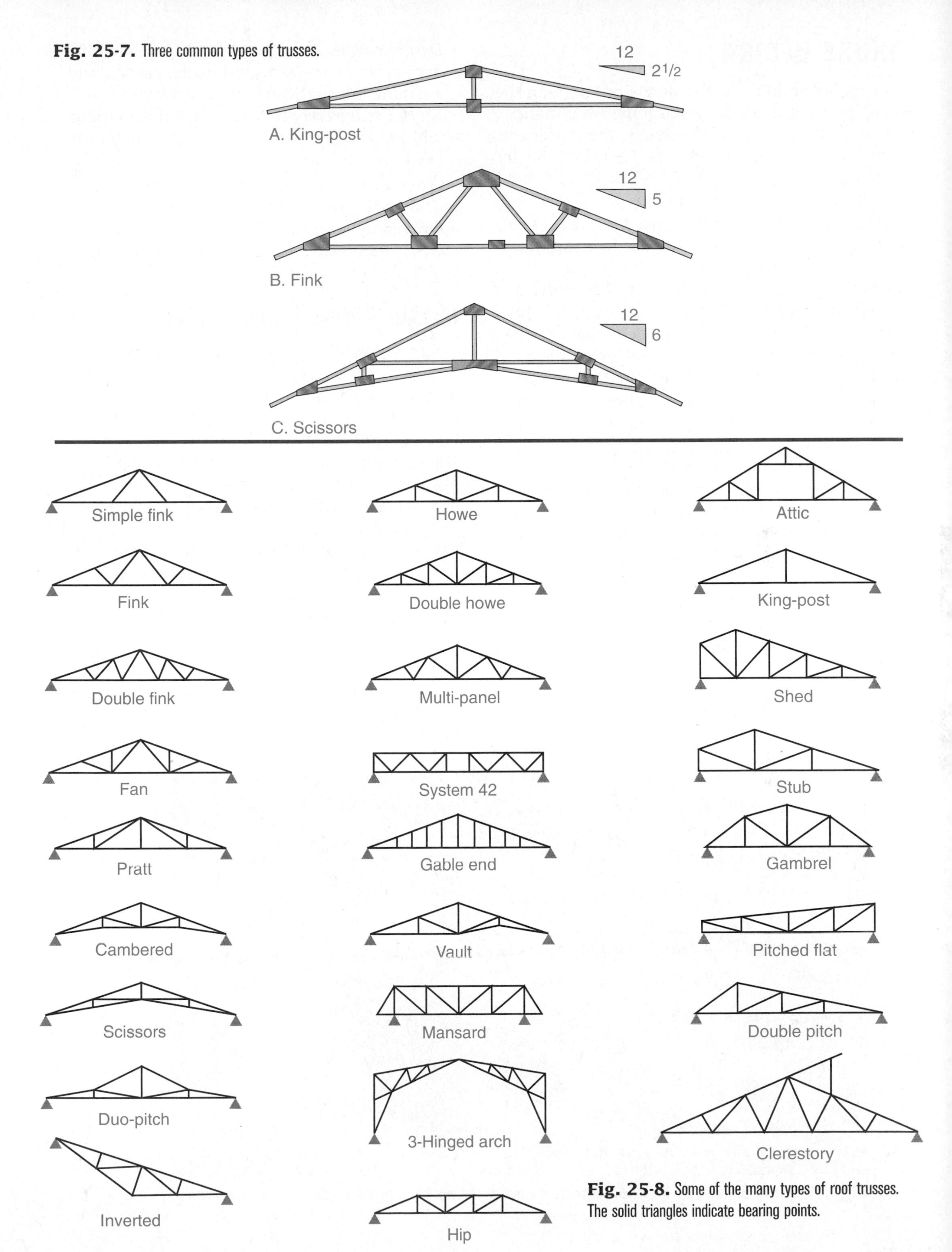

Fig. 25-7. Three common types of trusses.

Fig. 25-8. Some of the many types of roof trusses. The solid triangles indicate bearing points.

TRUSS DESIGN

The design of a truss depends not only on the loads it must carry but also on the weight and slope of the roof itself. Generally, the flatter the slope, the greater the stresses. Therefore, flatter roofs require trusses with larger members and stronger connections.

Many lumber dealers can provide the builder with completed trusses ready for installation. Often, however, the builder orders trusses directly from a truss manufacturer. To order a series of trusses, the builder must supply a precise description of what is needed. Much of the information is on the set of building plans. Ordering information includes the following:

- *Nominal span.* Generally, the **nominal span** is the length of the bottom chord.
- *Overhang length.* The overhang length is the horizontal distance from the end of the bottom chord to the bottom edge of the rafter (extension of the top chord).
- *Quantity.* The number of trusses required, including gable-end trusses, must be specified.
- *End cut of rafter.* Will the ends be plumb cut, square cut, or untrimmed?
- *Roof "pitch."* State the vertical unit rise per 12″ of run. Strictly speaking, this is the roof's slope, but the term *pitch* is often used instead.
- *Type of truss.* See Figs. 25-7 and **25-8** for different types of trusses.
- *Design parameters.* These would include information about the expected loads, particularly anything unusual, such as very heavy snow.
- *Special requirements.* These include anything unusual about the use of the truss, such as the need for it to cantilever past a wall.

When the trusses have been designed, drawings made by the manufacturer must be approved by local building officials. These drawings are then made a part of the approved set of building plans.

Machine Stress-Rated Lumber

Stress-rated lumber is structural lumber that has been graded electronically and stamped to indicate the specific load it will support. Because the grading is done with a machine, lumber rated in this way is called **machine stress-rated lumber** (MSR). When strength properties are critical, an architect or engineer may specify machine stress-rated lumber of a certain species and grade. Manufacturers of roof trusses often use MSR lumber since trusses are so important to the strength of the house.

Sheathing Requirements

Trusses are commonly designed for 24″ OC spacing. This spacing requires thicker interior and exterior sheathing or finish material than is needed for conventional 16″ OC spacing. **Fig. 25-9.**

Fig. 25-9. Roof sheathing ties the various elements of a roof system together. It should be installed as soon as possible.

Costs

A manufacturer delivers trusses to the job site and sets them on the rafter plate with a crane. They are then ready for workers to tip them into place for less than the cost of the material alone in conventional framing. To estimate exact costs, the truss fabricator reviews the building plans. When a bid is provided, the builder should know exactly what it covers. For example, is setting the trusses in place on the house included in the cost?

SECTION 25.1

Check Your Knowledge

1. What is a chord?
2. What three types of trusses are most commonly used for residential building?
3. What factors influence the design of a truss?
4. What is the nominal span of a truss?

On the Job

Contact a manufacturer of residential wood trusses. Find answers to the following questions. Then present the information to your class.

1. Which type of worker (engineer, architect, etc.) actually designs trusses? What qualifications and training are required for this job?
2. How long does it take to design a truss, and how far in advance should a builder order them?
3. What is the most important thing to know about installing a Fink truss (W-truss)?
4. How are computers used in the design of trusses?

SECTION 25.2

Installing Trusses

In handling and storing trusses, avoid placing unusual stresses on them. They are designed to carry roof loads in a vertical position. For this reason, they must be lifted and stored upright. However, it is important to prevent them from tipping and possibly injuring nearby workers. If they must be handled or stored in a flat position, they should be supported along their length to lessen bending. Never support the trusses only at the center or only at each end when they are in a flat position.

If the trusses will be stored outdoors before being installed, they should be supported above the ground to protect them from dampness or water. A tarp should cover them to prevent rain damage. The bands around bundles of trusses should not be cut or removed until just before the trusses are ready to be erected. Because every part of the truss has been specifically designed for a particular job, a truss must never be cut or altered.

Cutting Bands

The steel bands that secure trusses in bundles can be under considerable tension. Stand well to the side while cutting these bands. Make sure that others are standing well away.

RAISING TRUSSES

Completed trusses can be raised into place by hand or by crane. The truss fabricator may bring a truck-mounted crane when delivering the trusses. Because a large truss can be heavy and awkward to handle, a crane is the preferred method. **Fig. 25-10.** However, take great care to secure the truss properly as the crane is lifting it. A guide rope must be attached so that a worker on the ground can keep the truss from swinging out of control.

When raising small trusses by hand, care is needed to avoid damage to the trusses and accidental injury to workers. **Fig. 25-11.** One by one, the trusses should be laid across the building and swung up into place by two or more workers. Another worker should be at the roof level to brace the trusses as soon as they are tipped into place.

BRACING TRUSSES

Trusses must be braced temporarily while they are being installed. This helps to maintain precise spacing during installation and prevents them from tipping like dominoes. The manufacturer's drawings will accompany the trusses when they are delivered to the job site. These drawings should be studied for information about proper bracing.

Fig. 25-10. Lifting roof trusses into place with a crane is the easiest and safest method.

Fig. 25-11. Roof trusses are placed one at a time. The best method will depend on the situation.

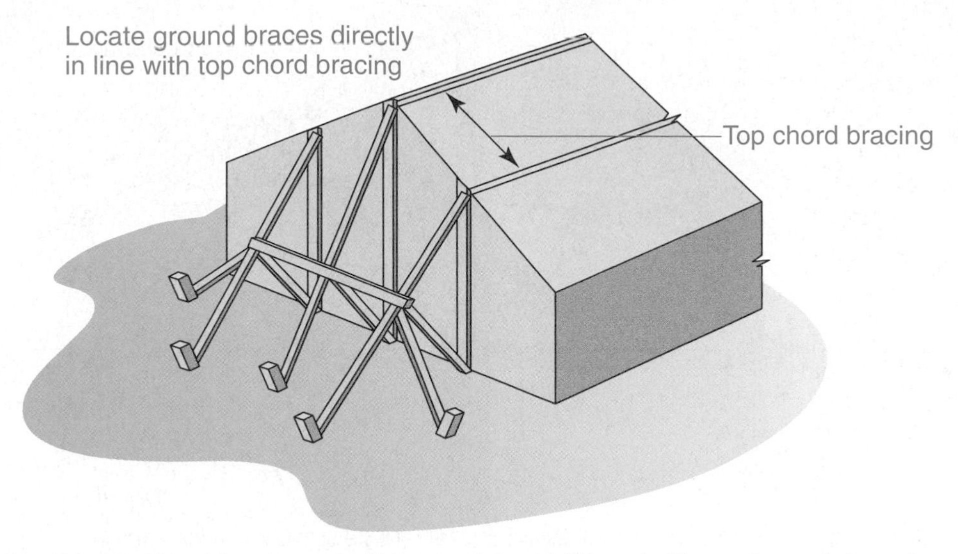

Fig. 25-12. The gable-end truss should be securely braced. This method is sometimes called *ground bracing*.

Temporary Bracing

The **gable-end truss** is the first truss on the building and the most important to brace. It should be braced with lumber standoffs anchored to stakes driven into the ground. **Fig. 25-12.** As each additional truss is put into place, it is braced temporarily to the adjacent trusses with a length of nominal 2″ lumber. The lumber is secured diagonally to the top chord with two 16d nails at every intersection. **Fig. 25-13.** Such diagonal bracing is sometimes called sway bracing. Lateral bracing may also be required.

Finally, a second gable-end truss is placed at the other end of the building. Top-chord bracing can be removed as the roof sheathing is installed.

Permanent Bracing

Permanent lateral metal bracing is available that ties the individual trusses into a rigid structural system. It also ensures precise spacing. **Fig. 25-14.** However, it does not eliminate the need for temporary gable-end and diagonal bracing with nominal 2″ lumber.

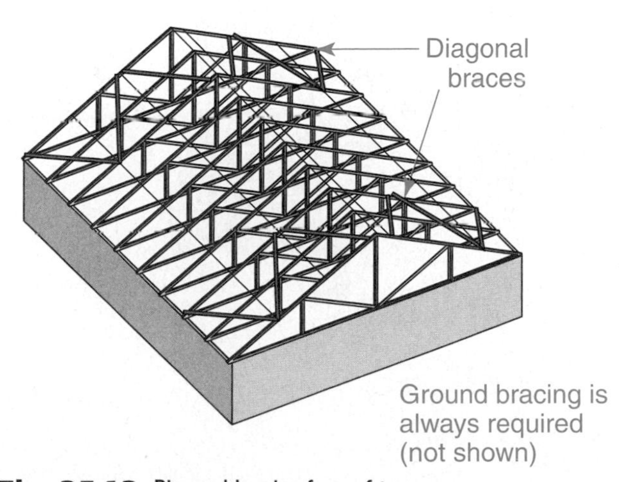

Fig. 25-13. Diagonal bracing for roof trusses.

Fig. 25-14. Prefabricated metal spacers help to brace trusses and ensure exact spacing.

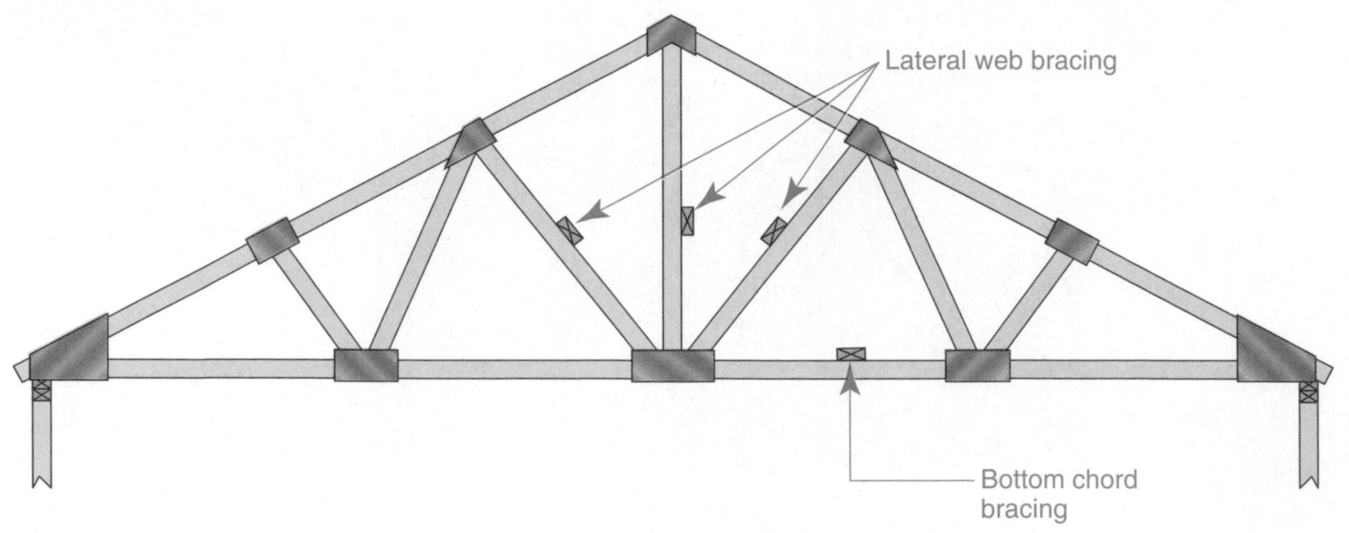

Fig. 25-15. Lateral bracing should run the entire length of the building. Here you see an end view of the bracing.

Permanent continuous lateral bracing consists of 2x4 or wider stock that is nailed to the web or lower chord of each truss. **Fig. 25-15.** The exact location of the lateral bracing is usually specified in the truss design.

On trusses with long spans, permanent bracing prevents the bottom chords from moving as the ceiling finish is applied. Nominal 2″ lumber is nailed to the top edge of the bottom chord and runs the length of the building. After the permanent bracing is in place, the roof should be sheathed as soon as possible. Temporary bracing is removed after sheathing is applied.

FASTENING TRUSSES

Trusses are fastened to the outside walls with nails or metal framing anchors. Resistance to wind uplift stresses and thrust must be considered. A ring-shank nail provides a simple connection that resists modest uplift. Toenailing is also sometimes done, but this is not always satisfactory because metal truss plates are located at the wall plate and make toenailing difficult.

A better system uses a metal bracket. **Fig. 25-16.** These brackets are available commercially in a variety of shapes. They are nailed to

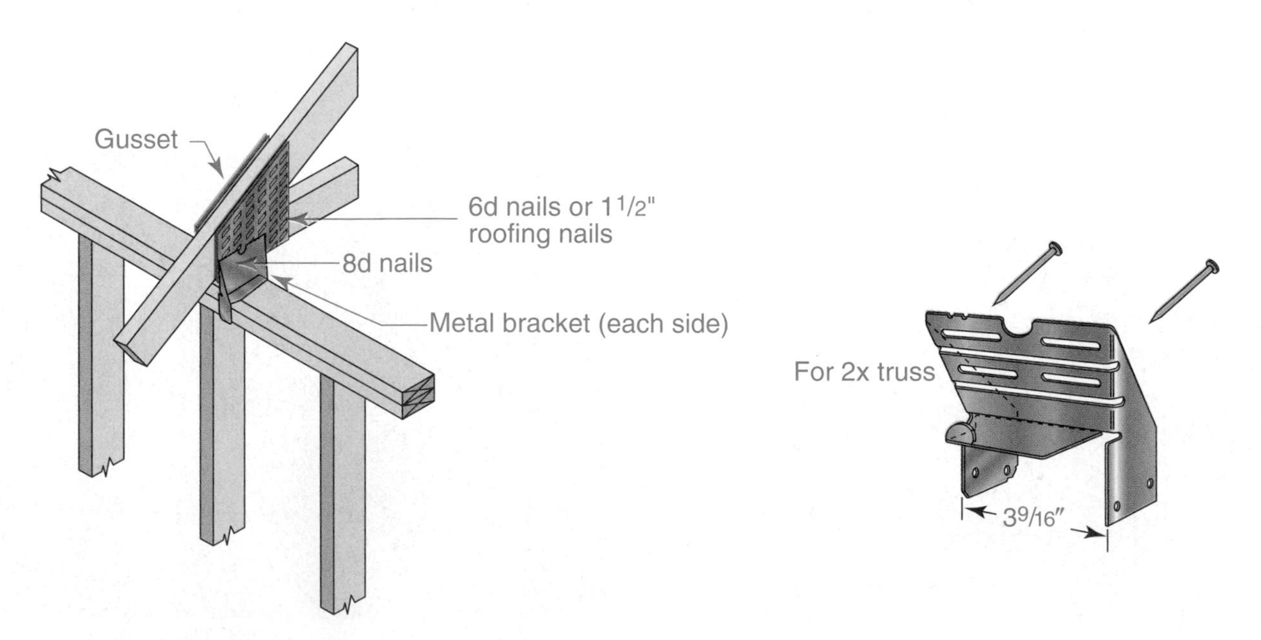

Fig. 25-16. Fastening trusses to the wall plate using metal brackets.

the top and sides of the wall plate and to the lower chord of the truss. They provide superior resistance against wind uplift and may be required by building codes.

Interior Partitions

Sometimes partitions run parallel to and between the bottom truss chords. When these partitions are erected before the ceiling finish is applied, install 2x4 blocking between the lower chords of the truss. **Fig. 25-17.** This blocking should be spaced not more than 4′ OC and nailed to the chords with two 16d nails in each end. To provide nailing for lath or drywall, nail a 1x6 or 2x6 continuous backer to the blocking. Set the bottom face level with the bottom of the lower truss chords.

When these partitions are erected after the ceiling finish is applied, 2x4 blocking is placed with its bottom edge level with the bottom of the truss chords. The blocking is fastened with two 16d nails in each end.

Metal brackets, called *clips*, should also be used to align and fasten the bottom chord of a truss where it passes over nonbearing partitions. **Fig. 25-18.** These clips prevent the

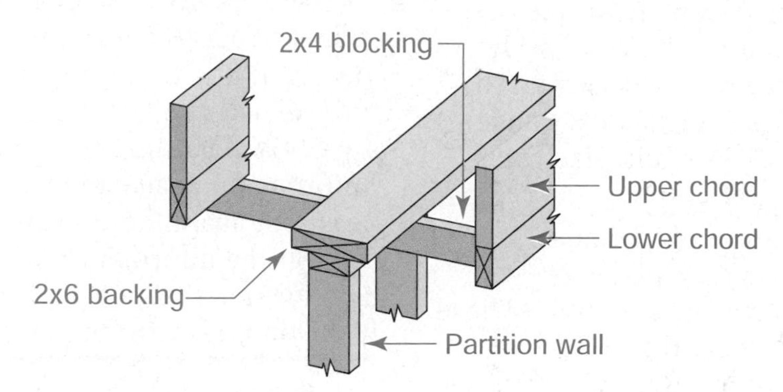

Fig. 25-17. Construction details for partitions that run parallel to the roof truss.

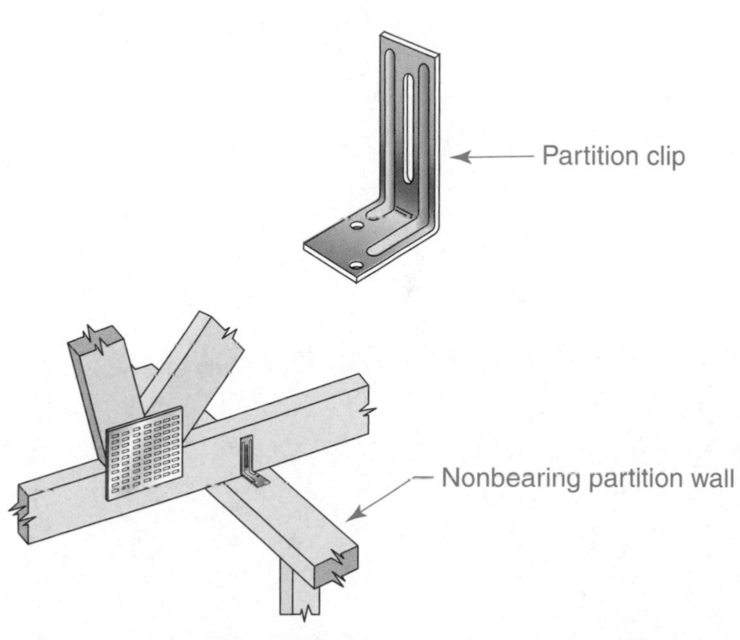

Fig. 25-18. A partition clip. Allow a 1/16″ gap between the nailheads and the clip to help prevent squeaking.

chords from moving from side to side. They also allow the bottom chord to flex upward slightly when the truss is loaded. This is important in order to prevent the walls from interfering with truss movement.

Problems with Framing

Unlike conventional framing, roof trusses are manufactured to precise tolerances before being delivered to the jobsite. For this reason, carpenters must take extra care when framing a house with a trussed roof. The trusses cannot be altered to make up for minor errors in framing.

If an interior partition wall is too high, it will prevent trusses from seating properly. A similar problem occurs when the top plate of one or more partition walls is not level. These problems might also put dangerous stresses on the bottom chord of the truss, which could cause the truss to fail. The stresses could also cause interior wall finishes to crack later.

Wall framing problems are sometimes caused by errors in reading the plans, or by mistakes made in measuring or assembly. These problems are fairly easy to correct. However, problems caused by a poorly constructed foundation or an unlevel floor system are much more troublesome.

SECTION 25.2 Check Your Knowledge

1. What precautions should be taken when handling and storing roof trusses?
2. What two methods can be used to raise roof trusses into place, and which one is preferable?
3. What is the first thing that should be done when a truss has been raised into place?
4. What is the procedure for temporary bracing of roof trusses?

On the Job

Trusses provide a strong and efficient way to frame a roof. However, many accidents have occurred due to improper installation and bracing. Review the latest safety guidelines provided by OSHA regarding roof truss installation. (This information is available online.) Also, locate at least one manufacturer of metal truss braces. Collect the information in a folder titled "Truss Bracing" and keep it for future reference. Share your findings with the class.

Chapter 25

Review

Section Summaries

25.1 Roof trusses are strong, efficient, and less costly than traditional framing. Common shapes include the Fink (W-truss), the king-post, and the scissors. Design of a truss depends on the loads it must carry and the weight and slope of the roof.

25.2 The proper installation of roof trusses helps to prevent accidents. Each truss should be solidly braced immediately after being lifted into place. Special metal clips should be used for attaching trusses to the wall plates.

Review Questions

1. Name three advantages of using roof trusses in residential construction.
2. Name and describe the three basic parts of a roof truss.
3. Name two other materials besides nominal 2x4 lumber that trusses can be made from.
4. What is the standard OC spacing for roof trusses?
5. How should roof trusses be stored on site?
6. What precaution should be taken when cutting the steel bands around groups of trusses?
7. Why is it important to brace trusses during installation?
8. What is the procedure for permanent bracing of roof trusses?
9. At what point in construction can temporary truss bracing be removed?
10. Roof trusses are sometimes toenailed to the top plate. However, there are some disadvantages to this method. What is a better method?

Hand Signals for Heavy Loads When cranes and other equipment are used to lift heavy loads such as trusses, the operator often relies on someone on the ground to help place the load in the right spot. Because voices cannot be heard over loud engine sounds and other noises, hand signals are often used to communicate. For example, a raised thumb is the signal for raising the load, and a closed fist is the signal to stop. Only people who are trained in the appropriate signals should be responsible for directing a crane. They should stay in one place so the operator knows where to look for them. If they can't see the operator clearly because framing or other objects are in the way, they should first make eye contact. Then the signals should be made close to the face. If signalers are wearing gloves that are the same color as their clothing, the signals should be made away from the body so the operator can distinguish them.

Unit 5

STEEL FRAME CONSTRUCTION

Careers in Construction

Construction Supervisor

Construction supervisors, also called *general construction managers*, plan and direct construction projects. Construction supervisors may own a construction company, or they may be salaried employees of a construction management or contracting firm. Construction supervisors oversee specialty construction supervisors and workers.

Construction supervisors monitor the progress of all construction activities, from the ordering and delivery of materials to the quality of construction and the completion of the project on time. They review engineering drawings and specifications, and they track expenses to avoid cost overruns. Construction supervisors prepare daily reports using computer software.

Experience with several construction activities is required to advance to the position of construction supervisor. Knowledge of the overall process of construction, from start to end, is especially important. Large construction firms increasingly employ persons with a combination of work experience and a bachelor's degree in construction science, construction management, or civil engineering.

For more information, check the *Occupational Outlook Handbook* or look up "construction manager" on the Internet.

Chapter

Steel Framing Basics

Objectives

After reading this chapter, you'll be able to:

- Describe the performance and prescriptive methods for steel framing design.
- Describe the three types of steel frame construction.
- Identify tools used in steel framing.
- Identify the head styles of steel framing screws.
- Tell the difference between welding and clinching.

Terms

clinching
cold-formed steel
feathering
mil
performance method
prescriptive method
pullout capacity
welding

Steel framing has been used for commercial and industrial structures for many years. As a framing material for residential construction, however, steel is fairly new. Apprentice carpenters usually learn how to do the job from skilled co-workers. However, because steel framing is new, few workers have a base of experience and knowledge from which to teach. This chapter is designed to help bridge the gap by providing basic information.

SECTION 26.1

Steel As a Building Material

The steel that is used for residential steel framing is cold-formed steel. **Cold-formed steel** is sheet steel that is bent and formed without using heat. This type of framing system is sometimes referred to as light-gauge steel framing. Unlike wood building materials, steel is not damaged by insects and moisture. Steel-framing materials are treated with a hot-dipped galvanized coating to resist rust and corrosion. Steel is 100 percent recyclable. New steel-framing materials contain at least 25 percent recycled content.

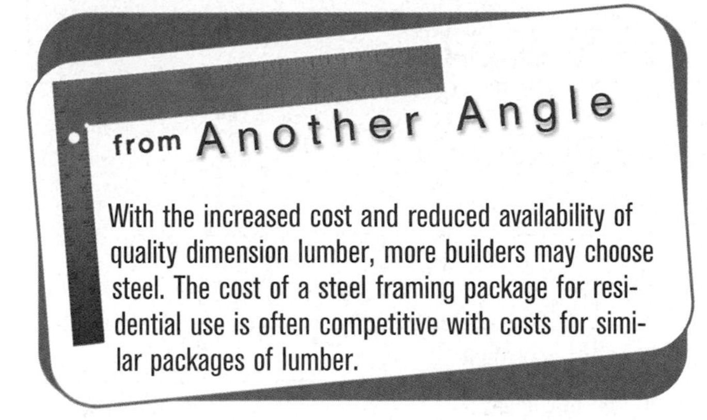

STEEL FRAMING DESIGN

Architects and engineers design steel frame houses using either the performance method or the prescriptive method.

Performance Method

The **performance method** depends upon established engineering principles and design-load specifications. Architects and engineers use these principles and specifications to calculate size and strength for individual steel-framing members.

The performance method is time consuming. Standard sizes of framing members are not always used, adding to costs and inefficiency.

Prescriptive Method

The **prescriptive method** uses standardized tables that give specifications and other information. These tables are created using regional or national design codes, regional design-load data, structural limitation data, and knowledge of engineering practices. **Table 26-A.** Data for such things as earthquake, snow, and wind load are also determined by using tables for specific geographic regions.

The prescriptive method provides architects and engineers with:

- Specifications for standard cold-formed steel members.
- An identification system for labeling the members.
- Minimum corrosion protection requirements.
- Floor joist, ceiling joist, and roof rafter span tables.
- Wall stud specifications.
- Wall bracing requirements.
- Connection requirements.
- Construction details.

The prescriptive method has several advantages. It helps reduce the engineering costs for steel frame houses. Builders can pre-select stud, joist, and rafter sizes. Building inspectors can easily check and identify stud, joist, and rafter sizes by their labeling. Manufacturers can determine the framing members that need to be supplied for specific markets and geographic areas.

The National Association of Home Builders (NAHB) Research Center developed the prescriptive method for residential cold-formed steel framing in 1995.

TYPES OF STEEL CONSTRUCTION

Residential steel-framing construction is categorized into three types: stick-built, panelized, and pre-engineered.

Stick-Built Construction

Stick-built steel framing is similar to wood framing. The names for the basic steel-framing members are the same as for wood members: stud, joist, and header. Spacing of studs and joists is set at the standard 16″ or 24″ OC intervals. **Fig. 26-1.**

Cutting and assembly are performed on the job site. Instead of being nailed, the steel pieces are screwed, welded, or pressed together.

Table 26-A. Prescriptive Method Applicability Limits

Attribute	Limitation
General	
Building dimension	Maximum width(a) is 36 feet Maximum length(b) is 60 feet
Number of stories	2 story
Design wind speed	110 mph maximum fastest-mile wind speed (except as noted for wall bracing)
Wind exposure	Exposures C (open terrain)
	Exposures A/B (suburban/wooded)
Ground snow load	70 psf(b) maximum ground snow load
Seismic zone	Zone 4 maximum (except as noted for wall bracing)
Floors	
Floor dead load	10 psf(b) maximum
Floor live load First floor Second floor (sleeping rooms)	 40 psf(b) maximum 30 psf(b) maximum
Cantilever 24 inches maximum	
Walls	
Wall dead load	10 psf(b) maximum
Load-bearing wall height	10 feet maximum
Roofs	
Roof dead load	12 psf(b) maximum total load (7 psf(b) maximum for roof covering only)
Roof live load	70 psf(b) maximum ground snow load
Ceiling dead load	5 psf(b) maximum
Roof slope	3:12 to 12:12
Rake overhang	12 inches maximum
Soffit overhang	24 inches maximum
Attic live load (for attics with storage) Attic live load (for attics without storage)	20 psf(b) maximum 10 psf(b) maximum

(a) Building width is in the direction of horizontal framing members supported by the wall studs.
(b) Building length is in the direction perpendicular to floor joists, ceiling joists, or roof trusses.

Panelized Construction

Panelized construction is used to pre-build flat components such as walls and floors. These components are built to engineering specifications and tolerances on platform tables and jigs. **Fig. 26-2.** Multiple components can be made using the same templates.

Fig. 26-1. Stick-built steel framing.

Components may be built at the job site or at an off-site production facility. The panelized components are set in place as units.

Wall panelization has several benefits. Straight walls can be consistently produced and are fairly easy to set in place. They can be completely constructed on a panel table. Assembly line methods allow faster construction and better quality control.

Fig. 26-2. A panelization table. Panels can be built to exact specifications and tolerances.

Pre-Engineered Construction

In pre-engineered construction, individual steel studs, joists, headers, and roof members are used to create pre-built columns, beams, and rafter assemblies. Each assembly is designed and constructed for a specific purpose. This method closely resembles metal-frame commercial construction using structural columns.

Pre-engineered construction may produce a rigid or semi-rigid frame. Engineered columns may be spaced at 4′ or 8′ OC.

Pre-engineered assemblies are designed using the American Iron and Steel Institute's specifications for the design of cold-formed steel structural members.

SAFETY FIRST

Personal Protection

Protective clothing and safety devices must be worn when working with steel framing members. Work gloves help to prevent cuts and punctures, burns from steel exposed to heat or direct sunlight, and freeze burns from steel exposed to cold weather. Thin protective gloves are recommended. Thick gloves make precise movements and placement of materials more difficult.

Ear protection, such as sound-reducing ear plugs, is required when noise levels are higher than normal conversational levels. The high-pitched noise caused by steel cutting saws can cause permanent hearing loss.

Safety glasses prevent injuries caused by flying bits of metal from chop saws, circular saws, drills, and grinders.

SECTION 26.1

Check Your Knowledge

1. What is cold-formed steel?
2. What two steel-framing design methods do architects and engineers use?
3. Panelized construction is used to pre-build which types of components?
4. What safety equipment must be worn when working with steel framing members?

On the Job

Make a list of the special safety equipment needed for steel framing. Find out how much it costs and where you can buy it locally.

SECTION 26.2

Steel Framing Tools

Before beginning any framing job, the framers should create a list of all the tools that may be needed. With the proper tools in place, framing can proceed quickly and efficiently. The tools used in steel framing may look like their wood-framing counterparts. However, their use and operation may differ greatly. Always follow the instructions and safety precautions supplied with the tools you use.

POWER TOOLS

Most tools used in steel framing are electrically, hydraulically, or pneumatically powered. In some situations, a gasoline engine may power larger tools, such as plasma cutters.

Screw Gun

An electric *screw gun* is specifically designed for attaching screws. It is not an electric drill, although the appearance is similar. Drills are not designed to apply screws to steel framing.

A screw gun has variable speeds. An industrial screw gun can operate at speeds as high as 4,000 rpm. This variable speed prevents damage from friction and overheating.

A screw gun has a clutch mechanism built into it that allows screws to be feathered. **Feathering** is the process of attaching a screw to the bit without stopping the screw gun. **Fig. 26-3.** The screw spins only when pressure is applied to the bit and the tip of the screw.

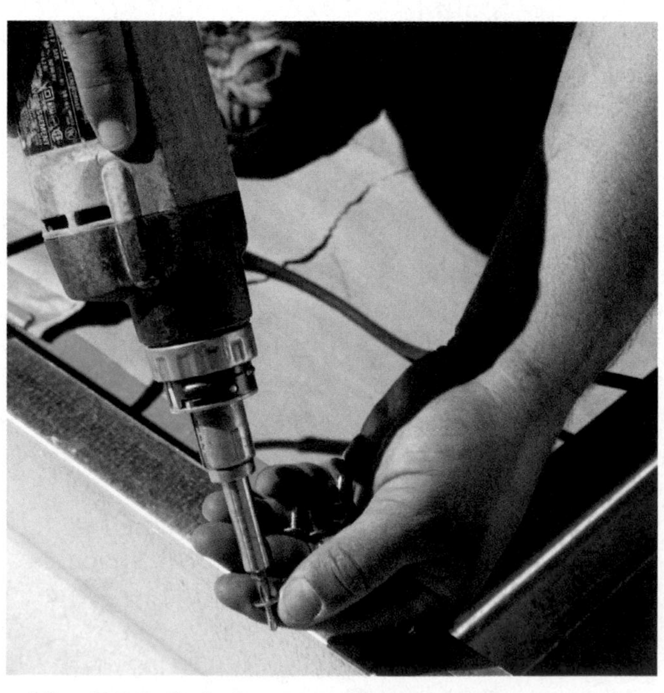

Fig. 26-3. Feathering screws with a power screw gun.

Attachments can feather strips of collated screws automatically into the bit. **Fig. 26-4.** Stand-up attachments are also available that allow the framer to remain standing while applying roof and floor sheathing. **Fig. 26-5.**

The two types of screw guns that are used on a construction site are the framing screw gun and the drywall screw gun. A *framing screw gun* is designed to connect steel members, such as studs, to bottom and top tracks. A *drywall screw gun* is designed to attach plywood, OSB sheathing, or wallboard to steel members. It operates at faster speeds than a framing screw gun. It also has a depth-sensitive nosepiece. **Fig. 26-6.** The nosepiece prevents the bit from damaging the surface of the sheathing or wallboard while seating the screw.

Nailer

Nailers are commonly used to attach plywood, oriented-strand board (OSB), and other sheathing materials to steel wall and roof members. **Fig. 26-7.**

Nailers are sometimes called *pneumatic nail guns.* They use compressed air to fire the nails and pins into the sheathing materials.

Portable Shears

Portable hydraulic shears are attached to a source of hydraulic power by high-pressure hoses. The hydraulic pressure powers a sharp blade that cuts through the steel. Shears produce a clean, straight cut.

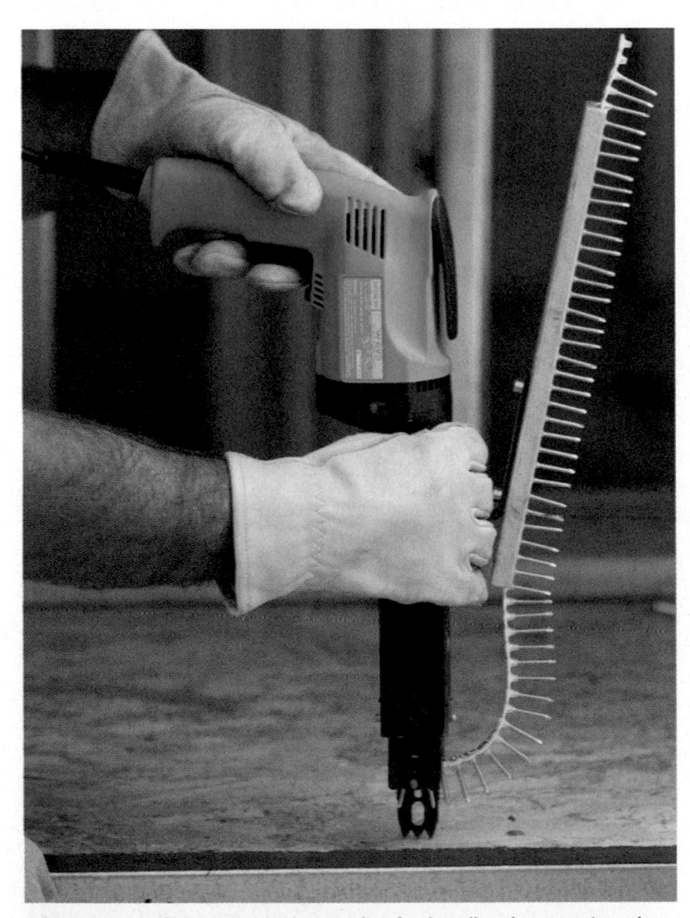

Fig. 26-4. Using an attachment that feeds collated screws into the screw gun.

Fig. 26-5. This drill attachment drives collated screws. It allows the worker to stand while drilling. After this worker positions the tool, she will straighten it to a perpendicular position. Screws should always be driven perpendicular to the floor sheathing.

Fig. 26-6. A drywall screw gun has a depth-sensitive nosepiece.

Fig. 26-7. A nailer used to attach sheathing to steel studs.

Electric hand-held shears are similar in operation to hydraulic shears. **Fig. 26-8.** An electric motor powers the sharp blades. Electric shears can cut steel as thick as 68 mil (about 1⁄16″).

Fig. 26-8. Electric shears can cut sheet steel.

SAFETY FIRST

Power Cords

When using electric power tools, be aware of the dangers of electrical shock. Check all power cords for exposed wiring. Check the cord's insulation for cuts and breaks. Be sure that a power cord is not wrapped around or passing over steel framing members. The sharp edges of the steel can snag and damage the insulation.

Fig. 26-9. A chop saw and an abrasive blade.

Steel framing is made from light-gauge galvanized steel. The smaller the gauge number the thicker the steel. For example, load-bearing structural studs for residential construction are usually 18 or 20 gauge. Nonload-bearing studs are usually 22 or 25 gauge.

The unit of measurement for measuring the thickness of thin steel is the **mil**. One mil equals one thousandth of an inch (1 mil = .001″). Common thicknesses of various steel framing members include the following:

12 gauge (97 mil)
14 gauge (68 mil)
16 gauge (54 mil)
18 gauge (43 mil)
20 gauge (33 mil)
22 gauge (27 mil)
25 gauge (18 mil)

Chop Saw

Chop saws resemble compound-miter saws used for cutting wood. **Fig. 26-9.** The chop saw for cutting steel can be mounted on a table.

Chop saws require an abrasive (non-toothed) blade for cutting steel. The cut made is very rough. Sharp burrs remain on the edge. It may be necessary to grind these rough edges to remove the burrs. In harsh environments the edge may be treated with a metallic coating to resist corrosion.

Chop saw blades cut quickly and produce hot metal chips that can be a safety hazard. They are effective for making square cuts and for cutting bundled studs. However, they are very noisy and ear protection is required.

Circular Saw

Circular saws for cutting steel are similar to those used for wood. **Fig. 26-10.** They must be equipped with a proper blade with carbide-tipped teeth. The carbide tips provide a very

Fig. 26-10. A circular saw used for cutting steel.

hard cutting surface. Abrasive blades are also available.

Blades with carbide-tipped teeth are expensive. Cost, safety, durability, and cutting ability are important considerations when choosing a blade.

Plasma Cutter

Plasma cutters produce a very hot arc of plasma between the tip of the cutter and the steel. The plasma cuts very quickly through steel stock like the flame of a welder's torch.

It may be necessary to grind the edges of a plasma cut. In harsh environments the edge may require treatment with a metallic coating to resist corrosion.

Press Brake

A *press brake* can create straight-line bends in steel. Builders and framers use a press brake to shape flat sheet steel for use as fascia material, ridge caps, and for other applications. **Fig. 26-11.**

Press brakes can bend flat stock as long as 10 feet.

Fig. 26-11. A press brake forms sheet steel.

Fig. 26-12. Hand seamers make small bends.

MANUALLY OPERATED TOOLS

Manually operated tools used in steel framing include hand seamers, clamps, aviation snips, and hole punches.

Hand Seamer

Hand seamers are used to make small bends in metal stock. They have a 3½″ flat jaw and are often called *duck-billed pliers.* **Fig. 26-12.** The tool is useful for bending steel webs or flanges. It is also useful when forming pieces of sheet steel around windowsills and door openings.

Clamp

Clamps are used to temporarily hold steel members together while they are fastened. When layers of steel are screwed together, the first layer can "climb" the threads of the screw and pull away from the second layer. This is called jacking. Locking C-clamps prevent jacking by holding the layers firmly together. **Fig. 26-13.** This allows the screw to penetrate both layers.

Bar clamps are often used to hold headers in place after they are fitted into the top track.

Aviation Snips

Aviation snips can cut steel as thick as 43 mil. They are especially useful for coping and making small cuts on such things as flanges. Snips are available in three different models to fit individual users. **Fig. 26-14.**

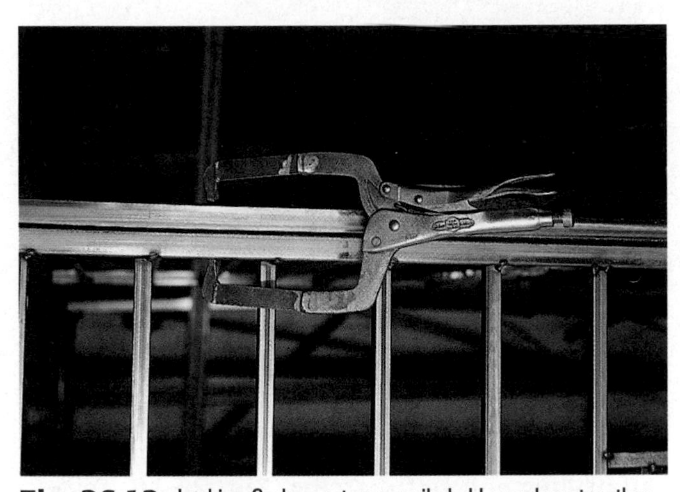

Fig. 26-13. Locking C-clamps temporarily hold members together.

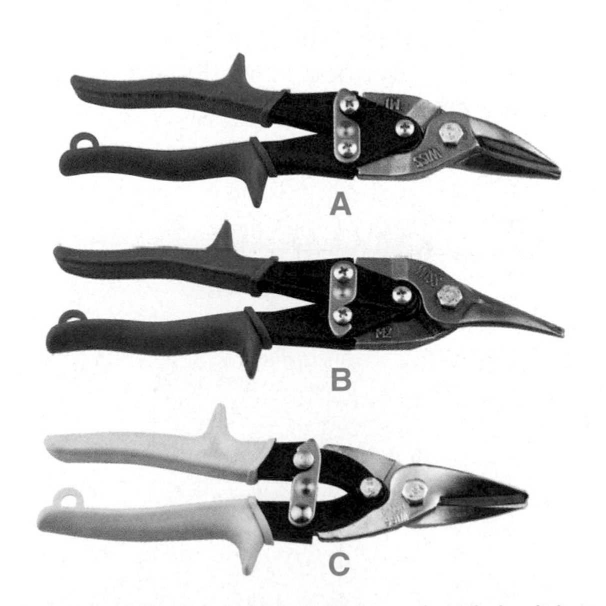

Fig. 26-14. *A.* Red-handled aviation snips are for right-handed people. *B.* Green-handled snips are for left-handed people. *C.* Yellow-handled snips should be used for straight cuts.

Hole Punch

Hole punches are used to create holes in steel as thick as 33 mil. **Fig. 26-15.** They are designed to fit around the flange of C-shaped members.

Holes can measure up to 1″ in diameter. The holes are often used as access openings for pipe or wiring. In this case, they must be lined with a grommet to prevent rough edges from causing damage.

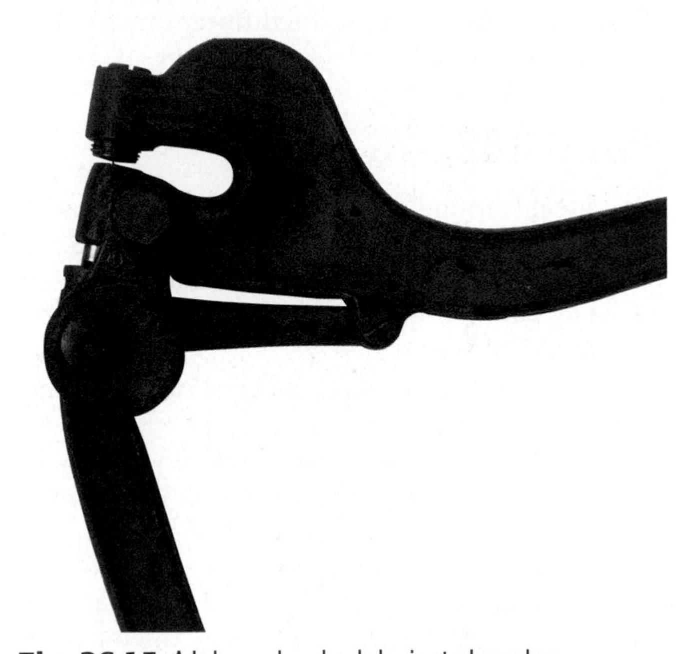

Fig. 26-15. A hole punch makes holes in steel members.

SECTION 26.2

Check Your Knowledge

1. What is feathering?
2. What is special about the nosepiece of a drywall screw gun and why?
3. What material is used for harder teeth on circular saw blades?
4. What is jacking?

On the Job

At your local tool supplier, research the differences among the various electric drills, framing screw guns, and drywall screw guns. Also research the difference between a metal chop saw and a compound-miter saw for wood.

SECTION 26.3

Fastening Methods

Steel framing members can be attached with mechanical fasteners such as screws, nails, and pins. They can also be joined by welding or clinching.

More time is needed to join steel members than wood members. Selecting the correct fastening method for the task is important. If the wrong one is used, the connection may fail. The framer must know about the different methods that are available.

USING SCREWS

All steel framing screws have a point, a head, a drive type, threads, and plating. **Fig. 26-16.** They are sized according to length and diameter. They come in many sizes, shapes, and head and thread styles.

Screws are rated on their pullout capacity. The **pullout capacity** is the screw's ability to resist pulling out of the connection. Pullout capacity is based on the number of threads penetrating and holding the connection. **Fig. 26-17.**

Framing screws are used to fasten steel to steel. Sheathing screws attach exterior sheathing, such as plywood or OSB, to steel members. The tip of the screw penetrates both the sheathing and the steel. The head and the threads hold the sheathing tight against the steel.

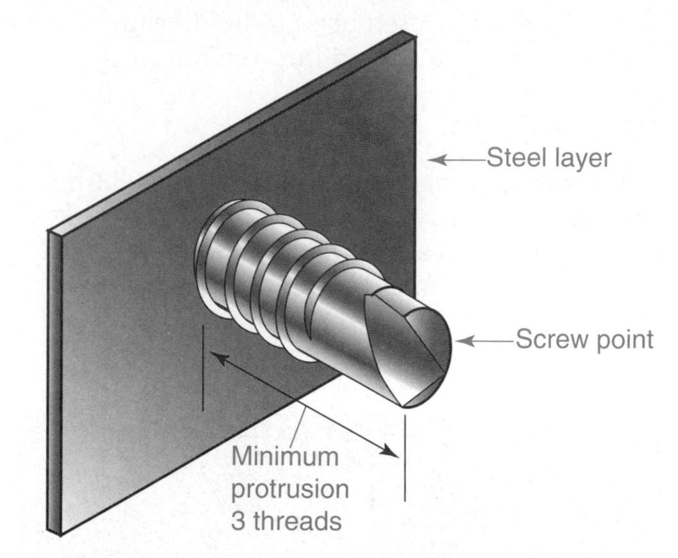

Fig. 26-17. Screw penetration indicates pullout capacity.

Point Types

Steel framing screws are self tapping. *Self-tapping screws* create their own holes. A predrilled hole is not needed.

Two types of self-tapping points are used: self-drilling and self-piercing. **Fig. 26-18.** *Self-drilling points* have drill tips. The point must be as long as the steel is thick. If the point is too short, the top layer of steel will climb the threads of the screw. *Self-piercing points* are sharp and can pierce thin steel layers. They are used to attach plywood or wallboard to steel studs that are up to 33 mil thick.

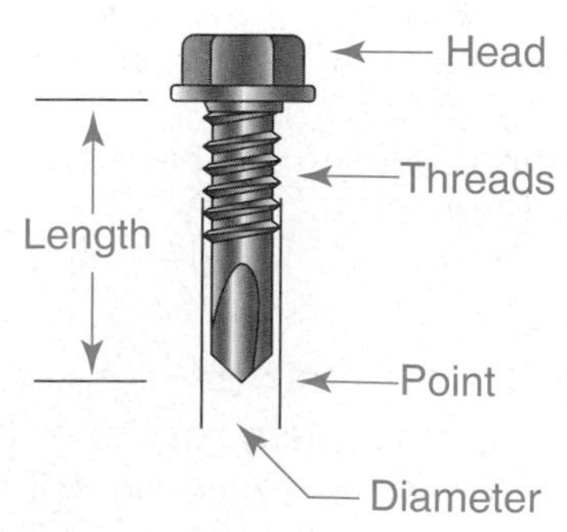

Fig. 26-16. Parts of a steel framing screw.

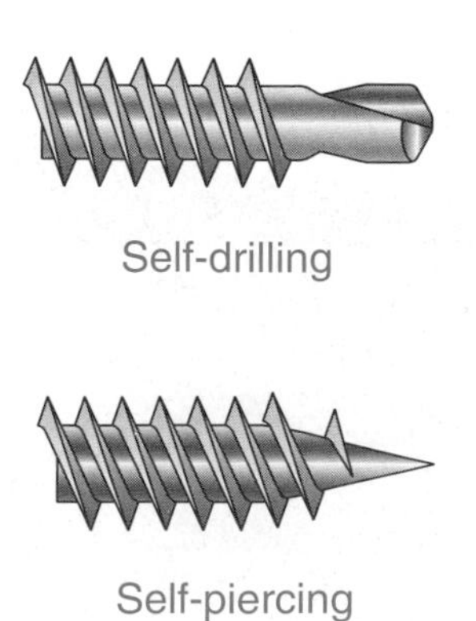

Fig. 26-18. Self-drilling and self-piercing points.

Head Types

Common head styles for steel framing screws are shown in **Fig. 26-19**. The hex washer head is the most common style for steel-to-steel connections. It provides the most *positive drive connection.* This means that the tool used to drive it fits securely and will not easily slip.

When sheathing and wallboard are applied over a screw head, the modified truss or pancake head styles are preferred. They have a very thin profile. A thin profile allows the sheathing to lie flat.

Always use the correct bit for the screw head style. A bit that is incorrect in size and shape will damage the head. A damaged head will prevent the screw from being seated properly. A poorly seated screw cannot be properly tightened and may be difficult to remove.

Drive Types

The type of head determines the bit used to drive and turn the screw. **Fig. 26-20.** The bit needs to fit securely and release quickly. An incorrect bit can become lodged in the screw head.

The most common drive types are Phillips and hex washer. Phillips-head bits are used with modified-truss head screws.

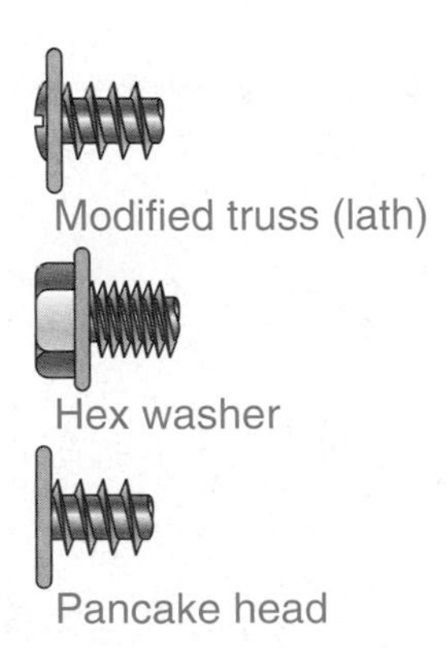

Fig. 26-19. Steel framing screw head types.

Phillips Square Slotted

Hex washer Torx“ Quadrex°

Fig. 26-20. Screw head design determines the type of driving tool used.

USING DRIVE PINS AND NAILS

Drive pins and nails are applied with a pneumatic nailer. **Fig. 26-21.** Instead of being screwed into the layers, the pins and nails are fired with air pressure. They are used to attach sheathing materials to steel members.

Fig. 26-21. Collated drive pins used with a pneumatic nailer.

Plywood and OSB sheathing for walls and roofs can be applied using 1 to 1½″ pins. Sheathing is usually attached with screws along its edges and with pins or nails in its field. Sheathing attached to walls must be held firmly against the steel during installation. This is because the fasteners do not draw the sheathing against the steel as a screw does.

WELDING AND CLINCHING

Welding and clinching are used to attach steel to steel.

Welding is the process of melting the steel and adding filler metals to fuse the pieces at the point of attachment. Welding is permanent.

Clinching is the process of joining two layers of steel with pressure. A powered clinching tool is used. A clinched joint takes more time and is also permanent.

SECTION 26.3 Check Your Knowledge

1. What is meant by the pullout capacity of a screw?
2. What is a self-tapping screw?
3. Why must sheathing be held tightly against the steel member before firing a pin or nail?
4. How is a weld formed?

On the Job

Screw together two scrap pieces of steel framing stock with one or two screws of the same size and length. The flat sides of the pieces should be together and the open side should face out. Test the pullout capacity of the screws by trying to pry the two pieces apart. Try this same test again with screws of a different length and diameter. Be sure to wear safety glasses and use good safety practices. Report the results to the class.

Chapter 26

Review

Section Summaries

26.1 Steel frame houses are designed using the performance or the prescriptive method. Residential steel framing is either stick-built, panelized, or pre-engineered.

26.2 Most tools used in steel framing are electrically, hydraulically, or pneumatically powered. In some situations, a gasoline engine may power larger tools. A few hand tools, such as clamps, are also used.

26.3 Mechanical fasteners, such as screws, nails, and pins, attach steel framing members. Framing screws attach steel to steel. Sheathing screws attach exterior sheathing to steel. Processes such as welding and clinching are also used.

Review Questions

1. How are steel framing members treated to resist corrosion?
2. Describe the performance and prescriptive methods of framing design.
3. Tell the difference between stick-built and panelized construction.
4. Describe the cut made by a chop saw blade.
5. What is the purpose of a press brake?
6. What is another name for a hand seamer?
7. What is the most common screw head type used in steel framing?
8. Name the two types of self-tapping screw tips.
9. What type of tool is used to apply drive pins and nails?
10. What is the difference between welding and clinching?

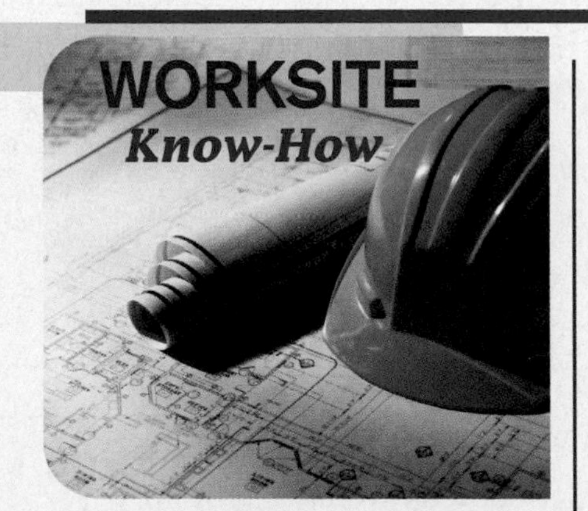

Software for Steel Framing Takeoffs and estimating for steel framing are made easier with computer software programs. The user can often perform takeoffs and estimates for all framing materials, not just steel. The data needs to be entered only once. The numbers of all steel and wood products, fasteners, and accessory items needed are then calculated automatically. Software can also create labor time and cost estimates, labor time budgets, and steel order and check-in sheets. Mistakes can be reduced, and the software ensures compliance with the prescriptive method. It can determine the highest gauge of steel needed, reduce the chance of material shortages, and allow for supplier data to be entered for easy price comparisons.

Chapter 27

Steel Framing Methods

Objectives

After reading this chapter, you'll be able to:

- Lay out steel floor joists.
- Describe the process for installing embedded or epoxied anchor bolts.
- Explain how to assemble a panelized wall.
- Explain how to set steel ceiling joists.

Terms

axial load
clip angle
in-line framing
joist tracks
roof rake

As in wood construction, the frame is the supporting structure of a steel-frame house. It supports the weight of the house and defines its shape. The frame includes the side walls, end walls, floor and ceiling joists, and roof frame.

In-line framing (shown in the photo on this page) is typically used in steel-frame construction. **In-line framing** aligns all vertical and horizontal load-bearing structural members. A detail is shown in **Fig. 27-1**. Because the members are aligned, all axial loads are transferred from the roof through the walls and floor joists to the foundation. The **axial load** is the load carried along the length of a structural member.

The foundation acts as an anchor, as well as a support, for the frame of the house. The foundation may be a concrete slab-on-grade, poured concrete walls, or concrete block walls. **Fig. 27-2.**

SECTION 27.1

Floors

Steel joists, like wood joists, are used to frame floors. The joists are supported by the foundation and by posts and girders. Joists are attached to the foundation with C-shaped members called **joist tracks**. Each end of the joist is inserted into the track and screwed in place. **Figs. 27-3** and **27-4.** Joist tracks may also be called *rim tracks* because they are attached to the rim of a foundation (or a header).

Track splices are used whenever a single section is not long enough to extend the entire length of a foundation wall or header. The minimum length of a track splice is 6″. **Fig. 27-5.** This allows for 3″ of lap on each section.

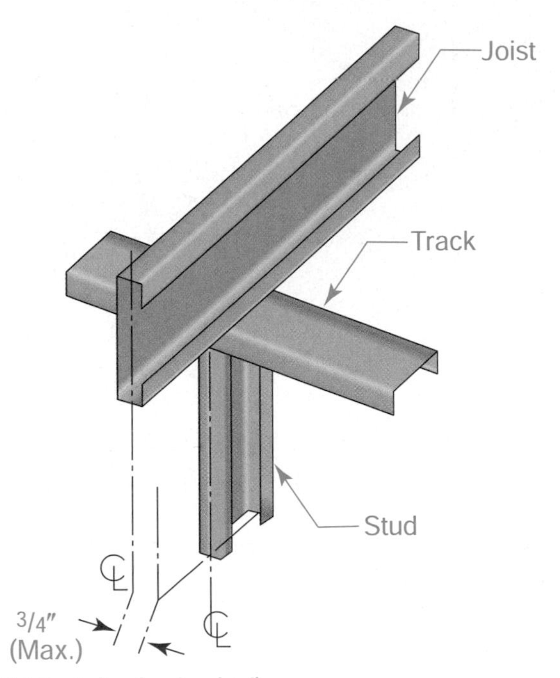

Fig. 27-1. In-line framing detail.

Fig. 27-2. A basement foundation with steel floor joists in place.

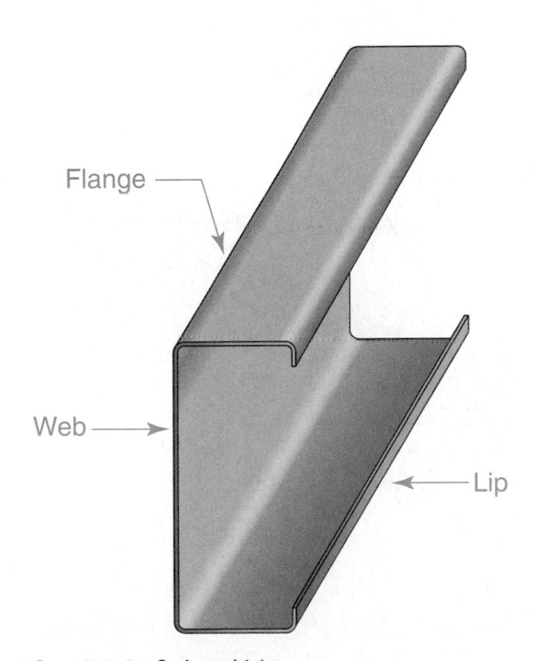

Fig. 27-3. C-shaped joist.

Fig. 27-4. This drawing shows how the joists and studs will be placed in relation to each other.

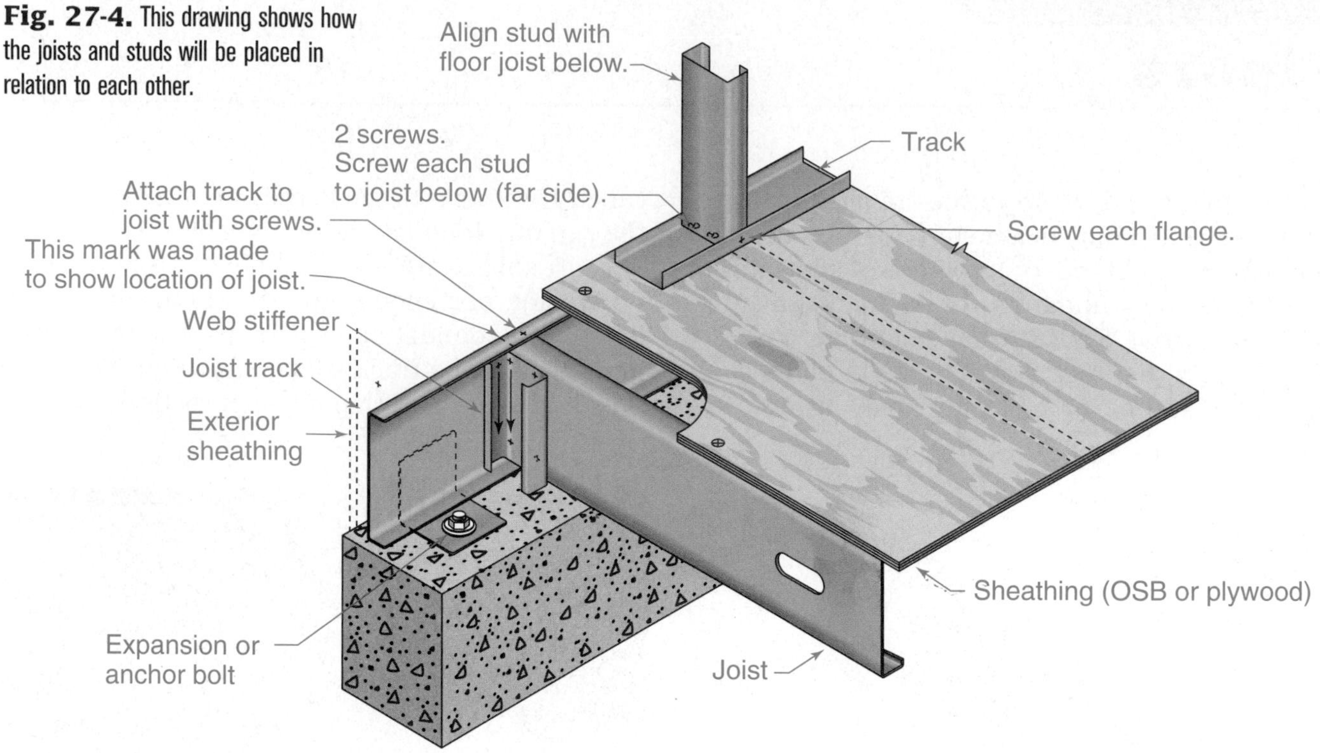

Align stud with
floor joist below.
Track
2 screws.
Screw each stud
to joist below (far side).
Attach track to
joist with screws.
Screw each flange.
This mark was made
to show location of joist.
Web stiffener
Joist track
Exterior
sheathing
Sheathing (OSB or plywood)
Expansion or
anchor bolt
Joist

LAYING OUT FLOOR JOISTS

Floor joists may be laid out from one end wall to another or from one side wall to another. The floor joists should run in the same direction that the roof trusses or rafters will.

When beginning the joist layout, place joist tracks for both sides on one side of the structure. Temporarily clamp their webs together. This allows you to mark both tracks for layout at the same time.

4 #8 screws through web or
flanges, each side of splice
C-shape inside track
6″ minimum
Track

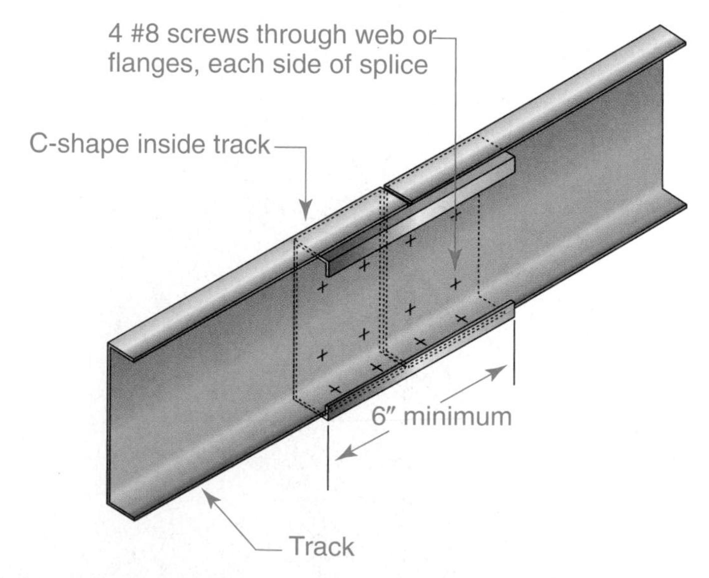

Fig. 27-5. A track splice showing the 3″ lap of each section.

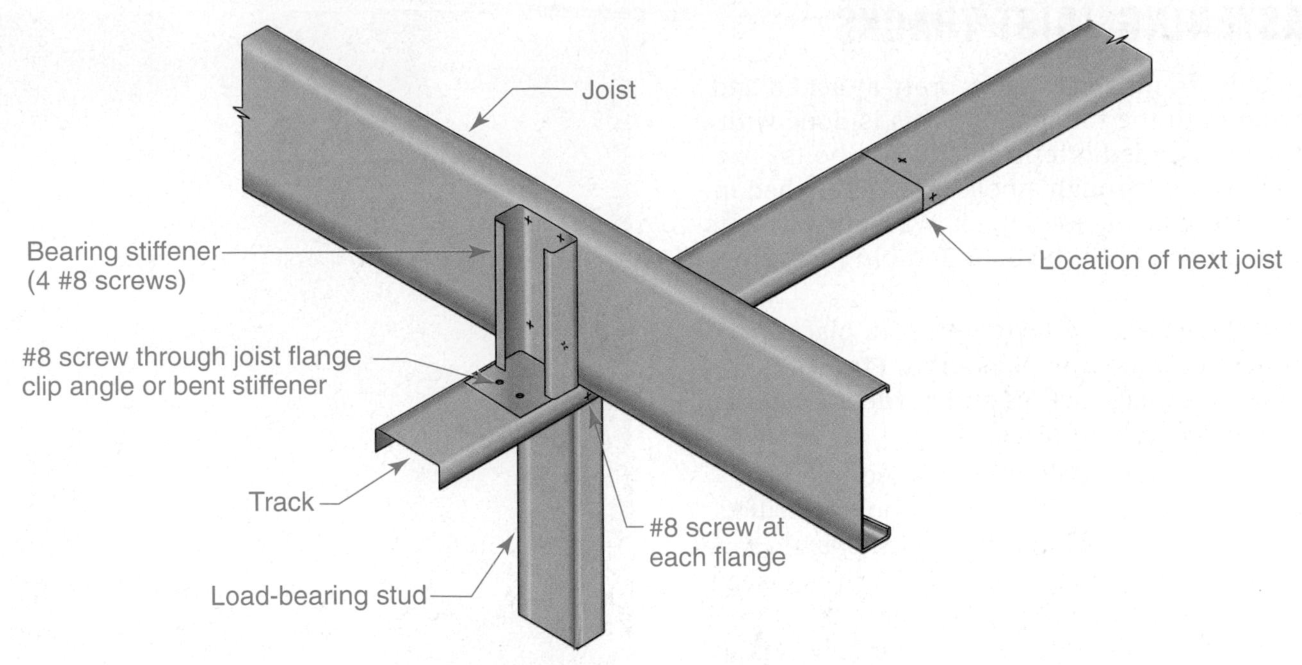

Fig. 27-6. Continuous-span joist.

Start the layout by marking for a joist at one end. Mark the location of the next joist on the joist track so it will be in line with the first roof member. It will be 24″ or less from the end joist.

Continue from that mark along the length of the joist tracks, making a new mark every 24″. Place an *X* on the side of each mark where the flange of that joist will be. The flanges must all be oriented in the same direction, or *on layout.* The open side of the joist should face away from the starting point.

Continuous-span joists span the entire floor opening. The *X*s are all on the same side of the joist location marks. **Fig. 27-6.**

A *non-continuous*, or *lapped, joist* is in two pieces. The pieces meet and overlap over an intermediate support. **Fig. 27-7.** The *X*s for the opposing track are on the side opposite the joist location marks.

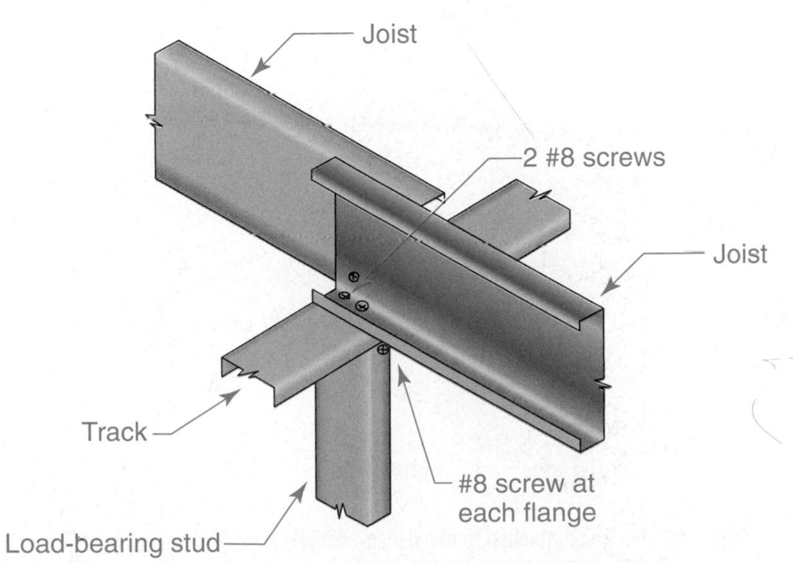

Fig. 27-7. Lapped joist across a load-bearing stud (intermediate support).

FASTENING JOIST TRACKS

A steel frame must be securely attached and anchored to the foundation. This is done with either embedded or epoxied anchor bolts. The bolts extend through a hole that is punched in the bottom of the joist track. Washers and nuts are tightened onto the bolts to hold the frame in place.

Embedded anchor bolts are set in place before a concrete foundation is poured. **Fig. 27-8.** When the concrete cures and hardens, it holds the bolt securely in place.

Epoxied anchor bolts are installed in cured concrete or in concrete block. A hole is drilled into the foundation and filled with *epoxy*. Epoxy is a type of adhesive. A threaded bolt is placed into the hole. When the epoxy hardens, it provides a strong bond that holds the bolt in place.

The joist tracks must then be fastened to the foundation. Place one track on each end wall or side wall. Stand the track on one flange with the web toward the outside of the foundation wall. **Fig. 27-9.** Keep the web of the joist track aligned with the edge of the foundation wall by tacking the track to the wall. Place a clip angle (see Fig. 27-9) over the anchor bolts at each anchor bolt location. A **clip angle** is a small piece of angle iron attached to a structural member to accept a structural load. Clamp the clip angles to the joist track to hold them in place. Attach them to the joist track with eight #8 screws. Place a washer and nut over the anchor bolt to secure the clip angle to the foundation.

Fig. 27-8. Embedded anchor bolt.

SETTING THE JOISTS

The joists are set into the track after the track is secured. **Fig. 27-10.** Turn the joist at an angle to fit between the flanges of the joist track. Twist the joist into position and set it inside the track. Keep the web sides of the joists oriented in the same direction. Position them on the same side of the mark on the track.

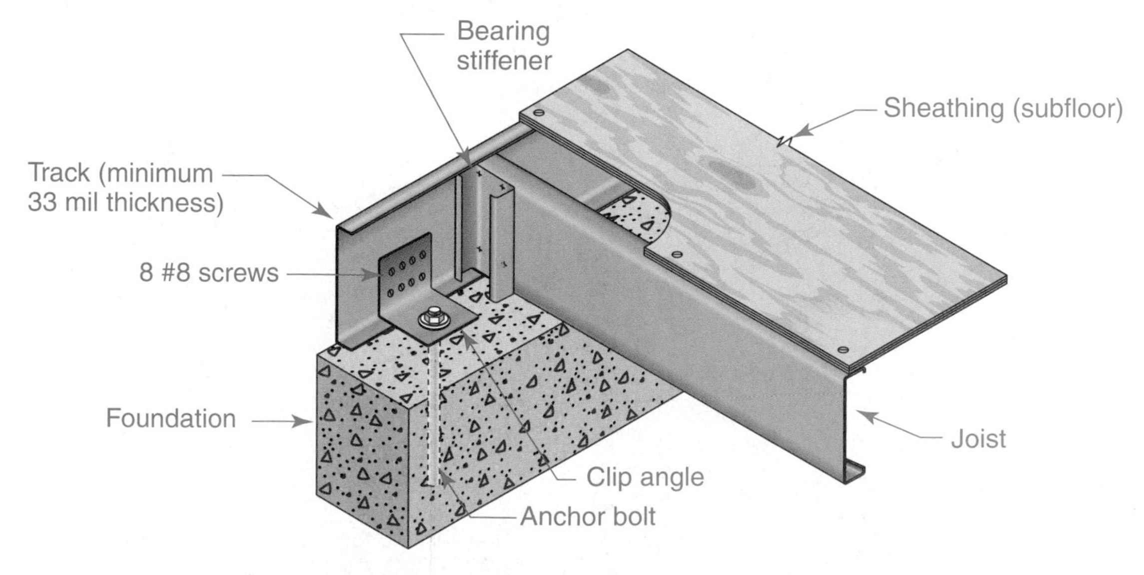

Fig. 27-9. Track attached to foundation with clip angle and anchor bolt. The web faces the outside of the foundation wall.

Fig. 27-10. Fastening the floor joists in the joist tracks.

Use a triangular framing square to adjust the end of each joist so it is perpendicular to the track. Allow a ⅛″ gap between the track and the end of the joist to prevent squeaks.

Screw the joist into position through its top and bottom flanges and the top and bottom track flanges. Use a minimum of one #8 screw at each point. Use screws with low-profile heads on the top flange to allow for the subflooring.

For lapped joists, lap the second joist toward the wall from which the layout was started. Otherwise, the distance between the starting point and the lapped joists will be greater than 24″. That would cause problems when laying the subfloor. Check the layout at the intermediate supports and screw the lapped joist into the support.

Set the remaining joists across the entire structure.

BRACING THE JOISTS

Braces prevent joists from rolling or twisting in the tracks. **Fig. 27-11.** The top flanges are braced with sheathing or subflooring. The bottom flanges are braced with gypsum board or a steel strap and blocking or bridging. Floor spans of 12′ or less do not require bracing on bottom flanges.

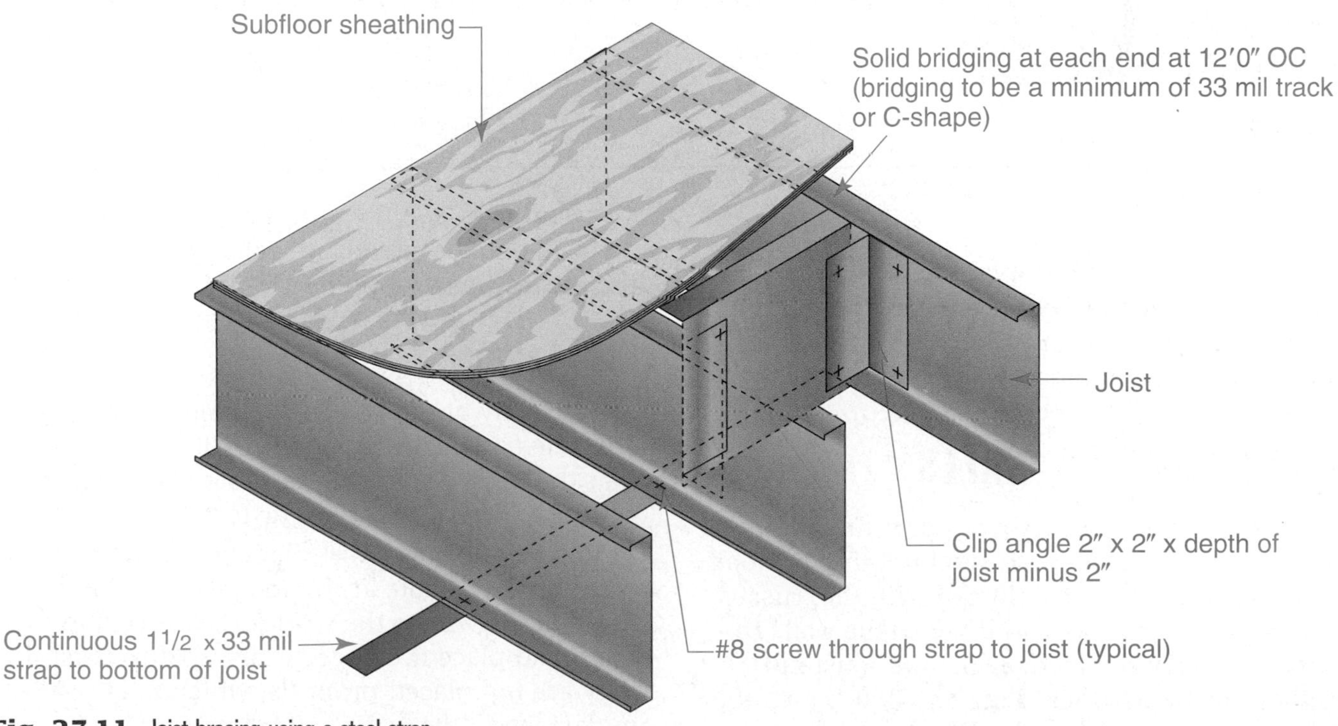

Fig. 27-11. Joist bracing using a steel strap.

Web Stiffeners

Web stiffeners are added to joists to prevent them from bending under the weight of floor loads. A web stiffener is made from stud or track material. It is the same thickness and depth as the floor joist.

Stiffeners must be added when the joists and joist tracks are installed. The stiffener is screwed to either side of the web. A stiffener is required under every load-bearing wall. Stiffeners are also required where non-continuous joists lap at an intermediate support.

Steel joists are much straighter than wood joists. When setting them, there is no need to compensate for a crown or bow.

Subflooring

Be sure to check your local building code for the type of material to use for the subflooring and how it should be attached. When the joists are spaced 24″ OC, $\frac{23}{32}$″ tongue-and-groove APA-rated sheathing plywood is used. Generally, the sheets of plywood are attached to the floor joists with #8 screws, 6″ OC on the edges, and 10″ OC on the joists in between. The sheathing should be tight against the joists. Use bugle-head screws and a drywall screw gun with an adjustable depth setting.

SECTION 27.1

Check Your Knowledge

1. What is the difference between continuous-span and non-continuous joists?
2. What is used to attach a steel frame to a foundation?
3. Why must joists be braced?
4. What are web stiffeners?

On the Job

Suppose you are going to space joists at 12″ or 16″ on center instead of 24″. Discuss how this will affect the rest of the structure.

SECTION 27.2

Walls

Construction and placement of the walls can begin after the floor joists, joist bracing, and subflooring are installed. Walls are either load bearing or nonload bearing (partitions).

LOAD-BEARING WALLS

Load-bearing walls help support the weight of the house above them. In steel framing, all load-bearing studs must be aligned with the trusses, joists, or rafters above and below the wall. To properly carry the load, each stud must butt tightly inside its track. **Fig. 27-12.** If the stud is not tight, the load is placed directly on the screws that attach the stud to the track. (Special instructions for panelized walls are included at the end of this section.)

Wall Length

Walls may be framed in full lengths as long as 40′. The advantages of full-length framing are that the walls are kept straight and square, and setting and placement are faster.

Actual wall length may depend upon the workforce available at the job site. The longer the wall, the larger the workforce needed to build and place it. Longer walls tend to twist if they are not placed properly, which may result in damage to the wall.

Fig. 27-12. A properly installed stud is butted firmly inside the track.

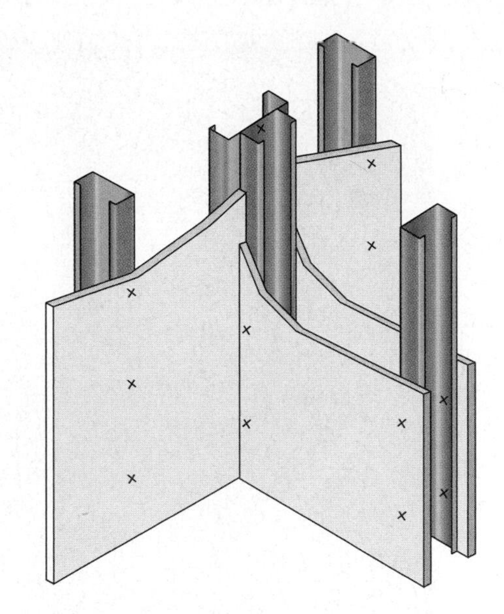

Fig. 27-13. Two walls meet at an intersection.

Walls are easier to frame in short sections and require a smaller workforce to put in place. Tracks for short sections are often spliced together to make longer walls. Care must be taken when splicing wall sections. The tracks must be kept aligned and straight.

Steel-frame structures can be as energy efficient as wood-frame structures. Thermal efficiency is dependent upon several things. Construction must be of good quality. All joints must be tight to prevent air infiltration. Steel studs must be spaced properly, not clustered or grouped. Clustering forms cold spots. Extra insulation should be placed in the exterior walls where practical. Insulation should fill the entire wall cavity, including the open sides of the C-shaped steel studs. Additional exterior foam sheathing should be used in colder climates. Refer to Chapter 39, "Thermal and Acoustical Insulation," for complete insulation procedures.

Intersections

Intersecting walls occur at the corners of the house where wall sections meet. A detail is shown in **Fig. 27-13**. Depending on the stud sizes being used—3½″ or 5½″—the bottom track will be shorter than full length.

To form an intersecting wall, cut the top and bottom tracks to the correct length. The bottom track should be 7 or 11 inches shorter (2 times 3½″ or 5½″).

Setting and Placement

Load-bearing walls must be prepared, placed, spliced, and connected.

Preparing and Placing Walls. When anchor bolts are used, measure their locations in the foundation. Make holes in the bottom track of the wall panels at these locations.

Place temporary bracing material near the foundation so it is ready. Move the wall section into position. Tilt the wall up and position the bottom track over the foundation bolts.

Clamp the temporary bracing material to the wall studs in two or three locations. **Fig. 27-14.** Install a brace every 8′ to 12′ along the wall. Secure each brace to a stud with a #10 hex-head screw before removing the clamps. Secure the bottom of the braces to a stake driven into the ground to hold them in place. Adjust the bracing to plumb the walls. Repeat this process until all load-bearing walls are in place.

Fig. 27-14. Temporary wall bracing.

SAFETY FIRST

Raising and Placing Walls

Raising and placing long wall sections require extra safety precautions. Be sure the on-site workforce is adequate to lift the length of wall being placed. Have temporary bracing and support beams readily available. Do not raise walls when strong winds could cause a lack of control. Securely brace the wall after it is in position.

Splicing and Connecting Sections. Splicing wall sections must conform to accepted engineering practices.

Center a 6″ or larger piece of C-shaped material inside the two sections of track to be spliced. **Fig. 27-15.** Screw the splice material through the flanges on both sides of the track with #8 screws.

When each section is properly positioned, plumb it. Attach the walls to the frame at the corners with #10 screws. Leave the bracing and bottom track in any door openings until roof framing and permanent bracing are completed.

Attaching Sheathing. After the wall is up and braced, Type II plywood or OSB sheathing can be attached. If openings in the wall are not extensive, the sheathing can act as bracing and protect the wall from racking and twisting. *Racking* occurs when the wall shifts and studs are forced out of plumb.

To be effective the sheathing must cover the full height of the wall from top track to bottom track. **Fig. 27-16.** It should be installed with the long dimension parallel to the stud framing. It should also be fastened tightly to the steel members with #8 self-piercing screws to draw the sheathing tight against the studs.

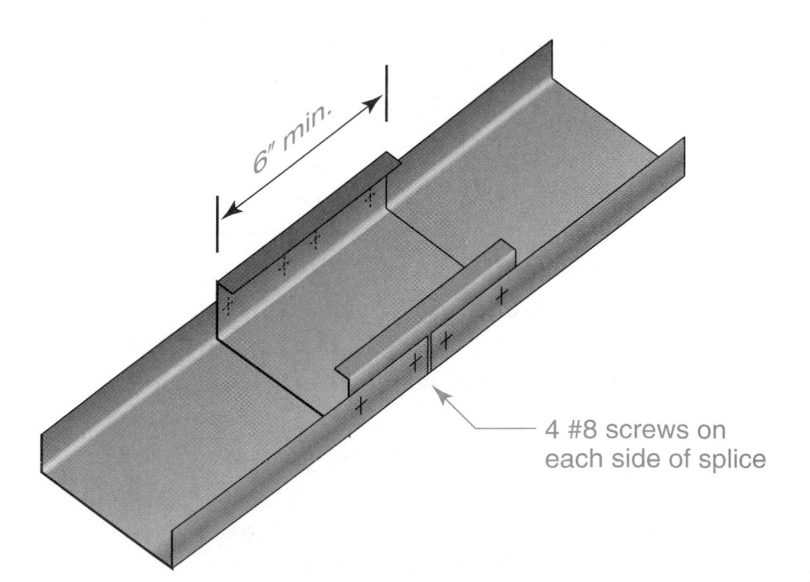

Fig. 27-15. Splicing two wall sections together.

Fig. 27-16. Sheathing can brace an exterior wall and prevent twisting and racking.

NONLOAD-BEARING WALLS

Interior nonload-bearing walls, or *partitions*, do not support or carry the weight of the structure. They are built to enclose rooms, closets, and other spaces. In-line framing is not required for these walls.

The structural members of nonload-bearing walls can be of a thinner gauge than those of load-bearing walls. However residential structures may need 33-mil (20 gauge) studs to prevent bending or damage during construction.

Nonload-bearing wall framing is similar to load-bearing wall framing. Generally, walls are stick built. However, they may also be panelized and then raised into position.

Cabinets and shelving may be attached directly to partition studs and to blocking materials in the walls with #8 2″ self-drilling screws. Wall studs must be 20 gauge or thicker. Wood cabinet blocking is installed as shown in **Fig. 27-17**. One end of the wood block is notched so it fits over the lip of the stud. When steel blocking is used, the flanges of the track material are notched.

INTERIOR LOAD-BEARING WALLS

Interior load-bearing walls increase the capacity of the house to resist shear forces, such as those that occur during earthquakes. That is because they stiffen the structure. They may also help increase the load capacity of the floors above the main floor.

Mark the top and bottom track for layout. Anchor the bottom track in place. Then secure studs in each end of the bottom track. Next, position the top track at the ends with intermediate studs. Install the remaining wall studs. After the wall is standing and properly positioned, install headers, X-bracing, or sheathing.

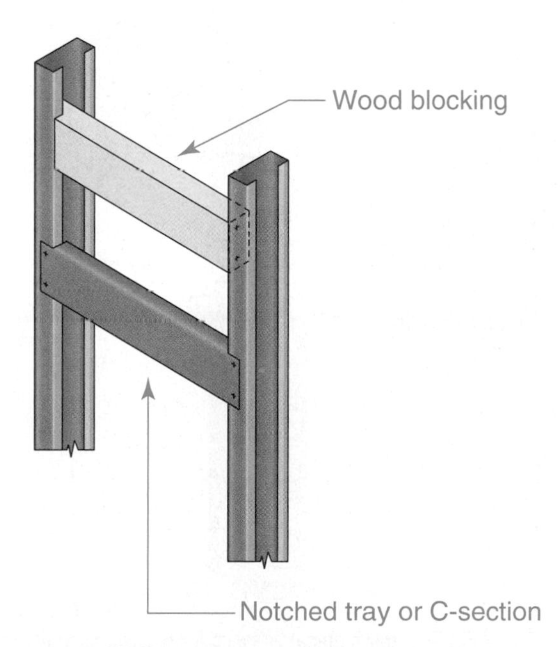

Fig. 27-17. Blocking material installed between studs.

Stick-Built Framing

Stick-built framing of a nonload-bearing wall begins with attaching the bottom wall track to the floor. The top track of the wall is positioned using a stud and a level. (The location of the top track for sloped walls or a cathedral ceiling can be set with a plumb bob.) The top track is screwed to the ceiling joists, the bottom chord of a truss, or a second-story floor joist.

Where interior walls run parallel to the joists or trusses, pieces of track or stud material are placed every 24″ as blocking material. **Fig. 27-18.** Blocking material should be cut 2″ longer than the distance between the trusses. One inch is then clipped from the flanges on each side of the blocking material. This allows the webs to overlap. The blocking is screwed on both ends with #8 self-drilling screws. The track is then marked for a stud spacing of 16″ to 24″.

The C-shaped studs must open toward the starting point of the layout, especially if they are 18-mil studs. The studs are twisted into the wall layout and the flanges on both sides of the tracks are secured with #6 or #8 self-piercing screws.

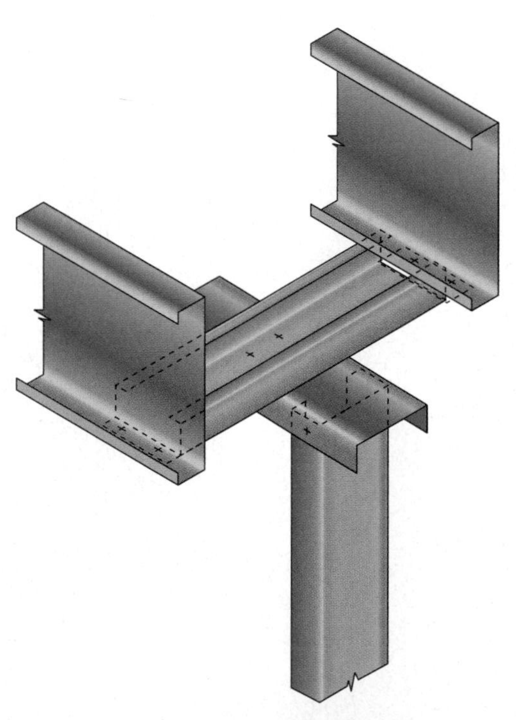

Fig. 27-18. Blocking material between joists used when the wall is parallel to the joists or trusses.

Holes and punch-outs are placed in steel studs to provide paths for utilities. When placing these paths, make sure both pre-punched and new holes line up. Place punch-outs in the studs under windows if utilities will be run through them. Remember that the number of holes and punch-outs will reduce the strength of a stud. Never punch a hole in the flange of a stud, joist, or track. Use grommets to cover the edges of holes and punch-outs. The grommets prevent damage to wires. They also prevent the electrolytic corrosion of steel caused by contact with copper pipe or pipe hangers.

Rough Openings

The rough openings in nonload-bearing walls do not need to be as strong as those in load-bearing walls.

When framing rough openings, allow 1½″ on each side of a door opening to install wood studs. Line all interior and closet door openings with wood studs to provide extra support at the hinge and strike plate. Place steel studs behind the wood studs with the flat side facing the opening.

Use wood or steel for the header of the opening. When using steel, cut the web back so the flanges provide an extra inch on each side. Install the cripple studs above the rough opening as necessary.

PANELIZED WALLS

As discussed in Chapter 26, "Steel Framing Basics," panelized walls are pre-assembled. The location of the studs in the wall is governed by the roof and floor layout. It is important to accurately lay out the wall studs with reference to the roof and joist framing.

The following information applies only to panelized walls. Setting and placement are the same as for stick-built walls.

Wall Layout

Panelized walls are built to engineering specifications and tolerances on templates such as platform tables and jigs. **Fig. 27-19.**

When laying out a panelized wall on a platform table, place the top and bottom tracks on the straight edge. Start with a stud at one end of the wall. Place a line on the flanges of the top and bottom tracks where the web of the stud will be located. Place an *X* on one side of this line to indicate the location of the stud flanges. **Fig. 27-20.** Continue marking the locations of all studs every 16″ or 24″ on center.

Arrange and temporarily clamp wall members with all of the webs facing in the same direction. The studs must fit tightly against the straight edge at the end of the wall.

Fig. 27-19. These panelized wall sections were built on a flat surface.

Rough Openings

After the wall is laid out, the rough openings for doors and windows are marked. **Fig. 27-21.**

Locate the door and window locations on the architectural drawings. Check the size of the openings. Mark the center of each opening on the top and bottom tracks. Add 12″ to the width of the window openings. Using a tape measure, center the dimensions over the marks on the track. Mark the location at each end of the tape to indicate the location of the king studs. Place an *X* on the side of the mark away from the window. The webs of the king studs will be on the rough-opening side.

Adding 12″ of width simplifies header assembly. It allows for two trimmer (jack) studs, one on each side of the header, and a wood stud on each side of the opening.

Framers may vary the length of the headers. Two trimmer studs may not be required at every opening. However, standardizing header length helps to simplify cut lists.

For wall stud assembly, see the Step-by-Step feature on page 540.

Fig. 27-20. Stud location. Note the line and the *X*.

Fig. 27-21. Rough opening for a window. Note position of header in wall.

STEP BY STEP

Wall Stud Assembly

After the layout is complete, assembly of the panelized wall can begin.

Step 1 Separate the top and bottom track members that were placed on the straight edge of the platform table.

Step 2 Install a stud at each end of the wall between the top and bottom tracks.

Step 3 Temporarily clamp the stud flanges to the track flanges at each end with locking C-clamps.

Step 4 Tap the tracks with a hammer to seat the top and bottom of the studs as tightly as possible.

Step 5 To prevent the studs from twisting, attach the flange of each stud to the flange of the track on each side of the wall using a #8 low-profile screw.

Step 6 Install the studs so open sides all face the same direction on parallel load-bearing walls.

Step 7 Align the punch-outs in the studs to provide straight paths for plumbing and electrical runs. **Fig. 27-22.**

Step 8 Install the king studs at the rough openings. Do not install studs at the markings between the king studs. These markings indicate the position of the cripple studs.

Step 9 Continue down the length of the wall until all studs are screwed into place. Do not remove the wall panel from the table until the header framing is complete.

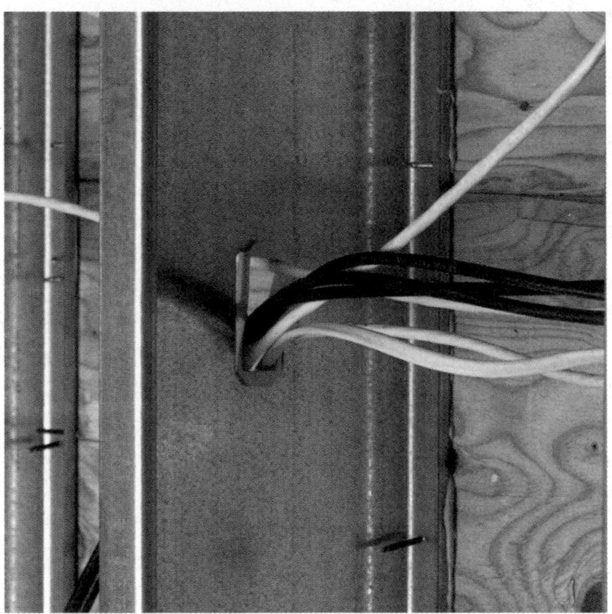

Fig. 27-22. Punchouts are aligned for straight runs of electrical wiring. Notice the grommets that cover rough edges.

Box Header Assembly

A *box header* is a common header that is built from standard C-shaped steel framing members. **Fig. 27-23.** A header jig is used to support the steel members and to keep them straight during assembly. A header jig can be built from C-shapes attached to a table and placed at the exact dimensions of the rough opening. The header can be built between these members.

To frame a box header, cut a section of wall track 2″ longer than the header. Snip the flanges of the track back 1″ at each end. Bend the web toward the flanges with a hand seamer. Make sure the bend is clean and straight.

Clamp the header track to the jig. Screw the web of the header track to the flanges of the C-shapes with two #8 screws, 24″ OC.

Cut web stiffeners from 3½″ stud material. Install the stiffeners in each end of the header with the flat side of the stiffener facing out. Attach four #8 screws through the web of the header pieces into each side of the stiffener flanges.

Insulate the header before it is installed in the wall.

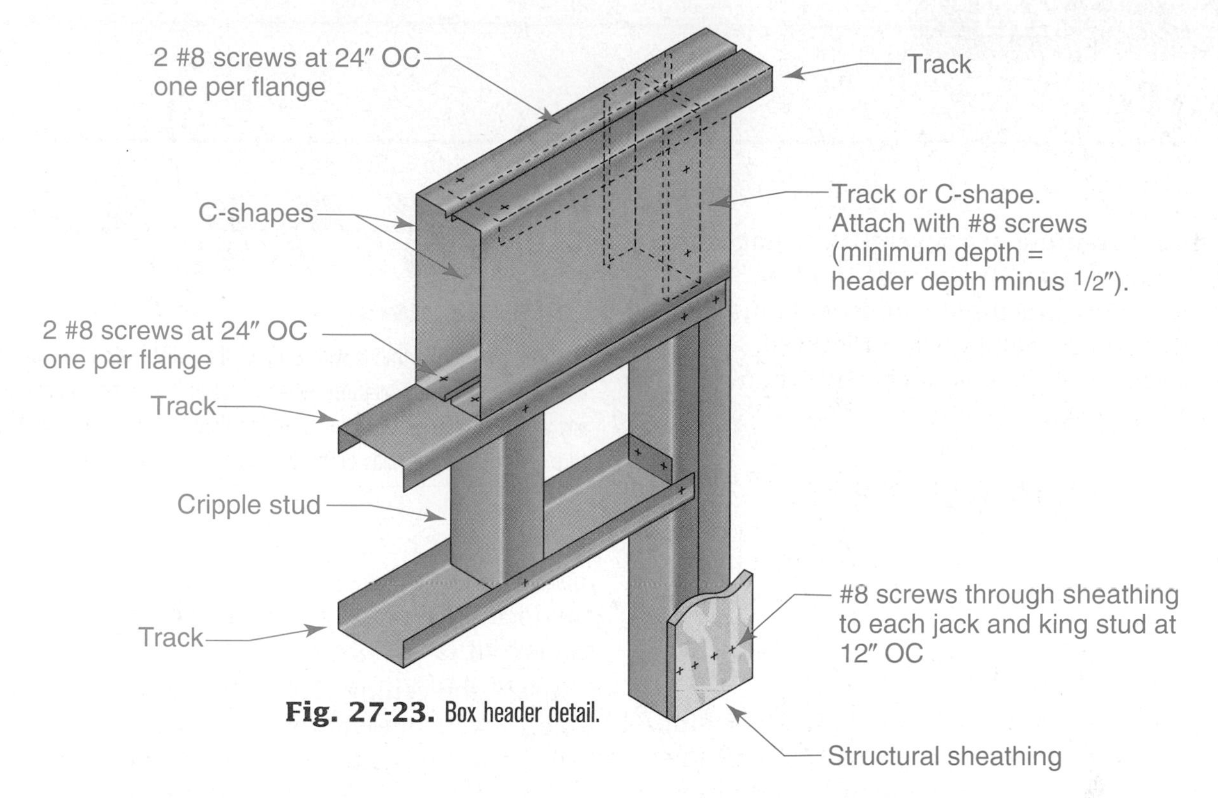

Fig. 27-23. Box header detail.

Bracing

Before a panelized wall is removed from the platform table, it must be checked for squareness. Then it must be braced. Measure the panel diagonally from corner to corner. If these measurements are the same, the wall is square.

Fig. 27-24. X-bracing using steel straps.

Lay extra bracing, studs, or truss material across the opening. X-bracing is the most effective at this stage. X-bracing consists of diagonal steel straps. **Fig. 27-24.** The bracing is attached to the walls with gusset plates and screws so it is permanent. Installation of the bracing straps must be inspected to ensure that the correct number of fasteners is used.

SECTION 27.2 Check Your Knowledge

1. What is an intersection?
2. At what intervals should temporary bracing be installed?
3. How is wind a factor in wall placement?
4. What type of stud is installed above a rough opening in nonload-bearing walls?

On the Job

Search the Internet for information about steel framing. Find an answer to one of the following questions:

1. What percentage of homes in the United States are built with steel framing?
2. What does a typical steel-frame package cost? How does that compare to the price of a wood-frame package?

SECTION 27.3

Roofs

Steel roof framing has several advantages over traditional wood-frame construction. With minimal support bracing it can provide more attic space. Fewer members are required. Complex roof designs cost less than when framed with wood.

Ceiling Joists

Once secured to the tracks with screws, the ceiling joists may be used temporarily as a work platform when installing the rafters. Before placing any weight on the joists, make sure that they are properly braced. Make sure all load-bearing walls below the ceiling joists are secured in place.

FRAMING WITH RAFTERS

Using steel joists and rafters has much in common with using their wood counterparts.

Installing Ceiling Joists

The procedure for setting ceiling joists is similar to that for floor joists. **Fig. 27-25.** Mark the layout for the top track. Start your layout at the same end for both sides. Next, measure and mark the layout over the headers. Also, mark any locations where there are no wall studs and the layout is not obvious.

Install the ceiling joists in the tracks one at a time. Move from where you began the layout to the end of the structure. Anchor the joists at the top of the track using two #10 screws. Install

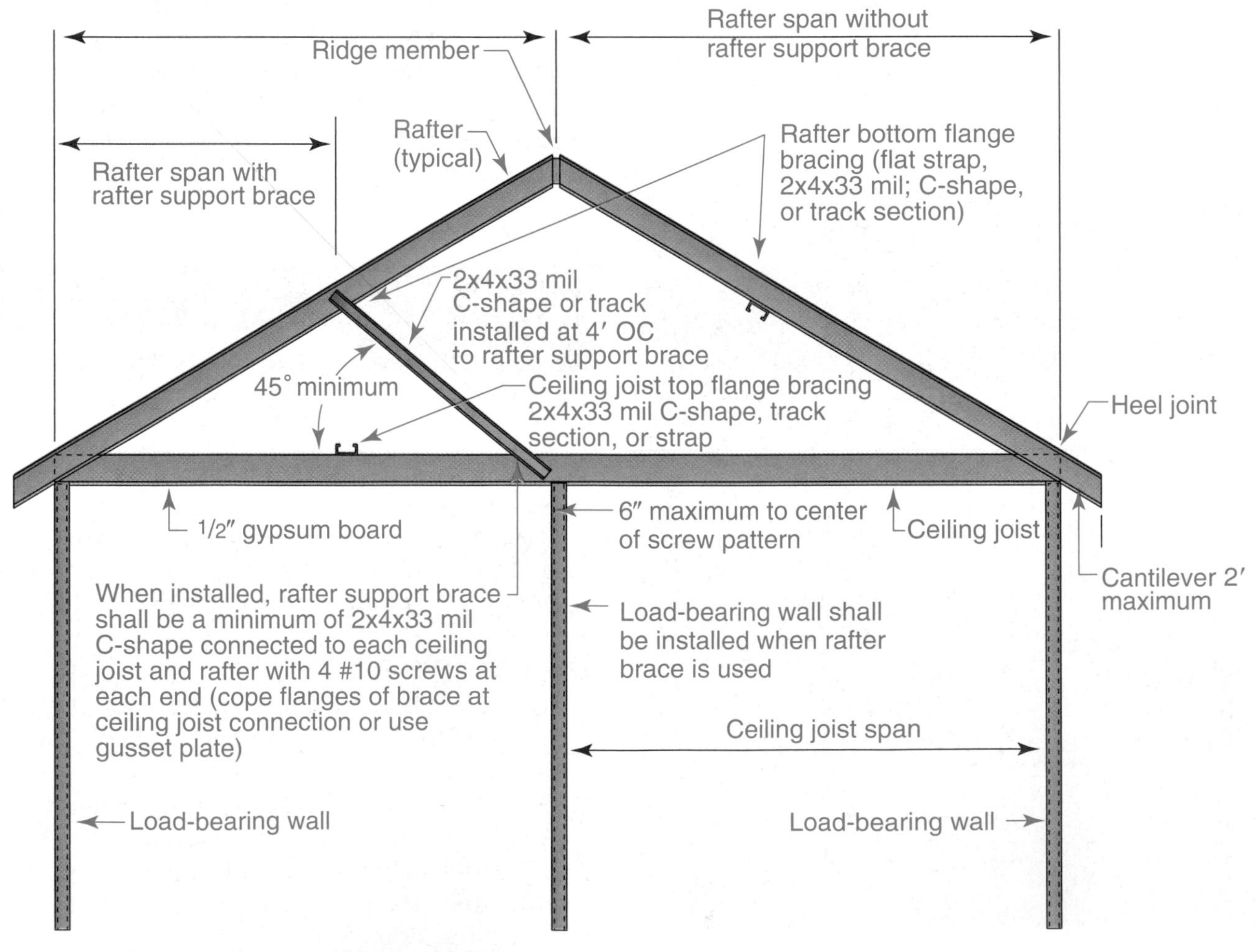

Fig. 27-25. Steel roof construction with joists and rafters.

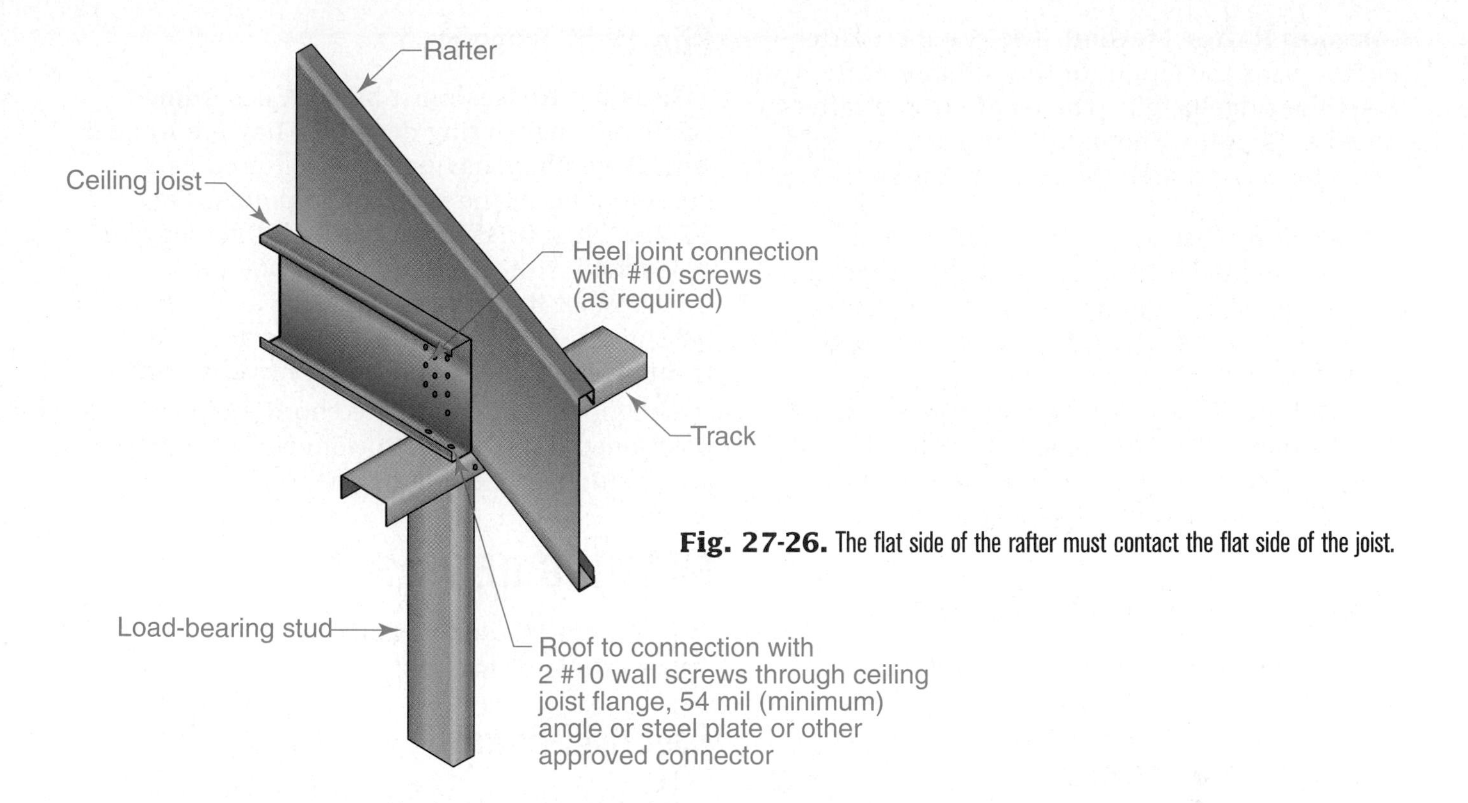

Fig. 27-26. The flat side of the rafter must contact the flat side of the joist.

2x4x33 mil C-shape top-flange bracing on the joists. Blocking must be installed every 12′ OC. The blocking keeps the joists from rolling in the tracks.

Preparing the Rafters

All rafters must be installed with the flat sides facing the same direction. The flat side of the rafter at the top track must be in contact with the flat side of the ceiling joist. **Fig. 27-26.**

Cut the rafters to length. Cut the top end of the rafter to match the slope of the roof. The ridge plumb cut allows the rafter to lie flush against the ridge member. Next, use 2″ by 2″ clip angles to attach the rafters to the ridge member. **Fig. 27-27.**

Rafter tails may be cut in advance or after roof framing is complete. However, the fascia material will remain straighter if the tail cuts are made after the roof is framed.

Setting Ridge Height

The ridge height can be determined by the same methods as for wood construction. See Chapter 22, "Basic Roof Framing," for complete instructions.

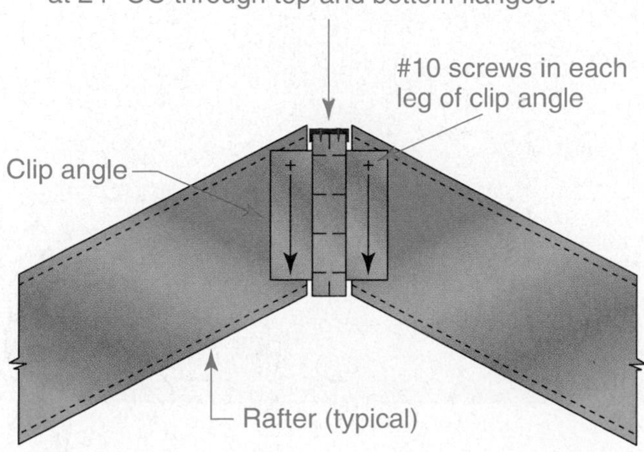

Fig. 27-27. Attaching the rafters to the ridge member with clip angles.

Common Rafter Method. The common rafter method uses the length of the common rafters to set the ridge height. The length of the rafters must be accurate. The plumb cut at the top of the rafter must match the slope of the roof.

Calculation Method. With the calculation method the pitch of the roof and the rafter length are used to determine the ridge height. The steel rafters rest on the top outside edge of the top track. See Fig. 27-26.

A steel rafter must *not* be notched as is done with a wood rafter. Notching will reduce its strength. The lack of a notch must be considered when calculating ridge height.

FRAMING WITH TRUSSES

Steel roof trusses can be manufactured off site or custom built on site.

Manufactured Trusses

Manufactured steel trusses are made in many different shapes and styles. **Fig. 27-28.** Several factors are important when choosing them. They should be as cost effective as wood trusses. They must be durable enough to withstand normal shipping and handling. They must be able to support the weight of workers framing and finishing the roof. They must be light enough for work crews to lift, move, and place.

Site-Built Trusses

Site-built trusses must be built according to approved engineering designs. They are framed with C-members having either mitered cuts or gusset plates at the connection points. **Fig. 27-29.** When trusses are mitered, they may be assembled with the members in one plane. The thickness of the truss is the same as the thickness of a C-member. Gusset plates are made from pieces of track and have only one flange.

The top and intermediate chord members are positioned flat side up. Bottom chord members are positioned flat side down.

FRAMING DETAILS

The following details apply to framing with either rafters or trusses.

Roof Hold-Downs

The roof framing is fastened to the top plate with screws. The number and type of screws making this connection are determined by wind-load data. Two #10 screws are sufficient for 70 mph Exposure *C* wind loads or 90 mph Exposure *A* or *B* wind loads.

Uplift connectors or hold-down clips are required in higher wind conditions. **Fig. 27-30.** Prescriptive-method tables and charts should be used to determine uplift load and connector requirements.

Fig. 27-28. Roof trusses are built in many styles and shapes.

Fig. 27-29. Using a heel gusset to join the chords.

Roof Fascia

The roof fascia provides a finished look to the end of the rafter tails. The fascia can be installed so that it is parallel to the side of the house (perpendicular to the ground). **Fig. 27-31.** It can also be installed so that it is perpendicular to the rafters. **Fig. 27-32.**

Fig. 27-31. Perpendicular fascia framing parallel to the side of the house.

Fig. 27-30. Roof hold-downs.

Roof Rake

The **roof rake** is that portion of the roof frame that extends beyond the walls on the gabled ends. **Fig. 27-33.** The rake may overhang as much as 12″. Rakes are formed using standard C-shaped members.

Fig. 27-32. Fascia framing that is perpendicular to the rafters.

Fig. 27-33. A roof rake extends beyond the house.

The rake supports the roof sheathing. Uplift loads determine its size. Longer rakes require that an engineer approve the length using uplift load data.

Using lookouts is another way of framing a rake. They are installed 2′ on center from the gable end to the barge rafter. **Fig. 27-34.**

Fig. 27-34. Lookouts can be used to form a rake.

Enclosed Soffits

Soffits cover the truss or rafter tails. Enclosed soffits are usually covered with aluminum, vinyl, or wood. The enclosure may be formed to match the pitch of the roof. **Fig. 27-35.** The bottoms of other enclosed soffits may be horizontal and parallel to the ground.

Fig. 27-35. An enclosed soffit with ventilation openings.

SECTION 27.3

Check Your Knowledge

1. What are the advantages of steel roof framing over traditional wood-frame construction?
2. What is the purpose of blocking material for ceiling joists?
3. Name the two methods used to determine roof ridge height.
4. Why must an engineer approve a roof rake longer than 12″?

On the Job

For a simple gable roof, compare the costs of one set of steel joists and common rafters to those for a steel truss that has a 5/12 pitch and a span of 28′. Then calculate the difference in cost if 25 trusses or rafters are needed to build the house.

Chapter 27 Review

Section Summaries

27.1 Floor joists are laid out starting from the same end of the building as the roof members. The layout may be from one end wall to another or from one side wall to another. Joist flanges must all be oriented in the same direction. The open side of the C-shaped member should face away from the starting point of the layout.

27.2 Load-bearing walls support the weight of the house above them. Each stud must butt tightly inside its track to properly carry the axial load. Interior nonload-bearing walls are built to enclose rooms, closets, and other spaces.

27.3 All rafters must be cut with the flat sides facing in the same direction. The flat side of the rafter at the top track must contact the flat side of the ceiling joist. Either the common rafter method or the calculation method can determine the height of the roof ridge.

Review Questions

1. Briefly describe the procedure for laying out floor joists.
2. When beginning the floor joist layout, what is the purpose of placing both joist tracks on one side of the structure?
3. How must the open side of a floor joist be placed with relation to the layout?
4. How are embedded and epoxied anchor bolts installed in a foundation?
5. Why is clustering wall studs not a good idea?
6. How are rough openings framed in panelized walls?
7. What type of bracing is most effective for panelized walls before they are installed?
8. Describe the process for setting ceiling joists.
9. When determining roof ridge height using the common rafter method, what must the plumb cut at the top of the rafter match?
10. What factor determines the extension of roof rakes?

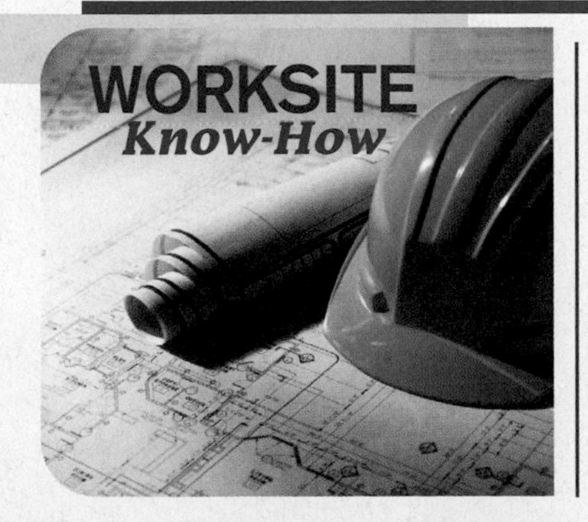

SFA The Steel Framing Alliance (SFA) was established by the American Iron and Steel Institute. The Alliance seeks to encourage and increase the use of light-gauge steel framing in construction. Currently, steel framing has a small share of the residential framing market. Through publications, a Web site, and various programs, SFA hopes to increase that share to 25 percent by 2007.

Unit 6

CLOSING IN THE STRUCTURE

Brick Mason

Brick masons build and repair walls, floors, partitions, fireplaces, chimneys, and other structures. Some brick masons specialize in installing firebrick linings in industrial furnaces. Brick masons and block masons work in closely related trades, and they are often both called *bricklayers*.

Brick masons must know how to work with a variety of materials. Besides brick, they must be able to work with concrete block, precast masonry panels, and specialty materials such as insulated wall panels and masonry accessories. They must know the types and characteristics of mortar and be able to work with a high degree of precision.

Most brick masons learn their trade on the job by watching and learning from experienced bricklayers. Whether learning strictly on the job or in an apprenticeship program, workers start out as helpers and laborers. They carry materials, build and move scaffolding, and mix mortar. As time goes by, they learn to spread mortar and to lay, line up, and join bricks.

For more information, check the *Occupational Outlook Handbook* or look up "brick mason" on the Internet.

Chapter 28

Windows and Skylights

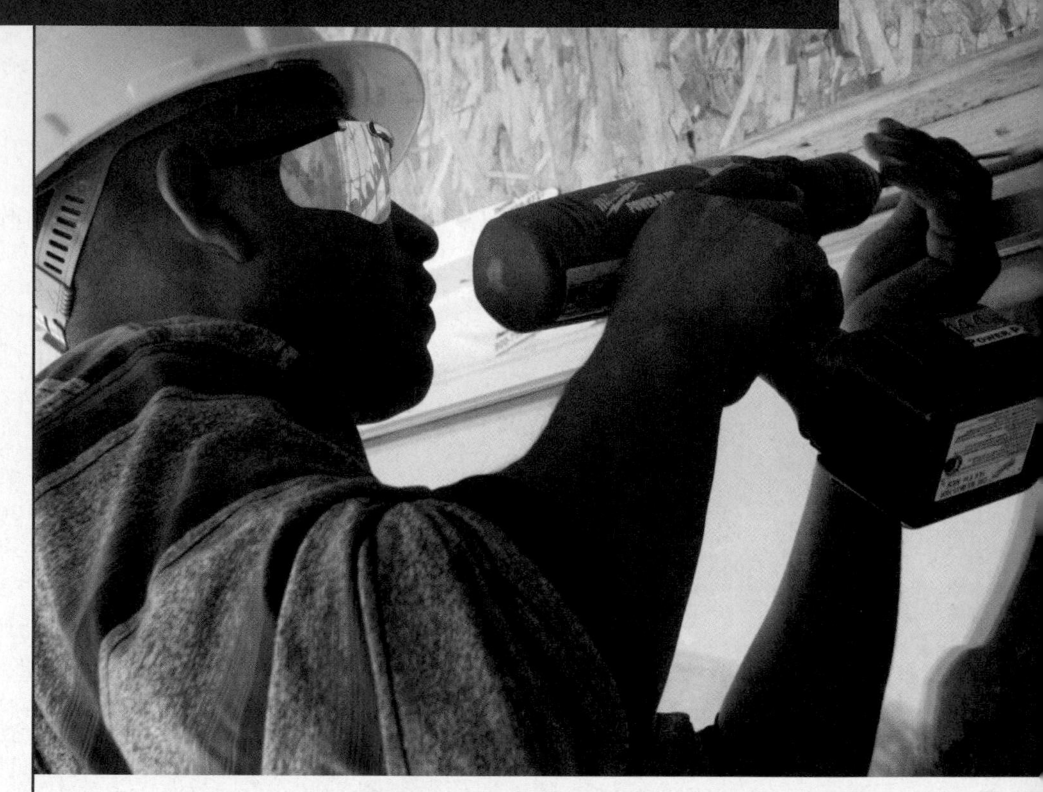

Objectives

After reading this chapter, you'll be able to:

- Describe the basic types of windows.
- Identify the ways in which windows are made energy efficient.
- Read a window schedule and a manufacturer's size table.
- Install a standard double-glazed or casement window.

Terms

glazing
mullion strip
muntin
sash
unit dimension
window schedule

Windows let light and air into a house. They are also an important part of its architectural design. However, 20 to 30 percent of the heat lost from some houses is through the windows. This loss is due to air leaking around the window or by heat being radiated through the glass. In hot climates, cool indoor air can be lost in a similar fashion. As heating and cooling costs have climbed, manufacturers have greatly improved the energy efficiency of windows.

A house requires several types and sizes of windows. After they have been chosen and delivered to the site, they must be installed with care. This prevents air leakage, which reduces energy efficiency, and water leakage, which encourages rot.

SECTION 28.1

Choosing Windows

The window style and size should suit the style of the house. **Fig. 28-1.** However, not every room will need the same size and type of window. For example, in bedrooms, light and ventilation are especially important. Privacy and wall space for furniture are also important. A row of narrow windows placed high on two walls can provide light and ventilation as well as privacy and wall space. Convenient window operation is another important consideration.

DESIGN REQUIREMENTS

Generally, the total area of window glass in a room should be not less than 8 percent of the floor area. This ensures enough natural light. The total window area that can be opened for ventilation should be not less than 4 percent of the floor area, unless mechanical air conditioning and ventilation are provided. Bathrooms must have no less than 3 sq. ft. of glazing, unless the room is ventilated with a fan. In the kitchen, windows should provide good ventilation of cooking odors.

One purpose of windows that is often overlooked is that they provide a way for rescuers to enter the room in an emergency. They also allow emergency exit from the room, particularly during a fire. According to building codes, every bedroom must have at least one window (or exterior door) that is suitable for *egress*, or emergency escape. It must have the following characteristics:

- Sill height no more than 44″ above the floor.
- Height of opening no less than 24″.
- Width of opening no less than 20″.
- Unblocked open area no less than 5.7 sq. ft. except those on grade floor openings. These can have an open area of no less than 5.0 sq. ft.

(Note that a window with the minimum opening height and the minimum opening width will have an unblocked open area of only 3.3 sq. ft. This will not meet code. However, a window with the minimum opening height that is also 48″ wide would have an unblocked open area of 8 sq. ft. That would be acceptable.)

Fig. 28-1. Windows can dramatically affect the look of a house.

WINDOW TYPES

Windows are factory assembled as complete units, often with the exterior casing in place. The basic parts are the glazing, the sash, and the frame. **Fig. 28-2.** **Glazing** refers to the clear glass or plastic portions of a window. The glass within each section of window is also called a *pane* or *light*. The **sash** is the part that holds the glazing. The *frame* is the fixed part of the assembly that receives the sash. It consists of a *sill, side jambs*, and a *head jamb*.

There are six major types of windows: double hung, casement, stationary, awning, hopper, and horizontal-sliding. **Fig. 28-3.**

Double-Hung Windows

The *double-hung window* consists of an upper and a lower sash that slide up and down in channels in the side jambs. **Fig. 28-4.** A *jamb* is an exposed upright member on each side and at the top of the frame. Each sash has springs or balances to hold it in any position. Some types allow the sash to be removed or pivoted away for easy cleaning, painting, or repair. A single-hung window is a variation. The upper sash is fixed in place, and only the lower sash slides up and down. Only half of a double-hung or single-hung window can be opened at one time.

A sash may have muntins (see Fig. 28-2). A **muntin** is a short vertical or horizontal piece used to hold a pane of glass. Some manufacturers sell preassembled muntins that snap in place over a single light, dividing it into six or more portions. These are not true muntins, but they simplify painting and other maintenance.

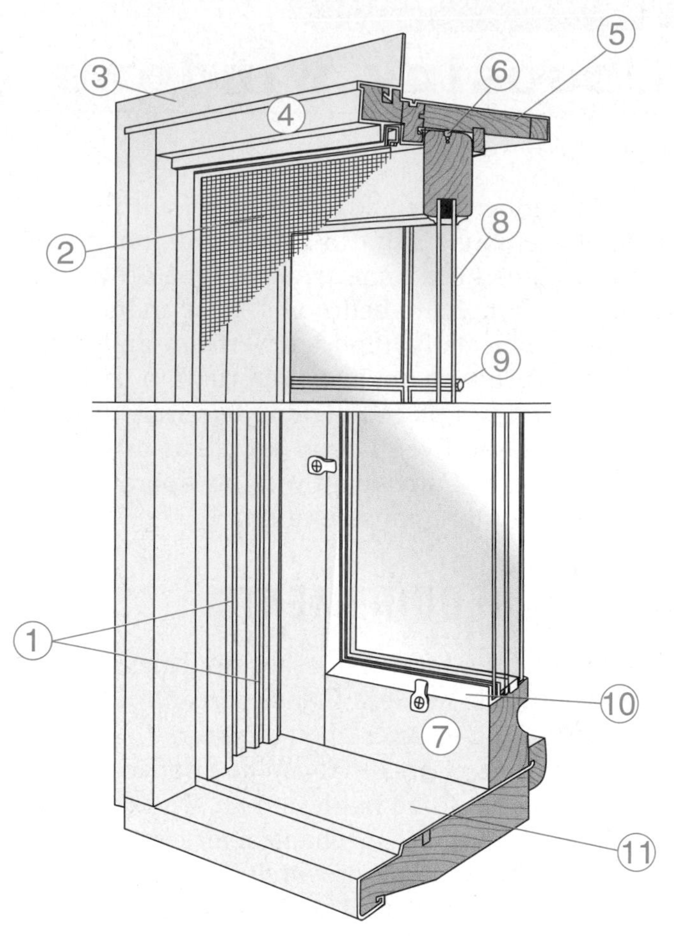

Fig. 28-2. Parts of an assembled double-hung window: 1. Tracks. 2. Screen. 3. Mounting flange. 4. Exterior casing. 5. Head jamb. 6. Weatherstripping. 7. Sash. 8. Glazing. 9. Muntins (installed on the inside when insulated glass is used). 10. Removable storm panel. 11. Sill.

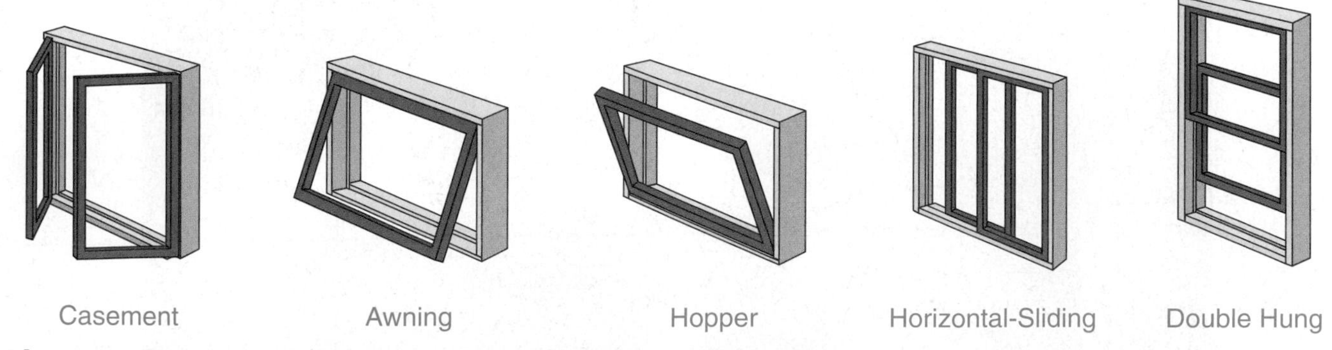

Fig. 28-3. Five basic window styles. Stationary windows do not open and are not shown here.

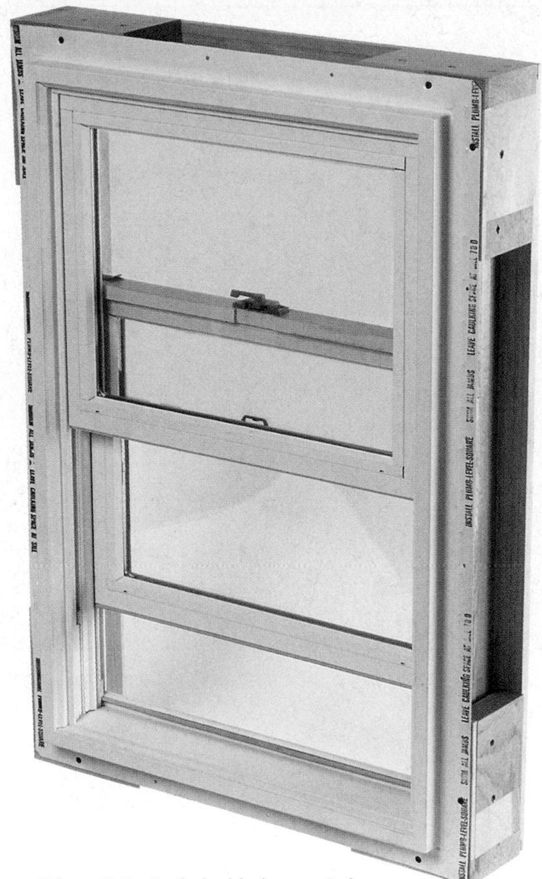

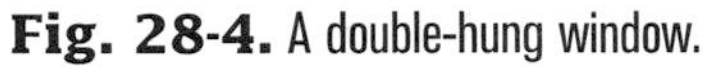

Fig. 28-4. A double-hung window.

Fig. 28-5. A wood casement window.

Hardware for a double-hung window includes one or two metal sash locks. These can be turned to prevent the sash from being opened from the outside. They also draw the sash together at the meeting rails to reduce air infiltration.

Casement Windows

Casement windows have a side-hinged sash that swings inward or outward. **Fig. 28-5.** An outward-swinging sash does not get in the way of furniture. Also, wind tends to push an outward-swinging sash against the weatherstripping, making a stronger seal. One advantage of the casement window over the double-hung type is that the entire window area can be opened for ventilation. Hardware consists of a rotary opener, a hinge assembly, and a sash lock.

Stationary Windows

Stationary windows are used alone or combined with other types. **Fig. 28-6.** They consist of a single light of insulated glass fastened permanently

Fig. 28-6. The two-story window wall on this house was assembled using stationary windows of various sizes.

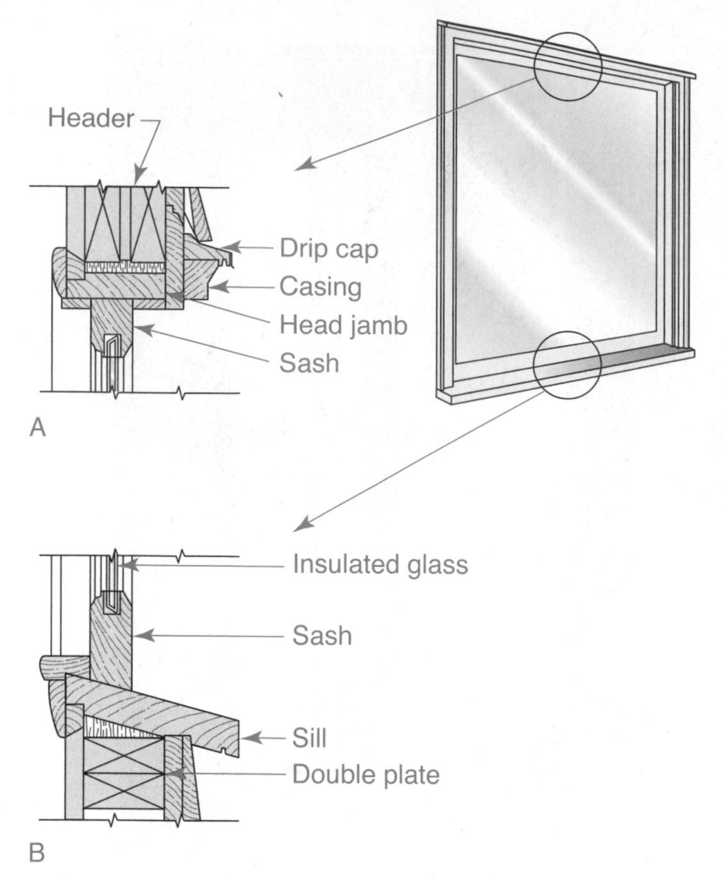

Fig. 28-7. Stationary window cross sections. *A.* Head jamb. *B.* Sill.

Fig. 28-8. Glass blocks can be used to admit light where ventilation is not required.

into the frame. They cannot be opened. **Fig. 28-7.** Stationary windows may also be installed without a sash. The glass is set directly into the frame members and held in place with stops.

Glass blocks are sometimes used for admitting light in places where transparency and ventilation are not required. **Fig. 28-8.** The individual blocks are held in place with mortar.

Awning and Hopper Windows

The sash of an *awning window* swings outward at the bottom. **Fig. 28-9.** Awning windows are sometimes grouped in pairs. A *hopper window* is similar, except that the sash swings inward at the top. Both types provide protection from rain while open. They are sometimes combined with stationary windows. Hardware includes hinges, pivots, and sash supporting arms. Various types of operating hardware are available. **Fig. 28-10.**

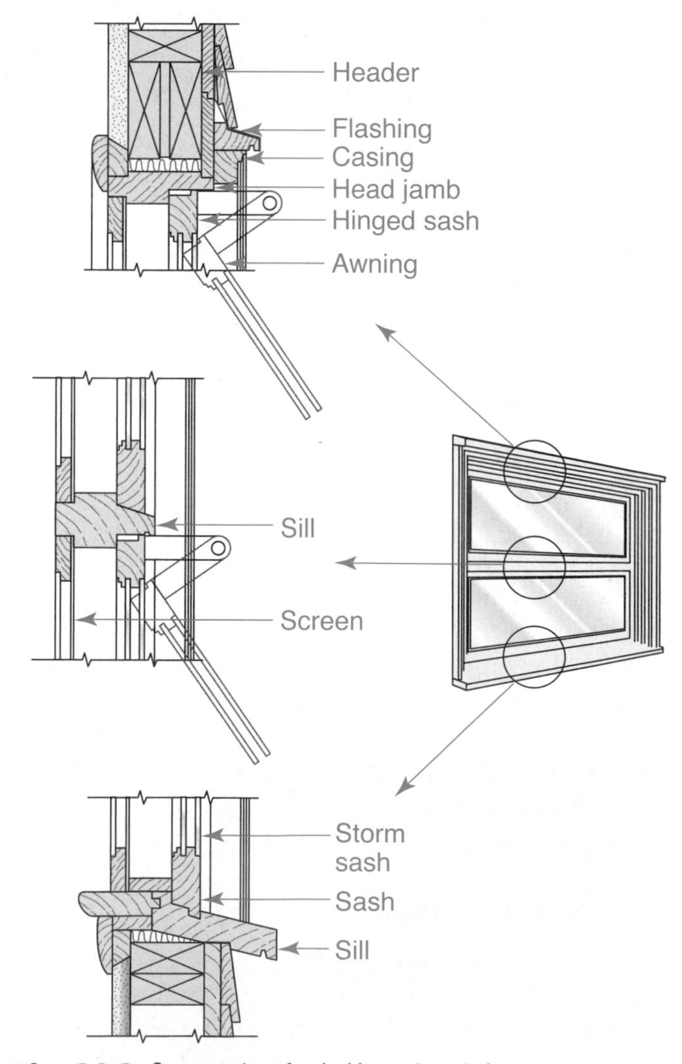

Fig. 28-9. Cross section of a double awning window.

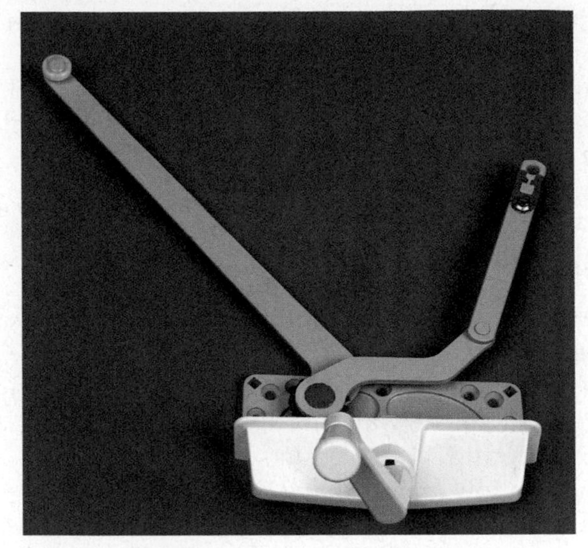

Fig. 28-10. One type of operating hardware for awning windows.

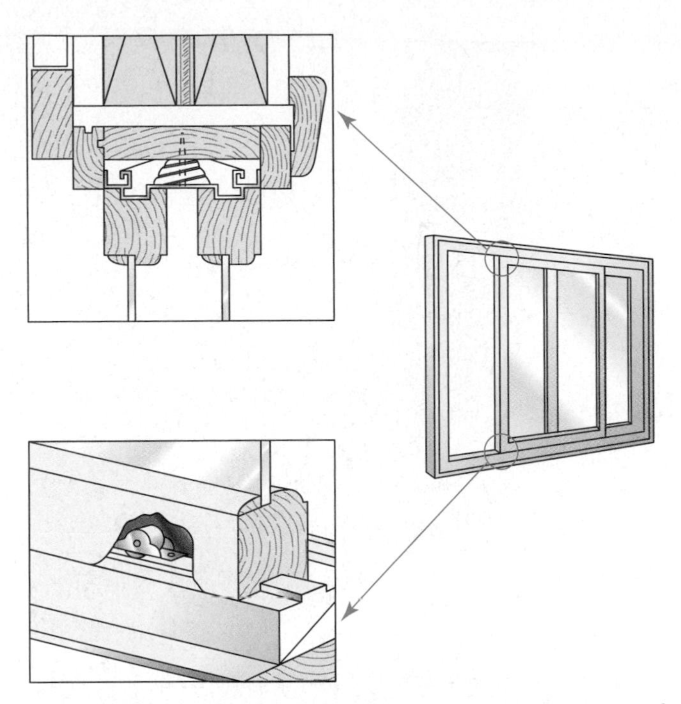

Fig. 28-11. A horizontal-sliding window unit. The track at the top of the sash is spring loaded. This provides a weathertight seal and also permits lifting the sash out of the window frame. Along the sill, the sash travels on a nylon roller for easy operation.

Horizontal-Sliding Windows

Horizontal-sliding windows resemble casement windows in appearance. However, the sashes (in pairs) slide horizontally in separate tracks, or guides, located on the sill and head jamb. **Fig. 28-11.**

Screens

Most windows can be fitted with screens to keep insects out when the window is open. Screens used with double-hung, sliding, and hopper windows are installed on the outside of the window. For casement and awning windows that open out, the screen is installed on the inside.

FRAME AND SASH MATERIALS

Any of the basic types of windows can have sashes and frames made of wood, metal, vinyl, fiberglass, or wood composites. *Hybrid windows* are a combination of two or more materials.

Wood

Wood window frames and sashes should be made from a clear grade of all-heartwood stock. **Fig. 28-12.** The wood should be decay resistant or given a preservative treatment. Species commonly used include ponderosa and other pines, cedar, cypress, and spruce. All wood components should also be treated with a water-repellent preservative at the factory to provide protection before and after they are placed in the walls.

Fig. 28-12. This cutaway view of a double-hung window shows how the wood components fit together.

Fig. 28-13. A cutaway of a clad-wood window.

The wood parts of a *clad-wood window* are covered, or clad, with vinyl or aluminum. **Fig. 28-13.** The wood provides strength, and the cladding protects the wood. This type of wood window never needs painting.

Metal

Metal window frames and sash are also made of steel or aluminum. They are generally lighter and less costly than windows made of other materials. Frames and sash are more narrow than those of wood windows. This allows a larger glass area for a given rough opening. Unlike wood windows, metal windows are not subject to insect attack. Also, they require less maintenance than wood windows. They are available with a baked-on or anodized finish. Painting is not required.

Metal windows, particularly those made of aluminum, are very common in some parts of the country. They are less popular where winters are cold. This is because heat loss through metal frames and sash is much greater than through similar wood units. A related problem is that moisture-laden air inside a house can condense on metal surfaces exposed to cold outside air. Windows that have a thermal break reduce these problems. A t*hermal break* is a material such as rubber or dense foam insulation that slows the transmission of heat and cold. The most energy-efficient metal windows have two-piece frames separated by a thermal break.

Most metal windows have a nailing flange on all sides. This makes them easy to install. Manufacturer's instructions should be followed carefully. However, the techniques generally follow those required for other flanged windows (see Fig. 28-20).

Vinyl, Fiberglass, and Composites

Windows with structural PVC (polyvinyl chloride) sashes and frames are easy to maintain, and they resist heat loss. **Fig. 28-14.** The vinyl is colored all the way through, so it does not need painting. It also resists attack by insects. Vinyl window frames have hollow channels beneath the surface. In insulated vinyl windows, these cavities are filled with insulation for greater energy efficiency.

Window frames can also be made of fiberglass, which is a polyester-based material reinforced with very thin glass strands. Like vinyl frames, they come in hollow and insulated types. However, fiberglass is stiffer and stronger than vinyl.

Another material used for windows consists of polymers (plastics) mixed with wood particles. This mixture is made into various shapes under pressure. Composites have properties similar to those of solid wood, but they are more decay resistant.

ENERGY EFFICIENCY

The energy efficiency of a window depends on more than one component. For example, a window with the most energy-efficient glazing

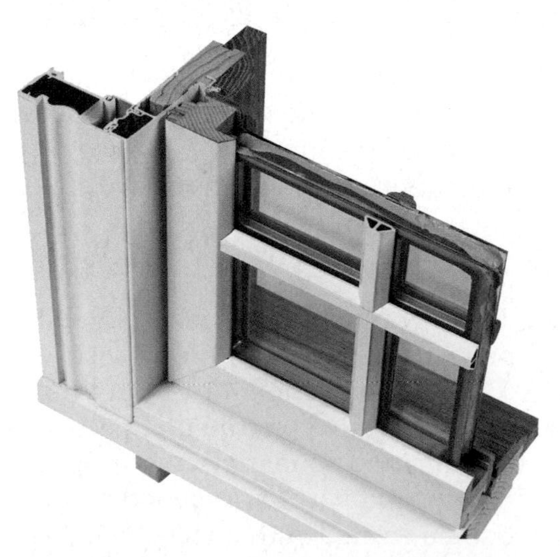

Fig. 28-14. A cutaway view of a structural PVC window.

would still be inefficient if faulty weatherstripping allowed heat loss around the sash.

Ratings

When choosing windows, compare independent ratings of overall performance. The most accurate ratings consider glazing, weatherstripping, materials, and construction. The National Fenestration Rating Council (NFRC) has developed a window rating system that considers solar heat gain, R-value (a measure of resistance to heat transfer), and air leakage. **Fig. 28-15.**

The rating numbers indicate the percentage of heating or cooling energy the window saves compared to an inefficient window with single glazing and an aluminum frame. The higher the number, the greater the savings.

Glazing

In most areas of the United States, building codes require that *insulating glass windows* be installed in new houses. Sometimes called *double-glazed windows*, they are made with two or more sheets of glass separated by an air space. The edges are sealed to trap the air between the sheets, which provides the insulation. **Fig. 28-16.** This type of window has more resistance to heat loss than one with a single sheet of glass. Insulating glass is used in both stationary and movable-sash windows.

In very cold climates, windows may even be triple glazed. The added airspace improves the energy efficiency of the window. Because triple-glazing can be expensive, it is important to balance its cost against the energy savings it delivers.

HEAT GAIN
SHGC = 0.39
39 percent of solar heat gain transmitted
VISIBLE LIGHT
VT = 0.70
70 percent of visible light transmitted

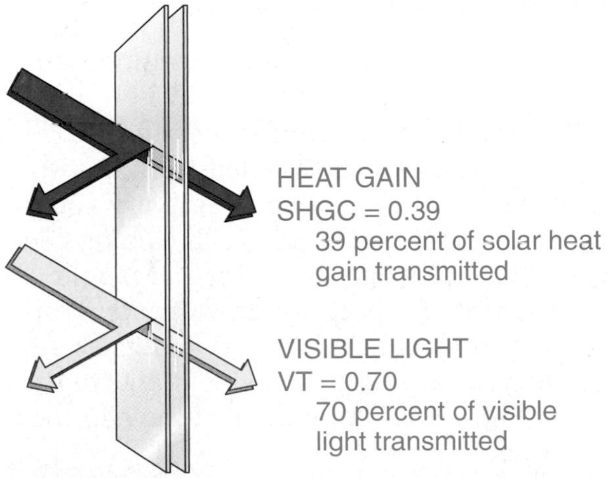

Fig. 28-15. Characteristics of one type of high-efficiency window. SHGC stands for solar heat gain coefficient, and VT stands for visible light transmission.

The type of glass used also affects energy performance. The following are available:

- *Low-e glazing.* Many window manufacturers offer *low-emissivity*, or *low-e, glazing.* Low-emissivity means that the glass radiates less heat to the outdoors than regular glass. For one common type, a special coating is applied directly to one of the glass surfaces facing the airspace. This coating reduces energy flow through the glazing by as much as 50 percent. Low-e glass can be useful in both warm and cool climates. **Fig. 28-17.**

Fig. 28-16. A cross-section view of an insulating glass window.

Fig. 28-17. Windows with low-e glazing come in many styles.

- *Heat-absorbing glazing.* This type of glass contains special tints (dyes) that enable it to absorb large amounts of solar energy. This is particularly helpful in cool climates.
- *Gas-filled glazing.* Energy efficiency is improved if the air between double-glazed panes is replaced with a denser gas that insulates better. Colorless gases such as argon and krypton are sometimes used.

Low-Conductance Spacers

In the 1960s and '70s, manufacturers used aluminum spacers to separate the two panes of double-glazed windows. Because aluminum is a good conductor of heat, these windows were not very efficient. Modern double-glazed windows use materials such as silicone foam or thermoplastics. These materials are sometimes referred to as *warm edge spacers.* They conduct less heat and improve the overall efficiency of a window.

Weatherstripping

The main purpose of *weatherstripping* around a window is to prevent air from leaking between the sash and the frame. Weatherstripping is made of various flexible materials, including foam and fibrous pile. Over time, weatherstripping can lose its effectiveness due to wear. Worn or damaged weatherstripping should be replaced. Weatherstripping should not be painted or stained.

SECTION 28.1 Check Your Knowledge

1. Why is it important for every bedroom to have at least one window or an exterior door?
2. Name the six basic types of windows.
3. What is a hybrid window?
4. What makes double-glazing more energy efficient than single-glazing?

On the Job

Interview someone at a local store that sells windows. Ask which types of window weatherstripping are most effective at reducing air leakage. Which types are easiest to replace if they become damaged? During the interview, be courteous and be sure to thank the person who helped you. Record your findings in a computer database that the class can access.

SECTION 28.2

Installing Windows

A **window schedule** is a portion of the building plans that contains descriptions of the windows, plus sizes for the glass, the sash, and sometimes the rough opening. The location of each window in a house is found by matching the number of the window in the window schedule with the corresponding number on the house plan. **Fig. 28-18.**

The width of a window's jambs must be the same dimension as the thickness of the wall, including the exterior sheathing and the interior finished wall covering. Window jambs are made of nominal 1″ or thicker lumber. The sills are made from nominal 2″ lumber and are sloped for good drainage. The sash is normally 1¾″ thick.

ROUGH-OPENING SIZES

Information about the rough-opening sizes for all windows in a house is needed when the walls are framed. When the rough-opening size is not on the plans, it can be obtained from the window manufacturer's catalog. Sizes vary somewhat among manufacturers. Each catalog contains tables showing four width and height measurements for each window: masonry opening, rough opening, frame size, and glass size. Some may also list the sash size. Refer to the table in **Fig. 28-19**. Note the headings in the top left corner:

- *Masonry* refers to the masonry opening. This is the size of the opening that should be used if the house is built using brick or stone.

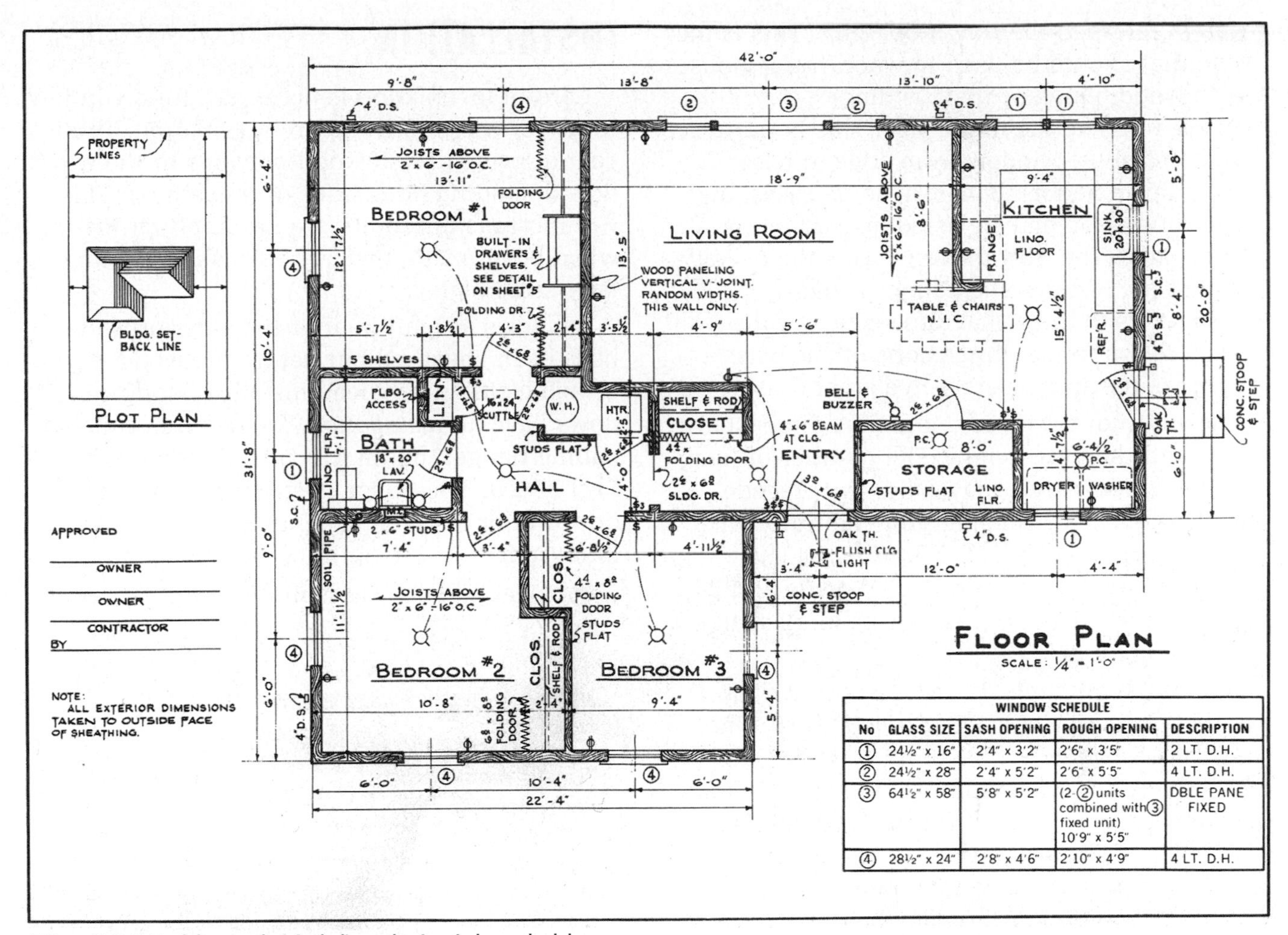

No	GLASS SIZE	SASH OPENING	ROUGH OPENING	DESCRIPTION
①	24½" x 16"	2'4" x 3'2"	2'6" x 3'5"	2 LT. D.H.
②	24½" x 28"	2'4" x 5'2"	2'6" x 5'5"	4 LT. D.H.
③	64½" x 58"	5'8" x 5'2"	(2-② units combined with ③ fixed unit) 10'9" x 5'5"	DBLE PANE FIXED
④	28½" x 24"	2'8" x 4'6"	2'10" x 4'9"	4 LT. D.H.

Fig. 28-18. A house plan, including a basic window schedule.

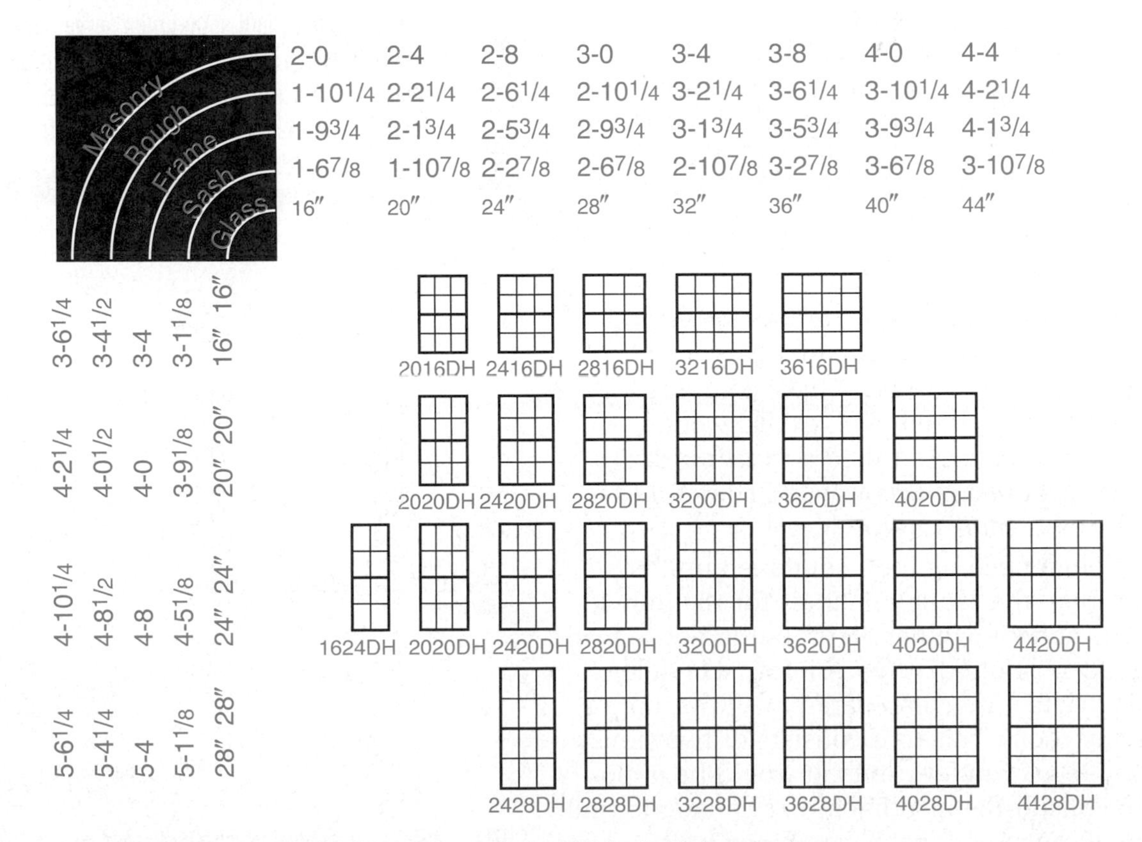

Fig. 28-19. An example of a manufacturer's size table for double-hung windows.

- *Rough* refers to the rough opening. This is the size that should be used in wood-frame houses with wood, vinyl, or metal siding.
- *Frame* refers to the frame size. This is the measurement of the window from edge to edge, excluding exterior casings. In some cases, the unit dimension may be listed instead of the frame size. The **unit dimension** is the overall size of the window, including casings.
- *Sash* refers to the actual dimensions of the sash.
- *Glass* refers to the dimensions of the glass, both visible and covered, in a single sash.

The width of the glass is the first dimension given, and then the height. The number of lights and the window style may follow or precede these dimensions. Consider, for example, this specification: *28½″ x 24″, 2 lights D.H.* This means that the glass itself is 28½″ wide and 24″ high and that there are two pieces of glass in a double-hung unit.

The rough opening size of a wood window can be figured if the glass size is known. The rough opening should be about 6″ wider and 10″ higher than the window glass size. To figure the rough-opening width for our example, add 6″ to the glass width: 28½″ + 6″ = 34½″, or 2′-10½″. To obtain the rough-opening height, add the upper and lower glass heights. Then add 10″: 24″ + 24″ + 10″ = 58″, or 4′-10″. These allowances are fairly standard. They provide room for plumbing, squaring, and normal adjustments. However, when the window manufacturer is known, use its recommended rough-opening sizes. Fig. 28-19. They will be more precise.

Combination Windows

Many times, windows of various styles and sizes are combined to make up a larger unit for a particular room and use. These combined units are separated only by vertical wood pieces. Such a piece is called a **mullion strip**. Windows grouped in this way are sometimes referred to as *mulled windows*.

The rough opening for a combined unit is smaller than the rough openings for the individual units added together. Refer to the house plan in Fig. 28-18. Note that the window schedule on the plan calls for a combination window unit in the living room. This unit consists of two No. 2 and one No. 3 window units. It would be important to consult the manufacturer's catalog to find the rough opening for this combined unit.

INSTALLATION

Careful installation is necessary for a window to perform properly. Before installation, apply a coat of primer to all wood portions of the window (including both sides of the jambs). This will increase durability. Do not apply primer to wood portions that will be varnished or similarly sealed later.

Windows are put in after the exterior walls have been sheathed but before the wood, vinyl, or metal siding has been installed. Many windows have an *installation flange*, often called a nailing flange, that makes installation easier. **Fig. 28-20.** The flange is either part of the window unit or made of separate pieces inserted into grooves in the outer face of the jamb.

See page 561 for steps in installing a window.

from Another Angle

During the manufacture of some windows, thick wood molding is permanently attached to the outer edges of the jambs. This molding is called brick mold or brick molding. Depending on the type of window, brick mold sometimes serves as a nailing flange. Casing nails may be driven through the brick mold and into the sheathing. Later, siding will be installed so that it butts up to the outer edges of the brick mold.

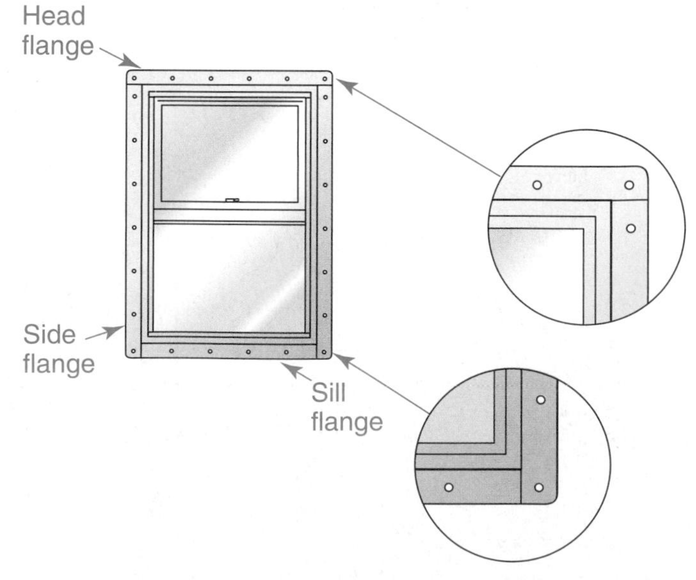

Fig. 28-20. Individual installation flanges on a double-hung window.

STEP BY STEP

Installing a Window

Window installation is a two- or three-person job. One installer works inside the house, while the others work outside.

Step 1 Prepare the window. Inspect the sash and frame for damage. If nailing flanges are separate pieces, insert them into their grooves. Tap them into place with a wood block and hammer. The head flange should overlap the side flanges. The side flanges should overlap the sill flange.

Step 2 The house might have been covered with housewrap. If so, make a horizontal knife cut in the housewrap just above the window. Then slip the top flange of the window under the resulting flap. If there is no housewrap in place, some builders staple lengths of felt paper (8″ x 12″ wide) to the sheathing around the opening. These are called *splines*. The upper splines must overlap those that are lower. This helps to drain any moisture that might later get behind the siding.

Step 3 Insert the window. Large or heavy windows should be lifted by at least two people. Place the frame in the opening from the outside, allowing the subsill to rest in the rough opening. Hold the window in place against the sheathing. Center it from side to side in the opening.

Step 4 Level the window sill by inserting blocks or tapered shims beneath it from inside the house. Place the shims or blocks near the corners of the window. **Fig. 28-21.** Check the window for plumb.

Step 5 When the window is plumb and level, nail through the flange at one corner, using a 1¾″ roofing nail. Check the window again to be sure it is plumb and level. Check it for squareness by measuring diagonally across the corners. If the two measurements are the same, the window is square. **Fig. 28-22.** If the window is not square, shim the side jambs as needed. Then recheck plumb and level. Measure across the window at the top, bottom, and center. Measurements should be equal. **Fig. 28-23.**

Step 6 Nail each corner of the installation flange to secure the window. Check the window for easy operation. Then nail the entire perimeter of the installation flange. Space roofing nails every 6″ to 8″ or as recommended by the manufacturer. Remove any packing.

Step 7 From inside, fill gaps between the jamb and the framing with fiberglass insulation or expanding foam sealant. Do not use too much insulation or the jambs will bow inward, and the window will not open properly.

Standard Windows

Most window frames are installed in the same general way, regardless of style or manufacturer. However, always refer to the manufacturer's instructions for recommendations. For example, some manufacturers recommend that the sash be removed from the frame to prevent breakage and allow easier handling. Others specify not only that the sash be left in the frame but also that diagonal braces and, in some cases, reinforcing blocks be left in place. This ensures that the frame remains square and in proper alignment during installation. The sash locks must also be engaged.

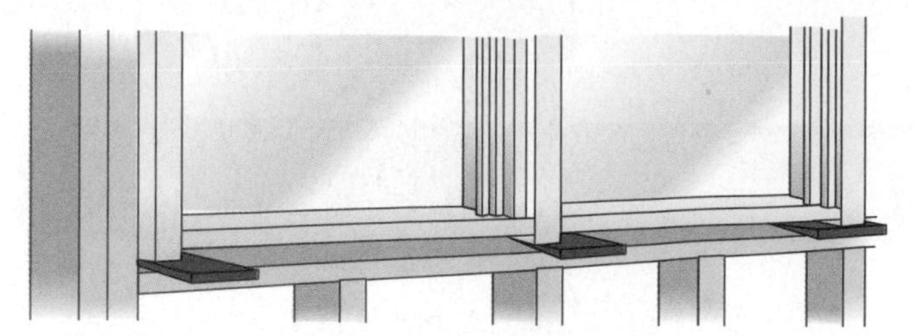

Fig. 28-21. Shim under the raised jamb legs and at the center of wide windows.

Fig. 28-22. When the diagonal measurements are equal, the unit is square.

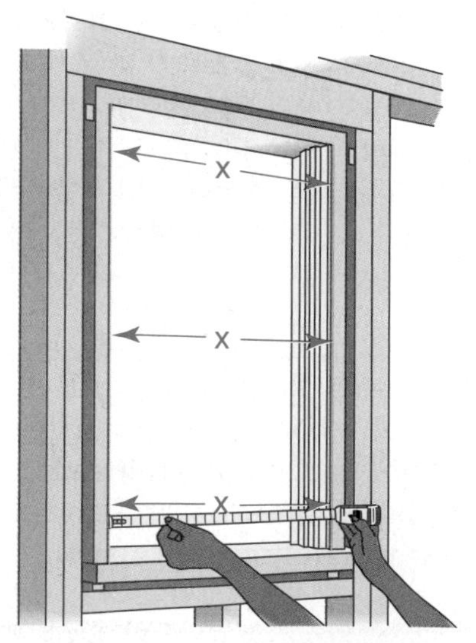

Fig. 28-23. Measure the distance between the side jambs to be sure they are equidistant at all points.

Fig. 28-24. Using metal jamb clips for masonry.

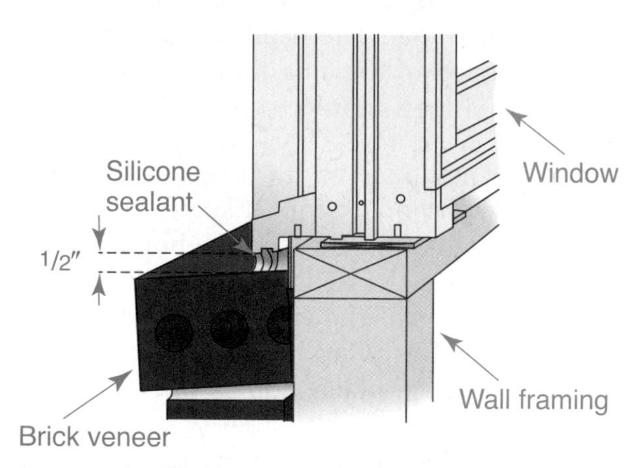

Fig. 28-25. Window installation in brick-veneer construction.

Another difference concerns the method for adding flashing to a window. The traditional technique is to use 8″ wide splines of 15 lb. building paper. The bottom spline is installed first, then the sides, then the top piece. These are overlapped and stapled around the opening before the window is installed. However, many builders are now using strips of flexible, self-adhesive flashing instead. These strips are made of either butyl rubber or modified bitumen (*rubberized asphalt*). Check with the window supplier to see which method is recommended.

Windows in Masonry Walls

Window manufacturers specify methods for installing their windows into masonry walls, such as those of brick veneer. A common method is to replace the installation flanges on the windows with metal jamb clips. **Fig. 28-24.** The clips are screwed to the window jambs. They are then nailed into furring strips or connected directly to masonry fasteners. There should be at least ½″ clearance from the top of the masonry to the bottom of the sill. **Fig. 28-25.**

Basement Windows

Basement window units are made of wood, plastic, or metal. In most cases, the sash is removed from the frame. The frame is set into the concrete forms for a poured wall. The wall is poured with the window frame in place. If the windows are to be set into a concrete block wall, special blocks accommodate the various types of frames. The floor framing is then constructed. The sills are usually installed later.

Skylights

Skylights can be installed in either pitched or flat roofs to provide ventilation and light. **Fig. 28-26.** There are two basic types: fixed skylights and ventilating skylights. *Fixed skylights* cannot be opened. They are generally less expensive and easier to install. *Ventilating skylights* swing open on hinges. They can allow heated air to escape the house in hot weather. They can also funnel cooling breezes inside.

The glazing in a skylight is glass or plastic that is either flat or domed. A skylight with flat glazing is sometimes called a *roof window*. Skylights should be double glazed to reduce heat loss. Some skylights include triple glazing or high-performance glazing with a low-e coating.

Some skylights are complete units, ready to set into the roof. Others must rest on a lumber *curb* that lifts them above the level of the roof. **Fig. 28-27.**

Fig. 28-26. A ventilating skylight. Note that the flashing extends over the shingles below the skylight.

Because skylights are often high in a ceiling, they can be fitted with small motors that open and close them. The motors are controlled electronically from below. Rough wiring is put in before finished wall and ceiling surfaces are installed. Skylights without motors can be opened and closed with long poles or cranks. **Fig. 28-28.**

Fig. 28-27. Some skylights rest on a wood curb. The curb may be supplied by the skylight manufacturer, or it may be constructed on site from 2x6 lumber.

Fig. 28-28. This ventilating skylight can be opened and closed from below with a telescoping hand crank.

Skylight Flashing. Because of the skylight's position on the roof, proper flashing is very important to prevent leaks. The most durable flashing is made of copper, but aluminum flashing is more commonly used because it is much less expensive.

There are two methods of installing skylight flashing. *Step flashing* uses small pieces of L-shaped metal that are interwoven with the roof shingles. **Fig. 28-29.** For *pan flashing*, a one-piece metal assembly called a *pan* fits over the skylight curb. **Fig. 28-30.** It must be fabricated by a sheet metal shop for a specific size of skylight. After pan flashing is in place, the roof shingles are installed.

It is also possible to install a skylight in a tile roof. In such cases, flexible lead step flashing is often used.

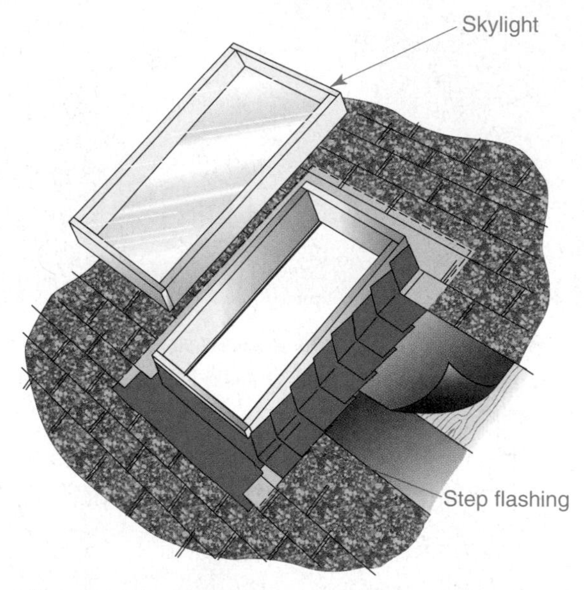

Fig. 28-29. Like shingles, each piece of step flashing overlaps another to shed water.

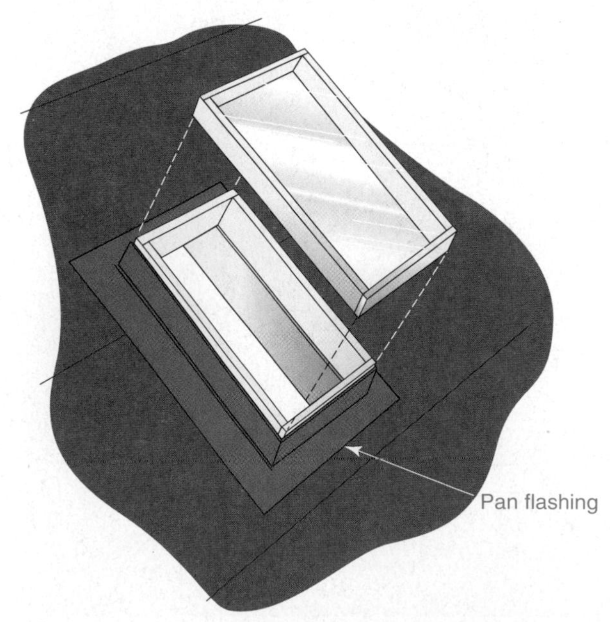

Fig. 28-30. Seams in pan flashing should be soldered to prevent leakage.

ESTIMATING COSTS

The cost of an individual window unit depends on its quality, style, glass, frame material, and any factory-applied finish. To determine an accurate cost, a complete list of the windows should be submitted to the supplier for pricing.

The labor required for installing and setting windows depends on their size and style. The approximate time can be estimated as follows based on window size:

- Up to 10 sq. ft. of glass area: 1 hr.
- Up to 20 sq. ft. of glass area: 1½ hrs.
- Over 20 sq. ft. of glass area: 2 hrs.

These estimates include only the preparation of the opening and the actual installation of the window unit. They do not include installation of interior trim.

SECTION 28.2 Check Your Knowledge

1. Name two places where you can find dimensions for the rough opening of a window.
2. Describe the two types of installation flange.
3. What is a mullion strip?
4. Describe the difference between step flashing and pan flashing for skylights.

On the Job

Choose two manufacturers from among those advertising in a consumer or professional building-industry magazine. Contact them either by mail or via the Internet to obtain a rough-opening table for their line of double-hung windows. Use the correct form for your letter. Check spelling and grammar. Keep the material you receive in a file folder titled "Window Rough Openings." Photocopy the table and place the copy in a notebook that the class can use for reference.

Chapter 28 Review

Section Summaries

28.1 A single house has various types and sizes of windows. The six basic types include double-hung, casement, stationary, awning, hopper, and horizontal-sliding windows. The energy efficiency of a window depends not just on the glazing, but also on other features.

28.2 A window schedule gives important specifications. Window installation requires two or more people. The care with which a window is installed has a large impact on its ability to prevent air and water leaks.

Review Questions

1. The total area of window glass in a room should be not less than what percentage of the floor area?
2. List at least two of the four basic characteristics required of an egress window.
3. List the six major types of windows.
4. How are casement windows similar to awning and hopper windows?
5. List the disadvantages of metal windows for cold climates.
6. Define the term *low-e*.
7. What can be done to improve the performance of double-glazing?
8. Window manufacturers often list *glass size* in their size tables. What does this refer to?
9. What is the difference between a mullion and a muntin?
10. What type and dimension of fastener is used to secure the nailing flanges of a window?

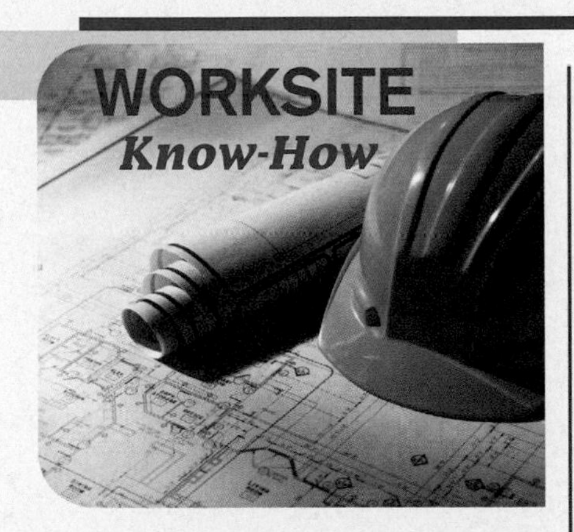

Window Ratings Heat transfer through windows is expressed in U-values, or U-factors. U-values are like the R-values for insulation, except they are reversed. A lower U-value indicates *less* heat loss or gain and *greater* insulating performance. The solar-heat-gain coefficient (SHGC) is another useful rating. It expresses the amount of solar heat that passes through a window. Its scale goes from 0 (zero), for none, to 1, for 100 percent of available solar heat. Numbers in between are given in decimals, such as 0.55. Visible transmittance (VT) is a number that indicates how easy a window is to see through and how well it admits daylight. For example, tinted glass may be rated as 15 percent VT and clear glass as 90 percent VT.

Chapter 29 Residential Doors

Objectives

After reading this chapter, you'll be able to:

- Identify the various types of interior and exterior doors and door hardware.
- Handle a door properly at a job site.
- Identify the hand of any door.
- List at least three aspects of exterior door construction and installation that improve energy efficiency.
- Install an interior prehung door.

Terms

door frame
gain
hollow-core construction
lockset
passage door
rails
solid-core construction
stiles
strike plate

A door has many functions. It guards a building and its possessions, ensures privacy, protects against the weather, and lends beauty and character to the home's architecture.

At one time there were few kinds of residential doors. Today, however, builders and carpenters can choose from many different designs, materials, assembly techniques, and sizes.

SECTION 29.1

Door Basics

All doors require mounting hardware, such as hinges and tracks. They also require hardware for using them, such as knobs or pulls.

TYPES OF DOORS

Doors can be categorized by the following:

- Location (exterior or interior).
- Material from which they are made (wood, fiberglass, vinyl, metal, and so on).
- Operation (hinged doors, sliding doors, folding doors).
- End use (new construction or replacement).
- Purpose (closet doors, garage doors, fire doors).
- Construction (solid core, foam core, hollow core).
- Style (raised panel, flat panel, arched top).
- Installation method (pre-hung, hung on site).

Any door can be described using a combination of these characteristics. For example, a door may be a pre-hung, exterior, hinged, wood door having a raised panel.

The most common type is a flat-panel or raised-panel passage door. A panel is a wide piece of solid wood or plywood. A **passage door** swings open and closed on two or more leaf hinges mounted along one side. It allows passage from one area into another. It has two doorknobs, a latching mechanism, and sometimes a locking mechanism. The *latch* slips into a hole in a metal **strike plate**, which is inserted into an opening in the door jamb. The latch holds the door closed.

An exterior passage door is often surrounded by moldings that emphasize the architectural style of the house. This is particularly common on houses with traditional styling. **Fig. 29-1.**

A

B

Fig. 29-1. Styles of doors. *A.* A double door with glazing. *B.* An entry door with sidelights and an arched transom.

Flat-Panel Doors

Flat-panel doors are sometimes referred to as *flush doors* or *slab doors.* Their entire surface is flat. They are made with plywood, hardboard, metal, or some other suitable facing applied over a light framework and core.

Cores are either solid or hollow. **Fig. 29-2.** **Solid-core construction** consists of strips of wood, particleboard, rigid foam, or other core material covered with a thin outer material, such as wood veneer. Solid-core construction reduces warping and is generally preferred for exterior doors. It is also more fire-resistant than hollow-core doors. **Hollow-core construction** consists of a light framework of wood or corrugated cardboard faced with thin plywood or hardboard. Plywood-faced flush doors usually have surface veneers of birch, oak, or mahogany. Most of these are suitable for natural finishes. Other wood veneers are usually painted, as are hardboard-faced doors.

Raised-Panel Doors

Raised-panel wood doors have panels that are thicker at the center than at the edges. They consist of **stiles** (vertical side members), **rails** (horizontal crosspieces), and the raised panels that fill the spaces between. **Fig. 29-3.**

Stiles and rails are generally made of solid wood. The panels may be made of solid wood or plywood.

Door Frames

A door is mounted on a door frame, which is attached to the wall framing. The **door frame** consists of two side jambs and a head jamb. **Fig. 29-4.** It is the surrounding assembly into which the door fits. Exterior door frames may also include a sill or threshold. Molding is usually nailed to the door frame on the inside of the house after the frame is installed. Exterior molding and wood stops are sometimes attached by the door manufacturer. However, they are often installed on site.

The door jambs fit inside the rough opening. They are installed so that their outer edges will be flush with the finished wall surface. A standard interior jamb is 4$\frac{9}{16}$" wide. **Fig. 29-5.** Jambs are manufactured in standard widths to suit various wall thicknesses. However, wood jambs may be easily cut to fit. If the wall is unusually thick, strips of wood called *jamb*

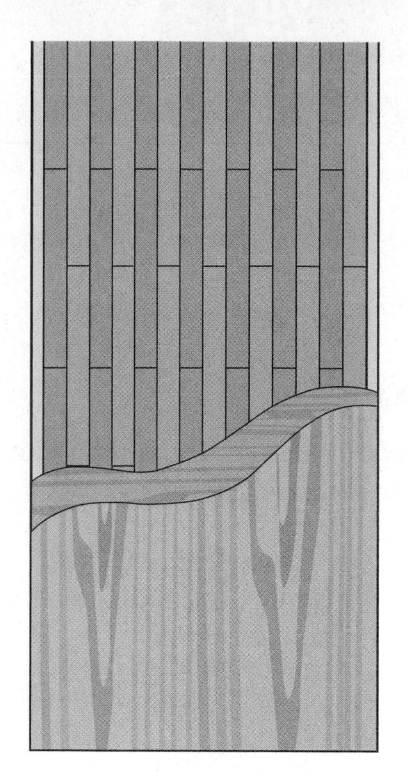

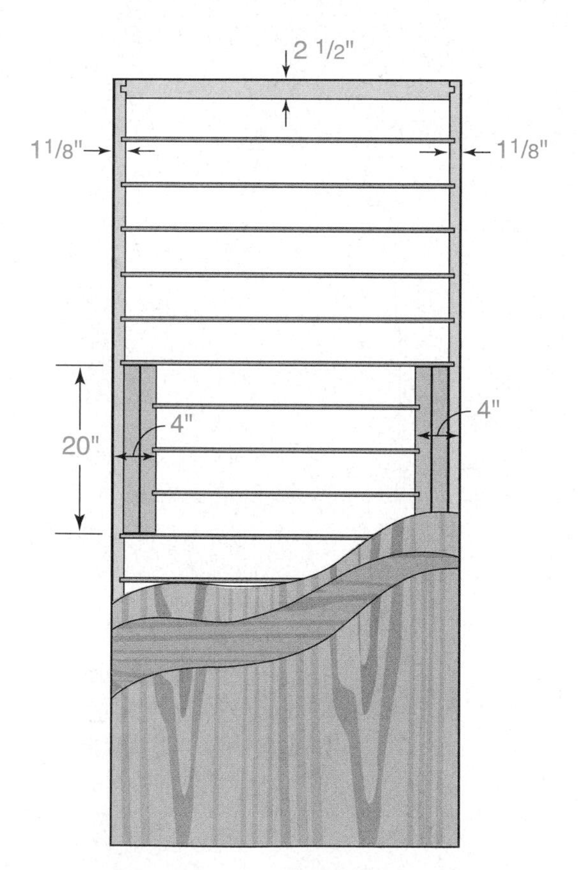

Fig. 29-2. The core construction of a flat-panel door varies with the manufacturer. Note the built-up areas at the edges near the middle of the hollow-core door. These provide solid backing for the lock. Solid wood around the edge allows a carpenter to trim the door to fit the opening.

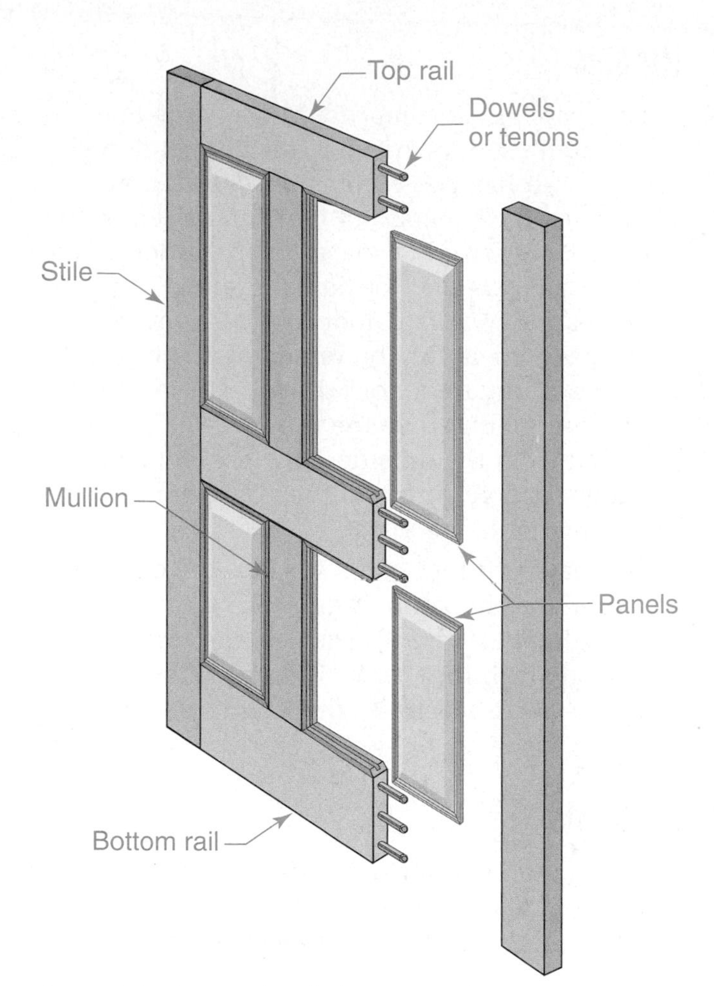

Fig. 29-3. Anatomy of a raised-panel wood door.

extensions are nailed to the edges of the jamb to make it wider. Jambs may also be custom-made to any size.

Wood is the traditional material used for jambs. However, metal is not uncommon in a residential building, particularly when the door itself is metal. When exterior door frames include a sill, it is usually made of oak (for wear resistance) or aluminum.

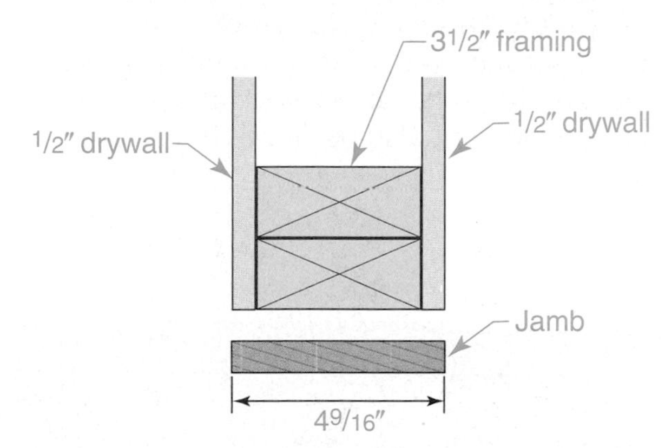

Fig. 29-5. The width of an interior door jamb should match the overall thickness of the wall.

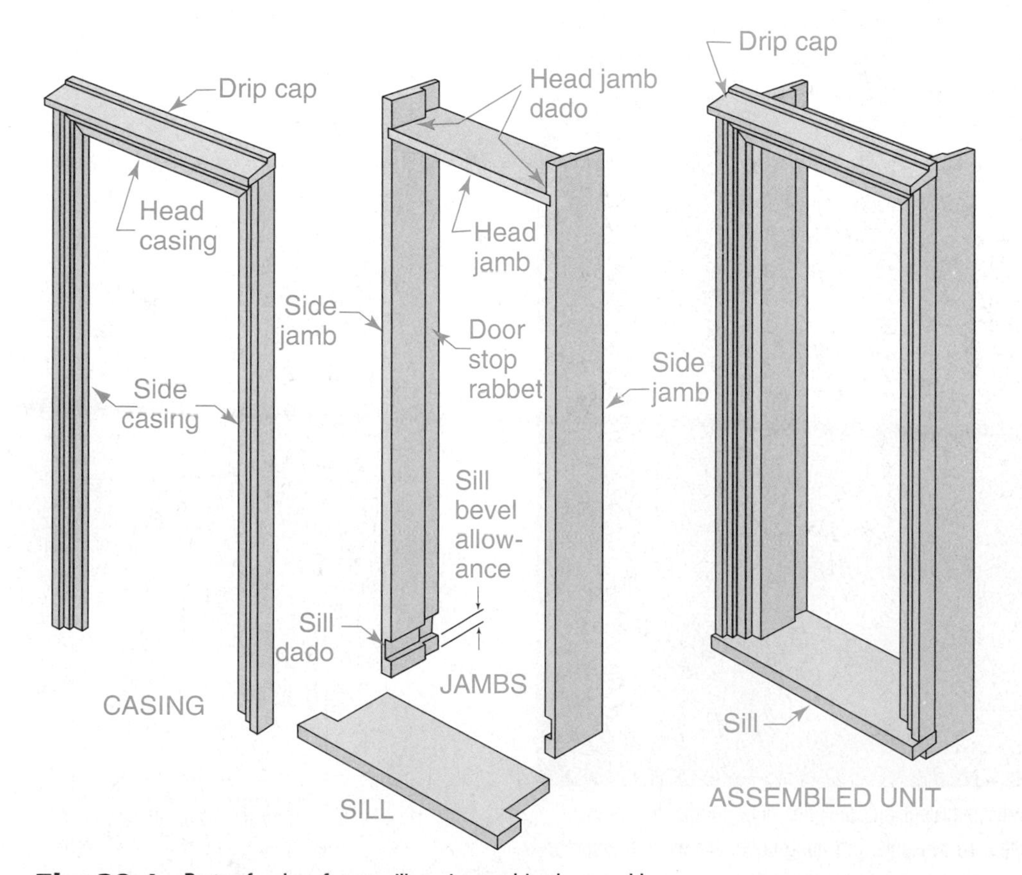

Fig. 29-4. Parts of a door frame: sill, casing, and jamb assembly.

Door frames may be purchased knocked down or preassembled with just the exterior casing or brick molding applied. Brick molding is a type of exterior casing. In some cases, door frames come preassembled with the door already hung in the opening. **Fig. 29-6.** These are called *pre-hung doors.*

HARDWARE

Hardware for doors is made using various metals and finishes. Steel, brass, bronze, and nickel are perhaps the most common. The type of metal and its finish affect not only how the hardware looks, but also its durability and cost.

Fig. 29-6. A pre-hung door unit includes door, jambs, and hinges. Many sizes and styles are available. Pre-hung doors are used in commercial construction as well as residential construction.

Hinges

The *loose-pin butt mortise* hinge is the one most often used for hanging residential doors. **Fig. 29-7.** It has two rectangular *leaves* that pivot on a loose metal pin that can be removed. One leaf is screwed to the edge of the door. The other leaf is screwed to the door jamb. The pin connects the two. The door may be removed from the jamb simply by removing the hinge pins and lifting the door out. On exterior doors, hinges are mounted so the pins cannot be removed from the outside. This prevents an intruder from getting into the house simply by removing the hinge pins.

The leaves fit into gains cut into the edge of the door and the jamb. A **gain** is a mortise (notch) that has a depth equal to the thickness of a single leaf. **Fig. 29-8.** The size of a loose-pin butt mortise hinge is the length of a leaf in inches.

Locksets

Passage doors are fitted with different types of opening hardware. **Fig. 29-9.** The assembly of knobs, latch, and locking mechanism is called

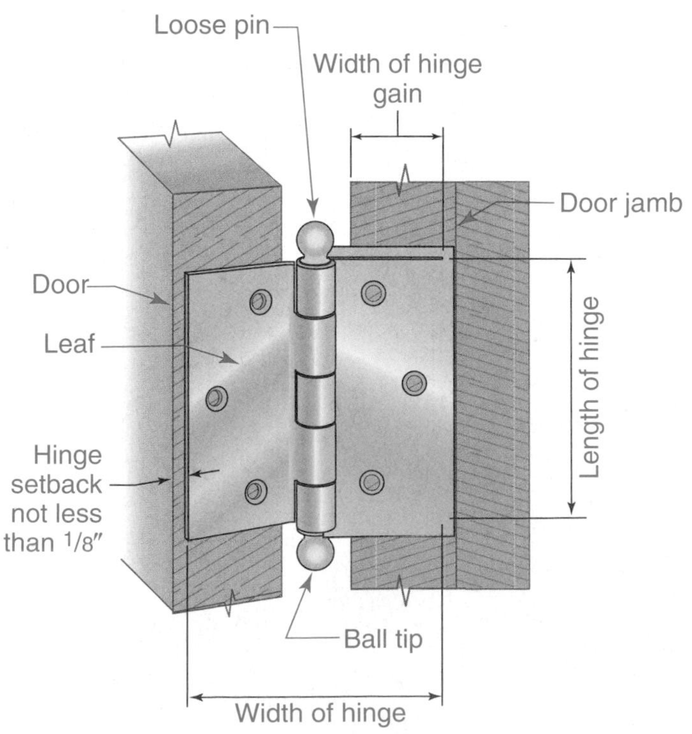

Fig. 29-7. A loose-pin butt mortise hinge.

a **lockset**. In some cases, lever handles replace the knobs. Lever handles are easier to use for people with limited strength or dexterity.

Locksets are available in three basic types: entry, privacy, and passage. *Bored locks* fit into a large hole bored into the face of the door stile. *Mortise locks* fit into a large notch cut into the edge of the door stile.

Entry Locksets. These are used on exterior doors and contain a locking mechanism and key. They may be of the bored or mortise type.

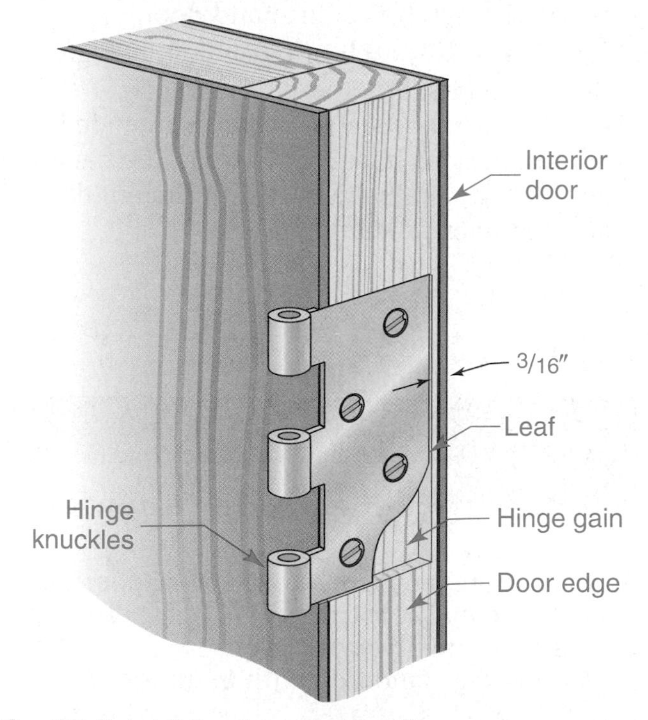

Fig. 29-8. Installation of a standard door hinge.

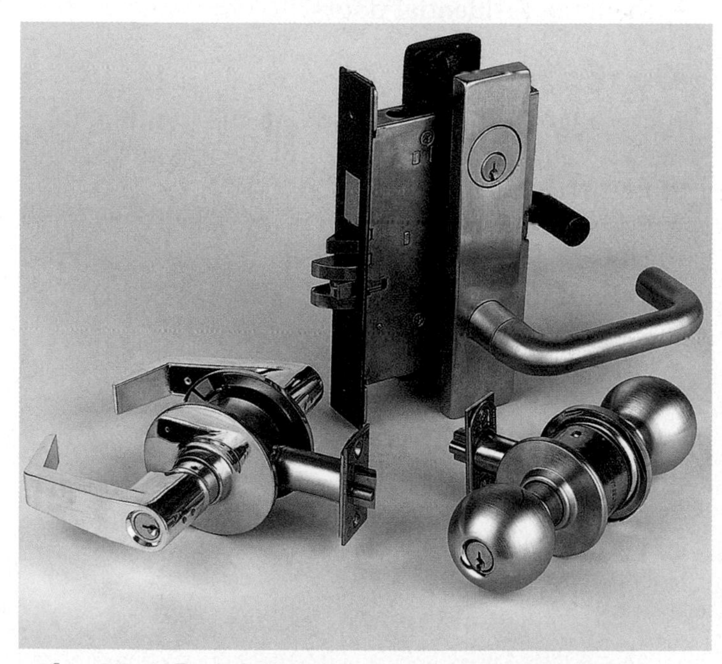

Fig. 29-9. Two locksets with lever handles and one with knobs.

Privacy Locksets. These light-duty locksets are used on doors leading to bedrooms and bathrooms. They can be locked from the inside by pressing or turning a button in the knob. There is usually a small slot or hole in the non-locking knob. A small screwdriver inserted in the hole pops the lock open. This is a safety feature that allows the door to be opened from the outside in an emergency. All privacy locksets are of the bored type.

Passage Locksets. These are sometimes referred to as *latchsets*. They are similar in design to privacy locksets but do not include a locking mechanism. They are often used on closet doors.

STORAGE AND HANDLING

Proper care and finishing of a door will ensure the most service and satisfaction. Proper door care includes the following:

- Wood doors should not be delivered to the house until wet materials, such as plaster and concrete, have given up most of their moisture. Otherwise, the doors can swell and will not fit properly.
- Keep all doors away from unusual heat or dryness. Sudden changes, such as heat forced into a building to dry it out, should be avoided.
- Store doors under cover in a clean, dry, well-ventilated area.
- Condition wood doors to the average local moisture content before hanging (see Chapter 16, "Wood As a Building Material").
- Store doors on edge on a level surface.
- Handle doors wearing clean gloves. Bare hands leave finger marks and soil stains on surfaces that have not yet been sealed or painted. When moving a door, carry it. Do not drag it.
- Seal the top and bottom edges of wood doors immediately to prevent moisture from reaching end grain. Seal the wood as soon as possible after the doors have been installed.

SAFETY FIRST

Carrying a Door

All doors are unwieldy to carry, particularly pre-hung units. Solid-core doors are very heavy. Get help when moving a door. This will reduce the chance of strained muscles and any damage to the door or finished wall surfaces.

DIRECTION OF SWING

When ordering and installing a door, it is important to know the direction in which the door should swing. A door that opens in the wrong direction may interfere with wall switches, cabinetry, and traffic patterns. The direction in which a door swings is called its *hand*. Doors are either left hand or right hand.

SINGLE DOOR

Hand of door may be determined by referring to sketches below. Door must always swing away from the point from which it is viewed.

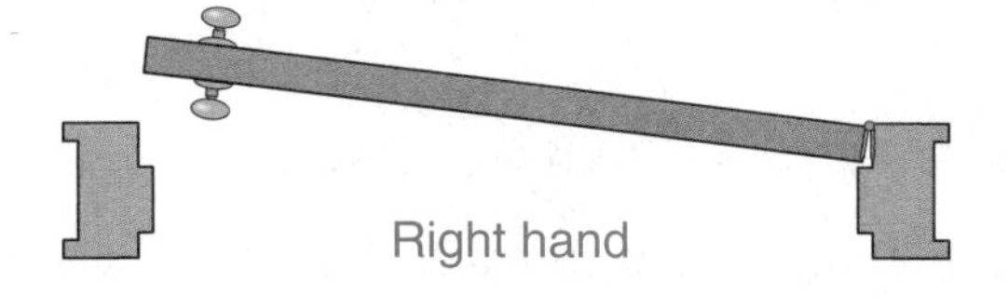

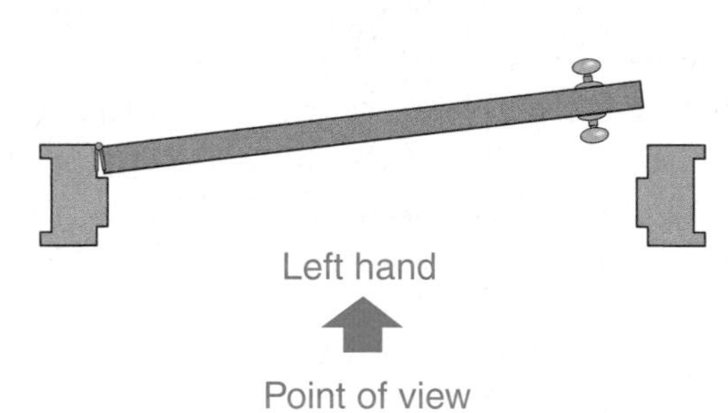

PAIRS OF DOORS

Hand of doors is determined by location of active leaf when doors swing away from point viewed.

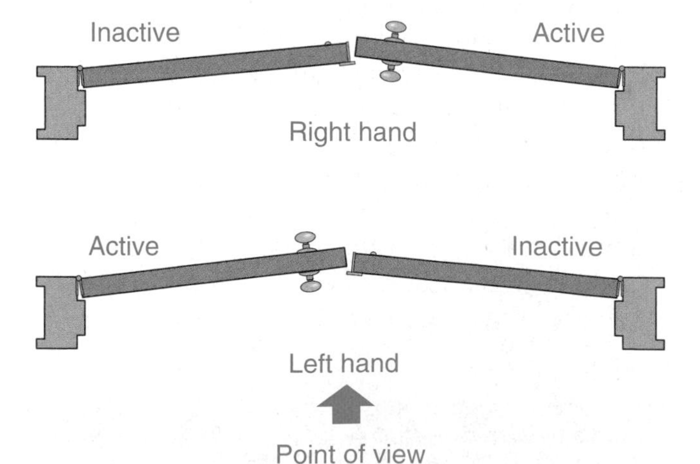

Fig. 29-10. Determining the hand of a door.

Unfortunately, there are several methods commonly used to determine the hand of a door. Some of them contradict each other.

- *Method 1.* Stand with your back against the hinge jamb. A door that swings toward your right is a right-hand door. One that swings to your left is a left-hand door. **Fig. 29-10.**
- *Method 2.* Face the inside of a closed door. In general, the inside of the door is the side from which the hinge knuckles are visible when the door is closed. If the hinges are on the right side of the door, it is a right-hand door. If they are on the left, it is a left-hand door.

As you can see, each of these methods gives different results. It is therefore important to make sure you understand what is intended when ordering or installing a door. The hand of a door will generally be noted on the building plans and door schedules.

SECTION 29.1 Check Your Knowledge

1. What is the most common type of door used in residential construction?
2. Describe a hollow-core door.
3. What is the standard width of an interior door jamb?
4. What type of hinge is most often used for hanging residential doors?

On the Job

Make a table listing the doors in the building in which you live. Include the following information for each door listed:

- Type of lockset.
- The hand of the door.
- Type of door.
- Location of door.
- Purpose of door.

Compare your table with the table of a classmate. What do the types of doors tell you about the use of the structure?

Exterior Doors and Frames

Many combinations of door and entry designs, trim, and decorative elements are available. **Fig. 29-11.** Care should be taken to select a door that is correct for the architectural style of the house. Strength, durability, and energy efficiency are also important characteristics of exterior doors.

Metal exterior doors are durable. They usually have cores made of rigid insulation. In cold weather, they greatly reduce the amount of heat loss. In hot weather, they reduce the amount of heat gain. **Fig. 29-12.**

Exterior doors are usually 1¾″ thick and not less than 6′-8″ high. The main entrance door is required by building codes to be at least 3′ wide, but a side or rear service door may be 2′-8″ wide. A hardwood or metal threshold helps to prevent water from getting under a door. It also serves as a base for weatherstripping. **Fig. 29-13.**

Fig. 29-12. Energy-efficient steel or fiberglass exterior doors are insulated with rigid foam. In this door wood stops hold glazing in place.

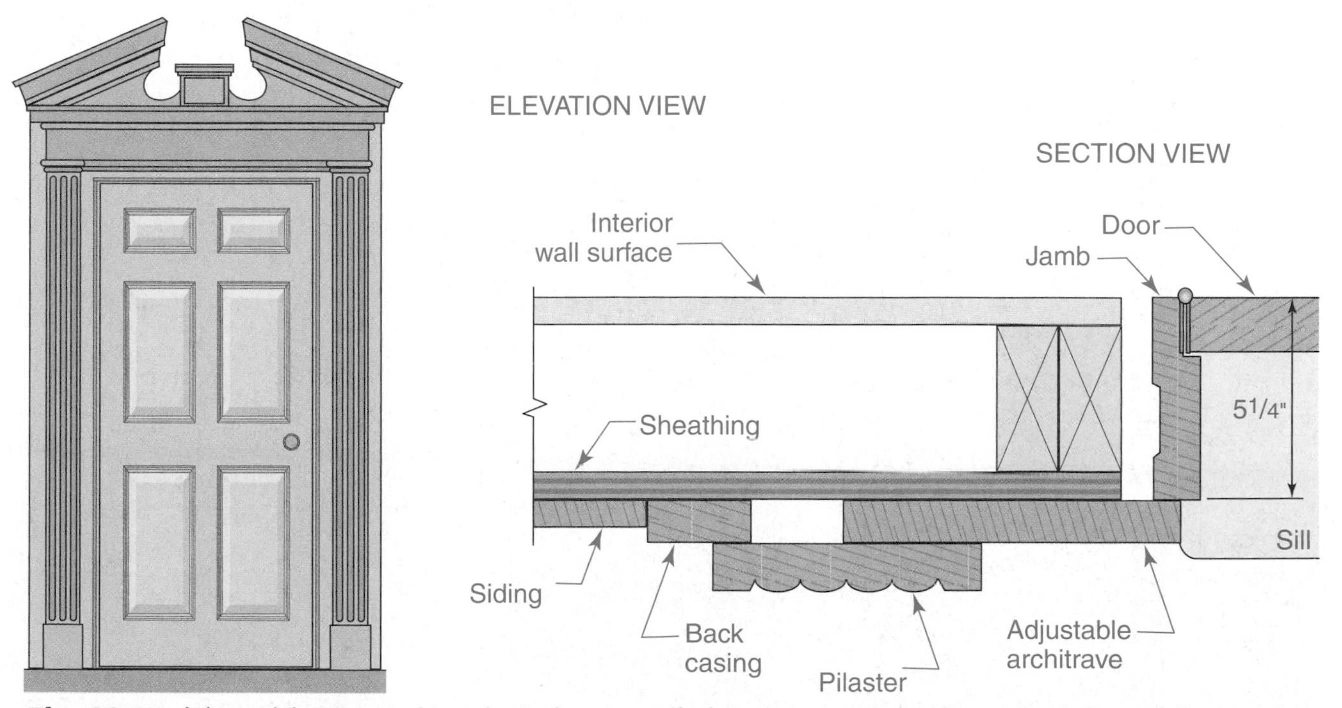

Fig. 29-11. A door and the trim around it can be simple or ornate. (A pilaster is a column built within a wall and often extending beyond the wall. An architrave is a beam that rests atop columns.)

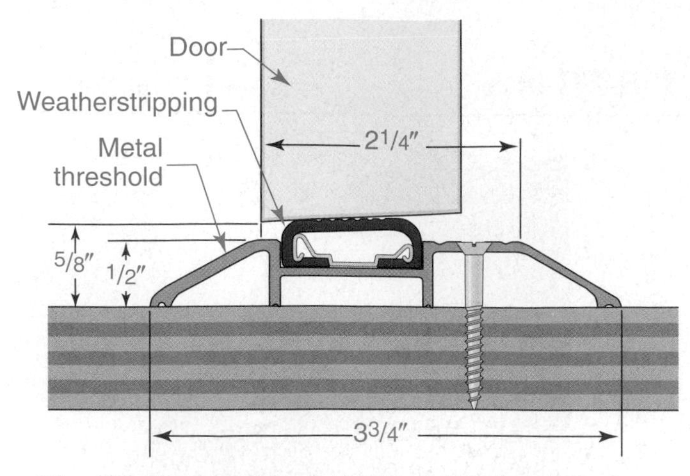

Fig. 29-13. A metal threshold with a vinyl weatherstripping insert.

Lightweight screen or storm doors are often attached to the frame of an exterior door. Screen doors allow extra ventilation during hot weather. Storm doors protect the main door from weather damage and reduce heat loss in cold weather. Combination storm and screen doors are the most common. The screen panel and the storm panel may be exchanged as needed. **Figure 29-14** shows design details that include a combination door.

TYPES OF EXTERIOR DOORS

Exterior doors share styling and many features with interior doors. However, some features are found only in exterior doors.

Following are several special types of exterior doors.

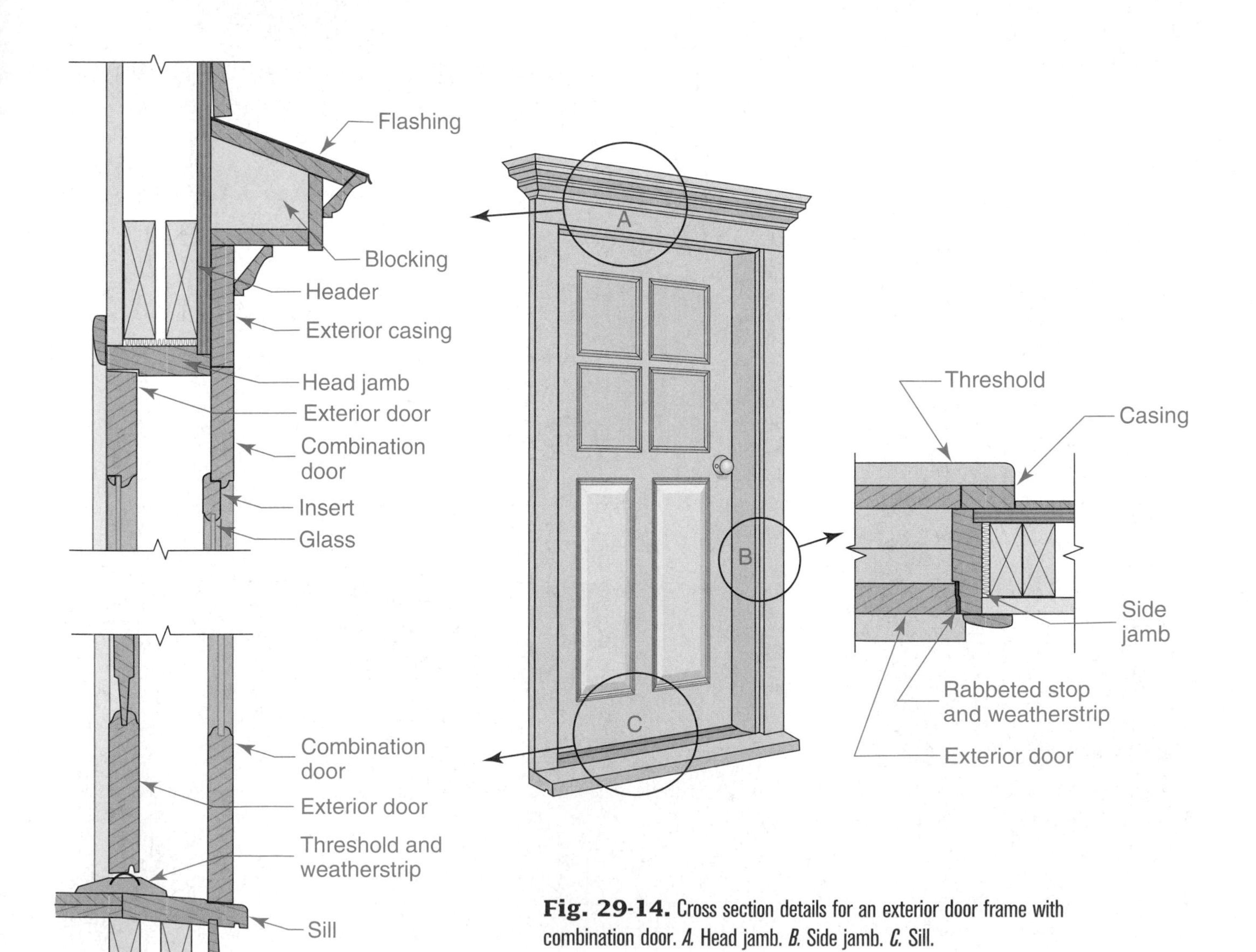

Fig. 29-14. Cross section details for an exterior door frame with combination door. *A.* Head jamb. *B.* Side jamb. *C.* Sill.

Sliding-Glass Doors

Sliding-glass, or *patio, doors* are available with either wood, vinyl, or metal frames. **Fig. 29-15.** Insulating glazing helps limit heat loss, but these doors are not as energy efficient as other types.

One side of the door is usually stationary; the other side slides. Door operation may be right- or left-hand (as viewed from the outside). Doors are available in widths from 30″ to 120″.

French Doors

French doors are hung in pairs on hinges located at each side of the door opening. The doors swing toward each other and meet at the center. **Fig. 29-16.** French doors are usually fully glazed and often lead to a deck or patio. They can swing into the room or out. When both sides of the door are open, the area between the jambs is unobstructed and unusually wide.

Molding with a T-shaped profile is attached to the edge of one of the doors. This provides a stop against which the other door closes. Because there is no framing in the middle of the opening, sealing exterior French doors against the weather can be difficult.

Glazed Doors

Glazed doors consist of a framework of stiles and rails. The space in between is divided into lights by bars called *muntins.* (A *light* is a panel of glass, like that used in window construction.) Glazed doors are often used wherever daylight is needed in the area near the door. For example, in a house with no windows in the entry hall, it is often helpful to have glass in the main door. The glass portion is often decorative. **Fig. 29-17.**

Fig. 29-16. A pair of French doors.

Fig. 29-15. A wood sliding-glass door with muntins.

Fig. 29-17. A glazed solid-wood entry door with two side lights.

According to building codes, doors are a hazardous location for glazing. For this reason, glazing in any door must be shatter resistant. Each light must be permanently marked at the factory to indicate its suitability for use in hazardous locations. The mark is etched or sandblasted into a corner of the glass, where it will not be covered by muntins.

Fire-Rated Doors

Fire-rated doors are built to *resist* the passage of fire. These doors are not fireproof. They withstand fire only long enough for occupants to reach safety. Though more commonly used in commercial construction, fire-rated doors are suitable for some places in a house. For example, building codes require that any door between a house and an attached garage have one of the following characteristics:

- A 20-minute fire rating.
- Solid wood construction not less than 1⅜″ thick.
- Solid-core or honeycomb-core steel construction not less than 1⅜″ thick.

Fire doors generally should not be trimmed in the field. This could affect their fire-rating.

Garage Doors

The unusually large openings in garages require special types of doors. The standard single garage door is 9′ wide and 7′ high. Double garage doors are usually 16′ wide. The opening is lined with wood jambs, much as the opening for other doors. However, the jambs are made from 2x6 or sometimes ¾x6 lumber. The jambs are nailed directly to the rough opening.

The most widely used garage door in new construction is the overhead sectional door shown in **Fig. 29-18**. The four or five sections are hinged together. They may be made of wood, steel, or fiberglass. Some models contain a core of rigid foam insulation. This protects the garage from severe temperature swings as well as too much heat or cold. Rollers on the ends of each section ride in a metal track at the side of the opening. **Fig. 29-19.** Mounting clearance required above the top of sectional overhead doors is usually about 12″. However, low-headroom brackets are available when such clearance is not possible. Overhead doors are usually installed by the door supplier.

The bottom edge of a garage door should be scribed and cut to conform to the garage floor. Weatherstripping is recommended for the bottom rail. It seals any minor irregularities in the floor and acts as a cushion in closing. The header over the door opening may be a steel I-beam, built-up framing lumber, a glulam beam, or laminated-veneer lumber (LVL). Sizing charts for garage-door headers are found in building code books and in instructions provided by header manufacturers.

Fig. 29-18. An overhead sectional garage door.

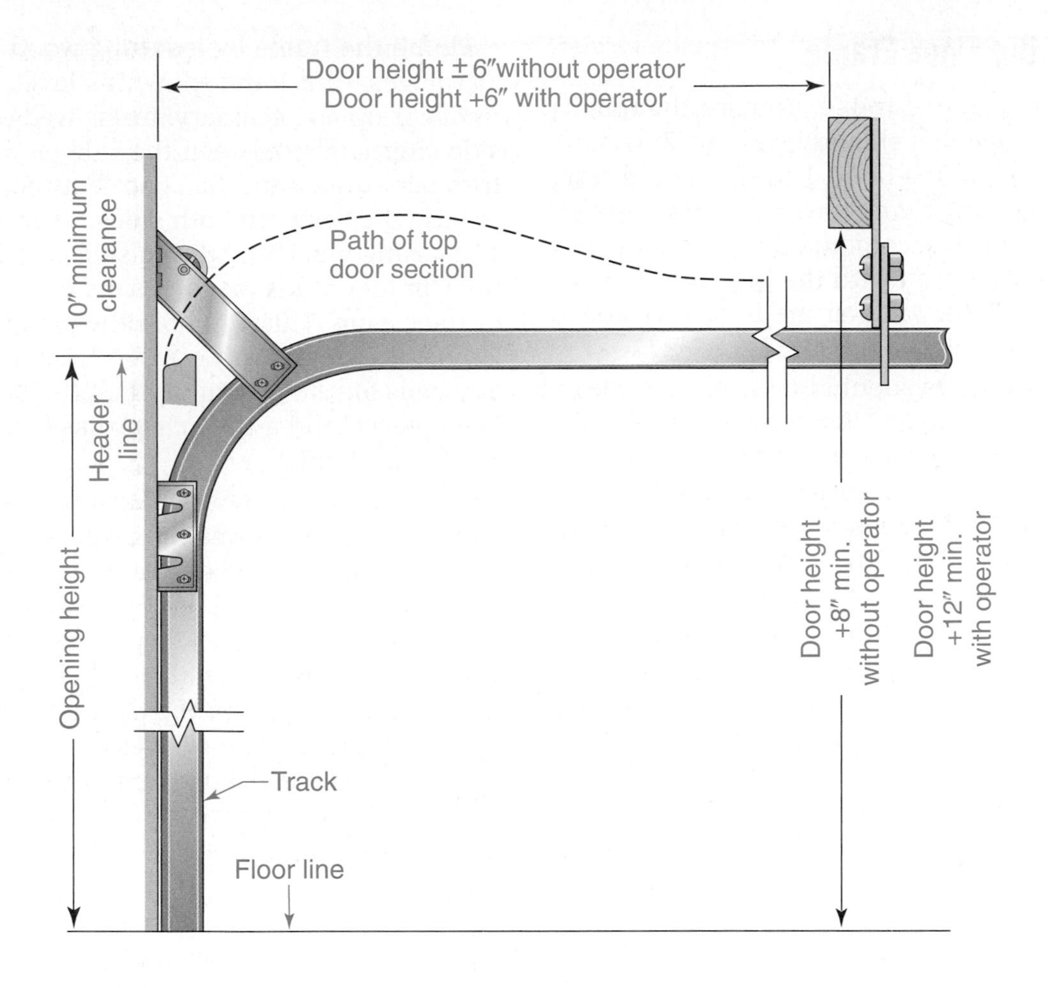

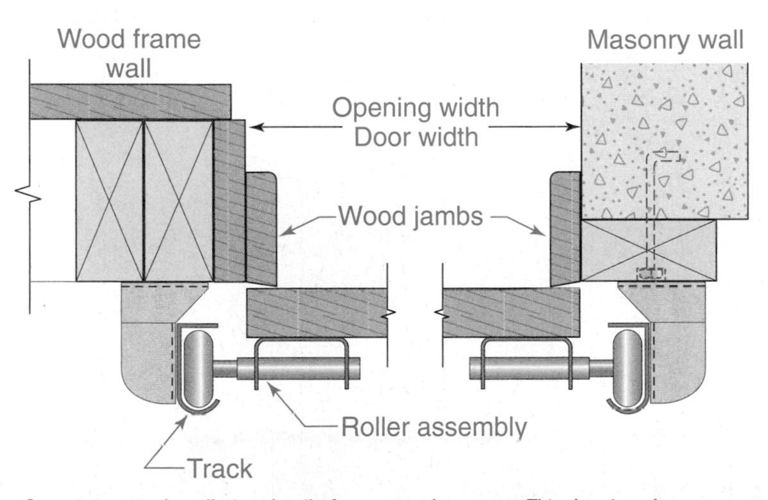

Fig. 29-19. Installation details for garage doors vary. This drawing shows one manufacturer's guidelines.

Sectional doors may be raised manually, but it is common to install an electric door opener. For safety, building codes require sensors on all newly installed garage doors fitted with electric openers. These sensors, one on each side of the opening, detect the presence of a person or object beneath the door. Then they will not allow the door to close.

INSTALLING EXTERIOR DOORS

Installing an exterior door requires a high level of ability. In terms of technique, there are two basic types: pre-hung doors and those hung on site. Hanging a door on site is described here. Hanging an interior door on site is much the same.

Installing the Door Frame

Before installing the frame, prepare the rough opening. The opening should be about 2″ wider and 2″ higher than the door. The sill should rest firmly on the floor framing, which must sometimes be cut out to accommodate it. The top of the sill should be even with the finished floor surface. **Fig. 29-20.** Another method would be to use an adjustable metal sill. **Fig. 29-21.**

The trimmer studs should be set so that they are plumb and straight. This is conveniently done with a long level. Once the trimmers are plumbed, they should be secured to the king studs in a way that prevents them from moving. Many carpenters "clinch" trimmers. They drive a 16d nail partway into the trimmer at various points. They then bend it over horizontally so that the edge of the nail head is embedded in the edge of the king stud. Then they drive a second nail partway into the king stud and bend it downwards to secure the first nail. Another method is to use wood shims to plumb each trimmer. The trimmer is then face-nailed to the king stud through the shims.

Line the rough opening with a strip of 15 lb. asphalt felt, 10″ or 12″ wide. Then set the sill of the assembled frame on the trimmed-out area in the floor framing. Tip the frame into place, and brace it to keep it from falling out during adjustment. **Fig. 29-22.**

Plumb the frame by inserting wood shingles as wedges. Check the sill with a level, and wedge it up as necessary. Insert wedges on each side alternately between the side jambs and the trimmer studs until the space between them is exactly the same on both sides. Then drive a 16d casing nail through the side casing and into the trimmer studs on each side, near the bottom of the casing. This will hold the sill in position. Drive the nails in only part way. Do not drive any nails all the way in until all the nails have been placed and a final check has been made for level and plumb.

Next, place your level against one of the side jambs. Adjust the remaining wedges on that side until the jamb is perfectly true and plumb. Repeat on the other side. Make a final check for level and plumb. Fasten the frame in place with 16d casing nails driven through the casings into the trimmer studs and the door header. Place nails ¾″ from the outer edges of the casings and space them about 16″ on center. Set all nails with a nail set. When the frame is complete, install interior and exterior casing.

After the finish flooring is in place, a hardwood or metal threshold with weatherstripping should cover the joint between the floor and the sill. Thresholds are used to close the space allowed for clearance. Weatherstripping should be installed around exterior door openings to reduce air infiltration.

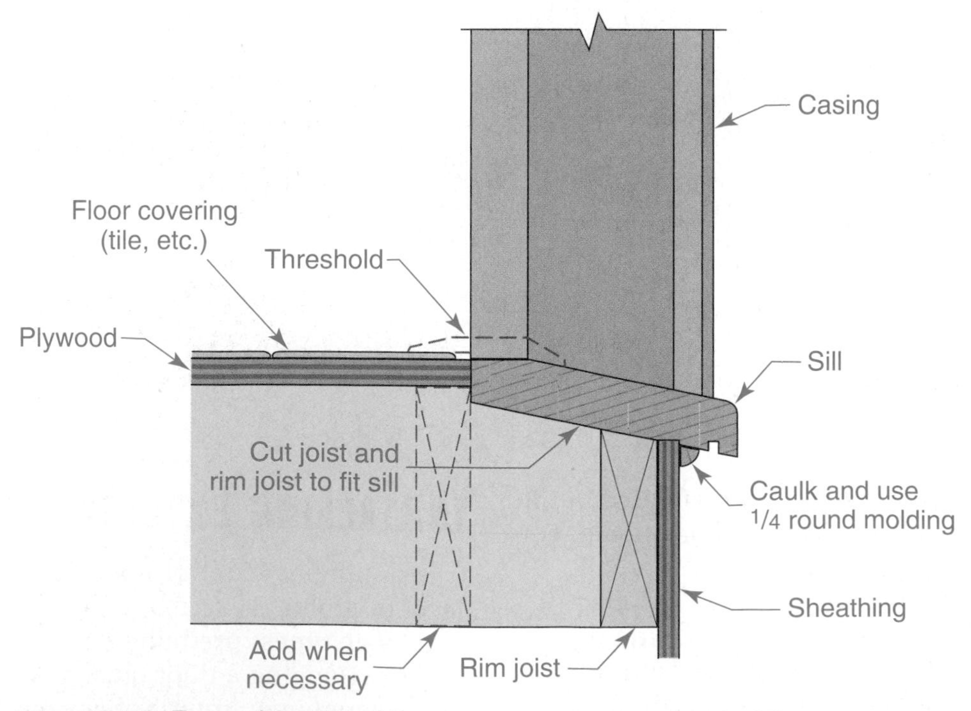

Fig. 29-20. The top of the sill should be set even with the surface of the finish floor.

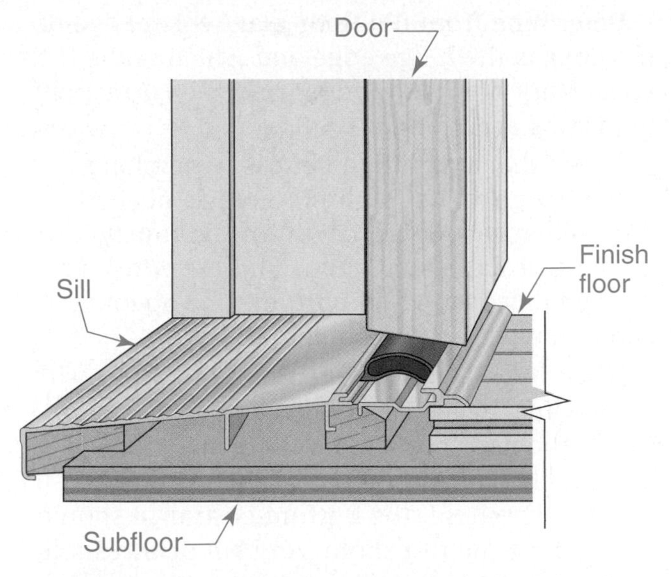

Fig. 29-21. This preassembled door frame features a sill that is adjustable. This eliminates the need for trimming the floor joists.

Fig. 29-22. Installing an exterior door frame.

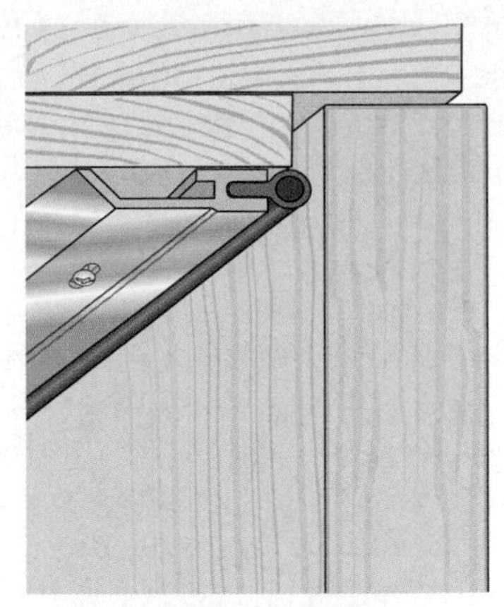

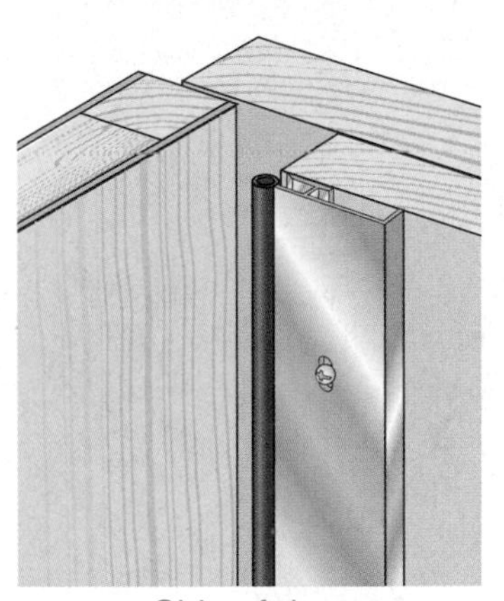

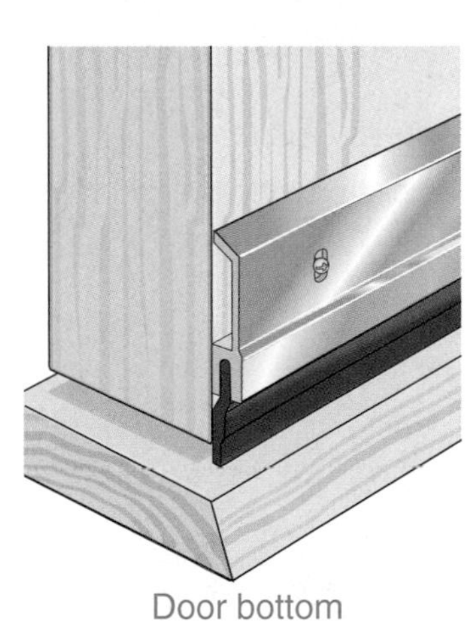

Fig. 29-23. Many kinds of weatherstripping are available to reduce air infiltration. Two types are shown here: one for the head and side of the door and a second for the bottom.

Weatherstripping

An exterior door provides a barrier to the weather. It must also prevent heated indoor air from being lost in the winter and cooled air from being lost in the summer. The construction of the door helps. Even more important is weatherstripping.

Weatherstripping consists of flexible lengths of rubber, vinyl, polypropylene pile, flexible metal, or other materials that are attached to the edge of the door or its frame. These materials must close air gaps around the door without interfering with door operation. **Fig. 29-23.**

Over time, weatherstripping wears down and becomes less effective. It should be replaced as a regular part of door maintenance. Weatherstripping should not be painted.

Preparing the Door

Check the door for imperfections as you remove any protective packaging. The door should be square and flat, with smooth and unmarked surfaces. You may notice a minor warp or bow caused by unequal moisture conditions on the two sides. The door will usually straighten when the moisture equalizes.

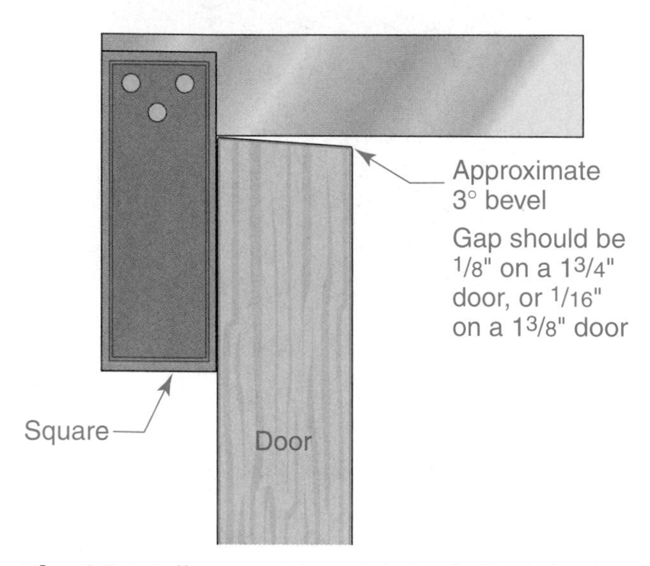

Fig. 29-24. Use a square to check the bevel while planing the edge of a door.

Determine from the floor plan which edge of the door is the hinge edge and which is the lock edge. Mark both door edges and the corresponding jambs accordingly.

Check the jambs for trueness with a long straightedge and straighten them as needed. Carefully measure the height of the finished opening on both side jambs and the width of the opening at top and bottom. The opening should be perfectly rectangular.

When hung properly, the door should fit with an opening clearance of 1/16″ at the sides and on top. If the door has a sill but no threshold, the bottom clearance should be 1/16″ above the sill. If it has a threshold, the bottom clearance should be 1/8″ above the threshold. Any sill or threshold should be in place before the door is hung. Lay out the dimensions of the finished opening, less clearance allowances, on the door.

Plane the door edges to the lines. Set the door in the opening frequently to check the fit. Bevel the lock edge so that the inside edge will clear the jamb. This angle is about 3°. **Fig. 29-24.**

As an aid in fitting the door, you might want to build a *door jack*, or *door stand*. **Fig. 29-25.** The jack holds the door upright for planing edges and for the installation of hardware. Commercially made jacks are also available.

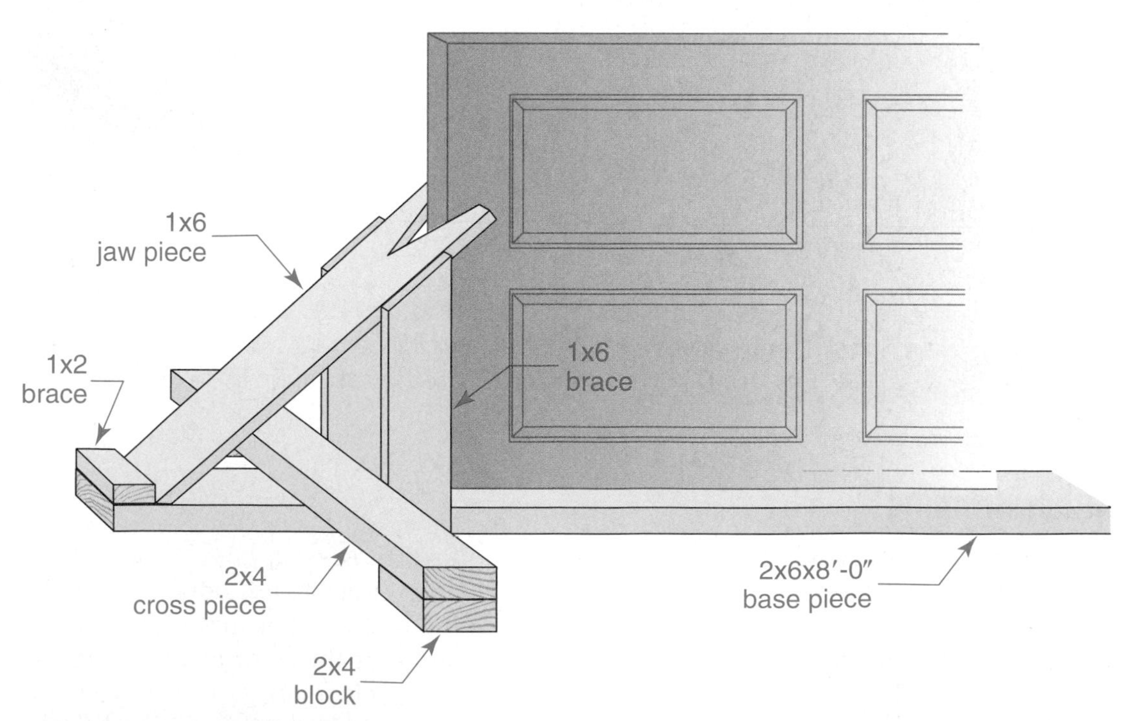

Fig. 29-25. A site-built door jack or stand.

from Another Angle

Some carpenters prefer to scribe a door to the jamb opening directly. This removes the need to move the door frequently to check its fit. Instead, the door is held against the opening and marked. A simple tool called a door hook can be used to hold the door in position as it is marked. **Fig. 29-26.**

Hanging the Door

After the door has been properly fitted, lay out the locations of the hinges on its edge and on the hinge jamb. Exterior doors usually have three hinges. If the exact positions aren't specified, the measurements used are those shown in **Fig. 29-27**. For an exterior door a 3½″ or 4″ hinge is recommended.

Set the door in the frame and force the hinge edge of the door against the hinge jamb with a wedge. See wedge *A* in Fig. 29-27. Then insert a 4d finish nail between the top of the door and the head jamb. Force the top of the door up against the nail with another wedge (wedge *B* in Fig. 29-27). Since a 4d finish nail has a diameter of 1⁄16″ (the standard top clearance), the door is now at the correct height.

Measure the distance from the top of the door to the top of the upper hinge and from the floor up to the bottom of the lowest hinge. Mark these locations.

When marking for the middle hinge, remember that the mark must locate the center of the hinge. If a 4″ hinge is used, measure 2″ from each side of the location line and make a mark. The gain will be cut between the marks.

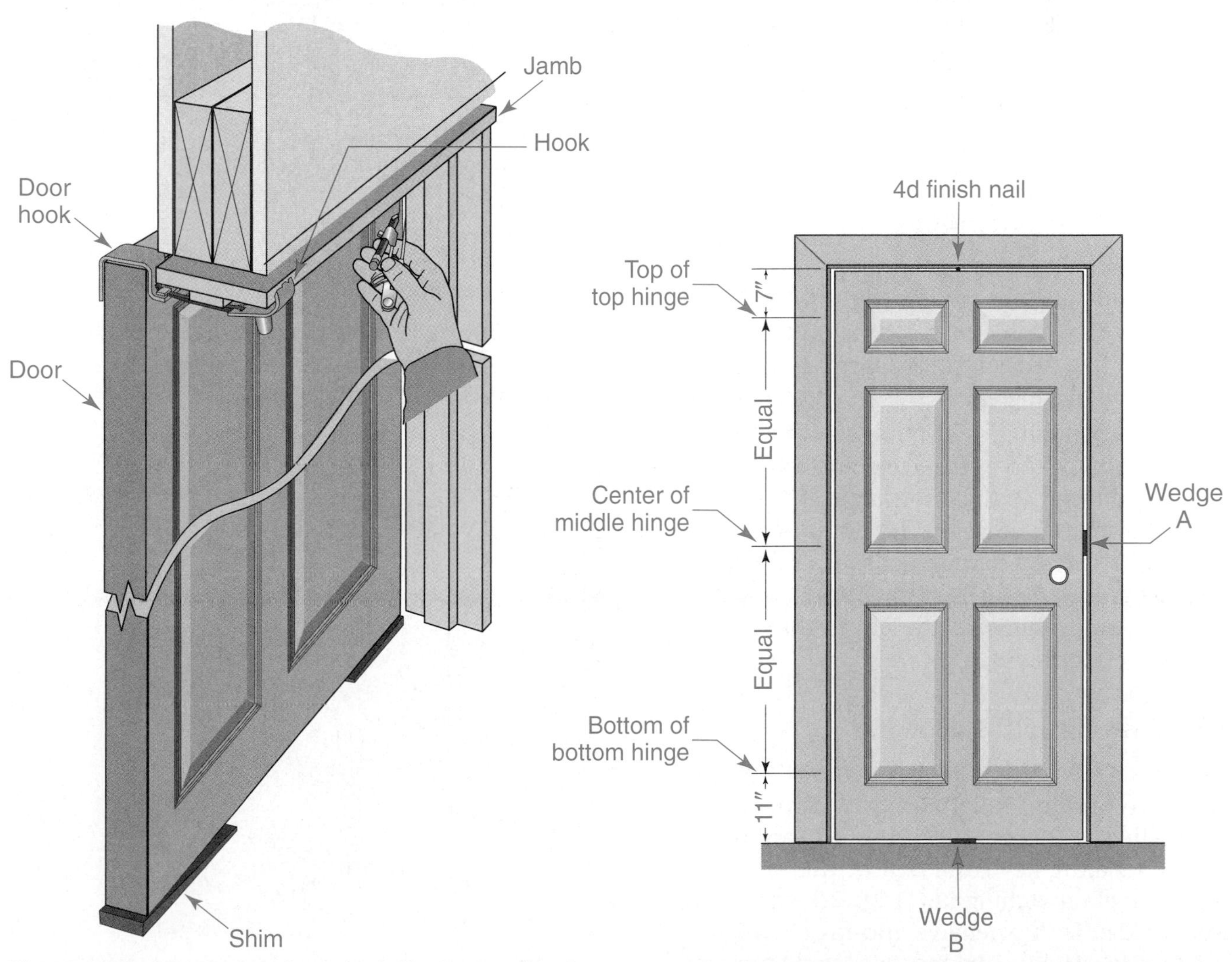

Fig. 29-26. A door hook can be used to hold a door in position for scribing.

Fig. 29-27. Measurements commonly used in laying out hinge locations on the exterior door and door jambs.

Remove the door from the opening. Place it in a door jack and lay out the outlines of the gains on the edge of the door using a hinge leaf or a butt-hinge marking gauge as a marker. **Fig. 29-28.** The door-edge hinge setback (see Fig. 29-7), should not be less than ⅛″. It is usually about ¼″. **Fig. 29-29.** Lay out gains of exactly the same size on the hinge jamb. Chisel out the gains to a depth equal to the thickness of a single hinge leaf.

Separate the hinge leaves by removing the pin. Screw the leaves into the gains on the door and the jamb. Make sure that the leaf into which the pin will be inserted is in the uppermost position when the door is hung in place.

Hang the door, insert the pins, and check the clearances at the side jambs. If the clearance along the hinge jamb is too large (more than 1⁄16″) and that along the lock jamb is too small (less than 1⁄16″), remove the pins from the hinges and remove the door. Then remove the hinge leaves from the gains and deepen the gains slightly. If the clearance along the hinge jamb is too small and that along the lock jamb is too large, the gains are too deep. This can be corrected by shims of stiff paper stock, such as a business card, placed in the gains.

Routing for a Butt Hinge

A special metal template is available for locating the gains for butt hinges. **Fig. 29-30.** The butt-hinge template may be adjusted for most common hinge spacings. It is easily mounted on the door by driving small pins into the door edge.

The template guides a router, and the gains are cut quickly and accurately. The template is then transferred to the door jamb for cutting the gains that match those on the door. Because router bits leave a rounded corner, the corners must be chiseled square. **Fig. 29-31.** An alternative is to use hinges with leaves that have rounded corners.

Installing an Entry Lockset

Entry locksets come in many styles, from very simple to ornate. Sometimes a separate deadbolt is installed to increase security. A deadbolt can have a separate key from that of the lockset, or it can have a matching key. **Fig. 29-32.** A bored-hole lockset is inexpensive and fairly easy to install. **Fig. 29-33.** The mortise type is expensive and challenging. However, it generally offers better security. Steps for installing a lockset are given on page 584.

Fig. 29-28. A butt-hinge marking gauge is struck with a hammer to create incised layout marks for a hinge gain.

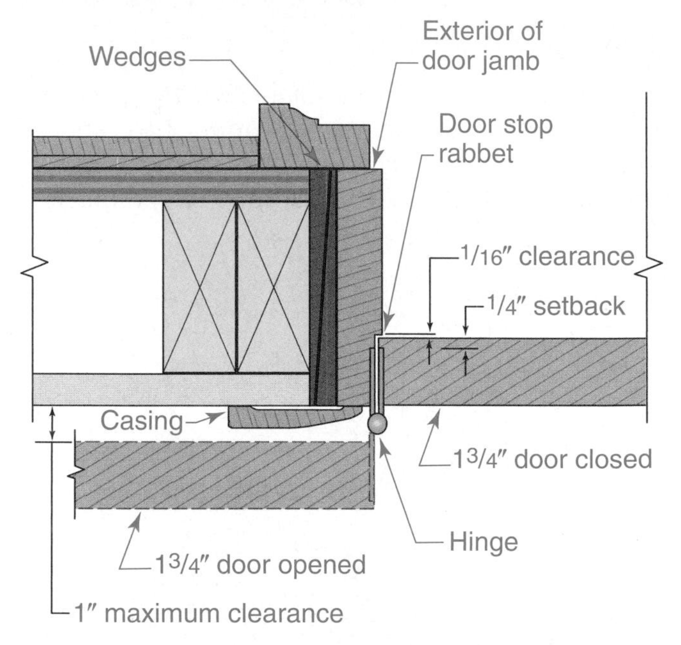

Fig. 29-29. The door hinge should be set back sufficiently to allow the door to clear the casing when it is swung wide open. For a 1¾″ exterior door and 4″ butt hinges, the maximum clearance is 1″.

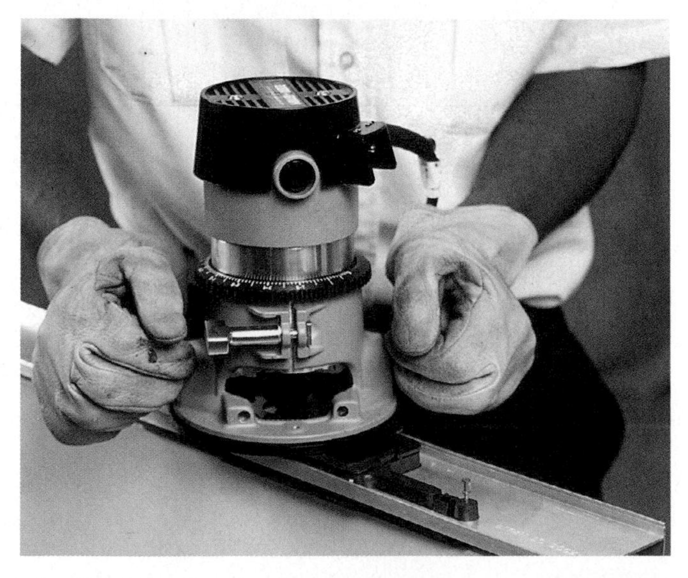

Fig. 29-30. Using a butt-hinge template and a router to cut hinge gains.

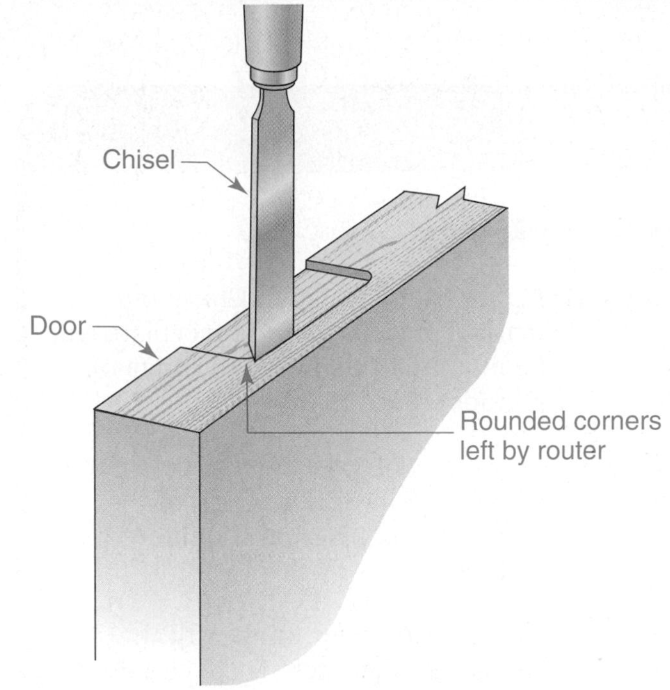

Fig. 29-31. If needed, use a sharp chisel to square-up corners left by a router. (Some hinges have round corners.)

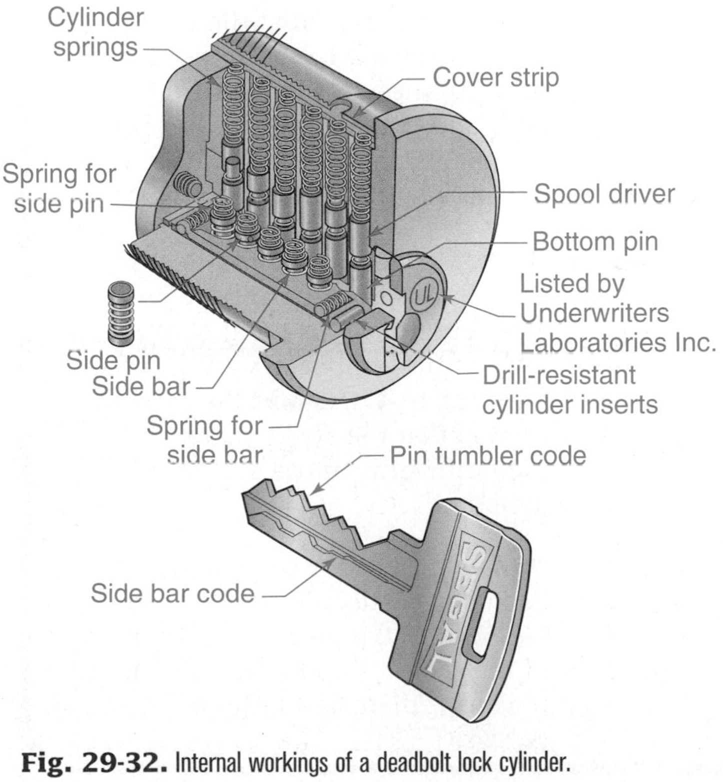

Fig. 29-32. Internal workings of a deadbolt lock cylinder.

ESTIMATING MATERIALS AND TIME

The cost of materials for an exterior door and frame depends on the style and trim. An accurate price should be obtained from a local supplier.

A conventional exterior frame and brick molding with an oak sill requires about two hours to assemble and install. It requires one extra hour to hang the door and half an hour to install the lockset. Combination storm and screen doors require about one hour for installation.

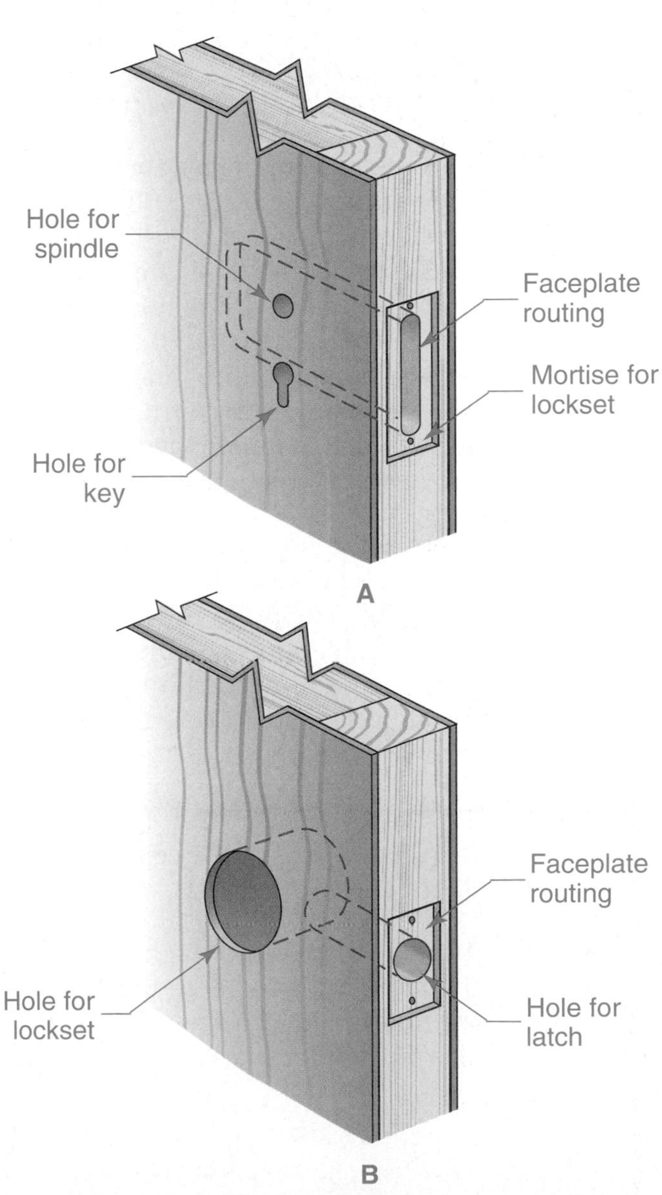

Fig. 29-33. Installation of a lockset. *A.* Mortise lock. *B.* Bored-hole lock.

STEP BY STEP

Installing A Bored-Hole Lockset

Methods for installing locksets vary with the manufacturer. Always refer to the instructions. A general procedure is explained here. The same method is used for interior doors.

Step 1 Open the door to a convenient position. Place wedges under the bottom near the outer edge to hold it steady. You may prefer to place the door on padded sawhorses.

Step 2 Measure up 36″ from the bottom of the door to locate the lockset.

Step 3 Fold the marking template (which comes with the lockset). Place it on the beveled edge of the door. **Fig. 29-34.** Using the template guides, mark the center of the door edge and the center of the hole. (If a special boring jig is used, no template is needed.) The distance from the door edge to the center of the hole is called the *backset*. It is typically 2⅜″ or 2¾″.

Step 4 Using a 2⅛″ hole saw, bore a hole of the correct size in the face of the door. **Fig. 29-35.** To prevent splitting of the faces, bore the hole on one side until the point of the bit breaks through. Then complete the boring from the other side.

Step 5 Using a ⅞″ hole saw, bore a hole of the correct size in the center of the door edge for the latch.

Step 6 Insert the latch into the hole. Keep the faceplate parallel to the edge of the door and mark around it with a sharp pencil or marking tool.

Step 7 Remove the faceplate. Chisel out the marked area so that the faceplate will be mounted flush with the edge of the door. **Fig. 29-36.**

Step 8 Install the latch with its curved surface facing in the direction of the door closing. Insert and tighten the screws.

Step 9 Insert the exterior knob with the stems into the latch. Make certain that the stems are positioned correctly inside the latch holes. **Fig. 29-37.**

Step 10 Install the interior knob by placing it over the stems and aligning the screw guides. Push the assembly flush with the door. Insert the screws and tighten them until the lockset is firm.

Step 11 To locate the strike plate, place it over the latch in the door. Then carefully close the door against the stops. The strike plate will hang on the latch in the clearance area between the door edge and the jamb. Push the strike plate in against the latch. With a pencil, mark its position on the jamb.

Step 12 Open the door and hold the strike plate in position against the jamb. Make sure that it is parallel to the edge of the jamb. Mark around the strike plate. Chisel out the marked area so that the strike plate will mount flush with the surface of the jamb.

Step 13 Drill a 15/16″ clearance hole for the latch bolt ½″ deep in the door jamb. **Fig. 29-38.** Locate it on the centerline of the screws (top to bottom). Install the strike plate and tighten the screws.

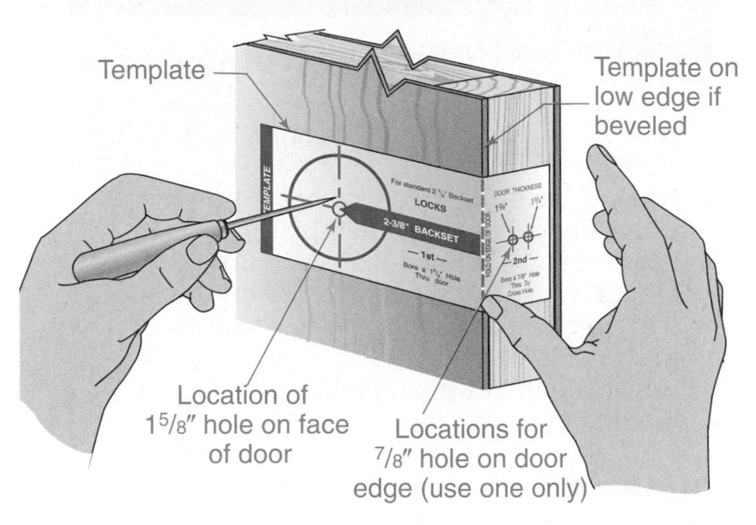

Fig. 29-34. Fold the template on the dotted line and place it on the door edge. Mark the door through the template with an awl or nail.

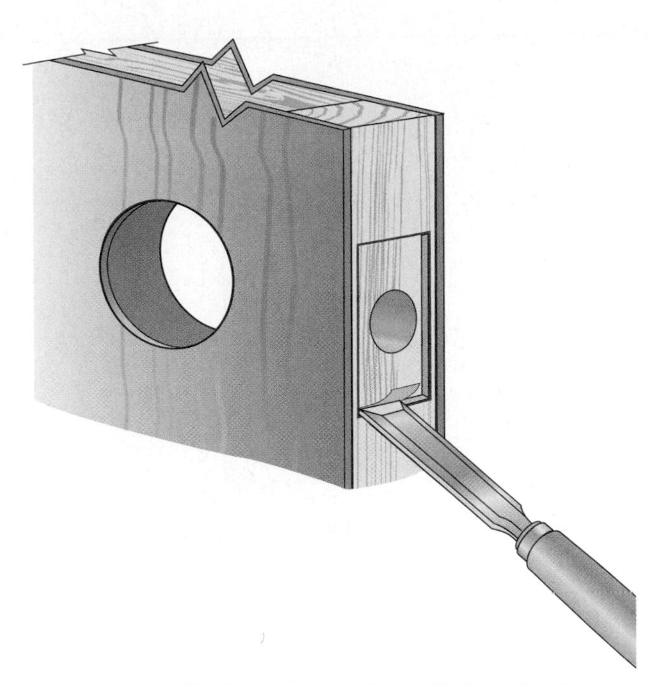

Fig. 29-36. Chisel out the marked area. The latch faceplate should mount flush with the edge of the door.

Fig. 29-35. Two different sizes of holesaws are required when installing locksets. The smaller one ($^7/_8''$) is for the latch assembly. The larger one ($1^5/_8''$) is for the knob assembly.

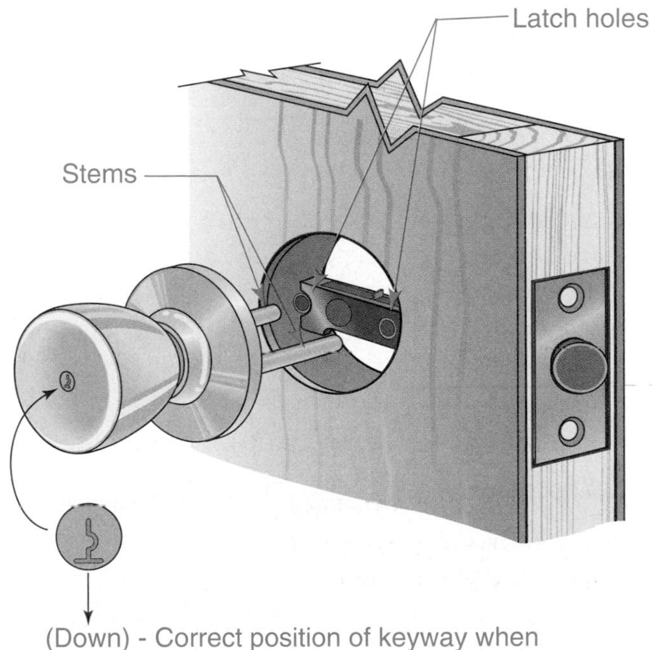

Fig. 29-37. Installing the exterior knob assembly. Stems and screws must go through the proper holes.

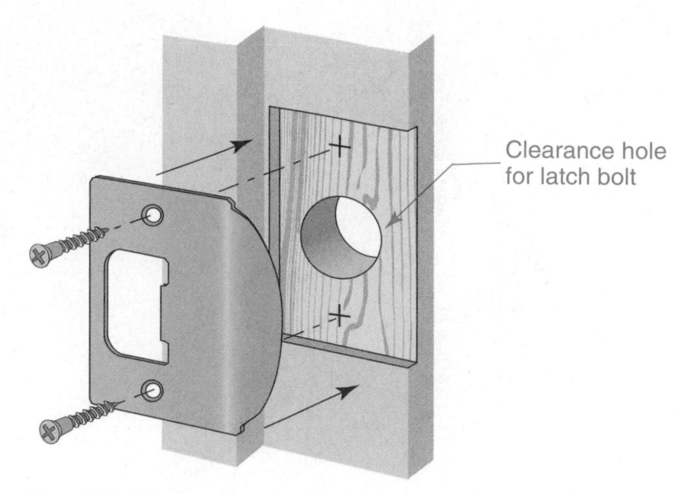

Fig. 29-38. Installing the strike plate on the door jamb.

SECTION 29.2 **Check Your Knowledge**

1. How much larger should a rough opening be for an exterior door?
2. What is the difference between a butt-hinge gauge and a butt-hinge template?
3. Exterior doors should be hung on three hinges. One should be centered on the door's length. Where should the other two be positioned?
4. How many holes must be bored in a door to mount a typical entry lockset?

On the Job

Obtain installation instructions for any type of bored-hole entry lockset for an exterior door. What types of drill bits does the manufacturer recommend for installation? Do you think these bits would be suitable for all types of exterior doors? Write a paragraph explaining your reasoning.

SECTION 29.3

Interior Doors and Frames

Most interior passage doors are 1⅜″ thick. Standard interior door height is 6′-8″. Common minimum widths for single doors are as follows:

- Bedrooms and other habitable rooms: 2′-6″.
- Bathrooms: 2′-4″.
- Small closets and linen closets: 2′.

In most cases, jambs, a stop, and a casing are used to frame and finish the opening.

Hinged doors should swing in the direction of natural entry, against a blank wall whenever possible. They should not be obstructed by other doors. For safety reasons, interior doors should never swing into a hallway. See Fig. 29-10 for determining the hand, or swing, of a door.

TYPES OF INTERIOR DOORS

In addition to basic flush or panel styles, other types of interior doors are available to solve special problems.

Louvered Doors

A *louvered door* is used for closets because it provides some ventilation. It is essentially a standard passage door in which the panels have been replaced by louvers (angled slats).

Sliding Doors

The bypass *sliding door* is designed for closets and storage walls with wide openings. **Fig. 29-39.** It requires no open swinging area, so it does not interfere with furniture placement. Access to the storage area is obtained by sliding the doors right or left. Only half of the opening is exposed at one time. The exterior surface of sliding doors is sometimes covered with a shatter-resistant mirror.

Sliding doors are usually installed in a door frame. The track is attached to the underside of the head jamb and can be hidden from view with a piece of trim. The doors are guided at the bottom by a small piece of hardware screwed into the floor where the doors overlap.

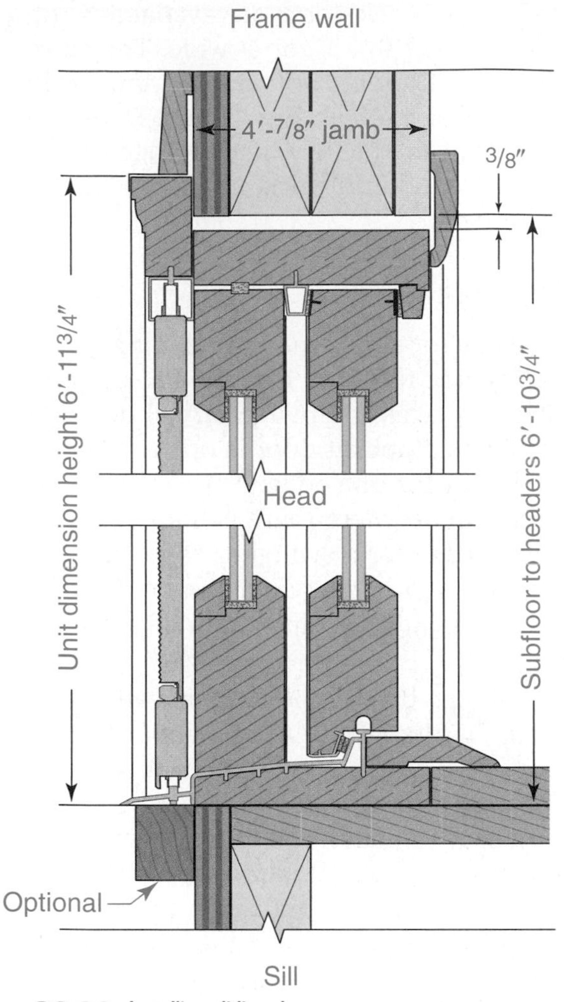

Fig. 29-39. Installing sliding doors.

Doors are available 1⅜″ thick, 6′-8″ or 7′-0″ high, and in many widths. Most sliding door hardware will also adapt to 1¾″ or 1⅛″ door thicknesses. The rollers are adjustable so the door may be plumbed and aligned in the opening. Rough opening sizes for sliding doors differ among manufacturers. Be sure to consult the specifications.

Bifold Doors

Bifold doors are often used to enclose a closet, pantry, or laundry area. The doors may be wood, metal, or a composite such as wood covered with vinyl. **Fig. 29-40.** Unlike sliding doors, bifold doors can be opened so the entire opening is exposed at one time.

Fig. 29-40. Wood bifold doors.

The doors are available in 6′-8″, 7′-6″, and 8′-0″ heights and in widths of 3′, 4′, 5′, and 6′. Each individually-hinged portion of the door is called a panel. If desired, the tracks may be cut in half and only two panels installed. For example, two panels from a 3′-0″ door could be used for a 1′-6″ linen closet opening.

A bifold door is installed in a conventional door frame. The frame may be trimmed with casing to match the trim in the rest of the house, or the jamb may be finished the same as the walls. The rough opening is framed in the same way as for a conventional swinging door. The finish opening size, however, varies with the manufacturer.

To install a bifold door, install the top track first. Then fasten the lower track to the floor, directly under the top track. The doors pivot on pins inserted in their top and bottom edges. **Fig. 29-41.** The pins fit into adjustable metal sockets in the tracks. Install the doors by inserting the bottom pivot pin into the bottom track socket. Then insert the upper pivot pin into the top track socket. Adjust the panels to the opening by adjusting the position of the sockets. To make the tops of the panels even, raise or lower the panels by adjusting the lower pins.

Folding Doors

A *folding door* may be used as a room divider or to close off a laundry area, closet, or storage wall. Folding doors are made from wood, reinforced vinyl, or plastic-coated wood. Folding doors with a metal framework covered with vinyl are sometimes called *accordion-fold* doors.

Folding doors are compact when opened. They hang on nylon rollers that glide smoothly in a metal track that may be concealed with matching wood molding.

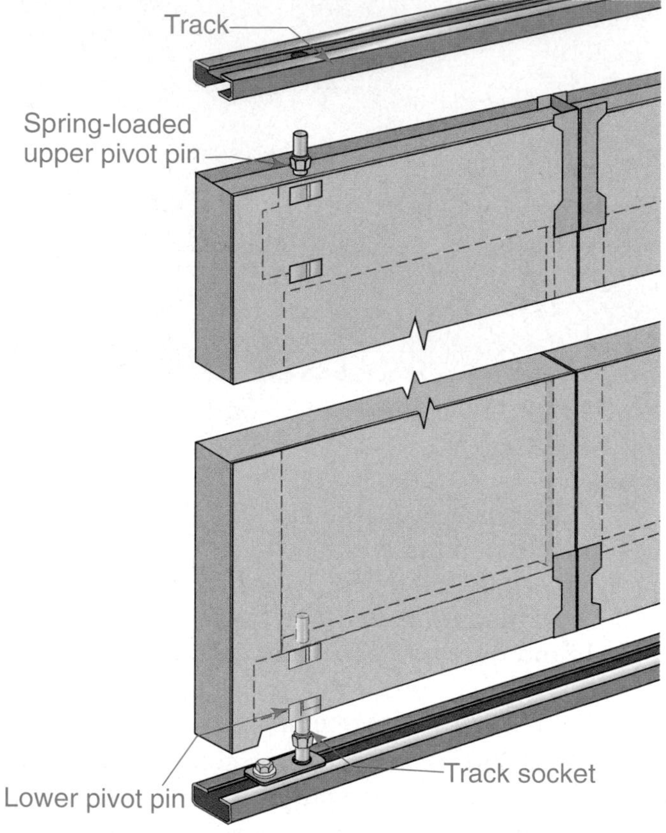

Fig. 29-41. Installation details for a bifold door. The track at the top is hidden by wood molding.

Standard or stock doors are available 6′-8″ high and 2′-4″, 2′-8″, 3′, or 4′ wide. They are installed in a standard frame and trimmed in a conventional manner. **Fig. 29-42.** Doors are shipped from the factory in a package containing hardware, latch fittings, and installation instructions.

Pocket Doors

A *pocket door* slides into an opening or "pocket" inside the wall. **Fig. 29-43.** It is often installed in places where a door will be seldom closed. When a pocket door is open, it is concealed except for one edge. A pocket door is also convenient where there is not enough clearance space for a swinging door. One disadvantage is that a pocket door can be difficult to repair or adjust because the tracks are inaccessible.

The unit can be bought complete with special mounting hardware and trim. Standard widths are 2′-0″, 2′-4″, 2′-6″, 2′-8″, and 3′-0″. Any style of door with a thickness of 1⅜″ can be installed in the pocket to match the other doors in the home. However, special hardware is required when the door itself is unusually heavy.

Framing carpenters must be made aware of special framing needs for pocket doors. Before the opening for the pocket unit is roughed in, the manufacturer should be consulted for specifications. The rough opening is usually 6′-11½″ or 7′ high and twice the door width plus 2″ or 2½″. The wall header above the pocket must be adequate to support any weight on the wall so there will be no weight on the door itself.

The pocket frame comes complete and ready for installation into the rough wall opening.

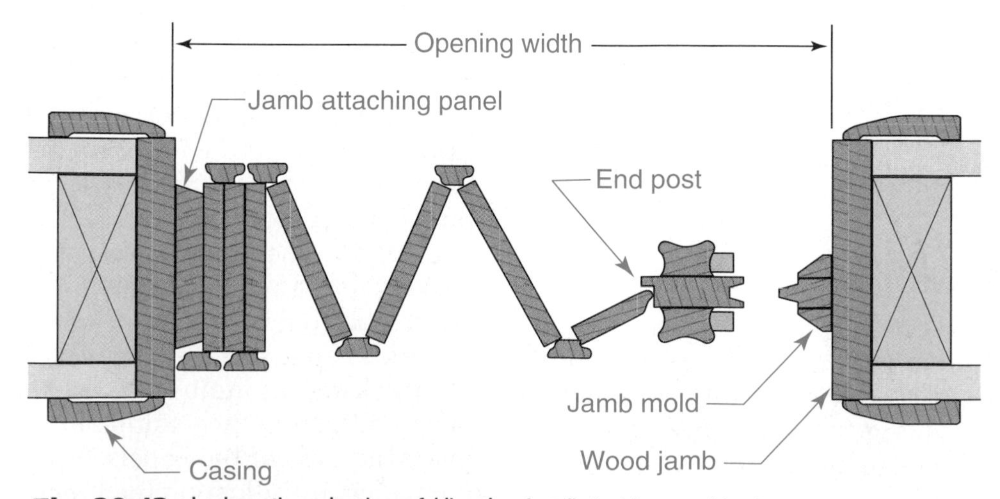

Fig. 29-42. Jamb sections showing a folding door installed with a wood jamb.

After the wall covering has been applied, hang the door and install the stops. When installing the wall covering, make sure nails or screws will not interfere with door movement.

Use the correct nails when applying the wall covering over a pocket door pocket. If the nails used are too long and project into the opening, they may scratch the surface of the door or prevent it from entering the pocket. Take the same care when installing the door casing and base molding.

INSTALLING INTERIOR DOORS

Rough openings in the stud walls for interior doors are usually 2″ higher than the door and 2″ wider. This provides room for plumbing and leveling the frame in the opening.

Interior door frames are made of two side jambs, a head jamb, and stop moldings that the door closes against. **Fig. 29-44.** One-piece jambs are the most common. They are available in 5¼″ widths for plaster walls and 4⁹⁄₁₆″ widths for walls with ½″ drywall finish. Wider jambs are required for thicker wall coverings. Two- and three-piece adjustable jambs (also called split jambs) are available. Their chief advantage is in being adaptable to different wall thicknesses.

Some manufacturers produce interior door frames with the door fitted and pre-hung, ready for installation. Adding the casing completes the job.

Installing the Door Frame

If a door unit is not pre-hung, the jambs must be cut to length, assembled, and installed. The side jambs should be nailed through the notch into the head jamb with three 7d or 8d coated nails (see Fig. 29-44). Cut a spreader to a length exactly equal to the distance between the jambs at the head jamb. **Fig. 29-45.** A spreader ensures that the side jambs will be a consistent distance apart.

Fig. 29-43. A sliding pocket door unit.

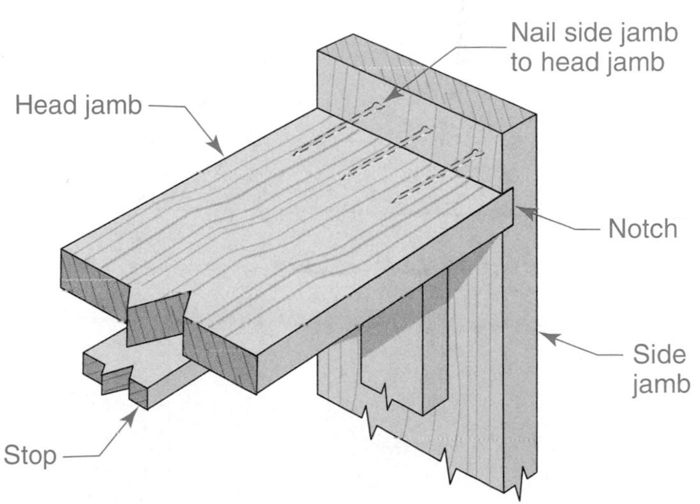

Fig. 29-44. Interior door frame details.

Plumb the assembled frame in the rough opening using pairs of shingle shims placed between the side jambs and the studs. **Fig. 29-46.** One jamb, usually the hinge jamb, is plumbed using four or five sets of shims along the height of the frame. Two 8d finishing nails are installed at each wedged area, one driven so that the door stop will cover it.

Place the spreader in position at the floor line. Fasten the opposite jamb in place using shingle shims and finishing nails. Use the first jamb as a guide in keeping a uniform width. This can be done by using a second precut spreader as a gauge, checking several points. It can also be done by carefully measuring at various points along the height of the door frame between the side jambs.

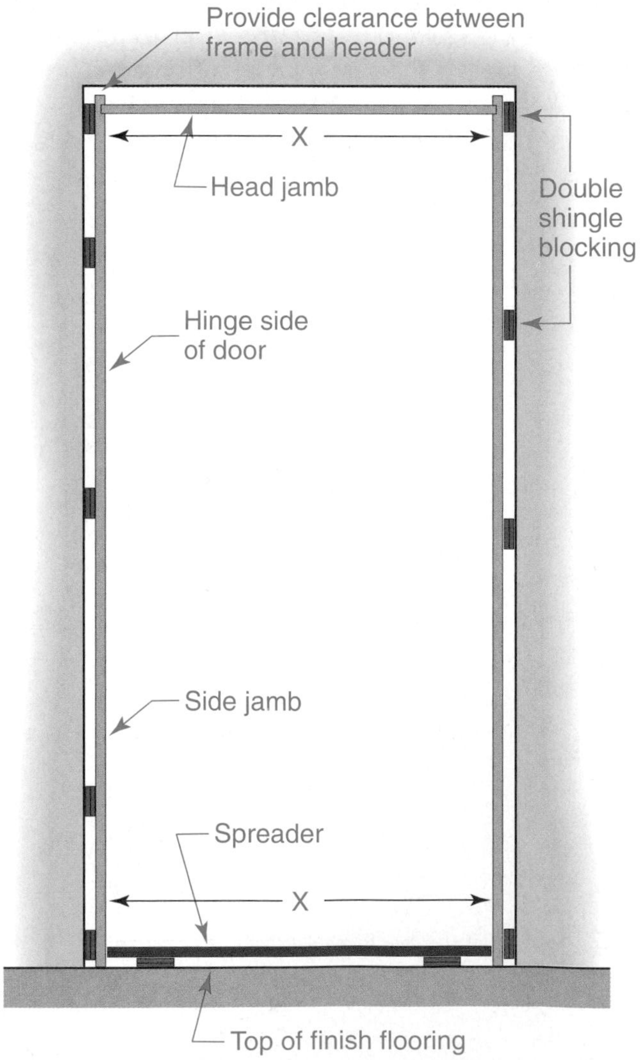

If the door unit *is* pre-hung, installing the frame follows much the same process as for one that is not pre-hung. However, spreaders may not be necessary if the unit has already been squared and braced at the factory. If so, leave the braces on and fit the entire unit into the rough opening.Then shim the frame and nail it as before. When the frame is secure, remove the braces and double-check the fit of the door.

Hanging an Interior Door

Interior doors are often hung with two 3½″ by 3½″ loose-pin butt hinges. However, three hinges will strengthen the door and help to prevent it from warping. Gains should be routed into the edge about 3⁄16″ from the door back (see Fig. 29-8).

The door is fitted into the opening with the clearances shown in **Fig. 29-47**. Clearances and locations for hinges, lockset, and doorknob may vary. The dimensions in Fig. 29-47 are generally accepted and conform to most standards.

Provide clearance between frame and header
X
Head jamb
Double shingle blocking
Hinge side of door
Side jamb
Spreader
X
Top of finish flooring

Fig. 29-45. Cut the spreader equal to the distance (X) between the side jambs just below the head jamb. Place the spreader at the floor line to hold the side jambs parallel.

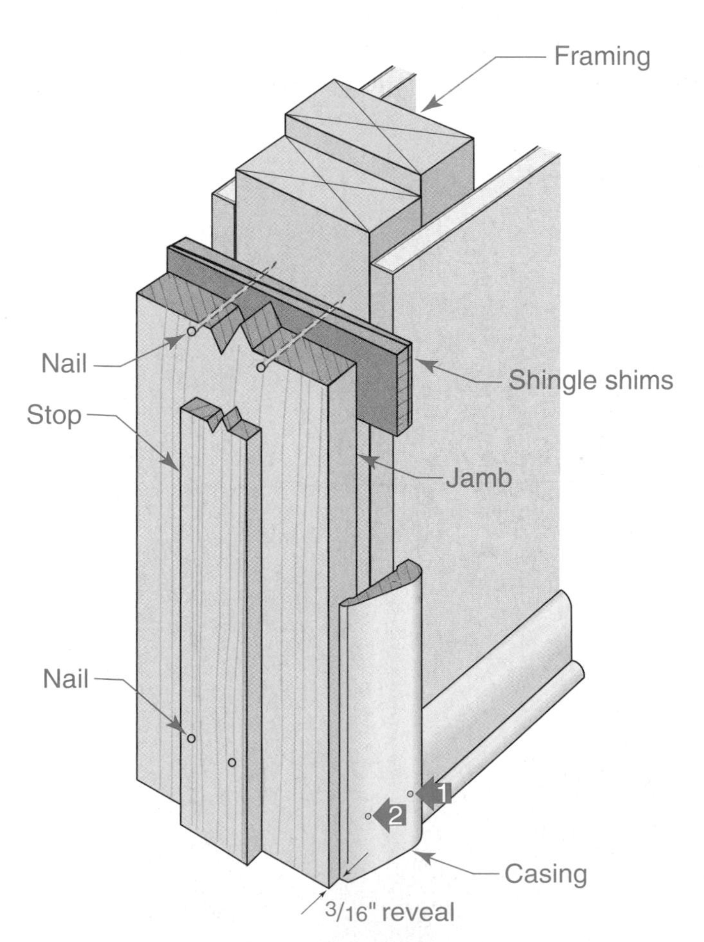

Fig. 29-46. Door frame and trim details. Use a 6d or 7d finish nail at arrow 1 to nail through the casing into the wall stud. At arrow 2, use a 4d or 5d finish nail to fasten the casing to the jamb.

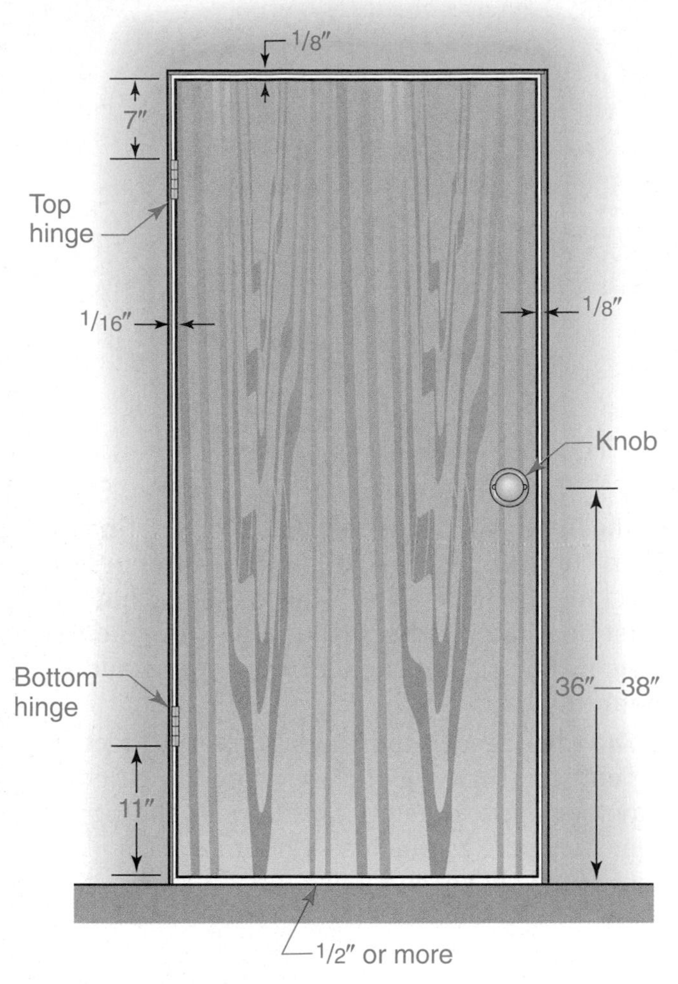

Fig. 29-47. Clearances for interior doors.

The lock stile is the door stile on which the lock will be located. The door stile on which the hinges are located is sometimes called the hinge stile. The edge of the lock stile should be beveled slightly to permit the door to clear the jamb when swung open. If the door is to swing across heavy carpeting, the bottom clearance should be increased.

When fitting doors, the stops are usually temporarily nailed in place until after the door has been hung. Stops for doors in single-piece jambs are generally 7⁄16″ thick and may be ¾″ to 2¼″ wide. They are installed with mitered joints at the junction of the side and head jambs.

To prevent the veneer from splintering when the door is trimmed, some carpenters use a cutting guide like the one shown in **Fig. 29-48**.

Door Stops

After the door is in place, permanently nail the stops with 1½″ finish nails. Nail the stop on the lock side first, setting it tightly against the door face while the door is latched. Space the nails 16″ apart in pairs. **Fig. 29-49.**

Nail the stop behind the hinge side next. Allow a 1⁄32″ clearance from the door face to prevent scraping as the door is opened. Finally, nail the head-jamb stop in place. Note that when the doors and trim are painted, some of the clearances will be taken up.

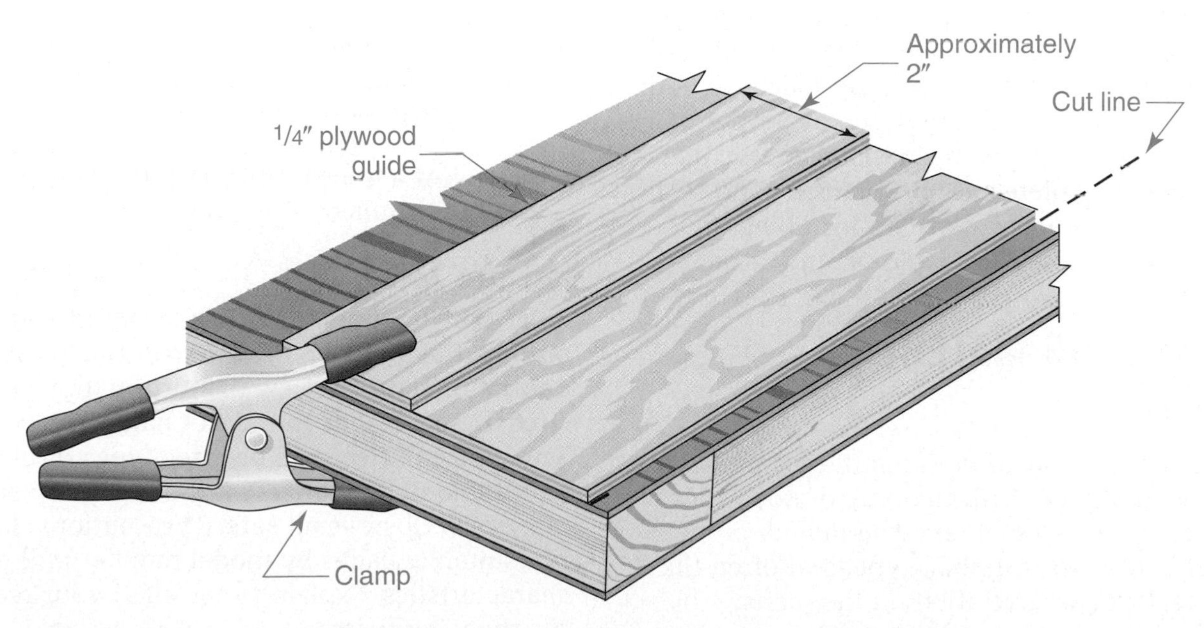

Fig. 29-48. A cutting guide for use when trimming doors to length. It must be clamped to the door.

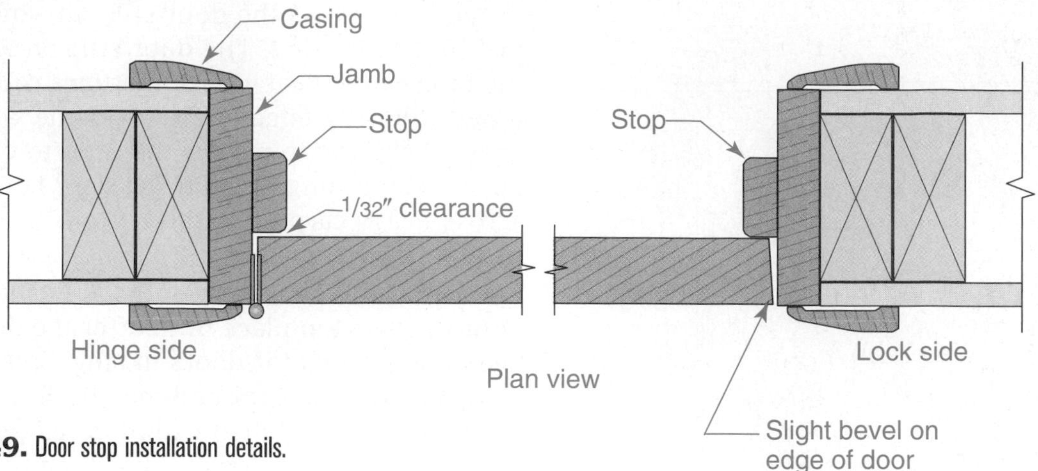

Fig. 29-49. Door stop installation details.

Many interior doors feature hollow-core construction and a wood-veneer surface. To prevent the veneer from splintering when the door is trimmed, some carpenters use a cutting guide like the one shown in Fig. 29-49. It can be made on site. The guide prevents wood fibers from being lifted by the blade of a circular saw. Using a blade specifically designed for crosscutting plywood also reduces splintering. Another method is to score the cut line with a utility knife before trimming the door.

Door Trim

Door trim, or casing, is nailed around openings and is also used to finish the room side of exterior door frames. Casings are nailed to both the jambs and the framing studs or header. When the casings have been installed, the door opening is complete except for fitting and securing the hardware. For more on installing door casing, see Chapter 35, "Molding and Trim."

ESTIMATING MATERIALS AND TIME

The cost of interior doors and door frames varies a great deal with the type of door, the materials it is made of, and the quality of its manufacture. The number, type, and often the manufacturer are specified on the plans.

Check the door schedule and specifications. Then confirm the number and type of doors by checking the floor plans. The cost of each door must be established separately. Be sure to determine if the cost includes the door frame and mounting hardware.

The time needed to install an interior door depends on the type of door. A pre-hung door may take approximately 1½ hours. A sliding door may take as much as 3 hours. Pocket doors may take even longer.

SECTION 29.3 Check Your Knowledge

1. What is the standard thickness of an interior passage door?
2. What is a pocket door?
3. When installing an interior door frame, what is the purpose of a spreader?
4. What can be done to prevent the surface veneer of a door from splintering when the door is trimmed to length?

On the Job

What type of circular saw blade would you recommend to a carpenter who had to trim many doors to length? Review the information about circular saw blades found in Chapter 7, "Power Saws." Then select two or three types of blades you think might work. Test the blades on scrap materials. Observe all safety precautions. Identify suitable blades by model number and tooth characteristics. Explain to the class your reasons for choosing them.

Chapter 29

Review

Section Summaries

29.1 Flat-panel or raised-panel passage doors are the most common in houses. They may be made of various materials, though wood is the traditional favorite. Door quality depends upon its construction and hardware.

29.2 An important feature of any exterior door is its energy efficiency, which depends on construction and weatherstripping. Exterior doors can be part of a preassembled package that includes the hinges and jambs. One of several types of keyed locksets may be used, depending on the level of security required.

29.3 Various types of sliding and folding doors are available for closets, storage areas, and other locations. They are sometimes mounted on metal tracks instead of on hinges. Installation of an interior door is less complicated than installation of exterior doors because it does not include a sill or weatherstripping.

Review Questions

1. Name three types of exterior doors and three types of interior doors.
2. Name the basic parts of a raised-panel door.
3. List at least five measures that can be taken to protect a door after it is delivered to the job site.
4. Explain how to determine the direction of a door's swing.
5. In a typical house, where is a fire-rated door, or its equivalent, required?
6. If maximum energy efficiency was important for a house you were building, what features would you want for an exterior door?
7. A well-fitted exterior door, when hung, should fit within the frame with what clearance at the sides and top?
8. What is the standard height for interior doors?
9. What are folding doors made from?
10. What clearances are needed when installing a pre-hung interior door?

Work Orders If you have been asked to make a repair to a newly completed house, such as replacing door trim, you may be given a work order. Work orders describe work that needs to be done. They help maintenance departments schedule jobs and keep track of work in progress. They include the date the request is made, the date by which the work should be completed, where the problem or task is located, and a description of it. A list of necessary materials and parts may also be included, as well as any special safety warnings. Most work orders require that you, too, enter information on them. They may ask for your name, the date you received the order, the date you finished the work, your diagnosis of the problem, what you did to correct it, and the hours it required.

Chapter 30

Roof Coverings

Objectives

After reading this chapter, you'll be able to:

- Recognize different roofing products.
- List the basic steps for installing a strip shingle roof covering.
- Describe the various types of flashing and explain where they are used.
- Tell the difference between shakes and wood shingles.

Terms

butt edge
closed valley
exposure
ice dam
open valley
side lap
square
top lap
underlayment

The roof covering must provide long-lasting waterproof protection for a house. The choice of materials and methods of application is influenced by cost, roof slope, expected service life of the roofing, fire resistance, wind resistance, and climate. Because a roof is so large and visible, appearance is also important.

The most common type of roof covering is the *shingle*. It can be made from many materials, including asphalt, wood, fiberglass, and stone. All shingles are applied to roof surfaces in an overlapping fashion in order to shed water.

Some of the material in this chapter was adapted from *Construction: Principles, Materials & Methods*, courtesy of the American Savings & Loan Institute Press.

Roofing Basics

The installation of a roof covering includes more than just shingles. It also involves metal flashing at roof openings such as chimneys, skylights, and vents. *Flashing* is a piece that protects against water seepage. It must be installed carefully to prevent water from getting behind the roofing itself.

Roofing is usually installed by a roofing contractor. These specialists are familiar with the different types of standard products. They sometimes specialize in a particular type. For example, some contractors install only wood shingles. Others may install only metal roof panels.

Roofing is estimated and sold by the square. One **square** of roofing is the amount required to cover 100 sq. ft. of roof surface. The amount of weather protection provided by the overlapping of shingles is called *coverage*. Coverage depends on the kind of shingle and the method of application. Shingles may furnish one (single coverage), two (double coverage), or three (triple coverage) thicknesses of material over the surface of the roof.

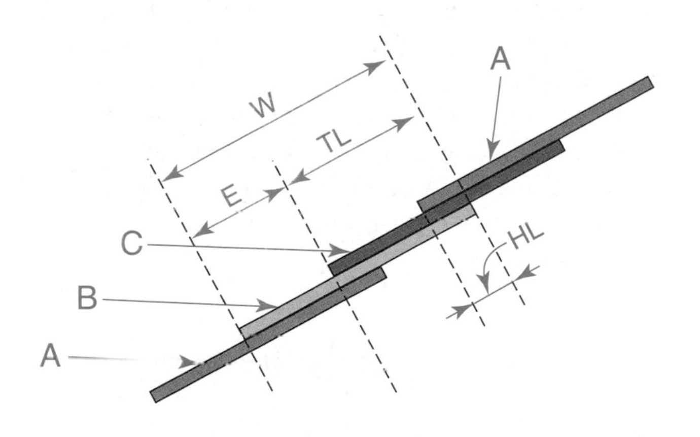

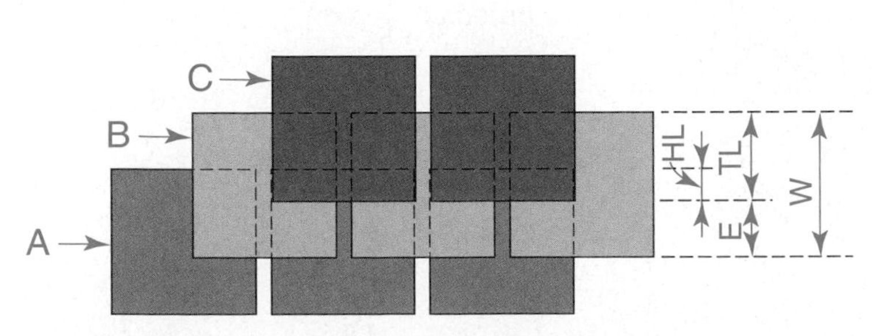

Fig. 30-1. Terms used to describe shingle placement: *E* = exposure, *TL* = top lap, *HL* = head lap, *W* = width of strip shingles or length of individual shingles.

Some terms used with shingles are illustrated in **Fig. 30-1**. **Exposure** is the amount of a shingle that shows after installation. The exposed edge of the shingle is called the **butt edge**. The portion of the shingle not exposed to the weather is the **top lap**. The *head lap* is the shortest distance from the lower edge of an overlapping shingle to the upper edge of the shingle in the second course below. **Side lap**, or *end lap*, is the amount that adjacent roofing sheets overlap each other horizontally. This applies primarily to rolled roofing and underlayment. **Underlayment** is a material, such as roofing felt, applied to the roof sheathing before shingles are installed.

ROOF SLOPE

The slope of a roof is expressed as a ratio of vertical rise to horizontal run. **Fig. 30-2.** It is written as a number "in 12." For example, a roof that rises at the rate of 4″ for each foot (12″) of run has a 4-in-12 slope. The triangular symbol above the roof in Fig. 30-2 conveys this information.

Slope is important because some roofing products are suited for use only on roofs with a slope that is great enough to provide proper drainage. In terms of building codes, there are three basic types of roofs based on the amount of slope. The three basic slope categories are:

- *Flat:* Roof slope is below 2.5-in-12.
- *Low slope:* Roof slope is between 2.5-in-12 and 4-in-12.
- *High slope:* Roof slope is 4-in-12 or greater.

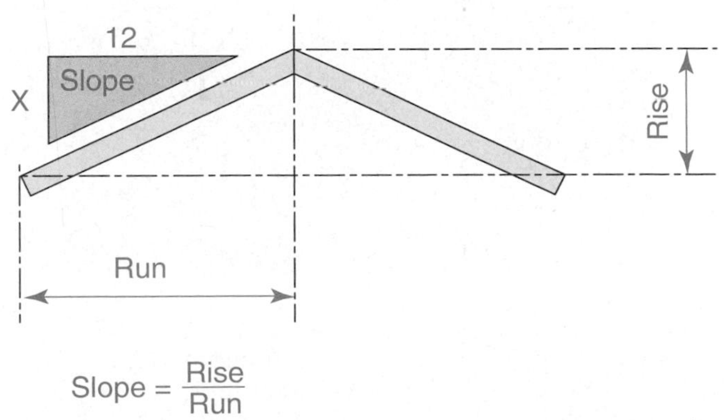

Fig. 30-2. The slope is expressed as a ratio of rise to run.

Most shingled roofs are high-slope roofs. The roof slope should never be less than the minimum specified by the shingle manufacturer. Figuring roof slope is discussed in Chapter 22, "Basic Roof Framing."

ROOFING PRODUCTS

Roofing products sold in single units, such as shingles and tiles, are applied to the roof in an overlapping fashion to keep water out. Sheet products cover much larger areas. They include roll roofing, built-up roofing, metal sheets, and single-ply roofing. Single-ply and built-up roofing are used only on flat roofs. Roll roofing is sometimes used on pitched roofs.

Fig. 30-3. Shingles are suitable for most styles of pitched roofs.

Shingles

Most residential roofs are covered with shingles. **Fig. 30-3.** They are easy to transport and install. They are offered in a wide variety of colors and shapes. Shingles may be made of asphalt, fiberglass, wood, cement, or slate.

Asphalt roof shingles are available in three styles: strip, individual, and large individual. A strip shingle is shown in **Fig. 30-4**. Strip shingles are widely available and installed on many homes. Individual shingles interlock or are stapled down. Large individual shingles are applied using either the American or Dutch lap methods.

One shingle that is becoming increasingly popular is the architectural shingle, sometimes called a laminated shingle. Two layers of strip-type shingles are bonded together by the manufacturer. Random, wide cutouts in the top layer give the roof a more textured appearance than that given by standard strip shingles. Architectural shingles should be installed according to manufacturer's instructions.

Interlocking (lock-down) asphalt shingles are designed to resist strong winds. They have locking tabs that vary in detail. **Fig. 30-5.** Interlocking shingles do not require adhesives, although roofing cement may be needed along rakes and eaves. However, the locking device on each shingle must be engaged properly and nails properly located. The shingle manufacturer's instructions specify where nails should be located for best results. Standard (non-interlocking) three-tab shingles that are used in high-wind areas must be installed using extra nails.

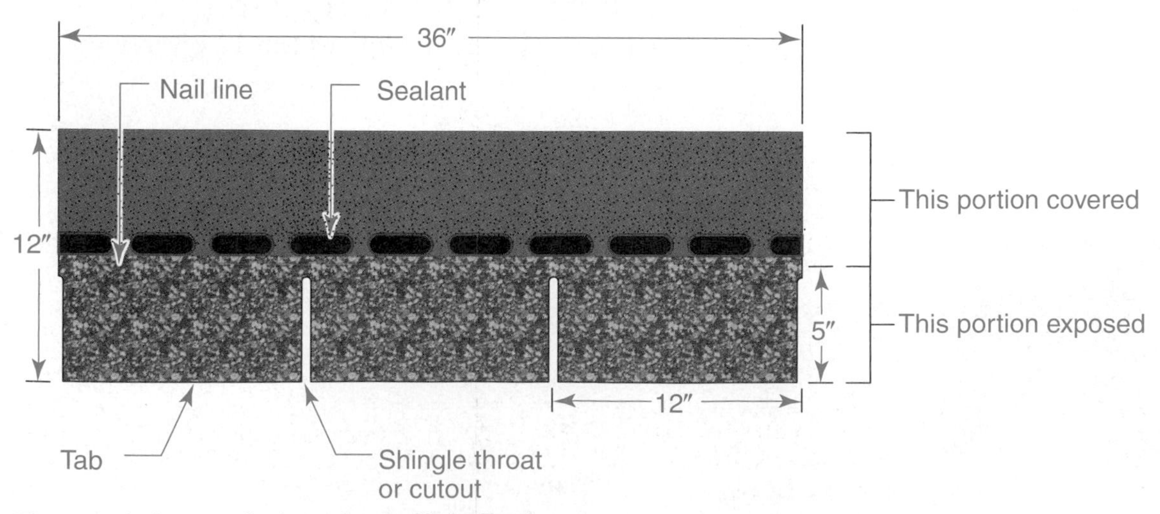

Fig. 30-4. Anatomy of a three-tab strip shingle. The dimensions shown are approximate and may vary.

from Another Angle

Strip shingles are common in every region of the country, but use of other products varies by region. Metal sheet roofing is common in the snowy Rocky Mountain region. Slate roofing is common in Pennsylvania, where slate quarries are nearby. Wood shingles are common in the Northwest because of the nearness of vast forests. Where fire hazard is significant, wood shingles may be treated with fire-retardant chemicals.

Roll Roofing

When cost is a factor, such as when roofing utility buildings, mineral-surfaced *roll roofing* is often suitable. It can be applied quickly over large areas. Roll roofing should be installed over a double-coverage underlayment.

Apply the first course using galvanized roofing nails. Apply the remaining courses with a full 19″ overlap, leaving just the mineral surface exposed. **Fig. 30-6.** Next, lift the mineral surface of each course. Apply a quick-setting lap cement to the underlying sheet to within ¼″ of the exposed edge. Apply firm pressure over the entire cemented area.

Fig. 30-5. Interlocking asphalt shingles are joined by locking tabs.

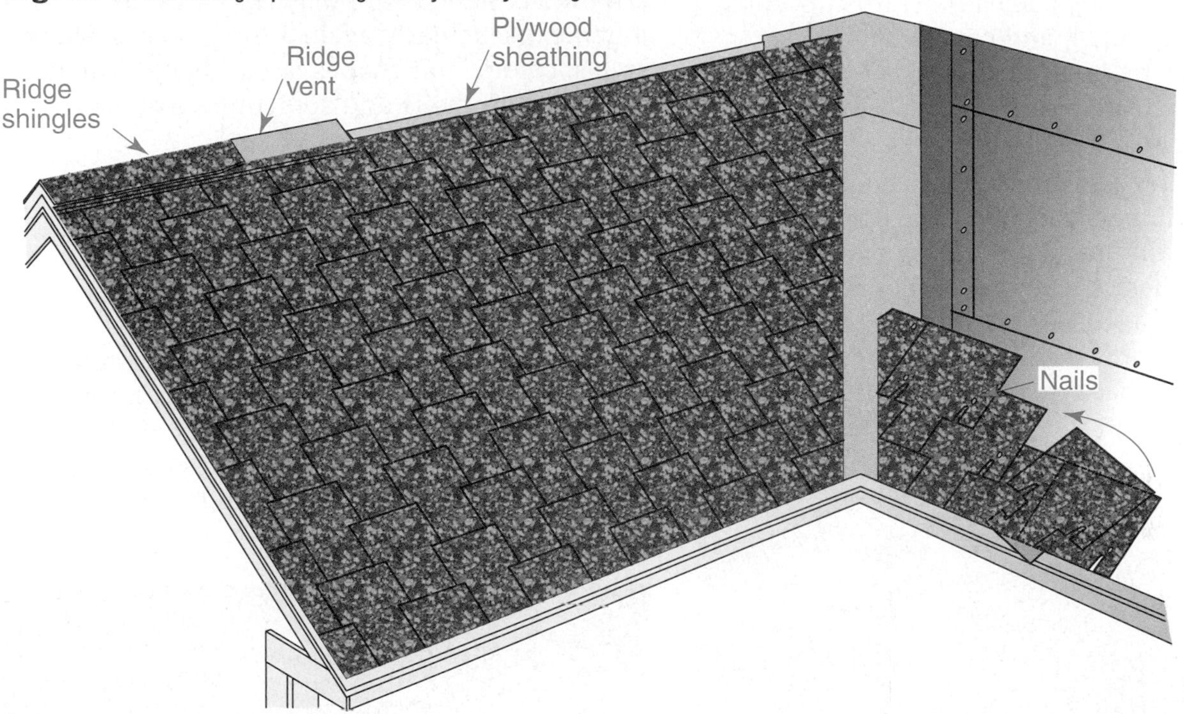

Fig. 30-6. Application details for roll roofing.

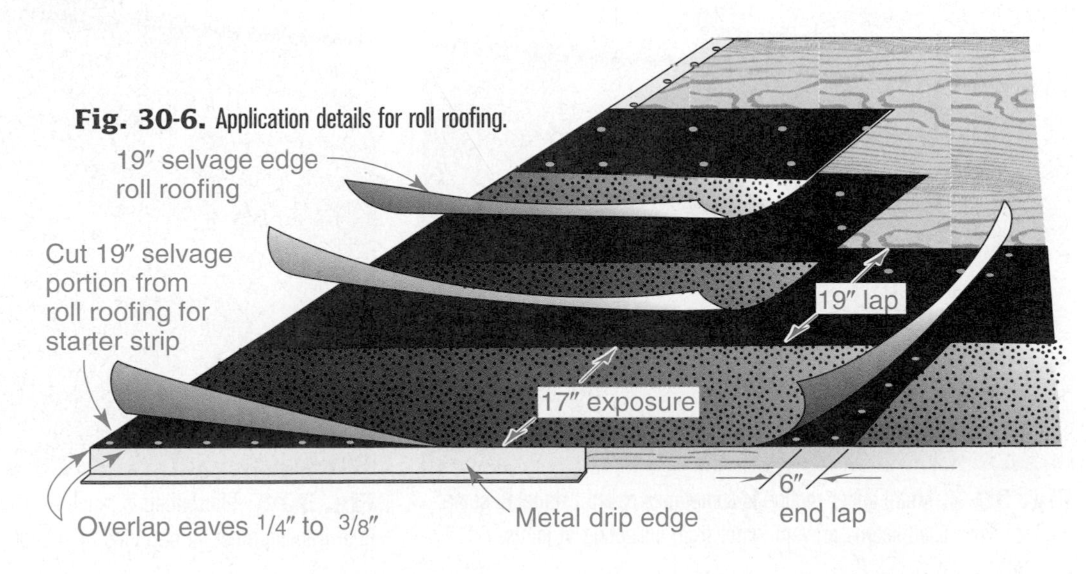

Built-Up Roofing

Built-up roof coverings are installed by roofing companies that specialize in this field. Roofs may receive three, four, or five layers of roofer's felt, each mopped down with tar or asphalt. The final surface may be coated with asphalt and gravel embedded in asphalt or tar, or it may be covered with a cap sheet. The *cap sheet* is a sheet of roll roofing or roofing felt that becomes the top layer.

The cornice or eave line of projecting roofs is usually finished with metal edging or flashing, which acts as a drip edge. A *drip edge* conducts water away from the eaves and cornice.

Metal Sheets

Metal sheet roofing comes in widths up to 4′ and lengths up to 24′ and covers large areas quickly. It can be used on slopes as low as 4-in-12 or, if a single panel will cover from eave to ridge, as low as 3-in-12.

Inexpensive, corrugated metal sheets are ideal for utility buildings such as storage sheds. However, high-quality metal roofing is more suitable for houses. These sheets have an enameled top surface that is available in a variety of colors. This type of roof is installed by a specialized contractor who has the tools needed. **Fig. 30-7.**

Fig. 30-7. Metal sheet roofing is sometimes called "standing seam" roofing. The raised seams prevent water from collecting at joints.

Single-Ply Roofing

Single-ply roofing is used primarily to cover the large, flat roofs of commercial buildings. However, it is increasingly used in residential construction as a surface for flat or very low-slope roofs. Single-ply roofing is made of various materials, but EPDM (ethylene propylene diene monomer) is common. Such sheets are very wide and are generally 45 or 60 mils thick. Single-ply roofing is installed by specialized roofing contractors.

Tile

Clay and lightweight concrete tile roofing products are very common in southern California, Florida, and parts of the southwestern United States. Both materials are very durable, particularly against fire hazards. Many styles, colors, and shapes are available. Tile is installed with nails and sometimes also with mortar. **Fig. 30-8.**

TOOLS AND EQUIPMENT

Traditionally, the basic tool required for installing most types of asphalt, fiberglass, or wood shingles has been the *shingling hatchet*. It is also called a *roofing hatchet* or *roofing hammer.* **Fig. 30-9.** A sharp blade on one end is used for scoring or cutting shingles. (Many roofers, however, use a utility knife for this

Fig. 30-8. Tile roofing is much heavier than other types of roofing. Roof framing must be designed to support the extra weight.

Fig. 30-9. Shingling hatchet with an adjustable gauge for measuring the amount of shingle exposure.

purpose.) A V-shaped notch on the underside of the blade is used to remove nails. Most shingling hatchets also have an adjustable gauge used to measure the exposure of shingle courses.

Many roofers now use pneumatic nailers instead of shingling hatchets. Nailers speed installation and reduce strain on the roofer's arm and hand. Various types of nailers are available. **Fig. 30-10.**

In addition to shingles, other materials are required, including underlayment, various types of flashing, roofing cement, drip edge, and roofing nails. Starter shingles and special hip and ridge shingles may also be required. Roofers must also be familiar with various types of ridge vents. These vents are part of a system that exhausts hot air from attic areas (see Chapter 39, "Thermal and Acoustical Insulation").

Regardless of the type of shingle to be installed, always check instructions provided by the shingle manufacturer. This will ensure that you have the correct tools and materials.

Ladders, Lifts, and Brackets

It is extremely important to reduce the safety risks of working on and around a roof. Whenever possible, use a hoist or a lift to transport shingles to the roof or have the shingles delivered directly to the roof. **Fig. 30-11.** This speeds the work and minimizes back strain. Also, strong ladders are important. You should inspect a ladder regularly for damage or signs of wear. Do not use it until any problems have been corrected.

Roof brackets (sometimes called *safety guards* or *roof jacks*) should be used to increase safety while working on the roof. These temporary brackets are secured by nails driven through the sheathing and into the rafters. They hold one or more boards at a right angle to the roof surface. The boards prevent workers and tools from sliding off. For more on roof brackets, see Chapter 11, "Ladders and Scaffolds."

Fig. 30-10. The nails in this pneumatic roofing nailer are coiled in a circular magazine located below the operator's hand.

Fig. 30-11. A truck-mounted hoist is a safe and efficient device for loading a roof with bundles of shingles.

SAFETY FIRST

Guard against Falls

Working on a roof is one of the most dangerous occupations in residential construction. Many workers, particularly roofers, are killed or injured each year in falls. Falls from roofs tend to result in serious injury, too. One study found that over 85 percent of those who fell from a roof were fatally or seriously injured. Take every precaution to prevent falls. Always follow appropriate OSHA requirements for wearing safety harnesses. A harness must fit properly and be tied off securely. Falls from ladders are another danger faced by roofers. Do not take chances. Make sure the ladder will not slip out of position while you are on it. Always keep your weight centered along the axis of the ladder. For more on ladder safety, see Chapter 11, "Ladders and Scaffolds."

Nails

No single step in applying roof shingles is more important than proper nailing. This depends on several factors, including the following:

- Selecting the correct nail for the kind of shingle and type of sheathing.
- Using the correct number of nails.
- Locating the nails in the shingle correctly.
- Choosing nails of a metal compatible with the metal used for flashing.

Specific recommendations for the type, size, number, and spacing of roofing nails are given in Sections 30.3 and 30.4.

Cements

Roofing cements include plastic asphalt cements, lap cements, quick-setting asphalt adhesives, roof coatings, and primers. They are used for installing eaves flashing, for flashing assemblies, for cementing tabs on asphalt shingles and laps in sheet material, and for roof repairs. The materials and methods used should be those recommended by the manufacturer of the roofing material.

SECTION 30.1 Check Your Knowledge

1. What term is used for the amount of roofing required to cover 100 sq. ft.?
2. Define shingle *coverage* and *exposure*.
3. Give two advantages of using a pneumatic nailer instead of a shingling hatchet.
4. Why is roofing one of the most dangerous occupations in residential construction?

On the Job

Suppose you will be roofing a large house. You wish to reduce the amount of time spent lifting bundles of shingles to the roof. Using any available resources, locate manufacturers of roofing products. Find at least three types of tools or equipment that would help. Note the advantages and disadvantages of each type. Report your findings to the class.

SECTION 30.2

Underlayment and Flashing

Before the roofing can be installed, underlayment is attached to the sheathing. Then metal flashing is added. Both of these products are needed for keeping water out of the roof system.

Underlayment and flashing are installed in various ways, depending on the type of roofing.

UNDERLAYMENT

Underlayment should be a material with low vapor resistance, such as asphalt-saturated felt. Felt comes in rolls and is installed easily and quickly. Underlayment is normally required for all types of shingles, as well as for some other roofing products. Roof underlayment generally has four purposes.

- It protects the sheathing and the house interior from moisture until the shingles can be applied. In some parts of the country, builders refer to this stage as "drying-in" the house.
- It provides a second layer of weather protection. If wind drives rain or snow under the shingles, the underlayment protects the sheathing.
- It prevents asphalt shingles from sticking to the sheathing, which can damage the shingles over time.
- It prevents condensation on the sheathing.

Valleys

An underlayment strip of No. 15 asphalt-saturated felt that is 36″ wide provides extra protection for valleys. **Fig. 30-12.** The strip is centered in the valley and secured with just enough nails to hold it in place. Horizontal courses of underlayment are cut to overlap this valley strip by at least 6″.

Eaves

In cold climates, ice dams can occur. An **ice dam** is formed by melting snow that freezes at the eave line. As more snow melts, the water backs up behind the ice and seeps beneath the shingles. **Fig. 30-13.** Proper attic insulation can prevent ice dams. However, the eaves should also be protected with flashing. Building codes require eaves flashing (sometimes called *eaves protection*) in areas where the average daily temperature in January is 25°F [-4°C] or less. This flashing can be provided by one of the following:

- Two layers of underlayment cemented together.
- A single layer of self-adhering bitumen sheet that acts as an ice and water shield beneath the shingles.
- Exposed metal flashing sheets with soldered joints.

Do not use materials such as coated felts or laminated waterproof papers for underlayment. They act as a vapor barrier. Moisture or frost then accumulates between the underlayment and the roof sheathing. This moisture encourages rot in the sheathing.

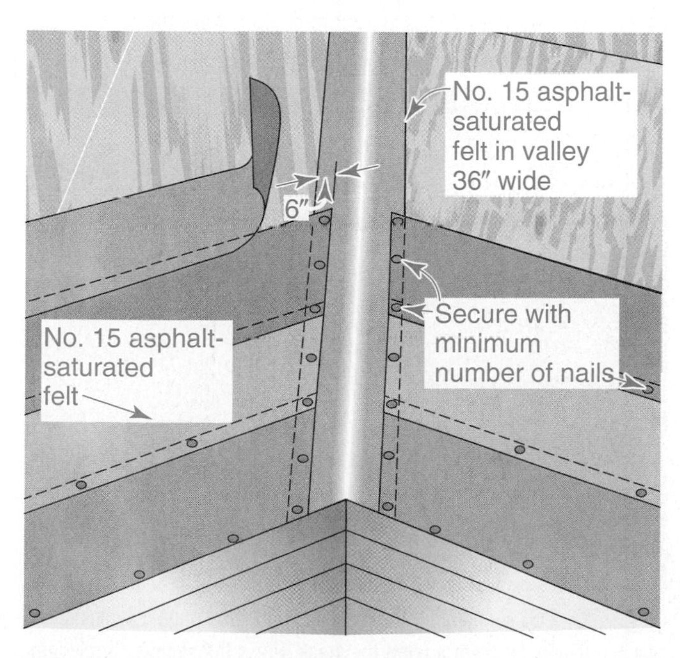

Fig. 30-12. Applying underlayment in the valley.

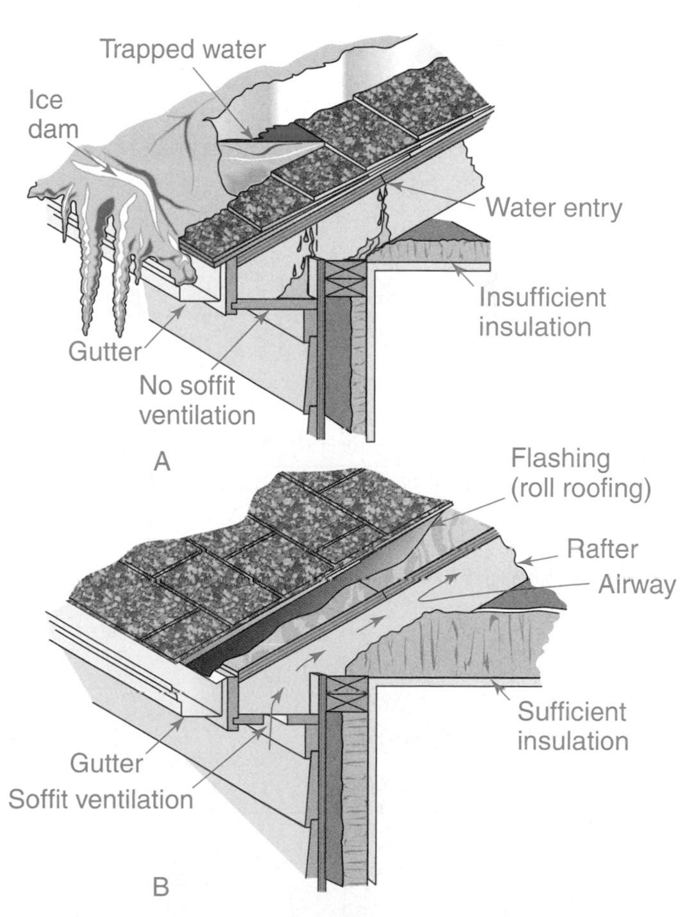

Fig. 30-13. Preventing ice dams. *A.* Snow and ice dams build up on the overhang of roofs and gutters. Damage to interior ceilings and walls and to exterior paint can result. *B.* Protection is provided by eaves flashing. Ventilation vents in the soffit and sufficient insulation prevent ice dams.

Eaves protection should extend from the end of the eaves (the edge of the roof) to a point at least 2′ inside the exterior wall line of the house. **Fig. 30-14.**

FLASHING

Flashing is a thin metal sheet or strip used to protect the building from water seepage. It is required wherever the roof covering intersects another surface, such as a wall, chimney, skylight, or vent pipe. It is sometimes also used in the valleys.

Flashing must be made watertight and water shedding. Metal used for flashing must be corrosion resistant. Galvanized steel (at least 26 gauge), 0.019″ thick aluminum, 16 oz. copper, or lead-coated copper can be used.

It is important not to use a variety of flashing metals on the same roof. This can cause a process called *electrolytic corrosion.* This is corrosion caused by electrolysis. Electrolysis is the creation of tiny electrical currents when different metals are in contact with each other and with water. Electrolysis can also occur where water washes first over one metal and then over another. For example, it might result when one type of metal is used for skylight flashing and another at the eaves.

SAFETY FIRST

Sharp Edges

The edges of flashing are sharp, particularly where it has been cut. When working with flashing, protect your hands with leather work gloves.

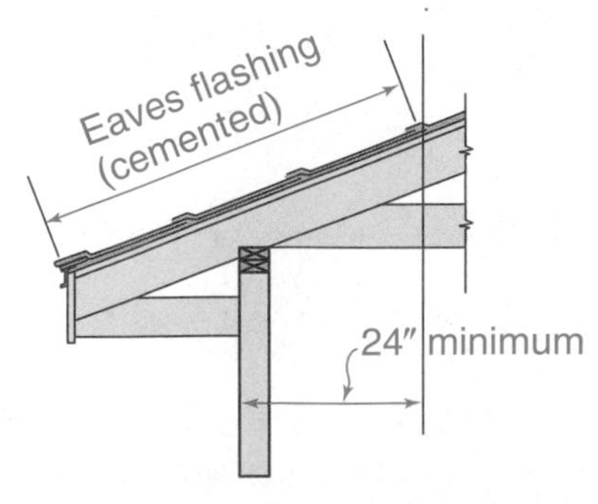

Fig. 30-14. Eaves flashing protects the roof system from leaks caused by ice dams. Shingles are usually laid over the flashing.

Soil Stacks

Roofing is applied up to a soil stack, then cut to fit. **Fig. 30-15.** The flashing consists of a corrosion-resistant metal sleeve that slips over the stack. An adjustable flange fits any roof slope. **Fig. 30-16.** Shingles are placed over the top and sides of the flange. They are cut to fit around the stack and pressed firmly into roofing cement. However, shingles should always fit under the bottom of the flange.

Open Valleys

In an open valley, flashing is used to cover the valley. Shingles overlap the edges of the flashing. An **open valley** is a type of roof valley on which shingles are not applied to the intersection of two roof surfaces. This leaves the underlying roofing material exposed along the length of the valley. (Closed valleys are discussed in the next section.) Open valley flashing can be strips of metal or mineral-surfaced asphalt.

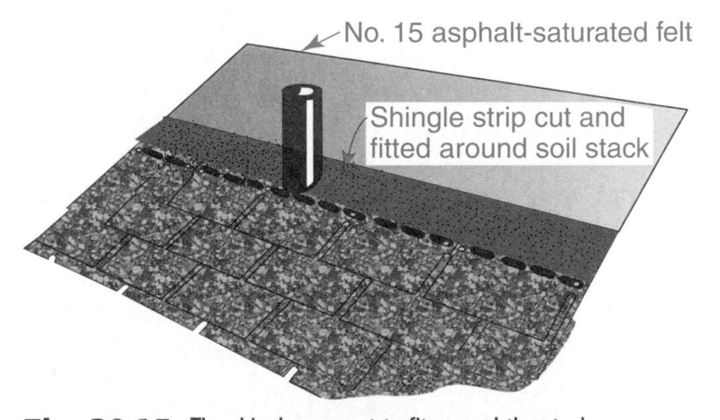

Fig. 30-15. The shingles are cut to fit around the stack.

Fig. 30-16. Completing the installation of the flange. Lay shingles over the flange. Fit them around the stack. Press the shingles firmly into the cement. No nails should be exposed.

Metal Flashing. This product consists of strips of copper or galvanized steel. It has a splash-diverting rib down the center. **Fig. 30-17.** The rib reduces the tendency for water to pour down one side of the roof and splash up on the adjacent side. The flashing is held in place with metal cleats nailed to the roof. These cleats allow the flashing to expand and contract. They do not puncture it as nails would. Valley flashing should be made of at least 26-gauge galvanized metal or an equivalent noncorrosive metal.

Each section of metal valley flashing should lap at least 4″ over the next lowest section. The sides must extend at least 8″ up each side of the intersecting roof. A 36″ wide layer of underlayment should run the full length of the valley under the flashing. Special underlayment similar to that used for eaves protection may be required in areas where ice dams are often a problem.

Mineral-Surfaced Asphalt Flashing. When mineral-surfaced roll roofing is used to flash a valley, it is matched to the color of the shingles. An 18″ wide strip of roll roofing is placed over the underlayment, with the mineral-surfaced side down. **Fig. 30-18.** When it is necessary to splice the material, the ends of the upper segments overlap the lower segments by 12″. They are then secured with asphalt plastic cement. Only enough nails are used in rows 1″ in from each edge to hold the strip smoothly in place.

Another strip, 36″ wide, is then placed over the first strip. It is centered in the valley with the surfaced side up and secured with nails. If necessary, it is lapped the same way as the underlying strip. As shingles are applied later, they are cut at an angle to fit against chalked lines snapped on either side of the valley. No exposed nails should appear along the valley flashing. No nails should be placed within 6″ of the valley's centerline.

Fig. 30-17. The center of metal valley flashing is raised to prevent heavy volumes of water from flowing down one side and up the other.

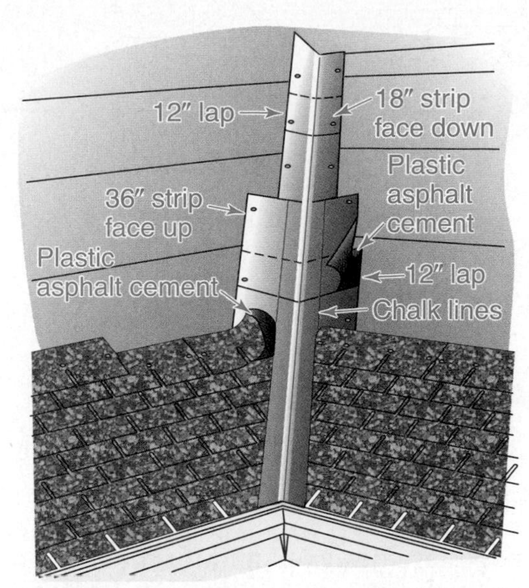

Fig. 30-18. Roll roofing used as open valley flashing. *Note:* The upper corners of each shingle at the valley should be cut off to prevent them from obstructing water flow.

Vertical Intersections

Where a vertical surface, such as a chimney or a second-story wall, meets the roof, *step flashing* is used. Step flashing consists of individual L-shaped pieces of metal.

Where the roof meets a wall, one leg of a piece of step flashing fits under a shingle. The other leg fits under the siding. **Fig. 30-19.** Where the roof meets a chimney, the top edge of the step flashing fits under metal cap flashing. The cap flashing is inserted 1½″ into the joints between bricks. The joints are then filled with mortar.

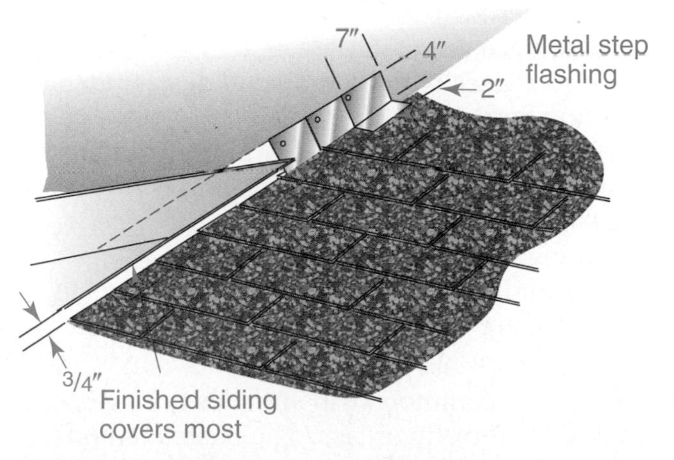

Fig. 30-19. Flashing the intersection of a roof and wall sided with clapboards.

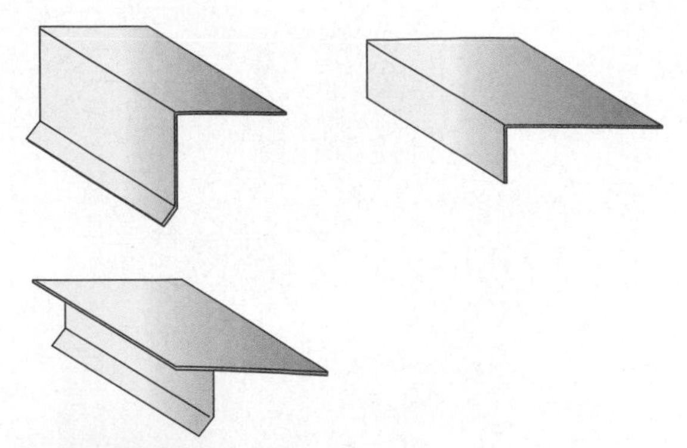

Fig. 30-20. Various drip edge shapes.

DRIP EDGES

Drip edges are designed and installed to protect the edges of the roof. They prevent leaks by causing water to drip free of underlying eave and cornice construction. Shapes of some preformed drip edges are shown in **Fig. 30-20**. A drip edge is recommended for most shingle roofs. It is applied to the sheathing and under the underlayment at the eaves, but over the underlayment up the rake.

SECTION 30.2

Check Your Knowledge

1. List the four purposes of underlayment.
2. How much of the roof should be covered with eaves protection?
3. What is the purpose of a splash-diverting rib on valley flashing?
4. Describe step flashing and explain where it is used.

On the Job

Gather information about the durability of the following flashing materials: uncoated copper, lead-coated copper, aluminum, and galvanized steel. Then locate a price for 100 lineal feet of each type. Prepare a table that compares the purchase price, expected lifetime, and cost per year of life for each of the flashings.

SECTION 30-3

Installing Strip Shingles

Strip shingles, sometimes called *three-tab shingles*, are the most common roofing product used on houses. Before applying shingles make sure that:

- The underlayment, drip edge, and flashings are in place.
- The roof deck is tight and provides a suitable nailing base.
- The chimney is completed and the counterflashing installed. *Counterflashing* is metal flashing that covers the top edge of base flashing.
- Vents and other items requiring openings in the roof are in place, with counterflashing where necessary.

The most common strip shingles are made from asphalt or fiberglass. The basic methods for installing them are the same.

INSTALLING UNDERLAYMENT

Apply the underlayment as soon as the roof sheathing has been completed. For single coverage, start at the eave line with 15 lb. felt. **Fig. 30-21.** Roll it across the roof with a top lap of at least 2″ at all horizontal joints and a 4″ side lap at all end joints. Lap the underlayment over all hips and ridges for 6″ on each side.

Double coverage can be started with two layers at the eave line, flush with the fascia board or molding. **Fig. 30-22.** For the remaining strips, allow 19″ head laps and 17″ exposures. Cover the entire roof in this manner.

Use only enough fasteners to hold the underlayment in place until the shingles can be applied. Fasteners may be nails or staples. Some roofers use a tool called a *hammer tacker* to attach roofing felt. Others use pneumatic equipment.

LAYING SHINGLES

Bundles of shingles are carried to the roof and distributed evenly. **Fig. 30-23.** This is sometimes called *stacking* or *loading the roof.* Spreading the weight around prevents damage to the house structure. It is also convenient for roofers. There are usually three bundles of shingles in a square of roofing.

Shingles should be applied over dry underlayment, never over wet. The sealant will not adhere to a wet surface. Strip shingles may be laid from either rake.

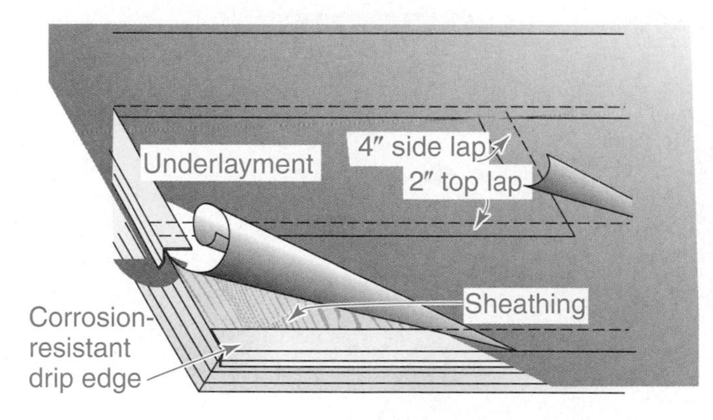

Fig. 30-21. Applying the underlayment for single coverage.

Fig. 30-23. Bundles of shingles should be laid out for maximum safety and efficiency. They should not be in the way as roofers work. Also, bundles should not be stacked where they will overstress roof framing. Notice how these shingles were installed around vent flashings.

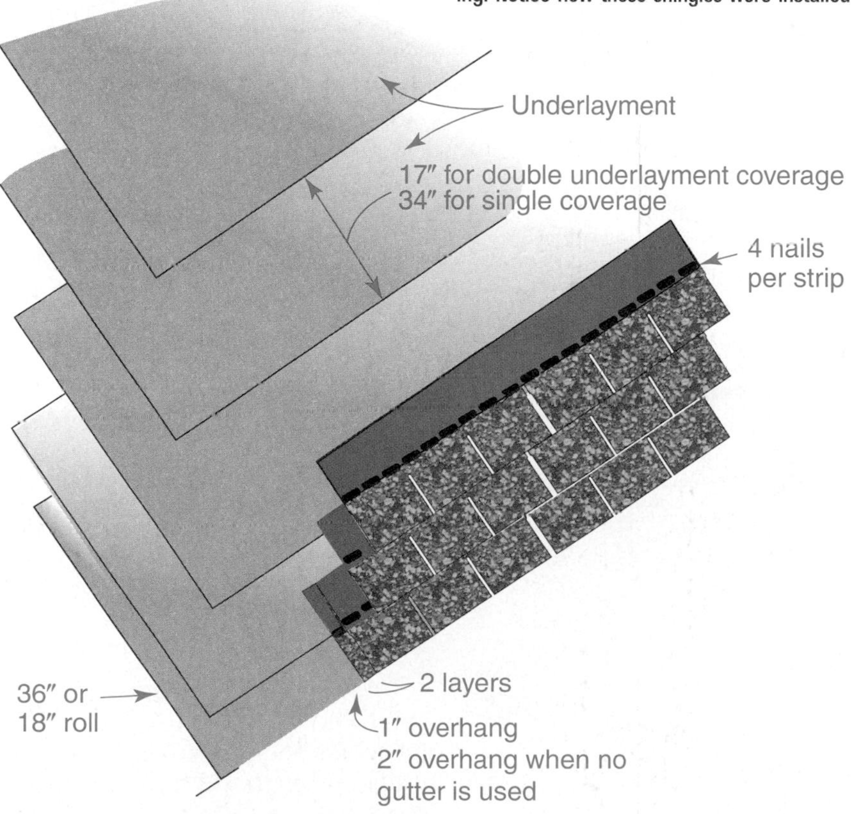

Fig. 30-22. Double coverage of underlayment.

Apply the first course of shingles, called the *starter course*, over the eaves flashing. Roll roofing or portions of shingles can be used. **Fig. 30-24.** This first course and starter strips should project ¼″ to ⅜″ and past the roof edge or edge metal. When applying shingles, cut off the tabs so that the sealant will secure the tabs of the next course. Fasten the starter strip with roofing nails placed about 3″ or 4″ above the eave edge and spaced so that the nail heads will not be exposed at the cutouts between the tabs on the first course. If square-butt strip shingles are used as a starter strip, cut 3″ off the first starter course shingle to be laid at the rake. Then start the first course laid right side up with a full shingle. Start succeeding courses with full or cut shingles, depending upon the look desired:

First method: This approach aligns the cutouts of every other course. **Fig. 30-25.** Start the first course with a full shingle. For the second course,

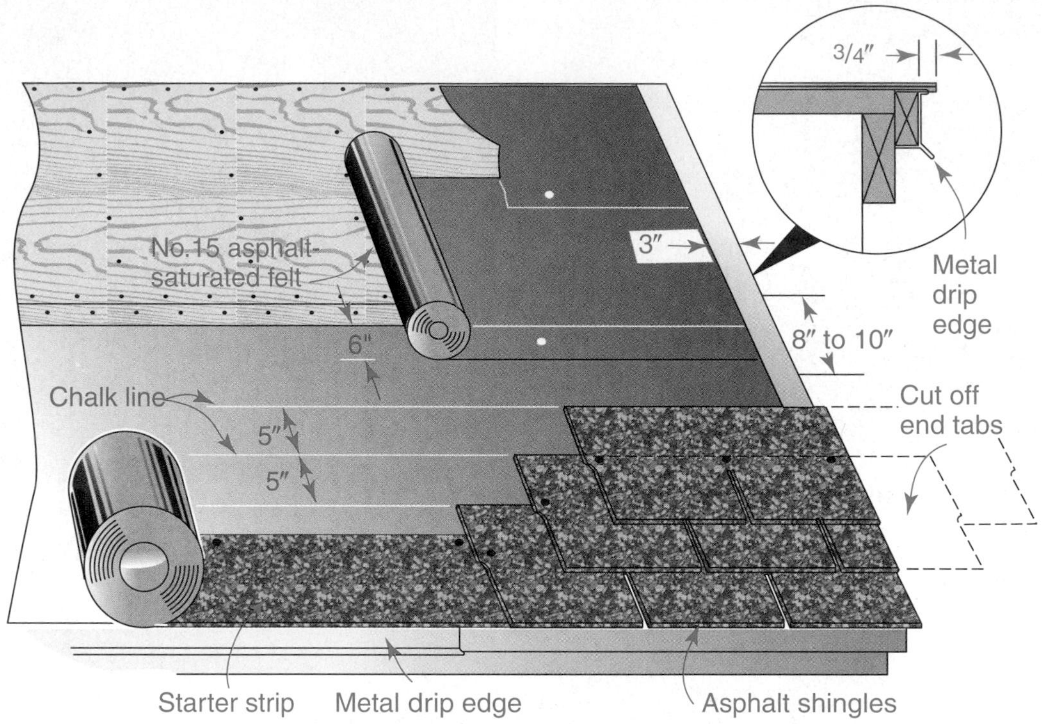

Fig. 30-24. Laying asphalt strip shingles.

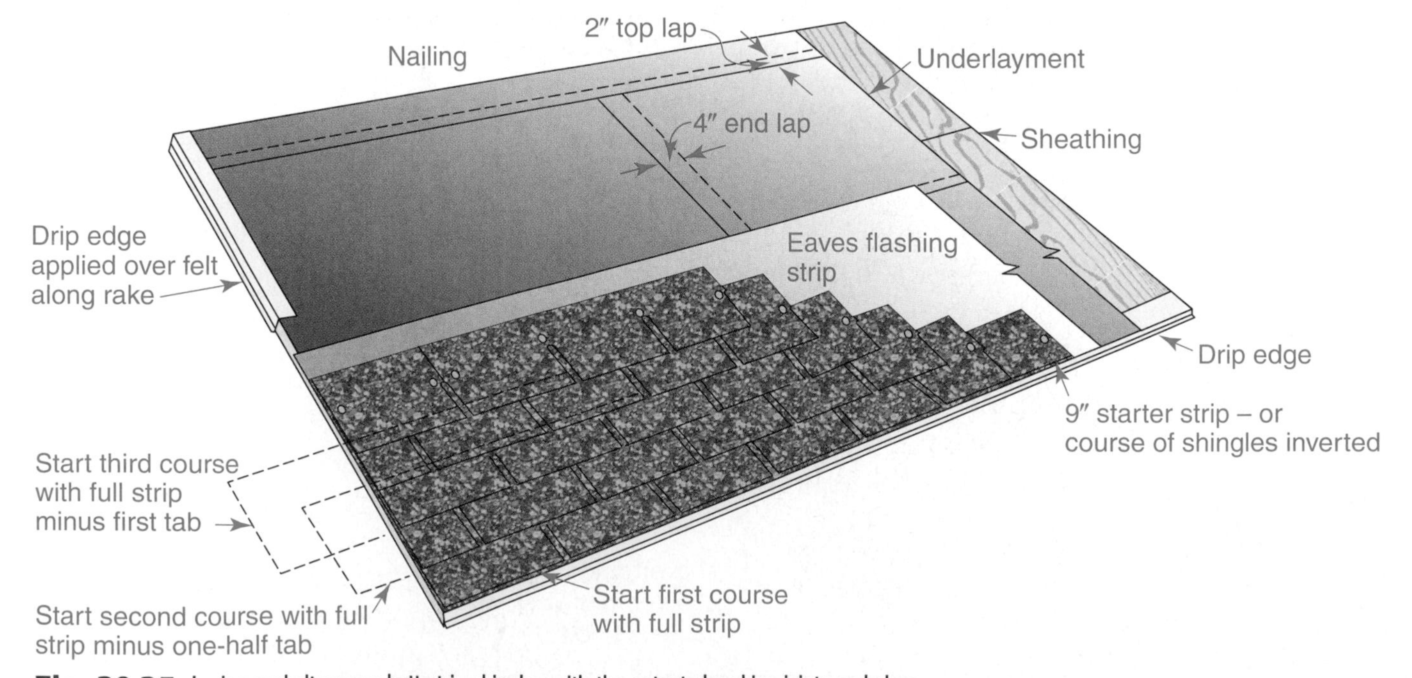

Fig. 30-25. Laying asphalt square-butt strip shingles with the cutouts breaking joints on halves.

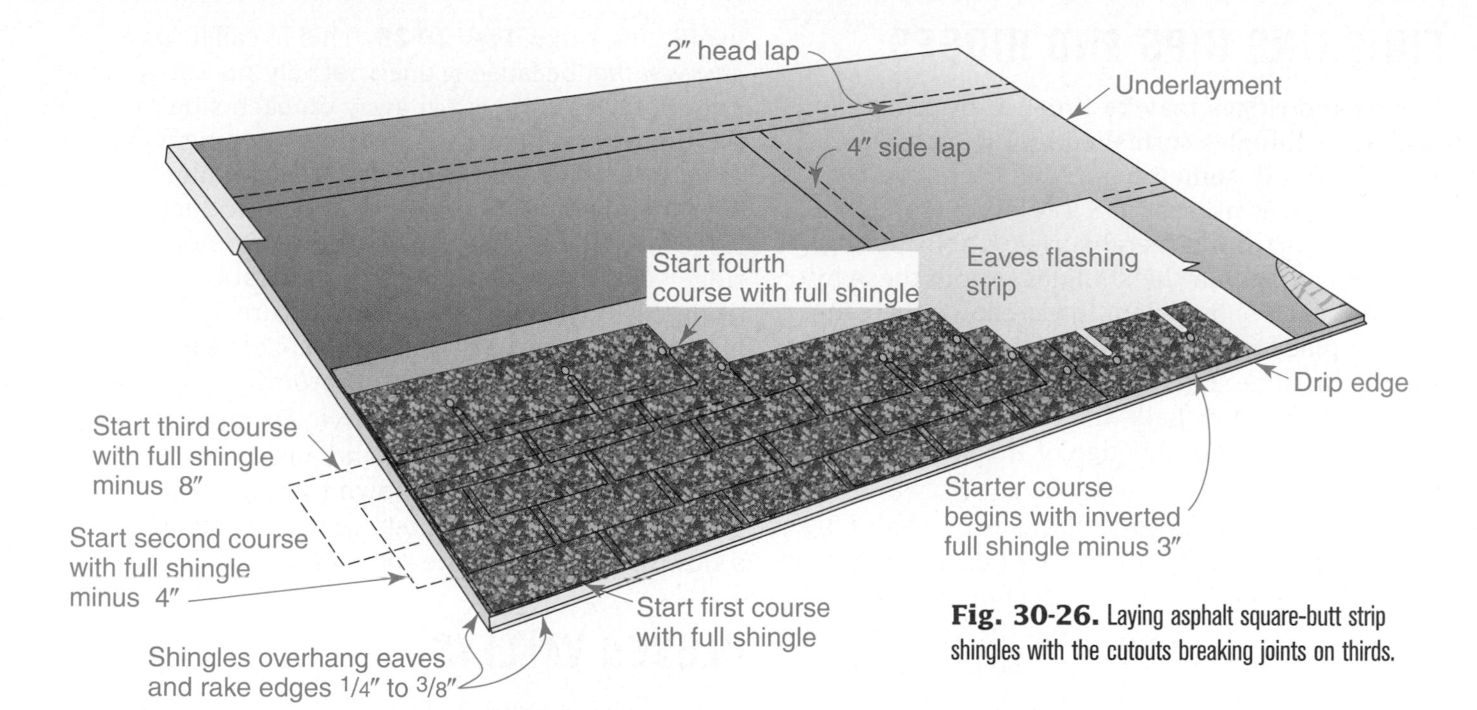

Fig. 30-26. Laying asphalt square-butt strip shingles with the cutouts breaking joints on thirds.

cut 6″ (one-half of a tab) off the end of a full shingle and use the shingle to start the course. For the third course, cut 12″ (a full tab) off the end of a full shingle and use the shingle to start the course. For the fourth course, cut 18″ (1½ tabs) off the end of a full shingle and use the shingle to start the course. This process is sometimes called *breaking the joints on halves.*

Second method: This approach separates aligned cutouts by two courses. **Fig. 30-26.** Start the first course with a full shingle. Start the second course with a full shingle cut 4″ short (one-third of a tab). Start the third course with a full shingle cut 8″ short (two-thirds of a tab). Start the fourth course with a full shingle. This is sometimes called *breaking the joints on thirds.*

Regardless of the method chosen, place each succeeding course of shingles so that the lower edges of the butt ends are aligned with the top of the cutouts on the underlying course.

To ensure proper alignment of the shingle courses, snap a chalk line periodically from one end of the row to the other at the top of the cutouts. Align the courses with the chalk line.

NAILING

Nails should be made of hot-dipped galvanized steel, aluminum, or stainless steel. **Fig. 30-27.** A roofing nail has a sharp point and a large, flat head at least ⅜″ in diameter. Shanks should be 10- to 12-gauge wire. They may be smooth or threaded for increased holding power. Nails should be long enough to penetrate roof sheathing that is ¾″ thick or less.

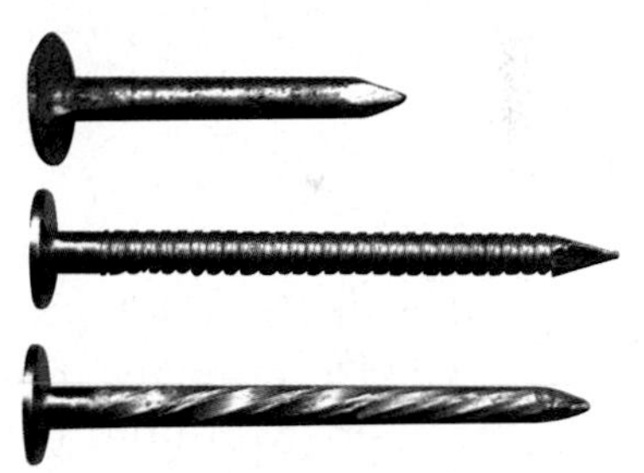

Fig. 30-27. Asphalt shingle nails.

The number and the placement of nails are important. Nailing should start at the end nearest the shingle last applied and proceed to the opposite end. To prevent buckling, be sure each shingle is in perfect alignment before driving any nails. Drive the nail straight to avoid cutting the shingle with the edge of the nail head. The nail head should not be sunk below the surface of the shingle.

Three-tab shingles require four nails for each strip. In areas where wind hazards are high, local codes may require six nails per shingle. When the shingles are applied with a 5″ exposure, the four nails are placed ⅝″ above the top of the cutouts. The nails are located horizontally with one nail 1″ back from each end and one nail on the centerline of each cutout. To provide extra resistance to uplift in high wind areas, use six nails for each strip.

FINISHING HIPS AND RIDGES

Hips and ridges may be finished by using hip and ridge shingles furnished by the manufacturer. They are sometimes called caps. You can also cut pieces at least 9″ x 12″ either from shingle strips or from mineral-surfaced roll roofing of a color to match the shingles. Apply these by bending each shingle lengthwise down the center and placing an equal amount on each side of the hip or ridge. **Fig. 30-28.** To ensure proper alignment, snap a chalk line down one side of the ridge and align the edge of the shingle with it as you nail.

Apply the hip and ridge shingles by beginning at the bottom of a hip or one end of the ridge. Use a 5″ exposure. Secure each shingle with one nail at each side 5½″ back from the exposed end and 1″ up from the edge. When laying the shingles on the ridge, always lay the exposed edge away from the prevailing winds.

VENTS

Proper ventilation of the roof is very important. It removes hot air from the attic that could damage shingles. It also removes moisture that could damage the roof sheathing. There are various ventilation methods. One that has become very common is the use of the full-length ventilating ridge. **Fig. 30-29.** This is called *passive venting*, because it does not rely on fans. The roof sheathing is cut away on each side of the ridge board, creating a narrow opening. One of various ridge-vent products is then nailed over the opening. Depending on the product, ridge shingles are often nailed to the top of the ridge vent. Ridge vents vary considerably in design. Always follow the manufacturer's instructions when installing them. This will ensure that the vent is weatherproof.

For a ridge vent to be effective, air must be drawn in through the eaves and soffit vents. As this relatively cool air is drawn in, warmer air is exhausted through the ridge vent. This ensures a flow of air through the roof cavities or attic.

CLOSED VALLEYS

For a closed valley (*woven valley*), strip shingles are interwoven as flashing to protect the valley from seepage. A **closed valley** is a roof covering in a roof valley laid so the flashing is not visible. **Fig. 30-30.** No metal flashing is necessary. This method doubles the coverage of shingles throughout the length of the valley. A valley lining made from a 36″ wide strip of 55 lb. (or heavier) roll roofing should be placed over the valley underlayment and centered in the valley.

Fig. 30-28. Properly applied hip and ridge shingles.

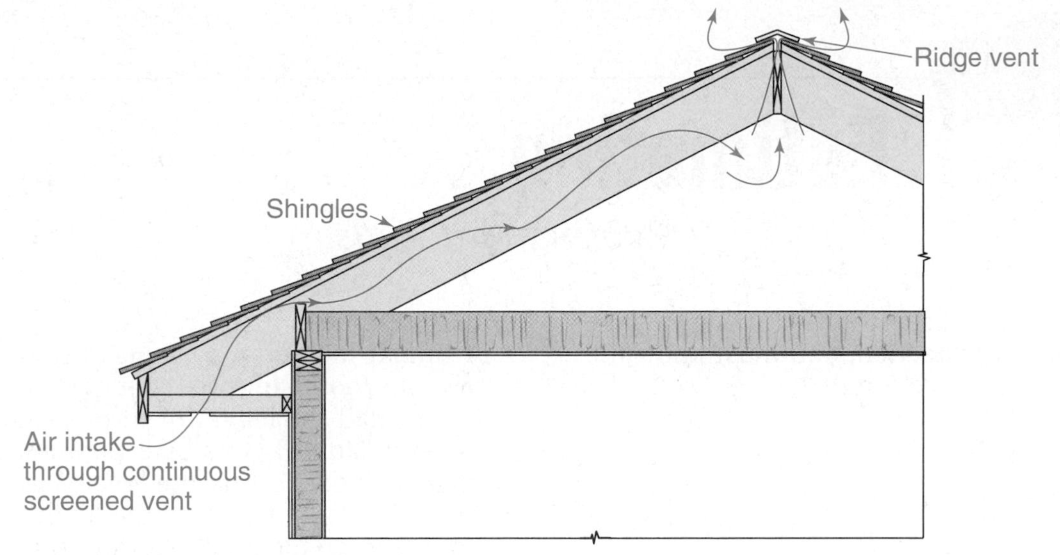

Fig. 30-29. A ridge vent releases air drawn in at the eaves.

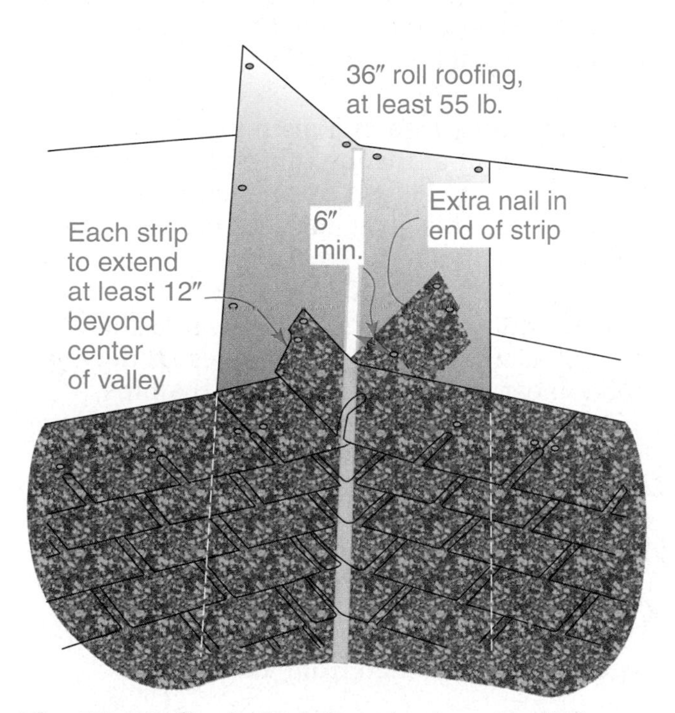

Fig. 30-30. Closed valley flashing using woven strip shingles.

Valley shingles are laid over the lining by either of two methods. In the first, they are applied on both roof surfaces at the same time, with each course in turn woven over the valley. In the second, each surface is covered to a point approximately 36″ from the center of the valley. The valley shingles are woven in place later.

In either case, the first course at the valley is laid along the eaves of one surface over the valley lining. It is then extended along the adjoining roof surface for at least 12″. The first course of the adjoining roof surface is then carried over the valley on top of the previously applied shingle. Succeeding courses are then laid alternately, the valley shingles being laid over each other.

Each shingle is cemented to the valley lining with asphalt cement and pressed down to ensure a tight seal. The shingles are then nailed in the usual manner, except that no nail should be located closer than 6″ to the valley centerline and no joints should occur within 12″ of the valley centerline. Also, two nails are used at the end of each terminal strip.

SECTION 30.3 Check Your Knowledge

1. What does *stacking the roof* mean?
2. What is often used as a starter course on shingled roofs?
3. What is the typical exposure of ridge shingles?
4. What is a closed valley?

On the Job

Obtain a supply of strip shingles and a piece of scrap plywood. Demonstrate for the class how to lay the start of first, second, and third courses.

Estimating...

Roofing Materials

To determine the amount of shingles and underlayment needed, you must know the total area to be covered.

ROOF AREA

To figure the roof area without actually getting on the roof to measure it, use **Table 30-A**.

Step 1 Look at the building plans to find the roof rise. The rise is given on Table 30-A in inches per horizontal foot.

Step 2 The area of the roofline (including the overhang) is then multiplied by the factor shown in the table. For example, if a home is 70′ long and 30′ wide, including the overhang, the roof area is 2,100 sq. ft. Look at Table 30-A. If the rise of the roof is 5½″, the factor needed is 1.100. The 2,100 sq. ft. multiplied by 1.100 results in a total roof area of 2,310 sq. ft.

Step 3 One square of shingles covers 100 sq. ft. of roof surface. To determine the number of squares needed to cover the roof, divide the total area by 100 and add 10 percent for waste and cutting.

$$2{,}310 \div 100 = 23.1$$
$$23.1 \times 0.10 = 2.31$$
$$23.1 + 2.31 = 25.41$$
or about 25 squares of shingles

Step 4 Be sure to subtract for openings in the roof such as the chimney. Subtract also for the area where a dormer intersects the roofline so that you do not include the dormer area twice.

Another method of figuring the area of a plain gable roof is to multiply the length of the ridge by the length of a rafter. This gives one-half the roof area. Then multiply by 2 to obtain the total square feet of roof surface.

HIP ROOFS

A similar method may be used to find the area of a hip roof. Multiply the length of the eaves by one-half the length of the common rafter at the end. Multiply this by 2 to obtain the area of both ends. To find the area of the sides, add the length of the eave to the length of the ridge and divide by 2. Multiply this by the length of the common rafter to obtain the area of one side of the roof. Multiply by 2 to find the number of square feet on both sides of the roof. Add this to the area of the two ends and divide the total area by 100 to get the number of squares.

To obtain the area of a plain hip roof running to a point at the top, multiply the length of the eaves at one end by one-half the length of the rafter. This gives the area of one end of the roof. To obtain the total area, multiply by 4.

Quantities of starter strips, eaves flashings, valley flashings, and ridge shingles all depend upon linear measurements along the hips, rakes, valleys, eaves, and ridge. Measurements for horizontal elements can be taken from the roof plan. The rakes, hips, and valleys run on a slope. The actual length of rakes, hips, and valleys must therefore be measured on the roof.

NAILS

The number of nails needed for asphalt roofing can be determined from **Table 30-B**.

Step 1 In our example, 25 squares of three-tab shingles are required to cover the roof area. Read down the table from the heading "Pounds per Square" to the line "3 tab sq. butt on new deck."

Step 2 If 11-gauge nails are used, 1.44 lbs. are required for each square. The total number of pounds of nails needed would then be 36.

$$25 \times 1.44 = 36 \text{ lbs. of nails}$$

The number of nails required for wood shingles can be determined from the information in **Table 30-C**.

(Continued)

Estimating...

(continued)

ESTIMATING ON THE JOB

Using Table 30-A, estimate the number of squares of shingles that would be required to cover a house that is 82′ long and 28′ wide, including overhang. The rise is 7″. Round your answer to the nearest whole number.

Table 30-A. Determining Roof Area from a Plan

Rise (inches)	Factor	Rise (inches)	Factor
3	1.031	8	1.202
3½	1.042	8½	1.225
4	1.054	9	1.250
4½	1.068	9½	1.275
5	1.083	10	1.302
5½	1.100	10½	1.329
6	1.118	11	1.357
6½	1.137	11½	1.385
7	1.158	12	1.414
7½	1.179		

Table 30-C. Estimating Wood Shingles

Wood Shingles Laid to Weather (inches)	Nails per 100 Square Feet	
	3d Nails	4d Nails
4	3¾ lbs.	6½ lbs.
5	3 lbs.	5¼ lbs.
6	2½ lbs.	4¼ lbs.

Note: Nails based on using 2 nails per shingle.

Table 30-B. Nail and Labor Requirements for Asphalt Roofing Products

Type of Roofing	Shingles per Square	Nails per Shingle	Length of Nails[(a)] (inches)	Nails per Square	Pounds per Square (approximate)		Labor Hours per Square
					12 ga. by 7/16″ head	11 ga. by 7/16″ head	
Roll roofing on new deck	–	–	1	252[(b)]	0.73	1.12	1
Roll roofing over old roofing	–	–	1¾	252[(b)]	1.13	1.78	1¼
19″ selvage over old shingle	–	–	1¾	181	0.83	1.07	1
3 tab sq. butt on new deck	80	4	1¼	336	1.22	1.44	1½
3 tab sq. butt reroofing	80	4	1¾	504	2.38	3.01	1⅝
Hex strip on new deck	86	4	1¼	361	1.28	1.68	1½

(a) Length of nail should always be sufficient to penetrate at least ¾″ into sound wood. Nails should show little, if any, below underside of deck.

(b) This is the number of nails required when spaced 2″ apart.

Wood Shingles and Shakes

Wood shingles and *shakes* are often installed when a traditional look is desired. Wood shingles are thinner than wood shakes. The surface of each may be sawed, for a relatively smooth appearance, or split, for a more rustic look. The installation methods are similar. Only the method for shingles will be described here.

GENERAL INSTALLATION

Wood shingles and shakes are generally laid over spaced sheathing boards, sometimes called *open sheathing*. This allows the shingles to dry uniformly. **Fig. 30-31.** However, shingles and shakes may also be laid over solid sheathing. This is sometimes required in earthquake areas. It is also recommended where wind-driven snow is common.

Underlayment protects the sheathing and reduces air infiltration. For underlayment, No. 15 asphalt-saturated felt may be used. However, underlayment is not installed over the entire roof in one layer, as with strip shingles. Instead, it is overlapped with successive courses.

TYPES AND GRADES

Shakes and shingles are graded according to the quality of the wood, considering any imperfections. The most common material is red cedar. Other types of cedar, along with oak and other woods, are sometimes used.

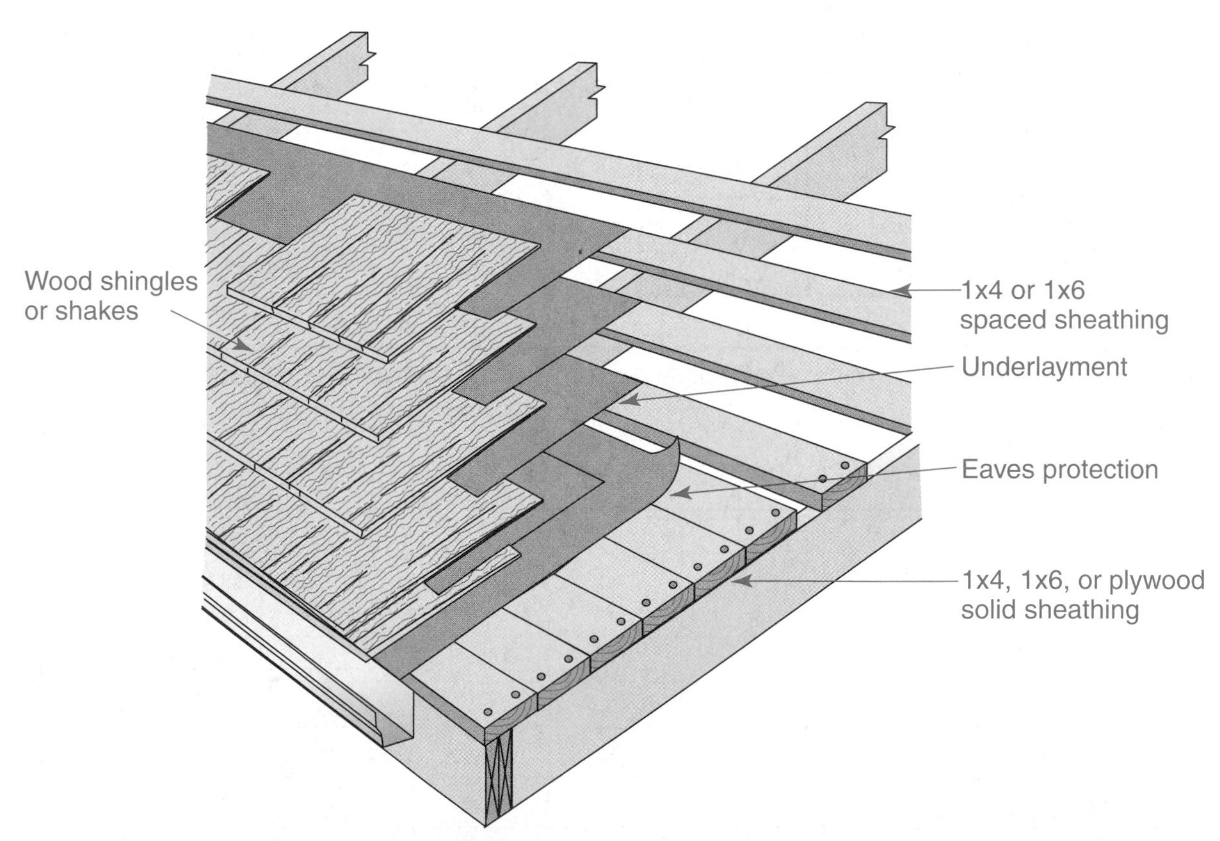

Fig. 30-31. The manufacturer's installation requirements should be closely followed when installing wood shingles and shakes.

Shakes

There are three types of wood shakes:

- *Handsplit-and-resawed shakes* have split faces and sawed backs. Blanks or boards are split and then run diagonally through a band saw to produce two tapered shakes.
- *Tapersplit shakes* are produced largely by hand, using a sharp-bladed steel froe and a wooden mallet. (A *froe* is a hand tool with a sharp blade and a wood handle at a right angle to the blade.) The taper is achieved by reversing the block end-for-end with each split.
- *Straightsplit shakes* are similar to tapersplit shakes. However, because they are split from the same end of the block, the shakes are not tapered.

Shakes are available in three lengths: 16″, 18″, and 24″. The maximum exposure recommended for double coverage is 13″ for 32″ shakes, 10″ for 24″ shakes, and 7½″ for 18″ shakes. Triple coverage can be achieved by reducing these exposures to 10″ for 32″ shakes, 7½″ for 24″ shakes, and 5½″ for 18″ shakes. Shakes are not recommended for roofs with slopes of less than 4-in-12.

Wood Shingles

Wood shingles are manufactured in lengths of 24″ (Royals), 18″ (Perfections), and 16″ (Fivex). They are available in No. 1 grade (sometimes called *blue label*), No. 2 grade (sometimes called *red label*), No. 3 grade (sometimes called *black label*), and undercourse grade used for underlying starter courses.

The exposure of wood shingles is dependent on the slope of the roof. **Table 30-D.**

In addition, decorative *fancy-butt shingles* are available. The *butt edge* (the thickest part of the shingle) is curved, beveled, or cut into any number of other shapes.

Some wood shingles are pressure-treated with fire-retardant chemicals at the factory. They may be required by code where fire danger limits the use of untreated shingles. Generally only No. 1 grade shingles are treated.

EAVES PROTECTION

In some areas, there is the possibility of ice dams forming along the eaves and causing a backup of water. In such areas, solid (plywood) sheathing should be applied above the eave line to a point at least 24″ inside the interior wall line of the building. The solid sheathing should then be covered with a double layer of No. 15 asphalt-saturated felt. A comparable product such as self-adhering bitumen sheet can also be used.

FLASHING

If copper flashing is used with wood shingles or shakes, take special precautions. Early deterioration of the copper may occur when the metal and wood are in direct contact in the presence of moisture.

On slopes up to 12-in-12, metal valley sheets should be wide enough to extend at least 10″ on each side of the valley centerline. **Fig. 30-32.** The open portion of the valley should be at least 4″ wide.

Table 30-D. Wood Shingle Exposure

	Maximum Exposure Recommended for Roofs Length (inches)								
	No. 1 Blue Label			No. 2 Red Label			No. 3 Black Label		
Slope	16	18	24	16	18	24	16	18	24
3:12 to 4:12	3¾	4¼	5¾	3½	4	5½	3	3½	5
4:12 and steeper	5	5½	7½	4	4½	6½	3½	4	5½

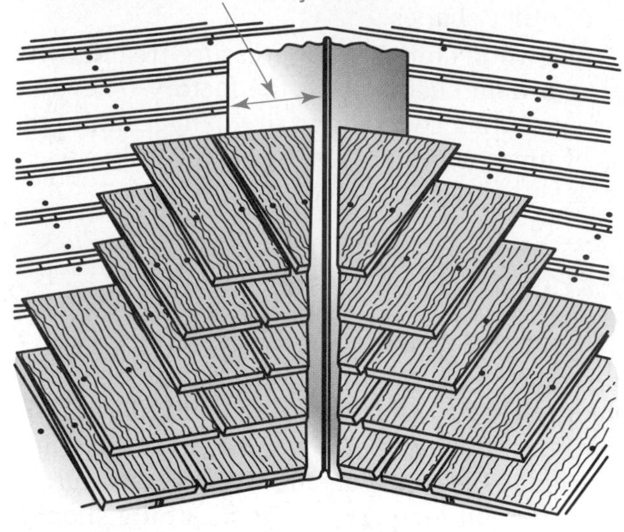

Fig. 30-32. Open valley flashing construction with wood shingles.

APPLYING WOOD SHINGLES

Double or triple the first course of shingles at the eaves. It should project l″ to 1½″ beyond the eaves to provide a drip edge.

Nail the second layer of shingles in the first course over the first layer to provide a minimum side lap of at least 1½″ between joints. **Fig. 30-33.** A triple layer of shingles in the first course provides additional insurance against leaks at the cornice. Undercourse shingles or No. 3 grade shingles frequently are used for the starter course.

Space shingles at least ¼″ apart to provide for expansion. Joints between shingles in any course should be separated not less than 1½″ from joints in the adjacent course above or

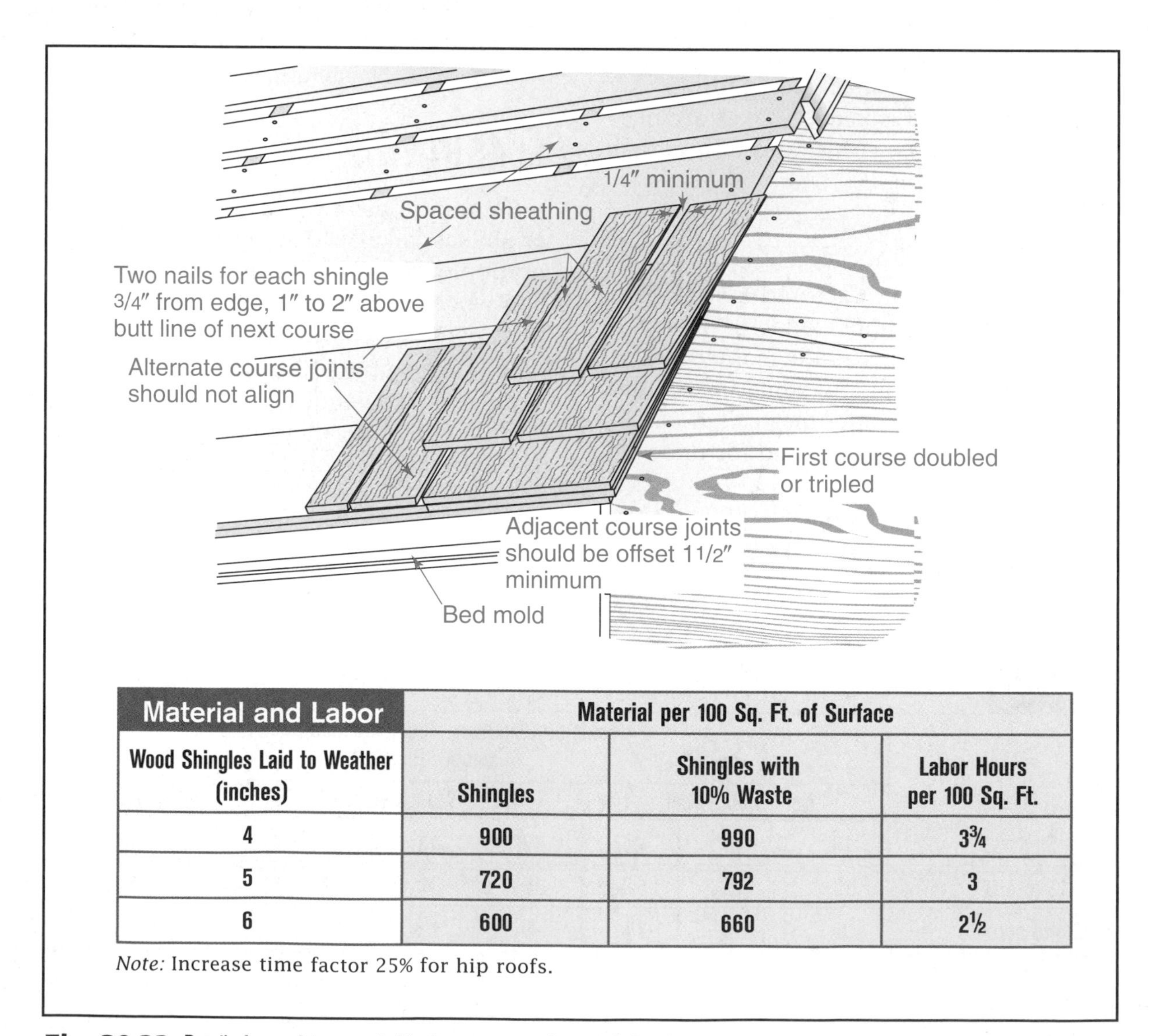

Material and Labor	Material per 100 Sq. Ft. of Surface		
Wood Shingles Laid to Weather (inches)	Shingles	Shingles with 10% Waste	Labor Hours per 100 Sq. Ft.
4	900	990	3¾
5	720	792	3
6	600	660	2½

Note: Increase time factor 25% for hip roofs.

Fig. 30-33. Details for applying wood shingles over spaced or solid sheathing.

below. **Fig. 30-34.** Joints in alternate courses should not be in direct alignment. When shingles are laid with the recommended exposure, triple coverage results.

When the roof terminates in a valley, carefully cut the shingles for the valley to the proper miter at the exposed butts. Nail these shingles in place first so that the direction of shingle application is away from the valley. This permits valley shingles to be carefully selected. It also ensures that shingle joints will not break over the valley flashing.

Nailing

To ensure that shingles will lie flat and give maximum service, use only two nails to secure each one. Place nails not more than ¾″ from the side edge, at a distance of not more than 1″ above the exposure line. Drive nails flush, but take care that the nail head does not crush the wood. The recommended nail sizes for the application of wood shingles are shown in **Table 30-E.**

Hips, Ridges, and Rakes

Hip and ridge shingles should overlap in a fashion sometimes referred to as a modified *Boston ridge.* **Fig. 30-35.** This calls for alternating the joint position in each pair of intersecting cap shingles. The top edges of the cap shingles should be beveled for a neat appearance. This also eliminates projections that would encourage water to seep into the joint. Nails at least two sizes larger than those used to apply the shingles are required.

Hips and ridges should begin with a double starter course. Either site-applied or pre-formed factory-constructed hip and ridge units may be used. Shingles should project 1″ to 1½″ over the rake.

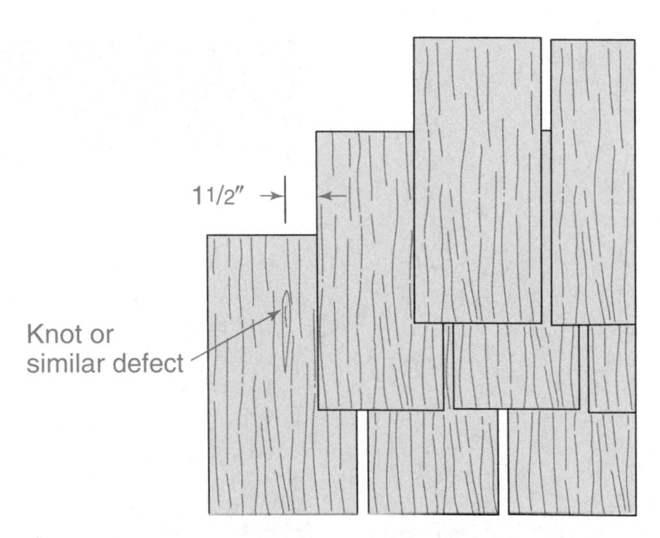

Fig. 30-34. Some shingle grades contain small defects, such as knots. Shingles should be laid so that the edges of the nearest shingles in the course above are at least 1½″ away from the defect.

Table 30-E. Recommended Nail Sizes for Application of Wood Shingles and Shakes

For 16″ and 18″ Material		For 24″ Material	For 16″ and 18″ Material	For 24″ Material
1¼″ long	1¼″ long 14½ gauge	1½″ long 14 gauge	1¾″ long 14 gauge	2″ long 13 gauge
Approx. 376 nails per lb.	Approx. 515 nails per lb.	Approx. 382 nails per lb.	Approx. 310 nails per lb.	Approx. 220 nails per lb.

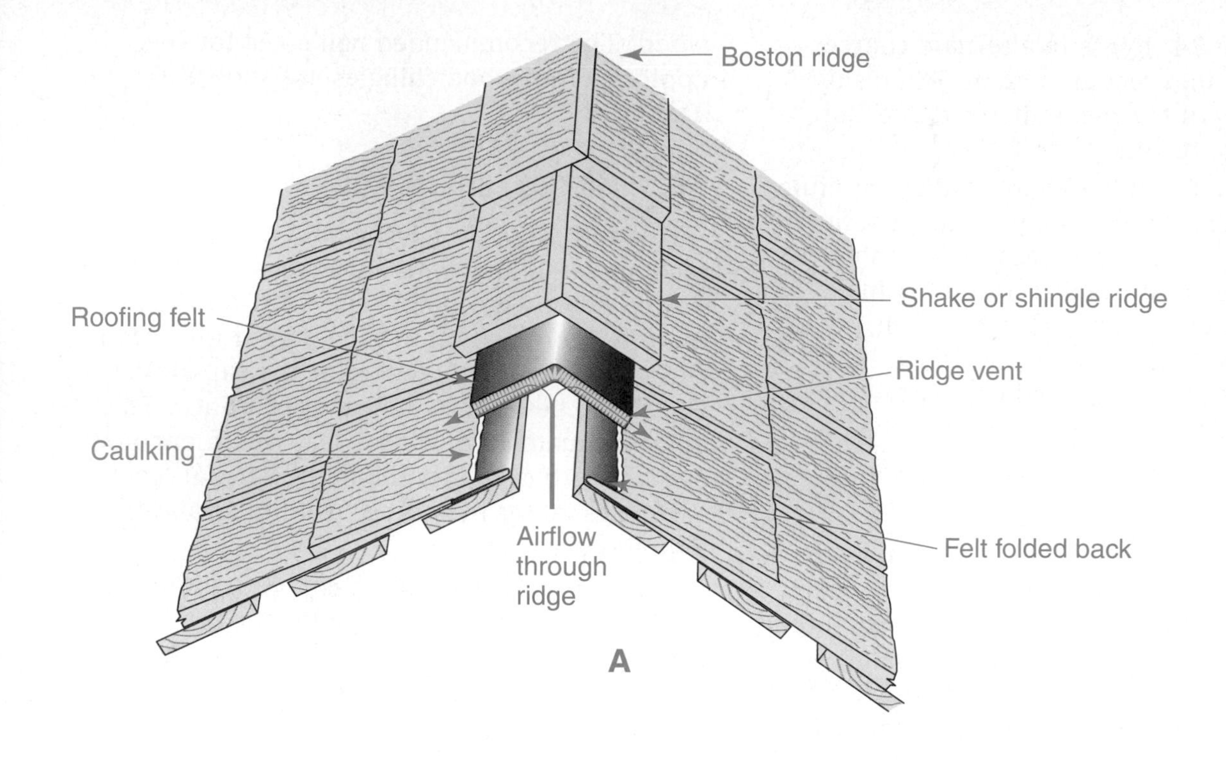

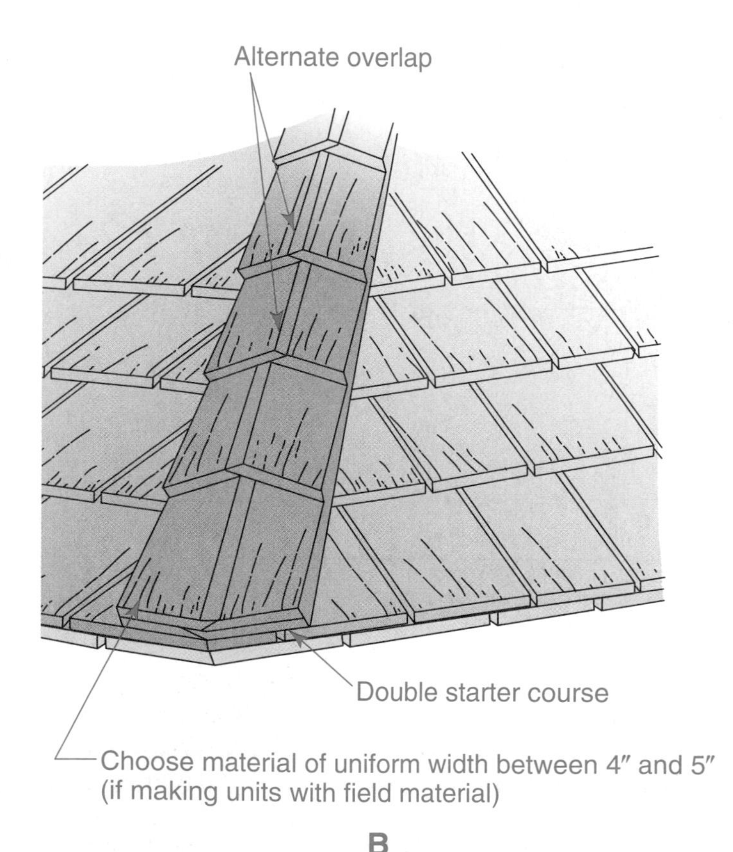

Fig. 30-35. Wood shingle construction. *A.* Boston ridge construction. *B.* Hip construction.

SECTION 30.4 Check Your Knowledge

1. What type of sheathing is most commonly used beneath wood shingles and shakes?
2. What grades of wood shingles are often used for starter courses?
3. How far should wood shingles be spaced from each other and why?
4. What length of nails should be used to secure wood ridge shingles?

On the Job

Red cedar is considered a renewable resource. However, there are concerns about how our forests are withstanding the great demand for wood products. Locate information about the location, growth, and harvesting of red cedar used for roof shingles. How are these forests managed? Gather information from organizations that have different, or even opposing, opinions about current forest management practices. Which point of view do you think is correct and why?

Chapter 30

Review

Section Summaries

30.1 Each type of roofing product has different characteristics that make it suitable for a particular house. The choice of a roofing material depends in part on the climate in which the house is located. Safety is of critical importance when working on a roof.

30.2 Underlayment and flashing prevent water from reaching the sheathing and causing damage. Underlayment also prevents damage from shingles sticking to the wood.

30.3 Installing strip shingles starts at the eaves of a roof and works up to the ridge. Shingles should be installed in an orderly fashion. Proper nailing is very important for the durability of the shingle and to maintain the manufacturer's warranties.

30.4 Wood shingles and wood shakes can be installed in similar ways. Various grades and types of shingles and shakes are available. They are installed over spaced sheathing.

Review Questions

1. What is the number used to describe a high-slope roof?
2. Name three types of roofing that might be suitable for covering large areas quickly.
3. If you needed to buy shingles for a high-wind area, which two kinds might you consider?
4. What precautions must be taken to minimize damage caused by ice dams?
5. In general, where should flashing be placed on a roof?
6. What is electrolytic corrosion?
7. Of what materials should nails be made that are used with shingles?
8. Describe the nailing pattern required for three-tab strip shingles.
9. What is the primary difference between a wood shingle and a wood shake?
10. In a cold climate, what precautions should be taken to protect the eaves of a wood-shingled house from leakage caused by ice dams?

Installing Flashing Roofers install most of the flashing on a roof. However, a mason may install step flashing if the chimney is made of brick or stone. This is because this work is readily done as the chimney is being built. In any case, the general contractor should be informed as to which contractor will take responsibility for installing chimney flashing.

Chapter

31 Roof-Edge Details

Objectives

After reading this chapter, you'll be able to:

- Identify different types of cornice construction and name the parts.
- Assemble a simple box cornice.
- Explain the purpose of a cornice return.
- Identify the main parts of a gutter system.

Terms

cornice
cornice return
eaves
fascia
fly rafter
lookout
rake
soffit

In many houses, the roof framing extends past the walls. The architectural style of a house is often revealed by the details at the edge of the roof.

The **eaves** are those portions of a roof that project beyond the walls. On a house with a hip roof, the eaves are the same width and height around the entire house. On a house with a gable roof, the eaves at the ends of the house follow the slope of the roof. They may be a different width than eaves at the sides of the house or may be omitted entirely. The upward slope of the eaves at a gable end is called the *rake angle.*

The roof-edge details can take many forms, depending on tradition and local preferences. They can include molding, gutters, and decorative cuts in exposed rafter tails.

Ventilation of the attic is an important factor to consider when planning and constructing roof-edge details. For more on that topic, see Chapter 39, "Thermal and Acoustical Insulation."

SECTION 31.1

Cornices

The eaves are often finished with molding, trim, and other details. **Fig. 31-1.** This collection of parts is called the cornice. A **cornice** consists of a fascia, a soffit, and various types of molding. **Fig. 31-2.** The **fascia** is a board that is nailed to the ends of the rafter tails. It protects the end grain of the rafters and serves as a mounting surface for gutters. The **soffit** is the underside of the eaves. It is sometimes enclosed with plywood, prefabricated vinyl panels, or aluminum sheets. It can also be left open, exposing the rafter tails.

Some cornice work may be done as soon as the roof has been framed. However, the cornice is more often built after the roof covering is in place. Cornice construction details are shown on the wall sections of the house plans. Detail drawings are usually included as well.

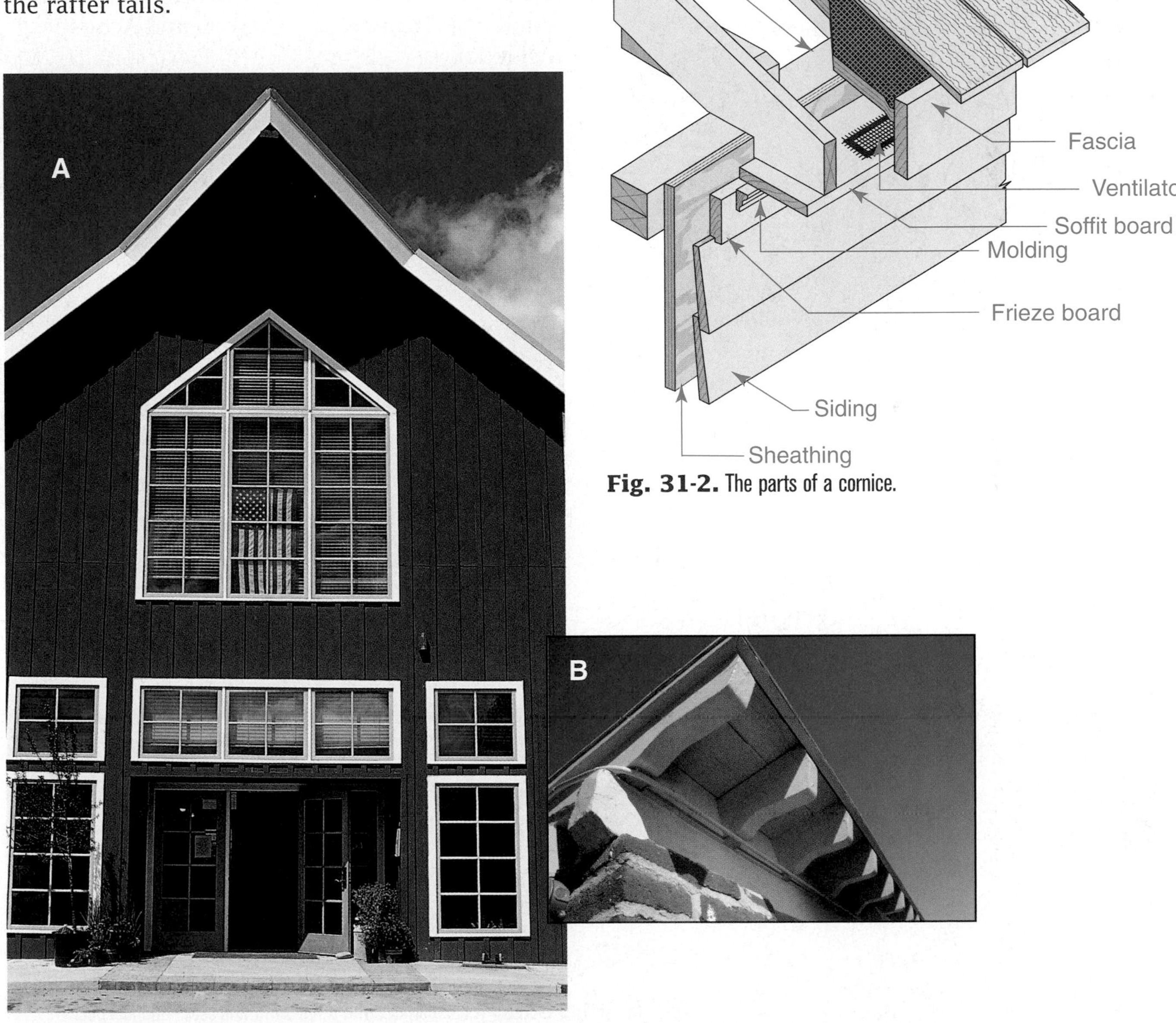

Fig. 31-2. The parts of a cornice.

Fig. 31-1. Distinctive uses of trim. *A.* The gable trim on this barn-style house finishes the edges of the roof. *B.* The rafter tails of this open soffit on an older building were cut by hand.

TYPES OF CORNICES

There are three basic types of cornices: open, box, and closed. An *open cornice* consists of frieze blocks, molding, and a fascia. The underside of the roof sheathing and the rafters are exposed. **Fig. 31-3.** It is simple to construct. One variation includes a continuous *frieze board*, which runs above the top course of siding. **Fig. 31-4.** Unlike a frieze board, a *frieze block* is strictly functional. It is a short piece of 2x framing lumber nailed between the roof rafters to seal off the attic space.

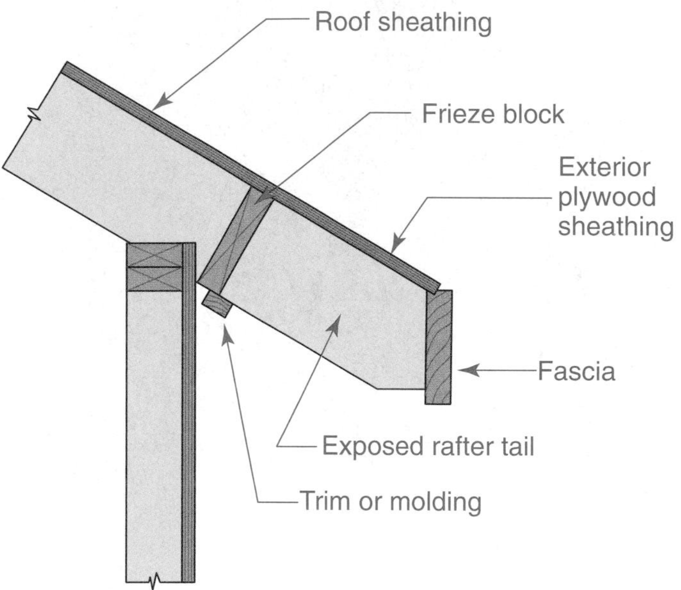

Fig. 31-3. An open cornice.

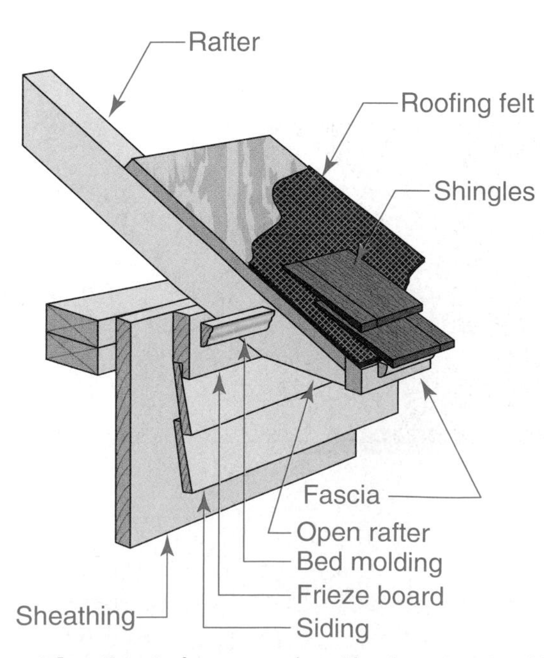

Fig. 31-4. An open cornice with a fascia board and frieze board.

A *box cornice* entirely encloses the rafter tails. It is built of roof sheathing, fascia, and a soffit. There are several ways of building a box cornice. The soffit can be nailed directly to the underside of the rafters. More often, however, it is nailed to lookouts. **Fig. 31-5.** A **lookout** is a horizontal member that extends from a rafter end to a nailer or the face of the wall sheathing. Lookouts form a horizontal surface to which the soffit material is attached.

A *closed cornice* appears on a house with no rafter overhang. **Fig. 31-6.** One version consists of a frieze board and one or more pieces of molding. This type of cornice is common on older houses in some parts of the United States. However, it is seldom used on newer houses because of the difficulty in providing attic ventilation (see Chapter 39, "Thermal and Acoustical Insulation").

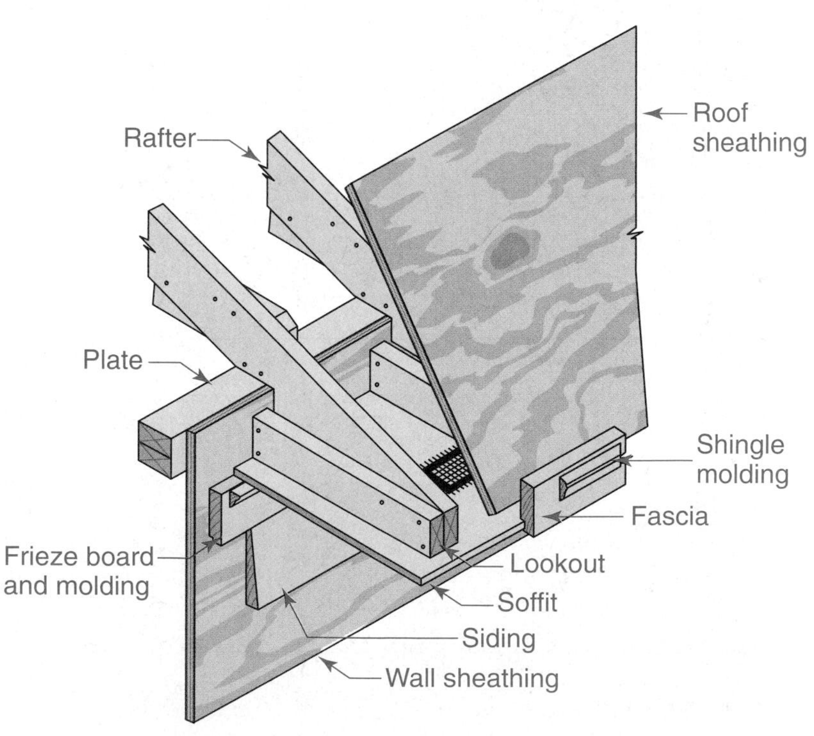

Fig. 31-5. A box cornice with a flat soffit enclosure and lookouts.

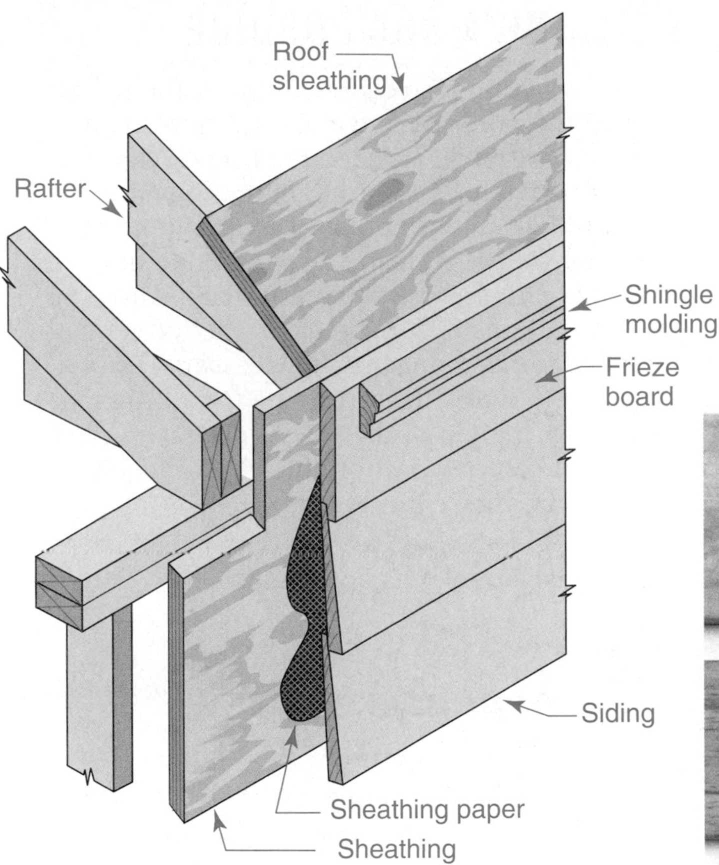

Fig. 31-6. A closed cornice.

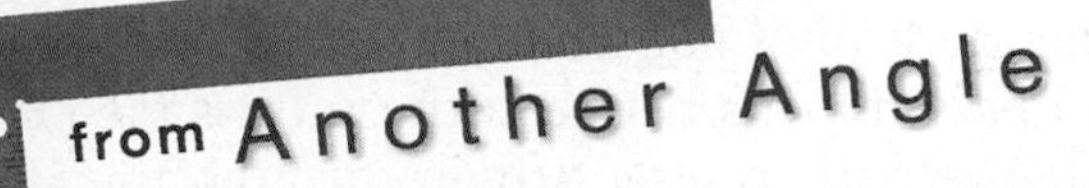

The availability of solid-wood and engineered-wood trim varies from region to region. Local builders generally rely on materials that have proven durability in a particular climate.

Fig. 31-7. Several examples of finger-jointed wood products.

CORNICE MATERIALS

Solid wood is the traditional material used for cornices. Because portions are exposed to the weather, choose a rot-resistant wood such as redwood or cedar. Other good choices include cypress and eastern white pine. The cornice is very visible, so top grades of lumber should be used. Avoid any board that contains sapwood, surface cracks, or loose knots. The fascia may be nominal 1x or 2x stock.

Engineered Wood

The use of new engineered-wood materials is becoming common. These materials are more uniform than solid lumber, free of defects, and of consistent quality. They are also available in long lengths. Many are pre-primed at the factory on all surfaces and edges. This saves labor at the job site and improves durability. Some of these products are composite blends of wood fiber and plastic. Others are made from finger-jointed lumber. Still others are made from LVL lumber. **Fig. 31-7.**

Like LVL lumber, LVL trim is stiff and uniform. It also has smooth surfaces, which make it easy to paint. LVL trim can be used wherever solid-wood trim would be used. One product is sprayed with a preservative during manufacture. One face is then covered with a smooth, water-resistant paper. The edges are sealed with a water-resistant coating and the whole board is sprayed with primer. The result is a straight, durable product that shows no traces of veneer on the edges.

When using engineered materials, it is extremely important to follow the manufacturer's guidelines. For example, some products must not be fastened with countersunk nails. Other products require a small expansion gap between adjoining lengths. If the manufacturer's guidelines are not followed, any warranty on the product is void.

BUILDING AN OPEN CORNICE

One method of constructing an open cornice is to install blocks between the rafters (see Fig. 31-3). The nails can be driven through the side of the rafter into the end of a block on one side. Nails have to be toenailed on the other side. **Fig. 31-8.** Then the vents are located and the necessary holes are bored. A piece of window screen is stapled or tacked on the back of the vent openings. Manufactured vents that fit into holes drilled in the blocking can also be used. Their screening is built in. Screens can be easily replaced if damaged.

A disadvantage of an open cornice is that the underside of the roof sheathing is exposed. The material used for roof sheathing may have surface imperfections that are unattractive. To counter this problem, carpenters may install a higher grade of plywood sheathing where it will show. Another solution is to install tongue-and-groove boards as sheathing in this area (see Fig. 24-44). The groove is removed from the starter sheathing board. Then the material is nailed to the rafters with the good surface down because it will be visible from below.

Cornice workmanship, too, is readily visible from the ground. For this reason, all joints in the construction of an open cornice should fit together tightly. Moldings should be mitered at outside corners and mitered or coped on inside corners.

BUILDING A BOX CORNICE

Before adding a box cornice, check the plumb cuts on the rafter tails to make certain they are all in line with one another. This check can be done by stretching a line along the top ends of the rafters from one corner of the building to the other. However, many carpenters do not make the plumb cut on the rafter tails when the rafter is cut. Instead, they install the rafters with the tails running longer than necessary. Then they snap a chalk line across the top of the tails to indicate the top of the cut. After drawing a plumb line downward from the chalk line on every rafter, they cut it to length.

See the Step-by-Step feature on page 623 for how to install lookouts and fascia.

The frieze block between rafters in an open cornice is sometimes positioned at an angle to the walls (see Fig. 31-3). However, some carpenters prefer to install the block so that it is parallel to the walls and at an angle to the rafters. In this case, the block must be a size larger than the nominal dimension of the rafters. It may have to be cut to a width that will fit the space and beveled to the slope of the roof.

Fig. 31-8. Nailing the blocking in place on an open cornice. The bottom edge of the ledger should be even with the level cut on the rafter tails.

STEP BY STEP

Installing Lookouts and Fascia

Install lookouts first and then the fascia.

Step 1 Use a piece of lx4 material as a ledger. Temporarily nail it tight against the wall and against the rafters, and align it with the inside edge of the first rafter. The bottom edge of the ledger should be even with the bottom of the rafter tail. (A *ledger* is a horizontal length of lumber used to support other structural elements.) **Fig. 31-9.** With a straightedge against the side of the rafter, draw a line on the ledger. Place an *X* on the side of the line away from the underside of the rafter to indicate the location of the lookout. Do this along the entire length of the building.

Step 2 Determine the length of the lookouts. Measure on a level line from the plumb cut on the rafter tail to the wall. Subtract ¾″ from this measurement to allow for the thickness of the ledger. Subtract another ¾″ to make sure that the lookouts do not project beyond the end of the rafters. Otherwise, if there is any deviation in the wall, such as a slight bow or a crooked stud, the lookout may extend beyond the end of the rafter tail. This will interfere later with installation and alignment of the fascia.

Step 3 Lookouts are generally made from 2x4 lumber. After they have been cut to length, remove the ledger from its temporary position. Nail the lookouts to the ledger over the *X*s. Nail through the back of the ledger into the end of each lookout with two 16d coated nails. **Fig. 31-10.** Some carpenters toenail the ends of the lookouts to the ledger instead.

Step 4 Locate the ledger on the wall by leveling from the rafter tail in toward the wall and placing a mark on the sheathing (point *B* in **Fig. 31-11**). Do this at each end of the building. Snap a chalk line along the length of the building on the sheathing.

Step 5 Place the bottom edge of the ledger on this line. Nail it through the sheathing and into the studs. Nail each lookout to the side of a rafter tail, except the end lookout. The end lookout should be cut to fit against the underside of the rafter. Level each lookout as it is nailed.

Step 6 If the soffit is narrow, as in Fig. 31-2, the connection between the fascia and the soffit may be a butt joint. If the soffit is wide, as in Fig. 31-5, one edge of the soffit material can be fitted into a groove sometimes cut in the back of the fascia. That method is described in Steps 7 and 8.

Step 7 Lay out, rip (if necessary), and groove the fascia to receive the soffit. Cut the groove about ⅜″ up from the bottom edge. This creates a drip edge.

Step 8 Nail the fascia to the ends of the rafter tails with the top of the groove even with the bottom edge of the lookouts. **Fig. 31-12.** If the fascia must be spliced, the joint should fall on the end of a rafter tail and be mitered. **Fig. 31-13.** The top edge of the fascia may be beveled to the same angle as the pitch of the roof. If it is not, its top outer edge should be in line with the top surface of the roof sheathing. Make certain that the fascia is straight along its length. If necessary, straighten the fascia by driving shims between it and the rafter tail ends.

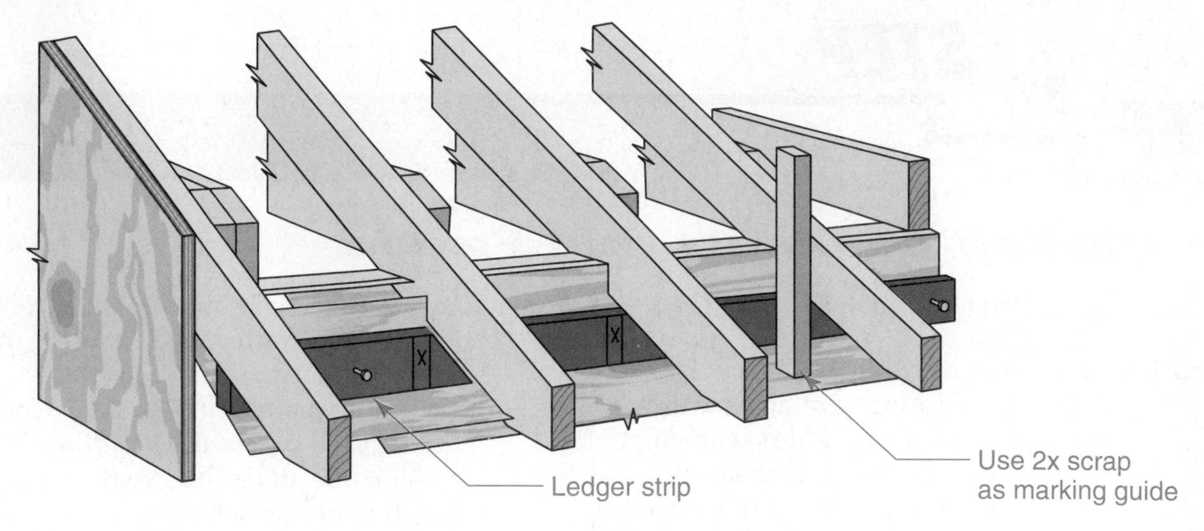

Fig. 31-9. Temporarily nail the ledger strip up under the rafters. Then mark the location of the lookouts.

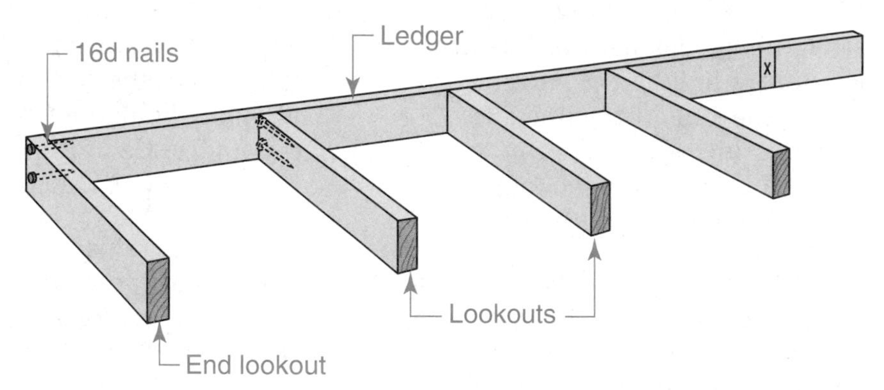

Fig. 31-10. The lookouts are nailed to the ledger strip next to the line and over the *X* made earlier. Note that the end lookout is nailed into the end of the ledger strip. This means that the end lookout has to be of the same thickness as the rafter and longer than the rest of the lookouts. It will have to be cut to fit under the rafter tail.

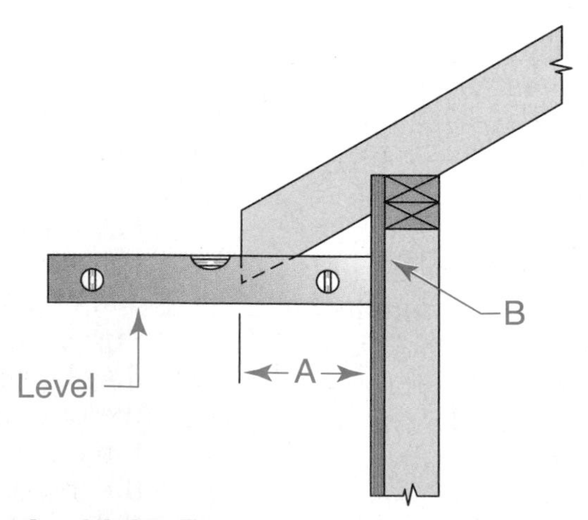

Fig. 31-11. The rafters are usually cut off before the ledger strip is located on the building. However, in some cases, point *B* is located on the building first. The cutoff line on the bottom of the rafter tail is then marked by leveling out from point *B*.

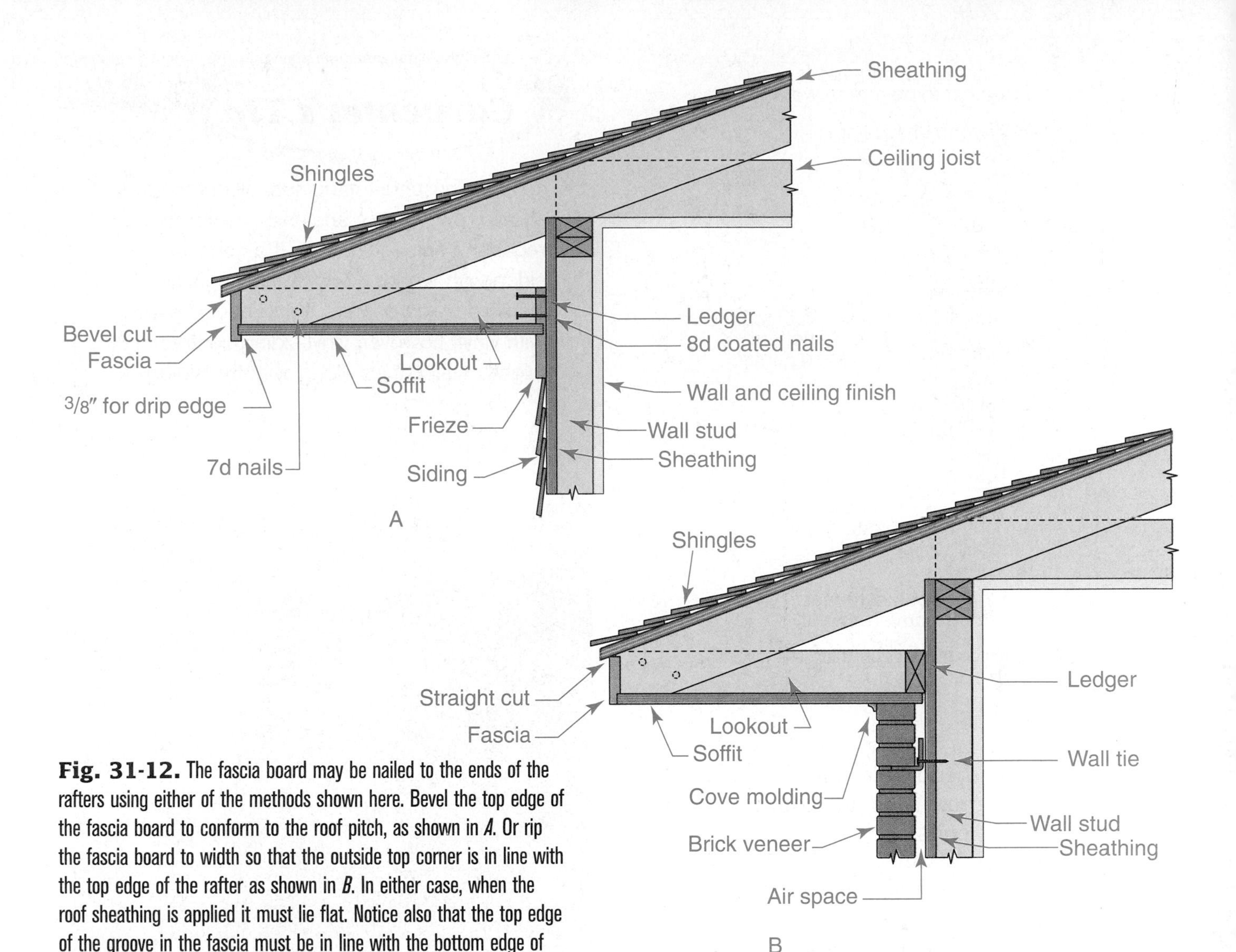

Fig. 31-12. The fascia board may be nailed to the ends of the rafters using either of the methods shown here. Bevel the top edge of the fascia board to conform to the roof pitch, as shown in *A*. Or rip the fascia board to width so that the outside top corner is in line with the top edge of the rafter as shown in *B*. In either case, when the roof sheathing is applied it must lie flat. Notice also that the top edge of the groove in the fascia must be in line with the bottom edge of the lookout for proper installation of the soffit material.

Soffits

Several materials may be used for the soffit of a box cornice. Because wide overhangs are popular, materials available in large sheets are often used. These include plywood, hardboard, vinyl, and aluminum.

Exterior plywood is one of the most popular soffit materials on a box cornice. It simplifies construction and presents a smooth, attractive surface. **Fig. 31-14.**

To install a plywood soffit, rip the plywood to width and slip the outer edge into the fascia groove. Then push the inside edge up against the lookouts and ledger. Nail the plywood securely to the ledger and to each lookout with 4d galvanized nails. Space the nails about 6″ apart. If the soffit material has to be made of several pieces, joints should be made under lookouts (see Fig. 31-13).

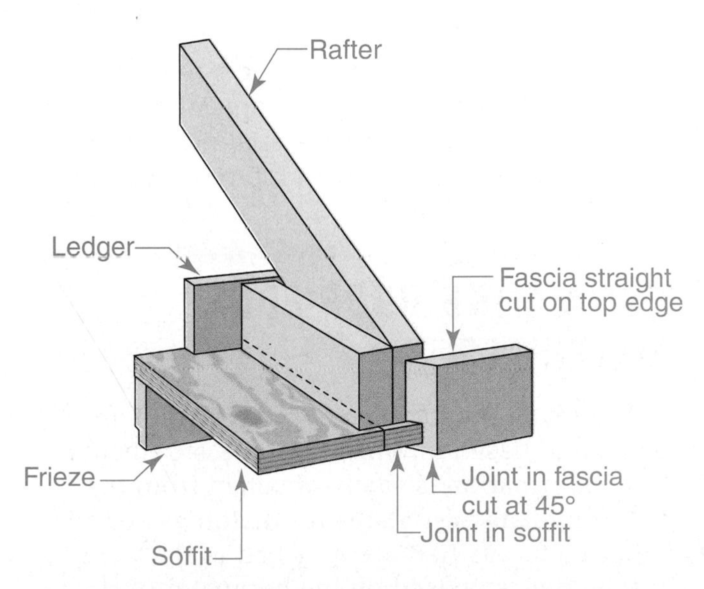

Fig. 31-13. The joint should fall on the end of a tail. Seams in the fascia and soffit board must occur over solid backing.

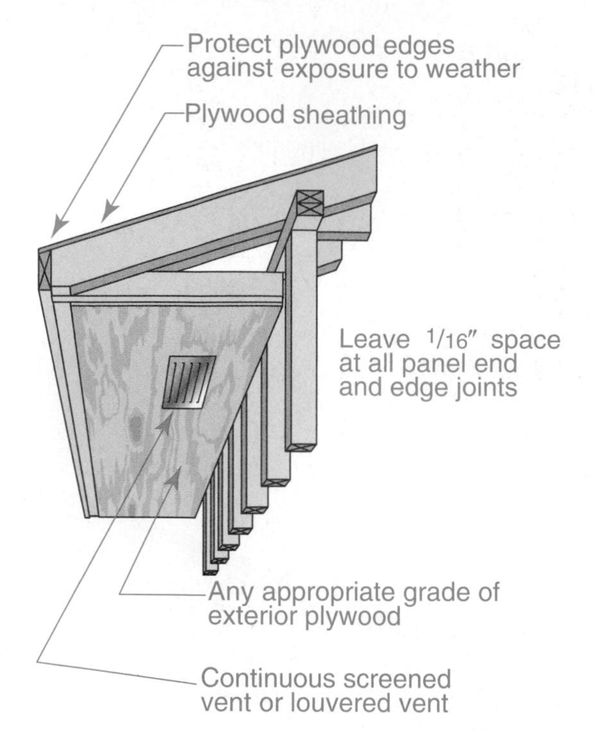

Fig. 31-14. Plywood is frequently used for soffit material on a box cornice.

When hardboard and other thin materials are used, the framing must provide continuous support at the edges, ends of panels, and joints. Intermediate supports may also be required. The manufacturer's instructions should always be followed.

Aluminum or vinyl soffit materials require little maintenance. **Fig. 31-15.** They are entirely prefinished and are available solid or perforated for ventilation. Light in weight, they come in small sectional panels or in sheets that are 12′ long. Installation is easy and convenient. Where aluminum or vinyl soffit material must turn a corner, as on a house with a hip roof, the panels can be mitered. **Fig. 31-16.**

Carpenter's Tip

To avoid misunderstandings, all contractors should review the plans and specifications regarding finish materials. If a house is sided with wood, wood soffits might be installed by carpenters. If the house is sided with vinyl, however, vinyl siding contractors might install panels along with the siding.

Fig. 31-15. An aluminum soffit board at the rake of a roof.

ESTIMATING ROOF-EDGE MATERIALS

The materials for cornice construction are estimated based on lineal foot measurements. This information is easily obtained from the building plans. Estimates for moldings and most other materials that are attached to the walls can be figured based on the perimeter of the house. The amount of soffit material required is also based on the perimeter measurement. You then need to refer to the house plans for the width and thickness.

The amount of material required for the fascia board and any molding attached to the fascia is figured by determining the perimeter of the roof at the rafter ends (not the perimeter of the walls). The lineal footage for rake moldings is figured in the same way as the length of the gable-end rafter. The amount of material needed for the lookouts is obtained by multiplying the projection times the number of rafters.

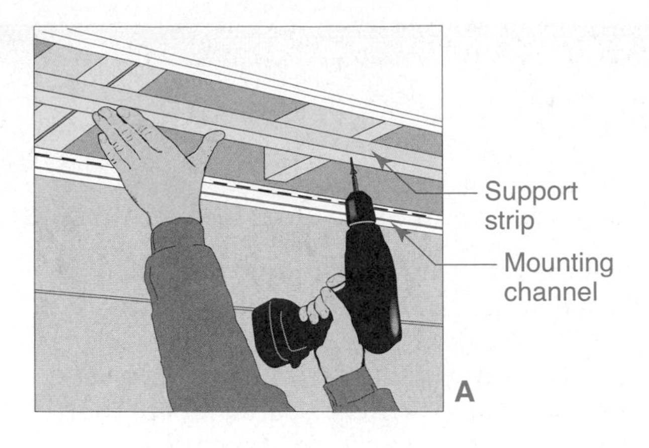

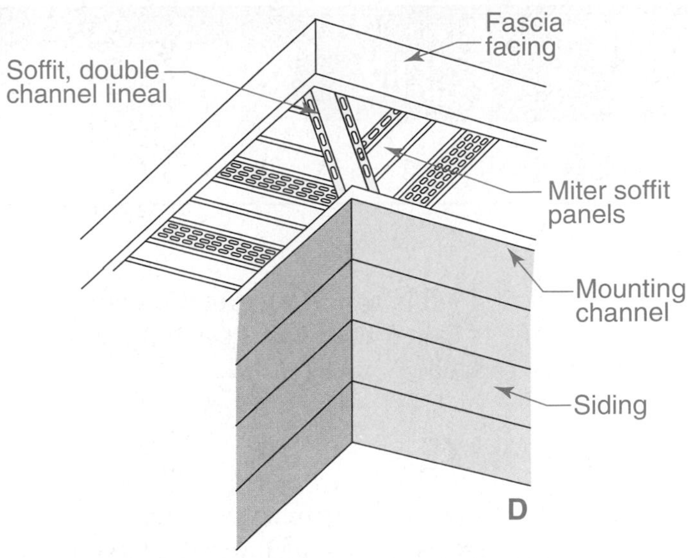

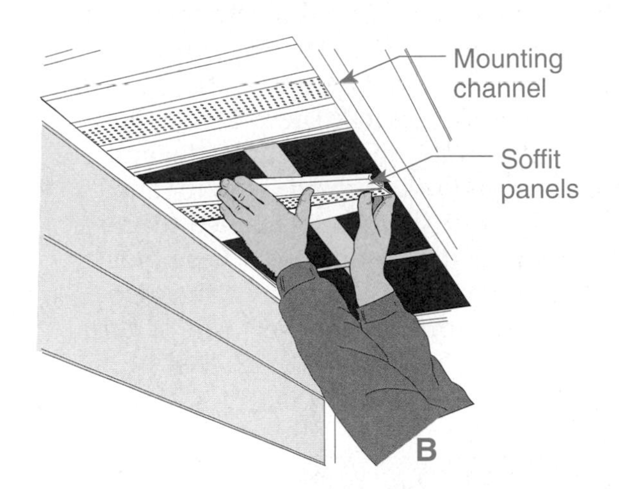

Fig. 31-16. Installing vinyl soffit material. *A.* Attach the mounting channel to the wall and a continuous support strip to the eave framing. *B.* Attach another mounting channel to the fascia, then flex the soffit panel as you slip it into place. *C.* Add fascia facing if called for. *D.* Where corners occur, miter the soffit material and support it with suitable trim.

SECTION 31.1 Check Your Knowledge

1. Name the three basic types of cornice.
2. What is the disadvantage of open cornices?
3. What must a carpenter check before beginning box cornice construction?
4. Name the four advantages of using aluminum or vinyl soffit material instead of plywood.

On the Job

A house measures 20′ by 35′. It has a hip roof, and the rafters project 18″ from the walls. Calculate how many lineal feet of frieze board and fascia it will require. Add 10 percent to each figure. Round up to the nearest even number of feet. Hint: First, sketch a plan-view diagram of the house.

SECTION 31.2

Rakes

The part of a gable roof that extends beyond the end walls is called the **rake**. It may be either closed or extended.

CLOSED RAKE

A *closed rake* consists primarily of the frieze board and moldings. Some additional protection and overhang can be provided by using a 2x3 or 2x4 fascia block over the sheathing. **Fig. 31-17.** This member acts as a frieze board. The siding can be butted against it. The fascia, often lx6 stock, then serves as trim. Metal roof edging is used along the rake to seal out water.

Rakes with little or no overhang are inexpensive and simple to build. However, extending the rake helps to protect side walls from weathering, which reduces maintenance costs.

EXTENDED RAKE

An *extended rake* may be as narrow as 6″ or as wide as 2′. If the underside of the roof sheathing is exposed, it is called an *open rake*. If it is not exposed, it is called a *boxed rake*.

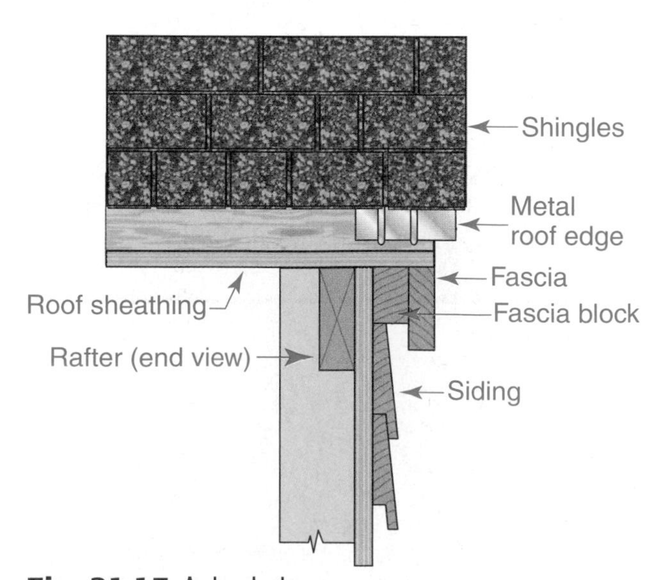

Fig. 31-17. A closed rake.

When the rake extension is only 6″ to 8″, the fascia and soffit can be nailed to a series of short lookout blocks. **Fig. 31-18A.** The fascia is further secured by nailing through the projecting roof sheathing. A frieze board and appropriate moldings complete the construction.

In a moderate overhang of up to 20″, both the sheathing and a fly rafter aid in supporting the rake section. **Fig. 31-18B.** The **fly rafter** extends from the ridge board to a structural fascia. It is made of 2x stock. The roof sheathing should extend from inner rafters to the end of the gable projection to provide rigidity and strength. The roof sheathing is nailed to the fly rafter and to the lookout blocks. These blocks help to support the rake extension and also serve as nailing surfaces for the soffit material.

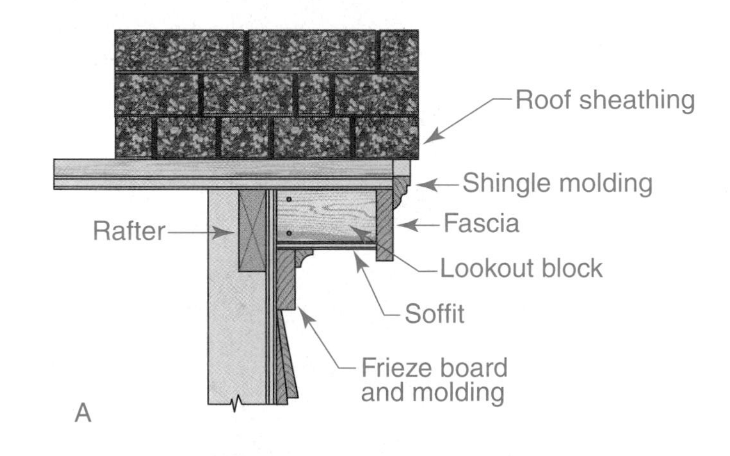

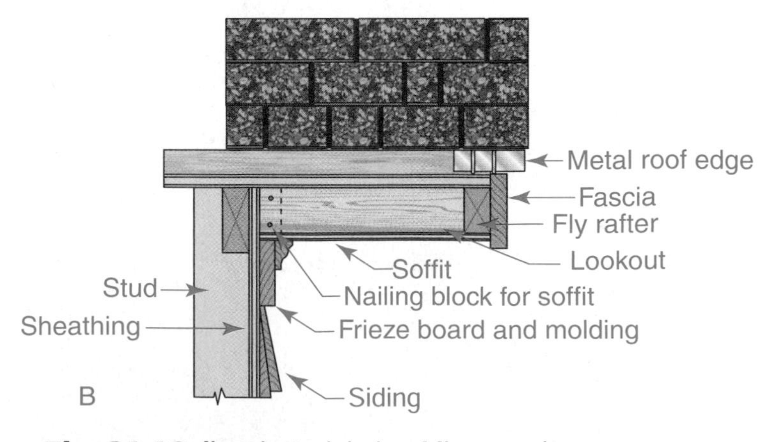

Fig. 31-18. Normal extended rakes. *A.* Narrow overhang. *B.* Moderate overhang.

Wide rake extensions require rigid framing to prevent deflection. This is usually done by installing a series of lookout rafters that cantilever over the end walls. **Fig. 31-19.** This is often called *ladder framing.* It may be constructed in place or built on the ground and hoisted into place. The lookouts are usually spaced 16″ or 24″ OC.

When ladder framing is preassembled, it is usually made with a header rafter on the inside and a fly rafter on the outside. Each is nailed to the ends of the lookouts that bear on the gable-end wall (rake wall). When the header is the same size as the rafter, it should be cut just as a standard rafter, including the bird's mouth. The header rafter is face-nailed directly to the standard rafters with pairs of 12d nails spaced 16″ to 20″ apart. Each lookout should be toenailed to the rake wall plate.

CORNICE RETURNS

The **cornice return** provides a transition between the rake and a cornice. **Fig. 31-20.** How it is built depends on how the cornice is built and on how far the rake projects beyond the side walls. In any case, it calls for a high level of carpentry skill.

SAFETY FIRST

Lifting Ladder Framing

Preassembled ladder framing can be heavy and unwieldy. Be sure to install it with plenty of help. Do not rely on stepladders for lifting the ladder framing into place because they can tip easily. Use scaffolding or properly anchored extension ladders instead.

When the cornice is boxed and there is some rake extension, the cornice return is also boxed. A boxed return is often used in houses of Cape Cod or Colonial design. Fig. 31-20A. The fascia board and shingle molding of the cornice are carried around the corner of the rake projection.

When a house has open cornices, the cornice return is sometimes handled quite simply. Fig. 31-20B. A curved piece of wood can be attached to the underside of the rake trim. This piece is sometimes called a *pork chop.* Fig. 31-20C.

Yet another method of building a cornice return is used on houses with narrow cornices and a closed rake. The fascia and trim details on the cornice are "turned" at the corner, without following the angle of the rake. To protect this area from weather, the top of the return must be covered with metal flashing. Some carpenters also slope the top surface to prevent water from accumulating against the siding.

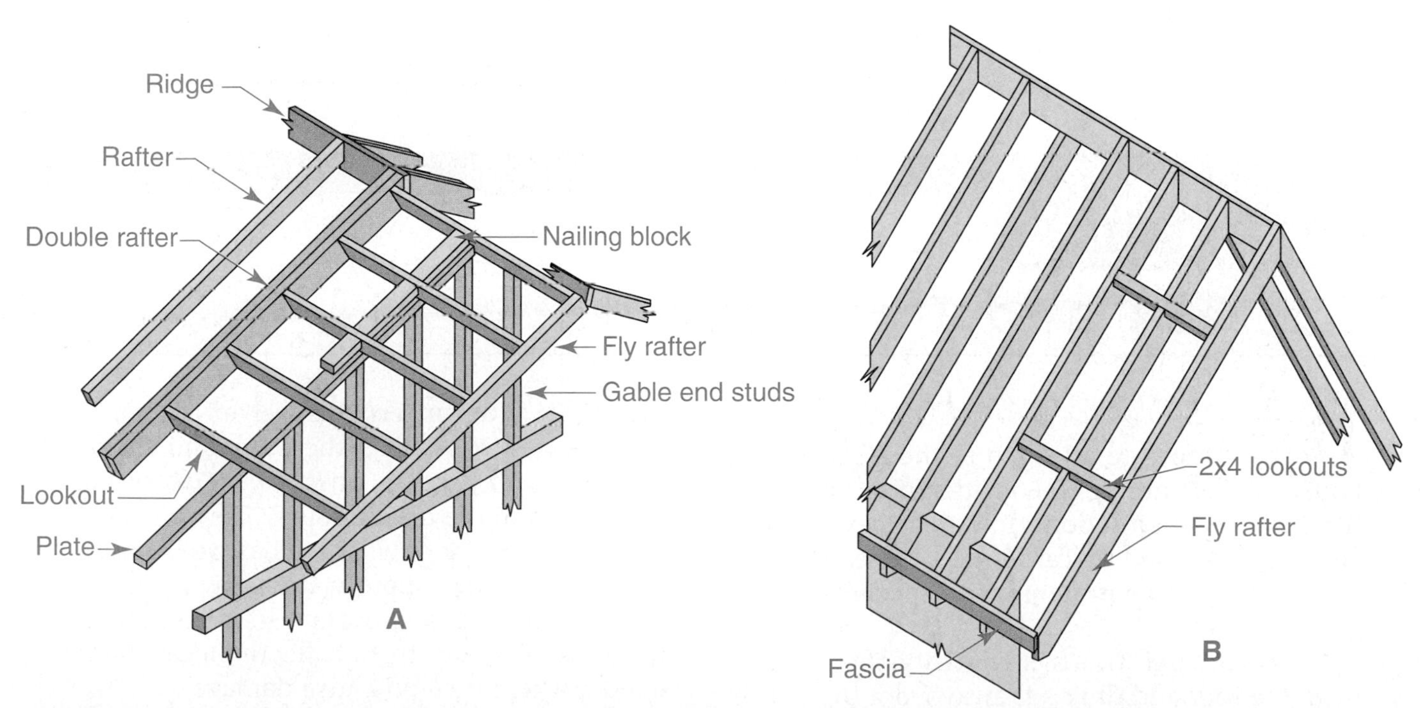

Fig. 31-19. Two methods for framing wide eaves at gable ends. *A.* Lookouts can rest directly on the top plate of the gable wall. They may be the same dimension as rafters. *B.* Lookouts fit into notches cut into the end rafter. They are typically made from 2x4 stock.

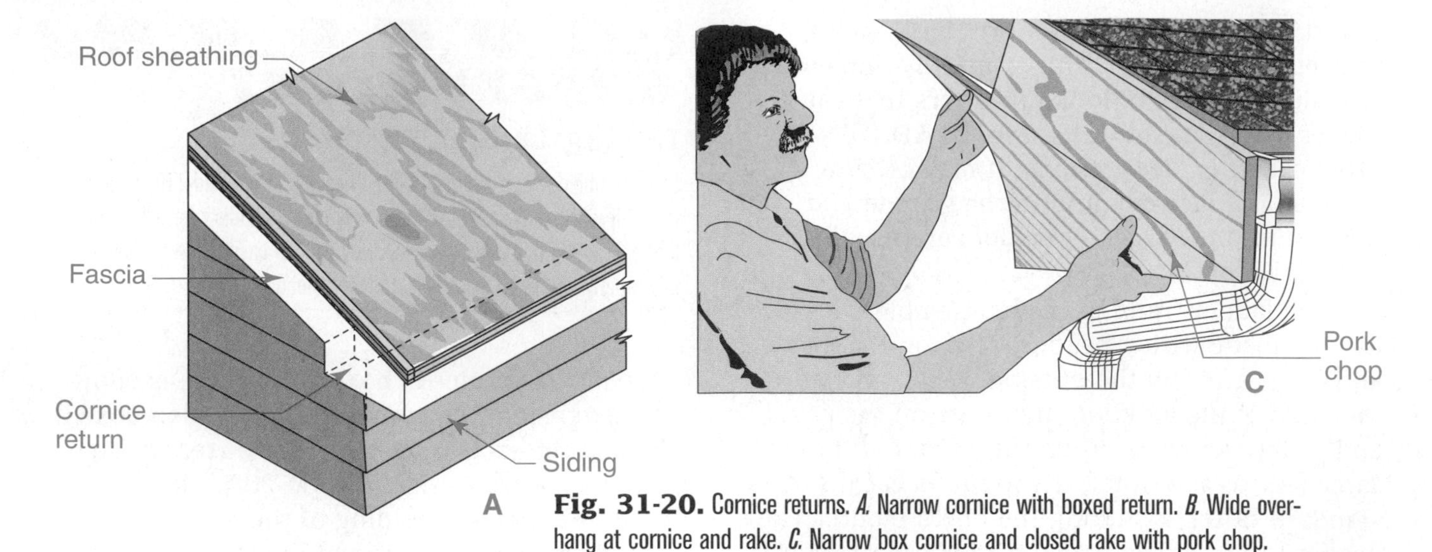

Fig. 31-20. Cornice returns. *A.* Narrow cornice with boxed return. *B.* Wide overhang at cornice and rake. *C.* Narrow box cornice and closed rake with pork chop.

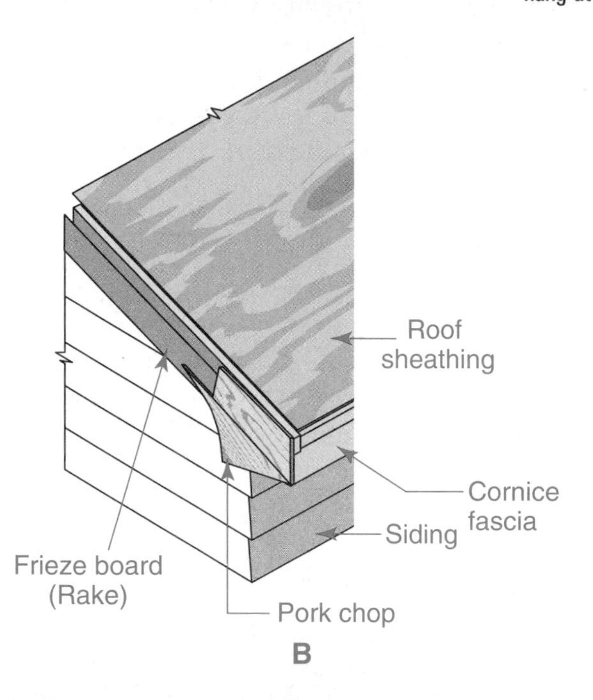

SECTION 31.2

Check Your Knowledge

1. What is the purpose of a fly rafter?
2. Describe the construction of preassembled ladder framing.
3. What is a cornice return?
4. What is a pork chop?

On the Job

Study the roof-edge details on five to ten houses in your community. Is one type of detail more common than others? Sketch one of the roof edges and analyze how it might be built. Present your sketch and a brief description of your analysis to the class.

SECTION 31.3

Gutters and Downspouts

Because they are attached to the fascia of a house, gutters are often considered to be part of the cornice construction. However, they are not generally installed by carpenters. Instead, they are the work of contractors who specialize in gutters.

Gutters are part of a system that collects water from the roof and drains it away from the house. **Fig. 31-21.** The gutters themselves are horizontal members that collect the water and channel it to vertical *downspouts*, or *leaders*. *Elbows* join the gutters to the downspouts. They are used at the bottom of the downspouts as well. *Splash blocks* direct downspout water away from the foundation. This is important in preventing large quantities of water from collecting near the foundation, where it could cause damage.

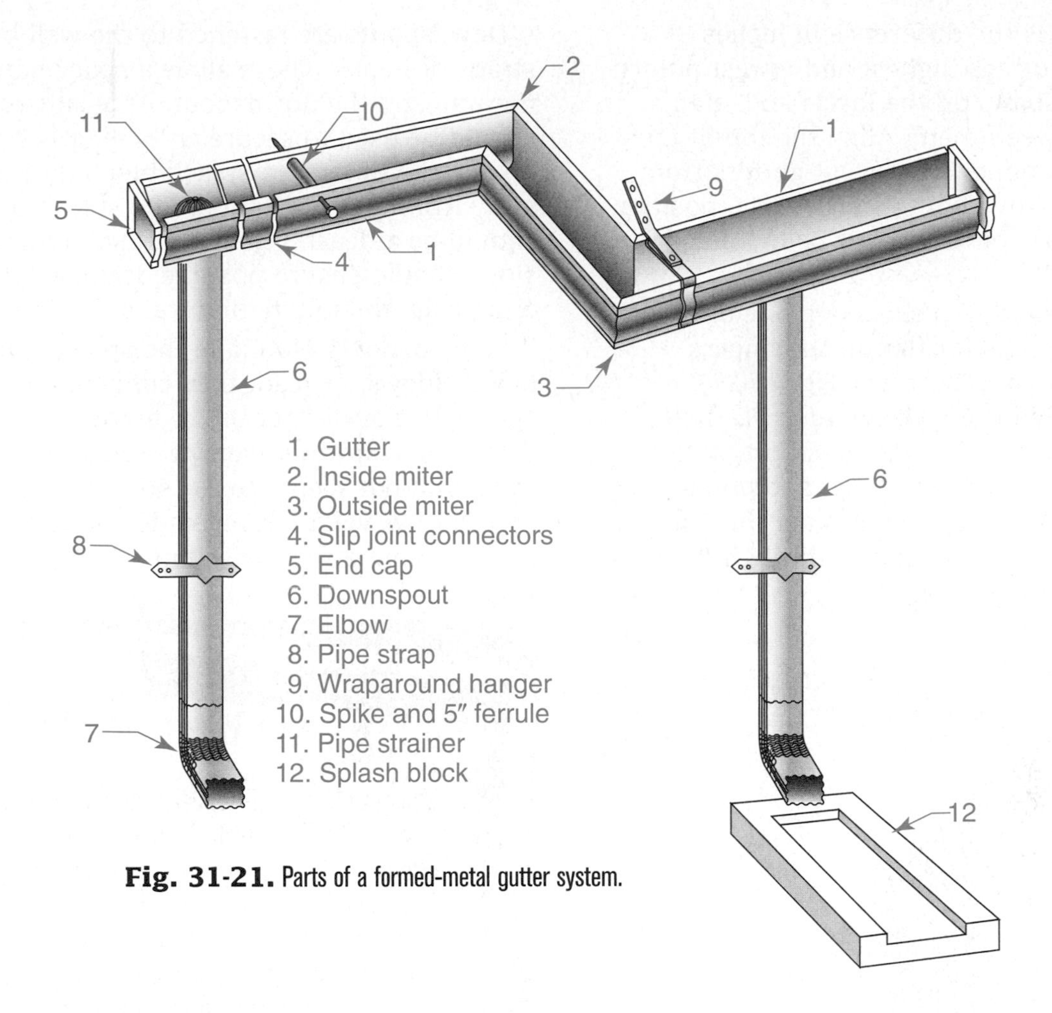

Fig. 31-21. Parts of a formed-metal gutter system.

Sharp Edges

The edges of metal gutters are very sharp. Wear leather gloves when handling and cutting them.

TYPES OF GUTTERS

Wooden gutters were once widely used but are very rare now. Today, most gutters are made of aluminum, copper, or vinyl. The two general types are the *formed-metal gutter* and the *half-round gutter*. **Fig. 31-22A** and **B.**

Downspouts are round or rectangular. The round downspout is ordinarily used with the half-round gutter. Both types are usually corrugated for added strength. **Fig. 31-22C.** Corrugated downspouts are less likely to burst if plugged with ice.

Gutters can be purchased in 10′ sections and joined with slip joint connectors. However, it is common for gutters to be fabricated on site using machines. Gutters of almost any length can then be formed from continuous coils of flat aluminum stock. These are sometimes called *seamless*, or *continuous, gutters*. They are less likely to leak because they are not assembled from many shorter lengths. In either case, the basic material is generally coated with a baked-on finish in one of several common colors.

INSTALLATION

Metal gutters on a house appear to be level. However, they actually slope at least 1″ every 16′ toward the downspouts (1⁄16″ per foot). This is essential for proper drainage. The maximum distance between the gutter's high point and the downspout should not ordinarily exceed 25′.

To ensure the correct slope, measure the distance in feet from one end of the fascia to the other. Round up to the nearest whole foot. Multiply this number by 1⁄16″. For example, a measurement of 20′-4″ is rounded up to 21′.

$$21 \times \tfrac{1}{16}'' = 1'\text{-}\tfrac{5}{16}''$$

The answer is the difference in inches between the gutter's highest and lowest points. Locate these points on the fascia and snap a chalk line between them. Align the top of the gutter with this line. To prevent gutters from being damaged by sliding snow or ice, position them so that the outer edge is below the plane of the roof.

Gutters are held in place using one of several methods. One calls for flat metal hangers spaced 3′ to 4′ on center (see Fig. 31-21). Another is called the *spike-and-ferrule method* (also in Fig. 31-21). *Ferrules* are short metal tubes placed between the inner and outer faces of the gutter. Aluminum spikes are then driven through the face of the gutter, through the ferrule, and into the fascia.

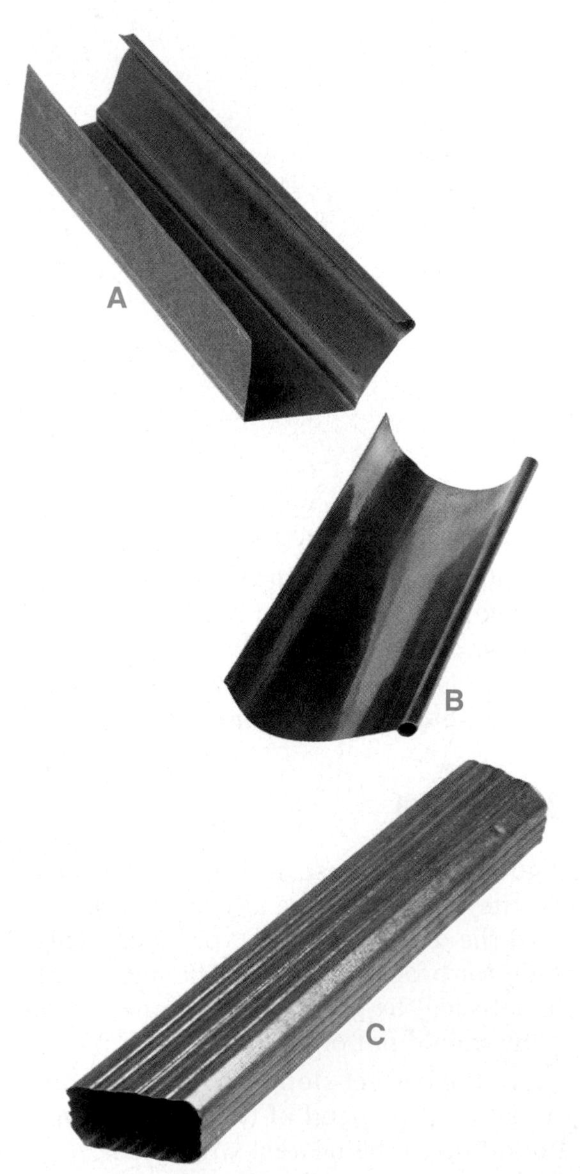

Fig. 31-22. Gutters: *A.* Formed. *B.* Half-round. *C.* Rectangular corrugated downspout.

Downspouts are fastened to the wall by leader straps or hooks. These allow a space between the wall and the downspout. At least two straps should be used to secure an 8′ length. An elbow directs the water to a splash block that carries it away from the foundation. The splash block should be at least 3′ long. In final grading the slope should ensure positive drainage of water away from the foundation walls.

Some builders eliminate the splash blocks and lower elbows. Instead, they connect the downspouts to a system of below-grade pipes that drain into a storm sewer. This ensures that water will not seep into the soil around the house. However, building codes prohibit drainage into a septic system.

from Another Angle

The depth of eaves depends on architectural style and the climate in which the house is located. A house in a mild or tropical climate might have deep eaves. They shield the walls from rain and allow windows to remain open for ventilation. A house in a cold climate might have short eaves, or none at all, to reduce the amount of snow that collects on the roof.

SECTION 31.3 Check Your Knowledge

1. Name the two general types of gutters.
2. Downspouts often have a corrugated shape. What purpose does this serve?
3. What is the minimum slope required to ensure that gutters drain properly?
4. What is a ferrule and how is it used?

On the Job

A common complaint of homeowners is that gutters clog easily with dead leaves, sticks, and other debris. Do some research to locate at least three products that reduce this problem. Study the manufacturer's performance claims. In a short paper, explain the advantages and disadvantages of the products. Which one do you think might be the most effective? Give your reasons.

Chapter 31 Review

Section Summaries

31.1 Cornices can be constructed in various ways, based on the architectural style of the house and the climate. They can be built of solid wood, but it is increasingly common for builders to use materials such as engineered wood and vinyl. The three types of cornices are open, box, and closed.

31.2 A rake is the part of a gable roof that extends beyond the end walls. Careful detailing is required at the rake, particularly at the cornice returns. The joints must be tight to prevent water from getting through.

31.3 Gutters and downspouts are part of a system that drains water away from the house. Gutters must be sloped toward downspouts. They are often installed by specialty contractors.

Review Questions

1. How is a box cornice different from an open cornice?
2. What are the advantages of using engineered wood when constructing a cornice?
3. Describe two methods for attaching wood soffit material to a wood fascia on a box cornice.
4. What is a pork chop?
5. What is the typical spacing of lookouts?
6. What is the purpose of a cornice return?
7. Name the main parts of a gutter system.
8. What two materials are most common in the construction of gutters?
9. How are seamless gutters commonly fabricated?
10. How many support straps are required for an 8′ length of downspout?

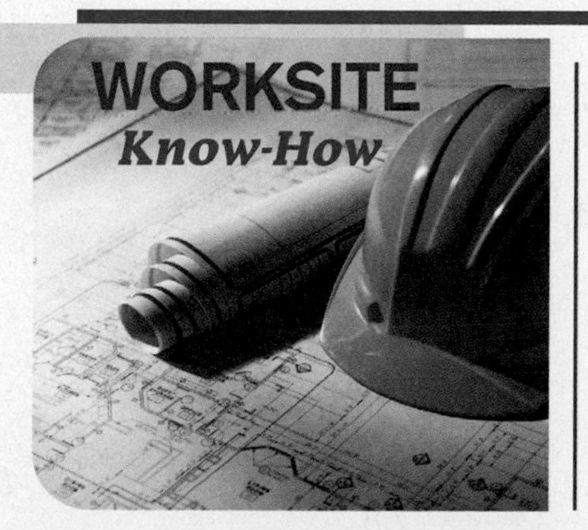

Timing of Gutter Installation Some types of gutter systems are best installed before the roofing has been applied. Others are best installed afterward. However, the roofers and the gutter installers should never be working simultaneously. The general contractor supervising the project must coordinate the work of the two trades so that conflicts can be avoided.

Chapter 32

Siding

Objectives

After reading this chapter, you'll be able to:

- Prevent moisture from seeping into or behind siding.
- Install plain-bevel wood siding.
- Describe the four coursing styles for wood shingles.
- Use good nailing technique on vinyl siding.

Terms

back-priming
J-channel
scarf joint
undercourse

The exterior wall covering of a house–the *siding*–should be selected with great care. It has an important effect on the overall appearance of the home, as well as on the ease of maintaining the house. A homebuilder today can select from a wide variety of siding materials. Many are available prefinished. This eliminates the need to paint or stain them after installation.

SECTION 32.1

Siding Basics

Depending on the material, siding is installed by either a carpenter or a siding specialty contractor. In either case, the process normally begins after windows and doors are in place and after the roofing has been installed.

Siding is available in a wide variety of materials, including solid wood, vinyl, plywood, steel, aluminum, stucco, and fiber cement. Another popular siding material is brick, which is discussed in Chapter 33, "Brick-Veneer Siding." Solid wood siding is the traditional favorite in most areas, but vinyl siding has become nearly as popular.

SOLID WOOD SIDING

The material most characteristic of North American houses is solid-wood siding. **Fig. 32-1.** Many other siding materials, including fiber cement, engineered wood, and vinyl, are formed to look like wood siding.

Wood Grades

Woods used for siding should have the ability to accept paint or stains, be easy to work with, and be dimensionally stable. These properties are present to a high degree in the cedars, eastern white pine, western white pine, sugar pine, cypress, and redwood. They are present to a good degree in western hemlock, ponderosa pine, spruce, and yellow poplar.

Fig. 32-1. Horizontal wood siding is common in all regions of the country.

Exterior siding materials should be of a premium grade that is free from knots. The moisture content at the time of application should be the same that the wood will have during service. This is about 12 percent, except in the dry southwestern United States. There the moisture content should average about 9 percent.

Types of Wood Siding

The following basic types of wood siding are shown in **Fig. 32-2**.

- **Vertical.** Solid wood boards with a uniform thickness are sometimes placed vertically over sheathing. The boards may be formed with a shiplap or tongue-and-groove edge to keep water out. When square-edge board siding is used, joints between boards must be covered with slender pieces of solid wood called *battens*.
- **Horizontal.** The most common type of solid wood siding is available as boards placed so that each piece overlaps the one below. A common type is plain-bevel siding (see Section 32.2).
- **Panel.** Exterior-grade plywood panels may also be used for siding. The exposed surface is covered with a high-grade wood veneer that may have a smooth or rough-sawn surface and may have grooves cut into it. The edges of panels may be covered with battens or have a tongue-and-groove or shiplap joint to seal out water.
- **Shingle.** In some parts of the country, wood shingle siding is common. The individual shingles are nailed to the wall sheathing in much the same way as wood roof shingles are nailed to the roof sheathing.

PREVENTING MOISTURE PROBLEMS

Poor construction enables moisture to seep into or behind any type of siding. This will eventually damage the paint or finish. It can

Fig. 32-2. Types of wood siding.

Name	Board		Bevel	Bungalow	Dolly Varden	Panel
Version	Board and Batten	Board on Board	Plain	Plain	Rabbeted Edge	
Description	Available surfaced or rough textured.		Plain bevel may be used with smooth face exposed or sawn face exposed for textured effect.	Thicker and wider than bevel siding. Sometimes called *colonial.* Plain bungalow may be used with smooth face exposed for textured effect.	Thicker than bevel siding. Rabbeted edge.	Typically 4′x8′ or 4′x9′ in size. May include decorative grooves.
Application and Nailing	Recommended 1″ minimum overlap. Use 10d siding nails as shown. Installed vertically or horizontally.		Recommend 1″ minimum overlap on plain bevel siding. Use 6d siding nails as shown. Installed horizontally.	Same as for bevel siding, but use 8d siding nails. Installed horizontally.	Same as for rabbeted bevel, but use 8d siding nails. Installed horizontally.	Exterior-grade plywood sheets are applied vertically directly to studs. Horizontal joints are flashed. Vertical joints may be covered with wood battens.

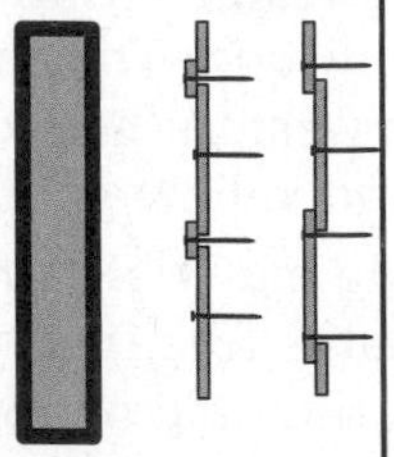

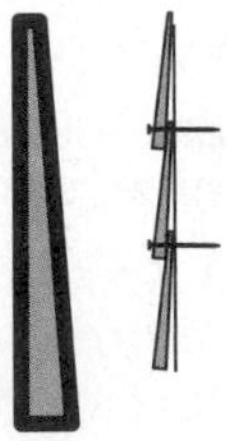

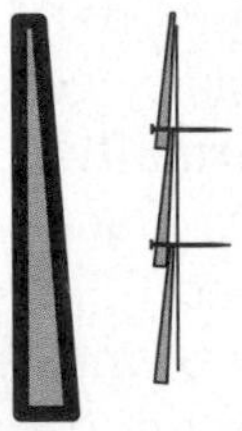

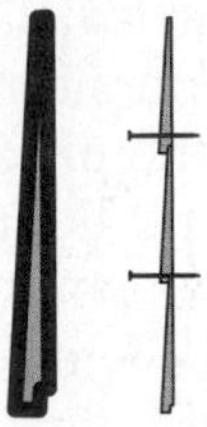

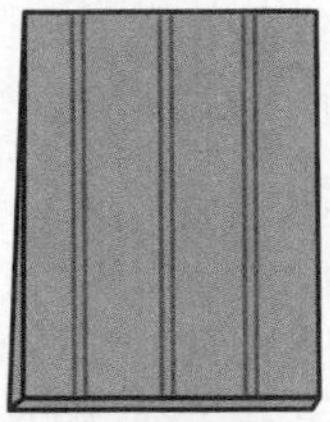

Name	Channel Rustic	Drop	Log Cabin	Tongue & Groove	Wood Shingle
Version	Board and Gap	Shiplap Patterns		Plain	
Description	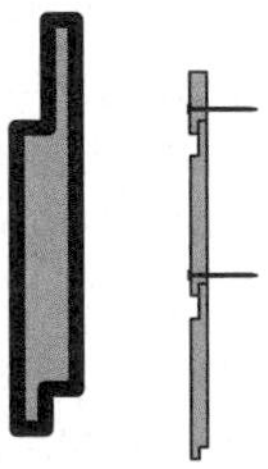 Available in roughsawn or smooth surface. Several thicknesses.	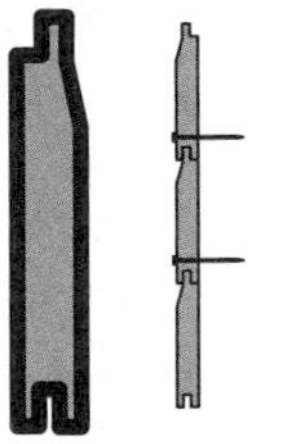 Available in various patterns.	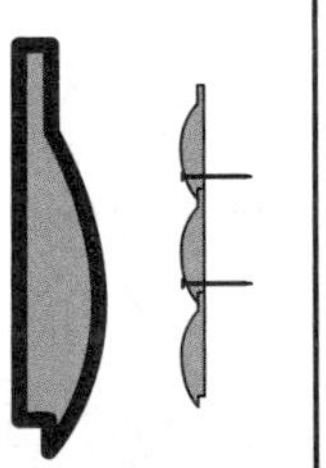 1½″ at thickest point.	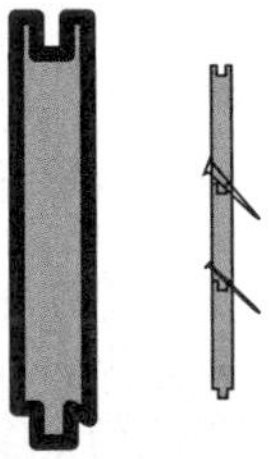 Available in smooth surface or rough surface.	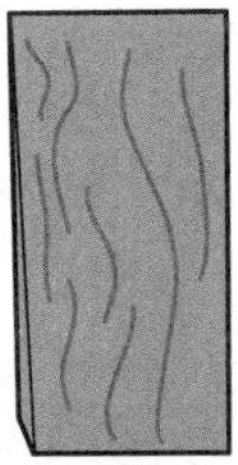 Available in random widths of 4″ to 14″. Lengths are 16″, 18″, and 24″.
Application and Nailing	May be applied horizontally or vertically. Has ½″ lap and 1¼″ channel when installed. Use 8d siding nails as shown for 6″ widths. Wider widths, nail twice per bearing. Installed horizontally or vertically.	Siding nails installed horizontally.	Nail 1½″ up from lower edge of piece. Use 10d casing nails. Installed horizontally.	Use 6d finish nails as shown for 6″ widths or less. Wider widths, face nail twice per bearing with 8d siding nails. Installed horizontally.	Applied in overlapping rows much like wood roof shingles.

also cause the sheathing to rot. The following methods are used to seal out water:

- **Proper detailing.** The siding must be installed so that water is directed away from joints. This is often done by lapping one piece of siding over another. Also, the lowest edge of any wood siding should be at least 8″ above grade level. This helps to keep it dry and reduces the chance of insect infestation.
- **Flashing.** Metal flashing is used to seal the joints where the siding meets a horizontal surface. These places include the areas over door and window frames. **Fig. 32-3.** Siding cannot dry out quickly where there is a tight fit. Flashing should extend well under the siding and sufficiently over edges and ends of a well-sloped drip cap to prevent water from seeping in.
- **High-quality caulking.** Caulking suitable for exterior use can be used to seal minor joints. Exterior caulking should be a type that remains permanently flexible. Vinyl or fiber cement sidings may require a special caulk recommended by the siding manufacturer.

The vertical joints between lengths of wood siding should be caulked with a durable, paintable sealant. However, the horizontal joints between courses of beveled siding should never be caulked. Caulking prevents moisture vapor from escaping from behind the siding, which can cause rot.

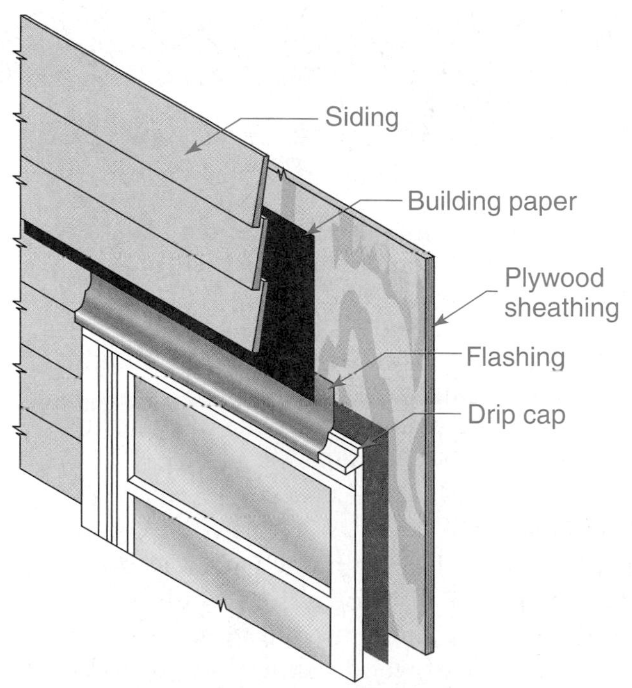

Fig. 32-3. Flashing should be used above windows and doors. The upper leg fits beneath the siding and building paper.

SHEATHING PROTECTION

The sheathing of a house is entirely covered by the siding and trim. However, wind-blown rain or water vapor can still reach it. The sheathing should be entirely covered by a barrier of building paper or housewrap. These materials are stapled to the sheathing just before the siding is installed. Additional layers are placed under trim, such as around windows and doors.

These barriers are water resistant but not moisture-vapor resistant. Vapor-resistant materials might trap moisture behind the siding or against the sheathing.

Building Paper

The traditional method for protecting sheathing is to cover it with horizontal courses of asphaltic felt, usually called *building paper* or *building felt.* This is a heavyweight paper combined with asphalt that comes in rolls 36″ wide. Building paper comes in two weights: 15 lb. and 30 lb. The lighter-weight paper is generally used beneath siding. Some manufacturers make a fiberglass-reinforced building paper that is less likely than standard paper to pucker if it gets wet.

Building paper should be applied smoothly to the sheathing using staples. Particular care should be taken around window and door openings. Succeeding layers should lap about 4″ over strips previously applied. Strips about 6″ wide should be installed behind all exterior trim.

Housewrap

Housewraps are made from high-density polyethylene fibers. These fibers interlock to allow water vapor to pass through, but not its liquid form. **Fig. 32-4.**

Fig. 32-4. A housewrap is often applied to the sheathing before siding the house. It reduces air infiltration.

A housewrap has some advantages over asphaltic felt. Because of its light weight, it comes in rolls 9′ wide. This speeds installation and reduces the number of seams. Also, a housewrap is difficult to rip, so it is less likely to be damaged during installation. However, it should *not* be used beneath stucco sidings. The stucco can bond to the housewrap in a way that can cause it to lose effectiveness.

Housewraps should be stapled to the wall sheathing before windows and doors are installed. Follow the manufacturer's recommendations for stapling the product and sealing the seams.

Siding Nails

Nails used to install siding should be rust resistant and must not cause the siding to discolor or stain. Three types with these characteristics are galvanized steel nails, stainless steel nails, and high-tensile-strength aluminum nails.

There are two kinds of galvanized nails: plated and hot-dipped. Mechanical plating provides a uniform coating, giving the nail predictable corrosion resistance. However, hot-dipped nails are generally more corrosion resistant. They are sometimes recommended by siding manufacturers.

Stainless steel nails are the most expensive. They are recommended when maximum weather resistance is required, as in areas affected by

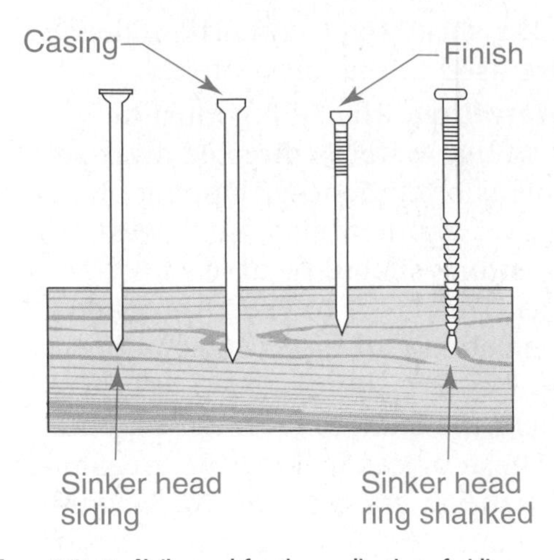

Fig. 32-5. Nails used for the application of siding.

salt spray. Aluminum nails can be difficult to apply by hand. They are readily installed by pneumatic nailers, however.

The basic types of siding nails are shown in **Fig. 32-5**. Nail heads are usually small so they won't show. Nail shanks may be smooth. However, ring-shank or spiral-threaded nails offer increased holding power.

Check Your Knowledge

1. List three characteristics of wood that are important when it is used for siding.
2. Name the woods that have a high degree of the properties noted in question 1.
3. Which portions of beveled siding should never be caulked and why?
4. What is the primary purpose of building paper and housewrap?

On the Job

If you were to build a home with a wood exterior, what type of wood siding would you choose? Find a home in your community that uses the type of wood siding that you have chosen. In a short paragraph, describe in detail the appearance of the home and the trim used. Conclude your paragraph with a statement that clarifies the reasons for your preference.

SECTION 32.2

Plain-Bevel Wood Siding

Beveled siding is a very common type of horizontal wood siding. The beveled shape allows the boards to be overlapped in horizontal courses that shed water effectively. **Fig. 32-6.** There are several types of beveled siding. The most common is plain-bevel siding, sometimes called clapboard or lap siding. It is made in nominal 4″, 5″, 6″, 8″, and 10″ widths. The butt edge (the thickest part of the board) ranges from 7⁄16″ to 11⁄16″, depending on the board's width. The top edge is 3⁄16″ thick in all sizes. Plain-bevel siding generally comes in random lengths from 4′ to 16′. One face of each board is rough sawn, while the other face is smooth. The siding can be installed with either surface exposed.

Fig. 32-6. The amount of overlap required on plain-bevel wood siding is specified in building codes as well as in the product literature.

PREPARATION AND LAYOUT

Before installing plain-bevel siding, allow it to reach a moisture content compatible with local conditions. This will prevent excessive shrinkage after the siding is in place.

Adding Protection

Wood siding that will be painted should be primed before it is installed. This ensures that all surfaces are protected and improves the durability of the siding as well as the final finish. If the siding has not been primed on all surfaces by the manufacturer (called *pre-priming*), the back surface of the boards should be primed on site. This is called **back-priming**. The front surface can then be primed after installation.

Another protective option is to treat the boards with a water repellent before installation. This may be done by brushing or spraying the water repellent on all surfaces. The ends of boards cut during installation should also receive treatment with water repellent.

Determining Exposure

The spacing for plain-bevel siding should be carefully laid out in advance. Siding starts at the foundation and progresses upward. Each new course overlaps the top edge of the previous course. **Fig. 32-7.**

Determine the number of courses by measuring from the underside of the soffit to a point 1″ below the sheathing. **Fig. 32-8.** Divide that distance by the maximum exposure of a single piece of siding. The *exposure* is the amount of surface exposed to the weather. To determine the exposure, deduct the minimum overlap (head lap) from the total width of the siding. The minimum overlap is 1″ for 4″ and 6″ widths and 1¼″ for widths over 6″.

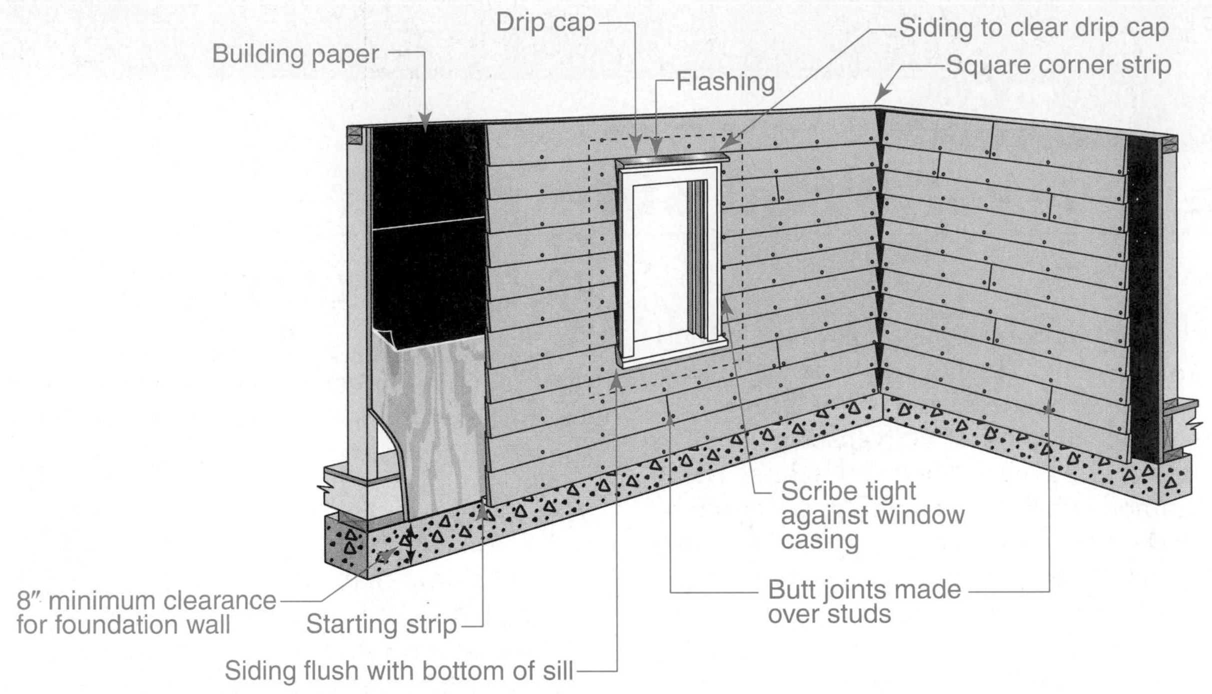

Fig. 32-7. An exterior wall with wood sheathing and beveled siding.

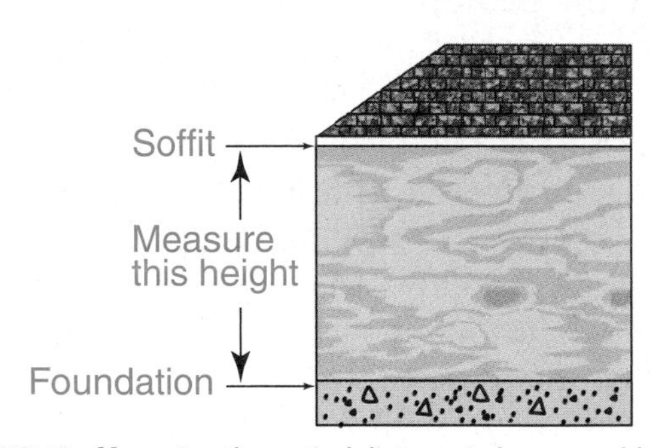

Fig. 32-8. Measuring the vertical distance to be covered by the siding.

For example, if nominal 10″ plain-bevel siding is used, its actual width is 9¼″. A minimum overlap of 1¼″ is required. Therefore, the maximum exposure is 8″ (9¼″ – 1¼″ = 8″). With a pair of dividers set at 8″, make a trial layout on the side wall. Begin at the bottom and "walk off" the height of the wall in 8″ increments. The bottom of the piece of siding that passes over the top of the first-floor windows should meet with the top of the window (see Fig. 32-7). If it does not line up properly, adjust the exposure distance until it does. Note, however, that in this case 8″ is the *maximum* exposure. Any adjustments must be to something less than 8″. Another way to make the layout work is to raise or lower the first piece of siding slightly.

Making a Story Pole

Many carpenters rely on a story pole. A *story pole* is a measuring device made on site to ensure a uniform layout all around the house. **Fig. 32-9.**

To make a story pole, select a straight piece of 1x2 stock approximately 8′ to 10′ long. Determine the number of courses and the spacing as described above. Lay out the spacing on the story pole. Additional information, such as the height of windowsills, can also be marked on the story pole.

APPLICATION

Siding can be installed after the house has been wrapped with building paper or housewrap. How well the first course of siding is applied determines how level and uniform the succeeding courses will be.

First, install all trim around windows and doors. Install *corner strips* at inside corners and *corner boards* at outside corners. These are lengths of solid wood trim that are placed vertically over the sheathing where walls intersect. They protect the corner joint from water seepage. **Fig. 32-10.** The size of this trim may be specified on the building plans. It varies according to the style of the house and the thickness

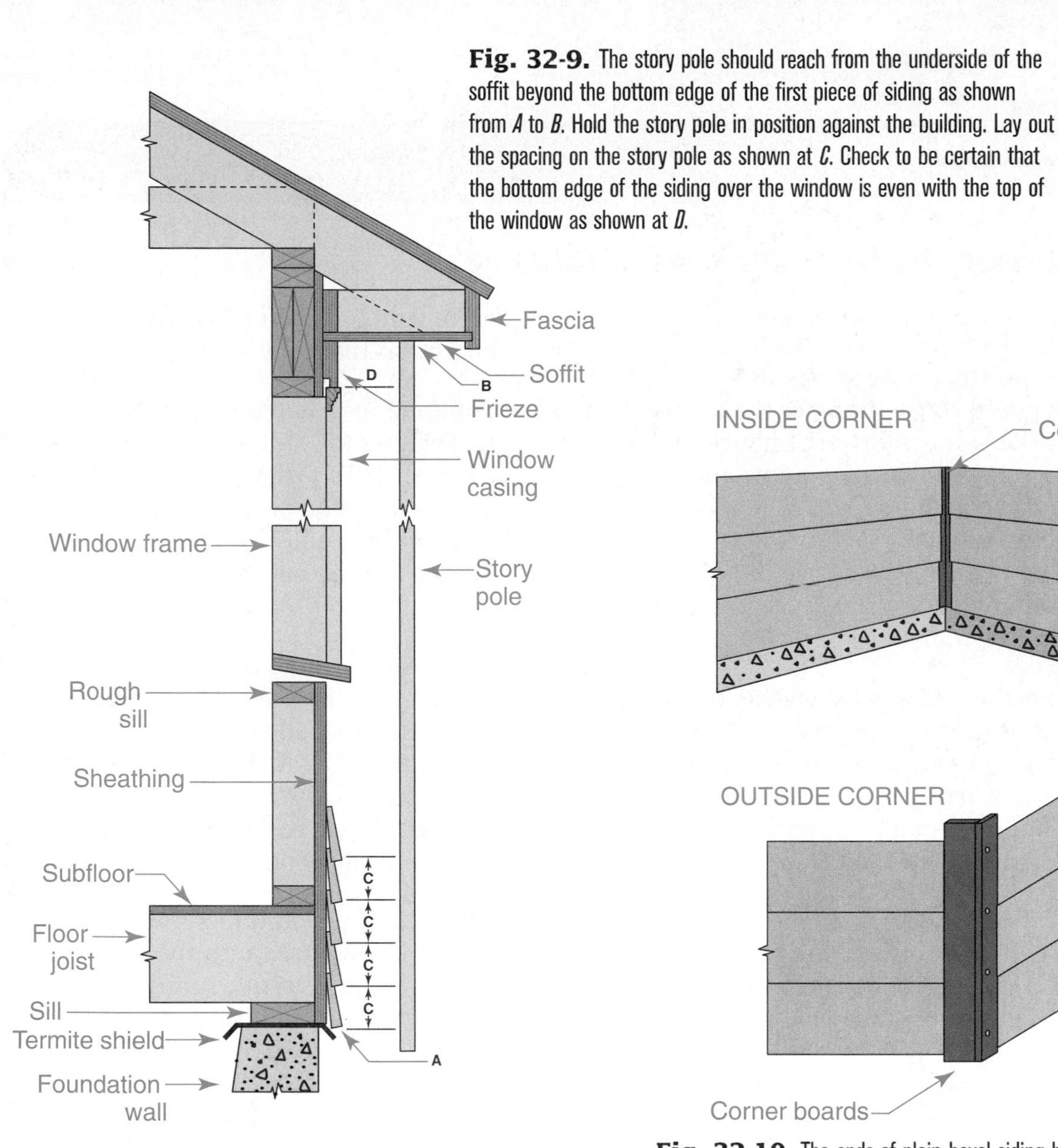

Fig. 32-9. The story pole should reach from the underside of the soffit beyond the bottom edge of the first piece of siding as shown from *A* to *B*. Hold the story pole in position against the building. Lay out the spacing on the story pole as shown at *C*. Check to be certain that the bottom edge of the siding over the window is even with the top of the window as shown at *D*.

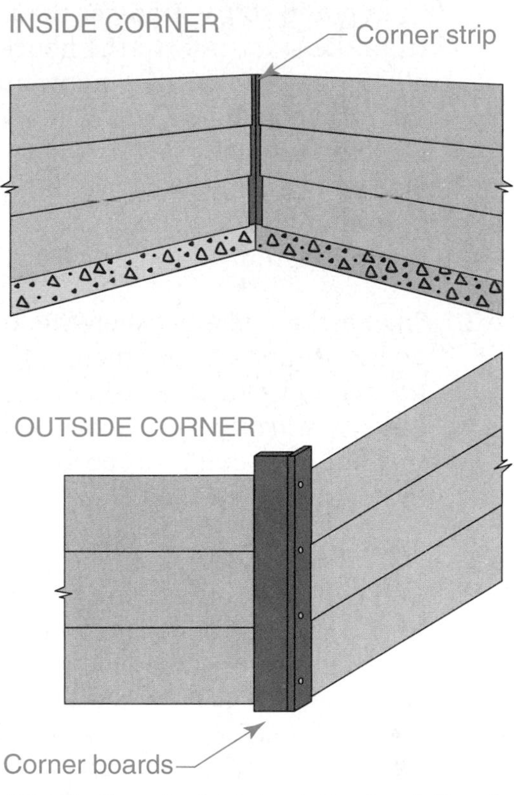

Fig. 32-10. The ends of plain-bevel siding boards fit against corner strips or corner boards.

Carpenter's Tip

Outside corner boards are nailed together before being nailed to the house. This ensures a tight joint and is much easier than nailing each board to the house separately.

of the siding. However, corner boards are generally made of nominal 1″ or 1¼″ stock. Corner strips are approximately 1⅛″ x 1⅛″ in size, depending upon the thickness of the siding.

Steps for installing plain-bevel siding are given on page 642.

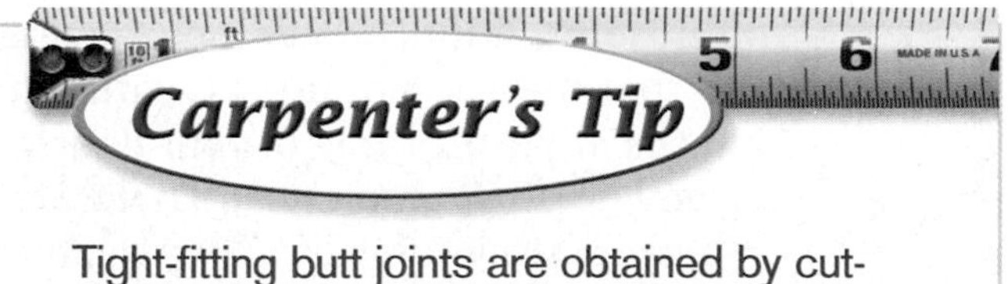

Carpenter's Tip

Tight-fitting butt joints are obtained by cutting the end board in each course (the closure board) approximately 1⁄16″ longer than the actual length measured. Bow the piece slightly to get the ends in position, and then push the middle into place. This works best on boards longer than about 8′.

STEP BY STEP

Installing Plain-Bevel Siding

Before you begin, make a story pole.

Step 1 Hold the story pole in position against the soffit. Transfer the marks from the story pole to the house on all corners and on all window and door casings. **Fig. 32-11.** On a long wall, intermediate layout marks may also be needed. Make sure that the bottom marks are clearly visible on the foundation.

Step 2 Snap a chalk line between the lowest marks around the perimeter of the house. Nail a furring strip (sometimes called a *starting strip*) about ⅜″ above this line to provide support for the first course. **Fig. 32-12.**

Step 3 Start the first course at one end of the wall and work toward the other end. Attach the first board to the bottom plate by placing nails just below each stud. **Fig. 32-13.** This marks the nailing locations for the succeeding courses. Use 6d siding nails for standard beveled siding. Use 8d siding nails for thicker siding.

Step 4 On long walls, two or more lengths of siding may be required for each course. Cut the ends of adjoining boards square to create a tight-fitting butt joint. Joints should be staggered so that they do not line up with joints in the adjacent three or four courses (see Fig. 32-7). Some carpenters prefer to use a scarf joint for extra weather tightness, but this is more time consuming. A **scarf joint** is formed by cutting an angle on the ends of boards so that they overlap.

Step 5 Continue to install additional courses by aligning the siding with your layout marks. To prevent splitting and to allow expansion clearance, never nail through the course underneath. **Fig. 32-14.** Tap the nail head flush with the surface.

Step 6 Where siding must be cut to fit against trim, hold a piece of siding in place. Use a small wood block gauge to accurately mark pieces that must fit against a vertical surface. **Fig. 32-15.** The gauge can be made from a scrap of plywood.

Step 7 Siding that passes under a windowsill should be cut to fit into the groove in the bottom of the sill. Siding installed over doors and windows should stop slightly above the window flashing to encourage drainage.

Step 8 Where siding meets a roof, as on a dormer, allow a 2″ clearance between the cut ends of the siding and the flashing. **Fig. 32-16 (page 645).** This ensures proper drainage. It also protects the vulnerable end grain of the siding from prolonged contact with water.

Step 9 Trim the last course of siding to fit under the eaves. Apply any molding or trim called for in the plans. After the face of the siding has been primed, but before it has been painted, caulk vertical joints between lengths of trim.

Fig. 32-11. Transferring the marks of the story pole to one corner of the house.

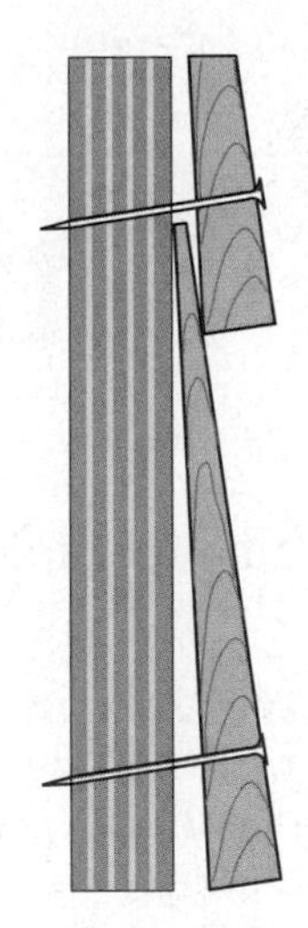

Fig. 32-14. Correct nailing procedure for plain-bevel siding. Note that the nails are perpendicular to the face of the siding. They do not pierce the siding on the course underneath.

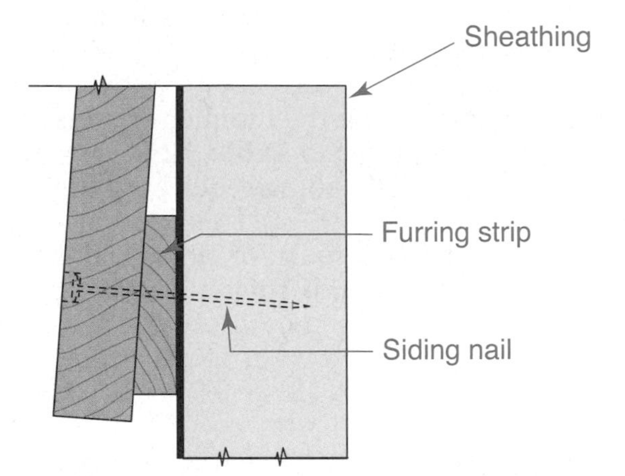

Fig. 32-12. The furring strip may be a length of wood ripped at an angle to support the bottom siding board along its length. An extra siding board may be used instead.

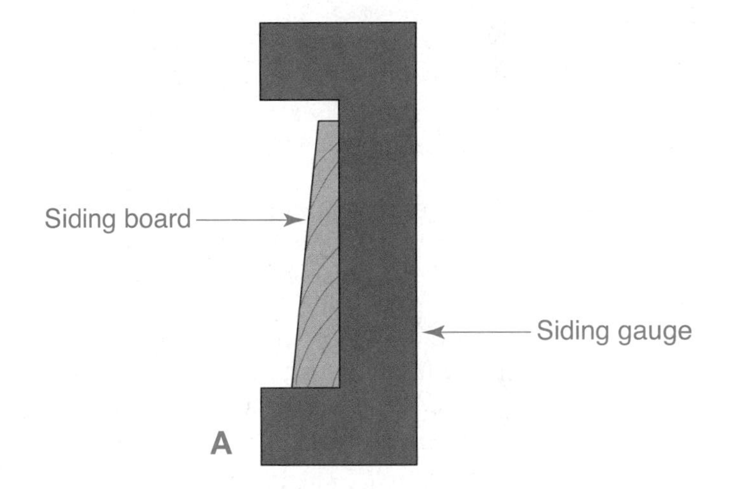

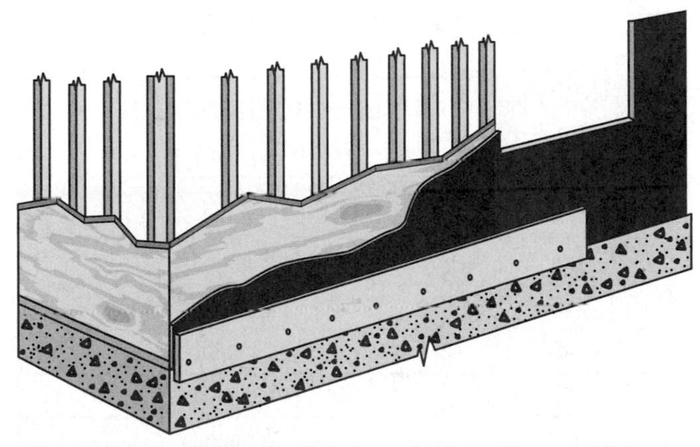

Fig. 32-13. Applying the first piece of siding with one nail below each stud.

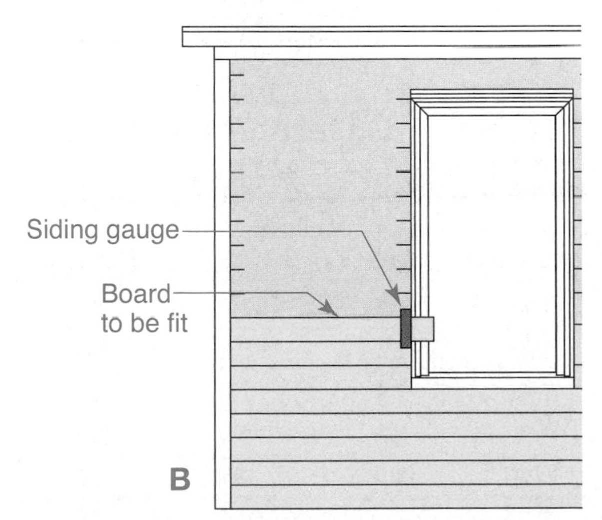

Fig. 32-15. A siding gauge can be made of scrap stock. *A.* To use it, cut a siding board slightly long and hold it in position on the house. Hold the siding gauge over the end of the board and against the side of the window casing. *B.* Mark the board to length.

Estimating...

Beveled Siding Materials

To estimate the amount of siding needed, you must determine the area to be covered.

Step 1 Find the area by multiplying the perimeter of the house by the wall height. For a house with a gable roof, figure the gable-end area separately and add the result to the side wall area. Subtract any areas greater than 50 sq. ft. that will not be sided, such as garage doors. You do not need to subtract smaller areas, such as windows and doors.

Step 2 See **Table 32-A**. This table includes factors for calculating different dimensions of beveled siding. The factors are based on actual exposures, including an allowance for trimming and waste.

Step 3 For example, consider a house 46′ long and 26′ wide with a hip roof. Its perimeter is 144′ (46 + 46 + 26 +26 = 144). With 8′ high walls, the total area to be covered is 1,152 sq. ft. (144 × 8 = 1,152). If the garage door openings total 112 sq. ft., the total area to be sided is 1,040 sq. ft. (1,152 − 112 = 1,040).

Step 4 Then multiply the area factor in Table 32-A by the square footage. If 1″ x 10″ beveled siding is to be used, 1,258.4 sq. ft. would be required (1,040 × 1.21 = 1,258.4).

Step 5 Round up the answer to the nearest hundred. In our example, that would be 1,300 sq. ft. Any siding left over after the project is complete should be left for the homeowner to use for future repairs.

Step 6 To determine the number of nails needed, refer to **Table 32-B**. For example, 1″ x 10″ siding requires ½ (0.5) lb. of nails per 100 sq. ft. In our example, about 1,300 sq. ft. of siding will be installed. Divide this by 100 (1,300 ÷ 100 = 13). Then multiply the resulting figure by the weight of nails required per 100 sq. ft. (13 × 0.5 = 6.5 lbs. of nails).

ESTIMATING ON THE JOB

A house is 58′ long and 27′ wide and has a hip roof. The walls are 8′ high. How many square feet of 1x8 siding will be required and how many pounds of nails?

Table 32-A. Coverage Estimator for Beveled Siding

Nominal Size	Width		Area Factor
	Dress	Face	
1x4	3½	3½	1.60
1x6	5½	5½	1.33
1x8	7¼	7¼	1.28
1x10	9¼	9¼	1.21
1x12	11¼	11¼	1.17

Table 32-B. Nails Required for Beveled Siding

Size	Nails (per 100 sq. ft.)
1x4	1½ pounds
1x5	1½ pounds
1x6	1 pound
1x8	¾ pound
1x10	½ pound
1x12	½ pound

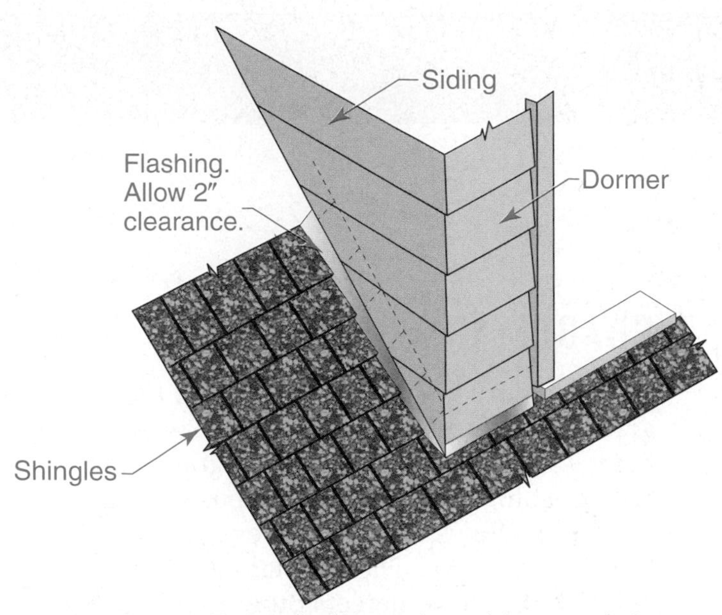

Fig. 32-16. Flashing should be used around dormers at the intersection of the siding and the roof.

Carpenter's Tip

When you are nailing near the end of wood siding, the wood may split. To prevent this, pre-drill the nail hole or blunt the point of the nail. Some siding nails already have a blunt tip and are thus much less likely to cause splitting.

Alternative Corner Treatment

At the outside corners of a house, plain-bevel siding is generally fitted snugly against the corner boards. However, the ends of the boards can be mitered instead. **Fig. 32-17.** Mitered corners, sometimes used with thicker siding, should be cut with a compound-miter saw. They must fit tightly and smoothly for the full depth of the miter. Nail mitered ends to the sheathing, not to each other.

SECTION 32.2 Check Your Knowledge

1. What is back-priming and why is it important?
2. What other finishing method can be used to improve the durability of siding?
3. Name two joints used where lengths of siding meet each other.
4. Explain the use of a small wood gauge when cutting siding.

On the Job

Suppose that the distance from the top of the foundation to the top of the window in a garage is 6′-6″. Beveled siding of 8″ nominal width is to be applied. Refer to the guideline for overlap of courses requiring that the bottom of the course just above the window meet the top of the window. Determine the number of courses required to reach this point.

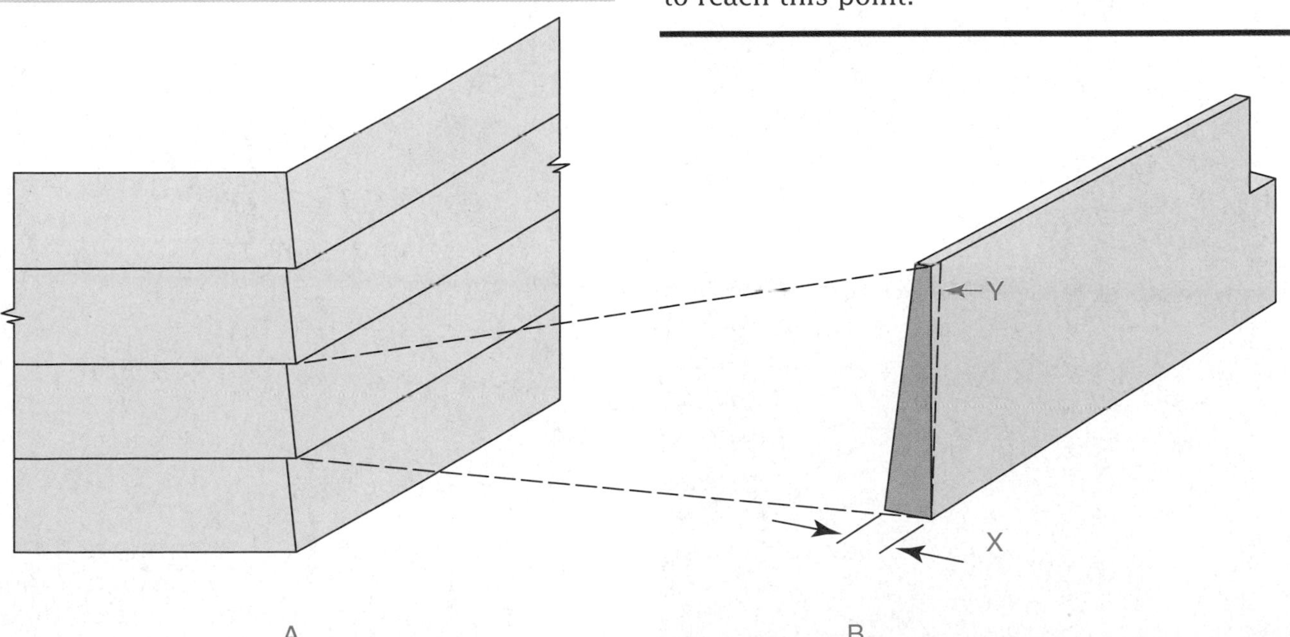

Fig. 32-17. Mitering plain-bevel siding. *A.* Mitering of plain-bevel siding corners must be done carefully to obtain a good joint. *B.* To lay out and cut the joint, measure the butt edge thickness (*x*). Measure back along the top edge a distance equal to the butt edge thickness. Then connect these two points as shown by the dashed lines (*y*). With the saw blade set at about a 47° angle, make the cut beginning at the butt end.

SECTION 32.3

Wood Shingles

When wood shingles are used as siding, they are sometimes referred to as *side-wall shingles.* **Fig. 32-18.** They are most commonly made from red cedar, but white cedar and other woods are also used.

Wood shingles are generally installed one by one. However, some companies manufacture a product that combines groups of shingles. **Fig. 32-19.** The shingles are attached at the factory to a plywood backing. The resulting shingle panel is then nailed into place.

Fig. 32-18. Shingle siding can be used by itself as shown here or combined with other types of siding.

GRADES AND SIZES

Shingles are usually classified into four grades. The first grade includes clear, all-heartwood shingles. The second grade consists of shingles with a clear exposed area (butt) and allows defects in the part that will be covered in use. The third grade includes shingles that have defects other than those permitted in the second grade. The fourth is a utility grade used for undercourses on double-coursed side walls. An **undercourse** is a low-grade layer of shingles that will not be exposed to the weather.

Shingles come in lengths of 16″, 18″, and 24″. They may be prefinished or finished after installation. They are made in random widths. In the first grade, they vary from 3″ to 14″ wide, with only a small proportion of the narrowest width permitted in each bundle. Shingles cut to uniform widths of 4″, 5″, or 6″ are also available. They are known as

Fig. 32-19. Shingle panels speed the installation of shingle siding.

dimension or *rebutted-and-rejointed shingles.* Their edges are machine trimmed so as to be exactly parallel; exposed ends are trimmed at 90° angles. Dimension shingles are applied with tight-fitting joints to create an unbroken horizontal line.

APPLICATION

Shingles are generally spaced ⅛″ to ¼″ apart. **Fig. 32-20.** This allows them to expand and prevents buckling. Maximum exposures vary. Spacing for the shingle courses is determined in the same way as for plain-bevel siding.

There are several methods for installing siding shingles. The method selected determines the overall look of the house.

- **Single coursing.** In single coursing, each course of shingles overlaps the one below so that every part of the wall is covered with two layers. Fig. 32-20. The same grade of shingle must be used throughout. Weather exposure is fairly small.
- **Double coursing.** One purpose of this method is to obtain deep shadow lines for appearance. High-grade shingles are laid over undercourse-grade shingles. **Fig. 32-21.** This method is less expensive than single-coursing

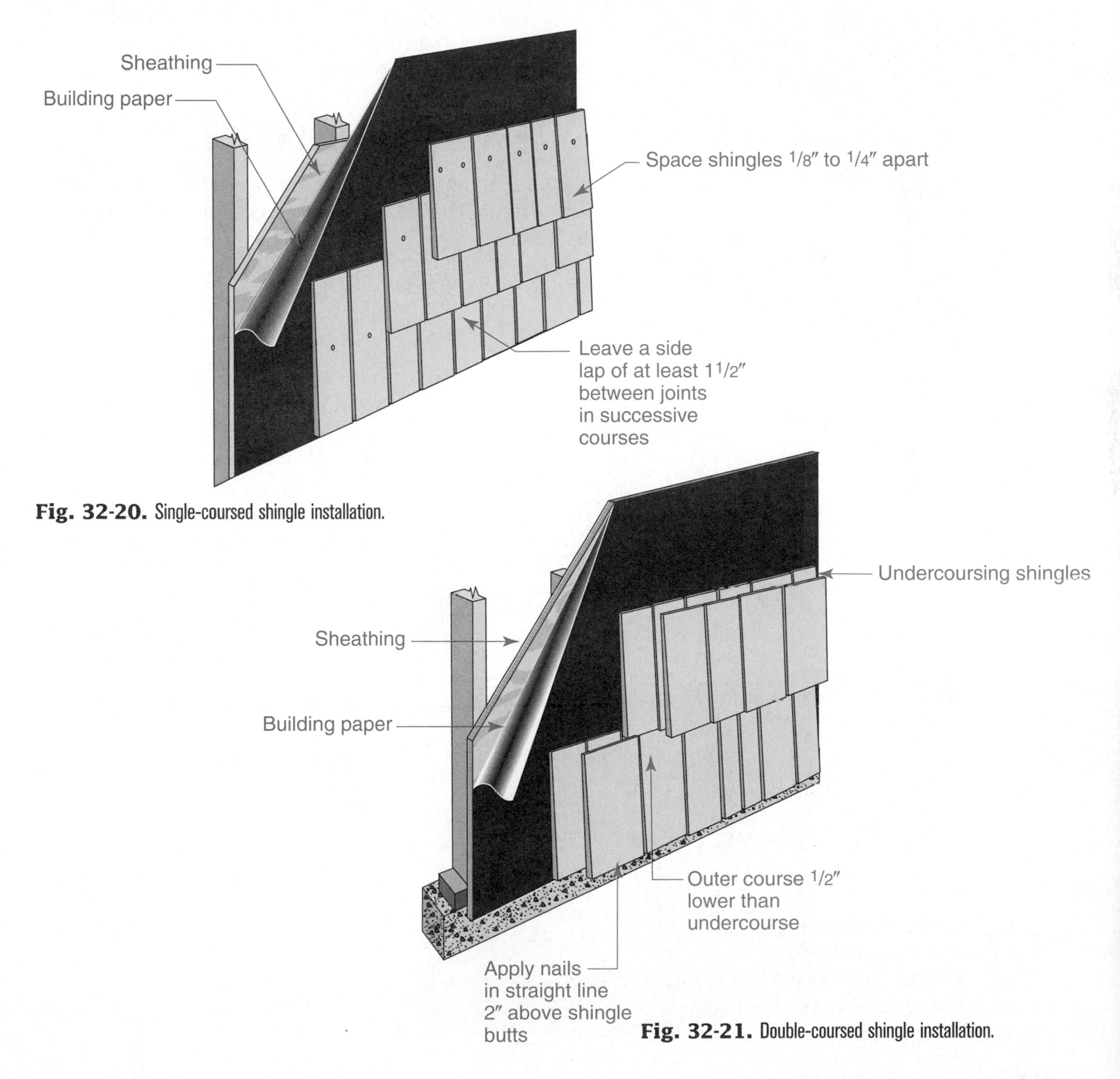

Fig. 32-20. Single-coursed shingle installation.

Fig. 32-21. Double-coursed shingle installation.

because fewer high-grade shingles are used. Rebutted-and-rejointed shingles are sometimes used as the outer course for length.

- **Ribbon coursing.** In this method, a double shadow line is created by raising the outer course slightly above the undercourse. **Fig. 32-22.** Because the undercourse is partially exposed, however, it should be the same grade of shingle as the outer course.
- **Decorative coursing.** A rustic effect can be created if the exposed ends of the shingles are placed at different distances from a horizontal layout line.

Nailing

For double coursing, secure each outer-course shingle with two small-head, rust-resistant, 5d nails driven about 2″ above the butt edges and ¾″ in from each side. Drive additional nails about 4″ apart across the face of the shingle. Single coursing involves the same number of nails, but they can be shorter, such as 3d. Blind nail them not more than 1″ above the butt edge of the next higher course. Never drive the nail so tight that its head crushes the wood.

Outside corners can be interlaced, mitered, or butted into corner boards. **Fig. 32-23.** Laced ends overlap in an alternating pattern. Inside corners may be mitered over metal flashing or butted to a corner strip similar to that used when installing plain-bevel siding.

ESTIMATING SHINGLES

To determine the number of shingles needed, figure the area to be covered plus a trim and

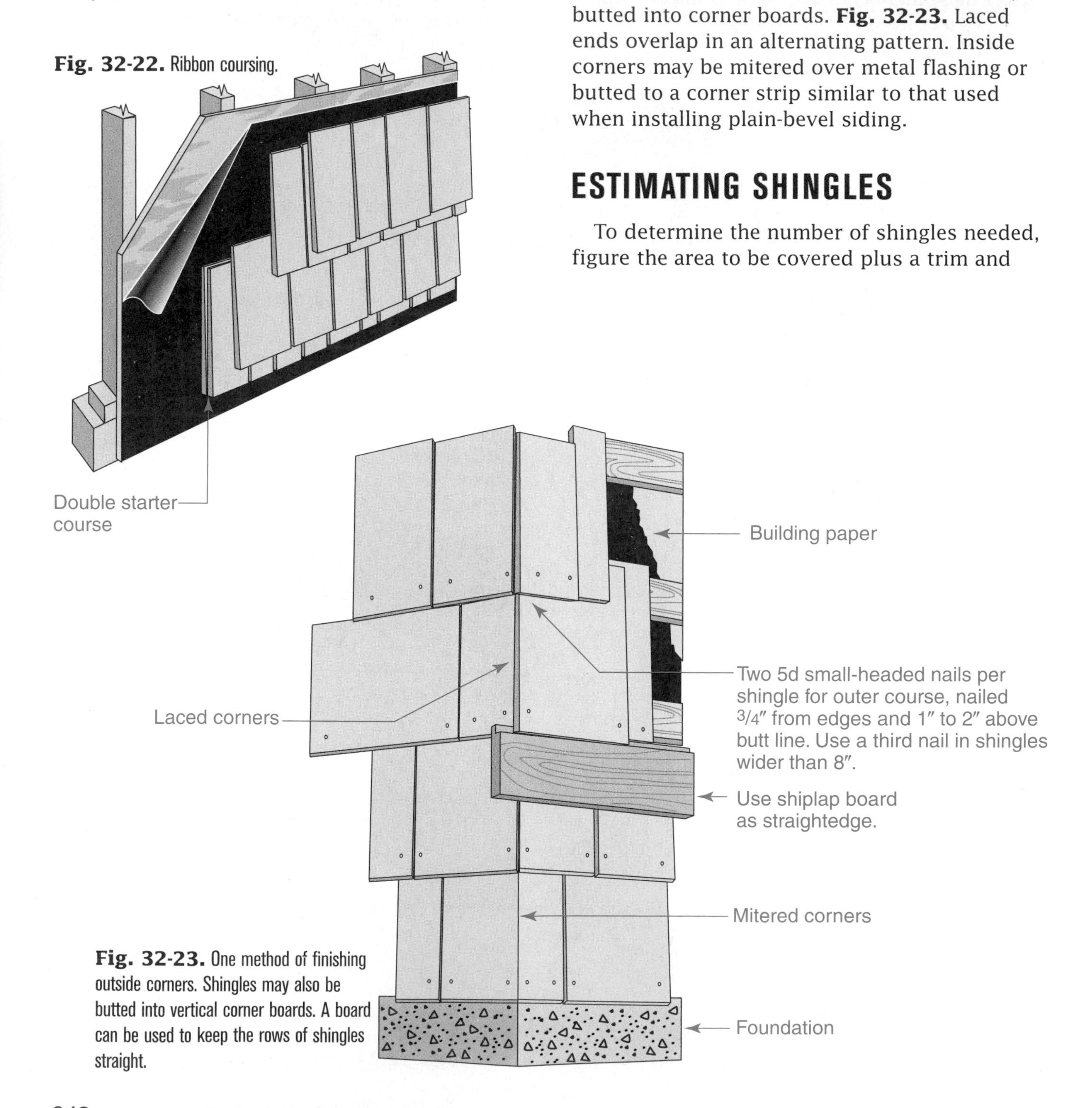

Fig. 32-22. Ribbon coursing.

Fig. 32-23. One method of finishing outside corners. Shingles may also be butted into vertical corner boards. A board can be used to keep the rows of shingles straight.

Table 32-C. Wood Shingle Exposure and Coverage

Length and Thickness (inches)	Approximate coverage in square feet of one square (4 bundles) of shingles based on the following exposures												
	3½″	4″	4½″	5″	5½″	6″	6½″	7″	7½″	8″	8½″	9″	9½″
16x5/2	70	80	90	100[a]	110	120	130	140	150[b]	160	170	180	190
18x5/2¼	-	72½	81½	90½	100[a]	109	118	127	136	145½	154½[b]	163½	172½
24x4/2	-	-	-	-	-	80	86½	93	100[a]	106½	113	120	126½
	10″	10½″	11″	11½″	12″	12½″	13″	13½″	14″	14½″	15″	15½″	16″
16x5/2	200	210	220	230	240[c]	-	-	-	-	-	-	-	-
18x5/2¼	181½	191	200	209	218	227	236	245½	254½	-	-	-	-
24x4/2	133	140	146½	153[b]	160	166½	173	180	186½	193	200	206½	213[c]

Note: The thickness dimension represents the total thickness of a number of shingles. For example, 5/2″ means that 5 shingles, measured across the thickest portion, when green, measure 2 full inches.

(a) Maximum exposure recommended for roofs.

(b) Maximum exposure recommended for single coursing on side walls.

(c) Maximum exposure recommended for double coursing on side walls.

waste allowance. For single coursing, one *square* (4 bundles) of 16″ shingles with a 7½″ exposure will cover 150 sq. ft. **Table 32-C.**

For example, suppose a house requires 902 sq. ft. of siding. Add 5 percent to this number for trim and waste. Then divide by 150 (the area covered by 1 square of shingles):

$902 \times 0.05 = 45.1$

$902 + 45.1 = 947.1$ sq. ft. to be covered

$947.1 \div 150 = 6.31$, or 6½ squares

Since there are 4 bundles in a square, 26 bundles will be required to shingle the house in this example ($4 \times 6.5 = 26$).

SECTION 32.3

Check Your Knowledge

1. Describe the top two grades of siding shingles.
2. What is an undercourse?
3. How is the undercourse for ribbon-coursed shingles different from that used for ordinary double-coursed shingles?
4. In what lengths do shingles come?

On the Job

A wood shake is similar to a wood shingle. What is the difference between the two? Research the use of wood shakes during the Colonial era. Write a paragraph explaining why shakes were such a popular exterior wall covering at that time.

SECTION 32.4

Other Types of Siding

The specific characteristics and durability of manufactured siding materials vary from manufacturer to manufacturer. This is particularly true of vinyl and fiber cement. Always follow the manufacturer's instructions for the product you are installing. This will ensure that the product warranty will cover the completed project.

VINYL SIDING

Vinyl siding is shaped to resemble horizontal wood siding. **Fig. 32-24.** It is applied in horizontal panels consisting of one or more beveled sections. **Fig. 32-25.** A slotted *nailing flange* (also called a *nail hem*) at the top of each section is used when securing the panel to sheathing. The bottom edge fits into the *lock* in the panel below.

Various textures, colors, and grades are available. The thickness of the vinyl itself ranges from 0.035″ to 0.055″. Wood trim is not used. Vinyl siding requires the use of vinyl trim, including starter strips, corner posts, and window trim. **Fig. 32-26.** This material must be ordered at the same time and from the same manufacturer as the siding.

Fig. 32-24. Vinyl siding can be installed quickly because each panel consists of two or more courses. The lower edge of a panel hooks onto the flange of a panel already installed.

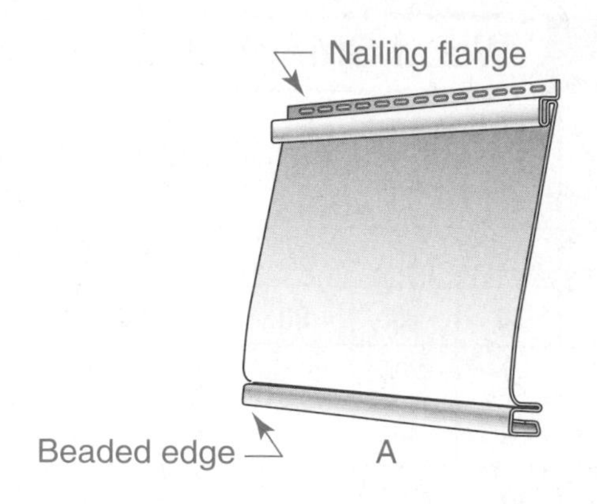

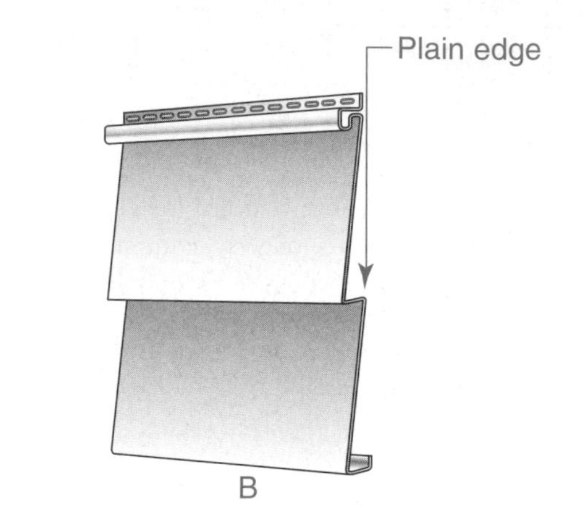

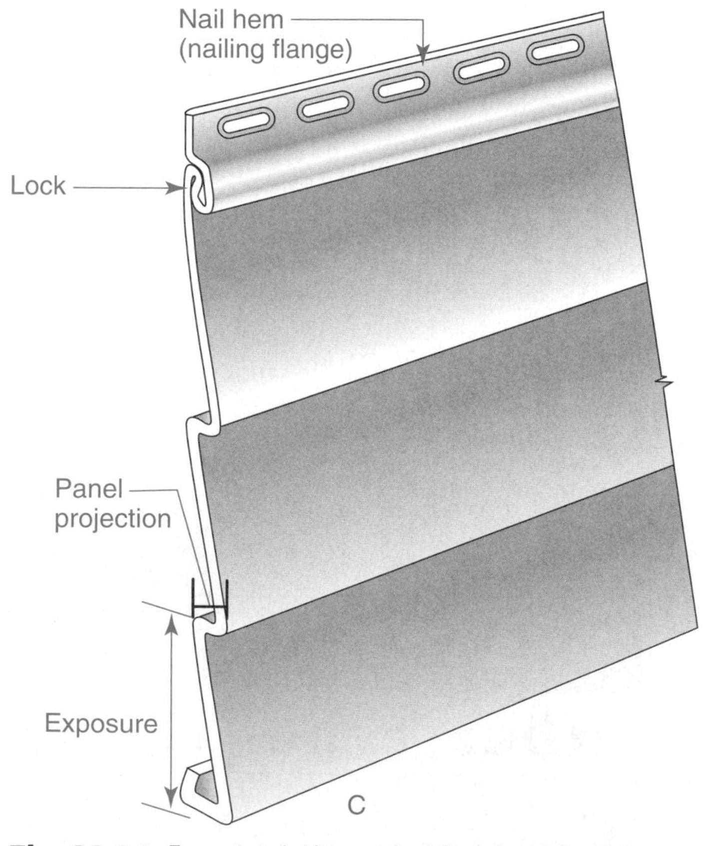

Fig. 32-25. Types of vinyl siding panels. *A.* Single lap. *B.* Double lap. *C.* Triple lap. The terminology used here applies to any vinyl siding panel.

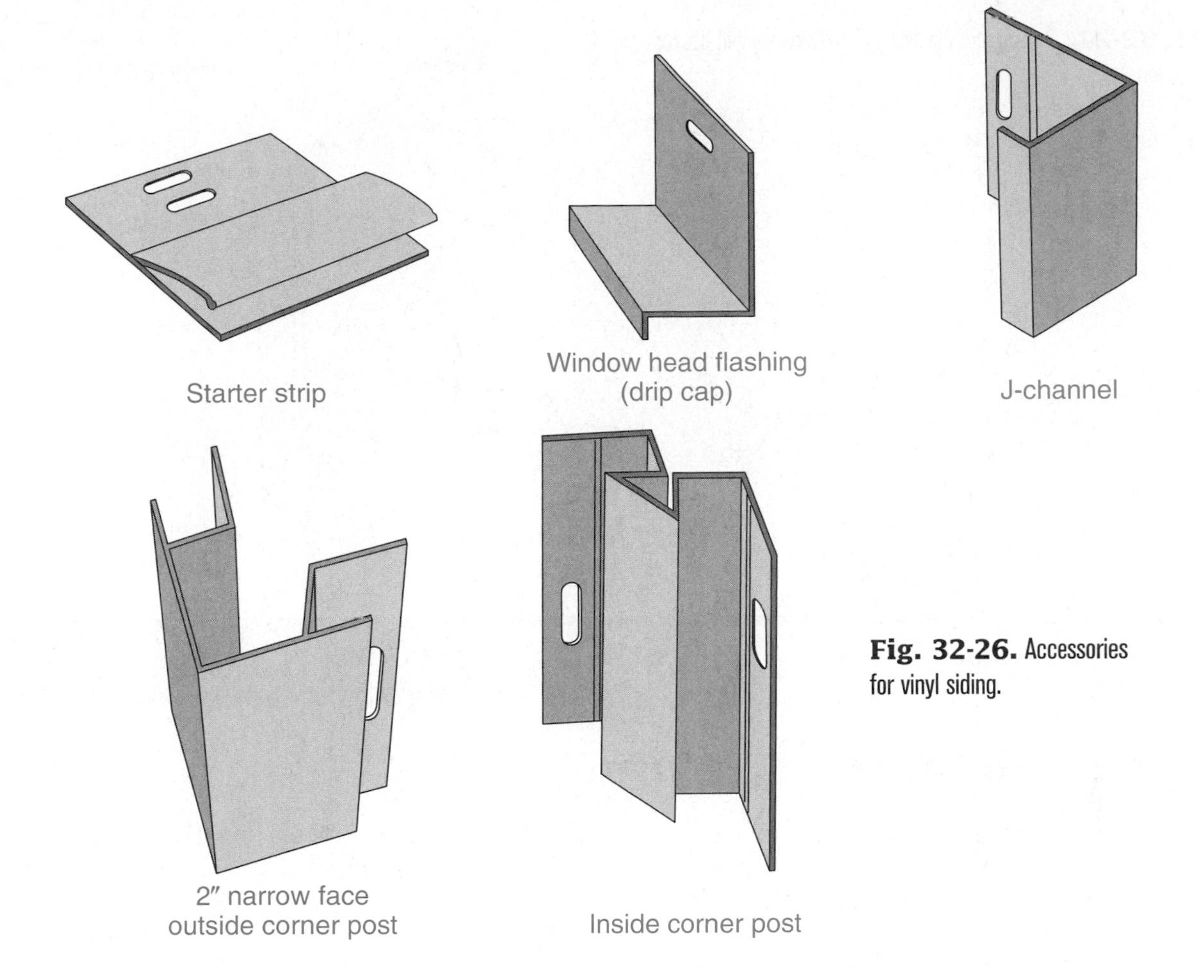

Fig. 32-26. Accessories for vinyl siding.

Vinyl siding has many advantages. Vinyl is colored throughout, not just on the surface, so scratches are not noticeable. It can be installed more quickly than wood siding. If damaged, it can be easily removed and replaced. It will not rot and requires little maintenance. However, it cannot be painted.

Application

Vinyl siding is installed by contractors who specialize in one or more product lines. They are sometimes trained by vinyl siding manufacturers.

Fastening Techniques. Vinyl siding expands and contracts much more than wood. For this reason, using the correct fastening technique is extremely important. Vinyl siding is generally nailed through the sheathing and into studs, though staples may be used instead. Nails should have heads at least 5⁄16″ in diameter, with a 1⁄8″ shank. Those used for panels should be 1½″ long. Those used for trim should be 1″ to 1½″ long. Good nailing technique includes the following:

- Never drive nails tight, unless manufacturer's instructions *specifically* recommend otherwise. Leave approximately 1⁄32″ (the thickness of a dime) between the underside of the head and the vinyl. This allows the vinyl to expand and contract and prevents it from buckling with changes in temperature.
- Always drive fasteners straight and level. This prevents the panel from distorting. **Fig. 32-27.** Start in the center of the panel and work toward the ends.

Step-by-Step instructions for installing vinyl siding are given on page 652.

SAFETY FIRST

Cutting Vinyl with a Power Saw

Vinyl siding is often cut on a radial-arm saw or power miter saw. The blade should have 12 to 16 steel teeth per inch. However, mount the blade so that the teeth face in the *opposite* direction from normal. In other words, the teeth at the bottom of the blade point *toward* you and away from the fence. This makes a smoother cut through vinyl. Never use this blade position to cut other materials. Always wear suitable eye protection.

Fig. 32-27. The careful placement of fasteners will prevent panel distortion.

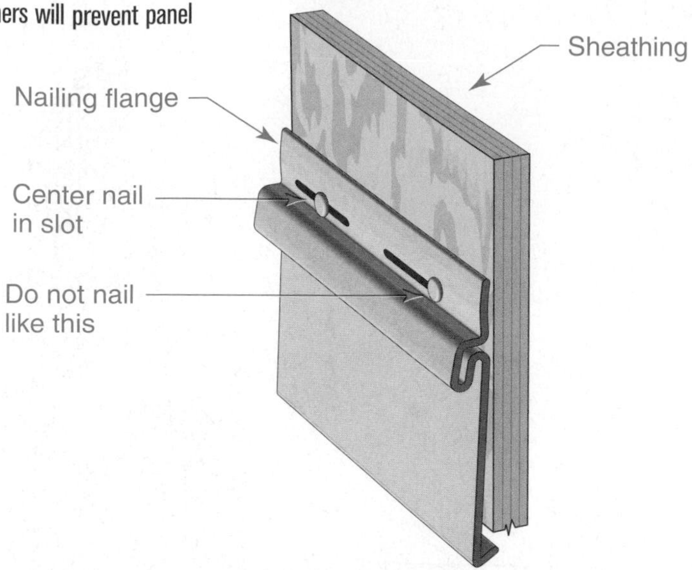

STEP BY STEP

Installing Vinyl Siding

The following is only a general guide. Instructions specific to a particular siding product must always be followed closely.

Step 1 Snap a level chalk line along the bottom of the sheathing. Align the starter strips with this line and nail them into place around the house. Leave room for corner posts at each inside and outside corner.

Step 2 The ends of the corner posts should be ¼″ below the bottom of the starter strips. Plumb each post carefully. Then nail it to the sheathing through the uppermost nailing slot on each side. The post should "hang" on these nails. Continue nailing down the length of the post on both sides. Install all inside and outside corner posts in similar fashion. **Fig. 32-28.**

Step 3 Apply housewrap or flexible self-adhesive flashing around windows, doors, exterior electrical boxes, and other openings. Overlap it as shown in **Fig. 32-29**. The flashing should be wide enough to extend past the nailing flange of any accessory.

Step 4 A **J-channel** is a plastic or metal channel shaped like a *J* that is used to support trim. Nail J-channel to the sheathing wherever necessary to hold the ends of siding panels. This would include areas around windows, at gable ends, and where dormer side walls meet a roof. Follow manufacturer's instructions carefully.

Step 5 Place the first panel in the starter strip and nail it into place. Subsequent panels can then be held in place, locked to the previous course, and nailed. **Fig. 32-30.** Leave a ¼″ gap between the siding and all corner posts and channels. (Increase the gap to ⅜″ when installing siding in temperatures below 40°F [4°C].)

Step 6 Cut the siding as needed to fit under windows. Be sure to include space for an expansion gap.

Step 7 The top course of siding may have to be cut to fit beneath the soffit. In this case, use a special siding tool called a *snaplock punch* to create a nailing flange along the cut edge. Use vinyl trim to cap the top of the wall as needed.

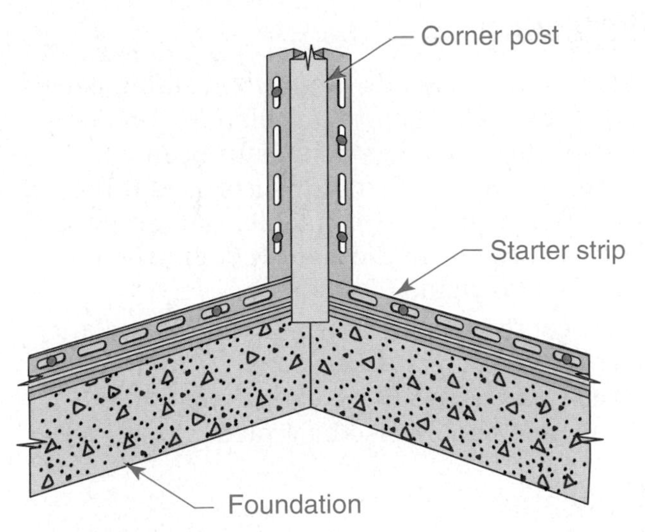

Fig. 32-28. The position of an inside corner post relative to the starter strip.

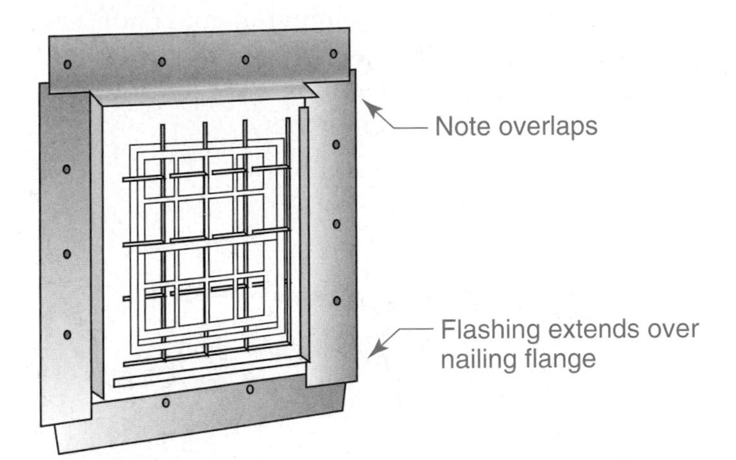

Fig. 32-29. Flashing should be overlapped to shed any water that gets behind the siding.

- Space fasteners no more than 16″ apart on panels and 8″ to 10″ apart on accessories.
- Center all fasteners in the nailing slots, except those at the very top of a corner post. This allows the siding to expand and contract. Also, leave a ¼″ space at joints, channels, and corner posts for expansion and contraction.
- For best appearance, locate any overlaps on panels in a way that minimizes their appearance. Stagger end laps a minimum of 24″ or as suggested by the manufacturer.

Estimating Vinyl Siding

Most manufacturers of vinyl siding indicate the number of pieces of a given size required to cover one square (100 sq. ft.) of wall area. For example, 12 pieces of 8″ siding might cover one square.

Figure the area to be covered by multiplying the perimeter measurement by the wall height. Divide this total by 100 to find the number of squares. Multiply the number of squares by 12 (the number of pieces needed to cover one square). For example, for a house having 947 square feet to be covered, you would need 114 pieces:

$$947 \div 100 = 9.47$$
$$9.47 \times 12 = 113.64, \text{ or } 114$$

Fig. 32-30. Installing vinyl siding panels. The ends fit into J-channel.

PLYWOOD SIDING

Plywood siding panels can also be used as an exterior wall covering. When this is done, sheathing is not required because the panels provide enough rigidity to the walls. **Fig. 32-31.** Using plywood sheet siding has several advantages. It comes in many grades and surface textures. **Fig. 32-32.** It covers large areas quickly, taking less time to install. Little material is wasted. By omitting sheathing, costs are reduced.

Fig. 32-31. Applying a plywood siding panel.

Preparation

The edges and ends of plywood siding panels should be sealed before installation. This prevents sudden changes in moisture content caused by wet weather. Primer is used if the siding will be painted. A paintable, water-repellent sealer is used if the siding will be finished with a solid-color stain.

To seal the panels, brush or roll the sealant over the edges of stacked panels. Any fresh edges created by cutting the panels during installation should also be sealed.

Application

Plywood siding is normally installed vertically but may be installed horizontally. All edges should be backed with framing members or blocking. **Fig. 32-33.** To prevent staining of the siding, galvanized, aluminum, or other noncorrosive nails are recommended.

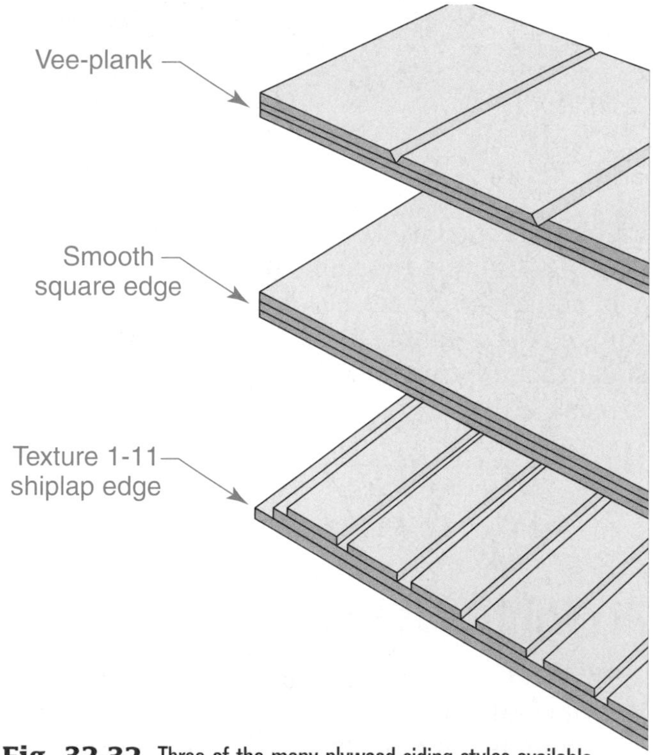

Vee-plank
Smooth square edge
Texture 1-11 shiplap edge

Fig. 32-32. Three of the many plywood siding styles available.

from Another Angle

Window shutters were first used for protection from fierce weather and other hazards. Shutters are still used on today's homes, but they are usually only decorative. They are screwed to the siding or held with special clips. Installation may fall to various trades. The siding contractor installs vinyl shutters. Wood shutters might be installed by the carpenter or by the painting contractor after the house is painted. Installation should be discussed in advance with the contractor. The work should then be figured in that contractor's bid.

Panels are 4′ wide. They come in standard 8′ lengths as well as 12′, 14′, and 16′ special lengths. Panels range in thickness from $\frac{11}{32}''$ to $\frac{3}{4}''$.

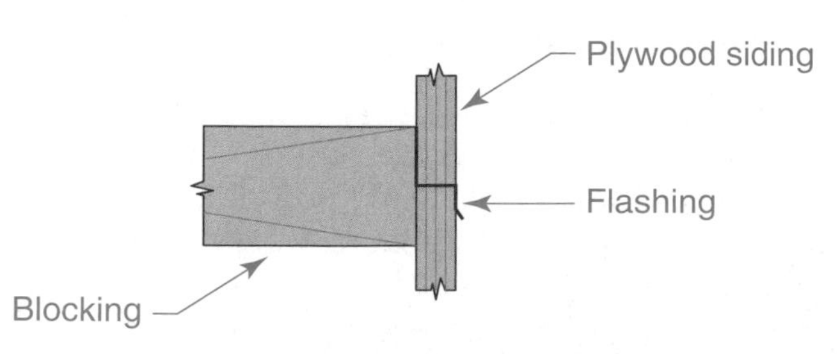

Fig. 32-33. There should always be blocking behind flashed joints.

Table 32-D.	Framing and Nailing Schedule for Plywood Panel Siding					
Panel Siding Thickness	5/16″	3.8″	½″ grooved	½″ flat	⅝″ grooved	⅝″ flat
Single-Wall Construction						
Maximum Stud Spacing		16″ OC	16″ OC	24″ OC	16″ OC	24″ OC
Nail Size		6d	8d	8d	8d	8d
Over ⅜″ Sheathing						
Maximum Stud Spacing	24″	24″	24″	24″	24″	24″
Nail Size	6d	6d	6d	6d	8d	8d
Approximate Nail Spacing[a]						
Edges	6″	6″	6″	6″	6″	6″
Intermediate Members	12″	12″	12″	12″	12″	12″

(a) Use non-corrosive casing, siding, or box nails.

Vertical joints between panels can be handled in a variety of ways to keep out water. Some panels have shiplap joints, for example. Vertical joints can also be covered with wood battens. Horizontal joints between panels should be protected with flashing.

Space panels ⅛″ apart at sides and ends to allow for expansion and contraction. Vertical joints need not be caulked if they are shiplapped, backed by building paper, or covered by battens. However, horizontal joints should be flashed, shiplapped, or overlapped.

Follow the nailing recommendations provided by the panel manufacturer or local codes. **Table 32-D.** Add corner boards and trim around windows after the siding is in place. **Fig. 32-34.** Building paper or housewrap is usually not required by code. However, always check local codes to be sure.

STUCCO

In some parts of the country, a stucco finish is common. *Stucco* is a durable cementlike product that is applied over reinforcing wire called *lath.* It forms a hard coating that is all of one piece. It is particularly suitable for use in hot or mild climates. **Fig. 32-35.** Stucco may have a natural cement color or be colored as desired.

If stucco is to be applied on houses more than one story high, balloon framing (see Chapter 19, "Framing Methods") or steel framing should be used for the exterior walls. This reduces expansion and contraction that could crack or otherwise damage the stucco. The framing should be sheathed according to local building codes. However, plywood is commonly used.

Portland-cement stucco that has been commercially prepared should be mixed and applied according to the manufacturer's instructions. If the material is mixed on site, it is generally one part Portland cement, three parts sand, and a portion of hydrated lime equal to 10 percent of the Portland cement by volume.

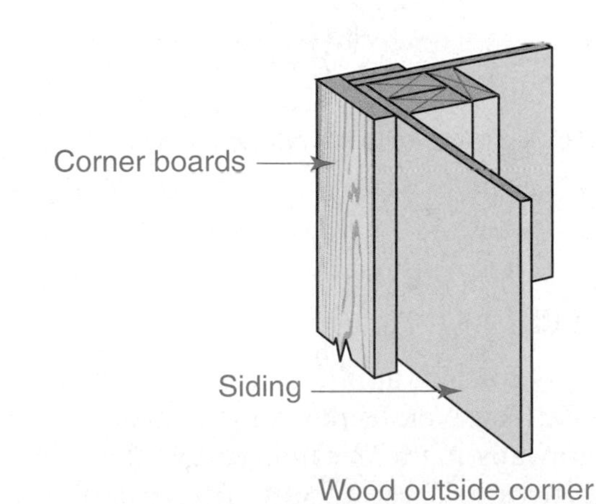

Fig. 32-34. Outside corner detail for plywood panel siding.

Fig. 32-35. The stucco exterior of this house provides a durable finish.

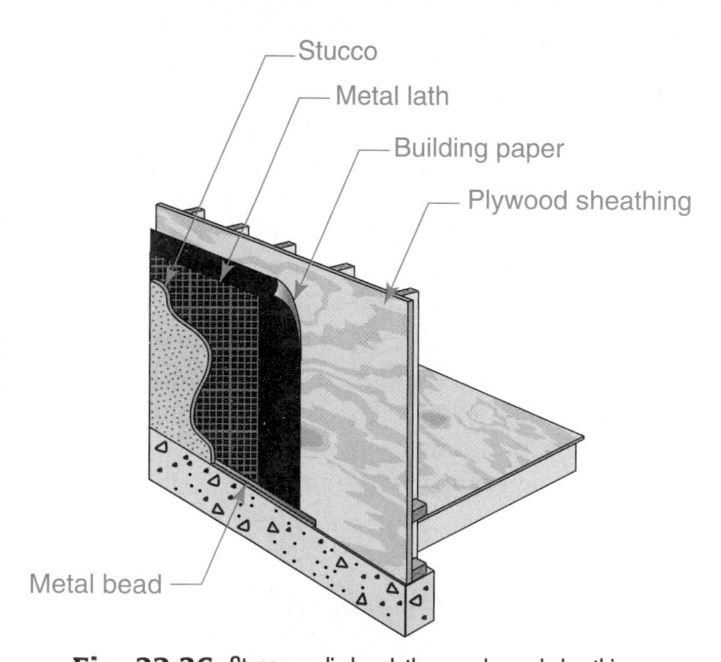

Fig. 32-36. Stucco applied on lath over plywood sheathing.

Application

Stucco is typically applied over metal lath. **Fig. 32-36.** However, it may also be applied directly to walls made of concrete block or poured concrete. Three acceptable types of lath include:

- *Zinc-coated or galvanized metal.* This may have large openings (1.8 pounds per square yard) or small openings (3.4 pounds per square yard).
- *Galvanized woven-wire fabric.* This material may be 18-gauge wire with 1″ maximum mesh, 17-gauge wire with 1½″ maximum mesh, or 16-gauge wire with a 2″ maximum mesh.
- *Galvanized welded-wire fabric.* This may be made of 16-gauge wire with 2″ x 2″ mesh and waterproof paper backing. It may also be made of 18-gauge wire with 1″ x 1″ mesh without paper backing.

The lath should be held at least ¼″ away from the sheathing so that the lath will be embedded completely as the stucco is forced through it. Galvanized furring nails, metal furring strips, or self-furring lath are used for this spacing.

The stucco should be applied in three coats to a total thickness of 1″. The first coat should be forced through the lath and worked so as to embed the lath at all points. Newly-applied stucco should be shaded and kept moist for three days. Do not apply stucco when the temperature is below 40°F [4°C]. It sets very slowly, and it may freeze before it has set.

FIBER CEMENT SIDING

Fiber cement is a fairly new type of siding material. It is made of Portland cement, ground sand, cellulose fiber, additives, and water. The ingredients are mixed, formed into siding boards, and cured in an autoclave. An *autoclave* is a chamber filled with steam under high pressure. The result is a product that will not burn, rot, or split. It resists mold, mildew, fungus, salt spray, UV rays, and pests such as termites. It contains no defects that must be removed before installation.

Though fiber cement can be formed into shingles, it is more commonly sold as planks. These planks are 5⁄16″ thick, 12′ in length, and available in widths from 5¼″ to 12″. The actual exposure is about 1¼″ less than the actual width. Planks are available pre-primed or unprimed.

SAFETY FIRST

Preventing Silicosis

Cutting, drilling, or sanding fiber cement releases a cloud of fine dust that may contain silica. Inhaling this dust over time can cause silicosis, a disabling lung disease (see Chapter 5, "Construction Safety and Health"). Work outdoors if possible. Always wear a dust mask. A NIOSH-approved respirator is recommended if exposure to the dust will exceed normal limits. Consult the product's material safety data sheet (MSDS) for additional information.

Handling and Cutting Fiber Cement

Fiber cement products should be stored flat and kept dry. Individual planks are dense and fairly heavy, so take care when lifting them. Long planks should be carried on edge to prevent them from snapping across their width.

Fiber cement can be cut using a circular saw fitted with a standard carbide-tooth blade. Extra-durable blades with diamond-tipped teeth are also available. To reduce dust created during cutting, circular saws can be fitted with plastic dust-collection housings. They can also be connected to vacuum equipment. **Fig. 32-37.** Another way to reduce dust is to use an electric, pneumatic, or hand shear that slices through the material.

Application

Fiber cement planks are installed much like plain-bevel siding. Each plank overlaps the one below and is nailed to the sheathing. **Fig. 32-38.** Building paper or housewrap may not be required by code, but fiber cement manufacturers generally recommend it. Joints between

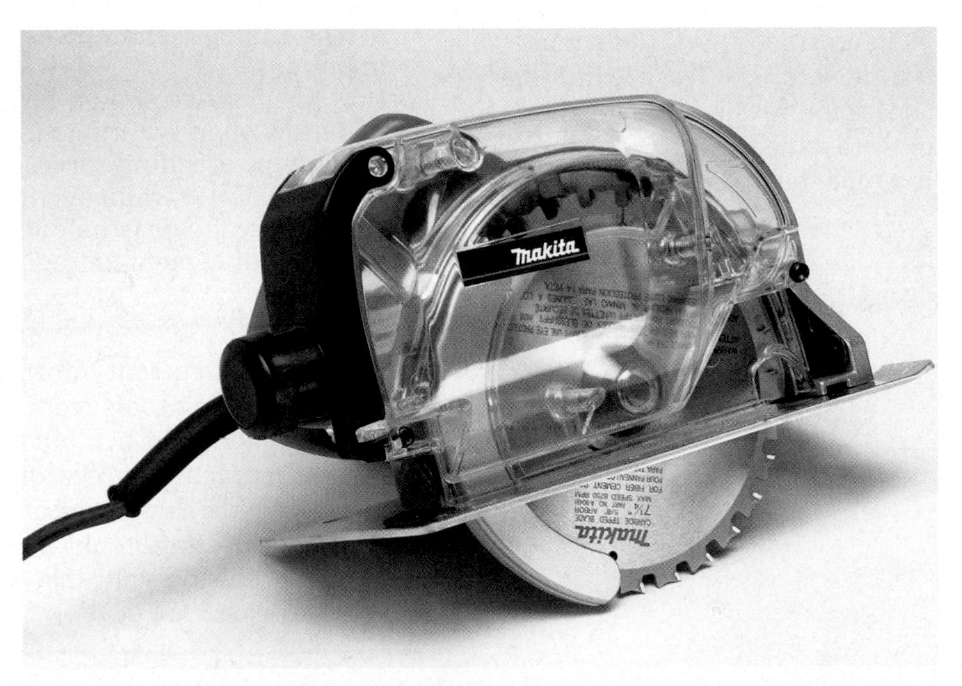

Fig. 32-37. The clear housing on this circular saw helps to contain the fine dust created when fiber cement products are cut.

Fig. 32-38. This house is sided with fiber cement planks. The inset on the lower right shows a detail of these planks.

planks should be no more than ⅛″ wide. Use a high-quality paintable caulk to seal butt joints and gaps between siding and trim.

Nails should be of 6d hot-dipped galvanized steel or stainless steel and have a blunt or diamond point. Local codes may allow the use of thinner siding nails in some cases. Nails must be long enough to penetrate at least 1″ into the wood. When metal framing is used instead of wood, the siding is installed with corrosion-resistant, Phillips-type, bugle-head screws.

SECTION 32.4 Check Your Knowledge

1. What characteristic of vinyl siding makes proper nailing technique extremely important?
2. How much space should be left under the nail head when securing vinyl siding?
3. Which type of siding serves as both sheathing and exterior wall covering?
4. What safety factor is unique to the installation of fiber cement siding?

On the Job

Obtain the most current information about recommended cutting tools from a manufacturer of fiber cement siding. Then obtain literature from the tool manufacturers regarding the specific models available. Finally, locate a local or mail-order source of these tools. Obtain prices for each of the tools on your list. Report your findings to the class.

Chapter 32

Review

Section Summaries

32.1 Siding is made from many materials, but solid-wood siding is the one most common on houses. It must be a high grade of material for maximum durability. Steps should be taken to prevent problems associated with water and water vapor.

32.2 Plain-bevel wood siding is installed in overlapping courses. The exposure of each course is important when determining the layout. Tight-fitting joints prevent water seepage.

32.3 Wood shingle siding may be installed in several ways that result in different looks. Various grades of shingles may be mixed, depending on the method used.

32.4 It is important with sidings such as vinyl, fiber cement, and plywood panels to follow manufacturer's instructions closely. This ensures the most durable results. Cutting and handling of fiber cement involves extra safety precautions. A dust mask should always be worn.

Review Questions

1. List several precautions that should be taken to prevent moisture from seeping into or behind any siding.
2. Why is it important for building paper and housewrap to be water resistant but not vapor resistant?
3. What does the term *exposure* refer to?
4. What is the advantage of using a story pole when installing plain-bevel siding?
5. How do carpenters cut tight-fitting butt joints in plain-bevel siding?
6. Name the four coursing styles used for wood shingles.
7. Where should nails be placed in vinyl siding panels?
8. What is the purpose of a J-channel and where is it used?
9. What sealing preparation is important before installing plywood panel siding?
10. What holds stucco in place?

Respecting Cultural Differences Many people work on a construction job, and often they come from diverse backgrounds. The United States is a nation of immigrants. People from many lands have contributed to the knowledge and skills that have made this country strong. Those who are looking for a better way of life continue to come here, and you may encounter them as coworkers or as customers.

American customs may seem strange to them at first, and it may take them a while to get used to new ways. They may also want to retain some of the old ways that feel comfortable and familiar. Give them time to adjust and respect their differences, as you would want them to respect yours if the situation were reversed.

Chapter 33

Brick-Veneer Siding

Objectives

After reading this chapter, you'll be able to:

- Identify the tools used in working with brick and mixing mortar.
- Cut brick with a mason's hammer.
- Name the type of mortar used most often for brick veneer.
- Explain why care should be taken when laying brick in cold weather.

Terms

jointer
lead corner
line block
retempering
weep hole

In residential construction, a layer of brick may be used for part or all of the exterior covering over wood-frame walls. This is called *brick-veneer siding.* In some regions of the country brick veneer is common, while in others it is rare. Brick is also sometimes used as a structural material, rather than as veneer. This chapter, however, will focus on brick veneer.

One advantage of brick veneer is that it reduces the transmission of sound to the inside of the house. Another advantage is brick's natural fire resistance. Although fairly high in cost, brick has low maintenance requirements and a long life. In addition, it is versatile and suitable for a variety of architectural styles.

SECTION 33.1

Tools and Materials

Brick comes in many colors and shapes. On some houses, it covers the entire surface of every exterior wall, while on others it is used on just some of the walls. **Fig. 33-1.** In every case, however, it should be applied by skilled brick masons. This ensures that the brick will properly protect the house. A brick mason may also install fireplaces, chimneys, and ornamental brickwork such as planters and walkways.

TOOLS

Many of the tools used in brick construction are similar to those used to install other types of masonry, such as concrete block (see Chapter 14, "Foundation Walls"). The following are the basic tools used in brick construction:

- The brick mason's basic tool is the *brick trowel.* The trowel has a steel blade and a wood handle. The end of the blade is called

Fig. 33-1. This house features brick-veneer siding on the front walls and wood siding on the side and back walls. The detail photo at right shows the garage wall. Note that the brick forms a layer (veneer) over the wood framing. Note also how the brick is interlocked at the corner. This strengthens the walls.

the toe, or point. The wide portion is called the heel. **Fig. 33-2.** Trowels are available in many sizes. However, short, wide trowels are most comfortable to use because their weight, when loaded with mortar, is centered nearer the handle. This puts less strain on the mason's wrist.

- A **jointer**, or *jointing tool*, is a simple metal bar with a shaped end. **Fig. 33-3.** It is run over the joints to pack the mortar into them and give them a particular shape.
- A good quality *mason's level* is another important tool for the brick mason. It should have horizontal and vertical leveling vials that can be read from both sides. The edges should be metal to withstand wear. **Fig. 33-4.**
- A *mason's rule* is used for measuring the height and spacing of brick courses (rows) as they are laid. **Fig. 33-5.** A folding rule is preferred over a tape measure because the tape can be damaged by contact with mortar. Two

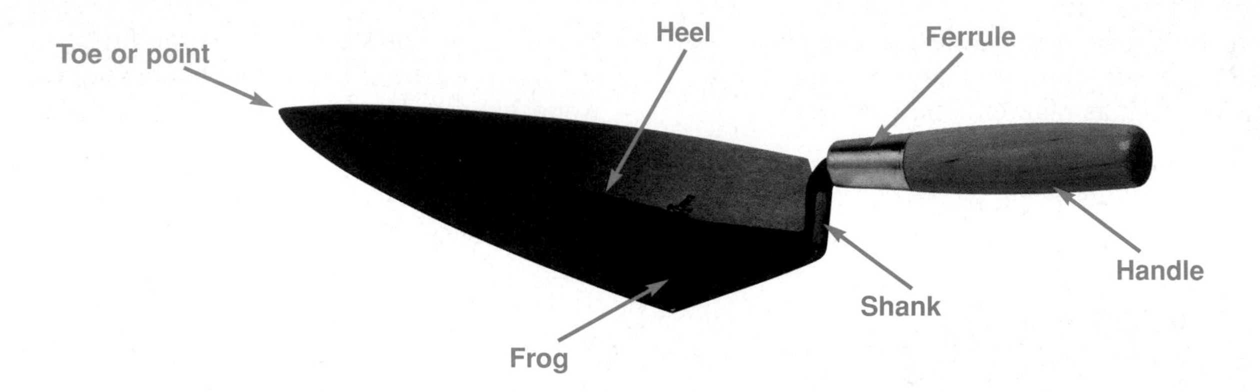

Fig. 33-2. The main parts of a brick trowel.

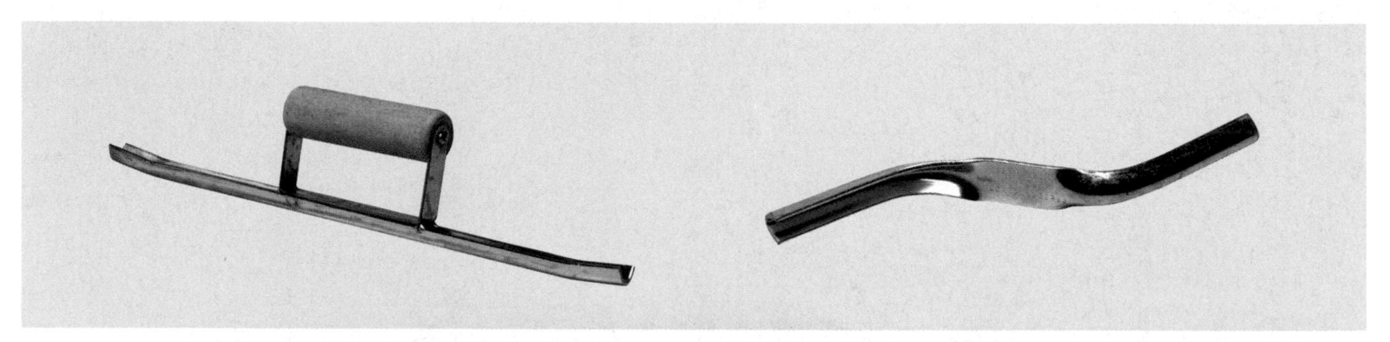

Fig. 33-3. A jointer is used to form and compact mortar joints. Various types are available.

Fig. 33-4. Mason's levels are available in various sizes. These are traditional mahogany levels.

types of folding rule are available. The standard mason's rule is white. It is used for measuring standard, or modular, brick. An oversized mason's rule is yellow. It is easier to use when working with oversized bricks.

- *Brick tongs* help masons carry small quantities of brick efficiently. **Fig. 33-6.** The metal tool clamps over a row of six to eleven bricks. The lever action of the handle holds the bricks in place. When the handle is lowered, the bricks are released. This tool reduces the damage that might occur to bricks if they were just dumped into a wheelbarrow.
- A *brick hammer* is used for splitting and rough-breaking bricks. **Fig. 33-7.** It often has a hardwood handle. The head has a chisel blade (sometimes called the *peen end*) and a square face.
- A *brick set* is a chisel-like tool made of tempered steel. One edge is beveled. Striking the brick set with a brick hammer cuts a brick cleanly. **Fig. 33-8.**

Handling Masonry Products

Masonry products are heavy. Whenever possible, use appropriate tools or machinery to carry even small numbers of bricks. This reduces the risk of back strain. Also, do not bend over as you lift. Always lift heavy loads by bending at the knees. When moving large numbers of bricks, transport them on pallets with the aid of a forklift. For more on moving materials safely, see Chapter 5, "Construction Safety and Health."

Fig. 33-5. A mason's rule. The front side of the rule reads in feet and inches. The back side of the rule is marked with brick coursing dimensions.

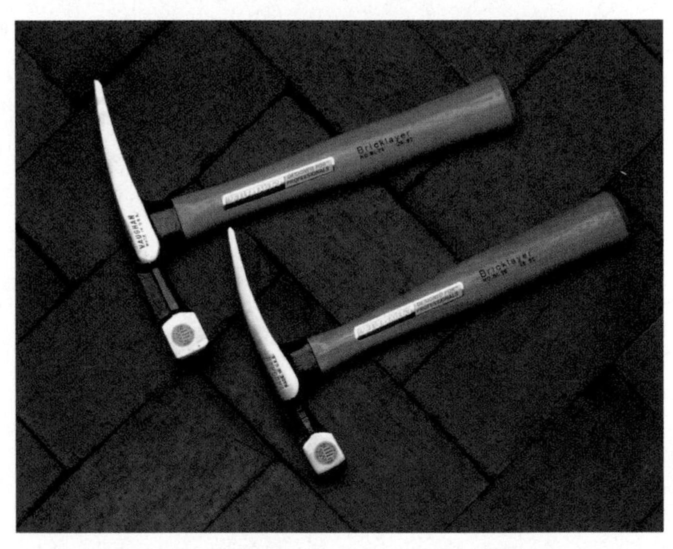

Fig. 33-7. These brick hammers have carbide chisel ends.

Fig. 33-6. Brick tongs.

Fig. 33-8. Using a brick hammer and brick set to cut brick.

Cutting Brick

Brick is sometimes cut with a masonry saw, but cutting it with hand tools is often the easiest and quickest method. To cut brick with a brick hammer, make a cutting line around the brick by striking it lightly and repeatedly with the square face. A sharp blow to one side of the completed cutting line will then split the brick along the line. **Fig. 33-9.** Rough surfaces can be cleaned up somewhat with the chisel blade. **Fig. 33-10.**

If a more accurate cut must be made, use a brick hammer and a brick set. If several bricks must be cut to the same size, line them up evenly. Then use a straightedge to scribe a line across them. This limits variations in the sizes of the cut brick.

Fig. 33-9. Cutting brick along the cutting line.

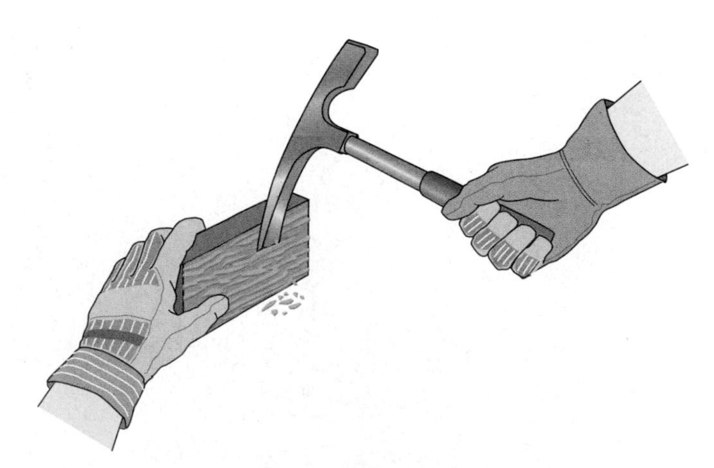

Fig. 33-10. Trimming brick with the chisel blade.

SAFETY FIRST

Brick Dust and Fragments

Cutting brick by hand can launch small pieces of brick toward you. Wear suitable eye protection. If cutting with a dry-cut masonry saw, wear a dust mask so as not to breathe in the fine brick dust.

BRICK

Brick is produced in factories by crushing clay and shale, tempering it with water, forming it into bricks, and then drying the bricks in large kilns (ovens). Other ingredients may be added during manufacture to improve some qualities of the brick.

The tempered material is formed into bricks in one of three basic ways:

- By extruding the material through dies and slicing it into individual bricks.
- By placing the material into individual molds.
- By *dry-pressing* the material under high pressure.

Types

The suitability of a brick for a particular use depends on several factors. These include the type and source of the clay and how the brick was manufactured.

Many types of bricks are available. Following are the three basic types:

- *Building brick* is a strong, general-purpose brick. Its color varies from brick to brick. Sizes are somewhat inconsistent.
- *Facing brick* is used primarily for exposed exterior surfaces such as veneer walls. Because manufacturing is carefully controlled, the resulting bricks are consistent in size, texture, and color.
- *Fire brick* is usually pale yellow or buff in color. It is used specifically for lining fireplaces and other heating units. It is sometimes referred to as refractory brick.

Bricks with holes (*cores*) through them are called *hollow bricks*, and those without holes are called *solid bricks*. Hollow and solid bricks are both suitable for veneer walls. During firing, the cores enable the bricks to dry and harden more evenly. *Firing* is a process that heats the brick to temperatures as high as 2,400°F [1316°C]. Bricks with cores are also less expensive to produce, because they use less clay and the firing process uses less fuel. Because they weigh less, they are less expensive to ship and easier to lay. One other advantage is that when mortar oozes into the cores, it makes a very strong mechanical connection.

Some hollow bricks have three fairly large cores. Others have ten or more smaller cores. The exact arrangement is determined by the manufacturer. However, the overall area of coring must not be more than 60 percent of the brick's surface.

A depression in one bedding surface of a solid brick is called a *frog*. A frog serves the same purposes as a core. Frogs are limited to a specified depth and a specified distance from the brick's face. Bricks should always be laid with the frogged surface down.

Sizes

For many years, only three sizes of bricks were available: standard, Roman, and Norman. Today there are hundreds. **Fig. 33-11.** When specifying the size of a brick, always list the dimensions in the following order: thickness by height by length.

All brick can be classified into two size groups: *modular* and *nonmodular*. The length of a modular brick is based on multiples of 4″. It is a nominal size that includes an allowance for the thickness of a standard mortar joint. The actual dimensions of a modular brick are therefore smaller than the nominal dimensions, just as the actual dimensions of a 2x4 stud are smaller than its nominal dimensions.

The size of nonmodular brick does not take the thickness of the mortar joint into account. The dimensions given for nonmodular brick are the actual dimensions.

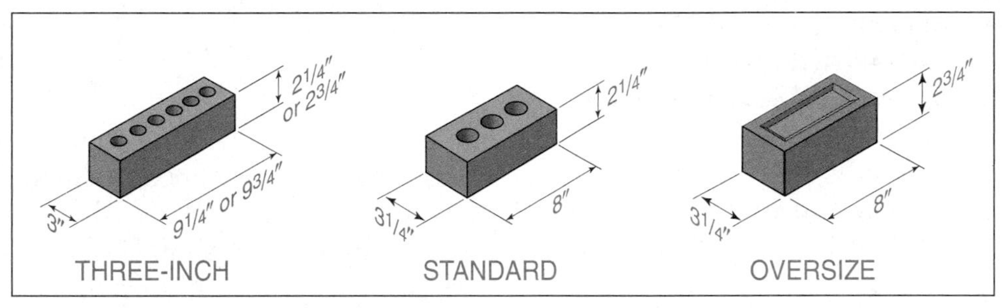

NONMODULAR BRICK
(actual dimensions)

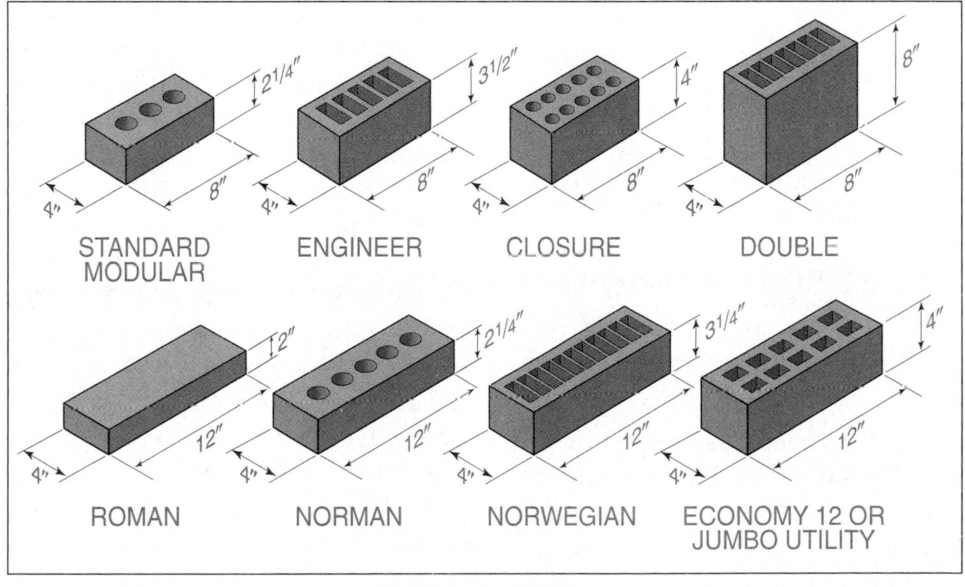

MODULAR BRICK
(nominal dimensions)

Fig. 33-11. Modular and nonmodular sizes of bricks, shown with nominal and actual dimensions.

Textures

Along with color and size, bricks vary in texture. The texture of a brick can significantly affect its appearance. Some bricks have smooth surfaces. Others may have a wirecut (velour), brushed, or other type of rough texture.

MORTAR

Mortar holds bricks together as they are laid. Its bond strength is its most important quality. Mortar must be durable and have enough bearing capacity to support the brick. It must also block the passage of water.

The basic dry ingredients of mortar are Portland cement, masonry cement, hydrated lime, and sand. When mixed with clean water, these ingredients form a durable and easily worked material.

Types of Mortar

Different types of mortar are needed for different types of brick construction. They vary as to ingredients and amounts. Following are the four basic types of mortar:

- Type M is recommended specifically for masonry below grade and in contact with soil. Uses include foundations, retaining walls, and walkways.
- Type S is recommended when the brick must resist high levels of lateral (sideways) force. It may be required in areas of high earthquake activity.
- Type N is a general-purpose mortar for brick-veneer walls. It is suitable for general use in exposed masonry above grade. It is recommended specifically for exterior walls exposed to severe weather conditions.
- Type O is used for load-bearing walls that will not be subjected to moisture and freeze/thaw cycles.

Mixing Mortar

Mixing proportions for these basic types of mortar are shown in **Table 33-A**. Measurements should be made carefully. A common mistake is to add too much sand. Colorants may also be added to change the appearance of mortar. This is sometimes done to complement the color of the brick.

Table 33-A. Mortar Proportions by Volume

Type	Portland Cement-Lime Mortars		Sand
	Portland Cement	Hydrated Lime or Lime Putty	
M	1	¼	3
S	1	½	4½
N	1	1	6
O	1	2	9
Type	**Masonry Cement Mortars**		**Sand**
	Portland Cement	**Masonry Cement Type II**	
M	1	1	6
S	½	1	4½
N	–	1	3
O	–	1 (Type I or II)	3

Note: Numbers represent parts. For example, "1 part lime to 6 parts water."

The proper amount of water to use in mixing mortar is a factor that is often misunderstood. Mortar should not be confused with concrete. Concrete is mixed with the least amount of water possible in order to maximize its ability to bear heavy loads. Mortar, on the other hand, requires workability and high bond strength. Mortar is considered workable if it spreads easily and will readily stick to vertical surfaces.

Unlike concrete, mixed mortar may be retempered. **Retempering** is adding water to a batch of mortar that has become too stiff to work. Only enough water is added to replace that lost by evaporation, however. Also, mortar should be used within 2½ hours after initial mixing when the air temperature is 80°F [27°C] or higher. Cooler weather allows a somewhat longer working time.

If a large volume of mortar is required, it may be mixed in a *mortar mixer* (sometimes called a *power mixer* or *mechanical mixer*). **Fig. 33-12.** It is similar to a concrete mixer, except that the mixing drum does not rotate. Instead, mixing paddles inside the drum are turned by a heavy-duty electric motor or a gas engine. Mortar ingredients are added to the drum and blended by the rotating paddles. All the dry ingredients should be measured and placed in the mixing drum and mixed for one minute before clean water is added. The mixer should continue to run until the ingredients are thoroughly blended.

Maintenance is required for a mortar mixer. This includes cleaning the mixing drum thoroughly after use. Any drive belts should be checked for proper tension, and the retractable guard over the mixing drum must be seen to work smoothly. Mortar should not be allowed to dry on the mixer's moving parts, particularly on the drive gears.

Small amounts of mortar may be mixed in a wheelbarrow. However, a steel *mortar box* is less likely to tip over. **Fig. 33-13.** A heavy-duty *mortar hoe* is used to blend the ingredients. It has holes in the blade to make mixing easier. Blend all the dry ingredients, and then add clean water as needed. Do not let the hoe or any other mixing tools come into contact with dirt.

Fig. 33-12. Mortar mixers come in capacities of 7, 9, and 12 cubic feet.

Fig. 33-13. A mortar hoe and a small mortar box.

SECTION 33.1 Check Your Knowledge

1. What is the term used to describe the wide portion of a brick trowel blade?
2. Name two safety precautions to be taken when cutting brick.
3. How should a mortar mixer be maintained?
4. What must be done before adding water to a mortar mixture?

On the Job

Consult the catalog of a company that supplies masonry tools. Price out the tools described in this section and total the costs. If the catalog includes various grades, divide your price totals into two categories: least expensive and most expensive. Date your summary and place the information in a file for future use.

Building a Brick-Veneer Wall

For brick veneer to protect the house, it must be installed with skill. All mortar joints must be fully filled because partially filled joints allow water to pass through. This encourages cracks to form in the joints, among other problems. However, if too much mortar is used, it will squeeze out and stain the bricks below. This also makes the job site more difficult to clean up. It is equally important to keep mortar out of areas intended to let moisture drain from behind the wall. Brick courses should be straight and level. In addition, vertical joints must fall in regular patterns that are plumb.

CONSTRUCTION DETAILS

A brick-veneer wall must be supported by a masonry or concrete foundation as well as be tied into the framework of the house. **Fig. 33-14.** The brick rests on a supporting ledge or shelf formed into the main house foundation. This ledge is approximately 5″ wide.

The first course of brick is a leveling course intended to make up for any irregularities in the support ledge. Subsequent courses should be checked frequently for level and plumb.

Flashing and Drainage

Base flashing is used at the brick course below the bottom of the sheathing and framing. Fig. 33-14. The top edge of the flashing should be slipped behind the building paper or building felt already attached to the sheathed walls. Various flashing materials are acceptable, but copper is highly durable and is often preferred.

A series of weep holes must be built into the wall. A **weep hole** provides drainage near the bottom of the walls. Weep holes are often formed by omitting some of the mortar in a vertical joint every 18″ to 24″ along the wall. Moisture that builds up behind the veneer can then escape to the outside. Weep holes are located in the lowest mortar joints above grade. They may be formed by leaving out certain head joints, by inserting plastic tubing into the wall, or by creating a hole using a metal rod.

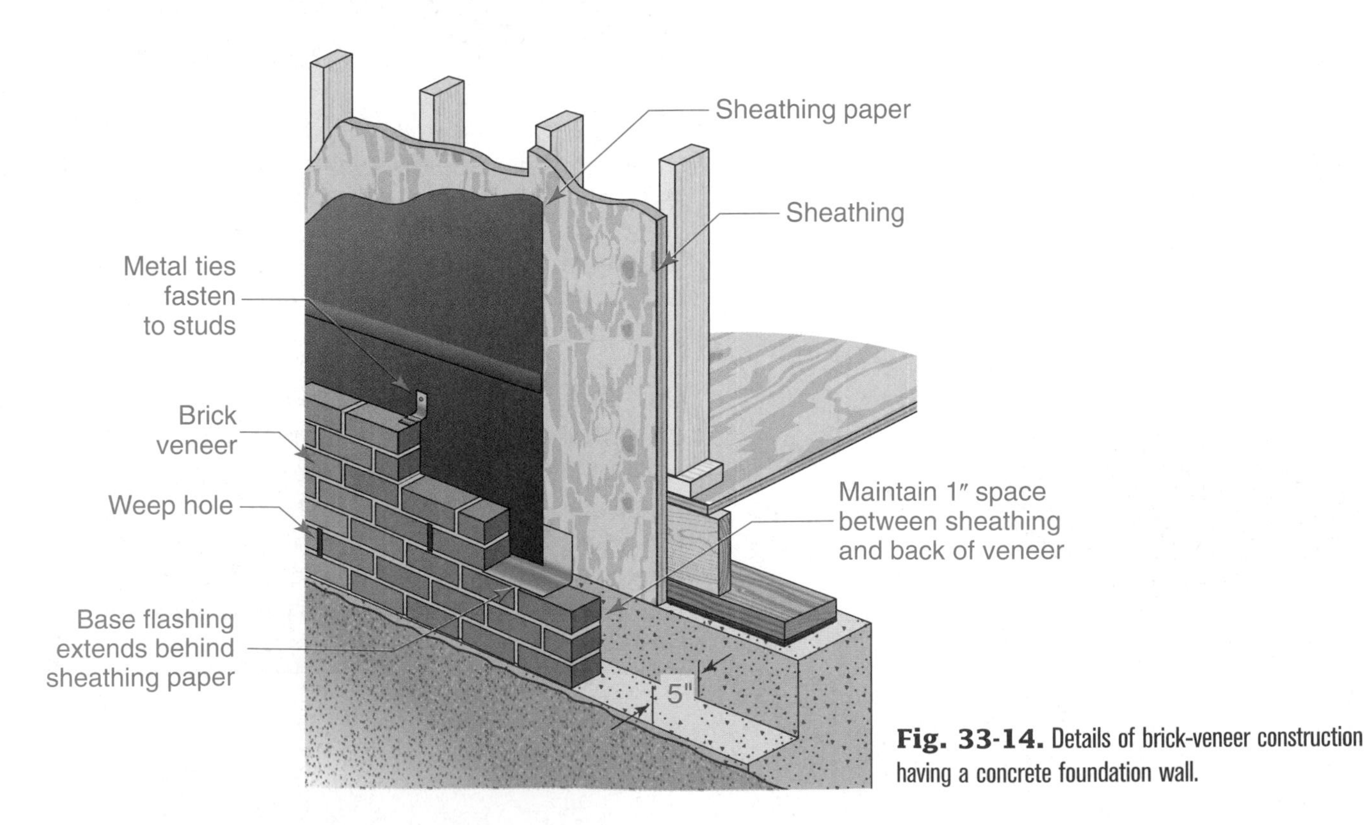

Fig. 33-14. Details of brick-veneer construction having a concrete foundation wall.

Wall Ties

The veneer wall must be tied to the frame of the house with corrosion-resistant fasteners, called *wall ties*, secured with galvanized nails. Several types of wall ties are available. **Fig. 33-15.** Corrugated metal straps ⅞″ wide and 6″ long are traditional for brick-veneer walls. However, wire-type ties are more corrosion resistant.

The ties are nailed through the sheathing and into the studs and covered in mortar as the wall goes up. The ties should be embedded 2″ into the mortar joint. Check local codes for the required spacing and type of ties. Generally, there should be one tie for every 2 sq. ft. of wall area. However, other requirements may apply in areas of earthquake activity.

Window and Door Openings

Special care is required around windows and doors to maintain weather resistance. The sill of a window, for example, is often made of a row of bricks slanted downward to shed water. Flashing provides a second layer of protection. Bricks above an opening must be supported by a lintel. **Fig. 33-16.**

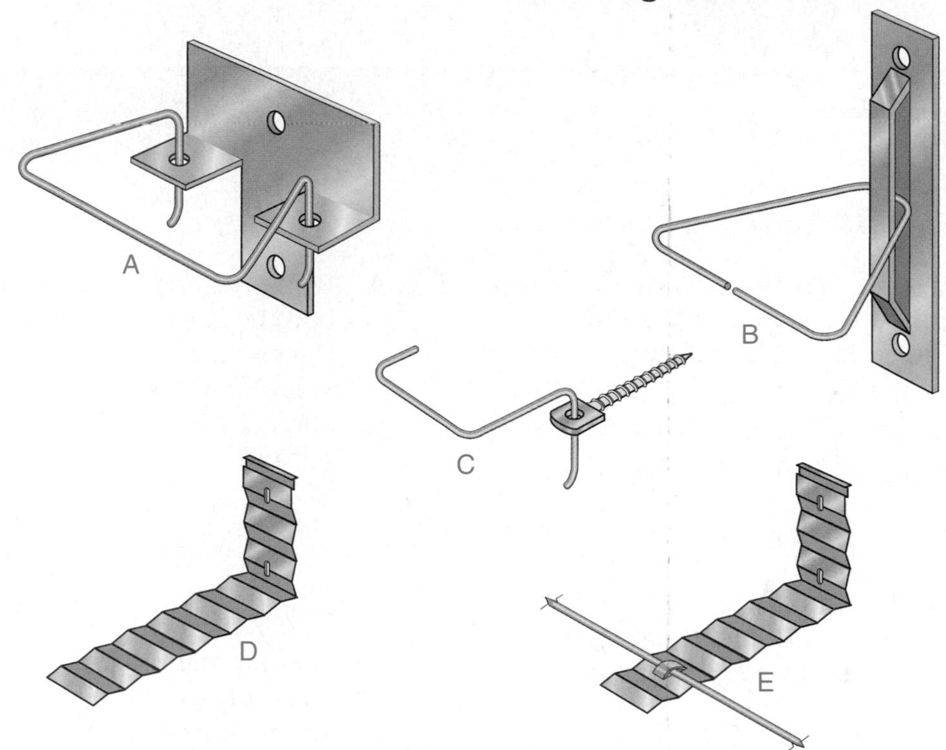

Fig. 33-15. Brick-veneer wall ties. *A*, *B*, and *C* are wire-type ties. *D* and *E* are strap-type ties.

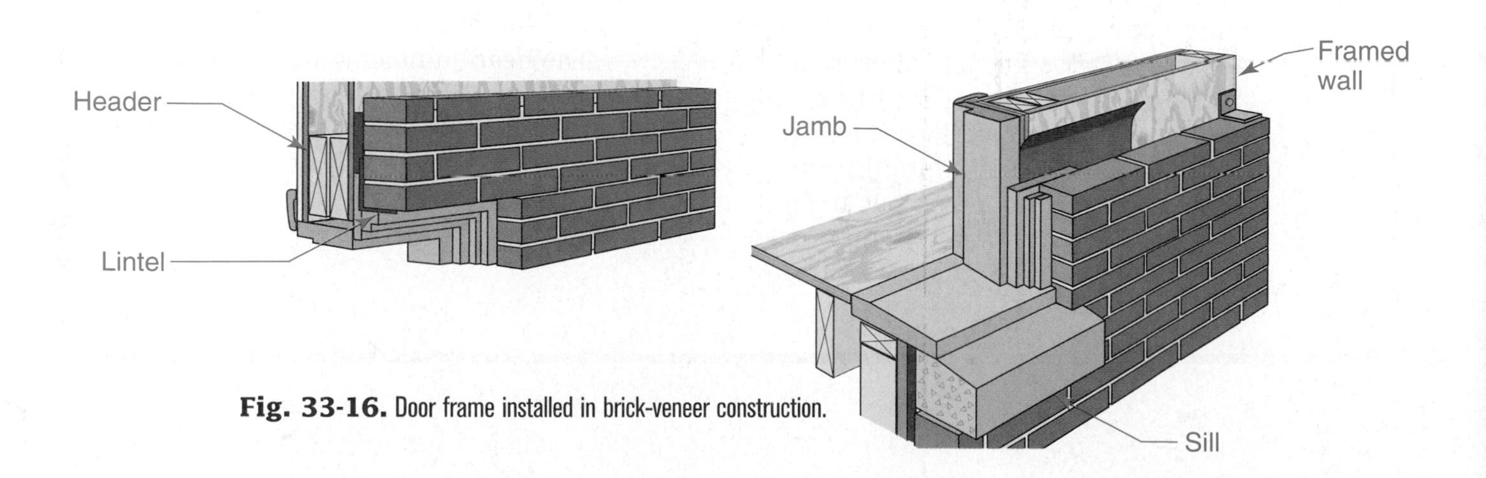

Fig. 33-16. Door frame installed in brick-veneer construction.

BUILDING THE WALL

Before actually laying brick, the mason should review the plans for the house. This will reveal any special details called for, such as arches or decorative coursing. Also, the mason should plan the courses of brick so that they line up with the top and bottom of window and door openings wherever possible. This reduces the need to cut brick and results in a better overall appearance. On a small project, a mason may mix mortar as well as lay brick. On larger projects, he or she may have a helper, or *tender*. This person mixes mortar and provides a steady supply to the mason. The mason can then focus on laying brick.

Step-by-Step instructions for laying brick appear below.

STEP BY STEP

Laying Brick

It is important for a mason to work efficiently. Each brick should be laid using the fewest possible motions. This reduces physical stress and increases speed.

Following are the basic steps for laying brick for a wall that has already been started.

Step 1 Scoop up a portion of mortar with the trowel. Spread it over three to five bricks by sliding the mortar off the trowel with one smooth sweeping motion. **Fig. 33-17.** This creates a mortar bed.

Step 2 Furrow the mortar by drawing the point of the trowel across it. This provides better coverage for the brick.

Step 3 Pick up a brick with one hand and *butter* one end. **Fig. 33-18.** Buttering means to swipe a small amount of mortar over the end of the brick. This mortar will fill the vertical (head) joint. Shove the brick into place so that the mortar squeezes out the top of the head joint. An alternate method is to butter the end of a brick already in place.

Step 4 Using the end of the trowel handle, bed the brick by tapping the top of the brick into place. Make sure that it is level with the adjoining brick and aligned with, but not touching, the mason's line.

Step 5 Slide the edge of your trowel across the bed and head joints to cut off mortar that has squeezed out. **Fig. 33-19.** This prevents the mortar from staining the bricks below. Mortar that is cut off can be reused. Continue to lay brick in this fashion until reaching the end of the mortar bed. Apply a new bed and repeat the process.

Step 6 After several complete courses of brick have been laid, use a jointer to tool (compact) bed and head joints. The head joints should always be tooled before the bed joints. Finally, brush the wall with a mason's brush to remove stray bits of mortar.

Fig. 33-17. Laying the mortar bed. Note the direction of motion of the trowel.

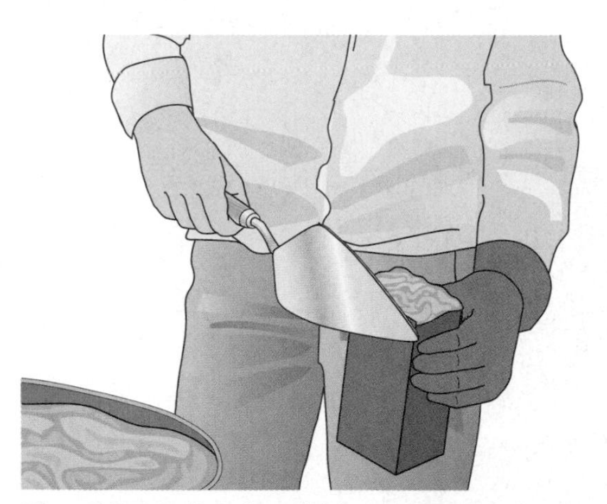

Fig. 33-18. Buttering a brick.

Fig. 33-19. Cleaning a mortar joint.

Laying Brick to a Line

To ensure that a course of brick is level and straight, masons align it with a string line that is tightly stretched across the wall. **Fig. 33-20.** The line identifies the top outside edge of each course. To begin a wall, a mason sometimes secures the line to stakes driven into the ground at each end of the wall. As the wall gains height, the line is then stretched between line blocks

Fig. 33-20. When the mason is laying bricks, a leveled string line helps keep the courses straight.

instead. A **line block** is a small L-shaped device made of wood or plastic. It hooks over the edge of a brick and is held in place by the tension of the string. Opposing pairs of line blocks are moved upward as the wall grows.

Another method of aligning a mason's string line is to stretch it between *corner poles* (also called *adjustable masonry guides* or *corner story poles*). **Fig. 33-21.** The poles are nailed to the sheathing at each end of a wall. They provide an accurate guide to course height and can be adjusted quickly. Corner poles come with fittings that allow them to be attached to either inside corners or outside corners.

Building Lead Corners

A **lead corner** is a partially constructed corner of brick. After lead corners are established at both ends of a wall, the remaining brick is laid between them. **Fig. 33-22.** The first course of each corner is placed into a thick bed of mortar laid on the foundation wall. Additional courses are stepped upward toward the corner. Work then proceeds toward the center of the wall. This technique helps to maintain straight and level courses. Line blocks may be hooked onto the outside edges of each lead corner.

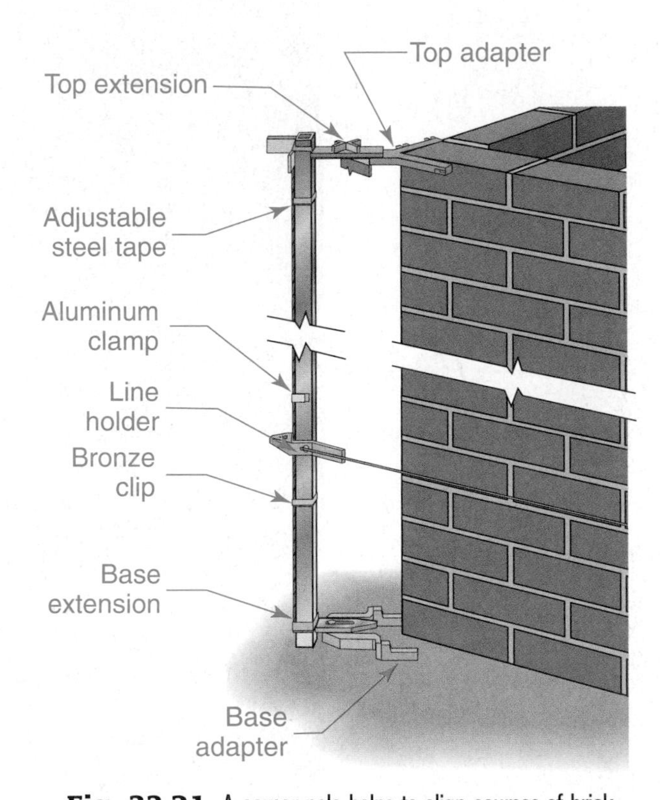

Fig. 33-21. A corner pole helps to align courses of brick.

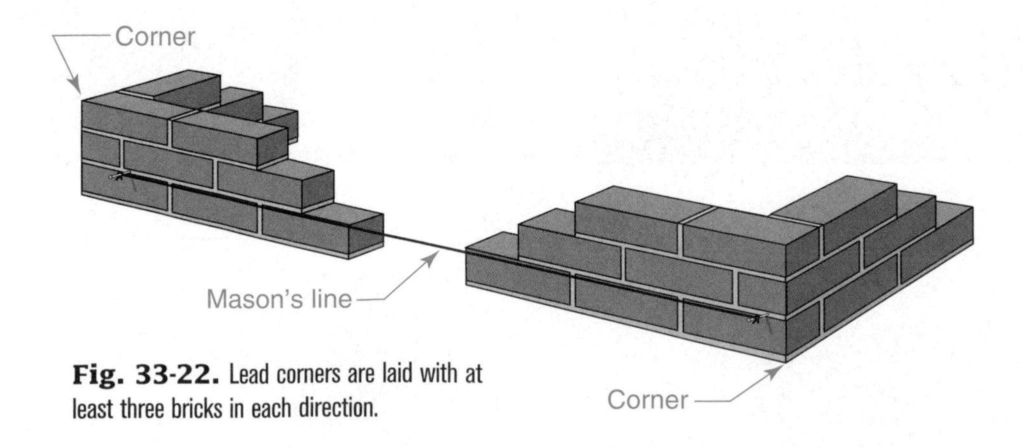

Fig. 33-22. Lead corners are laid with at least three bricks in each direction.

Tooling the Joints

Properly finished mortar joints help to create a strong, tight bond between the mortar and the brick. This is important when the wall will be exposed to the weather. Joints should be tooled with a jointer (Fig. 33-3) as soon as the mortar is thumbprint hard. The shape of the joints can have an impact on how a wall looks. **Fig. 33-23.** Concave joints, V-joints, and grapevine joints resist rain well and are recommended for brick-veneer walls.

WORKING IN COLD WEATHER

Building codes include rules for the installation of masonry in cold weather. Bricks that are cold affect curing. When outdoor temperatures are below 20°F [-7° C], bricks should be warmed before use. However, it is rarely necessary to warm them to more than 40°F [4°C]. If wet brick has become frozen, it must be thawed and dried completely before use.

Cold weather slows the hydration process in mortar and may affect the strength of the wall. When mixing mortar in cold weather, you may need to heat the sand and water before mixing them with the other ingredients. Mortar should never be allowed to freeze. This makes it less weather resistant. It can even reduce or destroy the bond between brick and mortar. For this reason, masons often work beneath protective tents in cold weather.

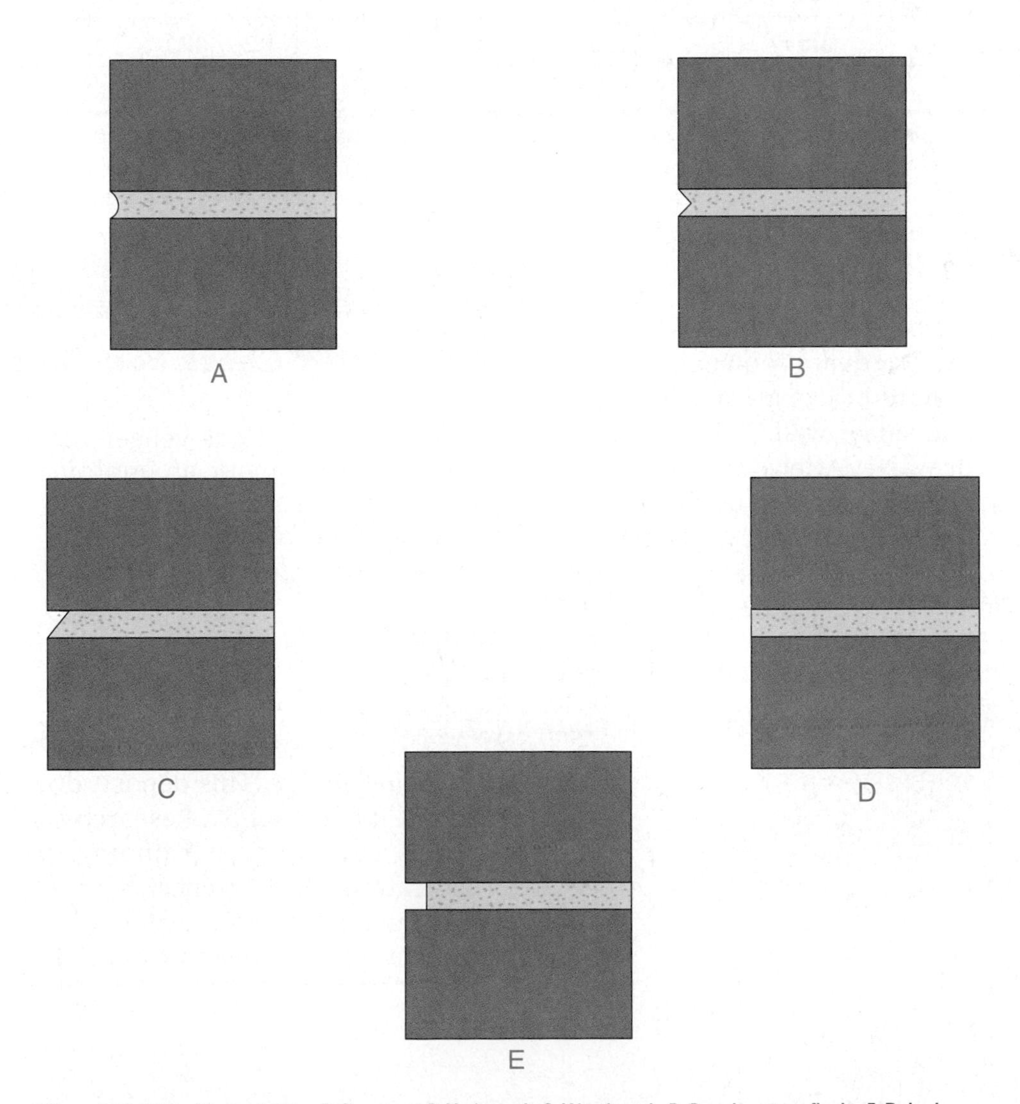

Fig. 33-23. Mortar joints. *A.* Concave. *B.* V-shaped. *C.* Weathered. *D.* Rough cut or flush. *E.* Raked.

Table 33-B. **Modular Brick and Mortar Required for Single-Wythe Walls in Running Bond**

Nominal Size of Bricks (inches)	Number of Bricks per 100 Sq. Ft	Cubic Feet of Mortar			
		Per 100 Sq. Ft.		Per 1,000 Bricks	
T H L		$\frac{3}{8}$″ Joints	$\frac{1}{2}$″ Joints	$\frac{3}{8}$″ Joints	$\frac{1}{2}$″ Joints
4 x $2\frac{2}{3}$ x 8	675	5.5	7.0	8.1	10.3
4 x $3\frac{1}{5}$ x 8	563	4.8	6.1	8.6	10.9
4 x 4 x 8	450	4.2	5.3	9.2	11.7
4 x $5\frac{1}{3}$ x 8	338	3.5	4.4	10.2	12.9
4 x 2 x 12	600	6.5	8.2	10.8	13.7
4 x $2\frac{2}{3}$ x 12	450	5.1	6.5	11.3	14.4
4 x $3\frac{1}{5}$ x 12	375	4.4	5.6	11.7	14.9
4 x 4 x 12	300	3.7	4.8	12.3	15.7
4 x $5\frac{1}{3}$ x 12	225	3.0	3.9	13.4	17.1
6 x $2\frac{2}{3}$ x 12	450	7.9	10.2	17.5	22.6
6 x $3\frac{1}{5}$ x 12	375	6.8	8.8	18.1	23.4
6 x 4 x 12	300	5.6	7.4	19.1	24.7

Note: Running bond is a particular arrangement of brick. No allowances are made for breakage or waste.

ESTIMATING BRICK

A rough estimate of bricks needed may be made based on the wall's square footage. Approximately 7 standard bricks are needed for every square foot of a veneer wall. This includes a small allowance for waste. After calculating the square footage of walls, minus any openings, multiply this figure by 7 to get the number of bricks required. Another method is to consult a table such as **Table 33-B**.

Check Your Knowledge

1. What supports a brick-veneer wall?
2. Why is a wire-type tie an improvement over the corrugated strap tie?
3. What is a lead corner?
4. Why is brick laid to a line?

On the Job

In some instances when a brick wall has been completed, a white, crystalline deposit forms on portions of the exterior surface. This deposit is called *efflorescence.* This deposit does not harm brick, but it is unsightly. Research the following questions and report your findings to the class:

- What causes efflorescence?
- What can be done to prevent it?
- How can it be removed from brick?

Chapter 33 Review

Section Summaries

33.1 Important brick-laying tools include the brick trowel and the jointer. Brick comes in three main types: building brick, facing brick and fire brick. Brick sizes are either modular or nonmodular. The four types of mortar are M, S, N, and O. Mortar may be mixed by hand or by machine.

33.2 Weep holes provide drainage for veneer walls. Wall ties secure the wall to the framing. Line blocks and corner poles help masons align courses. A wall is begun at the corners. Joints are tooled for strength and appearance.

Review Questions

1. What are the two types of folding mason's rules used for?
2. Name three methods for cutting a brick.
3. List the three basic types of brick.
4. When specifying brick, in what order should the dimensions be listed?
5. What does the size of a modular brick allow for?
6. What type of general-purpose mortar is used for brick-veneer walls?
7. What is the difference between a mason's hoe and a standard hoe?
8. How should the top edge of base flashing be installed?
9. What are weep holes and where are they located?
10. What effect does cold weather have on mortar?

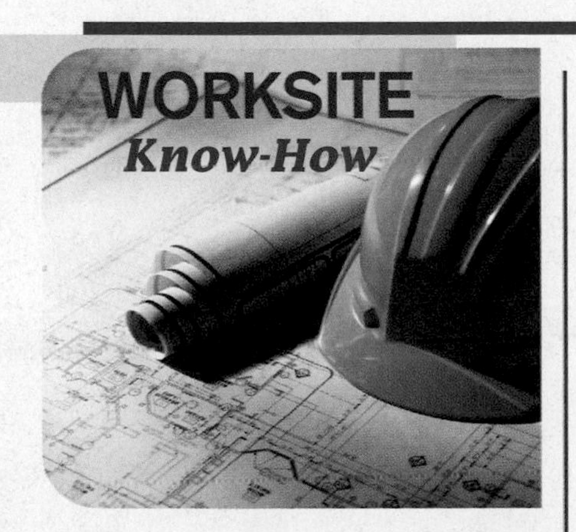

What Your Driving Record Tells an Employer Your driving record is public information that an employer can obtain as part of a background check. What would your record reveal about you? Take accidents, for example. If you've had any and if you were deemed even partially at fault, that can indicate carelessness, an unsafe attitude, and irresponsibility. It may mean you can't be trusted with trucks and other company equipment.

Have you ever been arrested or stopped for driving under the influence? That makes an employer wonder if you'll drink or take drugs during working hours or if you'll fail to show up at all. Do you have several moving violations? That suggests that you don't obey the rules.

Being a good driver can pay off, not only in your own safety and the safety of others, but also in the reputation it helps you build.

Unit 7

FINISH CARPENTRY

Careers in Construction

Finish Carpenter

Finish carpenters are another type of finishing worker. These specialty carpenters work on the detailed final stages of the construction project. While knowledge of framing is helpful in their work, finish carpenters usually pick up where framing carpenters leave off.

Finish carpenters install stairs, wood floors, kitchen cabinets, countertops, doors, and windows. Finish carpentry also includes both outside and inside work on the trim elements of a building. Trim elements include various types of molding (door casings, window trim, ceiling trim, and baseboard), as well as handrails for porches and stairs.

While most finish carpenters learn on the job, an apprenticeship provides more thorough training in layout, tool use, and the overall construction process. Employment with a large general contractor can also provide more exposure to different carpentry tasks. The more skills a carpenter has, the greater the opportunities for work.

For more information, check the *Occupational Outlook Handbook* or look up "finish carpenter" on the Internet.

Chapter 34

Stairways

Objectives

After reading this chapter, you'll be able to:

- Identify the method of construction used on any stairway.
- Understand the building code requirements that apply to stairs.
- Tell the purpose of the different parts of a stairway.
- Tell how to lay out a cut-stringer stairway.
- Install a cleat-stringer stairway.

Terms

headroom
skirtboard
stairway
step
winder

Quality wood stairway construction is often considered the hallmark of fine finish carpentry. Building a stairway is entrusted to experienced carpenters because stairways must be durable and safe, as well as attractive. Because of stairway accidents, building codes tightly regulate the design of stairways. To reduce the possibility of injury, the carpenter must work to close tolerances and must understand the local building codes for stairway design and construction.

Stairways are typically built by carpenters on site. They use a combination of structural lumber and millwork items such as treads, balusters, and trim. However, stairs are sometimes assembled in a cabinet shop and delivered to the site for installation. In other cases, specialists may custom-build the stairway on site. This is frequently the case when an expensive or unusual stair has been specified.

This chapter covers primarily the construction of interior stairways. Many houses also have exterior stairways that lead to decks. Those are discussed on page 694 of this chapter and in Chapter 45, "Decks and Porches."

SECTION 34.1

Stairway Basics

Some houses have two interior stairways. The stairway that connects the main levels is called a *main stairway, primary stairway,* or *finish stairway.* The stairway that leads to the basement is called a *service stairway.* A stairway may be built completely by hand or assembled from prefabricated parts. All parts can be purchased from a lumberyard as stock millwork items. **Fig. 34-1.**

Fig. 34-1. Stairs can be custom built or assembled from a collection of stock parts.

PARTS OF A STAIRWAY

Most interior stairways require a stairwell. An exception would be a stairway to an open loft. A *stairwell* is the vertical shaft inside of which a stairway is built. **Fig. 34-2.** Framing of stairwells is explained in Chapter 20, "Floor Framing." When the stair builder starts work, this framing has already been completed.

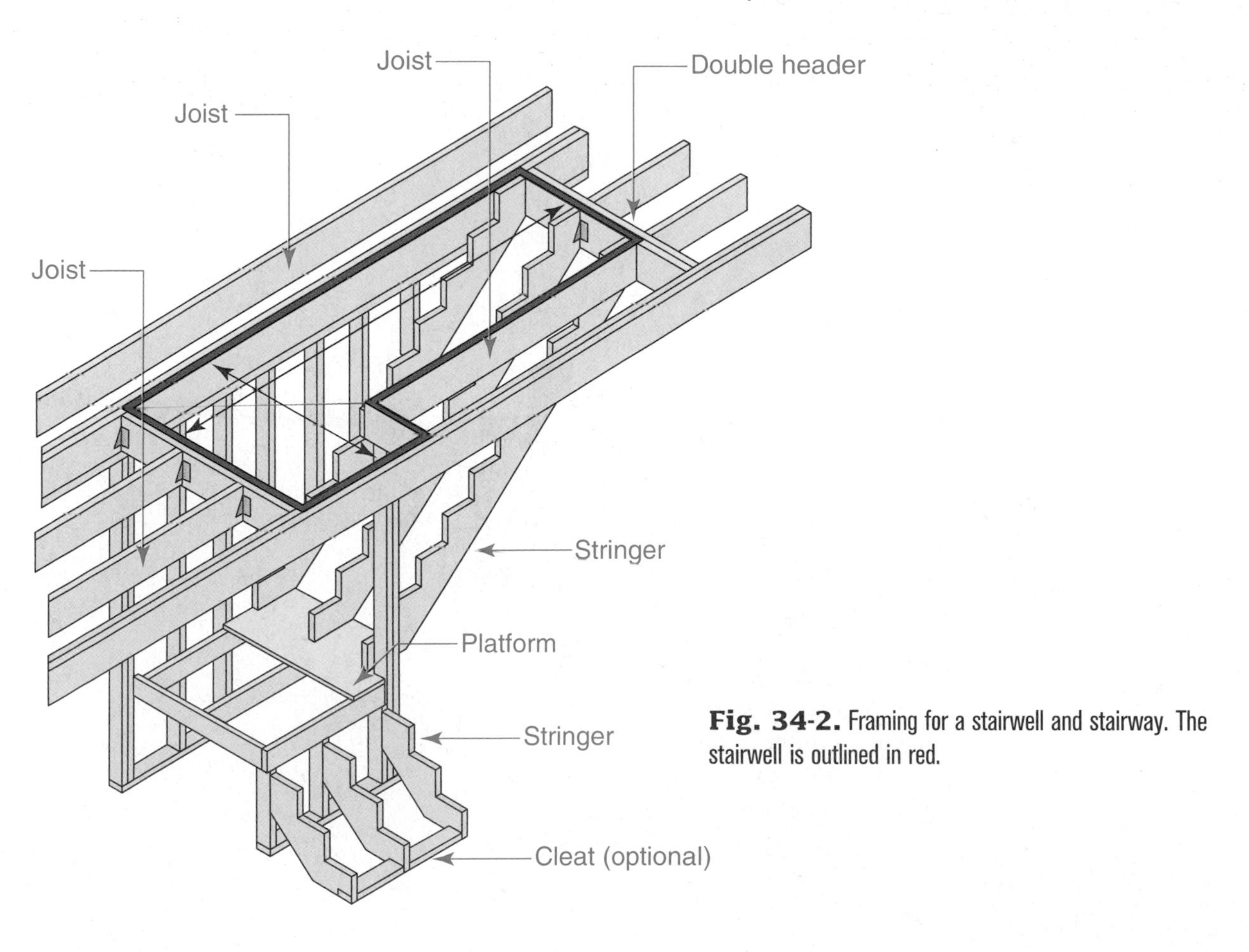

Fig. 34-2. Framing for a stairwell and stairway. The stairwell is outlined in red.

Though stairways vary in their construction, all have three common elements. The *treads* are the parts on which people step. The *stringers* support the treads, and a *handrail* is required for safety. On some stairways, the spaces between treads are enclosed by vertical boards called *risers.*

In this book, the term **step** refers to a tread and riser. The term **stairway** refers to a series of steps along with all the related elements, including stringers and handrail. A stairway may be completely enclosed, or it may be partially open on one or both sides. Open sides of the stairway must include a railing and balusters for safety reasons. *Balusters* are the slender vertical members that support the handrail.

The simplest stairway has two stringers and a series of plank treads. It is called a *cleat-stringer stairway* because the treads are supported by cleats attached to the sides of each stringer. **Fig. 34-3.** Cleat-stringer stairways are fairly easy to build. They are usually made of inexpensive materials.

Cut-stringer stairways are the most common type of stairway found in houses. The treads and risers are attached to notches sawn into the upper edge of each stringer. **Fig. 34-4.** A cut-stringer stairway may have two or three stringers. A primary stairway usually has three.

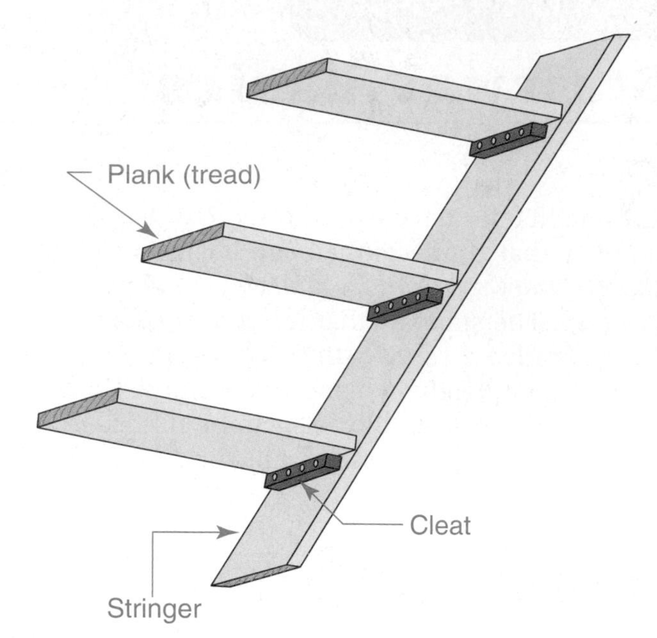

Fig. 34-3. Cleat-stringer stairways are sometimes used as service stairs because they are inexpensive and easy to build.

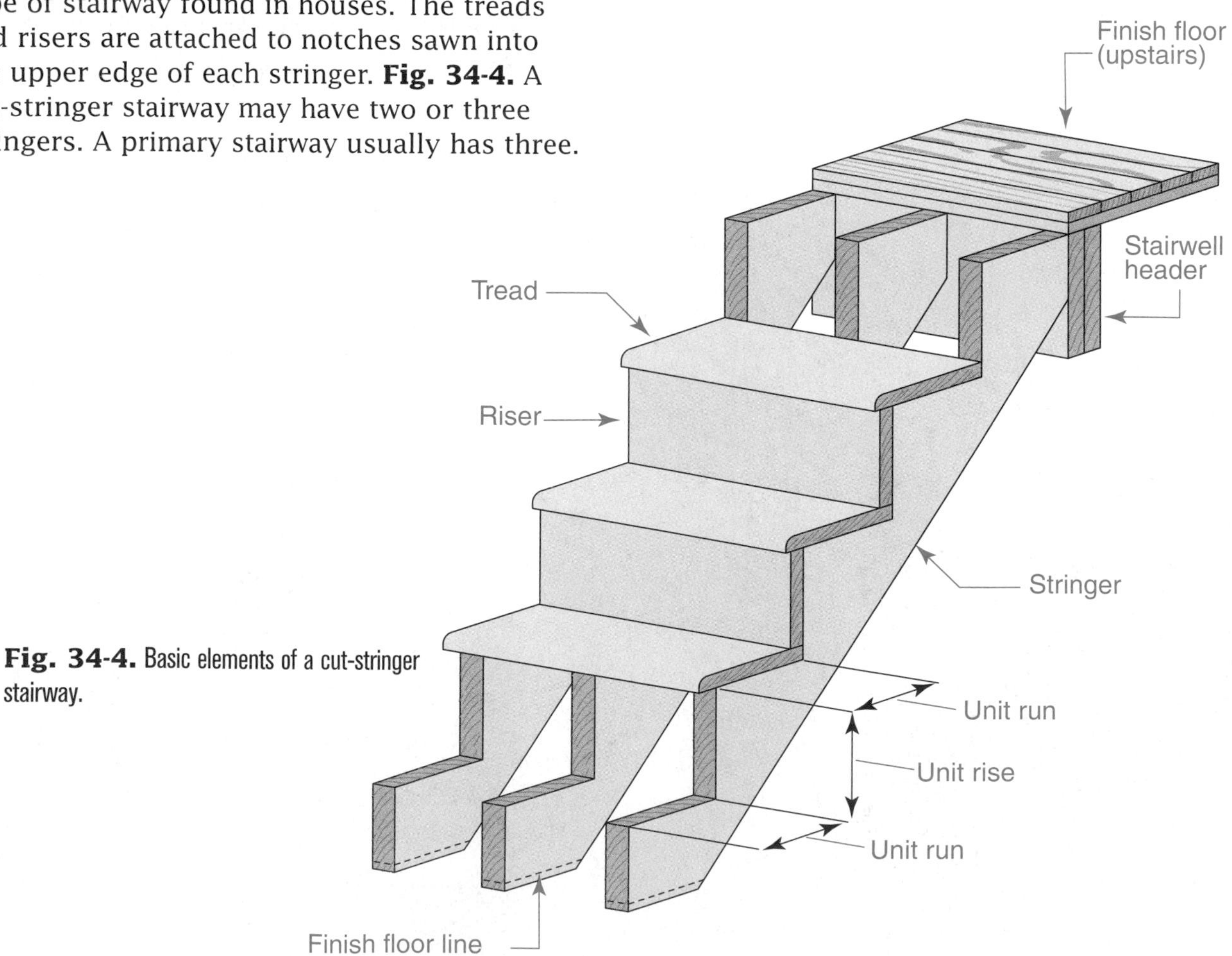

Fig. 34-4. Basic elements of a cut-stringer stairway.

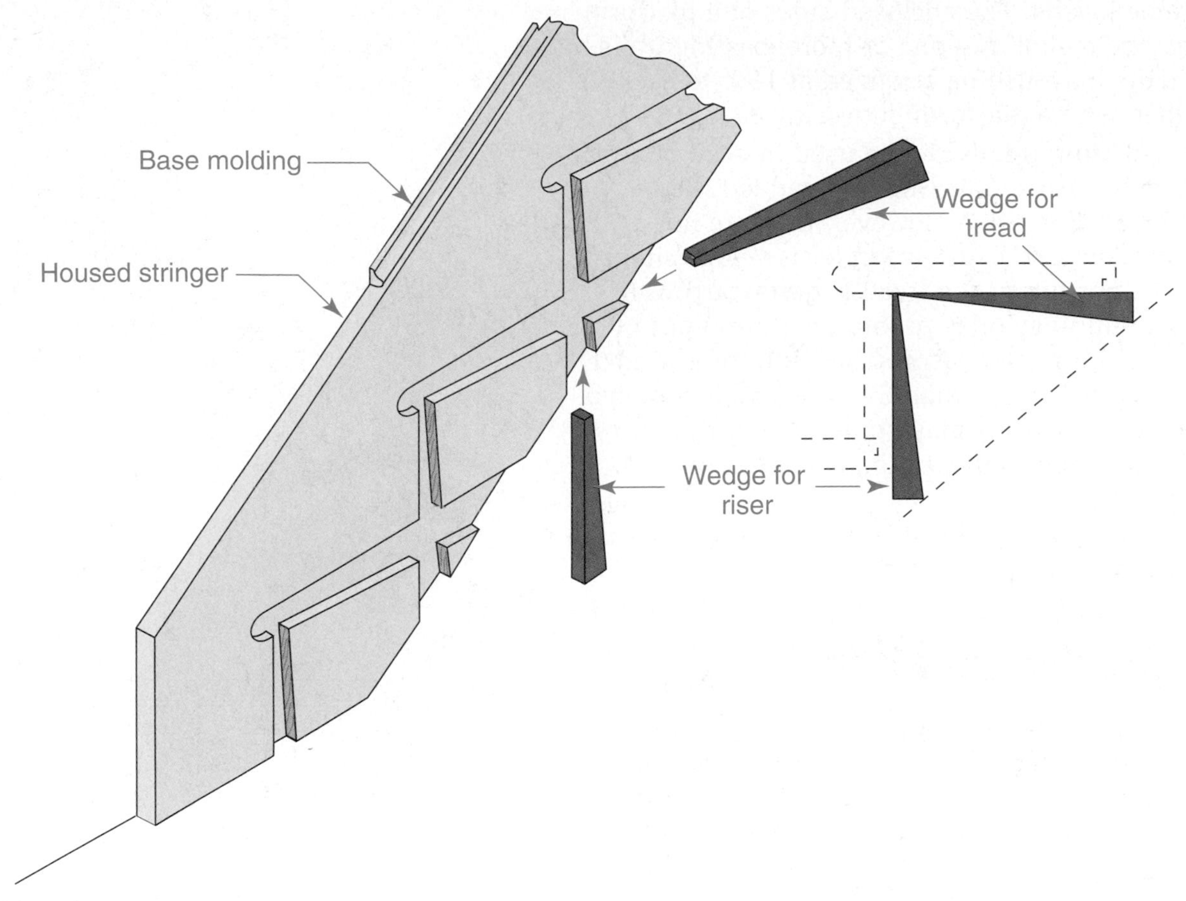

Fig. 34-5. A housed stringer.

Open (plain) stringers are cut to follow the lines of the treads and risers (see Fig. 34-4). *Housed stringers,* or *closed stringers,* have recesses for wedges mortised into them that support risers and treads. **Fig. 34-5.**

STAIRWAY LAYOUT

In most houses, a stairway makes a straight, continuous run. This straight run is called a *flight.* A flight goes from one landing to another. The *landing* is the floor area where a flight ends or begins. **Fig. 34-6.** However, a stairway may make a turn to conserve space. Stairways that turn usually include a platform, as shown in Fig. 34-6. This platform can also be considered a landing because it is the start of one flight and the end of another.

The stair shown in Fig. 34-6 is an example of an L-shaped stair. It contains two flights arranged at 90° to each other and separated by a platform. The platform is built with short joists covered by floor sheathing and is supported by

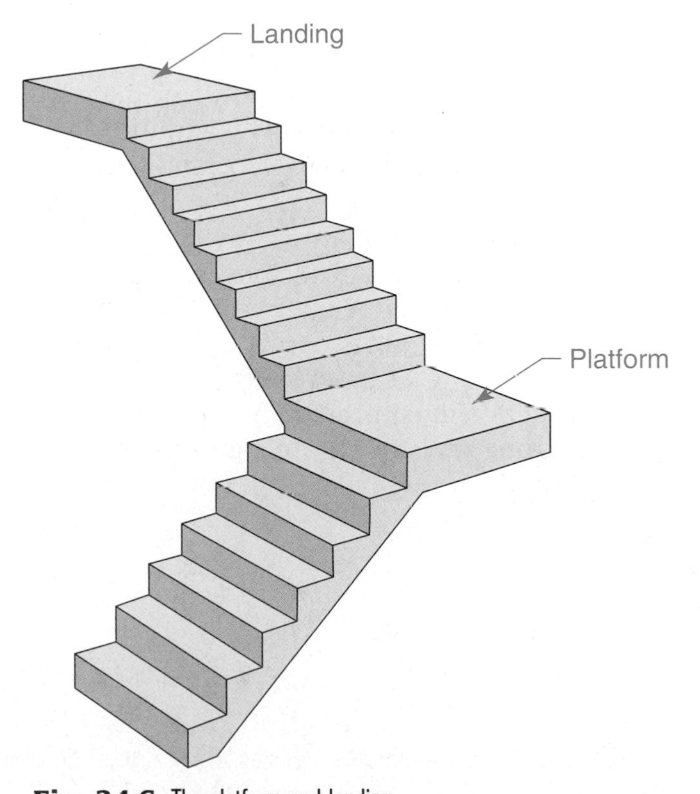

Fig. 34-6. The platform and landing.

framed walls. The enclosed sides of a platform may be nailed into one or more existing walls. Flights may also be arranged at 180° to each other, with a platform between. See Fig. 34-1.

Radiating treads can be used instead of a platform to turn a stair. Such a tread is called a **winder**. **Fig. 34-7.** However, they are not as safe. This is because a winder is wedge-shaped, and a portion of the tread is quite narrow. In fact, building codes prohibit certain types of winders for this reason. The width of a winder should be no less than 6″ at the small end, and other restrictions may apply. Due to cost or design, some stairways may be built off-site. **Fig. 34-8.**

Learn the important stairway terms shown in **Figs. 34-9** and **34-10**.

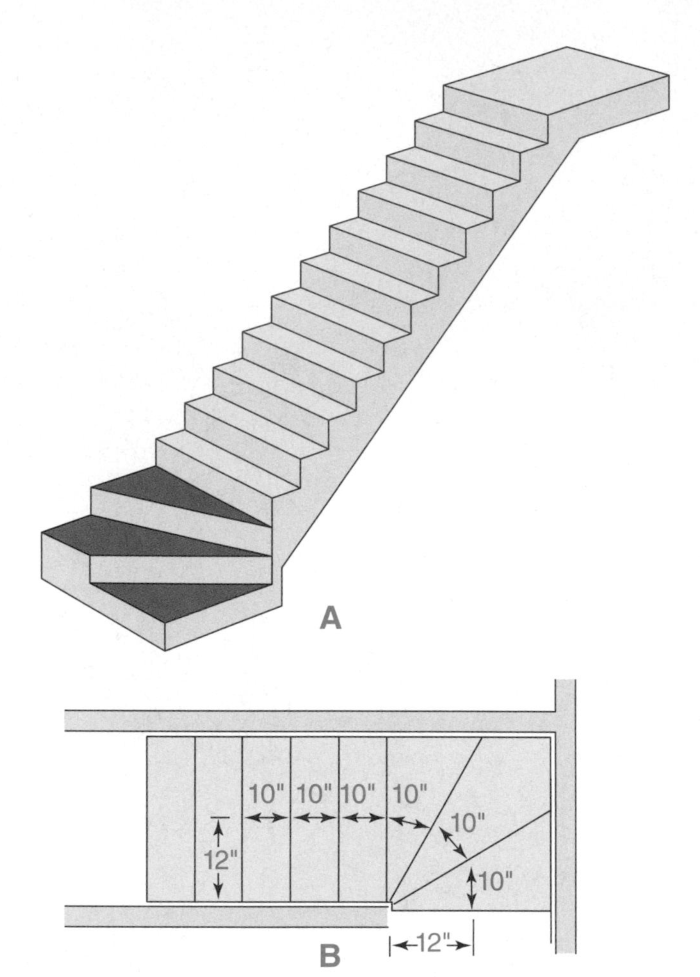

Fig. 34-7. A stairway with winders. *A.* The winders are the shaded steps at the bottom. Some building codes prohibit this type of stair. *B.* The width of treads at a point not more than 12″ from the narrowest side must not be less than 10″ wide.

STAIRWAY LOCATION

Determining the location of a stairway is a very important decision for several reasons. In addition to being a functional element of the house, a stairway can be a very important architectural feature. This is due in part to the size of the stair. It is due also to the fact that it is typically the only portion of a house that contains walls two stories high.

The stairway location also has an impact on the size and location of rooms on both floors. In fact, many architects start their floorplan sketches by determining the location of the stairway. The stairway is usually centrally located. This makes it equally accessible from various rooms.

Finally, the location of a stairway has an impact on the structure of the house. Because the stairway opening (the stairwell) interrupts the spacing of floor joists, structural reinforcement is required to channel loads to the foundation. Carpenters must provide framing details that are strong and unlikely to squeak as the stair is used.

Fig. 34-8. A stairway may be built off-site to fit a specific location.

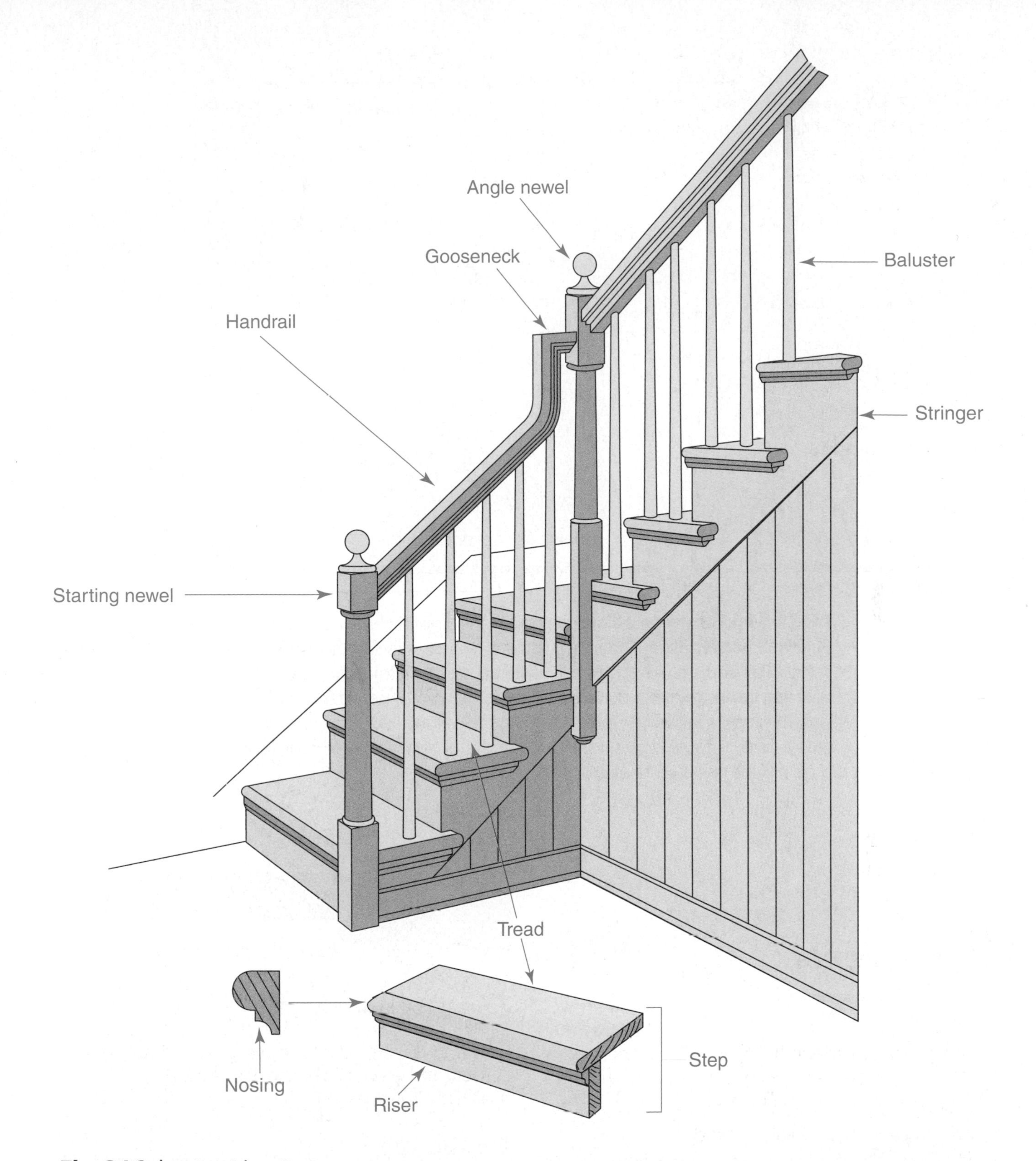

Fig. 34-9. Important stairway terms.
Baluster. A vertical member that supports the handrail on open stairs. **Gooseneck.** The curved piece between the main handrail and a newel post. **Handrail.** The portion of the stair that is grasped when going up or down. **Headroom.** Clearance above a step. **Newel.** A post that supports the handrail at the top and bottom. A landing newel is located at the bottom of a stair. It is often more elaborate than other newels and can serve as an architectural feature. **Nosing.** The part of a tread that projects beyond the face of the riser. **Riser.** The vertical portion of a step. **Step.** One tread or a tread and riser. The first step of a stair is often called the starting step. If the starting step is lengthened and rounded at one or both ends, it is referred to as a bullnose starting step. The landing newel can then be located on the bullnosed portion. This gives the handrail a decorative curve. **Stringer.** The piece of lumber that supports the treads and risers. A stringer may also be called a string, a carriage, or a horse. **Tread.** The horizontal portion of a step.

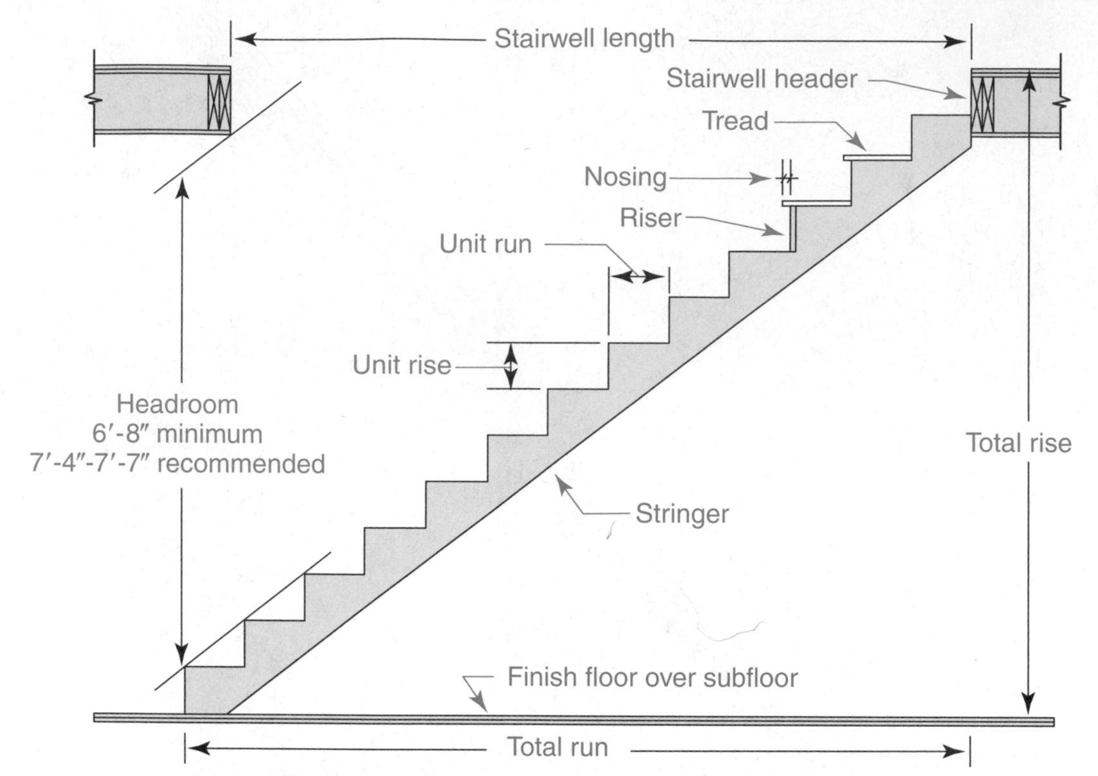

Fig. 34-10. Stairway terms. Headroom should be a minimum of 6′-8″ for a main stair. **Stairwell header.** The doubled framing that forms the ends of the stairwell opening. It supports the floor joists that were cut to create the stairwell opening. **Total rise.** The vertical distance from the finished surface of one floor to the finished surface of the next floor. **Total run.** The horizontal length of the stairs. **Unit rise.** The vertical distance from the top of one tread to the top of the next highest tread. **Unit run.** The horizontal distance between the face of one riser and the face of the adjacent riser.

The space beneath a stair is often enclosed to provide storage. Building codes require that drywall ½″ or thicker be installed on the inside of all walls. Drywall should also be attached to the underside of the stair stringers. The drywall provides a measure of fire protection in these spaces. This requirement should be taken into account when framing the platform walls.

SECTION 34.1 Check Your Knowledge

1. What is a stairwell?
2. What is a riser?
3. Name the two basic types of stair construction and explain their differences.
4. Define *total rise.*

On the Job

Write a paragraph describing the construction of the stairway shown in Fig. 34-9. In your description, use the following terms: *platform, nosing, risers, railing,* and *open* and *closed stringers.*

SECTION 34.2

Design Requirements

The following factors are important to consider when designing and building a stair. The code dimensions found in this chapter are from *The International Residential Code for One- and Two-Family Dwellings* (2000 edition). Before designing a stair, however, be sure to find out what building codes have been adopted in your area.

HEADROOM

The clearance directly above a step is called **headroom**. It is measured from the outside edge of the nosing to the ceiling directly overhead. Sometimes two or more flights of stairs are arranged one above the other in the same stairwell. An example would be a basement stairway under the main stairway. In this case, headroom above the lower stair must be carefully calculated. Although the minimum headroom required by code is 6′-8″, main stairways generally have between 7′-4″ and 7′-7″ of headroom.

STAIRWAY WIDTH

A stairway must be wide enough to allow two people to pass comfortably and to permit furniture to be carried up and down. The minimum width for a main stairway is generally 36″, measured between the finished walls of the stairwell. However, a width of 42″ makes moving furniture easier. The handrail should not project more than 4½″ on either side.

RISERS AND TREADS

The height of the riser and the depth of the tread determine the ease with which the stairs are used. If the risers are too high, climbing the steps can be tiring. If the treads are too shallow, toes will bump the riser at each step. **Fig. 34-11.** The building code allows a maximum riser height of 7¾″ and a minimum tread depth of 10″. Safety research indicates that the ideal riser is 7″ high and the ideal tread is 11″ deep.

Whatever dimensions are chosen, the height and depth of each step must be uniform. Perfect uniformity is difficult, but the code allows a variation of no more than ⅜″ between maximum and minimum riser heights. Likewise, the difference between the deepest and the shallowest tread must be no more than ⅜″. Warped or poorly secured treads reduce uniformity. As a result, they are a tripping hazard.

Treads should have a slip-resistant surface. Materials such as polished stone and glazed tile can be dangerous on a stair and should be avoided.

HANDRAILS

One of the most important features of good stair design is the handrail. A solid, easily grasped handrail can prevent falls and serious injuries. A continuous handrail must be provided on at least one side of every stairway.

Fig. 34-11. A stairway should be built with the proper rise and run. On this stairway, the tread is too shallow and the riser is too high.

You should be able to curl your fingers around a handrail with ease. Handrails are easiest to grasp when they are made from metal tubing or solid wood shaped like a cylinder. The diameter should be between 1¼″ and 2⅝″. Handrails with a larger diameter and those with a rectangular shape are more difficult to hold.

The edges of the handrail must have a minimum radius of ⅛″ for comfort. They should be rounded over and have no sharp edges. There should be at least 1½″ of space between the handrail and the wall on which it is mounted.

A handrail should be 34″ to 38″ high. This distance is measured vertically from the upper edge of the nosing to the top of the handrail.

BALUSTERS

The purpose of balusters is to prevent anyone, particularly children, from slipping under the handrail and falling. A *balustrade* is the assembly of balusters with the handrail. The railing around a stairwell is also called a balustrade. A *newel*, or *newel post*, supports each end of the handrail.

Balusters should be spaced so that a sphere 4″ in diameter cannot pass between them. The only exception is at the triangular opening sometimes formed between adjacent steps. In that case, a sphere 6″ in diameter should not be able to pass through.

SECTION 34.2 Check Your Knowledge

1. What is the minimum headroom required by building codes?
2. Where is the minimum width of a main stairway measured?
3. What role do the dimensions of risers and treads play in the ease with which a stair can be used?
4. What is the proper height for a handrail? How is this height measured?

On the Job

Evaluate the riser-tread dimensions for a stairway in your school or home. Decide whether the stairway is too steep, just right, or too shallow. Measure the handrail height. How does it compare with the code requirements noted in this chapter? Sketch the basic dimensions of the stairway.

SECTION 34.3 Stair Layout and Installation

Carpenters should know how to construct two basic types of stairs: those with cut stringers and those with cleated stringers. A cut-stringer stairway is the most common type. Both types can be used indoors or to provide access to wood decks outdoors.

MAKING CALCULATIONS

The calculations for a basic stairway can be easily done with pencil and paper. However, some builders use a construction calculator instead. This hand-held calculator can display results in fractions of an inch and is programmed to solve stair problems.

The first task in stairway layout is to determine the unit rise and unit run per step. **Fig. 34-12.** The *unit rise* is the height of one riser. It is based on the total rise of the stairway and the fact that the unit rise for stairs should be about 7″. The *unit run* is the distance from the face of one riser to the face of the next riser, or the depth of a tread less the depth of the nosing. The *total rise* is the vertical distance between the surface of the finish floor on one level and the surface of the finish floor on the next level. It is shown on the plans in elevations and wall sections.

It is important to actually measure the total rise before stair construction starts. It may vary

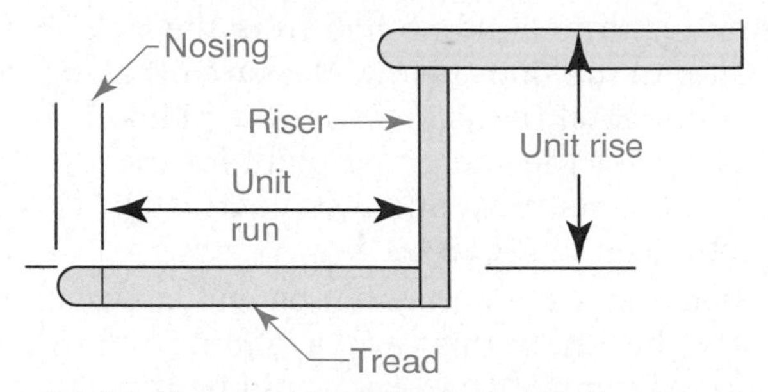

Fig. 34-12. The unit run is the distance from the face of one riser to the face of the next riser. It does not include the nosing. The unit rise is the distance from the top of one tread to the top of the next tread.

slightly from the distance specified on the plans. For example, suppose you are building a service stairway from the basement, and the concrete basement floor is already finished. You must then add the thickness of the upper floor's finish flooring to your total-rise measurement in order for it to match the measurement on the plans.

Calculating Unit Rise and Unit Run

Here is an example of how a floor calculation is made. Assume that the total rise for a stairway is 8′-11″. You can derive the unit rise from the total rise as follows:

1. Convert the total rise to inches. That number is 107″ (96 + 11 = 107).
2. Divide 107″ by 7″, the ideal riser height. The result is 15.28 (107 ÷ 7 = 15.28).
3. Round 15.28 to the nearest whole number, which is 15. This gives you the total number of risers in the stairway.
4. To find the unit rise, divide the total rise (107) by the number of risers (15) for a result of 7⅛″ (107 ÷ 15 = 7.13, or 7⅛″).
5. As a general rule, the sum of one riser and one tread should be between 17″ and 18″. If you subtract the unit rise from this sum, you can find the unit run. For example, if the sum of one riser and one tread is 17½″ and the unit rise is 7⅛″, the unit run will be 10⅜″ (17½″ – 7⅛″ = 10⅜″).

Calculating Total Run

The *total run* is a measurement equal to the unit run times the number of treads in the stairway. The total number of treads depends on the manner in which the upper end of the stairway is anchored to the upper landing. Three common methods are shown in **Fig. 34-13**.

A complete tread at the top of the stairway is shown in Fig. 34-13A. It requires a larger stairwell opening, yet it allows the stringer to bear solidly against the header. This means that the number of treads in the stairway is the same as the number of risers. If there are 15 treads and the unit run is 10⅜″, the total run of the stairway is 12′-11⅝″ (15 × 10⅜″ = 155⅝″, or 12′-11⅝″).

Only part of a tread at the top of the stairway is shown in Fig. 34-13B. In this case, the number of complete treads is one less than the number

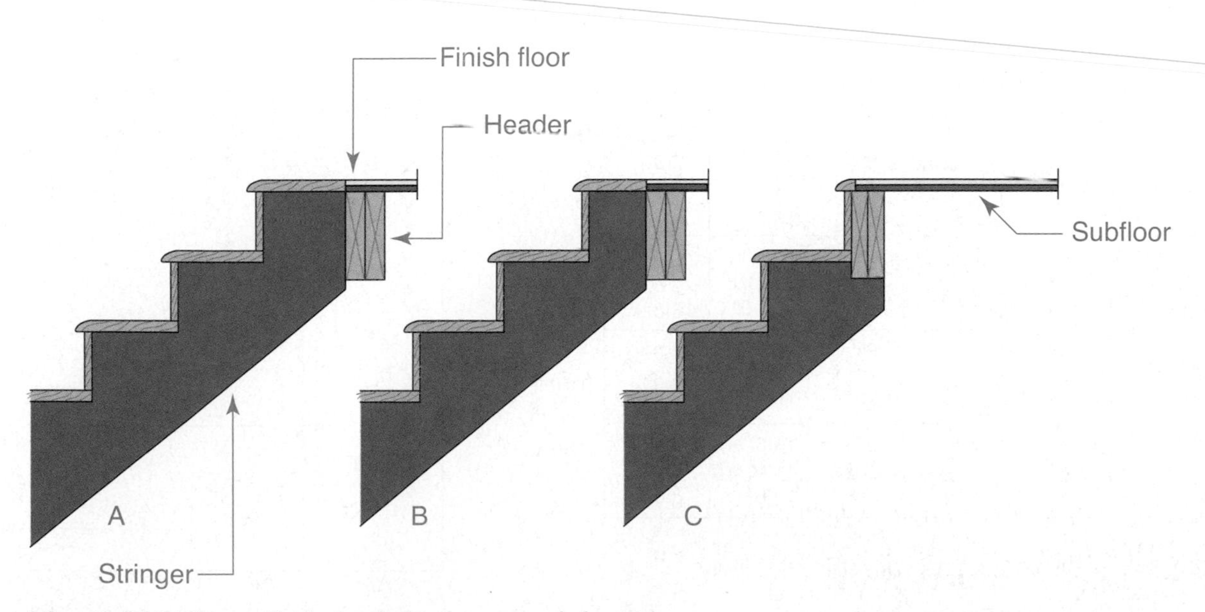

Fig. 34-13. Three methods of anchoring the upper end of a stringer.

of risers. Using the earlier example, that would mean 14 treads. The total run of the stairway would then be 14 × 10⅜″, plus the run of the partial tread at the top. This partial tread may be dimensioned in detail on the plans. If not, you will have to estimate it as closely as possible. If we assume that it is about 7″, the total run is 12′-8¼″ (14 × 10⅜″ = 145¼″; 145¼″ + 7″ = 152¼″, or 12′-8¼″).

In Fig. 34-13C, the upper finish flooring serves as the top tread. In this case the number of treads is one less than the number of risers. Using our example, the total run would be 12′-1¼″ (14 × 10⅜″ = 145¼″, or 12′-1¼″).

After you have figured the total run of the stairway, drop a plumb bob from the stairwell header to the floor below. Measure off along the floor the total run, starting at the plumb bob. This locates the anchoring point for the lower end of the stairway. Some standard stair layouts can be seen in **Fig. 34-14**.

Sometimes there may not be enough room for a straight run. In this case, a landing and two or more sections of stairway would be needed.

CUT-STRINGER STAIRWAYS

A cut-stringer stairway is very versatile. It can be built of expensive materials or common

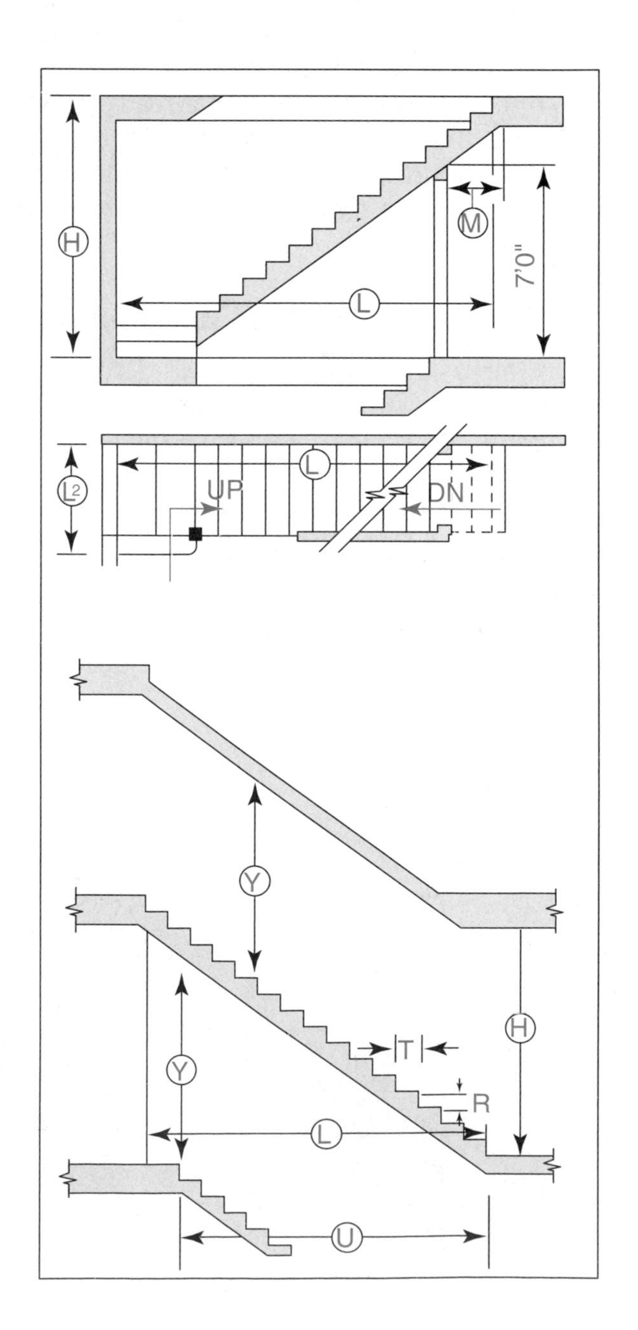

Height Floor to Floor H	Number of Risers	Height of Risers R	Width of Tread T	Run		Run	
				Number of Risers	L	Number of Risers	L2
8′0″	13	7 3/8″ +	10"	11	8′4″ + W	2	0′10″ + W
8′6″	14	7 5/16″ -	10"	12	9′2″ + W	2	0′10″ + W
9′0″	15	7 3/16″ +	10"	13	10′0″ + W	2	0′10″+ W
9′6″	16	7 1/8″-	10"	14	10′10″ + W	2	0′10″ + W

Height Floor to Floor H	Number of Risers	Height of Risers R	Width of Treads T	Total Run L	Minimum Head Rm. Y
8′0″	12	7 3/8″ +	9″	8′3″	6′8″
	13	7 3/8″ +	9 1/2″	9 6″	6′8″
	13	7 3/8″ +	10″	10 0″	6′8″
8′6″	13	7 3/8″ +	9″	9′0″	6′8″
	14	7 3/8″ +	9 1/2″	10′3 1/2″	6′8″
	14	7 3/8″ +	10″	10′10″	6′8″
9′0″	14	7 3/8″+	9″	9′9″	6′8″
	15	7 3/8″ +	9 1/2″	11′1″	6′8″
	15	7 3/8″ +	10″	11′8″	6′8″
9′6″	15	7 3/8″ +	9″	10′6″	6′8″
	16	7 3/8″ +	9 1/2″	11′10 1/2″	6′8″
	16	7 3/8″ +	10″	12′6″	6′8″

Fig. 34-14. Layout dimensions for some standard stairways.

lumber. It can have treads and risers, or just treads. (If it has no risers, it is called an *open-riser* stairway.) It can be a permanent part of the house or be used only during the construction phase. All of these variations, however, rely on the same basic concepts.

The building of a stair involves a series of operations. These must be carefully and accurately done.

Laying Out the Stringers

The treads and risers are supported by two stringers that are solidly fastened in place. When the treads are less than 1⅛″ thick, or if the stairs are more than 2′-6″ wide, a third stringer should be installed in the middle of the stairs.

Cut stringers for main stairways are usually made from 2x12 stock. To lay out the stringer, you must first determine how long a piece of stock you will need. Let's use the same figures used in the calculation examples. Assume that the method of anchoring the stair is the one shown in Fig. 34-13C. The total rise is 8′-11″. The total run is 12′-1¼″.

1. On the framing square twelfth scale, measure the distance between a little over 12 ¹⁄₁₂″ on the blade and 8¹¹⁄₁₂″ on the tongue. You will find that it comes to just about 15″. Therefore, you will need a piece of stock at least 15′ long. You should allow extra stock for waste (about 3′ more in this case).
2. Select or cut a piece about 18′ long. You will lay out the stringer from the lower end.
3. Set the framing square to the unit run and unit rise as shown in **Fig. 34-15**. Draw line *AB* along the blade and line *BC* along the tongue. *AB* indicates the first tread, *BC* the second riser.
4. Reverse the square and starting at *A*, draw line *AD* perpendicular to *AB*. It should be equal in length to the unit rise. Line *AD* indicates the first riser.

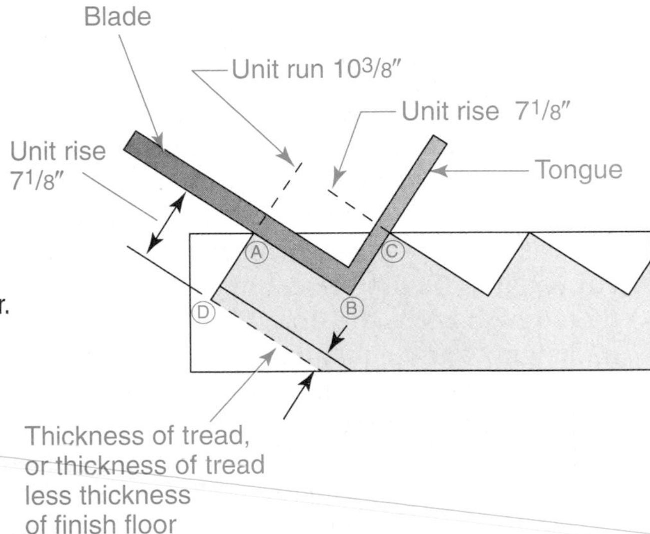

Fig. 34-15. Laying out the lower end of a cut stringer.

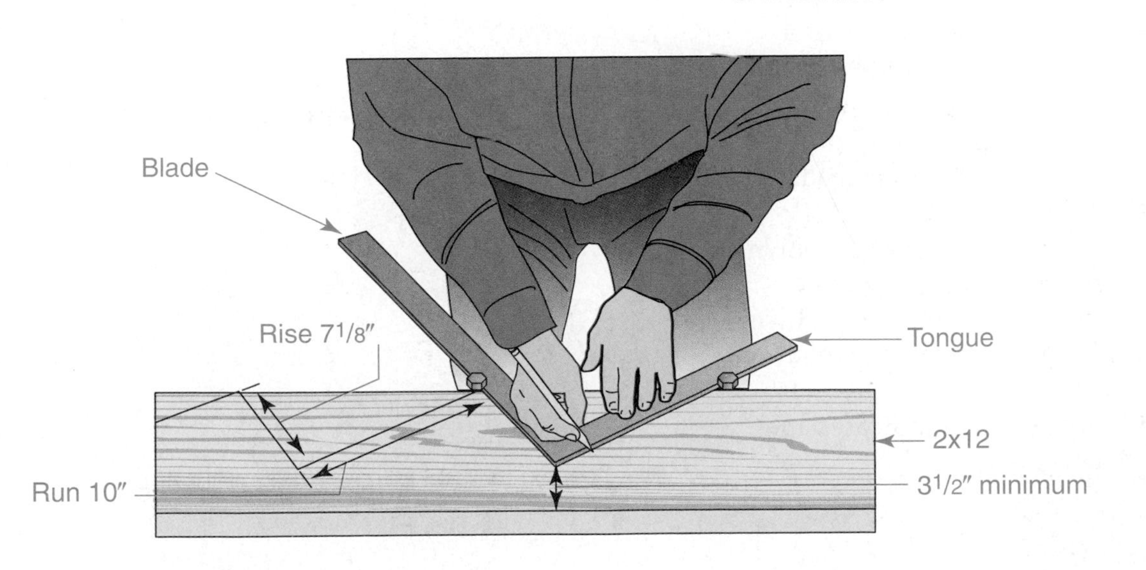

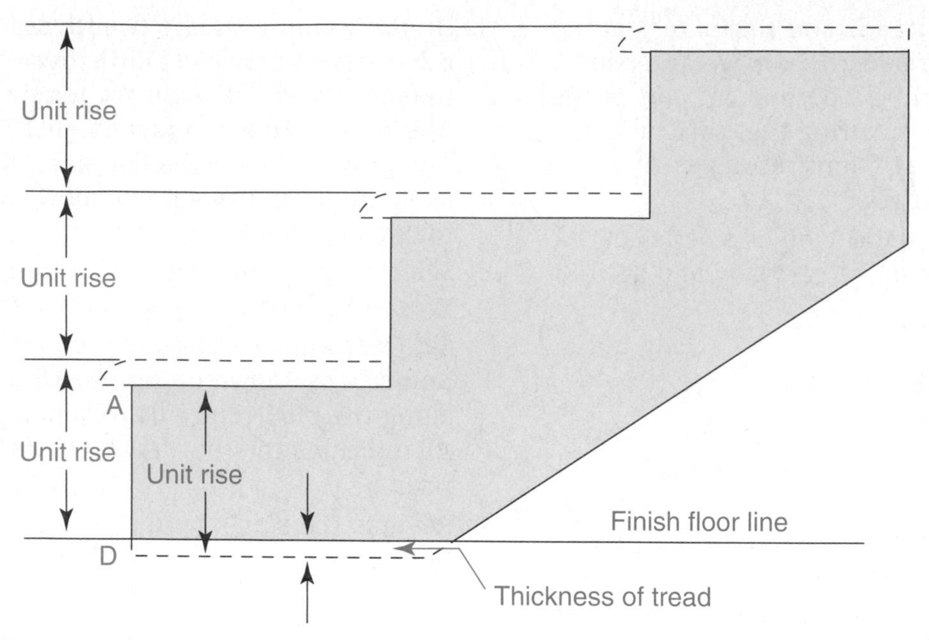

Fig. 34-16. Dropping the stringer to compensate for the thickness of the first tread keeps the unit rise uniform throughout.

5. The first riser has to be shortened, a process that is called *dropping* the stringer. **Fig. 34-16.** In the completed stair, the unit rise is measured from the top of one tread to the top of the next. Assume that the bottom of the stairway is to be anchored to a finished floor, such as a concrete basement floor. If *AD* were cut equal to the unit rise, the first step would be too high when the first tread was put on. Its height would equal that of the unit rise plus the thickness of the tread. To make the height of the first step equal to just the unit rise, shorten *AD* by the thickness of a tread. If the bottom of the stringer is to be anchored on a subfloor to which finish flooring will be applied, shorten *AD* by the thickness of a tread less the thickness of the finish flooring.
6. When you have shortened *AD* as required, proceed to step off the unit run and unit rise as many times as the stairway has treads. In our example, that would be 14.
7. Finish the layout at the upper end as shown in **Fig. 34-17**. Remember, we are going to anchor the upper end by the method shown in Fig. 34-13C. First lay out line *AB*, which represents the last of the treads.
8. Lay out dotted line *BC*, which indicates the face of the header.

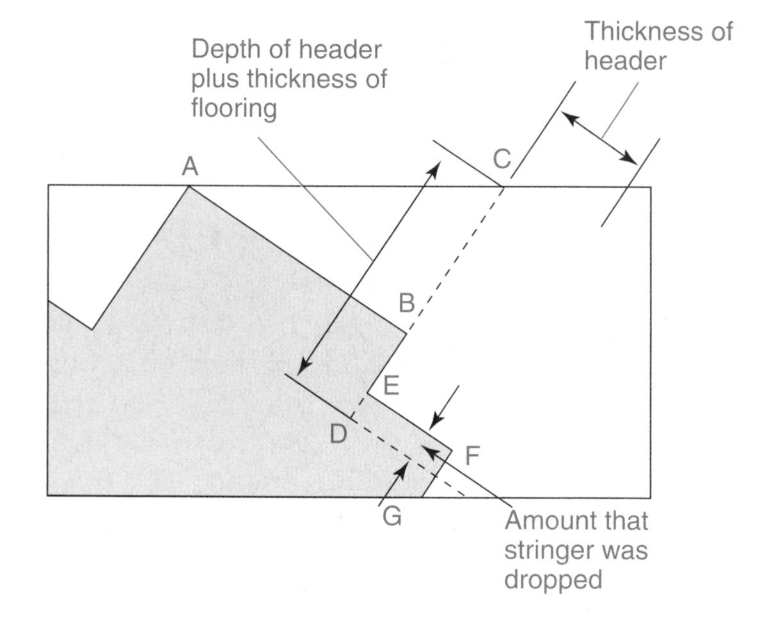

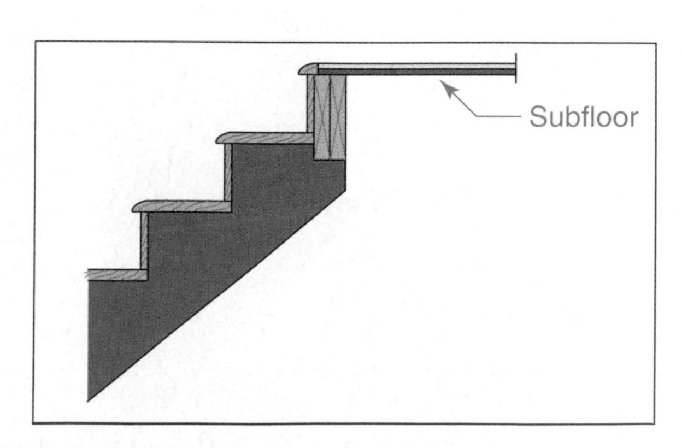

Fig. 34-17. Laying out the upper end of a cutout stringer.

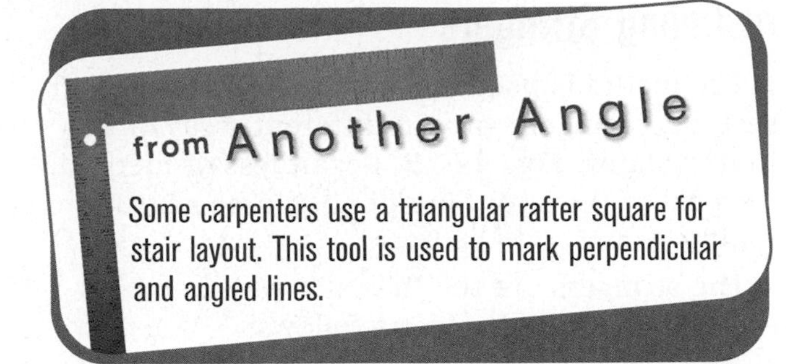

from Another Angle

Some carpenters use a triangular rafter square for stair layout. This tool is used to mark perpendicular and angled lines.

9. Extend *BC* down to *D*, so that *BC* plus *BD* will equal the depth of the header.
10. To make the stringer fit close under the lower edge of the header, you must shorten *BD* by the amount the stringer was dropped (Fig. 34-17). Draw *EF* equal in length to the thickness of the header. Draw line *FG* to square off the stringer.
11. Carefully cut out the first stringer with a circular saw. **Fig. 34-18.** Do not overcut intersecting cuts, which will weaken the stringer. Instead, finish with a handsaw or jigsaw. Then set the stringer in position, and check it. Use this stringer as a pattern for cutting others.

SAFETY FIRST

Tight Joints

Careful construction techniques improve the safety of a stair. A wobbly stairway can cause falls. Be sure to make all cuts square and even. This makes joints tight and prevents stair parts from wobbling or rocking over time.

Fig. 34-18. With the stringer resting on sawhorses, use a circular saw to cut just along the layout lines. To avoid overcutting, use a handsaw or jigsaw to finish the cut.

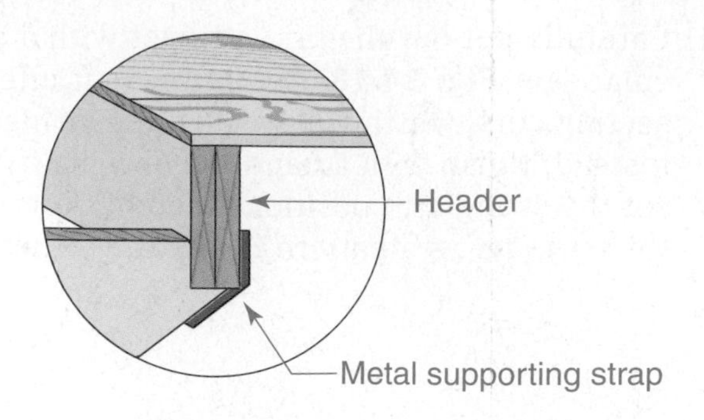

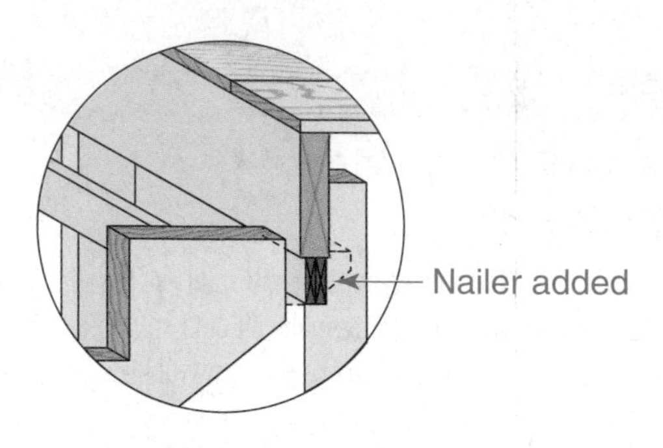

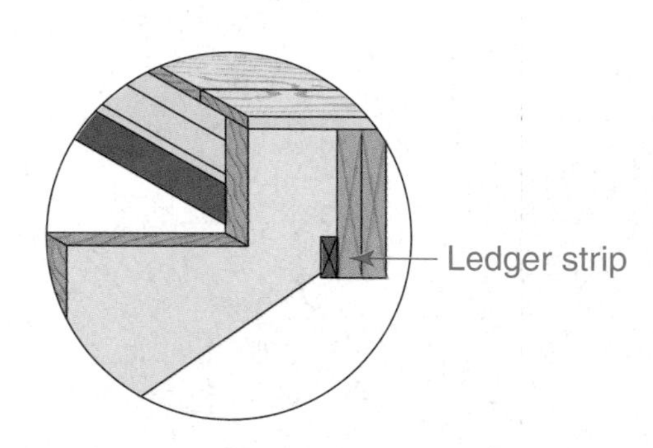

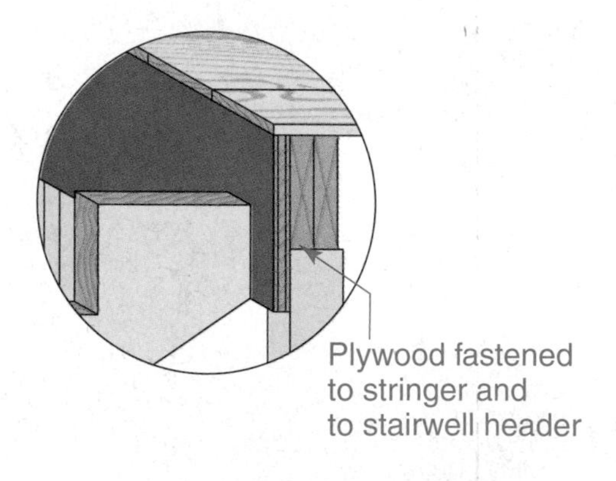

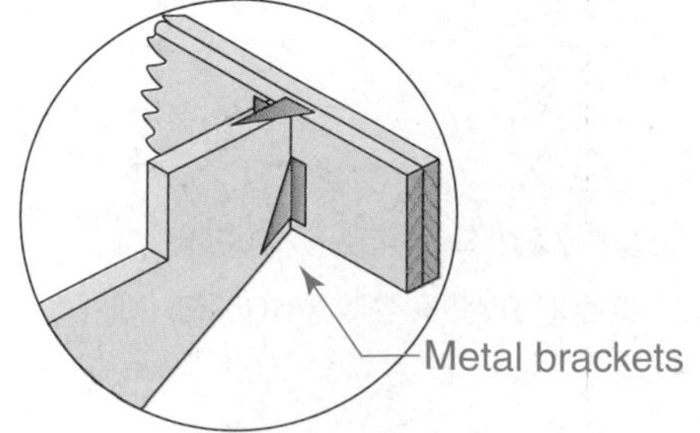

Fig. 34-19. Methods of securing stringers.

Installing Stringers

The methods used for framing stairways and securing stringers vary in different areas of the United States. **Fig. 34-19.** Regardless of method, the goal of the stair builder should be a structurally strong, safe stairway.

The stringers are the first stairway members erected. Install stringers as follows:

1. Tack the stringers into position.
2. Check each stringer for plumb by holding the carpenter's level vertically against a riser cut.
3. Check if each stringer is level with the other stringers by setting a carpenter's level across the stringers on the tread cuts.
4. When the stringers are level and plumb, nail them into place. A stringer that lies against a trimmer joist should be nailed to the joist with at least three 16d nails. The bottom of a stringer that is anchored on subflooring should be toenailed with 10d nails, four to each side if possible. The nails should be driven into the subflooring and, if possible, into a joist below. Some carpenters also anchor the stairway with a kick plate. See Fig. 34-22.

Installing Risers and Treads

After you have placed the stringers, you will install the treads and risers.

1. Cut the treads and risers to length.
2. Nail the bottom riser to each stringer with two 6d, 8d, or 10d nails, depending on the thickness of the stock.
3. If the first tread is 1$\frac{1}{16}$″ thick, nail it to each stringer with two 10d finish nails and to the riser below with at least two 10d finish nails.

If the first tread is 1⅝″ thick, a 12d finish nail may be required. Use three nails at each stringer, but do not nail to the riser below. When using hardwood stock, nail holes should be pre-drilled to prevent the stock from splitting. Set all finish nails.

4. Proceed up the stair in this same manner.

Sometimes the treads and risers are assembled with interlocking joinery. **Fig. 34-20.** This is often the case when the stairway is being assembled from manufactured parts.

Other Step and Stringer Methods

In some stair construction, the outer stringers are routed out to the exact profile of the tread, riser, and nosing, with sufficient space at the back for wood wedges (see Fig. 34-5). This produces a closed stringer, or housed stringer. The top of the riser is rabbeted to fit into a groove in the bottom front of the tread. The back of the tread is rabbeted to fit into a groove in the bottom of the next riser. (A rabbet is a cut or groove along or near the edge of a piece of wood. It allows another piece to fit into it to form a joint.) The treads and risers are fitted together and slipped into place. They are then tightened by driving and gluing wood wedges behind them. With this method, the outer stringers are visible above the steps, so the stringer must be of very good quality.

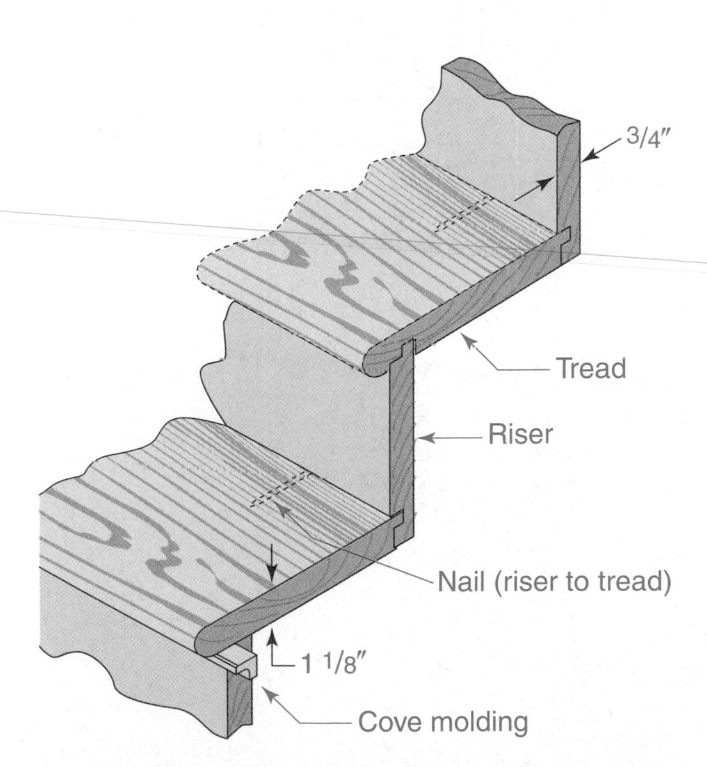

Fig. 34-20. Interlocking joinery provides a tight fit between treads and risers. Cove molding can be added under the nosing to conceal the joint there.

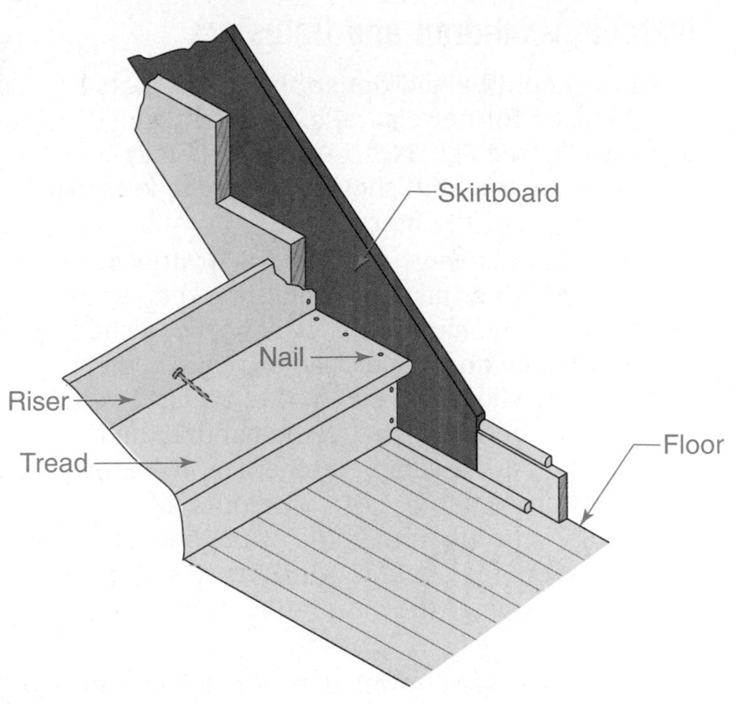

Fig. 34-21. A skirtboard and a rough stringer nailed in place.

Sometimes, a finished board called a **skirtboard** is nailed to the wall before the stringers are installed. **Fig. 34-21.** The risers and treads are nailed to the stringers and butted to the skirtboard. The skirtboard protects the wall from damage. It also provides a finished edge against the wall, which makes it easier to paint or wallpaper the adjacent areas.

With basement stairs, the lower end of the stairway rests on concrete. To prevent the stringers from moving, a kick plate is screwed or nailed to the concrete. **Fig. 34-22.** The stringers can then be toenailed to the kick plate.

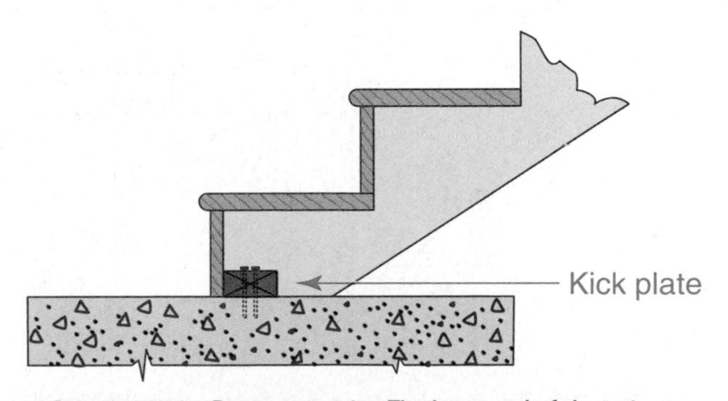

Fig. 34-22. Basement stairs. The lower end of the stringer should be anchored against a kick plate that has been bolted or nailed to the concrete floor.

Installing Handrail and Balusters

Stairs should be laid out so that stock parts may be used for newels, rails, balusters, and goosenecks (see Fig. 34-9). These parts may be plain or elaborate, but they should be in keeping with the style of the house.

For closed stairways, the handrail is attached to the wall with adjustable metal brackets. After the height of the handrail is established, a chalk line is snapped and the brackets are aligned with it. They should be screwed to the stairwell framing. For open stairways, the handrail and the balusters are assembled together. If the top of a baluster is cylindrical, it often fits into a hole drilled into the underside of the handrail. If the baluster is rectangular, it may be toenailed to the underside of the handrail with finishing nails.

The balusters are doweled or dovetailed into the treads. **Fig. 34-23.** For the dovetail method, a strip called a *nosing return* is cut to fit the end of the tread, as shown in the plan view of Fig. 34-23. Dovetails on the lower ends of the balusters fit into dovetail recesses in the end of the tread. The dovetails are glued into the recesses. The nosing return is then nailed into place to conceal the dovetails.

It is important to understand that balusters are not the primary support for a handrail. That is the function of the newel posts at each end. For this reason, the newel posts should be firmly anchored. Where half-newels are attached to a wall, blocking should be provided at the time the wall is framed.

CLEAT-STRINGER STAIRWAYS

For a cleat-stringer stairway, the stringers are not cut in order to support treads. This stairway does not normally have risers, and the treads are usually made of thick softwood planks. Layout of the stair is straightforward.

Steps for installing a cleat-stringer stairway are given on page 696.

EXTERIOR STAIRWAYS

Exterior stairs are made using preservative-treated lumber or a naturally decay-resistant wood such as redwood. They may be of the cut-stringer type or the cleat-stringer type. Stringers can be cut on site, but pre-cut pressure treated stringers are also available. This ensures that treatment chemicals will protect the cut edges

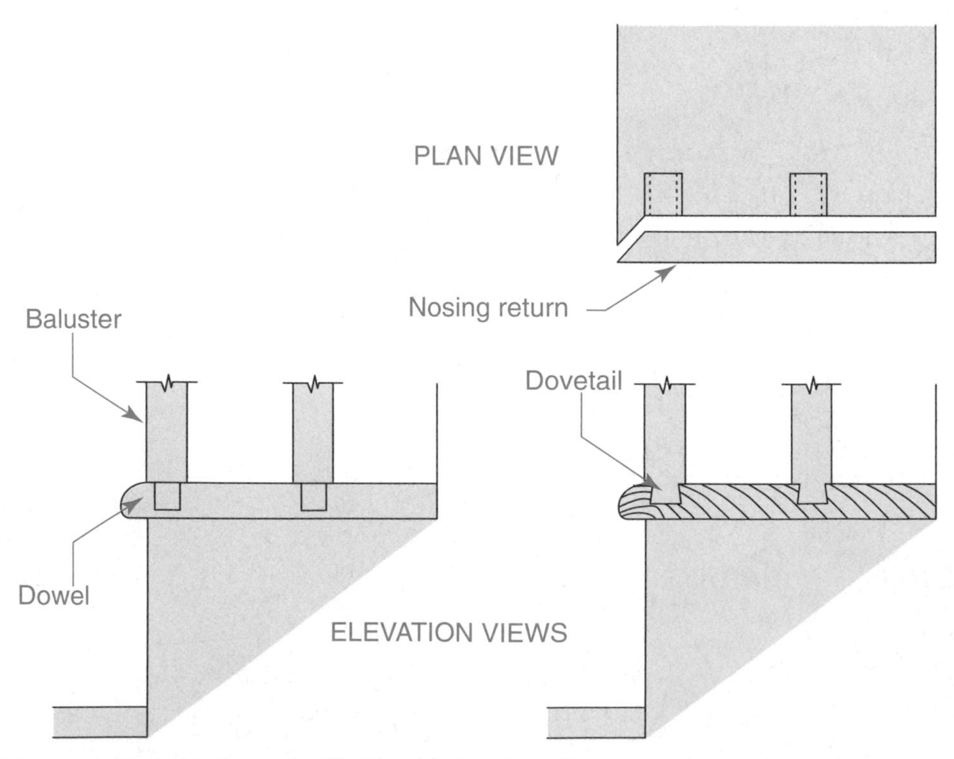

Fig. 34-23. Balusters are attached to the treads with either dowels or dovetails.

Estimating...

Stairway Materials and Labor

MATERIALS

Estimating the quantity of materials for a stairway is done on a piece-by-piece basis.

Step 1 Determine the design of the stairs, along with the rise, run, and baluster details.

Step 2 The quality of the materials will affect the cost, so next make a complete materials list.

Step 3 Total the cost of the items. In the case of a stairway built primarily of manufactured components, the manufacturer may furnish a package price.

LABOR

Labor costs can be only roughly estimated because of the many variables that will affect construction time. Here's an example.

For an open stairway less than 12′ long and 42″ wide:

Step 1 Estimate construction time at 8¾ hours. This includes rough-cutting the stringers and framing and installing the stringers, treads, and risers.

Step 2 Add 3 hours if there is a turn in the stairway involving a platform or landing.

Step 3 Add one hour to install a handrail.

Step 4 Add 2½ hours for the installation of the newel posts, rails, and balusters.

For a pre-cut stairway less than 12′ long and 42″ wide:

Step 1 Estimate 6 hours for assembly.

Step 2 If this stairway has a turn that includes a platform, add about 3 more hours.

Step 3 Add one hour for a handrail.

Step 4 For an open stairway with newel posts, rails, and balusters, add 2½ more hours.

These are very rough approximations. All estimates depend on the carpenter's experience, the style of the stairway, and the type of wood.

ESTIMATING ON THE JOB

Suppose your company is to build an open stairway that is 10½′ long and 40″ wide. It will have one platform. Estimate the time and labor cost if you hire one worker to do the job and pay him or her $22.50 an hour. Round your answer to the nearest dollar.

of the stringer. Stringers are often attached to adjacent structures using metal brackets (see Fig. 34-19). However, an exterior stair often does not have risers. This allows water to drain quickly and snow to be removed with relative ease. To aid drainage, each tread can slope up to 2 percent. For example, for a tread with a depth of 12½″, the back of the tread would be ¼″ higher than the front.

The hardware used to assemble exterior stairs must be weather resistant. This includes the following:

- Nails and bolts used to assemble the stairway.
- Brackets used to secure stairs to a building or a deck.
- Framing connectors used to support stringers (see Chapter 17, "Engineered Lumber").

Hot-dipped galvanized hardware is durable, readily available, and relatively inexpensive. However, where weathering conditions are severe, such as in and near coastal areas, hardware should be made of stainless steel.

The basic layout of exterior stairs generally follows that of interior stairs. However, building codes applicable to exterior stairs differ in some

STEP BY STEP

Installing a Cleat-Stringer Stairway

Step 1 Determine the total rise and run (see pages 686-688). Divide the rise by 7. If this does not result in even spacing, adjust the divisor until equal spacings are obtained. Try to keep this spacing between 6½″ and 7½″.

Step 2 Use a square to lay out a suitable angle at the bottom of the stair. This is shown in **Fig. 34-24**, line *B*. Set a T-bevel to this angle. Then cut each stringer along the layout line using a circular saw.

Step 3 To locate the position of the first cleat, measure up from the bottom of the stringer. Mark off a distance equal to the riser height minus the thickness of the tread. Use the T-bevel to draw a line parallel to the bottom of the stringer at this point (line *A* in Fig. 34-24). This line represents the top of the cleat and the bottom of the tread.

Step 4 Measure up from line *A* a distance equal to the riser height and establish point *C*. Position the T-bevel at point *C* and mark another line across the stringer. Continue this operation until all tread positions have been located.

Step 5 Lay out and cut the top of the stringer according to whatever method is used to support it (see Fig. 34-13 on page 687).

Step 6 Cut the cleats for each stringer from 1x2 or heavier stock. Screw them in position at each line using suitable woodscrews. Place the stringers in the stairwell and nail them in place.

Step 7 Cut the treads to length. Starting with the bottom tread, place each tread in position. Nail it securely to the cleat.

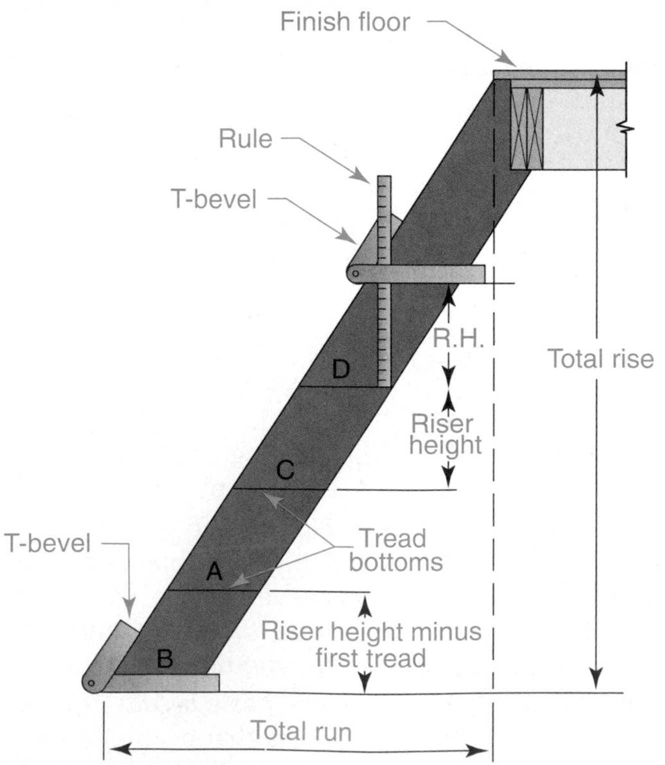

Fig. 34-24. Laying out a cleat stairway. Note the distance from *A* to *C* is the same as the distance from *C* to *D* and is equal to the riser height. The distance between the floor and line *A*, however, is less than the riser height to allow for the thickness of the first tread.

Wood exterior stairs are often assembled using lag bolts or through bolts. As the wood weathers, it shrinks somewhat. This can cause threaded fasteners to loosen over time. Fasteners should be tightened securely during construction. They should then be tightened again later. Tightening such bolts should be a part of annual maintenance for an exterior stair.

respects and should be checked. Proportioning of risers and treads in laying out porch steps or approaches to terraces should be carefully considered. Riser and tread dimensions similar to those for interior stairs can be used. However, the riser should be between 6″ and 7″ high.

The need for a good support or foundation for outside steps is often overlooked. **Fig. 34-25.** If the steps are located over backfill or disturbed ground, the foundation should be carried down to ground that is undisturbed.

The foundation can be a concrete wall or a concrete slab on grade. It can also be made from concrete columns called *piers.* In any case, stair stringers should never rest directly on the ground. This will encourage rot. Such placement would also allow the stair to move up and down slightly during weather cycles of freezing and thawing.

from Another Angle

Stairs are made of many different materials. The stairs in residential construction are usually of wood. In commercial construction, some stairs are sometimes built of wood, though fire-resistant metal service stairs may be required by code. Technical advances in metal forming and fabrication have improved the quality of metal service stairs. Such stairs may be classified as fire stairs.

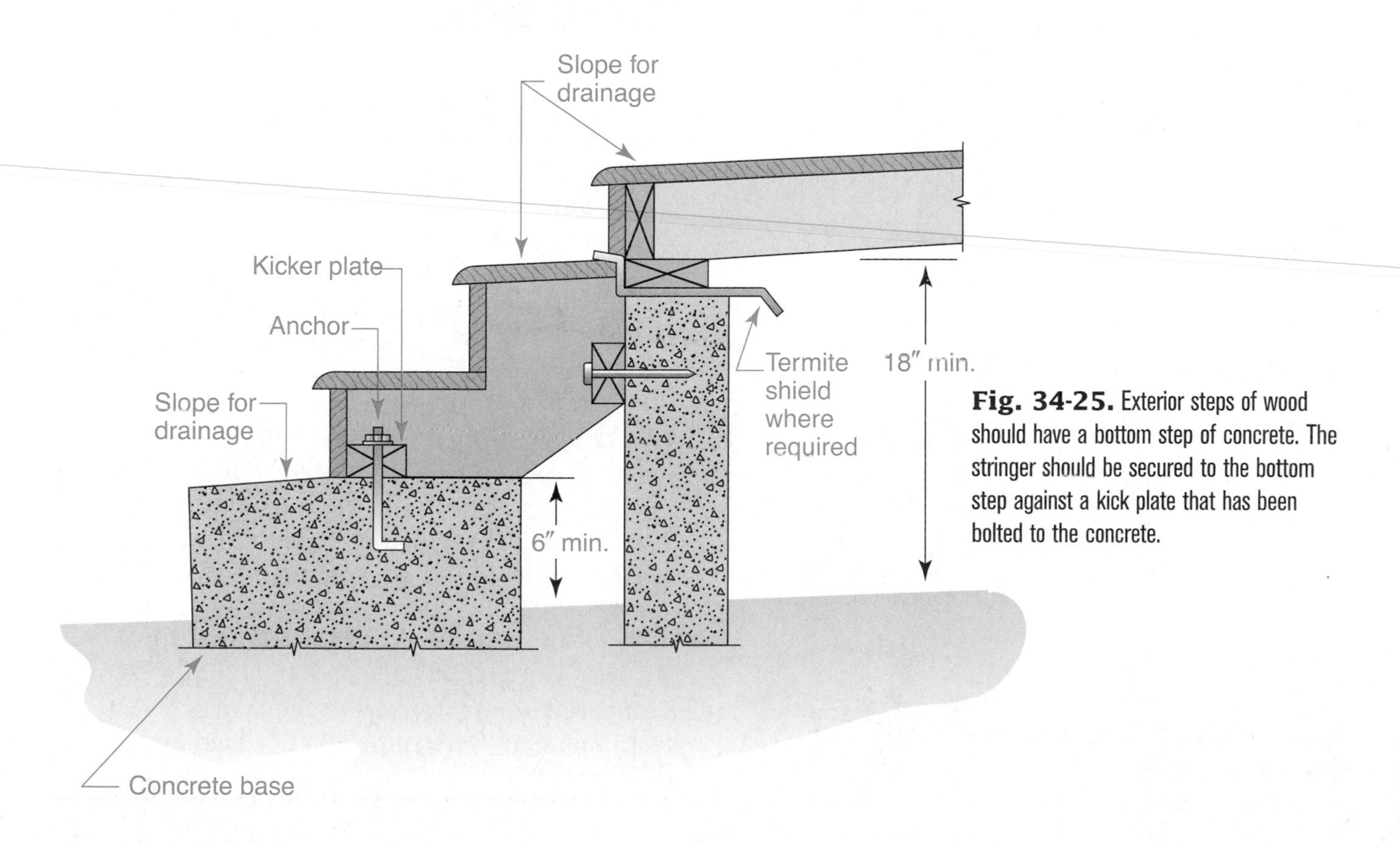

Fig. 34-25. Exterior steps of wood should have a bottom step of concrete. The stringer should be secured to the bottom step against a kick plate that has been bolted to the concrete.

SPECIALTY STAIRWAYS

Spiral stairways are prefabricated units made primarily of steel. **Fig. 34-26.** Steps and railings are shipped in pieces for easy handling at the job site. Stairwell dimensions and other framing requirements are provided by the stair manufacturer. Spiral stairways should not be used as primary stairs. The minimum width of a spiral stairway is 26″.

Hinged, or disappearing, stairs are often used for access to an attic. **Fig. 34-27.** They are installed as a complete unit, fitting into a framed opening in the ceiling. Disappearing stairs swing up into the attic space when not in use. They are suitable only for occasional attic access, not as access to a living area.

Fig. 34-26. Note the use of wood for the balusters and treads on this spiral stairway.

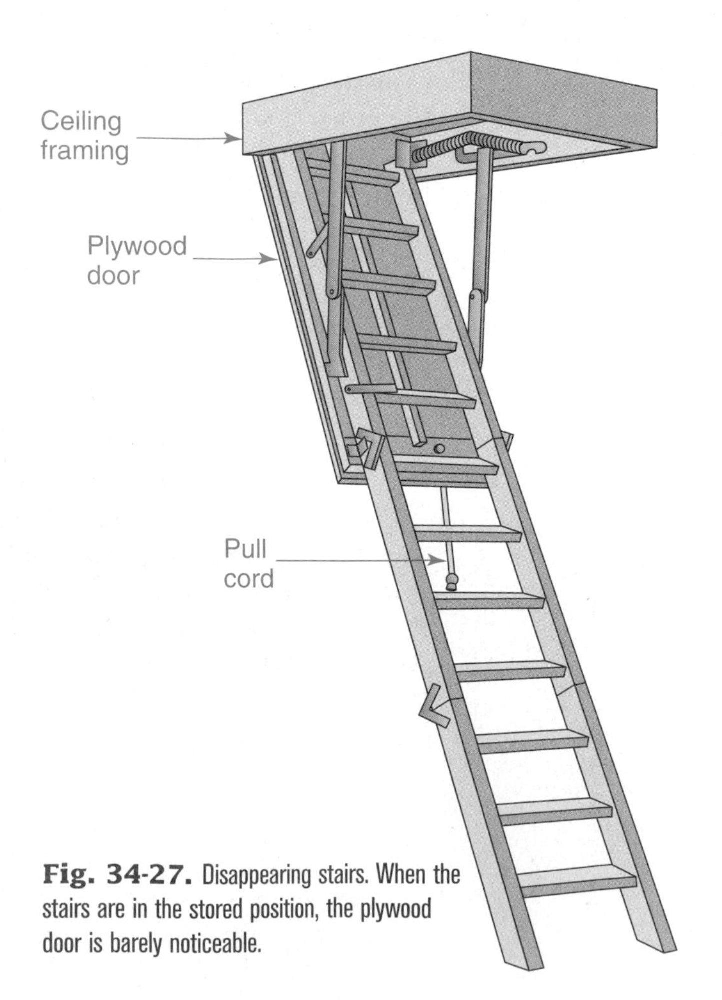

Fig. 34-27. Disappearing stairs. When the stairs are in the stored position, the plywood door is barely noticeable.

SECTION 34.3

Check Your Knowledge

1. The total rise of a stairway is the vertical distance between which two points?
2. The total run is equal to the unit run times the number of treads in the stairway. What framing factor affects the number of treads?
3. What precaution should you take when cutting out a stringer for a cut-stringer stairway?
4. On a closed stairway, what supports the handrail?

On the Job

A set of straight stairs is needed where the total rise is 7′-10″. The risers are to be a minimum of 7″ in height. Use the guidelines in this unit to:

1. Determine the number of risers.
2. Determine the size of each riser.
3. Determine the total run if the top of the stairs is attached as shown in Fig. 34-13A.

Compare your answers with those of a team member. Determine what caused any differences.

Chapter

34 Review

Section Summaries

34.1 The three main parts of a stairway include the treads, the stringers, and a handrail. The treads on cleat-stringer stairways are supported by cleats attached to the stringers. The treads on cut-stringer stairways are supported by notches cut into the stringers. In stairs with more than one flight, the flights are separated by landings.

34.2 Stair designers must consider headroom, width, riser and tread dimensions, handrails, and balusters. All are important to making a stairway safe and easy to use. In most cases, building codes specify maximum and minimum dimensions.

34.3 The first step in stairway construction is to calculate the unit rise and unit run. Total rise is given on the plans. Total run is based on the unit run. The next step is to lay out the stringers and install them. The third step is to install treads and risers (if any). Finally, the handrail and any balusters are put in place.

Review Questions

1. Why do building codes tightly regulate the dimensions and design of stairways?
2. What would you look for to identify a cut-stringer stair?
3. Describe the two types of stringers.
4. Why would a stairway make a turn and how is this done?
5. What is headroom and how is it measured?
6. What is the unit run?
7. What is the maximum riser height allowed by code?
8. How are cleats installed in a stairway?
9. When is a third stringer required for a stairway?
10. Tell how to lay out a cut-stringer stairway.

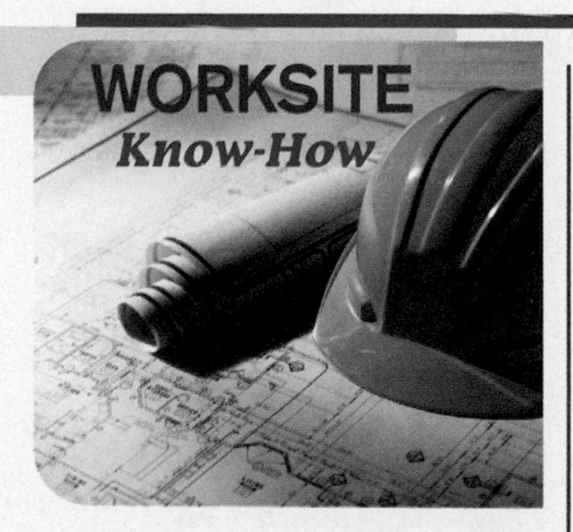

Teaching Others If you were asked to teach someone to frame a stairway, how would you go about it? First, approach the subject in a way that you yourself would find interesting. For example, you might explain how important the dimensions are to safety and ease of use. Next, organize the information so that it's easy to follow. If possible, take it step by step. Suggest that the learner take notes and ask lots of questions. Let the learner try different steps for him- or herself. Experience, more than anything else, is the best teacher. Be patient and supportive. Be sure any criticism is constructive and not personal. For example, don't say: "That's stupid. Do it this way." Instead, say something like: "Installing nails that way can split the board. You might want to try pre-drilling first."

Chapter

Molding and Trim

Objectives

After reading this chapter, you'll be able to:

- Identify uses for molding and trim other than decoration.
- Tell which joints are used for molding and trim and why.
- Identify different types of molding and trim.
- Tell how to scribe molding and trim to an uneven surface.
- Explain how to cut a coped joint.

Terms

baseboard
casing
coping
crown molding
molding
reveal
springing angle
trim

Careful trim carpentry is one sign of high-quality building construction. Generally, *trim carpentry* involves all the woodwork that is installed inside a building, with the exception of wood flooring. In the broadest sense, it includes doors and door frames, finished stairways, cabinetry, and molding.

SECTION 35.1

Molding and Trim Basics

The term **molding** usually refers to narrow lengths of wood with a shaped profile. The term **trim** refers more often to a straight length of wood such as a 1x4 that is also S4S, or *surfaced on 4 sides.* However, the two terms are often used interchangeably. *Trim* is also used as a verb. For example, a builder might "trim out" a window (attach molding and trim to it).

Trim and molding styles range from traditional to contemporary. They should match the style of the house in which they are used. **Fig. 35-1.** Although they are used decoratively, they often have more practical purposes. For example, window molding reinforces the window jambs and conceals the large gap between the jambs and the surrounding framing. Baseboard molding protects the lower portion of a wall from damage when the floors are cleaned. (For this reason, it was once known as *mop board.*)

Molding and trim can be made on the site from rough stock. This is sometimes done when unusual patterns and profiles are required. However, most molding and trim are purchased from local lumber dealers. Standard patterns and shapes are readily available. **Fig. 35-2** (see pages 702-703). They can be used individually or combined to form many interesting designs. An entire wall can be given a new look with wood moldings. **Figs. 35-3** and **35-4** (see pages 704-705).

Fig. 35-1. This room is accented by decorative door and window casing, baseboard trim, and wainscoting.

Fig. 35-2. Representative types of molding.

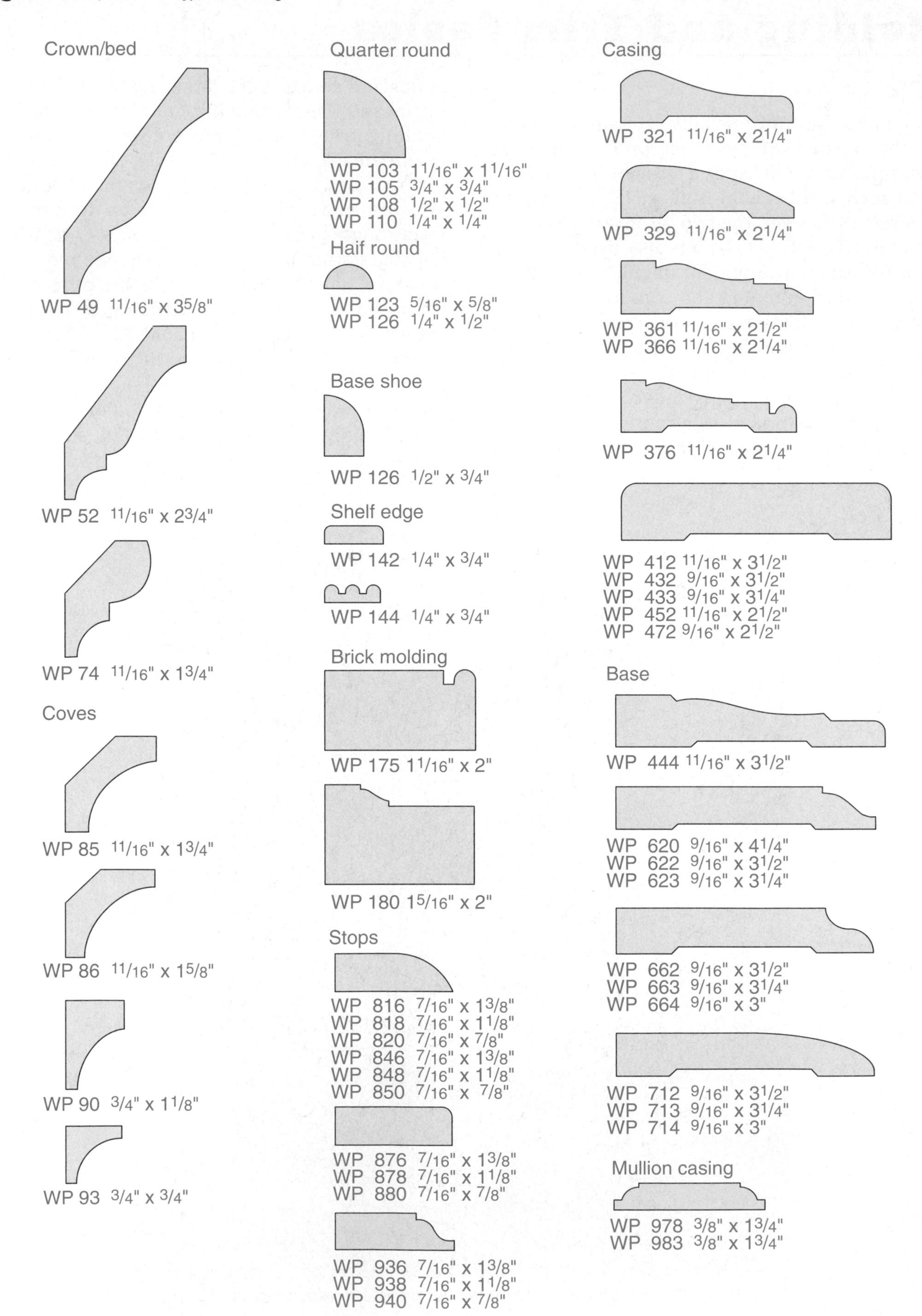

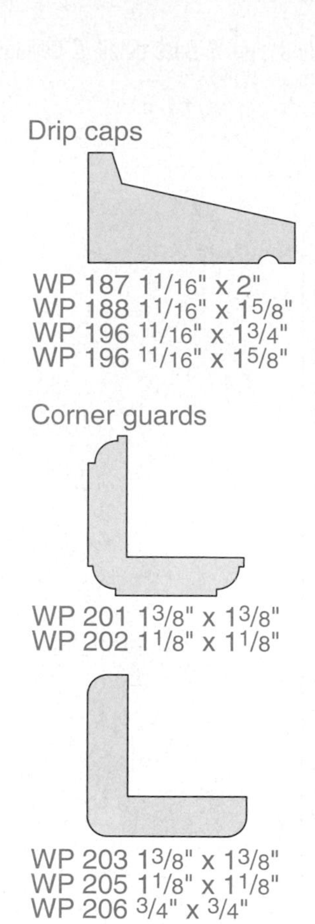
Drip caps
WP 187 1 1/16" x 2"
WP 188 1 1/16" x 1 5/8"
WP 196 11/16" x 1 3/4"
WP 196 11/16" x 1 5/8"
Corner guards
WP 201 1 3/8" x 1 3/8"
WP 202 1 1/8" x 1 1/8"
WP 203 1 3/8" x 1 3/8"
WP 205 1 1/8" x 1 1/8"
WP 206 3/4" x 3/4"

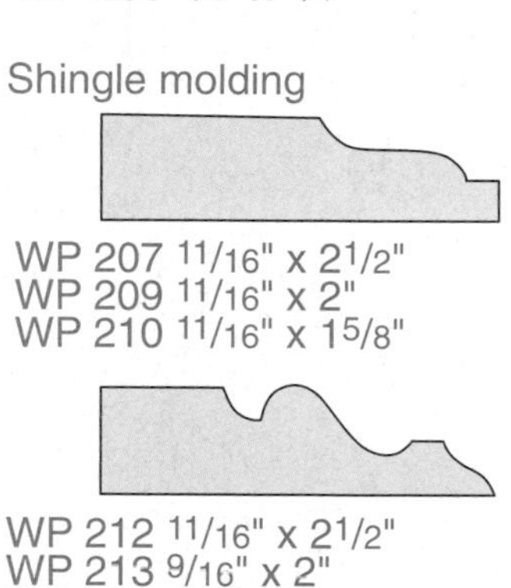
Shingle molding
WP 207 11/16" x 2 1/2"
WP 209 11/16" x 2"
WP 210 11/16" x 1 5/8"
WP 212 11/16" x 2 1/2"
WP 213 9/16" x 2"

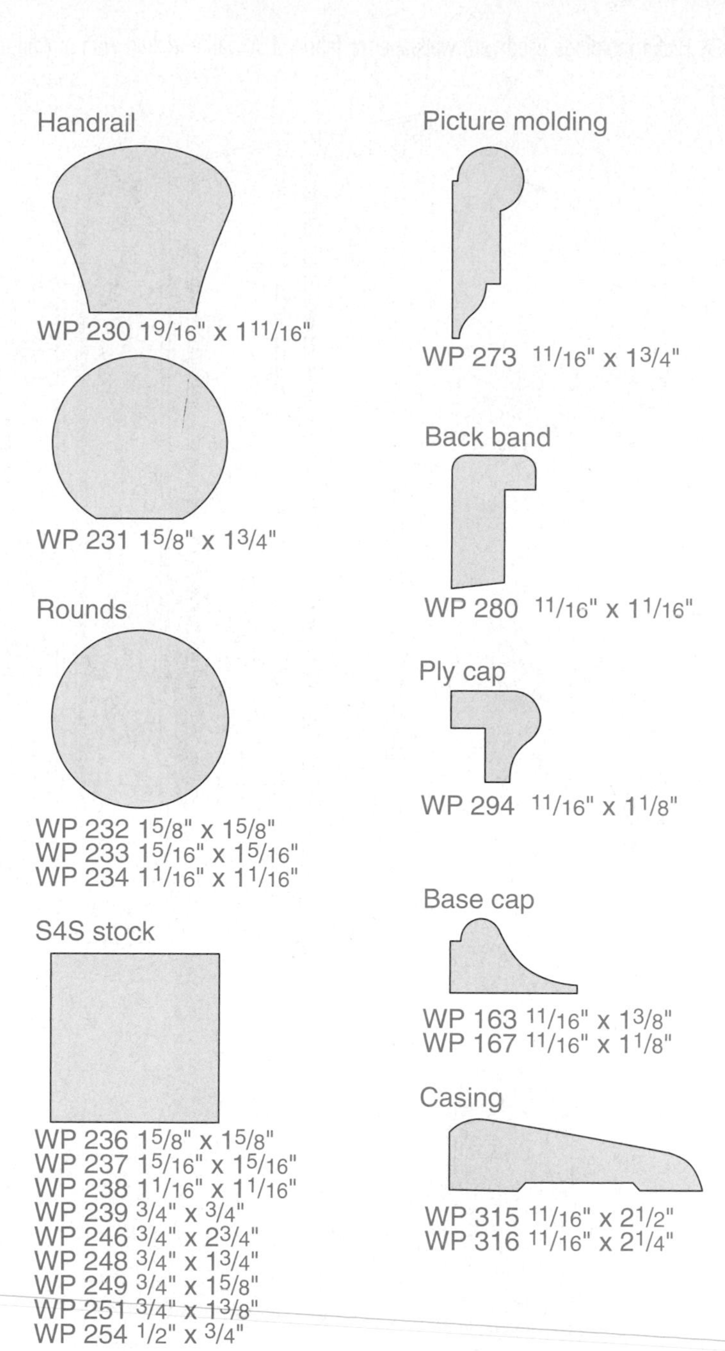
Handrail
WP 230 1 9/16" x 1 11/16"
WP 231 1 5/8" x 1 3/4"
Rounds
WP 232 1 5/8" x 1 5/8"
WP 233 1 5/16" x 1 5/16"
WP 234 1 1/16" x 1 1/16"
S4S stock
WP 236 1 5/8" x 1 5/8"
WP 237 1 5/16" x 1 5/16"
WP 238 1 1/16" x 1 1/16"
WP 239 3/4" x 3/4"
WP 246 3/4" x 2 3/4"
WP 248 3/4" x 1 3/4"
WP 249 3/4" x 1 5/8"
WP 251 3/4" x 1 3/8"
WP 254 1/2" x 3/4"
WP 265 9/32" x 1 3/4"
WP 266 9/32" x 1 5/8"
WP 267 9/32" x 1 3/8"
WP 268 9/32" x 1 1/8"
Picture molding
WP 273 11/16" x 1 3/4"
Back band
WP 280 11/16" x 1 1/16"
Ply cap
WP 294 11/16" x 1 1/8"
Base cap
WP 163 11/16" x 1 3/8"
WP 167 11/16" x 1 1/8"
Casing
WP 315 11/16" x 2 1/2"
WP 316 11/16" x 2 1/4"

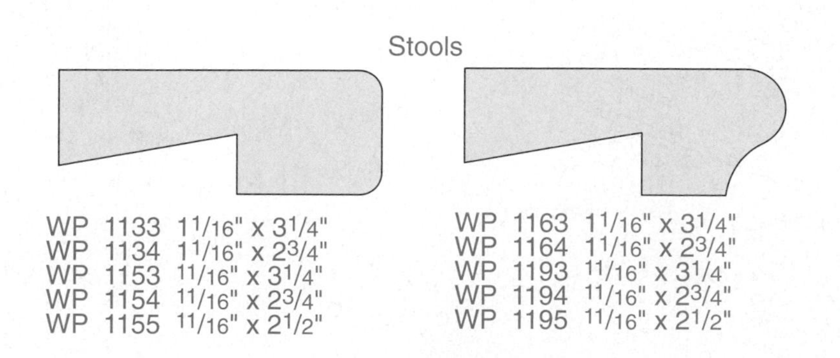
Stools
WP 1133 1 1/16" x 3 1/4"
WP 1134 1 1/16" x 2 3/4"
WP 1153 11/16" x 3 1/4"
WP 1154 11/16" x 2 3/4"
WP 1155 11/16" x 2 1/2"
WP 1163 1 1/16" x 3 1/4"
WP 1164 1 1/16" x 2 3/4"
WP 1193 11/16" x 3 1/4"
WP 1194 11/16" x 2 3/4"
WP 1195 11/16" x 2 1/2"

Fig. 35-3. Wood moldings used with wallpaper or fabric. *A.* A wall enriched with moldings in a traditional design. *B.* Base detail. *C.* Ceiling detail.

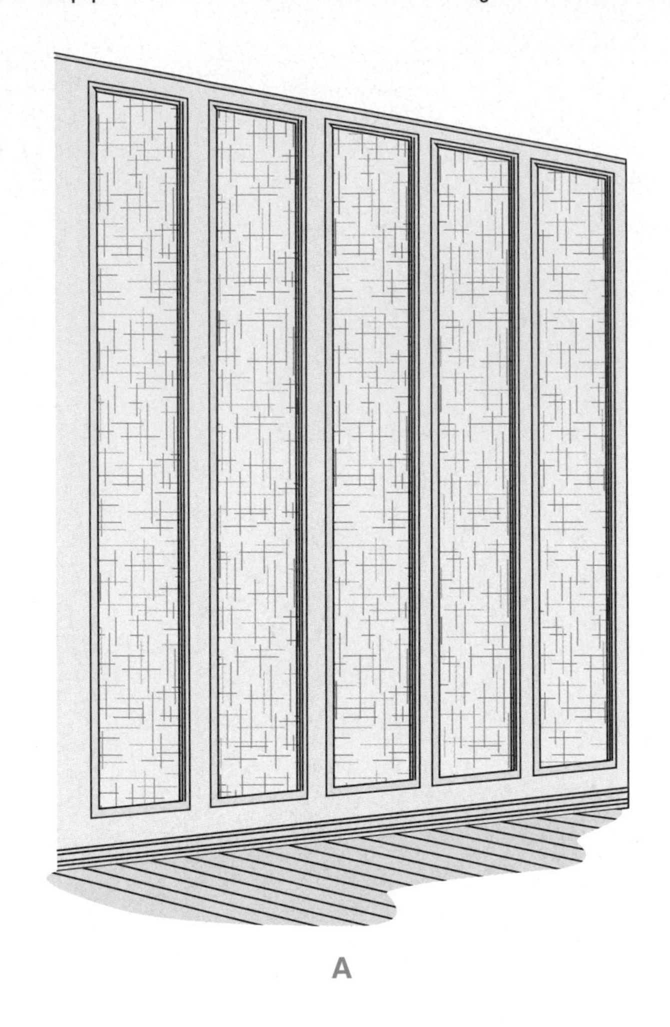

A

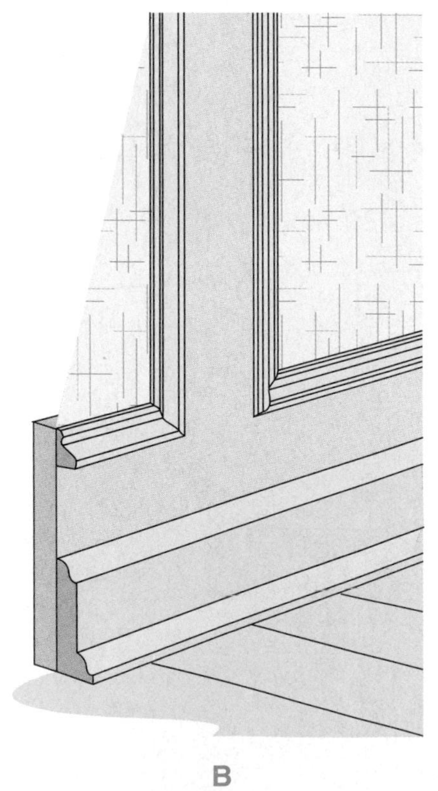

B

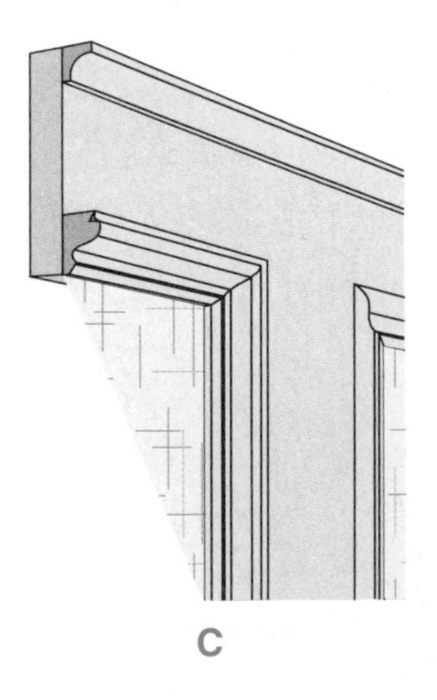

C

Fig. 35-4. Moldings and woodwork. *A.* A Spanish motif. *B.* Wall base detail. *C.* Nailing crown molding. *D.* Cutting miters in the molding to make the rosettes. *E.* Rosette detail.

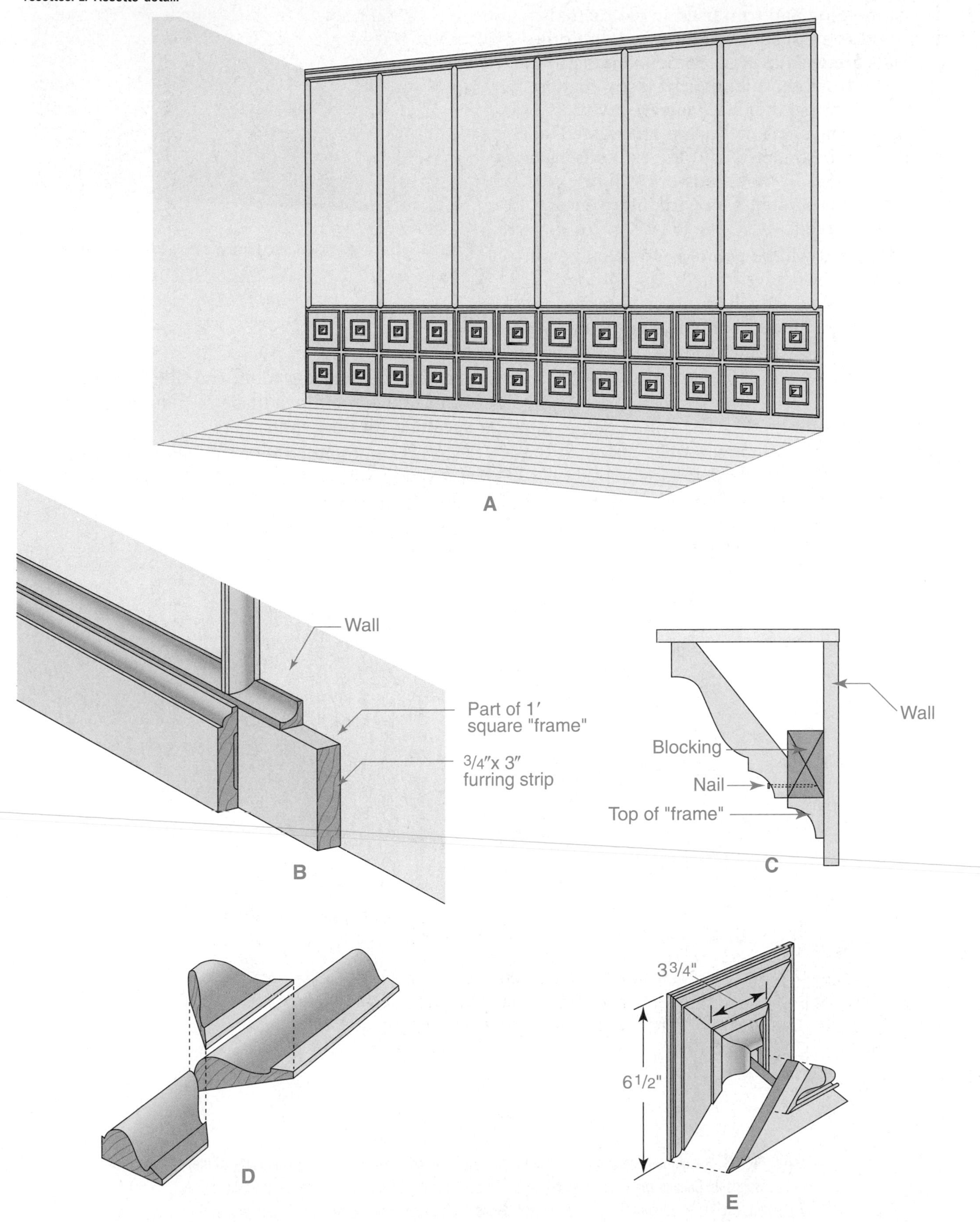

MATERIALS

Most molding and trim used in residential construction are made of solid wood, but other materials are used as well. Some manufacturers make trim from short lengths of wood that are finger-jointed together and veneered with a hardwood. The short pieces are not wasted, and the trim can be finished as if it were solid hardwood. **Fig. 35-5.** If the woodwork will be painted, finger-jointed trim without a veneer layer can be used.

Fig. 35-5. Finger-jointed pine window casing with a red oak veneer.

Molding that will be painted can often be purchased in lower grades, called *paint grades*, because painting will cover minor imperfections. Finger-jointed molding is a common paint-grade product. Such details are covered in the building plans and specifications.

The cost of interior trim varies a great deal with wood species and styles. For example, pine used for door and window frames may cost only half as much as some hardwood trims. The choice of materials is therefore based on where the trim is located and how it will be finished. For example, oak crown molding might be specified for a living room and dining room. Simple cove moldings made of pine might be specified for bedrooms.

The recommended moisture content for interior wood trim varies from 6 to 11 percent, depending on climate. The averages for various parts of the United States are shown in **Fig. 35-6**.

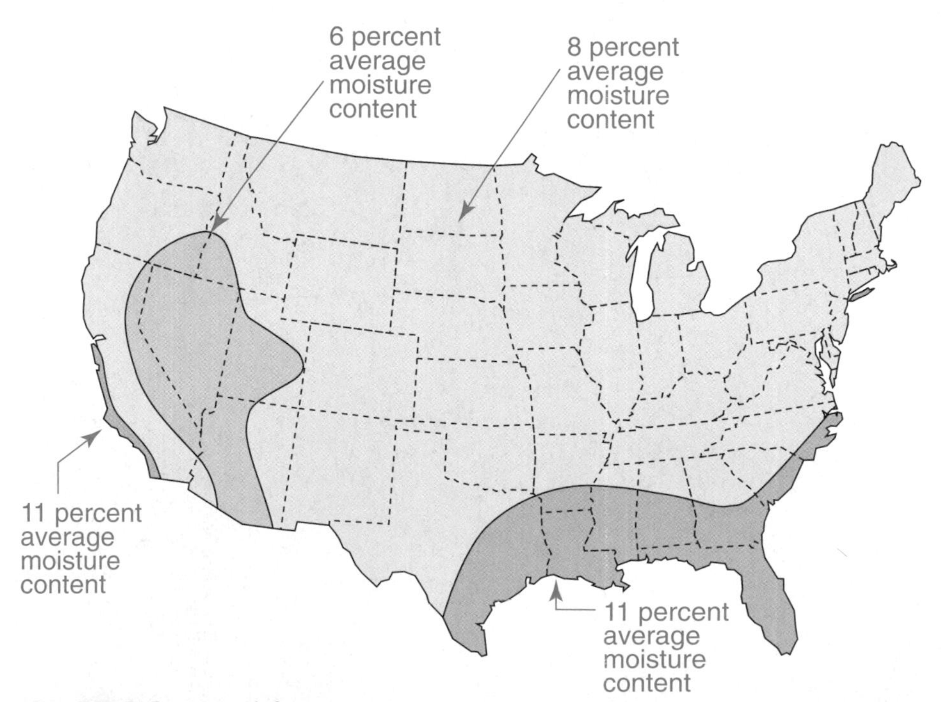

Fig. 35-6. Recommended average moisture content for interior wood trim in various parts of the United States. In Canada the recommended moisture contents are: Vancouver, 11 percent; Saskatoon, 7 percent; Ottawa, 8 percent; Halifax, 9 percent. (These cities represent the four major geographical areas.)

Fig. 35-7. This ceiling trim is a lightweight, synthetic product.

Some manufacturers produce trim made from synthetic materials that are much lighter than wood. However, they can be cut and nailed with standard woodworking tools and techniques. These materials are always painted. **Fig. 35-7.**

FINISHES

Interior molding and trim may be painted, stained, or given a clear finish such as varnish or polyurethane. In some cases, the wood is stained before it is coated with a clear finish. The type of finish desired often determines the species of wood to be used.

Woodwork to be painted should be smooth, close-grained, and free from pitch streaks. Two woods having these qualities in a high degree include northern white pine and yellow poplar. When the finish is to be clear, or natural, the wood should have a pleasing grain and uniform color. Woods with these qualities include ash, birch, cherry, maple, oak, and walnut.

from Another Angle

The woods used for interior trim that will not be painted can vary from region to region. In the Pacific Northwest, for example, high-quality grades of Douglas fir are sometimes used for baseboard as well as window and door trim. In Massachusetts, however, oak would be more common.

SECTION 35.1 **Check Your Knowledge**

1. Define trim carpentry.
2. What is the meaning of the abbreviation *S4S*?
3. What qualities are desired in wood that is to be painted?
4. What is the recommended moisture content for trim used in Minnesota?

On the Job

Refer to Figs. 35-2, 35-3, and 35-4. Make a sketch of your own decorative wall design that would use molding and trim. If possible, create your design on a computer using CAD software.

SECTION 35.2

Interior Door and Window Trim

The basic molding around a window or door is called the **casing**. Door and window frames are usually trimmed first because baseboard and some other moldings must fit against the door or window casing. Cabinets, built-in bookcases, and fireplace mantels are also installed before the trim work begins in earnest.

After interior wall covering has been applied and the finish floor laid, all floor and wall surfaces should be scraped clean and free of any irregularities. The location of all wall studs should be marked lightly on the floor (or on the wall, if the marks will be covered later by trim).

JOINTS

Where door casing meets the floor, it is given a square cut. When casing has a square edge, it can be assembled with butt joints. Casing with a molded shape must have mitered corner joints. **Fig. 35-8.** Mitering ensures that the shape will be continuous from side casings to head casing. As the wood dries, a mitered joint may open slightly at its outer edge. Nailing across the joint after pre-drilling the hole is one way to hold the joint together.

Many trim carpenters use compressed-wood biscuits to hold trim joinery together. A biscuit joiner (see page 178) is used to cut a shallow groove in the ends of both pieces. A compressed biscuit is inserted into the groove and glued in place to reinforce the joint. **Fig. 35-9.** When the pieces are brought together, the biscuit absorbs moisture from the glue and expands slightly, forming a tight joint. Biscuits are available in three standard sizes. **Table 35-A.**

Making a Miter Cut

The basic cuts made for window and door casings are the square cut and the miter cut. A square cut is made straight across the width of the casing. A miter cut is made at an angle. Because two pieces of trim are often joined to form a 90° corner, the angle for most miter cuts is 45°. Use a miter saw to make these and other cuts (see Chapter 7, "Power Saws").

If angles other than 90° or 45° are required, you must calculate them. To do this, divide 180 by the number of sides. Then subtract that answer from 90. The result will be the number of degrees for each miter cut. For example, to make cuts for a five-sided figure:

$$180 \div 5 = 36$$
$$90 - 36 = 54$$

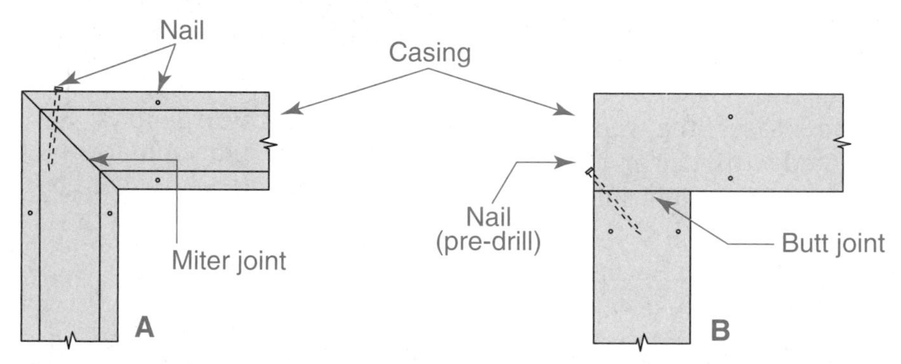

Fig. 35-8. Joining casing. *A.* Casing with a molded shape must have a mitered joint at the corner. *B.* Square-edged casing may be joined with a miter joint or a butt joint. In both cases, the joints may be reinforced by nailing at the locations shown by arrows.

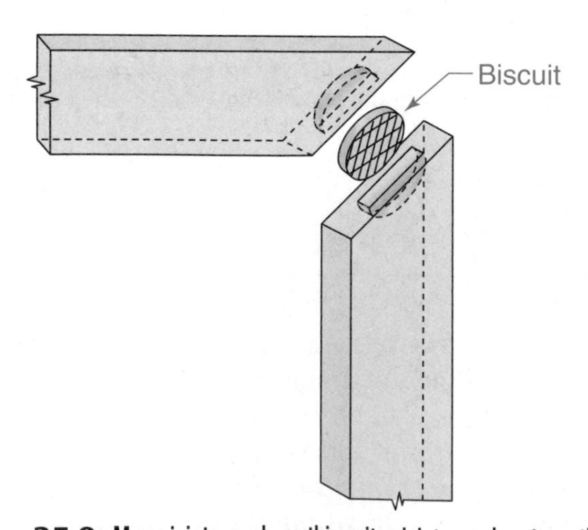

Fig. 35-9. Many joints, such as this miter joint, can be strengthened with a wood biscuit that is glued in place. The slot for the biscuit is cut by a biscuit joiner.

Table 35-A. Standard Sizes of Biscuit Joints

Biscuit Size	Dimension of Groove[a] (inches)
#0	⅝ wide x 1¾ long
#10	¾ wide x 2⅛ long
#20	1 wide x 2½ long

[a] Lengths are approximate.

INSTALLING DOOR CASING

The most commonly used casings for interior doors vary in width from 2¼″ to 3½″. Thicknesses vary from ½″ to ¾″. Two of the more common patterns are shown in **Fig. 35-10.**

Casings are nailed to the door jamb and to the framing around it, allowing about a 3⁄16″ reveal on the face of the jamb. **Fig. 35-11.** A **reveal** is a small offset between a piece of trim and the surface it is applied to. The small step this creates adds visual interest. It also allows the trim carpenter to adjust the fit of the casing if the door is not perfectly square.

Nails are located in pairs and spaced about 16″ apart around the opening. To nail into the framing, use either 6d or 7d finish nails, depending on the thickness of the casing, as shown in Fig. 35-11, arrow 1. To fasten the thinner edge of the casing to the jamb, use 3d, 4d, or 5d finishing nails as shown in Fig. 35-11, arrow 2. With hardwood, the holes should be pre-drilled to prevent the wood from splitting.

Carpenter's Tip

Miters are commonly used for joining molding at corners. However, molding can also be installed using rosettes and plinth blocks. These add a decorative element to the room. They eliminate the need to miter the molding. They also conceal differences in thickness between baseboard and door casing.

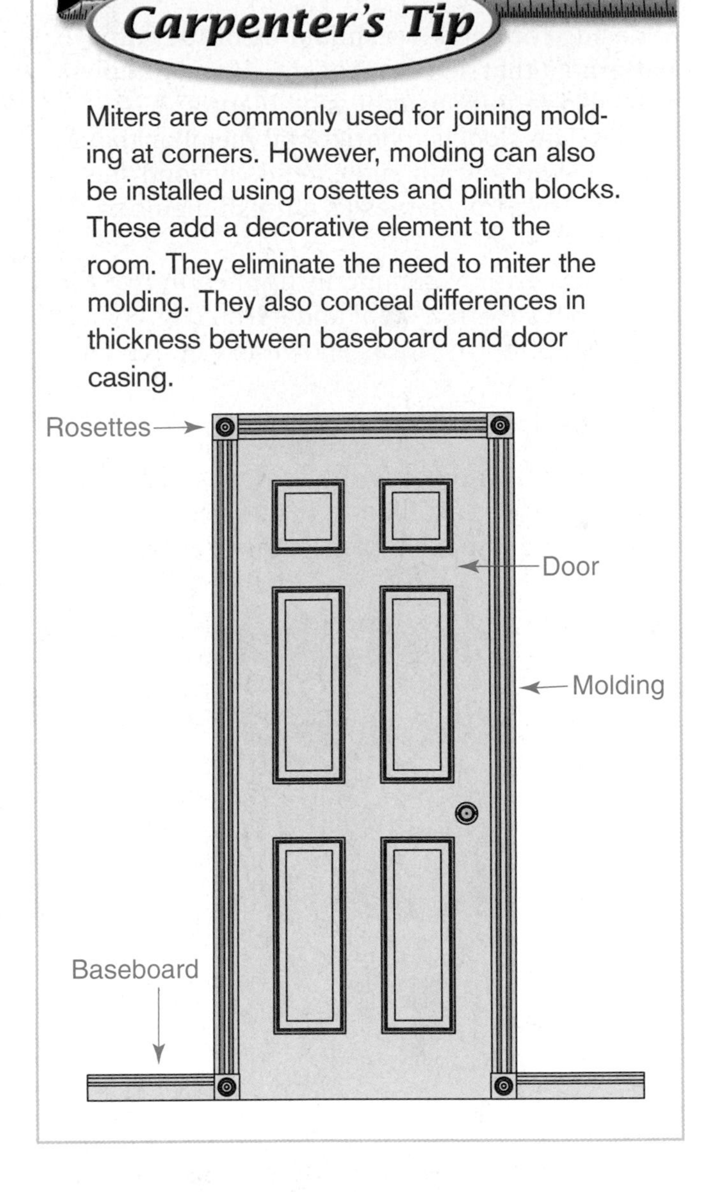

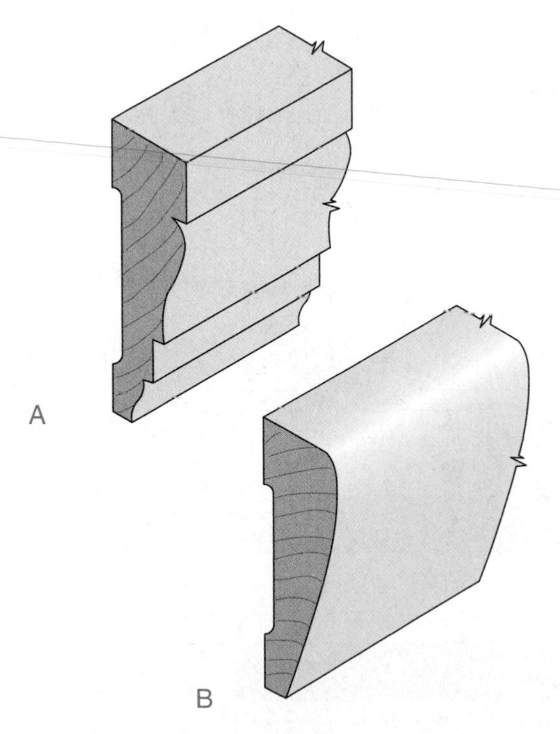

Fig. 35-10. Two common casings used for interior trim. *A.* Colonial. *B.* Ranch, or clamshell, casing.

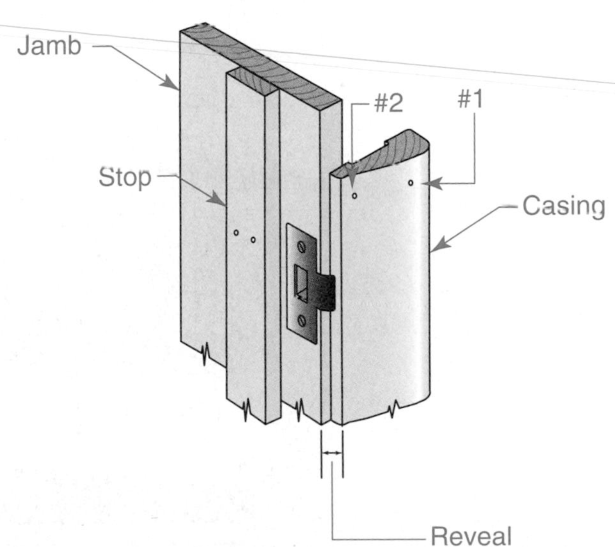

Fig. 35-11. A reveal is visible along the inside edge of this door casing.

INSTALLING WINDOW TRIM

Casing for windows should be of the same pattern as that selected for the door. Windows may also require a stool and an apron. **Fig. 35-12.** The *stool* is a horizontal member that laps the window sill and extends beyond the casing. An *apron* serves as a finish member below the stool.

Window trim is commonly applied in two different ways: with a stool and apron (Fig. 35-12) and with only casing, as shown in **Fig. 35-13**.

The Stool

The stool is normally the first piece of window trim to be installed. It is notched to fit between the jambs so that its inner edge contacts the lower rail of the lower sash. Refer to **Fig. 35-14**, which is a section view. The upper drawing shows the stool in place. The lower drawing shows it laid out and cut, ready for installation.

Note the three distances labeled *A*, *B*, and *C*. *A*, the overall length of the stool, is equal to the distance between the outer edges of the side casings, plus the amount that each end of the stool extends beyond the casing's outer edges. Distance *B* is equal to the width of the finished opening. Distance *C* is equal to the horizontal distance measured along the face of the jamb between its edge and the inside face of the lower sash. An allowance of about 1⁄32″ should be deducted for clearance between the sash and the stool. A notch is then cut at each corner of the stool along the layout lines.

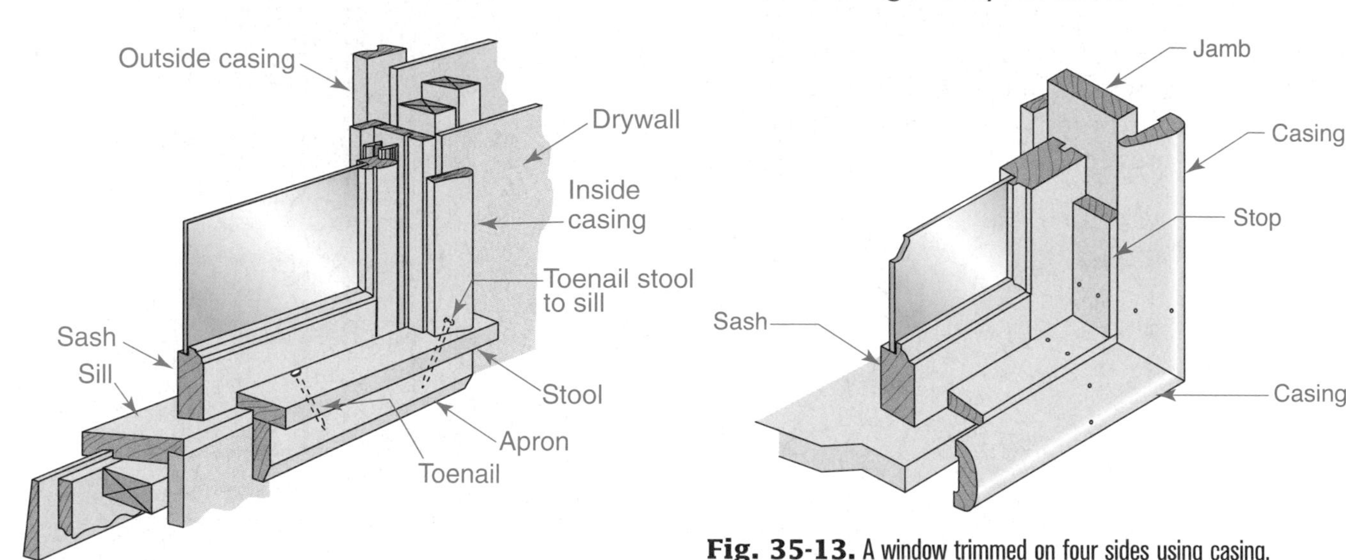

Fig. 35-12. Window trim installed with a stool and apron.

Fig. 35-13. A window trimmed on four sides using casing.

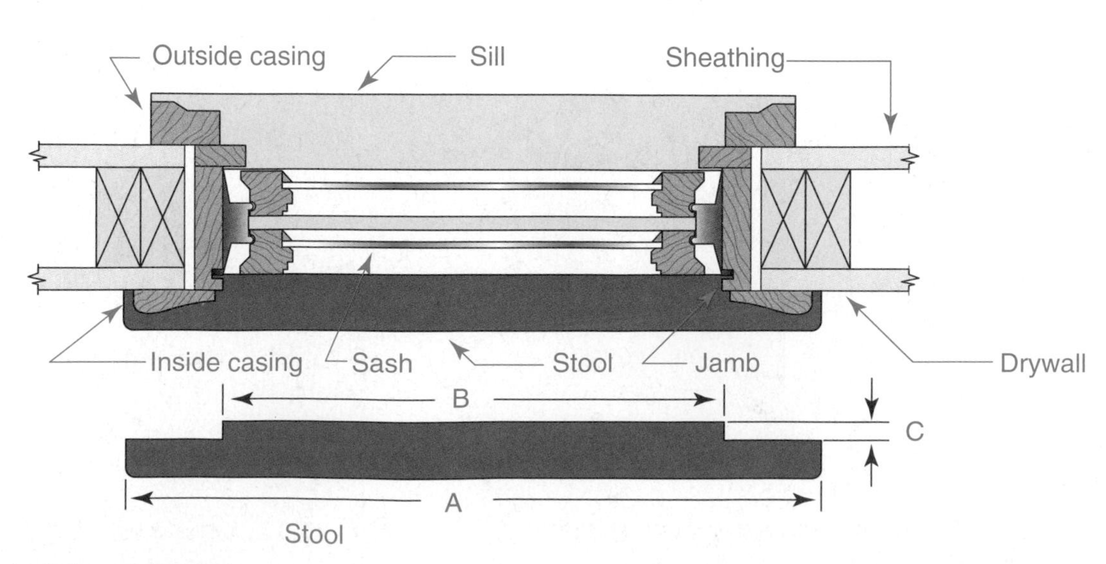

Fig. 35-14. Installation details for a window stool.

The stool is toenailed at the ends with 8d finish nails so that the casing at the sides will cover the nailheads. With hardwood, pre-drilling is required to prevent splitting. The stool should also be nailed at the center to the sill and to the apron when it is installed. Toenailing may be substituted for face-nailing to the sill (see Fig. 35-12).

The Casing

Apply the casing after installing the stool. Nail it as described for the door casing. Other types of windows, such as awning, hopper, or casement, are trimmed much like a double-hung window. Casings of the same type are used for all.

When just casing and no stool or apron is used to finish the bottom of a window frame, all four lengths are mitered (see Fig. 35-13). This is called *picture framing* a window. The four pieces can be nailed in place one by one. An alternative is to lay the pieces face down on a clean, smooth surface and fasten them together from the back with corrugated fasteners. The assembled casing, much like a picture frame, can then be nailed as a unit to the window jambs and studs.

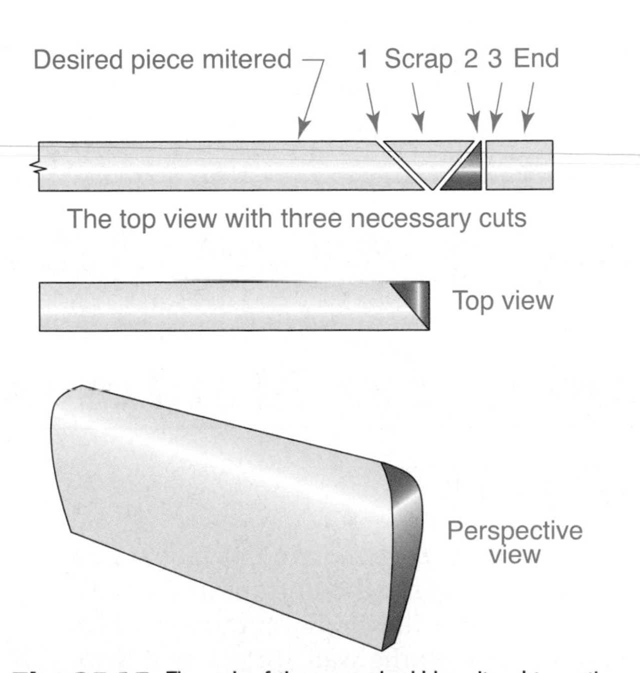

Fig. 35-15. The ends of the apron should be mitered to continue the profile of the apron and conceal its end grain.

The Apron

Cut the apron to a length equal to the distance between the outer edges of the side casings. Cut the ends of the apron with a coping saw at an angle to match the profile of the molding. You might also cut and nail a return in place. **Fig. 35-15.** A *return* is a piece that continues the profile of trim or molding around the corner. Attach the apron to the rough sill with 8d finish nails. Fig. 35-12.

Interior Shutters

Movable interior shutters were popular from about 1700 to the early part of the nineteenth century. They were used in the great mansions of New Orleans and in many other fine homes of America. Shutters are once again popular. **Fig. 35-16.** They are found most often in homes with traditional or country-style interiors.

Fig. 35-16. Louvered shutters may be used throughout a home. They allow light and air to pass through, yet ensure privacy.

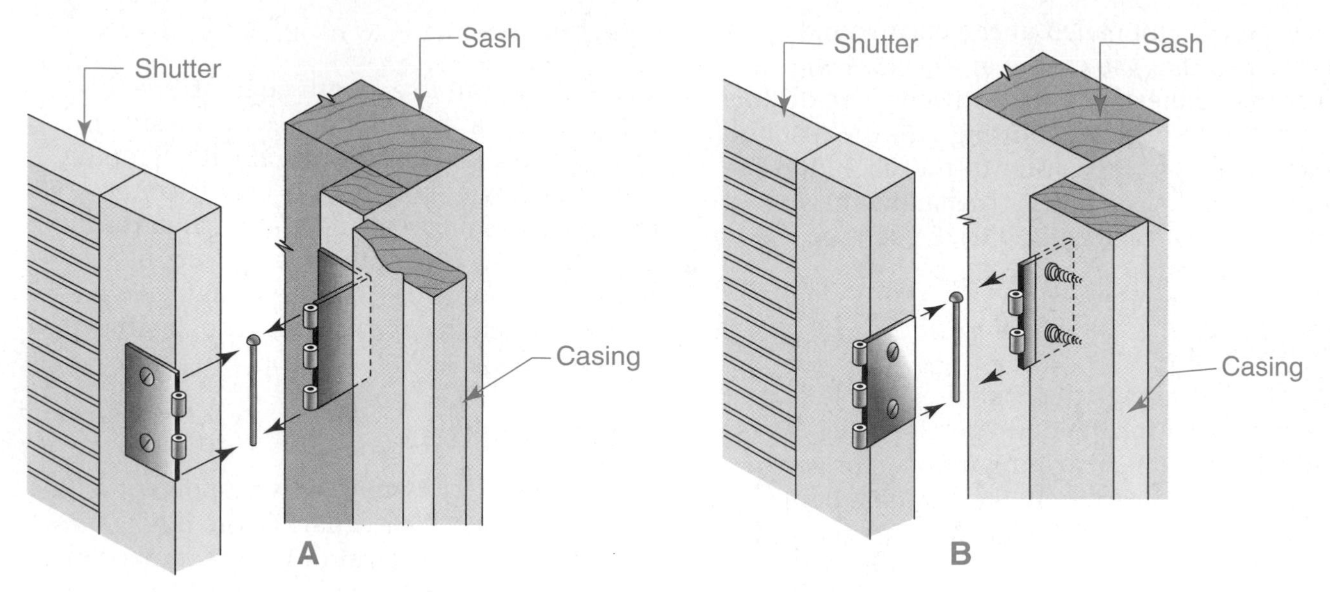

Fig. 35-17. Applying a hinge strip. *A.* A hinge strip for a shutter installed on a double-hung window. *B.* If the window jamb is not wood, a wood hinge strip is applied to the wall.

To determine the size of the shutters to be installed in a window, measure the width of the opening between the side jambs. Measure its height from the top of the sill to the inside surface of the top jamb. Various methods can then be used to install the shutter, as shown in **Fig. 35-17**.

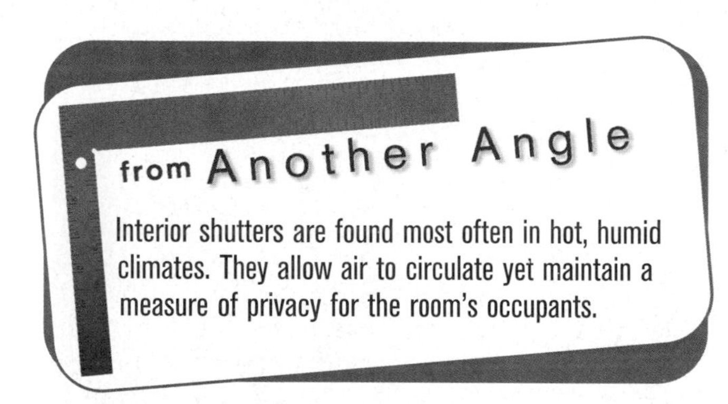

SECTION 35.2

Check Your Knowledge

1. What two basic cuts are used when installing door and window casing?
2. What is a reveal and why is it important?
3. How do you "picture frame" a window?
4. What determines the length to which the apron should be cut?

On the Job

Find out why recommended average moisture content for wood trim percentages vary according to climate. A builder, building code supervisor, or lumber supplier might be able to help you determine the recommendations for your area.

SECTION 35.3

Baseboard, Ceiling, and Other Moldings

After the window and door casings are complete, the trim carpenter installs the other moldings in a room. These include flat moldings, such as baseboard or chair rail, and sprung moldings, such as crown molding. *Sprung moldings* are moldings that project out from the wall surface.

BASEBOARD

Baseboard, or *base molding*, is a board or molding used against the bottom of walls to cover their joint with the floor. It serves as a transition between the wall surface and the floor. It also covers the gaps that often occur at this location. It can be added after all the doors are trimmed and the cabinets are in place. It should be installed after the finish flooring and before any carpeting.

Baseboard is made in a number of sizes and shapes and may have several parts. Two-piece baseboard consists of a base topped with a small cap. **Fig. 35-18.** When the wall covering is not straight and true, the base cap conforms more closely to the variations than a single wider baseboard would. A common size for two-piece baseboard is ⅝″ x 3¼″. One-piece baseboard varies in size from 7⁄16″ x 2¼″ to ½″ x 3¼″ or wider. Many baseboards include a ½″ x ¾″ *base shoe* (see Fig. 35-18). The shoe is nailed into the baseboard, not into the flooring. This prevents the shoe from being moved out of position as the flooring shrinks or expands.

When carpeting is to be installed, the baseboard is installed first, using temporary spacers to lift it slightly above the subfloor. **Fig. 35-19.** A consultation with the carpet installer can determine how much clearance is needed. The edges of the carpet are then tucked beneath the baseboard. When wall-to-wall carpeting is used, the shoe is usually omitted, and in some cases, the entire baseboard is omitted.

Square-edged baseboards should be installed with a butt joint at inside corners and a miter joint at outside corners. Molded baseboards are mitered at outside corners, but they are *coped* (shaped to fit each other) at inside corners (see Fig. 35-18). These joining methods are needed to provide tight joints because the walls may not be perfectly square or plumb at the corners.

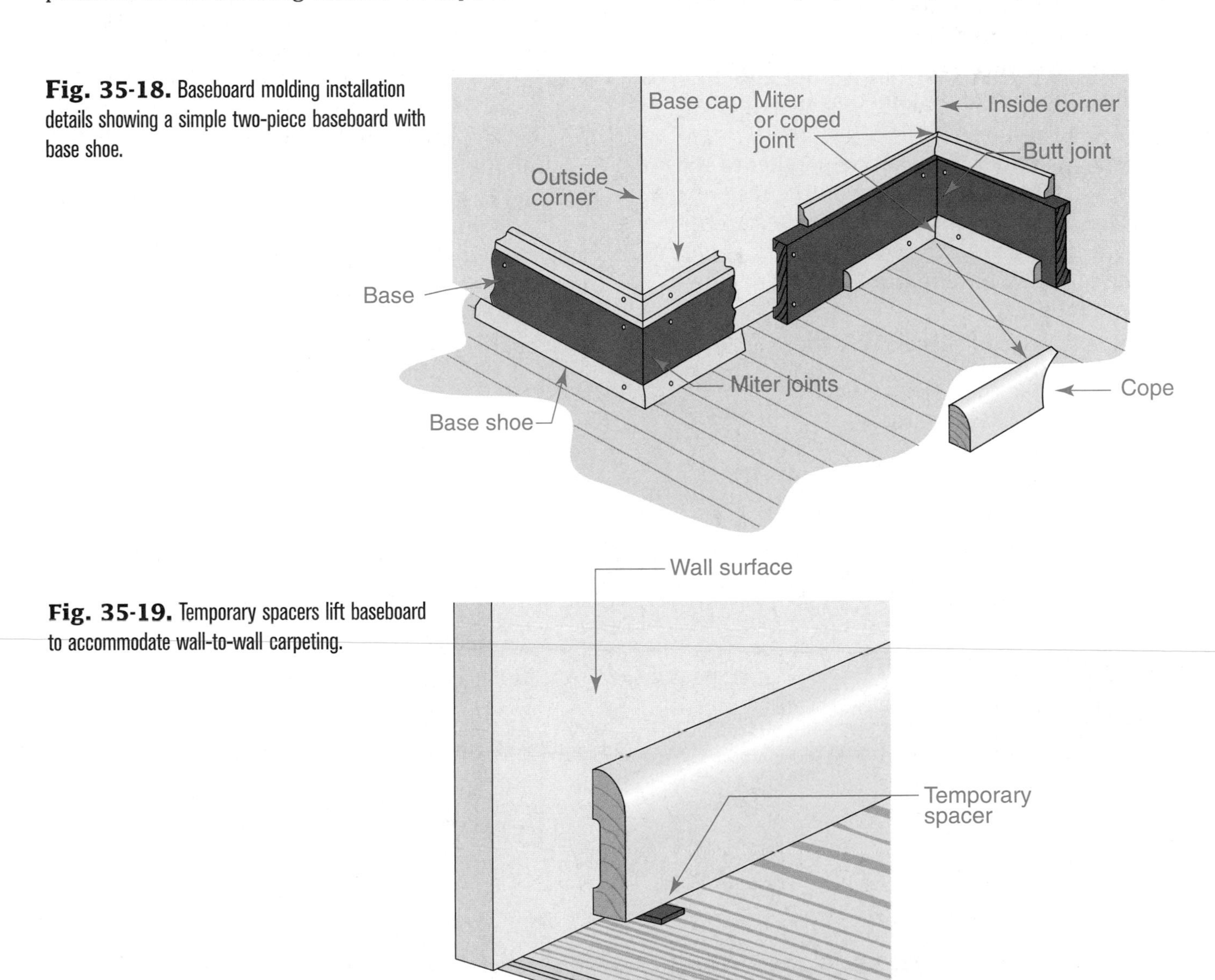

Fig. 35-18. Baseboard molding installation details showing a simple two-piece baseboard with base shoe.

Fig. 35-19. Temporary spacers lift baseboard to accommodate wall-to-wall carpeting.

Molding cut to fit between walls should always be cut a little long. The molding can then be bowed slightly and sprung into place. This ensures a tight fit. When more than one length of molding is needed along a wall, the pieces are joined over a wall stud with a mitered lap joint. The angle of the miter is typically 45°. **Fig. 35-20.** The baseboard is secured to each stud with two 8d finishing nails.

Scribing a Joint

When walls are out of plumb, two lengths of baseboard that intersect with a butt joint may have to be scribed and trimmed to fit tightly against each other. *Scribing* is a marking process that allows a piece of wood to be precisely fit against a surface that is irregular or not square.

1. Install the first piece.
2. Set the second piece in position on the floor. Place the end to be joined against or near the face of the piece already installed.
3. Using a scriber, draw a line parallel to the face of the installed piece on the face of the piece to be joined. **Fig. 35-21.** Be careful to hold the legs of the scriber at right angles to the installed baseboard. This will ensure a parallel line.
4. Cut the scribed piece along the line.

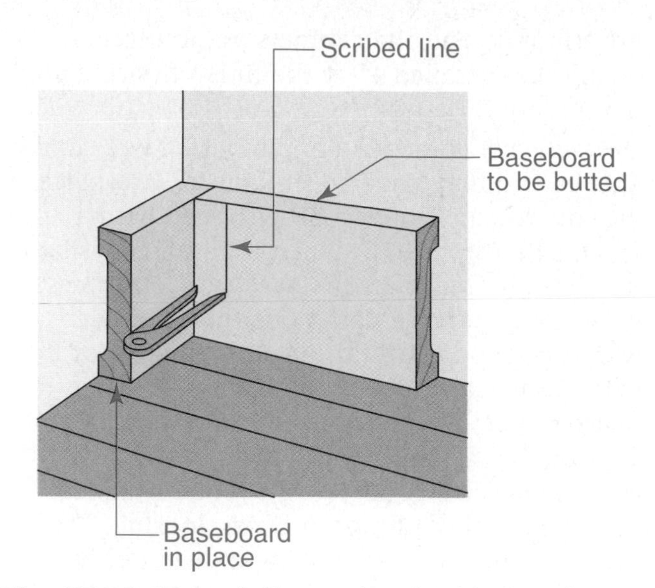

Fig. 35-21. When an inside corner has a butt joint, it may have to be scribed to ensure a tight fit if the wall surfaces are not plumb. The legs of the scriber should be held horizontally.

5. Test the fit. Recut as needed, or use a file to fine-tune the fit.

If the baseboard must fit against casing that is out of plumb, you can scribe it as noted above. However, some carpenters find it quicker to use a small piece of plywood scrap, sometimes called a *preacher*, to transfer the angle to the baseboard. **Fig. 35-22.**

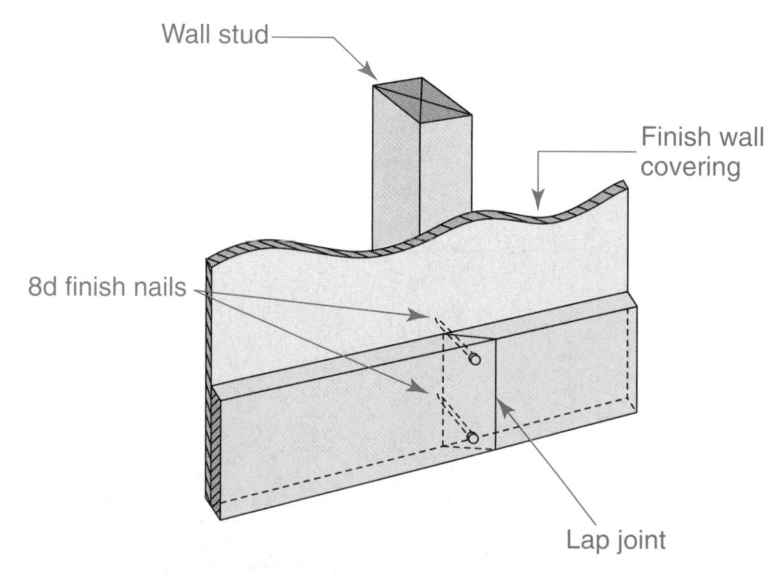

Fig. 35-20. When several pieces of molding are needed for length, they should be joined over a wall stud, using a mitered lap joint. Two 8d finish nails secure the joint. The bottom nail should be close enough to the floorline to be covered by the base shoe molding.

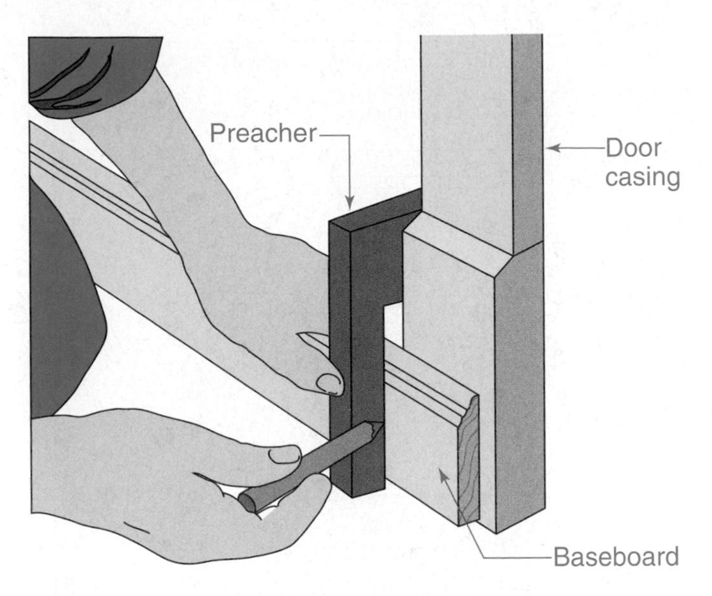

Fig. 35-22. If casing is not perfectly plumb, a small piece of plywood scrap called a preacher can be used to transfer its angle to the baseboard.

Mitering a Joint

Outside corners on baseboard are frequently mitered. The cut is made across the thickness of the material instead of across the width.

1. Set a piece of baseboard against the wall. **Fig. 35-23A.** Mark a layout line on the floor along the edge of the piece.
2. Repeat the process on the adjoining wall.
3. Hold the first piece to be mitered in place. Mark it where it intersects the layout line. **Fig. 35-23B.**
4. Set the miter saw to a 45° bevel angle and cut just outside the layout line.
5. Repeat Step 3 and cut the second piece at a 45° bevel angle.
6. Test-fit the pieces and trim them as needed. The completed corner is shown in **Fig. 35-23C.**

To get a good fit, it is often necessary to cut a tiny amount off the end of a piece of molding. To do this, lower the miter saw until the blade's teeth are at table height. Hold the molding against the fence with your fingers well away from the blade. Then slide the molding under the blade guard until one end touches the teeth of the blade. DO NOT TURN THE SAW ON YET. Push the molding against the teeth slightly. This will nudge the blade slightly out of position. Now raise the saw blade, but without moving the molding. Turn on the saw and make the cut. A small fraction of wood will be removed. Test-fit the cut. Repeat the process if necessary.

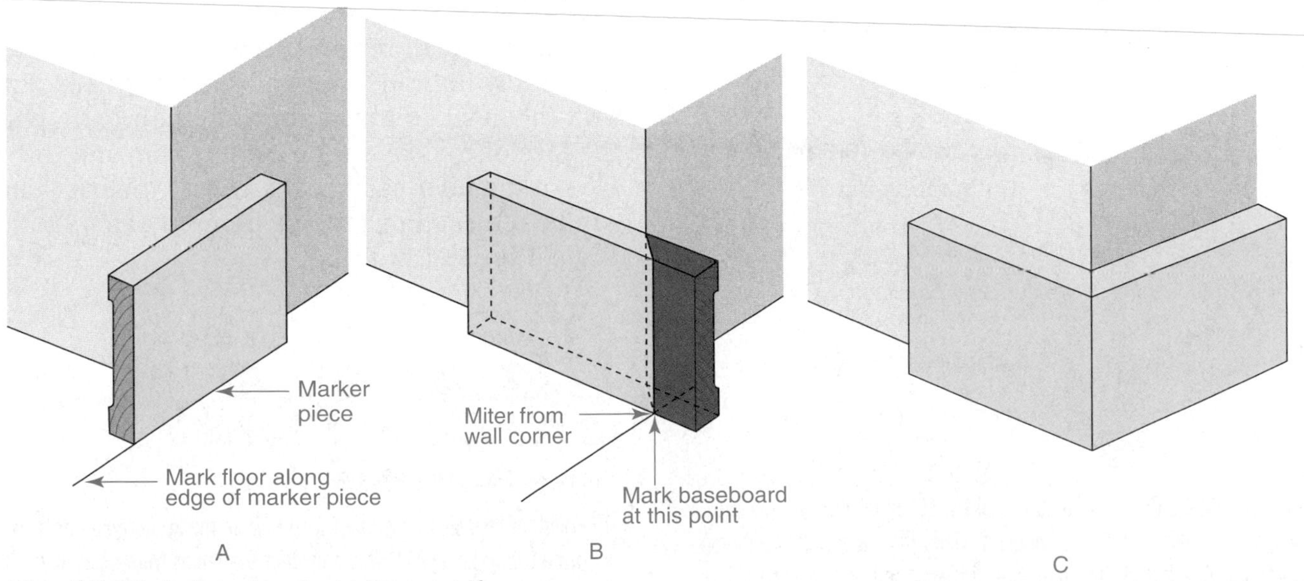

Fig. 35-23. Laying out a miter joint at an outside corner.

Coping a Joint

Inside corner joints between trim members are usually made by cutting the end of one member to fit against the face of the other. This shaping process is called **coping**. A coped inside joint looks better on baseboard than a mitered joint. **Fig. 35-24.** A coped joint will not open up when the molding is nailed in place. It is also less likely to show a gap if the molding shrinks after installation. Another view of a coped cut is shown in **Fig. 35-25**.

Baseboard is often coped at one end and butted into a wall at the other. If this is the case, the coped joint is cut first. Then the baseboard is square-cut to length.

1. To cope a molding, miter the end at 45°. Refer to *A* in Fig. 35-24.
2. Rest the coping saw blade against the edge of the miter cut. Hold the saw at 90° to the back of the molding and begin your cut. Then cut the molding along the inside edge left by the miter cut. As you cut, direct the saw slightly inward, away from the molding to be joined. This is known as back-cutting. Refer to *B* and *C* in Fig. 35-24.

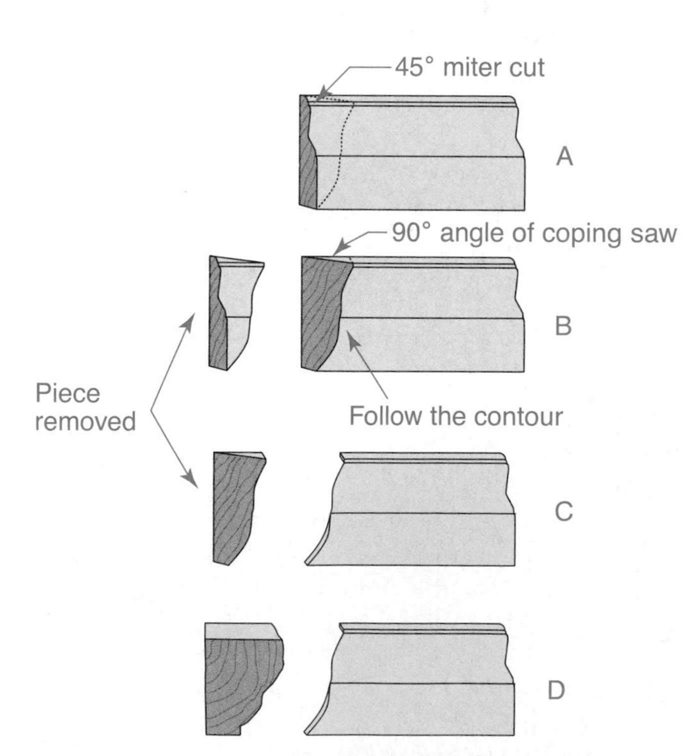

Fig. 35-24. Coping a joint. *A.* Make a 45° miter cut. *B.* Hold the coping saw at 90° to the back edge. *C.* Make the coping cut, following the contour line left by the miter cut. *D.* The coped end will fit tightly against the face of the other molding.

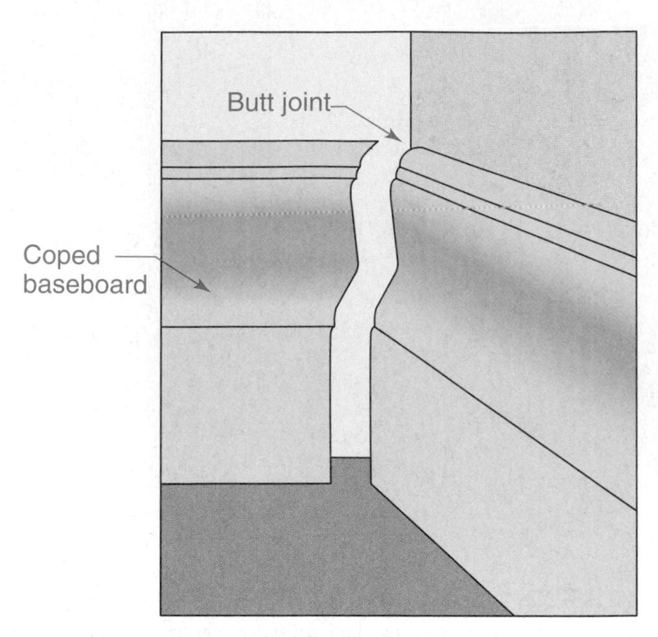

Fig. 35-25. The end of a coped baseboard matches the face of the intersecting baseboard.

3. The end profile of the coped member should match the face of the intersecting molding. Refer to *D* in Fig. 35-24. Fine-tune the fit as necessary for a tight joint.

Cutting Returns

Ideally, the outside edge of the door casing will be thicker than the baseboard molding. This will prevent the end grain of the baseboard from showing. However, sometimes the baseboard is thicker than the casing. To provide a finished detail, the baseboard can be returned where it meets the casing. There are two methods for doing this: face mitering and edge mitering. **Fig. 35-26.**

Glue the small return piece into position and fasten it with brads or small finishing nails. Predrill the holes to avoid splitting the wood. When the face of the base shoe projects beyond the face of the door casing, the end of the base shoe can be returned or reverse mitered at a 45° angle. **Fig. 35-27.**

Knee Protection

The work of installing baseboard trim can be made more comfortable with the use of kneepads. These protect the knees from injury caused by prolonged contact with hard floors.

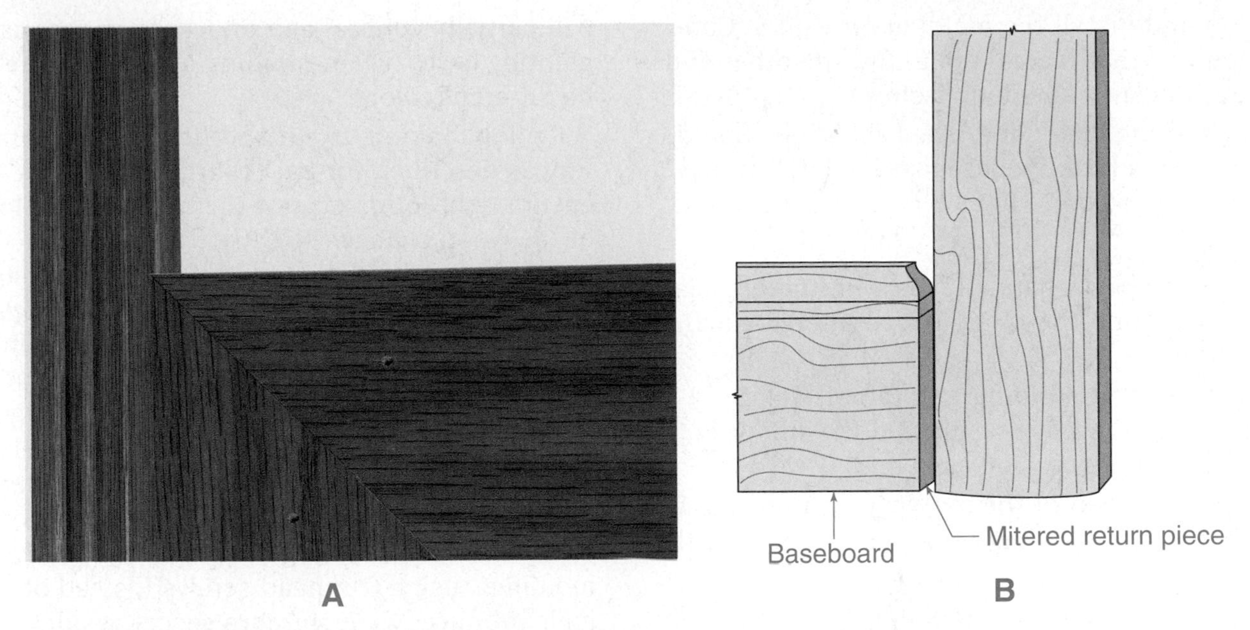

Fig. 35-26. Mitering returns a thicker baseboard to the casing. *A.* Face mitering. *B.* Edge mitering.

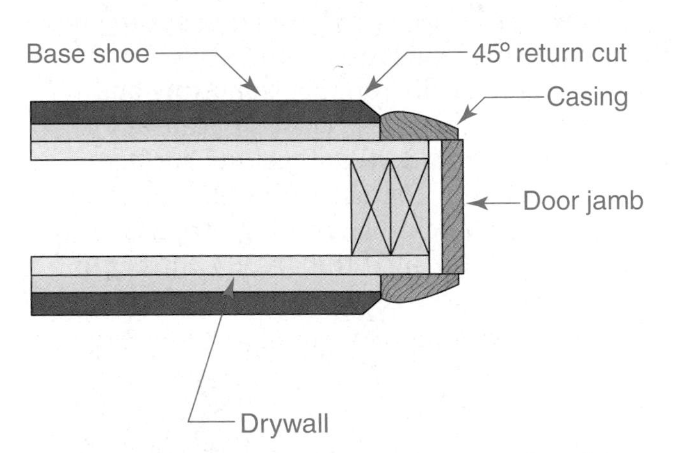

Fig. 35-27. When the face of the base shoe projects beyond the face of the casing, a 45° return cut can be made on the base shoe. This exposes end grain, however.

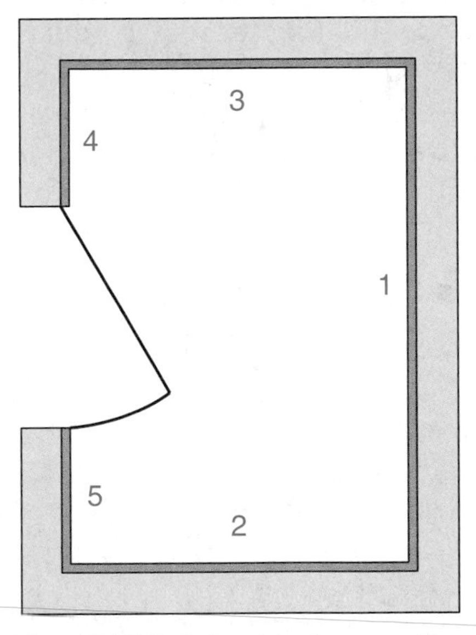

Fig. 35-28. A plan view of a room with one door.

Installing the Baseboard

Carefully plan the baseboard installation sequence before starting the job. This saves time later.

Square cuts fit against wall surfaces. If the walls are unusually irregular, square cuts should be scribed to fit. Coped cuts fit against adjacent lengths of baseboard. When fitting a baseboard, always make the coped cut first. It is the most difficult.

The outline of a room with one door is shown in **Fig. 35-28**. Following are two methods for installing base molding, using square cuts and coped cuts.

Method 1

1. Cut and install a piece of molding to go along wall 1. It should have a square cut on each end.
2. Cut and install the molding for wall 2. The end meeting wall 1 should be coped. The other end should be square.
3. Cut and install the molding for wall 3. The end meeting wall 1 should be coped. The other end should be square.
4. Cut and install the molding for wall 4. Cope one end to fit against wall 3. Cut the other end to fit against the door casing.

5. Cut and install the molding for wall 5. Cope the end that meets wall 2. Cut the other end to fit against the door casing.
6. Install the base shoe. The base shoe should be nailed into the baseboard itself, not into the finish floor.

Method 2

If you are right-handed, you will find it easiest to work around the room in a counterclockwise direction.

1. Cut the first molding to fit along wall 5 between the door casing and the end wall. Make square cuts on each end.
2. Cope one end of the molding for wall 2 to fit against the molding on wall 5. Square cut the other end.
3. Cope one end of the molding for wall 1 to fit against the molding on wall 2. Square cut the other end.
4. Cope one end of the molding for wall 3 to fit against the molding for wall 1. Square cut the other end.
5. Cope one end of the molding for wall 4 to fit against wall 3. Cut the other end to fit against the door casing.

CEILING MOLDING

Ceiling moldings are sometimes used at the junction of wall and ceiling for architectural effect. They are also used to cover any gaps between the wall and the ceiling. **Fig. 35-29.** If the edge is cut back at the top of the molding, it will partially conceal any unevenness and make painting easier when molding and ceiling are to be different colors.

Ceiling molding is cut and fitted in the same way as described for baseboard. Coped cuts ensure tight joints even if the moisture content of the wood changes slightly. To secure the molding, a finish nail should be driven through it and into the wall plates. For large moldings, a nail should be driven through the molding into each ceiling joist, if possible. It is also a good idea to use a solid wood or plywood backing. **Fig. 35-30.** This is because nailing through molding and into backing is much easier than nailing into framing hidden behind plaster or drywall. When installing certain types of wide moldings, using trimhead screws instead of nails produces a much more secure result.

Crown Molding

Crown molding is a fairly large sprung molding that usually includes both curved and angular surfaces. It calls for special cutting and installation techniques. This is because it is angled away from wall and ceiling surfaces, and its back is not in contact with either of them. The angle at which the molding projects away from the wall is called the **springing angle**. **Fig. 35-31.**

Steps for cutting crown molding are given on page 719.

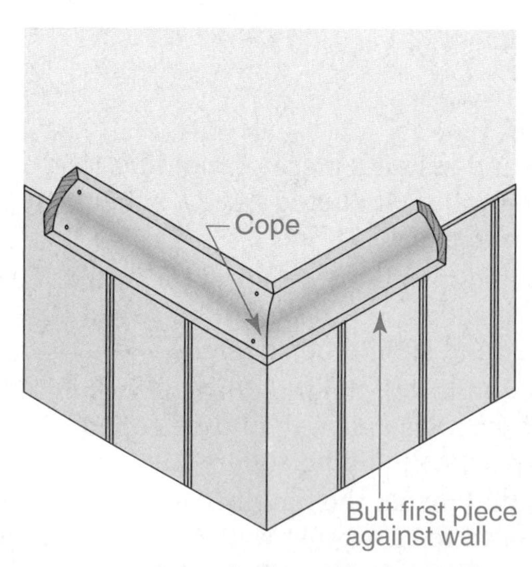

Fig. 35-29. Installation of ceiling molding at an inside corner.

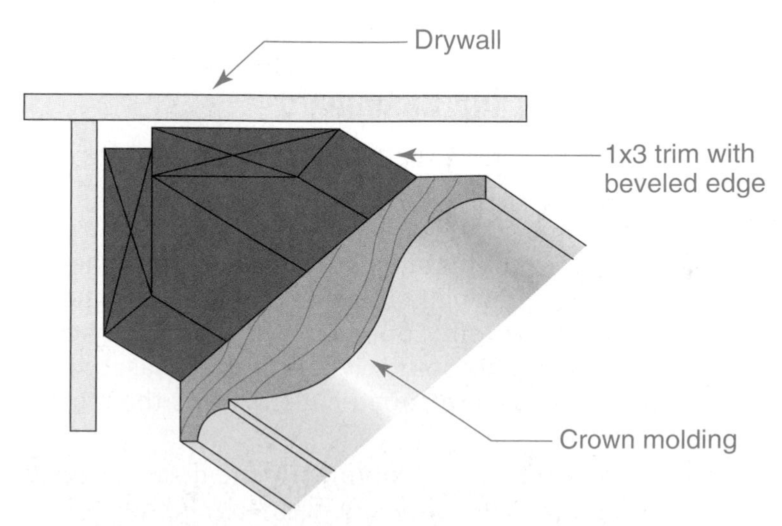

Fig. 35-30. Solid wood or plywood backing should be nailed to the wall framing to support wide moldings.

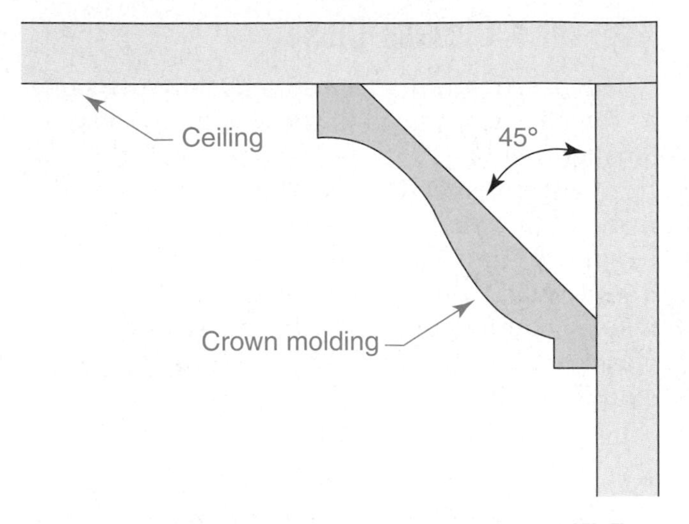

Fig. 35-31. This crown molding has a springing angle of 45°. The exposed face of the crown can be plain or molded.

Fig. 35-32. Coping a piece of crown molding.

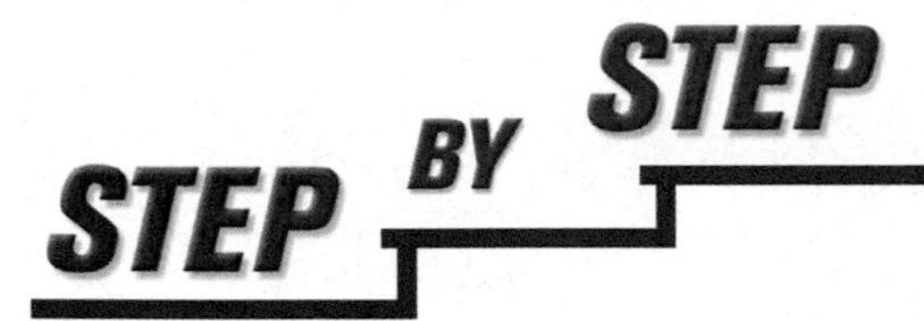

Cutting Crown Molding

Crown molding can be mitered to fit an inside corner. However, such a joint may open up over time and is not recommended. It is better to use a combination of coped and square cuts similar to those used for baseboard. Because of crown molding's shape, a compound-miter cut is required for a coped joint, instead of a simple miter cut. In a compound-miter cut, a miter and a bevel are cut simultaneously.

Make a compound-miter cut on crown molding as follows:

Step 1 The springing angle of the molding determines the correct saw settings. Set a compound-miter saw for the correct miter and bevel angles as shown in **Table 35-B**.

Step 2 Place the molding face up and flat on the saw table.

Step 3 After the molding is in position, make the compound-miter cut.

Step 4 Using the cut edge of the molding as a guide, complete the cut with a coping saw. **Fig. 35-32.**

Step 5 Test the fit against a scrap piece of crown molding. Fine-tune the fit as necessary with a file until it is tight.

Table 35-B. Compound-Miter Saw Settings for Crown Molding*

Type of crown molding	Miter angle	Bevel (tilt of blade)
Cope on right end (Top edge of crown against saw fence)		
45°	35.3° (right)	30°
38°	31.6° (right)	33.9°
Cope on left end (Bottom edge of crown against saw fence)		
45°	35.3° (left)	30°
38°	31.6° (left)	33.9°

*Crown molding is flat on the saw table.

OTHER MOLDINGS

Moldings are used for many other purposes in a house, such as for chair rails or shelving trim. An almost unlimited range of effects can be obtained.

Chair Rail

Chair rail is a molding that runs horizontally across walls at 3′ to 4′ from the floor. **Fig. 35-33.** It is often found in dining rooms, where it protects walls from damage caused by the backs of chairs. It may also serve as a transition between two different wall finishes. For example, a wall may be painted below the chair rail and wallpapered above. Chair rail can be installed in the same manner as baseboard.

Trim for a Clothes Closet

The baseboard in a closet is usually the same as the baseboard used in the adjoining room. Smaller moldings may be used to cover the front edge of shelving, especially if the shelf is made of plywood. Wood trim might also be used to support the closet shelf and clothes rod. **Fig. 35-34.** Such trim, often a piece of 1x3 stock, may be continued around the inside of the closet to provide a solid base for attaching clothes hooks.

Install closet trim as follows:

1. Cut the pieces of the hook strip to fit the closet. As you nail the hook strip into place, use a level to ensure correct position. Finish nails should be driven into the studs, not just into the drywall.

Fig. 35-33. Note the chair rail on the wall to the right of the opening.

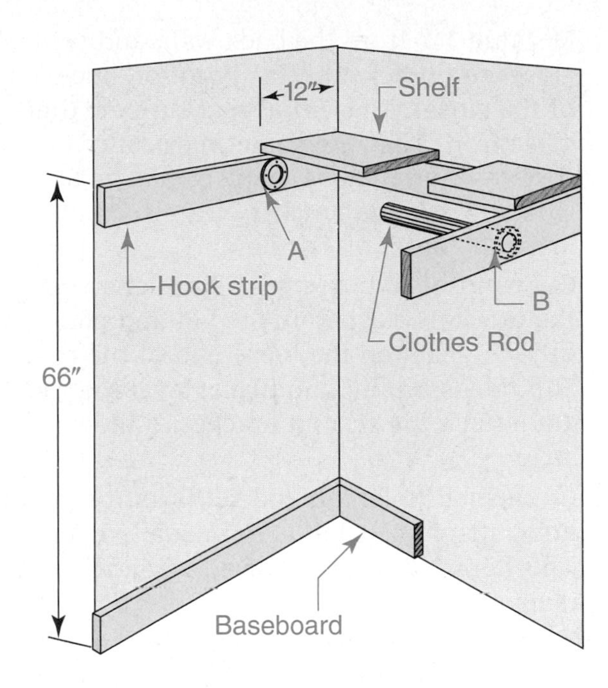

Fig. 35-34. Installation details for trimming a clothes closet. *A* and *B* are brackets.

Estimating...

Molding and Trim

Molding and trim are generally estimated by the lineal foot. However, they may sometimes be estimated based on board-foot calculations if large quantities are required.

The time needed to install molding depends on several factors. Following are some of the more important ones:

- Top-grade molding takes more time to install than paint-grade molding because joints must be fitted with great care. Molding that is applied low on the wall is easier to install than the same molding installed high on the wall, especially at heights greater than 8′.
- Installing wide crown molding takes more time than installing narrow crown molding. Narrow crown molding can often be nailed directly to the wall, but wide molding requires backing.
- Hardwood moldings are more difficult to install than softwood moldings because nail holes often must be pre-drilled.
- The style of trim also has a bearing on the installation time. For example, installing door and window casing with miter joints is more time consuming than installing trim that is butt jointed.

Trim carpenters sometimes base their rates on a per-lineal-foot figure. They may also charge on a per-window, per-door, and per-room basis.

In any case, measurements can be developed by studying the building plans. For example, a trim carpenter could review the floor plans to get a lineal-foot measurement for baseboard and ceiling molding. The carpenter could also check the interior elevation drawings or the window schedule to determine the lineal feet required for windows. Then he or she could review the finish schedule to find out exactly what types of woods and finishes have been specified.

ESTIMATING ON THE JOB

A living room has the following features: It measures 14′ x 15½′, has one 36″ wide door and two 32″ wide by 54″ tall windows. How many lineal feet of baseboard and crown molding will be required? Add 10% to your figure to account for waste, and round the answer up to the nearest even number.

2. Measure 12″ from the back wall, and center a closet rod bracket at this point on one side of the closet. These brackets support the closet rod. They are sometimes called rosettes, and may be made of plastic or wood. Screw one bracket into place but leave the other off for now.
3. Cut a closet rod to length. Place one end in the bracket attached in Step 2, and place the other bracket on the loose end of the rod. Slip the assembly into place, level the rod, and attach the second bracket to the hook strip.
4. Cut a shelf to length and set it on top of the hook strip. The shelf is not usually nailed. This allows it to be removed when the closet is painted.

If a closet is not needed for clothes, it can be put to other uses by adding shelving and table space, such as for a small home office. The doors can be closed when necessary to conceal office clutter.

SECTION 35.3 Check Your Knowledge

1. How should base shoe molding be nailed?
2. What two methods can be used to ensure that a mitered joint will not open up?
3. When should baseboard be scribed to a wall?
4. What is crown molding?

On the Job

Look for molding accents in your home or apartment. List at least four ways that molding is used there. In your inventory of moldings, try to identify the moldings by type, as shown in Fig. 35-2.

Chapter 35 Review

Section Summaries

35.1 Molding and trim are used both as decoration and for practical purposes, such as to protect walls. They are available in many patterns and shapes. Most are made of solid wood, but some are made from short pieces joined together or from synthetic materials. Cost varies depending on style and type of wood.

35.2 Casing refers to all the trim around doors or windows. Square cuts and miter cuts are commonly used for joints. Window trim may consist of the casing alone or of the casing plus a stool and apron. Shutters may also be added.

35.3 Baseboard moldings may consist of a base, a small cap, and a shoe. Walls that are not plumb may make scribing a joint necessary in order to achieve a tight fit. Joints are coped when one member is trimmed to fit against the face of another. Cutting a return is done to create a finished look when one member is thicker than another. Molding may also be placed along the ceiling, used for a chair rail, or used to trim a closet.

Review Questions

1. Define the terms *trim* and *molding.*
2. Name at least two uses for molding and trim other than decoration.
3. Identify *casing, stool,* and *apron.*
4. What are the three most common joints used when installing baseboard, and where are they placed?
5. If wall-to-wall carpeting is installed in a room, at what point should the baseboard be installed? What step must be taken to accommodate the carpeting?
6. If a wall is too long for a single length of baseboard to be used, how should the baseboard be installed?
7. Describe the process for cutting an outside miter in a length of baseboard.
8. How is scribing done on baseboard?
9. What is the springing angle, and to what type of molding does it refer?
10. Explain how to cope a joint in molding.

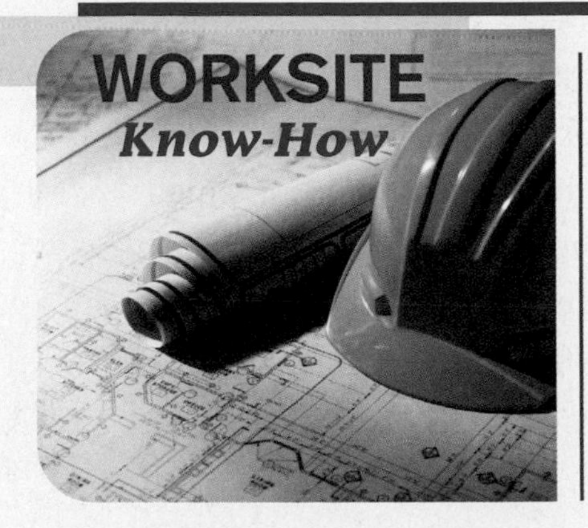

Planning for Molding and Trim Installation of molding and trim is one of the last steps in construction, but planning needs to start early. Orders for materials should be placed at least 6 to 8 weeks in advance. Everyone on the building team (the contractor, finish carpenters, etc.) should have drawings and specifications at the earliest possible stage. Any changes need to be communicated because they will affect the final installation as well as the budget.

Chapter 36

Cabinets and Countertops

Objectives

After reading this chapter, you'll be able to:

- Identify the five basic kitchen layouts.
- Explain the difference between frameless and face-frame cabinet construction.
- Explain how to install a base cabinet.
- Explain how to install a wall cabinet.
- Apply plastic laminate to a countertop surface.

Terms

carcase
face-frame cabinet
frameless cabinet
lower cabinets
soffit
substrate
universal design
upper cabinets
work triangle

Cabinets make a house more livable by providing storage as well as support for work surfaces. The kitchen usually contains more cabinetry than any other room. However, cabinets (sometimes called *casework*) are found also in bathrooms, laundry rooms, and family/recreation rooms.

Cabinetry is installed just before interior trim, or sometimes at the same time. This is usually after the finish floor is in place. In the past, most cabinets were built on site by finish carpenters. This is rarely done today. Instead, most cabinets are either custom built in small cabinet shops or mass produced by regional or national manufacturers. Cabinets are expensive, so kitchen and bath designs should make efficient use of them.

SECTION 36.1

Planning the Kitchen and Bathroom

The basic arrangement of cabinets in any room is shown on the building plans (see Chapter 3, "Reading and Drawing Plans"). In many cases, these plans provide only general information about the cabinets, appliances, and related plumbing. The choice of specific cabinets is then made at a later date by the builder or the client. A professional kitchen or bathroom designer might review the plans at this stage and make recommendations. The designer usually develops computer-generated renderings showing exactly how the kitchen would look with a particular style or brand of cabinetry. **Fig. 36-1.** Many home centers and cabinet suppliers can also do this. Once the layout has been agreed upon, the cabinets can be ordered.

Manufacturer's catalogs give stock numbers and dimensions. **Fig. 36-2.** A floorplan of the room will include these stock numbers and the exact location of upper and lower cabinets. These floor plan drawings showing cabinet details are often done at a scale of ½″ = 1′-0″. **Fig. 36-3.** **Upper cabinets**, also called *wall cabinets*, hang on a wall. **Lower cabinets**, often called *base cabinets*, rest on the floor and support the countertops.

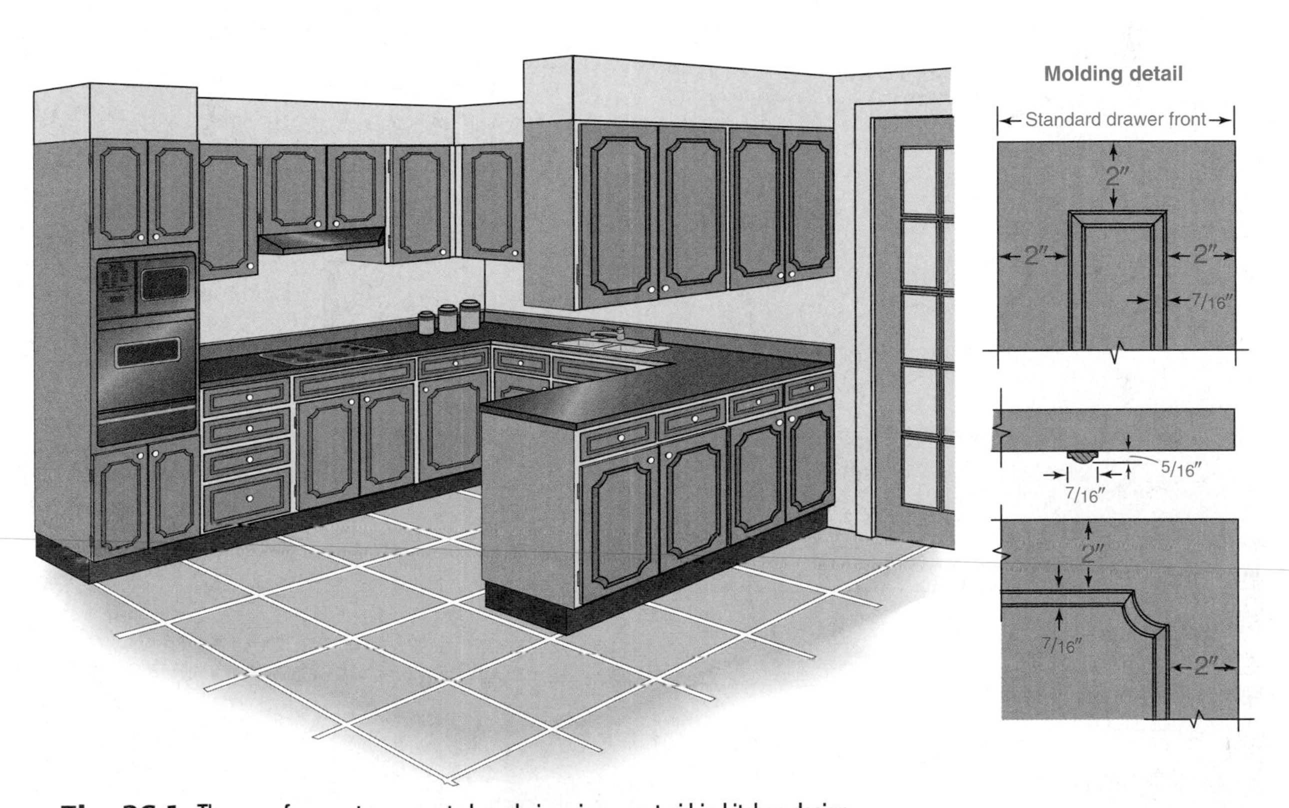

Fig. 36-1. The use of computer-generated renderings is a great aid in kitchen design.

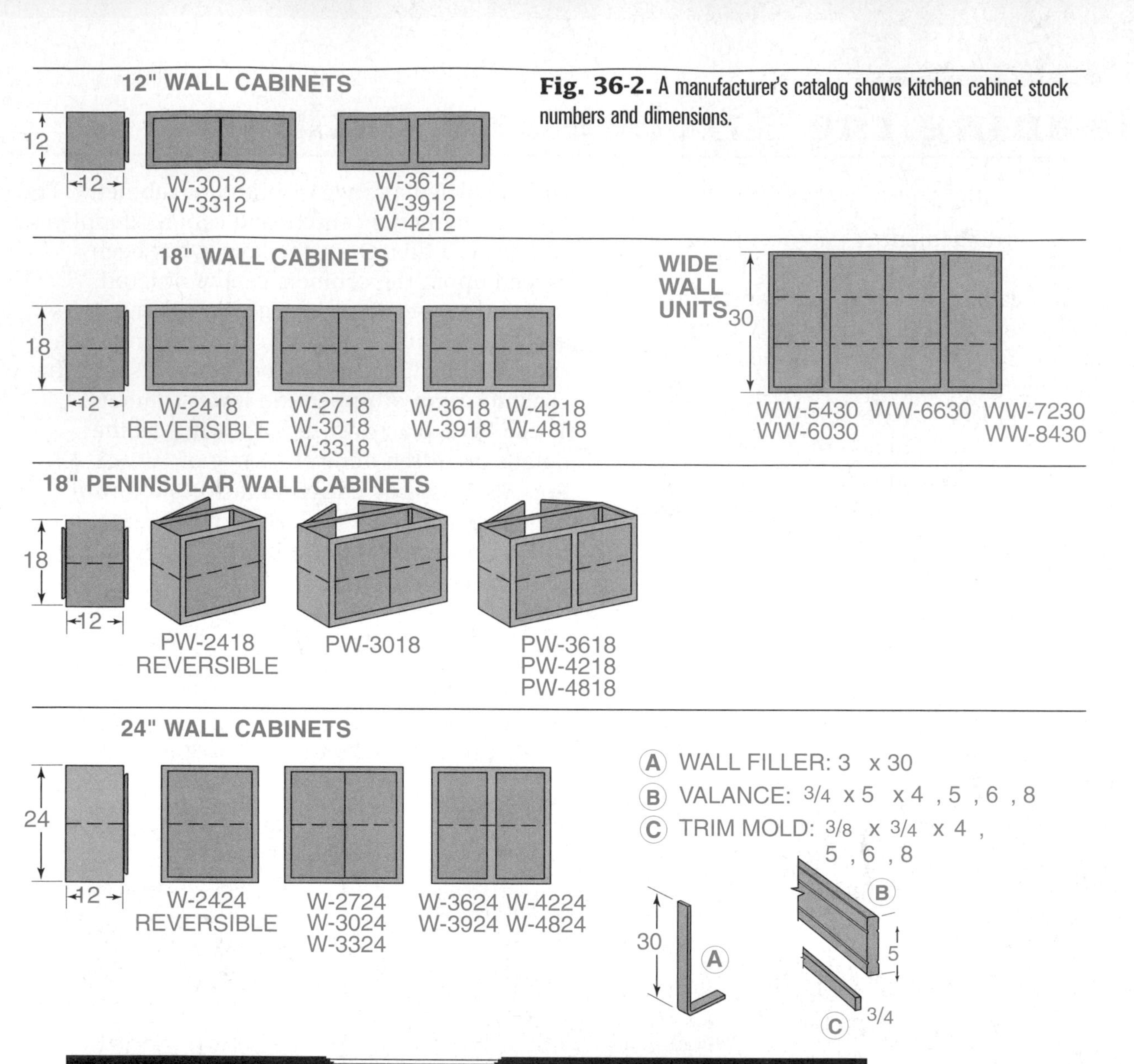

Fig. 36-2. A manufacturer's catalog shows kitchen cabinet stock numbers and dimensions.

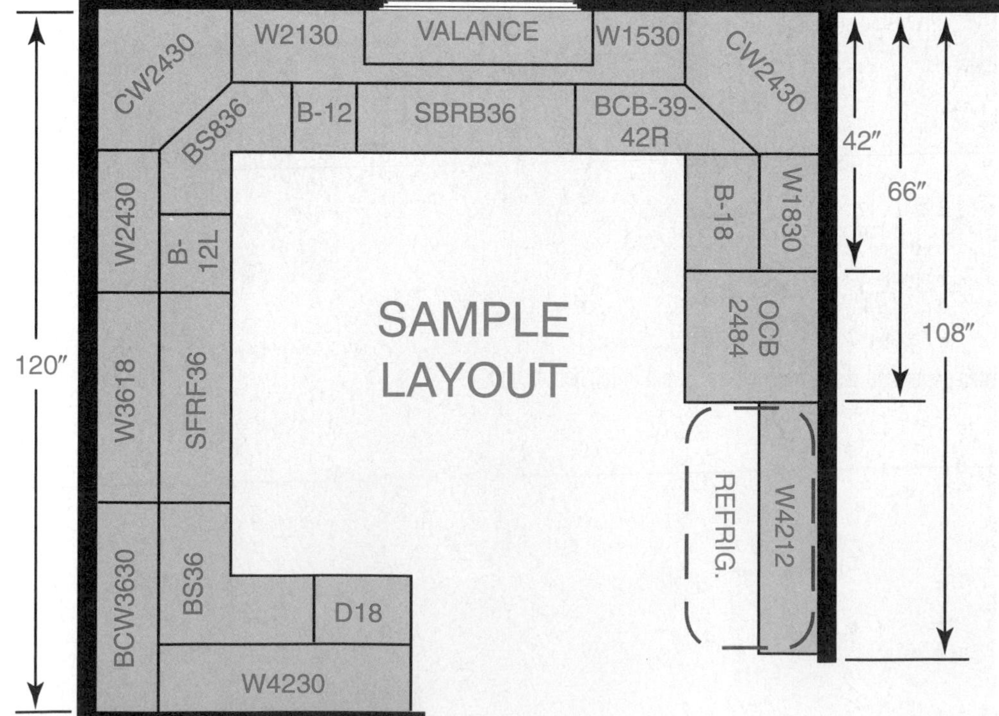

Fig. 36-3. The cabinets for this kitchen layout are identified by the manufacturer's stock numbers.

KITCHENS

Kitchen design concepts have changed a great deal over the years. At one time, the kitchen was set apart from all the other rooms. Today's kitchen is often combined with the family room to create a center for everyday living or informal entertaining. Kitchens are more beautiful, functional, and efficient than ever before.

Increasingly, kitchen designers are using the concept of universal design. **Universal design** is aimed at making a house usable and safe for the widest variety of people, including older adults and those with disabilities. Research indicates that by the year 2020, more than 20 percent of the population in the United States will be 65 years of age or older. A properly designed kitchen increases the ability of older adults to live independently. **Fig. 36-4.**

Kitchen Layouts

Five basic layouts are commonly used in kitchen design (**Fig. 36-5**):

- *U shape.* The U-shaped kitchen, with the sink at the bottom of the U and the range and refrigerator on opposite sides, is very efficient.

Fig. 36-4. Well-designed countertops at varying heights make it easier for people of different abilities to use a kitchen. The Americans with Disabilities Act (ADA) offers standards for accessible design. It is important to comply with these standards.

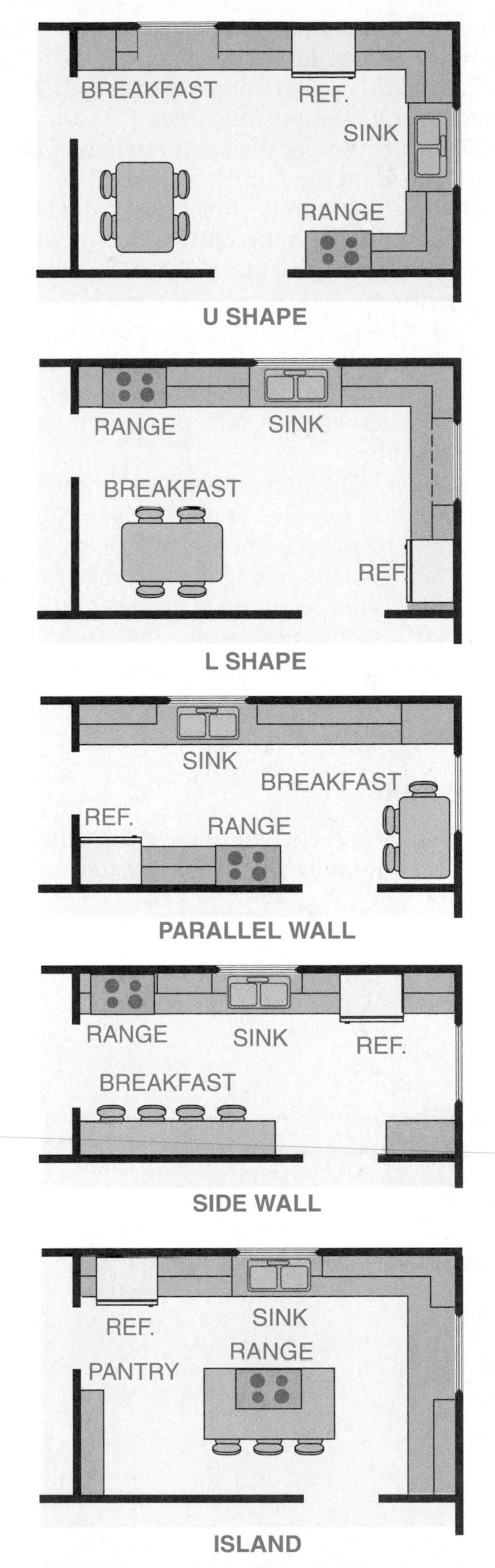

Fig. 36-5. Five of the most popular kitchen layouts.

- *L shape.* The L-shaped kitchen locates the sink and range on one leg of the L and the refrigerator on the other. Sometimes the dining space is located in the opposite corner.
- *Parallel wall.* The parallel-wall kitchen is often found where there is limited space. The parallel-wall kitchen is sometimes called a galley kitchen. It can be quite efficient with the proper arrangement of sink, range, and refrigerator.
- *Side wall.* The side-wall kitchen is usually preferred for small apartments. The cabinets, sink, range, and refrigerator are all located on one wall. When kitchens are small, counter space is limited.
- *Island.* The island kitchen features a cabinet "island" that is separate from the main cabinet runs in the rest of the room. A range is usually placed in the island, along with storage for pans. This layout sometimes makes it difficult to provide a ventilating fan for the range. To solve this problem, some ranges have built-in downdraft fans that exhaust air outdoors through ducts in the floor.

Work Centers

When planning a kitchen, three work centers must be kept in mind. **Fig. 36-6.** These work centers are:

- Food preparation center. This should be planned around the refrigerator and food storage area.
- Cooking center. This should be planned around the primary cooking surface.
- Cleanup center. Ideally, the cleanup center (sink and dishwasher) should be located between the food preparation center and the cooking center.

All equipment, storage space, and surface work areas for each activity should be located in the respective work centers. When upper cabinets are included, a small work center might look as arranged in **Fig. 36-7**. Whenever possible, counter space should be continuous between work centers.

Designers try to arrange the work centers in a way that allows a meal to be prepared efficiently. A **work triangle** represents the shortest walking distance between the refrigerator, the primary cooking surface, and the sink. **Fig. 36-8.** The three sides of the triangle should add up to no more than 26′. A triangle with 15′ to 22′ is desirable, with 12′ being the absolute minimum. No leg of the triangle should be shorter than 4′ or longer than 9′. The work triangle is a measure of a kitchen's efficiency.

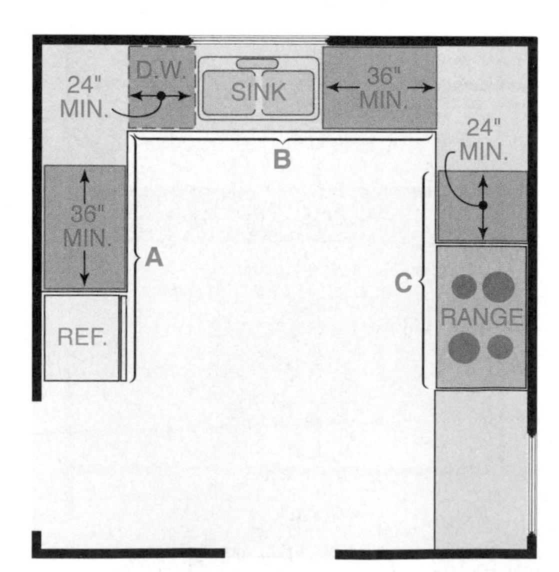

Fig. 36-6. The three basic work centers: *A.* Food preparation. *B.* Cleanup. *C.* Cooking. The minimum counter space needed for each area is shown.

Fig. 36-7. The cleanup center includes the dishwasher and the sink. It should provide a total of at least 60″ of counter space.

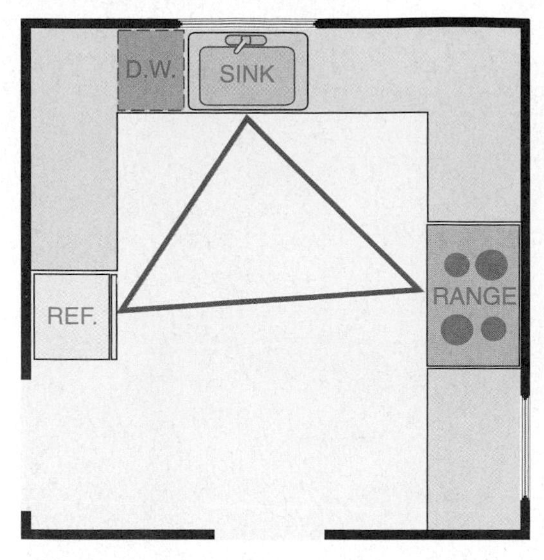

Fig. 36-8. In a work triangle, the sink or a major appliance is the focal point of each work center. The three sides of the triangle should add up to no more than 26′.

Table 36-A. Cabinet Storage Guidelines	Small Kitchen (under 150 s.f.)	Large Kitchen (over 150 s.f.)
Base cabinets[a] Lazy-Susan units count as 30″	156″	192″
Wall cabinets[a] Based on cabinets at least 12″ deep and 30″ high	144″	186″

[a] Minimum frontage.

Kitchen Cabinet Dimensions

Ample storage in a kitchen is a necessity. Though the amount of cabinet space often relates to the size of the home, some basic guidelines are available, as shown in **Table 36-A**.

It is essential to place the cabinets, countertops, and shelves at heights designed for efficiency, convenience, and comfort. Base and wall cabinets are usually installed at standard heights and depths. Clearances for wall cabinets over appliances and work centers are also standard. **Fig. 36-9.**

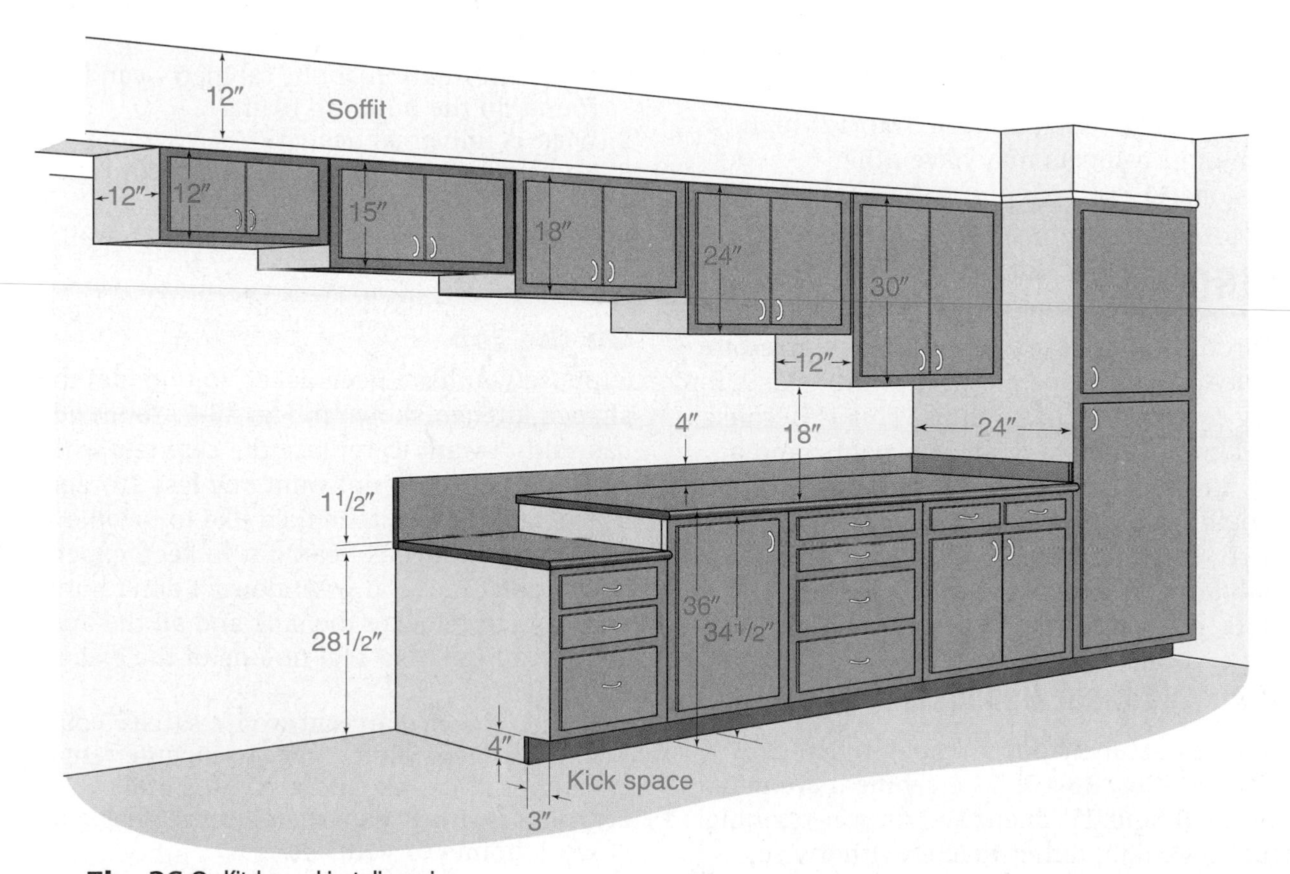

Fig. 36-9. Kitchen cabinet dimensions.

Fig. 36-10. An example of manufactured bathroom cabinets.

Wall cabinets vary in height. Depending on the type of installation, they may be from 12″ to 42″ high. Wall cabinets are usually 12″ deep and are often located beneath a soffit. A **soffit** is an area around the perimeter of a room that is lower than the rest of the ceiling. Kitchen soffits are usually 12″ below the rest of the ceiling. They may be 14″ to 28″ deep.

Base cabinets are typically 34½″ high, not including the countertop. They are usually 24″ deep. Drawer openings are 5″ to 12″ high. Custom-built cabinets may have other dimensions.

BATHROOMS

Bathroom cabinets are sometimes referred to as *vanity cabinets*. Much less flexibility exists for placing cabinetry in bathrooms. This is because the location of plumbing, drains, vents, and a tub or shower determines the cabinet layout. Also, bathrooms are much smaller than kitchens, and the need for storage is much less. Though large bathrooms may include upper cabinets, most feature only lower cabinets.

Bathroom Cabinet Dimensions

Bathroom cabinets differ from kitchen cabinets in size. **Fig. 36-10.** Base cabinets are usually 30″ high and 21″ deep. The drawer opening is usually 4″ high, rather than 5″. Otherwise, bathroom cabinets are built and installed in the same fashion as kitchen cabinets.

SECTION 36-1 Check Your Knowledge

1. What information about cabinetry can be found on the building plans?
2. What is universal design?
3. Name and describe the five basic kitchen layouts.
4. What is the usual depth of a kitchen wall cabinet?

On the Job

Suppose you have been asked to remodel the U-shaped kitchen shown in Fig. 36-5. Your client has said, "I want to replace the cabinets with new ones, but I do not want any less storage space in my new kitchen. I'd like to be able to see out a window as I eat, but to keep expenses down, don't move any windows. I don't mind if you have to relocate the sink and all the appliances. You can also seal up one of the existing doorways."

1. Sketch a floorplan that would satisfy your client's needs. Remember to include range, refrigerator, sink, and breakfast table.
2. Discuss with a team member the strong and weak points of your plan.

SECTION 36.2

Cabinets

Manufactured cabinets may be stock cabinets, semi-custom cabinets, or custom cabinets. The terms indicate how much input a client has in the final size and design of the cabinet.

Stock cabinets are built in standard sizes and stored in a warehouse until ordered. They are the least expensive type. The buyer has few choices regarding finishes and styles. He or she simply chooses the cabinets from a catalog. Stock cabinets are available in width increments of 3″. Because they are built ahead of time, they can be obtained fairly quickly.

Semi-custom cabinets are built only when they are ordered for a specific kitchen. A buyer has more choices about style, finish, and hardware. Also, the buyer may work with a designer instead of picking cabinets from a catalog. Semi-custom cabinets are generally available only in width increments of 3″.

Custom cabinets are usually the most expensive type of manufactured cabinet and usually take the longest to arrive. They can be built in any width to fit a kitchen exactly. Almost any size, style, finish, or hardware is possible. In this respect, manufactured custom cabinets are much like those made by local cabinetmakers.

ANATOMY OF A CABINET

The **carcase** is an assembly of panels that forms a cabinet's basic shape. It is often made of plywood. It may also be made of particleboard or medium-density fiberboard (MDF) covered with wood veneer or plastic laminate. The carcase is assembled with nails, staples, glue, or a combination of these. It is sometimes reinforced with wood corner blocks or stretchers.

The two basic types of cabinet construction are frameless (European-style) and face-frame (traditional). **Fig. 36-11.** Both types can be built from a variety of materials, using various types of joinery. Both types can be built on site or in a factory as stock, semi-custom, or custom cabinets.

A variation of frameless cabinet construction is sometimes referred to as the 32-mm system. The number refers to a modular dimension used to locate the position of various cabinet features, including shelves and hinges. All cabinets based on the 32-mm system are frameless, but not all frameless cabinets use the 32-mm module.

A

B

Fig. 36-11. Types of cabinetry. *A.* European-style (frameless) cabinetry does not require the use of a face frame. *B.* Face-frame cabinets are more common in the United States.

The face-frame cabinet is the traditional type used in the United States. In the **face-frame cabinet** the face frame fits around the front carcase opening and provides a mounting surface for hinges and drawer hardware. **Fig. 36-12.** A face frame is usually made of ¾″ thick hardwood. The joints of a face frame may be reinforced with dowels, biscuits, or screws.

A **frameless cabinet** has no framing around the opening. Hinges are concealed and mounted on the side walls. This requires a special type of hinge. **Fig. 36-13.**

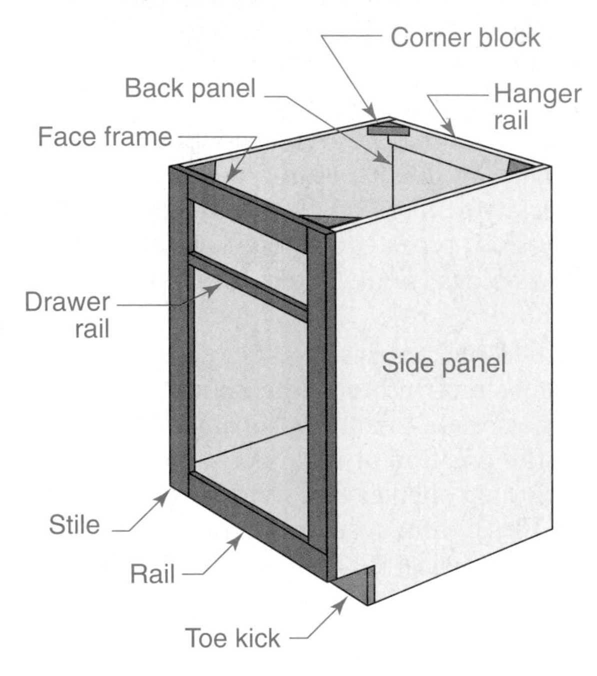

Fig. 36-12. The carcase of a face-frame cabinet.

The drawers of either type of cabinet can be assembled from plywood, particleboard, MDF, or a hardwood such as beech. The bottom panel of a drawer fits into a groove cut into the drawer sides, front, and back. Joinery details for drawers are shown in **Fig. 36-14**. The material and the methods used to assemble a drawer have a great impact on its strength and durability. The drawer front is sometimes a different type of wood than the body of the drawer.

Doors are the most visible part of a cabinet. They can be made of solid wood, plywood, MDF, or particleboard. The type, style, and finish of the doors affect the cabinet's appearance. There are two basic types of doors:

- *Inset doors*, or *flush doors*, fit entirely within the door opening. A small gap is required between the door and the face frame to provide clearance. **Fig. 36-15.**
- *Overlay doors* fit over the edge of the carcase or face frame. Overlay doors may be constructed in several ways, as shown in **Fig. 36-16**.

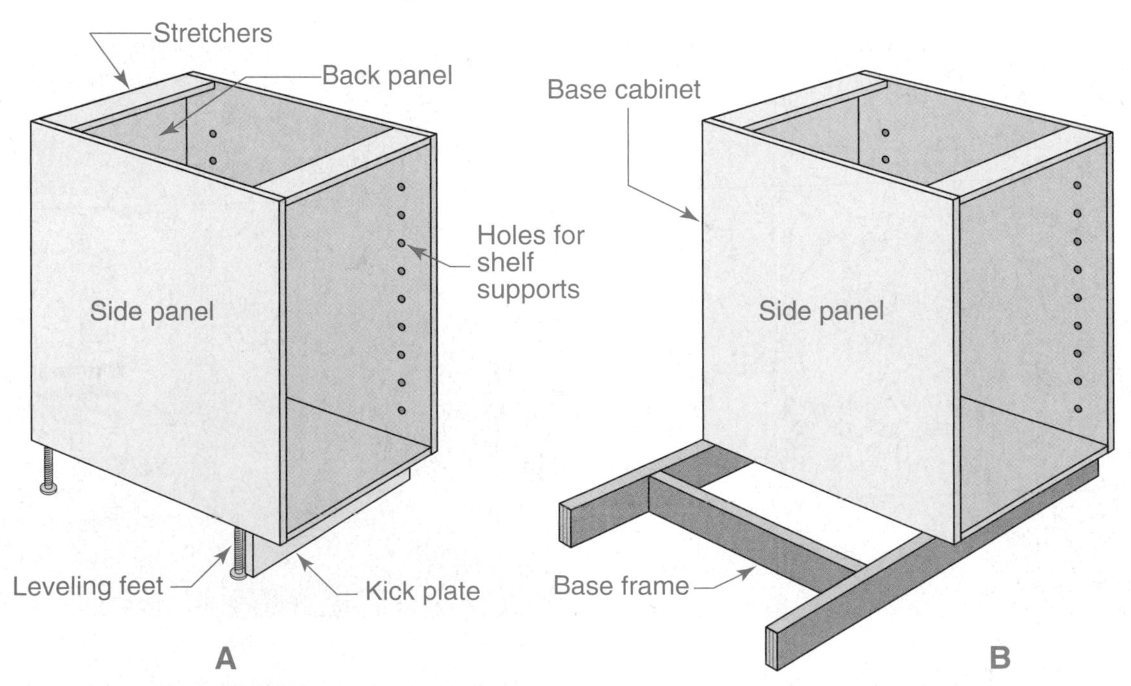

Fig. 36-13. Frameless cabinets. *A.* The base unit of a frameless cabinet. *B.* Frameless cabinets may rest on a base frame instead of leveling legs. The frame is often made of plywood.

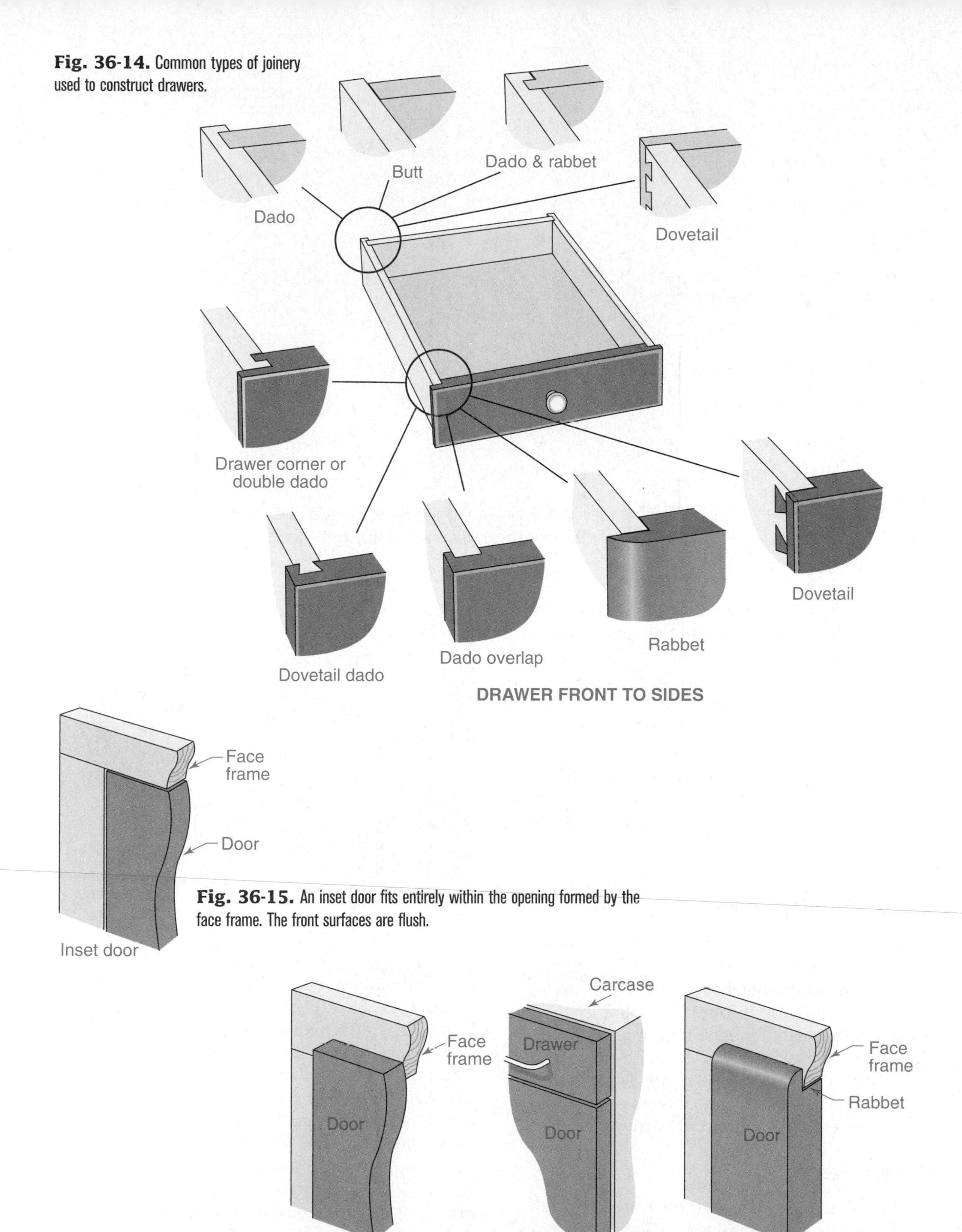

Fig. 36-14. Common types of joinery used to construct drawers.

Fig. 36-15. An inset door fits entirely within the opening formed by the face frame. The front surfaces are flush.

Fig. 36-16. The various types of overlay doors overlap the face frame or the carcase.

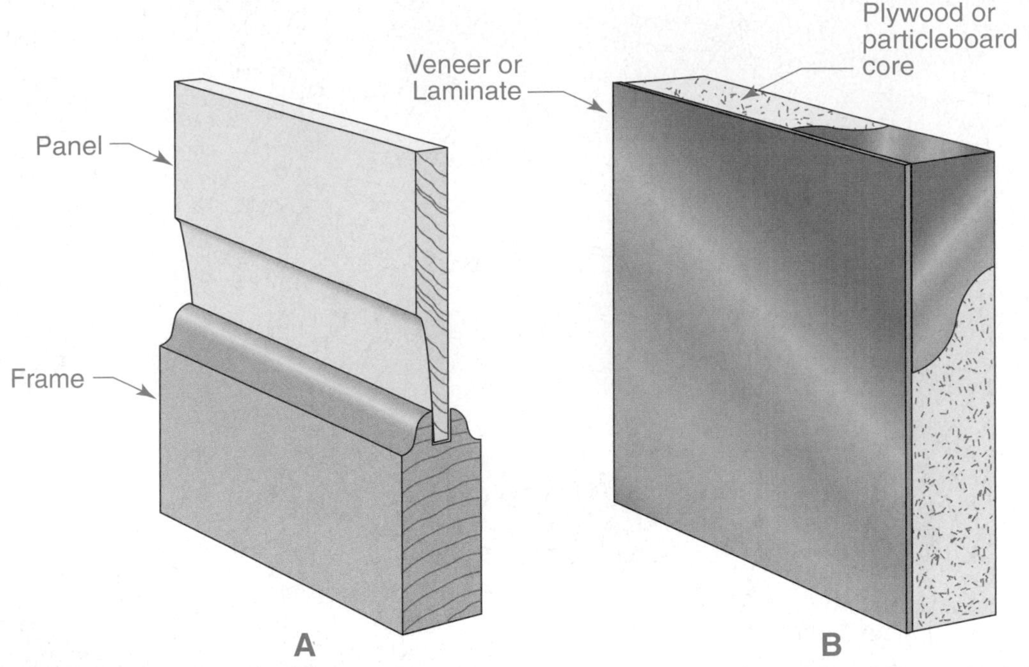

Fig. 36-17. Details of panel door construction. *A.* A raised-panel door is built from solid wood. The panel is held in place by the frame. *B.* A flat-panel door is often covered on all sides and edges with plastic laminate.

Doors may have flat or raised panels. **Fig. 36-17.** Both types can be used for inset doors or overlay doors. Both can be used on face-frame or frameless cabinets. Raised-panel doors have a more custom look, but the added labor and material increase the price. Flat-panel doors are economical and easy to keep clean.

Most cabinets may be made more useful with the addition of accessories. These include spice racks, drawer organizers, and slide-out storage trays.

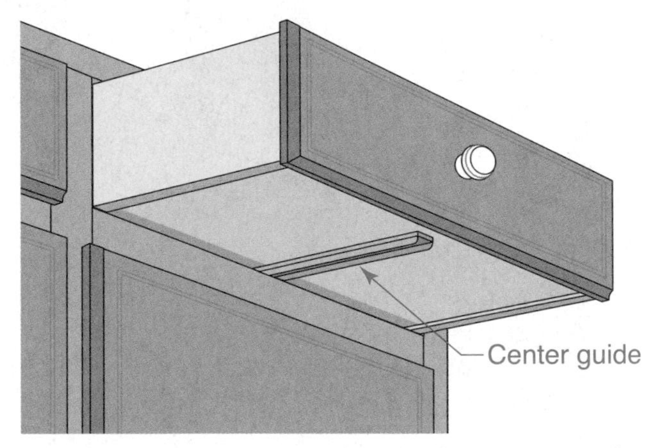

Fig. 36-18. A center-mounted drawer guide requires support by a face frame.

CABINET HARDWARE

To perform well over a long period of time, any cabinet must be fitted with quality hardware. Good door hinges and drawer guides are particularly important, but quality and cost vary widely. Some manufacturers offer several different grades of hardware for use with their cabinets. Others offer only one grade of hardware with each grade of cabinet. Makers of custom-built cabinets offer unlimited hardware choices.

Drawer Guides

Drawers may be mounted on one or two guides, which are sometimes called *slides.* A single, center-mounted guide is located beneath the drawer along its centerline. **Fig. 36-18.** It can be used only on cabinetry that has a face frame because the front of the guide needs support. It is generally attached to the inner surface of the face frame. To keep the drawer from tipping to either side, small rollers or plastic guides are attached to the face frame on the sides of the drawer opening. In manufactured cabinetry the center guide is usually made of metal.

Side-mounted guides are stronger than center guides because they support both sides of the drawer. They can be used on either face-frame or frameless cabinets. **Fig. 36-19.** Full-extension guides are the most useful because they allow the drawer to be pulled all the way out for full

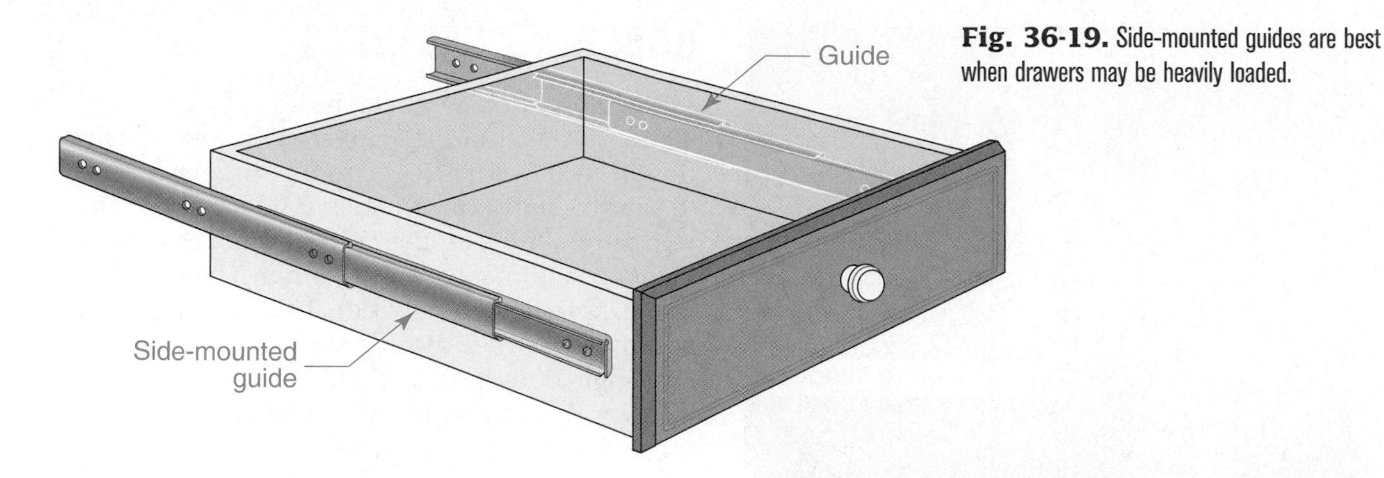

Fig. 36-19. Side-mounted guides are best when drawers may be heavily loaded.

access to the back. However, three-quarter extension slides are more common. The sliding mechanism may feature nylon wheels or ball bearings.

Door Hinges

Door hinges come in a variety of styles and designs. The three basic types include barrel hinges, knife hinges, and cup hinges.

Barrel hinges are a very common type of hinge used on cabinetry in the United States. The hinge consists of two plates connected with a pin. One plate is screwed to the face frame and the other is screwed to the cabinet door. Some plates are L shaped and wrap around the edge of the face frame. Barrel hinges are visible on the outside of the cabinet. They come in many styles and finishes. **Fig. 36-20.**

Knife hinges also have two plates. They are connected with a simple spring mechanism. **Fig. 36-21.** When the cabinet door is closed, the knife hinge holds the door against the face frame without needing a separate latch. One plate is screwed to the face frame, while the other is screwed into a small slot cut into the door.

Cup hinges, which are sometimes called *concealed hinges* or *European-style hinges*, were devised for use on frameless cabinetry. They have a mounting flange and a metal cup connected by a pivoting mechanism. **Fig. 36-22.** The cup is inserted into a 35-mm diameter hole bored into the door. The mounting flange is screwed to the inside wall of the cabinet. There is no need for a face frame. Cup hinges have several advantages. They can be adjusted in several planes (up/down, side-to-side, in/out) simply by turning one or more screws on the hinge.

A

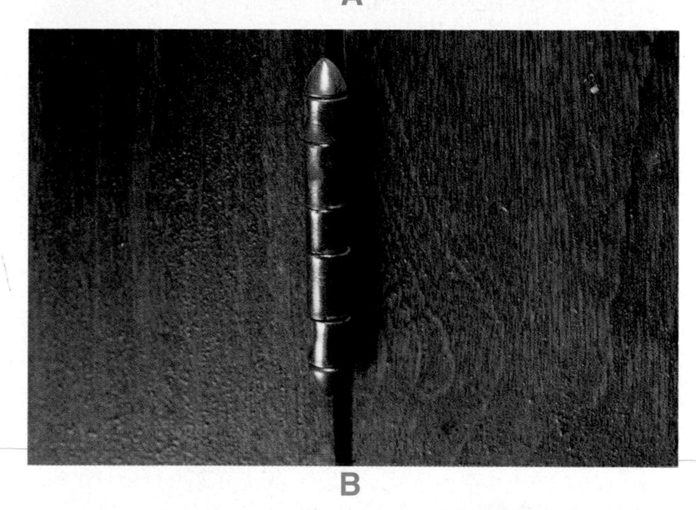

B

Fig. 36-20. Barrel hinges. *A.* The large plate of this barrel hinge wraps around the cabinet face frame. *B.* Barrel hinges are visible on the outside of the cabinet.

Fig. 36-21. A knife hinge is unobtrusive.

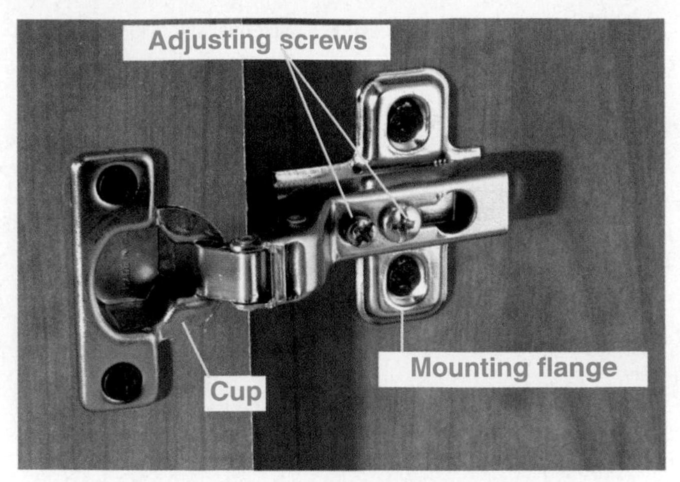

Fig. 36-22. A cup hinge. Some models have a cap that covers the hinge-adjusting screws. The hinge is not visible on the outside of the cabinet.

They are quite strong and can be installed quickly. Large doors might require three or more hinges. A cup hinge is not visible on the outside of the cabinet (see Fig. 36-11A).

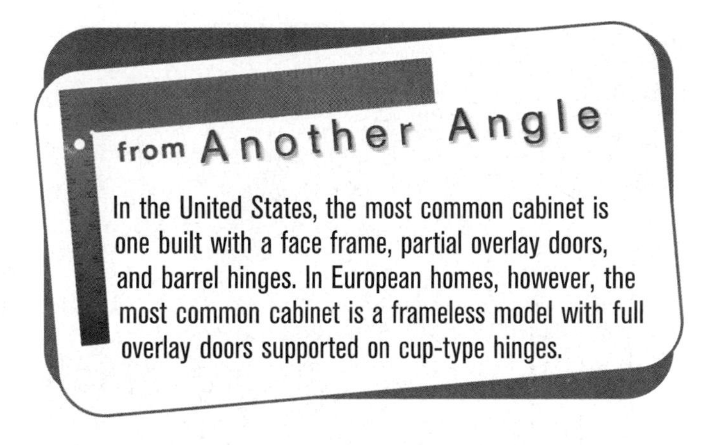

In the United States, the most common cabinet is one built with a face frame, partial overlay doors, and barrel hinges. In European homes, however, the most common cabinet is a frameless model with full overlay doors supported on cup-type hinges.

Knobs and Pulls

Knobs and pulls for drawers and doors are sometimes installed by the cabinet manufacturer. However, it is common for this hardware to be added after the cabinets are installed. This allows the client to have the greatest choice of style, color, and material.

Knobs and pulls are held in place by one or two bolts inserted through the back of the drawer front or door. The installer must carefully measure for the location of mounting holes. The holes for pulls may be 3″, 3½″, or 4″ OC.

ORDERING CABINETS

When ordering cabinets, be sure to use the correct product number listed with each illustration in the catalog. Most product numbers refer to the size and type of cabinet. **Fig. 36-23.** The first letters indicate the cabinet type. For example, *W* would mean a wall cabinet. The first two numbers indicate the width. The second pair of numbers, if any, indicates the cabinet height. For single-door base cabinets, always indicate whether the door is to be hinged on the right or the left side. Also, provide the manufacturer with the size of any sink and the opening needed for built-ins such as an oven, dishwasher, and refrigerator. This information can be obtained directly from the plumbing and appliance suppliers. Finally, be sure to include the style of the cabinet, the finish desired, and any accessories.

Depending on the type of cabinet ordered, it can take as little as one week to receive stock cabinets or as much as several months to receive custom cabinets. This is important information to consider when scheduling the construction of a house.

INSTALLING CABINETS

Factory-built cabinets may be installed in one of two ways. Some cabinetmakers prefer to install the base cabinets first and then the wall cabinets. Others prefer to install the wall cabinets first. This is sometimes more convenient because it allows the installer to stand close to the wall while working, rather than having to reach over or climb onto the base cabinets. With either approach, the end result must be cabinets that are plumb and level.

Base Cabinets

After the cabinets have been delivered, unpack them and check their dimensions against the plans and the original order. Store

Check Local Codes

When installing cabinets in earthquake zones, be sure to check local codes regarding the type and size of fastener.

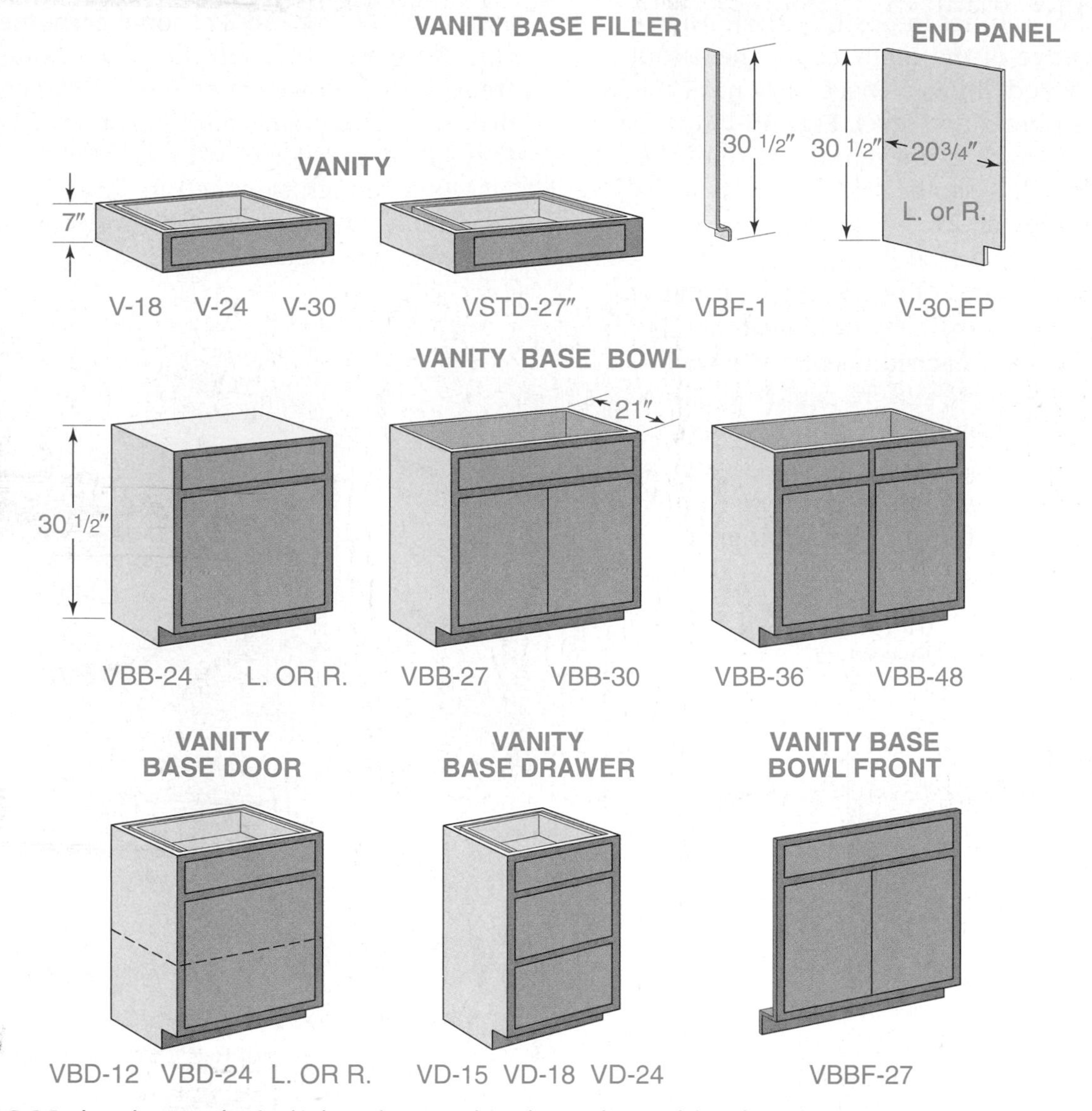

Fig. 36-23. A catalog page showing kitchen cabinets, stock numbers, and some of the cabinet dimensions available.

the cabinets near the room where they will be installed. Then begin thc layout.

1. Use a straightedge and a laser level, standard level, or water level to locate the highest part of the floor in the area where the cabinets will be placed. This will be the starting point for the layout.
2. Measure up the wall from this high point a distance equal to the height of the base cabinet. **Fig. 36-24.** This is usually 34½″ from the floor (allowing for a 1½″ thick countertop). Draw a mark.
3. Use the level to locate additional layout marks at the same elevation around the perimeter of the installation. Connect the layout marks with a pencil line or chalk line.
4. Locate the position of studs in the area. Mark their centerlines.

Fig. 36-24. Measure upward from the high point of the floor and draw a layout mark.

5. Set a corner cabinet in position first. Align the back edge of the cabinet with the layout line. Use wood shims as necessary until the cabinet is plumb and level. **Fig. 36-25.** If the floor and/or wall is uneven, the base of the cabinet may have to be scribed and material removed. **Fig. 36-26.**
6. Screw the cabinet to the studs with 2½″ or 3″ long wood screws. Run them through the mounting rail at the back of the cabinet. If studs cannot be reached, use hollow-wall anchors instead. Be sure to avoid any electrical wires or plumbing pipes in the wall.
7. Install the next cabinets in the same way. As you install each cabinet, clamp it to the previous cabinet and fasten the two together permanently. **Fig. 36-27.** Some carpenters run two screws through the edge of one face frame into the face frame next to it. They drill and countersink pilot holes first. Then they install slender trim-head screws that are just long enough to penetrate ¾″ into the face frame. Other carpenters prefer to bolt the cases together.

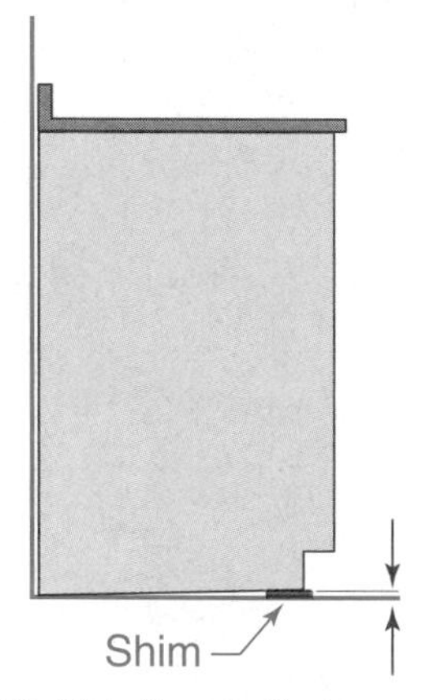

Fig. 36-25. To make the base cabinet set plumb and level, shims can be used as shown. They will be covered later by molding.

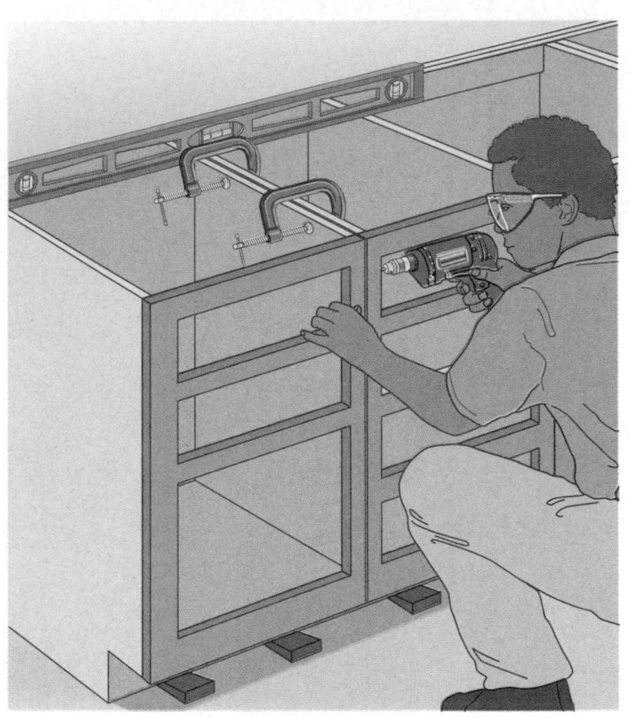

Fig. 36-27. When more than one cabinet is installed, fasten the cabinets together with ¼″ bolts or #10 wood screws.

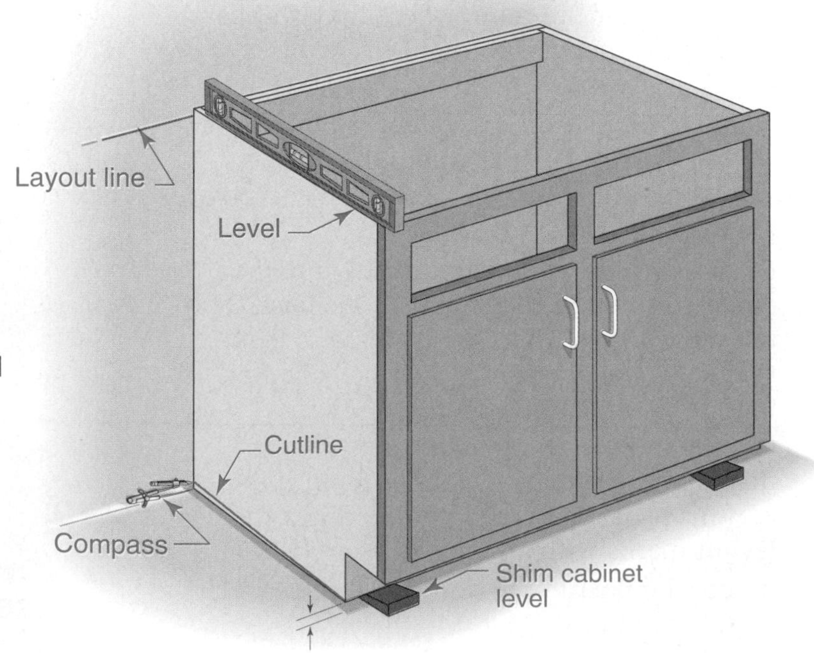

Fig. 36-26. As necessary, add shims to make the cabinet level. Then set the compass to the amount needed to lower the cabinet to the layout line.

8. Where a run of cabinets must fit between walls, it is often necessary to insert a filler strip at one or both ends of the run. The filler strip will close up any gap between the cabinet and the wall. It must have the same color and finish as the cabinets. Scribe the filler strip to fit the gap. To secure the strip, screw it to the side of the last cabinet to be installed.

Custom-built cabinets are often mounted on a separate continuous base. This eliminates joints in the base area. The base may be installed first. The finish flooring is then installed, and then the cabinets. This avoids possible damage to the cabinets during flooring installation.

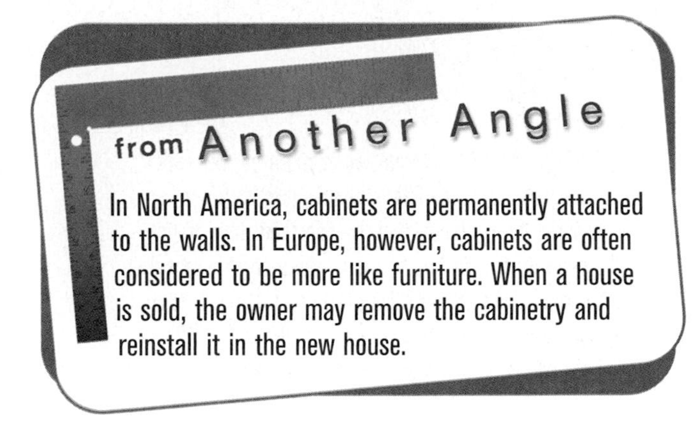

Wall Cabinets

A wall cabinet must be mounted securely so that it can bear heavy loads. It is attached to the wall with wood screws. Use at least #10 roundhead screws that are long enough to go through the ¾″ back rail and the wall covering and extend at least 1″ into the studs. A minimum of four screws should be used for each cabinet. Never rely on nails for hanging wall cabinets or on screws driven only into the wall covering. They will not hold securely. Also, do not use drywall screws, because the weight of the cabinet can cause them to shear off.

1. Measure up from the countertops (or down from the soffit) and draw a mark representing the bottom of the wall cabinet. Extend this line around the area where the wall cabinets will be installed. The most common distance between the countertop and the bottom of an upper cabinet is 18″. Cabinets over range tops require more clearance. Check local codes.
2. Locate the positions of the studs.
3. Determine where the cabinet mounting rails will cross over the centerlines of the studs. Drill through the rails at these points using a drill bit that matches the shank diameter of the mounting screw. The screw should slip through this hole with little resistance.
4. Place a cabinet in position and brace it securely. Make certain the cabinet is tight against the wall and the soffit. If there is no soffit, be sure the tops of the cabinets are level and aligned.
5. Drill pilot holes through the existing mounting rail holes and into the studs. **Fig. 36-28.** Use at least two screws in the upper rail and two in the lower rail. If it is impossible to screw directly into studs, some carpenters install wood blocking in the wall. If the cabinet spans only one stud, use wood screws to fasten it to the stud and 3/16″ by 3½″ toggle bolts to hold it against the wall surface.
6. Uneven walls sometimes make it difficult to obtain proper alignment and get a snug fit. If enough material is available on the back of the cabinet, the cabinet should be held in place, scribed, and cut to fit the irregular wall surface. Otherwise, it should be shimmed. **Fig. 36-29.** Molding can be used to cover any gaps.
7. Screw the cabinet to the wall. As the installation progresses, attach cabinets to each other as in Step 7 under "Base Cabinets." Small cabinets can be screwed together before being lifted into place. **Fig. 36-30.**

Fig. 36-28. Support the cabinet as holes are being drilled or fasteners installed.

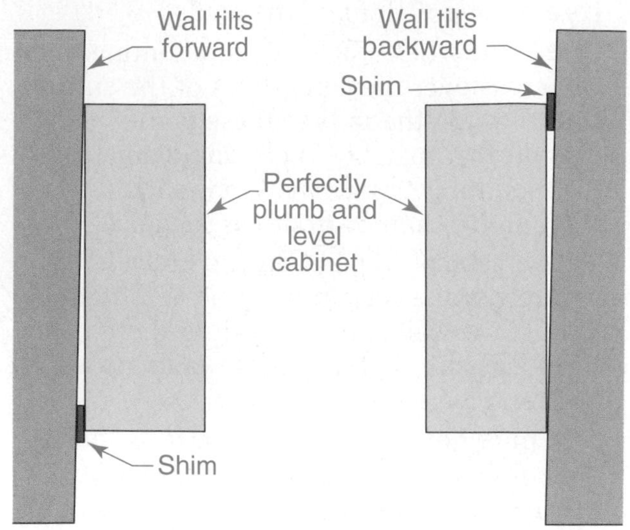

Fig. 36-29. If scribing the cabinet to the wall is not possible, place wood shims behind the wall cabinet so that it can be pulled up tight against the wall in a plumb and level position.

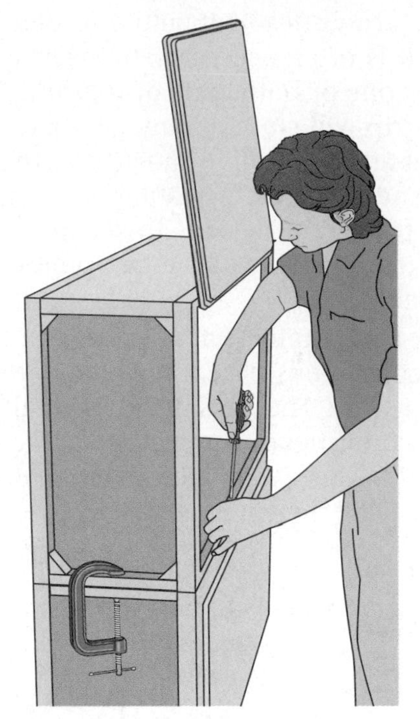

Fig. 36-30. When two or more narrow wall cabinets are placed side by side, it is better to fasten them together on the floor and then mount them on the wall as one unit. Make certain that the joining faces of the stiles are flush and the tops and bottoms of the cabinets are aligned before drilling. (A stile is the vertical portion of the face frame.)

You can use commercial cabinet jacks to support upper cabinets during installation. You can also make a sturdy support stand from plywood. Size the stand to rest on the lower cabinets and support the upper cabinets at a standard height. This will enable you to concentrate on fastening details without also having to hold up the cabinet.

LINEN CLOSETS AND BUILT-IN STORAGE

Built-in storage, such as a linen closet, reduces the amount of furniture needed in a house. Linen closets are usually in hallways near the bedrooms and bathrooms. They may be simply a series of shelves behind a flush or panel door. They might also consist of an open cabinet with doors and drawers built into a corner or wall area.

Shelves should be removable to make it easier to paint the closet. Shelves are typically made of plywood that has an edging of solid wood or of particleboard shelf stock with a rounded front edge. **Fig. 36-31.**

Wood shelves are supported by wood cleats nailed to the wall or by adjustable metal shelf brackets. Some builders use manufactured wire shelving. These shelving sections can be cut to fit using a hacksaw and mounted with special plastic brackets. Open wire shelving aids ventilation.

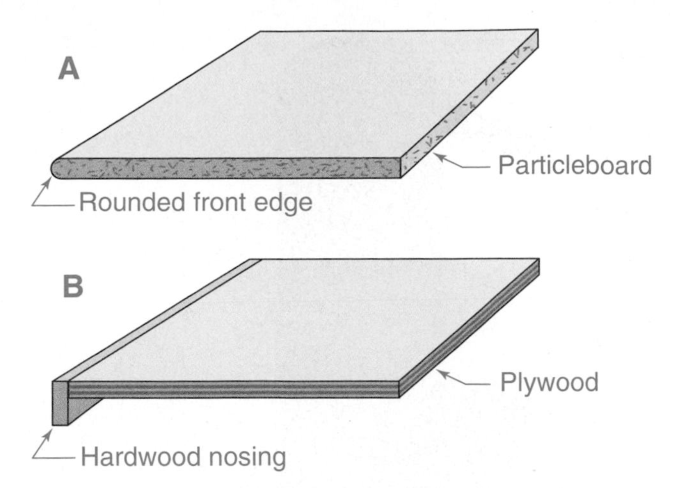

Fig. 36-31. Two types of shelving for closets and built-ins. *A.* Particleboard is inexpensive and ready to paint. *B.* Plywood requires a wood nosing to conceal the plies. This also stiffens the shelf.

SECTION 36.2

Check Your Knowledge

1. List and briefly describe the three types of manufactured cabinets.
2. What type of cabinet would be indicated by the catalog stock number W 2730?
3. Name the two types of drawer guides. Tell their advantages and disadvantages.
4. What are the advantages of cup hinges?

On the Job

Suppose you have decided to replace the porcelain knobs on all your kitchen cabinets with solid brass knobs. Using the Internet, locate three manufacturers of solid-brass kitchen cabinet knobs. Download information about the knobs, or write to the manufacturer to obtain a catalog. Compile this information in a folder.

SECTION 36.3

Countertops

Countertops for cabinets may be covered with plastic laminate, solid surfacing (synthetic materials such as Corian), stone, or ceramic tile. Ceramic tile, stone, stainless steel, and solid surfacing are installed by a contractor specializing in these products. The installation of plastic laminate will be described here. This material is frequently used and does not require specialized contractors.

While the limits for countertop height range from 30″ to 38″, the standard height in a kitchen is 36″. However, a kitchen designed according to universal design principles might contain countertops at several different heights to encourage use by anyone, including someone using a wheelchair.

SAFETY FIRST

Countertop Materials

Fabricating and installing countertop materials often call for extra care. Sanding solid surfacing, for example, generates a very fine dust and small amounts of chemical vapor. Wear the appropriate respiratory protection. When a router is used to trim plastic laminate, small sharp bits of the material are ejected from the tool at high speed. Wear suitable eye protection. Some adhesives used to install ceramic tile are caustic. Wear protective gloves.

PLASTIC LAMINATE COUNTERTOPS

Also called *high-pressure laminate,* plastic laminate is a durable and versatile countertop material. Two common trade names for plastic laminates are Formica and Wilsonart. During manufacture, decorative surface papers soaked with melamine resins are pressed over kraft-paper core sheets soaked with phenolic resin. These papers are then bonded together at pressures of at least 1,000 pounds per square inch (psi) and at temperatures approaching 300°F [149°C]. After bonding, the sheets are trimmed to size. Because its surface papers can be printed before assembly, plastic laminate comes in a large number of colors and patterns.

The backs of the sheets are sanded to improve the bond with the substrate. A **substrate** is a material that serves as a base for another material. A substrate is used because plastic laminate is quite brittle. Common substrate materials are plywood and particleboard at least ¾″ thick with no defects or voids in the surface. In residential construction, the laminate is usually adhered to the substrate with contact cement.

Plastic laminates are sold by the square foot. Sheets are available in widths of 24″, 30″, 36″, 48″, and 60″. The most common width is 24″. The most common lengths range from 5′ to 12′. Most manufacturers provide enough extra material in the stock sizes to allow for trimming.

The following three grades of laminates are used in residential construction:

- *General purpose.* This is approximately 1⁄16″ thick and is used for countertops.
- *Vertical surface.* This is a somewhat thinner product designed for use on surfaces that will receive less wear and impact.
- *Postformed.* This thinnest grade can be used on vertical or horizontal surfaces, but it is usually used on prefabricated countertop sections. It is thin enough to follow curves, as on a bullnose edge.

Cutting Laminate to Size

Plastic laminates may be sawed, routed, and drilled. Because laminate dulls tools more quickly than wood, cutting edges must be sharpened often. Dull tools may chip the laminate. Whenever possible, use carbide-tipped cutting tools. Plastic laminates can also be cut to approximate size with special shears or by scoring with a carbide-tipped scoring tool. Uniform strips can be cut with an accurate tool called a *laminate slitter.* The slitter is often used to cut countertop edging. **Fig. 36-32.**

Fig. 36-32. A laminate slitter.

First measure the area to be covered. Allowing ½″ extra on all edges, score a cutting line deeply on the face of the laminate. Place a straightedge along the scored line. Bend upward evenly. **Fig. 36-33.**

Applying the Adhesive

For best results, all materials should be at room temperature (70°F [21°C] or more) before installation. The substrate should be clean, dry, and free of oil, grease, or wax. If you are using edge trim, apply the adhesive only to the edge and install the trim. After trimming is finished, apply the adhesive to other parts of the laminate.

1. Fill holes and cracks with a spackling compound and then sand it flush with the surface. Vacuum dust off all surfaces.

SAFETY FIRST

Using Contact Cement

When using contact cement, wear solvent-impervious gloves, goggles or safety glasses with side shields, and a NIOSH-approved respirator. Make sure the work area is well ventilated. Most brands of contact cement are flammable. Keep them away from heat, flame, and sparks.

Fig. 36-33. Main steps in cutting plastic laminate. *A.* Score the face side of the laminate, using a straightedge as a guide. *B.* With the straightedge placed along the scribed line, bend the laminate up to break it off.

2. Stir the adhesive thoroughly from the bottom of the can. Pour it onto the back of the laminate. Spread the adhesive evenly, using a roller or a brush. **Fig. 36-34.** A brush is recommended when applying adhesive to vertical surfaces or edges, or whenever the use of a roller is impractical. If you are using a brush, apply two coats to ensure proper coverage. Be sure to allow the adhesive adequate drying time between coats.
3. Apply the adhesive to the substrate, and spread it with a brush or roller.
4. Let the adhesive dry according to instructions on the product label. Test the dryness of the adhesive by pressing a piece of paper lightly against it and pulling it away. If the adhesive sticks to the paper, more drying time is needed.
5. To make certain that you have applied enough adhesive, look across the surface into the light after the adhesive is completely dry. With most products the surface will appear glossy. Spots that are dull after drying require additional adhesive.

Bonding and Finishing

Install the laminate as soon as possible after the adhesive is dry. Eye protection is especially important during trimming because the small pieces of laminate debris are sharp.

1. If the edge trim is plastic laminate, install it first. Position the trim carefully so that its bottom edge is flush with the bottom edge of the substrate. The top edge should extend about ¼″ or more above the substrate's surface.
2. Press the edge trim in place by sliding a soft wood block along it and tapping the block with a hammer to complete the bond. **Fig. 36-35.** A special roller can be used instead.

Fig. 36-34. Spreading contact adhesive with a roller.

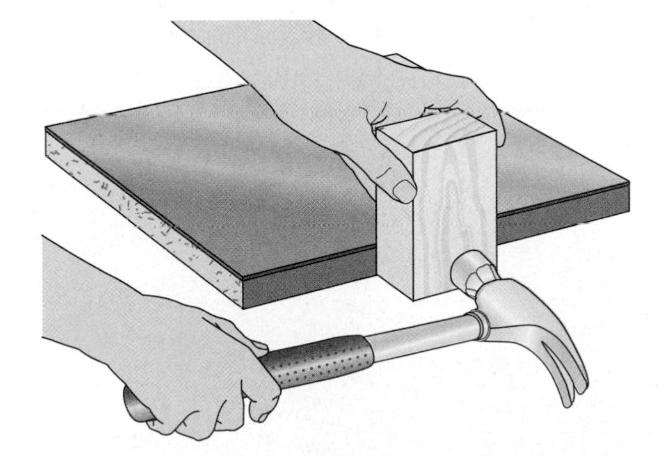

Fig. 36-35. Complete the bond between the plastic laminate and the core by sliding a softwood block along the trim. Then tap it with a hammer.

Fig. 36-36. A laminate trimmer is essentially a small router with a specialized base to guide the tool.

3. Using a laminate trimmer, carefully trim off excess material so the trim is flush with the substrate. Do not apply adhesive to other portions of the laminate until you have removed the debris from trimming.
4. When you are ready to bond the rest of the laminate to the substrate, place several dowel rods across the top of the substrate. **Fig. 36-37.**

Fig. 36-37. Use wood dowel rods to support the surface sheet of plastic laminate while aligning it with the substrate for bonding. Be sure to use enough dowel rods to prevent sagging.

5. Align the laminate with the substrate so that an equal amount of laminate hangs over all edges. Use extreme care, because bonding is immediate upon contact.
6. Gently slip the center dowel rod out from beneath the plastic laminate, leaving the others in place. The two adhesive surfaces will come in contact with each other. Press to complete the bond.
7. Remove the other dowel rods one at a time, working from the center toward the ends. This technique also helps to prevent air bubbles from being trapped beneath the laminate.
8. As you work, roll the surface outward from the center in all directions, using a wide, hard-rubber roller. If a roller is not available, use a block of soft wood. Place it at the center and work toward the edges, tapping sharply with a hammer. Tap or roll the entire surface to ensure a complete bond.
9. Use a router or plastic laminate trimmer to remove the excess laminate that hangs over the edges of the core.

POSTFORMED COUNTERTOPS

Postformed countertops consist of laminate that has been attached to a substrate at the factory. **Fig. 36-38.** This type of countertop is easy to install because it already incorporates both the backsplash and the countertop edge. If the end of a countertop will be exposed, pre-made end pieces are available. Postformed countertops are generally available in 8′, 10′, and 12′ lengths. The choice of patterns and colors is large.

Fig. 36-38. A cross section of a postformed countertop.

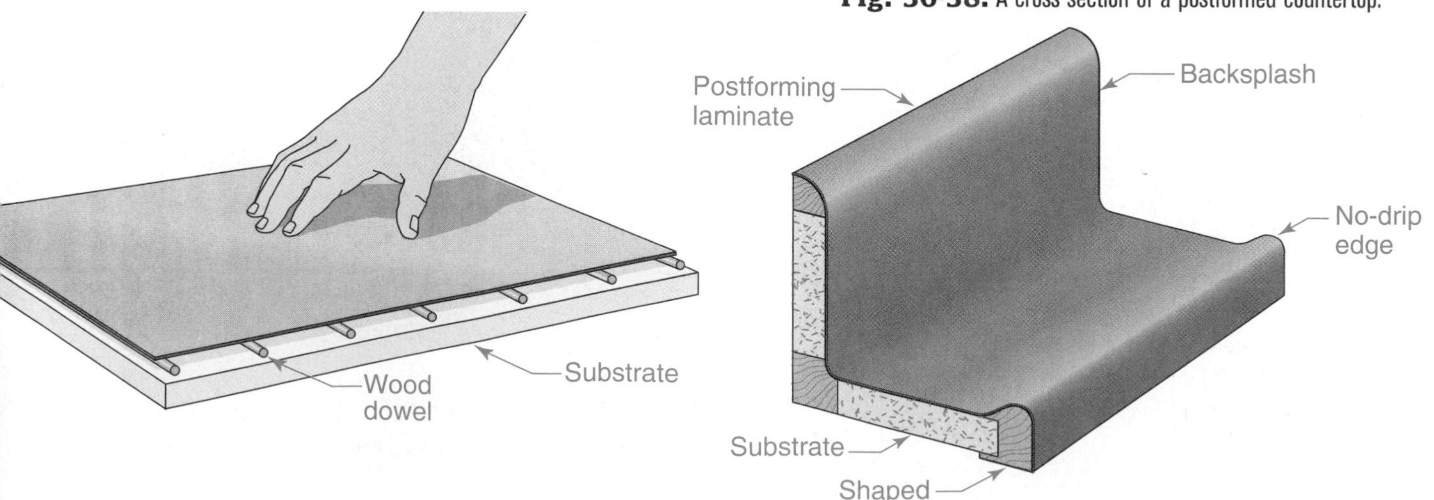

Estimating...

Cabinetry

Approximate costs for wall and base cabinetry can be obtained from lineal-foot measurements taken from the plans. These represent the length of the cabinetry as measured at its front edge. However, these figures are used only for general planning purposes. A more accurate estimate must be made when the style and grade of cabinetry have been chosen.

MATERIALS

The precise costs for manufactured cabinets can be found on the manufacturer's current price lists. If higher-grade hardware is available, the additional cost must be included. Site-built cabinets require a complete bill of materials with prices for each item, including hardware, glass, shelves, and any special trim.

Countertops are priced in various ways. Postformed countertops are sold by the lineal foot. If a laminate countertop is built on site, materials must be itemized. The list would include substrate material, plastic laminate, adhesive, moldings, and any other items that might be required. Other countertop materials are estimated based on square footage.

LABOR

The time required to install manufactured cabinets varies with the room layout and the cabinet type. An approximate labor cost can be determined by adding the times needed for installation and multiplying the total by the local hourly rate. The approximate times for installing various cabinets and countertops are listed in **Tables 36-B** and **36-C**.

ESTIMATING ON THE JOB

Refer to the L-shaped kitchen layout shown in Fig. 36-5. If the kitchen is 18′ long and 12′ wide:

1. How many square feet of plastic laminate would be needed to cover the countertop excluding edges? Assume that the countertop is 2′ wide.
2. If a postformed countertop with backsplash was used instead, how many lineal feet of material would be required? Assume that the two lengths of countertop will be joined with a 45° miter joint.

Table 36-B. Approximate Installation Times for Postformed Countertops

Countertops	Time (hours)
Postformed plastic laminate countertop	¼ (per lineal foot)
25″ wide plastic laminate countertop with a 4″ backsplash and self-edge	1 (per lineal foot)
Postformed plastic laminate mitered corner (L- or U-shaped kitchen)	1
End cap on a postformed plastic laminate countertop	⅓

Table 36-C. Approximate Installation Times for Factory-Built Cabinets

Type of Cabinet	Time (hours)
Base cabinet containing one door and one drawer	½
Base cabinet containing two doors and two drawers	¾
Base corner cabinet	1
Broom closet	1
Drawer cabinet with four drawers	½
Oven cabinet	1¼
Sink cabinet	1½
Wall cabinet with two doors (refrigerator cabinet)	½
Wall cabinet with two doors (standard height)	½
China case corner unit with 36″ front	2
Bathroom vanity up to 84″ long	2

To install postformed countertops:

1. Trim the countertop on site to fit the space exactly. You can do this using files or a power tool such as a jigsaw, router, or circular saw. You may have to scribe the top edge of the countertop backsplash to fit variations in the wall.
2. Once you trim the countertop to fit, fasten it in place by driving wood screws through cleats on the underside of the cabinet and into the underside of the countertop. First, drill the correct size pilot hole. *Take care not to drill entirely through the countertop.* Be sure to use a wood screw of the correct length so that it does not pierce the laminate when the countertop is pulled down snug against the top of the cabinets.
3. After the top is secured to the cabinets, apply a small bead of caulking compound at the joint between the wall and the back top edge of the backsplash. Some laminate manufacturers can supply caulk that is color-matched to the laminate.
4. Where sections of countertop meet, join them together with draw bolts and seal the joints with caulk.

Approximate installation times for postformed countertops are shown in Table 36-B.

Postformed countertops must sometimes be trimmed to fit between two existing walls that are not perfectly square. This happens frequently when installing bathroom countertops. To solve this problem, obtain a 2′ x 3′ piece of cardboard or hardboard. Use it to represent one end of the countertop. Lay it in place on the cabinets, scribe it to the wall, and cut it. Then transfer the pattern to the countertop. Repeat the procedure at the other end of the countertop. After the countertop is cut, it should fit precisely.

SECTION 36.3 Check Your Knowledge

1. What is the standard height of a countertop in a kitchen?
2. What gives plastic laminate its color and pattern?
3. What makes a postformed countertop easy to install?
4. What technique is often used when installing a postformed countertop between existing walls that are not perfectly square?

On the Job

Locate the websites for two different brands of plastic laminate. Compile a list of the grades available from each manufacturer. Include information about where these grades are typically used.

Chapter 36

Review

Section Summaries

36.1 The basic arrangement of cabinets for a room is shown on the building plans. Kitchen layouts include U shape, L shape, parallel wall, side wall, and island. Work centers include those for food preparation, cooking, and cleanup. Bathroom layouts are much less flexible because of plumbing requirements.

36.2 Manufactured cabinets may be stock cabinets, semi-custom cabinets, or custom cabinets. The carcase is the cabinet's basic framework. The face frame provides a surface for mounting hinges and other hardware. Doors may be of the inset or overlay type. Cabinet hardware includes drawer guides, door hinges, knobs, and pulls. Cabinets must be plumb, level, and securely attached to wall studs. Several cabinets that run together must be attached to one another.

36.3 Many countertops are made of plastic laminate glued to a substrate. Conventional laminates can be purchased separately and installed on site.

Review Questions

1. At what point in the construction of a house are cabinets installed?
2. Name the five basic kitchen layouts.
3. What is the work triangle?
4. What are the most common dimensions for bathroom base cabinets?
5. What is the difference between frameless and face-frame cabinet construction?
6. What are the two basic types of cabinet doors? Describe them.
7. Where should the layout of base cabinets begin?
8. What type and size of screw should be used to install wall cabinets?
9. What must be done if a cabinet does not fit tight against a wall?
10. What type of adhesive is used with plastic laminate and how is it applied?

Writing a Business Letter Before you begin a letter, think about what you're going to say and to whom you're saying it. Make some notes, if necessary. Then write a rough draft of your letter. In the first paragraph, state clearly the reason for your letter. Include any order numbers or dates that may be important. In the following paragraphs go into more detail until you've covered everything. In the last paragraph, state what, if anything, you would like to have done.

Check your letter for spelling and grammar. Make sure you've included the date, your return address, and the name and address of the person you're writing to. If possible, ask someone else to proofread your letter to be sure it's clear.

Chapter 37

Wall Paneling

Objectives

After reading this chapter, you'll be able to:

- Identify the three basic types of paneling.
- Explain how paneling should be stored and conditioned.
- Explain how to install sheet paneling.
- Estimate the amount of sheet paneling required for a room.

Terms

blind nailing
box extender
furring strip
sticker
wainscoting

The texture and versatility of wood paneling make it popular as an indoor wall finish. Wood paneling can dramatically change the look of a room, yet it is easy to install. It is often used in remodeling projects because it quickly covers flaws in wall surfaces. Wood paneling can be installed over drywall, plaster, and masonry surfaces. It can be painted or given a clear finish to highlight the color and grain of the wood. It can also be purchased prefinished.

SECTION 37.1

Paneling Basics

Paneling can be applied to walls in various ways, depending on the effect desired.

TYPES OF PANELING

Paneling that runs from floor to ceiling is referred to as *full-height paneling*. Paneling that runs partway up the wall from the floor is called **wainscoting**. It is usually about 32″ high. **Fig. 37-1.** A piece of wood molding runs along the top edge of wainscoting to conceal cut edges.

Wall paneling comes in three basic forms:

- *Sheet paneling.* This is the most common type of wall paneling. **Fig. 37-2.** Most sheet-panel products are made of plywood, hardboard, or *medium-density fiberboard* (MDF). MDF paneling is sometimes referred to as *panelboard.* Sheet paneling is most commonly found in 4x8 sheets, but 4x3, 4x6, and 4x10 sheets are also available. Thicknesses include 5⁄32″, 3⁄16″, 1⁄4″, 3⁄8″, 1⁄2″, 5⁄8″, and 3⁄4″. The edges along the panel's length may be square or rabbeted. The edges along the width are square.
- *Board paneling.* This type is made of solid wood, including Douglas fir, oak, and various species of pine. **Fig. 37-3.** It ranges from 3⁄8″ to 3⁄4″ thick and comes in lengths of 8′ to 12′ and longer. The edges of each board interlock with adjoining boards in either a lap joint or a tongue-and-groove (T&G) joint. Square-edged boards can also be used, but then the joints are often covered with molding.
- *Raised paneling.* Raised paneling is constructed much like raised-panel cabinet doors (see Chapter 36, "Cabinets and Countertops"). The panels are made of solid wood, such as oak or cherry. Individual raised panels are held in place by a grid of stiles and rails secured to

Fig. 37-1. Wainscoting protects the lower part of a wall. It leaves the upper part open for decorative treatments.

Fig. 37-2. The indentations of age can be felt as well as seen in this antiqued plywood paneling used as an accent wall.

Fig. 37-3. The interlocking edges of board paneling provide a gap-free joint. Boards come in various widths.

Fig. 37-4. Various types of molding can be applied to plywood or MDF to create custom paneling of any size or shape.

the walls with nails or screws. Raised paneling is very expensive, so it is sometimes simulated with wood molding applied to sections of sheet paneling. **Fig. 37-4.** Because raised paneling is not as common as the other types, its installation will not be covered in this chapter.

STORAGE AND CONDITIONING

Always store paneling indoors. Stack it on the floor, using stickers to separate the sheets or boards. A **sticker** is a long, slender piece of scrap wood that separates layers of wood products and allows air circulation. Stacking panels in this way prevents them from warping. If you must store sheet paneling on edge, make sure that the panels rest on a long edge. Place stickers beneath the panels to raise them off the floor.

Wood paneling must be conditioned before installation. *Conditioning* means that the paneling has been in the room in which it will be used for a certain period of time. This allows the paneling to become accustomed to the temperature and humidity of the room. Condition sheet paneling for at least 48 hours. Condition solid wood paneling for seven days, if possible.

from Another Angle

The woods used for board and raised paneling may vary based on local availability. In the Northwest, for example, Douglas fir and western red cedar are widely available. In northern California, redwood is sometimes used, particularly in period architecture. In the southern United States, cypress is more available than elsewhere. In New England, oak and white pine are popular. Each wood is generally less expensive within its home region.

SAFETY FIRST

Moving Sheet Paneling

Sheet paneling is unwieldy, and even thin sheets can be awkward to handle. Never move more than one sheet of paneling at a time unless you have help. When lifting panels, lift with your knees. To do this, lift while keeping your back straight. When carrying panels, avoid any twisting motion that may strain your lower back.

SECTION 37.1 **Check Your Knowledge**

1. What is a sticker?
2. What joints are used with board paneling?
3. What is sheet paneling made of?
4. Why should paneling be conditioned before installation?

On the Job

Using library or Internet resources, locate any statistics that would prove or disprove the following statement: "Sheet paneling uses less lumber than solid paneling for an equivalent coverage. This makes good use of timber resources." Report and explain your findings in a written paragraph.

SECTION 37.2

Sheet Paneling

Sheet paneling is available in many textures and patterns, including saw-textured, relief-grain, embossed, and grooved. Plywood and medium-density fiberboard (MDF) paneling are available with a wide variety of surface veneers, including domestic and tropical hardwoods.

Sheet paneling made of plywood shares characteristics with other plywood products, including strength and stability (see Chapter 17, "Engineered Lumber"). MDF panels can be damaged by moisture and high humidity. They should not be used in unheated rooms or in humid areas such as basements and bathrooms. Panels that are $\frac{5}{32}''$ thick or less should always be installed over a backing that will not catch fire, such as drywall. Thicker panels can be attached directly to studs if local building codes permit the practice. Panels $\frac{5}{32}''$ thick should never be placed over masonry. Other thicknesses can be installed over masonry according to the manufacturer's instructions.

The methods for handling and installing all types of sheet paneling are similar. It is always wise, however, to consult the manufacturer's instructions first for any special precautions. The following instructions cover the installation of plywood paneling.

CUTTING SHEET PANELING

Be sure the paneling has been stored and conditioned properly before installation.

When cutting panels with a crosscut handsaw or table saw, place the face side ("good" side) of the panel up. This reduces splintering. If you are using a circular saw or a saber saw, cut the panel with the face side down. The best blade to use in a circular saw or a table saw is a plywood-cutting blade (see Chapter 7, "Power Saws").

Carpenter's Tip

One way to reduce splintering is to place a strip of masking tape where you will make the cut. Then draw your cutting line and make the cut. Another method is to score the cutting line with a utility knife.

SAFETY FIRST

Avoiding Kickback

Sheet paneling is often cut using a table saw. However, thin panels are very flexible and may bend as they are being cut. This can cause the panel to pinch the saw blade, leading to a very dangerous condition called kickback. To prevent kickback, support thin paneling adequately across its width during the cutting operation. It must also be supported as it leaves the saw.

INSTALLING PANELING OVER DRYWALL

Local codes *may* allow the installation of ¼″ or thicker paneling directly to studs. However, it is often recommended that sheet paneling be applied over drywall. Drywall provides a fire-resistant base and solid support. It is generally required for paneling that is less than ¼″ thick.

Sheet paneling is secured to the wall with finishing nails, brads, or a combination of nails and panel mastic. *Mastic* is a thick adhesive that can be applied with a notched trowel or with a caulking gun.

The Step-by-Step instructions below and on the following pages cover the installation of sheet paneling over an existing drywall surface.

Carpenter's Tip

When removing trim that must be reused, pry it carefully away from the wall. Pull out any remaining nails through the backside of the trim, using nippers. This prevents the head of the nail from splintering the face of the trim as it exits. You can fill in the nail holes with wood putty.

STEP BY STEP

Wall Preparation and Paneling Layout

Drywall must be prepared before paneling is installed. Otherwise, irregularities in the surface will make installation difficult. Following is the general sequence for wall preparation and paneling layout. Note that Steps 2 and 3 relate to remodeling, rather than new construction.

Step 1 Walls must be clean and flat. Sand or scrape down high spots.

Step 2 Remove all plates around wall switches and receptacles and save them for reuse.

Step 3 Remove window, door, and baseboard trim. Though thin sheet paneling can be installed without removing existing trim, this method requires a high degree of precision. Removing it is often more convenient. It is nearly always best to remove baseboard trim. Trim can be reinstalled unless it is damaged during removal.

Step 4 Locate the position of studs in the existing wall. They are generally on 16″ centers. Lightly mark the stud center locations on the floor and ceiling to serve as a guide when nailing each panel in position. **Fig. 37-5.** If the panel has grooves, the grooves will usually be spaced to align with standard 16″ stud spacing. **Fig. 37-6.**

Step 5 Panels are generally applied with the long dimension running vertically. Stand the panels on edge side by side around the room. Arrange them by natural color variations into a pleasing pattern.

Step 6 For most rooms, it is practical to start paneling from one inside corner and then work around the room in only one direction. After you have established their order, number each panel on the back and set it aside.

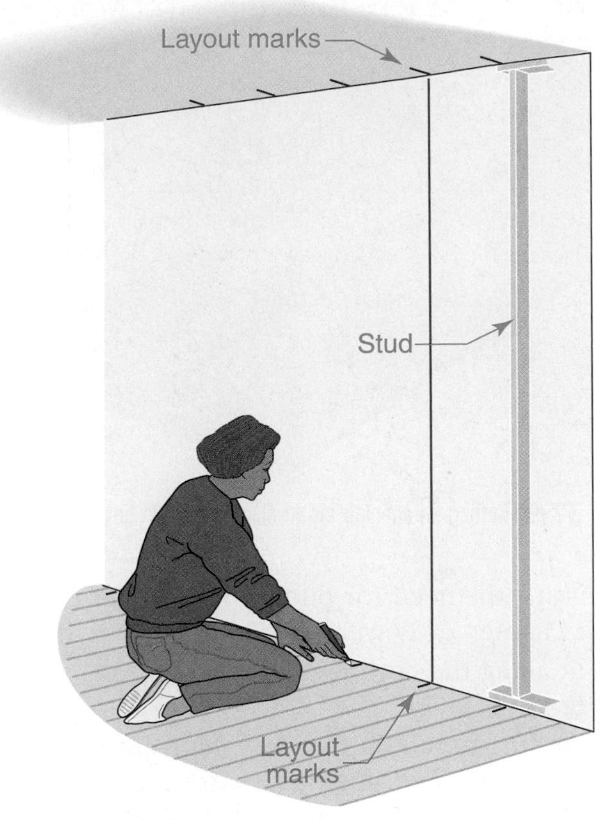

Fig. 37-5. Snapping a chalk line on the wall to indicate the center of each wall stud.

Fig. 37-7. Set the first panel in position, making certain that the edge is plumb.

Positioning the Panels

Positioning and fastening are usually done together. For ease in explanation, they are discussed separately here.

1. Measure the height of the wall in several places. If the height is less than 8′, subtract ½″ from this dimension and cut the 4x8 panels to length. This will provide ¼″ at top and bottom for expansion and contraction. If the height is greater than 8′, start with a 4x10 panel.
2. Place the first panel in position in a corner and butt it to the adjacent wall.
3. In many cases, the corners of a room are irregular. Make sure the panel is perfectly plumb and its outer edge is directly over the centerline of a stud. **Fig. 37-7.** (If you are using adhesive to fasten the panels to drywall, panel edges do not have to meet on a stud.) If this edge does not fall directly on the stud, trim the other side of the panel so that it will.
4. Position the panel at the proper height by shimming it to allow for ¼″ clearance at the bottom. When the panel is set perfectly plumb and at the correct height, check for gaps between the panel and the corner. Set a

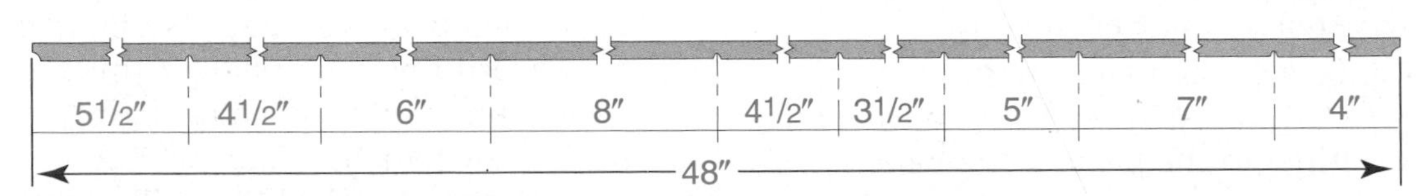

Fig. 37-6. A typical groove spacing for sheet paneling. The groove locations appear to be randomly spaced. However, when the dimensions are added together, the grooves fall on 16″ and 24″ centers. In this way, the panel can be nailed through the grooves and into the studs.

Fig. 37-8. To scribe the panel edge, hold the compass tip against the wall and move the compass downward. The tip will follow imperfections in the wall and the pencil will record them.

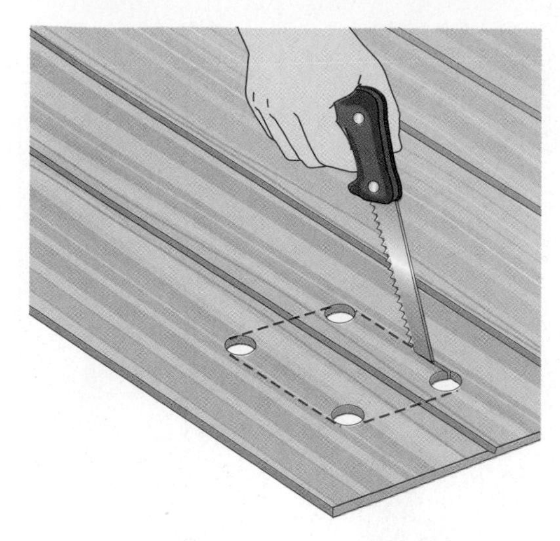

Fig. 37-9. Cutting an opening for an electrical outlet box.

compass for an amount equal to the widest gap. Scribe a line on the panel as shown in **Fig. 37-8**. Be sure to hold the compass as shown as you work.

5. Using a jigsaw or circular saw, cut the panel along this line so it will fit the corner.
6. Set the panel back in place against the wall and again shim it to the correct height. Now it should fit the corner exactly.
7. Fasten the first panel to the wall with nails or adhesive. This will be discussed in detail under "Fastening Panels."
8. Butt the second panel to the first. The panels should not be butted tightly together. To allow for expansion, a 1⁄16″ gap is recommended for hardboard and MDF panels. A smaller gap is recommended for plywood panels. If you are using nails, with the first panel properly positioned on the studs, the edges of the remaining 4′ wide panels will also land on stud centers. This assumes that the stud spacing is uniform across the wall.

Making Cutouts

A hole must often be cut in a panel to accommodate an electrical box.

1. Rub chalk against the edges of the box. Then hold the panel in place against it.
2. Strike the face of the panel sharply several times with the heel of your hand to transfer the box outline to the back of the panel.
3. Drill pilot holes in the corners of the marked outline. A plunge cut can also be made, eliminating the need for pilot holes (see page 148 in Chapter 7, "Power Saws").
4. Cut along the outline with a jigsaw. **Fig. 37-9.**

According to building codes, the front of any electrical box should be flush with the surface of the wood paneling when the job is complete. This prevents combustible materials from being exposed to possible short circuits within the box. If the box is not flush, it should either be repositioned or fitted with a box extender. A **box extender** is a metal or plastic fitting that is screwed to the front of the outlet box, bringing it forward.

Fastening Panels

The nailing patterns for plywood paneling depend on the spacing of supports and the thickness of the panels. **Table 37-A.**

1. Use colored ringshank nails that blend with the wood finish. This will eliminate the need for countersinking and puttying. Space the nails every 6″ along panel edges. Space them every 12″ along intermediate studs.
2. When nailing is complete, check that all nails are set properly and that the paneling is tight against the wall.

Prefinished paneling may also be nailed with standard finishing nails. If this technique is used, countersink the nails slightly below the surface of the paneling. Fill the holes using a putty stick that matches the color of the paneling.

Table 37-A. Nailing Recommendations for Interior Plywood Paneling

Plywood Thickness (inches)	Maximum Support Spacing (inches)	Nail Size (Use casing or finishing nails)	Nail Spacing (inches)	
			Panel Edges	Intermediate
1/4	16[a]	4d	6	12
5/16	16[b]	6d	6	12
3/8, 11/32	24	6d	6	12
1/2, 15/32	24	6d	6	12
5/8, 19/32	24	8d	6	12
3/4	24	8d	6	12

(a) Can be 20″ if face grain of paneling is across supports.
(b) Can be 24″ if face grain of paneling is across supports.

It is sometimes easier to find unset nails by lightly rubbing your hand over the paneling than it is to look for them.

Panel adhesive may be used instead of nails. Be sure to follow the adhesive manufacturer's instructions. Use only a latex, water-based adhesive with MDF paneling. Solvent-based adhesives may discolor finishes on this product.

1. After the panels have been properly cut and fitted, apply the adhesive to the wall surface or the back of the panel. Use a caulking gun to create a continuous 3/16″ – 1/4″ wide bead around the perimeter of the panel and around any cutouts. **Fig. 37-10.**
2. Apply additional adhesive in a zigzag pattern in the middle.
3. If the paneling is being installed directly to studs, place panel adhesive on intermediate studs in 3″ long beads spaced 6″ apart.
4. Position the panel and press it firmly against the adhesive.
5. Place three or four finishing nails across the top of the panel to hold it in place.
6. Place a padded block of wood against the panel and tap the block with a hammer or

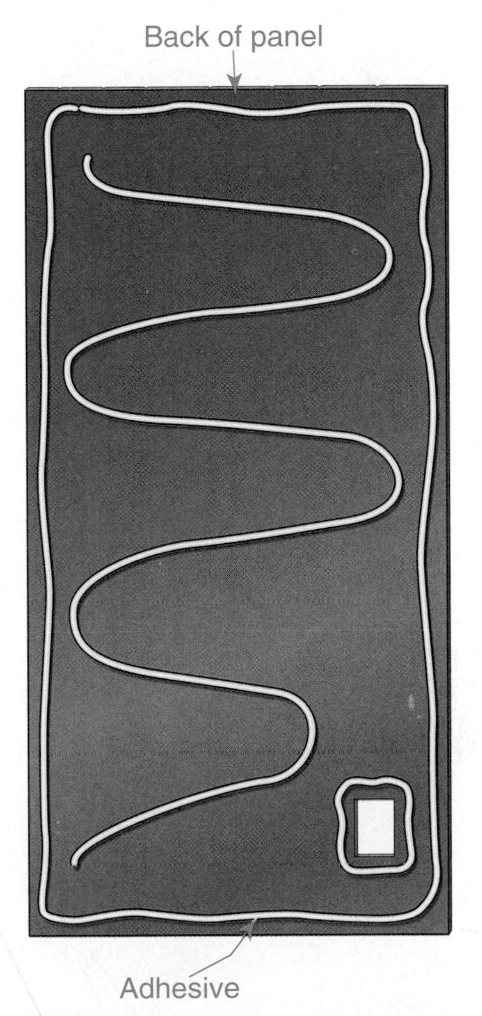

Fig. 37-10. Apply adhesive to the back of the panel. Keep it approximately 1″ or more from the edges to avoid adhesive squeeze-out.

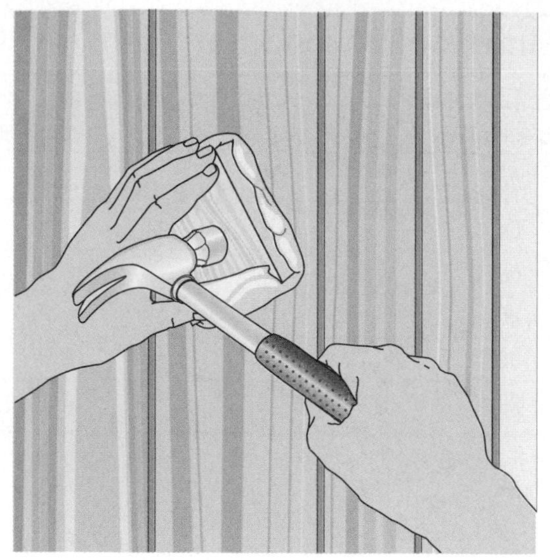

Fig. 37-11. Tapping the panel with a softwood block to press it firmly into place. You may put a cloth under the block to further protect the paneling.

rubber mallet to achieve full-surface contact. **Fig. 37-11.**

7. If necessary, use small finishing nails to hold the panel flat until the adhesive reaches full strength.

Installing Molding

Several styles of wood and plastic moldings can be used to cover joints or seams in paneling as well as at the ceiling line. Construction details for various methods are shown in **Fig. 37-12**.

Molding may also be used to cover corners. Prefabricated corner molding is sometimes available from the paneling supplier. It is often prefinished to harmonize. Solid wood molding can also be used. If molding is not desirable at the corners, they can be butt jointed or mitered as shown in **Fig. 37-13**.

For more information on moldings, see Chapter 35, "Molding and Trim."

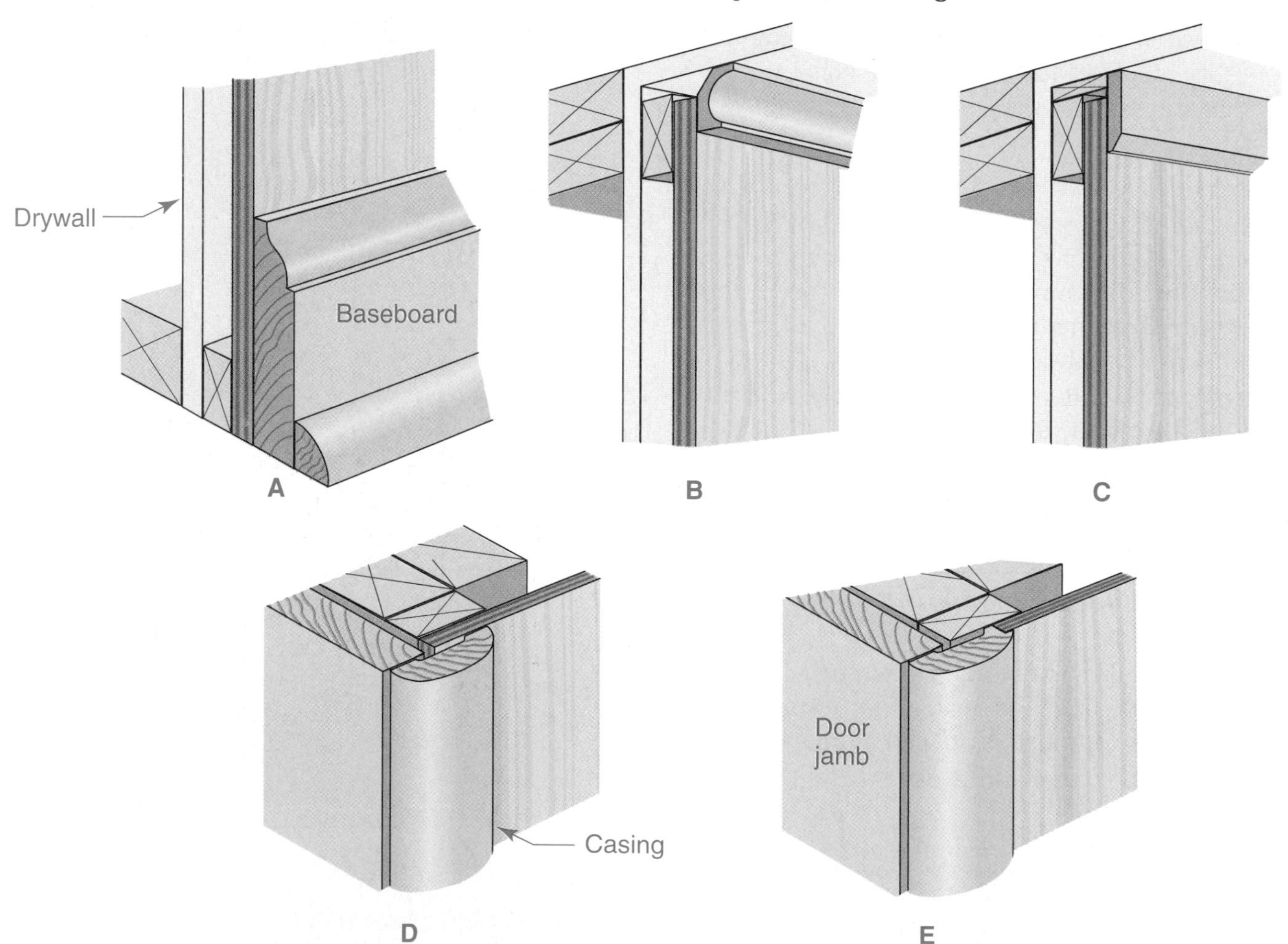

Fig. 37-12. Finishing details. Once the paneling is in place, molding and trim can be added. These details show a strapped wall. Details would be similar if paneling was applied directly to drywall. *A.* At the floor, baseboard covers any gaps at the bottom of the wall. *B.* At the ceiling, cove molding or crown molding serves the same purpose. *C.* Flat molding matched to the paneling provides an unobtrusive detail. *D.* Around doors and windows, paneling can run beneath the trim. *E.* Paneling can also butt against the trim around doors and windows.

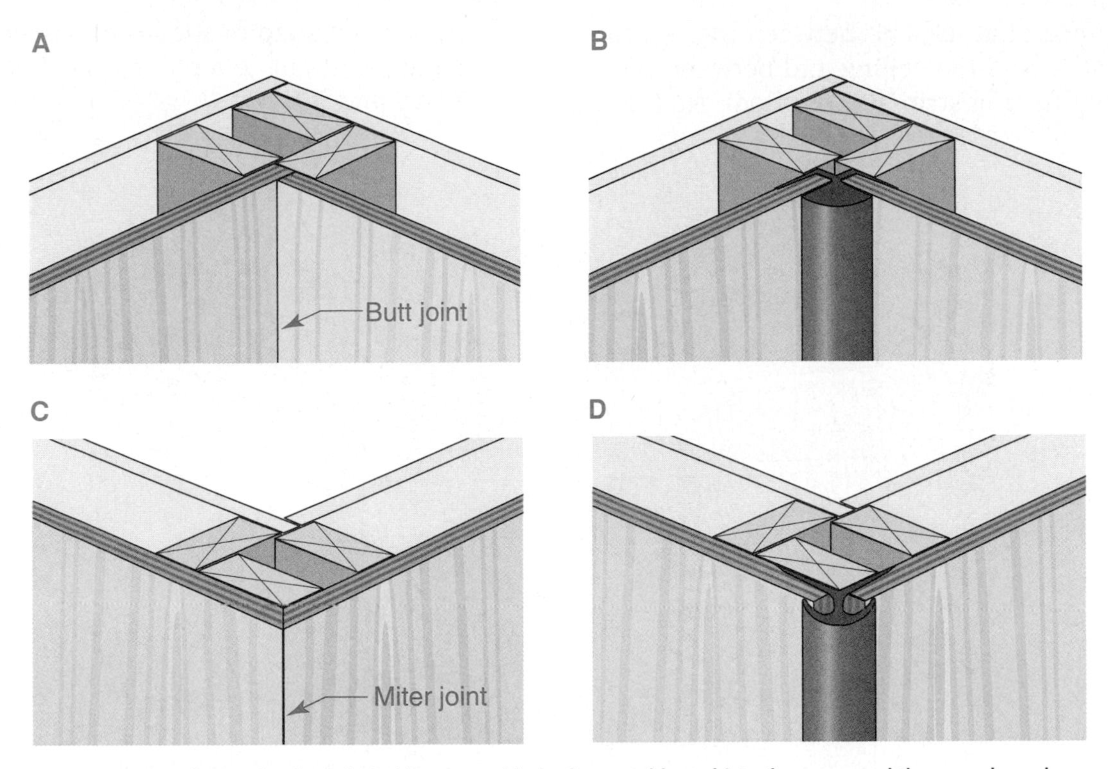

Fig. 37-13. Corner details. *A.* An inside corner with the first panel butted into the corner and the second panel scribed to the face of the first. *B.* An inside corner trimmed with aluminum molding. *C.* An outside corner mitered. *D.* An outside corner trimmed with aluminum molding.

INSTALLING PANELING OVER MASONRY

Some panels are sensitive to moisture. They are not recommended for use over masonry surfaces. Check the manufacturer's recommendations.

Panels that are approved for use over masonry are usually installed over furring strips. A **furring strip** is a thin strip of wood permanently installed to keep paneling and other materials from touching another surface. When used with paneling, they allow air to circulate behind the panel to reduce problems caused by trapped moisture. They also are often used to level an irregular surface.

The wall must be waterproofed before the furring strips are installed. Where extreme humidity may cause condensation on the inside of an exterior masonry wall, apply a vapor barrier. This will prevent moisture from penetrating to the panel.

1. Install furring strips horizontally every 16″. **Fig. 37-14.** Attach the furring strips to the masonry walls with masonry nails, screws, or fasteners driven into shields. Allow a

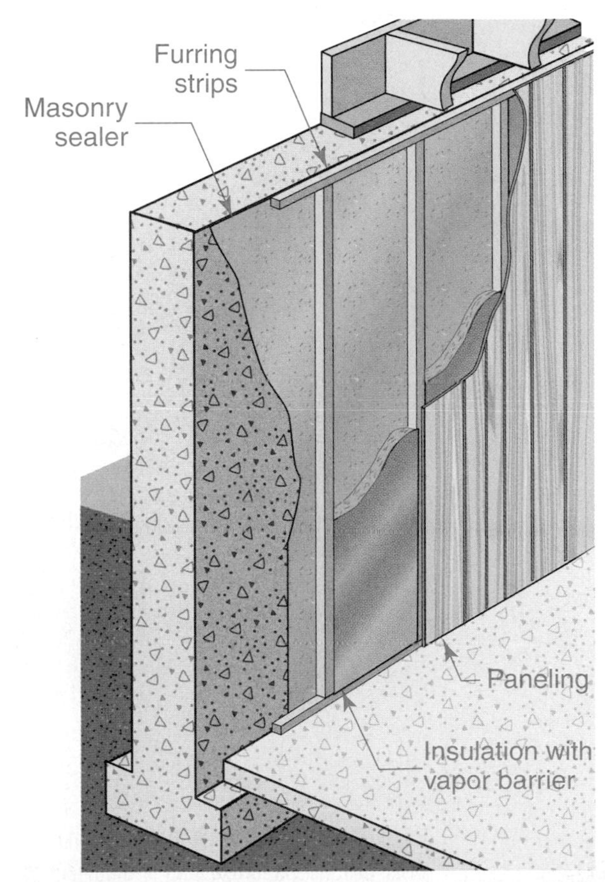

Fig. 37-14. Correct placement of furring strips in preparation for paneling.

clearance of at least ¼″ between the top furring strip and the ceiling and between the bottom furring strip and the floor. Nail the top furring strip to the bottom edge of the ceiling joists or to a nailing block. **Figs. 37-15** and **37-16.**

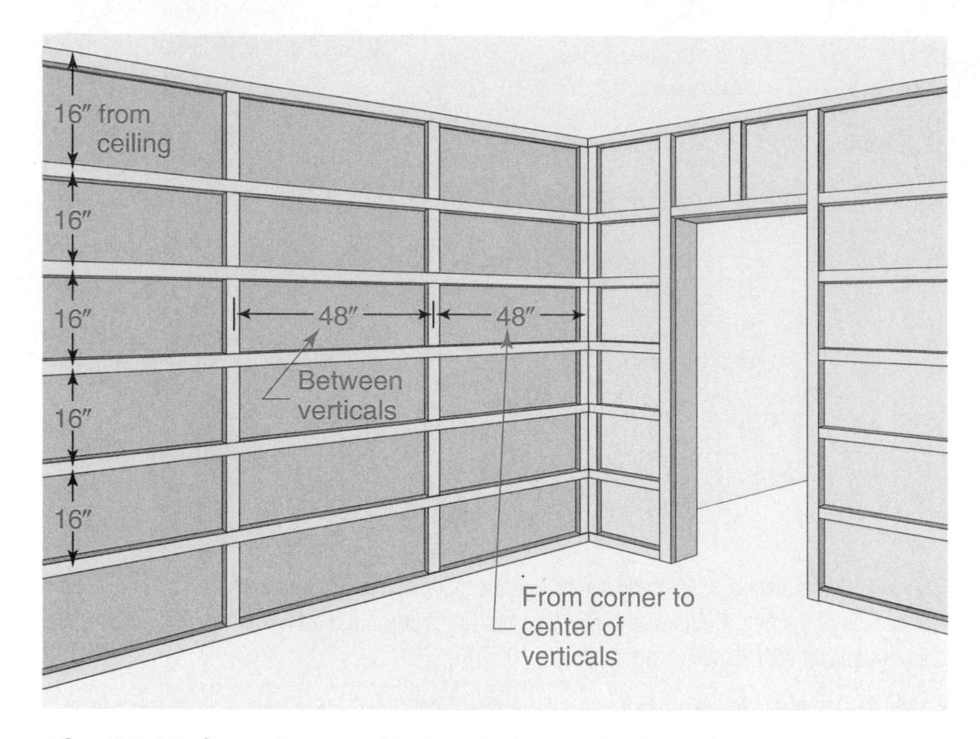

Fig. 37-15. Correct placement of furring strips in preparation for paneling.

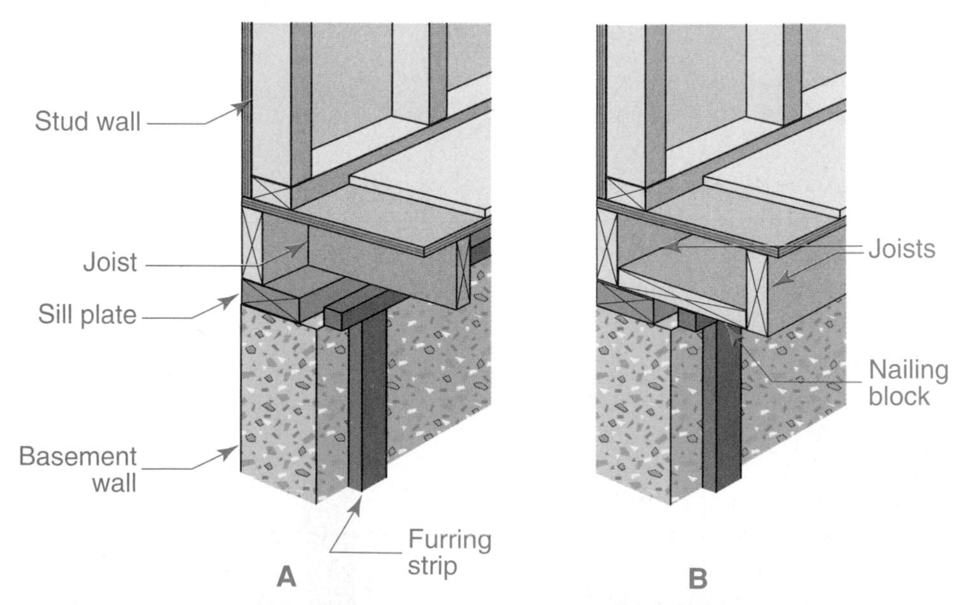

Fig. 37-16. Attaching the top furring strip. *A.* When the wall to be furred runs at right angles to the joists, nail the top furring strip to the underside of the joists. *B.* When the wall to be furred runs parallel to the joists, install a nailing block to which the top furring strip can be nailed.

2. Insert vertical strips every 48″ to support the panel edges.
3. Level furring strips if necessary by placing wood shims behind them in low spots. Drive a nail through the strip and the shim to hold them in place.
4. For walls over 8′ high, nail additional furring strips horizontally, with the center of one of the strips 8′ from the floor and another at the ceiling.
5. When wainscoting is installed, a furring strip must support its top edge.

SECTION 37.2

Check Your Knowledge

1. What material is often recommended as a backer for sheet paneling and why?
2. When is it not necessary for panel edges to meet at studs?
3. Describe the process of scribing a panel for an inside corner.
4. How must paneling fit around electrical outlet boxes?

On the Job

Using the placement of furring strips shown in Fig. 37-15, determine how many lineal feet of furring strips will be needed to panel a wall that is 8′ high and 8′ long. Add a waste allowance of 5 percent to your figures to determine the total amount of furring material that would be ordered.

SECTION 37.3

Board Paneling

Many kinds of wood are made into boards for paneling, including Douglas fir and various species of pine. Solid oak or cherry is also used. A rustic or informal look can be obtained with knotty pine or recycled barnwood. A more formal look can be achieved with a hardwood such as cherry, walnut, or mahogany.

Only thoroughly seasoned wood should be used. The boards should not be too wide, or the gaps created by expansion and contraction will be excessive. A nominal 8″ is the maximum width recommended in most parts of the United States. The boards are usually applied vertically but can be applied horizontally or diagonally.

Condition board paneling by storing it in the area in which it will be installed several days ahead of time. Be sure to stack and sticker the boards to promote air circulation.

from Another Angle

The moisture content of solid-wood paneling should be near the average it will reach in service–about 8 percent in most areas. However, in the dry southwestern United States, it should be about 6 percent. In the southern and coastal areas of the country, it should be about 11 percent. You can measure moisture content with an inexpensive moisture meter.

INSTALLING BOARDS VERTICALLY

Paneling installed vertically has a tongue-and-groove edge. **Fig. 37-17.** This lessens appearance problems caused by expansion and contraction. It also makes it easy to align the panels. When paneling is to be attached directly to studs (if allowed by code), adequate blocking must be placed between the studs to provide nailing support. **Fig. 37-18.** The blocking should not be more than 24″ OC.

A common practice is to nail a 1x8 board at the floor line to serve as a furring strip. A 1x4

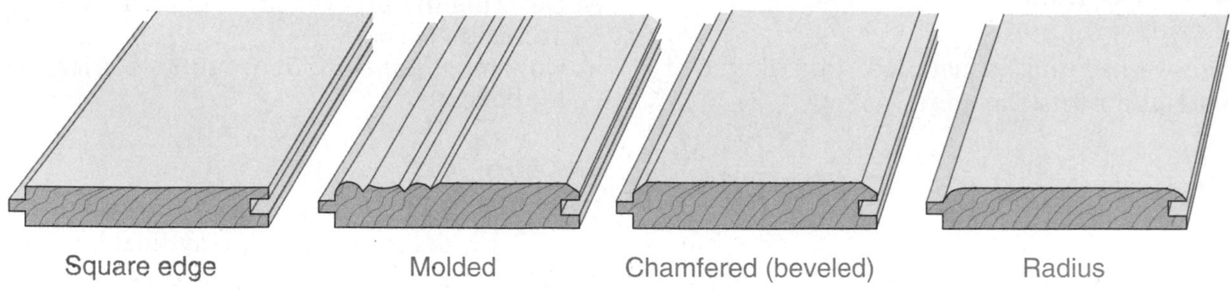

Fig. 37-17. Popular tongue-and-groove paneling patterns. Most retail lumberyards carry two or three patterns in stock.

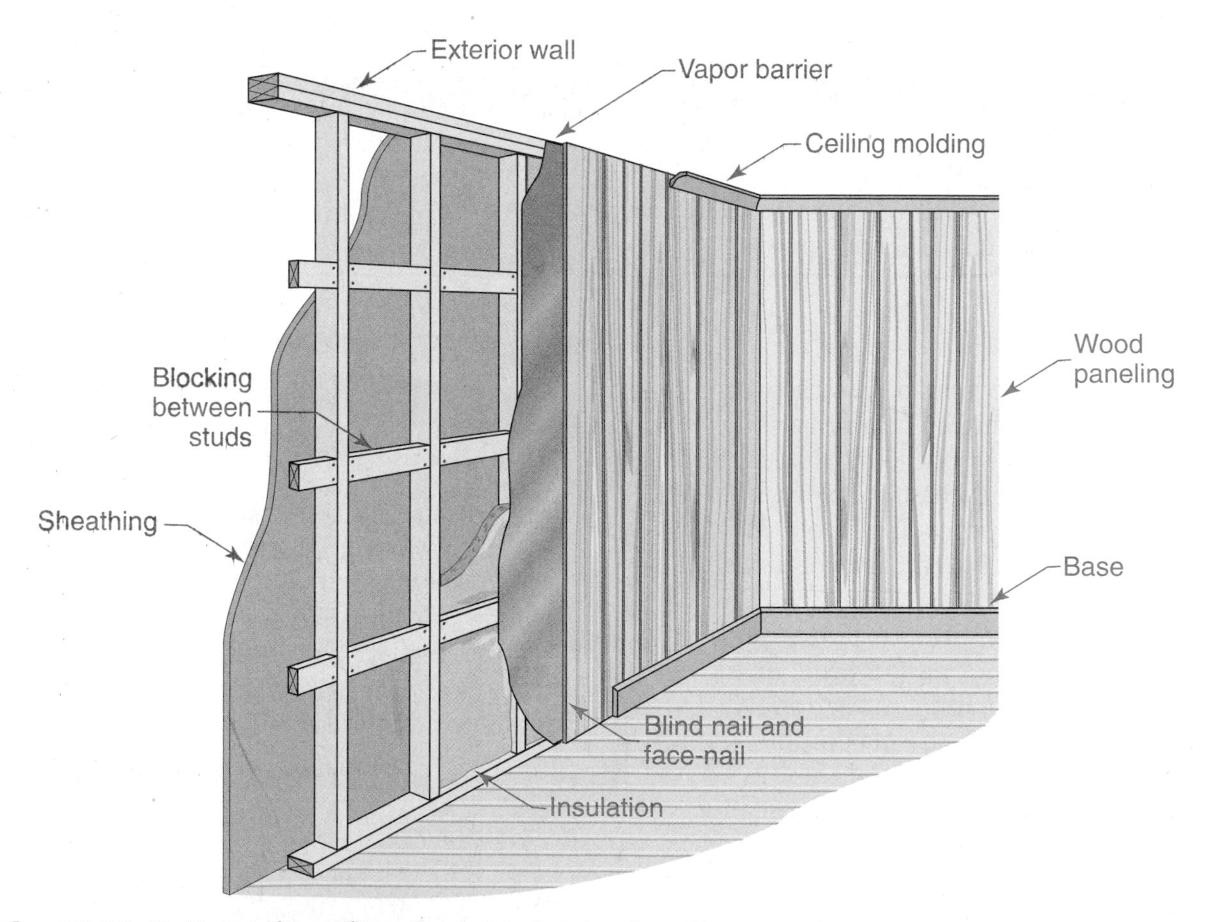

Fig. 37-18. Blocking provides a nailing surface for boards that are located between studs.

baseboard is then face-nailed to the 1x8 board. **Fig. 37-19.** The ends of the vertical paneling will rest on the top edge of the 1x4 base. This is a much cleaner application than resting the paneling ends on the floor and applying the base to the face of the paneling.

1. Starting at a corner, hold the first piece of paneling to the wall. Check that it is plumb.
2. Scribe the edge that fits into the corner and undercut the edge about 5° to ensure a snug fit. **Fig. 37-20.**

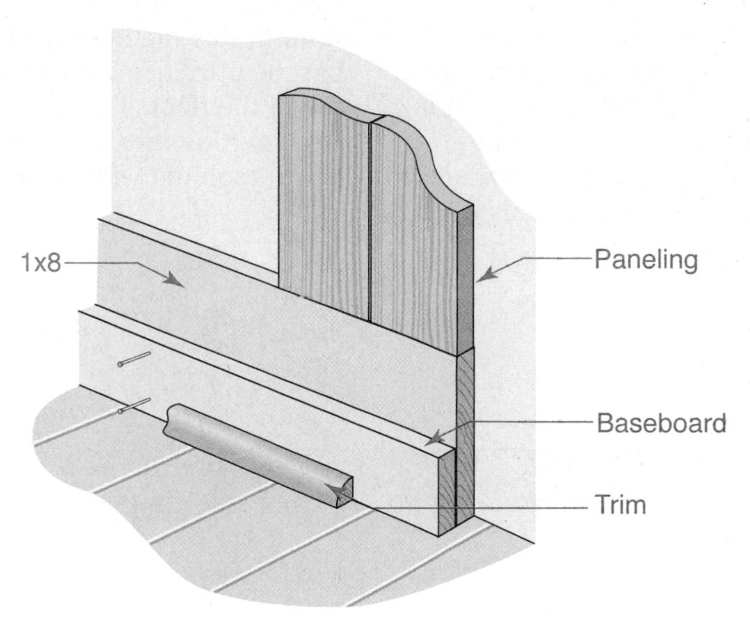

Fig. 37-19. The 1x4 baseboard is nailed to a 1x8 furring strip.

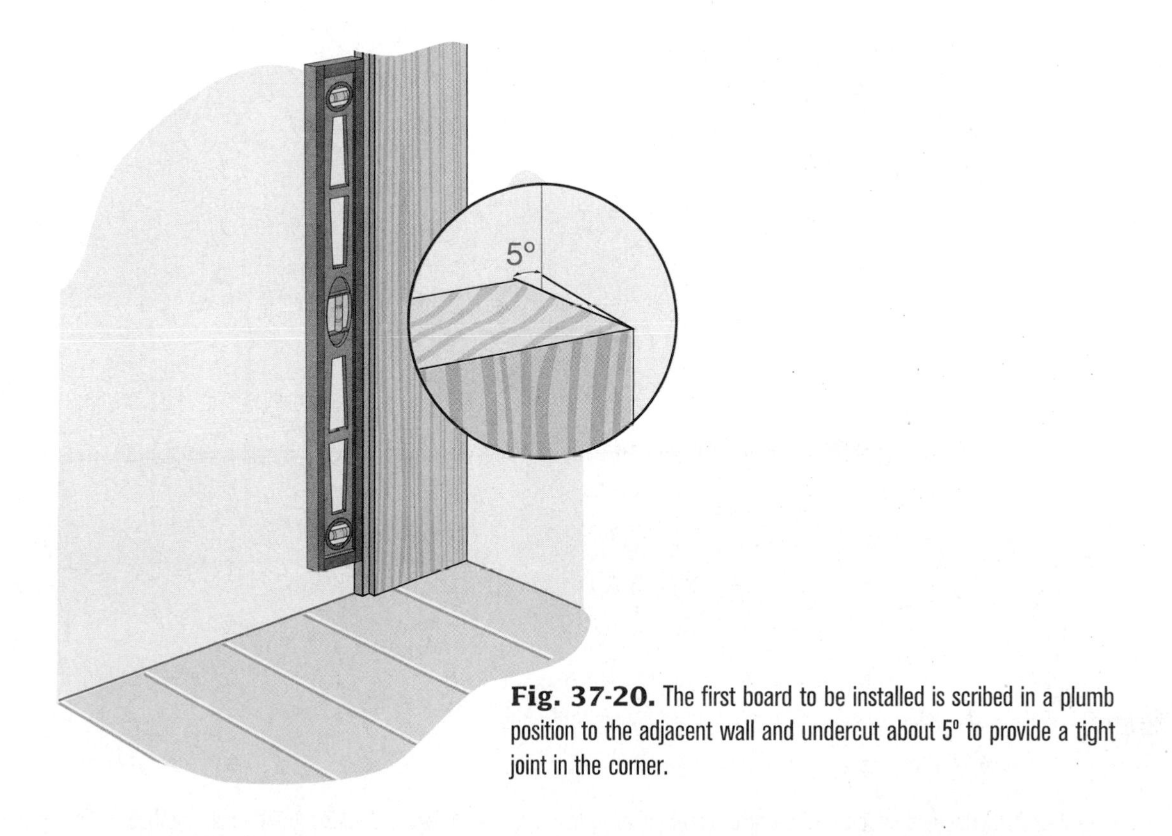

Fig. 37-20. The first board to be installed is scribed in a plumb position to the adjacent wall and undercut about 5° to provide a tight joint in the corner.

3. Blind nail all paneling in place using 5d or 6d finishing nails. **Fig. 37-21.** In **blind nailing**, the nails are driven at an angle through the tongue of the board and into framing or furring strips. It allows subsequent boards to conceal the nail heads.
4. Continue to install boards, checking them for plumb frequently. An out-of-plumb board can be repositioned until it is plumb.
5. When installing the last board on a wall, scribe the edge that is to fit into the corner and undercut it at an angle of about 5°. You can then slip the groove of the last board over the tongue of the preceding board and snap it into place. **Fig. 37-22.** This also ensures a snug fit at the corner.
6. Continue around the room in this fashion. Cut holes for outlets and other features as you encounter them. Where boards meet at outside corners, miter them or conceal the joint with molding.
7. Add ceiling and baseboard trim to complete the job.

Another method is to use the same size furring strip on the bottom as on the rest of the wall. In this method, the boards do not rest on a baseboard. They are installed so they almost touch the floor. The slight gap keeps moisture from getting into the ends of the boards. Baseboard molding will cover the gap. **Fig. 37-23.**

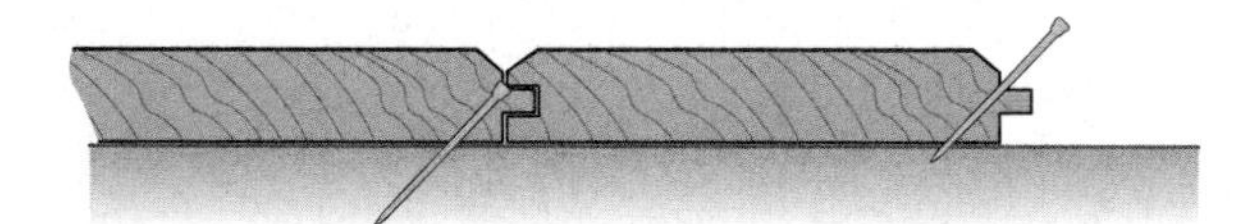

Fig. 37-21. Blind-nailing details for lumber paneling.

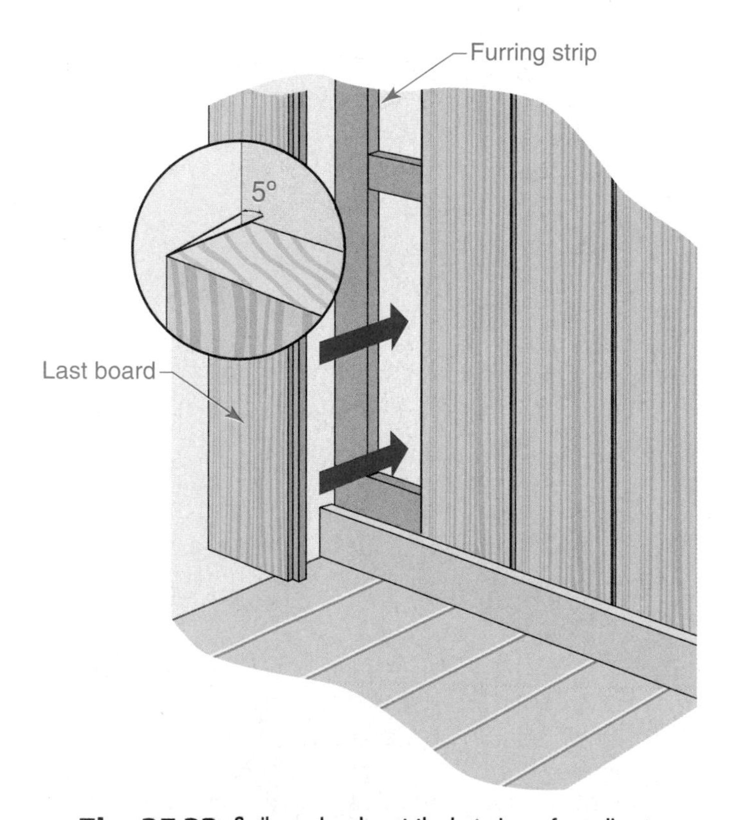

Fig. 37-22. Scribe and undercut the last piece of paneling to ensure a tight fit against the adjacent wall.

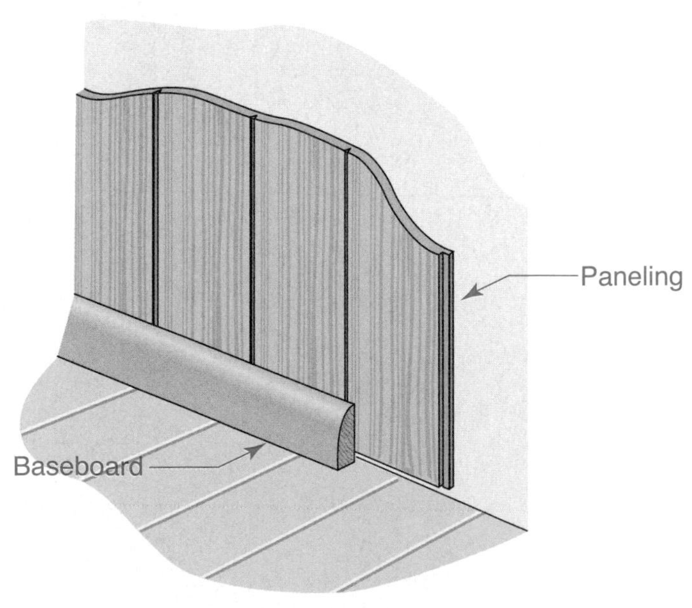

Fig. 37-23. An alternate method for installing board paneling vertically.

INSTALLING BOARDS HORIZONTALLY

Horizontal paneling, while not as common as vertical paneling, has some advantages. Blocking is not required. Instead, boards can span the distance between studs. Because longer boards can be used, it is less time-consuming to apply.

Measure from the ceiling to the floor in several places to make sure all measurements are equal. If they are not equal, make sure the narrower board will be at the bottom.

1. Begin the paneling at the floor line, making certain that the first piece is level and the tongue edge is up.
2. Scribe the bottom edge to the floor to eliminate any gaps. The gaps can also be covered later with baseboard or trim.
3. Undercut the ends of each board about 5° to provide a tight joint at the inside corners of the wall.
4. Miter the boards at the outside corners or trim them with molding. **Fig. 37-24.**
5. Blind nail each board, checking periodically to make certain the boards remain level.
6. If no molding is to be used at the ceiling, scribe and undercut the last panel edge at a 5° angle to ensure a snug fit.

Fig. 37-24. Wood paneling applied horizontally is mitered at outside corners. In this installation, instead of a baseboard, a reveal is shown.

INSTALLING BOARDS AT AN ANGLE

Application of boards in the herringbone (chevron) pattern is quite demanding. **Fig. 37-25.** The boards can be nailed to existing studs, although studs may not be in the right place to support the ends. Instead, you may have to apply vertical furring strips so the space between studs is evenly divided. For example, if the wall is 12′ long, you can place the strips 3′ on center as shown in *B*. Make sure that each furring strip is plumb. Installation steps are given on page 766.

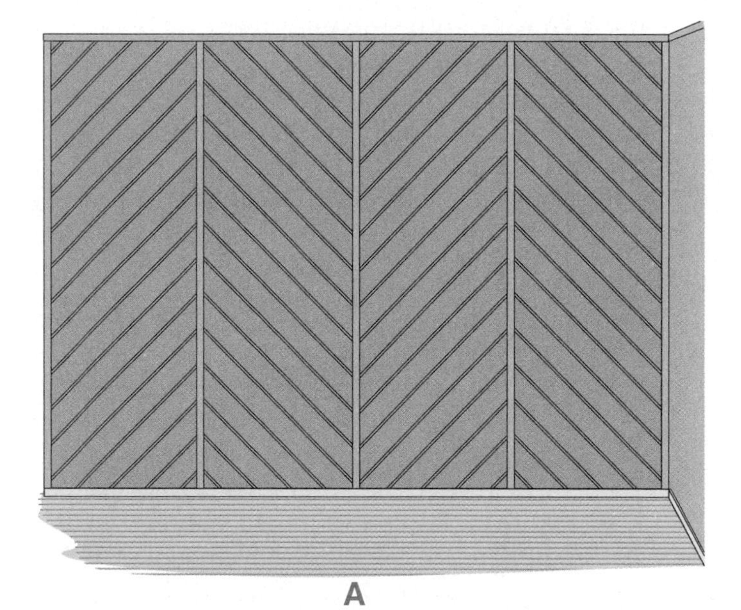

Fig. 37-25. Furring strip placement. *A.* Paneling can be installed in a herringbone style. *B.* To provide a symmetrical installation, locate furring strips accurately.

Estimating...

Paneling

SHEET PANELING

To estimate paneling, you first need to know the room's perimeter.

Step 1 Figure, in inches, the perimeter of the room to be paneled. **Fig. 37-A.**

Step 2 Divide the perimeter by the width of the panel in inches.

Step 3 Multiply this number by the waste allowance, which is usually 5 percent. Round up the result to the nearest whole number. This will be the number of panels you will need. In the eample shown here, 18 4x8 panels are required.

Step 4 If the ceiling height is more than 8′, determine the additional height. For example, if the room shown here has a 10′ ceiling, 2′ of additional height are required. You would use 10′ panels, if they are available, or cut four 2′ pieces from an 8′ panel. Since 18 panels are required to go around the room, 4½ (or, rounded up, 5) additional panels will be required (18 ÷ 4 = 4½). This makes a total of 23 panels.

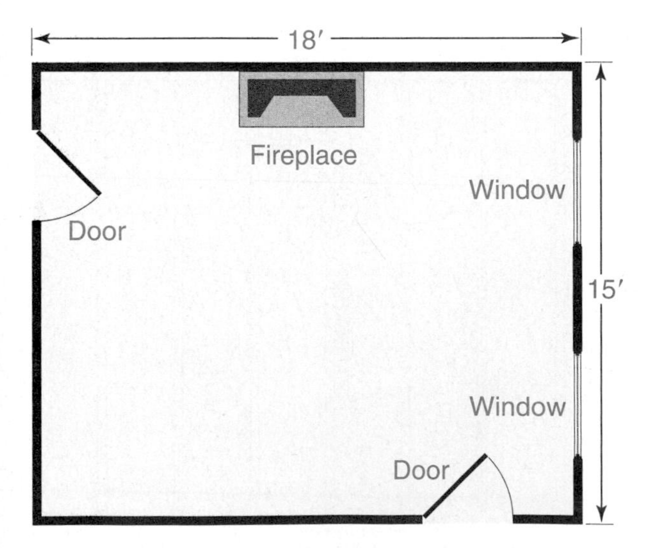

Fig. 37-A. The perimeter of a room is calculated by adding the lengths of the four walls together.

Step 5 Deduct from the panel count for any large areas that will not be paneled, such as a fireplace. Do not deduct for windows and doors.

BOARD PANELING

Board paneling may be estimated by the board foot or by the lineal foot.

Board-Foot Method

Step 1 Figure the wall area to be covered by multiplying the perimeter times the ceiling height. The room shown here has a perimeter of 66′ and a ceiling height of 8′. Its wall area is 528 sq. ft. (66 × 8 = 528).

Step 2 Subtract the area for windows, doors, and fireplaces. Assuming that those in our example total 112 sq. ft., a total of 416 sq. ft. is to be covered by wood paneling (528 – 112 = 416).

Step 3 Multiply the total area to be covered by the area factor shown in **Table 37-B**. For example, suppose we are using tongue-and-groove 1x8 paneling. Its area factor is 1.16. If we multiply that by the 416 sq. ft. of wall space, we need 483 board feet of paneling (416 × 1.16 = 482.56, or 483).

Step 4 Add an allowance for trim and waste. For straight paneling, add 5 percent; for herringbone, add at least 10 percent. In our example, 483 × 0.05 = 24.15, or 24. Then 483 + 24 = 507. The total amount of paneling required is 507 board feet.

(Continued)

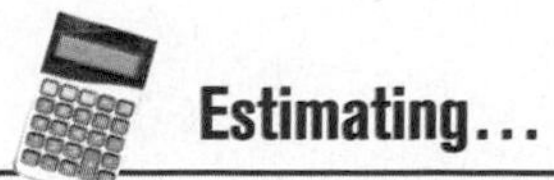

Estimating...

(continued)

Step 5 Multiply this figure by the cost per board foot to determine the total cost of the paneling.

Lineal-Foot Method

Step 1 Measure the height and length of the wall to be paneled.

Step 2 Determine the *face width* of the paneling. This is the portion of the board that will be visible when the paneling is in place. On a tongue-and-groove board, for example, this dimension does not include the tongue. The face width can be measured on a board. It is also given by the manufacturer or supplier in product specifications. For example, 1x6 boards have a face width of 5¼″.

Step 3 Assume that a wall 14′ long and 8′ high will be paneled vertically. Convert the wall length to inches, for a total of 168″ (14′ × 12 = 168″).

Step 4 Divide this total by the face width. The answer will be 32 (168″ ÷ 5.25 = 32). This is the number of boards you will need.

Step 5 Multiply the number of boards by their length: 32 × 8 = 256. This is how many lineal feet of wood you will use. If the wall is 8′-6″ high, however, you will have to order 10′ boards and cut them down to size. You will still need 32 boards, but your lineal-foot total will be 320. For each board, the waste will be 18″.

Step 6 Multiply the total lineal feet by the cost per foot to determine the total cost of the paneling.

ESTIMATING ON THE JOB

Using the board-foot method, estimate the amount of board paneling needed for a 15′ x 20′ room with 8′ ceilings. Assume 126 sq. ft. will be used for doors and windows. The 1x6 panels will be placed tongue-and-groove in the herringbone pattern. How many board feet of paneling are needed?

Table 37-B. Estimating Coverage

Paneling	Nominal Size	Width (inches)		Area Factor[a]
		Dress	Face	
Shiplap	1x6	5 7/16	4 15/16	1.22
	1x8	7 1/8	6 5/8	1.21
Tongue-and-groove	1x4	3 7/16	3 3/16	1.26
	1x6	5 7/16	5 3/16	1.16
	1x8	7 1/8	6 7/8	1.16
S4S	1x4	3 1/2	3 1/2	1.14
	1x6	5 1/2	5 1/2	1.09
	1x8	7 1/4	7 1/4	1.10

[a] Allowance for trim and waste should be added.

Note: For most installations, an allowance of 5 percent will be adequate for trim and waste. Sometimes, rather than add 5 percent, the area of the doors and windows is not subtracted but is used as a trim and waste allowance.

1. Draw a plumb line at the center of every other furring strip. For a 12′ wall, these lines should be 36″ apart, or as close to that as possible.
2. Cut two pieces of paneling in the shape of a 45° triangle, with the tongue on the long edge, as shown in **Fig. 37-26**.
3. Do not assume that the floor is level. Align the triangles with a vertical plumb line and to a level chalk line snapped across the wall at this point. The chalk line will serve to align this pair of starting triangles with other pairs. A molding strip will be applied later to cover the vertical joint.
4. Cut the next pair of boards at a 45° angle and fit them into place on the next centerline. Continue to work across the wall along the other centerlines, building toward the top. A miter saw is extremely useful for repetitive angle cutting such as this.
5. Blind nail the boards to each furring strip. Use the play in the tongue-and-groove joint to keep the boards aligned along the vertical joint. Check their horizontal alignment frequently.
6. After you have installed all the pieces, apply ceiling and baseboard molding. Then apply molding over the vertical joints in the paneling. **Fig. 37-27.** A cove or quarter-round may be used at the corners and a base shoe at the floor if necessary.

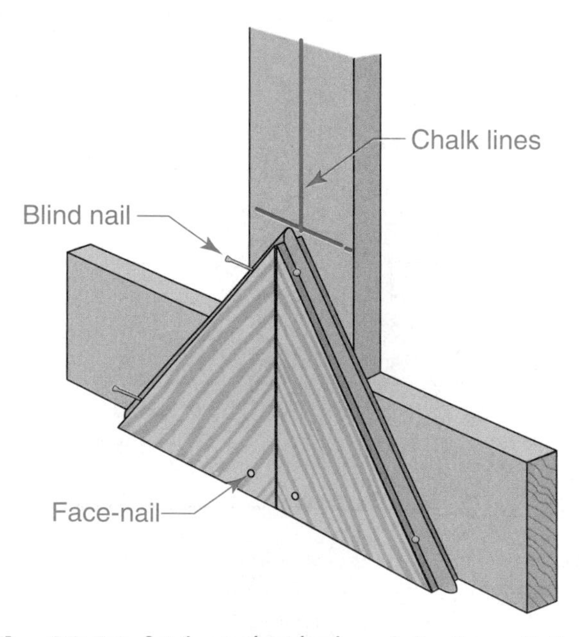

Fig. 37-26. Cut the starting triangles and align them with the chalk lines. Then nail the triangles into place.

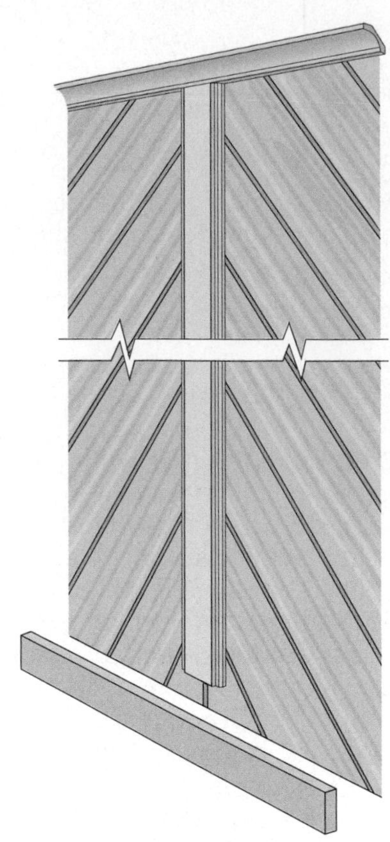

Fig. 37-27. Apply a molding strip at the vertical joint of the paneling. The molding should extend from the baseboard to the ceiling molding.

SECTION 37.3

Check Your Knowledge

1. What is the recommended maximum nominal dimension for solid-wood paneling?
2. When solid-wood paneling is applied vertically directly to studs (if allowed by code), what extra preparation is necessary?
3. What is blind nailing?
4. Is blocking required for horizontal paneling? Why or why not?

On the Job

Referring to Table 37-B, estimate the amount in lineal feet of 1x4 tongue-and-groove board paneling that would be required for wainscoting on two walls of a room. One wall is 12′ long. The other wall is 14′-6″ long. Assume that the wainscoting will be 36″ high, and that there are no doors or windows in these walls.

Chapter 37 Review

Section Summaries

37.1 Wainscoting is paneling that runs only part of the way up a wall. Sheet paneling is the most common and usually comes in 4x8 sheets. Board paneling is made of solid wood, and boards interlock with lap or tongue-and-groove joints. Raised paneling is made of solid wood. Paneling should be conditioned by placing it for at least 48 hours in the room in which it will be used.

37.2 Drywall makes the best backing for sheet paneling. Panels can be applied with nails or adhesives. Molding is used to cover joints and seams. When paneling is installed over masonry, furring strips keep the panels from contacting moisture.

37.3 Board paneling may be installed vertically, horizontally, or at an angle. Blind nailing allows for nails placed through the tongue of one board to be hidden by the next. Edges are undercut to ensure a tight fit in corners.

Review Questions

1. What is wainscoting, and what is its usual height?
2. Name and briefly describe the three basic types of paneling.
3. How should paneling be stored?
4. What are the restrictions for installing MDF paneling?
5. How much clearance should be allowed at the top and bottom of sheet paneling?
6. What spacing is recommended between the long edges of sheet paneling?
7. How should the adhesive be applied when attaching sheet paneling to drywall?
8. What precautions must be taken when applying paneling to masonry walls?
9. When solid-wood paneling is applied to a wall diagonally, what is this pattern called?
10. When estimating sheet paneling, how much is allowed for waste?

Personal Appearance and Hygiene Some people believe that personal appearance and hygiene should not matter on the job. All that should matter is your ability to do the work. Many employers disagree. Their experience has shown them that a worker's appearance and hygiene are a kind of message sent to customers and other workers. A sloppy, dirty, or radical appearance implies that you're not serious about what you're doing. It signals a careless attitude and, in some cases, a lack of self-respect and respect for others. Employers want workers whose appearance sends the message that they're professionals with a no-nonsense, businesslike attitude.

Unit 8

COMPLETING THE STRUCTURE

Careers in Construction

Plumber

Plumbing is one of the mechanical trades. Plumbers install and repair the water, waste disposal, drainage, and gas systems in residential, commercial, and industrial buildings.

Plumbers use building plans or blueprints to install pipes, plumbing fixtures, and appliances. First they lay out the job to fit the piping into the structure of the building. Then they measure and mark areas in which pipes will be installed and connected. To assemble a system, plumbers use special tools to cut and bend lengths of pipe. They connect lengths of pipe with fittings. After the piping is in place, plumbers install fixtures and appliances and connect the system to the outside water or sewer lines. Finally they check the system to ensure that the plumbing works properly.

Nearly all plumbers learn their trade through a 4- or 5-year apprenticeship program. On the job, apprentices first learn to identify types of pipe and use plumbing tools. Later, they learn how to work with various types of pipe and how to install different piping systems and plumbing fixtures.

For more information, check the *Occupational Outlook Handbook* or look up "plumber" on the Internet.

Chapter

38 Mechanicals

Objectives

After reading this chapter, you'll be able to:

- Describe or sketch a simple plumbing system.
- Recognize the various types of piping used for water supply and DWV systems.
- Describe the basic elements of an electrical system.
- Explain how split-system air conditioners work and identify basic parts.

Terms

ampere
circuit
drain field
fixture
infiltration
receptacle
service main
trap

The term *mechanicals* refers in general to plumbing, electrical, and heating/ventilating/air-conditioning (HVAC) systems. Mechanical systems are always installed by specialized subcontractors.

The mechanical trades work at different times during the construction process. For example, plumbers arrive during the rough framing stage to install rough drain lines. They return later to set finish plumbing. Because each trade requires multiple visits, their work must be carefully scheduled. The general contractor is responsible for coordinating the work of mechanical trades.

Each mechanical trade requires specialized tools and a great deal of knowledge. This chapter provides only a general introduction to mechanical systems.

SECTION 38.1

The Plumbing System

The plumber installs the piping system for water and drainage, including all of the fixtures. A plumbing **fixture** is any device that receives or drains water. A bathtub is one example. The plumber must know the sizes of fixtures so that pipes will be in the correct location for each one. **Fig. 38-1.**

Plumbers work with many different materials. Thus, they must possess a wide variety of skills. These include woodworking, metalworking, welding, brazing, soldering, caulking, and pipe threading. **Fig. 38-2.** Their hand tools include wrenches, reamers, drills, braces and bits, hammers, chisels, and saws. Plumbers also must be able to use power tools, such as portable drills and reciprocating saws. They also use oxyacetylene and propane torches for welding, brazing, and soldering.

Specifications for installing plumbing systems are outlined in the *Uniform Plumbing Code (UPC)* or the *International Plumbing Code (IPC)*, in addition to local codes. The installation must be checked by a plumbing inspector at two stages of construction: the rough-in stage and the finish stage.

Fig. 38-2. Plumbers work with various materials. Note that the plastic water-supply piping shown here is not code-approved in all areas.

Fig. 38-1. A full-sized bathroom contains a toilet, a tub or tub/shower, and at least one sink.

The house designer or architect determines the general location and type of fixtures. This information is shown on floor plans. **Fig. 38-3.** (A table titled "Plumbing Symbols" is in the Ready Reference Appendix.) Color, model number, and manufacturer can be found on the plumbing fixture schedule. However, the plumber determines the exact position of each fixture during installation. The plumber is also responsible for locating and installing the pipes to serve those fixtures.

PLUMBING SYSTEM BASICS

A plumbing system brings fresh water into the house and removes solid and liquid wastes. **Fig. 38-4.** The two portions of the system are referred to as the *supply side* and the *waste side.* The waste side is also called the *drain/waste/vent (DWV) system.*

A typical plumbing system consists of three basic types of pipes:

- *Supply pipes.* These are small-diameter pipes usually made of copper. They distribute hot and cold water to fixtures. They are pressurized at up to 160 psi to distribute the water evenly throughout the house.
- *Waste pipes.* These are large-diameter pipes made of plastic or cast iron. They convey liquid and solid wastes away from the house under atmospheric pressure only.
- *Vent pipes.* These are large-diameter plastic pipes. They encourage drainage and remove gases by balancing atmospheric pressure in the waste pipes.

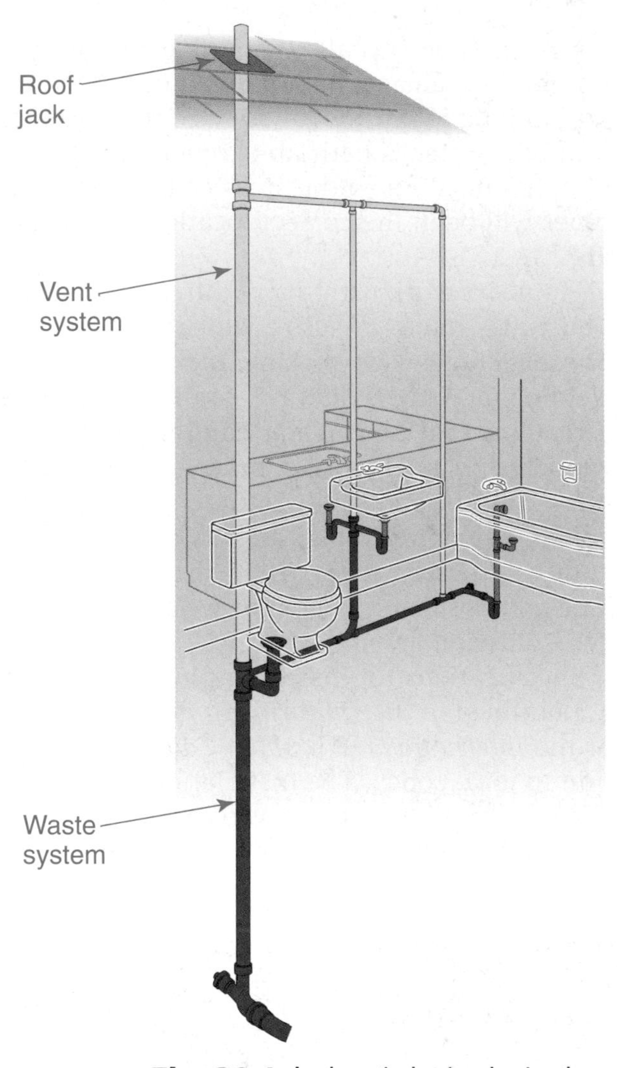

Fig. 38-4. A schematic drawing showing the rough-in plumbing with the finished fixtures set in place. In this installation, the plumbing is installed back to back on a partition wall. A countertop sink is on one side, with a smaller sink on the other side.

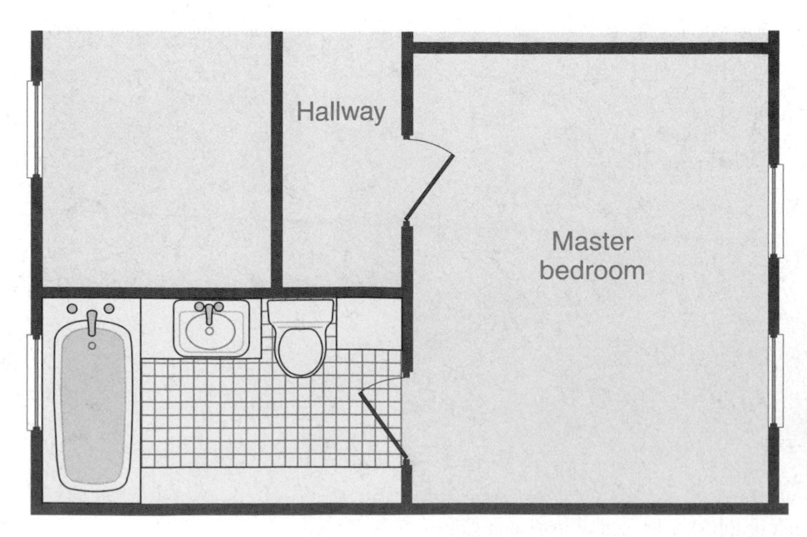

Fig. 38-3. The floor plan shows the location of the bathroom. *Note* the location of the fixtures.

A **service main** is a pipe that brings water to the house. It is connected at the street to the municipal water system. A *water meter* connected to the service main records the amount of water used.

Waste flows out of the house by means of gravity to the sewer or to a septic tank. Any horizontal lengths of waste pipe must be sloped to drain properly.

An important component of the DWV system is a collection of traps. A **trap** is a curved section of drainpipe that is located beneath a fixture. It prevents sewer gases in the waste pipes from entering the house but does not block drainage. A small amount of water in the bottom of each trap serves as a gas plug. **Fig. 38-5.**

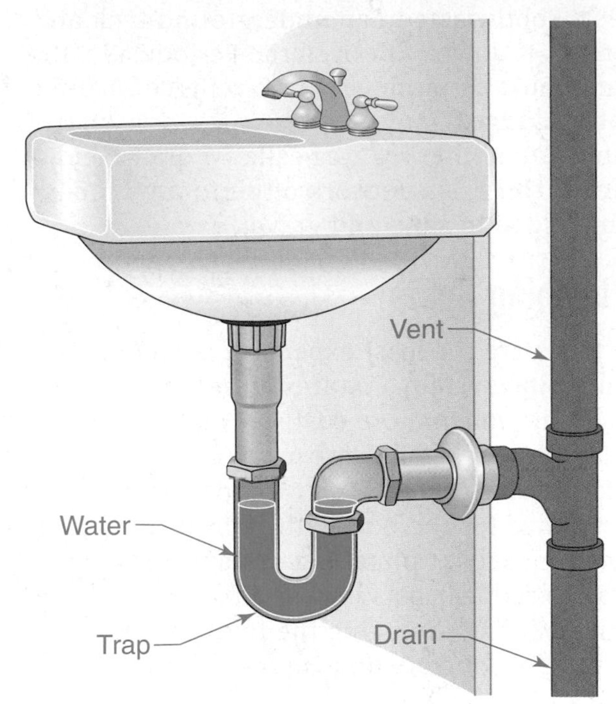

Fig. 38-5. A trap prevents gases from entering the house.

Wells and Septic Systems

Most houses in rural areas are not connected to a municipal water system. Instead, water is supplied by a water pump located near the bottom of a deep but narrow well. The well shaft is lined with pipe capped at the surface. Underground pipes lead from the pump to a tank located inside the house. Fresh water in the tank is kept under pressure and distributed by supply pipes as needed.

Houses served by a well are not usually connected to a sewer. Instead, wastes flow through the DWV system into a below-grade *septic system* on the property. **Fig. 38-6.** The system col-

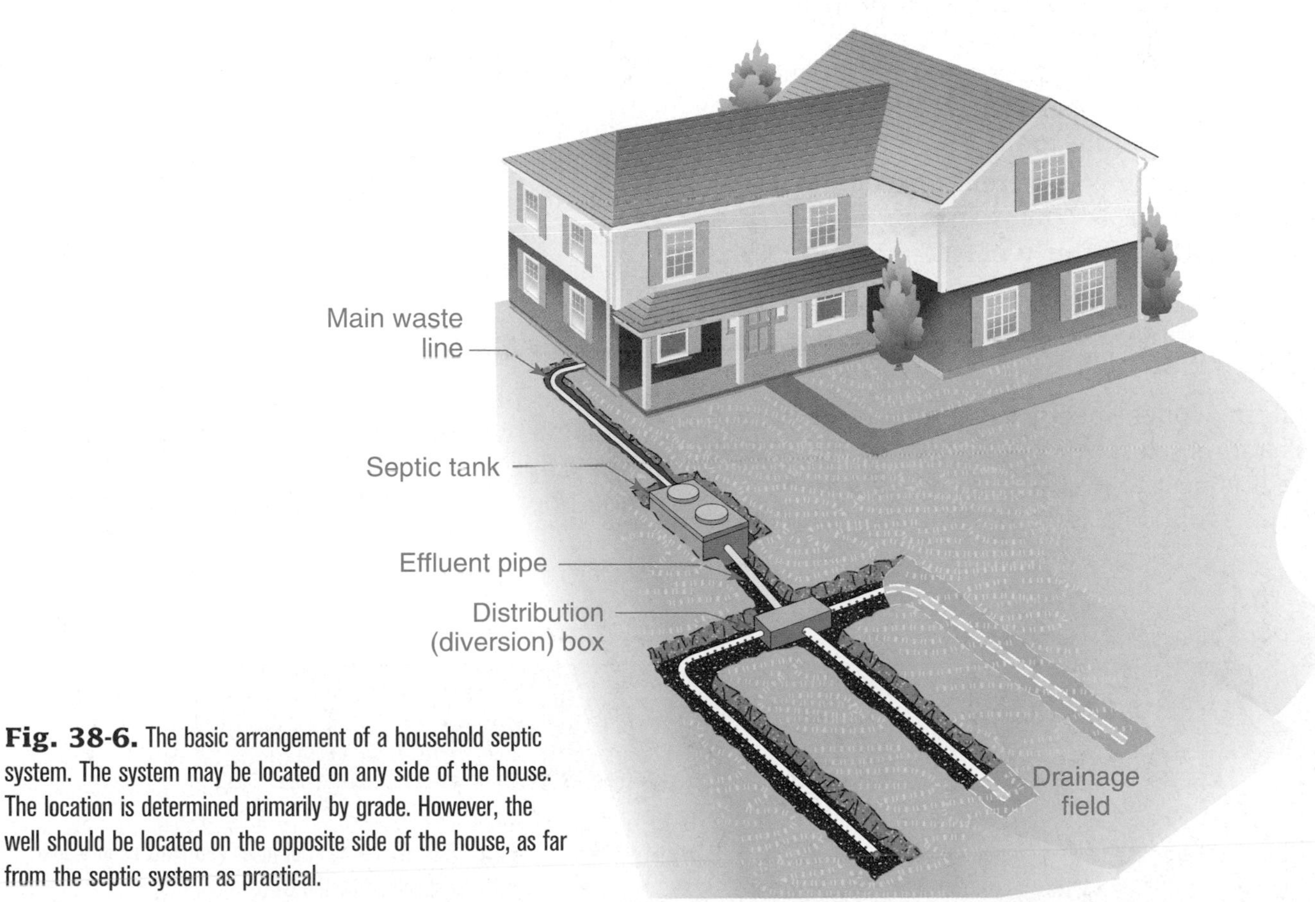

Fig. 38-6. The basic arrangement of a household septic system. The system may be located on any side of the house. The location is determined primarily by grade. However, the well should be located on the opposite side of the house, as far from the septic system as practical.

lects solid waste in an underground tank and breaks it down with bacteria. Periodically, the tank must be pumped out to remove accumulated sludge. Liquid wastes in a septic system flow into a filtering area called a drain field. A **drain field** is a network of perforated pipes embedded in sand and gravel.

Plumbing Costs

Pipes are the least expensive portion of a plumbing system. Fixtures and their related parts are much more costly. A deluxe faucet, for example, can easily cost ten times as much as a modest faucet. **Fig. 38-7.** When preparing cost estimates for the house, the contractor generally looks closely at plumbing system costs. One way to reduce costs is to use fixtures of lower quality. Also, arranging the fixtures efficiently can reduce installation costs.

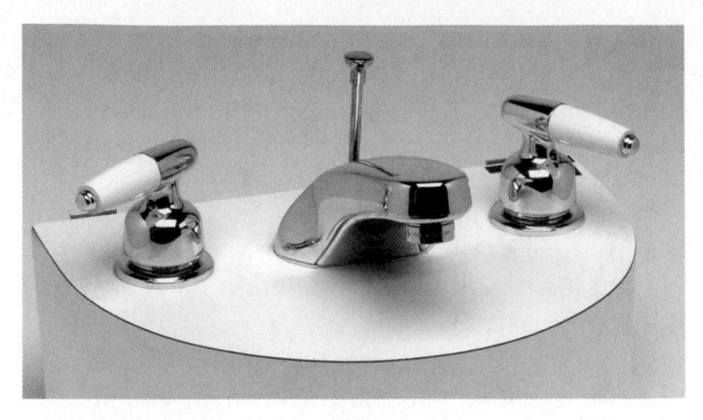

Fig. 38-7. Special plumbing hardware adds to the cost of the total system.

FRAMING REQUIREMENTS

Supply pipes are relatively easy for the plumber to position. Their diameter is small and they are pressurized. This means they can be run in a way that avoids obstacles. However, waste pipes are not as easy to position. The pipes are large and must slope for proper drainage. When framing a house, carpenters should provide adequate space for drain and waste pipes. This is particularly important at bathtub and toilet locations.

Special framing is sometimes needed to support unusually heavy items such as large bathtubs. For details of this type of framing, see Chapter 20, "Floor Framing."

Cutting Floor Joists

Building codes specify the limits for cutting holes and notches in joists and studs. **Fig. 38-8.** While it is best to avoid notching, it is sometimes unavoidable. Joists should then be reinforced by nailing a 2x scab to each side of the altered member, using 12d nails. A scab is a short length of wood used to reinforce another piece. In extreme cases, an additional full-length joist, called a *sister*, can be nailed to the notched joist.

Plumbers often need to bore large holes through a series of joists in order to install waste pipes. The size and location of these holes are limited by code (see Fig. 38-8). When a joist must be cut through completely, the cut ends must be supported by headers. **Fig. 38-9.** Proper planning during framing can usually eliminate the need to alter joists.

PLUMBING MATERIALS

Pipes and tubing used in plumbing systems are made of several different materials and are joined in different ways. Most new supply systems have copper piping, while most DWV pipes are made of plastic.

Supply Piping

Copper pipes are joined with copper fittings that slide over the pipes and are then soldered. Pipes come in 10′ and 20′ lengths. Main distribution lines are ¾″ or 1″ in diameter. Branch dis-

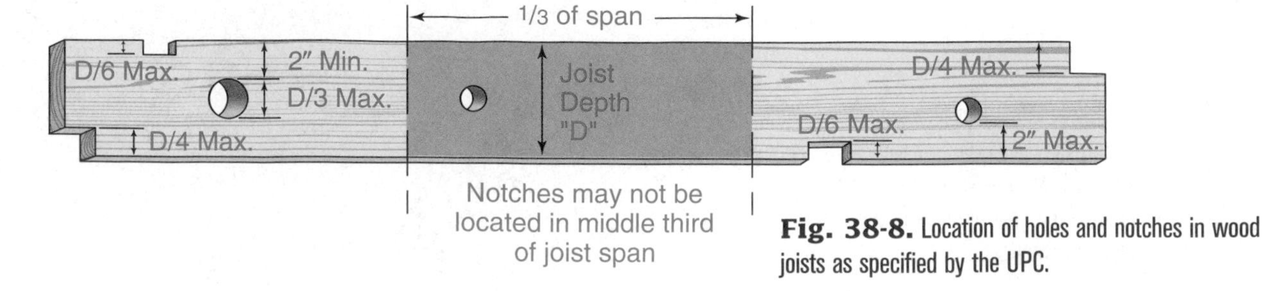

Fig. 38-8. Location of holes and notches in wood joists as specified by the UPC.

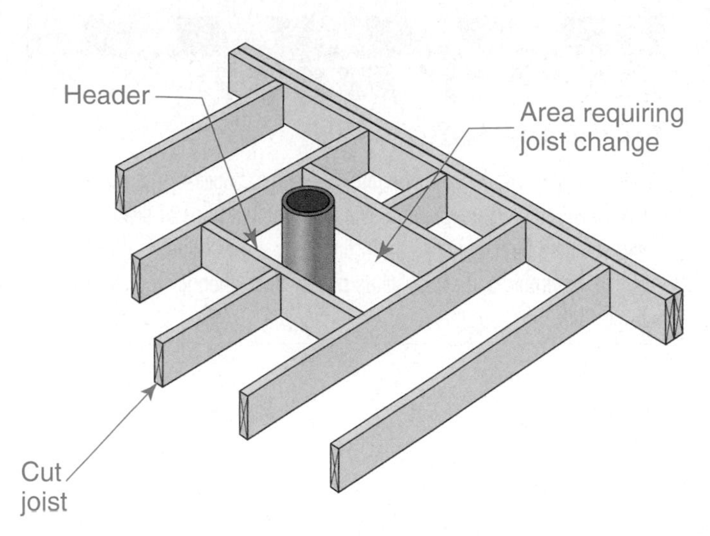

Fig. 38-9. Headers are used to support joists that must be cut through.

tribution lines lead to individual fixtures. **Fig. 38-10.** They are typically ½″ in diameter. Copper pipe comes in three wall thicknesses:

- Type M. Thin wall. This is most common in residential construction.
- Type L. Medium wall.
- Type K. Thick wall. Used for underground water lines.

Flexible copper tubing is much smaller in diameter than copper piping. It comes in coils up to 100′ long. It is used to supply appliances that use water, such as dishwashers and refrigerator icemakers. It is connected by friction fittings instead of being soldered.

Fittings for soldered connections come in many shapes and in each of the three pipe diameters. The joints between pipes and fittings are soldered (sweated) to seal the pipes and fittings together. **Fig. 38-11.** Solder was once a combination of lead and tin. However, lead in

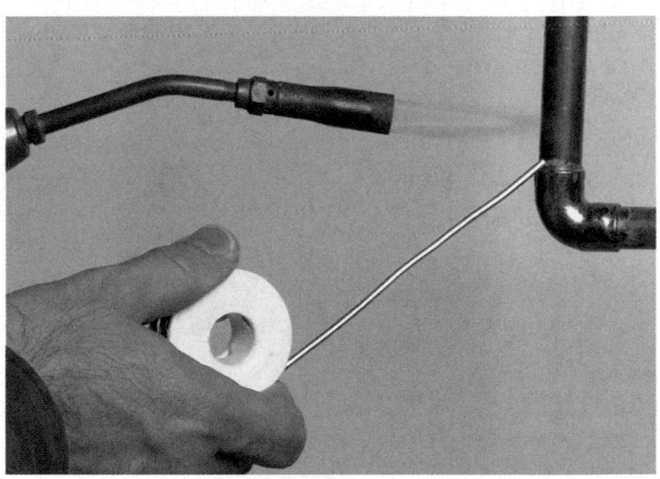

Fig. 38-11. Use a non-lead solder that is a combination of tin, copper, and silver to make a tight joint, with the heat supplied by a propane torch.

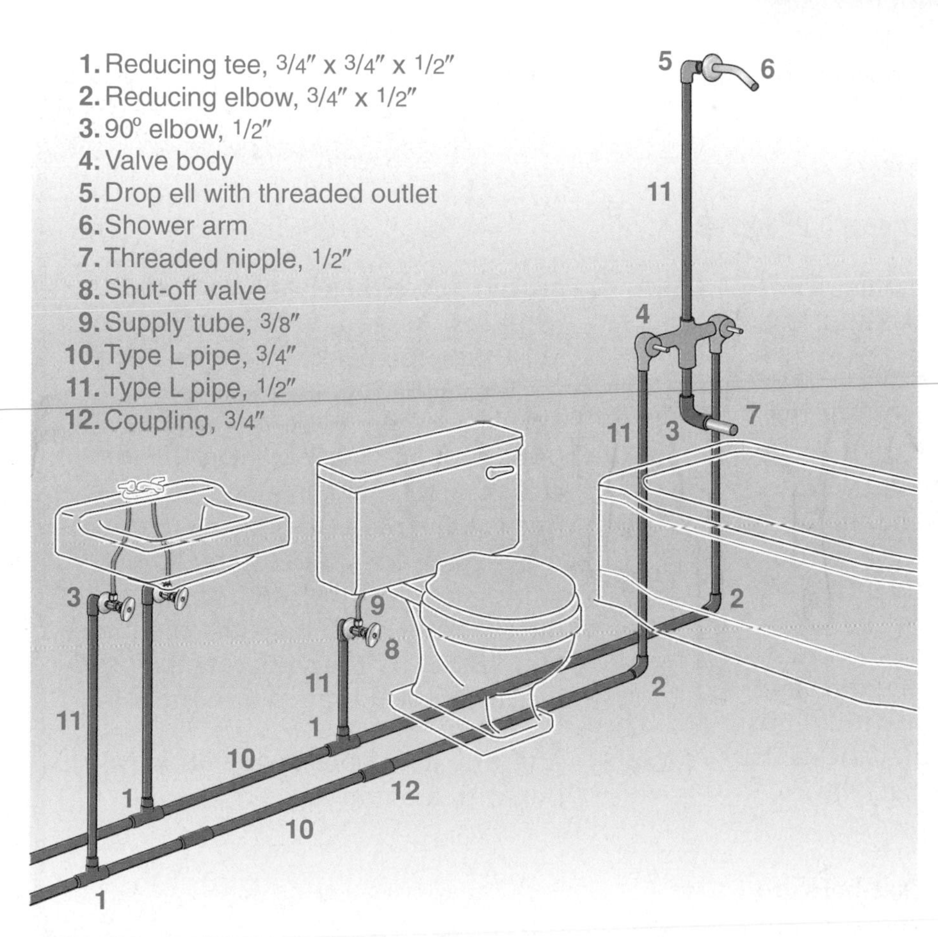

Fig. 38-10. Common pipe fittings required for a water supply system in a bathroom.

water supply systems is a health hazard. Lead-free solder has therefore been required since 1988. Galvanized steel pipe is common in the supply systems of older homes, but it is not used for new homes. Fittings connecting lengths of steel pipe are threaded, not soldered.

Plastic pipe can sometimes be used for water supply piping. However, always check for local code approval before using plastic supply pipe. Some materials are approved only in limited areas or for limited uses. They include chlorinated polyvinyl chloride (CPVC), polybutylene (PB), and polyethylene (PE). Plastic supply pipe is lightweight, easy to handle, and resists fracture in freezing conditions. Connections are threaded and/or solvent welded.

The basic technique for soldering copper pipe is described in the Step-by-Step feature below. The technique must be repeated for each joint in a supply system.

SAFETY FIRST

Soldering Safety

When installing copper supply piping, it is often necessary to solder overhead. Protect your eyes and skin from molten drips of solder. Avoid standing directly under the fittings you are working on. When possible, assemble and solder joints on the floor, then lift the assembly into position.

DWV Piping

Cast-iron drainpipe (sometimes called *soil pipe*) is used for waste systems in higher-quality construction. It is harder to install than plastic drainpipe but muffles the sound of water rushing through. The *bell end* of a cast-iron pipe is flared. The *spigot end* fits into the bell end. The joints are sealed using various methods.

STEP BY STEP

Soldering Copper Pipe

After the system has been assembled, it should be pressurized and checked for leaks. Faulty joints must be resoldered.

Step 1 Measure a length of pipe to fit the location, and cut it to length using a tubing cutter. **Fig. 38-12.** Use the reamer on the back of the tubing cutter to smooth out any burrs left on the inside of the pipe. Test fit the pipe into the fitting.

Step 2 The *outside* surface of the pipe and the *inside* surface of the fitting must be shiny-clean where they meet. Use fine emery cloth or a special wire brush to clean the surfaces.

Step 3 *Flux* is a special paste that helps to draw solder into the joint. Use a flux brush to coat the cleaned surfaces with flux. Assemble the joint and twist the pipe back and forth briefly to spread the flux evenly.

Step 4 Use a propane torch to heat the joint area evenly. Touch a length of lead-free solder to the area frequently. When the solder starts to melt, quickly turn off the torch and hold the tip of the solder against the joint. **Fig. 38-13.** As the solder melts, *capillary action* will draw it into the joint.

Step 5 After the joint cools, wipe off surplus flux with a damp rag.

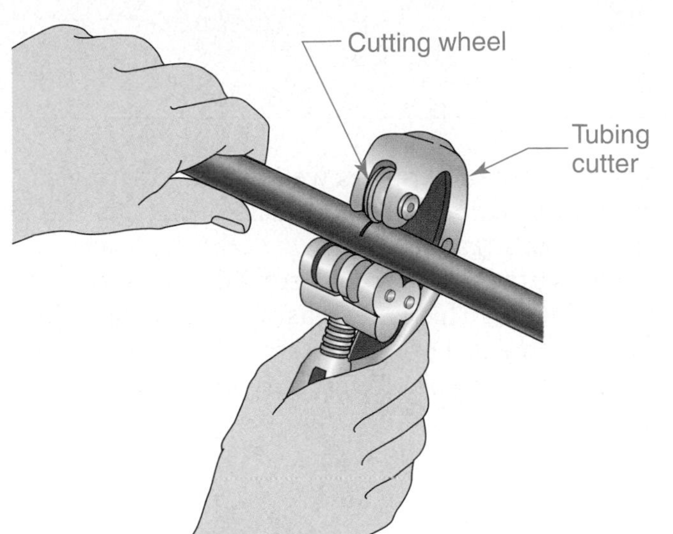

Fig. 38-12. Cut the pipe by rotating the tubing cutter. The cutter's wheel will gradually slice through the copper.

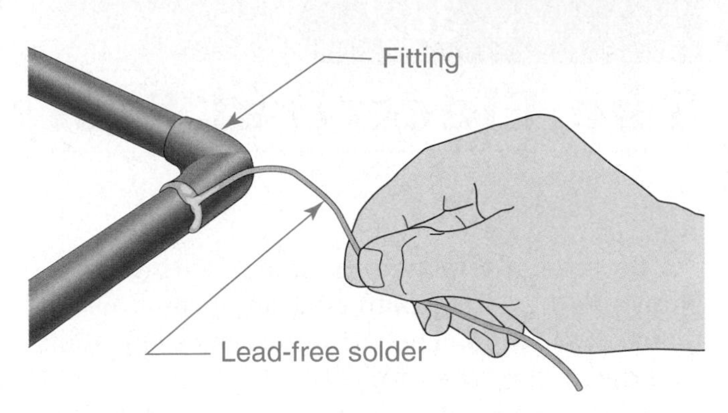

Fig. 38-13. Remove the torch and immediately touch the solder to the joint.

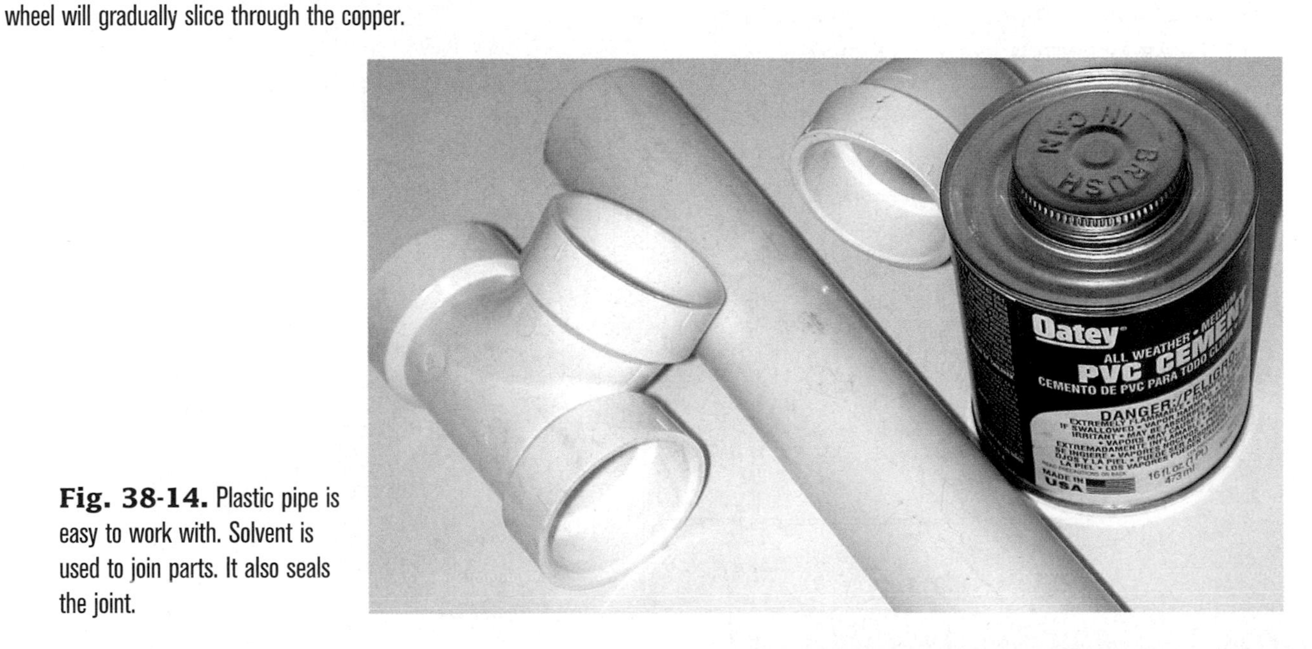

Fig. 38-14. Plastic pipe is easy to work with. Solvent is used to join parts. It also seals the joint.

The black plastic pipe most commonly used in DWV systems is acrylonitrile-butadiene-styrene (ABS). It is inexpensive, lightweight, and easy to cut. It is joined using a solvent cement.

White plastic pipe is made from polyvinyl chloride (PVC). It has considerably lower thermal expansion characteristics than ABS. This makes it suitable for long pipe runs. It is sometimes joined using a solvent-type primer followed by PVC cement. **Fig. 38-14.** One-step primer-cements are also available. Before connecting ABS or PVC pipe to a fitting, cut the pipe square with a fine-tooth saw. Plumbers use saws intended specifically for cutting plastic. A hacksaw will also work. Be sure to remove any burrs from the end of the pipe after cutting it.

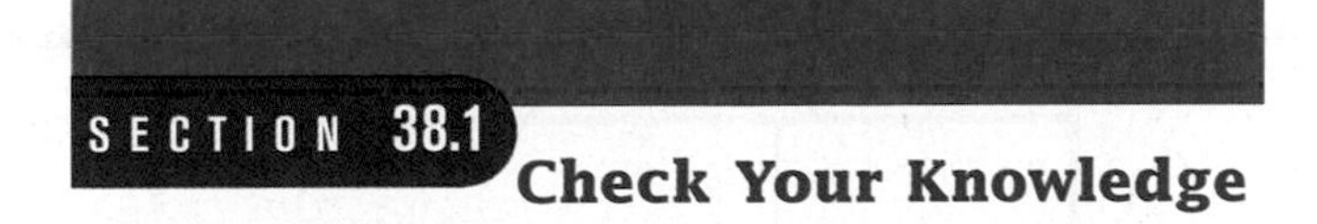

Check Your Knowledge

1. What does the abbreviation HVAC stand for?
2. At what stages must a plumbing inspector check a plumbing system while it is being installed?
3. What is a trap and what is its purpose?
4. How can joists be reinforced after notching?

On the Job

Research plumbing systems installed by the ancient Romans. What materials did they use for pipes? Based on what you've learned about solder, discuss the health implications of Roman pipe and present your findings to the class.

The Electrical System

The general scheme of a home's wiring is shown in the wiring plan portion of the floor plans. **Fig. 38-15.** The wiring plans use symbols to indicate the type of electrical devices to install at each location. (A table titled "Electrical Symbols" is in the Ready Reference Appendix.) The location of wires, as well as the exact placement of switches and receptacle outlets, is the electrician's responsibility.

The wiring plans should consider present and future needs. This is increasingly important due to the home use of computers and other electrical equipment once found only in office build-

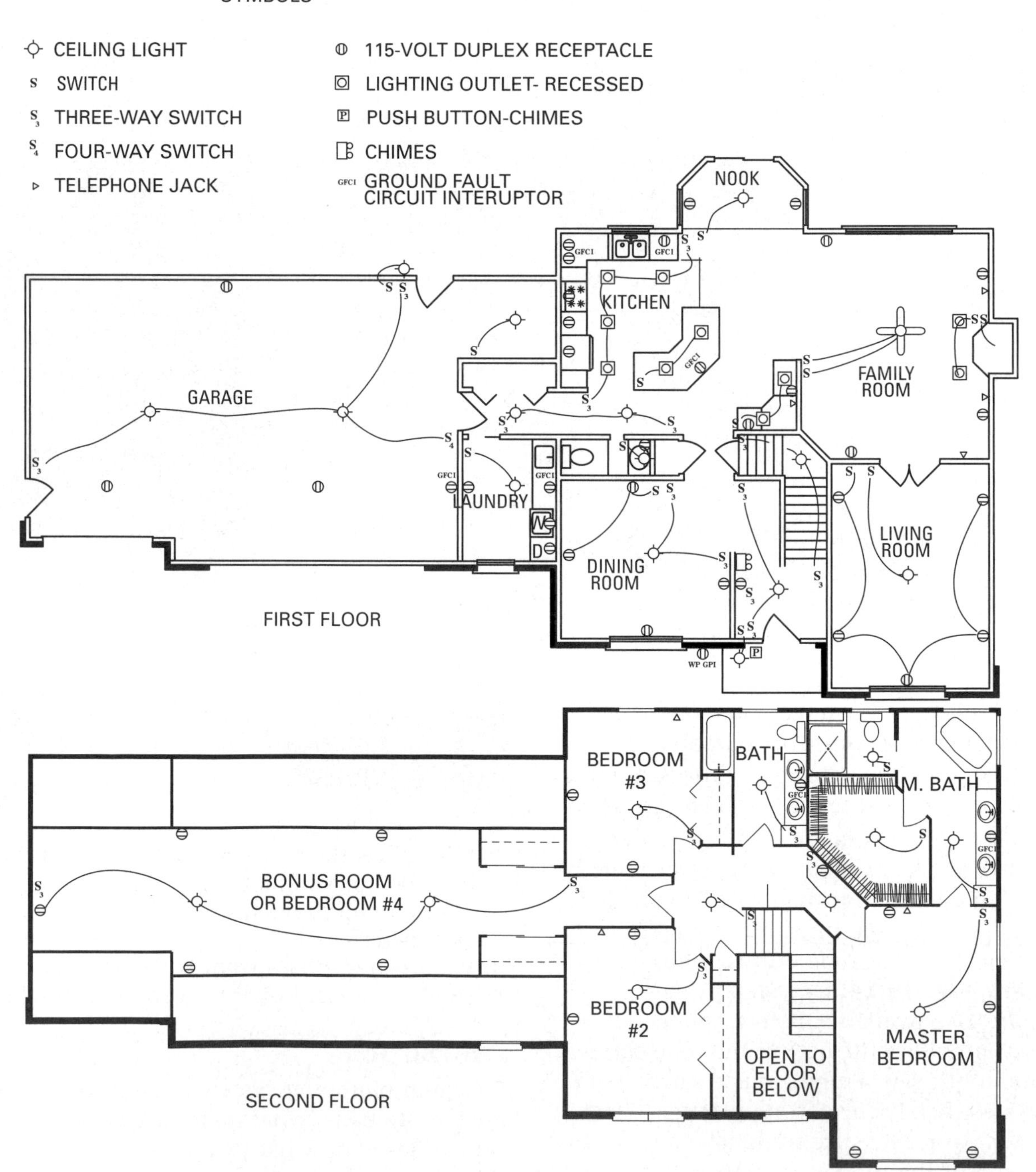

Fig. 38-15. A floor plan showing the electrical system. The electrician uses this plan to locate and install the various outlet (junction) boxes and the necessary wiring.

ings. Specialized wiring is often added during this phase. This includes cable for television, as well as high-speed Internet access. Additional wiring may serve phone, audio, intercom, and other systems. Electricians install the general electrical system. Other contractors may be called on to install specialized wiring. **Fig. 38-16.**

ELECTRICAL SYSTEM BASICS

All power comes into a building through the service entrance wires. These may be overhead wires or an underground cable. **Fig. 38-17.** New houses are supplied with 200-ampere service. An **ampere** (*amp*) is a measure of electrical current. The service entrance wires run first to the *watt-hour meter*. This records how much electricity is used within the house. In newer homes, digital watt-hour meters are installed to make recording usage easier.

From the meter, the wires run to a master distribution panel, called the *service panel*. The panel is usually located in the basement of the house. At the top of the service panel is a *master switch*. It is used to cut off all electricity in the house. This would be done in an emergency or when various parts of the wiring system are being worked on.

Smaller wires lead from the service panel to points throughout the house. The wires are organized into circuits. A **circuit** is a cable or group of cables that supplies electricity to a specific area or appliance. It can be connected or disconnected without affecting any other circuit. Each circuit is connected to an individual device called a *circuit breaker*. Circuit breakers are located inside the service panel. The circuit breaker is like a fast-acting switch. It shuts off power in a circuit if it detects overloads that might lead to a fire. The circuit breaker can also be turned off manually if maintenance work must be performed on the circuit.

A house could easily have as many as twenty-five or more separate circuits. There are three basic kinds of circuits:

- An *appliance circuit* is wired with No. 12 wire and connected to a 20-ampere circuit breaker. At least two appliance circuits are needed in the kitchen. An appliance circuit might also be added in a basement to provide electricity for shop tools.
- A *general-purpose circuit* is wired with No. 14 wire and connected to a 15-ampere circuit breaker. It also may use No. 12 wire and a 20-amp circuit breaker. These circuits lead to lighting and to all receptacles.
- A *special-purpose circuit* supplies the needs of stoves, air conditioners, furnaces, and other appliances that use large amounts of electricity. It often serves a single appliance. This circuit uses thicker wire than other circuits and is connected to a 30-ampere or greater circuit breaker.

Fig. 38-16. A typical home office requires receptacles for a variety of electrical and electronic devices. A second circuit serving just this room might be required. Jacks for phones and high-speed Internet access may also be desirable.

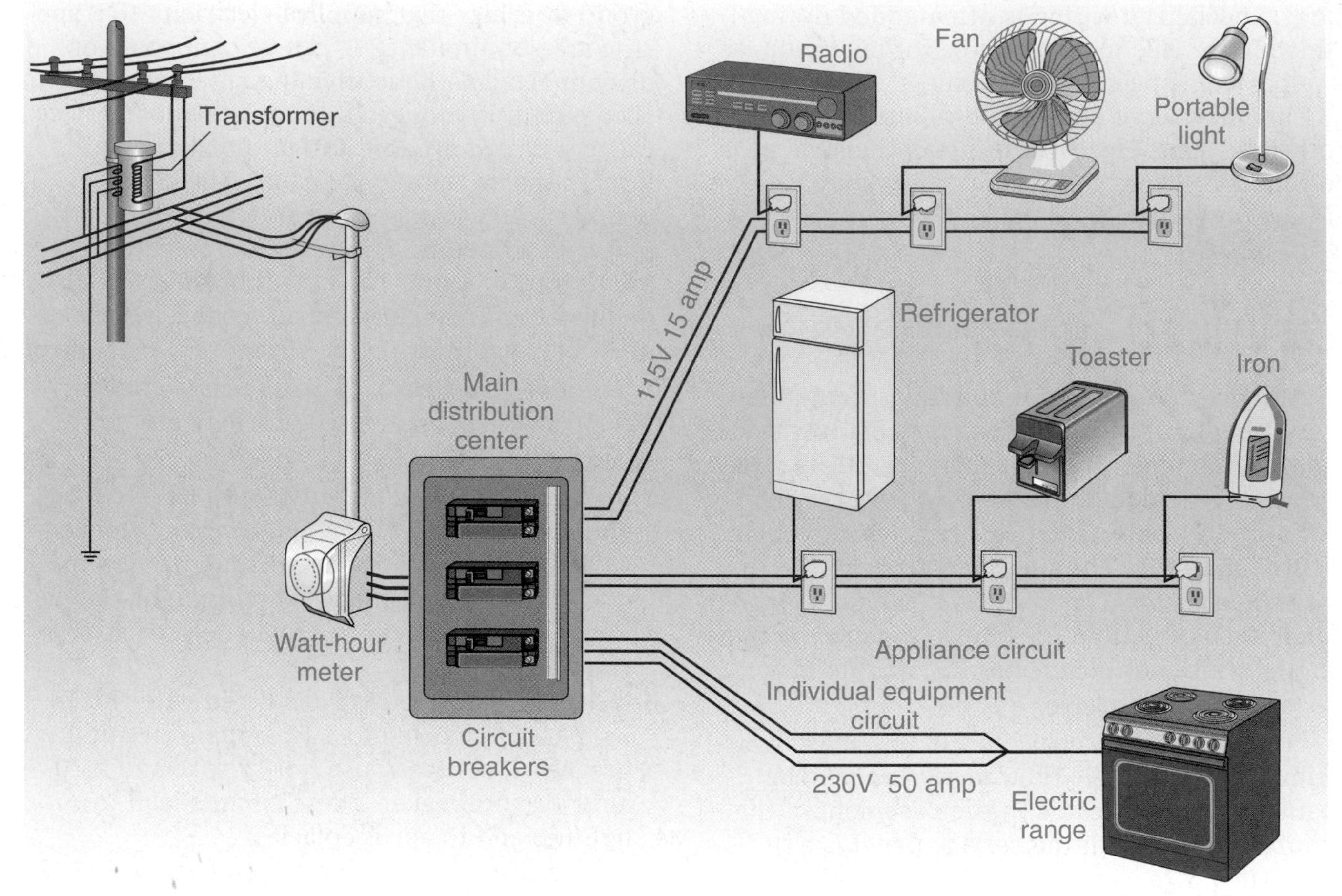

Fig. 38-17. A pictorial drawing of the electrical service to the house and the inside circuits. Circuits carry 115 and 230 volts. Minimums are 110 and 220 volts. Maximums are 120 and 240 volts.

Wire numbers are based on the American Wire Gauge (AWG) system. Each gauge number is associated with a particular diameter. For example, a No. 12 (12 gauge) wire is 0.081″ in diameter, and a No. 14 (14 gauge) wire is 0.064″ in diameter. The greater the diameter, the more current a wire can carry.

- *Nonmetallic sheathed cable wiring* is the most common, the simplest to install, and the least expensive. The cable consists of two or three insulated copper conductors and one bare copper conductor within a thermoplastic covering. All wires within a cable are always the same size.

ELECTRICAL MATERIALS

Several different kinds of wire and wiring systems are allowed by electrical codes. **Fig. 38-18.** Electrical wires are referred to as *conductors*. This distinguishes them from standard utility wire.

Dangerous Current

In cases of electric shock, current is what kills. A person can die from as little as one-tenth the amount of current needed to light a light bulb. Always follow all safety precautions when dealing with electricity.

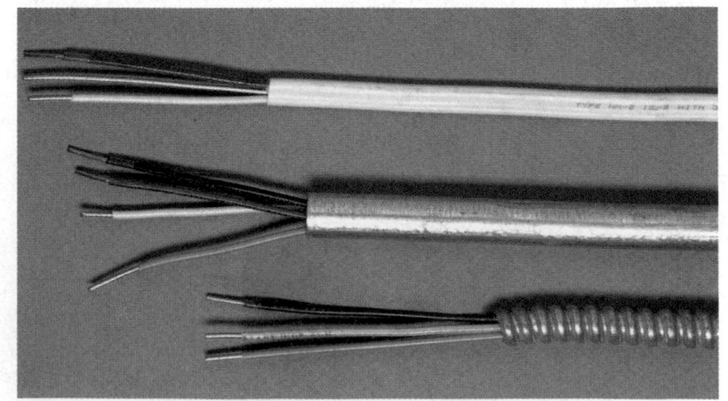

Fig. 38-18. Three kinds of wiring used between the circuit breakers and the outlet (junction) boxes: sheathed cable (top); conduit, or rigid (middle); and armored cable, or flexible (bottom).

- *Armored cable* is used in exposed locations where mechanical damage might be expected. This hollow cable, commonly called BX, has a flexible metal exterior. Individual insulated conductors are contained within the cable.
- *Rigid metal* or *plastic conduit* is used in exposed locations and sometimes underground. Like BX cable, it protects the conductors inside. Metal conduit can be bent around corners, using a special tool. **Fig. 38-19.** Plastic conduit is joined with solvent and plastic fittings.

Wiring leads from the service panel to various types and sizes of metal or plastic *outlet boxes.* **Fig. 38-20.** Outlet boxes provide a convenient location for joining wire and prevent dust and debris from collecting on the connectors. They limit damage from short circuits and other wiring faults that could cause fires. They provide a solid mounting surface for switches, receptacles, and other devices.

An outlet box is required wherever wiring will be connected to a device, such as a switch, a ceiling light, or a receptacle. A **receptacle** has a combination of slots and grounding holes sized to accept the prongs of an electrical plug. An outlet box is also required wherever lengths of wiring are spliced together. Wiring must never be spliced outside a box.

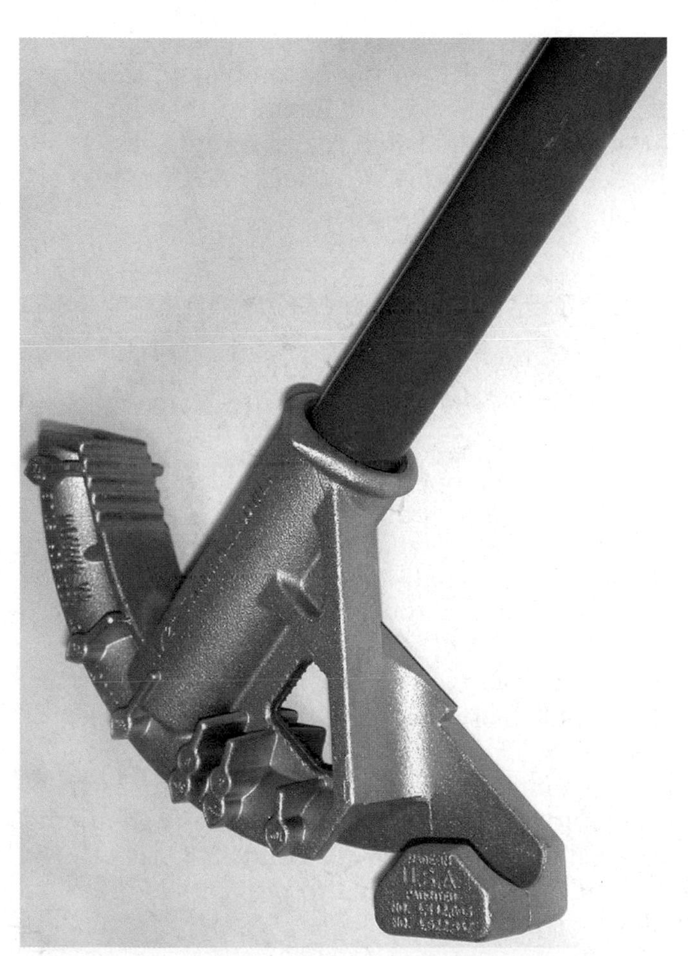

Fig. 38-19. A conduit bender is used to shape a length of conduit.

Fig. 38-20. Outlet boxes are available in a wide variety of sizes.

Wiring enters a box through pre-punched holes. Boxes are usually made of plastic but may also be made of metal. They are nailed securely to the framing. The electrician must position each box so that its front edge will be flush with the final wall covering.

WIRING A HOUSE

Wiring is done in two stages: the rough-in stage and the finish stage. The rough-in wiring is done after the exterior of the house has been completed but before the insulation has been installed. The electrician first installs the distribution panel and connects it to the service wiring. **Fig. 38-21.** Cables are run from the panel into outlet boxes throughout the house. Inside each outlet box the outer sheathing of the cable is stripped off to expose individual conductors. The conductors are left exposed until the finish wiring stage. **Fig. 38-22.**

After the rough-in wiring is completed and has been approved by a building inspector, insulation and wall finishes can be installed. After the interior of the house has been painted, the electrician returns to complete the finish wiring. All switches, receptacles, and lighting fixtures are connected at this stage, both inside and outside the house. **Fig. 38-23.** The electrician connects conductors by twisting their bare ends together and then twisting on a threaded cap called a *wire nut* or *wire connector.*

Fig. 38-21. Circuit breakers are located in the main distribution panel. Never work on the panel unless you are absolutely certain that power is not being supplied to it.

Fig. 38-22. Nonmetallic sheathed cable is run into the box and left exposed until the interior is completed. Note the crayon mark on the stud used to establish where the box is to be attached.

Fig. 38-23. Connecting a light switch. Power must not be turned on until the fixtures are ready to be tested. The V-shaped mark on the stud was made during the rough-wiring stage. It indicates to which side of the stud the box should be attached.

When the finish wiring is completed, the electrician tests it. Outlet covers must then be attached over all switches and receptacles. The inspector then returns to check and approve, or "final," the installation.

SECTION 38.2 Check Your Knowledge

1. What is an ampere?
2. What is the purpose of a circuit breaker?
3. What is a receptacle?
4. During the rough-in phase, what happens to cable after it is routed to the outlet boxes?

On the Job

The handles of tools used by electricians are insulated. This reduces the danger from accidental contact with a live conductor. Research the topic of electric shock. What steps should be taken if someone receives a shock? What safety precautions can be taken to prevent electric shock on a job site?

SECTION 38.3

Heating, Ventilating, and Air-Conditioning (HVAC) Systems

Without effective temperature control, houses in many parts of the country would be either too hot or too cold. However, heating, ventilation, and air-conditioning needs vary from region to region. Because these systems can be costly to operate, a great deal of research is under way to make them more energy efficient. This means getting more energy from less fuel. New HVAC systems are far more efficient than older systems. The thermostats controlling the systems are also more efficient. For example, digital thermostats can be programmed to turn on the system only at certain times of the day. **Fig. 38-24.**

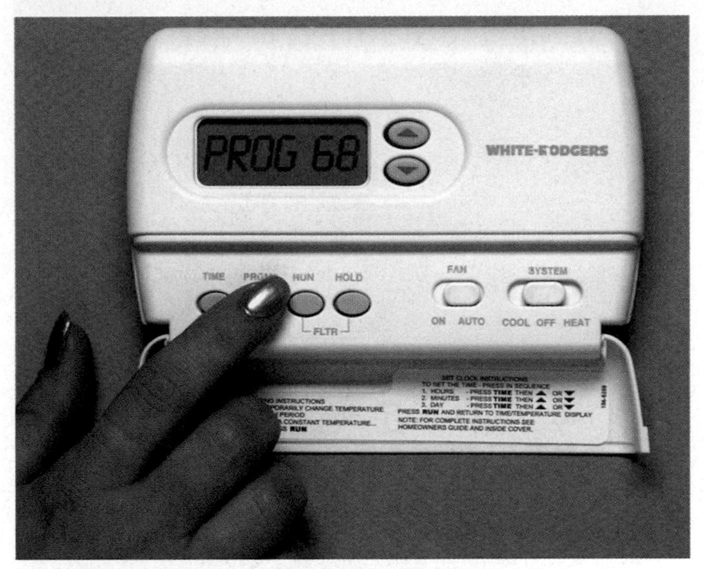

Fig. 38-24. A programmable electronic thermostat.

HEATING SYSTEMS

There are many types of heating systems. Some are combined with air-conditioning and ventilation systems. Heating systems are categorized primarily by the way the heat is distributed, not by the fuel they use. Various fuels can supply the power needed.

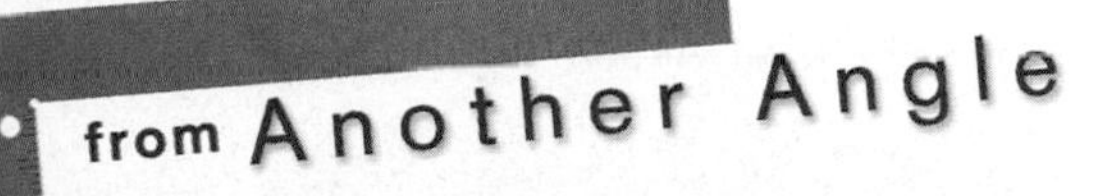

from Another Angle

Climate and the type of heating fuel used vary from region to region. These factors affect the type of heating system that is most common. In the eastern United States, for example, the oil-fired furnace is popular. In the Northwest it is common to heat with electricity. The climate is relatively mild, and electricity is fairly inexpensive (compared to oil) due to plentiful hydroelectric resources. In still other parts of the country, natural gas is the preferred fuel. In regions with consistently clear skies, solar-assisted heating systems are a workable option.

Forced Hot-Air Heating

A *forced hot-air heating system* consists of a furnace, ducts, and registers. The system is popular because it responds quickly to changes in outdoor temperatures. It can be used in many types of houses. The ducts and registers can also be used to distribute cool air created by a central air conditioner.

Fuel is burned inside the furnace. **Fig. 38-25.** A blower circulates the warm air to the rooms through *supply ducts.* The ducts may be made of sheet metal, flexible insulated tubes, or rigid fiberglass insulation. **Fig. 38-26.** *Supply registers* are located along the outside walls of the house. There is usually a *return-air register* in each room. It is usually located across the room from the supply registers. As air within the room cools, it sinks to the floor and flows into the return air register. Return registers and ducts carry cooled room air back to the furnace. There, it is reheated and recirculated. **Fig. 38-27.**

In houses with a slab foundation, *perimeter loop systems* may be used. Cylindrical ducts are located within the slab. They must be put into place after the foundation formwork is complete. **Fig. 38-28.**

Fig. 38-25. A gas-fired hot-air furnace. *A.* This one is fitted with an electronic air cleaner (attached to the left side of the furnace.) *B.* The inside of the furnace.

Fig. 38-26. Installing fiberglass heating ducts.

Fig. 38-27. Most forced hot-air systems have a cold-air return in each room (except the bathroom and the kitchen). When the basement is heated, additional ducts should deliver hot air near the basement floor along the outside walls.

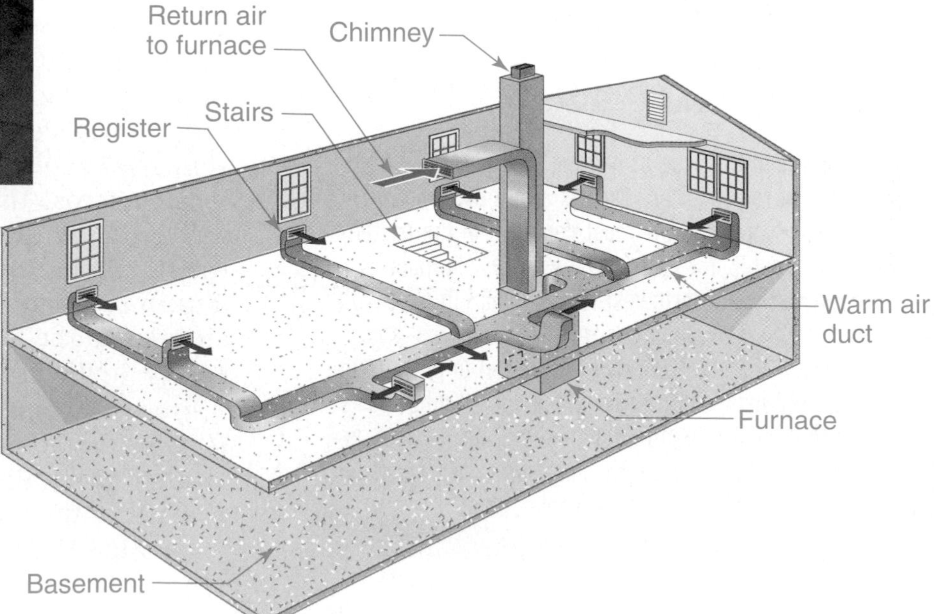

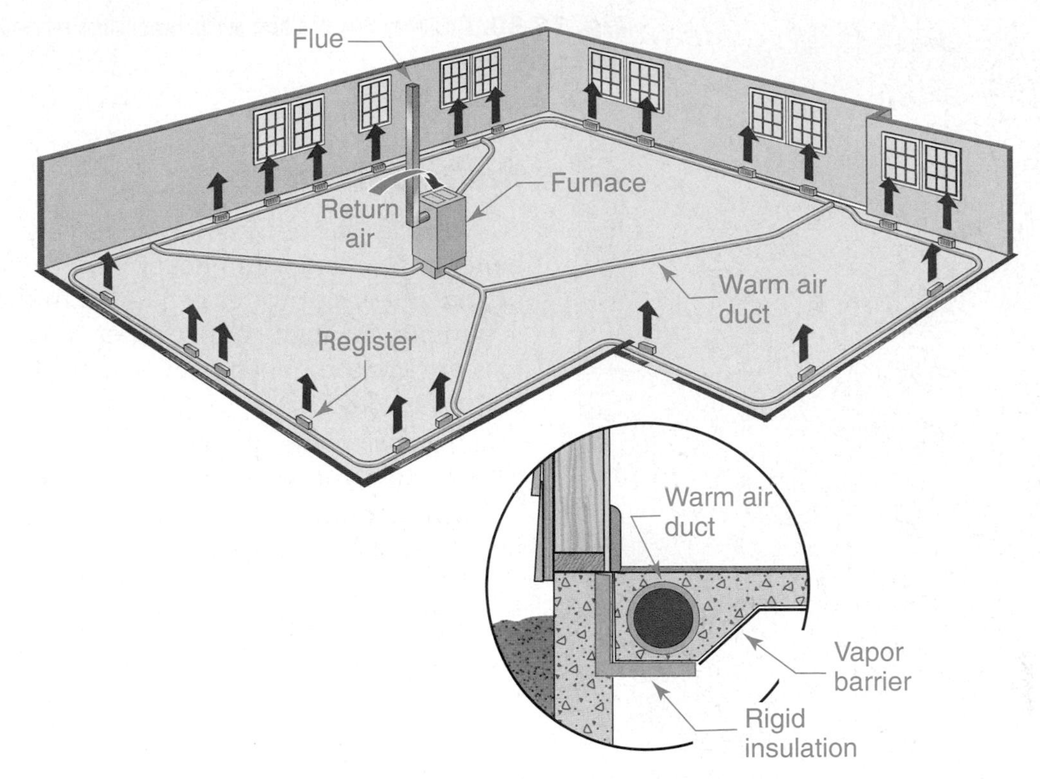

Fig. 38-28. Perimeter loop heating systems are often used in houses built on a concrete slab.

Heated air is filtered through replaceable or washable filters. Clogged filters reduce the effectiveness of the system. The homeowner can easily remove them for inspection on a regular basis during the heating season. *Electronic air cleaners* can be installed in some heating systems. They are very effective at removing pollen, fine dust, and other irritants that normally pass through standard filters. The part within the electronic air cleaner that actually removes contaminants is called a *cell.* **Fig. 38-29.** The homeowner should clean it periodically.

A *humidifier* is sometimes added to a hot-air system. A humidifier adds moisture to the air inside the house and counteracts the drying effects of hot air.

A *heat pump* is a device that can heat or cool the air. **Fig. 38-30.** It is useful in mild climates that do not experience extremely cold temperatures. The heat pump is connected to standard duct systems.

Fig. 38-29. This technician is installing cells for an electronic air cleaner. He is sliding the first cell into place. A side view of a second cell is visible to the right of the first one. Cells are removable for cleaning.

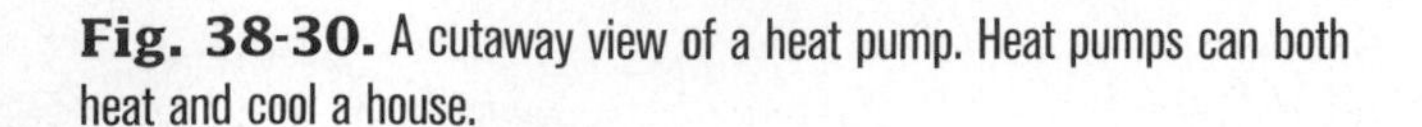

Fig. 38-30. A cutaway view of a heat pump. Heat pumps can both heat and cool a house.

Hydronic Heating

Hydronic, or *hot-water, systems* consist of a boiler, pipes, and room-heating units (*convectors* or *radiators*). Hot water generated in the boiler is pumped through copper pipes to the convectors or radiators. Then heat radiates into the room. **Fig. 38-31.**

Boilers are made of steel or cast iron. **Fig. 38-32.** They are designed for use with electricity, coal, natural gas, or oil. Boilers designed for remote areas can use wood as the basic fuel.

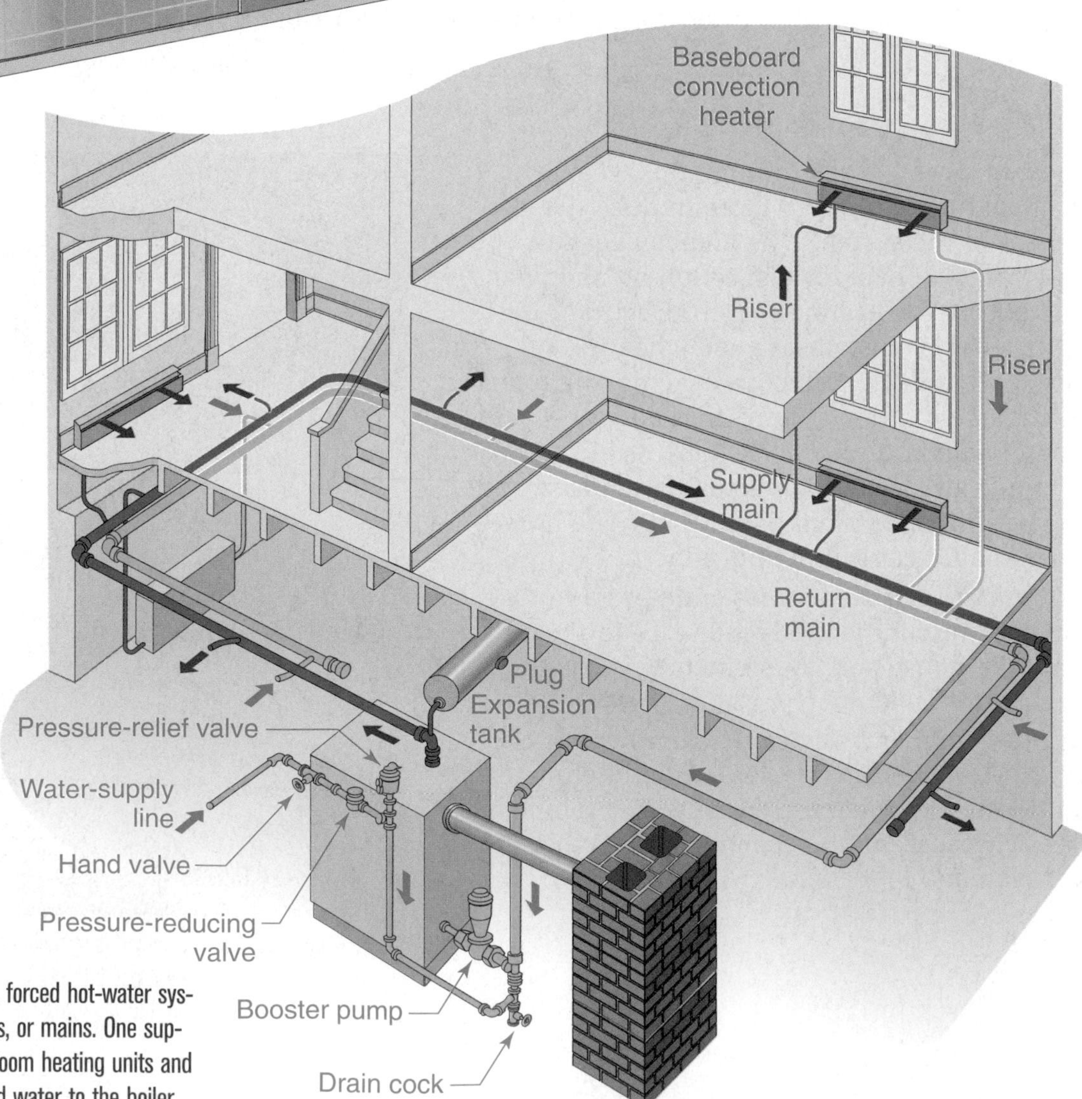

Fig. 38-31. Two-pipe, forced hot-water systems have two supply pipes, or mains. One supplies the hot water to the room heating units and the other returns the cooled water to the boiler.

One problem with any system based on a boiler is that corrosion can shorten boiler life. Boilers should be inspected at the beginning of each heating season.

Convectors usually consist of tubes with fins. They are enclosed in a housing that has openings at the top and bottom. Hot water circulates through the tubes. The fins maximize the transfer of heat to the surrounding air. Convectors usually run along the baseboards and are often placed under windows. Low-profile convectors can be placed in locations that would otherwise not be suitable. **Fig. 38-33.**

Radiant Heating

In *radiant heating systems*, heating coils, tubes, or cables are buried within ceilings, floors, or walls. No registers or ducts are required. This makes the system very quiet. Rather than heating air, as in a forced-air or hydronic system, a radiant system heats a material. This material then radiates the heat directly into the room. Many people find this type of heat very comfortable. There are two basic types of radiant systems: electric and hydronic.

Electric systems. Many types and designs of electric radiant heating systems are available. In one system, electric heating cable is laid back and forth across the ceiling surface. It is then covered with plaster or a second layer of drywall. As the cover material heats up, it radiates warmth to the room. Radiant panel units can also be placed directly on the finished surface of the ceiling. A thermostat located in each room generally controls heat levels.

Hydronic systems. In a radiant hot-water system, heated water is circulated through continuous coils of polyethylene tubing. The tubing is embedded in a masonry floor. **Fig. 38-34.** As the heated water circulates, it conducts its heat to the masonry. The floor then radiates heat to the room.

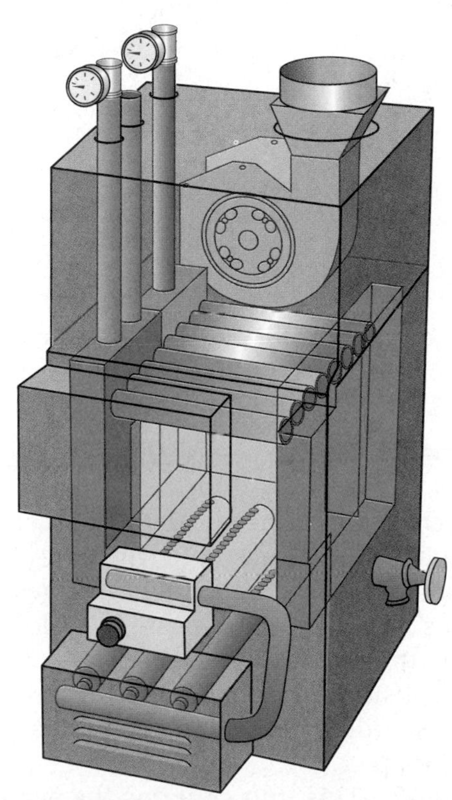

Fig. 38-32. Boilers heat water, which is then circulated through pipes to heat the house. Heat is extracted from the water as it flows through radiators or masonry floors.

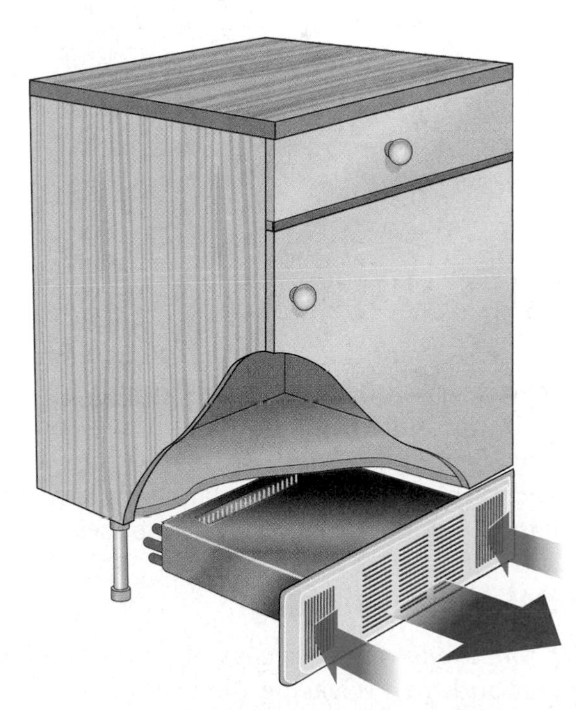

Fig. 38-33. This low-profile hydronic convector can be located in the kickspace of kitchen cabinetry. Intake air is indicated by the two small arrows. Heated air is indicated by the large arrow.

Fig. 38-34. Installing a radiant floor heating system. Concrete is poured over a network of hot water distribution tubing. The red material is epoxy-coated rebar.

COOLING SYSTEMS

In some parts of the country, cooling a house is as necessary as heating it. Energy efficiency is just as important when a house is being cooled as when it is being heated. Two types of systems—central air conditioning and whole-house ventilation—can be used to cool a house.

Central Air Conditioning

Air conditioning is a process of extracting heat from air and then releasing the heat outside the house. Small air-conditioning units can be placed in a window to cool a room. All the devices needed are contained in the unit. However, cooling an entire house calls for a central air-conditioning system. These units are sometimes called *split systems* because part is located outdoors and part is located indoors. **Fig. 38-35.**

There are three basic elements in a split system:

- *Refrigerant coils.* These coils of copper tubing hold a liquid refrigerant. Refrigerant is a material that changes from a liquid to a gas as it absorbs heat. The condenser coil is located outside the house. The evaporator coil is located inside the house. The coils are connected by additional tubing to form a closed loop.
- *Air handler.* This unit contains the evaporator coil. It also contains a blower to move air through an insulated duct system.

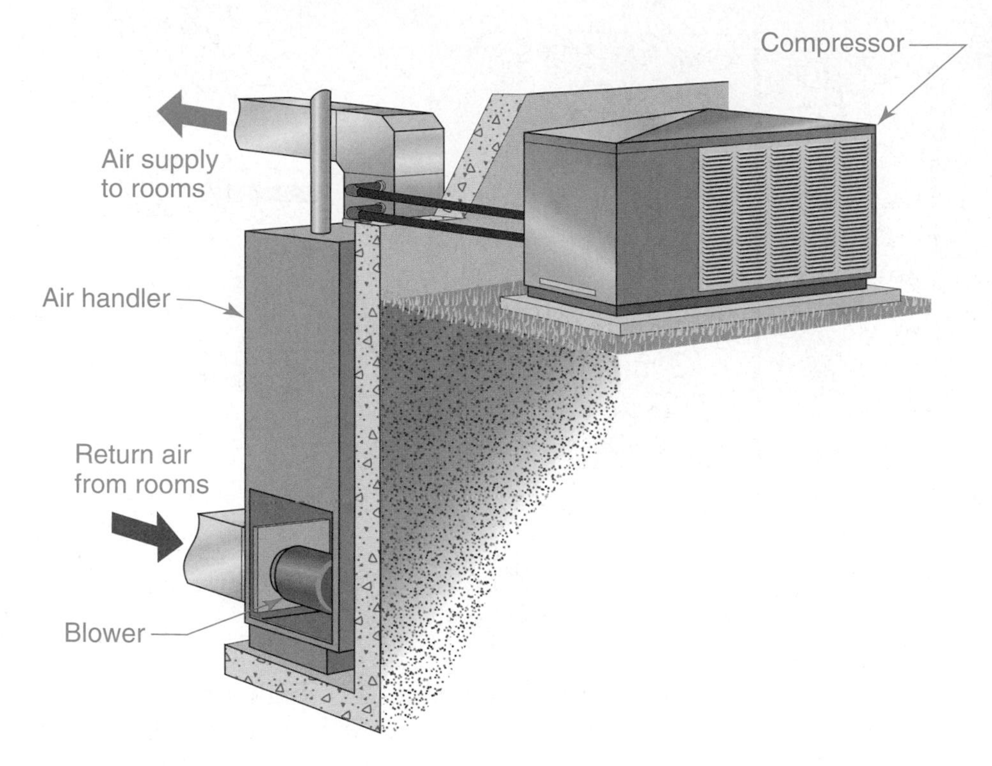

Fig. 38-35. Central air conditioning may be installed as part of the central heating system, using the same ductwork.

- *Compressor.* This unit contains the condenser coil. It includes a fan but no ductwork.

Here's how the system works:

1. The system is turned on when a thermostat indicates the temperature in a room has risen to a preset level.
2. The air handler draws in warmed house air through ducts and blows it over the evaporator coils. Refrigerant in the coils absorbs heat from the air. The cooled air is then distributed to the house.
3. As the refrigerant absorbs heat, it turns into a gas. The gas travels to the condenser coil outside the house, where it gives up its heat. The fan helps this process by circulating air over the condenser coil.
4. As the vapor cools, it condenses back to a liquid and returns to the evaporator coils. The process then repeats.

Whole-House Ventilation

In some parts of the country, a house may be cooled enough by mechanical ventilation instead of air conditioning. In such systems, a powerful enclosed fan is mounted in the highest ceiling in the house, often above a stairwell. **Fig. 38-36.** The fan draws relatively cool air into the house through open windows while exhausting hot air into the attic. Then vents release it to the outside. The system requires no ducts.

Fig. 38-36. This whole-house fan is mounted to the ceiling joists. Louvers beneath the fan blades can be closed when the fan is not operating.

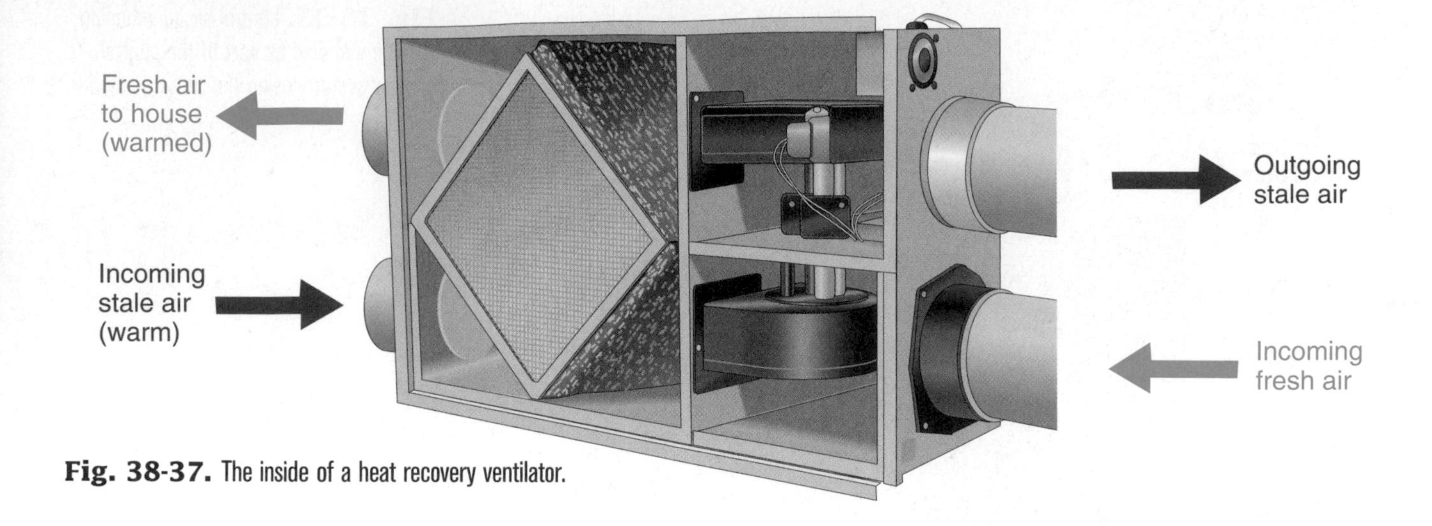

Fig. 38-37. The inside of a heat recovery ventilator.

Some whole-house ventilating fans are designed to be mounted on top of ceiling joists. This eliminates the need to cut joists for installation. However, the unit should be mounted on rubber pads. This limits any noise and vibration that might otherwise be transmitted through the framing. Some fans have variable speed controls.

HEAT RECOVERY VENTILATION

Fresh air leaks into a house through cracks around windows, doors, and framing. This process is called **infiltration**. This air must be heated in cold weather. However, heated air leaks out as easily as cold air leaks in. Builders reduce air infiltration by building "tight" houses. This means that there are few gaps in the house that can let in cold air. Of course, this also means that fresh air cannot get in. Moisture and indoor pollutants such as formaldehyde, tobacco fumes, and combustion by-products can build to unhealthy levels in a tight house. One solution is to install a device called a *heat recovery ventilator (HRV).* Heat recovery ventilators are sometimes called *air-to-air heat exchangers* or *energy recovery ventilators.* **Fig. 38-37.**

An HRV removes the heat from stale indoor air before exhausting the air outdoors. That heat is transferred to fresh air drawn into the house. To accomplish this, a fan within the HRV pulls in fresh air from outdoors through a duct. A second fan removes stale air from inside the house through a separate duct. Both sets of ducts meet at the HRV. There, heat is transferred from one air stream to the other. Each air stream is kept separate. By using heat from the outgoing air to warm the incoming air, less energy is required to raise the temperature of the incoming air. For more on energy efficiency, see Chapter 39, "Thermal and Acoustical Insulation."

SECTION 38.3 Check Your Knowledge

1. Name four types of heating fuel used in various parts of the country.
2. In a forced-air system, what happens after heated air is delivered to a room?
3. Describe the purpose of fins on a convector.
4. Describe the interaction of the air handler and the evaporator coils in a split-system air conditioner.

On the Job

Research the requirements in your state for furnace or air-conditioning installers. Find out what training, experience, and licensing are required to become an installer in your state. Report your findings to the class.

Chapter 38

Review

Section Summaries

38.1 A basic plumbing system consists of a supply side and a DWV side. Supply pipes are pressurized, while DWV pipes are not. Traps are simple devices that prevent sewer gases from entering the house.

38.2 An electrical system consists of wires, called conductors, which lead from circuit breakers in a service panel to individual outlet boxes. Each set of wires connected to a circuit breaker is called a circuit and leads to a particular portion of the house.

38.3 Heating systems are classified according to how they distribute heat, not by what fuel they use to create it. Air-conditioning systems are sometimes incorporated with forced-air heating systems so that they can use the same ducts.

Review Questions

1. What three types of pipes are found in a typical plumbing system?
2. Which side of the plumbing system is pressurized and which side is not?
3. What portion of a floor joist must not be notched to accommodate pipes?
4. How are cast-iron drainpipes joined together?
5. What is a circuit?
6. Name at least three purposes for outlet boxes.
7. In what part of a hydronic system is the water heated?
8. How does a radiant heating system differ from other heating systems?
9. Name the parts of a split-system air conditioner.
10. What is the purpose of an HRV?

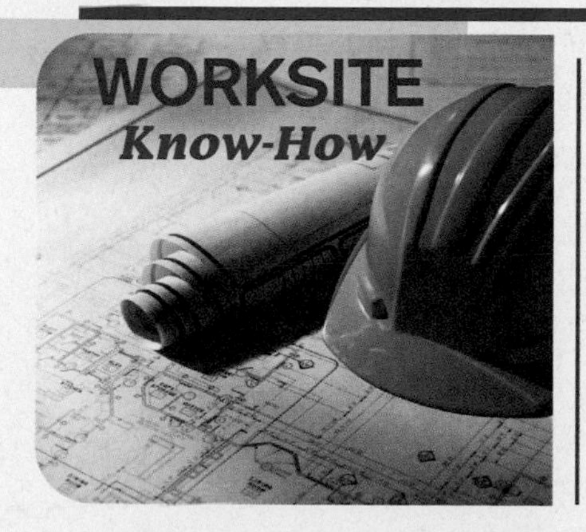

Plumbers and Carpenters Most plumbers want to cut their own holes and notches for fitting the rough plumbing into the structure. It is important that the plumber work closely with the carpenter so that the work will be neat and not weaken the joists or studs. Holes should be smooth and cut clean—just large enough for the pipe.

Chapter 39

Thermal and Acoustical Insulation

Objectives

After reading this chapter, you'll be able to:

- Identify several types and forms of insulation.
- Interpret an insulator's R-value in determining its effectiveness as insulation.
- Identify the best uses for common types of insulating materials.
- Explain the importance of vapor barriers and ventilation.
- Describe several types of wall construction that reduce noise transmission.

Terms

emissivity
Impact Noise Rating (INR)
radiant heat
R-value
Sound Transmission Class (STC)
thermal envelope
vapor barrier

Insulation is a material that slows the transmission of heat, sound, or electricity. Different uses require specific types of material. For example, the material that insulates electrical wires wouldn't be suitable for insulating walls.

More efficiently insulated homes are being built to please quality-conscious buyers. Upgrading of insulation beyond the minimum standards increases comfort. It also reduces heating and air conditioning costs because smaller, less expensive furnaces, cooling equipment, and ductwork are needed.

This chapter will cover primarily thermal insulation. Thermal insulation slows the transmission of heat through walls, floors, and ceilings. Acoustical (sound) insulation will also be discussed.

SECTION 39.1

Thermal Insulation

Most building materials and even the air space between studs have some insulating properties. **Table 39-A.** However, to meet current standards for energy efficiency, additional insulation is needed. The amount of thermal insulation required in a house varies greatly by region. Houses in mild climates need less, while houses in severe climates need more.

Materials are rated as to their insulating abilities. The most common method is to rate materials according to R-value. **R-value** is a measure of a material's ability to resist heat transmission. **Table 39-B** shows how R-value relates to insulation needs. R-value varies according to a material's thickness, but it is cumulative. One type of insulation, for example, might have a value of R-5 per inch. Two inches would have a total R-value of R-10. This is why R-value figures are often given per inch of material thickness.

When choosing the type and amount of insulation, climate is the primary factor to consider. The map in **Fig. 39-1** shows the lowest temperatures throughout the United States during an average winter. Such information is useful in figuring the amount of insulation needed for walls, ceilings, and floors. Generally, local codes specify the minimum amount of insulation required. **Fig. 39-2.**

TYPES OF INSULATION

Insulation is manufactured in a variety of types, each with advantages for specific uses. Types include flexible, loose-fill, rigid sheet, and spray-foam insulation.

Flexible Insulation

Flexible insulation comes in rolls called *blankets* or bundles called *batts*. Blankets are contin-

Table 39-A. Thermal Properties of Various Building Materials per Inch of Thickness

Material	Thermal Resistance (R)
Wood	1.25
Air space[1]	0.97
Cinder block	0.28
Common brick	0.20
Face brick	0.11
Concrete (sand and gravel)	0.08
Stone (lime or sand)	0.08
Steel	0.0032
Aluminum	0.00070

[1] Thermal properties apply to air spaces ranging from ¾ to 4 inches in thickness.

Table 39-B. R-Values for the Chicago Region

Maximum Comfort	
Ceilings	R-38 to R-42
Walls	R-19
Floors over unheated spaces	R-22
Moderate Comfort	
Ceilings	R-30 to R-33
Walls	R-19
Floors over unheated spaces	R-19 to R-22
Minimum Comfort	
Ceilings	R-19
Walls	R-11
Floors over unheated spaces	R-19

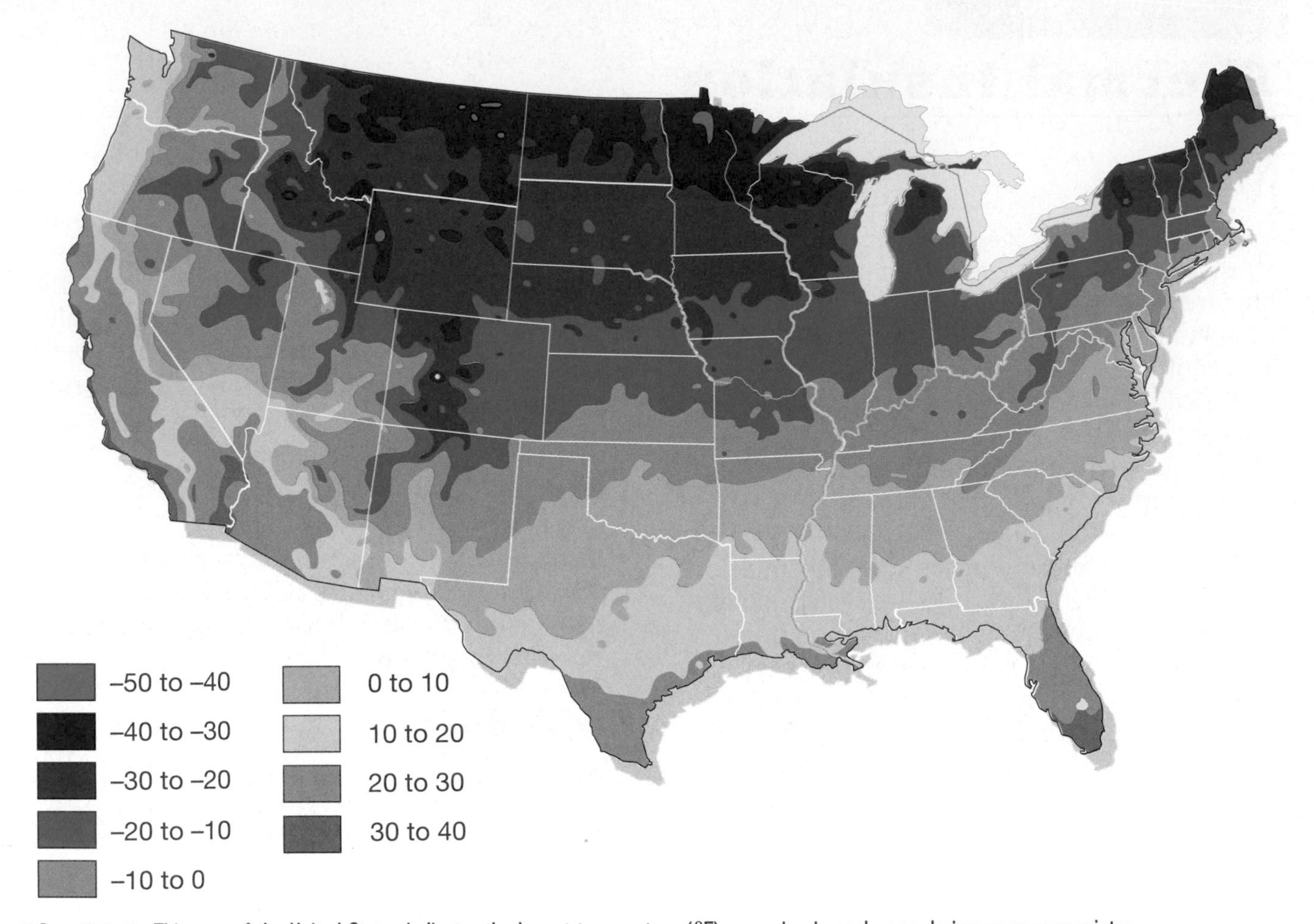

Fig. 39-1. This map of the United States indicates the lowest temperature (°F) occurring in each zone during an average winter.

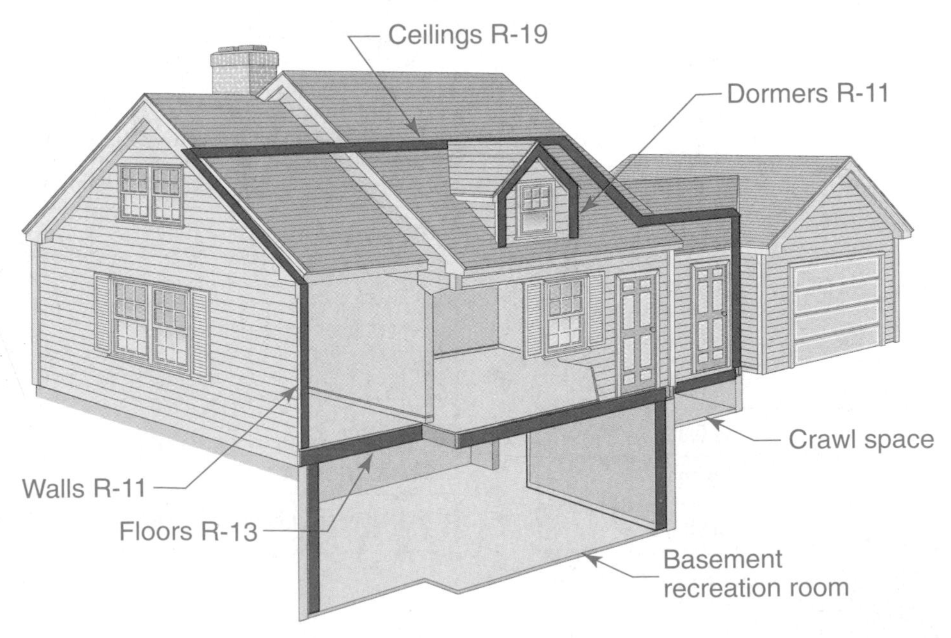

Fig. 39-2. Minimum insulation standards are established by local building codes. The R-values suggested for this house indicate that it would be located in a relatively mild climate.

uous lengths of insulation. They are typically used to insulate ceilings and roofs. Batts are essentially blankets that have been pre-cut to specific lengths for use in walls. Flexible insulation is the most common type used in houses. **Fig. 39-3.** The material is usually fiberglass, often with a kraft paper facing on one side. Continuous tabs on the sides of the facing allow the batts to be stapled to studs or joists. **Fig. 39-4.** Another version, called *unfaced insulation,* has no facing. It is sometimes referred to as *friction-fit insulation* because it is simply pressed into the wall cavities and not stapled. **Fig. 39-5.** A third and newer type of flexible insulation is completely enclosed in a thin plastic sheath. This makes it easier to handle.

The facing on flexible insulation also serves as a vapor barrier. A *vapor barrier* prevents moist air that is generated inside the house from reaching the insulation. In cold weather, this moisture could condense inside the wall and reduce the insulation's effectiveness. Moisture trapped inside the walls can also cause framing and sheathing to rot. A vapor barrier should always face the warm (heated) side of the wall.

Flexible insulation comes in different thicknesses and in widths suited to 16″ and 24″ OC stud and joist spacing. It can be easily cut to fit openings. **Fig. 39-6.**

Fig. 39-3. Fiberglass insulation in blankets and batts is the most common type used in residential construction.

Fig. 39-5. Insulating a room using friction-fit batts and a continuous plastic vapor barrier. The plastic should be stapled to the studs just enough to hold it in place.

Fig. 39-4. Installing batt insulation between studs.

Fig. 39-6. To cut insulation, place it on a piece of scrap plywood. Compress the material with a 2x4 or straightedge and cut it with a utility knife. When cutting faced insulation, keep the facing up.

Fiberglass insulation has a value of about R-3 per inch. Low-density batts intended to insulate 2x4 walls, for example, are usually rated R-11; high-density batts are rated R-15. Low-density batts intended for 2x6 walls are rated R-19; high-density batts are rated R-21. Blankets intended for floors and ceilings may be rated as high as R-38.

Loose-Fill Insulation

Loose-fill insulation is usually supplied in bags or bales and is poured or blown into place. **Fig. 39-7.** Materials used include shredded fiberglass, mineral wool, and cellulose-based products. Loose-fill insulation is often used in attic floors where HVAC pipes and wiring make it difficult to install blanket insulation. It can also be pumped into the walls of older houses that were not insulated during construction.

Rigid Insulation

Rigid insulation is manufactured in 4x8 solid panels. **Fig. 39-8.** Panels often have a reflective surface on one side. These thin panels pack more R-value into a smaller space than most other types of insulation. Rigid insulation is sometimes used as a nonstructural sheathing on walls during construction. It also serves as a substrate for other materials. Some types of rigid insulation are suitable for use below grade for the exterior surfaces of basement walls.

Fig. 39-8. Rigid insulation applied to the outside of a house prior to installation of the siding.

Fig. 39-7. Always wear appropriate protective clothing when installing loose-fill insulation.

Rigid insulation is made from one of the following materials:

- Expanded polystyrene (EPS). Polystyrene is formed into beads that puff up when exposed to steam. The beads are then molded into blocks of insulation and sliced into sheets. EPS is rated from R-3.6 to R-4.2 per inch.
- Extruded polystyrene (XEPS). This material is similar to EPS but has greater compressive strength for use as foundation insulation below grade. It is rated at R-5 per inch.
- Polyurethane and polyisocyanurate. These materials are often faced with foil to slow the loss of the blowing agent used in their manufacture. They are rated at R-5.6 per inch.

Spray-Foam Insulation

Closed-cell spray-foam insulation is made from polyurethane. It is sprayed as a wet material into open wall cavities before finished wall surfaces have been installed. Exposed to air, the foam rapidly expands to seal and fill the cavity.

After it has cured (within an hour), excess hardened material is sliced off flush with the surface of the framing. The foam is water vapor permeable (it does not trap moisture), remains flexible, and will not draw moisture into the wall. Because it is applied as a liquid and then expands, it seals the cavities better than other types of insulation. Its R-value is R-6.5 per inch.

One type of spray-foam insulation is made to expand more slowly. It can be pumped into the walls of existing construction where there is no insulation. This foam is rated at approximately R-3.6 per inch.

PLACEMENT

To reduce heat loss during cold weather in most climates, all walls, ceilings, roofs, and floors that separate heated from unheated spaces should be insulated. Fig. 39-2. This continuous insulation layer is referred to as the **thermal envelope**, or *conditioned space.* Everything inside the thermal envelope will be heated and/or cooled. Everything outside the envelope is exposed to outdoor temperatures.

Walls

All walls that separate living space from outdoor air must be insulated. In a one-and-a-half-story house, however, it is sometimes difficult to establish the thermal envelope. In such cases, second floor knee walls should be treated just as if they were exterior walls. **Fig. 39-9.** Knee walls are half-height walls often found in attics.

Floor Systems

In houses with unheated crawl spaces, insulation should be placed between the floor joists. **Fig. 39-10.** If blanket insulation is used, it should be well supported by a galvanized wire mesh or a rigid board. The vapor barrier should be installed toward the subflooring. Press-fit or friction insulation fits tightly between joists and requires only a small amount of support to hold it in place.

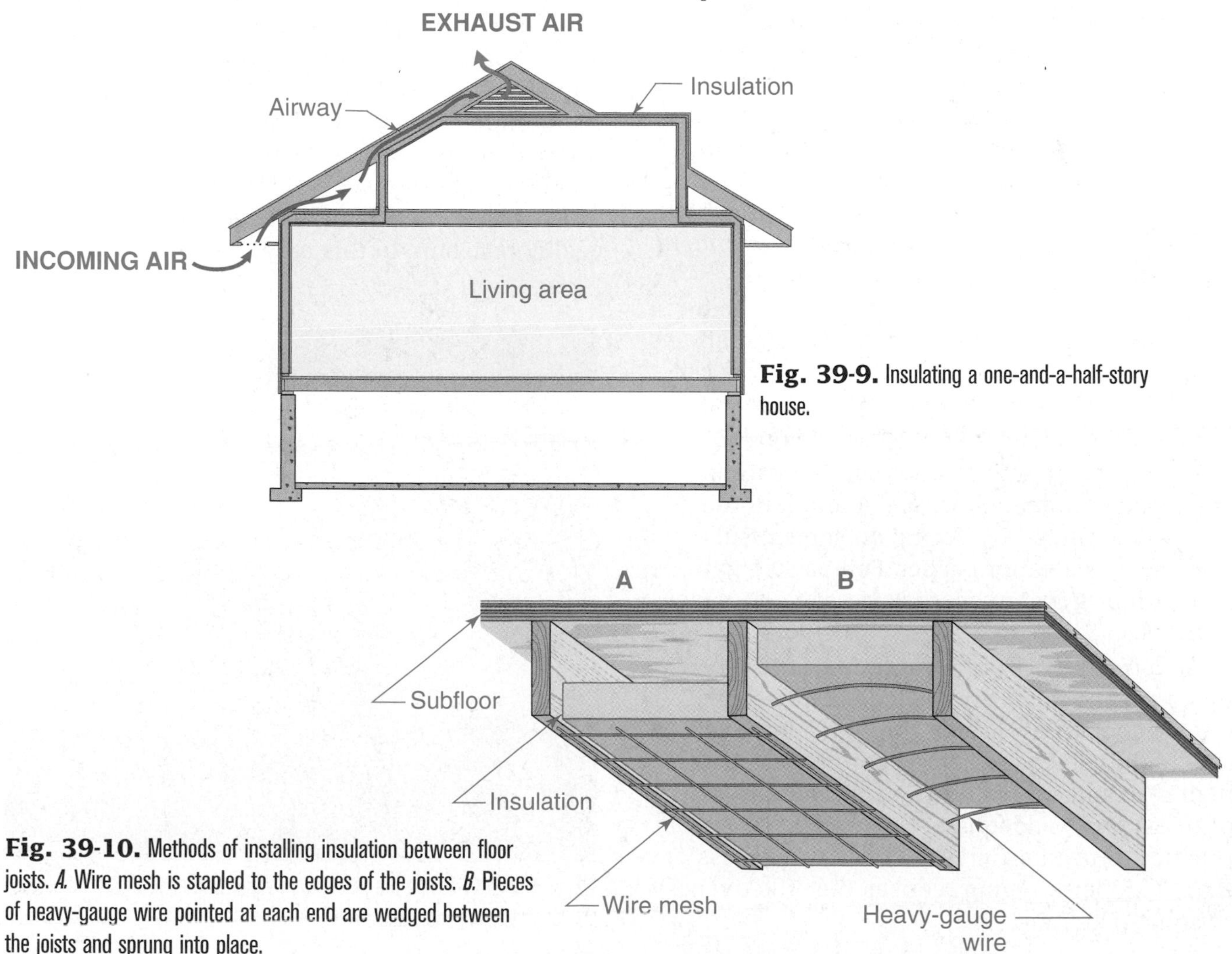

Fig. 39-9. Insulating a one-and-a-half-story house.

Fig. 39-10. Methods of installing insulation between floor joists. *A.* Wire mesh is stapled to the edges of the joists. *B.* Pieces of heavy-gauge wire pointed at each end are wedged between the joists and sprung into place.

Attics

Heat rises, so it is important to slow down heat loss during cold weather by insulating the attic. Where attic space is unheated and a stairway leads to the attic, insulation should be installed around the stairway as well as in the first-floor ceiling. The door or hatchway leading to the attic should be weatherstripped and insulated to prevent heat loss. Walls adjoining a garage or unheated porch should also be insulated.

In the summer, outside surfaces exposed to direct sunlight may reach temperatures of 50°F [10°C] or more above shade temperatures. These surfaces tend to transfer this heat toward the inside of the house. Insulation in the attic slows the flow of heat, improving summer comfort and reducing the need for air conditioning.

VAPOR BARRIERS

Most building materials allow water vapor to pass through them. This presents problems because much water vapor is generated in a house from cooking, dish washing, laundering, bathing, and other activities. During cold weather, this vapor may pass through wall and ceiling materials and condense in the wall or attic space. As a result, in severe cases, it may damage the exterior paint and interior finish. It may even promote decay in structural members. For protection, a vapor barrier should be installed. A **vapor barrier** is a material highly resistant to vapor transmission. It should always be installed on the heated side of a wall or ceiling. Otherwise, moisture entering the wall and ceiling cavities would be trapped there.

Among the effective vapor barrier materials are asphalt laminated papers, aluminum foil, and plastic films. The facing on some insulations acts as a vapor barrier. Foil-backed gypsum lath or gypsum boards also serve as vapor barriers.

The effectiveness of a vapor barrier is rated by its *perm value.* Perm value is a measure of water vapor transmission through a material. Low perm values indicate vapor barriers with high resistance to vapor transmission. A value of 0.50 perm is adequate. However, it is good practice to use barriers that have values less than 0.25 perm. Aging reduces the effectiveness of some materials.

Wall-high rolls of plastic-film vapor barriers are often applied over studs, plates, and window and door headers. This is called *enveloping* and is used over insulation that does not already include a vapor barrier. The plastic should be fitted tightly around outlet boxes and sealed if necessary. **Fig. 39-11.** A ribbon of sealing compound around an outlet or switch box limits vapor transmission at this area.

No vapor barrier resists all vapor. Some leakage into the wall can be expected. Therefore, the flow of vapor to the outside should not be slowed by materials of high resistance on the cold side of the barrier. For example, sheathing paper should be waterproof but not highly vapor resistant.

VENTILATION

During cold weather, water vapor in air leaking from heated sections of the house may condense when it comes in contact with cold surfaces in the attic. Even when vapor barriers have been installed, some vapor will work through spaces around pipes and other poorly sealed areas. Some vapor will also work through the vapor barrier itself. Although the amount may be unimportant if it is evenly distributed, it can cause damage if concentrated in cold spots. Wood shingle and wood shake roofs do not resist vapor movement, but asphalt shingles are highly resistant. In this case, the most practical

Fig. 39-11. Staple the plastic film vapor barrier to the wood so the insulation is completely sealed.

method of removing moisture is by ventilating the attic or roof.

Another reason to ventilate an attic or roof is to reduce the formation of ice at the eaves. An attic that is poorly ventilated and poorly insulated tends to be warmer than outside air in the winter. The warmth melts snow on the roof. Water running down the roof freezes when it reaches the colder surfaces of the eaves, often forming into ice at the gutter. This ice dam may cause water to back up at the eaves and into the wall and ceiling cavities. With a well-insulated ceiling and enough ventilation, attic temperatures are low. This greatly reduces the melting of snow on the roof.

In hot weather, ventilation of attic and roof spaces allows hot air to escape. This lowers the attic temperature and helps the house to stay cooler.

It was once a common practice to install louvered ventilation openings in the end walls of gable roofs. However, air movement through this system varies and is often inefficient. A much more effective approach is to provide openings in the soffit as well as a ridge vent at the top of the roof. **Fig. 39-12.** As heated air rises, it is exhausted through the ridge vent. This process draws cooler air in through the soffit vents. Where a sloped ceiling is insulated, there should be a free opening of at least 1½″ between the sheathing and the insulation to encourage air movement. (For more on ventilating roofs, see Chapter 30, "Roof Coverings," and Chapter 31, "Roof Edge Details.")

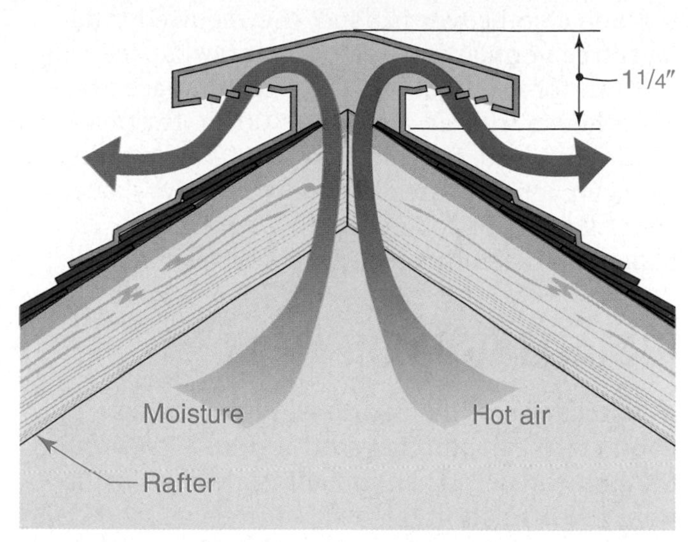

Fig. 39-12. A ridge vent. Some continuous vents can be capped with shingles. This helps blend the vent with the roof.

Crawl-Space Ventilation

The crawl space below a house and under a porch should be protected from ground moisture by a soil cover and ventilated. **Fig. 39-13.** The soil cover is most often a 6-mil or 8-mil thick plastic film. Such protection prevents decay of wood framing members. It also prevents insulation from becoming saturated with moisture.

from Another Angle

In regions where a house must be cooled for much of the year, thermal insulation helps the house to stay cool. Shade trees are also important in such climates. By shading walls and roof surfaces, trees can reduce a home's annual heating and cooling bill by 20 percent or more. Shading the west side of a house is particularly effective in reducing cooling needs. This is because the west side catches the afternoon sun.

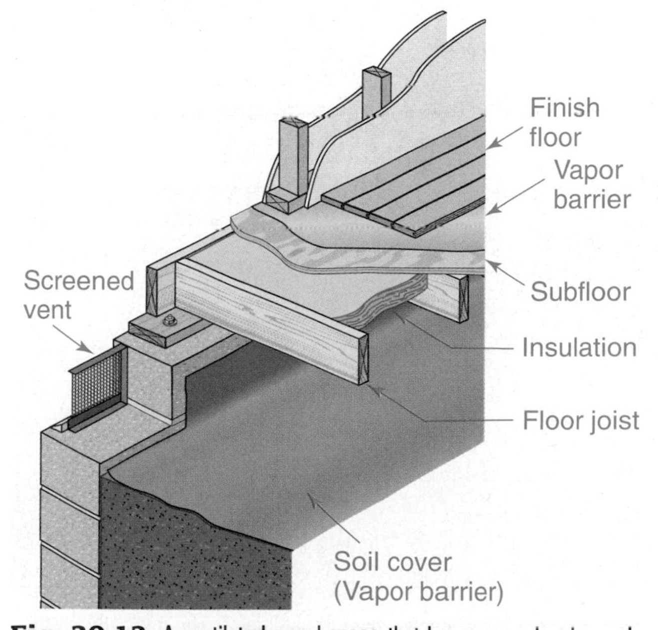

Fig. 39-13. A ventilated crawl space that has a vapor barrier and soil cover.

When a soil cover is used, the required total (net) free ventilating area of the crawl space is 1 sq. ft. for each 150 sq. ft. of crawl-space area. For a house with an area of 1,500 sq. ft., this would be 10 sq. ft. This area should be divided between vents located around the crawl space. Vents should be covered with a corrosion-resistant screen to keep insects out. Fig. 39-13.

INSTALLING INSULATION

Installation of insulation is a job in which good craftsmanship pays off in money saved for the homeowner. When installing flexible insulation, the insulation must fill all the wall and ceiling cavities. There should be no gaps between the insulation and the framing around electrical boxes. Gaps form a ready passage through which heat can escape. **Fig. 39-14.**

Flexible Insulation

Blanket or batt insulation with a vapor barrier should be placed between framing members so that the tabs of the facing lap the edges of the studs as well as the top and bottom plates. **Fig. 39-15.** This is generally preferred to stapling the tabs to the sides of the studs. A hand stapler or hammer tacker is commonly used to fasten the insulation and the barriers in place.

Flexible insulation is generally cut with a utility knife. Batts and blankets should always be compressed while being cut. This ensures that cut edges will be smooth, improves cutting accuracy, and prevents too many fiberglass fibers from escaping into the air. Something as simple as a 2x6 board can be used to compress the insulation near the cutting area. It can also serve as a straightedge for guiding the utility knife.

When friction-fit insulation is installed, a plastic-film vapor barrier such as 4-mil polyethylene is commonly used to envelop the entire exposed wall and ceiling. It covers the openings as well as window and door headers and edge studs. This system is one of the best for resisting vapor movement. After the drywall is installed or plastering has been completed, the film is trimmed around the window and door openings.

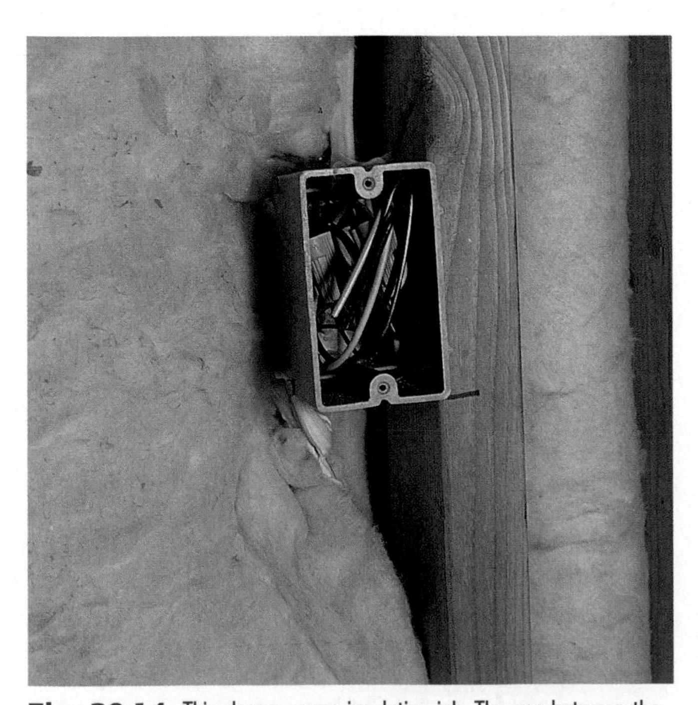

Fig. 39-14. This shows a poor insulation job. The gap between the insulation and the electrical box will allow heat to escape easily.

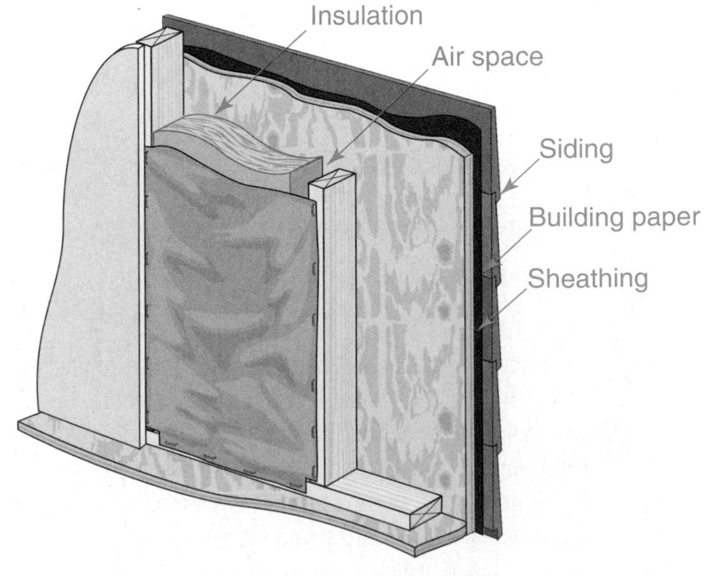

Fig. 39-15. The insulation tabs should be stapled to the edge of the stud.

Blanket insulation is often used in ceilings. **Fig. 39-16.** The vapor barrier is placed against the back of the ceiling finish. Unfaced blankets may be layered to provide enough thickness. Some contractors place one layer of insulation at 90° to the first. This also insulates the ceiling framing.

Insulation should be placed behind electrical outlet boxes and other utility connections in exposed walls to limit condensation. Areas around doors and windows also require insulation. This is best done with expanding foam sealant. **Fig. 39-17.**

Fig. 39-17. Gaps around windows and doors should be filled with expanding foam sealant. The product insulates and reduces air infiltration.

SAFETY FIRST

Handling Fiberglass

Fiberglass is a skin and lung irritant. Always wear protective clothing, including a long-sleeve shirt, gloves, long pants, high-top work boots, and a cap. In addition, wear a suitable dust mask or respirator and eye protection. Follow all safety precautions suggested by the insulation manufacturer.

Loose-Fill Insulation

Loose-fill insulation is commonly used in ceiling areas. A vapor barrier should first be placed on the warm side of the wall. Then the insulation is poured or blown into place. Use of a leveling board makes the insulation thickness uniform. **Fig. 39-18.** Loose-fill insulation is often installed by contractors who have the specialized equipment needed to blow it into attic spaces.

Fig. 39-16. Wear the appropriate safety gear when installing batt insulation.

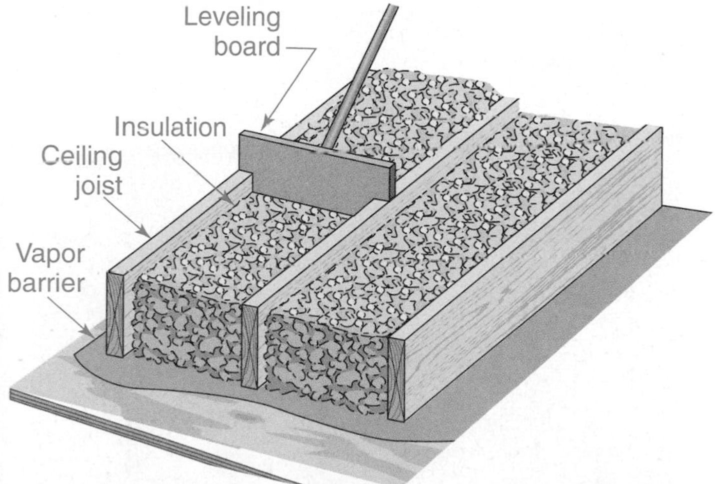

Fig. 39-18. Installing loose-fill insulation in a ceiling. Note the use of the leveling board.

RADIANT-HEAT BARRIERS

In climates where the cost of air conditioning is the main concern, additional steps are sometimes taken to reduce radiant heat gain. **Radiant heat** travels in a straight line away from a hot surface and heats anything solid it meets. Installing a radiant-heat barrier in a home's attic is one way to stop radiant heat gain.

A radiant-heat barrier is a thin, flexible sheet material with at least one reflective surface, usually of aluminum. **Fig. 39-19.** Some radiant-heat barriers have a reflective coating on both sides. Installed properly, a radiant-heat barrier can reduce heat transfer into the attic by about 95 percent. In climates where saving heating energy is the main concern, however, radiant-heat barriers are rarely cost-effective.

How Radiant-Heat Barriers Work

All materials emit energy by thermal radiation. The amount emitted depends on the surface temperature and the material's **emissivity**. Emissivity is expressed as a number between 0 and 1. The higher the emissivity, the greater the emitted radiation. Another important property is reflectivity. *Reflectivity* measures how much radiant heat is reflected by a material. It is expressed as a number between 0 and 1 or as a percentage between 0 and 100. A material with high reflectivity has low emissivity, and vice versa. To perform properly, radiant-barrier materials must have high reflectivity (usually 0.9 or 90 percent, or more), low emissivity (usually 0.1 or less), and face an open air space.

Fig. 39-19. A radiant-heat barrier reduces heat gain in a house.

For example, on a sunny day a roof absorbs solar energy. This heats the roof sheathing, which causes the underside of the sheathing and the roof framing to radiate heat downward toward the attic floor. Placing a radiant-heat barrier on the underside of the rafters reflects much of the heat back toward the roof. Thus the top surface of the attic insulation stays cooler and so do the rooms below.

Radiant-heat barriers may be installed in attics in two ways. One method is to attach the barrier to the underside of the rafter framing. Another method is to drape the barrier loosely over the rafters just before the roof sheathing is applied. In this method, the barrier should droop so that there is at least 1″ of air space between it and the underside of the sheathing. The air space makes the barrier more effective. It also creates an air channel that allows the soffit and ridge vents to work more effectively.

Do not install a radiant-heat barrier by spreading it over attic insulation. Dust accumulating on the barrier can reduce its effectiveness. Also, it might trap moisture rising through the ceiling. This could cause other problems, such as reducing the effectiveness of the insulation.

ESTIMATING FLEXIBLE INSULATION

To estimate the amount of insulation required, you must first figure the area to be insulated. Refer to the house plan in **Fig. 39-20**. Round off the outside dimensions of the heated portion of the home to a width of 28′ and a length of 52′. The perimeter of the house is thus 160′.

(2 × 28) [+] (2 × 52) [=] 160

If the wall height is 8′, the walls will have an area of 1,280 sq. ft.

8 × 160 [=] 1,280

Subtract the area of the window and door openings, which equals about 150 sq. ft., from the total area.

1,280 [−] 150 [=] 1,130

The total wall area to be insulated is 1,130 sq. ft.

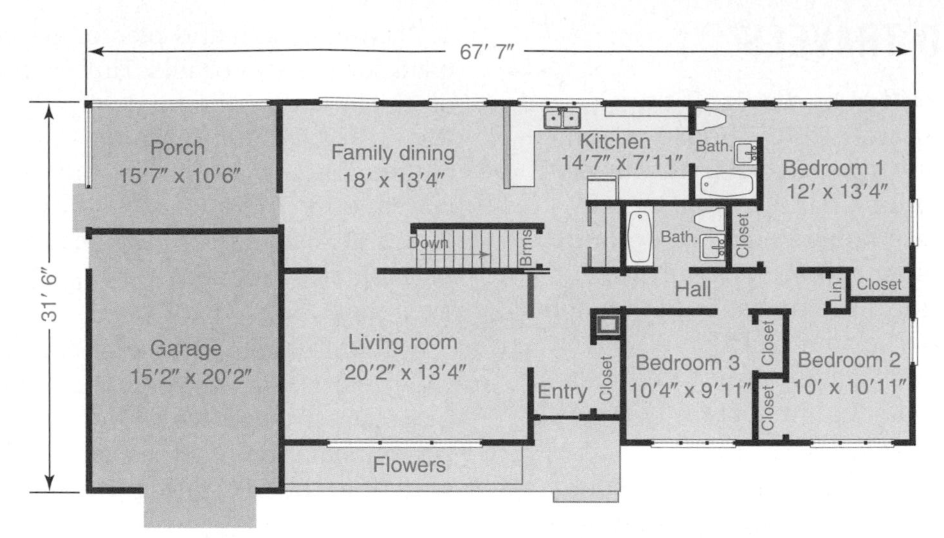

Fig. 39-20. Estimate the amount of insulation required to insulate the outside walls and the ceiling of this house.

Using figures supplied by the insulation manufacturer, determine how many square feet each roll or bundle of insulation will cover. Divide the area to be covered by the coverage per roll or bundle. The answer will be the number of rolls or bundles required. Add approximately 5 percent to this figure to allow for waste.

The ceiling must also be insulated. Figure the area of the ceiling by multiplying the width times the length. Divide the number by the number of square feet in each roll. The answer will be the number of rolls needed.

SECTION 39.1

Check Your Knowledge

1. What must be done after installing unfaced insulation that is not required when installing faced insulation?
2. What is the typical R-value for low-density batt insulation for 2x4 and 2x6 walls?
3. What is the thermal envelope?
4. Define *emissivity.*

On the Job

A rectangular house with outside dimensions of 26′ x 44′ is to be insulated. For the 8′ exterior walls, 4″ thick batts measuring 15″ x 48″ are to be used. Assume that the area of the doors and windows is 15 percent of the floor area. How many batts will be needed?

SECTION 39.2

Acoustical Insulation

Acoustical, or sound, insulation has always been important in apartments, motels, and hotels. However, the use of household appliances, television, radio, and stereo systems has increased the noise levels in homes. Today, sound insulation between the active areas (such as recreation rooms and home theaters) and sleeping areas is often desirable. Insulation against outdoor sounds is also important where houses are close together or where they are near highways. As a result, sound control has become a vital part of house design and construction.

HOW SOUND TRAVELS

Sound is transmitted by waves. It travels readily through the air and also through some materials. A noise inside a house, such as music, a loud conversation, or a barking dog, creates sound waves. These radiate outward until they strike a wall, floor, or ceiling. The surface vibrates as a result of the pressure of the sound waves. When airborne sound strikes a conventional wall, the studs act as sound conductors unless they are separated in some way from the covering material.

The resistance of a building element, such as a wall, to the passage of airborne sound is described by its **Sound Transmission Class (STC)**. The higher the STC number, the better it is as a sound barrier.

Flanking Paths

Faulty construction, such as poorly fitted doors, can allow sound to pass around a material without actually going through it. This type of sound transmission follows what is called a flanking path. Heating ducts, wiring chases, and plumbing runs can also allow sound to travel freely through the air within wall and ceiling assemblies. In fact, a hole as small as 1 sq. in. in a wall rated at STC 50 can reduce that wall's performance to STC 30. Plumbers, electricians, and others who regularly cut holes in framing should keep this fact in mind as they work.

SOUND INSULATION IN WALLS

Thick walls of dense materials such as masonry can stop sound. In a wood-frame house, however, an interior masonry wall results in increased costs and in structural problems created by the weight. To provide a satisfactory sound-resistant wall economically has been a problem. At one time, sound-resistant frame construction for the home involved much higher costs because it usually meant double walls. However, a fairly simple system has been developed using sound-deadening insulating board and gypsum board outer covering. This provides good sound control at only slight additional cost. A number of combinations, providing different STC ratings, are possible with this system.

Drywall or lath and plaster are commonly used for partition walls. However, an STC rating of 45 cannot be obtained with this construction. **Fig. 39-21, A** and **B.** Good STC ratings can be obtained in a wood-frame wall by using the combination of materials shown in **Fig. 39-21, D** and **E.** A system of resilient channels nailed horizontally to studs can improve the STC rating even more. **Fig. 39-22.**

A double wall, which may consist of 2x6 or wider plate and staggered 2x4 studs, is sometimes constructed for sound control. **Fig. 39-23.** When insulation is added to double wall construction, the STC rating increases.

SOUND INSULATION IN FLOORS AND CEILINGS

Sound insulation between an upper floor and the ceiling of a lower story involves not only resistance to airborne sounds but also to impact noises. *Impact noise* results when an object strikes or slides along a wall or floor. Footsteps, dropped objects, and furniture being moved all cause impact noise. It may also be caused by the vibration of a dishwasher, food disposal, or other equipment. In all instances, the floor is set into vibration by the impact or contact, and sound is radiated from both sides of the floor.

The impact noise resistance of a floor system is described by its **Impact Noise Rating (INR)**. The INR is based on decibels (dB), a measure of sound intensity. The higher the INR, the better the impact sound reduction. Another rating, the Impact Insulation Class (IIC), is sometimes used instead because IIC figures are easier to determine.

The softest sounds humans can hear range from 0 to 1 decibel. Except for thunder and erupting volcanoes, nothing in nature exceeds 100 dB. Noise levels produced by saws, routers, and other tools and equipment range from 87 to 108 dB.

WALL DETAIL	DESCRIPTION	STC RATING
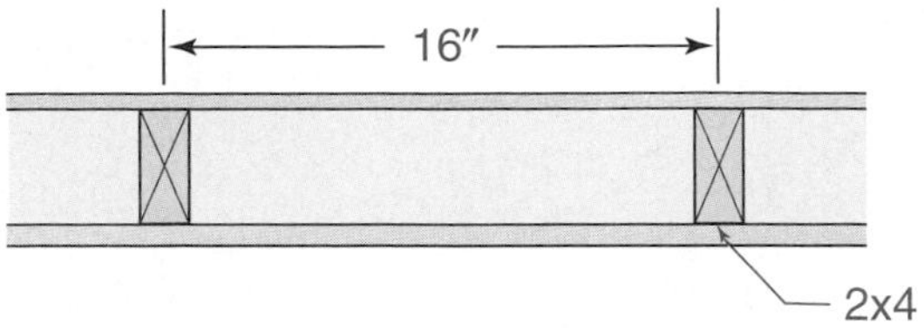 A (16″; 2x4)	1/2″ gypsum wallboard 5/8″ gypsum wallboard	32 37
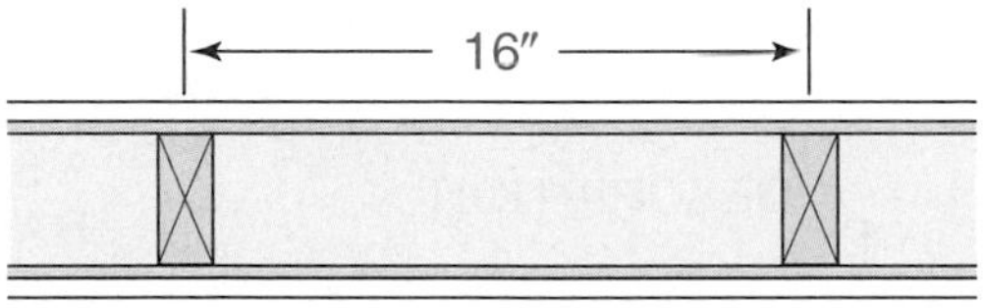 B (16″)	3/8″ gypsum lath (nailed) plus 1/2″ gypsum plaster with whitecoat finish (each side)	39
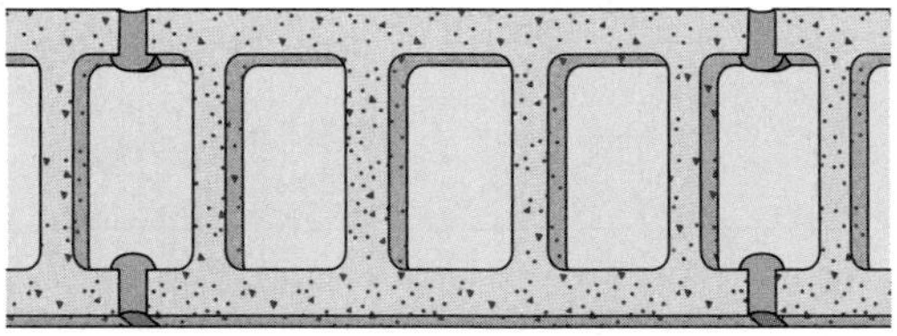 C	8″ concrete block	45
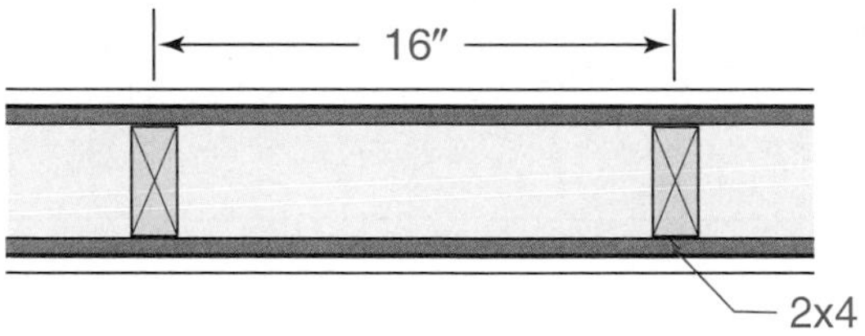 D (16″; 2x4)	1/2″ sound-deadening board nailed 1/2″ gypsum wallboard laminated (each side)	46
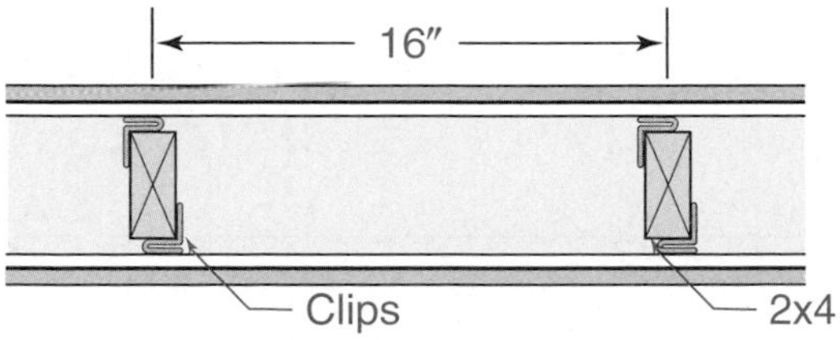 E (16″; Clips; 2x4)	Resilient clips to 3/8″ gypsum backer board 1/2″ fiberboard laminated (each side)	52

Fig. 39-21. Sound insulation of single walls.

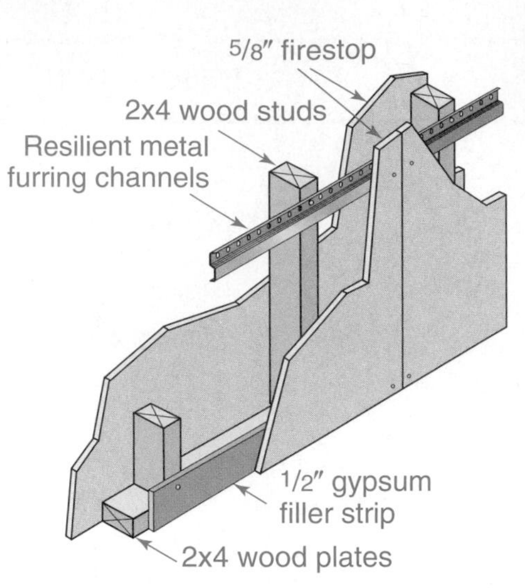

Fig. 39-22. Sound transmission can be reduced by fastening the interior wall covering to resilient metal furring channels.

Fig. 39-23. Sound insulation of double walls.

WALL DETAIL	DESCRIPTION	STC RATING
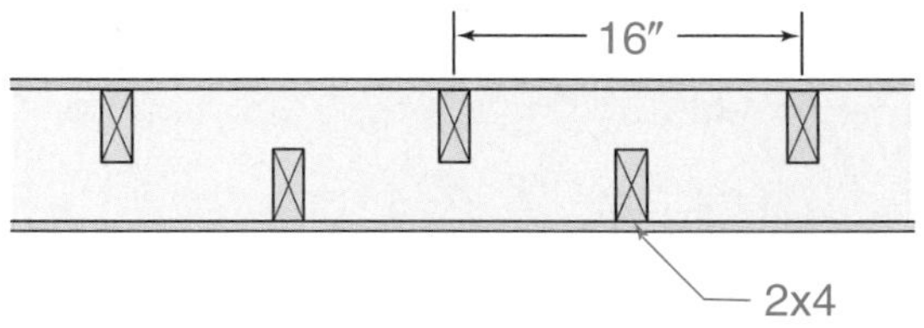 A (16″; 2x4)	1/2″ gypsum wallboard (each side)	45
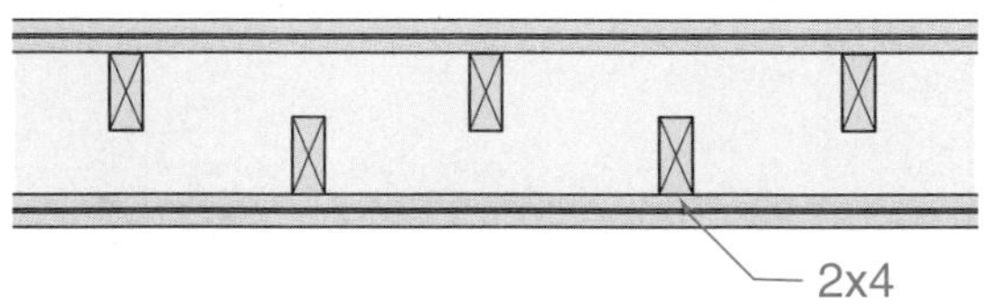 B (2x4)	5/8″ gypsum wallboard (double layer each side)	45
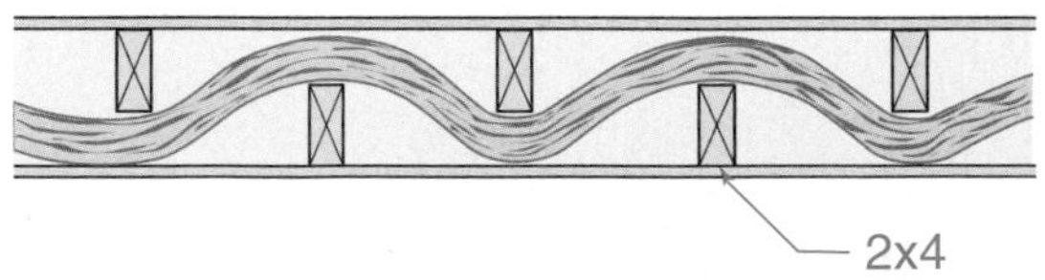 C (2x4)	1/2″ gypsum wallboard 1 1/2″ thick fibrous insulation	49
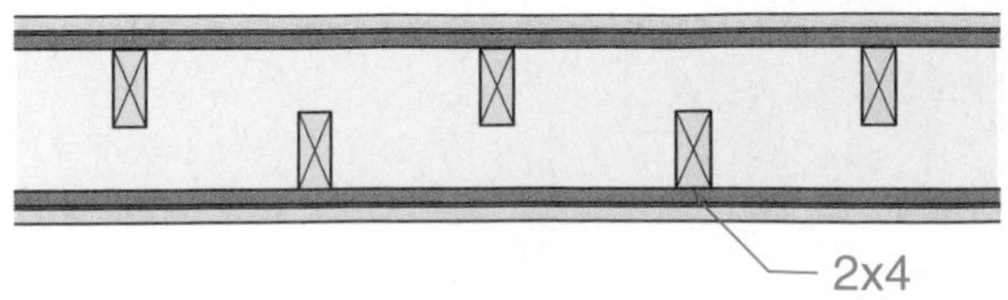 D (2x4)	1/2″ sound-deadening board nailed 1/2″ gypsum wallboard laminated (each side)	50

FLOOR DETAIL	DESCRIPTION	STC RATING	INR RATING
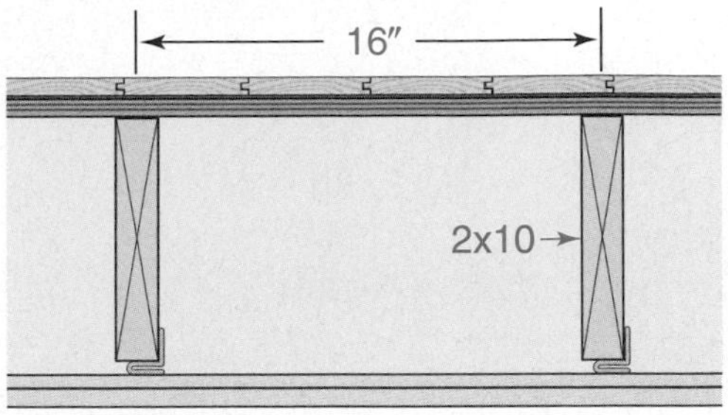 A (16″ spacing; 2x10)	FLOOR 3/4″ finish floor building paper 3/4″ subfloor CEILING 1/2″ gypsum plaster gypsum lath and spring clips	52	-2
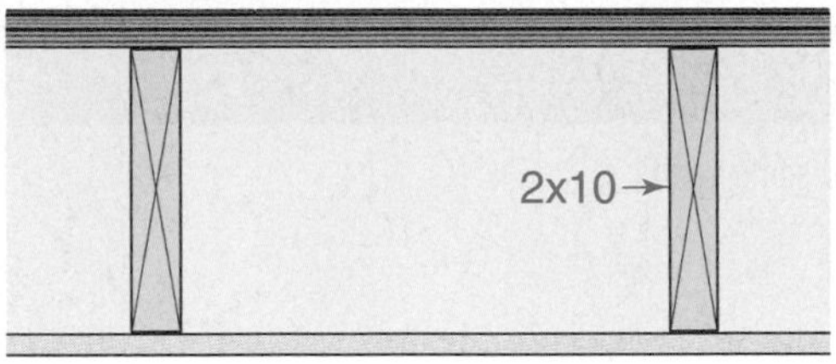 B (2x10)	FLOOR 1/8″ vinyl-asbestos tile 1/2″ plywood underlayment 5/8″ plywood subfloor CEILING 1/2″ gypsum wallboard	31	-17
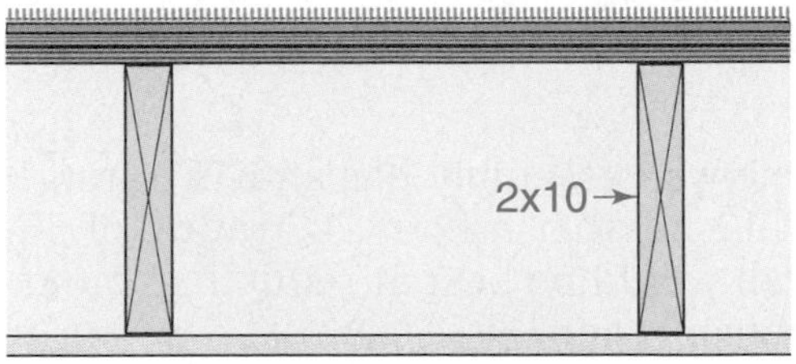 C (2x10)	FLOOR 3/8″ nylon carpet foam rubber pad 1/2″ plywood underlayment 5/8″ plywood subfloor CEILING 1/2″ gypsum wallboard	45	+5

Fig. 39-24. Estimated STC and INR ratings in floor-ceiling combinations using 2x10 joists.

Figure 39-24 shows estimated STC and INR values for three types of floor construction. The value of isolating the ceiling joists from a gypsum lath and plaster ceiling by means of spring clips is illustrated in *A*. Foam rubber padding and carpeting improve both STC and INR values.

SOUND ABSORPTION

The design of a quiet house can also include the use of sound-absorbing materials. Sound-absorbing materials do not necessarily resist air-borne sounds. However, they can reduce noise

Fig. 39-25. A suspended ceiling system with acoustical panel inserts will absorb some sound.

by preventing sound from being reflected back into a room. Perhaps the most commonly used sound-absorbing material is acoustical ceiling tile or panels. **Fig. 39-25.** Numerous holes or fissures on the surface, or a combination of both, trap the sound.

Acoustical tile and panels are most often used where they are not subject to too much mechanical damage, such as in the ceiling. Paint or other finishes that fill or cover the tiny holes or fissures greatly reduce their efficiency. For more on acoustical ceilings, see Chapter 40, "Walls and Ceilings."

SECTION 39.2 Check Your Knowledge

1. One wall assembly has an STC rating of 40, while another has an STC rating of 55. Which wall would be best at reducing sound transmission?
2. What is a flanking path?
3. Why is it important to limit the number and size of holes in walls?
4. On what unit is the INR rating based?

On the Job

Meet in a group with three other students. Discuss the noise levels where each of you lives. What are the sources of the noise? Remember to consider inside sources and outside sources. Which steps might you be able to take to reduce sound transmission?

Chapter 39 Review

Section Summaries

39.1 Thermal insulation is available as flexible batts and blankets, rigid board, loose fill, and spray foam. Insulation helps to reduce heat gain as well as cooling loss. R-value is the measure of an insulator's effectiveness. A vapor barrier limits water vapor penetration.

39.2 The amount of sound transmitted through a house can be reduced with the proper wall and ceiling construction. The STC and INR ratings measure a material's resistance to sound transmission.

Review Questions

1. What is the primary factor to consider when choosing the amount and type of thermal insulation?
2. Name the four basic types of thermal insulation.
3. What is meant by the term *R-value*?
4. What is the advantage of loose-fill insulation as compared to flexible insulation?
5. Which type of rigid insulation would be suitable for insulating the outside of a foundation wall below grade?
6. What is a vapor barrier?
7. Give three reasons why proper attic ventilation is important.
8. Describe radiant heat transmission.
9. Describe at least two types of wall construction used to reduce noise transmission.
10. How are sound-absorbing materials different from sound-insulating materials?

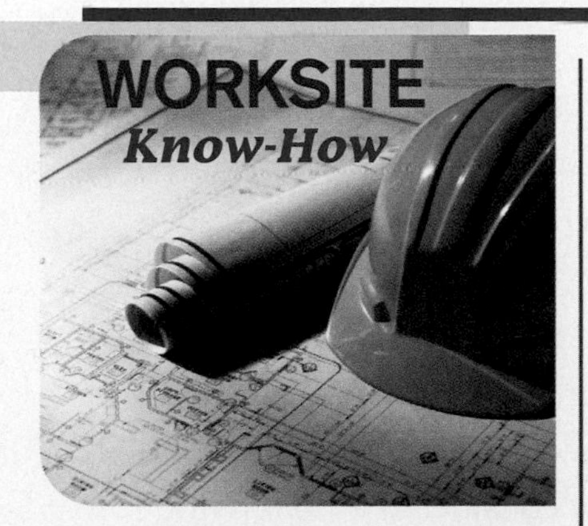

Your Health and Your Job Your health has an impact on the work you do. If you're sick or feeling below par, your stores of energy are low and your ability to concentrate is affected. You can't get as much done, and what you do accomplish is usually not your best work.

Everyone gets sick once in a while, but there are things you can do to prevent illness. You can eat a balanced diet. You can get plenty of sleep at night. You can exercise daily and obtain regular physical checkups from your doctor. You can refuse to abuse drugs of any kind, including alcohol. Doing all these things won't guarantee perfect health, but it will improve your body's ability to resist illness and help it recover faster when you do get sick.

Chapter 40

Walls and Ceilings

Objectives

After reading this chapter, you'll be able to:

- Identify and describe the various types of drywall.
- Describe a nail pop and explain the methods used to prevent it.
- Describe problems relating to safety and health when installing drywall and explain preventative measures.
- Identify the basic materials used in three-coat plaster work.
- Install a suspended ceiling.

Terms

acoustical ceiling
corner bead
feathering
ground
lath
suspended ceiling
veneer plaster

After the mechanical systems have been roughed in and the insulation is in place, interior wall and ceiling materials can be applied. Drywall is the material most commonly used, but plaster is sometimes preferred. The two materials can even be used in combination. Wood paneling, another finishing choice, is discussed in Chapter 37, "Wall Paneling."

There are advantages and disadvantages to plaster and drywall. The choice of one or the other should be made as the house is being designed. The short-term and long-term costs of each should be considered at that point. The choice will have a significant effect on the work schedule for the house.

SECTION 40.1

Drywall

Drywall has become the most popular interior wall and ceiling finish in residential construction.

DRYWALL BASICS

Drywall consists of sheets, or panels, made with a noncombustible *gypsum* core covered with paper. It is also known as *gypsum wallboard*, *gypsum board*, or by various trade names. Natural gypsum is a mineral rock. After it is mined, it is ground to a powder and baked. The resulting material, commonly called *plaster of Paris*, is mixed with water and other ingredients. It is then sandwiched between the sheets of special paper to form drywall panels. Manufacturers sometimes use synthetic gypsum as a substitute for natural gypsum. Synthetic gypsum is made in factories.

Unlike plaster, the large sheets of drywall can be applied quickly. They do not require lengthy drying time before other work can progress. Strongest in the long dimension, drywall is dimensionally stable and inexpensive. Like plaster, it has fire-resistant properties. It can serve as a substrate for other finish materials, such as paint, wood paneling, or wallpaper. (A *substrate* is a material that serves as a base for another material.) Drywall is installed by drywall contractors. **Fig. 40-1.**

Types of Panels

Drywall panels are available in many types, sizes, and thicknesses for a variety of conditions. The following three types of drywall panels are common in residential construction:

Standard Drywall. Drywall sheets are commonly 4′ wide and 8′ long. Panels are also available in lengths of 9′, 10′, 12′, and 14′. Long panels speed construction but can be unwieldy to work with. Panels that are 4′-6″ wide are sometimes applied horizontally to reduce installation costs where walls are 8′-6″ or 9′ tall. The most common thickness for drywall is ½″. However, ⅜″ and ¼″ panels are used for covering old surfaces, for curved walls, and when layering to reduce sound transmission. Drywall is also available in a thickness of ⅝″.

Face paper wraps around the long edges of the panel but does not cover the short edges. The edges along the length of a panel are tapered and, on some types, the ends are tapered also. Tapering allows the joints between panels to be filled and smoothed. Sheets with square-cut long and short edges are used as a substrate for paneling and other materials.

Fire-Code Drywall. When additives are mixed with the gypsum, drywall becomes more fire resistant. The resulting product is generally referred to as *fire-code drywall*. It is important to understand that a fire-resistant product slows the passage of fire but does not completely stop it.

Fig. 40-1. Installing drywall panels on a curved ceiling. Wall panels are installed after the ceiling is complete.

Type-X fire-code drywall is ⅝″ thick. It contains glass fibers that keep it from crumbling in extreme heat. This drywall is required by code on the outer surface of walls separating an attached garage from the house. This improves the fire resistance of the wall. *Type-C drywall* contains vermiculite and comes in thicknesses of ½″ and ⅝″. More fire resistant than Type-X drywall, it is sometimes used to provide extra fire resistance to ceilings.

Moisture-Resistant Drywall. In damp areas, such as bathrooms, *MR drywall*, or *green board* (for the color of its paper facing), should be used. The core is a water-resistant type of gypsum. The face and back paper are chemically treated to reduce moisture penetration. MR drywall comes in ½″ and ⅝″ thicknesses. *Fire-code MR drywall* (Type X and Type C) is also available.

Fasteners

Drywall panels must be securely fastened to wood or steel studs with special nails or screws. **Fig. 40-2.** Drywall nails have thin, flat heads for flush driving without damage to the surface of the panel. Standard drywall nails have smooth shanks, but *annular-ring* (*ring-shank*) drywall nails offer better holding power. Drywall ½″ thick requires a nail at least 1¼″ long.

Drive nails so that their heads are slightly below the surface. The head of a drywall hammer forms a small dimple in the drywall. If a nail is driven too hard and breaks the paper surface of the drywall, remove it and install another nail nearby. Later, you can fill both dimples with joint compound.

Screws provide better holding power than nails. Drywall screws are corrosion resistant. They have a Phillips-type bugle head and a sharp point. Type-W screws are used for wood framing and should be at least 1¼″ long for use with ½″ drywall. Type-S screws are used for steel framing and should be 1″ long for use with ½″ drywall. Neither type of screw requires a predrilled pilot hole.

Joint Compound

After installation, panel joints and edges must be finished. Be sure to use products compatible with the type of drywall being installed.

Joint compound is a thick, pastelike material. It is used in combination with *joint tape* made of perforated paper or self-adhesive fiberglass mesh to conceal the joints between panels. By itself, joint compound is used to fill nail dimples and sometimes for texturing the panel's surface. It can be purchased in ready mixed or powder form.

Ready-mixed joint compound has the best working qualities. Its quality is consistent from batch to batch. However, it is heavy to transport and will freeze if stored in a cold area. Frozen compound that is slowly thawed at room temperature will not be damaged. However, repeated freeze/thaw cycles make it more difficult to work with. Powdered compound must be mixed with clean water before use. It has a long shelf life and can be stored at any temperature.

Ready-mixed and powdered joint compound are each available in two basic types. The *drying type* cures as it gives up moisture. Differences in house humidity and temperature can slow or speed up drying time. The *setting type* cures through a chemical process. Less affected by humidity and temperature, it cures more quickly than drying compounds.

Some contractors use an all-purpose joint compound for every step in the finishing process. Others prefer to use separate compounds for different steps. For example, a *taping compound* can be used in the early stages. It offers greater bond strength and crack resistance than all-purpose compounds. A *topping compound* can then be used to complete the joints. It is easier to sand than all-purpose compound, shrinks very little, and finishes smoothly.

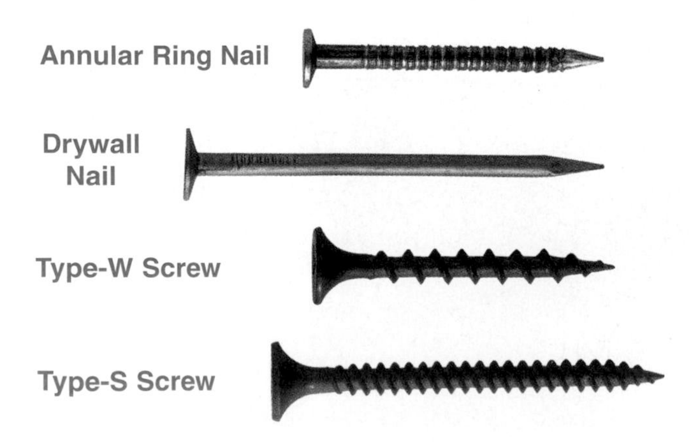

Fig. 40-2. Common types of drywall fasteners.

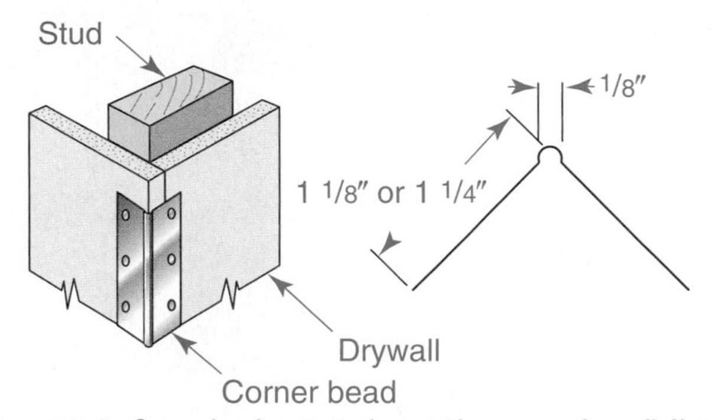

Fig. 40-3. Corner bead protects the outside corners of a wall. Note how the drywall panels overlap at the corner.

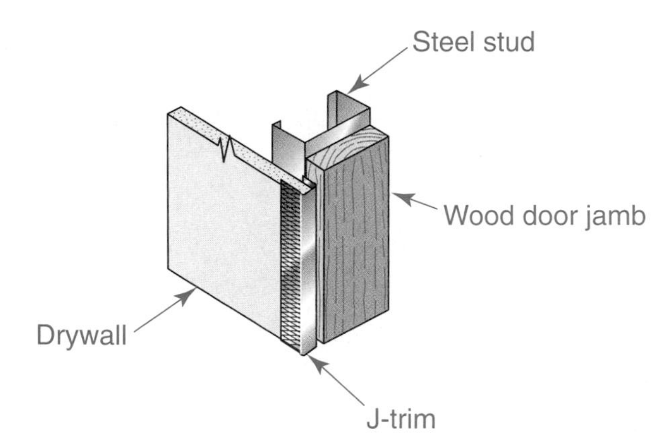

Fig. 40-4. J-trim can be used to provide a finished edge where drywall meets another material.

Trim Accessories

A variety of metal and vinyl shapes can be used to cover and protect the raw edges of the cut sheets. At outside corners, one edge of the drywall overlaps the intersecting edge. Corner bead is then nailed, screwed, or crimped (using a special tool) over the entire length of the corner. **Fig. 40-3. Corner bead** is a vinyl or galvanized metal strip that reinforces and protects the corner. It comes in lengths of 8′ and 10′. Standard corner bead forms a square 90° corner. *Bullnose corner bead* forms a rounded 90° corner.

Other trim can be used to finish or protect drywall edges near window and door jambs and where drywall meets another material. J-trim is an example. **Fig. 40-4.**

TOOLS

Special installation and finishing tools are required for drywall work. Drywall contractors also use various types of ladders and scaffolds. For some jobs, many drywall panels will be needed. In this case, power lifting equipment should be considered for carrying panels from the delivery truck directly into the house. This speeds up construction. It also improves safety because the heavy, awkward sheets do not have to be carried by hand. It also reduces the chance that sheets will be damaged as they are carried.

Installation Tools

Installation tools are used to lay out, cut, and attach drywall panels to structural members. **Fig. 40-5.**

Fig. 40-5. Drywall installation tools. *A.* Layout square. *B.* Chalk line. *C.* Tape measure. *D.* Drywall hammer. *E.* Screw gun. *F.* Drywall saw. *G.* Utility knife. *H.* Drywall router.

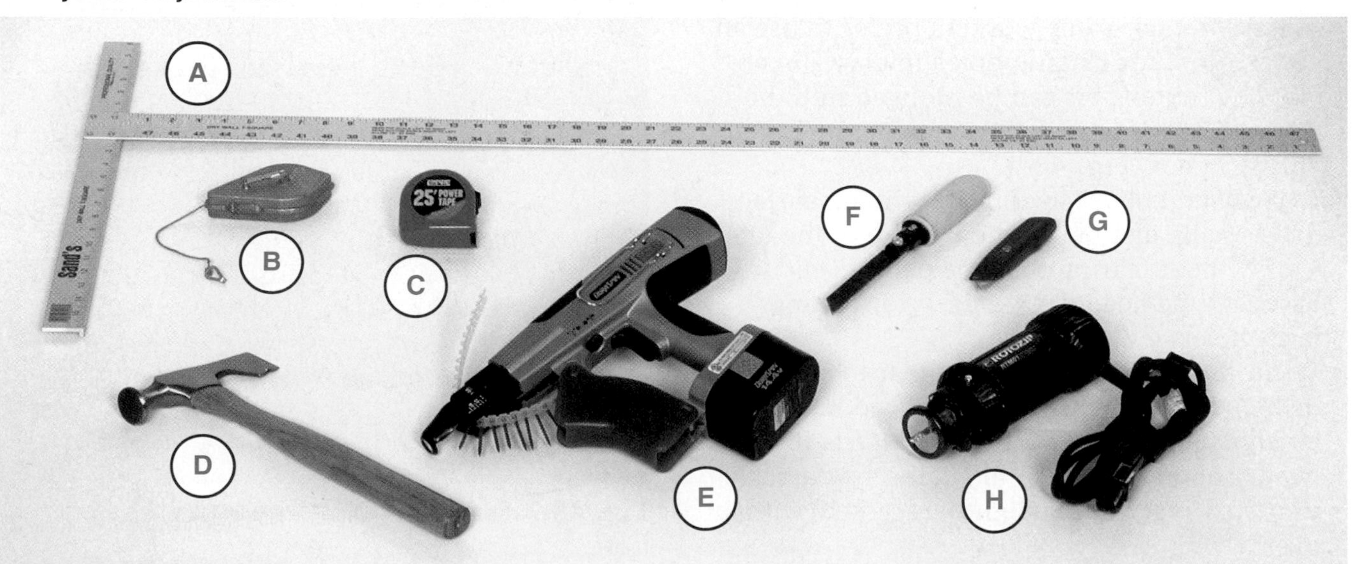

A

B

C

Fig. 40-6. Cutting drywall. *A.* Scoring with a utility knife. Note that the left hand is out of danger. *B.* Bending the panel. *C.* Snapping the panel apart after cutting through the backing paper.

- *Tape measure, chalk line, and drywall square.* These tools are used to measure and mark drywall panels for cutting. The metal drywall square can also be used to guide a utility knife.
- *Utility knife.* Drywall is easily cut with a utility knife. After scoring through the face paper with the knife, bend the drywall along the score line. **Fig. 40-6.** To complete the separation, slice through the backing paper and snap the board forward toward the face side for a clean, straight break. When extra accuracy is important, guide the utility knife with a drywall square.
- *Drywall utility saw.* Small cutouts for electrical boxes and other openings are made with a drywall utility saw. This tool is similar to a keyhole saw but has a stiffer blade and larger teeth.
- *Drywall router.* Some workers prefer to use an electric tool for making holes in drywall panels. The router's bit can be plunged into the drywall. The bit can follow the contours of an electrical box. **Fig. 40-7.**
- *Drywall hammer.* The domed striking surface drives nails just below the surface of the drywall without tearing the face paper. The hatchet-type head can be used for cutting large holes.
- *Screw gun.* A screw gun is similar to an electric drill but has a depth-sensitive head instead of an adjustable chuck. A Phillips bit fits into the head. The tool drives a drywall screw quickly to the correct depth (slightly recessed) without overdriving it.

SAFETY FIRST

Watch Your Fingers!

A utility knife is extremely sharp. Many workers are cut when a knife slips unexpectedly. When cutting drywall, keep your hands well away from the knife's path. Also, keep the knife in a leather sheath when not using it, not in a pocket.

Fig. 40-7. Holes for electrical boxes can be cut with a drywall router.

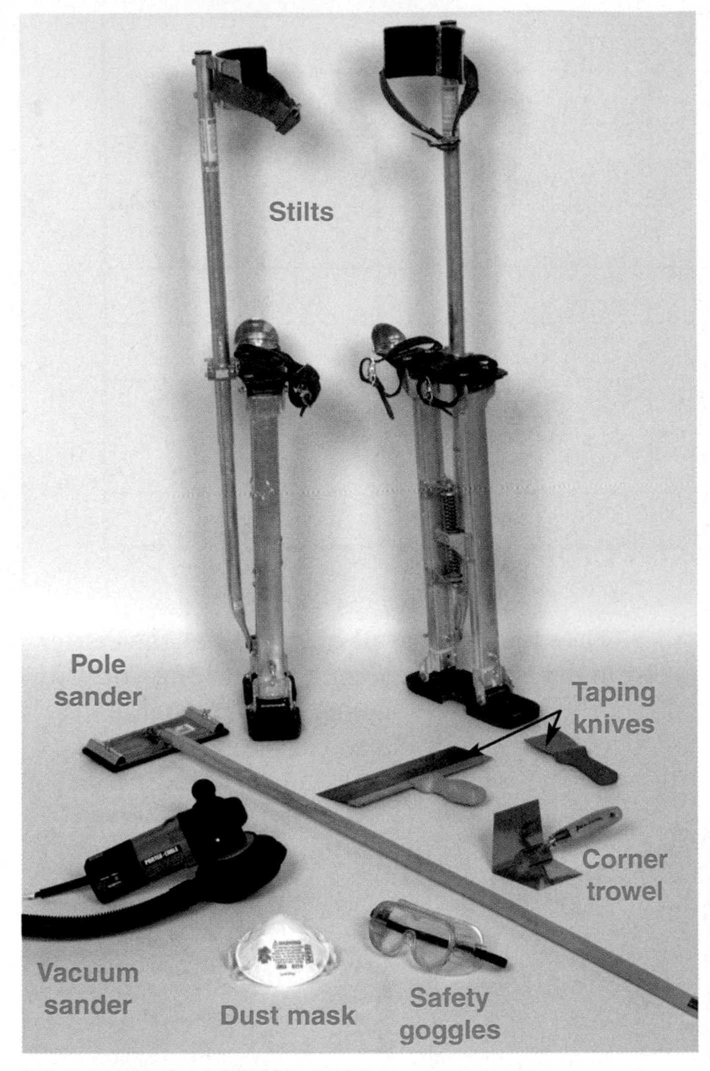

Fig. 40-8. Drywall finishing tools.

Finishing Tools

Finishing tools are used to conceal joints between panels. They can also be used to apply a decorative texture to the drywall surface. **Fig. 40-8.**

- *Taping knives.* Knives are used to spread and smooth joint compound. The flexible blades may be blue steel or stainless steel. They are available in depths of 2¼″ and 3″ and in various widths. Knives 6″ or 8″ wide are used for setting tape. Knives up to 20″ wide are used for applying finish coats.
- *Corner trowel.* The blade is angled at 103° and flexes to 90° for finishing inside corners.
- *Pole sander.* This sanding block has a foam rubber pad that is attached to a ¾″ diameter pole. It holds strips of sandpaper or sanding screen (an open grid coated with carbide grit). The wood pole enables the user to reach all parts of a wall or ceiling safely.
- *Dust mask/respirator.* A NIOSH-approved dust mask reduces exposure to sanding dust that can cause eye, nose, throat, or upper-respiratory irritation.
- *Safety glasses or goggles.* They protect eyes from sanding dust.
- *Vacuum sander.* This vacuum-assisted device is used to sand drywall and collect the dust.
- *Stilts.* Stilts allow the user to reach ceilings without repeatedly climbing a ladder or scaffold. **Fig. 40-9.**

INSTALLATION

Drywall is generally attached directly to framing in a single layer. The maximum spacing of framing members for various thicknesses of

Fig. 40-9. Drywall stilts in use while installing drywall.

Table 40-A. Maximum Spacing Recommended for Drywall

Long Direction of Sheet	Minimum Thickness (inches)	Maximum Spacing of Supports (on center)	
		Walls (inches)	Ceilings (inches)
Parallel to framing members	3/8	16	-
	1/2	24	16
	5/8	24	16
	3/8	16	16
Right angles to framing members	1/2	24	24
	5/8	24	24

drywall is shown in **Table 40-A**. Two layers can be used to reduce sound transmission between rooms. An undercourse of 3/8″ thick material is installed vertically. The second layer is applied horizontally using an adhesive and only enough nails to hold the uppermost panels in place. **Fig. 40-10.**

Always fasten drywall beginning at the center of the panel, and then work toward the ends. Hold the panel tight against the framing member as the fastener is driven. Butt all joints loosely. Never force panels into position.

Apply panels to the ceiling first. **Fig. 40-11.** In some areas, 5/8″ drywall is commonly used for

Fig. 40-10. Installing drywall horizontally over the sound-deadening panels, which were applied vertically. Openings for such things as electrical outlets and heating vents must be caulked carefully. Even a small hole lessens the sound-deadening ability of the wall.

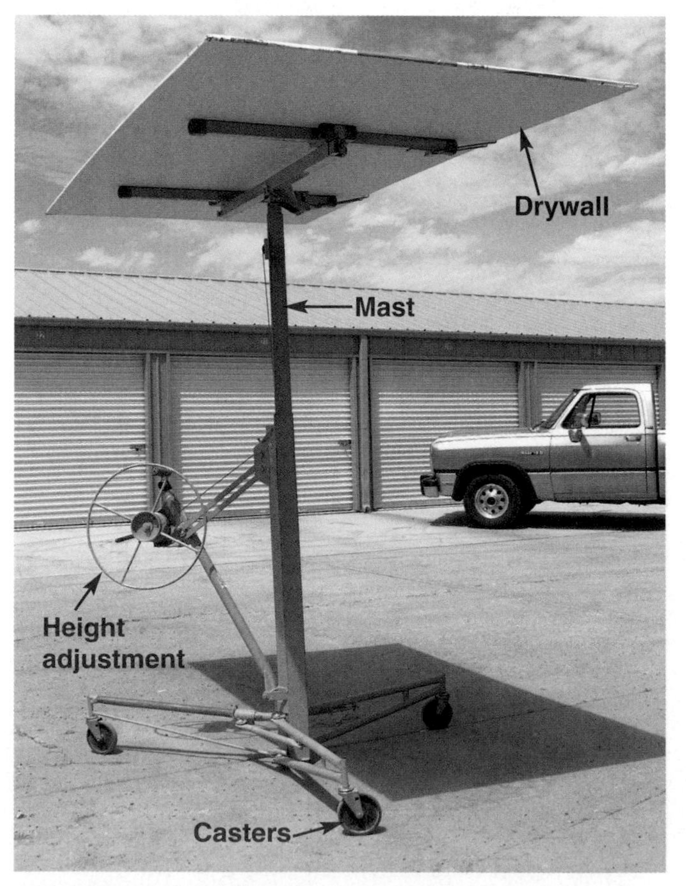

Fig. 40-11. A drywall jack can be used to hold panels against a ceiling as they are being fastened.

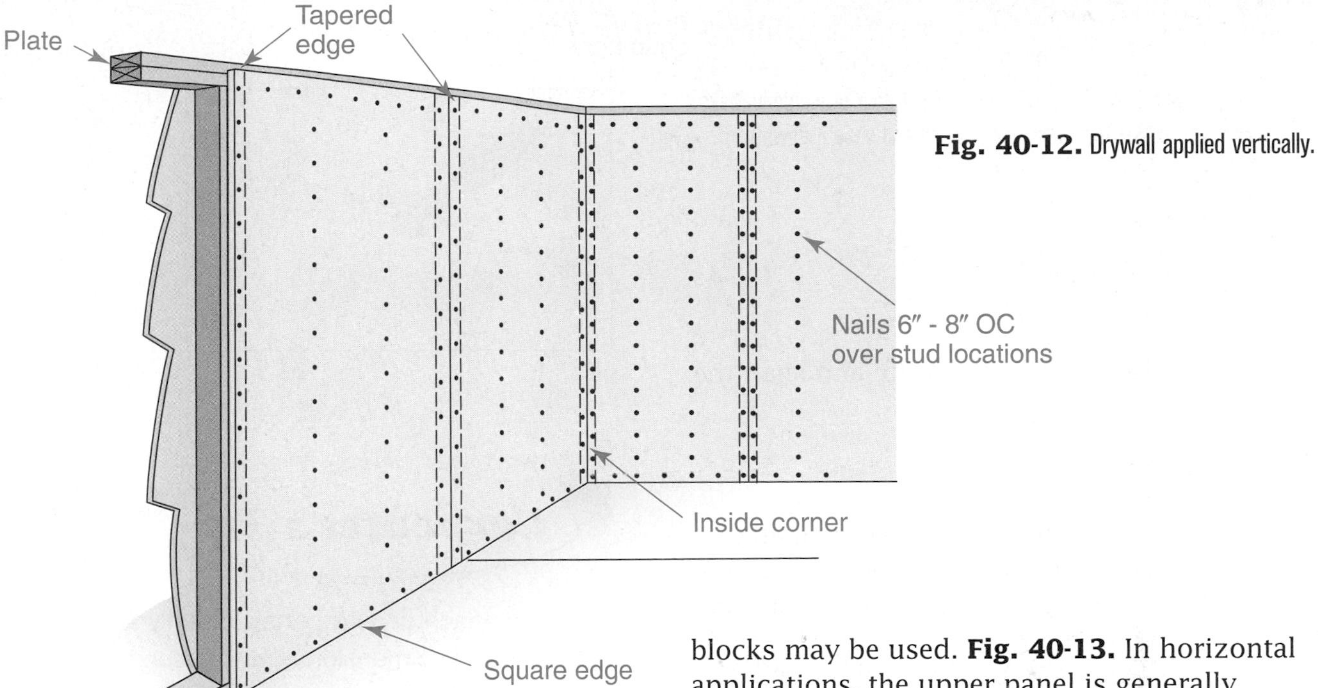

Fig. 40-12. Drywall applied vertically.

ceilings. When applying the panels vertically to walls, be sure to support all edges by framing or blocking. **Fig. 40-12.** When applying panels horizontally, blocking is not required behind ½″ or thicker drywall if it is applied to studs 16″ OC. However, if the stud spacing is greater or additional support at the joint is desirable, nailing blocks may be used. **Fig. 40-13.** In horizontal applications, the upper panel is generally installed first to provide the best fit at the ceiling/wall corner. Drywall edges at the floor are covered by baseboard. Horizontal application is generally preferred for the following reasons:

- The lineal footage of joints is reduced by up to 25 percent.
- Horizontal panels can more easily bridge studs that are not precisely aligned.
- The strongest dimension of the panel runs across the studs.
- Horizontal joints are at a convenient height for finishing.

Nail or screw spacing is the same for both horizontal and vertical applications. Some installers place a second nail within 2″ of the first for added holding power. This is called *double nailing* and allows greater distance between nails. However, it is not a common practice in all states.

When notching drywall to fit around obstructions, use a drywall saw to cut through the panel along one or more layout lines. Then score the

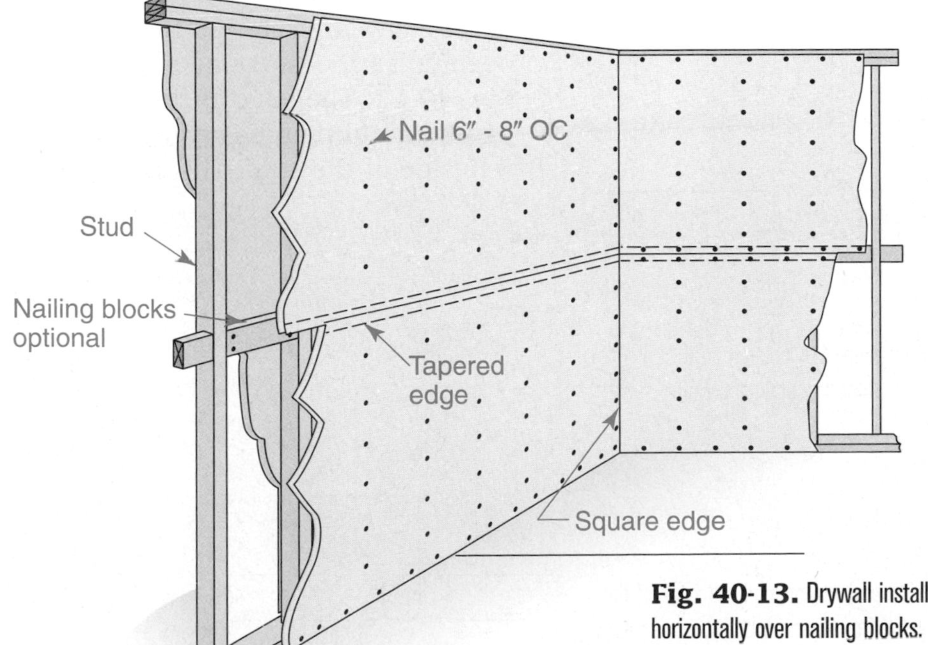

Fig. 40-13. Drywall installed horizontally over nailing blocks.

Fig. 40-14. Making a cutout for a door or window. Make two saw cuts. Then score the drywall and snap it downward.

intersecting line with a utility knife and snap the piece off. **Fig. 40-14.**

Wood Framing

Wall studs and ceiling joists must be in alignment to provide a smooth, even drywall surface. Bowed or twisted studs should not be used. **Fig. 40-15.** Also, the framing lumber must have a low moisture content to prevent nail "pops." These result if wood framing members dry out and shrink away from the nails. This can cause the nail head to pop above the drywall surface, causing a bump. Nail pops are greatly reduced if the moisture content of the framing is less than 15 percent when the drywall is applied. The use of screws nearly eliminates the problem.

Uneven framing, such as misaligned blocking, prevents the drywall from lying flat. This can damage the drywall as it is fastened. **Fig. 40-16.** Before installing drywall, inspect the framing and fix any such problems.

Do not attach drywall panels directly to the face of wide dimensional lumber such as floor joists and headers. Instead, "float" panels over them in case of wood shrinkage (do not nail directly into the wood). Otherwise, shrinkage might cause cracking or nail pops in the drywall.

Steel Framing

When drywall is placed over steel framing, the panels must be installed in a particular direction as the carpenter moves around the room. This direction depends on which way the stud flanges are facing. Plan the work so that drywall panel edges are screwed first to the open (unsupported) side of a stud. **Fig. 40-17.** The edge of the next panel should then be screwed to the web side of the stud. This prevents

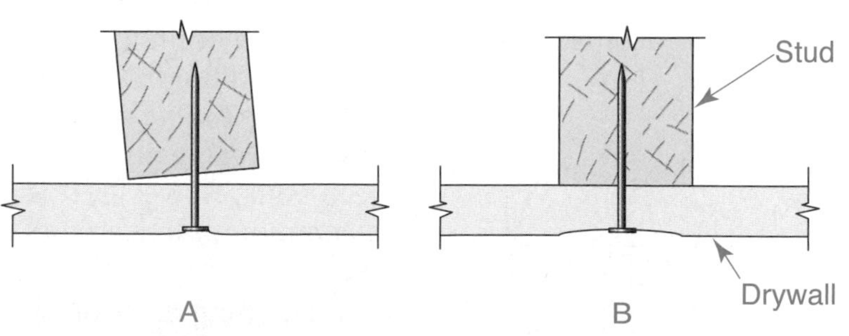

Fig. 40-15. Drywall must fit tightly against framing. *A.* A twisted stud increases the possibility of nail pops. *B.* A properly fastened connection. Note the slight dimple around the nail head.

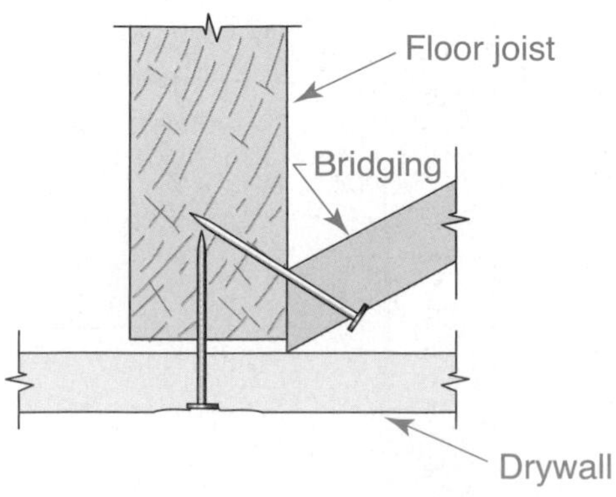

Fig. 40-16. This bridging, which projects beyond the edge of the joists, prevents the back of the drywall from being brought into contact with the nailing surface. A puncture can occur.

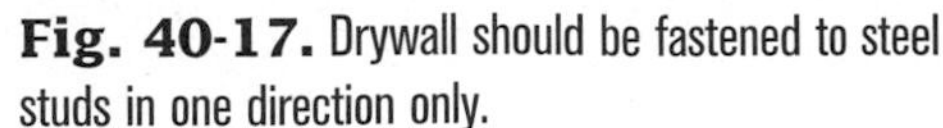
Fig. 40-17. Drywall should be fastened to steel studs in one direction only.

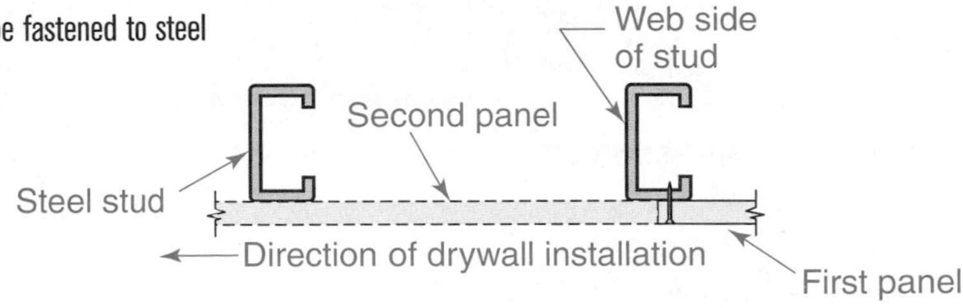

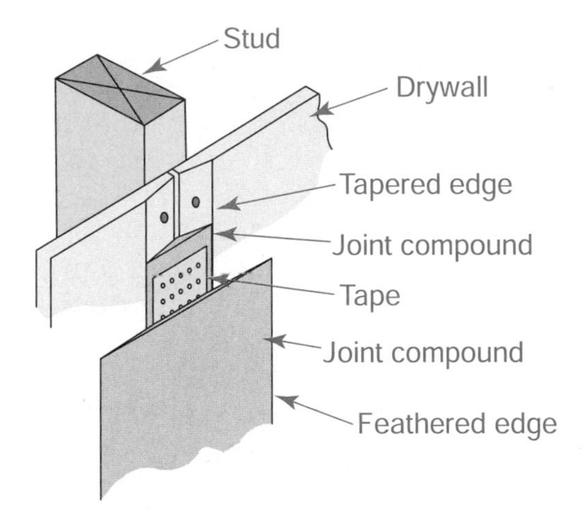

Fig. 40-18. The tapered edge of the drywall is filled with joint compound and tape. Additional joint compound is then applied and feathered out to provide a smooth surface.

the open side from deflecting as the screws are driven, which would result in uneven joints.

FINISHING

After all corner bead has been installed, joints between the panels and at inside corners are filled in a multi-step process called taping the joints. One or more layers of joint compound are applied over a single layer of joint tape. Tape reinforces the joint. **Fig. 40-18.** When the last layer of joint compound dries, it must be sanded smooth. One method for taping joints is described in the Step-by-Step feature on page 820.

Temperature and humidity have a direct effect on the drying time of joint compound. Each layer must be thoroughly dry before more coats are applied. In all cases, good ventilation speeds drying. **Table 40-B** shows the average drying periods for joint compound under different temperature and humidity conditions.

SAFETY FIRST

Breathe Easier

Joint compound sanding dust may contain harmful amounts of *silica.* When lodged in your lungs, silica can lead to serious health problems, such as cancer or silicosis (see Chapter 5, "Construction Safety and Health"). Limit your exposure to drywall dust by wearing a NIOSH-approved dust mask. Use a pole sander whenever possible instead of sanding by hand. The pole increases the distance between the worker and the sanding surface. The use of a vacuum-based sanding system can reduce dust exposure by 80 percent or more.

Veneer Plaster

Where walls will receive very hard wear, special *gypsum base drywall* can be used. It is then coated with a layer of veneer plaster. **Veneer plaster** is a specially formulated gypsum plaster. The plaster is applied by trowel in one layer 1/16″ to 3/32″ thick or in two layers totaling 1/8″.

Table 40-B. Approximate Drying Time for Joint Compound

	Relative Humidity								
Temperature (°F)	0%	20%	40%	50%	60%	70%	80%	90%	98%
40°	28H	34H	44H	2D	2½D	3½D	4½D	9D	37D
60°	13H	16H	20H	24H	29H	38H	2½D	4½D	18D
80°	6H	8H	10H	12H	13½H	19½H	27H	49H	9D
100°	3H	4H	5H	6H	8H	10H	14H	26D	5D

Note: H = Hours, D = Days (24 hours).

STEP BY STEP

Taping Joints

The following describes the use of all-purpose joint compound and paper reinforcing tape. Using other products would mean a change in the order of steps. Also, drywall contractors use specialized tools that make the work go faster.

TAPING FLAT JOINTS

Step 1 Use a 5″ wide taping knife or applicator to apply compound over the joint. **Fig. 40-19.**

Step 2 Press joint tape into the fresh compound with a 6″ or 8″ taping knife until the compound is forced through the holes in the tape. **Fig. 40-20.**

Step 3 Immediately cover the tape with additional compound, **feathering** (smoothing) the outer edges so there are no ridges.

Step 4 After the first layer of compound has dried, apply a second coat, using a wider knife.

Step 5 For best results, apply a third coat, feathering the edges beyond the second coat.

Step 6 After the final coat is completely dry, sand the joint smooth and even with the wall surface. **Fig. 40-21.**

TAPING CORNERS

Step 1 For an inside corner, apply joint compound along both sides of the corner.

Step 2 Cut joint tape to the length of the corner. Fold the tape lengthwise down the center and crease it to form a right angle. **Fig. 40-22.**

Step 3 Press the tape into the compound and follow Steps 2 through 5 for flat joints.

Step 4 For an outside corner, apply compound over the edges of the corner bead on both sides. Joint reinforcement tape is not necessary.

Step 5 Apply more layers as necessary, always feathering the edges.

Step 6 Sand the joint smooth.

FILLING NAIL DIMPLES

Step 1 To hide hammer indentations, fill them with joint compound using a 6″ knife. Apply additional layers as necessary.

Step 2 Sand the areas smooth when they are dry.

Gypsum-base drywall is sometimes called *blue board* for the color of its surface paper. The multiple layers of paper provide an excellent bond with veneer plaster.

Other Surface Finishes

The surface of standard drywall is smooth, but various products can be used to give it a decorative texture. **Fig. 40-23.** Ceilings, for example, are often sprayed with a product containing fine, medium, or coarse polystyrene aggregate. This results in a heavily textured surface creating what is sometimes called a *popcorn ceiling.* This finish masks minor surface defects and is usually left unpainted. Other finishes can be used on walls as well as ceilings. They should be painted when dry.

A

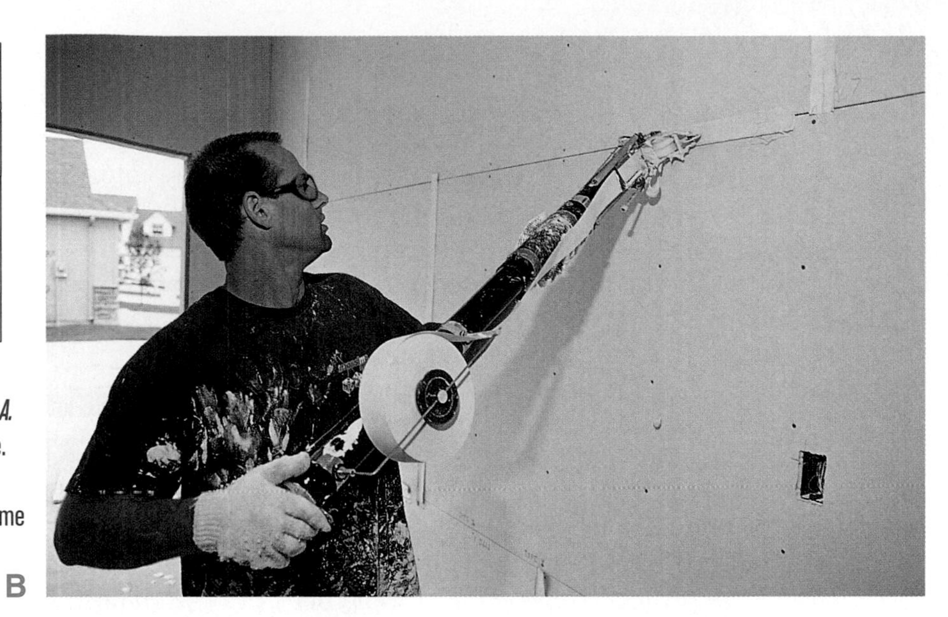

B

Fig. 40-19. Applying joint compound. *A.* Applying joint compound with a taping knife. Compound is dispensed from a mud box. *B.* Applying joint compound and tape at the same time with a mechanical applicator.

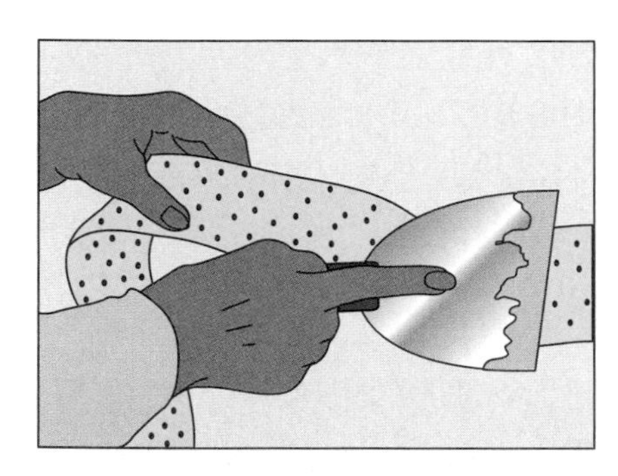

Fig. 40-20. Press the perforated tape into the compound, forcing the excess compound from under the tape.

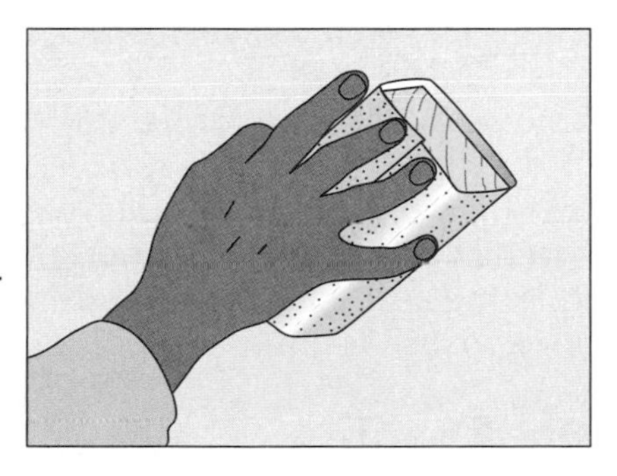

Fig. 40-21. Sanding the joints and nail dimples after the joint is completely dried. Use a pole sander or vacuum sander whenever possible.

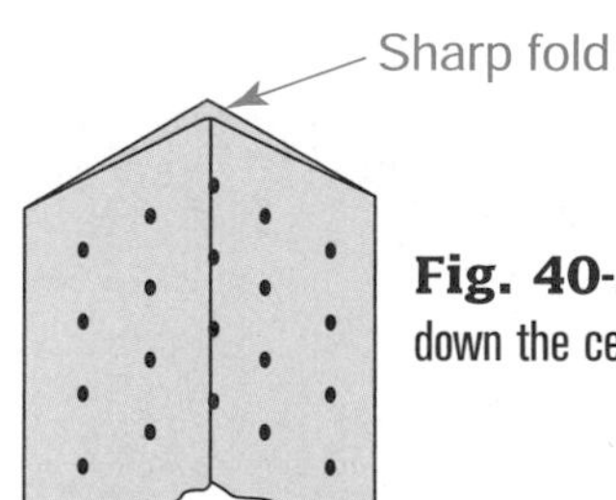

Fig. 40-22. Fold the perforated tape down the center to form a right angle.

A. Sand finish

B. Ceiling texture finish

C. Rough troweled finish

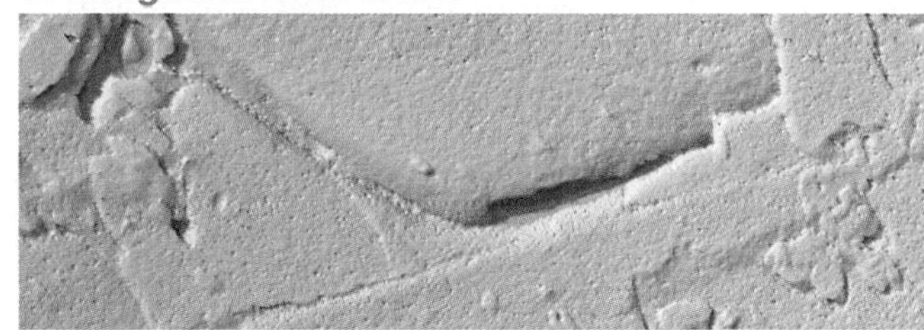

D. Stippled finish

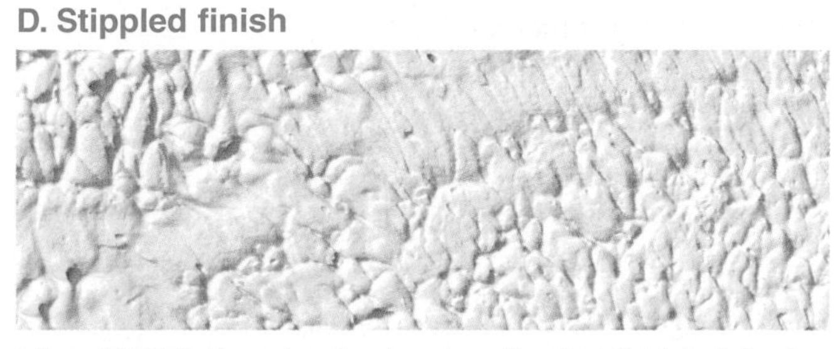

Fig. 40-23. Examples of various drywall surface finishes. *A.* Sand finish. *B.* Ceiling texture finish. *C.* Rough troweled finish. *D.* Stippled finish.

ESTIMATING DRYWALL MATERIALS

The amount of materials required for a room is based on the square footage of walls and ceilings to be covered. Contractors typically calculate the square footage and translate that into the number of panels. Each 4x8 panel represents 32 sq. ft, and each 4x10 panel represents 40 sq. ft. When calculating square footage, walls are often "figured solid." That means that the overall square footage of the wall is calculated without subtracting for door and window openings. This is done partly to simplify calculations and partly because the large cutouts required for doors and windows are generally considered waste. These pieces are often difficult to reuse elsewhere in the project. However, if a wall contains a large picture window, the estimator may decide to subtract its area from the overall square footage of the wall.

Panels

To determine square footage, multiply room perimeter by room height. (Obtain this information from the plans.) Do not subtract door and window openings from the figure. This provides a small allowance for waste.

For example, a 10′ x 12′ room with 9′ high ceilings would contain 516 sq. ft.:

Walls: $10 + 10 + 12 + 12 = 44$ ft.
$44 \times 9 = 396$ sq. ft.
Ceiling: $10' \times 12' = 120$ sq. ft.
$396 + 120 = 516$ sq. ft.

Each 4x8 drywall panel covers 32 sq. ft., so the total number required for this room would be approximately 17 panels:

$516 \div 32 = 16.12$

Fasteners

The quantity of nails is estimated by pounds per 1,000 sq. ft. of drywall. For example, ½″ drywall requires 4.5 lbs. per 1,000 sq. ft. when applied to wood framing 16″ OC. The room in our example would need about 2.5 lbs.:

$516 \div 1{,}000 = 0.516$
$0.516 \times 4.5 = 2.32$ lbs.

Joint Treatment

To finish 1,000 sq. ft. of drywall, 370 lineal feet of joint tape and 138 lbs. of ready-mixed all-purpose joint compound or 83 lbs. of conventional drying-type powder are required.

To determine the quantities, divide the total square footage of wall and ceiling by 1,000. Then multiply this figure by the amounts per 1,000 sq. ft.:

$516 \div 1{,}000 = 0.516$
$370 \times 0.516 = 190.9$ l.f. of joint tape
$138 \times 0.516 = 71.2$ lbs. of all-purpose joint compound

SECTION 40.1

Check Your Knowledge

1. Along which dimension is a drywall panel stronger?
2. *Type X* and *Type C* refer to which kind of drywall?
3. Which type of compound would be used when fast curing is important?
4. Name at least two methods for reducing exposure to joint compound sanding dust.

On the Job

A 12′ by 13′ bedroom has an 8′ ceiling. Find the area of the ceiling. Estimate the number of 4x8 panels of gypsum board needed to drywall the ceiling. Include 5 percent for trim and waste.

SECTION 40.2

Plaster

Plaster is a traditional wall and ceiling finish made from sand, lime or prepared plaster, and water. When applied properly, it has a smooth, dense surface. It can also be given a wide variety of textures. Because it is applied as a wet material, it must dry before other work can continue. This can be inconvenient when construction must be finished quickly. However, many builders and homeowners feel the inconvenience is worthwhile.

Plaster is applied by skilled contractors who specialize in its installation. Many of the tools used in plastering are similar to those used for drywall.

Fig. 40-24. Plaster is commonly installed over a substrate of gypsum lath.

LATH

Plaster must be applied to a base material, called **lath**. Lath usually consists of strips that are fastened to wood or steel framing members. It must have bonding qualities so that plaster sticks to it. Slender strips of wood were once used as lath. Wood lath is rarely used today, though remodelers frequently find it in old houses. The most common types of lath used today are made of gypsum or metal.

Openings in lath allow plaster to be pushed partially through the material. As the plaster dries, it adheres to the back side of the lath. This provides a strong mechanical connection, sometimes called a *keyed connection.*

Gypsum Lath

Gypsum lath has a core of gypsum surrounded by a multi-layered paper face specifically designed for plaster. Gypsum lath comes in 16″ by 48″ panels with square edges. It is applied horizontally across the framing members. **Fig. 40-24.** For stud or joist spacing of 16″ OC, a ⅜″ thickness is used. For 24″ spacing, the lath should be ½″ thick.

Over wood studs, lath can be attached with either flat head 13-gauge gypsum-lathing nails 1⅛″ long or 16-gauge galvanized staples. The staples have a flat 7⁄16″ wide crown and 1″ divergent-point legs. Gypsum lath can be secured to metal studs by 1″ long type-S screws.

Vertical joints should be made over the center of studs or joists. The nails should be spaced 5″ OC, or four nails for the 16″ height, and used at each stud or joist crossing. Joints over heads of openings should not occur at the jamb lines. **Fig. 40-25.**

Metal Lath

Metal lath is made from sheet metal. The metal is slit and expanded during manufacture to form various patterns, such as flat ribs or a diamond mesh. Openings in the lath create gaps for the plaster to "grip." **Fig. 40-26.** Metal lath is usually 27″ x 96″ in size and galvanized to resist rust. It is usually installed on studs or joists spaced 16″ OC.

Metal lath is often used around tub recesses and other bath and kitchen areas. In such cases, Portland cement plaster is sometimes used instead of gypsum plaster. It provides a substrate more suitable for ceramic tile. When used in wet areas, metal lath must be backed with water-resistant sheathing paper.

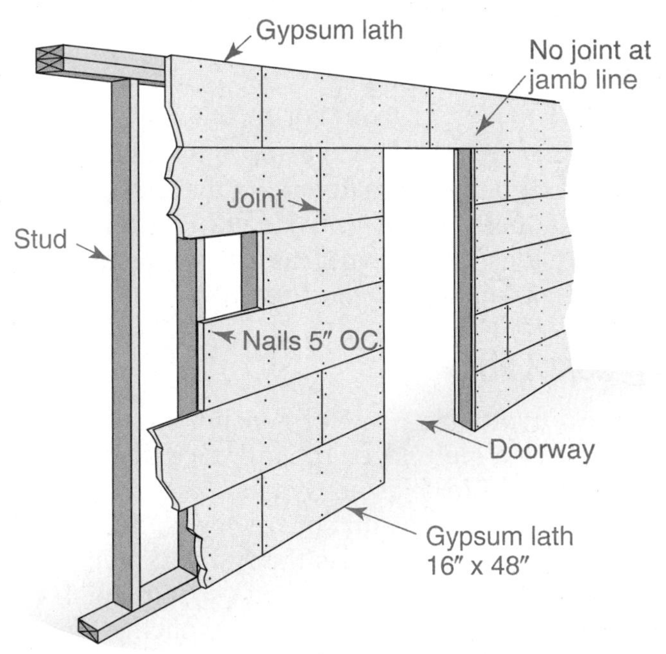

Fig. 40-25. Gypsum lath is nailed horizontally. Note that the joints are staggered and that there is no joint at the jamb line in the doorway.

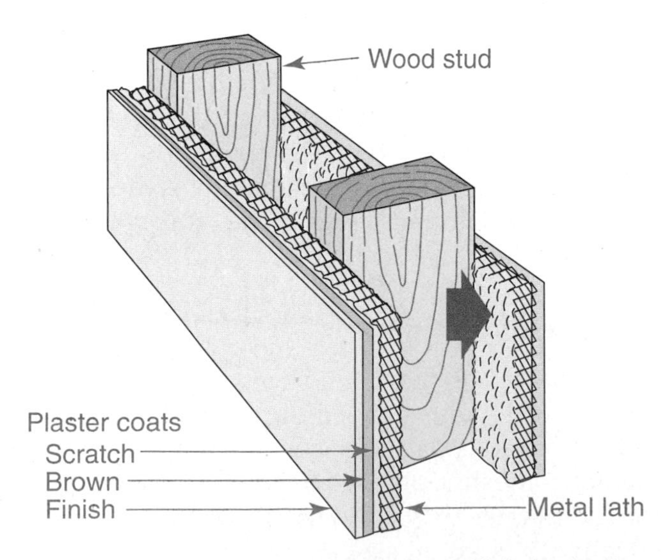

Fig. 40-26. A cross section of plaster on metal lath showing the buildup of the various coats. Notice how the plaster is keyed to the metal lath in the area indicated by the arrow.

TRIM ACCESSORIES

Like drywall edges, the edges of a plastered wall can be covered and protected by trim accessories. These accessories also provide a ground. A **ground** is a material permanently or temporarily attached to a surface to be plastered. It provides a straight edge and helps the plasterer gauge the thickness of the plaster. It may be made of wood but is most often made of metal. Common accessories include the following:

- Metal corner bead is required at all outside corners. It has a solid galvanized metal edge and expanded flanges. Each flange is approximately 2⅞″ wide. **Fig. 40-27.**
- *Cornerite* is an angled length of metal lath that is used to strengthen interior corners. **Fig. 40-28.**
- Casing bead is used around wall openings. It is also used where plaster meets other finishes. It can eliminate the need for wood trim around doors and windows.
- Reinforcing lath is a flat length of expanded lath 4″ or 6″ wide. It is used to reinforce areas that might crack, such as corners around doors and windows. **Fig. 40-29.**

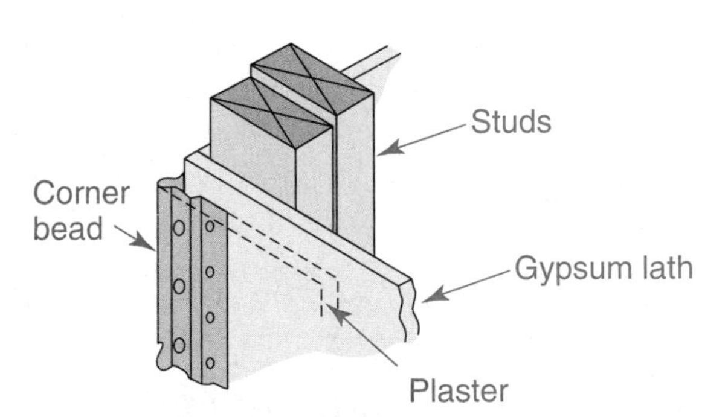

Fig. 40-27. A corner bead is installed at outside corners to serve as a leveling edge when the plaster is applied.

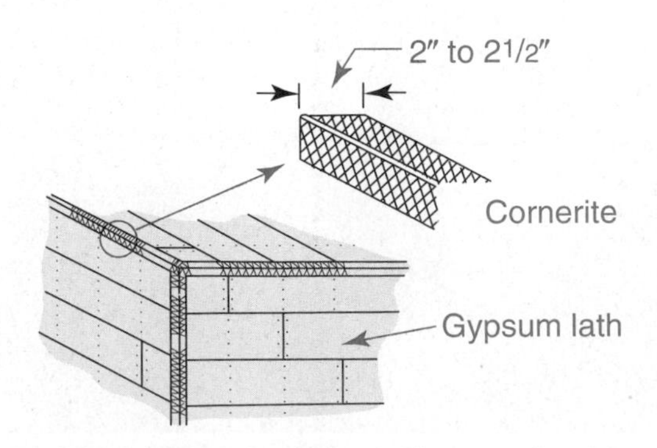

Fig. 40-28. Cornerite is installed at inside corners for reinforcement and to limit plaster cracks.

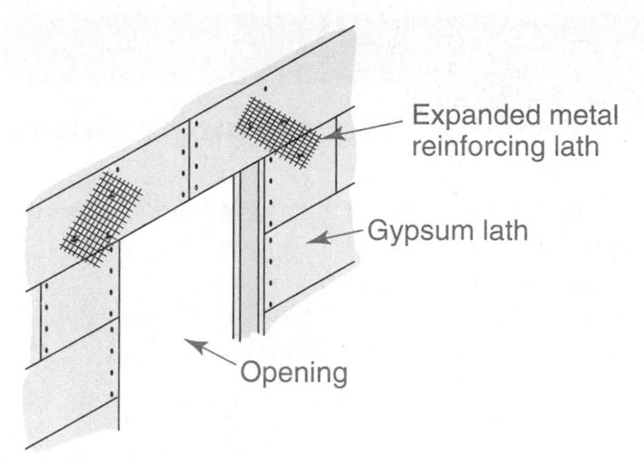

Fig. 40-29. Expanded metal lath is used to help limit plaster cracks.

INSTALLATION

Plaster is applied in three layers over metal lath. It is applied in two or three layers over gypsum lath. The minimum thickness over ⅜″ gypsum lath should be about ⅜″. Three-coat work (see Fig. 40-26) is usually at least ¾″ thick.

The first plaster coat is called the *scratch coat*. After a slight set has occurred, the plaster is scratched to ensure a good bond with the second coat. The second coat is called the *brown coat*, or *leveling coat*. The plaster is brought to level during its application. The third coat is the *finish coat*. It provides the finished wall surface.

Estimating...

Gypsum Lath, Nails, and Labor

Gypsum lath is packaged in bundles of eight 24″ x 48″ pieces. A standard lath bundle therefore contains 64 sq. ft. of lath.

Step 1 To determine the number of bundles required, divide 64 into the total area to be covered. For example, suppose that the walls and ceiling of the room in **Fig. 40-30** are to be finished with lath and plaster. Assume the ceiling is 8 ft. high. The total wall and ceiling area equals 798 sq. ft.:

Walls: $66 \times 8 = 528$
Ceiling: $15 \times 18 = 270$
$528 + 270 = 798$ sq. ft.

Step 2 Divide the number of square feet to be covered by the number of square feet in a bundle of gypsum lath (64) for a total of 12.46, or 13 bundles of gypsum lath.

$$798 \times 64 = 12.46$$

Step 3 To estimate the amount of nails required for installing the gypsum lath, figure that 5 lbs. are needed for every 100 sq. ft. About 800 sq. ft. of lath are to be installed. Therefore, $8 \times 5 = 40$ lbs. of nails.

Step 4 A plasterer calculates the labor cost of a job by the number of square yards to be covered. Convert the square feet in the room to square yards by dividing by 9 (1 sq. yd. equals 9 sq. ft.). In our example, $798 \div 9$ equals 88.66, or 89 sq. yd. This figure would then be multiplied by the plasterer's labor rate.

ESTIMATING ON THE JOB

Suppose a 9′ by 12′ room with 9 ft. ceilings must be plastered. How much gypsum lath and nails will be needed? If a plasterer charged $22 per square yard, how much would the labor cost?

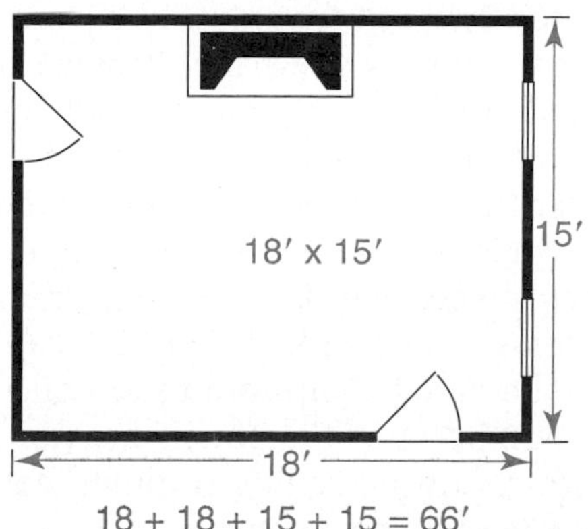

Fig. 40-30. Assume that the ceiling in this room is 8 ft. high.

Two-coat work over gypsum lath, sometimes called *double-up work*, combines the scratch and brown coats.

Plaster receives one of two basic finishes: the *sand-float* and the *putty finish*. For the sand-float finish, lime is mixed with sand, which produces a texture. The putty finish, made without sand, is smooth. It is common in kitchens and bathrooms where a gloss or enamel paint will be used.

Plastering should not be done in freezing weather without a source of constant, even heat. In normal construction, portable heating units are sometimes in place before plastering begins.

SECTION 40.2

Check Your Knowledge

1. Name three types of lath used as a base for plaster.
2. What is a plaster ground?
3. What is Cornerite and what is it used for?
4. Name the two plaster finishes.

On the Job

Plaster has a long history of use as an interior wall and ceiling surface. Research the historical development of plaster, particularly the evolution of ingredients used to reinforce or strengthen it. Report your findings to the class.

SECTION 40.3

Suspended and Acoustical Ceilings

Drywall and plaster are the most common materials used for residential ceilings. However, they prevent access to the areas above. If ducts and water pipes are routed between floor joists, a **suspended ceiling** is sometimes installed. A suspended ceiling consists of panels held in place by a metal or plastic grid at a distance from the floor joists. **Fig. 40-31.** An **acoustical ceiling** consists of panels glued directly to the ceiling surface or stapled to wood furring strips nailed to the ceiling joists.

A suspended ceiling conveniently covers bare joists, exposed pipes, and wiring. Panels can be removed easily for access to valves, switches, and controls. A suspended ceiling may also be used to lower the ceiling level. This is sometimes done when walls are unusually high.

Sometimes suspended ceilings are preferred to drywall ceilings because of their acoustical properties. The panels help to muffle noise between floors. Because the panels are not attached directly to the ceiling framing, noise transmission is reduced further. In houses, suspended ceilings are most common in finished basements. They are also common in commercial construction. In commercial construction, the exact layout of a suspended ceiling may be determined by a special drawing called a *reflected ceiling plan*. However, this drawing is rarely necessary in residential construction.

Fig. 40-31. A suspended ceiling system.

TYPES OF SUSPENDED CEILINGS

Ceiling panels are made of plastic or *mineral board*, which is a lightweight material. It consists of mineral components, binders, and inert filler materials, such as recycled newsprint and mineral wool. Each panel is 2′ x 2′ or 2′ x 4′. The grid system that supports these panels includes *main beams* (sometimes called *runners*), *cross tees*, and wall molding. Main beams are usually 12′ long and are spaced 2′ or 4′ OC. Cross tees are installed at right angles to the main beams. There are many types of suspended ceiling grid components. Two kinds are shown in **Fig. 40-32**. Others include the concealed zee bar system, exposed zee bar system, Hand T system, and furring bar system.

INSTALLATION

Before installing a suspended ceiling, establish the finished ceiling height. Some ceilings, such as those in basements, should be as high as possible to provide maximum headroom. Generally, however, the top edges of the grid system must be at least 3″ below the bottom of the ceiling framing. This space is necessary for the insertion of the panels after the grid system is in place.

A suspended ceiling looks best if the panels on opposite sides of the room are the same width. **Fig. 40-33.** To achieve this, you must accurately plan the layout of the system. Manufacturers provide planning instructions that include layout details. Follow these instruc-

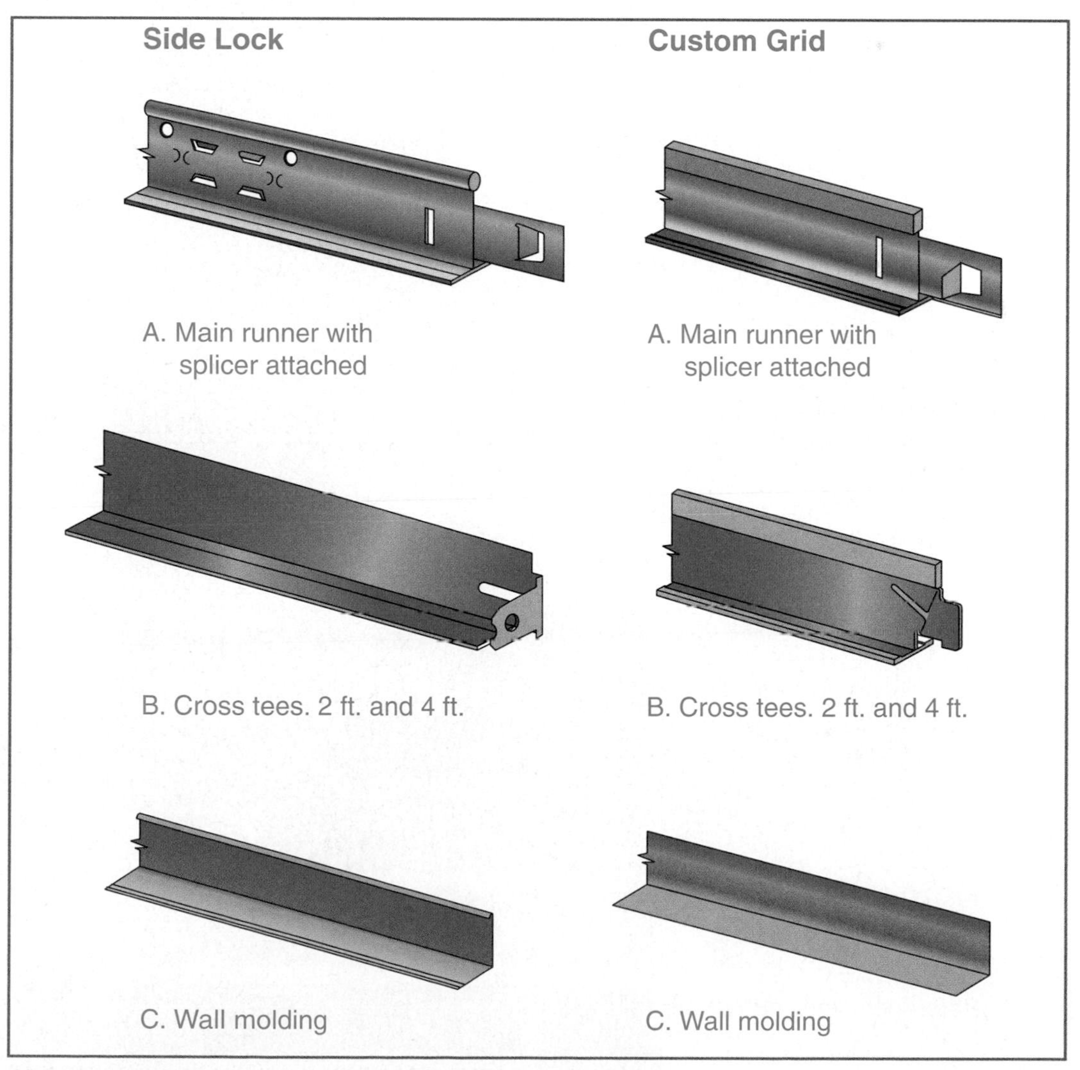

Fig. 40-32. Two of the many types of suspended ceiling grid components.

tions carefully. Once layout has been planned, installation can begin. Step-by-Step instructions are given on page 829.

Ceiling Lights

Recessed fluorescent lighting can be installed at most locations in a suspended ceiling. Fixtures are supported by the main beams. Any one of several styles of translucent panels can be placed over the fixture in place of a ceiling panel.

ACOUSTICAL CEILINGS

In rooms without enough height to hang a suspended ceiling, an acoustical ceiling may be installed instead. The panels consist of 12″ x 12″ squares, or sometimes 12″ x 24″ rectangles. Each panel has a tongue on two edges, and a groove on two edges. This allows the panels to interlock. Panels are typically made of fiberboard. The surface may be embossed or textured. Some panels are made specifically to reduce sound levels in a room.

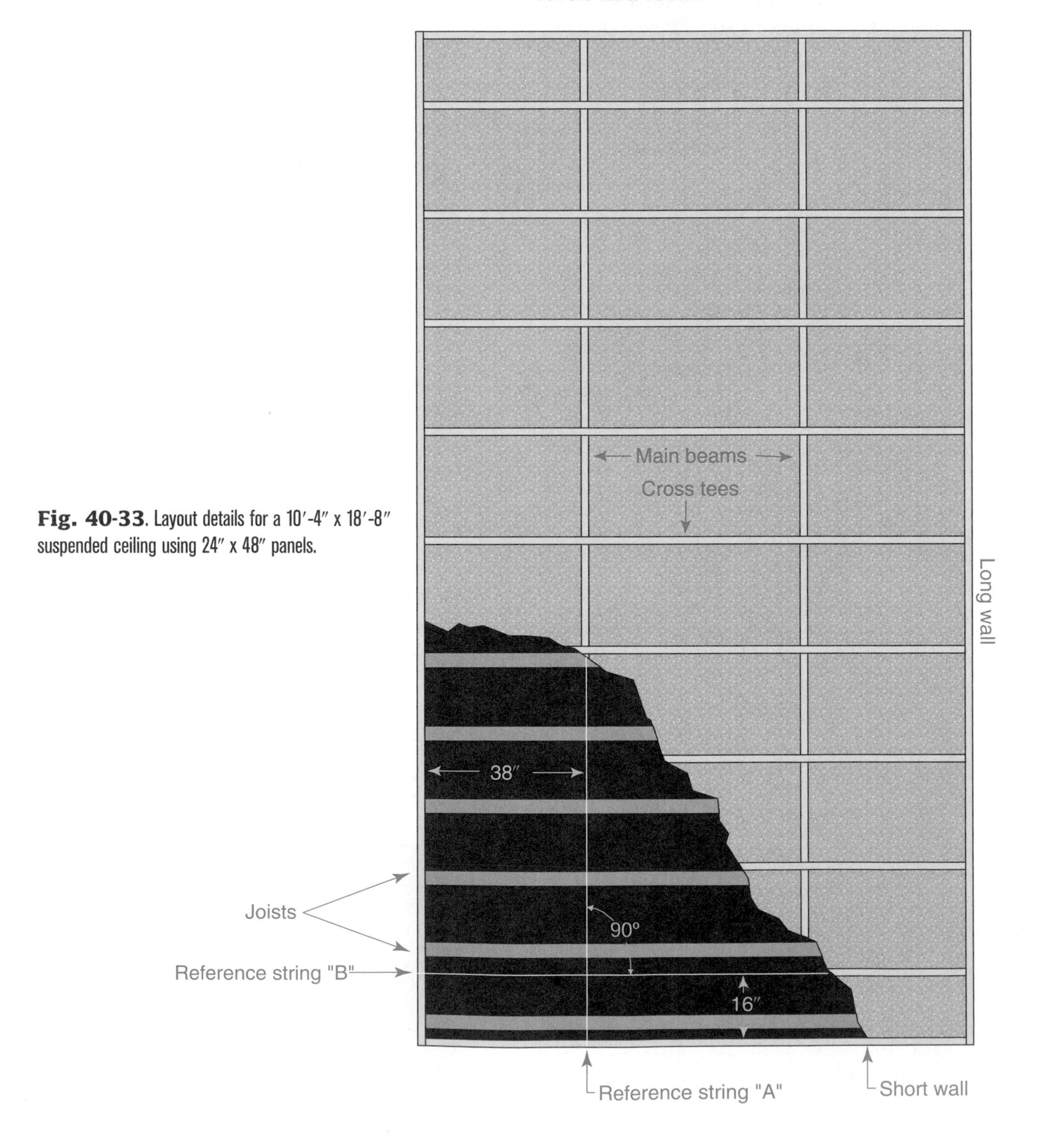

Fig. 40-33. Layout details for a 10′-4″ x 18′-8″ suspended ceiling using 24″ x 48″ panels.

STEP BY STEP

Installing a Suspended Ceiling

Be sure to plan the layout before you begin.

Step 1 Nail the wall molding to the walls, making certain that the top of the molding is aligned with a level chalk mark. For inside corners, lap one piece of molding over the other. Form outside corners by mitering the wall moldings together or by overlapping them.

Step 2 Mark the location of the hanger-wire screws by snapping a chalk line across the ceiling joists at 4′ intervals. Install a screw at each intersection, centering it on the joist edge. Now loop a length of hanger wire (or hanger strap) through every screw and wrap it back around itself three times. **Fig. 40-34.** These wires will be used in a later step to support the main beams.

Step 3 Check the ceiling layout for the location of the first main beam and the first row of cross tees. Stretch a string across the length of the room and another across the width to represent these locations. Keep the strings very tight. Check them with a framing square to ensure that they meet at a 90° angle. Adjust them as needed.

Step 4 Measure up 1⁵⁄₁₆″ from the bottom of the wall molding at several locations on all walls. Drive a nail into the wall at each location. Stretch leveling strings across the room between opposing nails and tie them to the nails. Now use pliers to make sharp 90° bends in every hanger wire where it intersects a leveling string. **Fig. 40-35.** When all the wires have been bent, remove the leveling strings. (Do not remove the two strings representing the main beam and cross tees.)

Step 5 Cut the beams one by one to fit into place, starting at the appropriate guide string. Slip the ends of the hanger wires into existing holes or slots in the beams. Repeat the process with the remaining beams.

Step 6 Starting at the appropriate guide string, install the first row of cross tees between the main beams. Lock the ends of each cross tee into slots in the main beams. **Fig. 40-36.** Install the remaining cross tees in the same way. Make sure they are spaced properly to accept the desired size of ceiling panel.

Step 7 Measure each of the border ceiling panels individually. Cut each panel face up, using a sharp utility knife. After all the border panels are in place, slip the remaining ceiling panels into place. **Fig. 40-37.** Take care when handling ceiling panels to avoid marring the surface. Handle the panels by the edges, keeping your fingers off the finished side as much as possible. Lightweight cotton gloves can be worn to prevent the panels from being smudged.

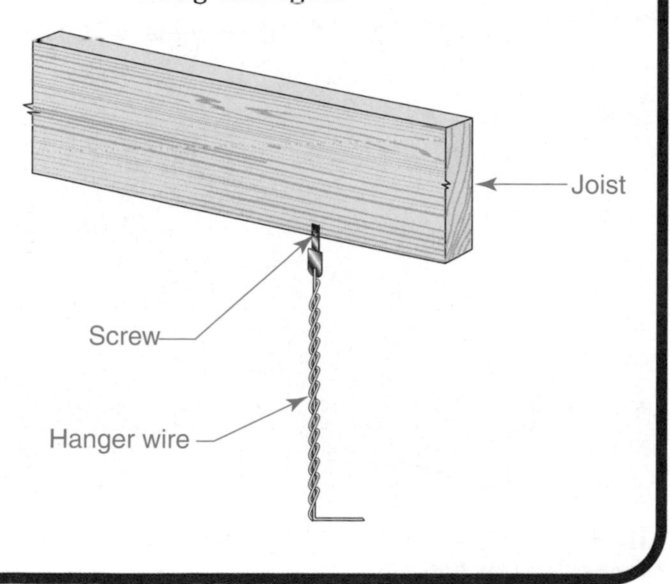

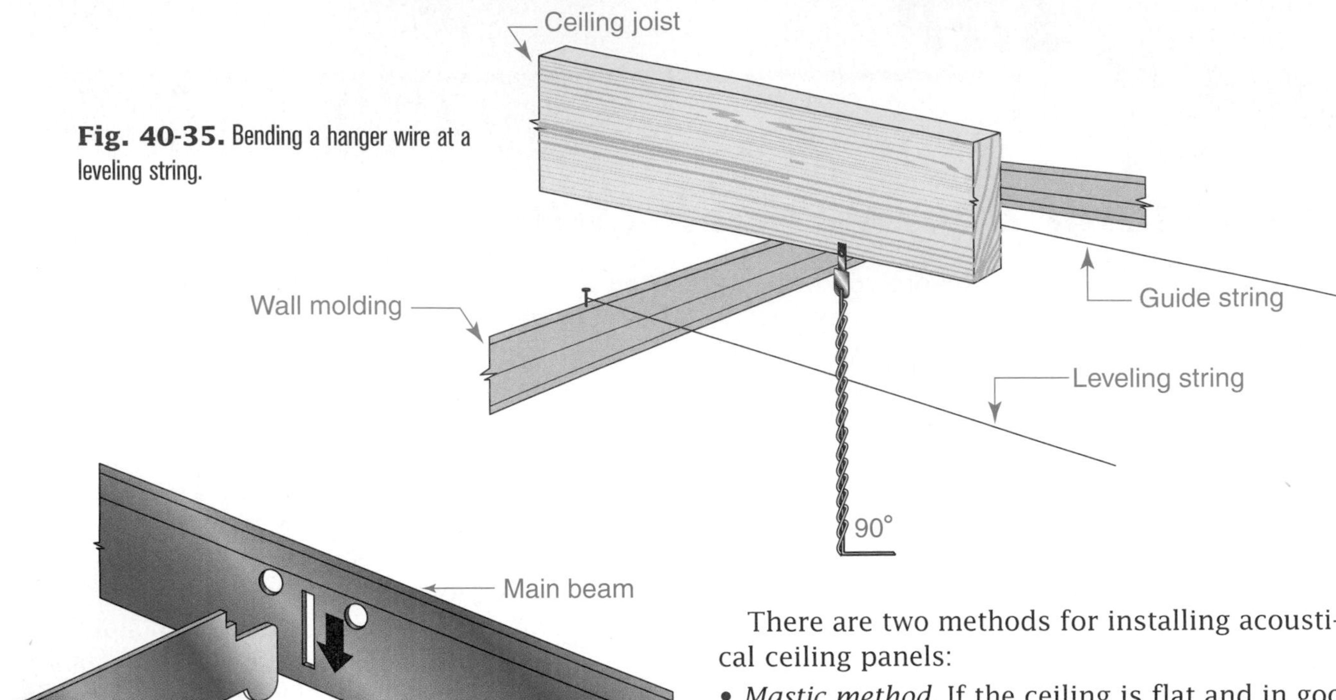

Fig. 40-35. Bending a hanger wire at a leveling string.

Fig. 40-36. Inserting a cross tee into a main beam.

Fig. 40-37. Lay the ceiling panels into the grid formed by the main runners and the cross tees.

There are two methods for installing acoustical ceiling panels:

- *Mastic method.* If the ceiling is flat and in good shape, each panel can be adhered directly to the ceiling surface. A dollop of mastic or construction adhesive placed near each corner and in the middle holds the panels in place.
- *Staple method.* Where a ceiling is uneven, or where there is no existing ceiling surface, panels must be stapled to wood furring strips. The strips are nailed to the joists and shimmed so that they are in the same plane.

SECTION 40.3 Check Your Knowledge

1. What are the advantages of suspended ceilings?
2. Name the basic parts of a suspended ceiling system.
3. What supports a suspended ceiling grid?
4. Which ceiling panels must be cut when installing a ceiling system?

On the Job

Some manufacturers of suspended ceiling systems provide estimating help on the Internet. They make it easy to determine how many ceiling panels, main beams, cross tees, and wall moldings will be required for a given room. Visit one of these sites and review the estimating method. Summarize its main points in a report to your class.

Chapter 40 Review

Section Summaries

40.1 Drywall is made of a gypsum core covered with special paper. It comes in three basic types: standard, fire code, and moisture resistant. Joint compound and tape are used to fill joints. Panels can be installed vertically or horizontally. Installation differs for wood or steel framing.

40.2 Plaster must dry before other work can progress. This can slow the construction schedule. Plaster is applied over gypsum or metal lath in two or more layers. It can be given a smooth or textured finish.

40.3 Suspended ceilings consist of panels held in place by a metal or plastic grid. They cover joists, pipes, and wiring. They are also used to lower a ceiling or to provide sound insulation.

Review Questions

1. Why are the long edges of drywall tapered?
2. In what location do building codes require the use of Type-X drywall?
3. What type of drywall would be used on walls in a moisture-prone area?
4. Name two factors that reduce the problem of nail pops.
5. What does it mean to *feather* a joint?
6. What substance does joint compound contain that can be harmful when drywall joints are sanded?
7. What material is placed behind metal lath when the plastered wall surface will be in a wet area?
8. What are the basic ingredients in plaster?
9. Name each layer in a three-coat plaster job.
10. When installing a suspended ceiling, what is used to mark the placement of the first main beam and cross tees?

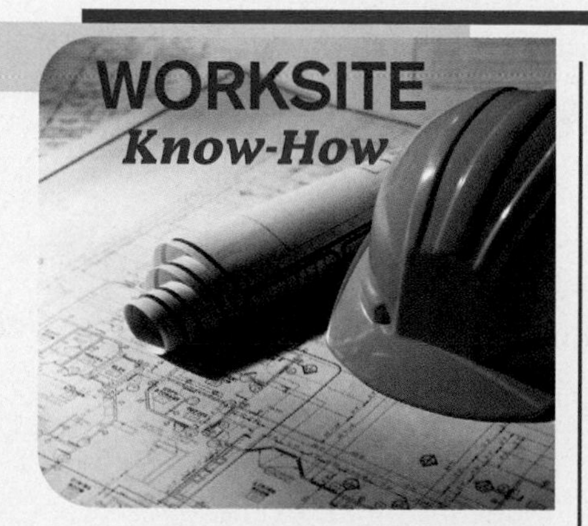

Accident Reports Many employers keep track of accidents by means of forms called accident reports. Also, OSHA may require them to do so. An accident report asks for basic information such as your name, sex, age, and Social Security number. It also asks for a description of what you were doing at the time, how the accident happened, what caused it, and how it could have been prevented. Also important are the location of the accident, the date and time it occurred, and the names of any witnesses. If you required medical attention, you will need to state the date and time it was sought and the name of the hospital or doctor.

Chapter

Exterior and Interior Finishes

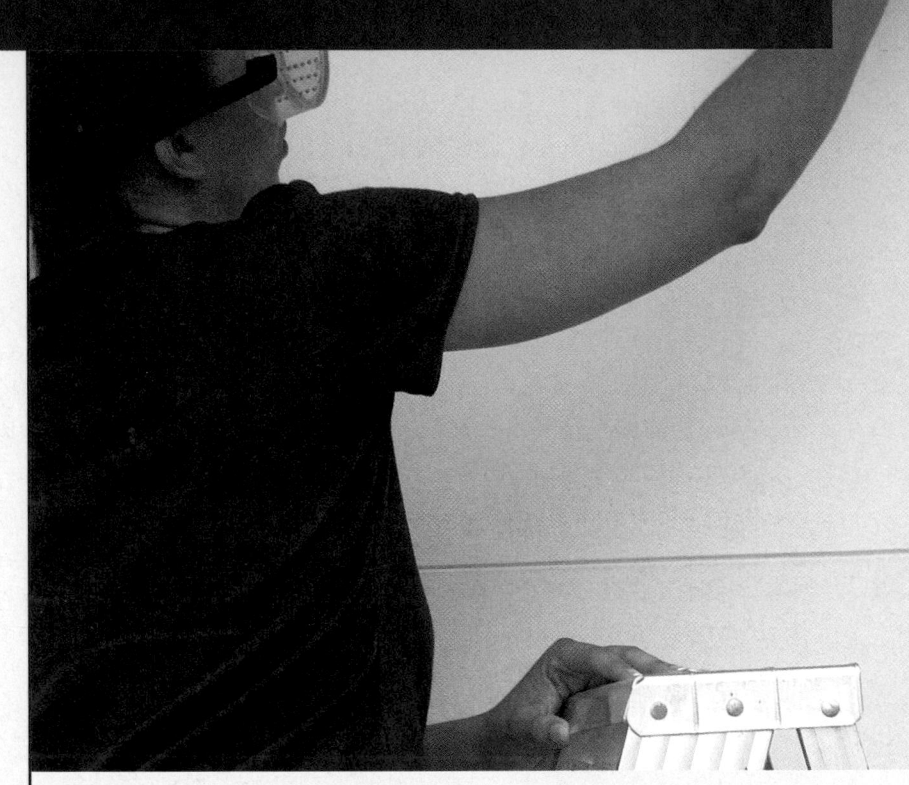

Objectives

After reading this chapter, you'll be able to:

- Describe the differences between the two basic types of finish.
- List the basic ingredients of paint.
- Give the steps in painting a house exterior.
- Give the steps in painting an interior.
- Diagnose problems with painted finishes.

Terms

binder
edging
flagged bristles
primer
sheen

Paints, coatings, and other finishes have been used for thousands of years to decorate and protect surfaces. Finishes are particularly important for wood. They can prolong the life of wood and improve its appearance. For example, exterior surfaces of a home require finishes that will protect against weathering, sunlight, and moisture. Interior finishes must be durable and easy to clean. As a general rule, hardwoods are given a clear finish, while softwoods are given either an opaque (not clear) finish or a clear finish.

Wood is the most common building material. Therefore, this chapter is about paint and painting techniques for wood. The information generally applies to new construction.

When repairing, removing, or recoating an existing finish, many additional surface preparation steps are required that are not covered here.

SECTION 41.1

Finishing Basics

Many types of finishes can be used to protect and beautify wood. Finishing technology is constantly improving. New products are introduced to the market each year. It is therefore important to review manufacturer's recommendations for each type that you use. Pay particular attention to any instructions about health and safety.

Finishes might be clear or opaque. They might be suited for exterior use or only for interior use. However, all finishes fall into two basic categories. *Film-forming finishes* coat the wood surface. *Penetrating finishes* soak into the wood.

FILM-FORMING FINISHES

Many finishes protect wood by leaving a coating, or film, on the wood surface. The most common type of film-forming finish is paint. **Fig. 41-1.** Some clear finishes, such as varnish and polyurethane, also fit into this category. The film protects the wood against moisture and seals in natural resins. Pigments may be added to protect wood from ultraviolet (UV) rays. They also add color.

Fig. 41-1. Paint allows a variety of decorative schemes.

Paint

Any paint contains ingredients that make it suitable for a particular use. However, all paints contain the following:

- *Pigments.* These are either finely ground natural minerals or synthetics. A pigment gives paint color and makes it opaque. A greater percentage of pigment increases opacity.
- *Binder.* A **binder** is a resin that holds particles of pigment together. The particles form a film after the liquid evaporates.
- *Carrier.* Sometimes called the *vehicle*, a carrier is a liquid that keeps the pigments and binders in suspension. It also keeps them evenly dispersed (spread out) during application.

Oil-Base Paint. Paints that have oil-base binders suspended in a mineral spirit carrier are referred to as *oil-base paints*, or *oil paints.* There are two types of oil-base binders. *Vegetable oil binders* are chiefly linseed oil, a yellowish oil pressed from flaxseed. *Alkyd binders* are synthetic. They are sometimes mixed with linseed oil.

Oil-base paints are less flexible than latex paints. This is an advantage where a tough, stable surface is required. However, oil-base paints tend to become brittle over time. This can cause the paint film to crack. Solvents are needed to clean tools and equipment used with oil-base paints. Solvents include mineral spirits (made from petroleum distillates) and turpentine (made from the resin of pine trees).

Check the paint label for manufacturer's recommendations for suitable thinners or solvents.

Latex Paint. *Latex paints* have latex-base binders suspended in water. There are two types of latex-base binders. *Acrylic latex* is a synthetic resin that is flexible and very durable. *Vinyl latex* is a synthetic resin that is somewhat less durable than acrylic latex.

Latex paints were first developed for interior use but are now readily available for exterior painting. In fact, research indicates that a good-quality acrylic latex outdoor house paint will generally outlast a good-quality oil-base outdoor house paint. In general, latex paints have the following characteristics:

- Easy to apply, even on slightly damp surfaces.
- Flexible. The paint film expands and contracts slightly with wood movement. It is less likely to crack than an oil-base film.
- Do not trap moisture within the wood. This makes it unlikely that water vapor will cause the paint to bubble.
- Dry rapidly.
- Easy cleanup. Tools can be washed clean with water before the paint on them dries.

Exterior latex paints have one disadvantage. Siding woods such as redwood and cedar contain water-soluble extractives that can bleed through latex paint. This sometimes creates dark stains. To prevent this, paint all surfaces of the wood with an oil-base primer before installation. Then top coat it with acrylic latex paint.

Primer

Most paint manufacturers make a primer, or undercoat, for use with their house paints. A **primer** is a paint that has a higher proportion of binder than standard paint. This enables it to hold particularly well to unpainted wood surfaces. Because a primer does not block UV radiation, it must be covered with two coats of standard paint.

Primers are available in oil-base or latex forms. They are typically white but may be tinted slightly for use under dark-colored paints. When painting metal, use a special rust-preventative primer.

Fig. 41-2. A penetrating finish allows the grain of the wood to show. It can be coated with a clear finish for greater protection.

Solid-Color Stain

Solid-color stain is similar to a thin paint. It comes in latex and oil-base forms and is applied in almost the same way as paint. It is not as durable as paint, however. Solid-color stains are used mainly where they can be recoated frequently.

PENETRATING FINISHES

Unlike film-forming finishes, penetrating finishes actually soak into the wood. **Fig. 41-2.** They fill the wood's surface pores. Some are clear, while others contain pigments. Penetrating finishes are very easy to apply. They allow the wood grain to show.

There are several types of penetrating finishes. Some are used primarily on exterior wood. These include oil-base semi-transparent stains and clear water-repellent finishes. (Latex semi-transparent stains are available. They are actually a type of film-forming finish and do not soak into the wood.) Some penetrating finishes are used primarily on interior wood, including furniture. These include Danish oil and tung oil.

Semi-transparent stains work very well on rough surfaces, such as plywood siding and some types of beveled siding. They can also be applied to weathered surfaces without much surface preparation. The pigment in semi-transparent stain protects the wood from UV damage. Penetrating finishes that do not contain pigment are not as effective in protecting wood from UV radiation. High-quality products also contain wood preservatives and water repellents.

FINISHING WOOD

While all woods can be finished, some take finishes better than others. The ability of a wood to accept a finish is determined by four basic factors: species, grade, grain, and manufacture.

Fig. 41-3. The use of pre-primed or pre-finished trim speeds the installation. Nail holes should be filled prior to putting on the finish coat.

Species

In general, denser species of woods are less accepting of finish than less dense woods. Tests have shown that cedar and cypress hold paint best of all the woods used for siding and trim. Northern white pine, western white pine, and sugar pine are almost as good. Western yellow pine, white fir, and hemlock come next. Serious flaking of paint occurs soonest on southern yellow pine, Douglas fir, and western larch.

Grade

Top-quality grades of wood accept finishes better than lower-quality grades that contain defects such as knots and pitch pockets. The knots of yellow and white pines cause more trouble than the knots of such woods as cedar, hemlock, white fir, and larch.

Grain

Quartersawn boards hold paint much better than plain-sawn boards because the bands of *summerwood* are very narrow. Summerwood is the dense, dark-colored portion of the wood. Its cells have thick walls and small cavities. The more porous, light-colored springwood accepts finish more readily. Flat-grained boards hold paint better on the bark side than on the pith side.

Manufacture

The natural expansion and contraction of solid wood can reduce the durability of a finish. Engineered-wood products, however, are manufactured in ways that reduce this problem. From a finishing standpoint, engineered wood has some advantages over solid wood, particularly when used for exterior trim. It behaves predictably and its surface is uniform. It is dimensionally stable over a wide range of widths and thicknesses. It does not have the defects commonly found in solid lumber.

Some engineered-wood trims are primed at the factory. **Fig. 41-3.** Others may have an unusually smooth finish that takes paint well. For more on this topic, see Chapter 17, "Engineered Lumber."

SECTION 41.1 Check Your Knowledge

1. What is the purpose of pigments?
2. What is a binder and how does it behave?
3. What is the basic difference in mixtures between oil-base paint and latex paint?
4. Why is it important to cover primer with standard paint?

On the Job

Obtain two similar scraps of softwood. Apply a single coat of a film-forming finish to one sample. Apply a single coat of a penetrating finish to the other. In each case, follow all instructions on the finish containers, particularly with regard to safety. Let the samples dry for at least seven days, then perform the following tests:

1. Scrape each sample with the point of a nail.
2. Place several drops of water on each sample.
3. Use 120-grit sandpaper, mounted on a sanding block, to remove as much of the finish as you can.

Keep notes of what you observe during and after each test. Report your findings to the class.

SECTION 41.2

Painting the Exterior

The most common type of exterior finish is paint. In part, this is because paint is available in many colors. Light-colored paints reflect heat away from the house. This can reduce interior temperatures. **Fig. 41-4.** See **Table 41-A** for differences in how colors reflect light.

Paint lasts longer than other exterior finishes. In general, it lasts seven to ten years before requiring recoating. A solid-color stain generally lasts only three to seven years.

For best appearance and maximum durability, three coats of exterior paint are best over bare wood. This means a primer followed by two finish coats of standard paint. To ensure compatibility between primer and finish coats, choose a primer and finish paint of the same brand and type.

Many manufacturers make several paints of differing quality and cost. However, the cost of the paint is a fairly small portion of the total cost of painting a home, and problems can be expensive to correct. It is therefore wise to use only top-quality products.

Fig. 41-5. An extension ladder is an essential painter's tool. Drop cloths prevent paint from splattering the lawn and plants.

Fig. 41-4. This white house will reflect 90 percent of the sun's rays, reducing heat gain in hot weather.

Table 41-A. Light Reflectivity of Colors

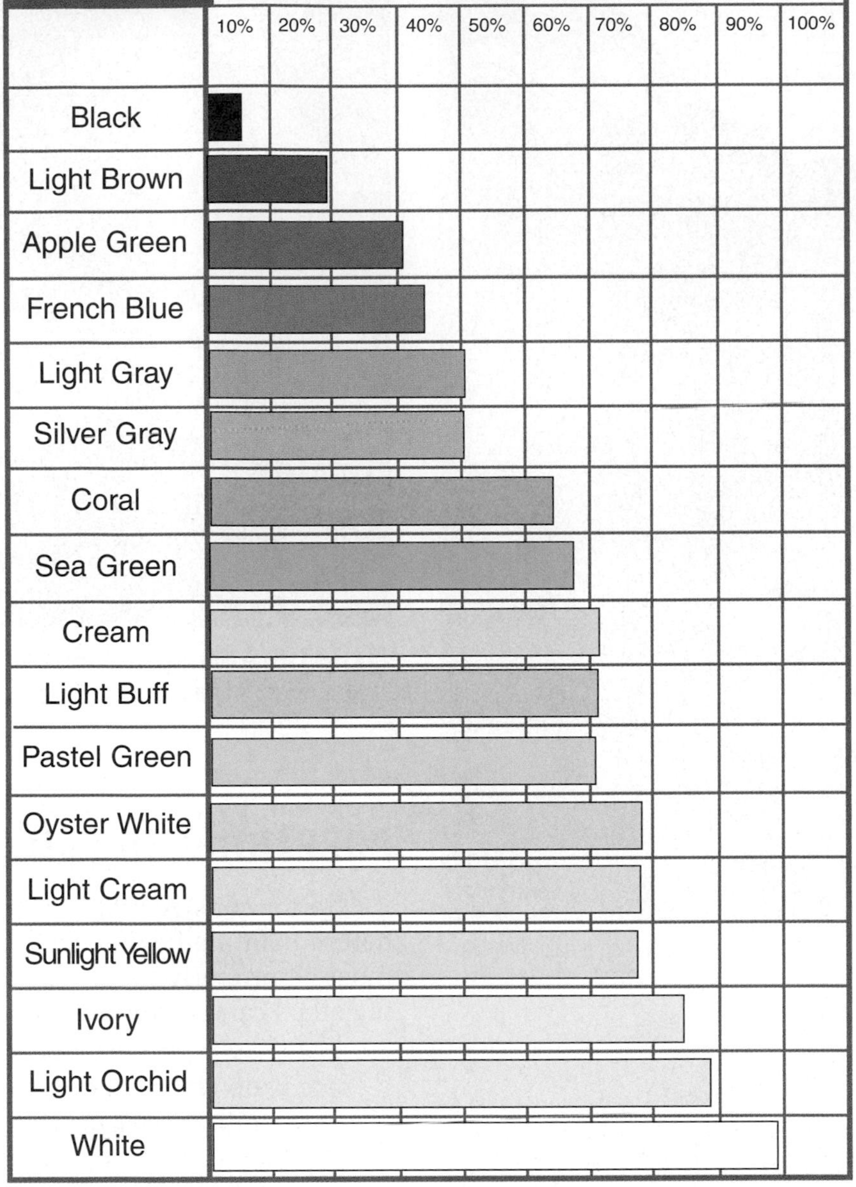

	10%	20%	30%	40%	50%	60%	70%	80%	90%	100%
Black										
Light Brown										
Apple Green										
French Blue										
Light Gray										
Silver Gray										
Coral										
Sea Green										
Cream										
Light Buff										
Pastel Green										
Oyster White										
Light Cream										
Sunlight Yellow										
Ivory										
Light Orchid										
White										

SUPPLIES AND EQUIPMENT

Equipment needed for painting exteriors includes the following basic items. **Fig. 41-5.**

- A stepladder for lower areas and an extension ladder for the highest spots. Include attachments like a paint hook. **Fig. 41-6.**
- Drop cloths.
- Caulking gun for sealing joints.
- Hammer, nail set, putty, and putty knife.
- Mixing pails.
- Brushes.
- Solvents for cleaning brushes and other equipment.
- Cleaning cloths.
- Rubber or latex gloves for use when using solvents.
- Safety glasses or goggles for use with solvents or when preparing surfaces.

Exterior paint can also be sprayed on using a compressor, a paint pot, and a spray gun. **Fig. 41-7.** Use a roller and tray for painting masonry, such as brick. **Fig. 41-8.**

Fig. 41-6. When brush painting from a ladder, use a paint hook to support the paint can.

Fig. 41-7. A commercial-grade rig for spray-painting. Notice that there is a pressure gauge on the compressor (at right) as well as on the paint pot.

Fig. 41-8. A deep nap roller works best for applying paint to a textured or rough surface such as a brick wall.

PREPARING TO PAINT

Exterior construction should be complete before painting begins. Surfaces to be painted must be properly prepared. Usually, the following steps can be completed before the primer is applied.

Place drop cloths under the area you are about to paint. Cover nearby walks and shrubs. This will shorten cleanup time.

Nail heads may be left at the surface of the wood or sunk below it. Use a nail set and hammer to sink nail heads. Fill them with an exterior-grade wood putty. **Fig. 41-9.** Seal any knots with shellac to prevent brown stains later. **Fig. 41-10.**

Use paintable caulk around door and window frames where necessary. Tightly caulked joints help weatherproof the house and prevent moisture damage. **Fig. 41-11.**

APPLYING THE FINISH

Primer and finish coats are brushed on. This works paint into the wood surface and ensures that every surface and edge is coated. However, the large, flat areas of panel siding may be painted using rollers.

Fig. 41-9. Set all exposed nails and putty the heads to prevent rust spotting.

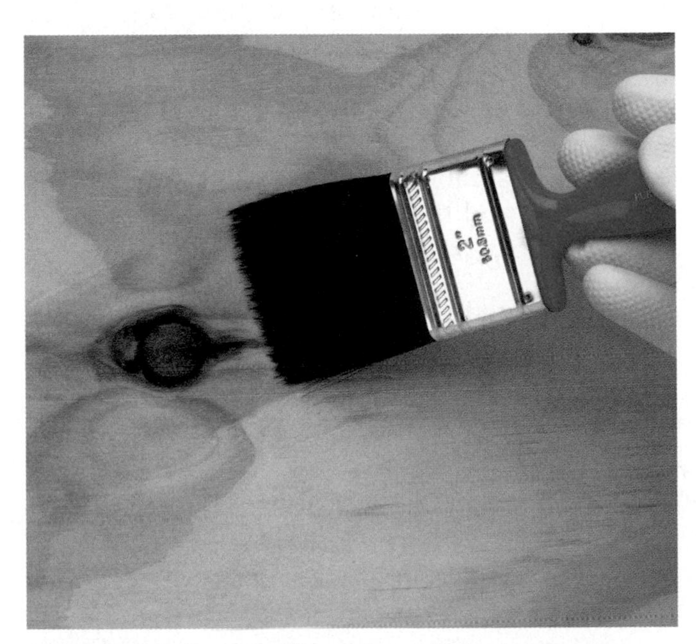

Fig. 41-10. Knots must be sealed to avoid discoloration of the finished surface.

Spray application is faster but tends to deposit paint only on the very top of the wood. To ensure proper coverage on rough surfaces (such as plywood siding), "roll in" sprayed paint by going over the area with a roller. This works the paint into the uneven surface. Rolling in should be done a section at a time immediately after spraying.

Morning dew or water from a brief shower should be wiped off and at least an hour of warm sunshine should follow before any painting is done. After a hard rain, several days may be needed for drying. Always avoid painting when a surface will be heated by full sun.

The outdoor temperature must stay above 40°F [4°C] for at least twenty-four hours after oil-base paints are applied. The temperature must stay above 50°F [10°C] for at least twenty-four hours after latex paints are applied. When using paintable water-repellent wood preservatives prior to painting, best results are obtained when the temperature is above 70°F [21°C].

See the Step-by-Step instructions for painting on page 840.

SAFETY FIRST

Extension Ladders

An extension ladder makes painting high areas of the house more convenient. However, always check for what's overhead before moving a ladder or tilting it up. An aluminum extension ladder that comes into contact with power lines could conduct electricity with deadly results. Even a wood ladder can conduct electricity, particularly when wet.

Fig. 41-11. Caulk around the window and door moldings to weatherproof the house. Joints between dissimilar materials require extra attention.

STEP BY STEP

Basic Painting Technique

Primer and finish coats call for the same basic techniques.

Step 1 Even if the paint dealer has mixed the paint mechanically, mix it again just before and during painting. Stir the contents of the can from the bottom up. Then "box" the paint by pouring it back and forth from one can into another. **Fig. 41-12.** This evens out any slight variations in color.

Step 2 Load the brush by dipping it about two inches into the paint and tapping the excess off against the inside of the can. **Fig. 41-13.** Repeat several times.

Step 3 Start painting at the top of the house and work down. This prevents drips and splatters from spoiling previously painted areas. **Fig. 41-14.** Wearing safety glasses will protect your eyes from paint splatters.

Step 4 Apply the paint generously along siding joints, distributing it evenly. Do not bear down too hard. "Feather" the ends of your brush strokes. This helps avoid a distinct edge and ensures smoothness where one painted area meets another. Always paint with the grain.

Step 5 After painting the gable end of the house, start at a corner and work across. It makes no difference whether you work from the left or right. However, before you move or shorten the ladder, finish an area about four or five feet square.

Step 6 Paint windows with a narrow sash brush. Paint the mullions first, then the rails, and then the stiles. **Fig. 41-15.** Paint the casing and trim last. Move the sash up and down before the paint dries to prevent sticking.

Step 7 For a panel door, first paint the molding and then the panels. Paint the rails next and finally the stiles.

Step 8 Paint shutters separately. Install them after the rest of the job has been completed.

Fig. 41-12. After the paint has been mixed, it should be boxed. To box paint, pour it back and forth from one container into another.

Fig. 41-13. Work the paint into the brush by dipping it about 2″ into the paint and then tapping off the excess against the inside of the can.

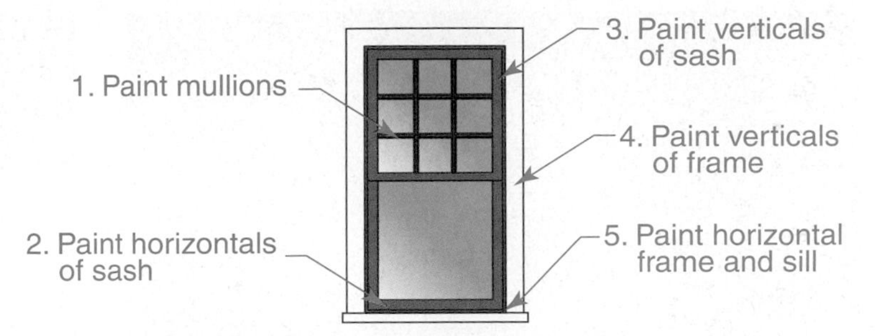

Fig. 41-15. When painting a double-hung window, use the sequence shown above.

Fig. 41-14. Always start at the top and work down. This will keep paint from dripping onto the freshly painted area. Hold the brush as shown whenever possible. This minimizes stress in your wrist.

CLEANUP

Protect your tools by cleaning them immediately after use, especially brushes and rollers. After using oil paints, work solvent into the brush bristles with gloved fingers. Squeeze out as much paint and solvent as possible. Repeat this operation until the paint disappears. **Fig. 41-16.** Give the brushes a final rinse in clear solvent. Then wash them in soapy water, rinse thoroughly, and spin them dry. **Fig. 41-17.**

To clean a roller cover, remove it from the roller frame and scrape off as much paint as possible. **Fig. 41-18.** Then immerse the cover in a generous amount of the correct solvent. Work the solvent into the roller cover until it is clean. Then wash the cover in a mild detergent solution and rinse it in clear water. Disposable roller covers have cardboard cores and generally cannot be cleaned.

Solvents used for cleanup of oil-base paints are flammable. Always use them in a well-ventilated area away from pilot lights and other

Fig. 41-16. Work solvent into the bristles thoroughly. Wear rubber gloves to protect your skin.

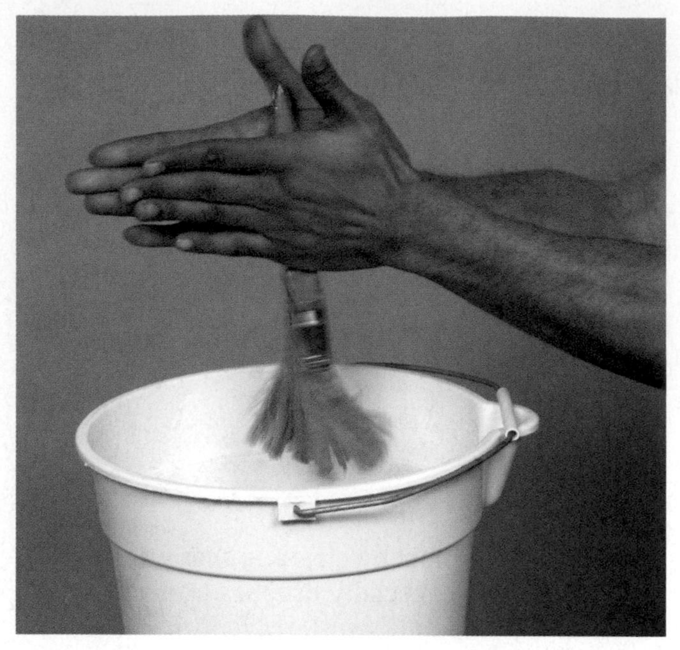

Fig. 41-17. Spin brushes to remove excess water or solvent. Center brush in a bucket to contain the spray.

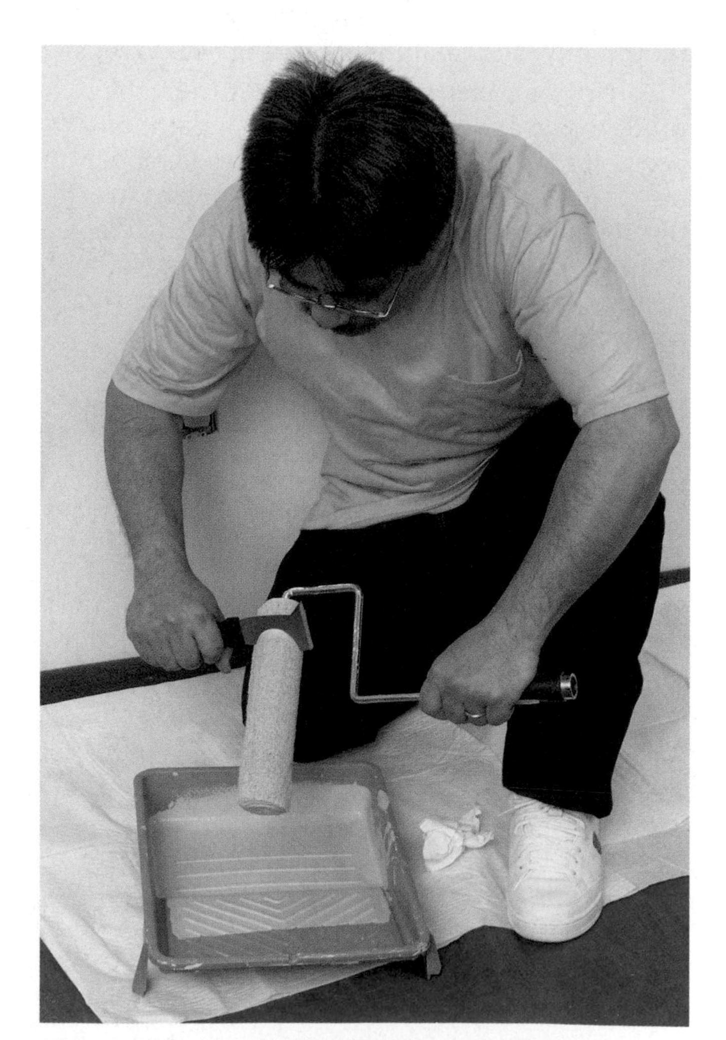

Fig. 41-18. A 5-in-1 tool can be used to scrape excess paint from a roller cover prior to cleaning.

Fig. 41-19. A loose-fitting cardboard sheath protects bristles as they dry. Good brushes are well worth this extra care.

flames. Store all rags used for cleaning in an airtight metal container. An alternative is to soak them thoroughly in water and leave them outdoors to air dry. This also applies to rags and newspaper saturated with oil-base or alkyd-base paints and stains. Proper storage or disposal will reduce the risk of spontaneous combustion.

For latex paints, follow the same steps, using soapy water instead of solvent. Rinse the brushes with clear water. Allow them to dry thoroughly before storing.

To protect bristles as they dry, wrap brushes in heavy paper or a cardboard sheath and lay them in a dry place. **Fig. 41-19.** Some painters hang brushes to dry. Store roller covers on end so that their nap is not flattened. Allow drop cloths to dry, if damp, before folding them for storage.

If paint has fallen on walkways, scrub it out with a suitable solvent and a stiff brush. Scrub off spatters from latex paint with soapy water before the paint dries.

COMMON PROBLEMS AND SOLUTIONS

Problems caused by improper painting may not show up for months or even years. To avoid these problems, it is important to understand the ways in which paint fails. This section describes some common problems, their causes, and their solutions. Before applying any primer or house paint, always check the label. You will

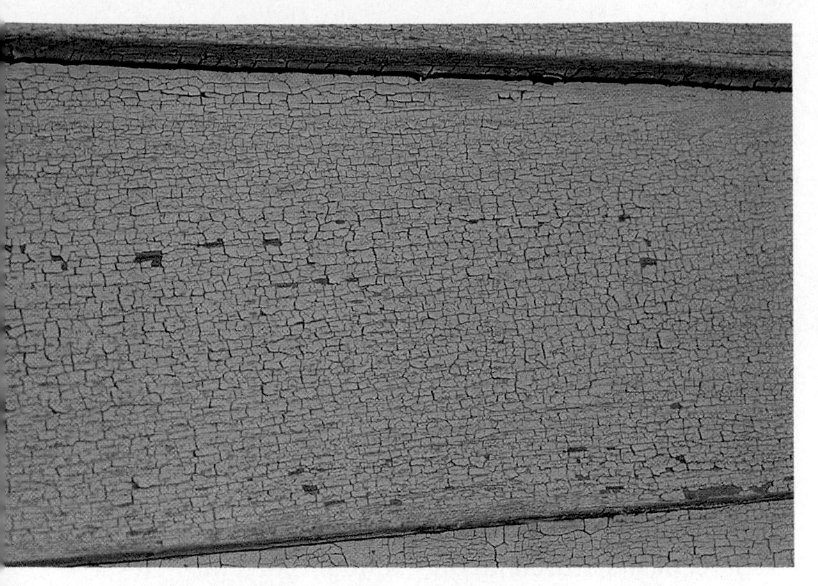

Fig. 41-20. Cracking and alligatoring.

Fig. 41-21. Localized peeling.

find there recommendations on surface preparation and compatibility with caulks, sealants, and primers.

Cracking and Alligatoring

If paint cracks, it may have been applied in several heavy coats without sufficient drying time between coats. Also, the primer may not be compatible with the finish coat. **Fig. 41-20.** To correct the problem:

1. Sand the cracked or alligatored surface smooth.
2. Apply one coat of primer and one top coat of house paint.

Localized Peeling

Peeling results when moisture trapped in siding is drawn from the wood by the sun's heat and pushes the paint from the surface. **Fig. 41-21.** One cause is improper installation of a vapor barrier beneath the siding. To correct the problem:

1. Locate and eliminate sources of moisture. Is the area near a poorly ventilated bathroom or a kitchen? Is there seepage or leakage from eaves, roof, or plumbing?
2. Reduce future moisture by installing bathroom and kitchen exhaust fans.
3. Scrape off the old paint. Scrape down to the wood over the entire board or for a distance of 12″ around the peeling area.
4. Sand the surface to fresh wood and spot prime with a recommended primer.
5. Apply a top coat of house paint.

Flaking

Flaking is caused by the alternate swelling and shrinking of siding as the moisture behind it is absorbed and then evaporates. Brittle paint cracks under the strain and pulls away from the wood. **Fig. 41-22.** To correct the problem:

1. Locate and eliminate sources of moisture. Is the affected area near a bathroom or kitchen? Is there seepage or leakage from eaves, roof, or plumbing?

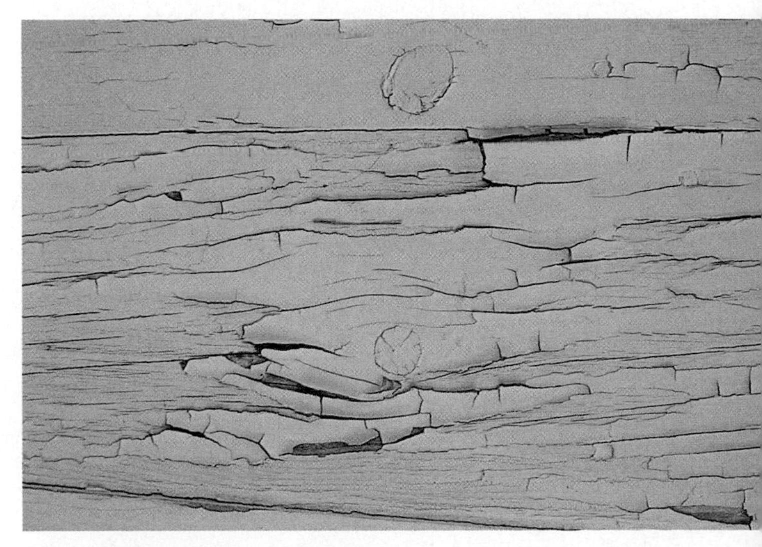

Fig. 41-22. Flaking.

2. Scrape off the flaking paint to expose the wood for about 12″ around the area.
3. Sand the surface to fresh wood and spot prime with a recommended primer.
4. Seal all seams, holes, and cracks against moisture, using suitable caulk.
5. Apply a top coat of house paint.

Mildew

Mildew is a microscopic fungus that thrives on many household surfaces, including painted siding. **Fig. 41-23.** A warm, wet, or humid environment provides the best conditions for its growth. Although mildew is unattractive, it does not cause the wood to decay. However, if painted over, it will grow through the new coat of paint. To correct the problem:

1. Gently scrub the entire surface with a solution of ⅓ cup of trisodium phosphate (TSP) or a comparable substitute, ½ cup of household bleach, and 4 quarts of warm water.
2. Apply one coat of primer. Add mildew-resistant additives to a primer if the likelihood of mildew is high.
3. Apply one top coat of mildew-resistant latex house paint.

Extractive Staining

Staining is caused by moisture in redwood and cedar siding that dissolves extractives in the wood. *Extractives* are natural chemicals that tend to be dark in color. The colored moisture seeps into the paint through breaks in the paint film. A stain forms when the water dries. To prevent the problem:

1. Locate and eliminate moisture sources before painting.
2. Back prime the siding boards before installation.

To correct the problem:

1. Wash stained surfaces with a mixture of 50 percent denatured alcohol and 50 percent clean water.
2. Allow the surface to dry for forty-eight hours. Then apply two coats of the house paint.

Blistering

Blistering, like peeling, is caused when moisture trapped in the siding is drawn from the wood by the sun's heat. This pushes paint from the surface. **Fig. 41-24.** To correct the problem:

1. Locate and eliminate the sources of moisture.
2. Scrape off the old paint for a distance of about 12″ around the blister condition.

Fig. 41-23. Mildew.

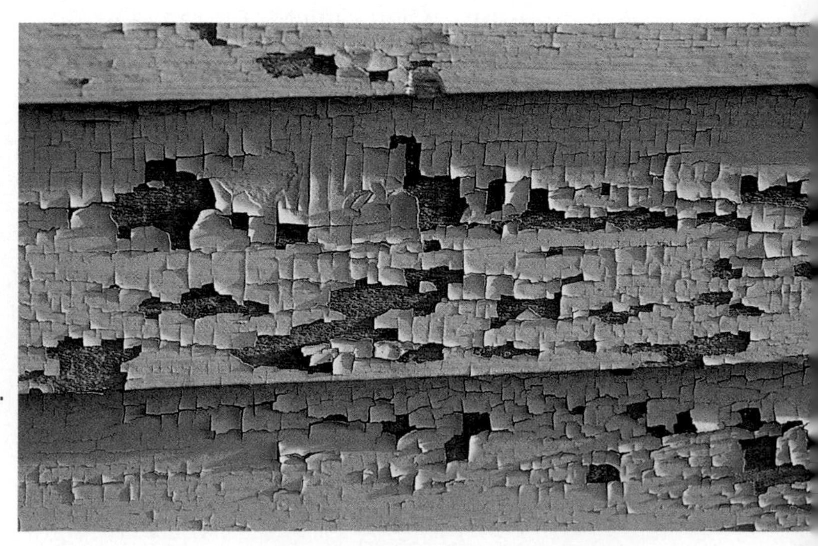

Fig. 41-24. Blistering.

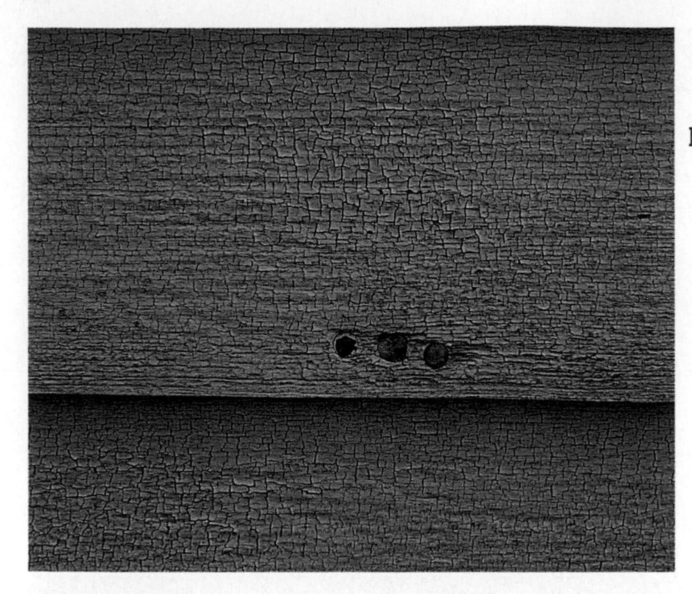

Fig. 41-25. Nail head staining.

3. Sand the surface to fresh wood and spot prime with primer.
4. Use caulk to seal all seams, holes, and cracks against moisture entry.
5. Apply a top coat of house paint.

Nail Head Staining

Nail head stains are caused when excessive moisture rusts uncoated or poorly coated steel nails used to install the siding. **Fig. 41-25.** To correct the problem:

1. Sand the stained paint and remove the rust down to the bright metal of the nail head.
2. Countersink the nail head ⅛″ below the surface of the siding. Immediately spot prime the nail head.
3. Fill primed, countersunk holes with exterior-grade putty. Apply two top coats of house paint.

ESTIMATING

Both materials and labor needed for exterior paint should be estimated.

Materials

To estimate the amount of paint needed for the exterior of a house, first determine the number of square feet to be covered.

Figure the siding area below the roofline by measuring the total distance around the house and multiplying this figure by the height. For the house shown in **Fig. 41-26**, the perimeter is 120′; 40′ + 40′ + 20′ +20′ = 120′. Multiply this number by the height to determine the area: 120′ × 12′ = 1,440 sq. ft.

For the gables, multiply the height of the gable at its highest point by half the width of the gable. Do this for each gable. In the example, 6′ (gable height) × 10′ (half the gable width) × 3 (number of gables) = 180 sq. ft.

Add the area for gables to the area for siding below the roofline: 180 + 1,440 = 1,620 sq. ft.

Primer and topcoats typically cover different amounts per gallon. Divide the total number of square feet by 450 to find how many gallons of primer will be needed. Divide by 500 to find the number of gallons required for each finish coat:

1,620 ÷ 450 = 3.6 gal. of primer
1,620 ÷ 500 = 3.24 gal. of paint

Labor

To estimate labor for exterior painting, refer to **Table 41-B** to determine the number of hours required. Multiply this number by your local labor cost per hour to find the total cost.

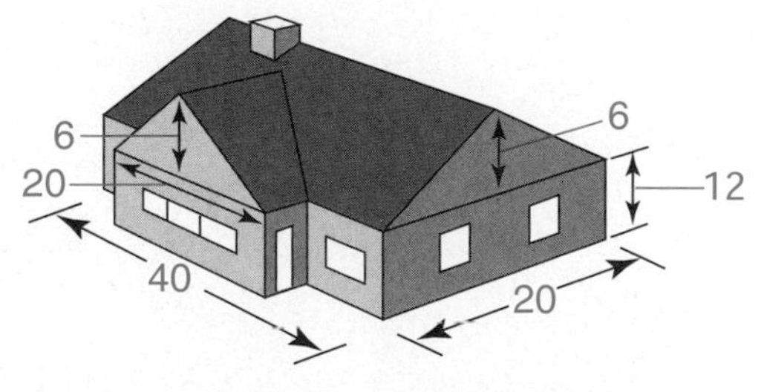

Fig. 41-26. Determine the number of gallons of primer and finish coat required to paint this house.

Table 41-B. Estimating Labor: Exterior Painting

Preparation of siding and trim (sanding and puttying)	175 sq. ft. per hr.
Preparation of trim only (brick veneer or masonry construction)	100 sq. ft. per hr.
Brushing windows and door frames	175 lineal ft. per hr.
Brushing wood siding	175 sq. ft. per hr.
Brushing asbestos shingle siding	75 sq. ft. per hr.
Brushing wood shingle siding	150 sq. ft. per hr.

Note: No allowance is included for preparatory work or for setting up scaffolding.

Exterior and interior brick surfaces may be painted. Exterior brick surfaces will generally require repainting every three to five years. Proper surface preparation is very important. Follow the recommendations of the paint manufacturer. Water-base paints are alkali-resistant and easily applied to brick. Cement-base paints can also be used. Oil-base paints are not recommended for exterior brick masonry.

SECTION 41.2 Check Your Knowledge

1. Why is it important to use good-quality exterior paint?
2. What is meant by "boxing" paint and why is boxing important?
3. What type of paintbrush is used to paint the mullions of a window?
4. How should paintbrushes and roller covers be stored after they are cleaned?

On the Job

Using the most current sources available to you, find information about recycling used paint. Answer the following questions: What types of paints can be recycled? Is there anyplace in your town where paint can be recycled? What is done with the paint after it is turned in for recycling? If there is no place to recycle paint in your town, what do you think is done with old paint?

SECTION 41.3

Painting the Interior

Many different kinds of interior paints are available. The most popular are latex paints, which are easy to apply and dry quickly. Interior paints can make surfaces easy to clean and give them wear resistance. They seal surfaces against moisture and vapor penetration. They also add to the room's attractiveness.

Interior paints are available in various sheens. **Sheen** describes how shiny, or glossy, they are when dry. High-sheen paints are easier to clean, but low-sheen paints have a softer, less glaring appearance. High-sheen paints are used where cleanup is important, such as in kitchens and baths. Low-sheen paints are used in living rooms and bedrooms. Following is a list of paint types in order of their sheen, from greatest to least:

- Enamel.
- Semi-gloss enamel.
- Pearl.
- Eggshell.
- Flat.

SUPPLIES AND EQUIPMENT

Brushes and rollers are the primary interior painting tools. Other items may be needed to prepare the surface, protect floors and furniture, mix the paint, and cleanup.

Good-quality brushes are expensive but worth the money. **Fig. 41-27.** With a good brush you get better results with less effort. A 3″ or 4″ wide brush is recommended for painting trim and for "cutting in" corners and edges. Cutting in means to brush paint carefully along a straight line, such as along the edge of trim. Brushes should be 5″ to 7″ long and have dense bristles with flagged, not square-cut, ends. **Flagged bristles** are slightly splayed at the tips.

Rollers are easier to use and faster than brushes for painting large flat areas. Paint is held in a tray instead of a can. Short-nap roller covers are suitable for most paints and surfaces. Lambswool covers are used for flat finishes on rough or imperfect surfaces. **Fig. 41-28.** Mounting the roller on an extension pole has

Fig. 41-28. Roller covers come with naps of various lengths, such as 1¼″, 1″, ¾″, and ½″. Longer naps are best for surfaces with a rough texture. Shorter naps are best for smooth surfaces.

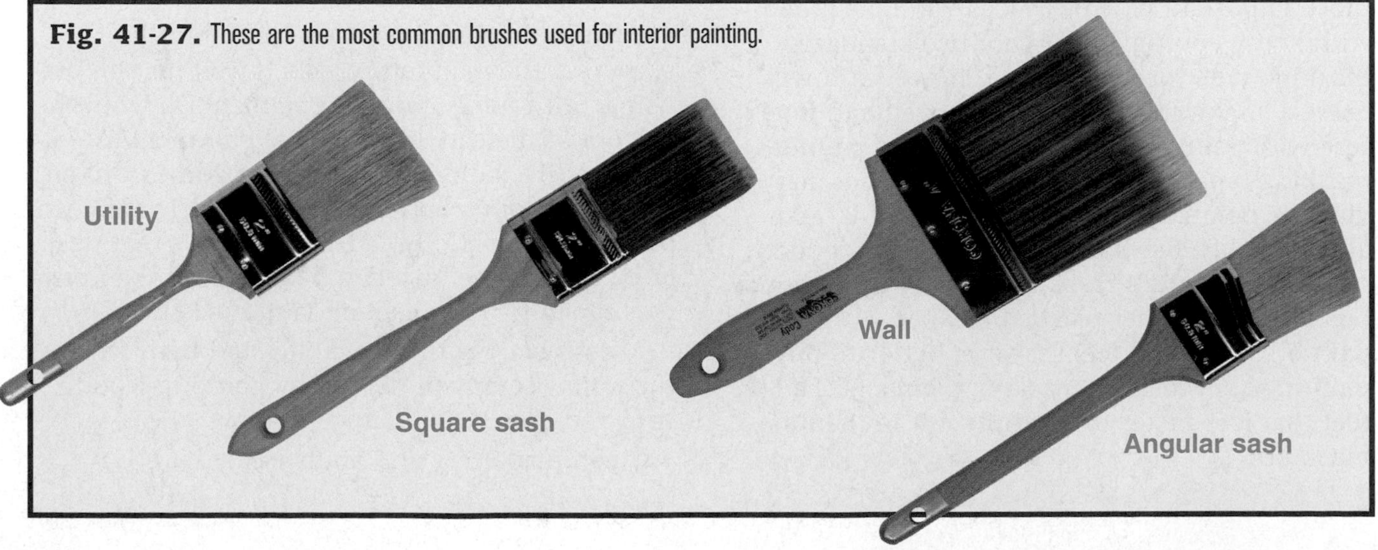

Fig. 41-27. These are the most common brushes used for interior painting.

several advantages. The painter stands several feet away from the surface being painted, so he or she can better see areas that have not yet been covered properly. Loading the roller or painting low portions of the wall do not require bending over. A ladder is not needed to reach high portions of most walls.

Avoid Falls

Drop cloths are often used to protect floor surfaces when walls and ceilings are being painted. Plastic sheets can be used but can be slippery. For this reason, many painters prefer to use canvas tarps as drop cloths. Canvas is more durable and slip resistant than plastic.

PREPARING TO PAINT

Good preparation makes the painting job much easier and faster. Be sure the room is dry, well ventilated, and at a comfortable temperature. Cover finished floors with drop cloths. Mask hardware such as doorknobs and hinges. Also mask wall switches and receptacles. If ceiling fixtures are in place, lower the canopy (the domed portion covering the electrical box) so that you can paint under it.

Start with a clean surface. On new construction, the walls do not have to be washed. A thorough dusting of the surfaces is usually enough. Fine cracks in walls or nail holes in wood trim should be filled with spackling compound or painter's putty.

When painting ceilings and walls, protect windows and other areas from being splattered with paint by "masking off" with tape. This is even more important when surfaces will be painted with spray equipment. Do not use standard masking tape for masking off, however. It will leave a sticky residue when removed and interfere with paint adhesion. Instead, use painter's masking tape. Easily removed, it will not mar glass or painted surfaces. To mask off large areas quickly, use masking rolls. This product combines painter's masking tape with a continuous length of either plastic or paper. Many painters, however, feel that it is better to rely on painting skill than on masking products. They feel that it is faster to carefully cut in than to mask off.

Fig. 41-29. Paint mixing paddle for use with an electric drill. A detail of the paddle is shown in the inset on the right.

PAINTING THE ROOM

When surfaces have been prepared and the room is clean, painting can begin. Brushes are used to paint trim and to paint into corners. Rollers are generally used to paint all other surfaces. Sometimes paint may be applied to a room with a combination of spray equipment, rollers, and brushes.

Even if the paint has been mechanically shaken at the paint store, mix it well just before using. Stir rapidly, working pigment up from the bottom of the can. Professional painters buy paint in five-gallon pails. Mixing paddles driven by a heavy-duty, variable-speed electric drill can be used to stir it. **Fig. 41-29.** When a great deal of paint must be mixed, a heavy-duty mixer can be clipped to a five-gallon paint bucket.

Always start with the ceiling, and then paint the walls. Complete the job by painting wood trim and doors. Clean up as follows:

- Wipe up spatters and spills immediately.

- Clean brushes, rollers, and other tools as soon as you finish using them.
- Wear rubber gloves when cleaning brushes and rollers. The gloves will protect your hands and make cleanup faster.

Interior surfaces are normally under longer and closer observation than are exterior surfaces. Hence, the brushing on, smoothing out, and leveling off of the paint must be done with care. Most plaster and drywall surfaces are finished with two coats of flat paint over a single coat of primer or sealer. Primers and sealers reduce penetration of succeeding coats, so less paint will be needed for good coverage.

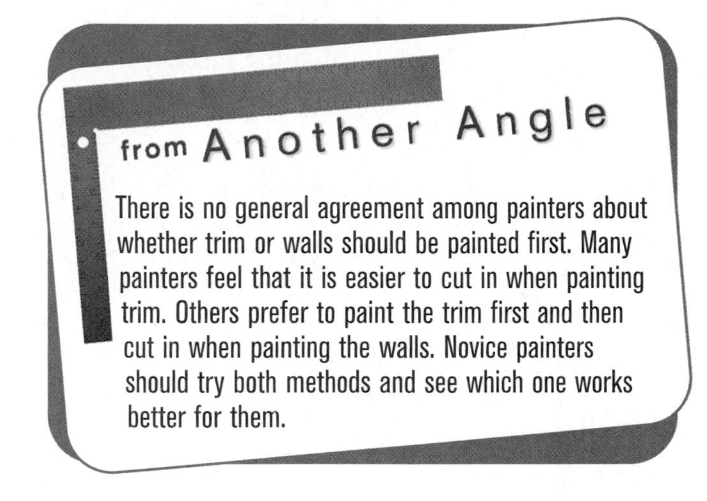

There is no general agreement among painters about whether trim or walls should be painted first. Many painters feel that it is easier to cut in when painting trim. Others prefer to paint the trim first and then cut in when painting the walls. Novice painters should try both methods and see which one works better for them.

Ceiling

Scaffolding or stepladders may be needed if ceilings are unusually high. However, a paint roller mounted on an extension pole is often all that is needed. You will need a small brush for edging the ceiling. **Edging** is using a brush to paint into the corners between large flat surfaces, where a roller cannot reach. **Fig. 41-30.**

Fig. 41-30. A roller cannot get into corners. Use a small brush for edging.

Fig. 41-31. After the wall has been edged, roll paint on the wall in a W pattern. Note the use of an extension handle.

Roll paint in two- or three-foot strips across the shortest dimension of the ceiling. By doing this, you can paint the next strip before the last edge is dry. Overlapping a dry edge sometimes leaves a mark that shows later. Light strokes help to eliminate lap marks.

Walls

Cut in the edges of a wall by first painting a narrow strip around doors, windows, baseboards, and any other adjoining surfaces. Then fill in the large areas with a roller. Finish one entire wall before beginning the next one.

Dip brush bristles only one-third their length into the paint. Tap the brush gently against the inside edge of the can to release drips. Starting at the ceiling line, paint down in three-foot wide strips, brushing from the unpainted into the painted areas.

When using a roller, pour paint into the deep portion of the tray. Work the paint into the roller by moving it back and forth in the tray until the paint is evenly distributed on the roller. Start on one side of the wall and paint a *W* on the surface. **Fig. 41-31.** Use slow, smooth strokes. Quick strokes and heavy uneven pressure may cause bubbles or spatters. When you have covered a few square feet, use parallel vertical strokes to spread the paint evenly.

Estimating...

Interior Paint Needs

Calculating material requirements for interior painting is a two-part process. Wall and ceiling areas are calculated based on square footage. Trim is calculated based on lineal footage. Primer or sealer over smooth walls will cover 575 to 625 sq. ft. per gallon. The first and second coats of paint will cover 500 to 550 square feet. Trim may require a different paint, such as enamel.

Labor costs are based on hourly wage rates or figured as a portion of square footage rates.

MATERIALS

To determine the amount of paint for a room, first calculate the total wall area.

Step 1 To find the area of one wall, multiply the length of the wall by the height. If the entire room is to be painted, multiply the perimeter of the room by the height. Windows and doors are not usually subtracted from the total paint requirement unless they are unusually large or numerous.

As an example, see the bedroom in the lower right corner of the floor plan in Fig. 41-32. Assume that the ceiling height is 8′ and that the entire room is to be painted. The end walls are each 10′ long and the front wall and closet wall are each 14′ long. The perimeter of the room is therefore 48 lineal feet (10 + 10 + 14 + 14 = 48). Multiply this figure by the room height to obtain the total wall area: 48 × 8 = 384 sq. ft. This room will require 1½ to 2 gallons of paint, depending on the coverage.

Step 2 A window's trim and frame require ¼ pint of paint. The bedroom has three windows, for a total of ¾ pint. A doorframe and door require ½ pint. The closet door is equal to two doors. A total of three doors would then require 1½ pints of paint. Doors and windows together require a total of 2¼ pints (¾ + 1½ = 2¼).

Like the walls, the trim will need both primer and finish coats. For our example, the trim will take one coat of primer (2¼ pints) and two coats of finish (4½ pints). Since paint is sold in cans no smaller than 1 quart, it will be necessary to buy 2 quarts of primer and 3 quarts of finish. However, this will provide enough extra for painting the baseboard, with some left over to allow for future touch-ups by the homeowner.

Step 3 To determine the amount of paint needed for the ceiling, calculate the area by multiplying the length of the room by its width. In the example, the bedroom ceiling area is 140 sq. ft. (10 × 14 = 140).

LABOR

Step 1 To estimate labor for interior painting, refer to **Table 41-C**. For example, the time needed to apply one coat of paint to one window is about ¾ of an hour. If there are ten windows and two coats of finish paint are to be applied, the total time will be 15 hours:

$$10 \times \frac{3}{4} = \frac{30}{4}$$

$$\frac{30}{4} \times 2 = \frac{60}{4} \text{ or } 15$$

Step 2 Multiply this figure by the labor rate per hour to find the total labor cost.

ESTIMATING ON THE JOB

Calculate the amount of paint needed for a room that measures 9′ x 12′. The ceilings are 9′ high, and it has one door and two windows. Include one coat of primer and two coats of finish paint for walls, ceiling, doors, and windows.

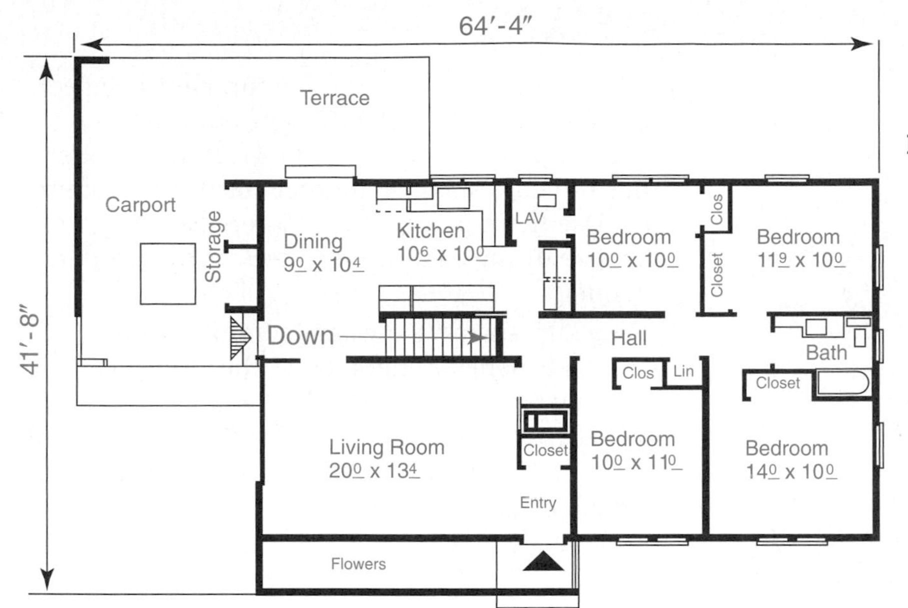

Fig. 41-32. Floor plan.

Trim

Paint interior trim and woodwork using a 1½″ sash brush for windows and a 2″ brush for other parts of the trim. Completing a small area at a time, brush on the paint with back-and-forth strokes. Level the paint with even strokes in one direction. Work quickly but carefully. Never go back to touch up a spot that has started to dry, because this will mar the surface.

In general, trim is painted from the top down. For example, crown molding would be painted first and baseboards last. This prevents finished work from being splattered by paint from above. A cardboard, metal, or plastic guard held flush against the bottom edge of the baseboard protects the floor. It will also prevent the brush from picking up dirt. **Fig. 41-33.**

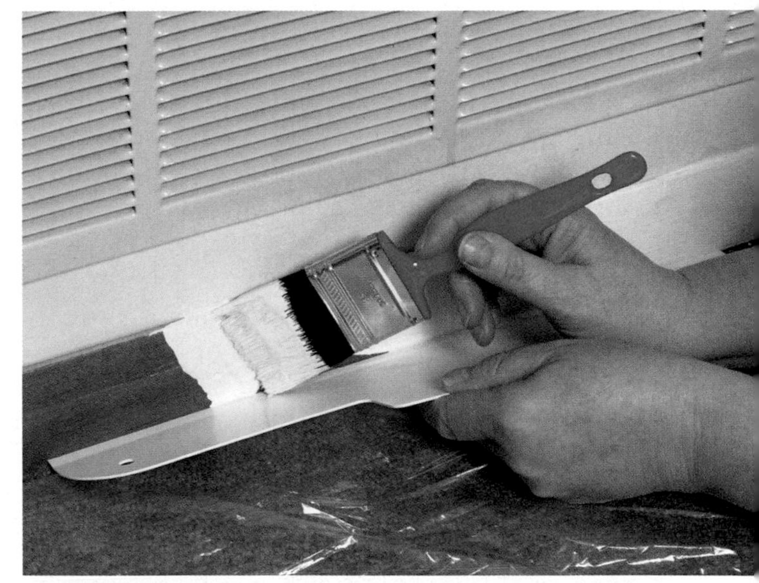

Fig. 41-33. When painting the baseboard, use a guard to keep the paint off the floor and to keep the brush clean.

Table 41-C. Estimating Labor for Interior Painting

Preparation of trim (including sanding and spackling)	115 lineal ft. per hr.
Molding (chair rails and other trim up to 6″ wide)	150 lineal ft. per hr.
Windows (including sash, trim, sills, and apron)	Each coat ¾ hr. per window
Paneled door (including door and trim)	Each coat ¾ hr. per door
Flush door (including door and trim)	Each coat ½ hr. per door
Finishing walls and ceiling:	
Brush	150 sq. ft. per hr.
Roller	300 sq. ft. per hr.

Note: No allowance for preparatory work or for setting up scaffolding is included.

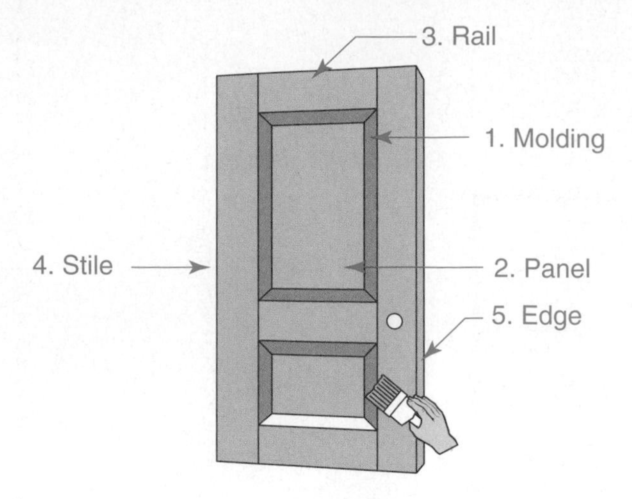

Fig. 41-34. To paint a raised-panel door, follow this sequence. In general, try to work from the center out, and paint rails before stiles.

Adjust a double-hung window so that you can first paint the lower part of the upper sash. Then raise the upper sash almost to the top to finish painting it. Paint the lower sash next. With the window open slightly at the top and bottom, it can be finished easily. Paint the recessed part of the window frame next, then the frame, and finally the windowsill.

When painting a door, paint the jambs and casing first. Then paint the edges of the door itself. Finally, paint the front and back face of the door. When painting the face of a raised-panel door, paint the panel molding first, starting at the top. **Fig. 41-34.** Keep a clean cloth handy to wipe off any paint that gets on the area surrounding the panels. Then paint the remainder of the door.

CLEANUP

The cleanup of tools and equipment used for interior painting is no different than that for exterior painting (see Section 41.2). Remember that solvents such as mineral spirits are flammable. Use them in a well-ventilated area. Store or dispose of rags and newspapers in the proper manner.

- Wipe up spatters and spills immediately.
- Clean brushes, rollers, and other tools as soon as you finish using them.
- Wear rubber gloves when cleaning brushes and rollers. The gloves will protect your hands and make cleanup faster.

SECTION 41.3 Check Your Knowledge

1. What does the sheen of paint refer to?
2. What is edging?
3. When painting baseboard, describe two ways to prevent the brush from picking up dirt from the floor.
4. Which part of a raised-panel door should be painted first and which part second?

On the Job

Visit a paint supply store or the paint section of a hardware store. Make a list of all the solvents that can be used to thin or remove paint. Note the precautions for handling each type of solvent and disposing of used solvents. Prepare a table that compares your findings.

Chapter 41 Review

Section Summaries

41.1 Film-forming finishes coat the wood surface. Penetrating finishes soak into the wood. In each type of finish are pigments, binders, and carriers that make it suitable for a particular use. Paint is the most common type of film-forming finish.

41.2 Surface preparation is important when painting wood. To get the best results, finishes are best applied by brush. On new wood, the first coat of paint should be primer, followed by two top coats of standard paint. Paint should not be applied if temperatures are not suitable. Proper application of paint avoids many problems that are difficult to correct.

41.3 Interior painting procedure should minimize paint splatter and cleanup. Various tools, such as rollers, can be used to make the work go more quickly. They can improve the quality of the job as well and minimize strain on the painter.

Review Questions

1. Name and briefly describe the two basic types of finish.
2. What three ingredients does every paint contain?
3. What is a primer and why is it important?
4. What characteristics of a penetrating finish might make it preferable to paint in some cases?
5. In terms of taking a finish, what advantages does engineered wood have over solid wood?
6. On a two-story house, which is painted first, the top or the bottom?
7. What are the minimum temperatures at which oil-base and latex paints can be applied?
8. Name the two most likely causes of cracked or alligatored paint.
9. Name the five types of interior paints based on their sheen.
10. In what order should the parts of a room be painted?

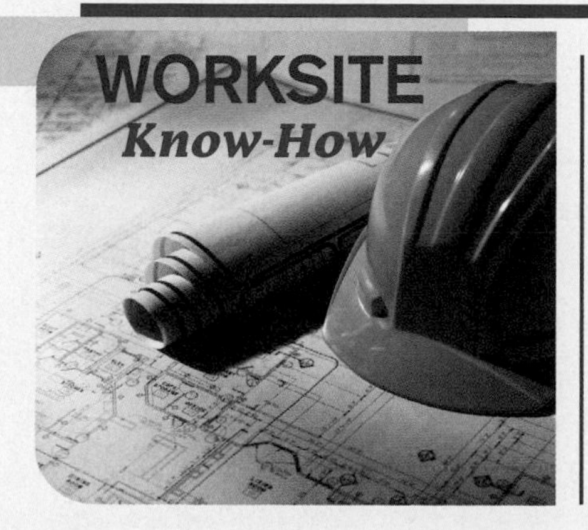

Scheduling Painters Painters are usually among the last contractors to work on a house. Thus any delays in the construction schedule have a significant impact on the painting schedule. The general contractor must keep this in mind when managing the construction schedule. If the schedule has changed significantly, the painters originally scheduled to be available may be working on other projects. This could delay completion of the project.

Chapter

Wood Flooring

Objectives

After reading this chapter, you'll be able to:

- List the three most common forms of wood flooring.
- Identify tree species used to create hardwood flooring.
- Secure wood flooring to a plywood subfloor.
- Describe two methods for applying wood flooring to a concrete subfloor.

Terms

acclimation
parquet
plank
sleeper
wear layer

Finish flooring is the topmost surface of a floor system. Installation of the finish flooring is the last large construction operation in a house. All plumbing, electrical wiring, and plastering are completed first. Only the final interior trim work remains.

Many materials are used as finish flooring. In each case, durability and ease of cleaning are essential. Other properties are important as well, including wear-resistance, comfort, and attractive appearance.

Solid wood is very popular as a finish floor material. Hardwoods and softwoods from various species are available in a variety of widths, thicknesses, and styles. The most common hardwoods used include oak, maple, beech, and birch. Oak is the most plentiful and the most popular flooring wood in the United States. Other species used include cherry, walnut, and plantation-grown tropical hardwoods. No two wood floors are exactly alike. Each has a different character and beauty.

SECTION 42.1

Wood Flooring Basics

Wood flooring is generally attached to a subfloor in a way that conceals the fasteners. Solid wood is the most common material used in many parts of the country, but engineered wood is becoming popular.

SOLID-WOOD FLOORING

Strips or planks of solid wood can be fastened to a subfloor to create different effects. Generally, the wood is applied in rows that run in the long dimension of a room. **Fig. 42-1.** This arrangement is efficient and cost effective. The flooring can also be installed in other patterns. For example, it can be applied diagonally, with a mitered or stacked border. Decorative borders can make use of contrasting woods.

Solid-wood lengths generally have tongue-and-groove edges and ends that interlock with adjoining lengths. This flooring is most often installed by blind nailing it to the subfloor. *Blind nailing* is the process of driving fasteners at an angle through the edge of each board, so that the fasteners will be concealed by the next board.

Forms

Solid-wood flooring is available in three basic forms.

- *Strips.* Strip flooring is the most widely used type. As the name implies, it consists of narrow strips of wood. They are generally no more than 3½″ wide. **Fig. 42-2.** Many wood species are available in this form. Because it is so popular, its installation will be discussed in detail in the next section.

Fig. 42-2. Hardwood strip flooring can be used throughout a house.

Fig. 42-1. Wood flooring patterns: *A.* Standard installation. *B.* Mitered border. *C.* Stacked border.

Fig. 42-3. A plank floor. Planks are fastened with screws, which are then covered with plugs.

Fig. 42-4. Parquet flooring comes in a variety of patterns.

- *Planks.* One of the oldest forms of hardwood flooring is the plank. A **plank** is any solid-wood board that is at least 3″ wide. Plank flooring was widely used in Europe in the 1500s. In the 1700s, it became popular in American colonial homes. Modern plank flooring usually comes in random widths. The edges of the planks may be beveled slightly to reproduce the effect of early hand-hewn planks. The wood pegs that fastened the old plank floors are simulated by gluing wood plugs into shallow holes in the ends of the planks. **Fig. 42-3.**
- *Parquet.* **Parquet** (par-KAY) refers to any flooring assembled with small, precisely cut pieces of wood into a geometric pattern. **Fig. 42-4.** Parquet floors appeared as early as the fourteenth century in Europe. Today's parquet floors are formed with squares, rectangles, and herringbone patterns to achieve a wide variety of effects. Parquet can also be used to form borders around other forms of wood flooring. **Fig. 42-5.** Though parquet flooring can be made from individual pieces, prefabricated parquet tiles are more common and much easier to install. The individual pieces of solid wood are glued to a plywood backing at the factory. The assembly is then machined to form tongued or grooved edges. In this respect, parquet tiles are similar to engineered-wood flooring.

Grading

Through trade associations, the principal American producers of solid-wood flooring have adopted grading rules for various species of wood. Every bundle of flooring identified by this grading system is guaranteed to meet minimum specifications for quality and uniformity.

Oak. Oak is graded according to its general appearance and how sawing methods reveal the grain during manufacturing. The three main types are:

- *Plain sawn.* The end grain of the board is nearly parallel to its face.
- *Quarter sawn.* The end grain runs between 60° and 90° to the board's face.
- *Rift sawn.* The end grain runs between 30° and 60° to the board's face

Grading for appearance refers to how the top face of a board looks. It does not address the board's strength. Red oak and white oak are graded to the same standards. There are five appearance grades:

- *Clear.* This wood has the best appearance and the most uniform color. It is mostly heartwood. Limited small character marks are permitted.
- *Select.* The face may contain color variations typical of heartwood and sapwood. It can include slight milling imperfections, small tight knots, and a modest number of slightly open checks.
- *No. 1 Common.* Prominent variations of color are allowed, as well as broken knots less than ½″ wide and other imperfections.
- *No. 2 Common.* A greater number and degree of natural and manufacturing imperfections are allowed. This grade is used for a utility floor or where character marks and contrasting appearance are acceptable.
- *Shorts.* Pieces 9″ to 18″ long are bundled together in either of two subgrades: No. 1 Common & Better and No. 2 Common. These pieces can be used to fill in rows to avoid cutting longer pieces.

Maple, Beech, and Birch. Grading rules governing maple, beech, and birch are almost the same. In order of general quality, these grades are First, Second, Third, Second & Better, and Third & Better. Neither sapwood nor varying natural color is considered a defect in standard grades.

Each of these woods also is available in a special grade selected for uniformity of color. For maple flooring, this is First Grade White. It is the finest grade of maple flooring. For beech and birch flooring, the special grade is First Grade Red.

Size

Oak strip flooring is commonly ½″ or ¾″ thick. Maple, beech, and birch flooring come in thicknesses of ¾″, 25⁄32″, and 33⁄32″. Face widths for all species range from 1½″ to 3¼″. Flooring ⅜″ thick is sometimes available by special order, but only in widths up to 2″.

Strip flooring is packaged in bundles. A bundle contains strips of various lengths, positioned end to end. Lengths in a bundle vary, but average lengths are specified for each grade. For example, clear oak averages 60″ long. Select oak averages 48″ long, and No. 1 common oak averages 33″ long.

Moisture Content

One of the factors that most affects the durability of wood flooring is its moisture content. Hardwood flooring is kiln dried at the factory to a low moisture content. However, **acclimation** occurs when the wood reaches a moisture content equal to that inside the building where it is installed. The change in width in a single floorboard at various levels of moisture content is shown in **Table 42-A**. For this reason the flooring should always be stored in the building in which it will be installed at least four or five days before being laid to permit acclimation.

Fig. 42-5. Decorative parquet borders.

Table 42-A. Changes Based on Moisture Content

In a 2¼″ Board, a Moisture Content Difference of . . .	May Result in an Approximate Width Change of . . . (inches)
1%	1⁄128
3%	1⁄64
5%	1⁄32
7%	3⁄64
9%	1⁄16
18%	⅛

Other changes can occur when flooring contacts objects with different moisture contents. For example, if flooring absorbs moisture from the subfloor, the underside of the flooring expands. This causes boards to cup slightly. **Fig. 42-6.** If the boards are then sanded flat, they will become crowned when moisture later equalizes. For more on moisture and wood behavior, see Chapter 16, "Wood As a Building Material."

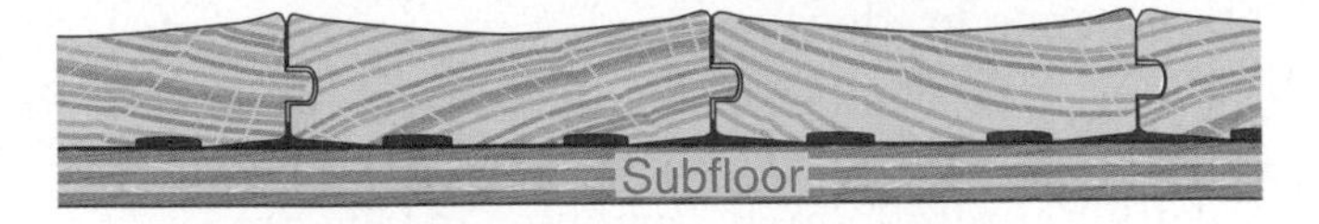

Fig. 42-6. Solid-wood flooring boards can become cupped or crowned.

from Another Angle

The proper moisture content of wood flooring depends on where in the country it will be installed. For example, in houses along the Gulf Coast in the United States, it acclimates between 11 and 13 percent. In central Texas, moisture content is between 8 and 10 percent. In the western Rocky Mountain area, it is between 4 and 8 percent. Acclimation tables are available from flooring manufacturers or from flooring trade associations. Consult these to determine percentages for your region. Wood's moisture content can be determined with a moisture content meter.

Storage and Handling. Wood flooring must be protected from the weather during storage and delivery. This prevents excessive shrinkage or expansion, which could cause the floor to crack or buckle after it has been laid. Manufacturers recommend the following precautions:

- Never unload wood flooring when it is raining or snowing. Cover it with a tarp in foggy or damp conditions.
- Store wood flooring in a well-ventilated and weather-tight building.
- Do not store or lay wood flooring in a damp building. Wait until the plaster and concrete work have given off most of their moisture.
- The building in which the flooring is to be used should first be heated to 70°F [21°C]. Do not lay flooring in a cold building.

ENGINEERED-WOOD FLOORING

Engineered-wood flooring has become quite popular. It is made of three, five, seven, or more layers of wood veneer or thin wood strips that have been bonded together much like plywood. Unlike plywood, however, the top layer of engineered flooring may be ⅛″ to nearly ¼″ thick. **Fig. 42-7.** This top layer is called the **wear layer**.

The assembly is formed into strips or planks that appear similar to solid wood. Because its thin layers are arranged with their grains at right angles to each other, a strip or plank is extremely stable. Engineered-wood flooring is less likely than solid-wood flooring to be affected by excess moisture. The total thickness is less than ½″. It can be sanded and refinished like solid-wood flooring. It is graded under separate rules but by the same organization that grades oak flooring.

Carefully follow the manufacturer's recommended installation methods. This will ensure

Fig. 42-7. Cross section of an engineered flooring plank.

coverage by any warranty on the product. There are three basic methods:

- *Nail-down method.* This technique is almost the same as that used for solid wood floors. The planks or strips are blind nailed (or blind stapled) to a wood subfloor.
- *Floating method.* Each length of flooring is secured to adjacent lengths with aliphatic resin (yellow) glue. None of the boards is nailed or glued to the subfloor. The entire floor "floats" atop a thin sheet of closed-cell foam padding.
- *Glue-down method.* Each length of flooring is glued to the subfloor with a thick adhesive, called *mastic,* that is spread with a notched trowel. The technique is sometimes used to apply engineered-wood flooring directly to a concrete subfloor.

SECTION 42.1 Check Your Knowledge

1. List the appearance grades of oak strip flooring in order.
2. Which of the following woods—birch, oak, maple, and beech—are graded using the same system?
3. What happens if wood flooring absorbs moisture from the subfloor?
4. How is engineered-wood flooring like plywood?

On the Job

Find out more information about any three of the four species of wood discussed in this section. Present your findings in a written report that includes drawings. Include answers to these questions: Where in North America can you find the most abundant growth of these trees? How can you identify the trees by features, such as the shape of the leaf, the texture of the tree bark, and the height of the tree?

SECTION 42.2

Installing Hardwood Strip Flooring

Most hardwood strips are of uniform width. Attractive designs may be achieved using strips of random widths. Interesting patterns can be formed by using stock selected for variations in color or other natural irregularities. Most hardwood strip flooring today has tongue-and-groove edges. Each piece is snug against the next one. **Fig. 42-8.**

FASTENING TECHNIQUES

Proper nailing of the floorboards is absolutely essential. Too few nails may result in annoying squeaks. Tongue-and-groove flooring is blind nailed, except for the first course (row) or two. These are difficult to blind nail, so the boards are face-nailed. In blind nailing, the nails are driven at an angle of 45° to 50°. Nails are placed at the point where the tongue leaves the shoulder.

Wood flooring was once blind nailed by hand. Now, however, installers often use a power nailer. **Fig. 42-9.** The power nailer holds a strip of nails. The installer slides the nailer along the tongue of a floorboard and strikes the tool's plunger with a mallet. This drives a nail at an angle through the tongue of the board. A pneumatic power nailer includes parts that are similar to those of other pneumatic nailers, including a magazine. **Fig. 42-10.** The tool ensures consistent placement of the nails.

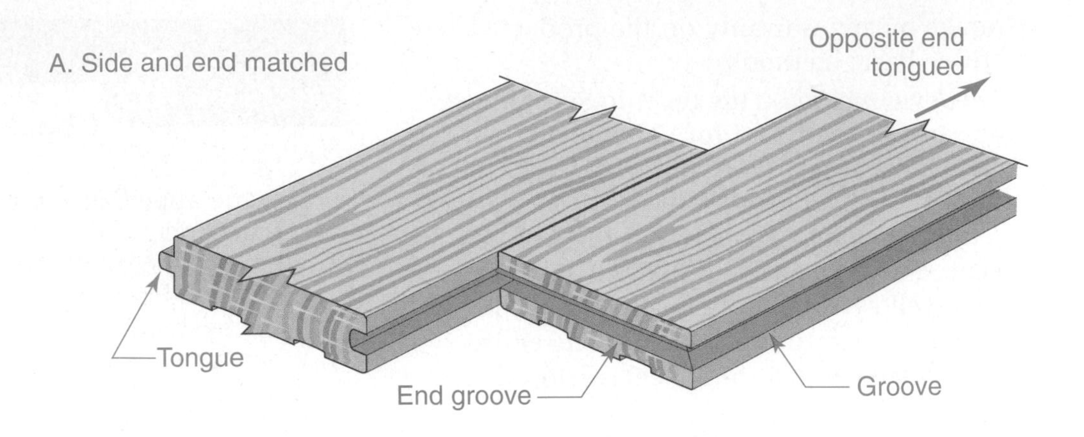

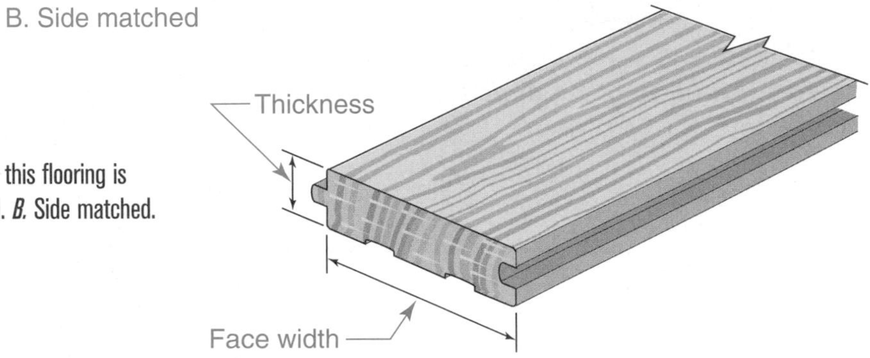

Fig. 42-8. Strip flooring. Note that this flooring is quarter sawn. *A.* Side and end matched. *B.* Side matched.

Fig. 42-9. Using a pneumatic nailer. Note that the installer's hammer has two different faces.

Fig. 42-10. A close-up view of a pneumatic nailer. The lip on the nailer's base plate enables it to be quickly positioned at a precise location.

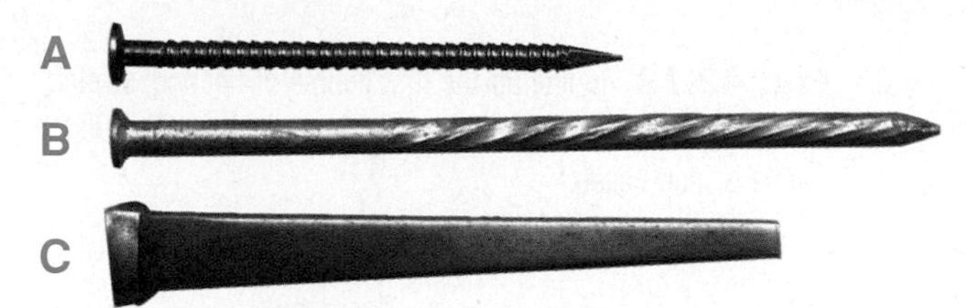

Fig. 42-11. Flooring nails: *A.* Barbed. *B.* Screw. *C.* Cut steel.

Types of Fasteners

Three types of flooring nails are shown in **Fig. 42-11**. Always follow the nailing recommendations of the flooring manufacturer. However, with flooring 25⁄32″ thick and 1½″ or more wide, 7d or 8d screw nails or cut steel nails are best. If steel wire flooring nails are used, they should be 8d and preferably cement coated.

INSTALLATION OVER A WOOD SUBFLOOR

Strip flooring is generally laid over a plywood subfloor. Examine the subfloor carefully and correct any defects. Raised nails, for instance, should be driven down. Scrape any globs of plaster, joint compound, or dried adhesives off the subfloor. Then sweep the area thoroughly.

Staple 15 lb. asphalt building paper to the subfloor. Lap seams from 2″ to 4″. The paper protects the flooring from moisture that might come from below and helps to prevent squeaks. **Fig. 42-12.** After the building paper is in place, snap chalk lines to indicate the position of floor joists. Flooring boards should be nailed into joists, not just into the floor sheathing.

Planning

Strip flooring should be laid at right angles to the floor joists. Plan the work so that the flooring flows from one room to another. Be sure to consider closets and hallways when planning.

When floor coverings in adjoining rooms are different, the flooring should end under the center of a doorway. In this way, only the flooring of the room in which someone is standing will be seen by that person when the door is closed. In some cases, finish floors of different materials may meet at a large opening that has no door. Then the wood floor is usually laid through the opening to a point even with the wall line of the adjacent room.

Fig. 42-12. Laying the asphalt building paper over the subfloor in preparation for the finish floor. ***Note:*** Mark the location of the floor joists on the walls first. Chalk lines may be snapped to indicate the location of joists for nailing the strip flooring.

Laying Strip Flooring

Many walls are not perfectly true, even in new construction. To ensure a straight course, stretch a string the length of the room between two nails placed 8″ from a side wall. Line up the first courses at a uniform distance from the string rather than from the wall itself. **Fig. 42-13.** Some installers snap a chalk line on the floor instead of measuring to a string.

Place a long piece of flooring with the grooved *edge* ½″ to ⅝″ from a side wall and the grooved *end* nearest an end wall. The space allows the flooring to expand without binding against the wall. It will be hidden later by baseboards or shoe molding. Face-nail the board into place. **Fig. 42-14.** Maintain the same distance from the guide string as you install each board in the first course. Drive one nail at each joist crossing, or every 10″ to 12″ if the joists run parallel to the flooring. Fit the groove end of each board over the tongue end of the previous board.

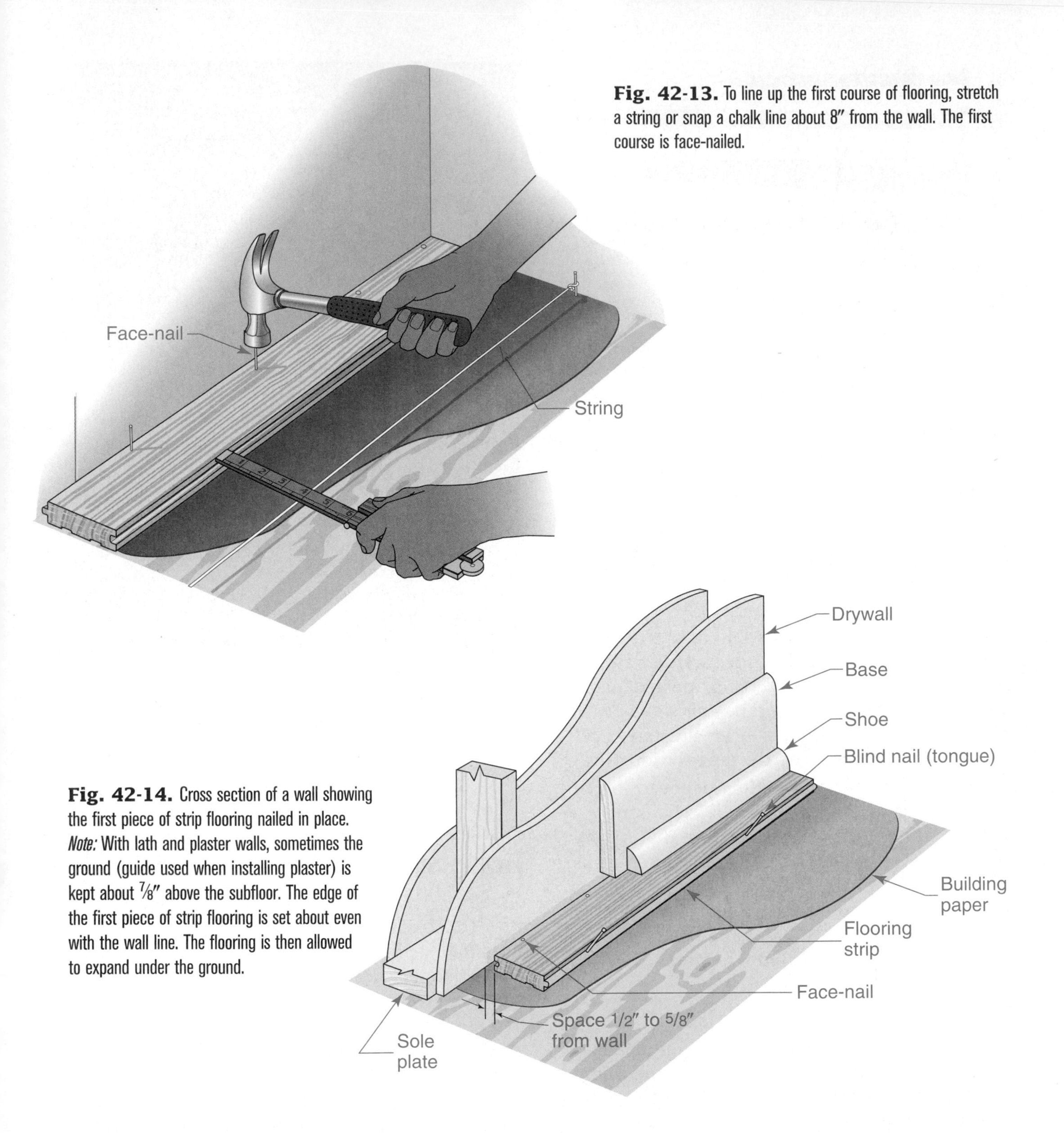

Fig. 42-13. To line up the first course of flooring, stretch a string or snap a chalk line about 8″ from the wall. The first course is face-nailed.

Fig. 42-14. Cross section of a wall showing the first piece of strip flooring nailed in place. *Note:* With lath and plaster walls, sometimes the ground (guide used when installing plaster) is kept about 7/8″ above the subfloor. The edge of the first piece of strip flooring is set about even with the wall line. The flooring is then allowed to expand under the ground.

Depending on the width of the flooring, the second course may also have to be face-nailed. However, subsequent courses can be installed with a power nailer or pneumatic nailer. Hold a board in place against the previous course and use either device to blind nail through the board's tongue. Slide the device along the board's tongue and nail at each joist location. The best nailing procedure is to stand on the strip, with toes in line with the outer edge, and strike (or fire) the nailer from a stooped position.

When a length of flooring cannot be readily found to fit the remaining space in a course, cut one to approximate length. Lay the piece down in a position reversed from that in which it will

Fig. 42-15. Fitting a piece of flooring to the remaining space in a course.

Fig. 42-16. Laying out the strip flooring so that the joints are staggered. This is called racking the floor.

be when nailed. Draw a line at the point where it should be cut. **Fig. 42-15.** When the piece is reversed, the tongue end is cut off. The groove end is needed for joining with the tongue end of the previous piece.

Take care to stagger the end joints of the flooring pieces so that joints are not grouped closely together. A joint should be no closer than 6″ to another in a previous course. Arranging the strips in this way is called *racking*. **Fig. 42-16.** Two people usually work together to install a wood floor. One racks the pieces and cuts end boards to length. The other fits the racked boards together and nails them.

SAFETY FIRST

Safe Leverage

Never use chisels or screwdrivers to lever floorboards into place. These tools are not designed to take lateral loads and could snap suddenly under stress. Instead, use a prybar or make the device shown in **Fig. 42-17.**

Installing Closing Boards

On reaching the opposite side of the room, you will find there is no space between the wall and the flooring to permit blind nailing of the last two or three courses. Instead, face-nail them, at the same time pulling the flooring up tightly by exerting pressure against it with a prybar or a piece of scrap. **Fig. 42-18.** The last course may have to be ripped to width on a table saw in order to fit. Remember to leave a space for expansion. If the last course is narrow, drill holes for the nails to prevent splitting.

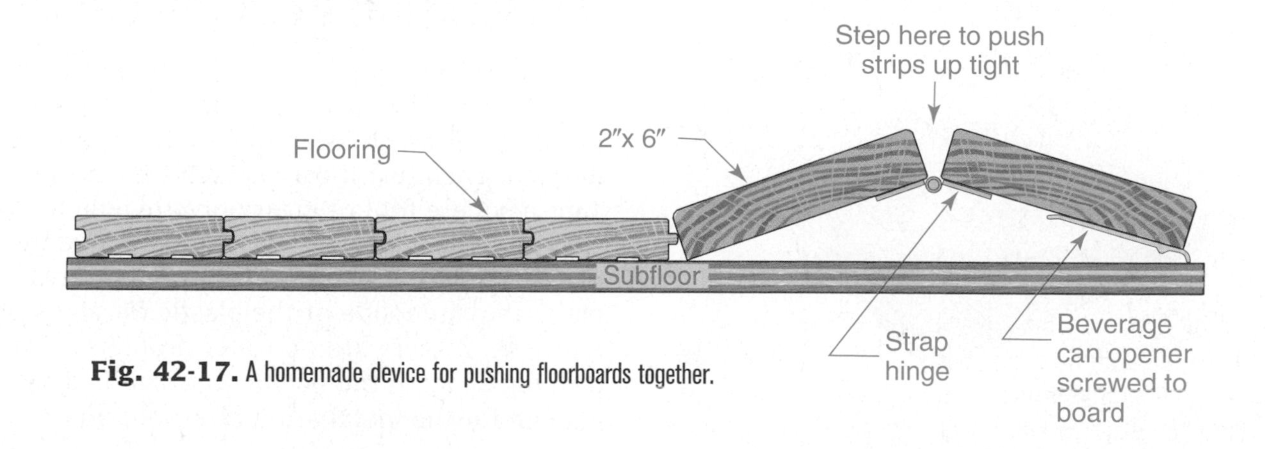

Fig. 42-17. A homemade device for pushing floorboards together.

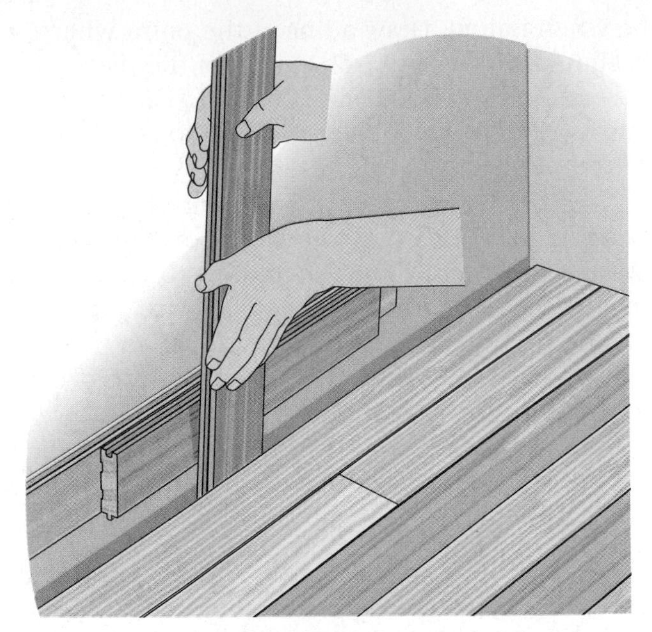

Fig. 42-18. Place the last few courses in position, and pull the flooring up tightly when face-nailing. When prying the pieces with the crowbar or scrap length of flooring, put scrap stock against the wall to protect the wall surface. The scrap should span several wall studs.

If flooring continues into the adjacent room, fit floorboards around openings as needed. Generally, the orientation of tongues and grooves can be continued. However, there may be cases where the installer wishes to change this orientation for the sake of convenience. In such cases, a spline can be slipped into place to connect the grooves of two boards. **Fig. 42-19.**

Fig. 42-19. A spline can be used to change the direction in which the flooring is installed.

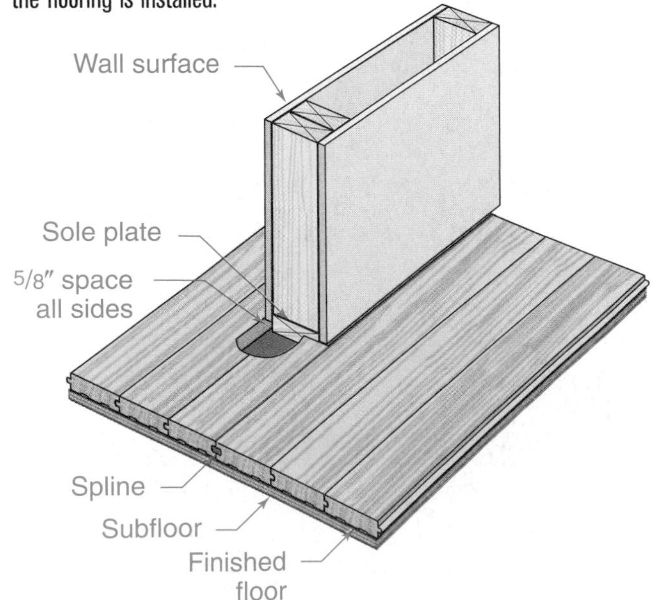

Carpenter's Tip

To notch a floorboard to fit a door opening, place it flush against the framing. **Fig. 42-20.** Measure the gap between the face of the previous piece and the groove edge of the new piece. Where the framing begins, draw a straight line on the flooring to the same distance as the width of the gap. Do the same on the other side of the door frame. Draw a straight line connecting the ends of these lines. Using a jigsaw, cut the flooring along the lines.

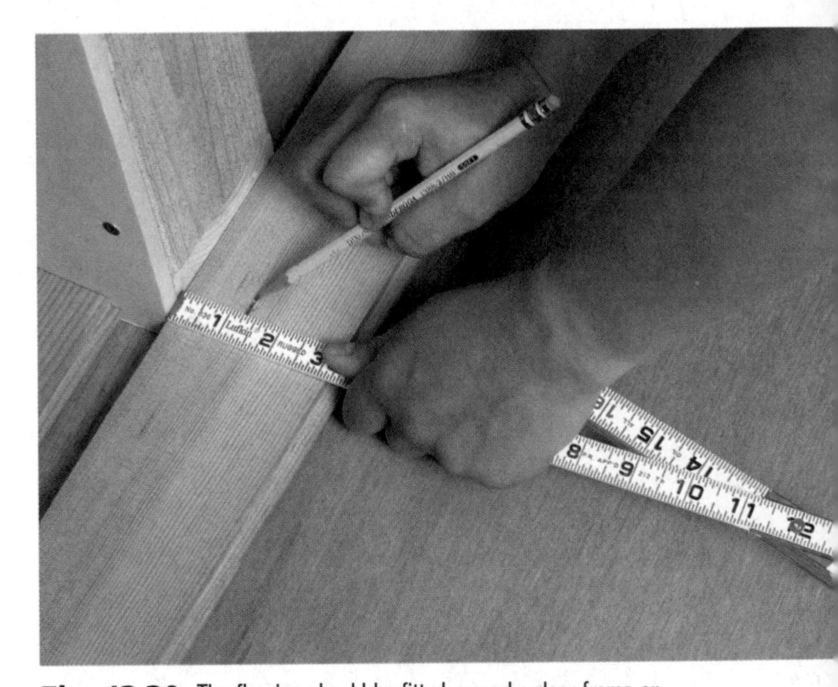

Fig. 42-20. The flooring should be fitted around a door frame or other projection.

INSTALLATION OVER CONCRETE

Concrete gives off moisture as it cures, which can be harmful to wood flooring. To prevent problems, allow the slab to cure for at least two months. Then test it for excessive moisture. Tape a square foot of clear polyethylene to the slab. Seal the edges with duct tape. Leave the plastic in place for twenty-four hours. Then check the underside of the plastic for signs of moisture. If there are no water droplets or moisture fog beneath the plastic, the slab is dry enough for the installation of a wood floor.

Two methods are used to install strip flooring over concrete: flooring over sleepers and flooring over plywood. Before you begin, however, install a vapor barrier.

Vapor Barriers

Even small amounts of moisture should be kept away from wood flooring. Asphalt felt building paper or polyethylene plastic provides a suitable vapor barrier between concrete and wood.

To use asphalt felt, sweep the slab clean. Then apply cut-back asphalt mastic to the slab with a notched trowel. *Cut-back mastic* has been thinned slightly with a solvent. About two hours after spreading the mastic, roll out strips of 15-lb. asphalt felt over the entire slab. Lap the edges 4″. Spread a second layer of mastic over the felt. Then add a second layer of felt on top of that. Both layers of felt should run in the same direction, but the rows should be offset.

To use a polyethylene plastic vapor barrier, sweep the slab clean. Then spread cut-back mastic over the slab with a notched trowel. After the mastic has dried, spread 4-mil or 6-mil polyethylene over the slab. Use a weighted floor roller to press it into the mastic.

Flooring Over Sleepers

A **sleeper** is a length of lumber that supports wood flooring over concrete. It should be preservative-treated.

1. Snap chalk lines 12″ apart at right angles to the direction the flooring will run. Cover the lines with rivers of asphalt mastic about 4″ wide.
2. Embed 2x4 sleepers in the mastic. **Fig. 42-21.** Lap the ends of sleepers at least 4″. Leave ¾″ between the ends of sleepers and the walls. It is not necessary to nail the sleepers in place.
3. After the mastic has cured, spread a 6-mil polyethylene vapor barrier over the sleepers. Lap all edges. This adds a layer of moisture protection to the system.
4. Install the strip flooring at right angles to the sleepers. Two adjoining courses of flooring should not have joints on the same sleeper. Where a flooring board runs over a lapped sleeper joint, nail the board into both sleepers. Provide at least ½″ of clearance between flooring and the walls to allow for expansion.

Flooring Over Plywood

1. Lay ¾″ exterior grade plywood over the vapor barrier. Stagger the end joints 4″.
2. When all the plywood is in place, fasten it to the slab with concrete nails or powder-actuated fasteners. **Fig. 42-22.** Use at least nine nails per panel. To ensure that the panels stay flat, nail them at the center first. Then work toward the edges. To allow for

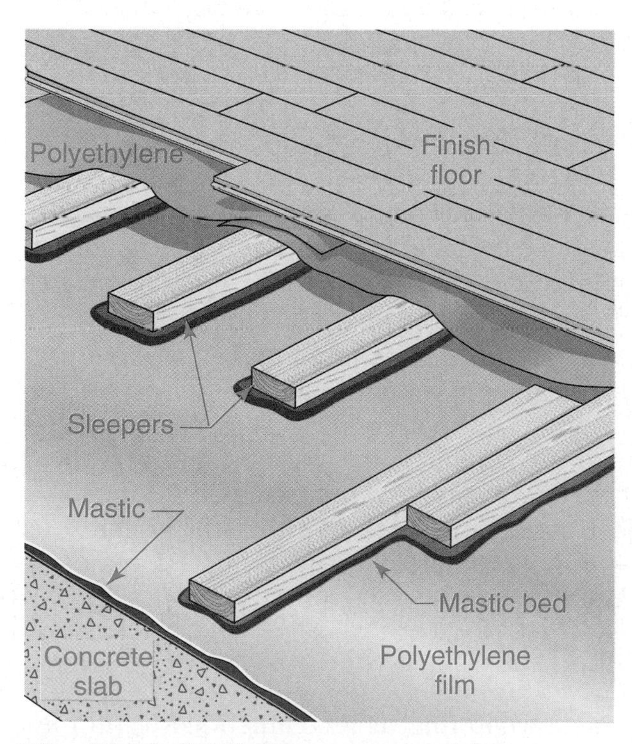

Fig. 42-21. Strip flooring over concrete and sleepers.

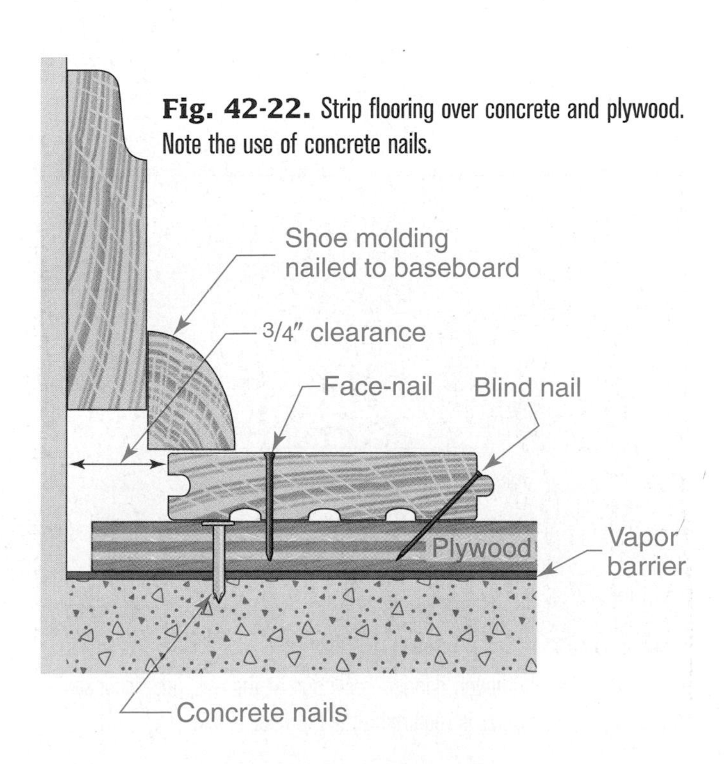

Fig. 42-22. Strip flooring over concrete and plywood. Note the use of concrete nails.

expansion, leave a gap of about 3/8″ between each panel and a gap of 3/4″ at the walls.
3. Install the strip flooring as you would over a standard plywood subfloor. Nails should be slightly less than 1½″ long.

APPLYING A FINISH

After the flooring is in place, the floor is finished. Finishing is a time-consuming process that stretches over several days.

Sanding

Although unfinished hardwood flooring is smoothly surfaced by the manufacturer, scratches and other marks caused by handling usually show after the floor has been laid. Also, it is common to see slight differences in the height of adjacent boards. This difference is called *overwood*. All these imperfections must be removed. A drum-type floor sander is used. **Fig. 42-23.** A smaller electric sander called an *edger* is also needed. **Fig. 42-24.** Finishing a new floor calls for several sandings, called *cuts*. The first cut uses coarse sandpaper. Subsequent cuts use progressively finer sandpaper.

Fig. 42-23. Although flooring is sanded at the mill, additional sanding with a drum sander is required after the floor is laid.

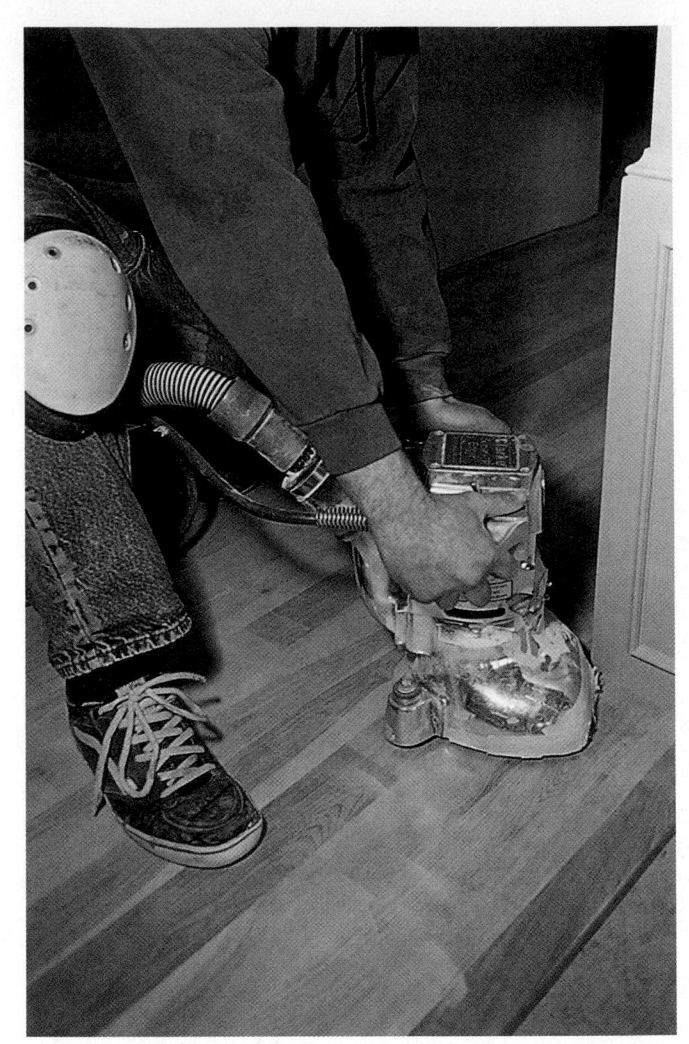

Fig. 42-24. A small power sander called an edger is used for sanding floors near walls, in closets, and in other small areas where the drum sander cannot reach. Note the vacuum attachment.

The drum sander should make overlapping passes along the wood grain, not across it. The edger is used to sand close to the walls, where the drum sander cannot reach. Hand sanding or scraping may be required to work around obstructions that interfere with the edger. After sanding is complete, all dust must be removed with a vacuum.

Filling

Paste wood filler is recommended to fill the tiny surface crevices in oak and other hardwoods that have large pores. It gives the floor the perfectly smooth surface required for a lustrous appearance. Depending on circumstances, filler may be applied either before the last sanding cut or after the floor is stained. It should be allowed to dry twenty-four hours before the next operation is begun. Wood filler may be colorless or it may contain pigment to bring out the grain of the wood.

Staining

To give the floor a color different from that of the natural wood, stains may be used. The first coat of stain or other finish should be applied on the same day as the last sanding. This prevents the grain from becoming raised, a condition that roughens the surface slightly. Stain should be applied before other finishes. It should be put on evenly, preferably with a high-quality brush that is 3″ or 4″ wide.

Types of Finishes

In recent years, modern synthetic finishes have replaced a number of traditional finishes. Varnish, for example, has given way to polyurethane. The ideal finish should be attractive and durable. It should be easy to apply and maintain. Also, it should be capable of being retouched in worn spots without producing a patched appearance.

However, no finish has all these characteristics. Some are more durable than others. Some cannot be retouched easily. Others are so toxic prior to curing that they should be applied only by specialists. When choosing a finish, make sure it has the characteristics you feel are most important for the situation.

In some parts of the country, particularly in large cities, restrictions limit the use of floor finishes containing solvents made from *volatile organic compounds* (VOCs). This is due to environmental concerns. Many floor finishes have therefore been reformulated to reduce or eliminate VOCs.

Penetrating Finishes. Penetrating finishes differ from other finishes in one important respect. Rather than forming a surface coating, the finish penetrates the wood fibers. In effect it becomes a part of the wood itself. It wears only as the wood wears and does not chip or scratch. It does not provide as shiny an appearance as other finishes. However, it has the advantage of being easily retouched. Refinishing worn spots does not create a patched appearance. Penetrating finishes are available either clear or slightly tinted with color.

A wide brush, a squeegee, or a wool applicator may be used to apply penetrating finishes. **Fig. 42-25.** Excess material should be wiped off with clean cloths or a rubber squeegee. For best results the floor then should be buffed with No. 2 steel wool. Penetrating finishes may also be used as a base for a surface finish such as varnish.

SAFETY FIRST

Dangerous Vapors

The chemicals and solvents that make some synthetic finishes very durable are also hazardous to installers. It is important to follow the manufacturer's instructions carefully. In general, these instructions call for plenty of ventilation and the use of a respirator. The respirator must be fitted with filter cartridges suitable for the specific finish being applied.

Fig. 42-25. A penetrating finish is tough and wear resistant. It can be applied easily with long- or short-handled tools.

Estimating...

Strip Flooring

Both flooring materials and labor can be estimated.

MATERIALS

To estimate the quantity needed, determine the number of square feet to be covered.

Step 1 Multiply the length of the room times the width of the room. Any offsets or closets should be figured separately by multiplying their length times their width and adding the product to the total number of square feet. For example, a room that is 10′ by 12′ has 120 sq. ft. of floor area ($10 \times 12 = 120$). If the closet is 2′ wide by 8′ long, the closet contains a total of 16 sq. ft. ($2 \times 8 = 16$). The total is therefore 136 sq. ft. ($120 + 16 = 136$).

Step 2 To determine the amount of strip flooring needed, refer to **Table 42-B**. In the Strip Flooring Size column, select the size to be used. Then read across for material needed. For example, if $\frac{25}{32}$″ x $2\frac{1}{4}$″ strip flooring is selected, it will take 138.3 bd. ft. to cover 100 sq. ft. of floor area. The room in our example has 136 sq. ft. of floor space. Divide that number by 100:

$$136 \div 100 = 1.36$$

Step 3 Multiply the result by 138.3:

$$1.36 \times 138.3 = 188.09 \text{ bd. ft.}$$

Therefore, 188.09 bd. ft. of strip flooring will be required.

Step 4 To figure the cost of the material, multiply the cost per board foot times the total number of board feet required.

Step 5 Table 42-B also has information for determining the quantity of nails needed. The table shows it will take 3 lbs. of nails to lay 100 sq. ft. of $2\frac{1}{4}$″ strip flooring. The floor in our example contains 136 sq. ft., which will require a little over 4 lbs. of nails.

$$136 \div 100 = 1.36$$
$$1.36 \times 3 = 4.08 \text{ lbs.}$$

Step 6 Multiply the cost per pound times the number of pounds to find the cost of the nails.

LABOR

Table 42-B also shows hours of labor.

Step 1 Refer to the column headed Labor Hours per 100 Sq. Ft. The table shows that a worker can lay 100 sq. ft. of $\frac{25}{32}$″ x $2\frac{1}{4}$″ strip flooring in 3 hours.

Step 2 Using the table, you can determine that the floor in the room in our example will require 4.08 hours to lay.

$$136 \div 100 = 1.36$$
$$1.36 \times 3 = 4.08 \text{ hrs.}$$

Step 3 Multiply this figure by the hourly rate to determine total labor cost.

ESTIMATING ON THE JOB

Estimate the quantity of $\frac{25}{32}$″ x 2″ strip flooring needed for the bedroom and closet shown in **Fig. 42-26**. Then estimate the hours of labor required to lay, sand, and finish the floor. Round your answers.

Table 42-B. Estimating Strip Flooring Materials and Labor

Strip Flooring Size (inches)	Material		Nails	Labor Hours per 100 Sq. Ft.		
	Bd. Ft. per 100 Sq. Ft.	1,000 Bd. Ft. Will Lay (Sq. Ft.) . . .	per 100 Sq. Ft. (Lbs.)	Laying	Sanding*	Finishing*
25/32 x 1½	155.0	645.0	3.7	3.7	1.3	2.6
25/32 x 2	142.5	701.8	3.0	3.4	1.3	2.6
25/32 x 2¼	138.3	723.0	3.0	3.0	1.3	2.6
25/32 x 3¼	129.0	775.2	2.3	2.6	1.3	2.6
⅜ x 1½	138.3	723.0	3.7	3.7	1.3	2.6
⅜ x 2	130.0	769.0	3.0	3.4	1.3	2.6
½ x 1½	138.3	723.0	3.7	3.7	1.3	2.6
½ x 2	130.0	769.2	3.0	3.4	1.3	2.6

*Sanding and finishing times are averages.

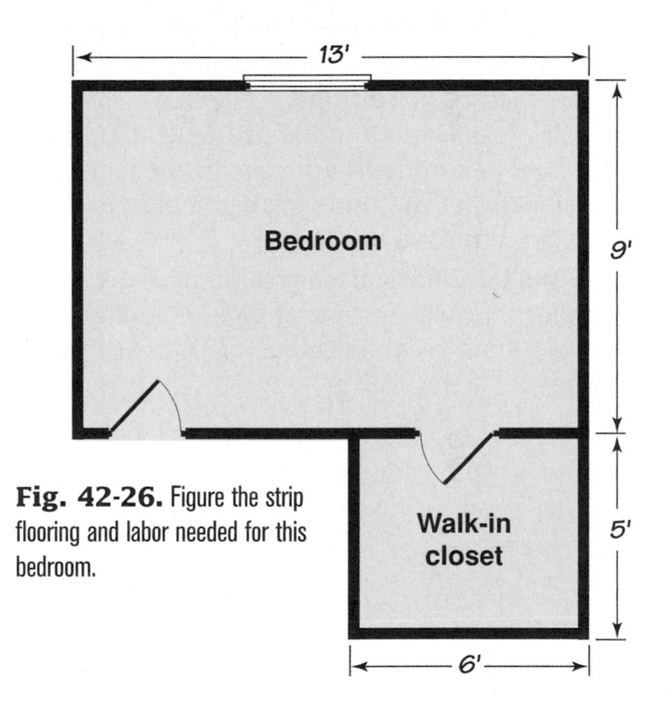

Fig. 42-26. Figure the strip flooring and labor needed for this bedroom.

Urethane Finishes. A number of floor finishes are included in the general category of *urethanes.* These are durable finishes that cure to a hard film. They are fairly resistant to moisture.

Moisture-cured urethanes are the hardest and most moisture resistant. They offer a glossy look that resists abrasion. They cure by reacting with humidity in the air. The proper amount of humidity is critical, however. This makes these finishes difficult to apply, except by professional floor finishers.

Oil-modified urethanes (sometimes called *polyurethanes*) are easier to apply than moisture-cured urethanes. They provide a durable coating with a gloss, semigloss, or matte finish. Widely available, they are commonly used.

Water-based urethanes are fairly new. The solid portions of the product are suspended primarily in water, rather than in a volatile solvent. Water-based urethanes are durable but require more coats to build up a thickness that compares to other urethanes.

Other Finishes. *Varnishes* were once widely used to finish floors but are seldom used now. They have been replaced by synthetic finishes that are easier to install and more durable.

Natural oil finishes can be used on a floor, though they require much time to fully cure. Oils are less durable than other finishes but are easy to repair. Linseed oil and tung oil are common types.

Carpenter's Tip

Prefinished wood flooring is easier to install than unfinished wood flooring. However, estimating requires greater care. Special trim such as thresholds, border strips around fireplace hearths, and transition pieces must be prefinished to match. If they are not ordered with the rest of the flooring, trim may not match the color and finish of the floorboards. This will detract from the overall appearance of the floor.

Though *shellac finishes* are thought by some to result in floors of great beauty, a shellac finish is difficult to maintain. Shellac water-spots easily and does not hold up against common household solvents.

Wax is usually applied over some other type of finish. It not only gives a lustrous sheen to a floor but also forms a film that protects the finish beneath. When wax becomes dirty, it is easily removed and new wax applied. However, wax can make a floor slippery. It should be used with care.

Prefinished Flooring. Many manufacturers now produce wood flooring that is completely prefinished at the factory. It has the following advantages:

- It is ready for use immediately after being laid.
- The finish is uniform because it is applied under factory conditions.
- Finish types that would be difficult to apply on site may be applied with ease in the factory.
- Special curing methods available only in a factory can improve durability.

Prefinished floors are available in many styles and colors. However, the range of colors and finishes is not as great as those for floors finished on site.

SECTION 42.2 Check Your Knowledge

1. Which floor-nailing tool must be struck by a mallet?
2. Why is wood flooring laid atop building paper?
3. What standard tools should be used to lever floorboards into place? Which should not be used?
4. What impact do VOCs have on the choice of a floor finish?

On the Job

Using library or Internet resources, find out what basic materials lacquer and polyurethane are made of. How would you compare the overall environmental impact of each finish? Be sure to consider such factors as durability, availability of raw materials, and the level of VOCs in each.

Chapter 42

Review

Section Summaries

42.1 Solid-wood flooring is available in several forms, including strips, planks, and parquet. The grade of the wood depends on the wood species, as well as on how the material was manufactured and how the surface appears. Allowing flooring to acclimate before installation prevents warping.

42.2 Hardwood strip flooring is installed by blind nailing it into the floor joists. It is most often installed over a wood subfloor. It may also be installed over concrete as long as no moisture problems exist. Sanding a floor removes imperfections. After all sanding dust has been removed, the floor can be finished with any one of several types of products.

Review Questions

1. What is the difference between a flooring plank and a flooring strip?
2. Define blind nailing.
3. Describe parquet flooring.
4. Name the three methods used to install engineered-wood flooring.
5. Name the tree species used to create hardwood flooring.
6. Wood flooring should be stored in the building in which it will be installed before being laid. What is the term for this process?
7. Give at least three recommendations for storing wood flooring.
8. Describe two methods for ensuring that the first course of flooring will be straight.
9. Why must you be cautious when installing solid-wood flooring over a concrete subfloor?
10. What is a sleeper?

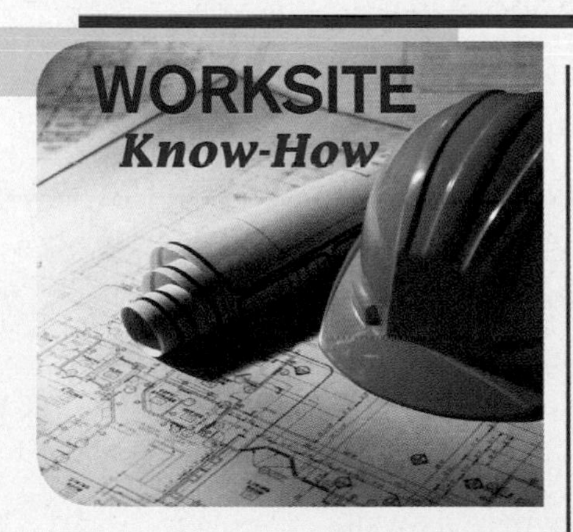

Responding to Customer Complaints New homeowners may know little about construction. They may also be concerned about rising costs. These things can contribute to a feeling of irritability and sometimes even rude behavior.

Many carpenters never have to deal directly with a project's owners. However, suppose an owner is visiting the site and complains that you've damaged something.

The first thing to remember is not to take a complaint personally. The problem may not be your fault, and even if it is, we all make mistakes. The best response would be to say, "I'll check it right away," and to do so while the owner is there. If the owner is still not satisfied, call your supervisor, explain the problem, and wait for instructions. Never get into an argument with a client or behave disrespectfully. Even if you're in the right, your boss may wonder about your ability to handle yourself in difficult situations.

Chapter

Resilient Flooring and Ceramic Tile

Objectives

After reading this chapter, you'll be able to:

- Describe the basic method for laying sheet vinyl flooring.
- Estimate the quantity of resilient flooring needed for any room.
- Identify the basic tools used for installing ceramic tile.
- Identify a ceramic tile by its characteristics.

Terms

backerboard
bisque
grout
underlayment

In addition to the solid-wood flooring discussed in Chapter 42, many other types of flooring are available. Among these, vinyl and ceramic tile flooring are the most common. Vinyl flooring belongs to a category of materials called *resilient flooring*. Resilient materials are flexible and are installed as tiles or in wide sheets.

Ceramic tile can be used throughout the house to provide a durable, colorful, and easy-to-clean surface. Though found primarily in kitchens and bathrooms, ceramic tile can be used elsewhere as well.

SECTION 43.1

Resilient Flooring

Resilient flooring refers to a broad group of manufactured products. Some of them, such as vinyl flooring, are made of synthetic materials. Others, such as linoleum, are made primarily of natural materials. All resilient flooring, however, is flexible and less than 3⁄16″ thick. It is available in various forms and in many different colors, patterns, and textures.

The most common type of resilient flooring is made of vinyl. Vinyl flooring is often used in kitchens, bathrooms, and recreation rooms because it is durable, stain resistant, and fairly inexpensive.

Vinyl flooring comes in sheet and tile form. Sheet vinyl comes in large rolls 12′ wide. **Fig. 43-1.** In many cases, it can be laid without the need for seams. It is usually installed by professionals. Vinyl tiles are usually 9″ or 12″ square. **Fig. 43-2.** Their size makes them easy to work with and easier for homeowners to install themselves.

Fig. 43-2. Vinyl flooring in tile form.

Fig. 43-1. The range of colors and patterns in sheet vinyl flooring makes it extremely versatile.

Sheet vinyl and vinyl tiles are usually applied to a wood subfloor using mastic. However, vinyl can be laid over almost any solid, dry surface, including concrete.

INSTALLING A SHEET VINYL FLOOR

The following procedure is generally followed when installing a sheet vinyl floor. However, manufacturers often have specific recommendations for their products. Those should always be followed closely.

A wood subfloor should be covered with plywood underlayment first. **Underlayment** is a thin panel product with a surface smoother than standard plywood or OSB subflooring. Underlayment prevents small flaws in the subfloor from showing through resilient flooring. It also provides firm, clean, and void-free support. Underlayment should be at least ¼″ thick and have a sanded face.

Nails or staples should be 6″ apart in the field and 4″ apart at the edges. The *field* is the center area of the panel that is away from the edges. The joints between underlayment panels should be staggered and butted together. **Fig. 43-3.** Any gaps larger than 1⁄32″ should be filled with latex patching compound and sanded flush.

Sweep the floor thoroughly to remove any dust and debris. Check to ensure that fasteners are flush with the surface of the underlayment. One way to check this quickly is to run a wide-blade putty knife over the floor. You will hear a metallic ring when the blade hits protruding fasteners.

Measure the room and determine if the sheet vinyl will require seams. Because of the width of vinyl sheets, it is often possible to avoid a seam. If a seam is required, snap a chalk line where it will fall. Then snap two parallel lines about 8″ away and on either side of the first line. These chalk lines identify the width of the seam area.

Unroll the flooring and cut as many pieces as needed to cover the floor. Each piece should be about 3″ longer than the length of the room. A utility knife works well for cutting vinyl flooring. Flooring that is cold is more difficult to work with than flooring that is at room temperature.

Spread mastic with a notched trowel over half of the area to be covered by a single strip. **Fig. 43-4.** Keep mastic out of the seam area. Place the flooring in the wet mastic and roll it smooth with a weighted floor roller. One edge should overlap the center seam line by about 1″. Lift the second half of the vinyl. Apply mastic to the underlayment beneath it. Lower this vinyl into the mastic and roll it smooth. Trim the ends of the vinyl to final length.

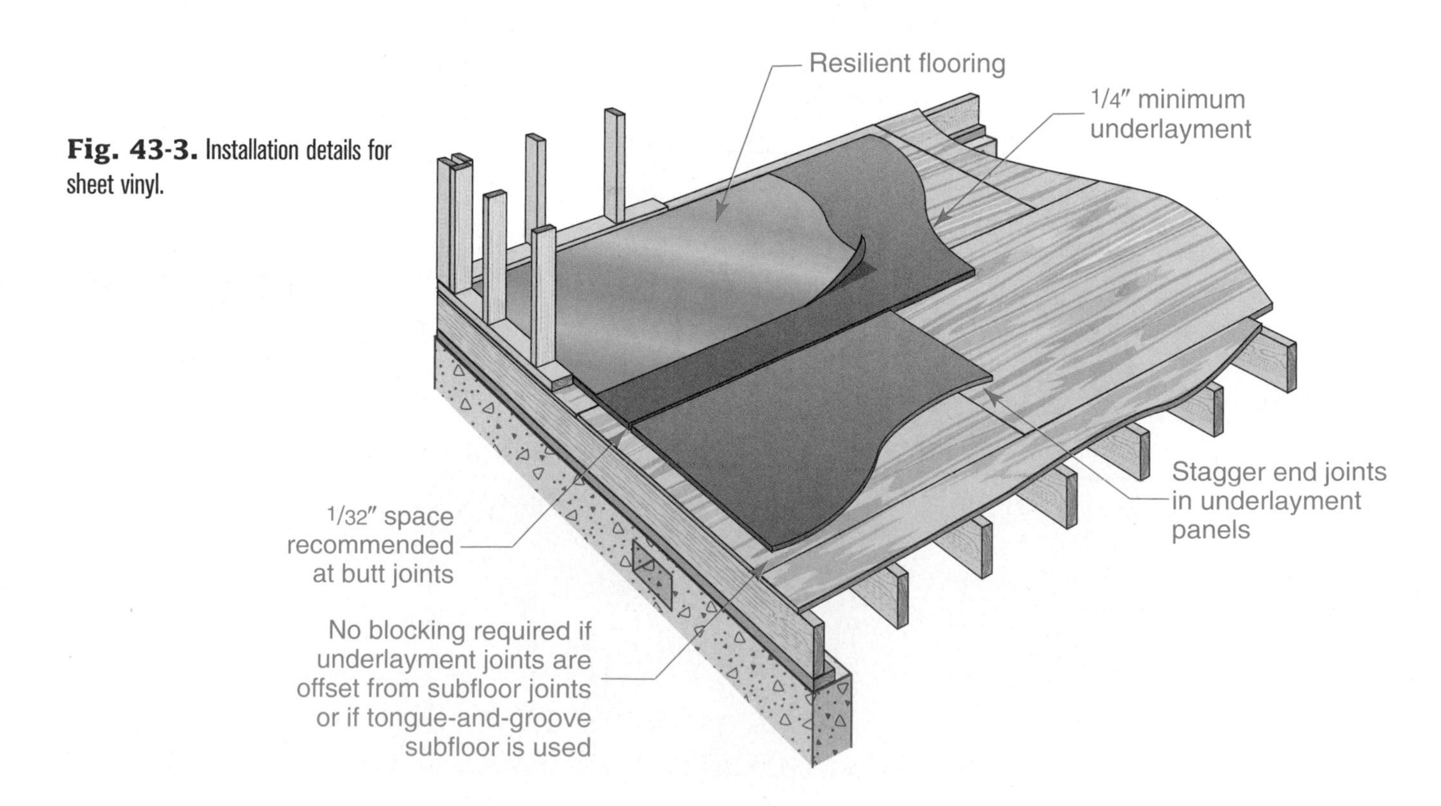

Fig. 43-3. Installation details for sheet vinyl.

Fig. 43-4. Mastic should be spread with a notched trowel. This ensures that the adhesive will be a uniform thickness. Excess mastic should be removed with the trowel.

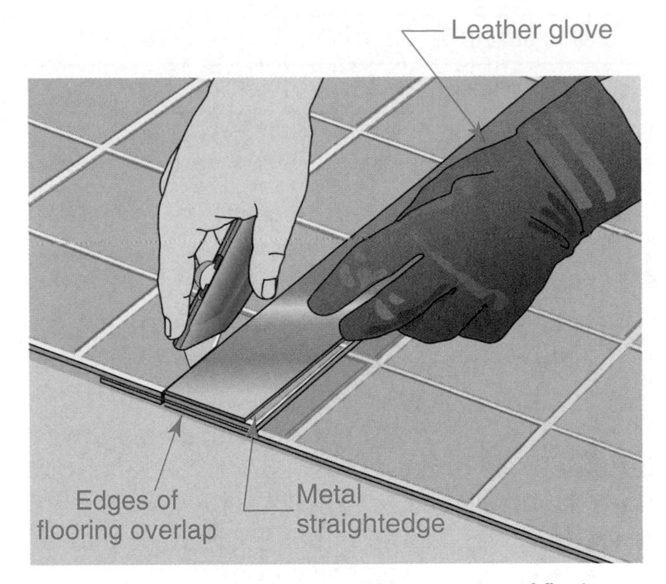

Fig. 43-5. Double-cutting a seam. Adjacent sections of flooring should be overlapped. After the overlapped area is cut through, excess flooring is removed.

Repeat the procedure with the next strip of vinyl. When placing this piece, one edge should overlap the previous piece by several inches. After adjoining strips of vinyl flooring are in place, there will be a 16″ wide "dry zone" beneath the overlapping edges. Cut through the overlapping edges with a utility knife. **Fig. 43-5.** Guide the cut with a steel straightedge. Lift each edge of the flooring. Apply mastic to the underlayment, and roll the seam smooth.

Estimating Sheet Vinyl

Estimating the amount of sheet vinyl needed is a matter of determining the square footage of floor to be covered. An extra amount must be figured in to account for waste, seams, and pattern matching. How much will depend on the type of flooring and the pattern. The manufacturer or distributor should be consulted.

Tables 43-A and **43-B** can be used to estimate labor requirements and waste allowances for resilient tile products.

Table 43-A. Estimating Resilient Tile Flooring

Resilient Flooring Type	Labor Hours per 100 sq. ft.						Gallons of Mastic per 100 sq. ft.
	4 x 4	6 x 6	9 x 9	6 x 12	12 x 12	9 x 18	
Rubber Tile	5.0	3.3	2.2	2.2	1.8	1.3	0.75
Asphalt Tile		3.3	2.0	2.0	1.3	1.3	0.75
Linotile			7.0	6.4		5.7	1.50
Plastic Tile			2.4				1.35
Cork Tile		6.0	3.5		2.5		1.50

Table 43-B. Tile Waste Allowances	
Size of Area (sq. ft.)	Add for Waste
1 to 50 sq. ft.	14%
50 to 100 sq. ft.	10%
100 to 200 sq. ft.	8%
200 to 300 sq. ft.	7%
300 to 1,000 sq. ft.	5%
Over 1,000 sq. ft.	3%

INSTALLING A VINYL TILE FLOOR

Vinyl tile can be laid directly over wood flooring or over a plywood floor. **Fig. 43-6.** However, flooring in adjacent rooms must be at the same height. The underlayment must make up any difference. In other words, the thickness of the underlayment plus the thickness of the vinyl tile (and adhesive) should equal the thickness of the finish floor in the adjacent room.

Correct layout of the tile is important. After measuring the room, determine how many tiles will fit across its length and width. Then snap chalk lines indicating one of the two basic layouts shown in **Fig. 43-7**. They will govern the rest of the installation. Lay tiles in adhesive as the work progresses. Cut tiles to fit around obstructions. **Fig. 43-8.**

Fig. 43-6. Plywood is frequently used as an underlayment for a vinyl tile floor.

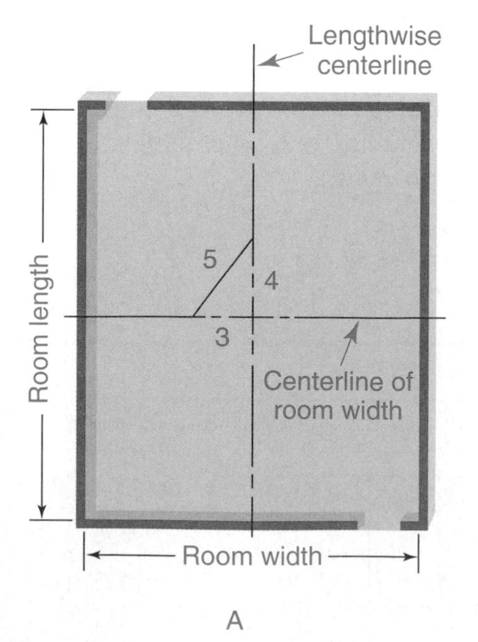

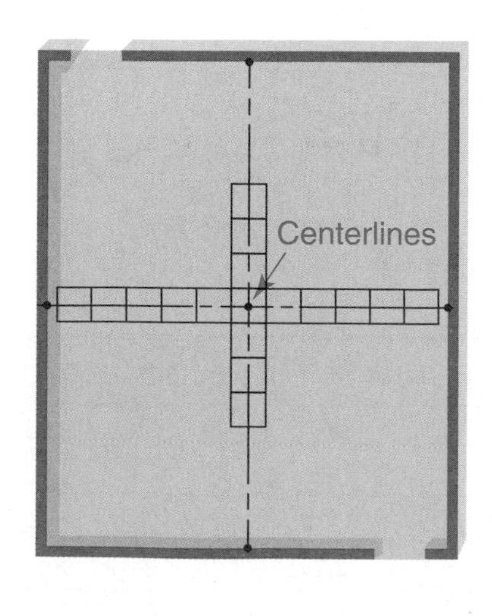

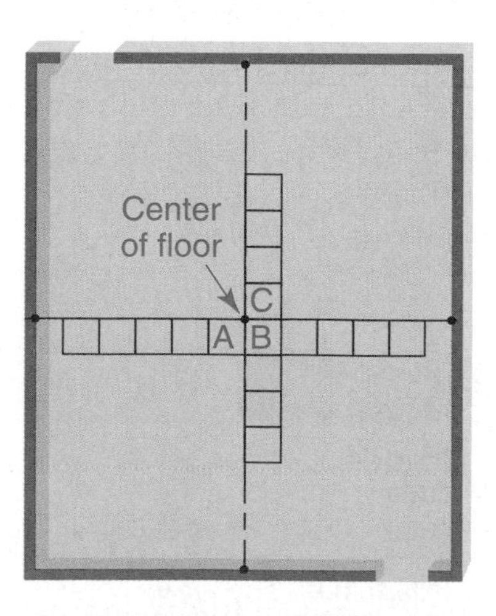

Fig. 43-7. Room layout for vinyl tile. Locate the center of the floor and establish centerlines as shown at *A*. Check the centerlines for square by using the 3-4-5 formula and adjust them as needed. Determine how many tiles will be required across the length and width of the room. If an odd number is required, establish a layout as at *B*. If an even number is required, use *C* as your model.

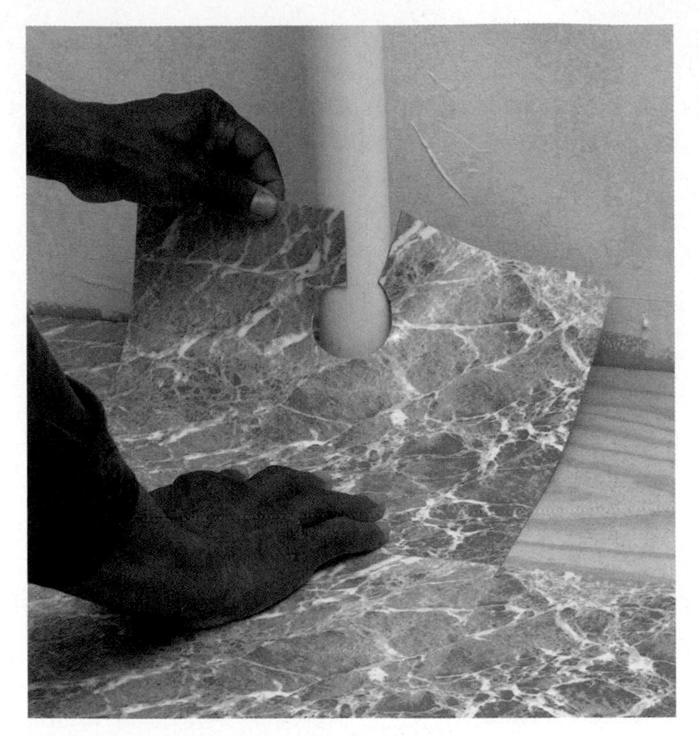

Fig. 43-8. Fitting tile around a pipe.

SECTION 43.1 **Check Your Knowledge**

1. List the characteristics that are common to all types of resilient flooring.
2. Which type of flooring is synthetic, vinyl or linoleum?
3. Which type of adhesive is used to install resilient flooring?
4. When installing sheet vinyl flooring, why are three chalk lines sometimes snapped across the underlayment?

On the Job

Standard 9x9 vinyl tiles are to be used on a rectangular 14′-6″ x 24′-3″ floor. Calculate the area of the floor in square feet. Assuming that 178 9x9 tiles will cover 100 sq. ft., estimate the number of tiles needed. Using Table 43-B, allow the correct percentage for waste and trim.

SECTION 43.2

Ceramic Tile

Ceramic tile is often used where a highly durable, scratch-resistant flooring is desired, such as a kitchen. **Fig. 43-9.** However, it may be used in any room of the house. It is available in a large variety of shapes, sizes, and colors. **Fig. 43-10.**

The earliest known use of ceramic tiles having colored glazes dates to 4,000 B.C. At that time, the Egyptians used tile to decorate important structures. The American tile industry dates to 1647, when production of roofing and paving tile began in the colonies. During the 1700s, small quantities of floor and decorative wall tile were produced, usually in connection with pottery

Fig. 43-9. The ceramic tile in this kitchen is used on floors, countertops, and backsplashes. Note the trim tile along the edges of the countertops.

Fig. 43-10. Ceramic tiles come in a wide variety of patterns, shapes, sizes, and colors.

manufacturing. Ceramic tile was first mass produced in the United States in 1853 in Bennington, Vermont.

This chapter introduces ceramic tile installation in general. In new construction, tile is usually installed by tile contractors or tile setters.

TILE MANUFACTURE

Custom lots of ceramic tile are still made by hand, but most tile is made in highly automated factories. Commonly, it is made from a combination of pure clay or pure gypsum and other ingredients that extend the clay and control shrinkage. After the clay has been refined and mixed with water and these additives, it is shaped into a bisque. A **bisque** is a tile without the glaze. To form a bisque, the clay mixture may be extruded, dust-pressed, cut from a sheet, or formed by hand. Most commercial tile is made by the *dust-press method.* In this method the ingredients are mixed with so little water that only high pressure can bond them together.

The bisque is then dried before being fired in a kiln at temperatures up to 2,200°F [1,204°C]. A glaze (glassy finish) may be applied at this time. The glazed surface of a tile is waterproof after firing.

from Another Angle

The amount of ceramic tile found in a house varies from region to region. In cold climates it is found primarily in bathrooms and kitchens. In hot climates it can often be found throughout the house. Houses in hot climates are often built on a concrete slab foundation. This type of foundation is an excellent base for the installation of ceramic tile. Also, tile is not affected by humid conditions.

TILE CLASSIFICATION

Tile can be classified according to permeability, where is it placed, how it is used, and other characteristics.

Permeability

The basic types of tile are classified by their permeability after firing. *Permeability* is the ability of a substance to allow water to pass through. The temperature and firing time determine permeability. Highly permeable tiles are the least waterproof because they absorb the most water. Slightly permeable tiles absorb less water. From most permeable to least permeable, the four types of tile are *nonvitreous, semi-vitreous, vitreous,* and *impervious.* (*Vitreous* means glasslike.)

Permeability is important because it determines the best use of the tile. Tiles that will be exposed to water in a bathroom, for example, should be less permeable. To test for permeability, turn a tile over and put a drop of water on the unglazed (back) portion. If the drop is absorbed immediately, the tile would be rated toward the nonvitreous side of the scale. If the drop remains on top of the tile, the tile would be rated toward the impervious side of the scale.

Placement

Tile is often categorized by where it is used, either on walls or floors. Wall tile is generally a nonvitreous tile with a relatively soft glaze. The softness of the glaze makes the tile unsuitable for foot traffic. It is usually about ¼″ thick and is commonly made in sizes 4″ or 6″ square.

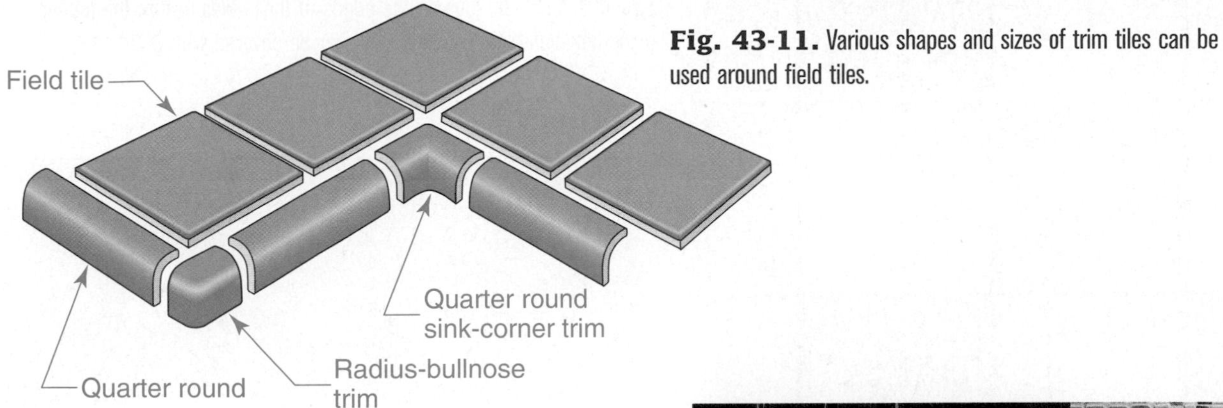

Fig. 43-11. Various shapes and sizes of trim tiles can be used around field tiles.

Fig. 43-12. Mosaic tile used on a countertop and backsplash.

Floor tile can be any kind of tile (from nonvitreous to impermeable, glazed or unglazed) that is strong enough to hold up in use on the floor. A floor tile can, of course, be used on walls. However, a wall tile should not be used for flooring.

Use

Another way to categorize tile is by use either in the field or as trim. Trim tile is specially shaped to form a border. The shape is often bullnosed. It may also be radiused to form more of a curve or ridged to form a pattern. **Fig. 43-11.** Trim tile is glazed on one or more edges.

Field tile is the tile contained within the borders formed by trim tile. Field tile is flat rather than shaped. It is glazed on the top surface only.

Other Characteristics

The following types of tile are commonly used in residential construction.

- *Paver tiles* may be glazed or unglazed. They are at least ½″ thick and intended for use on floors. Machine-made pavers may be up to ⅝″ thick and are usually semi-vitreous or vitreous. They range in size from 4″ by 6″ to 12″ square. Handmade pavers are generally nonvitreous and have a slightly uneven surface. They range in size from 4″ square to 24″ square and in thickness from ½″ to 2″. Handmade, unglazed pavers are commonly known as *Mexican tiles* or *Mediterranean tiles.*
- *Quarry tile* is generally semi-vitreous or vitreous clay tile that is unglazed. The tiles range in thickness from ½″ to ¾″. Quarry tile is excellent for use on floors because of its density.
- *Mosaic tile* is considered to be any tile that is 2″ square or smaller. It is usually vitreous and ranges in thickness from ³⁄₃₂″ to ¼″. **Fig. 43-12.**
- *Lugged tile* is any tile that has spacing lugs built into its sides. When the tiles are placed edge-to-edge, the lugs automatically determine the proper spacing. **Fig. 43-13.**

SUBSTRATES

Tile must be installed over a suitable substrate. The substrate must be stiff enough to prevent too much flexing, which could crack tiles or joints.

In some cases tile can be adhered directly to plywood. However, this is generally not recommended, particularly on floors. Tile can also be adhered directly to a drywall surface. In areas

Fig. 43-13. The lugs on the edges of these tiles ensure the proper spacing between tiles. The lugs will later be covered with grout.

that might become wet, such as bathroom walls, moisture-resistant drywall should be used (see Chapter 40, "Walls and Ceilings").

Cement-based sheets called **backerboard**, or *cement board*, provide an excellent base for tile, particularly on floors and in wet installations such as shower stalls. **Fig. 43-14.** Backerboard can be nailed or screwed to a subfloor or to a plywood countertop. It comes in sheets ½″ or ⅝″ thick. The sheets are 32″, 36″, or 48″ wide and 4′, 5′, 6′, or 8′ long. They are applied to a wood subfloor with 1½″ hot-dipped roofing nails or 1¼″ corrosion-resistant screws. These screws, sometimes called *cementboard screws*, have small fins on the underside of the head that help to countersink it.

Fig. 43-14. Backerboard on a subfloor should be embedded in dry-set mortar and screwed into place.

INSTALLATION MATERIALS

Adhesives, grout, and waterproofing membranes are needed for proper installation of ceramic tile.

Adhesives

Ceramic tile is adhered to the substrate with dry-set mortar or mastic. **Fig. 43-15.** Either adhesive is applied with a trowel, then "combed out" evenly with a notched trowel. This distributes the adhesive to an even thickness. The even thickness helps to support the tile, preventing breakage caused by point loads.

Fig. 43-15. Adhesive is spread on a surface and then combed out to produce uniform coverage.

Dry-set mortar, also called *thin-set mortar*, is a very effective adhesive. It is a mixture of Portland cement, sand, and additives that strengthen the bond. Dry-set mortar may be mixed with water, with a latex- or acrylic-modified liquid, or with epoxy resins. **Table 43-C.**

Mastic is an organic adhesive. It comes premixed in cans and is often preferred by non-professionals because of its ease of use.

Grout

After tiles have been attached to a substrate with adhesive, the spaces between the tiles must be filled with grout. **Fig. 43-16. Grout** is a thin mortar used for filling spaces. It can be mixed with water, latex- or acrylic-modified liquids, or epoxy resin. It prevents moisture and dirt from getting between the tiles. Grout comes in a wide array of colors.

Tile grout comes in two forms: plain and sanded. Plain grout is mixed with additives to make it smooth and creamy. It is generally used when the spaces between tiles are less than 1⁄16″ wide. Sanded grout is simply plain grout to which sand has been added. This improves its strength. Sanded grout is used for joints wider than 1⁄16″.

Table 43-C. Adhesives for Ceramic Tile

Adhesive	Characteristics
Mastic	Good grip strength (useful for setting wall tiles) Lacks the strength or flexibility of mortar Not heat resistant Least expensive and easiest to use adhesive Suitable for use on drywall No mixing required
Dry-set mortar mixed with water	Good bond strength Good compressive strength Not flexible Heat resistant Inexpensive Easy to use
Dry-set mortar mixed with latex- or acrylic-modified liquid	Excellent bond strength Excellent compressive strength Somewhat flexible Heat resistant Can be applied to most surfaces except steel Resistant to frost damage
Dry-set mortar mixed with epoxy resin	Very high bond strength Somewhat flexible Heat resistant Expensive Can be applied to almost any surface, including plastic laminate and steel Can be hard to work with Very high resistance to impact

Fig. 43-16. Grout is spread over the entire tiled surface with a grouting trowel. Once it has been packed into the joints, most of the excess grout can be removed using the trowel. Any grout that remains on the tile can be removed with a sponge.

SAFETY FIRST

Guard against Dust and Vapors

Dry-set mortars and grout are very fine powders that must be mixed with a liquid. Wear a suitable dust mask when mixing these materials. Some mastics give off fumes that may be harmful. Check instructions on the can for any health warnings. Take care to work in a well-ventilated area. Be aware that a standard dust mask offers no protection against vapors.

Waterproofing Membranes

Properly installed, ceramic tile creates a durable and water-resistant surface. However, where the installation will be exposed to large amounts of water, such as around a bathtub, water may penetrate. To prevent this, a *waterproofing membrane* must be placed beneath the substrate. Such a membrane is any flexible, waterproof sheet material. Tarpaper is commonly used. It is nailed or stapled in place. Its edges may be sealed with asphalt adhesive.

Other products, such as chlorinated polyethylene (CPE) may be used where more durability is required. CPE is a flexible material 30 mils thick. It comes in large rolls and is attached directly to the substrate with dry-set mortar. A roller is used to ensure a proper bond.

TOOLS FOR CUTTING AND SETTING TILE

Cutting and setting tile does not require a large number of expensive tools. Some of the basic tools are shown in **Fig. 43-17**. Not all of them are required for every installation.

- *Portable snap cutter.* This is used to cut tiles in a straight line. The tile is placed on the bed of the tool (beneath the two rails) and against the guide. The long handle of the tool is lifted and pulled toward the user. This forces a small scoring wheel against the tile and draws it across the tile's surface. The tile may then be snapped apart at the scored line.
- *Knee pads.* These pads help to protect the tile setter's knees from injury during long hours of setting floor tiles.
- *Trowels.* A tile setter uses a variety of flat and notched trowels with steel blades. Trowels with notched edges are used to spread adhesive. The size of the notch gauges the depth of the adhesive.

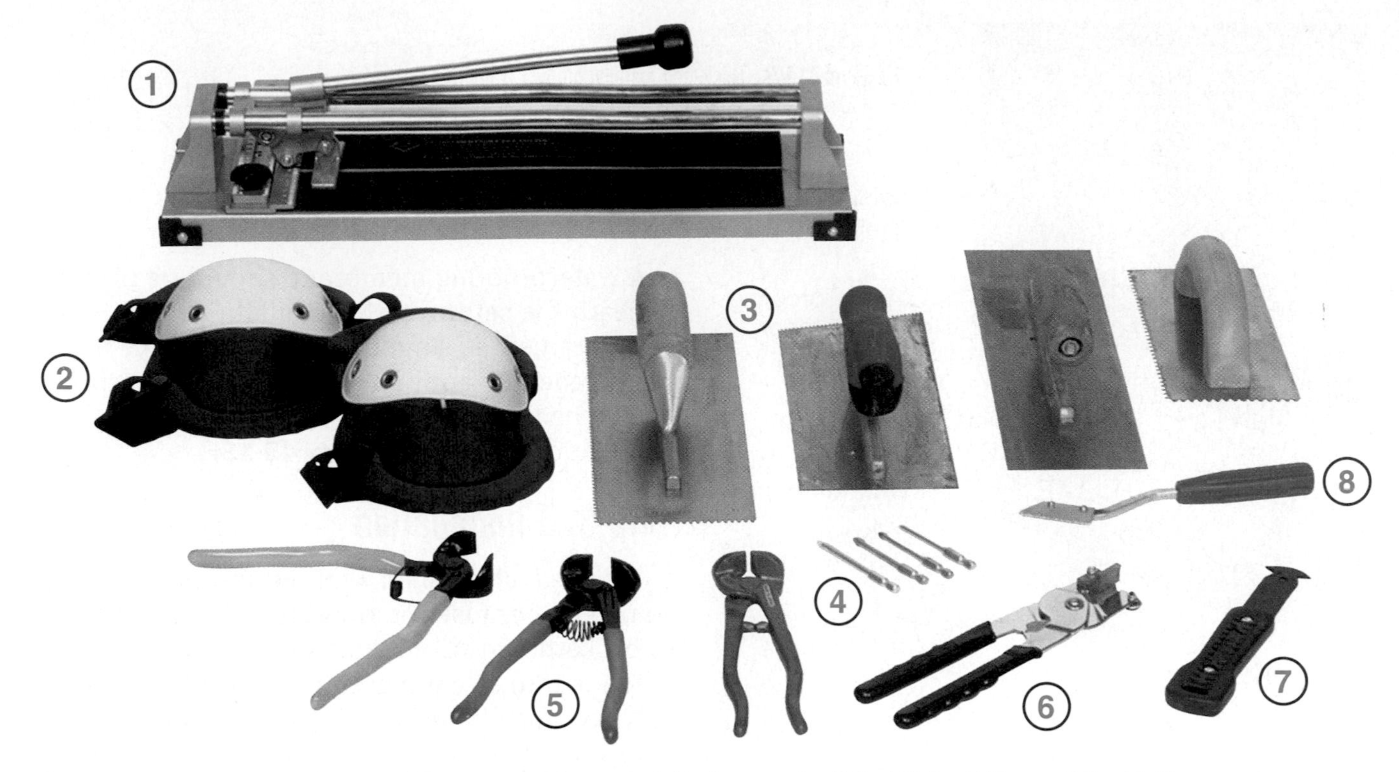

Fig. 43-17. Tools used in tilesetting. *1.* Snap cutter. *2.* Kneepads. *3.* Notched trowels. *4.* Tile drill bits. *5.* Nippers. *6.* Hand-held snap cutter. *7.* Laminate cutter. *8.* Grout saw.

- *Tile drill bits.* These carbide-tipped drill bits are used for cutting holes near the center of a ceramic tile. This is sometimes needed when water supply pipes must pass through. Carbide-tipped hole saws may also be used.
- *Nippers and nibblers.* These tools look something like pliers or small nail pullers, but they have straight, hardened edges. They are used to cut shapes in tile by "nibbling" away at the edges.
- *Hand-held snap cutter.* This tool cuts tiles in a straight line. It is easier to carry than the portable snap cutter. It is used where accuracy of the cut is less important.
- *Scoring tool.* This hand tool has a carbide tooth mounted on a steel blank. It is used to score through the fiberglass reinforcement of cement board. This weakens the cement board so that it can be snapped in two.
- *Grout saw.* This small tool has teeth or a grinding edge and is used for cleaning cured grout from between tiles. It is primarily used in remodeling and repair work.

Other tools used by tile setters include levels, straightedges, grouting trowels, and wet saws. A grouting trowel has a cushioned working surface that allows the tile setter to spread grout without damaging the tile surface. Fig. 43-16. A wet saw is often used to cut tile, particularly when large quantities must be cut accurately. The tool includes a circular diamond-grit blade, a water pump, and a moisture-proof motor. The pump sprays a continuous stream of water on the blade during the cut. This lubricates and cools the blade. It also prevents the diamond abrasive from becoming clogged with clay particles. The edge of a tile cut in this way is very smooth.

SAFETY FIRST

Wet Saw Precautions

Water and electricity are a dangerous combination. A wet saw's motor is protected from water, but extension cords and nearby power tools may not be. Keep other electrical tools away from the area in which the wet saw is being used. Make sure all power tools, including the wet saw, are plugged into GFCI-protected circuits.

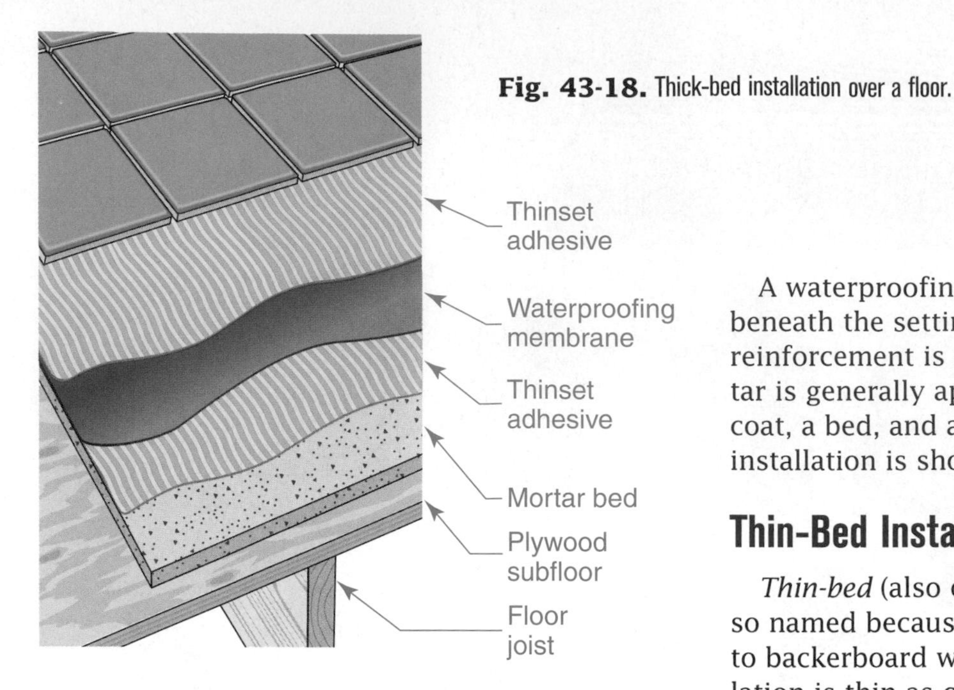

Fig. 43-18. Thick-bed installation over a floor.

INSTALLING CERAMIC TILE

There are many methods for installing tile. Each job requires a different combination of tile, adhesive, grout, and setting methods. The proper methods and materials depend on several factors, including the stiffness of the floor system.

Thick-Bed Installation

Using the *thick-bed method*, tiles are applied over a mortar setting bed that is ¾″ to 1¾″ thick. After the setting bed has cured, tiles are applied to it with dry-set adhesive. This allows for accurate slopes and planes in the finished work. The result is structurally strong and is not affected by prolonged contact with water. This method can be used to level uneven substrates.

A waterproofing membrane should be placed beneath the setting bed. Metal lath or wire mesh reinforcement is sometimes included. The mortar is generally applied in three layers: a scratch coat, a bed, and a bond coat. A typical thick-bed installation is shown in **Fig. 43-18**.

Thin-Bed Installation

Thin-bed (also called *thin-set*) *installations* are so named because the tiles are adhered directly to backerboard with adhesive. The overall installation is thin as compared to a thick bed. The adhesive may be mastic or dry-set mortar. Thin beds are less costly than thick beds, relatively light, and easier and quicker to install. One limitation of the thin-set method, however, is that the substrate must be very flat and very well prepared. Surfaces cannot be easily sloped.

SECTION 43.2 Check Your Knowledge

1. What is a bisque?
2. List four types of tile based on water permeability.
3. What is mosaic tile?
4. What is sanded grout used for and why?

On the Job

Using the resources of your local library or the Internet, research the manufacture and use of ceramic tile in ancient times. What were the principal uses? Do those uses differ at all from the main uses for ceramic tile today? Present your research in a short essay.

Chapter 43

Review

Section Summaries

43.1 Resilient flooring includes a broad group of products that are flexible and thin. They are attached to a smooth, solid underlayment using mastic. The most common types are made of vinyl and include sheet vinyl and vinyl tile.

43.2 Ceramic tile can be classified by its water permeability, where it is placed, and how it is used. It can be applied to various substrates, including drywall, but cement backerboard has many advantages. Tile can be attached with mastic or various types of dry-set mortar. After the tile is attached, the spaces are filled with grout.

Review Questions

1. What is the purpose of underlayment for resilient flooring?
2. How is the quantity of sheet vinyl flooring determined?
3. Why is ceramic tile often found in houses located in hot climates?
4. How is ceramic wall tile different from ceramic floor tile?
5. Describe a lugged tile and tell why it is made that way.
6. One type of tile substrate is made with cement. What is it called and how thick is it?
7. What is a nibbler used for?
8. What is grout and why is it used?
9. What safety precautions should be taken when working with a wet saw?
10. Name the three layers of mortar in a thick-bed tile installation.

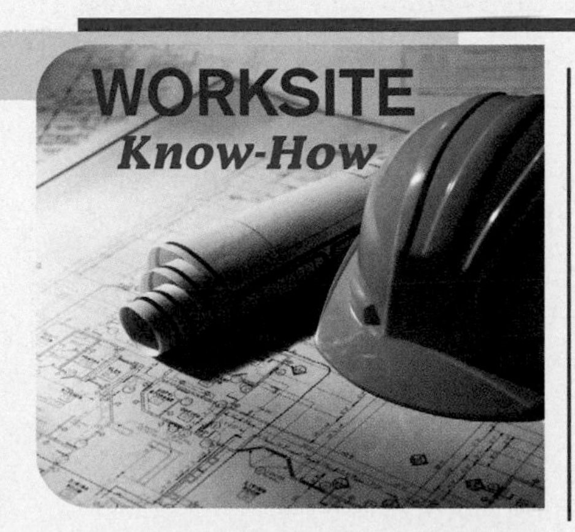

Finish Flooring A typical house contains several types of finish flooring. The thicknesses may vary considerably. However, the surfaces should all be at the same level. This requires advance planning by the general contractor and the flooring subcontractors. Each trade should be consulted about the installation requirements for a particular product.

Other trades should not create conditions that cause unnecessary work for the flooring contractors. This includes leaving dried globs of joint compound, paint, or adhesives on the subfloor.

Chapter 44 Chimneys and Fireplaces

Objectives

After reading this chapter, you'll be able to:

- **Identify the main parts of a chimney.**
- **Identify the main parts of a fireplace.**
- **Explain how chimneys and fireplaces are installed to limit fire hazards.**

Terms

corbel
draft
flue
lintel
makeup air
refractory cement

In addition to their practical uses, fireplaces and chimneys have a major effect on the look of a house. Both can be designed to complement or emphasize any architectural style.

Fireplaces may be hand-built from solid masonry, or they may be prefabricated from metal and masonry. Likewise, chimneys may be built of masonry or other fireproof materials. Whatever the construction material, it is essential for safety to follow all local building codes when installing chimneys and fireplaces. This reduces fire hazards. It also ensures that dangerous combustion gases are not released into the house.

Chimneys

A chimney is required for any fuel-burning appliance, such as a fireplace, wood stove, or furnace. The purpose of a chimney is to produce sufficient draft. **Draft** is the upward movement of air within the chimney. Draft draws air into the appliance. This aids in combustion (burning) and expels smoke and harmful gases. The greater the difference in temperature between chimney gases and the outside air, the stronger the draft. An interior chimney will usually have a better draft than an exterior chimney of the same height because it is better able to retain heat.

Chimneys are generally constructed of brick or other masonry units supported by a concrete foundation. However, lightweight metal chimneys can be used when approved by local building codes. They usually do not require a foundation.

DESIGN AND PLANNING

The design of a chimney is very important for its safety and effectiveness. It may be well constructed, but if it is not designed properly it will not work well. The following information is meant only as a general guide to the subject. Always consult local building codes.

Flue Size

The **flue** is the passage inside the chimney through which the air, gases, and smoke rise. Its dimensions, height, shape, and interior smoothness determine how effective the chimney is in creating enough draft. When a fuel-burning unit is connected to a chimney, consult the unit's specifications to establish the flue size.

Height

The height of a chimney above the roofline is usually based on its location in relation to the ridge. **Fig. 44-1.** On a pitched roof, the top of the flue lining should be at least 2′ above any portion of the roof that is within 10′ (measured horizontally) of the chimney. One reason for this is to ensure that burning embers leaving the chimney will cool before they can ignite roofing materials. Another reason is to encourage proper draft. A chimney shielded from the wind by a nearby ridge may not draw well.

In addition, codes may require that the top of the chimney be above any operable window within 20′. This helps to prevent smoke from being drawn into the house when the window is open.

Earthquake Protection

Where earthquake activity is a serious risk, building codes require masonry chimneys to be reinforced vertically and horizontally. The exact size and type of reinforcement depend on the size of the chimney. However, chimneys up to 40″ wide must contain at least four continuous lengths of No. 4 reinforcing bar. Horizontal reinforcements must be located no farther apart than every 18″ along the height of the chimney.

In addition, a masonry chimney located outside the house walls must be anchored to the framing. This must be done with metal straps at each floor, ceiling, and roofline that is more than 6′ above grade.

Clearances

Any portion of a chimney located within the house must have a 2″ clearance between its walls and the wood framing. **Fig. 44-2.**

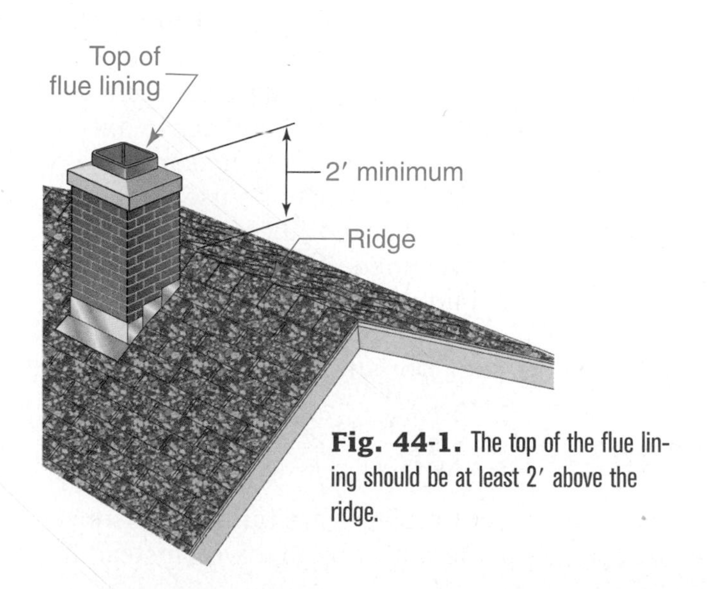

Fig. 44-1. The top of the flue lining should be at least 2′ above the ridge.

Fig. 44-2. Ceiling joists and other framing must not touch the chimney walls.

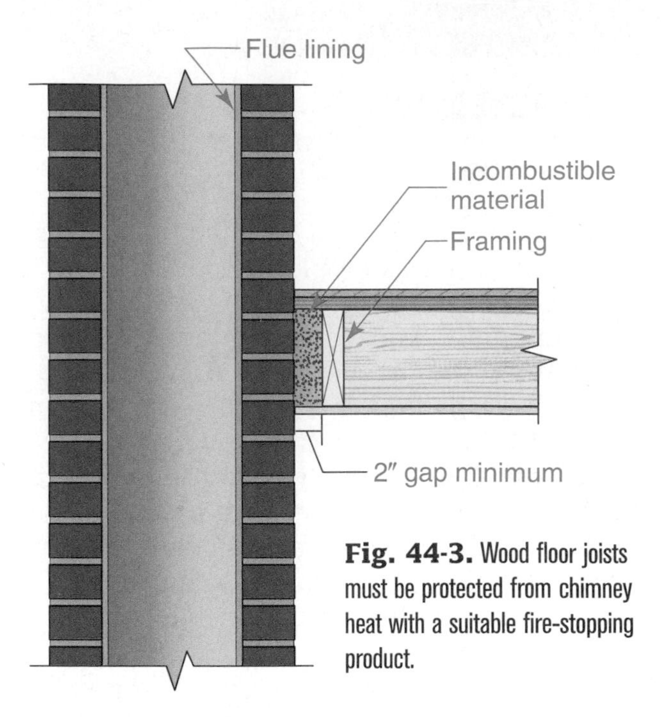

Fig. 44-3. Wood floor joists must be protected from chimney heat with a suitable fire-stopping product.

Subflooring and finish flooring can be laid within ¾″ of the masonry. If the chimney is located entirely outside the exterior walls, the gap must be at least 1″. Exterior wood sheathing, siding, and trim can touch the side walls of the chimney, but only where they will be at least 12″ from the nearest flue liner.

The space between wall and floor framing must be filled with a code-approved fire-stopping material. **Fig. 44-3.** This prevents shavings or other flammable material from building up in these areas. It also keeps combustible materials away from the masonry. Several types of materials may be used, including mineral wool. Unbacked fiberglass insulation is not recommended. Brickwork or standard mortar should not be used because they conduct heat. Fire-stopping materials should be added before the floor sheathing is installed.

CONSTRUCTION

Chimneys and fireplaces are built by masons. However, carpenters may be involved instead if the chimney is a lightweight metal unit supported by wood framing.

The main parts of a chimney include the foundation, flue liners, walls, and cleanout opening.

Foundation

The chimney is usually the heaviest part of a building. It must rest on a foundation and footings to prevent uneven settling and to avoid exceeding the load-bearing capacity of the soil. The foundation is usually built at the same time as the house foundation walls. It must extend at least 6″ beyond the chimney on all sides and be at least 12″ thick. **Fig. 44-4.** Steel reinforcement is added as required by local codes.

Flue Liners

Building code now requires that all chimneys be lined during installation. A separate flue liner is needed for each fireplace, furnace, and boiler. A *flue liner* is a fire-clay or stainless-steel pipe assembled from individual sections that sit within the chimney brickwork. Without a liner, mortar and bricks directly exposed to heat and flue gases can crack. This creates a fire hazard.

Rectangular fire-clay flue liners or round glazed (vitrified) tile can normally be used in all chimneys. Glazed tile or a stainless steel liner is usually required for gas-burning equipment. Local codes outline specific requirements.

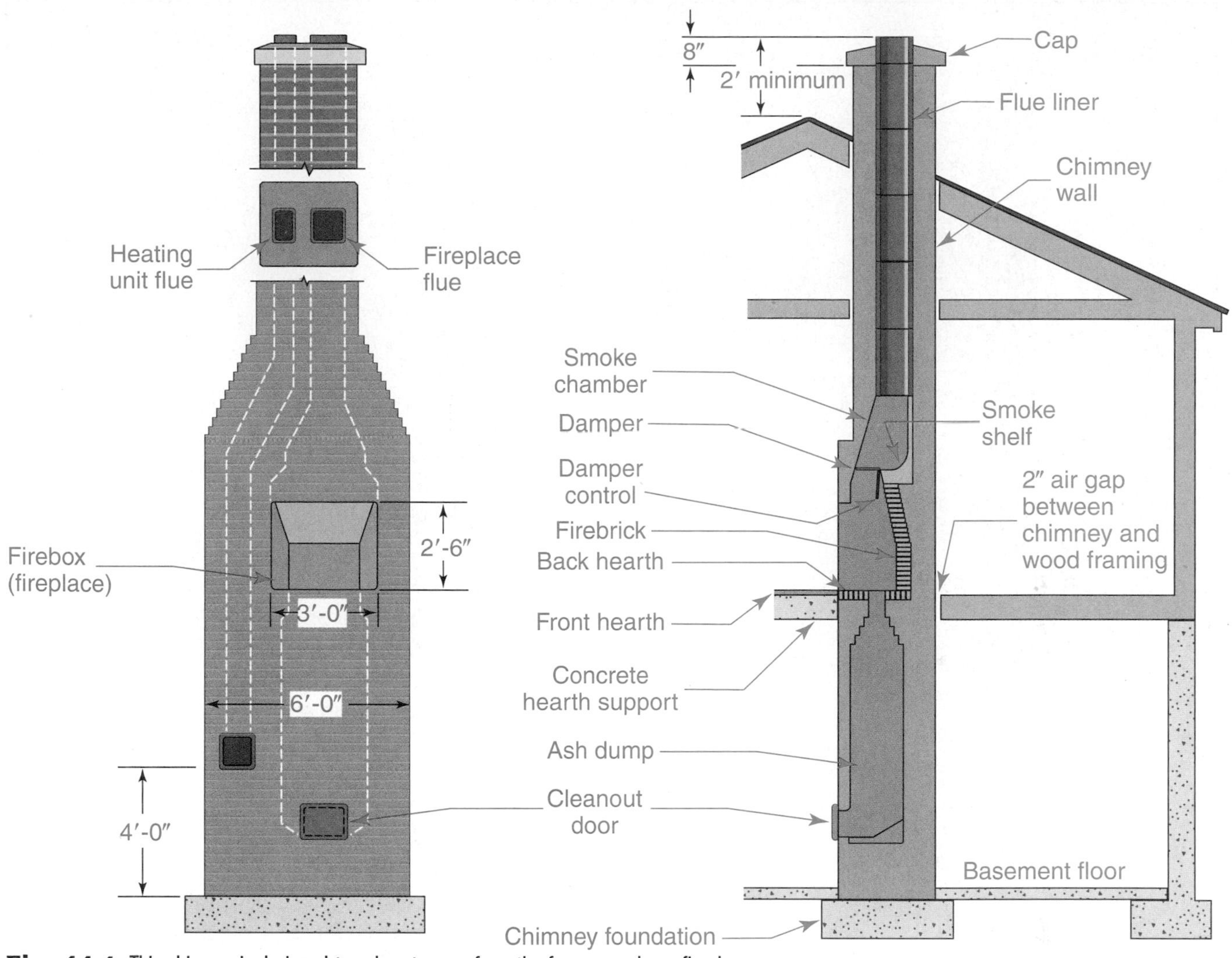

Fig. 44-4. This chimney is designed to exhaust gases from the furnace and one fireplace.

Each length of fire-clay or glazed-tile liner should be set in refractory cement with the joint struck smooth on the inside. (**Refractory cement** is resistant to high temperatures.) The liner and brick are installed together as the chimney is built. In masonry chimneys with walls less than 8″ thick, there should be an air space between the liner and the chimney walls. This space should not be blocked by mortar.

The flue liner above a fireplace starts at the top of the throat and extends to the top of the chimney. If a chimney contains three or more lined flues, each group of two must be separated from the others by a layer of brick called a *wythe* (pronounced "with"). **Fig. 44-5.** Joints in the liners of two flues grouped together without a wythe between them should be staggered at least 7″.

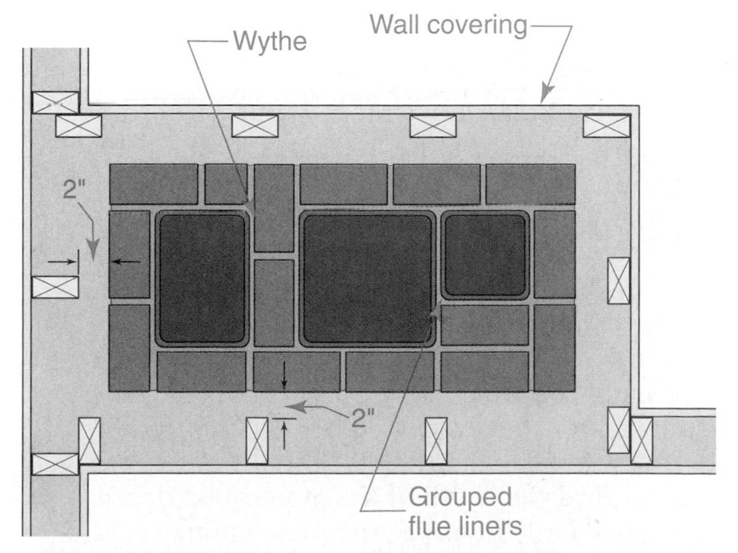

Fig. 44-5. A three-flue chimney. The joints of successive courses of brick should be staggered. This strengthens the chimney. Wood framing should be at least 2″ from the masonry.

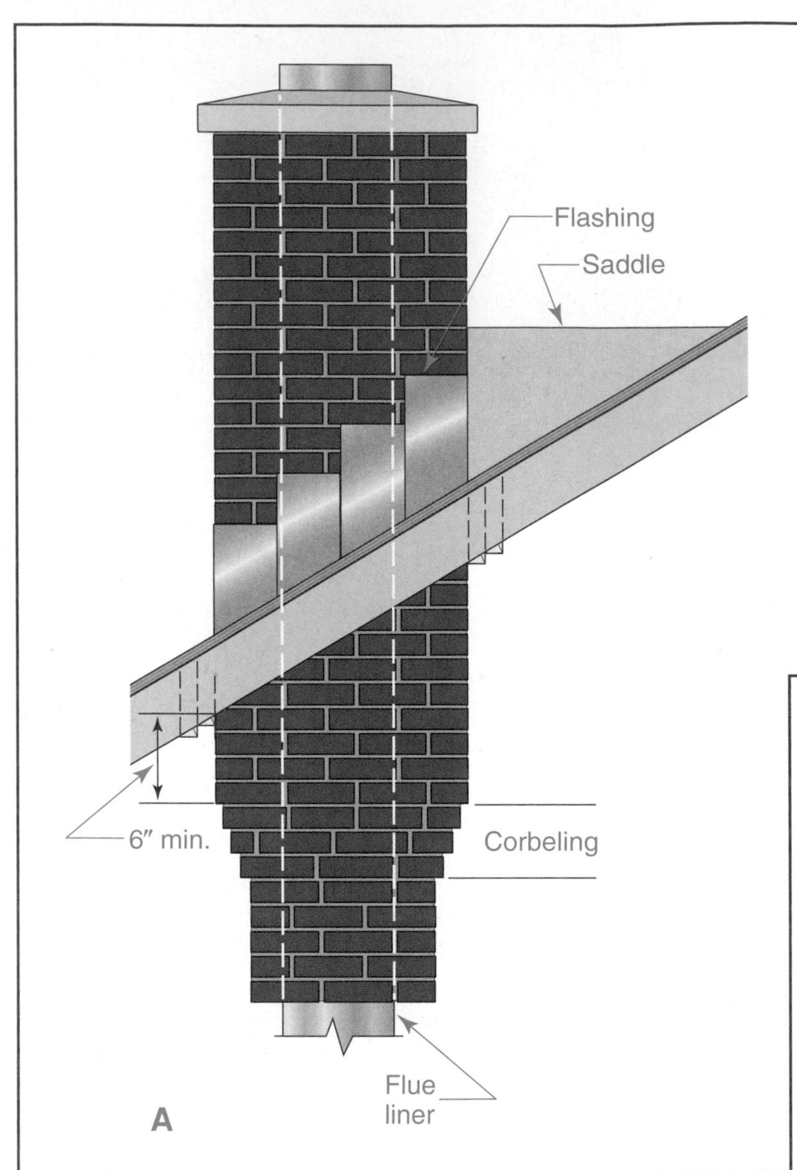

Fig. 44-6. *A.* Corbeling (offsetting the bricks) to provide a larger chimney above the roof line. *B.* Offsetting a chimney. For structural safety, the centerline of the upper flue should not fall beyond the center of the lower chimney wall.

Chimney Walls

Walls of masonry chimneys must have a nominal thickness of at least 4″. This is about the width of one brick. Greater thickness may be required if the chimney is unusually tall or located in an earthquake zone.

To strengthen the exposed portion of an interior chimney, the bricks are sometimes corbeled in the portion around the roofline. **Fig. 44-6.** A **corbel** is a course of brick offset to extend past the course below it. A corbel must not project more than one-half the height of the brick or one-third the width of the mortar bed depth, whichever is less. The top of a chimney is also sometimes corbeled, though this is done purely for decoration. Corbeling can be used to alter the position of a chimney, as when avoiding framing that cannot be relocated. Local codes may specify other requirements.

The chimney wall and its flue liner must not change dimension within 6″ above or below where the chimney passes through a floor, ceiling, or roof assembly. This reduces the risk of leaving gaps in the masonry that might allow sparks to reach the framing.

Joints. Brickwork around chimney flues and fireplaces should be laid with cement mortar. It is more resistant to the action of heat and flue gases than lime mortar. All bricks and blocks require full, push-filled mortar joints having no gaps anywhere. A *push-filled joint* is one created by pushing the brick into a thick bed of mortar and then striking off the excess that squeezes out.

Cleanout Opening

Soot and ash that build up in a chimney can be removed through a small cleanout. **Fig. 44-7.** A cleanout is required within 6″ of the base of each flue. A cleanout should serve only one flue. If two or more flues are connected to the same cleanout, air drawn from one to the other will

Fig. 44-7. Installing a cleanout door.

affect the draft in all the flues. The cast-iron door on the cleanout should fit snugly and be kept tightly closed to keep air out.

ROOF DETAILS

Care must be taken where the chimney meets the roofing system. The area must resist heat from the chimney, but it must also resist water leakage. Wood and masonry expand and contract at different rates, so construction must allow for this movement.

At the Roof

Where the chimney passes through the roof, a 2″ clearance between the wood framing and the masonry is required for fire protection. This clearance also permits expansion due to temperature changes, settling, and slight movement of the chimney during heavy winds.

Chimneys must be flashed and counterflashed to make the junction with the roof watertight.

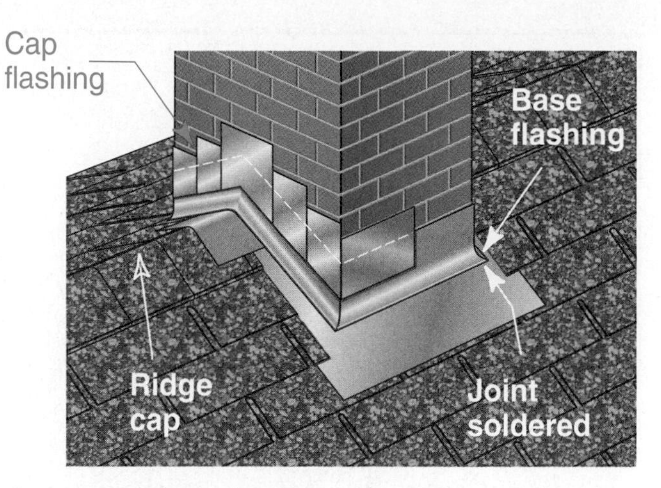

Fig. 44-8. A chimney located on a ridge calls for cap flashing that fits over base flashing.

Fig. 44-8. Corrosion-resistant metal, such as copper, galvanized steel, or lead-coated copper, should be used for flashing. (For more on chimney flashing, see Chapter 30, "Roof Coverings.")

When a chimney rises through a sloped roof, a *chimney saddle* (sometimes called a *chimney cricket*) may be required. **Fig. 44-9.** A saddle diverts water around the chimney. Building code requires a saddle when the chimney dimension parallel to the ridge line is greater than 30″ and does not intersect the ridge. The required saddle dimensions are shown in **Table 44-A.** For installation information, see Chapter 24, "Roof Assembly and Sheathing."

Above the Roof

A mortar or precast concrete *cap* should be placed over the top course of brick to prevent moisture from seeping between the brick and flue liner. **Fig. 44-10.** The cap should be sloped away from the flues on all sides to drain water away. The flue liner should extend at least 4" above the top course of brick. Any gaps between the flue liner and the cap should be sealed with mortar.

A metal or stone hood over the flue openings helps to keep rain out of the chimney. **Fig. 44-11.** It also prevents wind downdrafts from causing a fireplace to smoke. *Spark arresters* may be required around the hood when chimneys are on or near flammable roofs, or in areas where fire hazards are high. Spark arresters do not eliminate sparks, but they greatly reduce the hazard. A spark arrester also prevents birds and small animals from getting into the chimney.

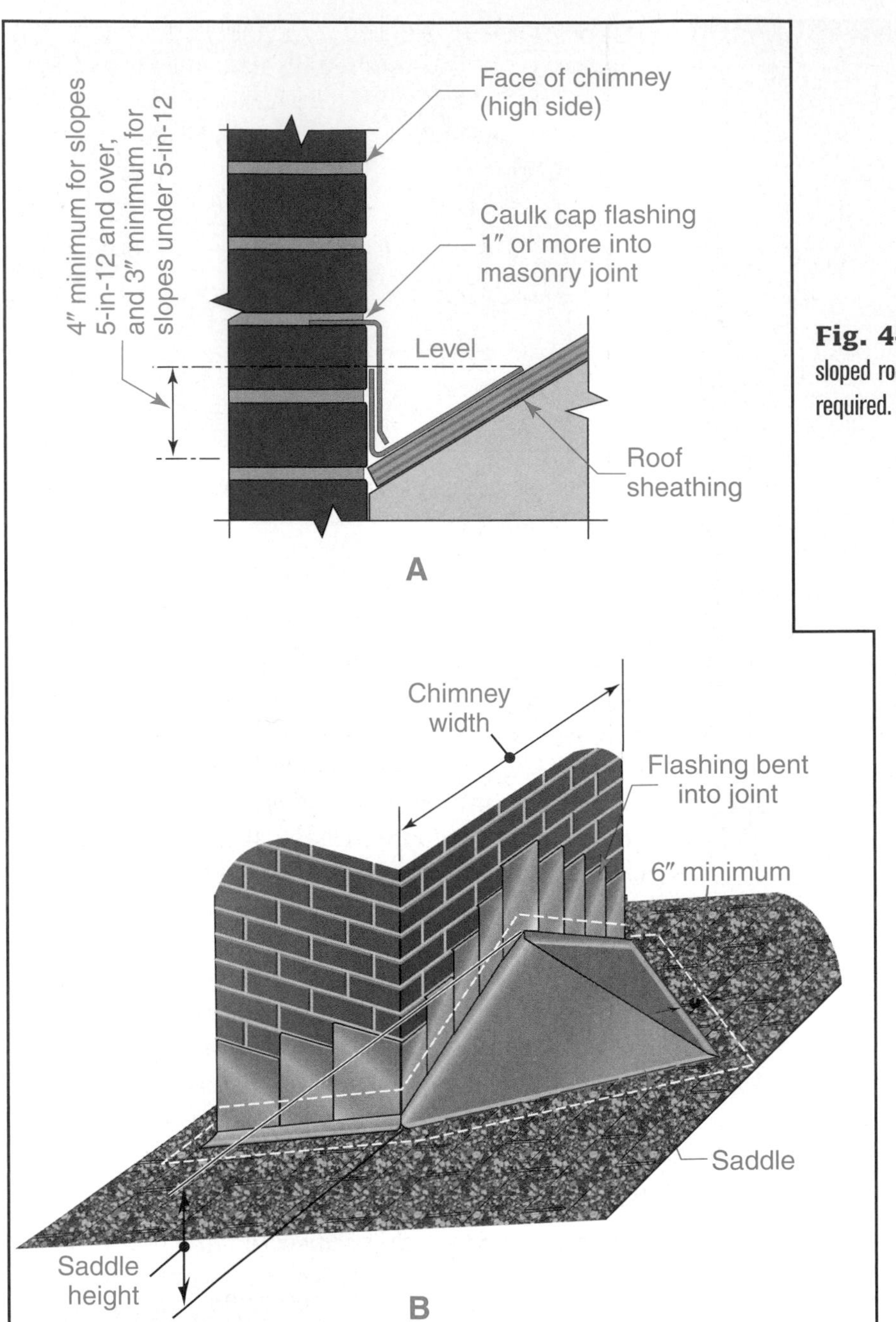

Fig. 44-9. Flashing a chimney that rises through a sloped roof. *A.* A narrow chimney where no saddle is required. *B.* A wide chimney with a saddle.

Table 44-A. Saddle Dimensions

If Roof Slope Is:	Height of Saddle Equals:
12-in-12	½ of chimney width
8-in-12	⅓ of chimney width
6-in-12	¼ of chimney width
4-in-12	⅙ of chimney width
3-in-12	⅛ of chimney width

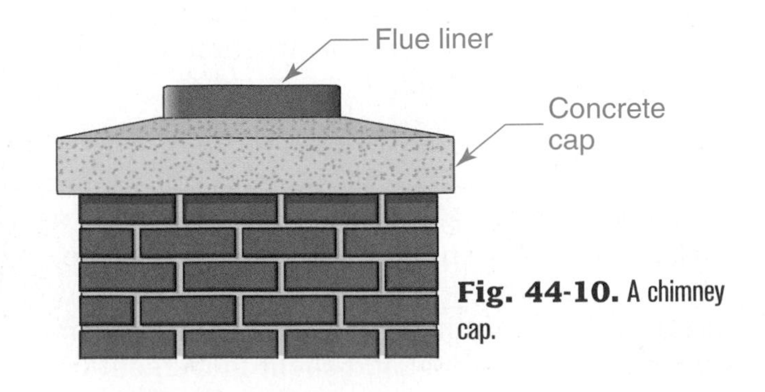

Fig. 44-10. A chimney cap.

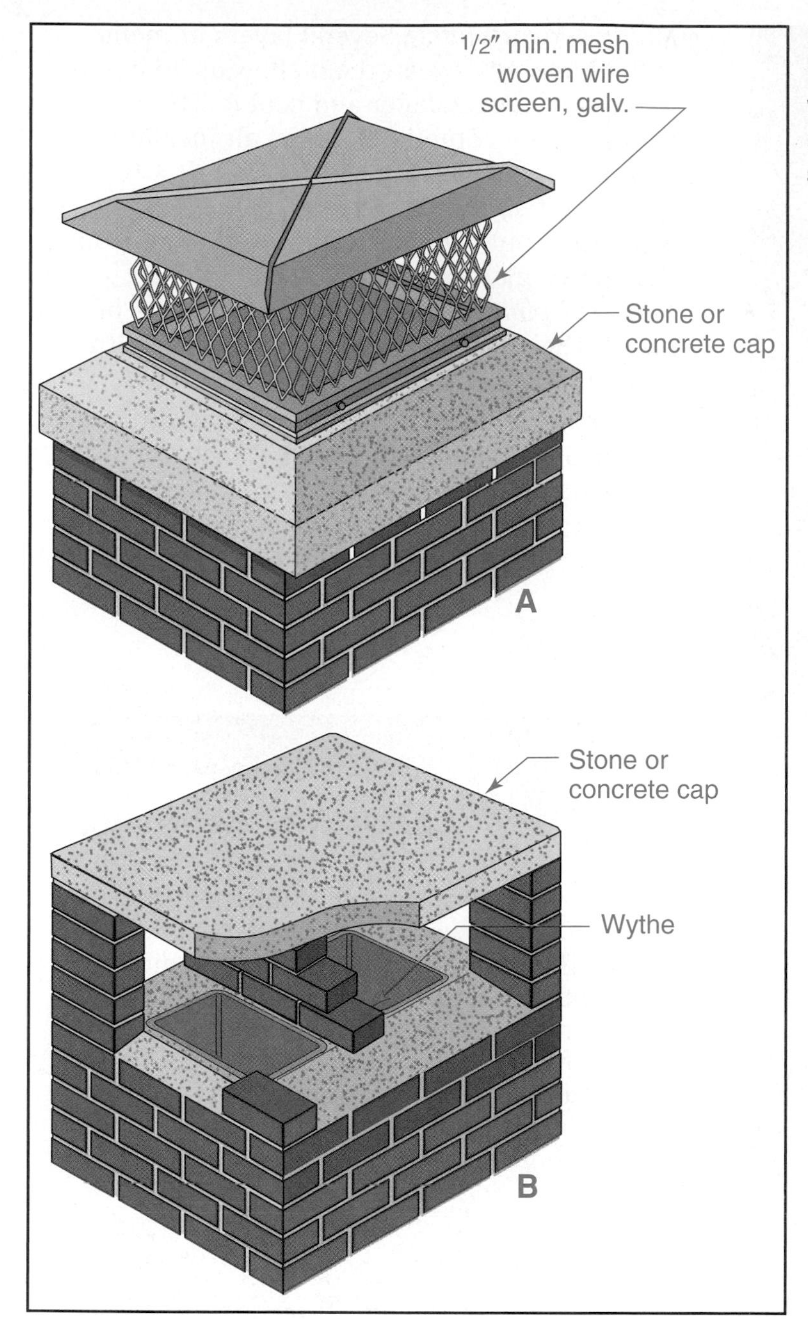

Fig. 44-11. A chimney is often topped with a metal or stone hood to prevent downdrafts and keep water out. *A.* A metal hood with spark-arrester screening also keeps small animals out of the chimney. *B.* A stone hood is often found on houses with traditional styling.

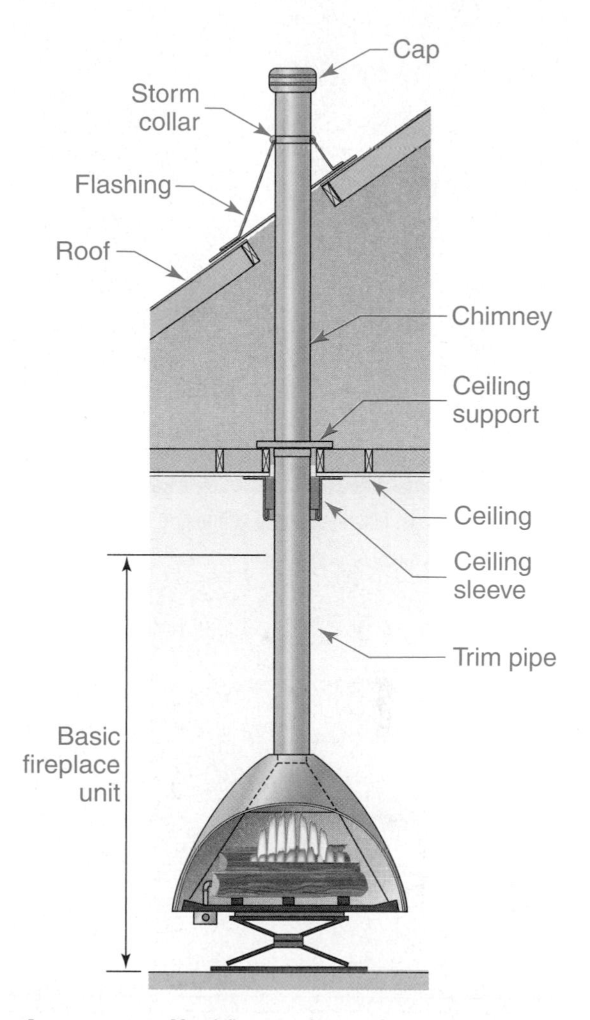

Fig. 44-12. Metal flues are frequently used for factory-built fireplaces. Special care must be taken where the flue passes through floor, ceiling, and roof framing.

SAFETY FIRST

Scaffolding Safety

When completing the top of a chimney, work from scaffolding whenever possible. This is safer than trying to work standing on the roof itself. Scaffolding offers a flat, stable surface from which tools and materials will not slide. It is also a more comfortable surface from which to work.

PREFABRICATED CHIMNEYS

Lightweight metal chimneys require no masonry protection and no footing. They are often referred to as *prefabricated chimney systems.* These systems are often used with fireplaces that are also prefabricated (see Section 44.2). **Fig. 44-12.** The metal chimney may consist of one or more types of piping:

Fig. 44-13. An insulated metal chimney.

Fig. 44-14. Prefabricated metal chimneys are often contained within wood-framed chimney surrounds. The surround may be covered with siding to match the house.

- *Multiple-layer piping.* Several layers of metal with airspace between them allow air to circulate between each layer and cool it. These chimneys are sometimes called air-insulated or triple-wall flues. **Fig. 44-13.**
- *Single-wall piping.* This piping is the least expensive, but it must be kept well away from flammable materials.
- *Insulated piping.* This pipe has two layers of metal. The space between them is filled with nonflammable insulation.

Prefabricated chimney systems should match the style of the house. **Fig. 44-14.** Install a prefabricated chimney in strict accordance with the manufacturer's instructions. Also, make sure the unit conforms to all local building codes.

SECTION 44.1 Check Your Knowledge

1. Why is draft important to a chimney?
2. Name at least two important characteristics of the flue that affect the draft of a chimney.
3. How much clearance should there be between the chimney walls and wood framing members if the chimney is located within the house?
4. Why is cement mortar preferred to lime mortar for joints around chimney flues and fireplaces?

On the Job

In recent years a new type of chimney lining system has become available. It is often used when remodeling an older house that has an unlined masonry chimney. Find out more about this type of system. Would it also be suitable for use in new construction? Be sure to consider building code requirements as well as such factors as cost and ease of installation. Present your findings and explain your answer to the class.

Fireplaces

An ordinary fireplace has a heating efficiency of only about 10 percent. Its value as a heating unit is low compared with its decorative value and the cheerful and homelike atmosphere it creates. **Fig. 44-15.** However, its heating efficiency can be increased with a factory-made metal unit that is built into the fireplace structure. This unit circulates the heated air throughout a room.

Fig. 44-15. Unless a fireplace is fitted with a factory-made insert, its heating efficiency will be very low.

DESIGN AND PLANNING

The design and construction of a fireplace require a great deal of thought and a high degree of craft. A fireplace should harmonize in detail and proportion with the room, but safety and utility should not be sacrificed for appearance. Many fireplace designs are possible.

Fireplace openings are usually from 2′ to 6′ wide. **Fig. 44-16.** Their height can range from 18″ for an opening 2′ wide to 28″ for one that is 6′ wide. In general, the wider the opening, the greater the fireplace depth. A deep opening holds larger, longer-burning logs. A shallow opening throws out more heat than a deep one, but it requires smaller pieces of wood. A minimum depth of 16″ lessens the danger of firebrands falling out on the floor. However, for a special type of fireplace called a Rumford, it may be as narrow as 12″. Suitable screens or glass doors can be placed in front to minimize the danger from brands and sparks.

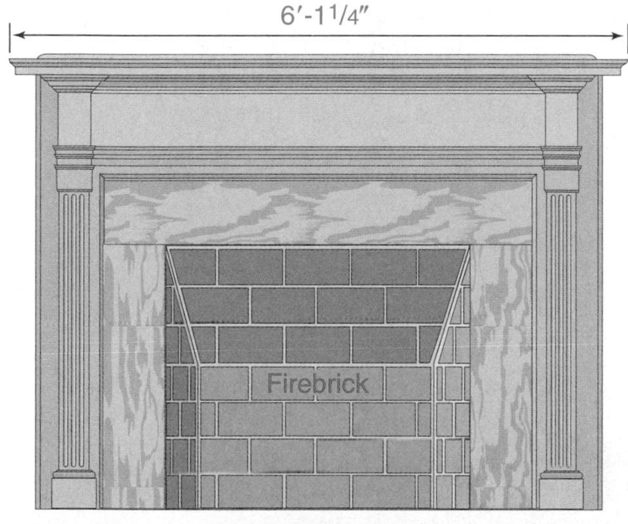

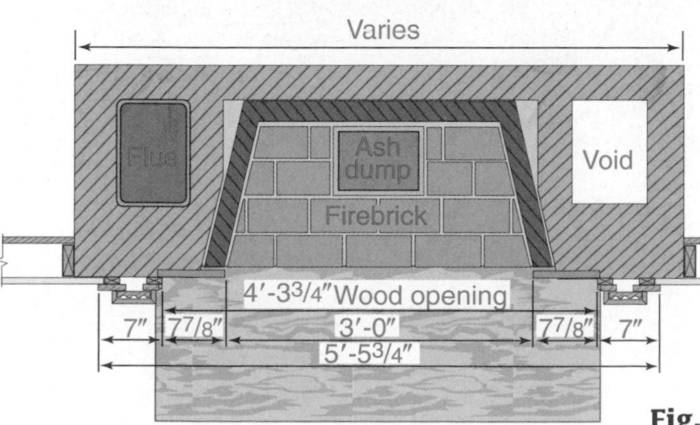

Fig. 44-16. This opening is 3′ wide.

Makeup Air

Combustion requires a source of air. In many cases, air for a fireplace is drawn from inside the house. That air is in turn replaced by outside air filtering in. In cold weather, this means that heated household air is drawn up the chimney and replaced by cold outside air. In houses built to reduce air infiltration, the fire may not burn well because it cannot get enough air, and the chimney may smoke.

To reduce this problem, makeup air should be drawn into the firebox directly from outdoors. (The *firebox* is where burning takes place.) **Makeup air** replaces air exhausted by a combustion appliance. Increasingly, local codes require that all types of fireplaces be supplied with makeup air. The makeup air passageway must have a cross section of at least 6 sq. in. and be covered with a corrosion-resistant screen. It may be located in the back or sides of the firebox, or within 24″ of the firebox opening on or near the floor. It cannot be located in a basement or garage. The outlet must be closable.

MASONRY CONSTRUCTION

The construction of a typical fireplace is shown in **Fig. 44-17**. The relationships among the depth, height, and width of the firebox are important for proper operation. The cross-sectional size of the flue is also important. Building codes contain charts and graphs as an aid to fireplace design.

The main parts of a fireplace include the firebox, hearth, lintel and throat, damper, smoke shelf, and smoke chamber.

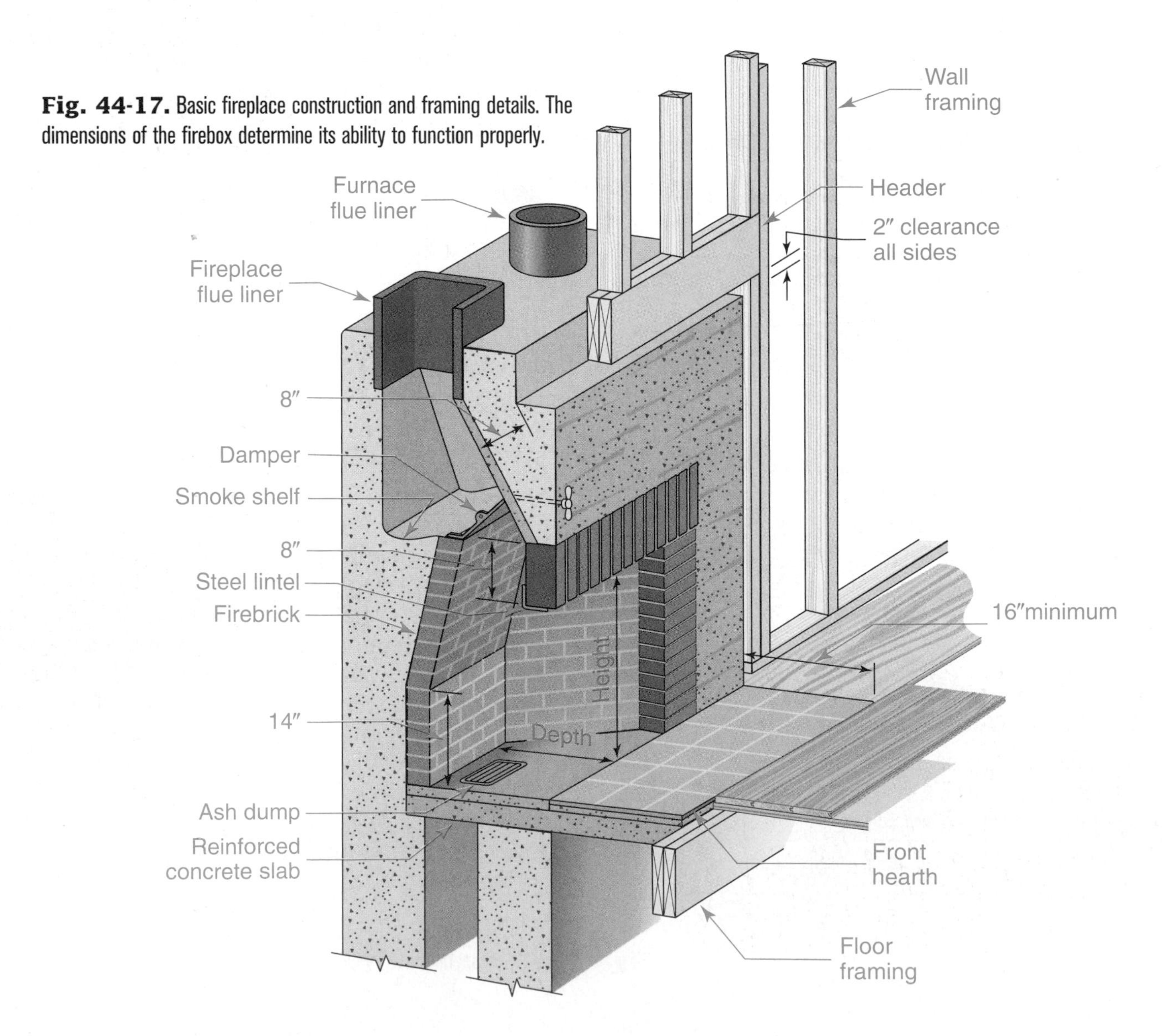

Fig. 44-17. Basic fireplace construction and framing details. The dimensions of the firebox determine its ability to function properly.

> **from Another Angle**
>
> Though many houses have chimneys, fewer also have fireplaces. They are much less popular where the climate is mild. However, a masonry or prefabricated fireplace is common in cold climates and in cool, rainy climates, such as in the Northwest. In rural areas, a woodstove may provide all the heating needs of an entire house.

Firebox

Building codes generally require that the backs and sides of fireboxes be constructed of solid masonry, stone, reinforced concrete, or hollow masonry units grouted solid. When lined with at least 2″ of firebrick, the walls should be at least 8″ thick. The firebrick must be laid using refractory mortar, with joints no greater than ¼″ wide.

Hearth

The *hearth* is the floor of the firebox, plus the fireproof area in front of the fireplace. The hearth has two parts: the *front hearth* (sometimes called the *hearth extension* or the *finish hearth*) and the *back hearth*, under the fire. Because the back hearth must withstand intense heat, it is built of or lined with firebrick. It should be at least 4″ thick. The front hearth protects against flying sparks. While it must be noncombustible, it does not have to resist intense prolonged heat. It should be at least 2″ thick.

If the fireplace opening is less than 6 sq. ft. in area, the front hearth should extend at least 16″ in front of it and at least 8″ on both sides. If the fireplace opening is 6 sq. ft. or more, the hearth should extend 20″ in front of the opening and at least 12″ to either side.

The hearth can be flush with the floor or it can be raised. Raising and lengthening the hearth is presently common practice, especially in contemporary design. If there is a basement, a convenient ash dump can be built under the back of the hearth. (See Fig. 44-17.)

In wood-framed buildings, the front and back hearths are sometimes supported by steel-reinforced concrete poured in place. If this method is used, any wood formwork must be removed after construction is complete. No combustible material can remain against the underside of the back or front hearths. One method of installing floor framing around the fireplace is shown in **Fig. 44-18**.

Lintel and Throat

Every standard masonry fireplace includes a lintel. A **lintel** is a length of steel angle iron installed across the top of the firebox opening to support the masonry (Fig. 44-17). It cannot be seen from the front of the fireplace. Angle iron measuring ¼″ thick and having 3½″ legs is commonly used. However, the actual dimensions depend on the width of the opening and the load to be supported.

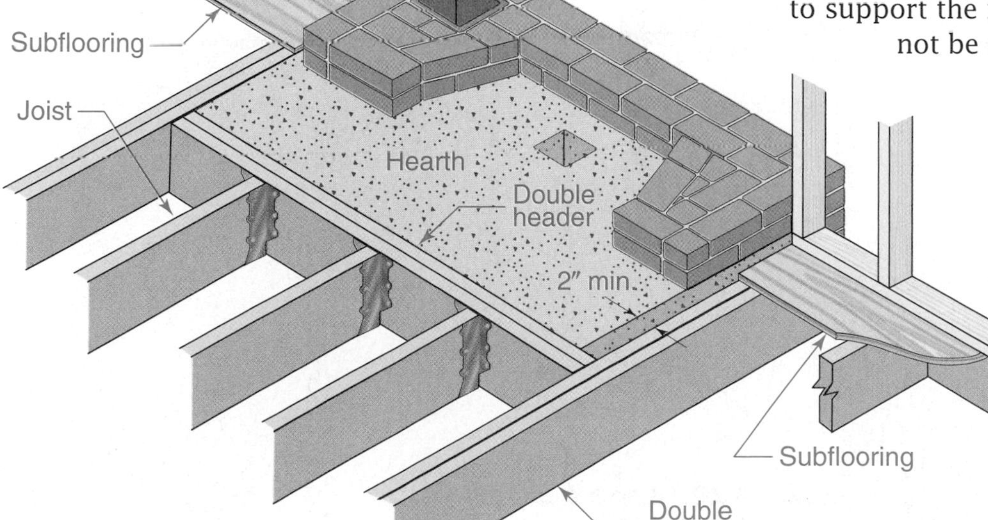

Fig. 44-18. Floor framing details around a fireplace.

Fig. 44-19. Approved installation details for the chimney throat and surrounding areas must be followed closely. This assures fire safety and improves the draw of the fireplace and chimney.

Proper construction of the throat is essential for a satisfactory fireplace. **Fig. 44-19.** The throat is the narrowest part of the firebox, where the damper is located. The sides of the firebox must be vertical up to the throat, which should be 8″ or more above the bottom of the lintel. The area of the throat must not be smaller than that of the flue.

Damper

A *damper* consists of a cast iron frame with a hinged lid. It opens or closes to vary the size of the throat opening. Fig. 44-17. In cold weather, closing the damper reduces heat loss when the chimney is not in use. In warm weather, a closed damper prevents insects and small animals from entering the house.

Dampers of various designs are available. However, it is important that the size of the damper opening equal the cross-sectional area of the flue.

Smoke Shelf and Smoke Chamber

The *smoke shelf* is on the back wall of the smoke chamber. It helps to prevent downdrafts from driving smoke back down into the firebox. Fig. 44-17. It is made by setting the brickwork at the top of the throat back to the line of the flue wall for the full length of the throat. The depth of the shelf may be 6″ to 12″ or more, depending on the depth of the fireplace. The smoke shelf is concave to hold any slight amount of rain that may enter.

The *smoke chamber* is the area from the top of the throat to the bottom of the flue. Fig. 44-17. Its sidewalls slope inward to meet the flue, and its front is formed by corbeled bricks. To make the surfaces of the smoke shelf and the smoke chamber walls smooth, they should be plastered with cement mortar at least ½″ thick.

Clearances

It is the front, or *surround*, of a fireplace that can have the greatest effect on the architectural style of a room. Many different materials can be used. These include brick, ceramic tile, wood molding and trim, and wood mantels. However, any combustible material must be installed with care and according to building codes. **Fig. 44-20.**

- No woodwork can be placed within 6″ of the firebox opening.
- Woodwork, including any mantel located between 6″ and 12″ from the firebox opening, must not project forward more than ⅛″ for every inch above the opening. For example, a mantel located 9″ above the firebox opening can be no more than 1⅛″ wide (9 × ⅛″ = 1⅛″).

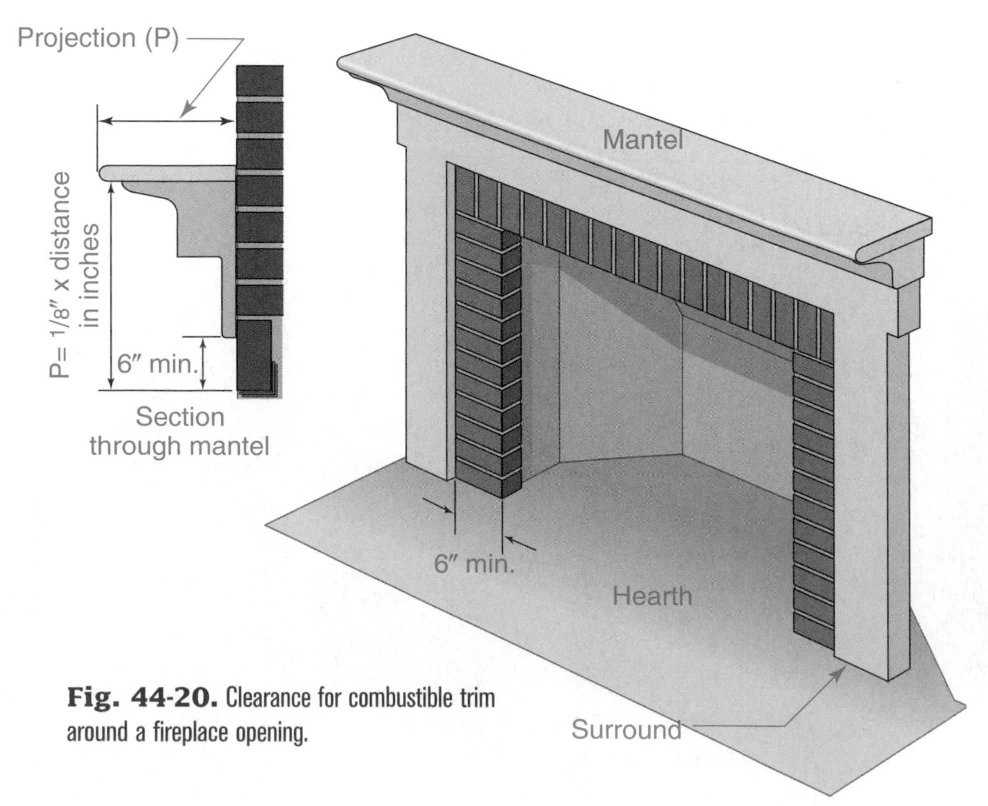

Fig. 44-20. Clearance for combustible trim around a fireplace opening.

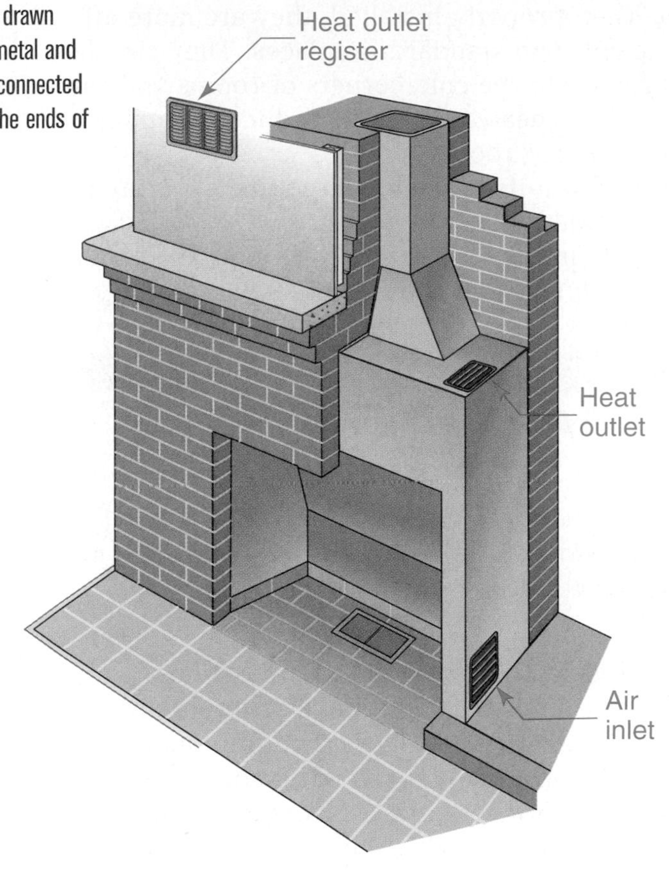

Fig. 44-21. A prefabricated firebox. Air from the room is drawn through the air inlet. The air is heated upon contact with the metal and discharged through the heat outlet. The inlets and outlets are connected to registers that may be located at the front, as shown, or at the ends of the fireplace.

PREFABRICATED FIREPLACES

Some fireplaces are made with a heavy-gauge metal firebox. Some of these are designed to be concealed by brickwork or other materials. **Fig. 44-21.** Others can be set into a wood-framed opening and connected to a prefabricated metal chimney system. In either case, a prefabricated fireplace includes all the essential parts: firebox, damper, throat, smoke shelf, and smoke chamber.

These units are available in a variety of styles for different room locations. **Fig. 44-22.** Different installations are possible through the use of chimney offsets, elbows, and various types of roof terminations. **Fig. 44-23.**

Prefabricated fireplaces offer several advantages:

- The correctly designed and proportioned firebox provides a ready-made form for masonry. This reduces the chance of faulty construction.

Fig. 44-22. A prefabricated fireplace installed with a traditionally styled wood and ceramic tile surround.

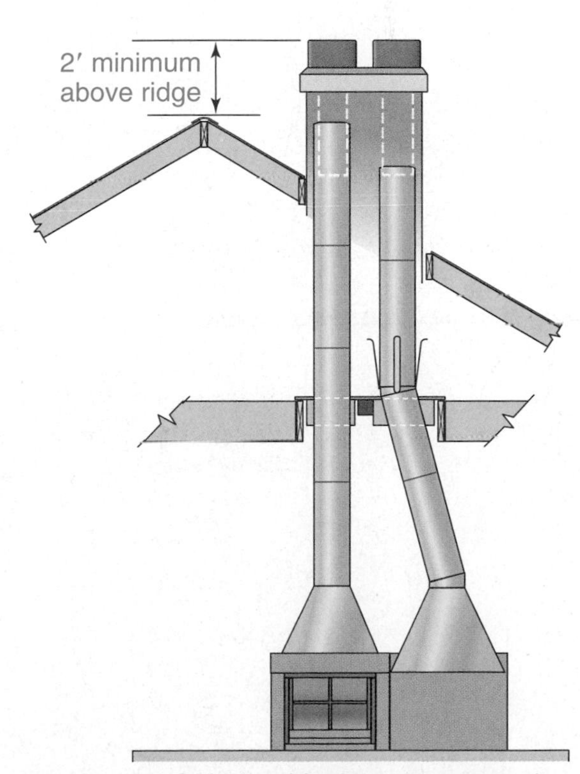

Fig. 44-23. Prefabricated fireplace components can be arranged in various ways, including side by side and back to back.

- When properly installed, they are more efficient than standard fireplaces. They circulate heat into the cold corners of rooms and can deliver heated air through ducts to upper or adjoining rooms.
- The unit itself does not require a footing or foundation.
- The firebox and chimney do not take up as much space as those made from masonry.

SAFETY FIRST

Don't Lift Alone

A prefabricated fireplace or firebox is much lighter than one of masonry construction, but it is still quite heavy. Always work with one or more helpers when moving or positioning the unit.

When a conventional masonry chimney is used, proper construction is as important as it is for masonry fireplaces. The framing required to enclose these units is not complex. **Fig. 44-24.** However, proper clearances should be observed. Some units are called *zero-clearance* fireplaces because they can be placed directly against wood framing. The manufacturer's specific framing instructions should be followed.

Fig. 44-24. A fireplace framed with headers ready for the application of the interior wall covering.

Fig. 44-25. A freestanding fireplace.

Another type of prefabricated fireplace is called a *freestanding fireplace.* **Fig. 44-25.** The basic element is a specially insulated metal firebox shell. Like other prefabricated units, it can rest on standard floor framing. However, it must be placed far enough away from combustible wall surfaces to prevent a fire hazard.

SECTION 44.2 Check Your Knowledge

1. What is makeup air?
2. What are the minimum dimensions for a front hearth?
3. Which interior portion of a fireplace is corbeled?
4. How close can woodwork come to the firebox opening?

On the Job

The early 1970s saw a rebirth in the use of wood-burning stoves. Lately, however, there has been controversy over their use because of pollution problems. Find out what the controversy is all about by researching this topic using the *Reader's Guide to Periodical Literature* or your library's periodical research system.

Chapter 44 Review

Section Summaries

44.1 Chimneys may be made of masonry or prefabricated parts. It is extremely important to construct a chimney so that it does not create a fire hazard. Height above the roofline and clearance to wood framing must be considered. A chimney saddle diverts water around the chimney. A cap keeps moisture from seeping between the brick and the flue.

44.2 The interior portions of a masonry fireplace must be properly designed and carefully constructed. This ensures proper working of the fireplace. It also ensures that smoke and harmful gases are drawn out of the house efficiently. The main parts of a fireplace include the firebox, damper, throat, lintel, smoke shelf, smoke chamber, and hearth.

Review Questions

1. Why will a chimney in the interior of a house have better draft than a chimney built on an exterior wall?
2. Name the main parts of a chimney.
3. What type of material should be used to join flue sections?
4. What determines the number of flues in a chimney?
5. What is a corbel?
6. What is the purpose of a concrete cap on a chimney?
7. Name the main parts of a fireplace.
8. What factors are most important for proper operation of a fireplace?
9. What is the purpose of a damper?
10. What is a zero-clearance fireplace?

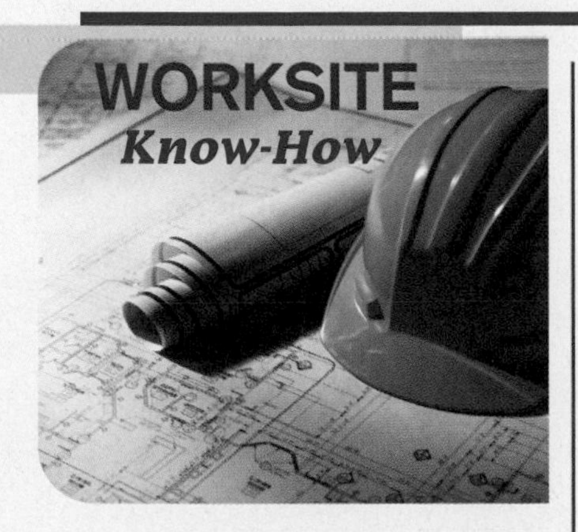

Teamwork The installation of a masonry chimney and fireplace calls for close coordination among masons, carpenters, and roofing contractors. The work of each of these trades affects the others. Scheduling must be monitored carefully because masonry often proceeds in several stages separated by days or weeks. It is also affected by weather extremes. The various trades should contact each other directly and be cooperative. They should notify the general contractor or project supervisor when they have technical questions or scheduling problems that may affect the other trades.

Decks and Porches

Objectives

After reading this chapter, you'll be able to:

- **Name the basic types of materials used for decking.**
- **Name the basic elements of a deck.**
- **Lay out piers for a rectangular attached deck.**
- **Plumb a post.**
- **Handle and cut preservative-treated wood safely.**
- **Describe two methods for installing concrete porch steps.**

Terms

ACQ
galvanizing
heartwood
ledger
pier
sapwood
stoop

Many homeowners want an outdoor deck. It does not require wiring, insulation, or expensive finish surfaces. This makes it fairly inexpensive to build, compared with the rest of the house. It also allows homeowners to enjoy their yards.

A deck is generally the last major assembly completed during new house construction. Decks are built by the carpenters who framed the house or by contractors who specialize in the construction of decks.

A porch is another desirable feature. Depending on the architectural design of the house, it may be built in various ways. It may resemble a deck with a roof over it, or it may be more enclosed.

SECTION 45.1

Deck Materials

A *deck* is an uncovered platform made from wood members fastened with nails, screws, bolts, and metal brackets. Construction techniques and structural needs are straightforward. The primary requirements are weather resistance, strength, and a safe design. Because a deck is entirely exposed to the weather, joints must not trap water and the structure must resist wind uplift forces.

There are two basic types of decks. A *freestanding*, or *grade-level, deck* is not attached to the house. It is low to the ground and does not require a foundation. It is usually on only one level. **Fig. 45-1.** An *attached*, or *elevated deck* has at least one side permanently connected to the structure of the house. This type of deck may have one or two levels. It is partly supported by the house and partly by a network of concrete piers that extend below the frost line. **Fig. 45-2.**

Fig. 45-1. A grade-level deck is not attached to the house.

DECKING AND STRUCTURAL MATERIALS

Materials used for structural elements beneath the decking are chosen primarily for their strength and durability. Appearance is usually a lesser concern. The decking itself is the most visible portion. It has a large impact on the appearance of the deck. Many new types of decking materials have become available in recent years. These include tropical hardwoods as well as a wide variety of plastics and composites.

Softwoods

The most popular types of decking are made from softwood lumber. Three different softwoods are commonly used.

- Redwood. This wood is highly resistant to decay and insect attack. However, it is fairly expensive and not readily available in all parts of the country.

Fig. 45-2. An attached deck is supported by posts and anchored to the house. A strong and well-designed railing makes a deck safe to use.

- Cedar. Several species of cedar are resistant to decay and insect attack. Western red cedar is the species used most often for decking. It is medium priced and readily available throughout the country.
- Preservative-treated wood. Preservative-treated wood is inexpensive and readily available. It is frequently used for structural members as well as for decking itself. The wood is usually southern yellow pine. By itself, such wood is not nearly as durable as redwood and cedar. However, preservatives forced into the wood under pressure make it very resistant to decay and insect attack. Several treatment levels are available, depending on the degree of protection required. Lumber that will be in direct contact with soil, such as for posts, should have the highest level of treatment.

Softwood decking lumber is specified by its nominal size. The most commonly available sizes are 2x4 and 2x6 (actual thickness 1⅝″). Wider stock is used less often because it is more likely to cup as it weathers. In some areas, preservative-treated decking lumber is also available in an actual thickness of 1¼″. Decking lumber is readily available in lengths of 8′, 10′, 12′, and 14′. Softwood structural lumber is readily available in sizes from 2x6 through 2x12 and in lengths up to 14′.

Grades. Grading for exterior lumber is not uniform. Redwood lumber is available in over 30 different grades, for example. Cedar lumber is graded with a different system and preservative-treated with yet another. In general, however, exterior softwood lumber is graded according to the following characteristics:

- Appearance. This describes the size, type, and number of knots permitted in a board. Other surface flaws may be identified as well. Wood of the highest appearance grade is completely free from knots and is sometimes referred to as *clear*. This grade is often used for deck railings and skirt boards and sometimes for the decking itself.
- Strength. This describes the lumber's ability to support loads. Higher strength grades are important for joists and beams.
- Moisture content. Deck lumber is often kiln-dried to a moisture content of either 19 or 15 percent. This reduces the tendency of the wood to shrink after installation. Some preservative-treated lumber is kiln-dried twice: once before and once after treatment. This grade is stamped KDAT (Kiln-Dried After Treatment).
- Decay resistance. The most decay-resistant portion of a tree is the heartwood. **Heartwood** is the portion of a tree nearest the core. It is dark in color. The least decay-resistant part of the tree is the sapwood. **Sapwood** is the outer growth layer. It is lighter in color than heartwood. When maximum decay resistance is required, grades containing larger proportions of heartwood should be used. Because heartwood and sapwood differ in color, decay resistance also has some bearing on appearance grading. The highest grades are the most uniform in color.

Preservatives

Until recently, the most common preservative for decking wood was CCA (chromated copper arsenate). Wood treated with CCA is greenish in color. Studies have indicated that the arsenic in CCA-treated wood could leach out and contaminate soil and ground water under some circumstances. In 2002, the U.S. Environmental Protection Agency announced that residential use of this material should be gradually phased out.

Other non-arsenic preservatives can replace CCA in the wood treatment process. One that is already used extensively is **ACQ** (ammoniacal copper quaternary ammonium compound). Wood treated with ACQ does not contain arsenic. It is sometimes brownish in color.

SAFETY FIRST

Avoiding Toxic Chemicals

Preservative-treated woods contain toxic chemicals. Always wear work gloves when handling them and a dust mask when cutting them. To prevent chemicals in the sawdust from leaching into the soil, cut preservative-treated wood over a tarp. Dispose of the collected sawdust as directed by local regulations. Avoid sanding preservative-treated wood. Always wash your hands thoroughly with soap after working with it, particularly before eating.

Hardwoods

Many tropical hardwoods, such as mahogany, teak, and Ipe, are strong and highly resistant to decay and insect attack. These trees grow in Central and South America but are increasingly sold in North America.

Most hardwood decking ranges from ¾″ to 1¼″ thick. No special tools are required when cutting these woods. However, holes for nails and other fasteners must be pre-drilled because the wood is so dense.

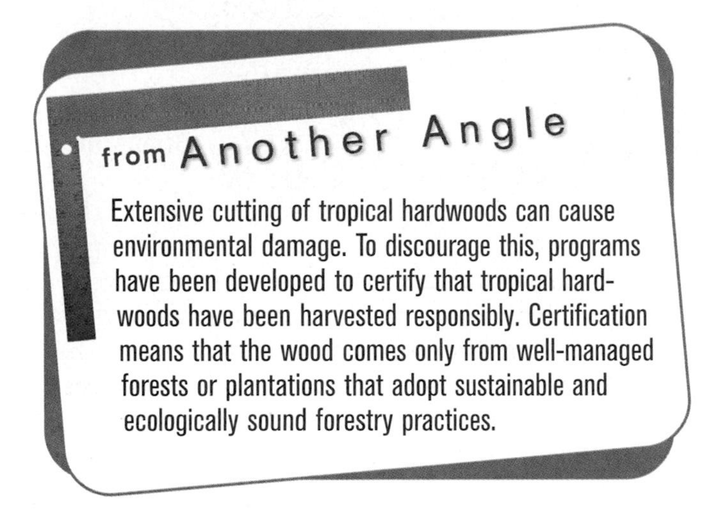

from Another Angle

Extensive cutting of tropical hardwoods can cause environmental damage. To discourage this, programs have been developed to certify that tropical hardwoods have been harvested responsibly. Certification means that the wood comes only from well-managed forests or plantations that adopt sustainable and ecologically sound forestry practices.

Other Decking Materials

Many synthetic decking products are now available. These products may be less expensive than solid wood and require little maintenance. However, they can be used only for decking, not for the substructure of the deck. Synthetic decking should be approved by local building codes before being used.

There are two basic types of synthetic decking products. *Plastic decking* is made entirely of plastic. Products are shaped into boardlike planks that are hollow or partially hollow. **Fig. 45-3.** Chemical additives in the plastic improve

Fig. 45-3. Plastic decking consists of hollow extrusions. Each type uses a fastening system supplied by the manufacturer.

Fig. 45-4. Composite decking is available in various dimensions, shapes, and colors. Skirt boards or special end caps are used to conceal the open ends of hollow composite decking.

its durability outdoors. Concealed fastening systems supplied by the manufacturer secure the decking to wood joists. Decking ranges from about 4″ to 8″ in width. *Composite decking* is a blend of recycled plastic and wood dust or fibers. **Fig. 45-4.** It is denser and heavier than solid wood but usually not as stiff. Boards are solid and can be attached to wood joists with nails or screws. Boards should be cut with carbide-tipped saw blades. Sizes include 5/4 x 6, 2x4, 2x6, and 2x8.

FASTENERS

The parts of a deck are fastened together with nails, screws, lag bolts, through bolts, and structural metal connectors. Structural connections should be made in a way that maintains the strength of the connections over time.

Types of Fasteners

The most common fastener used to assemble a deck is the nail, but screws and bolts are also commonly used. **Fig. 45-5.** Connections between posts and beams or joists and rim joists are often made with metal connectors, such as brackets or joist hangers. These provide a stronger connection than nails or screws alone. They may be required in areas exposed to earthquakes or severe weather.

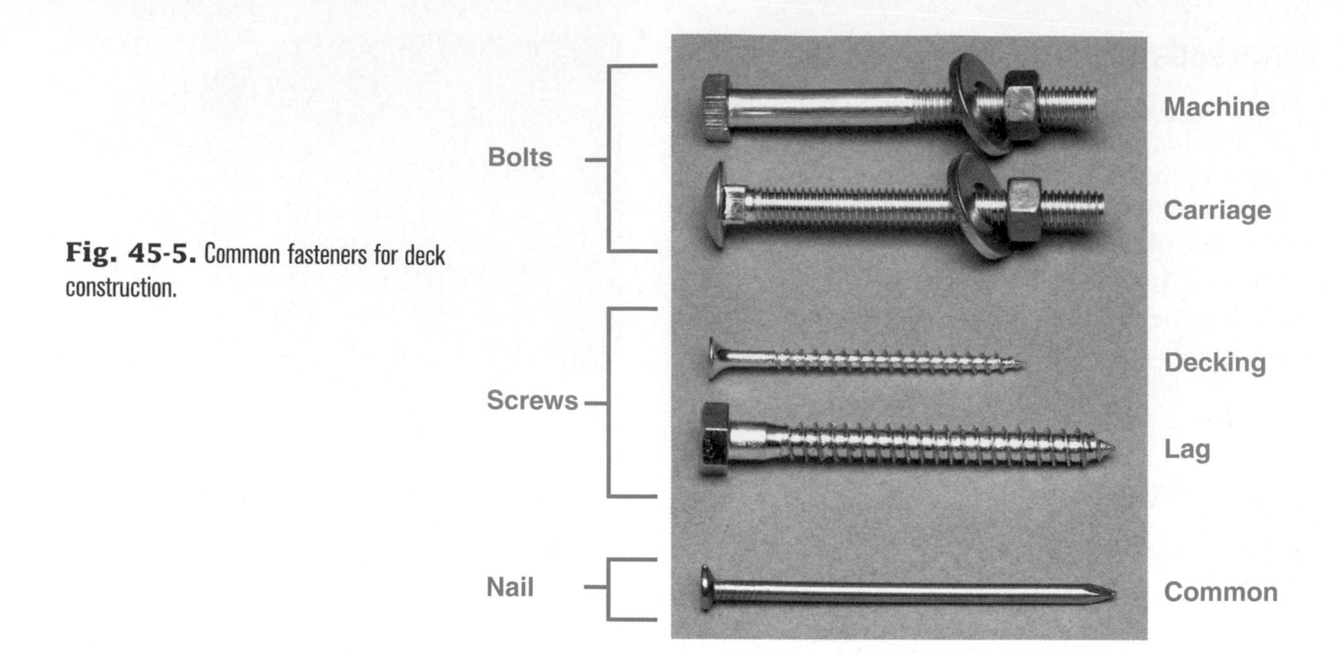

Fig. 45-5. Common fasteners for deck construction.

Through bolts used to make a connection should be approximately 1″ longer than the combined thickness of the lumber. This ensures that threads on the nut will be fully engaged. Always place a flat washer under each nut. This prevents the nut from crushing wood fibers and reduces the chance that the connection will loosen over time.

Corrosion Resistance

All metal hardware used on a deck must be corrosion resistant. The least expensive and most common type of corrosion resistance is provided by **galvanizing**. This process coats the steel with a protective layer of zinc.

Two types of galvanized hardware are strong as well as durable. Electroplated galvanizing coats the steel with a thin, smooth, and very uniform layer of zinc. It is available on all metal products, including metal connectors. Hot-dipping produces a slightly irregular layer of zinc that is thicker than an electroplated finish. It offers greater protection but is more expensive than electroplating. It is not used on through bolts because the thicker coating clogs threads.

Hardware made of stainless steel does not require galvanizing. Stainless steel is used where maximum corrosion resistance is necessary. It is ideal for use in coastal areas, particularly where salt spray is a factor. It is available in many forms, including through bolts and framing connectors. However, stainless steel is much more expensive than galvanized steel. Stainless steel structural connectors should always be fastened using stainless steel fasteners.

SECTION 45.1 Check Your Knowledge

1. What supports an attached deck?
2. Name the three basic types of softwood lumber used for decking.
3. What preservative has been phased out of use for residential construction?
4. What is the purpose of galvanizing metal?

On the Job

Locate two manufacturers of structural metal connectors. Obtain product literature and compare the products used for constructing decks. Do both companies offer various grades of galvanized hardware for deck construction? Do both companies offer stainless steel hardware and fasteners? Mark the pages that contain decking products. Start a file on structural metal connectors for decking.

SECTION 45.2

Planning and Construction

The elements of a simple attached deck are shown in **Fig. 45-6**. Decking usually runs parallel to the house. However, this is primarily for installation convenience and appearance. It is not a requirement. Decking is supported by joists and usually runs perpendicular to them.

BUILDING CODE AND ZONING REQUIREMENTS

Decks are governed by local building codes as well as zoning restrictions. Building codes are concerned with such details as:

- The span of beams, joists, and decking.
- The diameter and depth of foundation piers.
- The design of railings and steps.
- The deck's connection to the house.

Construction details for the deck should be included in the construction drawings for the house. The location of the deck would show up in a plan view. Assembly details would be included on a detail sheet.

Zoning ordinances affect deck location. These restrictions differ from community to community. However, they specify the minimum allowable distance between the deck and such features as streets, lot lines, septic systems, wells, and utility easements. They may also limit the height of a deck.

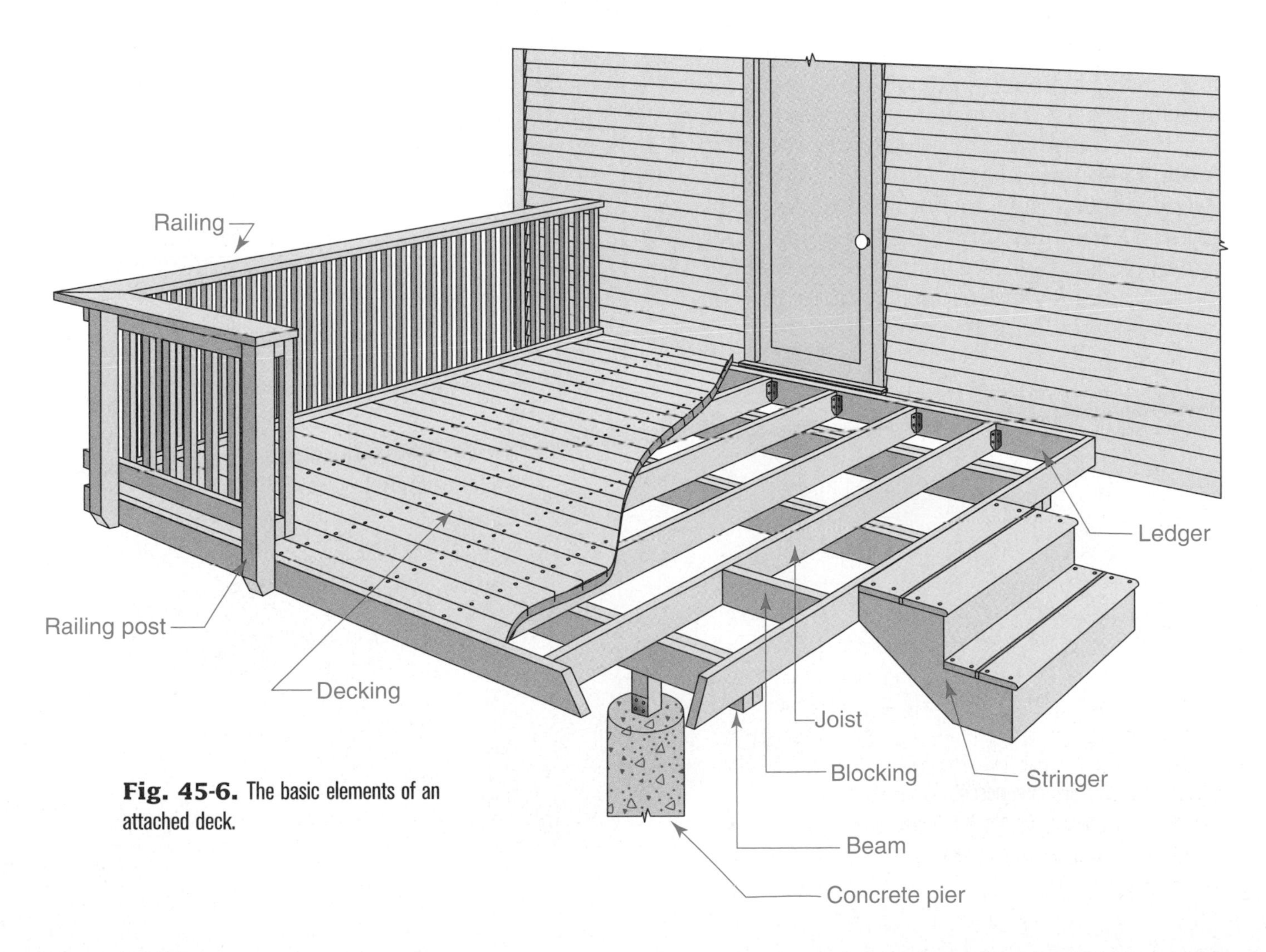

Fig. 45-6. The basic elements of an attached deck.

Fig. 45-7. Formwork for footings must be braced properly to prevent it from moving when concrete is placed.

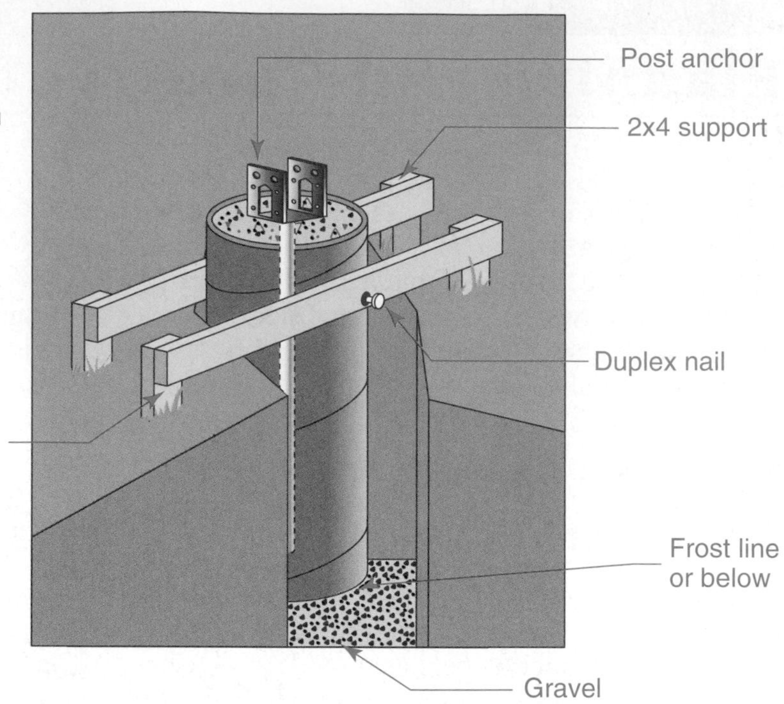

INSTALLING FOOTINGS AND PIERS

A deck does not require a continuous concrete foundation. Instead, it rests on piers. A **pier** is a concrete column that supports a concentrated load, such as a post. Each pier rests on a concrete footing that distributes loads to the soil. The bottom of the footing should be approximately 6″ below the frost line. The frost line is determined by local climate and its depth can be found in local building codes.

One common method of forming a pier is to use a Sonotube. **Fig. 45-7.** A Sonotube is an inexpensive cylinder made of laminated, waxed paper products. It comes in various lengths and diameters and serves as a form for concrete. **Table 45-A.** Immediately after the concrete is placed, a metal post anchor should be embedded in it. Sonotube forms are left in place permanently. However, portions that are visible above grade may be stripped off after the concrete has cured for a few days.

Table 45-A. Estimating Concrete for Sonotube Forms

Column Diameter (inches)	Concrete Required per Lineal Foot (cubic yards)
6	.0073
8	.0129
10	.0202
12	.0291
14	.0396
16	.0617
18	.0654

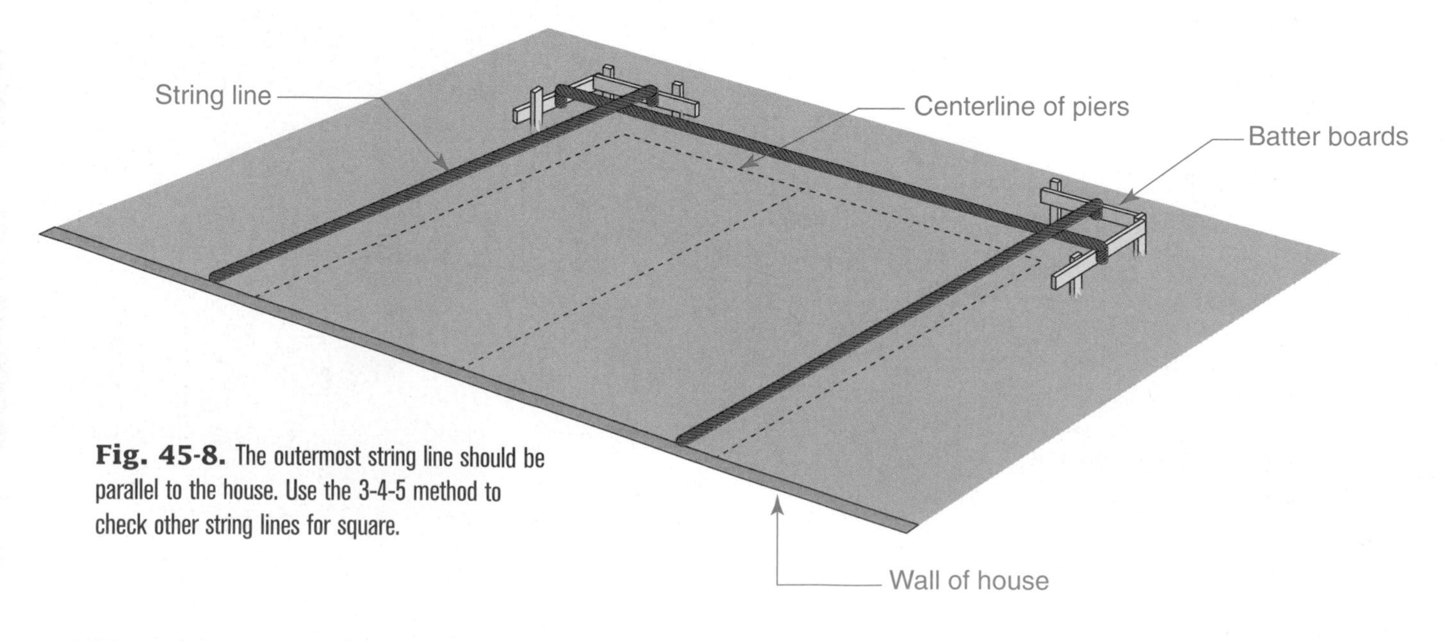

Fig. 45-8. The outermost string line should be parallel to the house. Use the 3-4-5 method to check other string lines for square.

Fig. 45-9. After string lines have been set up, use a tape measure and a plumb bob to locate the center point of individual piers.

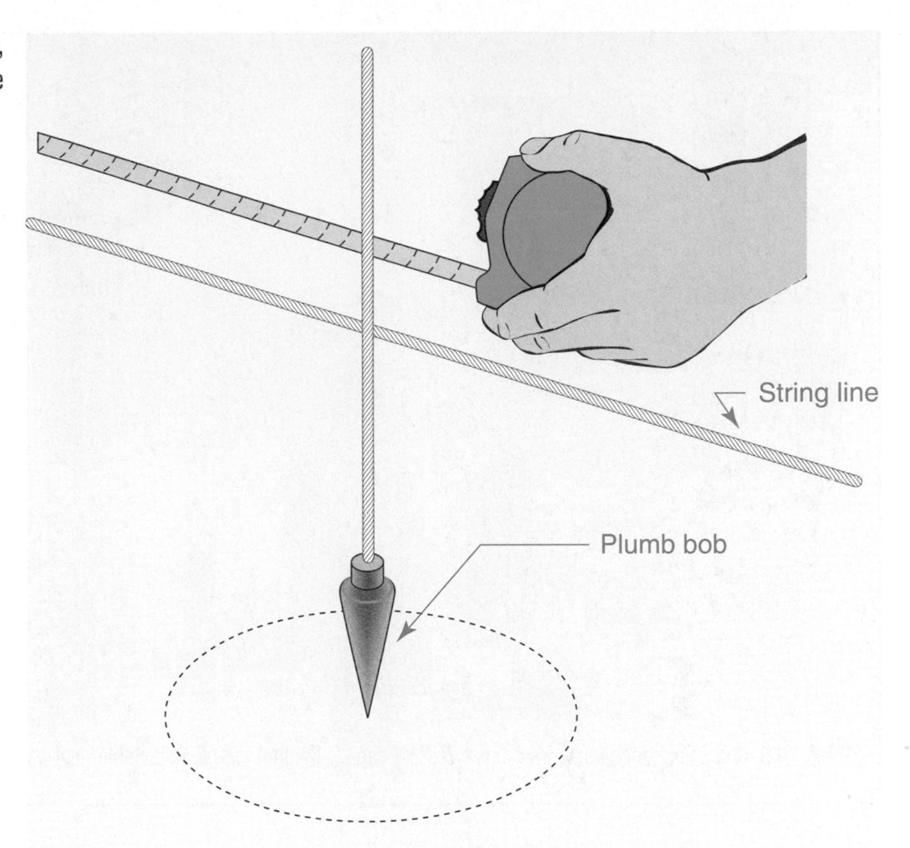

The general location of piers is determined by the plan of the deck. An exact location is determined by using the 3-4-5 method to ensure a right-angle layout in relation to the house. (See Chapter 13, "Locating the House on the Building Site.") String lines can then be used to locate the centerlines of piers. **Fig. 45-8.** To plot the location of individual piers, use a tape measure and a plumb bob. **Fig. 45-9.**

Excavation for piers may be done with shovels, post-hole diggers, or mechanical equipment. The tools used will depend on the depth of the footing, the diameter of the pier, and the number of piers. Power equipment is generally preferred when more than a few piers will be needed. **Fig. 45-10.**

BUILDING THE SUBSTRUCTURE

The substructure of an attached deck consists of all the elements above the piers and below the decking itself. It supports the decking as well as railings and the upper ends of attached stairs (see Fig. 45-6).

Posts

Posts should be made of solid lumber graded for structural use. Common dimensions are 4x4, 4x6, and 6x6. Most often posts are made from preservative-treated lumber, but redwood is common in some areas of the country. The bottom of a post is secured by a metal post anchor embedded in a pier. The top is secured to a beam with a metal post cap. **Fig. 45-11.** Step-by-Step instructions for plumbing a post are given on page 910.

Fig. 45-10. The use of heavy equipment to "drill" holes for piers improves their accuracy and speeds the work when many holes are required.

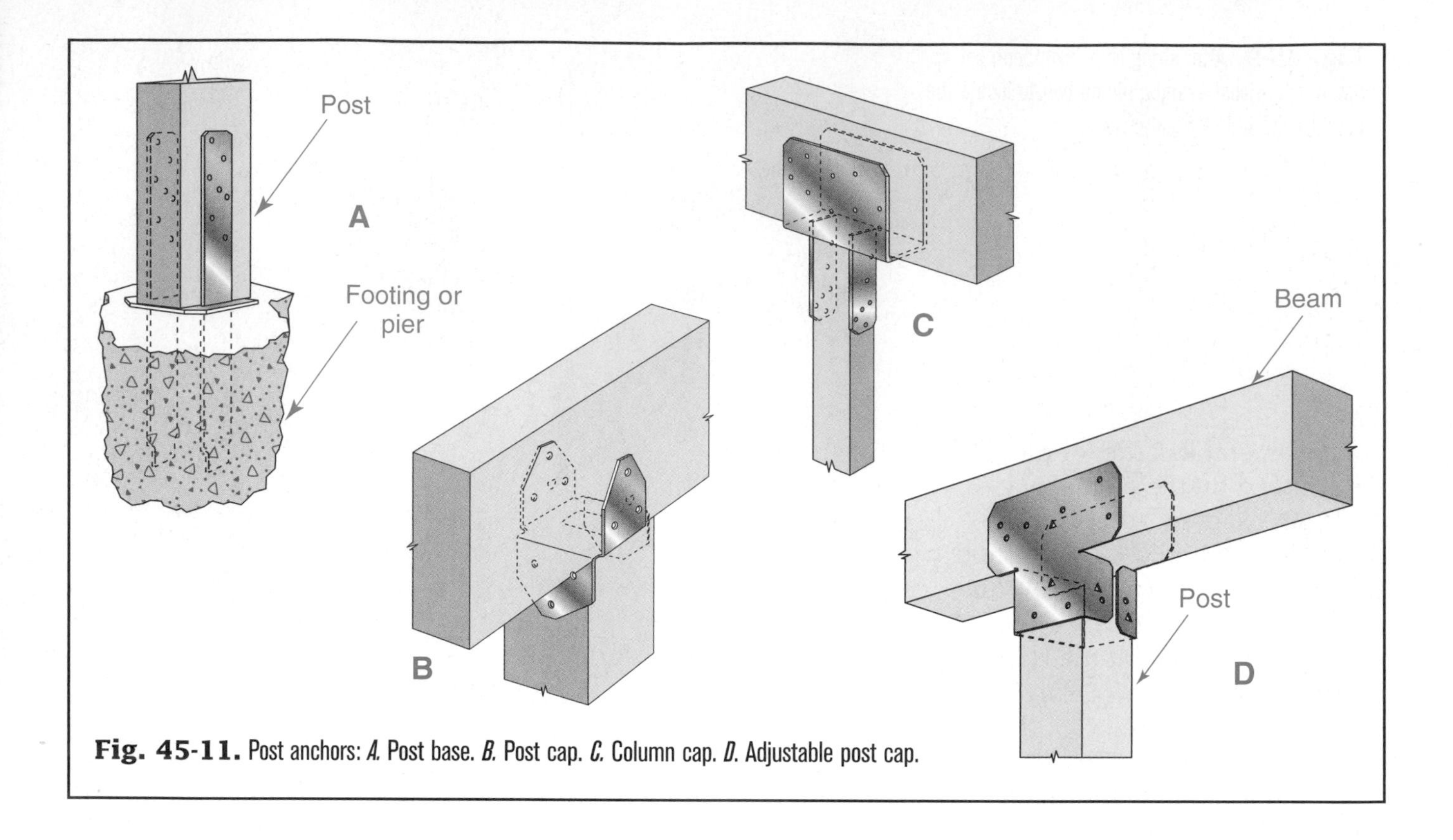

Fig. 45-11. Post anchors: *A.* Post base. *B.* Post cap. *C.* Column cap. *D.* Adjustable post cap.

STEP BY STEP

Plumbing a Post

Posts must be plumbed to ensure that they will bear vertically on the piers. An out-of-plumb post puts unnecessary stresses on the deck structure. Plumb the posts with a 3′ level or by using the following method:

Step 1 Tack a wood block to the side of the post at its top. Then hang a plumb line over the block. **Fig. 45-12.**

Step 2 At the bottom of the post, measure the distance from the post to the line. If the distance is not the same as the thickness of the block, the post is not plumb.

Step 3 Tilt the post as needed until the distance from the post to the line is exactly the same along the entire length of the line.

Step 4 Nail a temporary brace to the post to hold it in position. Repeat Steps 1 through 3 on an adjacent face of the post. When this face is plumb, secure a second brace.

Step 5 Double-check the post on two adjacent faces. If they are both plumb, the post is plumb.

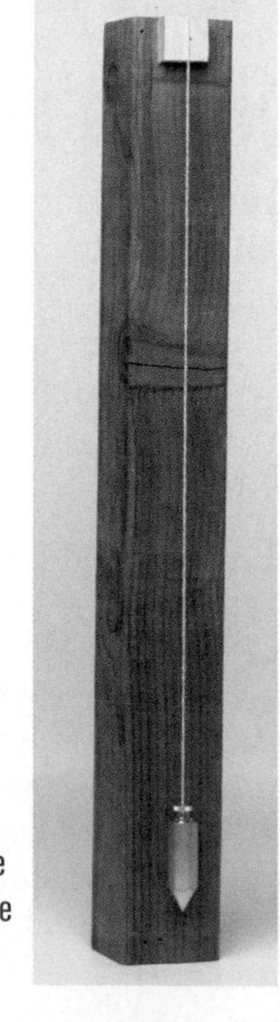

Fig. 45-12. To plumb a post, drape a plumb line over a scrap block. Measure between the line and the post.

Beams

Beams may be solid wood or a built-up assembly of 2x lumber. Building up beams can produce a beam of any length. Another advantage is that a built-up beam is easier to position because it can be assembled in place. The cut ends of solid or built-up beams should be coated with a water repellent to increase their durability.

The width of a solid-wood beam should match the width of the posts that support it. However, the beam's depth is always greater than its width. Nominal beam depths of 6″ and 8″ are common. Built-up beams are made of two or three layers of 2x8, 2x10, or other dimension lumber. The layers should be spiked or bolted together.

One disadvantage of a built-up beam is that water can be trapped between the pieces of stock. This can cause rot. To eliminate this problem, two-layer beams are often assembled with an airspace between the pieces. This can be done by inserting treated-wood spacers or stacked washers between the pieces as they are nailed or bolted together.

Ledger

One of the most important but least understood parts of a deck's substructure is the ledger. The **ledger** is the length of lumber that connects the deck to the house. **Fig. 45-13.**

Proper installation of the ledger is critical. Metal flashing prevents water from rotting the siding, the sheathing, or the structural framing of the house. If not attached properly, the ledger can rip away from the house when stressed. This can cause the entire deck to collapse.

Never secure a ledger to a house with nails alone. Nails are not strong enough to prevent the ledger from pulling away. Instead, use lag bolts or through bolts connected to studs, plates, or rim joists. Do not rely on any connections made to the sheathing alone. Such connections do not provide sufficient strength.

Joists

Deck joists are laid out and installed much like floor joists (see Chapter 20, "Floor

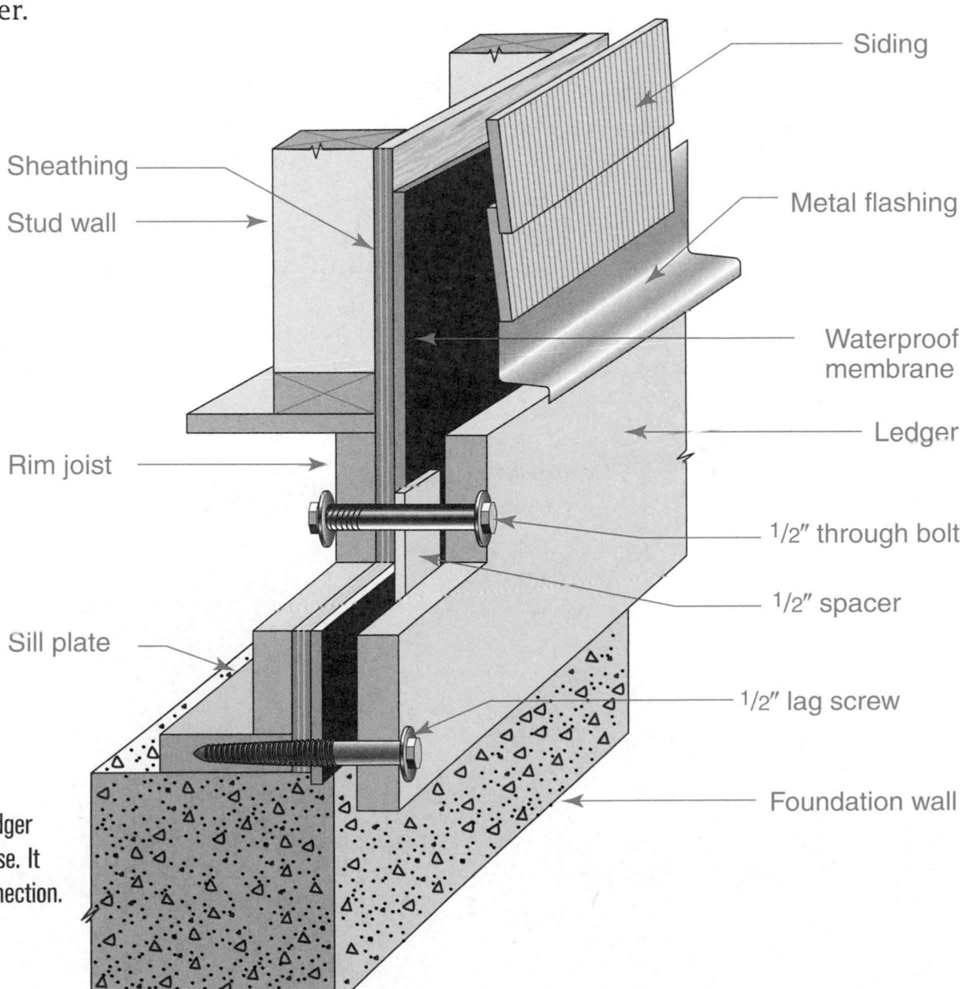

Fig. 45-13. A properly installed ledger provides a strong connection to the house. It also channels water away from the connection.

Fig. 45-14. Decking fasteners are available in various materials, finishes, and head types. The fastener should be matched to the type and thickness of decking being used.

Framing"). They are usually spaced 16″ OC but may also be 12″, 20″, or 24″ OC. When synthetic decking is used, always consult the manufacturer's instructions for joist requirements.

Joists are generally connected to other structural elements using metal joist hangers. Continuous solid blocking is often required between joists that are more than 8″ in depth.

INSTALLING DECKING

Softwood decking with a nominal 2″ thickness is nailed with 10d galvanized or stainless steel nails. Use one nail at every joist connection when installing 2x4 decking. Use two nails when installing 2x6 decking. Use 8d nails to install 1¼″ thick decking.

Galvanized or stainless steel screws make a tighter connection than nails. Screws made especially for attaching decking have a slender shaft, a sharp self-drilling point, and a fairly small head that sinks flush with the surface of the decking. **Fig. 45-14.** They should be long enough to penetrate at least 1″ into the joists. When installing synthetic decking, follow manufacturer's instructions carefully for using nails or screws.

Spacing

Gaps between deck boards ensure that water will drain freely. Generally this space is about ⅛″. If hardwood, composite, or kiln-dried decking is used, gaps must be created as the boards are installed. However, when installing preservative-treated lumber, butt boards tightly during installation. As the boards shrink, suitable gaps will eventually open up between them.

The thickness of a 12d or 16d nail can be used to gauge gaps between decking boards. Drive a nail through a small scrap of thin plywood to create a spacing jig. **Fig. 45-15.** Use several of these reusable devices to maintain a uniform gap thickness.

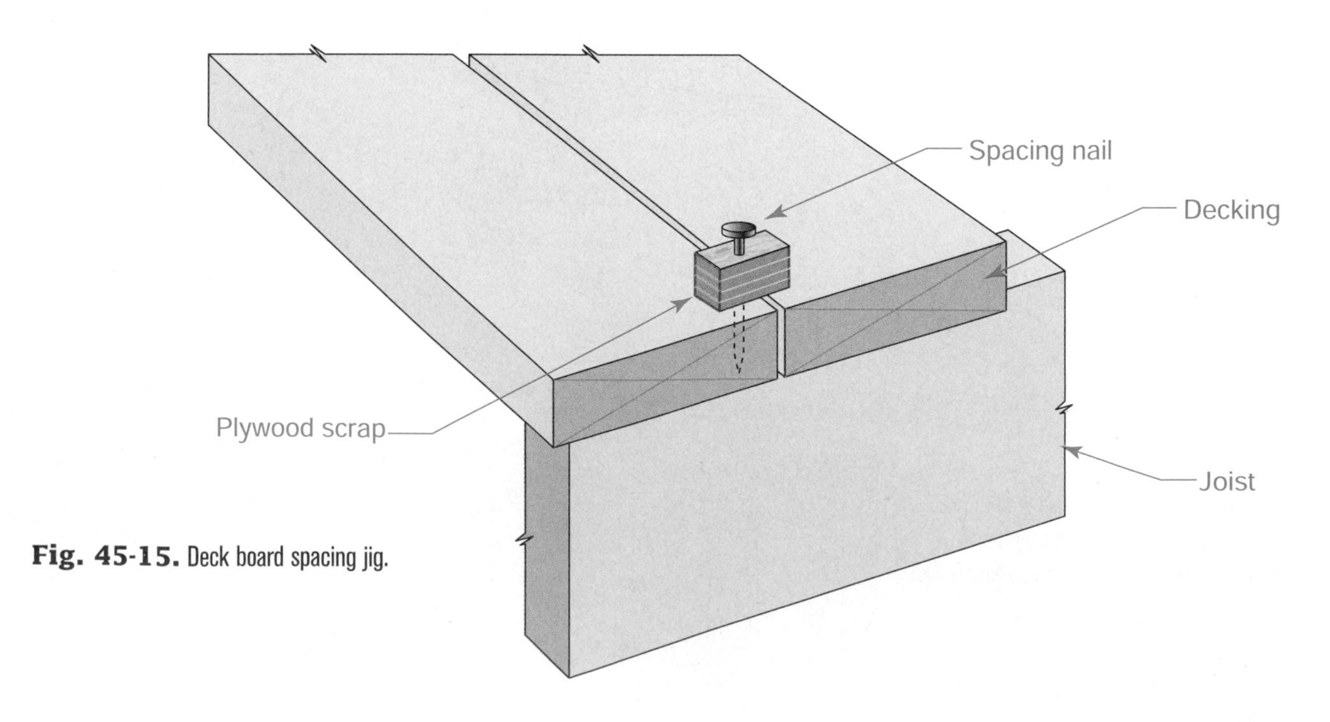

Fig. 45-15. Deck board spacing jig.

Fig. 45-16. Hidden deck nailing systems allow decking to be fastened without surface nailing: *A.* Continuous metal strip. *B.* Individual metal clips.

Hidden Fastening Systems

Instead of driving nails or screws through the face of decking, many builders use hidden fastening systems. These are sometimes called *blind-nailing systems.* Blind nailing prevents the fasteners from showing. It also reduces the chance that water will get into the wood around fastener heads. Several types of blind-nailing systems are available. **Fig. 45-16.**

INSTALLING STAIRS AND RAILINGS

All elevated decks require stairs and railings. Because these elements play a large role in the safety of a deck, local codes should be followed carefully.

Stairs

A low deck may not require stairs. However, most decks will require at least a few steps down to grade level. Steps are supported by treated-wood stringers. **Fig. 45-17.** These stringers are laid out just as those for interior stairs (see Chapter 34, "Stairways"). However, the degree of finish work is not as great. This is because stairs to a deck are exposed to the weather. Stringers are frequently attached to the deck substructure with joist hangers.

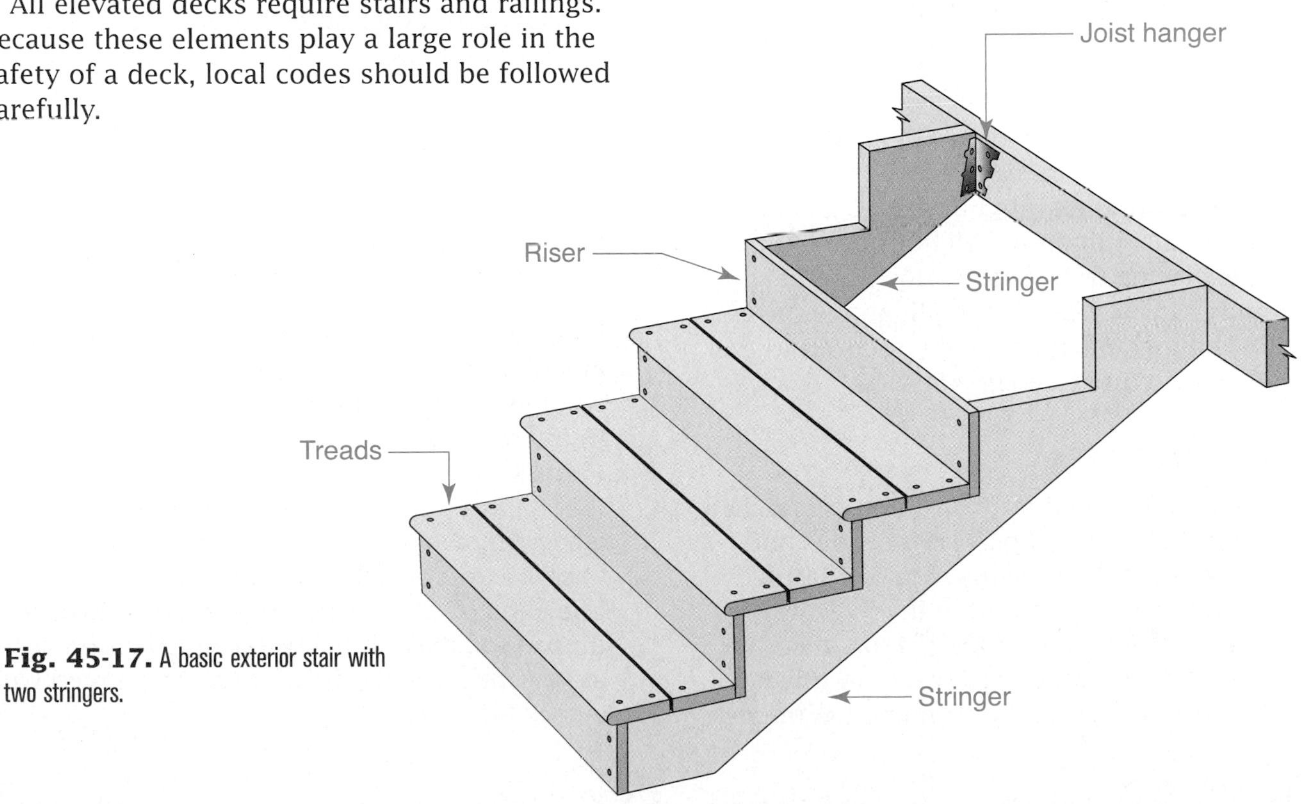

Fig. 45-17. A basic exterior stair with two stringers.

Fig. 45-18. A platform stair can improve access to a deck.

Another type is the platform stair. **Fig. 45-18.** It is much wider than a standard stair and often incorporates a landing. However, it is constructed much as a standard stair.

Railings

The primary purpose of a railing is safety. It should be installed on both sides of a stairway, as well as around elevated decks. Local codes determine the minimum height of the railing and the spacing of balusters. However, height generally ranges from 32″ to 38″ above the decking. All railings must be solidly secured to the deck substructure (see Fig. 45-6).

PORCHES

A porch is a roofed structure that is attached to a house. It is often open on the sides and may serve as the main entry. **Fig. 45-19.** Construction of a porch often involves wall framing, roof framing, roofing, and concrete slab methods described elsewhere in this book. Porch construction can be combined with deck construction. This is often the approach taken with screened porches. Consider the following when building a porch:

- Porches supported on continuous foundation walls should have a clearance of at least 8″ above the exterior finish grade. Floor joists and beams should have a clearance of 18″ or more from the bottom of the joists to the grade, unless preservative-treated lumber is used.
- Horizontal concrete surfaces should be sloped to promote runoff of water.
- Porch columns should be designed to avoid any details or joints that might trap water. Treated structural posts are often cased with untreated finish lumber for better appearance. **Fig. 45-20.**
- It is important to protect the end grain of finished trim wood at joints, because this area absorbs water easily and is prone to rotting. The ends of porch flooring should be brushed, dipped, or soaked in a water-repellent preservative. Once dry, the boards can be painted with a deck enamel.

Fig. 45-19. This porch fits the architectural style of the house. It serves primarily as a protected main entry. It is also large enough for sitting outdoors.

Concrete Steps

Many porches, particularly those that serve as the main entrance, feature concrete steps. Concrete is a durable, low-maintenance material that is ideal for this use.

Many builders prefer to install precast steps. **Fig. 45-21.** These units are cast in a factory, cured under controlled conditions, and then delivered to the job site. They are lifted into place by a small crane mounted on the delivery truck. Precast units are hollow to reduce their weight. They are available in various sizes but are usually 48″ wide. They may include a stoop. A **stoop** is an enlarged landing at the top of the steps.

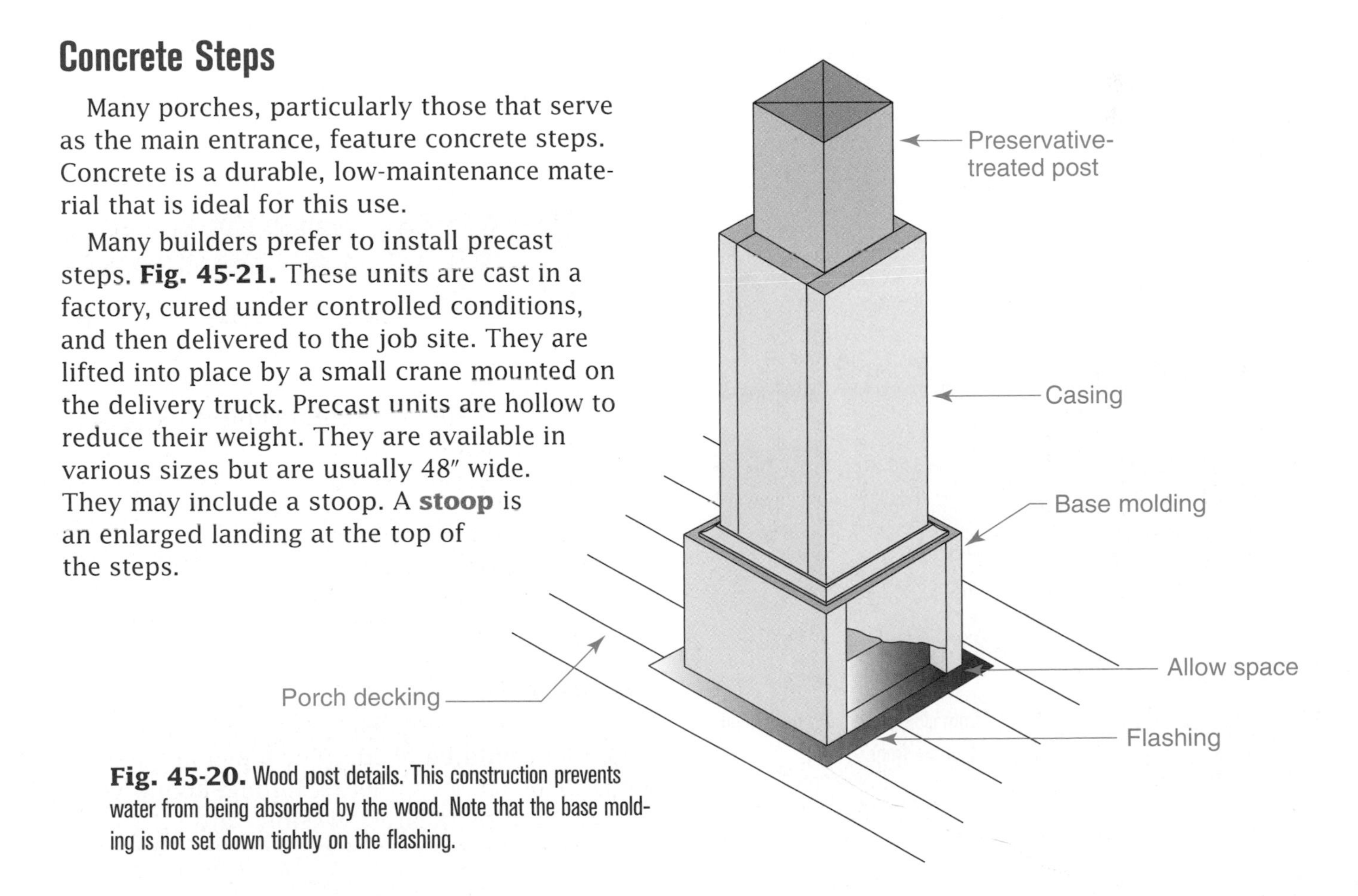

Fig. 45-20. Wood post details. This construction prevents water from being absorbed by the wood. Note that the base molding is not set down tightly on the flashing.

Fig. 45-21. Precast step units are hollow to reduce weight. However, they are still heavy enough to require placement by crane. The unit rests on footings or piers.

Porch steps may instead be cast in place. This work is done by masons or carpenters who build the formwork for risers and treads on site. After the concrete is placed and has partially cured, the forms are removed. Formwork may be made of wood or metal. Wood formwork calls for a high degree of craftsmanship to ensure that the forms are strong and properly designed. For example, each tread and the stoop should be sloped forward slightly to encourage drainage. **Fig. 45-22.** Risers are sometimes slanted inward toward the next lower tread. Like the nosing of a wood step (see Chapter 34, "Stairways"), this provides clearance for using the step.

Fig. 45-22. The risers are leveled from side to side and positioned so the back of each tread is ¼″ higher than the front.

SECTION 45.2 Check Your Knowledge

1. Name two advantages that built-up beams have as compared to solid beams.
2. What step should be taken with the cut ends of built-up or solid beams to increase their durability?
3. When installing a ledger, what are the two most important installation factors?
4. What is the advantage of using a blind-nailing system to install decking?

On the Job

Using Table 45-A, estimate the amount of concrete that would be needed for 6 piers that are 12″ in diameter. Each pier is 4′ long. Round your answer up to the nearest ¼ cubic yard.

Chapter 45 Review

Section Summaries

45.1 In addition to traditional softwoods, decking materials include hardwoods, plastic decking, and composite decking. The materials should be weather and decay resistant. The hardware used to install decking must be corrosion resistant.

45.2 Construction of a deck calls for several layers of structural support. All construction details must be installed to minimize decay caused by trapped water. A ledger is a very important element of an attached deck. It must be installed with great care. Porches are built with the same framing, roofing, and concrete-slab work as other parts of a house.

Review Questions

1. What are the primary requirements of a deck?
2. Name the actual thicknesses most common for softwood decking.
3. What are the four characteristics by which deck construction lumber is graded?
4. What is the difference between heartwood and sapwood?
5. What is a pier?
6. When cutting preservative-treated wood, how can you prevent chemicals from leaching into the surrounding soil?
7. Name the basic types of materials used for decks.
8. Name the basic parts of a deck's substructure.
9. Explain how to plumb a post.
10. Why are porch steps sloped when they are cast in place?

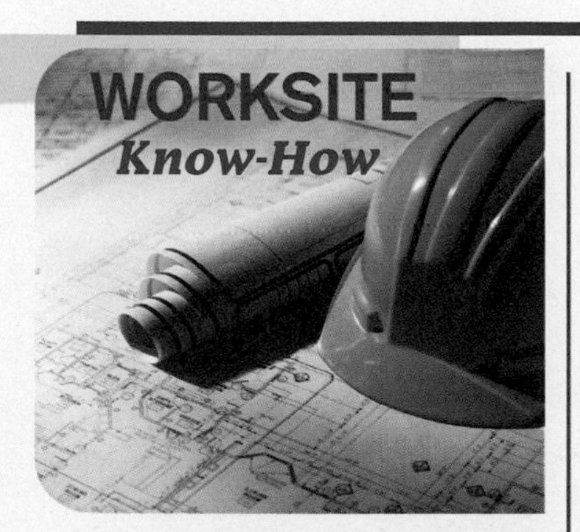

Carpentry Is a System A system is a group of parts that work together to achieve a goal. A system's parts are input, process, output, and feedback. Input includes those resources put into the system. An example would be the materials, money, information, and labor needed to do a particular job, such as construct a porch. The process includes all the activities that have to take place to build the porch, such as nailing the parts together. Output is the result of the system, which in our example would be the finished porch and the benefits it provides. Feedback is information sent back to the system that indicates whether or not the output is satisfactory. If you've installed a porch railing and someone tells you it's not straight, you have received feedback.

Ready Reference Appendix

TABLE OF CONTENTS

ARCHITECTURAL ABBREVIATIONS

These are common abbreviations found on drawings. Abbreviations on drawings are written in all capital letters. No period is needed after an abbreviation unless it might be confused with a whole word. Note that some abbreviations, such as AC, can stand for more than one term. Some terms, such as *beam*, may have more than one acceptable abbreviation.

A

AB—Anchor bolt
AC—Air condition; alternating current
ADH—Adhesive
AG—Above grade; against the grain
AGGR—Aggregate
AL—Aluminum
ALLOW.—Allowance
ALT—Alternate
AP—Access panel
APPROX—Approximate
ASPH—Asphalt
AVG—Average

B

B—Bathroom; beam
BALC—Balcony
BATT—Batten
BD—Board
BET.—Between
BF—Board feet
BL—Building line
BLDG—Building
BLK—Block
BLKG—Blocking
BLR—Boiler
BM—Beam
BOT—Bottom
BR—Bedroom
BRG—Bearing
BRK—Brick
BS—Both sides
BSMT—Basement

C

CAB.—Cabinet
CAT.—Catalog
C CONC—Cast concrete
CEM—Cement
CER—Ceramic
CHIM—Chimney
CI—Cast iron
CIR; CKT—Circuit
CIR BKR—Circuit breaker
CIRC—Circumference
CKT; CIR—Circuit
CL—Centerline
CLG—Ceiling
CLKG—Caulking
CLO—Closet
CLR—Clear
CO—Cleanout
COL—Column
COMB.—Combination
COMP—Component; composition
CONC—Concentric, concrete
CONST—Construction
CONT—Continue
CONTR—Contractor
CORR—Corrugate
CS; X-SECT—Cross section
CSG—Casing
CSK—Countersink
CTD—Coated
CTR—Center; counter
CW—Cold water

D

D—Dryer
DBL—Double
DC—Direct current
DEG—Degree
DET—Detail
DH—Double-hung
DIAG—Diagonal
DIM.—Dimension
DISP—Disposal
DK—Decking
DL—Dead load
DMPR—Damper
DN—Down
DP—Damp-proofing
DR—Dining room; door; drain
DS—Downspout
DW—Dishwasher

E

EA—Each
ELEC—Electric
ENAM—Enamel
ENT—Entrance
EQ—Equal
EST—Estimate
EXC—Excavate
EXT—Extension; exterior

F

FA—Footing area
FAB—Fabricate
FD—Floor drain
FDN—Foundation
FIN.—Finish
FIX.—Fixture
FL—Flashing; floor
FLG—Flooring
FLUOR—Fluorescent
FOS—Face of studs
FPRF—Fireproof
FR—Frame
FS—Full size
FTG—Footing

G

G—Gas; girder
GA—Gauge
GALV—Galvanize
GAR—Garage
GB—Glass block
GFCI—Ground-fault circuit interrupter
GL—Glass; grade line
GND—Ground
GR—Grade
GYP—Gypsum

H

H—Hall
HD—Head
HDR—Header
HDW—Hardware
HOR—Horizontal
HTR—Heater
HVAC—Heating, ventilating, air conditioning
HW—Hot water

I

I—I-beam; iron
IB—I-beam

ARCHITECTURAL ABBREVIATIONS, continued

ID—Inside diameter
INCL—Include
INS—Insulate
INT—Intake; interior; internal
IR—Inside radius

J

JST—Joist
JT—Joint

K

KIT—Kitchen
KD—Kiln-dried; knocked down
KO—Knockout
kW—Kilowatt

L

LAM—Laminate
LAU—Laundry
LAV—Lavatory
LBR—Lumber
L CL—Linen closet
LH—Left hand
LIN—Linear
LL—Live load
LOA—Length overall
LR—Living room
LT—Light
LTL—Lintel
LV—Louver

M

MATL—Material
MAX—Maximum
MECH—Mechanical
MEMB—Membrane
MET.—Metal
MIN—Minimum
MIX.—Mixture
MLDG—Molding
MN—Main
MOD—Model
MRTR—Mortar
MULT—Multiple

N

NAT—Natural
NO.—Number
NOM—Nominal
NTS—Not to scale

O

OA—Overall
OC—On center
OD—Outside diameter
OPNG—Opening
OPP—Opposite
OR—Outside radius
OVHD—Overhead

P

PAR.—Parallel
PC—Piece; pull chain
PERM—Permanent
PERP—Perpendicular
PL—Plaster; plate; property line
PLMB—Plumbing
PLYWD—Plywood
PNL—Panel
PRCST—Precast
PREFAB—Prefabricated
PROP—Property
PT—Part; pressure-treated
PTN—Partition

R

R—Radius, range; riser
RAD—Radiator
RD—Round
RECP—Receptacle
REF—Reference; refrigerator
REG—Register
REINF—Reinforce
REQD—Required
RET—Return
RF—Roof
RFG—Roofing
RH—Right hand
RM—Room
RO—Rough opening

S

SCH—Schedule
SDG—Siding
SECT—Section
SERV—Service
SEW.—Sewer
SH—Sheet; shower
SHTHG—Sheathing
SIM—Similar
SP—Soil pipe
SPEC—Specification
SST—Stainless steel
ST—Stairs; steam; street
STD—Standard
STG—Storage
STK—Stock
STL—Steel
SUP—Supply
SUR—Surface
SYM—Symbol; symmetrical
SYS—System

T

T&G—Tar and gravel; tongue and groove
TC—Terra-cotta
TEMP—Temperature
TER—Terrazzo
THERMO—Thermostat
THRU—Through
TOL—Tolerance
TOT.—Total
TR—Tread
TUB.—Tubing
TYP—Typical

U

UNFIN—Unfinished

V

V—Vacuum, valve; volt
VAP PRF—Vapor-proof
VENT.—Ventilate
VERT—Vertical
VP—Vent pipe
VS—Vent stack

W

W—Watt
W/—With
WC—Water closet
WD—Wood
WDW—Window
WH—Water heater; weep hole
WI—Wrought iron
WM—Washing machine
W/O—Without
WS—Weatherstripping

X, Y, Z

X-SECT; CS—Cross section

PLUMBING SYMBOLS

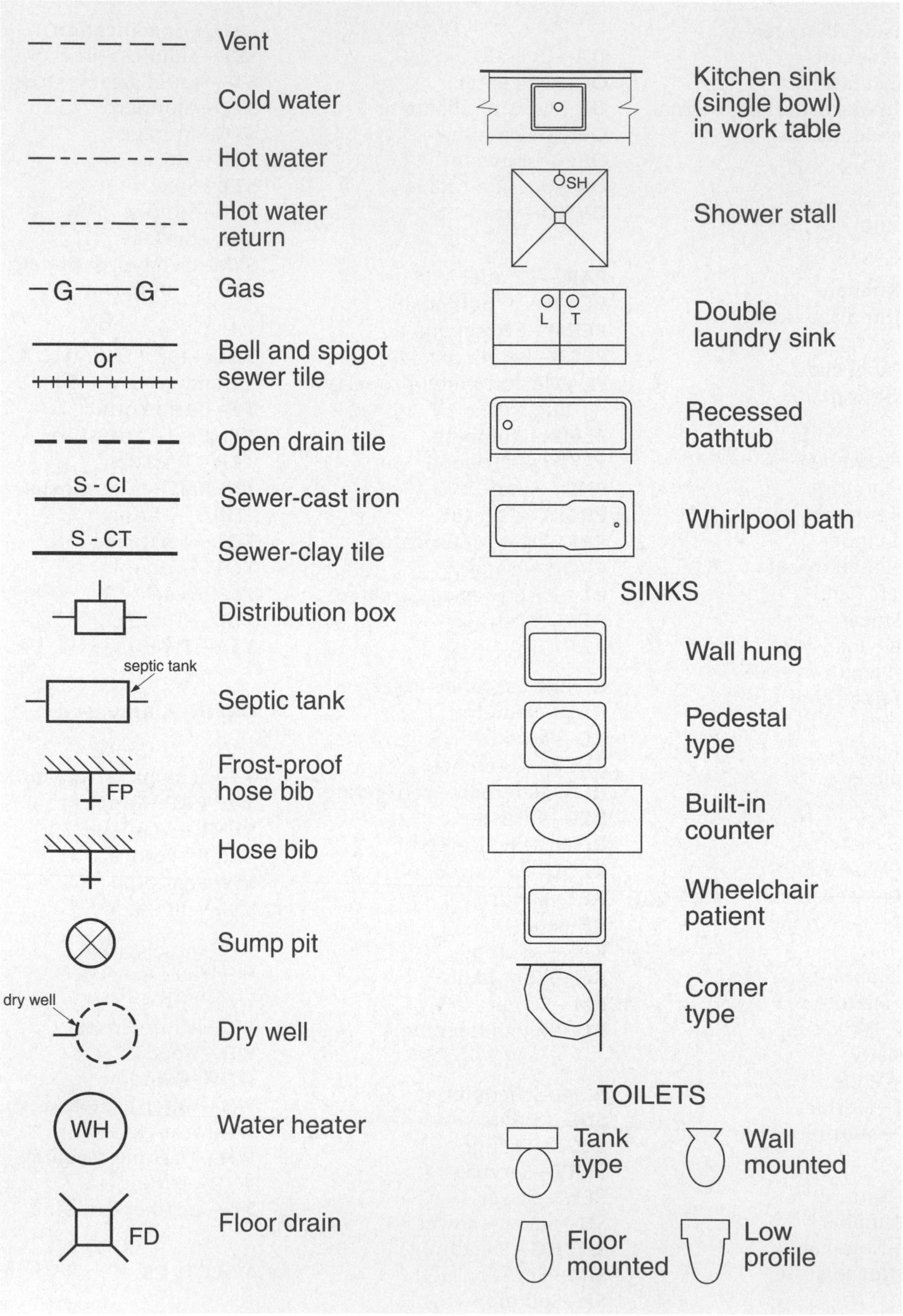
Vent
Cold water
Hot water
Hot water return
G
G
Gas
or
Bell and spigot sewer tile
Open drain tile
S - CI
Sewer-cast iron
S - CT
Sewer-clay tile
Distribution box
septic tank
Septic tank
FP
Frost-proof hose bib
Hose bib
Sump pit
dry well
Dry well
WH
Water heater
FD
Floor drain
Kitchen sink (single bowl) in work table
SH
Shower stall
L
T
Double laundry sink
Recessed bathtub
Whirlpool bath
SINKS
Wall hung
Pedestal type
Built-in counter
Wheelchair patient
Corner type
TOILETS
Tank type
Wall mounted
Floor mounted
Low profile

ELECTRICAL SYMBOLS

Symbol	Description
	Wall fixture outlet
B	Blanked ceiling outlet
B	Blanked wall outlet
D	Drop cord
F	Ceiling fan outlet
F	Wall fan outlet
J	Ceiling junction box
J	Wall junction box
L	Ceiling lamp holder
L	Wall lamp holder
L_{PS}	Ceiling lamp holder with pull switch
L_{PS}	Wall lamp holder with pull switch
S	Ceiling pull switch
S	Wall pull switch
O	Surface or drop individual fluorescent fixture
OR	Recessed individual fluorescent fixture
O	Surface or drop continuous fluorescent fixture
OR	Recessed continuous fluorescent fixture

Symbol	Description
	Duplex convenience outlet
1, 3	Convenience outlet other than duplex 1=single, 3=triple, etc.
WP	Weatherproof convenience outlet
GR	Grounded outlet
	Split wired outlet
R	Range outlet
AC	Air conditioner outlet
S	Switch and convenience outlet
R	Radio and convenience outlet
	Special purpose outlet (design in specifications)
	Floor outlet
	Floor single outlet
	Floor duplex outlet
	Lighting panel
	Power panel
	Branch circuit; concealed in ceiling or wall
	Branch circuit; concealed in floor

Symbol	Description
	Branch circuit; exposed
	Home run to panel board; indicate number of circuits by number of arrows
	Feeders
	Push button
	Buzzer
	Bell
S	Single-pole switch
S_2	Double-pole switch
S_3	Three-way switch
S_4	Four-way switch
S_D	Automatic door switch
S_P	Switch and pilot lamp
S_K	Key-operated switch
S_{CB}	Circuit breaker
S_{WCB}	Weatherproof circuit breaker
S_{RC}	Remote-control switch
S_{WP}	Weatherproof switch
S_L	Low-voltage switch
S_T	Time switch

METRIC CONVERSION FACTORS

When you know:	You can find:	If you multiply by:
Length		
inches	millimeters	25.4
feet	centimeters	30.48
yards	meters	0.91
miles	kilometers	1.6
millimeters	inches	0.04
centimeters	inches	0.4
meters	yards	1.09
kilometers	miles	0.62
Area		
square inches	square centimeters	6.45
square feet	square meters	0.09
square yards	square meters	0.84
square miles	square kilometers	2.59
acres	hectares	0.4
square centimeters	square inches	0.16
square meters	square yards	1.2
square kilometers	square miles	0.4
hectares	acres	2.5
Mass		
ounces	grams	28.3
pounds	kilograms	0.45
short tons	metric tons	0.9
grams	ounces	0.04
kilograms	pounds	2.2
metric tons	short tons	1.1
Liquid Volume		
ounces	milliliters	30
pints	liters	0.47
quarts	liters	0.95
gallons	liters	3.8
milliliters	ounces	0.03
liters	pints	2.1
liters	quarts	1.06
liters	gallons	0.26
Temperature		
degrees Fahrenheit	degrees Celsius	0.6 (after subtracting 32)
degrees Celsius	degrees Fahrenheit	1.8 (then add 32)

CUSTOMARY/METRIC CONVERSIONS

Customary/ English (inches)	Metric (millimeters)
1/32	0.8
1/16	1.6
1/8	3.2
3/16	4.8
1/4	6.4
5/16	7.9
3/8	9.5
7/16	11.1
1/2	12.7
9/16	14.3
5/8	15.9
11/16	17.5
3/4	19.1
13/16	20.6
7/8	22.2
15/16	23.8
1	25.4
5	127.0
12	304.8
18	457.2
24	609.6
36	914.4
48	1219.2

RELATIVE NAIL SIZES

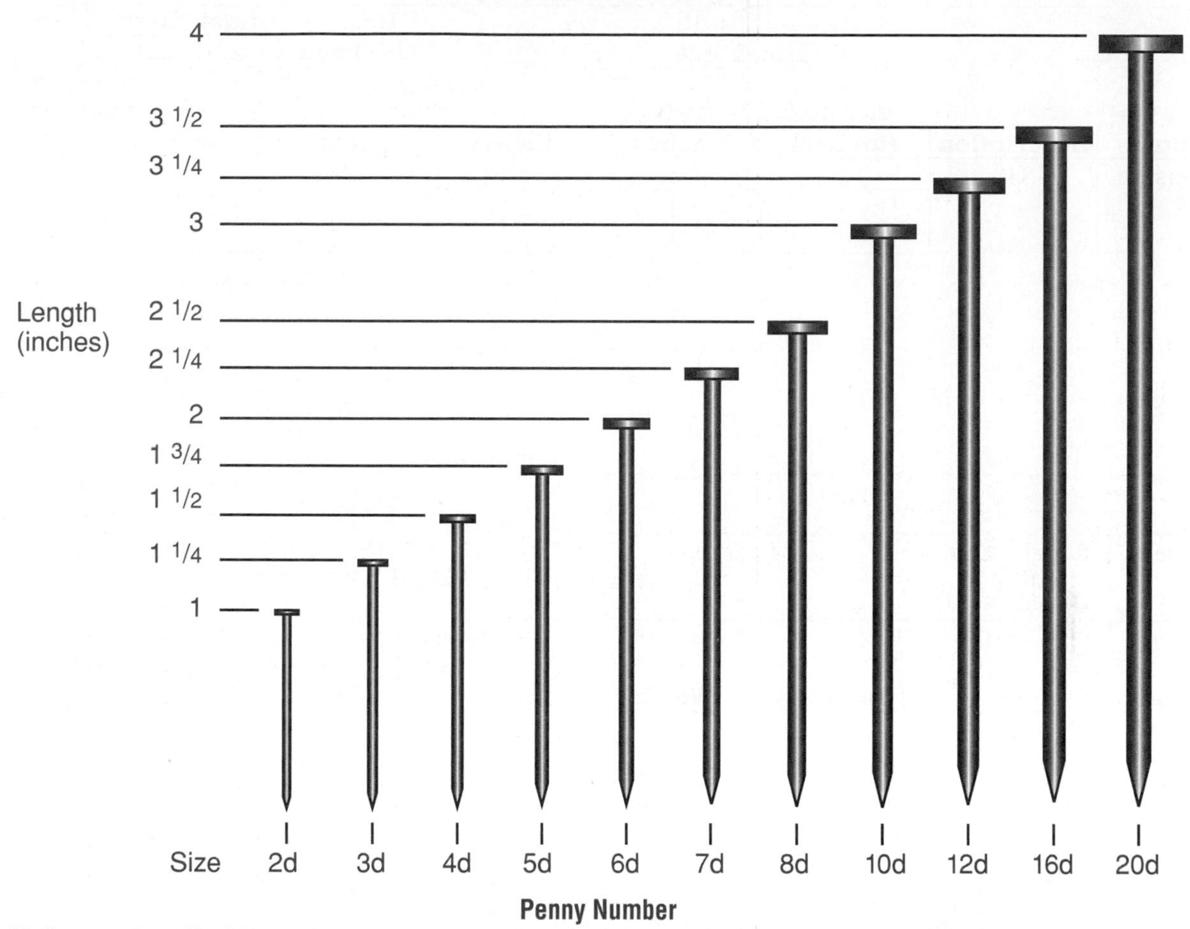

Nails are classified by pennyweight and ordered by penny, or pennyweight, number. Note the lower-case *d* following the number below each nail in the above illustration. This number (for example, 2d) is the penny number. The *d* stands for "penny" and is the abbreviation for the Latin word *denarius*, a small coin that was the Roman equivalent of a penny. As you can see, penny number is related to nail length. The penny number increases with nail length: the larger the number, the longer the nail.

TYPES OF NAILS

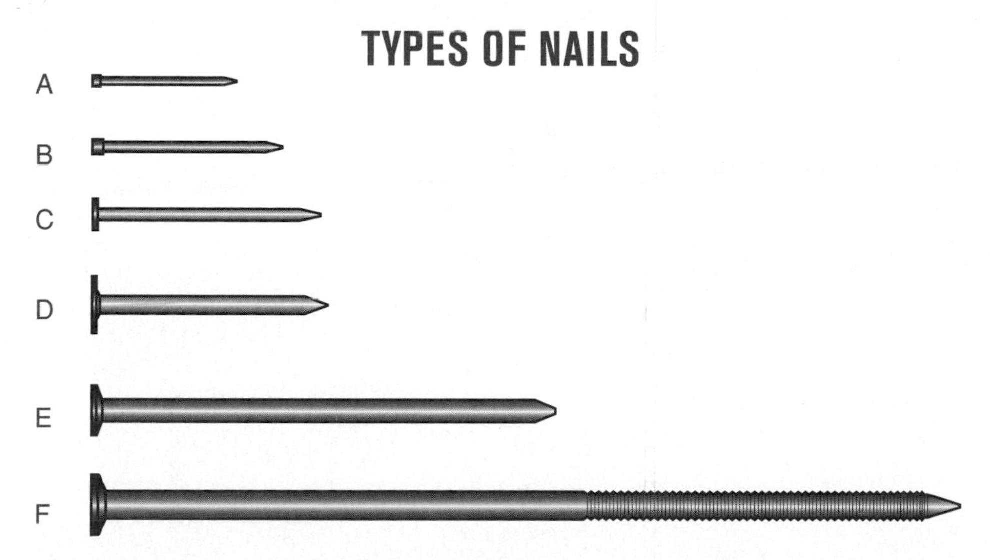

A few of the more commonly used nails. *A.* Wire brad. *B.* Finish nail. *C.* Box nail. *D.* Roofing nail. *E.* Common nail. *F.* Spike.

STANDARD SIZES FOR FRAMING LUMBER, NOMINAL AND DRESSED

Product	**Description**	**Nominal Size**		**Dressed Dimensions Thicknesses and Widths**			
				Surfaced Dry		**Surfaced Unseasoned**	
		Thickness (inches)	**Width (inches)**	**inches**	**mm**	**inches**	**mm**
Dimension	S4S	2	2	1 ½	38	1 9⁄16	40
		3	3	2 ½	64	2 9⁄16	65
		4	4	3 ½	89	3 9⁄16	90
			5	4 ½	114	4 ⅝	117
			6	5 ½	140	5 ⅝	143
			8	7 ¼	184	7 ½	191
			10	9 ¼	235	9 ½	241
			12	11 ¼	289	11 ½	292
			over 12	¾ off nominal	19 off nominal	½ off nominal	13 off nominal
				Thickness (unseasoned)		**Width (unseasoned)**	
Timbers	Rough or S4S (shipped unseasoned)	5 and larger		½" (13 mm) off nominal (S4S) [See 3.20 of WWPA Grading Rules for Rough.]			
				Thickness (dry)		**Width (dry)**	
		Thickness	**Width**	**inches**	**mm**	**inches**	**mm**
Decking	2" (Single T&G)	2	5	1 ½	38	4	102
			6			5	127
			8			6 ¾	172
			10			8 ¾	222
			12			10 ¾	273
	3" and 4" (Double T&G)	3	6	2 ½	64	5 ¼	133
		4		3 ½	89		

Western Wood Products Association

Notes: Based on Western Lumber Grading Rules
Metric equivalents are provided for surfaced (actual) sizes.
Abbreviations: FOHC–Free of Heart Center
Rough Full Sawn–Unsurfaced lumber cut to full specified size
T&G–Tongued-and-grooved
S4S–Surfaced four sides

ESTIMATING MATERIAL FOR EXTERIOR WALL STUDS

Size of Studs	Spacing on Centers (inches)	Bd. Ft. per Sq. Ft. per Area	Lbs. Nails per 1000 Bd. Ft.
2×4	12	1.09	22
	16	1.05	
	20	0.98	
	24	0.94	
2×6	12	1.66	15
	16	1.51	
	20	1.44	
	24	1.38	

Note: This table tells you how you can figure the number of board feet and nails for exterior wall framing.

ESTIMATING MATERIAL FOR PARTITION STUDS

Size of Studs	Spacing on Centers (inches)	Bd. Ft. per Sq. Ft. per Area	Lbs. Nails per 1000 Bd. Ft.
2×3	12	0.91	25
	16	0.83	
	24	0.76	
2×4	12	1.22	19
	16	1.12	
	24	1.02	
2×6	16	1.48	16
	24	1.22	

Note: With this table you can figure the board feet of lumber needed for partition studs. In addition to giving the amount of material for the partition construction, this table also gives consideration to the need for extra lumber for headers, trimmers, and other special framing.

MAXIMUM SPANS FOR HEADERS

Nominal depth of headers made of two thicknesses of nominal two-inch lumber installed on edge	Interior Partitions or Walls				Exterior Walls		
	Limited attic storage	Full attic storage, or roof load, or limited attic storage plus one floor	Full attic storage plus one floor, or roof load plus one floor, or limited attic storage plus two floors	Full attic storage plus two floors, or roof load plus two floors	Roof, with or without attic storage	Roof, with or without attic storage, plus one floor	Roof, with or without attic storage, plus two floors
4"	4'	2'	Not permitted	Not permitted	4'	2'	2'
6"	6'	3'	2' 6"	2'	6'	5'	4'
8"	8'	4'	3'	3'	8'	7'	6'
10"	10'	5'	4'	3' 6"	10'	8'	7'
12"	12' 6"	6'	5'	4'	12'	9'	8'

Note: Supported loads include dead loads and ceiling. These header widths (lintel spans) may be used for most residential buildings.

PARTITION STUDS NEEDED

Partition Length in Feet	Number of Studs Required
2	3
3	3
4	4
5	5
6	6
7	6
8	7
9	8
10	9
11	9
12	10
13	11
14	12
15	12
16	13
17	14
18	15
19	15
20	16

Notes: This table shows studs required for framing 16" OC
with single top and bottom plates.
For dbl. plate, add per sq. ft.
For 2×8 studs, double above quantities.
For 2×6 studs, increase above quantities 50 percent.

STAPLING SCHEDULE

Plywood Thickness (inches)	Size of Staple (length)	Spacing	
		Edges (inches)	Intermediate supports (inches)
5/16	Staple 15 ga. (1 3/8)		
	Staple 16 ga. (1 3/4)		
3/8	Staple 15 ga. (1 3/8)	6	12
	Staple 16 ga. (1 3/4)	6	12
15/32 and 1/2	Staple 15 ga. (1 1/2)	6	12
	Staple 16 ga. (1 3/4)	6	12

Note: Be sure to follow local building codes.

PLYWOOD WALL SHEATHING APPLICATION DETAILS

Panel Identification Index	Minimum Thickness (inches)	Maximum Stud Exterior Covering Nailed to:		Nail Size (a)	Nail Spacing (inches)	
		Stud	Sheathing		Panel Edges (when over framing)	Intermediate (each stud)
12/0, 16/0, 20/0	5/16	16	16[b]	6d	6	12
16/0, 20/0, 24/0	3/8	24	16, 24[b]	6d	6	12
24/0, 32/16	1/2	24	24	6d	6	12

[a] Common smooth, annular, spiral thread, galvanized box or T-nails of the same diameter as common nails (0.113" dia. for 6d) may be used. Staples also permitted at reduced spacing.

[b] When sidings such as shingles are nailed only to the plywood sheathing, apply plywood with face grain across studs.

Notes: This is a general guide. Be sure to follow local building codes.

Look for these APA grade-trademarks on wall sheathing.

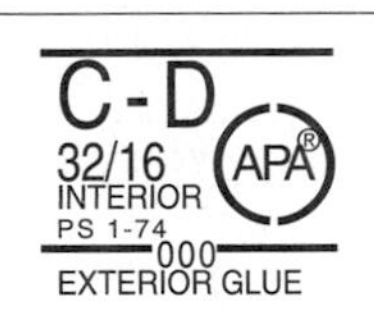

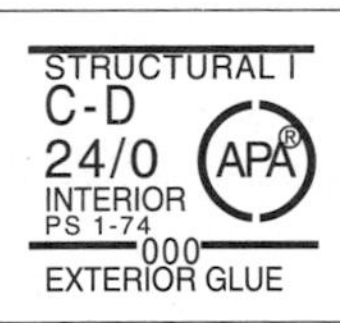

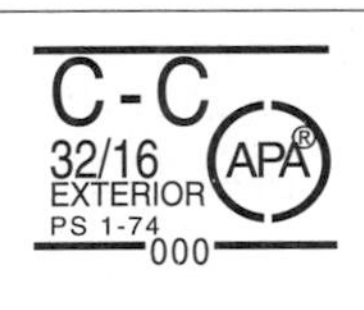

BOARD-FOOT MEASURES

Nominal Size (inches)	Actual Length in Feet								
	8	**10**	**12**	**14**	**16**	**18**	**20**	**22**	**24**
1×4	2 ⅔	3 ⅓	4	4 ⅔	5 ⅓	6	6 ⅔	7 ⅓	8
1×6	4	5	6	7	8	9	10	11	12
1×8	5 ⅓	6 ⅔	8	9 ⅓	10 ⅔	12	13 ⅓	14 ⅔	16
1×10	6 ⅔	8 ⅓	10	11 ⅔	13 ⅓	15	16 ⅔	18 ⅓	20
1 ¼×4		4 ⅙	5	5 ⅚	6 ⅔	7 ½	8 ⅓	9 ⅙	10
1 ¼×6		6 ¼	7 ½	8 ¾	10	11 ¼	12 ½	13 ¾	15
2×4	5 ⅓	6 ⅔	8	9 ⅓	10 ⅓	12	13 ⅓	14 ⅔	16
2×6	8	10	12	14	16	18	20	22	24
2×8	10 ⅔	13 ⅓	16	18 ⅔	21 ⅓	24	26 ⅔	29 ⅓	32
2×10	13 ⅓	16 ⅔	20	23 ⅓	26 ⅔	30	33 ⅓	36 ⅔	40
4×4	10 ⅔	13 ⅓	16	18 ⅔	21 ⅓	24	26 ⅔	29 ⅓	32
4×6	16	20	24	28	32	36	40	44	48
4×8	21 ⅓	26 ⅔	32	37 ⅓	42 ⅔	48	53 ⅓	58 ⅔	64
4×10	26 ⅔	33 ⅓	40	46 ⅔	53 ⅓	60	66 ⅔	73 ⅓	80

NONSTRESS-GRADED LUMBER

Species	Minimum Grade	Uniform Building Code Standard Number
Group I		
Douglas fir and larch[a]	Construction	25-3, 25-4
Group II		
Bald cypress (tidewater red cypress)	No. 2	25-2
Douglas fir (south)[a]	Construction	25-4
Fir, white	Construction	25-3, 25-4
Hemlock, eastern	No. 1	25-5
Hemlock, West Coast and western[a]	Construction	25-3, 25-4
Pine, red (Norway pine)	No. 1	25-5
Redwood, California	Select heart	25-7
Spruce, eastern	No. 1	25-8
Spruce, Sitka	Construction	25-3
Spruce, white and western white	Construction	25-4[b]
Group III		
Cedar, western	Construction, West Coast studs	25-3
Cedar, western red and incense	Construction	25-4
Douglas fir and larch[a]	Standard, West Coast studs	25-3, 25-4
Douglas fir (south)[a]	Standard	25-4
Fir, balsam	No. 1, Standard	25-8
Fir, white	West Coast studs	25-3, 25-4
Hemlock, eastern	No. 2, Standard	25-5
Hemlock, West Coast and western[a]	West Coast studs	25-3, 25-4
Pine, ponderosa, lodgepole, sugar, Idaho white	Construction	25-4
Redwood, California	Construction	25-7
Redwood, California (studs only)	Two Star	25-7
Spruce, Engelmann	Construction, standard	25-4
Spruce, Sitka	West Coast studs	25-3
Spruce, white and western white	Standard	25-4[b]
Group IV (See Section 2501 (e) Uniform Bldg. Code)		
Cedar, western	Utility	25-3
Cedar, western red and incense	Utility	25-4
Douglas fir and larch	Utility	25-3, 25-4
Douglas fir (south)	Utility	25-4
Fir, white	Utility	25-3, 25-4
Hemlock, West Coast and western	Utility	25-3, 25-4
Pine, ponderosa, lodgepole, sugar, Idaho white	Utility	25-4
Redwood, California	Merchantable	25-7
Redwood, California (studs only)	One Star	25-7
Spruce, Engelmann	Utility	25-4
Spruce, Sitka	Utility	25-3
Spruce, white and western white	Utility	25-4[b]

[a] 2×4 only.

[b] Spruce (white and western white) shall be graded under the requirements of Section 25.409 of U.B.C. Standard No. 25-4.

SPAN TABLE

This is an example of a span table.
You should refer to the span tables appropriate for your area.

TABLE R502.5(1) GIRDER SPANS[a] AND HEADER SPANS[a] FOR EXTERIOR BEARING WALLS
(Maximum header spans for douglas fir-larch, hem-fir, southern pine and spruce-pine-fir[b] and required number of jack studs)

		GROUND SNOW LOAD (psf)[e]											
		30						50					
		Building width[c] (feet)											
		20		28		36		20		28		36	
HEADERS SUPPORTING	SIZE	Span	NJ[d]	Span	NJ[d]	Span	NJ[d]	Span	NJ[d]	Span	NJ[d]	Span	NJ[d]
Roof and Ceiling	2-2×4	3-6	1	3-2	1	2-10	1	3-2	1	2-9	1	2-6	1
	2-2×6	5-5	1	4-8	1	4-2	1	4-8	1	4-1	1	3-8	2
	2-2×8	6-10	1	5-11	2	5-4	2	5-11	2	5-2	2	4-7	2
	2-2×10	8-5	2	7-3	2	6-6	2	7-3	2	6-3	2	5-7	2
	2-2×12	9-9	2	8-5	2	7-6	2	8-5	2	7-3	2	6-6	2
	3-2×8	8-4	1	7-5	1	6-8	1	7-5	1	6-5	2	5-9	2
	3-2×10	10-6	1	9-1	2	8-2	2	9-1	2	7-10	2	7-0	2
	3-2×12	12-2	2	10-7	2	9-5	2	10-7	2	9-2	2	8-2	2
	4-2×8	7-0	1	6-1	2	5-5	2	6-1	2	5-3	2	4-8	2
	4-2×10	11-8	1	10-6	1	9-5	2	10-6	1	9-1	2	8-2	2
	4-2×12	14-1	1	12-2	2	10-11	2	12-2	2	10-7	2	9-5	2
Roof, ceiling and one center-bearing floor	2												1
	2												2
	2												2
	2-												2
	2-												3
	3												2
	3-												2
	3-												2
	4												2
	4-												2
	4-												2
Roof, ceiling and one clear span floor	2												1
	2												2
	2												2
	2-												3
	2-												3
	3												2
	3-												2
	3-												2
	4												2
	4-												2
	4-												2
Roof, ceiling and two center-bearing floors	2-2×4	2-7	1	2-3	1	2-0	1	2-6	1	2-2	1	1-11	1
	2-2×6	3-9	2	3-3	2	2-11	2	3-8	2	3-2	2	2-10	2
	2-2×8	4-9	2	4-2	2	3-9	2	4-7	2	4-0	2	3-8	2
	2-2×10	5-9	2	5-1	2	4-7	3	5-8	2	4-11	2	4-5	3
	2-2×12	6-8	2	5-10	3	5-3	3	6-6	2	5-9	3	5-2	3
	3-2×8	5-11	2	5-2	2	4-8	2	5-9	2	5-1	2	4-7	2
	3-2×10	7-3	2	6-4	2	5-8	2	7-1	2	6-2	2	5-7	2
	3-2×12	8-5	2	7-4	2	6-7	2	8-2	2	7-2	2	6-5	3
	4-2×8	4-10	2	4-3	2	3-10	2	4-9	2	4-2	2	3-9	2
	4-2×10	8-4	2	7-4	2	6-7	2	8-2	2	7-2	2	6-5	2
	4-2×12	9-8	2	8-6	2	7-8	2	9-5	2	8-3	2	7-5	2

READING SPAN TABLES

A span is the horizontal distance between supports. In carpentry, various framing members are used across openings. Span tables enable a carpenter to determine what dimension of header, girder, joist, or rafter will be needed over a given opening or area. For example, this span table gives the dimensions of the girders and headers needed to span a given opening in an exterior bearing wall. Many span tables carry notes at the bottom. For a fuller understanding of the table, always refer to these notes. To use this table, you will need the following information:

- The Ground Snow Load in your location. This may be found on a map or chart in the code book.
- The Building Width. This will be given on the building floor plans.
- The Span of the header. This will be given on the building floor plans.

Refer to the highlighted cells in this table. The highlighted information identifies the construction project as having:

- A Ground Snow Load of 30 psf (pounds per square feet).
- A Building Width of 28 feet.

If a header must span 7'3" in this house, the table indicates that it should be made of two 2×10s.

Four other representative span tables follow this one. These tables are provided only as examples. On an actual construction project, refer to the span tables in your local code.

For SI: 1 inch = 25.4 mm, 1 pound per square foot = 0.0479 kN/m^2.

a. Spans are given in feet and inches.

b. Tabulated values assume #2 grade lumber.

c. Building width is measured perpendicular to the ridge. For widths between those shown, spans are permitted to be interpolated.

d. NJ – Number of jack studs required to support each end. Where the number of required jack studs equals one, the headers are permitted to be supported by an approved framing anchor attached to the full-height wall stud and to the header.

e. Use 30 psf ground snow load for cases in which ground snow load is less than 30 psf and the roof live load is equal to or less than 20 psf.

Copyright 2000, International Code Council, Inc., Falls Church, Virginia. 2000 International Residential Code. Reprinted with permission of the author. All rights reserved.

SPAN TABLE

This is an example of a span table.
You should refer to the span tables appropriate for your area.

TABLE R502.5(2) GIRDER SPANS[a] AND HEADER SPANS[a] FOR INTERIOR BEARING WALLS
(Maximum header spans for douglas fir-larch, hem-fir, southern pine and spruce-pine-fir[b] and required number of jack studs)

HEADERS AND GIRDERS SUPPORTING	SIZE	BUILDING WIDTH[c] (feet)					
		20		28		36	
		Span	NJ[d]	Span	NJ[d]	Span	NJ[d]
One floor only	2-2×4	3-1	1	2-8	1	2-5	1
	2-2×6	4-6	1	3-11	1	3-6	1
	2-2×8	5-9	1	5-0	2	4-5	2
	2-2×10	7-10	2	6-1	2	5-5	2
	2-2×12	8-1	2	7-0	2	6-3	2
	3-2×8	7-2	1	6-3	1	5-7	2
	3-2×10	8-9	1	7-7	2	6-9	2
	3-2×12	10-2	2	8-10	2	7-10	2
	4-2×8	5-10	1	5-1	2	4-6	2
	4-2×10	10-1	1	8-9	1	7-10	2
	4-2×12	11-9	1	10-2	2	9-1	2
Two floors	2-2×4	2-2	1	1-10	1	1-7	1
	2-2×6	3-2	2	2-9	2	2-5	2
	2-2×8	4-1	2	3-6	2	3-2	2
	2-2×10	4-11	2	4-3	2	3-10	3
	2-2×12	5-9	2	5-0	3	4-5	3
	3-2×8	5-1	2	4-5	2	3-11	2
	3-2×10	6-2	2	5-4	2	4-10	2
	3-2×12	7-2	2	6-3	2	5-7	3
	4-2×8	4-2	2	3-7	2	3-2	2
	4-2×10	7-2	2	6-2	2	5-6	2
	4-2×12	8-4	2	7-2	2	6-5	2

For SI: 1 inch = 25.4 mm, 1 foot = 304.8 mm.

a. Spans are given in feet and inches.

b. Tabulated values assume #2 grade lumber.

c. Building width is measured perpendicular to the ridge. For widths between those shown, spans are permitted to be interpolated.

d. NJ – Number of jack studs required to support each end. Where the number of required jack studs equals one, the headers are permitted to be supported by an approved framing anchor attached to the full-height wall stud and to the header.

Copyright 2000, International Code Council, Inc., Falls Church, Virginia. 2000 International Residential Code. Reprinted with permission of the author. All rights reserved.

SPAN TABLE

This is an example of a span table.
You should refer to the span tables appropriate for your area.

TABLE R502.3.1(2) FLOOR JOIST SPANS FOR COMMON LUMBER SPECIES
(Residential living areas, live load = 40 psf, L/Δ = 360)

JOIST SPACING (inches)	SPECIE AND GRADE		DEAD LOAD = 10 psf				DEAD LOAD = 20 psf			
			2×6	2×8	2×10	2×12	2×6	2×8	2×10	2×12
			Maximum floor joist spans							
			(feet - inches)	(feet - inches)	(feet - inches)	(feet - inches)	(feet - inches)	(feet - inches)	(feet - inches)	(feet - inches)
12	Douglas fir-larch	SS	11-4	15-0	19-1	23-3	11-4	15-0	19-1	23-3
	Douglas fir-larch	#1	10-11	14-5	18-5	22-0	10-11	14-2	17-4	20-1
	Douglas fir-larch	#2	10-9	14-2	17-9	20-7	10-6	13-3	16-3	18-10
	Douglas fir-larch	#3	8-8	11-0	13-5	15-7	7-11	10-0	12-3	14-3
	Hem-fir	SS	10-9	14-2	18-0	21-11	10-9	14-2	18-0	21-11
	Hem-fir	#1	10-6	13-10	17-8	21-6	10-6	13-10	16-11	19-7
	Hem-fir	#2	10-0	13-2	16-10	20-4	10-0	13-1	16-0	18-6
	Hem-fir	#3	8-8	11-0	13-5	15-7	7-11	10-0	12-3	14-3
	Southern pine	SS	11-2	14-8	18-9	22-10	11-2	14-8	18-9	22-10
	Southern pine	#1	10-11	14-5	18-5	22-5	10-11	14-5	18-5	22-5
	Southern pine	#2	10-9	14-2	18-0	21-9	10-9	14-2	16-11	19-10
	Southern pine	#3	9-4	11-11	14-0	16-8	8-6	10-10	12-10	15-3
	Spruce-pine-fir	SS	10-6	13-10	17-8	21-6	10-6	13-10	17-8	21-6
	Spruce-pine-fir	#1	10-3	13-6	17-3	20-7	10-3	13-3	16-3	18-10
	Spruce-pine-fir	#2	10-3	13-6	17-3	20-7	10-3	13-3	16-3	18-10
	Spruce-pine-fir	#3	8-8	11-0	13-5	15-7	7-11	10-0	12-3	14-3
16	Douglas fir-larch	SS	10-4	13-7	17-4	21-1	10-4	13-7	17-4	21-0
	Douglas fir-larch	#1	9-11	13-1	16-5	19-1	9-8	12-4	15-0	17-5
	Douglas fir-larch	#2	9-9	12-7	15-5	17-10	9-1	11-6	14-1	16-3
	Douglas fir-larch	#3	7-6	9-6	11-8	13-6	6-10	8-8	10-7	12-4
	Hem-fir	SS	9-9	12-10	16-5	19-11	9-9	12-10	16-5	19-11
	Hem-fir	#1	9-6	12-7	16-0	18-7	9-6	12-0	14-8	17-0
	Hem-fir	#2	9-1	12-0	15-2	17-7	8-11	11-4	13-10	16-1
	Hem-fir	#3	7-6	9-6	11-8	13-6	6-10	8-8	10-7	12-4
	Southern pine	SS	10-2	13-4	17-0	20-9	10-2	13-4	17-0	20-9
	Southern pine	#1	9-11	13-1	16-9	20-4	9-11	13-1	16-4	19-6
	Southern pine	#2	9-9	12-10	16-1	18-10	9-6	12-4	14-8	17-2
	Southern pine	#3	8-1	10-3	12-2	14-6	7-4	9-5	11-1	13-2
	Spruce-pine-fir	SS	9-6	12-7	16-0	19-6	9-6	12-7	16-0	19-6
	Spruce-pine-fir	#1	9-4	12-3	15-5	17-10	9-1	11-6	14-1	16-3
	Spruce-pine-fir	#2	9-4	12-3	15-5	17-10	9-1	11-6	14-1	16-3
	Spruce-pine-fir	#3	7-6	9-6	11-8	13-6	6-10	8-8	10-7	12-4
24	Douglas fir-larch	SS	9-0	11-11	15-2	18-5	9-0	11-11	14-9	17-1
	Douglas fir-larch	#1	8-8	11-0	13-5	15-7	7-11	10-0	12-3	14-3
	Douglas fir-larch	#2	8-1	10-3	12-7	14-7	7-5	9-5	11-6	13-4
	Douglas fir-larch	#3	6-2	7-9	9-6	11-0	5-7	7-1	8-8	10-1
	Hem-fir	SS	8-6	11-3	14-4	17-5	8-6	11-3	14-4	16-10[a]
	Hem-fir	#1	8-4	10-9	13-1	15-2	7-9	9-9	11-11	13-10
	Hem-fir	#2	7-11	10-2	12-5	14-4	7-4	9-3	11-4	13-1
	Hem-fir	#3	6-2	7-9	9-6	11-0	5-7	7-1	8-8	10-1
	Southern pine	SS	8-10	11-8	14-11	18-1	8-10	11-8	14-11	18-1
	Southern pine	#1	8-8	11-5	14-7	17-5	8-8	11-3	13-4	15-11
	Southern pine	#2	8-6	11-0	13-1	15-5	7-9	10-0	12-0	14-0
	Southern pine	#3	6-7	8-5	9-11	11-10	6-0	7-8	9-1	10-9
	Spruce-pine-fir	SS	8-4	11-0	14-0	17-0	8-4	11-0	13-8	15-11
	Spruce-pine-fir	#1	8-1	10-3	12-7	14-7	7-5	9-5	11-6	13-4
	Spruce-pine-fir	#2	8-1	10-3	12-7	14-7	7-5	9-5	11-6	13-4
	Spruce-pine-fir	#3	6-2	7-9	9-6	11-0	5-7	7-1	8-8	10-01

For SI: 1 inch = 25.4 mm, 1 foot = 308.4 mm, 1 pound per square foot = 0.0479 kN/m^2.

[a] Check sources for availability of lumber in lengths greater than 20 feet.

[b] End bearing length shall be increased to 2 inches.

Copyright 2000, International Code Council, Inc., Falls Church, Virginia. 2000 International Residential Code. Reprinted with permission of the author. All rights reserved.

SPAN TABLE

This is an example of a span table.
You should refer to the span tables appropriate for your area.

TABLE R802.4(1) CEILING JOIST SPANS FOR COMMON LUMBER SPECIES
(Uninhabitable attics without storage, live load = 10 psf, L/Δ = 240)

CEILING JOIST SPACING (inches)	SPECIE AND GRADE		DEAD LOAD = 5 psf			
			2×4	2×6	2×8	2×10
			Maximum ceiling joist spans			
			(feet - inches)	(feet - inches)	(feet - inches)	(feet - inches)
12	Douglas fir-larch	SS	13-2	20-8	Note[a]	Note[a]
	Douglas fir-larch	#1	12-8	19-11	Note[a]	Note[a]
	Douglas fir-larch	#2	12-5	19-6	25-8	Note[a]
	Douglas fir-larch	#3	10-10	15-10	20-1	24-6
	Hem-fir	SS	12-5	19-6	25-8	Note[a]
	Hem-fir	#1	12-2	19-1	25-2	Note[a]
	Hem-fir	#2	11-7	18-2	24-0	Note[a]
	Hem-fir	#3	10-10	15-10	20-1	24-6
	Southern pine	SS	12-11	20-3	Note[a]	Note[a]
	Southern pine	#1	12-8	19-11	Note[a]	Note[a]
	Southern pine	#2	12-5	19-6	25-8	Note[a]
	Southern pine	#3	11-6	17-0	21-8	25-7
	Spruce-pine-fir	SS	12-2	19-1	25-2	Note[a]
	Spruce-pine-fir	#1	11-10	18-8	24-7	Note[a]
	Spruce-pine-fir	#2	11-10	18-8	24-7	Note[a]
	Spruce-pine-fir	#3	10-10	15-10	20-1	24-6
16	Douglas fir-larch	SS	11-11	18-9	24-8	Note[a]
	Douglas fir-larch	#1	11-6	18-1	23-10	Note[a]
	Douglas fir-larch	#2	11-3	17-8	23-0	Note[a]
	Douglas fir-larch	#3	9-5	13-9	17-5	21-3
	Hem-fir	SS	11-3	17-8	23-4	Note[a]
	Hem-fir	#1	11-0	17-4	22-10	Note[a]
	Hem-fir	#2	10-6	16-6	21-9	Note[a]
	Hem-fir	#3	9-5	13-9	17-5	21-3
	Southern pine	SS	11-9	18-5	24-3	Note[a]
	Southern pine	#1	11-6	18-1	23-1	Note[a]
	Southern pine	#2	11-3	17-8	23-4	Note[a]
	Southern pine	#3	10-0	14-9	18-9	22-2
	Spruce-pine-fir	SS	11-0	17-4	22-10	Note[a]
	Spruce-pine-fir	#1	10-9	16-11	22-4	Note[a]
	Spruce-pine-fir	#2	10-9	16-11	22-4	Note[a]
	Spruce-pine-fir	#3	9-5	13-9	17-5	21-3
24	Douglas fir-larch	SS	10-5	16-4	21-7	Note[a]
	Douglas fir-larch	#1	10-0	15-9	20-1	24-6
	Douglas fir-larch	#2	9-10	14-10	18-9	22-11
	Douglas fir-larch	#3	7-8	11-2	14-2	17-4
	Hem-fir	SS	9-10	15-6	20-5	Note[a]
	Hem-fir	#1	9-8	15-2	19-7	23-11
	Hem-fir	#2	9-2	14-5	18-6	22-7
	Hem-fir	#3	7-8	11-2	14-2	17-4
	Southern pine	SS	10-3	16-1	21-2	Note[a]
	Southern pine	#1	10-0	15-9	20-10	Note[a]
	Southern pine	#2	9-10	15-6	20-1	23-11
	Southern pine	#3	8-2	12-0	15-4	18-1
	Spruce-pine-fir	SS	9-8	15-2	19-11	25-5
	Spruce-pine-fir	#1	9-5	14-9	18-9	22-11
	Spruce-pine-fir	#2	9-5	14-9	18-9	22-11
	Spruce-pine-fir	#3	7-8	11-2	14-2	17-4

For SI: 1 inch = 25.4 mm, 1 foot = 304.8 mm, 1 pound per square foot = 0.0479 kN/m^2.

[a] Check sources for availability of lumber in lengths greater than 20 feet.

Copyright 2000, International Code Council, Inc., Falls Church, Virginia. 2000 International Residential Code. Reprinted with permission of the author. All rights reserved.

SPAN TABLE

This is an example of a span table.
You should refer to the span tables appropriate for your area.

TABLE R802.5.1(2) RAFTER SPANS FOR COMMON LUMBER SPECIES
(Roof live load = 20 psf, ceiling attached to rafters, L/Δ = 240)

RAFTER SPACING (inches)	SPECIE AND GRADE		DEAD LOAD = 10 psf					DEAD LOAD = 20 psf				
			2×4	2×6	2×8	2×10	2×12	2×4	2×6	2×8	2×10	2×12
			Maximum rafter spans[a]									
			(feet - inches)	(feet - inches)	(feet - inches)	(feet - inches)	(feet - inches)	(feet - inches)	(feet - inches)	(feet - inches)	(feet - inches)	(feet - inches)
12	Douglas fir-larch	SS	10-5	16-4	21-7	Note[b]	Note[b]	10-5	16-4	21-7	Note[b]	Note[b]
	Douglas fir-larch	#1	10-0	15-9	20-10	Note[b]	Note[b]	10-0	15-4	19-5	23-9	Note[b]
	Douglas fir-larch	#2	9-10	15-6	20-5	25-8	Note[b]	9-10	14-4	18-2	22-3	25-9
	Douglas fir-larch	#3	8-7	12-6	15-10	19-5	22-6	7-5	10-10	13-9	16-9	19-6
	Hem-fir	SS	9-10	15-6	20-5	Note[b]	Note[b]	9-10	15-6	20-5	Note[b]	Note[b]
	Hem-fir	#1	9-8	15-2	19-11	25-5	Note[b]	9-8	14-11	18-11	23-2	Note[b]
	Hem-fir	#2	9-2	14-5	19-0	24-3	Note[b]	9-2	14-2	17-11	21-11	25-5
	Hem-fir	#3	8-7	12-6	15-10	19-5	22-6	7-5	10-10	13-9	16-9	19-6
	Southern pine	SS	10-3	16-1	21-2	Note[b]	Note[b]	10-3	16-1	21-2	Note[b]	Note[b]
	Southern pine	#1	10-0	15-9	20-10	Note[b]	Note[b]	10-0	15-9	20-10	25-10	Note[b]
	Southern pine	#2	9-10	15-6	20-5	Note[b]	Note[b]	9-10	15-1	19-5	23-2	Note[b]
	Southern pine	#3	9-1	13-6	17-2	20-3	24-1	7-11	11-8	14-10	17-6	20-11
	Spruce-pine-fir	SS	9-8	15-2	19-11	25-5	Note[b]	9-8	15-2	19-11	25-5	Note[b]
	Spruce-pine-fir	#1	9-5	14-9	19-6	24-10	Note[b]	9-5	14-4	18-2	22-3	25-9
	Spruce-pine-fir	#2	9-5	14-9	19-6	24-10	Note[b]	9-5	14-4	18-2	22-3	25-9
	Spruce-pine-fir	#3	8-7	12-6	15-10	19-5	22-6	7-5	10-10	13-9	16-9	19-6
16	Douglas fir-larch	SS	9-6	14-11	19-7	25-0	Note[b]	9-6	14-11	19-7	24-9	Note[b]
	Douglas fir-larch	#1	9-1	14-4	18-11	23-9	Note[b]	9-1	13-3	16-10	20-7	23-10
	Douglas fir-larch	#2	8-11	14-1	18-2	22-3	25-9	8-6	12-5	15-9	19-3	22-4
	Douglas fir-larch	#3	7-5	10-10	13-9	16-9	19-6	6-5	9-5	11-11	14-6	16-10
	Hem-fir	SS	8-11	14-1	18-6	23-8	Note[b]	8-11	14-1	18-6	23-8	Note[b]
	Hem-fir	#1	8-9	13-9	18-1	23-1	Note[b]	8-9	12-11	16-5	20-0	23-3
	Hem-fir	#2	8-4	13-1	17-3	21-11	25-5	8-4	12-3	15-6	18-11	22-0
	Hem-fir	#3	7-5	10-10	13-9	16-9	19-6	6-5	9-5	11-11	14-6	16-10
	Southern pine	SS	9-4	14-7	19-3	24-7	Note[b]	9-4	14-7	19-3	24-7	Note[b]
	Southern pine	#1	9-1	14-4	18-11	24-1	Note[b]	9-1	14-4	18-10	22-4	Note[b]
	Southern pine	#2	8-11	14-1	18-6	23-2	Note[b]	8-11	13-0	16-10	20-1	23-7
	Southern pine	#3	7-11	11-8	14-10	17-6	20-11	6-10	10-1	12-10	15-2	18-1
	Spruce-pine-fir	SS	8-9	13-9	18-1	23-1	Note[b]	8-9	13-9	18-1	23-0	Note[b]
	Spruce-pine-fir	#1	8-7	13-5	17-9	22-3	25-9	8-6	12-5	15-9	19-3	22-4
	Spruce-pine-fir	#2	8-7	13-5	17-9	22-3	25-9	8-6	12-5	15-9	19-3	22-4
	Spruce-pine-fir	#3	7-5	10-10	13-9	16-9	19-6	6-5	9-5	11-11	14-6	16-10
19.2	Douglas fir-larch	SS	8-11	14-0	18-5	23-7	Note[b]	8-11	14-0	18-5	22-7	Note[b]
	Douglas fir-larch	#1	8-7	13-6	17-9	21-8	25-2	8-4	12-2	15-4	18-9	21-9
	Douglas fir-larch	#2	8-5	13-1	16-7	20-3	23-6	7-9	11-4	14-4	17-7	20-4
	Douglas fir-larch	#3	6-9	9-11	12-7	15-4	17-9	5-10	8-7	10-10	13-3	15-5
	Hem-fir	SS	8-5	13-3	17-5	22-3	Note[b]	8-5	13-3	17-5	22-3	25-9
	Hem-fir	#1	8-3	12-11	17-1	21-1	24-6	8-1	11-10	15-0	18-4	21-3
	Hem-fir	#2	7-10	12-4	16-3	20-0	23-2	7-8	11-2	14-2	17-4	20-1
	Hem-fir	#3	6-9	9-11	12-7	15-4	17-9	5-10	8-7	10-10	13-3	15-5
	Southern pine	SS	8-9	13-9	18-1	23-1	Note[b]	8-9	13-9	18-1	23-1	Note[b]
	Southern pine	#1	8-7	13-6	17-9	22-8	Note[b]	8-7	13-6	17-2	20-5	24-4
	Southern pine	#2	8-5	13-3	17-5	21-2	24-10	8-4	11-11	15-4	18-4	21-6
	Southern pine	#3	7-3	10-8	13-7	16-0	19-1	6-3	9-3	11-9	13-10	16-6
	Spruce-pine-fir	SS	8-3	12-11	17-1	21-9	Note[b]	8-3	12-11	17-1	21-0	24-4
	Spruce-pine-fir	#1	8-1	12-8	16-7	20-3	23-6	7-9	11-4	14-4	17-7	20-4
	Spruce-pine-fir	#2	8-1	12-8	16-7	20-3	23-6	7-9	11-4	14-4	17-7	20-4
	Spruce-pine-fir	#3	6-9	9-11	12-7	15-4	17-9	5-10	8-7	10-10	13-3	15-5

(continued)

Copyright 2000, International Code Council, Inc., Falls Church, Virginia. 2000 International Residential Code. Reprinted with permission of the author. All rights reserved.

SPAN TABLE

This is an example of a span table.
You should refer to the span tables appropriate for your area.

TABLE R802.5.1(2) — continued RAFTER SPANS FOR COMMON LUMBER SPECIES
(Roof live load = 20 psf, ceiling attached to rafters, L/Δ = 240)

RAFTER SPACING (inches)	SPECIE AND GRADE		DEAD LOAD = 10 psf					DEAD LOAD = 20 psf				
			2×4	2×6	2×8	2×10	2×12	2×4	2×6	2×8	2×10	2×12
			Maximum rafter spans[a]									
			(feet - inches)	(feet - inches)	(feet - inches)	(feet - inches)	(feet - inches)	(feet - inches)	(feet - inches)	(feet - inches)	(feet - inches)	(feet - inches)
24	Douglas fir-larch	SS	8-3	13-0	17-2	21-10	Note[b]	8-3	13-0	16-7	20-3	23-5
	Douglas fir-larch	#1	8-0	12-6	15-10	19-5	22-6	7-5	10-10	13-9	16-9	19-6
	Douglas fir-larch	#2	7-10	11-9	14-10	18-2	21-0	6-11	10-2	12-10	15-8	18-3
	Douglas fir-larch	#3	6-1	8-10	11-3	13-8	15-11	5-3	7-8	9-9	11-10	13-9
	Hem-fir	SS	7-10	12-3	16-2	20-8	25-1	7-10	12-3	16-2	19-10	23-0
	Hem-fir	#1	7-8	12-0	15-6	18-11	21-11	7-3	10-7	13-5	16-4	19-0
	Hem-fir	#2	7-3	11-5	14-8	17-10	20-9	6-10	10-0	12-8	15-6	17-11
	Hem-fir	#3	6-1	8-10	11-3	13-8	15-11	5-3	7-8	9-9	11-10	13-9
	Southern pine	SS	8-1	12-9	16-10	21-6	Note[b]	8-1	12-9	16-10	21-6	Note[b]
	Southern pine	#1	8-0	12-6	16-6	21-1	25-2	8-0	12-3	15-4	18-3	21-9
	Southern pine	#2	7-10	12-3	15-10	18-11	22-2	7-5	10-8	13-9	16-5	19-3
	Southern pine	#3	6-5	9-6	12-1	14-4	17-1	5-7	8-3	10-6	12-5	14-9
	Spruce-pine-fir	SS	7-8	12-0	15-10	20-2	24-7	7-8	12-0	15-4	18-9	21-9
	Spruce-pine-fir	#1	7-6	11-9	14-10	18-2	21-0	6-11	10-2	12-10	15-8	18-3
	Spruce-pine-fir	#2	7-6	11-9	14-10	18-2	21-0	6-11	10-2	12-10	15-8	18-3
	Spruce-pine-fir	#3	6-1	8-10	11-3	13-8	15-11	5-3	7-8	9-9	11-10	13-9

For SI: 1 inch = 25.4 mm, 1 foot = 304.8 mm, 1 pound per square foot = 0.0479 kN/m^2.

[a] The tabulated rafter spans assume that ceiling joists are located at the bottom of the attic space or that some other method of resisting the outward push of the rafters on the bearing walls, such as rafter ties, is provided at that location. When ceiling joists or rafter ties are located higher in the attic space, the rafter spans shall be multiplied by the factors given below.

H_C/H_R	Rafter Span Adjustment Factor
2/3 or greater	0.50
1/2	0.58
1/3	0.67
1/4	0.76
1/5	0.83
1/6	0.90
1/7.5 and less	1.00

where: H_C = Height of ceiling joists or rafter ties measured vertically above the top of the rafter support walls.
H_R = Height of roof ridge measured vertically above the top of the rafter support walls.

[b] Check sources for availability of lumber in lengths greater than 20 feet.

Copyright 2000, International Code Council, Inc., Falls Church, Virginia. 2000 International Residential Code. Reprinted with permission of the author. All rights reserved.

GLOSSARY

A

abstract of title. A history of the deeds and other papers affecting the ownership of the property.

acclimation. A condition that occurs when wood reaches a moisture content equal to that inside the building where it is installed.

acoustical ceiling. A ceiling consisting of panels glued directly to the ceiling surface or stapled to wood furring strips nailed to the ceiling joists.

ACQ. A chemical compound used to treat wood. Wood treated with ACQ (ammoniacal copper quaternary ammonium compound) does not contain arsenic.

ADA. *See* **Americans with Disabilities Act.**

admixture. An ingredient other than cement, aggregate, or water that is added to a concrete mix to change its physical or chemical characteristics.

aggregate. Granular material, such as sand, gravel, or crushed stone.

Allen wrench. A hexagonal steel bar with a bent end that fits inside a hexagonal recess in the top of a screw.

allowance. A dollar figure representing the cost of products that have not yet been chosen when a detailed estimate is made.

Americans with Disabilities Act (ADA). Legislation that contains provisions regarding new construction. The design of public buildings and certain multi-family dwellings must meet these provisions to ensure that the building is accessible to people who have disabilities.

amperage. A measure of the strength of an electric current expressed in *amperes*, or *amps*.

ampere. A measure of electrical current. Often referred to as an *amp*.

anchor bolt. A bolt, usually L-shaped, used in wood-frame construction to securely fasten the sill plate to the foundation.

annual rings. Rings visible in a cross section of a tree stump. In temperate climates, the tree adds one annual ring during each year of growth. Most annual rings consist of a light band formed in the spring (early wood) and a dark band formed in the summer (late wood).

apprentice. A person who works under the guidance of a skilled worker to learn a particular trade. In the construction industry, an apprentice carpenter learns under an experienced carpenter.

apron. In a window, a finish member below the stool.

architect's scale. A measuring instrument that allows the measurements in reduced-scale drawings to be measured in feet and inches.

architectural plans. A set of more formal drawings showing more precisely how an entire structure should be built.

armored cable. Hollow cable with a flexible metal exterior. Individual insulated conductors are contained within the cable. Also called *BX*.

articulated ladder. A folding ladder that can be adjusted to fit into such spots as stairwells.

asbestosis. A medical condition that can occur when asbestos fibers are inhaled or swallowed. This can cause scarring of the lungs and various types of cancer.

awning window. A window in which the sash swings outward at the bottom.

axial load. The load carried along the length of a structural member.

B

backerboard. Cement-based sheets, They provide an excellent base for tile, particularly on floors and in wet installations. Often called *cement board.*

backfilling. The process of filling in the excavated area around a foundation with dirt.

backing the hip. Beveling the upper edge of the hip rafter. This allows the roof sheathing to be installed without hitting the corners of the hip rafter.

back-priming. Priming the back surface of the board on site if the siding has not been primed on all surfaces by the manufacturer.

backsaw. A fine-tooth crosscut saw with a heavy metal band across the back that strengthens the blade.

balloon-frame construction. Framing in which the studs run from the sill attached to the foundation to the top plate of the second floor. Also called *balloon framing.*

balloon framing. *See* **balloon-frame construction.**

baluster. A slender vertical member that supports the handrail.

bar clamp. A clamp with a stationary head, a sliding tailstop, and an adjustable screw assembly, all mounted on a flat bar.

base cabinets. *See* **lower cabinets.**

base molding. *See* **baseboard.**

baseboard. A board or molding used against the bottom of walls to cover their joint with the floor. It serves as a transition between the wall surface and the floor. It also covers the gaps that often occur at this location. Also called *base molding.*

batter board. A board fastened horizontally to stakes placed to the outside of where the corners of the building will be located. These boards and string tied between them locate and mark the outline of the building.

battery pack. Batteries sealed within a plastic case inside or at the end of the handle of a portable power tool, such as a drill.

bearing wall. A wall that supports loads in addition to its own weight.

bed joint. A horizontal mortar joint.

bench mark. A basic starting point from which measurements in building layout can be made using a transit or level. Also called a *point of reference* (POR).

bevel cut. A cut made at an angle through the thickness of a board or panel. Most saws can be adjusted to make bevel cuts at angles between 45° and 90°.

bid. A signed proposal to do work and/or supply a material for a specified price.

binder. A resin that holds particles of pigment together.

bird's mouth. A notch made in a rafter with an overhang so that the rafter will fit against a plate.

biscuit. A small flat piece of compressed wood glued into crescent-shaped grooves to form a joint with another workpiece in which matching grooves have been cut. The crescent shaped grooves are cut by a portable power tool called a plate joiner or a biscuit joiner.

bisque. A piece of tile without the glaze.

blind nailing. Driving nails at an angle through the tongue of the board and into framing or furring strips. It allows subsequent boards to conceal the nail heads.

blind-nailing system. A hidden fastening system used by many deck builders in which the fasteners do not show.

block plane. A small (about 6″ long) plane with a blade that cuts bevel-side up.

board foot. A unit of measure that represents a piece of lumber having a flat surface area of 1 sq. ft. and a thickness of 1″ nominal size.

bottom plate. The plate that ties the bottom ends of the studs together. It also provides a nailing surface for the bottom edge of wall coverings and wall sheathing. Also called the *sole plate.*

box cornice. Exterior trim that entirely encloses the rafter tails. It is built of roof sheathing, fascia, and a soffit.

box extender. A metal or plastic fitting that is screwed to the front of the outlet box, bringing it forward.

box header. A common header built from standard C-shaped steel framing members.

box-joint utility pliers. Large pliers with a slip joint at four or more positions.

box sill. A type of sill consisting of a sill plate (also called a *mudsill*, or just the *sill*) that is anchored to the foundation wall, floor joists and rim joist and subflooring.

box wrench. A metal wrench with two enclosed ends.

brace. A vertical or diagonal length of 2x4 or 2x6 lumber that stiffens or supports an individual rafter at mid-span. One end is nailed to the rafter. The other end is nailed to wall framing below the rafter.

brick mold. Thick wood molding permanently attached to the outer edges of the jambs. Also called *brick molding.*

brick molding. *See* **brick mold.**

brick tongs. A metal tool that clamps over a row of six to eleven bricks. The lever action of the handle holds the bricks in place. When the handle is lowered, the bricks are released.

brick-veneer siding. A layer of brick used for part or all of the exterior covering over wood-frame walls.

bridging. A method of bracing between joists. It is done to distribute loads, prevent the joists from twisting, and add stability and stiffness.

building code. A set of regulations that governs the details of construction.

building paper. Heavyweight paper combined with asphalt that comes in rolls 36″ wide.

building permit. A formal, printed authorization for the builder to begin construction.

business plan. A document that gives specific information about the business, including a vision, goals, strategies, and a plan of action.

butt edge. The exposed edge of the shingle.

BX. *See* **armored cable.**

butt wall. A wall that fits between the by-walls.

by-wall. A wall that runs from the outside edge of the subfloor at one end of the building to the outside edge of the subfloor at the opposite end.

C

camber. A slight upward curve in a glulam beam. The beam is installed with the curve oriented up.

cambium. A layer of living tissue that produces new wood, called *sapwood*, along the inner surface of the bark of a tree.

cantilever. A supporting member that projects into space and is itself supported at only one end.

carcase. An assembly of panels that forms a cabinet's basic shape.

carpenter's level. A long wood, metal, or fiberglass instrument with several glass leveling vials. Sometimes called a spirit level. Some levels measure electronically instead.

carpenter's square. *See* **framing square.**

casement window. A window with a side-hinged sash that swings inward or outward.

casing. The basic molding around a window or door.

cement board. *See* **backerboard.**

certificate of occupancy (CO). A document issued after the house has been finally inspected stating the house is ready for occupancy.

certification. Written proof of skill.

chair. A small device that supports the wire fabric at a particular height as concrete is poured.

chair rail. A molding that runs horizontally across walls at 3′ to 4′ from the floor.

chalk line. Powdered chalk and a reel of string in a steel or plastic case.

chamfer. A beveled edge. Also a bit that is used to produce a beveled edge.

change order. A document signed by the builder and the client that exactly describes the changes to be made after construction has begun and estimates the cost for the extra work.

cheek cut. *See* **side cut.**

chord. The top or bottom outer member of the truss.

circuit. An electrical cable or group of cables that supplies electricity to a specific area.

claw hammer. A hammer with a curved claw.

cleat-stringer stairway. The simplest stairway, having two stringers and a series of plank treads.

clinching. The process of joining two layers of steel with pressure in steel frame construction. A powered clinching tool is used.

clip angle. A small piece of angle iron attached to a structural member to accept a structural load.

clipped nail. *See* **D-head nail.**

closed cornice. Exterior trim appearing on a house with no rafter overhang. It is seldom used on newer houses because of the difficulty in providing attic ventilation.

closed valley. A roof covering in a roof valley laid so the flashing is not visible. Also called a *woven valley.*

closure block. The block that fills the final gap in a course between corners.

CMU. *See* **concrete masonry unit.**

CO. *See* **certificate of occupancy.**

cold chisel. A tool-steel chisel with a hardened and tempered edge for cutting metal.

cold joint. A joint occurring where fresh concrete is poured on top of or next to concrete that has already begun to cure.

cold-formed steel. Sheet steel that is bent and formed without using heat. Such steel is used for residential steel framing.

collar tie. A horizontal framing member that prevents opposing rafter pairs from spreading apart. It also prevents the rafters from bowing inward when weight is placed upon them.

collated fasteners. Fasteners arranged into strips or rolls, with each fastener connected to the fasteners on either side.

collet. That part of a router that holds the bit.

combination square. A hand tool with a blade that slides along its handle or head.

common difference. Gable-end studs have the same on-center spacing as standard wall studs. However, each stud is a different length than the studs on either side. Their differences in length are based on a single figure that depends on the pitch of the roof. This figure is called the common difference.

complete construction cost estimate. *See* **quantity takeoff.**

component–cost estimate. *See* **unit–cost estimate.**

composite decking. Synthetic decking material made from a blend of recycled plastic and wood dust or fibers.

composite panel product. A panel product made from pieces of wood mixed with adhesive.

compound-bevel cut. A cut made when a bevel is added to a miter cut.

concrete masonry unit (CMU). Any hollow masonry unit, such as concrete block.

conditioning. In working with paneling, placing the paneling in the work area before work begins to allow it to adjust to the temperature and humidity of the room.

conductor. A material that allows electricity to flow through it readily.

coniferous tree. A tree that produces seeds in cones and has needlelike or scalelike leaves. Softwoods come from coniferous trees.

connector plate. A prepunched metal plate with stamped teeth. It is pressed into the wood under hydraulic pressure to splice the joint on each side.

construction loan. A short-term loan used to pay expenses during construction.

Construction Specifications Institute (CSI). A professional association that develops standards for writing specifications.

continuous joist. A joist that spans the entire floor opening. The *X*s are all on the same side of the joist location marks.

contract of sale. A document that usually describes all the details relating to the purchase.

contractor's saw. A power saw on which the motor is perpendicular to the blade. The blade is usually mounted on the right side of the motor and is driven by a spindle connected directly to it. Sometimes called a *sidewinder*.

control joint. In a concrete slab, a joint that helps to minimize random cracks. In a wall, a joint that controls movement caused by stress.

coping. The process of shaping inside corner joints between trim members by cutting the end of one member to fit against the face of the other.

coping saw. A saw with a U-shaped frame having a deep throat.

corbel. A course of brick offset to extend past the course below it.

corner bead. A vinyl or galvanized metal strip that reinforces and protects the corner. It comes in lengths of 8′ and 10′. Standard corner bead forms a square 90° corner. Bullnose corner bead forms a rounded 90° corner.

corner post. An assembly of full-length studs at the corner of a building. A corner post is usually built from three or more studs to provide greater strength.

cornice. The exterior trim of a structure consisting of a fascia, a soffit, and various types of molding.

cornice return. The continuation of a cornice. Its construction depends on how the cornice is built and on how far the rake projects beyond the side walls.

corporation. A business organization created when a state grants an individual or a group of people a charter with legal rights. The owners buy shares, or parts of the company. These owners, called shareholders, earn a profit based on the number of shares they own. If the business fails, the owners lose the money they have invested in the business.

countersink. A bit with beveled cutting edges. It creates a funnel shape at the top of a drilled hole. This funnel shape allows the head of a wood screw to be flush with the wood surface.

course pole. *See* **story pole.**

CPM. *See* **critical path method.**

cripple. *See* **cripple stud.**

cripple stud. A stud that does not extend all the way from the bottom plate to the top plate, due to an opening in the wall. Also called a *cripple*.

critical path method (CPM). A method of scheduling that shows the relationships among tasks as well as how long each task takes.

crosscut. A cut made *across* the grain of a board.

crown. The outermost curve of the bow. Any joists having a slight edgewise bow should always be placed with the crown on top.

crown molding. A fairly large sprung molding that usually includes both curved and angular surfaces. It is angled away from wall and ceiling surfaces, and its back is not in contact with either of them.

CSI. *See* **Concrete Specifications Institute.**

cut-back mastic. Mastic that has been thinned slightly with a solvent.

cuts. The several sandings made in finishing a new floor.

cut-stringer stairway. A stairway in which the treads and risers are attached to notches sawn into the upper edge of each stringer.

cutterhead. A solid metal cylinder on a jointer on which three or four cutting knives are mounted. The cutterhead is mounted below the bed of the machine. As the cutterhead spins, the knives shear off small chips of wood, producing a smooth surface.

cutting plane. A *floor plan* is included for each level of the building. Each plan drawn as if the house was sliced horizontally at a level that would include all doors and window openings. This imaginary slicing is referred to as a cutting plane.

D

dead load. The total weight of the building. This includes the structural frame and anything permanently attached, such as wall coverings, cabinets, and roof shingles.

deciduous tree. A tree that sheds its leaves annually during cold or very dry seasons. Hardwoods are cut from broad-leaved, deciduous trees.

deed. The document that shows evidence of ownership.

deed restrictions. Restrictions that specify such things as the minimum-size house that can be built on the lot, requirements for certain architectural features, and setback distances.

design value. A number assigned to indicate how well each wood resists stresses.

detail drawing. A drawing used when precise information is needed about a small or complex portion of the building. Such drawings are used whenever the information given in elevations, plans, and sections is not clear enough. The construction at doors, windows, and eaves is often shown in detail drawings. Details are drawn at larger scales than plan views, such as ½″ = 1′-0″, ¾″ = 1′-0″, 1″ = 1′-0″, or 1¼″ = 1′-0″.

D-head nail. A nail used only with nailers. Part of the head has been removed giving it a *D* shape. This allows the nails to be packed closely together. Also called a *clipped nail.*

dimensions. Numbers that give the size of something.

direct costs. Costs related to a certain construction project. They include such costs as those for labor, materials, building permits, temporary power hookups, and some types of insurance. Also called *project costs.*

doghouse dormer. A gable dormer with side walls that protrudes horizontally outward from a sloping roof and has its own gabled ends.

door frame. The assembly around a door. It is attached to the wall framing and consists of two side jambs and a head jamb.

dormer. An upright window projection on a roof that adds light and ventilation to second-floor rooms or the attic.

double nailing. Placing a second nail within 2″ of the first for added holding power.

double plate. A second top plate nailed to the first top plate after the walls have been erected.

double-glazed window. *See* **insulating glass window.**

double-hung window. A window consisting of an upper and a lower sash that slide up and down in channels in the side jambs.

dovetail joint. A joint having interlocking pieces. Dovetail joints are used to assemble the drawers in high-quality cabinetry.

dovetail saw. A saw that is similar to a backsaw, but having a blade that is narrower and thinner and with very fine teeth.

draft. The upward movement of air within a closed space, such as a chimney. Draft draws air in, aiding in combustion and expelling smoke and harmful gases.

drain field. A filtering area within a septic system into which liquid wastes flow. A drain field contains a network of perforated pipes embedded in sand and gravel.

dressed sizes. Lumber sizes that apply after the wood has shrunk and been surfaced with a planing machine. The width and thickness of dressed lumber are considerably less than its nominal width and thickness.

drill index. A case that holds a group of twist bits in various sizes.

drip edge. Metal edging or flashing that conducts water away from the eaves and cornice.

dropping the hip. Deepening the bird's mouth to bring the top edge of the hip rafter in line with the upper ends of the jacks.

dry-set mortar. A mortar made from a mixture of Portland cement, sand, and additives that strengthen the bond.

duplex-head nail. A nail with a double head.

Dutch hip roof. A hip roof with a small gable at each end near the top. Like a hip roof, it has an even overhang around the entire building.

E

eaves. Those portions of a roof that project beyond the walls.

edging. Using a brush to paint into the corners between large flat surfaces, where a roller cannot reach.

electrical circuit. The circuit produced when electricity flows from a point of origin and returns to that point of origin through a conductor.

electrical plan. A plan drawn like a simplified floor plan showing the location and type of every electrical feature of the building. These include switches, ceiling lights, receptacles, and the service panel. It also indicates a schematic view of the electrical wiring that connects individual features to each other.

elevation. A side view that allows you to see the height of objects.

emissivity. A number symbolizing how much radiation something is emitting.

end lap. *See* **side lap.**

engineered lumber. Any manufactured product made of solid wood, wood veneer, wood pieces, or wood fibers in which the components have been bonded together with adhesives.

engineered panel. Any manufactured sheet product, including plywood, made of wood or wood pieces bonded with a natural or synthetic adhesive.

entrepreneur. A person who creates and runs his or her own business.

ergonomics. The science of designing and arranging things to suit the needs of the human body.

estimator. An individual who figures the cost of a project.

ethics. Your inner guidelines for telling right from wrong.

excavation. A cut, cavity, trench, or depression made by removing earth. Excavations are dug to prepare the site for footings, foundations, and the installation of pipes for site drainage.

expansion joint. A gap between portions of concrete that is filled with a flexible material. The concrete is thus able to expand and contract without damage to itself or to adjacent surfaces.

exposure. The amount of surface (as in a shingle or siding) exposed to the weather.

extension ladder. A common type of straight ladder that can be adjusted to various lengths.

F

face-frame cabinet. A cabinet having a face frame that fits around the front carcase opening, thus providing a mounting surface for hinges and drawer hardware.

face-nailing. A nailing technique in which a nail is driven straight through the thickness of the lumber and into another piece.

facing brick. Brick used primarily for exposed exterior surfaces such as veneer walls.

fascia. A board nailed to the ends of the rafter tails. It protects the end grain of the rafters and serves as a mounting surface for gutters.

featherboard. A piece of stock with a series of long saw kerfs on one end. It is used to hold narrow stock against the rip fence when making a rip cut with a table saw.

feathering. In taping drywall joints, the process of smoothing the outer edges of the joint compound so that there are no ridges. In using a screw gun, the process of attaching a screw to the bit without stopping the screw gun.

feed rate. The speed at which stock is pushed through the saw blade.

fiberboard. An engineered wood product. To make fiberboard, Wood fibers are refined and mixed with an adhesive. They are then compressed under heat and pressure to produce panels.

fiber-cement board. An engineered wood product. Its cellulose fibers are bound together with a mixture of Portland cement, ground sand, additives, and water.

fiber-saturation point. The point at which the cell walls of wood have absorbed all the water they can hold.

film-forming finish. A finish that coats the wood surface.

fines. Finely crushed or powdered materials.

finger joint. A joint having a closely spaced series of wedge-shaped cuts made in the mating surfaces of two pieces of wood. These cuts create a large surface area that improves the glue bond between the two parts.

finish flooring. The topmost surface of a floor system.

finished grade. The level of the ground when grading is completed.

fireblocking. Blocking meant to slow the passage of flames through wall cavities. It also strengthens the walls. It is made from short lengths of 2x framing lumber installed crosswise between studs.

fire brick. Brick used specifically for lining fireplaces and other heating units.

fire-code drywall. Drywall that is more fire resistant.

fire-rated door. A door built to resist the passage of fire. These doors are not fireproof. They withstand fire only long enough for occupants to reach safety.

fixture. Any device, such as a bathtub, that receives or drains water.

flagged bristles. Bristles, as on a paintbrush, having slightly splayed tips.

flashing. A thin sheet of material that prevents water from reaching wood framing.

flat-sawn lumber. Lumber cut from a log that is squared up lengthwise and then sawed into boards. The end grain of a flat-sawn board shows the growth rings running across the board's width. The face has a distinctive archlike pattern.

flight. In a stairway, a straight, continuous run.

floor joist. Any light beam that supports a floor.

floor plan. A plan included for each level of the building. It is drawn as if the house was sliced horizontally at a level that would include all doors and window openings. It shows the size and location of rooms on a given floor.

floor sheathing. The layer of material over the floor joists.

flue. The passage inside the chimney through which the air, gases, and smoke rise. Its dimensions, height, shape, and interior smoothness determine how effective the chimney is in creating draft.

flue liner. A fire-clay or stainless-steel pipe assembled from individual sections that sit within the chimney brickwork.

fly rafter. The rafter extending from the ridge board to a structural fascia. In a moderate overhang of up to 20″, both the sheathing and a fly rafter aid in supporting the rake section.

foam-core panel. *See* **structural insulated pane (SIP).**

folding rule. A rigid wood rule 6′ or 8′ long that folds into a compact size.

footing. A base providing a larger bearing surface against the soil for load-bearing parts of the structure. Footings are generally made of concrete poured into place.

form. Any framework designed to contain wet concrete. Forms can be made of steel, lumber, or a combination of lumber and plywood.

form-release agent. A liquid that prevents concrete from sticking to the forms.

Forstner bit. A bit having a brad point and a sharpened rim. It is excellent for boring smooth holes with flat bottoms in wood.

foundation plan. A plan showing a top view of the footings and foundation walls. It also shows the location of posts and other elements, such as pads needed to support an exterior deck. All openings in foundation walls are labeled and dimensioned. The type and location of foundation anchor bolts are identified.

frame. In a window, the fixed part of the assembly that receives the sash. It consists of a sill, side jambs, and a head jamb.

frameless cabinet. A cabinet having framing around the opening. Its hinges are concealed and mounted on the side walls.

framing connector. A connection that is often used to support and connect standard framing lumber. Such connectors consist of a formed metal bracket.

framing plan. A plan showing the size, number, and spacing of structural members. Separate framing plans may be drawn for the floors and the roof.

framing square. A large metal square consisting of a blade, or body, and a tongue. Also called a *carpenter's square*.

free enterprise. An economic system in which businesses and individuals may buy, sell, and set prices for goods and services.

French doors. Doors hung in pairs on hinges located at each side of the door opening.

frieze block. A short piece of 2x framing lumber nailed between the roof rafters to seal off the attic space.

full-height paneling. Paneling that runs from floor to ceiling.

furring strip. A thin strip of wood permanently installed to keep paneling and other materials from touching another surface. They are also used to level an irregular surface and to allow air to circulate behind paneling.

G

gable. A triangular wall enclosed by the sloping ends of the roof.

gable-end truss. The first truss on the building and the most important truss in bracing it. It should be braced with lumber standoffs anchored to stakes driven into the ground.

gable roof. A roof with two sloping sides that meet at the top to form a gable at each end.

gable wall. A wall that angles upward to meet the underside of the roof framing.

gain. A mortise (notch) with a depth equal to the thickness of a single leaf.

galvanizing. The process of coating steel with a protective layer of zinc.

gambrel roof. A variation of the gable roof. It has a steep slope on two sides. A second slope begins partway up and continues to the top.

gasket. A flexible material preventing air or liquid from moving between parts of a tool.

GFCI. *See* **ground fault circuit interrupter.**

girder. A large principal horizontal member used to support the floor joists.

glazing. The clear glass or plastic portions of a window.

glue-nailing. The use of adhesives to hold plywood in place when nails or screws are not enough. This combination produces a particularly strong bond.

glulam. An abbreviation for "glue laminated," as in "glue-laminated beam." When layers of lumber are glued together, their strength and stiffness are greater than that of solid lumber of equal size.

grade. The height or level of the surrounding soil.

grade stamp. A permanent mark that identifies a board's species, quality, mill source, and general indication of strength.

ground. In plastering, a material permanently or temporarily attached to a surface to be plastered. It may be made of wood but is most often made of metal. It provides a straight edge and helps the plasterer gauge the thickness of the plaster.

ground fault circuit interrupter (GFCI). A fast-acting circuit breaker that can protect people from electrical shock.

grounding. Providing a path for electricity to flow safely from an electrical device, such as an electrically powered tool, to the earth.

ground-support slab. *See* **independent slab.**

grout. A thin mortar used for filling spaces.

H

hacksaw. A saw with a U-shaped steel frame fitted with replaceable metal-cutting blades.

hammer drill. A specialized corded drill used to drill holes in masonry. While the chuck revolves, the drill creates a rapid, hammer-like, reciprocating action. This helps to drive a masonry bit into the masonry.

hammer tacker. A slender magazine for holding staples, with a handle at one end.

handsaw. A saw with a wide blade in lengths from 20″ to 28″.

hand sledge. A hammer with a two-faced head weighing between 2 and 4 lbs.

hardboard. A high-density fiberboard.

header. A horizontal member carrying loads from other members and directing the loads around an opening.

head joint. A vertical mortar joint.

head lap. The shortest distance from the lower edge of an overlapping shingle to the upper edge of the shingle in the second course below.

headroom. The clearance directly above a step. It is measured from the outside edge of the nosing to the ceiling directly overhead.

heartwood. The portion of a tree nearest the core. It is dark in color.

hip rafter. A rafter forming a raised area, or "hip," usually extending from the corner of the building diagonally to the ridge board. It extends diagonally from plate to ridge board.

hip roof. A roof that slopes at the ends of the building as well as at the two sides.

hold-down anchor. A fastening anchor installed at each corner of the house or as required by local codes.

hole saw. A cylindrical metal sleeve having a sawtooth edge.

hollow-core construction. Construction consisting of a light framework of wood or corrugated cardboard faced with thin plywood or hardboard.

horizontal-sliding window. A window in which the sashes (in pairs) slide horizontally in separate tracks.

housewrap. Material made from high-density polyethylene fibers. These fibers interlock to allow water vapor to pass through, but not its liquid form.

hybrid window. A window having sashes and frames made of a combination of two or more materials, such as wood, metal, vinyl, fiberglass, or wood composites.

hydration. A chemical reaction causing concrete to harden when combined with water.

hydrostatic pressure. Pressure created by water building up on one side of a foundation wall, forcing moisture through the concrete.

I

ice dam. Ice formed by melting snow freezing at the eave line. As more snow melts, the water backs up behind the ice and seeps beneath the shingles.

impact noise rating (INR). A measurement identifying the impact noise resistance of a floor system.

independent slab. A slab used in areas where the ground freezes fairly deep during winter. Also called a *ground-support slab.*

indirect costs. Costs not specifically related to a particular project. These costs relate to the organization and supervision of the project. Also called *overhead.*

infiltration. The passage of fresh air into a building through cracks around windows, doors, and framing.

in-line framing. Framing typically used in steel-frame construction, in which all vertical and horizontal load-bearing structural members are aligned.

INR. *See* **impact noise rating.**

inset door. In cabinets, a door that fits entirely within the door opening. A small gap is required between the door and the face frame to provide clearance.

inside diameter. The widest part of a circular opening, such as that in a hose.

insulating glass window. Windows having two or more sheets of glass separated by an air space. The edges are sealed to trap the air between the sheets, which provides the insulation. Sometimes called a *double-glazed window.*

insulation. A material that slows the transmission of heat, sound, or electrical energy.

internal cut. A hole cut in a material without starting at the edge.

International Residential Code (IRC). A building code designed to make up for regional variations. It covers detached one- and two-family dwellings and townhouses that are no more than three stories high.

internship. A form of on-the-job training that combines classroom instruction and work experience.

IRC. *See* **International Residential Code.**

J

jack plane. *See* **jointer plane.**

jack rafter. A shortened common rafter that may be framed to a hip rafter, a valley rafter, or both. There are hip jack rafters and valley jack rafters.

jack stud. *See* **trimmer stud.**

jamb. An exposed upright member on each side and at the top of the frame.

J-channel. A J-shaped piece of plastic or metal that is used to support trim.

joint compound. A thick, pastelike material used in combination with joint tape to conceal the joints between panels.

jointer. In masonry, a simple metal bar with a shaped end that is run over a mortared joint to pack the mortar into it and give it a particular shape. Also called a *jointing tool.*

jointer plane. A long (20″ to 24″) plane with a blade that cuts bevel-side down. Also called a *jack plane.*

jointing tool. *See* **jointer.**

joist hanger. A sturdy metal bracket used where floor or ceiling joists meet another framing member, such as a beam.

joist tracks. C-shaped members by which joists are attached to the foundation. Also called *rim tracks.*

journey-level worker. A worker with an intermediate level of skill.

K

kerf. The width of a cut made by the blade of a saw.

keyhole saw. A narrow saw with a 10″ long replaceable blade with fine teeth.

keyway. That part of a footing that locks the foundation walls to the footing.

kickback. A momentary stoppage of a spinning blade when it encounters something while the saw is under full power. Consequently, the saw is violently "kicked back" at the operator.

kiln. An oven, such as one used for removing moisture from wood, in which moisture, airflow, and temperature are carefully controlled.

king-post truss. A truss with upper and lower chords and a single vertical post in the center.

king stud. The full-length stud on either side of an opening.

kneeboards. Boards measuring about 12″ by 24″ placed on the concrete to support the weight of the finisher.

L

ladder stabilizer. A device that can be bolted to the top of the ladder. It has arms 4′ apart that steady the top of the ladder and prevent it from slipping.

laminated-strand lumber (LSL). An engineered wood product made of wood strands glued together and cut to uniform dimensions.

laminated-veneer lumber (LVL). An engineered wood product in which the basic element is wood veneer glued together.

landing. The floor area where a flight ends or begins.

latex paint. Paint that has latex-base binders suspended in water.

lath. In plastering, strips fastened to wood or steel framing members. They are usually of gypsum or metal. Lath serves as a base material for the application of plaster.

layout tape measure. A steel or fiberglass tape in a rust-resistant case with a reel-in crank.

lead carpenter. The most experienced carpenter on a team. This person is entrusted with reading the plans.

lead corner. A partially constructed corner of brick.

ledger. The length of lumber that connects the deck to the house.

lifeline. A rope intended to prevent a worker from falling more than 6′. The lifeline is fastened at one end to a secure point on the structure and at the other end to a harness worn by the worker.

lift. A compacted layer of fill.

line block. A small L-shaped wood or plastic device to which one end of a mason's string line is attached. It hooks over the edge of a brick and is held in place by the tension of the string. Opposing line blocks are moved upward as the wall gains height.

lineman's pliers. Pliers with stout, flattened jaws and long, slightly curved handles. Cutting edges are formed into one side of the jaws.

lintel. A horizontal supporting member installed above an opening such as a window, door, or masonry fireplace.

live load. Weight that is not permanently attached to the building. Examples of live loads include furniture, books, and people.

load. A force that creates stresses on a structure. Weight is one type of load. Wind is another.

load-bearing wall. A wall that also supports weight from portions of the house above, such as the roof.

locking pliers. An all-purpose tool with double-lever action that locks the jaws to clamp a workpiece.

lockset. An assembly of knobs, latch, and a locking mechanism.

lookout. A horizontal member that extends from a rafter end to a nailer or the face of the wall sheathing. A lookout forms a horizontal surface to which the soffit material is attached.

lookout rafter. A rafter that projects beyond the walls of the house, usually at 90° to the common rafters.

louvered door. A door in which the panels have been replaced by louvers (angled slats).

lower cabinets. Cabinets that rest on the floor and support the countertops. Often called *base cabinets.*

LSL. *See* **laminated-strand lumber.**

lumber. Pieces of wood having a uniform thickness and width and sawn from a log.

LVL. *See* **laminated-veneer lumber.**

M

machine stress-rated lumber (MSR). Structural lumber that has been graded electronically and stamped to indicate the specific load it will support.

magazine. The container on a tool that holds a ready supply of fasteners. In both pneumatic and cordless nailers and staplers, the fasteners are held in one of two types of magazine: strip loaded or coil loaded.

makeup air. Air that replaces the air exhausted by a combustion appliance. Increasingly, local codes require that all types of fireplaces be supplied with makeup air.

mallet. A two-headed hammer, often made of wood, rubber, or plastic. The handle is wood.

mansard roof. A variation of the hip roof. It has steep slopes on all four sides. Partway up, a shallow second slope is developed and continues to the top where it meets the slopes from the other sides.

mason's rule. A rule used for measuring the height and spacing of brick courses (rows) as they are laid.

master. A worker with the highest level of skill.

mastic. A thick adhesive that can be applied with a notched trowel or with a caulking gun.

material safety data sheet (MSDS). An information sheet that identifies potential health and safety hazards associated with handling or machining a material. It will suggest suitable precautions.

MDF. *See* **medium-density fiberboard.**

measuring box. In masonry, a bottomless box having a capacity of 1, 2, 3, or 4 cu. ft. The frame should be marked on the inside to show volume levels, such as 1 cu. ft., 2 cu. ft., or less. Handles on the side of the box make it easier to lift after the material has been measured.

mechanical plan. A plan showing the arrangement and location of plumbing and heating features.

mechanicals. The plumbing, electrical, and heating/ventilating/air-conditioning (HVAC) systems in a building.

medium-density fiberboard (MDF). A panel product made of compressed wood fibers mixed with urea-formaldehyde adhesive.

mentor. A more experienced worker who is able and willing to give guidance and advice to a less skilled (usually younger) worker.

metal framing ties. Metal fasteners used to hold pieces of wood together or to reinforce a joint.

metal snips. A cutting tool with scissors-like handles. Sometimes called *tin snips*.

mil. The unit of measurement for measuring the thickness of thin steel. One mil equals one thousandth of an inch (1 mil = .001″).

mildew. A microscopic fungus that thrives on many household surfaces, including painted siding.

miter cut. A type of crosscut made at an angle across the grain of a board.

model building code. A set of building regulations developed by an independent organization on which local governments can base their own building codes.

molding. A narrow length of wood with a shaped profile.

monolithic slab. A footing and floor slab that are formed in one continuous pour. Also referred to as a *unified slab*, a *thickened-edge slab*, or a *slab with a turned-down footing*.

mortgage. A long-term loan (usually 15-30 years) that is secured by property.

MSDS. *See* **material safety data sheet.**

MSR. *See* **machine stress-rated lumber.**

mud sill. *See* **box sill.**

mulled windows. Windows of various styles and sizes combined to make up a larger unit. These combined units are separated only by vertical wood pieces.

mullion strip. A vertical wood piece separating windows of various styles and sizes combined to make up a larger unit.

muntin. A short vertical or horizontal piece used to hold a pane of glass.

musculoskeletal disorder. A disorder of the muscles, tendons, ligaments, joints, cartilage, or spinal discs.

N

nail set. A steel shank 4″ long with a concave tip and a square striking surface used for driving nail heads below the surface of wood.

National Building Code. A building code published by the Building Officials and Code Administrators International (BOCA).

National Electrical Code. A building code covering work to install electrical service.

National Plumbing Code. A building code covering work done to install plumbing service.

needle-nose pliers. Pliers with a long, thin nose and cutting edges near the joint.

networking. Making use of all your personal connections to achieve your career goals.

newel. A member supporting each end of the handrail.

nodes. On a CPM diagram, the boxes or circles that represent events that can be recognized.

nominal span. The length of the bottom chord of a truss.

non-continuous joist. A joist that is in two pieces. The pieces meet and overlap over an intermediate support.

nonmetallic sheathed cable wiring. Cable consisting of two or three insulated copper conductors and one bare copper conductor within a thermoplastic covering.

O

Occupational Safety and Health Act. Federal legislation enacted " . . . to assure so far as possible every working man and woman in the Nation safe and healthful working conditions and to preserve our human resources." This act affects all employees who are working in the building trades where one or more workers are employed.

Occupational Safety and Health Administration (OSHA). The federal agency that administers the Occupational Safety and Health Act. It issues standards and rules for safe and healthful working conditions, tools, equipment, facilities, and processes. OSHA conducts workplace inspections to assure the standards are followed.

offcut. A waste piece of wood that can become wedged between the blade and the rip fence when wood is being crosscut with a miter gauge and a rip fence.

official survey. A document that shows the boundaries of the property.

oil-base paint. Paint that has an oil-base binder suspended in a mineral spirit carrier.

on center (OC). The distance from the centerline of one structural member to the centerline of the next closest member. Span tables list the maximum spacing allowed between different sizes of joists or rafters. This spacing is referred to as on center (OC) spacing.

open-end wrench. A nonadjustable wrench with accurately machined openings on either end.

open-riser stairway. A stairway having no risers.

open valley. A roof valley on which shingles are not applied to the intersection of two roof surfaces. This leaves the underlying roofing material exposed along the length of the valley.

oriented-strand board (OSB). A wood product made from wood strands bonded with adhesive under heat and pressure.

OSHA. *See* **Occupational Safety and Health Administration.**

overhead. *See* **indirect costs.**

overlay door. In a cabinet, a door that fits over the edge of the carcase or face frame.

P

paint grades. Lower grades of molding on which painting will cover minor imperfections.

pane. The glass within each section of window.

parallel-strand lumber (PSL). An engineered wood product made with veneers that are glued together.

parging. The process of damp proofing by spreading mortar or cement plaster over concrete block and forming a cove where the wall joins with the footing.

parquet. Flooring consisting of small precisely cut pieces of wood forming a geometric pattern.

particleboard. A wood product made of very small particles of wood bonded together.

partition wall. An interior wall. It can sometimes be a load-bearing wall.

partnership. A business in which two or more people share ownership. Control and profits of the business are divided among partners according to a partnership agreement.

passage door. A door that swings open and closed on two or more leaf hinges mounted along one side.

penetrating finish. A finish that soaks into the wood.

performance method. A technique that depends upon established engineering principles and design-load specifications to calculate size and strength for individual steel framing members.

performance standard. In construction, a standard that defines the required performance of a specified building component.

perm value. The measure of the effectiveness of a vapor barrier.

picture framing. In window construction, the use of only casing and no stool or apron to finish the bottom of a window frame, with all four lengths being mitered.

pier. A block of concrete that is usually separate from the main foundation. It is often used in girder floor systems or to support decks.

pilaster. A projection resembling a column that may be used to strengthen a wall under a beam or girder.

pilot hole. A hole drilled in wood to start and guide a screw.

pitch. On roof framing, the ratio of total rise to span.

plank. A solid-wood board that is at least 3″ wide.

plan of action. A plan that helps a business reach its goals by identifying a specific course of action.

plan view. A top view showing the width, length, and location of objects as if you were standing on a platform high above them and looking down. Also known as a "bird's-eye" view.

plate. A horizontal framing member used to tie together interior and exterior wall framing. The width of the plate corresponds to the thickness of the wall. Each wall has three plates: a bottom plate and two top plates.

platform-frame construction. A construction technique in which each level of the house is constructed separately. The floor is a platform built independently of the walls. Also called *platform framing.*

platform framing. *See* **platform-frame construction.**

pliers. A hand tool with opposing jaws that are designed to hold things.

plies. Very thin, pliable sheets of wood that have been sawed, peeled, or sliced from a log and used in plywood.

plot plan. *See* **site plan.**

plunge cut. An internal cut made without first drilling a hole.

pneumatic tool. A tool powered by compressed air.

pocket door. A door that slides into an opening or "pocket" inside the wall.

point of reference (POR). *See* **bench mark.**

Portland cement. A manufactured cement used in modern concrete. Its name derives from its similarity in color to Portland stone, a limestone quarried on the Isle of Portland, off the coast of England.

post. A wood or steel vertical member that provides intermediate support for a girder.

post-and-beam framing. Framing in which fewer, but larger, pieces of wood are spaced farther apart than those used in conventional framing.

postformed countertop. A countertop consisting of laminate that has been attached to a substrate at the factory.

pre-design estimate. An estimate made before the exact features of the house are known.

prescriptive method. A technique that uses standardized tables that give specifications and other information relating to steel frame construction.

primer. A paint that has a higher proportion of binder than standard paint. This enables it to hold particularly well to unpainted wood surfaces.

project costs. *See* **direct costs.**

pry bar. A steel bar 6″ to 14″ long, with a nail-removing claw at one or both ends.

PSL. *See* **parallel-strand lumber.**

pullout capacity. The holding capacity of a screw within a connection. Pullout capacity is based on the number of threads penetrating and holding the connection.

pump jack. A metal device with a foot pedal that a worker pumps to make it slide up and down on a wood or aluminum post. Two or more jacks in a row support planks that a worker can use as a scaffold. Pump jacks are commonly used to reach the side walls of a house during siding or painting operations.

punch list. A list identifying all the repairs that must be completed before the house is acceptable to the owner.

purchasing agent. An individual who buys materials according to current needs.

purlin. A horizontal structural member that supports roof loads and transfers them to roof beams.

Q

quantity survey. *See* **quantity takeoff.**

quantity takeoff. A cost estimate in which every piece of material required to build the house is counted and priced. Also called a *complete construction cost estimate* or a *quantity survey.*

quarter-sawn lumber. Premium lumber cut from a log that is first sawed lengthwise into quarters. Boards are then cut from the faces of each quarter. The end grain of a quarter-sawn board shows growth rings running across the thickness of the board. These growth rings generally form angles of 60° to 90° to the board's surface.

R

racking. In wall framing, a condition that occurs when the wall shifts and studs are forced out of plumb. In flooring, staggering the end joints of the flooring pieces so that joints are not grouped closely together. A joint should be no closer than 6″ to another in a previous course.

radiant heat. Heat that travels in a straight line from a hot surface and heats anything solid it meets.

radius wall. A curved wall.

radon. A colorless, odorless radioactive gas given off by some soils and rocks. In some parts of the United States, the seepage of radon into houses poses a health threat.

rafter. An inclined member of the roof framework. Rafters serve the same purpose in the roof as joists in the floor or studs in the wall.

rafter framing square. A square marked with degrees for fast layouts. Its small size makes it handy. Also called a *triangular framing square.*

rails. On a ladder, the vertical supports to which the rungs or steps are attached. On a raised-panel wood door, the horizontal crosspieces that form the outside frame of a door.

rake. The part of a gable roof that extends beyond the end walls. It may be either closed or extended.

rebar. Reinforcing steel can be purchased in the form of bars. It has a patterned surface that helps the concrete grip the steel.

receptacle. A contact device with a combination of slots and grounding holes sized to accept the prongs of an electrical plug.

reflected ceiling plan. A plan drawn as the ceiling would appear in a mirror placed on the floor below it. Reflected plans are used to show complex ceiling designs, such as tray ceilings and customized suspended ceilings, or to show the locations of multiple lighting fixtures.

refractory cement. Cement that is resistant to high temperatures.

regulator. A valve that controls the air pressure reaching a tool.

rendering. A drawing that is more like a picture of the structure than any other type of architectural drawing. Its purpose is most often to show the exterior of a house as it would look completed.

repetitive stress injury (RSI). Physical injury caused by repetitive tasks that cause minor irritation to nerves and tissues.

resilient flooring. Flooring made of flexible shock-absorbing materials. It can be installed as tiles or in wide sheets.

resources. The raw materials with which you do your work.

résumé. A summary of your career objectives, work experience, job qualifications, education, and training.

retempering. Adding water to mortar that has become too stiff to work.

return. A piece that continues the profile of trim or molding around the corner.

reveal. A small offset between a piece of trim and the surface it is applied to. It adds visual interest and allows the trim carpenter to adjust the fit of the casing if the door is not perfectly square.

ridge. A roof framing member placed at the intersection of two upward-sloping surfaces.

ridge beam. A horizontal framing member to which the tops of rafters are fastened. A ridge beam is made from LVL, glue-laminated, or nominal 4″ lumber. The rafters rest on top of the ridge beam or are supported by metal brackets nailed to its side. Also called a *structural ridge.*

ridge board. The horizontal piece that connects the upper ends of the rafters.

rift-sawn boards. Quarter-sawn boards with end grain at angles between 30° and 60°.

Right to Know laws. Regulations requiring that workers be notified of hazards.

rim board. A length of engineered stock that has the same depth as the I-joists.

rim joist. A joist at the edge of the floor system.

rim tracks. *See* **joist tracks.**

rip cut. A cut made with a saw *along* the direction of the grain.

rip hammer. A hammer that has a wedge-shaped claw. Also called a straight-claw hammer.

ripping bar. A bar with claws at each end.

riser. On a stairway, the vertical board enclosing the spaces between treads.

roll roofing. Mineral-surfaced roofing material available in rolls that can be applied quickly over large areas.

roof rake. That portion of the roof frame that extends beyond the walls on the gabled ends.

room finish schedule. A list identifying the materials and finishes to be used for floors, walls, and ceilings for each room, including hallways.

rough opening (RO). The space into which a door or window will fit. It allows room for the door or window and its frame.

rough sill. A horizontal member placed at the bottom of a window opening to support the window. It connects the upper ends of the cripple studs that are below the window.

RSI. *See* **repetitive stress injury.**

R-value. In insulation, measure of a material's ability to resist heat transmission.

S

saddlebag dormers. A back-to-back pair of long shed dormers.

sapwood. The outer growth layer of the tree. It is lighter in color than heartwood.

sash. The part of a window that holds the glazing. The *frame* is the fixed part of the assembly that receives the sash.

scab. A short length of wood used to reinforce another piece.

scaffold. A raised platform used for working at a height.

scale. The ratio between the size of the object as drawn and its actual size.

scarf joint. A joint formed by cutting an angle on the ends of boards so that they overlap.

schedule. A list that provides information too detailed to include elsewhere n the plans. An example is a *window schedule.*

screed. A long, straight length of metal or wood that is used to "strike off" (level) the concrete.

seasoning. The process of drying wood by air drying or kiln drying.

section view. A view providing important information about materials, fastening and support systems, and concealed features. It shows how an object looks when "cut" vertically by an imaginary cutting plane. The cut is not necessarily continuous but may be staggered to include as much construction information as possible.

self-tapping screw. A screw that creates its own hole. A pre-drilled hole is not needed.

service main. A pipe that brings water to the house. It is connected at the street to the municipal water system.

service panel. The master electrical distribution panel.

setback distance. The minimum distance allowed by local codes between a house and the property lines. Codes also specify setback distances between the house and utility lines, streams, and ponds.

shear wall. A wall engineered to withstand unusual lateral (sideways) stresses. Shear walls are often used in areas where earthquakes and severe storms are common. They may require hold-downs and/or special anchor bolts.

sheathing. Rigid 4x8 or larger panels that are attached to the outside surface of the exterior wall framing. Sheathing adds great stiffness and strength to the walls.

shed roof. A roof that slopes in one direction only.

sheen. The glossiness of paint when dry. High-sheen paints are easier to clean, but low-sheen paints have a softer, less glaring appearance.

side cut. The cut at the end of a hip rafter where it joins the ridge board (or the ends of the common rafters) at an angle. Also called a *cheek cut.*

side lap. The amount that adjacent roofing sheets overlap each other horizontally. This applies primarily to rolled roofing and underlayment. Also called *end lap.*

side-wall shingles. Wood shingles used as siding.

sidewinder. *See* **contractor's saw.**

sill. *See* **box sill.**

sill plate. The horizontal framing member anchored to the foundation wall.

sinkers. Nails that are slightly thinner and shorter than commons.

SIP. *See* **structural insulated panel.**

site layout. The process of marking the location of a building on the land itself. This may be done by a surveyor or by a builder familiar with basic surveying methods.

site plan. A plan that shows the building lot with boundaries, contours, existing roads, utilities, and other details such as existing trees and buildings. Also called a *plot plan.*

skirtboard. A finished board nailed to the wall before the stringers are installed. It protects the wall from damage and provides a finished edge against the wall, which makes it easier to paint or wallpaper the adjacent areas.

slab with a turned down footing. *See* **monolithic slab.**

sleeper. A length of lumber that supports wood flooring over concrete. It should be preservative-treated.

sliding T-bevel. A hand tool with a sliding metal blade that can be set at an angle and then locked into place to transfer angles.

slope. In roof framing, a ratio of *unit rise* to *unit run.*

slump test. A test to measure the consistency of concrete.

soffit. On the interior, an area around the perimeter of a room that is lower than the rest of the ceiling. On the exterior, the underside of the eaves. It is sometimes enclosed. It can also be left open, exposing the rafter tails.

sole plate. *See* **bottom plate.**

sole proprietorship. A business with only one owner.

solid-core construction. A type of construction used for exterior doors in which strips of wood, particleboard, rigid foam, or other core material are covered with a thin outer material, such as wood veneer.

sound transmission class (STC). A single number indicating the resistance of a building element, such as a wall, to the passage of airborne sound.

span. The distance between the outer edges of the top plates measured at right angles to the ridge board.

span table. A table listing the maximum spacing allowed between different sizes of joists or rafters. Using span tables, a carpenter can quickly find the right spacing for the species, grade, and dimensions of wood being used.

spec house. A house constructed by a builder before there is a buyer.

specifications. Written notes arranged in list form. They give instructions about materials and methods of work, especially those having to do with quality standards.

spirit level. *See* **carpenter's level.**

spline. A thin strip of wood used to reinforce a joint.

split-ring connector. A connector that allows truss stock, such as that in a heavy truss, to be built up into layers.

spreader. A device that holds the ladder open and prevents it from closing accidentally.

springing angle. The angle at which the crown molding projects from the wall.

springwood. The more porous, light-colored portion of a tree's wood.

square. The amount of roofing material required to cover 100 sq. ft. of roof surface.

stairway. A series of steps along with all the related elements, including stringers and handrail. A stairway may be completely enclosed, or it may be partially open on one or both sides.

stairwell. The vertical shaft inside of which a stairway is built.

Standard Building Code. A building code published by the Southern Building Code Congress International (SBCCI).

stationary window. A window consisting of a single light of insulated glass fastened permanently into the frame. It cannot be opened.

station mark. In layout, the point over which the level is directly centered. The layout is sighted (or shot) from this point. The station mark may be a bench mark or a corner of the lot, but it should be where the area can be conveniently sighted.

STC. *See* **sound transmission class.**

step. A tread and riser.

stepladder. A common type of folding ladder that has flattened steps instead of rungs.

sticker. A long, slender piece of scrap wood that separates layers of wood products and allows air circulation.

stiles. The vertical side members in raised-panel wood doors.

stock cabinet. A cabinet built in standard sizes and stored in a warehouse until ordered.

stock plan. A standard house plan that can be adapted to fit many different lots.

stool. In a window, a horizontal member that laps the window sill and extends beyond the casing.

stoop. An enlarged landing at the top of the steps.

story pole. In carpentry, a measuring device made on site to ensure a uniform layout all around the house. In masonry, a board with markings 8″ apart. It can be used to gauge the top of the masonry for each course. Also called a *course pole.*

straight-claw hammer. *See* **rip hammer.**

strike plate. A metal plate inserted into an opening in the door jamb into which the latch slips.

stringers. Those parts of a stairway that support the treads.

strongback. A member used with shorter spans to stiffen the ceiling joists.

structural insulated panel (SIP). A rigid panel of 3½″ thick expanded polystyrene (EPS) foam insulation between sheets of exterior plywood or oriented-strand board (OSB). Also called a *foam-core panel.*

structural ridge. *See* **ridge beam.**

structural timber. Lumber that is 5x5 or larger. It is used mainly for posts and columns.

stucco. A durable cementlike product that is applied over reinforcing wire.

stud. A vertical framing member. Conventional construction commonly uses 2x4 studs spaced 16″ on center (OC).

subflooring. Engineered wood sheets or construction grade lumber that is used to construct a subfloor, which is a rough floor laid on floor joists as a base for the finish floor.

subgrade. The earth below the slab. The subgrade must be well and uniformly compacted to prevent any uneven settlement of the floor slab.

substrate. A material, such as plywood or particleboard, that serves as a base for another material. Common substrate materials are plywood and particleboard at least ¾″ thick with no defects or voids in the surface.

summerwood. The dense, dark-colored portion of the wood. Its cells have thick walls and small cavities.

T

tail. The portion of the rafter that extends beyond the wall of the building to form the eave.

tail joist. A floor joist interrupted by a header.

template. A guide made from metal or thin wood.

temporary bracing. Bracing that has the following purposes: It prevents the walls from tipping as they are being erected or holds them in position after they have been plumbed and straightened.

theodolite. A transit that reads horizontal and vertical angles electronically. It displays the measurements on an LCD (liquid-crystal display) screen.

thermal break. A material such as rubber or dense foam insulation that slows the transmission of heat and cold in a window.

thickened-edge slab. *See* **monolithic slab.**

timber frame. A freestanding type of post-and-beam frame that rests on a foundation. The supporting members are fairly far apart. Made from either hardwood or softwood, the timbers are surfaced and connected with interlocking joinery. The joints are secured with wooden pegs.

tin snips. *See* **metal snips.**

toenailing. A nailing technique in which a nail is driven at an angle from the face through the edge of the lumber and into another piece. In general, toenailing calls for smaller nails than face-nailing.

toolbox saw. A general-purpose handsaw with a flexible blade and hardened teeth.

top lap. The portion of the shingle not exposed to the weather.

top plate. The plate nailed to the top ends of the studs to tie them together. It also provides a nailing surface for wall coverings and sheathing.

torpedo level. A small spirit level, approximately 9″ long.

total rise. The vertical distance from the top of the top plate to the upper end of the measuring line.

total run. One-half the span (except when the slope of the roof is irregular).

trap. A curved section of drainpipe that is located beneath a fixture. It prevents sewer gases in the waste pipes from entering the house but does not block drainage.

tread. That part of a stairway on which people step.

trend. A general development or movement in a certain direction.

trestle. A portable metal frame with rungs that is used to support scaffold planks at various heights.

triangular framing square. *See* **rafter framing square.**

trim. A straight length of wood such as a 1x4 that is also S4S, or surfaced on 4 sides. *Trim* is also used as a verb. For example, a builder might "trim out" a window (attach molding and trim to it).

trimmer. *See* **trimmer stud.**

trimmer joist. A joist used to form the sides of a large opening.

trimmer stud. A short beam that supports the header over a window or door opening to transfer structural loads from the header to the bottom plate. Also called a *trimmer* or *jack stud.*

try square. A fixed-blade square with a metal blade and a wood or metal handle.

U

undercourse. A low-grade layer of shingles that will not be exposed to the weather.

underlayment. In roofing, a material, such as roofing felt, applied to the roof sheathing before shingles are installed. In flooring, a thin panel product with a surface smoother than standard subflooring. It prevents small flaws in the subfloor from showing through resilient flooring, and provides firm, clean, and void-free support.

unified slab. *See* **monolithic slab.**

Uniform Building Code. A building code published by the International Conference of Building Officials (ICBO).

unit-cost estimate. A detailed estimate of construction costs made by determining the cost for each component, such as a wall or a roof. Also called a *component-cost estimate.*

unit dimension. The overall size of the window, including casings.

unit of run. *See* **unit run.**

unit rise. The number of inches that a roof rises for every 12″ of run (the *unit run*). As the unit rise varies, the slope of the roof changes.

unit run. A set length that is used to figure the slope of rafters. The unit run for a rafter that is at a 90° angle to the ridge (a common rafter) is always 12″. The unit run for a rafter that is at a 45° angle to the ridge is 17″. Also called *unit of run.*

universal design. A design concept aimed at making a house usable and safe for the widest variety of people, including older adults and those with disabilities.

upper cabinets. Cabinets that hang on a wall. Also called *wall cabinets.*

utility drywall saw. A slender saw with a pointed tip, a stiff blade, and large, sharp teeth.

V

valley rafter. A sloping beam that forms a depression in the roof instead of a hip. Like the hip rafter, it extends diagonally from plate to ridge board. A hip rafter is called for only when framing a hip roof, but a valley rafter is needed on both hip and gable roofs whenever roof planes intersect.

vapor barrier. A material highly resistant to vapor transmission.

veneer match. The arrangement of pieces of veneer to create different patterns and effects.

veneer plaster. A specially formulated gypsum plaster.

W

wainscoting. Paneling that runs partway up the wall from the floor.

wale. A horizontal bracing member for a reusable form.

wall cabinets. *See* **upper cabinets.**

wall sheathing. A panel product nailed to the outside surface of exterior walls.

wall tie. A corrosion-resistant fastener secured with galvanized nails.

Warrington hammer. A hammer with a flattened peen instead of a claw.

wear layer. The top layer of engineered flooring. It may be ⅛″ to nearly ¼″ thick.

weatherstripping. Flexible materials such as foam and fibrous pile designed to prevent air leakage around an opening.

web. The member between the chords on a truss.

weep hole. A drainage hole located in masonry, usually formed by omitting the mortar in part of a vertical joint.

welding. The process of joining metals by melting the steel and adding filler metals to fuse the pieces at the point of attachment.

wind chill. A combination of temperature and wind speed that increases the chilling effect. For example, when the actual air temperature is 40°F [4°C], a wind of 35 mph creates weather conditions equivalent to those when the temperature is 11°F [-12°C].

winder. A radiating tread that can be used instead of a platform to turn a stair.

window schedule. A portion of the building plans that contains descriptions of the windows, plus sizes for the glass, the sash, and sometimes the rough opening. The location of each window in a house is found by matching the number of the window in the window schedule with the corresponding number on the house plan.

wood chisel. A tool with a steel blade sharpened to a fine edge at one end and a wood or plastic handle at the other.

wood rasp. A tool that is similar to a metal file but having raised teeth. On some models, the teeth are located on a replaceable, thin metal plate that is attached to the handle. In others, the teeth and handle are formed from a solid piece.

wood veneer. A very thin, pliable sheet of wood that has been sawed, peeled, or sliced from a log.

work ethic. Your personal commitment to doing your very best on the job. It includes exercising responsibility, flexibility, honesty, cooperation, and commitment.

work triangle. The shortest walking distance between the refrigerator, the primary cooking surface, and the sink. The size of the work triangle is a measure of a kitchen's efficiency.

woven valley. *See* **closed valley.**

wrench. A hand tool designed for turning a fastener such as a bolt or nut.

X, Y, Z

zoning. Regulations that divide land into areas, or zones, used for different purposes. Only certain types of buildings may be built within these defined zones.

INDEX

B

C

D

E

I

J

K

L

M

N

O

P

Q

R

S

T

U

V

W

X, Y, Z

CREDITS

Cover Design: SquareCrow Creative Services

Cover Images:
Photodisc, Spencer Jones/Getty Images, Stephen Marks Inc/The Image Bank/Getty Images, Gary Moon Photography

Interior Design: SquareCrow Creative Services

All interior illustrations by:

Art MacDillos/Gary Skillestad, Chapters 3, 5, 6, 7, 8, 9, 10, 11,13, 18, 21, 22, 28, 30, 40

Steve Karp, Chapters 2, 4, 12, 16, 17, 19, 24, 25, 26, 27, 31, 32, 34, 35, 41, 45, Appendix

Ian Warpole, Chapters 14, 15, 20, 22, 23, 29, 33, 36, 37, 38, 42, 43, 44, Appendix

Information for certain tables was provided by:

Western Wood Products Association,

Precision Panel Corporation, and

International Code Council, Inc.

Courtesy of Aearo Company, 108

Courtesy of The American Engineered Lumber Association, 313, 492, 325

Arnold & Brown, 9, 10, 17, 18, 19, 20, 21, 27, 29, 31, 34, 38, 40, 42, 54, 60, 65, 82, 101, 102, 106, 113, 114, 115, 118, 120, 121, 122, 123, 124, 126, 130, 134, 136, 137, 138, 139, 141, 143, 146, 147, 148, 149, 150, 151, 152, 155, 157, 158, 159, 160, 164, 166, 167, 168, 16, 171, 173, 175, 177, 180, 183, 187, 192, 197, 202, 221, 311, 321, 338, 368, 383, 390, 423, 430, 464, 501, 504, 548-549, 567, 599, 607, 650, 657, 660, 661, 662, 663, 667, 700, 701, 706, 711, 717, 719, 720, 730, 731, 735, 736, 737, 742, 744, 748, 749, 750, 774, 775, 780, 781, 782, 783, 784, 808, 812, 813, 814, 815, 816, 821, 826, 829, 830, 832, 834, 836, 838, 839, 840, 841, 842, 847, 848, 849, 851, 854, 856, 857, 861, 864, 873, 877, 878, 880, 883, 894, 902, 903, 905, 906, 910, 912, 913, 914, 915, 916

Roger B. Bean, 11, 17, 18, 87, 213, 265, 268, 334, 506, 634, 639, 678, 785, 676-677

Courtesy of Bullard, 108

Courtesy of Calculated Industries, 115

Courtesy of the Concrete Microscopy Laboratory at UIUC Paul E. Stutzman photo, 209

Courtesy of Construction Master, 434

Corbis
- Craig Aurness, 598
- Chris Daniels, 551
- Michael Keller, 11, 218
- Gehl Company, 909
- Philip Gould, 12, 288
- Chinch Gryniewicz, 219
- John Henley, 50
- Rodney Hyett, Elizabeth Whiting & Associates, 771
- Lester Lefkowitz, 51
- Bill Miles, 92-93
- Doug Wilson, 557
- Tim Wright, 219

Courtesy of The Custom Group of Companies, Custom Dry Kiln Company Ltd., 293

Luis Delgado, 727

Courtesy of Delta International Machinery Co., 133, 141, 143, 174, 176

Courtesy of Designed Stairs, 5, 679, 697, 698

Courtesy of DeWalt Industrial Tool Co., 127

Courtesy of Dreaming Creek Timber Framed Homes, 353, 354

Courtesy of Electrophysics Company, 294

David R. Frazier Photolibrary Inc., 4, 7, 8, 12, 13, 14, 15, 17, 18, 19, 20, 21, 26, 29, 30, 34, 35, 36, 37, 41, 48, 51, 53, 56, 57, 63, 74, 82, 83, 83, 95, 112, 207, 214, 221, 222, 223, 224, 235, 242, 245, 248, 249, 252, 253, 255, 257, 258, 259, 260, 261, 273, 275, 280, 281, 282, 283, 305, 306, 307, 311, 313, 317, 324, 326, 335, 336, 338, 339, 341,360, 365, 392, 399, 404, 408, 448, 470, 500, 502, 506, 567, 618, 619, 635, 638, 646, 654, 656, 658, 663, 667, 671, 707, 724, 731, 749, 768-769, 770, 771, 777, 779, 781, 782, 784, 795, 796, 798, 800, 801, 802, 810, 811, 815, 821, 833, 835, 838, 841, 860, 861, 863, 866, 867, 872, 875, 899, 900

Tim Fuller, 4, 10, 12, 13, 14, 15, 16, 19, 21, 203, 206, 212, 214, 243, 254, 258, 259, 260, 261, 262, 265, 269, 271, 272, 274, 280, 282, 283, 286-287, 304, 317, 321, 344, 422, 441, 502, 512-513, 514, 517, 518, 519, 520, 521, 522, 528, 532, 533, 539, 540, 541, 544, 545, 546 550, 554, 562, 566, 570, 579, 587, 594, 596, 598, 599, 602, 605, 608, 619, 622, 626, 788, 792, 795, 816, 823, 855, 856, 876, 877, 879, 880, 882, 886, 888, 891

Ann Garvin, 279, 873

Courtesy Karl Graffte - Woodzone.com, 296, 297

Courtesy Home Planners Inc., 69, 70, 559

Courtesy of ICF Builders, 243

Courtesy of James Hardie® Building Products, 658, 839

Courtesy Lab Safety Supply Inc., 106

Courtesy of Makita USA Inc., 128, 129, 142, 156, 156, 157, 166, 173, 174, 177, 178, 185, 190

Joe Mallon, 5, 207, 215, 241, 254, 265, 306, 340, 336, 479, 522, 523, 525, 553, 555, 556, 557, 567, 571, 573 575, 576, 582, 585, 603, 621, 632, 789, 838, 858, 895, 900

Kevin May Corporation, 108, 113, 114, 115, 116, 117, 118, 119, 120, 121, 122, 123, 124, 290

Courtesy of Mitek Inc., 507

Jon P. Muzzarelli, 4, 104, 111, 131, 135, 138, 168, 184, 296, 297, 302, 307, 312, 319, 529, 536, 537, 539, 545, 546, 690, 691

Courtesy of MVIS Group, University of Oulu, 297

Photo Edit
- Bill Aron, 154
- Spencer Grant, 222
- Bonnie Kamen, 24-25
- Elena Rooraid, 8, 94
- David Young-Wolff, 11, 229, 234

Photo Researchers, Inc.
- Vaughan Flemming/Science Photo Library, 298
- Holt Studios Int., 301
- James H. Robinson, 299
- Alice K. Taylor, 301
- Kenneth H. Thomas, 301

Courtesy of Porter Cable Corp., 10, 148, 182

Courtesy of Portland Cement Association, 48

Courtesy Precision Panel Structures, Inc., 354

Courtesy of Schieler and Rassi Quality Builders, 66, 67, 68*

Courtesy of Senco Inc., 860

Courtesy of SkillsUSA/VICA, 36

Courtesy Stanley Tools Inc., 105

Stock Boston
- Greg Probst, 348

Courtesy of Velux Corp., 563

Special Thanks to:

Alexander Lumber, Rushville, IL; A-1 Supply, Creve Couer, IL; Robert Caputo, Rushville, IL; Schieler and Rassi Quality Builders, Inc., Deer Lake, IL; Joy Doss of Designed Stairs, Sandwich, IL.

*These images are printed with permission and remain the exclusive property of Schieler and Rassi Quality Builders, Inc. These images should not be used without the express written permission of Schieler and Rassi Quality Builders, Inc., Deer Lake, IL.

Models and fictional names have been used to portray characters in stories and examples in this book.